JavaScript Programmer's Reference

For the
complete reference
see the CD.

List of all entries
in the book and on the CD,
by topic, at the back
of this book.

C
D
E
F
G
H
I
J
K
L
M
N
O
P
R
S
T
U
V
W
X
Symbols

JavaScript Programmer's Reference

Cliff Wootton

Wrox Press Ltd. ®

JavaScript Programmer's Reference

Published by Wrox Press Ltd,
Arden House, 1102 Warwick Road, Acocks Green,
Birmingham, B27 6BH, UK
Printed in the United States
ISBN 1-861004-59-1

Trademark Acknowledgements

Wrox has endeavored to provide trademark information about all the companies and products mentioned in this book by the appropriate use of capitals. However, Wrox cannot guarantee the accuracy of this information.

Credits

Author
Cliff Wootton

Category Manager
Dave Galloway

Technical Editors
Timothy Briggs
Howard Davies
Phillip Jackson
Amanda Kay
Simon Mackie
Chris Mills
Peter Morgan

Project Manager
Chandima Nethisinghe

Production Coordinator
Tom Bartlett

Additional Layout
Simon Hardware
Pippa Wonson

e-book Production
Tom Bartlett

Production Manager
Simon Hardware

Technical Reviewers
Alex Abacus
Jonny Axelsson
Chong Chang
Andrew Van Heusen
Martin Honnen
Ron Hornbaker
Kenneth Lo
Jim Macintosh
Jon Stephens
Peter Torr
Chris Ullman
Paul Vudmaska
Paul Wilton

Figures
Shabnam Hussain

Cover
Shelley Frazier

Proofreaders
Ian Allen
Christopher Smith
Agnes Wiggers

Index
Andrew Criddle

About the Author

Cliff Wootton lives in the south of England and works on multimedia systems and content management software for large data driven web sites. Currently he is developing interactive TV systems for BBC News Online in London (http://www.bbc.co.uk/news) and previously worked for other commercial broadcasters on their web sites. Before that he spent several years developing geophysical software and drawing maps with computers for oil companies.

Cliff is married with three daughters and a growing collection of bass guitars.

Acknowledgements

It's hard to believe I've actually reached the stage of writing the introductory pages to this book. It's been a long process and I don't think I would have reached this point without the help of Tim Briggs at Wrox, who very gently urged me onwards and gave me encouragement when I needed it. Tim's contribution to this project was vital to its success because he developed the process which converted my DOCBOOK output into something the Wrox editors could turn into a book. Tim also prepared the CD-ROM content from the same XML files; truly amazing!

Thanks also to all the other folks at Wrox who have helped, organised, checked and collated my material to present it in the form you now see it. Grateful thanks to my reviewers, who in a very short time provided me with some useful guidance and support; in particular Jon Stephens and Martin Honnen, who also provided some amazingly clever example code fragments for use as examples.

There are many other people who contributed without realising it. In particular Nick Cohen (formerly of the BBC and now at Turner Broadcasting) who provided some helpful insights into TV set-top-box workings. Also Matt Karas and Emyr Tomos (both ex-BBC, now at Talkcast) who threw down the gauntlet of several interesting challenges for me to implement on the BBC News Online web site. I also wouldn't be sitting here if it weren't for Bruce Morris at Carlton Online. It was through the happy chance of an article I wrote for Bruce's Web Developer's Journal (WDJ) web site that led to Wrox contacting me and the BBC inviting me to do some JavaScript work. What an amazing thing the web is.

Most importantly I dedicate this book to my family. To my wife, Julie and my daughters Hannah, Lydia and Ruth who kept me going with cups of coffee, hugs and the occasional giggle when they saw the photograph of me for the front cover.

about: URL (Request method)
AbstractView object (Object/DOM)
ActiveXObject object (Object/JScript)
Add (+) (Operator/additive)
Add then assign (+=) (Operator/assignment)

Table of Contents

Table of Contents

Table of Contents

Table of Contents

G   385

Table of Contents

J   465

Table of Contents

Table of Contents

Table of Contents

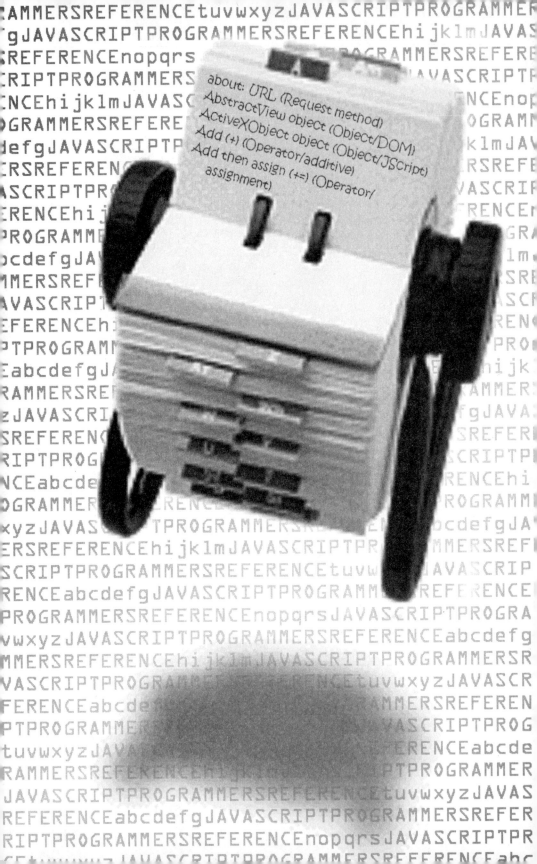

Introduction

The JavaScript language is constantly developing, and continues to increase in popularity. Its evolution into a general-purpose scripting language from what started life purely for scripting web browsers is indicative of its success. You can now find JavaScript interpreters in many different environments and there are sure to be other new and interesting uses for the language in the future, especially now that embeddable interpreters are available.

In this book, we have attempted to snapshot the web browser JavaScript implementations that exist currently, which need to be supported by web sites, and collate that information together in a form that has broad scope and is deep enough to be useful on a day-to-day basis. As the language is growing all the time, this is likely to be an ongoing task.

Who is This Book For?

The book is aimed at people who already have some knowledge of JavaScript and need a companion volume to their daily work. It is primarily aimed at the experienced practitioner, and so does not attempt to be a tutorial for the beginner.

For a tutorial book, we suggest Paul Wilton's Beginning JavaScript *(Wrox Press, ISBN 1-861004-06-0).*

Typical uses of the book include times when you:

❑ Need to check out the specific details of a particular language construct or object property

❑ Know what you want to do, but want to know how JavaScript helps you achieve that

❑ Want information on cross-browser compatibility issues for your script

❑ Have encountered a problem in your script and need help to debug it

One important motivation I had for writing this book was to reduce the amount of material I have to carry around when I'm working on projects in my clients' offices. My library now contains several shelves devoted purely to JavaScript, and in researching this book, I ended up with many megabytes of material. There have been many fine books written about JavaScript but I simply cannot carry them around on the train, even with a large rucksack! So, I set out to try to distil enough useful information into one book and organize it so that the information is easy to find. I've also put in material on issues that I've encountered in discussions with other programmers.

The Structure of the Book

To make it easy to navigate through the topics, titles describe the topic content and the topic type and are organized alphabetically. Where a topic might be referred to using several headings, a brief entry in the cross-reference at the end of the book shows the main topic for that subject.

I used a great deal of software automation to manage the book content and the whole thing was built in a database. There are now in excess of 3,500 individual topics in this work. That is more than twice as many as we have room for in the book so we have put a useful subset of the reference into the printed book and the complete set of material onto the CD-ROM, which is available both in 'e-book' PDF and HTML formats. Some additional reference information that is not strictly part of the JavaScript language, but that you may find useful, is also included, such as country codes and MIME types.

Where we discuss an object all the important properties, methods, events, and any supporting material are broken out into their own topics, and these detailed entries are included on the CD. Where objects inherit properties and methods, they are listed in the object coverage but to avoid duplication the information about the inherited properties is described as a member of the super-class. This slightly detracts from the lexical referencing but it saves space. In some cases these inherited properties/methods are deemed important enough to merit a cross-referencing entry of their own.

This allows us to indicate availability of features at a very fine level of detail. Within each topic we can also discuss bugs, gotchas, and areas of difficulty in a focused way.

Entries for objects summarize the support for important methods and properties. The Notes column in those tables notes any deprecations and other warnings – details of which can be found in that method or property's topic, on the CD.

Language syntax is illustrated by way of example code fragments that show how to access an object, method, or property. More extensive examples are given where necessary.

Because of the scoping rules, properties are available without the need for the `window` object to be specified as a prefix. Thus `navigator` as a topic is available under the `window.navigator` topic as well. Once you have found an entry topic, you can then use the cross-referencing listings to locate other related material.

The book content was developed inside a database system, which provided tools to relate topics. The benefit is a rich source of cross-referencing links between topics. The cross-reference in the printed book is complete; that is, it also includes entries found only on the CD. The italicized cross-references can be found in the book.

The cross-reference at the end of the book allows you to browse entries by their type. In particular, collections, events, methods, and properties are listed alphabetically, showing all the references to them in both the book and CD, and the objects to which those references belong.

We will now look at some of the 'features' of JavaScript programming, as an introduction to what topics in the book will address.

Differences between Browsers

For some time, the most popular browsers have been Netscape Navigator 4.7 and Microsoft Internet Explorer 5.0 (MSIE). Other, newer browsers make a point of being standards-compliant and so if your script conforms to the standards for core JavaScript as laid down by ECMA and the W3C DOM specifications, it should function correctly.

However, the dominant browsers have for a long time been competing with one another to add new features. Architecturally, this means their browsers have each gone in a completely different direction. The penalty has been that support for various language features has been implemented in each browser in ways that makes it difficult to use in a portable way. Indeed, to make use of some features requires twice the work, since the same code has to be written in two different ways and called after detecting which browser is being used.

Because of the proliferation of browser versions and platforms, features are generally referred to as being available in the revision in which they were first introduced. As the Netscape browser is available on so many different platforms, to test for compliance across all platforms would require a test suite of a dozen machines and 30 or more different installations of browser applications. Indeed, when building such a test suite just prior to starting on this book, I found more than a dozen distinctly different browser versions just for the Macintosh platform and many more than that for Windows. Similarly, MSIE comes in a bewildering variety of versions and platform variants. In addition, the JScript interpreter is a replaceable component that can be upgraded without changing the containing browser.

Browsers and Standards

There is still much that is ambiguous or not yet defined in the standards and the browser manufacturers continue to add new features in competition with one another. Even though they are standards-compliant at a functional level, there are still significant differences if you 'look under the hood'.

We have included coverage of the following standards:

❑ ECMAScript core language up to edition 3 of the standard

❑ DOM coverage to level 1

❑ Some DOM coverage of level 2 where implemented in Netscape 6

❑ Discussion of the features being added at DOM level 3

JavaScript implementations we cover include:

❑ Netscape 3.0, 4.0, 4.06, 6.0 (the final release came out as we went to press)

❑ MSIE version 3.0, 4.0, 5.0, 5.5

❑ Opera 3, 4, 5

❑ Netscape Enterprise Server

By implication that means we cover JavaScript versions up to 1.5 and JScript up to 5.5. The coverage of Netscape 6.0 is based on it supporting the W3C DOM standards and several bugs in the currently released version prevented the verification of some functionality although that may be platform-dependent. There are also some new and unexpected features.

We concentrate our discussions on the peculiarities of Netscape and MSIE because the other browsers that support JavaScript attempt to provide a fault-free standards-based implementation.

Features and Versions

There are now a wide variety of sources of information about JavaScript and they don't all agree. In particular there is some uncertainty over which release of JavaScript introduces certain features.

The source material was assimilated by examining the standards documents and by inspecting objects with fragments of JavaScript. Then, the availability of features was checked against several alternative reference works. Occasionally, when a consistency error showed up, it was necessary to go back to the browser and test for the availability of a property or method.

Where there is some room for doubt, we have documented the release at which the feature became useful. This is because in earlier releases it may have had a serious flaw or been significantly revised later to make it work properly. Any implementation prior to that may be unreliable. So where we may appear to disagree with other commentators our coverage is based on whether it is practical to use a particular feature at a certain release.

Some browser features are available at an earlier release on some platforms than others are. We take the Windows 32-bit release as our baseline although significant testing was also done on the Macintosh versions, which disappointingly lagged somewhat in performance and feature availability. Both platforms exhibited instabilities and crash-prone behavior but in quite different areas of the language.

As there are so many variants of the browsers, the availability matrix for objects and their member properties/methods is huge and requires a large amount of work to test on all the available combinations. So far, no single reference source has proven to be error free and while the information here has been examined and cross-checked it is still likely that there are errors. If, in your work, you disagree with the information provided here, please send feedback (see the end of the *Introduction* for how to do this).

Core JavaScript

At first glance, the JavaScript environment appears to be built around a small core of objects and it is easy to fall into the trap of assuming the language is small and compact. That is certainly true if you are only considering core JavaScript functionality. The core language is defined by ECMA and both Netscape and MSIE claim to be ECMA-compliant. They may well be, but you cannot write much useful JavaScript for deployment in a web page by confining yourself only to the functionality of the ECMA standard. It is at that point that the two browsers begin to diverge.

DOM Support

Likewise, both browsers (MSIE 5 upwards and Netscape 6) claim to be DOM-compliant. Browser support for the DOM is slowly converging but if you need to do any esoteric code development that involves DOM traversal and class names, they are still somewhat different.

MSIE implements a DOM model that is structurally right, but the class names of the objects that compose that model are certainly not correct and do not conform to the DOM standard. Netscape 6 implements a DOM-compliant model that does use the correct class names. Another slight difference is that MSIE implements distinctly different classes for some objects whereas Netscape Navigator instantiates the same class for several purposes.

These differences don't cause much grief to you when you are constructing simple scripts and web page enhancements but can be quite a problem if you need to manipulate the DOM structure and operate on objects by means of their class names. This difference did not become apparent until I used inspection scripts to examine internal document structures.

There are also areas where DOM specifies objects in a way that the browsers can implement ambiguously. For example, DOM describes documents as being a generic document class with an HTML document as a sub-class. Browsers simply provide a single document class with no access to the two separate class types.

Object Classes

You might also assume that there is a small and finite set of different object types. However if you inspect the constructor properties and examine the function names, you will find the opposite, there are a large number of object types. For example, the `applets` property that returns a list of applets in a document will give you an `AppletArray` object and not a `Collection` object in Netscape. Trying to work out class names on MSIE is a bit more problematic and it tends to provide generic `Collection` objects instead. By building fragments of JavaScript to inspect objects, you can determine these class names and learn a lot about how the browser maintains the internal model of the page.

The topics are constructed around a browser-centric model. The objects are defined based on their instantiation by an HTML tag in a web browser window. MSIE creates a distinct object class for each tag. Netscape does a similar trick, but not so convincingly in earlier versions. At version 6, the objects are DOM-compliant and named differently from those in MSIE and earlier Netscape browsers. Netcsape 6 is so different as to be a new browser with little similarity to the earlier versions of Netscape.

There is an emerging standards-based model that frames the object hierarchy much more logically and, while it is still evolving, it may become a more robust way of describing the catalog of available classes. For now, though, the web and browser dominate use of JavaScript, so this seems like the more appropriate model.

Document Objects

Another area of debate is the document object. Typically, the previous documentation describes access to it as if there is only one document object. This is true within the context of a single script within a page. However, it is not necessarily true of a window in a web browser. A window may contain many frames or layers. Each one will have its own private document object. If you are writing scripts that operate across multiple frames or windows, you may refer to several document objects, so the syntax examples are designed to accommodate the different ways in which objects can be accessed.

The Future

JavaScript is becoming available in an ever-wider variety of applications. It is used in:

❏ PDF forms for validation

❏ Developer tools for modifying the behavior of the GUI

❏ Embedded interpreters in cell phones and television set-top boxes

There was not space enough or time to cover these extensively. They are also changing continually and will not be stable enough to document for a while yet.

What Do I Need to Use This Book?

All that is needed to use this book is a text editor and a JavaScript-enabled browser, such as Microsoft Internet Explorer or Netscape Navigator.

To make use of the CD you will need:

❏ A browser to view the HTML version of the book

❏ A copy of Adobe Acrobat Reader to read the PDF e-book version of the reference. This is freely available from www.adobe.com.

❏ The Glassbook reader (http://www.glassbook.com) is an alternative e-book viewer

To make navigation easier, the e-book contains an interactive table of contents, bookmarks, thumbnails, and hyperlinks in the entries.

All of the code examples given in the book are available on the CD, and are also available to download from our web site, www.wrox.com.

Conventions Used in This Book

The convention used for syntax naming is that a variable created within the local scope is prefixed with my while a global variable is prefixed with the. Parameters passed into function and method calls are prefixed with a, an, or some.

The syntax description for an object shows how a reference to an object of that class can be retrieved via a property or method on another object. The syntax for properties and methods show them as members of an object that is referred to with a variable. This manifests itself as an object reference like this:

```
myDocument = document
myDocument = myElement.parentNode
myDocument = myFrame.document
myDocument = myLayer.document
```

Then a property reference looks like this,

```
myDocument.cookie
```

and not:

```
document.cookie
```

Of course you can omit the indirection through a referencing variable and any of these would be equally valid:

```
document.cookie
myElement.parentNode.cookie
myFrame.document.cookie
myLayer.document.cookie
```

But by using the indirection, the syntax descriptions for the member properties and methods are simplified.

In the tables, we have used the abbreviations N for Netscape, NES for Netscape Enterprise Server, and IE for Internet Explorer.

As for styles in the text:

❑ Filenames, and code in the text appear like so: dummy.xml

❑ Text on user interfaces, and URLs, are shown as: **File/Save As**...

❑ Italicized cross references refer to topics that can be found in the book

7

Customer Support

Wrox has three ways to support books. You can:

- ❑ Post and check for errata at **www.wrox.com**
- ❑ Enroll at the peer-to-peer forums at **p2p.wrox.com**
- ❑ E-mail technical support a query or feedback on our books in general

Errata

You can check for errata for the book at our web site, **www.wrox.com**. Simply navigate to the page for this book. There will be a link to the list of errata.

P2P Lists

You can enroll in our peer to peer discussion forums at **p2p.wrox.com**. The JavaScript list is available in the 'Web Design' section.

E-mail Support

If you wish to point out an erratum to put up on the website or directly query a problem in the book with an expert who knows the book in detail, then e-mail support@wrox.com. A typical e-mail should include the following things:

- ❑ The name of the book, the last four digits of the ISBN, and the entry name for the problem in the Subject field
- ❑ Your name, contact info, and the problem in the body of the message

You may want to tell us your opinion of this book, or you may have ideas about how it can be improved, in which case, e-mail feedback@wrox.com. We will do our utmost to act upon your comments.

about: URL (Request method)

This is a special kind of URL that fetches content from a storage area inside the Netscape browser instead of using HTTP to get it from a web server.

Availability:	JavaScript – 1.1 JScript – 3.0 Internet Explorer – 4.0 Netscape – 3.0

This is a special request method provided by the Netscape browser to gain access to local client-side resources. The resources are loaded from inside the application itself.

In the Macintosh version of Navigator, this means they are stored in the resource fork of the browser application. If you need to deploy a custom version of Navigator within an Intranet environment, with some care you can modify these resources with a resource-editing tool, such as ResEdit. Always work on a copy of the application and test the changes thoroughly.

On other platforms, the resources are likely to be stored in files located in folders adjacent to the application. You will need to study your own copy of Netscape to see what you can change.

These special URLs are mostly not present in early versions of MSIE, although there will be some internal resources which may provide customization opportunities. MSIE also supports an about:blank URL that provides a blank page. There may be others hidden away inside the application.

You may also be able to obtain administration tools from Netscape and Microsoft to carry out legitimate customizations on the browsers before deploying them throughout your organization.

The following special URLs seem to work when typed into the location box:

URL	Description
about:logo	Netscape logo
about:mozilla	A fire & brimstone quote from the book of Mozilla (Yes it's really there – at least on some versions)
about:authors	Shows a cryptic message about the page having been removed, although the authors.html file is still present inside the application
about:cache	Displays a disk cache report
about:document	Displays the document info console
about:fonts	Displays the font info console
about:global	A global history report
about:image-cache	A report on the internal image cache
about:license	A hyperlink to the Netscape license document
about:mailintro	Displays the Netscape mail info page
about:memory-cache	A report on the memory cache
about:pics	Generates a security exception
about:plugins	A page of information about the plugins
about:security?advisor=XXX	Brings up a security console where XXX indicates the window to operate on
about:security?banner-insecure	Serves an unlocked padlock image
about:security?banner-secure	Serves a locked padlock image
about:security?issuer-logo=XXX	Returns a graphic where XXX identifies which one
about:security?subject-logo=XXX	Returns a graphic where XXX identifies which one
about:coslogo2	Cosmo logo
about:fclogo	Full Circle software logo
about:hslogo	Beatnik logo
about:hype	An audio clip
about:insologo	Inso logo
about:javalogo	Java compatible logo
about:litronic	Litronic logo
about:mclogo	Marimba Castanet logo
about:mmlogo	Macromedia logo
about:ncclogo	Netcast logo
about:odilogo	Object Design logo
about:qtlogo	Apple QuickTime logo
about:rsalogo	RSA secure logo

URL	Description
about:symlogo	Symantec logo
about:tdlogo	TrueDoc logo
about:visilogo	VisiGenic logo
about:blank	Presents a blank page on Netscape Navigator 3 and MSIE version 5. It is used to create a blank page when a new window is opened.

Some of these URLs can be used in frames, but others can't. A few can be used as HREF values. JavaScript complains that the about: request method is illegal. This means you cannot change the location.href within a page to any of the "about:" URLs. However, you might be able to write some innerHTML content into a <DIV> or <SPAN> to place a link to these assets.

Many of the built-in assets are used as image sources in the about page. It's possible you might want to display the Netscape logo. If you are aware that you are using software provided by the other third parties, you might (if they give you permission) place their logo on the screen when you are using features of their software. You should ask first, although Netscape probably won't mind their logo being served like this.

The interesting thing about this is that you are effectively serving assets out of a static cache in the client file system.

The URL that points at the license document may be useful as it is possible you might want to display the Netscape license if you are redistributing the browser.

The about:plugins URL yields a page containing some useful JavaScript that displays the plugins page. You may find some useful techniques in here for managing plugin facilities although they may be Netscape compatible only.

Mostly, these special URLs will be useful for debugging. Getting details of the disk cache, for example, may be useful. Pulling up the JavaScript debugger page if you detect an error in your script might also be a cool trick.

The MSIE and Netscape browsers can both use the about:blank URL value as a default page when the browser is started up.

Warnings:

❑ The UniversalBrowserRead privilege is required for access to internal browser values and state information such as the cache contents.

See also:	javascript: URL, nethelp: URL, UniversalBrowserAccess, UniversalBrowserRead, URL

AbstractView object (Object/DOM)

An object that belongs to the DOM level 2 views module.

Availability:	DOM level – 2 JavaScript – 1.5 Netscape – 6.0	
JavaScript syntax:	N	`myAbstractView = myMouseEvent.view`
	N	`myAbstractView = myUIEvent.view`

This is part of a new suite of functionality introduced at DOM level 2 which provides a way of looking at documents from alternative points of view. At present only the Abstract and Document views are standardized and, because the capabilities are quite new, implementations may be incomplete at this stage.

See also:	*MouseEvent object,* `MouseEvent.initMouseEvent()`, *UIEvent object*

ActiveXObject object (Object/JScript)

A Windows and MSIE specific object that allows various document components to be embedded.

Availability:	JScript – 3.0 Internet Explorer – 4.0	
JavaScript syntax:	IE	`myActiveX = ActiveXObject`
	IE	`myActiveX = new` `ActiveXObject(anApplication)`
Argument list:	`anApplication`	References an external application
Collections:	Depends on the object created by the constructor	

This is an object for embedding other applications into web pages on the Windows platform. The example shows the creation of an object that is managed by the Word application.

This is also used to create `Dictionary` objects by using the Scripting application to create a new `Dictionary` object.

Warnings:

❑ This is totally non-portable and non-standard, but if your scripts are likely to be deployed in a Windows only environment, it may be useful.

❑ Using this construct in client-side scripting is subject to security restrictions. If a script in a web browser could just instantiate Word, then that implies that it has rights of access to the local file system. The normal IE security settings disallow that level of access.

Example code:

```
// An example that opens a Word document and writes
// text into it.
var myActiveX = new ActiveXObject("Word.Document");
myActiveX.Application.Visible=true;
myString="Some text to be written to the document";
// now write the text to the Word document
myActiveX.application.selection.typeText(myString);
```

See also:	*Dictionary object, OBJECT object*

Add (+) (Operator/additive)

Add two numeric operands together. See concatenation for Strings.

Availability:	ECMAScript edition – 2 JavaScript – 1.0 JScript – 1.0 Internet Explorer – 3.02 Netscape – 2.0 Netscape Enterprise Server – 2.0 Opera – 3.0	
Property/method value type:	`Number primitive`	
JavaScript syntax:	-	`anOperand1 + anOperand2`
Argument list:	*anOperand1*	An expression that evaluates to a number
	anOperand2	Another expression that evaluates to a numeric value

The addition operator adds two numeric values together or concatenates one string onto another.

When used with numeric operands, the plus sign adds the values together.

The addition is commutative, meaning that the order of the operands does not affect the outcome of the calculation. However, the calculation is not always associative (so `(a+b)+c` is not always the same as `a+(b+c)`) and so the precedence established with the grouping operator might affect the outcome.

The associativity is left to right.

Refer to the operator precedence topic for details of execution order.

If either operand is NaN, the result will be NaN.

The sum of infinity and minus infinity will be NaN, they do not cancel one another out.

The sum of two infinity values of the same sign will be the infinity of that sign.

The sum of infinity and a finite value is equal to the infinite operand.

Internally the sum of two negative zero values is -0. However, the sum of two positive zero values or a positive and negative zero value added together will be +0. At the scripting level however, you cannot determine whether a zero is positive or negative, but its sense may affect subsequent computations.

The sum of zero and a non-zero value will be the non-zero value.

The sum of two non-zero finite values of the same magnitude but opposite signs will be zero.

Provided neither an infinity, a zero or NaN is involved, adding two finite values results in the sum of the two values given that the result will be rounded to its nearest representable value. Where the result exceeds the largest presentable value, infinity will be substituted. A negative infinity may result from an underflow.

The addition/concatenation operator looks at the arguments and if either is a String already or preferentially converts to one, then a concatenation occurs. If neither operator prefers to be a String, then a Number conversion happens and the values are added.

See also:	*Add then assign (+=)*, Additive expression, Additive operator, Associativity, *Negation operator (-)*, Operator Precedence, *String concatenate (+)*, *Subtract (-)*, Type conversion, Unary expression, Unary operator

Cross-references:

ECMA 262 edition 2 – section – 11.6.1

ECMA 262 edition 2 – section – 11.13

ECMA 262 edition 3 – section – 11.6.1

Wrox *Instant JavaScript* ISBN 1-861001-27-4 – page – 37

Add then assign (+=) (Operator/assignment)

Add two numeric operands and assign the result to the first. See concatenation for Strings.

Availability:	ECMAScript edition – 2 JavaScript – 1.0 JScript – 1.0 Internet Explorer – 3.02 Netscape – 2.0 Netscape Enterprise Server – 2.0 Opera – 3.0	
Property/method value type:	`Number primitive`	
JavaScript syntax:	-	`anOperand1 += anOperand2`
Argument list:	`anOperand1`	An expression that evaluates to a number
	`anOperand2`	Another numeric value

Add the right operand to the left operand and assign the result to the left operand.

This is functionally equivalent to the expression:

```
anOperand1 = anOperand1 + anOperand2;
```

Although this is classified as an assignment operator, it is really a compound of an assignment and an additive operator.

It also works with string values and will concatenate the second onto the first.

The associativity is right to left.

Refer to the operator precedence topic for details of execution order.

The new value of *anOperand1* is returned as a result of the expression.

Warnings:

❑ The operand to the left of the operator must be an LValue. That is, it should be able to take an assignment and store the value.

Example code:

```
// Initialize with numeric values
myVar1 = 100;
myVar2 = 1000;
// After this myVar1 contains 1100, myVar2 is unchanged
myVar1 += myVar2;
```

See also:	*Add (+)*, Additive operator, *Assign value (=)*, Assignment expression, Assignment operator, Associativity, *Concatenate then assign (+=)*, *Increment value (++)*, LValue, Operator Precedence, *Subtract then assign (-=)*

Cross-references:

ECMA 262 edition 2 – section – 11.13

ECMA 262 edition 3 – section – 11.13

Anchor object (Object/HTML)

An object representing an HTML <A> tag.

Availability:	DOM level – 1 JavaScript – 1.2 JScript – 3.0 Internet Explorer – 4.0 Netscape – 4.0	
Inherits from:	*Element object*	
JavaScript syntax:	-	*myAnchor* = *myAnchorArray*[*aName*]
	-	*myAnchor* = *myAnchorArray*[*anIndex*]
	-	*myAnchor* = *myDocument*.anchors[*aName*]
	-	*myAnchor* = *myDocument*.anchors[*anIndex*]
	-	*myAnchor* = *myDocument*.getElementById(*anElementID*)
	-	*myAnchor* = *myDocument*.getElementsByName (*aName*)[*anIndex*]
	-	*myAnchor* = *myDocument* .getElementsByTagName("A")[*anIndex*]
	-	*myAnchor* = *myDocument*.links[*aName*]
	-	*myAnchor* = *myDocument*.links[*anIndex*]
	IE	*myAnchor* = *myDocument*.all.*anElementID*
	IE	*myAnchor* = *myDocument*.all.tags("A")[*anIndex*]
	IE	*myAnchor* = *myDocument*.all[*aName*]
	IE	*myAnchor* = *myDocument*.anchors.item (*aName*)[*anIndex*]
	IE	*myAnchor* = *myDocument*.links.item(*aName*)[*anIndex*]

HTML syntax:	<A> ... </A>	
Argument list:	aName	An associative array reference to the anchor object
	aName	The name property of the anchor object
	anIndex	An index into the anchors collection
	someText	The text (or innerText) property of the anchor
	anElementID	The ID value of an Element object
Object properties:	accessKey, charset, coords, dataFld, dataSrc, hash, host, hostname, href, hreflang, Methods, mimeType, name, nameProp, pathname, port, protocol, protocolLong, recordNumber, rel, rev, search, shape, tabIndex, target, text, type, urn, x, y	
Object methods:	blur(), focus()	
Event handlers:	onClick, onMouseDown, onMouseOut, onMouseOver, onMouseUp	

This object represents a named location in the HTML document. Only those <A> HTML tags that have a NAME attribute will have anchor objects created for them. All the anchors are listed in the anchors[] array object that belongs to the document object that represents the HTML.

Although the <A> tag is also used to create links using the HREF attribute, they are not anchors unless they are named. Any <A> tags that have HREF attributes (whether or not they have NAME attributes) will be listed in the links[] array.

In Netscape, you can construct new instances of the Anchor object, but there is no constructor property in MSIE to support this.

<A> tags and the objects that represent them are inline elements. Placing them into a document does not create a line break.

Warnings:

❑ If you put an anchor object into a document.write(), in Netscape you get a string containing the object class. In MSIE, you will get the HREF string if there is one and an empty string if there isn't.

❑ MSIE provides access to properties that would normally be considered part of the link object. Internally MSIE probably maintains a single object type for anchors and links, whereas Netscape implements two quite different classes.

❑ Netscape supports an associative reference to an anchor object within the anchors[] array according to the value of its NAME tag attribute. MSIE does not support this means of locating an anchor object in quite the same way.

❑ Note that although the syntax examples illustrate the use of an innerText property, Netscape does not support this mode of access and it will generate an error.

Example code:

```
<!-- Example showing how to dynamically replace -->
<!-- the anchor text -->
<HTML>
<HEAD>
</HEAD>
<BODY>
<A NAME="A1" HREF="www.apple.com">Click here</A><BR>
<A NAME="A2" HREF="www.wrox.com">Click here</A><BR>
<A NAME="A3" HREF="www.msdn.com">Click here</A><BR>
<BR>
<HR>
<SCRIPT>
myLength = document.anchors.length;
for (myEnumerator=0; myEnumerator<myLength; myEnumerator++ )
{
    document.anchors[myEnumerator].innerText =
document.anchors[myEnumerator].name;
}
</SCRIPT>
</BODY>
</HTML>
```

See also:	Document.anchors[], Document.links[], *Element object*, Element.all[], Input.accessKey, *LINK object*, *Location object*, String.anchor(), Subclasses, Superclasses, URL, *Url object*, Window.scrollTo()

Property	JavaScript	JScript	N	IE	Opera	DOM	HTML	Notes
accessKey	1.5 +	3.0 +	6.0 +	4.0 +	-	1 +	-	Warning
charset	1.5 +	5.0 +	6.0 +	5.0 +	-	1 +	-	-
coords	1.5 +	5.0 +	6.0 +	5.0 +	-	1 +	-	-
dataFld	-	3.0 +	-	4.0 +	-	-	-	-
dataSrc	-	3.0 +	-	4.0 +	-	-	-	-
hash	1.2 +	3.0 +	4.0 +	4.0 +	-	-	-	Warning
host	1.2 +	3.0 +	4.0 +	4.0 +	-	-	-	Warning
hostname	1.2 +	3.0 +	4.0 +	4.0 +	-	-	-	Warning
href	1.2 +	3.0 +	4.0 +	4.0 +	-	1 +	-	Warning
hreflang	1.5 +	5.0 +	6.0 +	5.0 +	-	1 +	-	-
Methods	-	3.0 +	-	4.0 +	-	-	-	-
mimeType	-	3.0 +	-	4.0 +	-	-	-	Warning, ReadOnly
name	1.2 +	3.0 +	4.0 +	4.0 +	-	1 +	-	Warning
nameProp	-	3.0 +	-	4.0 +	-	-	-	ReadOnly
pathname	1.2 +	3.0 +	4.0 +	4.0 +	-	-	-	Warning
port	1.2 +	3.0 +	4.0 +	4.0 +	-	-	-	Warning

Property	JavaScript	JScript	N	IE	Opera	DOM	HTML	Notes
protocol	1.2 +	3.0 +	4.0 +	4.0 +	-	-	-	Warning
protocol Long	-	3.0 +	-	4.0 +	-	-	-	ReadOnly
record Number	-	3.0 +	-	4.0 +	-	-	-	ReadOnly
rel	1.5 +	3.0 +	6.0 +	4.0 +	-	1 +	-	-
rev	1.5 +	3.0 +	6.0 +	4.0 +	-	1 +	-	-
search	1.2 +	3.0 +	4.0 +	4.0 +	-	-	-	Warning
shape	1.5 +	5.0 +	6.0 +	5.0 +	-	1 +	-	-
tabIndex	1.5 +	3.0 +	6.0 +	4.0 +	-	1 +	-	-
target	1.2 +	3.0 +	4.0 +	4.0 +	-	1 +	-	Warning
text	1.2 +	-	4.0 +	-	-	-	-	Warning, ReadOnly
type	1.5 +	3.0 +	6.0 +	4.0 +	-	1 +	-	-
urn	-	3.0 +	-	4.0 +	-	-	-	-
x	1.2 +	-	4.0 +	-	-	-	-	Warning, ReadOnly
y	1.2 +	-	4.0 +	-	-	-	-	Warning, ReadOnly

Method	JavaScript	JScript	N	IE	Opera	DOM	HTML	Notes
blur()	1.5 +	3.0 +	6.0 +	4.0 +	-	1 +	-	-
focus()	1.5 +	3.0 +	6.0 +	4.0 +	-	1 +	-	-

Event name	JavaScript	JScript	N	IE	Opera	DOM	HTML	Notes
onClick	1.2+	3.0 +	4.0 +	4.0 +	3.0 +	-	4.0 +	Warning
onMouseDown	1.2 +	3.0 +	4.0 +	4.0 +	3.0 +	-	4.0 +	Warning
onMouseOut	1.2 +	3.0 +	4.0 +	4.0 +	3.0 +	-	4.0 +	Warning
onMouseOver	1.2 +	3.0 +	4.0 +	4.0 +	3.0 +	-	4.0 +	Warning
onMouseUp	1.2 +	3.0 +	4.0 +	4.0 +	3.0 +	-	4.0 +	Warning

Inheritance chain:

Element object, Node object

AnchorArray object (Object/DOM)

An array of Anchor objects retrieved from the document.anchors property.

Availability:	DOM level – 1 JavaScript – 1.0 JScript – 3.0 Internet Explorer – 4.0 Netscape – 2.0
JavaScript syntax:	- *myAnchorArray* = *myDocument*.anchors
Object properties:	length

The AnchorArray object is a sub-class of the Array object but has no additional properties. It responds to the length property request as you would expect.

Any Anchor objects in this array can be accessed by index value because the Array class supports that. In Netscape, the individual Anchor objects are accessible associatively by their NAME attribute. However, MSIE does not make this associative mechanism available.

In MSIE, the AnchorArray object is a kind of Collection object and so it can be searched with the item() and tags() methods.

Warnings:

❑ Netscape adds a constructor property to this object class from which you can request the name to determine the object class. Actually Netscape provides constructors for virtually everything, but MSIE only supports them when it's necessary and useful.

❑ Be aware that renaming an anchor in MSIE will add a new item to the AnchorArray collection without destroying the old one. However, the length property remains the same. It does mean that you could have problems enumerating the collection. But then, why would you ever want to rename an anchor after it has been instantiated and named within the HTML tag?

Example code:

```
<!-- Catalog of anchors in an array -->
<HTML>
<HEAD>
</HEAD>
<BODY>
<A NAME="A1" HREF="http://www.apple.com/">Apple</A><BR>
<A NAME="A2" HREF="http://www.wrox.com/">Wrox</A><BR>
<A NAME="A3" HREF="http://www.msdn.com/">Microsoft</A><BR>
<BR>
<HR>
```

```
<TABLE BORDER=1>
<TH>Index</TH>
<TH>Name</TH>
<TH>Text</TH>
<TH>URL</TH>
<TH>Tab index</TH>
<TH>Protocol (long)</TH>
<SCRIPT>
myLength = document.anchors.length;
for (myEnumerator=0; myEnumerator<myLength; myEnumerator++ )
{
    document.write("<TR><TD>");
    document.write(myEnumerator);
    document.write("</TD><TD>");
    document.write(document.anchors[myEnumerator].name);
    document.write("</TD><TD>");
    document.write(document.anchors[myEnumerator].innerText);
    document.write("</TD><TD>");
    document.write(document.anchors[myEnumerator].href);
    document.write("</TD><TD>");
    document.write(document.anchors[myEnumerator].tabIndex);
    document.write("</TD><TD>");
    document.write(document.anchors[myEnumerator].protocolLong);
    document.write("</TD></TR>");
}
</SCRIPT>
</TABLE>
</BODY>
</HTML>
```

See also:	*Anchor object, Collection object,* `Document.anchors[]`

Property	JavaScript	JScript	N	IE	Opera	DOM	Notes
length	1.0 +	3.0 +	2.0 +	4.0 +	-	-	ReadOnly

Applet object (Object/HTML)

An object representing an HTML <APPLET> tag.

Availability:	DOM level – 0 JavaScript – 1.1 JScript – 3.0 Internet Explorer – 4.0 Netscape – 3.0 Opera – 3.0 Deprecated – HTML 4.0, DOM level 1
Inherits from:	*Element object*

JavaScript syntax:	-	`myApplet = aName`
	-	`myApplet = myAppletArray[aName]`
	-	`myApplet = myAppletArray[anIndex]`
	IE	`myApplet = myDocument.all.anElementID`
	IE	`myApplet = myDocument.all.tags ("APPLET")[anIndex]`
	IE	`myApplet = myDocument.all[aName]`
	-	`myApplet = myDocument.aName`
	-	`myApplet = myDocument.applets[aName]`
	-	`myApplet = myDocument.applets[anIndex]`
	-	`myApplet = myDocument.getElementById(anElementID)`
	-	`myApplet = myDocument .getElementsByName(aName)[anIndex]`
	-	`myApplet = myDocument.getElementsByTagName ("APPLET")[anIndex]`
HTML syntax:		`<APPLET> ... </APPLET>`
Argument list:	`aName`	The name of an applet
	`anIndex`	An element in the `applets` collection
	`anElementID`	The ID value of an `Element` object
Object properties:		`accessKey, align, alt, altHTML, archive, code, codeBase, dataFld, dataSrc, form, height, hspace, name, object, src, tabIndex, vspace, width`
Object methods:		`start(), stop()`
Event handlers:		`onAfterUpdate, onBeforeUpdate, onBlur, onClick, onDataAvailable, onDataSetChanged, onDataSetComplete, onDblClick, onErrorUpdate, onFocus, onHelp, onKeyDown, onKeyPress, onKeyUp, onLoad, onMouseDown, onMouseMove, onMouseOut, onMouseOver, onMouseUp, onReadyStateChange, onResize, onRowEnter, onRowExit`

The properties and methods of an `Applet` object are inherited from the public properties and methods of the `Java` object it represents. However, in addition to these, MSIE also supports some additional properties.

The Java applet itself is the concrete object whose properties are accessed.

In Netscape, Applets are encapsulated as instances of the `JavaObject` class and communicate by means of the LiveConnect support. The mechanisms are quite different in MSIE, which uses ActiveX facilities to access applets.

When you access an `Applet` (`JavaObject`) object, you are really interacting with the Java applet itself.

The publicly accessible properties and methods depend on the applet, although all applets must support the `start()` and `stop()` methods.

It is generally safer to interact with methods that you have provided as custom additions to the applet, rather than hope that the applet supports any particular methods.

Because Java is so much more strongly data typed than JavaScript, you must be careful with the kind of values you try and send to and receive from a Java applet. Java will also not forgive the omission of an argument. In JavaScript, all arguments are assumed to be optional as a general rule, although leaving them out will have strange side effects sometimes. Java will not allow you to do this and a run-time error will be generated if the arguments are not complete and all of the correct type.

In Netscape, you can build an enumerator loop to examine all the properties of an `Applet` object. Enumerating applet interfaces like this will yield a long list of function objects. Each function object represents an accessor for internal properties of the Java environment. Your applet may publish additional properties. With these functions, you can enquire about certain attributes of the applet and can change some of them from the script. Refer to the JavaObject topic for details about these generic capabilities, but bear in mind they only work in Netscape.

In MSIE, the `APPLET` object inherits its behavior from the `Element` object. Refer to the topic covering that for its generic properties and methods. MSIE supports many other properties and methods that are not generally available to `Element` objects and these are detailed here as properties and methods of the `Applet` object.

Warnings:

❏ MSIE implements this object as a member of the class `APPLET` rather than `Applet` as you would expect.

❏ Netscape implements it as a member of the class `JavaObject` , although this is masked by some shortcomings in the implementation that prevent it from displaying its class type.

❏ `<APPLET>` tags are deprecated in HTML 4.0 and DOM level 1, which suggests there may be some changes to the JavaScript support for them in subsequent implementations of JavaScript in browsers.

See also:	ActiveX, `Applet.start()`, `Applet.stop()`, *AppletArray object*, `Document.applets[]`, *Element object*, `Input.accessKey`, *JavaObject object*, LiveConnect

Property	JavaScript	JScript	N	IE	Opera	DOM	HTML	Notes
accessKey	1.1 +	3.0 +	3.0 +	4.0 +	3.0 +	0 +	-	Warning, Deprecated
align	1.5 +	3.0 +	6.0 +	4.0 +	-	1 +	-	-
alt	1.5 +	5.0 +	6.0 +	5.0 +	-	1 +	-	-
altHTML	-	3.0 +	-	4.0 +	-	-	-	-
archive	1.1 +	5.0 +	3.0 +	5.0 +	-	1 +	-	-
code	1.5 +	3.0 +	6.0 +	4.0 +	-	1 +	-	ReadOnly
codeBase	1.5 +	3.0 +	6.0 +	4.0 +	-	1 +	-	ReadOnly
dataFld	1.1 +	3.0 +	3.0 +	4.0 +	3.0 +	0 +	-	Warning, Deprecated
dataSrc	1.1 +	3.0 +	3.0 +	4.0 +	3.0 +	0 +	-	Warning, Deprecated
form	1.1 +	3.0 +	3.0 +	4.0 +	3.0 +	0 +	-	Warning, Deprecated
height	1.5 +	3.0 +	6.0 +	4.0 +	-	1 +	-	ReadOnly
hspace	1.5 +	3.0 +	6.0 +	4.0 +	-	1 +	-	-
name	1.5 +	3.0 +	3.0 +	4.0 +	-	1 +	-	ReadOnly
object	1.5 +	3.0 +	6.0 +	4.0 +	-	1 +	-	-
src	-	3.0 +	-	4.0 +	-	-	-	ReadOnly.
tabIndex	1.1 +	3.0 +	3.0 +	4.0 +	3.0 +	0 +	-	Warning, Deprecated
vspace	1.5 +	3.0 +	6.0 +	4.0 +	-	1 +	-	-
width	1.5 +	3.0 +	6.0 +	4.0 +	-	1 +	-	ReadOnly

Method	JavaScript	JScript	N	IE	Opera	DOM	HTML	Notes
start()	1.1 +	3.0 +	3.0 +	4.0 +	-	-	-	-
stop()	1.1 +	3.0 +	3.0 +	4.0 +	-	-	-	-

Event name	JavaScript	JScript	N	IE	Opera	DOM	HTML	Notes
onAfter Update	-	3.0 +	-	4.0 +	-	-	-	-
onBefore Update	-	3.0 +	-	4.0 +	-	-	-	-
onBlur	1.1 +	3.0 +	3.0 +	4.0 +	3.0 +	-	-	Warning
onClick	1.1 +	3.0 +	3.0 +	4.0 +	3.0 +	-	4.0 +	Warning
onData Available	-	3.0 +	-	4.0 +	-	-	-	-
onData SetChanged	-	3.0 +	-	4.0 +	-	-	-	-
onData SetComplete	-	3.0 +	-	4.0 +	-	-	-	-
onDblClick	1.2 +	3.0 +	4.0 +	4.0 +	3.0 +	-	4.0 +	Warning
onError Update	-	3.0 +	-	4.0 +	-	-	-	-
onFocus	1.1 +	3.0 +	3.0 +	4.0 +	3.0 +	-	-	Warning
onHelp	-	3.0 +	-	4.0 +	-	-	-	Warning
onKeyDown	1.2 +	3.0 +	4.0 +	4.0 +	3.0 +	-	4.0 +	Warning

Event name	JavaScript	JScript	N	IE	Opera	DOM	HTML	Notes
onKeyPress	1.2 +	3.0 +	4.0 +	4.0 +	3.0 +	-	4.0 +	Warning
onKeyUp	1.2 +	3.0 +	4.0 +	4.0 +	3.0 +	-	4.0 +	Warning
onLoad	1.1 +	3.0 +	3.0 +	4.0 +	3.0 +	-	-	Warning
onMouseDown	1.2 +	3.0 +	4.0 +	4.0 +	3.0 +	-	4.0 +	Warning
onMouseMove	1.2 +	3.0 +	4.0 +	4.0 +	-	-	4.0 +	Warning
onMouseOut	1.1 +	3.0 +	3.0 +	4.0 +	3.0 +	-	4.0 +	Warning
onMouseOver	1.1 +	3.0 +	3.0 +	4.0 +	3.0 +	-	4.0 +	Warning
onMouseUp	1.2 +	3.0 +	4.0 +	4.0 +	3.0 +	-	4.0 +	Warning
onReady StateChange	-	3.0 +	-	4.0 +	-	-	-	-
onResize	1.2 +	3.0 +	4.0 +	4.0 +	-	-	-	Warning
onRowEnter	-	3.0 +	-	4.0 +	-	-	-	-
onRowExit	-	3.0 +	-	4.0 +	-	-	-	-

Inheritance chain:

Element object, Node object

AppletArray object (Object/DOM)

A sub-class of the Array object that implements an applet collection.

Availability:	DOM level – 1 JavaScript – 1.0 JScript – 1.0 Internet Explorer – 3.02 Netscape – 2.0
JavaScript syntax:	- *myAppletArray* = *myDocument*.applets
Object properties:	length

Warnings:

❑ Although Netscape supports a constructor for this object type, it appears to point at the wrong thing. In any case, it's unlikely you'd want to create a new AppletArray.

See also:	*Applet object*, AppletArray.length, *Collection object*, Document.applets[]

Property	JavaScript	JScript	N	IE	Opera	DOM	Notes
length	1.0 +	1.0 +	2.0 +	3.02 +	-	1 +	ReadOnly

Area object (Object/HTML)

An object representing an <AREA> HTML tag.

Availability:	DOM level – 1 JavaScript – 1.1 JScript – 1.0 Internet Explorer – 3.02 Netscape – 3.0 Opera – 3.0
Inherits from:	*Element object*
JavaScript syntax:	IE `myArea = myDocument.all.aMapID` `.areas[anIndex]`
	IE `myArea = myDocument.all.anElementID`
	IE `myArea = myDocument.all.tags` `("AREA")[anIndex]`
	IE `myArea = myDocument.all[aName]`
	- `myArea = myDocument.getElementById` `(anElementID)`
	- `myArea = myDocument.getElementsByName` `(aName)[anIndex]`
	- `myArea = myDocument` `.getElementsByTagName("AREA")[anIndex]`
	- `myArea = myDocument.links[anIndex]`
HTML syntax:	`<AREA>`
Argument list:	`anIndex` A reference to an element in a collection
	`aName` An associative array reference
	`anElementID` The ID value of an Element object

Object properties:	`accessKey, alt, coords, hash, host, hostname,`
	`href, name, noHref, pathname, port, protocol,`
	`search, shape, tabIndex, target, text, x, y`

Object methods:	`add()`

Event handlers:	`onAfterUpdate, onBeforeUpdate, onBlur, onClick,`
	`onDataAvailable, onDataSetChanged,`
	`onDataSetComplete, onDblClick, onErrorUpdate,`
	`onFocus, onHelp, onKeyDown, onKeyPress, onKeyUp,`
	`onLoad, onMouseDown, onMouseMove, onMouseOut,`
	`onMouseOver, onMouseUp, onReadyStateChange,`
	`onResize, onRowEnter, onRowExit`

An `Area` object represents an area of an image map. They are generally referred to as `Link` objects, although Netscape and MSIE instantiate them as different classes.

Netscape supports these objects as objects of the `Url` class.

MSIE treats them as `Link` objects.

Event handling support via properties containing function objects was added to `Area` objects at version 1.1 of JavaScript.

See also: *Element object, HyperLink object,* `Input.accessKey`, *LINK object, LinkArray object, Location object, Map object, Url object*

Property	JavaScript	JScript	N	IE	Opera	DOM	HTML	Notes
accessKey	1.5 +	3.0 +	6.0 +	4.0 +	-	1 +	-	-
alt	1.5 +	3.0 +	6.0 +	4.0 +	-	1 +	-	-
coords	1.5 +	3.0 +	6.0 +	3.02 +	-	1 +	-	-
hash	1.1 +	1.0 +	3.0 +	3.02 +	3.0 +	-	-	-
host	1.1 +	1.0 +	3.0 +	3.02 +	3.0 +	-	-	-
hostname	1.1 +	1.0 +	3.0 +	3.02 +	3.0 +	-	-	-
href	1.1 +	1.0 +	3.0 +	3.02 +	3.0 +	1 +	-	-
name	1.1 +	3.0 +	3.0 +	4.0 +	-	-	-	-
noHref	1.5 +	3.0 +	6.0 +	4.0 +	-	1 +	-	-
pathname	1.1 +	1.0 +	3.0 +	3.02 +	3.0 +	-	-	-
port	1.1 +	1.0 +	3.0 +	3.02 +	3.0 +	-	-	-
protocol	1.1 +	1.0 +	3.0 +	3.02 +	3.0 +	-	-	-
search	1.1 +	1.0 +	3.0 +	3.02 +	3.0 +	-	-	-
shape	1.5 +	1.0 +	6.0 +	3.02 +	-	1 +	-	-
tabIndex	1.5 +	3.0 +	6.0 +	4.0 +	-	1 +	-	-
target	1.1 +	1.0 +	3.0 +	3.02 +	3.0 +	1 +	-	-
text	1.2 +	-	4.0 +	-	-	-	-	-
x	1.2 +	-	4.0 +	-	-	-	-	-
y	1.2 +	-	4.0 +	-	-	-	-	-

Method	JavaScript	JScript	N	IE	Opera	DOM	HTML	Notes
add()	-	3.0 +	-	4.0 +	-	-	-	-

Event name	JavaScript	JScript	N	IE	Opera	DOM	HTML	Notes
onAfterUpdate	-	3.0 +	-	4.0 +	-	-	-	-
onBeforeUpdate	-	3.0 +	-	4.0 +	-	-	-	-
onBlur	1.1 +	3.0 +	3.0 +	4.0 +	3.0 +	-	-	Warning
onClick	1.1 +	1.0 +	3.0 +	3.02 +	3.0 +	-	4.0 +	Warning
onDataAvailable	-	3.0 +	-	4.0 +	-	-	-	-
onDataSetChanged	-	3.0 +	-	4.0 +	-	-	-	-

Table continued on following page

29

Event name	JavaScript	JScript	N	IE	Opera	DOM	HTML	Notes
onData SetComplete	-	3.0 +	-	4.0 +	-	-	-	-
onDblClick	1.2 +	3.0 +	4.0 +	4.0 +	3.0 +	-	4.0 +	Warning
onError Update	-	3.0 +	-	4.0 +	-	-	-	-
onFocus	1.1 +	3.0 +	3.0 +	4.0 +	3.0 +	-	-	Warning
onHelp	-	3.0 +	-	4.0 +	-	-	-	Warning
onKeyDown	1.2 +	3.0 +	4.0 +	4.0 +	3.0 +	-	4.0 +	Warning
onKeyPress	1.2 +	3.0 +	4.0 +	4.0 +	3.0 +	-	4.0 +	Warning
onKeyUp	1.2 +	3.0 +	4.0 +	4.0 +	3.0 +	-	4.0 +	Warning
onLoad	1.1 +	1.0 +	3.0 +	3.02 +	3.0 +	-	-	Warning
onMouseDown	1.2 +	3.0 +	4.0 +	4.0 +	3.0 +	-	4.0 +	Warning
onMouseMove	1.2 +	3.0 +	4.0 +	4.0 +	-	-	4.0 +	Warning
onMouseOut	1.1 +	3.0 +	3.0 +	4.0 +	3.0 +	-	4.0 +	Warning
onMouseOver	1.1 +	1.0 +	3.0 +	3.02 +	3.0 +	-	4.0 +	Warning
onMouseUp	1.2 +	3.0 +	4.0 +	4.0 +	3.0 +	-	4.0 +	Warning
onReady StateChange	-	3.0 +	-	4.0 +	-	-	-	-
onResize	1.2 +	3.0 +	4.0 +	4.0 +	-	-	-	Warning
onRowEnter	-	3.0 +	-	4.0 +	-	-	-	-
onRowExit	-	3.0 +	-	4.0 +	-	-	-	-

Inheritance chain:

Element object, Node object

Arguments object (Object/core)

An object represented as an array containing the argument values passed to the function when it is called.

Availability:	ECMAScript edition – 2 JavaScript – 1.1 JScript – 5.5 Internet Explorer – 5.5 Netscape – 3.0
JavaScript syntax:	- *myArguments* = arguments
Object properties:	callee, caller, length

When you call a function, you can pass zero or more arguments to it from outside. These arguments are available as named variables whose name is defined in the function declaration.

However, they are also available as the elements in an array. The `arguments` array is referenced by the `arguments` property of the `call` object. Since the `call` object is added to the scope chain, you don't need to reference the `arguments` property with an object identifier prefix.

The array based mechanism is useful for those times when you want to implement a function that has a variable number of arguments passed to it according to how and when it is called.

A new `arguments` object is created for each execution context. When the flow of control enters an execution context for a function block, a new `arguments` object is created. Declared functions, anonymous code and implementation-specific code all use this technique.

When creating the `arguments` object, the initial conditions are set up like this:

❑   The internal `Prototype` property for the `arguments` object is that returned by calling Object.Prototype.

❑   A property is created with the name `callee`. The `callee` property cannot be enumerated. The initial value of the `callee` property is the `function` object being executed. Anonymous functions can then be executed recursively if you so desire.

❑   A property named `length` is created whose value is the number of arguments passed to the function. The `length` property cannot be enumerated.

❑   Each argument is associated with a property whose name is its integer position in an array of arguments. The arguments are accessed in presentation order. Although the names are strings, they represent purely numeric values and range from 0 to 1 less than the value in the `length` property. You can enumerate the arguments in a `for` loop.

Note that objects of this type can only exist within a function body in a web browser, because you cannot pass parameters to a script from outside. It is possible that an embedded JavaScript interpreter may provide a `host` object to the main entry point to perform the same function.

Warnings:

❑   In Netscape, the `arguments` array is implemented as an object of type `Arguments` but in MSIE its type is simply an `Object` object. In Netscape, the `arguments` object is extended with a `toString()` mechanism that returns the arguments as a comma separated list in a String. In MSIE, you get the object type.

❑   None of the properties of the `arguments` object are enumerable.

❑   Because the `arguments` object is meant to be used in a manner that is local to the function it was created in, you get unpredictable results if you pass it to another function as an argument itself.

❑   Note that at the time of writing the example given below did not seem to work on Netscape 6.0.

Example code:

```
<SCRIPT>
// Calls a function and uses its arguments array to find out the
// name of the function that called it.  Demonstrates a one
// level call tracer.

level1();

function level1()
{
   testArgs(1, "ONE", true);
}

function testArgs(a1, a2,a3)
{
   document.write(callerName(arguments));
   document.write("<BR>");
}

function callerName(a1)
{
   myCallerObject = a1.caller.callee;
   myCallerSource = String(myCallerObject);
   mySplitArray1  = myCallerSource.split(" ");
   mySplitArray2  = mySplitArray1[1].split("(");
   myCaller       = mySplitArray2[0];
   return(myCaller);
}
</SCRIPT>
```

See also: Argument, Argument list, Arguments.callee,
Arguments.caller, Arguments.length, arguments[],
Collection object, Execution context, Function arguments, Function call,
Function call operator ( ), *function(...) ...*, Function.arguments[],
Object inspector, Object.prototype, Parameter

Property	JavaScript	JScript	N	IE	Opera	NES	ECMA	Notes
callee	1.2 +	5.5 +	4.0 +	5.5 +	-	-	-	DontEnum
caller	1.1 +	5.5 +	3.0 +	5.5 +	-	-	-	Warning, DontEnum, Deprecated
length	1.1 +	5.5 +	3.0 +	5.5 +	-	-	-	ReadOnly, DontEnum

Cross-references:

ECMA 262 edition 2 – section – 10.1.6

ECMA 262 edition 2 – section – 10.1.8

ECMA 262 edition 2 – section – 15.2.3.1

ECMA 262 edition 3 – section – 10.1.6

ECMA 262 edition 3 – section – 10.1.8

Wrox *Instant JavaScript* – page – 27

Array index delimiter ([ ]) (Delimiter)

Access elements of an array with this delimiter.

Availability:	ECMAScript edition – 2 JavaScript – 1.1 JScript – 3.0 Internet Explorer – 4.0 Netscape – 3.0 Netscape Enterprise Server – 2.0 Opera – 3.0	
Property/method value type:	Depends on array content	
JavaScript syntax:	-	myArray[anIndex]
Argument list:	anIndex	A legal index value into the array, not greater than the array length

Array elements are indexed by selecting them numerically within the set of elements contained in the array. The length property of an array indicates how many indexable locations there are. Array elements begin with the zeroth item.

Storing values into indices that are higher than the current value of the length property will automatically extend the array and reset the length property. An array with only one entry in the 100th element (index value 99) is very sparsely populated but still should report a length value of 100.

In Netscape, referencing the array with no element delimiters will yield a comma-separated list of the contents of the array. So this:

```
myArray = new Array(6);
myArray[0] = 0;
myArray[1] = "XXX";
myArray[2] = 0;
myArray[3] = "XXX";
myArray[4] = 0;
myArray[5] = "XXX";
document.write(myArray);
```

...yields this when executed:

0,XXX,0,XXX,0,XXX

Accessing properties of an object by name simply requires the name to be added to the object reference with a dot separator between them. Numeric values cannot be used in this way. You must use a string to name the Array element when it is assigned.

The associativity is left to right.

Refer to the operator precedence topic for details of execution order.

Although JavaScript does not properly support multi-dimensional arrays, you can simulate them by storing references to one array in the elements of another. You need to create a separate array for each row and then one master array to arrange them into a column.

True multi-dimensional arrays would use a notation like this:

```
multiArray[1,2]
```

But in JavaScript we can at least manage this:

```
multiArray[1][2]
```

This is close enough that most programmers will be able to cope with it quite happily.

Another alternative way to do this is to use a single dimensional array, but calculate the indices. For example to make a 5 x 5 array, you would create a single dimensional array that is 25 elements long. Then to reach the rows you use the row number and multiply the value by 5 before adding the column number to access the desired cell. You need to be careful though because if you have an 'off-by-one' error, it all goes wrong.

Warnings:

❑ Be aware that your script is referring to array elements starting at zero. You can get subtle 'off-by-one' errors if you assume that the array begins at item 1.

❑ In Netscape 2.02, the length property of an array cannot be relied on to hold the right value.

❑ You should avoid putting spaces into associative names because it introduces a property whose name cannot be reached other than via an array index. Not all implementations will trap this error situation. A property name is an identifier and identifier names cannot contain spaces so it should throw an exception.

Example code:

```
<SCRIPT>
// Multidimensional array simulation
hExtent = 5;
vExtent = 6;
theExtent = hExtent * vExtent;
myArray = new Array(theExtent);
document.write("<TABLE BORDER=1>");
for(vEnum = 0; vEnum < vExtent; vEnum++)
{
    document.write("<TR>");
    for(hEnum = 0; hEnum < hExtent; hEnum++)
    {
        targetCell = (vEnum * hExtent) + hEnum;
        document.write("<TD>");
        document.write(vEnum);
        document.write(",");
        document.write(hEnum);
        document.write(" = ");
        document.write(targetCell);
        document.write("</TD>");
    }
    document.write("</TR>");
}
document.write("</TABLE>");
</SCRIPT>
```

See also: *Array object*, `Array.length`, Associativity, Multi-dimensional arrays, *Off by one errors*, Operator Precedence, `Postfix` operator, Property name

Cross-references:

ECMA 262 edition 2 – section – 7.6

ECMA 262 edition 2 – section – 11.2

ECMA 262 edition 3 – section – 7.7

Wrox *Instant JavaScript* – page – 16

Wrox *Instant JavaScript* – page – 32

Wrox *Instant JavaScript* – page – 33

Array object (Object/core)

An object of the class "Array".

Availability:	ECMAScript edition – 2 JavaScript – 1.1 JScript – 3.0 Internet Explorer – 4.0 Netscape – 3.0 Netscape Enterprise Server – 2.0 Opera – 3.0	
JavaScript syntax:	-	`myArray = Array`
	-	`myArray = myVBArray.toArray()`
	-	`myArray = new Array()`
	-	`myArray = new Array(aLength)`
	-	`myArray = new Array(anItem1, anItem2, anItem3, ...)`
Argument list:	`aLength`	An optional initial length to set the array to
	`anItemN`	A variable number of initial elements to insert into the array
Object properties:	`constructor, index, input, length, prototype`	
Object methods:	`concat(), join(), pop(), push(), reverse(), shift(), slice(), sort(), splice(), toLocaleString(), toSource(), toString(), unshift(), valueOf()`	

An array is basically an indexed collection of references to other objects or values.

In JavaScript version 1.0, arrays were simple objects and had limited functionality, scarcely enough really to be called arrays. Some commentators argue that the functionality was so limited that they should be flagged as available from version 1.1 of JavaScript only. They were usually simulated by creating an instance of the `Object` object and using its named properties as if the object was an array.

Much additional functionality was added for JavaScript version 1.1. JavaScript version 1.0 lacked the constructors and arrays had no special methods available. The ECMA standard enhances the functionality and Netscape 4 provides additional functionality.

An instance of the class "Array" is created by using the new operator on the `Array()` constructor. At JavaScript version 1.2, Arrays can be created with an Array literal as well. The new object adopts the behavior of the built-in prototype object through the prototype-inheritance mechanisms.

All properties and methods of the prototype are available as if they were part of the instance.

Note that the `index` and `input` properties are available only for Arrays that are produced as the result of a `RegExp` match. They are not generally available in Arrays or Collections.

An array is a collection of properties owned by an object and which can be accessed by name or by index position in the array. Because they are collected together and accessible as a set, they may be sorted into order of the array.

Array objects give special treatment to property names, which are numeric values. These are used as an index value and will affect the value of the `length` property. The length supported depends on the platform, but is usually based on a 32 bit integer being used for addressing. That limits the range to 4 billion array elements.

Array objects implement the `Put()` internal function slightly differently to non-array based objects.

The prototype for the `Array` prototype object is the `Object` prototype object.

In C language, an array is referred to as an aggregate type since it is made from a collection or aggregate of individual members.

Warnings:

❑ Although arrays were partially supported prior to JavaScript version 1.1, the support was not reliably or completely implemented. There was no way for the script developer to create and modify the arrays. Netscape 2 lacks any realistic Array support even though `Array` objects were returned by some object properties.

❑ The WebTV set top box limits the extent of the `Array` objects to contain only 32,768 elements instead of the 4 billion or so that is defined as the normal maximum. This is because WebTV uses 16 bit integers for addressing arrays rather than 32 bit integers.

Example code:

```
<SCRIPT>// Array object demonstration
var weekly_summary = new Array(7);
weekly_summary[1] = 10;
weekly_summary[2] = 25;
var day_names = new Array("Su","Mo","Tu","We","Th","Fr","Sa");
for(var i=0; i<7; i++)
{
    document.write("Summary for day (");
    document.write(day_names[i]);
    document.write(") = ");
    document.write(weekly_summary[i]);
    document.write("<BR>");
}
</SCRIPT>
```

See also:	Aggregate type, *Array index delimiter ([ ])*, Array literal, `Array()`, *Array.Class*, `Array.length`, `Array.prototype`, *Collection object*, *JavaArray object*, JellyScript, Native object, *Object object*, `String.split()`, *unwatch()*, `VBArray.toArray()`, *watch()*

Property	JavaScript	JScript	N	IE	Opera	NES	ECMA	Notes
constructor	1.1 +	3.0 +	3.0 +	4.0 +	-	-	2 +	-
index	1.2 +	5.5 +	4.0 +	5.5 +	-	-	-	-
input	1.2 +	5.5 +	4.0 +	5.5 +	-	-	-	-
length	1.0 +	3.0 +	2.0 +	4.0 +	-	-	-	ReadOnly
prototype	1.1 +	3.0 +	3.0 +	4.0 +	-	-	2 +	ReadOnly, DontDelete, DontEnum

Method	JavaScript	JScript	N	IE	Opera	NES	ECMA	Notes
concat()	1.2 +	3.0 +	4.0 +	4.0 +	-	3.0 +	3 +	Warning
join()	1.1 +	3.0 +	3.0 +	4.0 +	3.0 +	2.0 +	2 +	-
pop()	1.2 +	5.5 +	4.0 +	5.5 +	-	3.0 +	3 +	-
push()	1.2 +	5.5 +	4.0 +	5.5 +	-	3.0 +	3 +	-
reverse()	1.1 +	3.0 +	3.0 +	4.0 +	3.0 +	2.0 +	2 +	-
shift()	1.2 +	5.5 +	4.0 +	5.5 +	-	3.0 +	3 +	-
slice()	1.2 +	3.0 +	4.0 +	4.0 +	-	3.0 +	3 +	Warning
sort()	1.1 +	3.0 +	3.0 +	4.0 +	3.0 +	2.0 +	2 +	Warning
splice()	1.2 +	5.5 +	4.0 +	5.5 +	-	3.0 +	3 +	Warning
toLocale String()	1.5 +	5.5 +	6.0 +	5.5 +	-	-	3 +	Warning
toSource()	1.3 +	3.0 +	4.06 +	4.0 +	-	-	-	-
toString()	1.1 +	3.0 +	3.0 +	4.0 +	3.0 +	2.0 +	2 +	Warning
unshift()	1.2 +	5.5 +	4.0 +	5.5 +	-	3.0 +	3 +	-
valueOf()	1.1 +	3.0 +	3.0 +	4.0 +	-	-	-	-

Cross-references:

ECMA 262 edition 2 – section – 8.6.2.2

ECMA 262 edition 2 – section – 15.4

ECMA 262 edition 3 – section – 8.6.2.2

ECMA 262 edition 3 – section – 15.4

Wrox *Instant JavaScript* – page – 15

Array() (Function)

An Array object constructor.

Availability:	ECMAScript edition – 2 JavaScript – 1.1 JScript – 3.0 Internet Explorer – 4.0 Netscape – 3.0	
Property/method value type:	`Array object`	
JavaScript syntax:	-	`Array()`
	-	`Array(aLength)`
	-	`Array(anItem1, anItem2,` `anItem3, ...)`
Argument list:	`aLength`	An optional initial length for the array
	`anItemN`	A variable number of initial elements to insert into the array

Calling the `Array()` constructor as a function behaves exactly the same as if it had been called with the `new` operator.

The function call `Array()` is equivalent to the object creation expression `new Array()` with the same arguments. With other primitive objects, calling the constructor as a function carries out a type conversion instead of an object instantiation.

The arguments passed to the constructor affect the way that the array is initialized in the same way as they do with a `new Array()` expression.

See also:	*Array object*, `Array()`, `Array.prototype`, `Cast` operator, `Constructor` function, `constructor` property, Implicit conversion

Cross-references:

ECMA 262 edition 2 – section – 15.1.3.3

ECMA 262 edition 2 – section – 15.4.1

ECMA 262 edition 2 – section – 15.4.2

ECMA 262 edition 3 – section – 15.4.1

Array.Class (Property/internal)

Internal property that returns an object class.

Availability:	ECMAScript edition – 2

This is an internal property that describes the class that an `Array` object instance is a member of. The reserved words suggest that in the future, this property may be externalized.

See also:	*Array object, Class*

Property attributes:

DontEnum, Internal.

Cross-references:

ECMA 262 edition 2 – section – 8.6.2

ECMA 262 edition 2 – section – 15.4.2.1

ECMA 262 edition 3 – section – 8.6.2

ASCII (Standard)

A table of seven-bit binary numbers that encode the alphabet and other symbols.

ASCII stands for American Standard Code for Information Interchange. It describes an encoding for letters, numbers and punctuation symbols that can be realized in seven bits. It uses only 7 of the 8 bits for historical reasons to allow the eighth bit to be used for parity control when the characters are transmitted through serial interfaces.

Many of the character codes are reserved to send control signals to terminals and to manage the communications. Modern networking provides this capability outside of the character encoding.

There is an extended ASCII encoding that provides all 8 bits for character code mapping. This defines the upper 127 characters in addition to the lower 127 characters in the 7-bit representation.

There are many alternative interpretations of the ASCII character set that allow for national extensions to the character set. In some cases, this may only result in the replacement of a few currency symbols.

JavaScript uses the Unicode character set. The lower 127 characters of Unicode are purposely mapped to the ASCII character. ASCII is described here to provide help when you are exchanging data files with ASCII based systems or applications.

It may also be useful in some situations if you are using JavaScript to drive a serial interface to control some external system. Whether you could do that would depend on the hosting environment. A browser wouldn't give you those capabilities, but an embedded JavaScript interpreter in a process control system may well allow you to do that sort of thing.

This table summarizes the lower 127 characters in the ASCII character set.

Dec	Hex	Unicode	Sym	Description
000	00	\u0000	NUL	<ctrl-@> Null character
001	01	\u0001	SOH	<ctrl-A> Start of header
002	02	\u0002	STX	<ctrl-B> Start of text
003	03	\u0003	ETX	<ctrl-C> End of text
004	04	\u0004	EOT	<ctrl-D> End of transmission
005	05	\u0005	ENQ	<ctrl-E> Enquiry
006	06	\u0006	ACK	<ctrl-F> Positive acknowledgement
007	07	\u0007	BEL	<ctrl-G> Alert (bell)
008	08	\u0008	BS	<ctrl-H> Backspace
009	09	\u0009	HT	<ctrl-I> Horizontal tab
010	0A	\u000A	LF	<ctrl-J> Line feed
011	0B	\u000B	VT	<ctrl-K> Vertical tab
012	0C	\u000C	FF	<ctrl-L> Form feed
013	0D	\u000D	CR	<ctrl-M> Carriage return
014	0E	\u000E	SO	<ctrl-N> Shift out
015	0F	\u000F	SI	<ctrl-O> Shift in
016	10	\u0010	DLE	<ctrl-P> Data link escape
017	11	\u0011	DC1	<ctrl-Q> Device control 1 (XON)
018	12	\u0012	DC2	<ctrl-R> Device control 2 (tape on)
019	13	\u0013	DC3	<ctrl-S> Device control 3 (XOFF)
020	14	\u0014	DC4	<ctrl-T> Device control 4 (tape off)
021	15	\u0015	NAK	<ctrl-U> Negative acknowledgement
022	16	\u0016	SYN	<ctrl-V> Synchronous idle
023	17	\u0017	ETB	<ctrl-W> End of transmission block
024	18	\u0018	CAN	<ctrl-X> Cancel
025	19	\u0019	EM	<ctrl-Y> End of medium
026	1A	\u001A	SUB	<ctrl-Z> Substitute

Table continued on following page

Dec	Hex	Unicode	Sym	Description
027	1B	\u001B	ESC	<ctrl-[> Escape
028	1C	\u001C	FS	<ctrl-\> File separator (Form separator)
029	1D	\u001D	GS	<ctrl-]> Group separator
030	1E	\u001E	RS	<ctrl-^> Record separator
031	1F	\u001F	US	<ctrl-_> Unit separator
032	20	\u0020	SP	Space
033	21	\u0021	!	Exclamation point (bang)
034	22	\u0022	"	Double quote
035	23	\u0023	#	Hash (number sign, pound sign, sharp)
036	24	\u0024	$	Dollar sign (buck)
037	25	\u0025	%	Percent sign
038	26	\u0026	&	Ampersand
039	27	\u0027	'	Apostrophe (single quote)
040	28	\u0028	(	Left parenthesis
041	29	\u0029	)	Right parenthesis
042	2A	\u002A	*	Asterisk (star)
043	2B	\u002B	+	Plus sign
044	2C	\u002C	,	Comma
045	2D	\u002D	-	Minus sign (hyphen)
046	2E	\u002E	.	Period (full stop, dot, point)
047	2F	\u002F	/	Slash (virgule, solidus)
048	30	\u0030	0	-
049	31	\u0031	1	-
050	32	\u0032	2	-
051	33	\u0033	3	-
052	34	\u0034	4	-
053	35	\u0035	5	-
054	36	\u0036	6	-
055	37	\u0037	7	-
056	38	\u0038	8	-
057	39	\u0039	9	-
058	3A	\u003A	:	Colon
059	3B	\u003B	;	Semi-colon
060	3C	\u003C	<	Left caret (less than, left angle bracket)
061	3D	\u003D	=	Equal sign
062	3E	\u003E	>	Right caret (greater than, right angle bracket)

Dec	Hex	Unicode	Sym	Description
063	3F	\u003F	?	Question mark
064	40	\u0040	@	Commercial at sign
065	41	\u0041	A	-
066	42	\u0042	B	-
067	43	\u0043	C	-
068	44	\u0044	D	-
069	45	\u0045	E	-
070	46	\u0046	F	-
071	47	\u0047	G	-
072	48	\u0048	H	-
073	49	\u0049	I	-
074	4A	\u004A	J	-
075	4B	\u004B	K	-
076	4C	\u004C	L	-
077	4D	\u004D	M	-
078	4E	\u004E	N	-
079	4F	\u004F	O	-
080	50	\u0050	P	-
081	51	\u0051	Q	-
082	52	\u0052	R	-
083	53	\u0053	S	-
084	54	\u0054	T	-
085	55	\u0055	U	-
086	56	\u0056	V	-
087	57	\u0057	W	-
088	58	\u0058	X	-
089	59	\u0059	Y	-
090	5A	\u005A	Z	-
091	5B	\u005B	[	Left square bracket
092	5C	\u005C	\	Backslash (reverse solidus)
093	5D	\u005D	]	Right square bracket
094	5E	\u005E	^	Circumflex accent
095	5F	\u005F	_	Underscore (low line)
096	60	\u0060	`	Grave accent (back quote, back tick)
097	61	\u0061	a	-
098	62	\u0062	b	-

Table continued on following page

Dec	Hex	Unicode	Sym	Description
099	63	\u0063	c	-
100	64	\u0064	d	-
101	65	\u0065	e	-
102	66	\u0066	f	-
103	67	\u0067	g	-
104	68	\u0068	h	-
105	69	\u0069	i	-
106	6A	\u006A	j	-
107	6B	\u006B	k	-
108	6C	\u006C	l	-
109	6D	\u006D	m	-
110	6E	\u006E	n	-
111	6F	\u006F	o	-
112	70	\u0070	p	-
113	71	\u0071	q	-
114	72	\u0072	r	-
115	73	\u0073	s	-
116	74	\u0074	t	-
117	75	\u0075	u	-
118	76	\u0076	v	-
119	77	\u0077	w	-
120	78	\u0078	x	-
121	79	\u0079	y	-
122	7A	\u007A	z	-
123	7B	\u007B	{	Left brace (left curly bracket)
124	7C	\u007C	|	Verical line (bar, pipe)
125	7D	\u007D	}	Right brace (right curly bracket)
126	7E	\u007E	~	Tilde
127	7F	\u007F	DEL	Delete

See also: Character set, Character-case mapping, Control character, *Equal to (==)*, *Greater than (>)*, *Greater than or equal to (>=)*, *Identically equal to (===)*, isLower(), isUpper(), *Less than (<)*, *Less than or equal to (<=)*, *NOT Equal to (!=)*, *NOT Identically equal to (!==)*

ASP (Object model)

The object model inside an ASP server module.

As of the time of writing the ASP object model is at version 3.0 and is now shipped with Windows 2000 as part of the core OS. It is a mechanism that enhances the Microsoft IIS product to provide server side dynamically generated pages and uses JScript 5.0 as its programming language. It also supports VBScript.

Code that is executed in an ASP page is delimited with a special tag pair that does not conform to the HTML standards, but nevertheless should be ignored by browsers if the unprocessed pages ever escape out of the server.

Here is an ASP tag pair with an example fragment of code:

```
<%
Response.Write('<HR>');
%>
```

More detailed and in-depth information on ASP can be found in the Wrox ASP 3.0 Programmer's Reference.

Assign value (=) (Operator/assignment)

Assign one operand to a left value.

Availability:	ECMAScript edition – 2 JavaScript – 1.0 JScript – 1.0 Internet Explorer – 3.02 Netscape – 2.0 Netscape Enterprise Server – 2.0 Opera – 3.0	
Property/method value type:	Depends on right value	
JavaScript syntax:	-	anLValue = anExpression
Argument list:	anExpression	Some operation that yields a suitable value to assign
	anLValue	A target that can be assigned to

The expression value on the right is assigned to the target operand on the left.

The associativity is right to left.

Refer to the operator precedence topic for details of execution order.

The source expression to the right is called an RValue, the target expression to the left is called an LValue. The LValue must be capable of having something assigned to it and the RValue must evaluate to a meaningful and compatible value or a run-time exception will be thrown.

Warnings:

❑ The operand to the left of the operator must be an LValue. That is, it should be able to take an assignment and store the value.

❑ Be careful not to confuse the single equals with the double equals. Placing a double equals in place of an assignment will do a comparison without assigning the result. This is less dangerous than mistakenly assigning a value where you intended to compare for equality. The interpreter may be forgiving enough that a run-time error isn't generated, but the side effects could be subtle and make it hard to diagnose the cause.

See also:	= (Assign), Add then assign (+=), Associativity, Concatenate then assign (+=), Equal to (==), Location.assign(), LValue, Multiply then assign (*=), Operator Precedence, Reference, Remainder then assign (%=), Subtract (-), var

Cross-references:

ECMA 262 edition 2 – section – 10.1.3

ECMA 262 edition 2 – section – 11.1.2

ECMA 262 edition 2 – section – 11.13

ECMA 262 edition 2 – section – 12.2

ECMA 262 edition 3 – section – 10.1.3

ECMA 262 edition 3 – section – 11.1.2

ECMA 262 edition 3 – section – 11.13

ECMA 262 edition 3 – section – 12.2

Attr object (Object/DOM)

This is implemented in MSIE as an `Attribute` object.

Availability:	DOM level – 1 JavaScript – 1.5 JScript – 5.0 Internet Explorer – 5.0 Netscape – 6.0	
Inherits from:	*Node object*	
JavaScript syntax:	-	`myAttr = myDocument.createAttribute(aName)`
Argument list:	aName	The name of the attribute to create

The DOM level 2 standard adds an `ownerElement` property to the `Attr` object specification. This is not yet supported in browsers.

See also:	*Attribute object,* `Document.createAttribute()`

Inheritance chain:

Node object

Attribute object (Object/DOM)

A DOM object that represents an HTML tag attribute.

Availability:	DOM level – 1 JavaScript – 1.5 JScript – 5.0 Internet Explorer – 5.0 Netscape – 6.0	
Inherits from:	*Node object*	
JavaScript syntax:	-	`myAttribute = myAttributes.` `aPropertyName`
	-	`myAttribute = myAttributes` `[anIndex]`
	-	`myAttribute = myAttributes` `[aName]`
	-	`myAttribute = myDocument.` `createAttribute(aName)`
Argument list:	`aPropertyName`	The name of the tag attribute
	`aName`	An attribute name
	`anIndex`	A valid numeric reference to an element in the collection
Object properties:	`name, nodeName, nodeType, nodeValue, specified, value`	

This is used by the browser to maintain property values for HTML tag instantiated objects.

This object represents a single HTML tag attribute. The properties of this object indicate whether the tag attribute has been specified or not, and if it has, what the current value is.

The `Element` object should contain enough information for you to be able to determine the instantiating source tag name. The attributes can be inspected with a script and the complete source HTML reconstructed from a combination of the information supplied by the element and its associated `attributes` collection.

47

The `attributes` collection that belongs to an object also tells you what the expected complete set of attributes are for the tag, although this may not be completely reliable.

The example script demonstrates how you can make an `Attribute` object inspector with a fragment of JavaScript. These inspectors can be put into a library and called in for debugging when you are experiencing problems.

Note that the example below does not work on Netscape 6.0 due to the use of the `all` property.

Example code:

```
<HTML>
<HEAD>
</HEAD>
<BODY alink=red>
<SCRIPT>
// An example attributes object inspector
myAttributeObject = document.all[3].attributes.aLink;
displayAttributes("BODY alink", myAttributeObject);

// Display attributes object
function displayAttributes(aTitle, anObject)
{
    document.write("<H3>");
    document.write(aTitle);
    document.write("</H3>");
    document.write("<TABLE BORDER=1 CELLPADDING=2><TR>");
    document.write("<TH>Description</TH>");
    document.write("<TH>Property</TH>");
    document.write("<TH>Value</TH></TR>");
    displayTableLine("Tag attribute name:", "name", anObject.name);
    displayTableLine("Tag attribute value:", "value",
anObject.value);
    displayTableLine("DOM node name:", "nodeName",
anObject.nodeName);
    displayTableLine("DOM node type:", "nodeType",
anObject.nodeType);
    displayTableLine("DOM node value:", "nodeValue",
anObject.nodeValue);
    displayTableLine("Specified flag:", "specified",
anObject.specified);
    document.write("</TABLE>");
}

// Display a table line
function displayTableLine(aDescription, aProperty, aValue)
{
    document.write("<TR><TH ALIGN=LEFT>");
    document.write(aDescription);
    document.write("</TH><TD>");
    document.write(aProperty);
    document.write("</TD><TD>");
    document.write(aValue);
    document.write("</TD></TR>");
}
</SCRIPT>
</BODY>
</HTML>
```

See also:	*Attr object*, *Attributes object*, Document.createAttribute(), Element.getAttributeNode(), Element.removeAttribute(), Element.removeAttributeNode(), Element.setAttributeNode(), *HasProperty()*, HTML tag attribute, MutationEvent.attrChange, MutationEvent.attrName

Property	JavaScript	JScript	N	IE	Opera	DOM	Notes
name	1.5 +	5.0 +	6.0 +	5.0 +	-	1 +	ReadOnly
nodeName	1.5 +	5.0 +	6.0 +	5.0 +	-	1 +	-
nodeType	1.5 +	5.0 +	6.0 +	5.0 +	-	1 +	-
nodeValue	1.5 +	5.0 +	6.0 +	5.0 +	-	1 +	-
specified	1.5 +	5.0 +	6.0 +	5.0 +	-	1 +	ReadOnly
value	1.5 +	5.0 +	6.0 +	5.0 +	-	1 +	-

Inheritance chain:

Node object

Attributes object (Object/DOM)

A sub-class of the Array object that contains a set of Element object attributes. This is a collection of all attribute objects that apply to an element.

Availability:	DOM level – 1 JavaScript – 1.5 JScript – 5.0 Internet Explorer – 5.0 Netscape – 6.0
JavaScript syntax:	- myAttributes = myElement.attributes
Object properties:	length

The Attributes array object is associated with an Element object as a container for a set of Attribute objects each of which relates to a property of the Element object. This is the correct implementation of the DOM specified Attr object class.

Not all Element object properties have an Attribute object, but those that do have related HTML tag attributes. Thus the Attributes array corresponds to the HTML tag attributes for a tag.

The Attributes array has a length property and a named property for each Element object tag attribute.

Properties are reserved to support event handlers and other tag attributes and so from the `Attributes` array for a particular `Element` object, you can establish what the supported features are for the HTML tag it represents. This means that the `length` property will vary from object to object.

The `Attributes` array seems to contain some properties that correspond to the imaginary HTML generic `Element` class. Although this is not really a genuine object class, it is a convenient way of documenting HTML object behaviors where they are common across a range of objects. The `Attributes` array does not support a complete set of properties that correspond to the `Element` class and therefore it is not true to say it is inherited from that class.

The example script shows how you can inspect the attributes of an object. In this example, the attributes of a `<BODY>` tag are exposed. Because they are enumerable, you can determine what properties and what events the object instantiated by the `<BODY>` tag can respond to. Note that the example does not work on Netscape 6.0 due to the use of the `all` property.

Example code:

```
<HTML>
<HEAD></HEAD>
<BODY alink=red vlink="blue" leftmargin="100">
<TABLE BORDER=1 CELLPADDING=2>
<SCRIPT>
myAttributesObject = document.all[3].attributes;
displayTableLine("Object class:", myAttributesObject, "");
displayTableLine("Number of attributes:", myAttributesObject.length,
"");
for(myEnumerator=0; myEnumerator<myAttributesObject.length;
myEnumerator++)
{
    myAttrib = myAttributesObject[myEnumerator];
    displayTableLine("Attribute ("+myAttrib.nodeName+"):",
myAttrib.specified, myAttrib.nodeValue);
}

// Output one line of a table
function displayTableLine(aHeading, aFlag, aValue)
{
    document.write("<TR>");
    document.write("<TH ALIGN=LEFT>");
    document.write(aHeading);
    document.write("</TH>");
    document.write("<TD>");
    document.write(aFlag);
    document.write("</TD>");
    document.write("<TD>");
    document.write(aValue);
    document.write("</TD>");
    document.write("</TR>");
}
</SCRIPT>
</TABLE>
</BODY>
</HTML>
```

See also:	*Attribute object*, `Attributes.length`, *Collection object, Element object,* `Element.attributes[]`, `Element.removeAttribute()`, *HasProperty(), HTML object,* HTML tag attribute

Property	JavaScript	JScript	N	IE	Opera	DOM	Notes
`length`	1.5 +	5.0 +	6.0 +	5.0 +	-	1 +	ReadOnly

ATVEF (Standard)

Advanced Television Enhancement Forum.

This extract from the ATVEF standard describes in outline the aims and scope of this web and TV convergence project. You should consult the specification for a complete description of how this is to be accomplished. There are several manufacturers already building and deploying these systems on a variety of broadcast mediums.

The Advanced Television Enhancement Forum (ATVEF) is a group of people from the broadcast TV and Internet industries who are working to specify a single public standard for delivering interactive television experiences. The intention is that these should be authored once using a variety of tools and deployed to a range of television, set-top, and PC-based receivers.

The Enhanced Content Specification defines the fundamental requirements that are necessary to enable creation of HTML-enhanced television content. This goes beyond normal Internet based delivery to describe how it can be reliably broadcast across any network to any compliant receiver. Because the broadcast requires that there is no bidirectional link, some changes to the delivery protocols are outlined.

The ATVEF specification for enhanced television programming uses existing Internet technologies. It describes how to deliver enhanced TV programming over both analog and digital video systems using terrestrial, cable, satellite and Internet networks. The specification can be used in both one-way broadcast and two-way video systems, and is designed to be compatible with all international standards for both analog and digital video systems.

See also:	Interpret, Liberate TV Navigator, Microsoft TV, URL, WebTV

Web-references:

http://atvef.com/library/spec1_1a.html

AuthentiCode (Security related)

This is a security model that applies digital signatures to ActiveX objects in MSIE.

Warnings:

❑   This technique does not currently support signed scripts in MSIE and only applies to ActiveX objects.

See also: Security policy, *Signed scripts*

about: URL (Request method)
AbstractView object (Object/DOM)
ActiveXObject object (Object/JScript)
Add (+) (Operator/additive)
Add then assign (+=) (Operator/
assignment)

Background object (Object/browser)

A background image object associated with a Netscape Nigator layer.

Availability:	JavaScript – 1.2 Netscape – 4.0	
JavaScript syntax:	N	*myBackground = myLayer*.background
Object properties:	src	

This object is used with a layer in Netscape Navigator and its properties correspond with properties of the Image object in Netscape Navigator.

See also:	Background.src, *BODY object, Image object,* Layer.background

Property	JavaScript	JScript	N	IE	Opera	HTML	Notes
src	1.2 +	-	4.0 +	-	-	-	-

Backquote (`) (External code call)

Call some external code during server-side execution.

The back-quote substitutions operate much like you may have seen them work in command line shells and Perl interpreters. The text enclosed inside the back-quotes is parsed out from the HTML and is then executed as JavaScript.

ASP provides a means of substituting the output of JavaScript code into a block enclosed in <%...%> markers which does a similar thing.

This allows us to include fragments of JavaScript into an HTML page and expect them to be parsed server-side.

This is somewhat analogous to JavaScript entities but they operate at the client-side.

The server-side example wraps its result inside quote symbols so that the HTML tag attribute syntax is preserved intact.

Example code:

```
<HTML>
<BODY>
<FORM>
<INPUT TYPE="text" VALUE=`server.hostname;`>
</FORM>
</BODY>
</HTML>
```

See also:	*JavaScript entity*, Netscape Enterprise Server

Bar object (Object/Navigator)

An object used to hold properties for toolbars, location bars etc.

Availability:	JavaScript – 1.2 Netscape – 4.0	
JavaScript syntax:	N	`myBar = locationbar`
	N	`myBar = menubar`
	N	`myBar = myWindow.locationbar`
	N	`myBar = myWindow.menubar`
	N	`myBar = myWindow.personalbar`
	N	`myBar = myWindow.scrollbars`
	N	`myBar = myWindow.statusbar`
	N	`myBar = myWindow.toolbar`
	N	`myBar = personalbar`
	N	`myBar = scrollbars`
	N	`myBar = statusbar`
	N	`myBar = toolbar`
Object properties:	`visible`	

This object is used to represent various items of window furniture (otherwise called chrome or adornments) in Netscape Navigator. It isn't supported by MSIE although the control facilities it offers are available when a new window is created with the `window.open()` method.

It only has one usable property. That is the visible property, which can be set to a Boolean value. Some early documentation referred to this as the visibility property but that is the wrong property name.

See also:	Bar.visible, Window.locationbar, Window.menubar, Window.personalbar, Window.scrollbars, Window.statusbar, Window.toolbar

Property	JavaScript	JScript	N	IE	Opera	Notes
visible	1.2 +	-	4.0 +	-	-	-

Bar.visibility (Pitfall)

An erroneous name for the visible property of a Bar object.

Warnings:

❑ Some reference works refer to the visibility property of the Bar object, possibly due to early prototype versions of the Netscape browser or in an attempt to document forthcoming features of the browser. In between publishing and release of the browser, the property changed its name to the visible property.

❑ You may even then have some difficulty in getting it to work on some platforms but you do need to make sure you are trying to set the correct property value when changing the visibility of Bar objects.

See also:	Bar.visible

BASE object (Object/HTML)

Represents the <BASE> HTML tag that describes a base URL for the document.

Availability:	DOM level – 1 JavaScript – 1.5 JScript – 3.0 Internet Explorer – 4.0 Netscape – 6.0
Inherits from:	*Element object*

JavaScript syntax:	IE	`myBASE = myDocument.all.anElementID`
	IE	`myBASE = myDocument.all.tags("BASE")` `[anIndex]`
	IE	`myBASE = myDocument.all[aName]`
	-	`myBASE = myDocument.getElementById` `(anElementID)`
	-	`myBASE = myDocument.getElementsByName` `(aName)[anIndex]`
	-	`myBASE = myDocument` `.getElementsByTagName("BASE")[anIndex]`

HTML syntax:	`<BASE>`	
Argument list:	`anIndex`	A valid reference to an item in the collection
	`aName`	The name attribute of an element
	`anElementID`	The ID attribute of an element

Object properties:	`href, target`

Event handlers:	`onClick, onDblClick, onHelp, onKeyDown,`
	`onKeyPress, onKeyUp, onMouseDown,`
	`onMouseMove, onMouseOut, onMouseOver,`
	`onMouseUp`

The `<BASE>` tag must appear inside the `<HEAD>` block of a document and is used to define a base URL for the document; this can be useful if the document is not served from the same server that subsequent pages need to be served from.

See also:	*Element object*

Property	JavaScript	JScript	N	IE	Opera	DOM	HTML	Notes
`href`	1.5 +	3.0 +	6.0 +	4.0 +	-	1 +	-	-
`target`	1.5 +	3.0 +	6.0 +	4.0 +	-	1 +	-	-

Event name	JavaScript	JScript	N	IE	Opera	DOM	HTML	Notes
`onClick`	1.5 +	3.0 +	6.0 +	4.0 +	-	-	4.0 +	Warning
`onDblClick`	1.5 +	3.0 +	6.0 +	4.0 +	-	-	4.0 +	Warning
`onHelp`	-	3.0 +	-	4.0 +	-	-	-	Warning
`onKeyDown`	1.5 +	3.0 +	6.0 +	4.0 +	-	-	4.0 +	Warning

Event name	JavaScript	JScript	N	IE	Opera	DOM	HTML	Notes
onKeyPress	1.5 +	3.0 +	6.0 +	4.0 +	-	-	4.0 +	Warning
onKeyUp	1.5 +	3.0 +	6.0 +	4.0 +	-	-	4.0 +	Warning
onMouse Down	1.5 +	3.0 +	6.0 +	4.0 +	-	-	4.0 +	Warning
onMouse Move	1.5 +	3.0 +	6.0 +	4.0 +	-	-	4.0 +	Warning
onMouseOut	1.5 +	3.0 +	6.0 +	4.0 +	-	-	4.0 +	Warning
onMouse Over	1.5 +	3.0 +	6.0 +	4.0 +	-	-	4.0 +	Warning
onMouseUp	1.5 +	3.0 +	6.0 +	4.0 +	-	-	4.0 +	Warning

Inheritance chain:

Element object, Node object

BASEFONT object (Object/HTML)

A <BASEFONT> HTML tag is represented by this object and defines some generic font information to be used as a default in this page.

Availability:	DOM level – 1 JavaScript – 1.5 JScript – 3.0 Internet Explorer – 4.0 Netscape – 6.0	
Inherits from:	*Element object*	
JavaScript syntax:	IE	myBASEFONT = myDocument.all.anElementID
	IE	myBASEFONT = myDocument.all.tags ("BASEFONT") [anIndex]
	IE	myBASEFONT = myDocument.all[aName]
	-	myBASEFONT = myDocument.getElementById(anElementID)
	-	myBASEFONT = myDocument.getElements ByName(aName)[anIndex]
	-	myBASEFONT = myDocument.getElements ByTagName("BASEFONT")[anIndex]
HTML syntax:	<BASEFONT>	
Argument list:	anIndex	A valid reference to an item in the collection
	aName	The name attribute of an element
	anElementID	The ID attribute of an element

Object properties:	color, face, size
Object methods:	getAttribute()
Event handlers:	onClick, onDblClick, onHelp, onKeyDown, onKeyPress, onKeyUp, onMouseDown, onMouseMove, onMouseOut, onMouseOver, onMouseUp

Historically web developers will have used the <FONT> tag to set the attributes of blocks of text. Latterly, they will be using style sheets to control this.

The <BASEFONT> tag provides a way to set the font presentation style from the position of this tag to the end of the document unless overridden by further <BASEFONT> tags or <FONT> settings.

See also:	Element object

Property	JavaScript	JScript	N	IE	Opera	DOM	HTML	Notes
color	1.5 +	3.0 +	6.0 +	4.0 +	-	1 +	-	-
face	1.5 +	3.0 +	6.0 +	4.0 +	-	1 +	-	-
size	1.5 +	3.0 +	6.0 +	4.0 +	-	1 +	-	-

Method	JavaScript	JScript	N	IE	Opera	DOM	HTML	Notes
getAttribute()	1.5 +	3.0 +	6.0 +	4.0 +	-	1 +	-	-

Event name	JavaScript	JScript	N	IE	Opera	DOM	HTML	Notes
onClick	1.5 +	3.0 +	6.0 +	4.0 +	-	-	4.0 +	Warning
onDblClick	1.5 +	3.0 +	6.0 +	4.0 +	-	-	4.0 +	Warning
onHelp	-	3.0 +	-	4.0 +	-	-	-	Warning
onKeyDown	1.5 +	3.0 +	6.0 +	4.0 +	-	-	4.0 +	Warning
onKeyPress	1.5 +	3.0 +	6.0 +	4.0 +	-	-	4.0 +	Warning
onKeyUp	1.5 +	3.0 +	6.0 +	4.0 +	-	-	4.0 +	Warning
onMouseDown	1.5 +	3.0 +	6.0 +	4.0 +	-	-	4.0 +	Warning
onMouseMove	1.5 +	3.0 +	6.0 +	4.0 +	-	-	4.0 +	Warning
onMouseOut	1.5 +	3.0 +	6.0 +	4.0 +	-	-	4.0 +	Warning
onMouseOver	1.5 +	3.0 +	6.0 +	4.0 +	-	-	4.0 +	Warning
onMouseUp	1.5 +	3.0 +	6.0 +	4.0 +	-	-	4.0 +	Warning

Inheritance chain:

Element object, Node object

BDO object (Object/HTML)

An object representing the <BDO> HTML tag for supporting bidirectional text algorithms.

Availability:	JScript – 5.0
	Internet Explorer – 5.0
Inherits from:	*Element object*
JavaScript syntax:	IE *myBDO = myDocument.all.anElementID*
	IE *myBDO = myDocument.all.tags("BDO")* *[anIndex]*
	IE *myBDO = myDocument.all[aName]*
	- *myBDO = myDocument.getElementById (anElementID)*
	- *myBDO = myDocument.getElementsByName (aName)[anIndex]*
	- *myBDO = myDocument .getElementsByTagName("BDO")[anIndex]*
HTML syntax:	<BDO>...</BDO>
Argument list:	*anIndex* A valid reference to an item in the collection
	aName The name attribute of an element
	anElementID The ID attribute of an element
Object properties:	dir
Event handlers:	onClick, onDblClick, onHelp, onKeyDown, onKeyPress, onKeyUp, onMouseDown, onMouseMove, onMouseOut, onMouseOver, onMouseUp

This is the Bi-Directional Override object. The LANG and DIR attributes of HTML tags in the document will cover most eventualities but there may be times when you need to explicitly override the direction of text flow.

Usage of this is likely to be confined to scripts that operate in multiple language environments and on pages containing text in more than one international language.

See also:	*Element object*

Property	JavaScript	JScript	N	IE	Opera	DOM	HTML	Notes
dir	-	5.0 +	-	5.0 +	-	-	-	-

Event name	JavaScript	JScript	N	IE	Opera	DOM	HTML	Notes
onClick	-	5.0 +	-	5.0 +	-	-	4.0 +	Warning
onDblClick	-	5.0 +	-	5.0 +	-	-	4.0 +	Warning
onHelp	-	5.0 +	-	5.0 +	-	-	-	Warning
onKeyDown	-	5.0 +	-	5.0 +	-	-	4.0 +	Warning
onKeyPress	-	5.0 +	-	5.0 +	-	-	4.0 +	Warning
onKeyUp	-	5.0 +	-	5.0 +	-	-	4.0 +	Warning
onMouseDown	-	5.0 +	-	5.0 +	-	-	4.0 +	Warning
onMouseMove	-	5.0 +	-	5.0 +	-	-	4.0 +	Warning
onMouseOut	-	5.0 +	-	5.0 +	-	-	4.0 +	Warning
onMouseOver	-	5.0 +	-	5.0 +	-	-	4.0 +	Warning
onMouseUp	-	5.0 +	-	5.0 +	-	-	4.0 +	Warning

Inheritance chain:

Element object, Node object

BGSOUND object (Object/HTML)

An object representing a <BGSOUND> HTML tag that defines an audio track to play while the page is displayed.

Availability:	JScript – 3.0 Internet Explorer – 4.0 (as HTML in IE 3.0)	
Inherits from:	*Element object*	
JavaScript syntax:	IE	myBGSOUND = myDocument.all.anElementID
	IE	myBGSOUND = myDocument.all.tags ("BGSOUND")[anIndex]
	IE	myBGSOUND = myDocument.all[aName]
	-	myBGSOUND = myDocument.getElementById (anElementID)
	-	myBGSOUND = myDocument .getElementsByName(aName)[anIndex]
	-	myBGSOUND = myDocument.getElementsBy TagName("BGSOUND")[anIndex]
HTML syntax:	<BGSOUND>	
Argument list:	anIndex	A valid reference to an item in the collection
	aName	The name attribute of an element
	anElementID	The ID attribute of an element
Object properties:	balance, loop, src, volume	
Event handlers:	onClick, onDblClick, onHelp, onKeyDown, onKeyPress, onKeyUp, onMouseDown, onMouseMove, onMouseOut, onMouseOver, onMouseUp	

This object is instantiated by the <BGSOUND> HTML tag and represents a sound effect that is to be played in the background. As the BGSOUND object is created during document loading and requires that a sound file be downloaded, there may be some noticeable delay before the sound starts to play.

See also:	Element object

Property	JavaScript	JScript	N	IE	Opera	DOM	HTML	Notes
balance	-	3.0 +	-	4.0 +	-	-	-	ReadOnly
loop	-	3.0 +	-	4.0 +	-	-	-	-
src	-	3.0 +	-	4.0 +	-	-	-	-
volume	-	3.0 +	-	4.0 +	-	-	-	ReadOnly

Event name	JavaScript	JScript	N	IE	Opera	DOM	HTML	Notes
onClick	-	3.0 +	-	4.0 +	-	-	4.0 +	Warning
onDblClick	-	3.0 +	-	4.0 +	-	-	4.0 +	Warning
onHelp	-	3.0 +	-	4.0 +	-	-	-	Warning
onKeyDown	-	3.0 +	-	4.0 +	-	-	4.0 +	Warning
onKeyPress	-	3.0 +	-	4.0 +	-	-	4.0 +	Warning
onKeyUp	-	3.0 +	-	4.0 +	-	-	4.0 +	Warning
onMouseDown	-	3.0 +	-	4.0 +	-	-	4.0 +	Warning
onMouseMove	-	3.0 +	-	4.0 +	-	-	4.0 +	Warning
onMouseOut	-	3.0 +	-	4.0 +	-	-	4.0 +	Warning
onMouseOver	-	3.0 +	-	4.0 +	-	-	4.0 +	Warning
onMouseUp	-	3.0 +	-	4.0 +	-	-	4.0 +	Warning

Inheritance chain:

Element object, Node object

Bitwise AND (&) (Operator/bitwise)

Bitwise AND of two operands.

Availability:	ECMAScript edition – 2 JavaScript – 1.0 JScript – 1.0 Internet Explorer – 3.02 Netscape – 2.0 Netscape Enterprise Server – 2.0 Opera – 3.0
Property/method value type:	Number primitive

JavaScript syntax:	-	*anOperand1* & *anOperand2*
Argument list:	*anOperand1*	A binary bit pattern
-	*anOperand2*	Another binary bit pattern

The result is the bitwise AND of both binary bit pattern values.

This operator performs a bit by bit AND of the 32-bit value derived from both operands. Effectively, each corresponding bit pair has a logical AND applied to it.

The truth table shows the result of this operator for two Boolean primitive values:

A	B	AND
false	false	false
false	true	false
true	false	false
true	true	true

Where a corresponding bit is 1 in both values, a 1 bit is inserted into the result otherwise the value is zero.

The associativity is left to right.

Refer to the operator precedence topic for details of execution order.

Example code:

```
<HTML>
<HEAD></HEAD>
<BODY>
<SCRIPT>
myValue1 = 0xFFFF;
myValue2 = 0xFF00;
myValue3 = myValue1 & myValue2;
document.write("Val 1 : " + binary32(myValue1) + "<BR>");
document.write("Val 2 : " + binary32(myValue2) + "<BR>");
document.write("AND : " + binary32(myValue3) + "<BR>");
// Binary convertor (ignore sign bit on MSIE)
function binary32(aValue)
{
myArray = new Array(32);

for(myEnum=0; myEnum<32; myEnum++)
{
if(aValue & Math.pow(2, myEnum))
    {
      myArray[31-myEnum] = "1";
    }
```

```
        else
        {
           myArray[31-myEnum] = "0";
        }
   }
   return myArray.join("");
}
</SCRIPT>
</BODY>
</HTML>
```

See also: Associativity, Binary bitwise operator, Bit-field, *Bitwise AND then assign (&=)*, Bitwise expression, Bitwise operator, *Logical AND (&&)*, Operator Precedence

Cross-references:

ECMA 262 edition 2 – section – 11.10

ECMA 262 edition 2 – section – 11.13

ECMA 262 edition 3 – section – 11.10

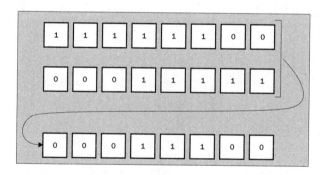

Bitwise AND then assign (&=) (Operator/assignment)

Bitwise AND two operands and assign the result to the first.

Availability:	ECMAScript edition – 2
	JavaScript – 1.0
	JScript – 1.0
	Internet Explorer – 3.02
	Netscape – 2.0
	Netscape Enterprise Server – 2.0
	Opera – 3.0

Property/method value type:	Number primitive
JavaScript syntax:	- anOperand1 &= anOperand2
Argument list:	anOperand1 A binary value
	anOperand2 Another binary value

Bitwise AND the right operand with the left operand and assign the result to the left operand.

This is functionally equivalent to the expression:

anOperand1 = anOperand1 & anOperand2;

Although this is classified as an assignment operator it is really a compound of an assignment and a bitwise operator.

The associativity is right to left.

Refer to the operator precedence topic for details of execution order.

The new value of anOperand1 is returned as a result of the expression.

The truth table shows the result of this operator for two Boolean primitive values:

A	B	AND
false	false	false
false	true	false
true	false	false
true	true	true

This is applied to each corresponding bit pair in the two values.

Warnings:

❏ The operand to the left of the operator must be an LValue. That is, it should be able to take an assignment and store the value.

See also:	Assignment operator, Associativity, Bit-field, *Bitwise AND (&)*, Bitwise expression, Bitwise operator, *Logical AND (&&)*, LValue, Operator Precedence

Cross-references:

ECMA 262 edition 2 – section – 11.13

ECMA 262 edition 3 – section – 11.13

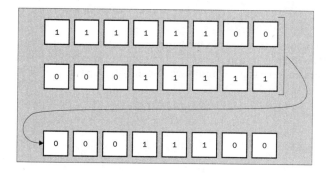

Bitwise NOT - complement (~) (Operator/bitwise)

Bitwise NOT of one operand.

Availability:	ECMAScript edition – 2	
	JavaScript – 1.0	
	JScript – 1.0	
	Internet Explorer – 3.02	
	Netscape – 2.0	
	Netscape Enterprise Server – 2.0	
	Opera – 3.0	
Property/method value type:	Number primitive	
JavaScript syntax:	-	~anOperand
Argument list:	anOperand	A numerical value

The operand is evaluated and then converted to a 32-bit integer value. Every bit is complemented and the result is a bitwise NOT.

The truth table shows the result of this operator for a Boolean primitive value:

A	NOT
false	true
true	false

This operation is applied to each individual bit in the operand, inverting them one by one.

Note that this could be classified as a unary operator but here we have called it a bitwise operator on account of its functionality rather than its placement.

The associativity is right to left.

Refer to the operator precedence topic for details of execution order.

67

Warnings:

❑ There are some deficiencies in the handling of bitwise operators in the MSIE 5.0 browser on the Macintosh platform. It does not properly handle the sign bit and so you should observe some caution when using this operator.

Example code:

```
<HTML>
<HEAD></HEAD>
<BODY>
<SCRIPT>

myValue1 = 0xFFFF;
myValue2 = ~myValue1
document.write("Val 1 : " + binary32(myValue1) + "<BR>");
document.write("NOT : " + binary32(myValue2) + "<BR>");
// Binary convertor (ignore sign bit on MSIE)
function binary32(aValue)
{
  myArray = new Array(32);

  for(myEnum=0; myEnum<32; myEnum++)
  {
    if(aValue & Math.pow(2, myEnum))
    {
      myArray[31-myEnum] = "1";
    }
    else
    {
      myArray[31-myEnum] = "0";
    }
  }
  return myArray.join("");
}

</SCRIPT>
</BODY>
</HTML>
```

See also:	Associativity, Bit-field, *Logical NOT – complement (!)*, Operator Precedence, Unary operator

Cross-references:

ECMA 262 edition 2 – section – 11.4.8

ECMA 262 edition 3 – section – 11.4.8

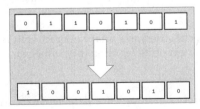

Bitwise OR (|) (Operator/bitwise)

Bitwise OR of two operands.

Availability:	ECMAScript edition – 2 JavaScript – 1.0 JScript – 1.0 Internet Explorer – 3.02 Netscape – 2.0 Netscape Enterprise Server – 2.0 Opera – 3.0	
Property/method value type:	Number primitive	
JavaScript syntax:	-	*anOperand1* | *anOperand2*
Argument list:	*anOperand1*	A numeric value
-	*anOperand2*	Another numeric value

Performs a bit by bit OR of the 32-bit value derived from both operands.

Where a corresponding bit is 1 in either of the two operands, a 1 is inserted into the result. A zero is inserted only when neither operand has a 1 bit at that position.

The associativity is left to right.

Refer to the operator precedence topic for details of execution order.

The truth table shows the result of this operator for two Boolean primitive values:

A	B	OR
false	false	false
false	true	true
true	false	true
true	true	true

This is applied to each corresponding bit pair in the operands.

Example code:

```
<HTML>
<HEAD></HEAD>
<BODY>
<SCRIPT>
myValue1 = 0x00FF;
myValue2 = 0xFF00;
```

69

```
myValue3 = myValue1 | myValue2;
document.write("Val 1 : " + binary32(myValue1) + "<BR>");
document.write("Val 2 : " + binary32(myValue2) + "<BR>");
document.write("OR : " + binary32(myValue3) + "<BR>");
// Binary convertor (ignore sign bit on MSIE)
function binary32(aValue)
{
  myArray = new Array(32);

  for(myEnum=0; myEnum<32; myEnum++)
  {
    if(aValue & Math.pow(2, myEnum))
    {
      myArray[31-myEnum] = "1";
    }
    else
    {
      myArray[31-myEnum] = "0";
    }
  }
  return myArray.join("");
}
</SCRIPT>
</BODY>
</HTML>
```

See also: Associativity, Binary bitwise operator, Bit-field, *Bitwise OR then assign (|=)*, Operator Precedence

Cross-references:

ECMA 262 edition 2 – section – 11.10

ECMA 262 edition 3 – section – 11.10

Bitwise OR then assign (|=) (Operator/assignment)

Bitwise OR two operands and assign the result to the first.

Availability: ECMAScript edition – 2
JavaScript – 1.0
JScript – 1.0
Internet Explorer – 3.02
Netscape – 2.0
Netscape Enterprise Server – 2.0
Opera – 3.0

Property/method value type:	Number primitive	
JavaScript syntax:	-	anOperand1 |= anOperand2
Argument list:	anOperand1	A numeric value that can be assigned to
-	anOperand2	Another numeric value

Bitwise OR the right operand with the left operand and assign the result to the left operand.

This is functionally equivalent to the expression:

anOperand1 = anOperand1 | anOperand2;

Performs a bit by bit OR of the 32-bit value derived from both operands.

Where a corresponding bit is 1 in either of the two operands, a 1 is inserted into the result. A zero is inserted only when neither operand has a 1 bit at that position.

Although this is classified as an assignment operator it is really a compound of an assignment and a bitwise operator.

The associativity is right to left.

Refer to the operator precedence topic for details of execution order.

The new value of anOperand1 is returned as a result of the expression.

The truth table shows the result of this operator for two Boolean primitive values:

A	B	OR
false	false	false
false	true	true
true	false	true
true	true	true

This is applied to each corresponding bit pair in the operands.

Warnings:

❑ The operand to the left of the operator must be an LValue. That is, it should be able to take an assignment and store the value.

See also:	Assignment operator, Associativity, Bit-field, Bitwise operator, *Bitwise OR (	)*, LValue, Operator Precedence

Cross-references:

ECMA 262 edition 2 – section – 11.13

ECMA 262 edition 3 – section – 11.13

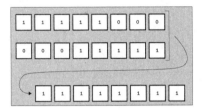

Bitwise shift left (<<) (Operator/bitwise)

Bitwise shift leftwards one operand according to another.

Availability:	ECMAScript edition – 2 JavaScript – 1.0 JScript – 1.0 Internet Explorer – 3.02 Netscape – 2.0 Netscape Enterprise Server – 2.0 Opera – 3.0	
Property/method value type:	Number primitive	
JavaScript syntax:	-	anOperand1 < anOperand2
Argument list:	anOperand1	A value to be shifted
-	anOperand2	A distance to shift anOperand1

The bitwise shift left operator converts its left operand to a 32 bit integer and moves it leftwards by the number of bits indicated by the right operand.

As the value is shifted leftwards, bits that roll out of the left end of the register are discarded. The right hand end of the register is filled with zero bits. Shifting leftwards by 32 bits will fill the buffer with all zero bits.

Because the value is converted to an integer, any fractional part is discarded as the shift begins.

The right hand operand is converted to a 5 bit value with a bitwise mask to limit the distance of the shift to 32 bits. This can cause unexpected results if the right hand side is derived from an expression that may yield a value larger than 32.

The associativity is left to right.

Refer to the operator precedence topic for details of execution order.

You can accomplish bitwise shift lefts by multiplying values using powers of 2. Multiplying a value by 2 shifts leftwards by one bit position.

Example code:

```
<HTML>
<HEAD></HEAD>
<BODY>
<SCRIPT>
myValue1 = 0x00FF;
myValue2 = myValue1 < 4;
document.write("Val 1 : " + binary32(myValue1) + "<BR>");
document.write("Result : " + binary32(myValue2) + "<BR>");
// Binary convertor (ignore sign bit on MSIE)
function binary32(aValue)
{
    myArray = new Array(32);

    for(myEnum=0; myEnum<32; myEnum++)
    {
        if(aValue & Math.pow(2, myEnum))
        {
            myArray[31-myEnum] = "1";
        }
        else
        {
            myArray[31-myEnum] = "0";
        }
    }
    return myArray.join("");
}
</SCRIPT>
</BODY>
</HTML>
```

See also:	Associativity, Bit-field, *Bitwise shift left then assign (<<=)*, Bitwise shift operator, *Bitwise shift right (>>)*, *Bitwise shift right and assign (>>=)*, *Bitwise unsigned shift right (>>>)*, *Bitwise unsigned shift right and assign (>>>=)*, Operator Precedence, Shift operator

Cross-references:

ECMA 262 edition 2 – section – 11.7.1

ECMA 262 edition 3 – section – 11.7.1

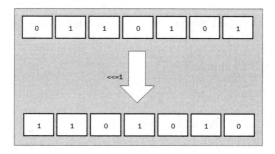

Bitwise shift left then assign (<<=) (Operator/assignment)

Destructively bitwise leftwards shift the first of two operands.

Availability:	ECMAScript edition – 2 JavaScript – 1.0 JScript – 1.0 Internet Explorer – 3.02 Netscape – 2.0 Netscape Enterprise Server – 2.0 Opera browser – 3.0
Property/method value type:	`Number primitive`
JavaScript syntax:	-	`anOperand1 <<= anOperand2`
Argument list:	`anOperand1`	A value to be shifted and assigned to
	`anOperand2`	A distance to shift `anOperand1`

Bitwise shift leftwards the left operand by the number of bits in the right operand and assign the result to the left operand.

This is functionally equivalent to the expression:

`anOperand1 = anOperand1 << anOperand2;`

The bitwise shift left operator converts its left operand to a 32 bit integer and moves it leftwards by the number of bits indicated by the right operand.

As the value is shifted leftwards, bits that roll out of the left end of the register are discarded. The right hand end of the register is filled with zero bits. Shifting leftwards by 32 bits will fill the buffer with all zero bits.

Because the value is converted to an integer, any fractional part is discarded as the shift begins.

The right hand operand is converted to a 5 bit value with a bitwise mask to limit the distance of the shift to 32 bits. This can cause unexpected results if the right hand side is derived from an expression that may yield a value larger than 32.

Although this is classified as an assignment operator it is really a compound of an assignment and a bitwise operator.

The associativity is right to left.

Refer to the operator precedence topic for details of execution order.

The new value of `anOperand1` is returned as a result of the expression.

74

Warnings:

❑ The operand to the left of the operator must be an LValue. That is, it should be able to take an assignment and store the value.

See also:	Assignment operator, Associativity, Bit-field, Bitwise operator, *Bitwise shift left (<<)*, Bitwise shift operator, *Bitwise shift right (>>)*, *Bitwise shift right and assign (>>=)*, *Bitwise unsigned shift right (>>>)*, *Bitwise unsigned shift right and assign (>>>=)*, LValue, Operator Precedence, Shift operator

Cross-references:

ECMA 262 edition 2 – section – 11.13

ECMA 262 edition 3 – section – 11.13

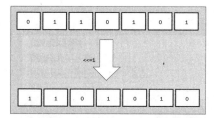

Bitwise shift right (>>) (Operator/bitwise)

Bitwise shift right one operand according to another.

Availability:	ECMAScript edition – 2 JavaScript – 1.0 JScript – 1.0 Internet Explorer – 3.02 Netscape – 2.0 Netscape Enterprise Server – 2.0 Opera – 3.0	
Property/method value type:	`Number primitive`	
JavaScript syntax:	-	`anOperand1 >> anOperand2`
Argument list:	`anOperand1`	A value to be shifted
	`anOperand2`	A distance to shift `anoperand 1`

This is sometimes called shift right with sign extension.

The bitwise shift right operator converts its left operand to a 32 bit integer and moves it rightwards by the number of bits indicated by the right operand.

As the value is shifted rightwards, bits that roll out of the right end of the register are discarded. The left hand end of the register containing the sign bit is duplicated to sign fill the value as it shifts. Shifting rightwards by 32 bits will fill the buffer with all zero or all one bits according to the value of the sign bit at the outset.

Because the value is converted to an integer, any fractional part is discarded as the shift begins.

The right hand operand is converted to a 5 bit value with a bitwise mask to limit the distance of the shift to 32 bits. This can cause unexpected results if the right hand side is derived from an expression that may yield a value larger than 32.

The associativity is left to right.

Refer to the operator precedence topic for details of execution order.

You can accomplish bitwise shift rights by dividing values using powers of 2. Dividing a value by 2 shifts rightwards by one bit position.

Example code:

```
<HTML>
<HEAD></HEAD>
<BODY>
<SCRIPT>
myValue1 = 0x00FF00;
myValue2 = myValue1 > 4;
document.write("Val 1 : " + binary32(myValue1) + "<BR>");
document.write("Result : " + binary32(myValue2) + "<BR>");
// Binary convertor (ignore sign bit on MSIE)
function binary32(aValue)
{
   myArray = new Array(32);

   for(myEnum=0; myEnum<32; myEnum++)
   {
       if(aValue & Math.pow(2, myEnum))
       {
           myArray[31-myEnum] = "1";
       }
       else
       {
           myArray[31-myEnum] = "0";
       }
   }
   return myArray.join("");
}
</SCRIPT>
</BODY>
</HTML>
```

See also: Associativity, Bit-field, *Bitwise shift left (<<)*, *Bitwise shift left then assign (<<=)*, Bitwise shift operator, *Bitwise shift right and assign (>>=)*, *Bitwise unsigned shift right (>>>)*, *Bitwise unsigned shift right and assign (>>>=)*, Operator Precedence, Shift operator

Cross-references:

ECMA 262 edition 2 – section – 11.7.2

ECMA 262 edition 3 – section – 11.7.2

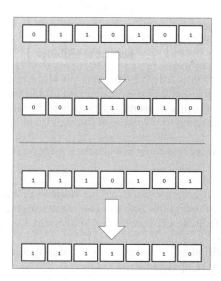

Bitwise shift right and assign (>>=) (Operator/assignment)

Destructively bitwise rightwards shift the first of two operands.

Availability:	ECMAScript edition – 2 JavaScript – 1.0 JScript – 1.0 Internet Explorer – 3.02 Netscape – 2.0 Netscape Enterprise Server – 2.0 Opera – 3.0	
Property/method value type:	Number primitive	
JavaScript syntax:	-	*anOperand1* >>= *anOperand2*
Argument list:	*anOperand1*	A value to be shifted and assigned to
	anOperand2	A distance to shift *anOperand1*

Bitwise shift rightwards the left operand by the number of bits in the right operand and assign the result to the left operand.

This is functionally equivalent to the expression:

```
anOperand1 = anOperand1 >> anOperand2;
```

The bitwise shift right operator converts its left operand to a 32 bit integer and moves it rightwards by the number of bits indicated by the right operand.

As the value is shifted rightwards, bits that roll out of the right end of the register are discarded. The left hand end of the register containing the sign bit is duplicated to sign fill the value as it shifts. Shifting rightwards by 32 bits will fill the buffer with all zero or all 1 bits according to the value of the sign bit at the outset.

Because the value is converted to an integer, any fractional part is discarded as the shift begins.

The right hand operand is converted to a 5 bit value with a bitwise mask to limit the distance of the shift to 32 bits. This can cause unexpected results if the right hand side is derived from an expression that may yield a value larger than 32.

Although this is classified as an assignment operator it is really a compound of an assignment and a bitwise operator.

The associativity is right to left.

Refer to the operator precedence topic for details of execution order.

The new value of *anOperand1* is returned as a result of the expression.

Warnings:

❑ The operand to the left of the operator must be an LValue. That is, it should be able to take an assignment and store the value.

See also:	Assignment operator, Associativity, Bit-field, Bitwise operator, *Bitwise shift left (<<)*, *Bitwise shift left then assign (<<=)*, Bitwise shift operator, *Bitwise shift right (>>)*, *Bitwise unsigned shift right (>>>)*, *Bitwise unsigned shift right and assign (>>>=)*, LValue, Operator Precedence, Shift operator

Cross-references:

ECMA 262 edition 2 – section – 11.13

ECMA 262 edition 3 – section – 11.13

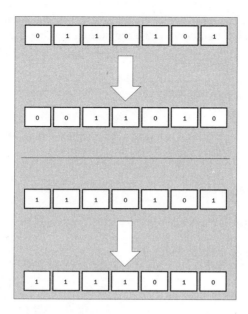

Bitwise unsigned shift right (>>>) (Operator/bitwise)

Bitwise shift right one operand according to another.

Availability:	ECMAScript edition – 2 JavaScript – 1.0 JScript – 1.0 Internet Explorer – 3.02 Netscape – 2.0 Netscape Enterprise Server – 2.0 Opera – 3.0	
Property/method value type:	`Number primitive`	
JavaScript syntax:	-	`anOperand1 >>> anOperand2`
Argument list:	`anOperand1`	A value to be shifted
	`anOperand2`	A distance to shift `anoperand 1`

This is sometimes called shift right with zero extension.

The bitwise unsigned shift right operator converts its left operand to a 32 bit integer and moves it rightwards by the number of bits indicated by the right operand. The sign bit is not propagated.

As the value is shifted rightwards, bits that roll out of the right end of the register are discarded. The left hand end of the register containing the sign bit is zero filled as the contents are shifted. Shifting rightwards by 32 bits will fill the buffer with all zero bits.

Because the value is converted to an integer, any fractional part is discarded as the shift begins.

The right hand operand is converted to a 5 bit value with a bitwise mask to limit the distance of the shift to 32 bits. This can cause unexpected results if the right hand side is derived from an expression that may yield a value larger than 32.

The associativity is left to right.

Refer to the operator precedence topic for details of execution order.

Example code:

```
<HTML>
<HEAD></HEAD>
<BODY>
<SCRIPT>
myValue1 = -0x00FF00;
myValue2 = myValue1 >> 4;
document.write("Val 1 : " + binary32(myValue1) + "<BR>");
document.write("Result : " + binary32(myValue2) + "<BR>");
// Binary convertor (ignore sign bit on MSIE)
function binary32(aValue)
{
   myArray = new Array(32);

   for(myEnum=0; myEnum<32; myEnum++)
   {
      if(aValue & Math.pow(2, myEnum))
      {
         myArray[31-myEnum] = "1";
      }
      else
      {
         myArray[31-myEnum] = "0";
      }
   }
   return myArray.join("");
}
</SCRIPT>
</BODY>
</HTML>
```

See also: Associativity, Bit-field, *Bitwise shift left (<<)*, *Bitwise shift left then assign (<<=)*, Bitwise shift operator, *Bitwise shift right (>>)*, *Bitwise shift right and assign (>>=)*, *Bitwise unsigned shift right and assign (>>>=)*, Operator Precedence, Shift operator

Cross-references:

ECMA 262 edition 2 – section – 11.7.3

ECMA 262 edition 3 – section – 11.7.3

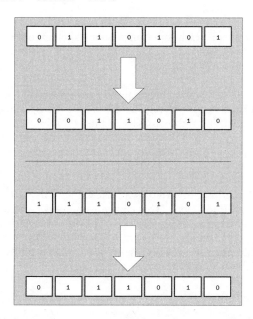

Bitwise unsigned shift right and assign (>>>=) (Operator/assignment)

Destructively bitwise rightwards shift the first of two operands.

Availability:	ECMAScript edition – 2 JavaScript – 1.0 JScript – 1.0 Internet Explorer – 3.02 Netscape – 2.0 Netscape Enterprise Server – 2.0 Opera – 3.0	
Property/method value type:	Number primitive	
JavaScript syntax:	-	anOperand1 >>>= anOperand2
Argument list:	anOperand1	A value to be shifted and assigned to
	anOperand2	A distance to shift anoperand 1

Bitwise unsigned shift rightwards the left operand by the number of bits in the right operand and assign the result to the left operand.

This is functionally equivalent to the expression:

```
anOperand1 = anOperand1 >>> anOperand2;
```

The bitwise unsigned shift right operator converts its left operand to a 32 bit integer and moves it rightwards by the number of bits indicated by the right operand. The sign bit is not propagated.

As the value is shifted rightwards, bits that roll out of the right end of the register are discarded. The left hand end of the register containing the sign bit is zero filled as the contents are shifted. Shifting rightwards by 32 bits will fill the buffer with all zero bits.

Because the value is converted to an integer, any fractional part is discarded as the shift begins.

The right hand operand is converted to a 5 bit value with a bitwise mask to limit the distance of the shift to 32 bits. This can cause unexpected results if the right hand side is derived from an expression that may yield a value larger than 32.

Although this is classified as an assignment operator it is really a compound of an assignment and a bitwise operator.

The associativity is right to left.

Refer to the operator precedence topic for details of execution order.

The new value of *anOperand1* is returned as a result of the expression.

Warnings:

❑ The operand to the left of the operator must be an LValue. That is, it should be able to take an assignment and store the value.

See also:	Assignment operator, Associativity, Bit-field, Bitwise operator, *Bitwise shift left (<)*, *Bitwise shift left then assign (<=)*, Bitwise shift operator, *Bitwise shift right (>)*, *Bitwise shift right and assign (>=)*, *Bitwise unsigned shift right (>>)*, LValue, Operator Precedence, Shift operator

Cross-references:

ECMA 262 edition 2 – section – 11.13

ECMA 262 edition 3 – section – 11.13

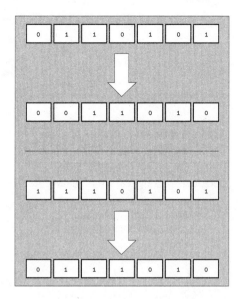

Bitwise XOR (^) (Operator/bitwise)

Bitwise XOR one operand with another.

Availability:	ECMAScript edition – 2 JavaScript – 1.0 JScript – 1.0 Internet Explorer – 3.02 Netscape – 2.0 Netscape Enterprise Server – 2.0 Opera – 3.0	
Property/method value type:	`Number primitive`	
JavaScript syntax:	-	*anOperand1 ^ anOperand2*
Argument list:	*anOperand1*	A numeric value
	anOperand2	Another numeric value

Performs a bit by bit XOR of the 32 bit value derived from both operands.

Where a corresponding bit is different in both operands, a 1 bit will be inserted into the result. If the corresponding bit is identical in both operands, regardless of whether they both have a 1 bit or a zero bit, a zero will be inserted at that bit position in the result.

The associativity is left to right.

Refer to the operator precedence topic for details of execution order.

83

This is the truth table for two Boolean primitive values being operated on with the XOR operator.

A	B	XOR
false	false	false
false	true	true
true	false	true
true	true	false

The bitwise operator performs this operation on each corresponding bit pair in the two operands.

Example code:

```
<HTML>
<HEAD></HEAD>
<BODY>
<SCRIPT>
myValue1 = 0xFFFF;
myValue2 = 0x0FF0;
myValue3 = myValue1 ^ myValue2;
document.write("Val 1 : " + binary32(myValue1) + "<BR>");
document.write("Val 2 : " + binary32(myValue2) + "<BR>");
document.write("XOR : " + binary32(myValue3) + "<BR>");
// Binary convertor (ignore sign bit on MSIE)
function binary32(aValue)
{
   myArray = new Array(32);

   for(myEnum=0; myEnum<32; myEnum++)
   {
      if(aValue & Math.pow(2, myEnum))
      {
         myArray[31-myEnum] = "1";
      }
      else
      {
         myArray[31-myEnum] = "0";
      }
   }
   return myArray.join("");
}
</SCRIPT>
</BODY>
</HTML>
```

See also: Associativity, Binary bitwise operator, Bit-field, *Bitwise XOR and assign (^=)*, *Logical XOR*, Operator Precedence

Cross-references:

ECMA 262 edition 2 – section – 11.10

ECMA 262 edition 3 – section – 11.10

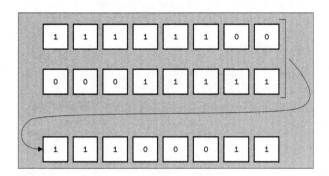

Bitwise XOR and assign (^=) (Operator/assignment)

Destructively bitwise XOR two operands and store the result in the first.

Availability:	ECMAScript edition – 2 JavaScript – 1.0 JScript – 1.0 Internet Explorer – 3.02 Netscape – 2.0 Netscape Enterprise Server – 2.0 Opera – 3.0	
Property/method value type:	Number primitive	
JavaScript syntax:	-	anOperand1 ^= anOperand2
Argument list:	anOperand1	A numeric value that can be assigned to
	anOperand2	Another numeric value

Bitwise XOR the right operand with the left operand and assign the result to the left operand.

This is functionally equivalent to the expression:

```
anOperand1 = anOperand1 ^ anOperand2;
```

Performs a bit by bit XOR of the 32 bit value derived from both operands.

Where a corresponding bit is different in both operands, a 1 bit will be inserted into the result. If the corresponding bit is identical in both operands, regardless of whether they both have a 1 bit or a zero bit, a zero will be inserted at that bit position in the result.

Although this is classified as an assignment operator it is really a compound of an assignment and a bitwise operator.

The associativity is right to left.

Refer to the operator precedence topic for details of execution order.

The new value of *anOperand1* is returned as a result of the expression.

This is the truth table for two Boolean primitive values being operated on with the XOR operator.

A	B	XOR
false	false	false
false	true	true
true	false	true
true	true	false

The bitwise operator performs this operation on each corresponding bit pair in the two operands.

Warnings:

❑ The operand to the left of the operator must be an LValue. That is, it should be able to take an assignment and store the value.

See also:	Assignment operator, Associativity, Bit-field, Bitwise operator, *Bitwise XOR (^)*, LValue, Operator Precedence

Cross-references:

ECMA 262 edition 2 – section – 11.13

ECMA 262 edition 3 – section – 11.13

blob object (Object/NES)

A special object that is designed to contain binary data extracted from a database or file.

Availability:	JavaScript – 1.1
	Netscape Enterprise Server – 2.0
JavaScript syntax:	NES *myBlob* = blob()
	NES *myBlob* =
	myCursor.colName.blobImage(...)
Object methods:	blobImage(), blobLink()

A blob object is so called because it encapsulates a Binary Large Object or BLOb. This is a block of data, often quite large, that is stored in a binary form and which is likely to contain many non-printable characters and probably some nulls as well.

You cannot instantiate a blob object directly in JavaScript but you can obtain one by fetching the data from a database as shown in the example code.

Example code:

```
<SERVER>
// Example derived from Wrox Professional JavaScript
// This opens a database, selects some records
// Traverses the collection that was selected
// and for each one, outputs an image tag.
database.connect("ODBC", "TargetDB", "", "", "");
myCursor = database.cursor("SELECT * FROM TARGET_TABLE");
while(myCursor.next())
{
    myBlob = myCursor.blobData;
    write(myBlob.blobImage("bmp"));
}
myCursor.close();
</SERVER>
```

See also:	Netscape Enterprise Server, *unwatch()*, *watch()*

Method	JavaScript	JScript	NES	Notes
blobImage()	1.1 +	-	2.0 +	-
blobLink()	1.1 +	-	2.0 +	-

BLOCKQUOTE object (Object/HTML)

An object that represents a `<BLOCKQUOTE>` text area.

Availability:	DOM level – 1 JavaScript – 1.5 JScript – 3.0 Internet Explorer – 4.0 Netscape – 6.0
Inherits from:	*Element object*
JavaScript syntax:	IE *myBLOCKQUOTE =* *myDocument.*all.anElementID
	IE *myBLOCKQUOTE = myDocument.*all.tags ("BLOCKQUOTE")[*anIndex*]
	IE *myBLOCKQUOTE = myDocument.*all[*aName*]
	– *myBLOCKQUOTE =* *myDocument.*getElementById(*anElementID*)
	– *myBLOCKQUOTE = myDocument.*getElements ByName(*aName*)[*anIndex*]
	– *myBLOCKQUOTE = myDocument.*getElements ByTagName("BLOCKQUOTE")[*anIndex*]
HTML syntax:	`<BLOCKQUOTE>` ... `</BLOCKQUOTE>`
Argument list:	*anIndex* A valid reference to an item in the collection
	aName The name attribute of an element
	anElementID The ID attribute of an element
Object properties:	`cite`
Object methods:	`click()`

Event handlers:	`onClick, onDblClick, onDragStart,`
	`onFilterChange, onHelp, onKeyDown,`
	`onKeyPress, onKeyUp, onMouseDown,`
	`onMouseMove, onMouseOut, onMouseOver,`
	`onMouseUp, onSelectStart`

This is used to set off a long quote inside a document and is intended to place an extract from a document into the displayed window with an active link to the document it quotes from. The style and appearance is that of a block quote text.

The `<BLOCKQUOTE>` tag is a block-level tag. That means that it forces a line break before and after unless the alignment and text flow around it are controlled very cleverly.

The DOM level 1 specification refers to this as a `QuoteElement` object.

See also:	*Element.object*

Property	JavaScript	JScript	N	IE	Opera	DOM	HTML	Notes
cite	1.5 +	3.0 +	6.0 +	4.0 +	-	1 +	-	-

Method	JavaScript	JScript	N	IE	Opera	DOM	HTML	Notes
click()	1.5 +	3.0 +	6.0 +	4.0 +	-	1 +	-	-

Event name	JavaScript	JScript	N	IE	Opera	DOM	HTML	Notes
onClick	1.5+	3.0 +	6.0 +	4.0 +	-	-	4.0 +	Warning
onDblClick	1.5 +	3.0 +	6.0 +	4.0 +	–	-	4.0 +	Warning
onDragStart	-	3.0 +	-	4.0 +	-	-	-	-
onFilterChange	-	3.0 +	-	4.0 +	-	-	-	-
onHelp	-	3.0 +	-	4.0 +	-	-	-	Warning
onKeyDown	1.5 +	3.0 +	6.0 +	4.0 +	-	-	4.0 +	Warning
onKeyPress	1.5+	3.0 +	6.0 +	4.0 +	–	-	4.0 +	Warning
onKeyUp	1.5 +	3.0 +	6.0 +	4.0 +	–	-	4.0 +	Warning
onMouseDown	1.5 +	3.0 +	6.0 +	4.0 +	–	-	4.0 +	Warning
onMouseMove	1.5 +	3.0 +	6.0 +	4.0 +	-	-	4.0 +	Warning
onMouseOut	1.5+	3.0 +	6.0 +	4.0 +	–	-	4.0 +	Warning
onMouseOver	1.5+	3.0 +	6.0 +	4.0 +	–	-	4.0 +	Warning
onMouseUp	1.5+	3.0 +	6.0 +	4.0 +	–	-	4.0 +	Warning
onSelectStart	-	3.0 +	-	4.0 +	-	-	-	-

Inheritance chain:

Element object, Node object

BODY object (Object/HTML)

An object that represents the body of a document.

Availability:	DOM level – 1 JavaScript – 1.5 JScript – 3.0 Internet Explorer – 4.0 Netscape – 6.0
Inherits from:	*Element object*

JavaScript syntax:	IE	`myBODY = myDocument.all.anElementID`
	IE	`myBODY = myDocument.all.tags("BODY")[anIndex]`
	IE	`myBODY = myDocument.all[aName]`
	-	`myBODY = myDocument.body`
	-	`myBODY = myDocument.getElementById(anElementID)`
	-	`myBODY = myDocument.getElementsByName(aName)[anIndex]`
	-	`myBODY = myDocument.getElementsByTagName("BODY")[anIndex]`

HTML syntax:	`<BODY> ... </BODY>`	
Argument list:	`anIndex`	A valid reference to an item in the collection (should be 0)
	`aName`	The name attribute of an element
	`anElementID`	The ID attribute of an element
Object properties:	`accessKey, aLink, background, bgColor, bgProperties, bottomMargin, leftMargin, link, noWrap, recordNumber, rightMargin, scroll, tabIndex, text, topMargin, vLink`	
Object methods:	`createControlRange(), createTextRange()`	
Event handlers:	`onAfterUpdate, onBeforeUnload, onBeforeUpdate, onChange, onClick, onDataAvailable, onDataSetChanged, onDataSetComplete, onDblClick, onDragStart, onErrorUpdate, onFilterChange, onHelp, onKeyDown, onKeyPress, onKeyUp, onMouseDown, onMouseMove, onMouseOut, onMouseOver, onMouseUp, onRowEnter, onRowExit, onScroll, onSelectStart, onUnload`	
Collections:	`controlRange[]`	

Although this generally represents the <BODY> tag, there are also properties that relate to the body which belong to the Document and Window objects. In MSIE, there is also a HEAD object which contains related information.

The <BODY> tag is a block-level tag. You can't place a <BODY> tag into the document but taken in the context of a framed environment it manifests itself as if it were a block-level tag.

See also:	*Background object, Document object,* Document.bgColor, Document.body, *Element object,* Element.isTextEdit, Element.offsetParent, *Frame object, HEAD object,* Input.accessKey, *Window object*

Property	JavaScript	JScript	N	IE	Opera	DOM	HTML	Notes
accessKey	1.5 +	3.0 +	6.0 +	4.0 +	-	1 +	-	-
aLink	1.5 +	3.0 +	6.0 +	4.0 +	-	1 +	-	-
background	1.5 +	3.0 +	6.0 +	4.0 +	-	1 +	-	Warning
bgColor	1.5 +	3.0 +	6.0 +	4.0 +	-	1 +	-	-
bgProperties	-	3.0 +	-	4.0 +	-	-	-	-
bottomMargin	-	3.0 +	-	4.0 +	-	-	-	Warning
leftMargin	-	3.0 +	-	4.0 +	-	-	-	Warning
link	1.5 +	3.0 +	6.0 +	4.0 +	-	1 +	-	-
noWrap	-	3.0 +	-	4.0 +	-	-	-	Warning
recordNumber	-	3.0 +	-	4.0 +	-	-	-	ReadOnly
rightMargin	-	3.0 +	-	4.0 +	-	-	-	Warning
scroll	-	3.0 +	-	4.0 +	-	-	-	Warning
tabIndex	1.5 +	3.0 +	6.0 +	4.0 +	-	1 +	-	-
text	1.5 +	3.0 +	6.0 +	4.0 +	-	1 +	-	-
topMargin	-	3.0 +	-	4.0 +	-	-	-	Warning
vLink	1.5 +	3.0 +	6.0 +	4.0 +	-	1 +	-	-

Method	JavaScript	JScript	N	IE	Opera	DOM	HTML	Notes
createControl Range()	-	5.0 +	-	5.0 +	-	-	-	-
createText Range()	-	3.0 +	-	4.0 +	-	-	-	-

Event name	JavaScript	JScript	N	IE	Opera	DOM	HTML	Notes
onAfter Update	-	3.0 +	-	4.0 +	-	-	-	-
onBefore Unload	-	3.0 +	-	4.0 +	-	-	-	-
onBefore Update	-	3.0 +	-	4.0 +	-	-	-	-
onChange	1.5 +	3.0 +	6.0 +	4.0 +	-	-	-	-
onClick	1.5 +	3.0 +	6.0 +	4.0 +	-	-	4.0 +	Warning
onData Available	-	3.0 +	-	4.0 +	-	-	-	-
onData SetChanged	-	3.0 +	-	4.0 +	-	-	-	-
onDataSet Complete	-	3.0 +	-	4.0 +	-	-	-	-
onDblClick	1.5 +	3.0 +	6.0 +	4.0 +	-	-	4.0 +	Warning
onDragStart	-	3.0 +	-	4.0 +	-	-	-	-
onErrorUpdate	-	3.0 +	-	4.0 +	-	-	-	-
onFilterChange	-	3.0 +	-	4.0 +	-	-	-	-
onHelp	-	3.0 +	-	4.0 +	-	-	-	Warning

Table continued on following page

Event name	JavaScript	JScript	N	IE	Opera	DOM	HTML	Notes
onKeyDown	1.5 +	3.0 +	6.0 +	4.0 +	–	-	4.0 +	Warning
onKeyPress	1.5 +	3.0 +	6.0 +	4.0 +	–	-	4.0 +	Warning
onKeyUp	1.5 +	3.0 +	6.0 +	4.0 +	–	-	4.0 +	Warning
onMouseDown	1.5 +	3.0 +	6.0 +	4.0 +	–	-	4.0 +	Warning
onMouseMove	1.5 +	3.0 +	6.0 +	4.0 +	-	-	4.0 +	Warning
onMouseOut	1.5 +	3.0 +	6.0 +	4.0 +	–	-	4.0 +	Warning
onMouseOver	1.5 +	3.0 +	6.0 +	4.0 +	–	-	4.0 +	Warning
onMouseUp	1.5 +	3.0 +	6.0 +	4.0 +	–	-	4.0 +	Warning
onRowEnter	-	3.0 +	-	4.0 +	-	-	-	-
onRowExit	-	3.0 +	-	4.0 +	-	-	-	-
onScroll	-	3.0 +	-	4.0 +	-	-	-	-
onSelectStart	-	3.0 +	-	4.0 +	-	-	-	-
onUnload	1.5 +	3.0 +	6.0 +	3.02 +	–	-	-	Warning

Inheritance chain:

Element object, Node object

Boolean (Primitive value)

A built-in primitive value.

Availability:	ECMAScript edition – 2
Property/method value type:	Boolean primitive

A Boolean value is a member of the Boolean type and may have one of two unique values, either true or false.

In some languages the values true and false also equate to numeric values. False is commonly 0 and true any non-zero value. In JavaScript this is not the case. The value false does not test equal against zero. However, a false Boolean value does become zero when converted to a number.

If you create a Boolean object and set it to the value true, you cannot convert it to a number with the toNumber() method, because this generates a run-time error. However, you can coerce the Boolean value into a numeric value by preceding it with a unary plus sign. So +true is a numeric primitive and yields the value 1, while false is converted to zero.

See also:	*false*, JavaScript to Java values, *true*

Cross-references:

ECMA 262 edition 2 – section – 4.3.13

ECMA 262 edition 3 – section – 4.3.13

Wrox *Instant JavaScript* – page – 14

boolean (Reserved word)

Reserved for future language enhancements.

The boolean keyword represents both a Java data type and the native Boolean primitive data type in JavaScript. This suggests some potential extensions of JavaScript interfaces to access Java applet parameters and return values.

See also:	*java.lang.Boolean*, LiveConnect, Reserved word

Cross-references:

ECMA 262 edition 2 – section – 7.4.3

ECMA 262 edition 3 – section – 7.5.3

Boolean (Type)

A native built-in type.

Availability:	ECMAScript edition – 2
Property/method value type:	Boolean primitive

Any object or expression that yields a result of type Boolean represents a logical entity.

Logical entities can only represent the true or false states.

These are useful as flags or conditional switches in your script.

See also:	Data Type, *false*, Fundamental data type, *true*, Type

Cross-references:

ECMA 262 edition 2 – section – 4.3.14

ECMA 262 edition 2 – section – 8.3

ECMA 262 edition 3 – section – 4.3.14

ECMA 262 edition 3 – section – 8.3

O'Reilly *JavaScript Definitive Guide* – page – 41

Boolean literal (Primitive value)

A literal constant whose type is a built-in primitive value.

Availability:	ECMAScript edition – 2
Property/method value type:	`Boolean primitive`

Boolean literals specify constant values for the true and false values used in relational expressions and are the only two values a Boolean primitive or object can resolve to.

See also:	*false*, Implicit conversion, Literal, Token, *true*

Cross-references:

ECMA 262 edition 2 – section – 7.7.2

ECMA 262 edition 3 – section – 7.8.2

Boolean object (Object/core)

An object of the class `"Boolean"`.

Availability:	ECMAScript edition – 2 JavaScript – 1.1 JScript – 3.0 Internet Explorer – 4.0 Netscape – 3.0 Netscape Enterprise Server – 2.0 Opera – 3.0	
JavaScript syntax:	-	`myBoolean = BooleanValue`
	-	`myBoolean = new Boolean()`
	-	`myBoolean = new Boolean(aValue)`
Argument List	`Boolean Value`	A Boolean value (either true or false)
	`aValue`	A value to be converted to a Boolean object.
Object properties:	`constructor, prototype`	
Object methods:	`toSource(), toString(), valueOf()`	

An instance of the class `"Boolean"` is created by using the new operator on the `Boolean()` constructor. The new object adopts the behavior of the built-in `Boolean` prototype object through the prototype-inheritance mechanisms.

All properties and methods of the prototype are available as if they were part of the new instance.

A `Boolean` object is a member of the type Object and is an instance of the built-in `Boolean` object.

Cloning the built-in `Boolean` object creates `Boolean` objects. This is done by calling the `Boolean()` constructor with the new operator. For example:

```
myBoolean = new Boolean(true);
```

A `Boolean` object can be coerced into a Boolean value and can be used anywhere that a Boolean value would be expected.

Programmers familiar with object oriented techniques may be happy to use the `Boolean` object, while procedural language programmers may prefer to implement the same functionality with a Boolean value instead.

This is an example of the flexibility of JavaScript in its ability to accommodate a variety of users from different backgrounds.

The prototype for the `Boolean` prototype object is the `Object` prototype object.

See also:	`Boolean.prototype`, Native object, *Object object, unwatch(), watch()*

Property	JavaScript	JScript	N	IE	Opera	NES	ECMA	Notes
constructor	1.1 +	3.0 +	3.0 +	4.0 +	-	-	2 +	-
prototype	1.1 +	3.0 +	3.0 +	4.0 +	3.0 +	2.0 +	2 +	-

Method	JavaScript	JScript	N	IE	Opera	NES	ECMA	Notes
toSource()	1.3 +	-	4.06 +	-	3.0 +	-	-	-
toString()	1.1 +	3.0 +	3.0 +	4.0 +	3.0 +	2.0 +	2 +	-
valueOf()	1.1 +	3.0 +	3.0 +	4.0 +	-	-	2 +	-

Cross-references:

ECMA 262 edition 2 – section – 4.3.15

ECMA 262 edition 2 – section – 10.1.5

ECMA 262 edition 2 – section – 15.6

ECMA 262 edition 3 – section – 4.3.15

ECMA 262 edition 3 – section – 15.6

Boolean() (Function)

A Boolean object constructor.

Availability:	ECMAScript edition – 2 JavaScript – 1.1 JScript – 3.0 Internet Explorer – 4.0 Netscape – 3.0	
Property/method value type:	Boolean primitive	
JavaScript syntax:	-	Boolean()
	-	Boolean(aValue)
Argument list:	aValue	A value to be converted to a Boolean result

When the Boolean() constructor is called as a function, it performs a type conversion on the value that is passed to it as a parameter.

The following results are yielded by the Boolean() constructor function:

Value:	Result:
No value	false
undefined	false
null	false
Boolean false	false
Boolean true	true
NaN	false
0	false
Non zero number	true
Zero length string ""	false
Non zero length string	true
Object	true

The result will be true or false depending on the parameter's value. If the parameter value is omitted, then false is returned by default.

See also:	Cast operator, Constructor function, constructor property, Implicit conversion, Type conversion

Cross-references:

ECMA 262 edition 2 – section – 15.1.3.5

ECMA 262 edition 2 – section – 15.6.1

ECMA 262 edition 2 – section – 15.6.2

ECMA 262 edition 2 – section – 15.6.3

ECMA 262 edition 3 – section – 15.6.1

Boolean.Class (Property/internal)

Internal property that returns an object class.

Availability:	ECMAScript edition – 2

This is an internal property that describes the class that an instance of a `Boolean` object is a member of. The reserved words suggest that this property may be externalized in the future.

See also:	`Boolean.constructor`, *Class*

Property attributes:

`DontEnum`, `Internal`.

Cross-references:

ECMA 262 edition 2 – section – 15.6.4

BR object (Object/HTML)

An object that represents the `<BR>` HTML tag.

Availability:	DOM level – 1 JavaScript – 1.5 JScript – 3.0 Internet Explorer – 4.0 Netscape – 6.0
Inherits from:	*Element object*

JavaScript syntax:	IE	myBR = myDocument.all.anElementID
	IE	myBR = myDocument.all.tags ("BR") [anIndex]
	IE	myBR = myDocument.all[aName]
	-	myBR = myDocument.getElementById (anElementID)
	-	myBR = myDocument.getElementsByName (aName) [anIndex]
	-	myBR = myDocument .getElementsByTagName ("BR") [anIndex]

HTML syntax:	

Argument list:	anIndex	A valid index reference to an item in the collection
	aName	The name attribute of an element
	anElementID	The ID attribute of an element

Object properties:	clear

Event handlers:	onClick, onDblClick, onHelp, onKeyDown, onKeyPress, onKeyUp, onMouseDown, onMouseMove, onMouseOut, onMouseOver, onMouseUp

This object represents a line break in the text. There are very few appearance modifying properties you could apply to such an object.

The <BR> tag is a block-level tag. That means that it forces a line break before and after itself.

See also:	Element object

Property	JavaScript	JScript	N	IE	Opera	DOM	HTML	Notes
clear	1.5 +	3.0 +	6.0 +	4.0 +	-	1 +	-	-

Event name	JavaScript	JScript	N	IE	Opera	DOM	HTML	Notes
onClick	1.5 +	3.0 +	6.0 +	4.0 +	3.0 +	-	4.0 +	Warning
onDblClick	1.5 +	3.0 +	6.0 +	4.0 +	3.0 +	-	4.0 +	Warning
onHelp	-	3.0 +	-	4.0 +	-	-	-	Warning
onKeyDown	1.5 +	3.0 +	6.0 +	4.0 +	3.0 +	-	4.0 +	Warning
onKeyPress	1.5 +	3.0 +	6.0 +	4.0 +	3.0 +	-	4.0 +	Warning
onKeyUp	1.5 +	3.0 +	6.0 +	4.0 +	3.0 +	-	4.0 +	Warning
onMouseDown	1.5 +	3.0 +	6.0 +	4.0 +	3.0 +	-	4.0 +	Warning
onMouseMove	1.5 +	3.0 +	6.0 +	4.0 +	-	-	4.0 +	Warning
onMouseOut	1.5 +	3.0 +	6.0 +	4.0 +	3.0 +	-	4.0 +	Warning
onMouseOver	1.5 +	3.0 +	6.0 +	4.0 +	3.0 +	-	4.0 +	Warning
onMouseUp	1.5 +	3.0 +	6.0 +	4.0 +	3.0 +	-	4.0 +	Warning

JavaScript Programmer's Reference

Inheritance chain:

Element object, Node object

break (Statement)

Exit unconditionally from a loop or switch.

Availability:	ECMAScript edition – 2 JavaScript – 1.1 JScript – 1.0 Internet Explorer – 3.02 Netscape – 3.0 Netscape Enterprise Server – 2.0 Opera – 3.0	
JavaScript syntax:	-	`break aLabelName;`
	-	`break;`
Argument list:	`aLabelName`	The name of a label associated with some code

The `break` keyword is a jump statement. It is used in an loop to abort the current cycle and exit from the smallest enclosing loop immediately. Execution continues at the line following the statement block associated with the loop.

A break statement can only legally exist inside a `while` or `for` loop in an ECMA compliant implementation. Implementations that provide additional iterator types may also honor the same behavior for the `break` statement.

The `break` statement would normally be executed conditionally, otherwise it would cause the remaining lines in the loop to be redundant, since no execution flow would ever reach them. Compilers generally warn you about this, but JavaScript would simply ignore it.

At version 1.2 of JavaScript, the `break` statement was enhanced to support a label as a breaking destination. When the break is processed, it will jump to the end of the statement that has been labeled. If an iterator is labeled, then the break is associated with that iterator. This mechanism works like a 'goto'. It can work with an `if` block and with a labelled block of brace delimited code.

See also:	Completion type, *continue*, *for(...)* ..., *for(...in...)* ..., Iteration statement, Jump statement, Label, *return*, Scope chain, Statement, *switch(...)* ... *case:* ... *default:* ..., *while(...)* ...

Cross-references:

ECMA 262 edition 2 – section – 10.1.4

ECMA 262 edition 2 – section – 12.8

ECMA 262 edition 3 – section – 10.1.4

ECMA 262 edition 3 – section – 12.8

Wrox *Instant JavaScript* – page – 25

Button object (Object/DOM)

An object representing an <INPUT TYPE="button"> HTML button in a form.

Availability:	DOM level – 1 JavaScript – 1.0 JScript – 1.0 Internet Explorer – 3.02 Netscape – 2.0 Opera – 3.0	
Inherits from:	*Input object*	
JavaScript syntax:	-	`myButton = myDocument.aFormName.anElementName`
	-	`myButton = myDocument.aFormName.elements[anItemIndex]`
	IE	`myButton = myDocument.all.anElementID`
	IE	`myButton = myDocument.all.tags("INPUT")[anIndex]`
	IE	`myButton = myDocument.all[aName]`
	-	`myButton = myDocument.forms[aFormIndex].anElementName`
	-	`myButton = myDocument.forms[aFormIndex].elements[anItemIndex]`
	-	`myButton = myDocument.getElementById(anElementID)`
	-	`myButton = myDocument.getElementsByName(aName)[anIndex]`
	-	`myButton = myDocument.getElementsByTagName("INPUT")[anIndex]`
HTML syntax:	`<INPUT TYPE="button">`	

Argument list:	*anItemIndex*	A valid reference to an item in the collection
	aName	The name attribute of an element
	anElementID	The ID attribute of an element
	aFormIndex	A reference to a single form in the forms collection
	anIndex	A valid reference to an item in the collection
Object properties:	type, value	
Object methods:	handleEvent()	
Event handlers:	onAfterUpdate, onBeforeUpdate, onBlur, onClick, onDblClick, onErrorUpdate, onFilterChange, onFocus, onHelp, onKeyDown, onKeyPress, onKeyUp, onMouseDown, onMouseMove, onMouseOut, onMouseOver, onMouseUp, onRowEnter, onRowExit	

Many properties, methods and event handlers for this object are inherited from the Input object class. Refer to topics grouped with the "Input" prefix for details of common functionality across all sub-classes of the Input object super-class.

There isn't really a Button object class in Netscape, but it is helpful when trying to understand the wide variety of input element types if we can reduce the complexity by discussing only the properties and methods of a button. In actual fact, the object is represented as an item of the Input object class.

In MSIE, there is a special BUTTON class that is used to represent a <BUTTON> tag. It is documented separately in its own topics. The Button object is the correct spelling for a DOM level 1 compliant implementation.

Event handling support via properties containing function objects was added to Button objects at version 1.1 of JavaScript.

Warnings:

❏ Note that on MSIE, Input objects are actually INPUT objects, because MSIE follows a general rule of naming object classes after the capitalized name of the HTML tag that instantiates them. However, in some special cases, MSIE creates other object types. For buttons, it uses the BUTTON class.

❏ Netscape does not support the defaultValue property for this sub-class of the Input object.

See also:	*Element object*, Element.isTextEdit, Form.elements[], *FormElement object*, *Input object*, Input.accessKey, onClick, *TextRange object*

Property	JavaScript	JScript	N	IE	Opera	DOM	HTML	Notes
type	1.1 +	1.0 +	3.0 +	3.02 +	3.0 +	1 +	-	ReadOnly
value	1.0 +	1.0 +	2.0 +	3.02 +	3.0 +	1 +	-	Warning

Method	JavaScript	JScript	N	IE	Opera	DOM	HTML	Notes
handleEvent()	1.2 +	-	4.0 +	-	-	-	-	-

Event name	JavaScript	JScript	N	IE	Opera	DOM	HTML	Notes
onAfterUpdate	-	3.0 +	-	4.0 +	-	-	-	-
onBeforeUpdate	-	3.0 +	-	4.0 +	-	-	-	-
onBlur	1.1 +	3.0 +	3.0 +	4.0 +	3.0 +	-	-	Warning
onClick	1.0 +	3.0 +	2.0 +	4.0 +	3.0 +	-	4.0 +	Warning
onDblClick	1.2 +	3.0 +	4.0 +	4.0 +	3.0 +	-	4.0 +	Warning
onErrorUpdate	-	3.0 +	-	4.0 +	-	-	-	-
onFilterChange	-	3.0 +	-	4.0 +	-	-	-	-
onFocus	1.0 +	3.0 +	2.0 +	4.0 +	3.0 +	-	-	Warning
onHelp	-	3.0 +	-	4.0 +	-	-	-	Warning
onKeyDown	1.2 +	3.0 +	4.0 +	4.0 +	3.0 +	-	4.0 +	Warning
onKeyPress	1.2 +	3.0 +	4.0 +	4.0 +	3.0 +	-	4.0 +	Warning
onKeyUp	1.2 +	3.0 +	4.0 +	4.0 +	3.0 +	-	4.0 +	Warning
onMouseDown	1.2 +	3.0 +	4.0 +	4.0 +	3.0 +	-	4.0 +	Warning
onMouseMove	1.2 +	3.0 +	4.0 +	4.0 +	-	-	4.0 +	Warning
onMouseOut	1.1 +	3.0 +	3.0 +	4.0 +	3.0 +	-	4.0 +	Warning
onMouseOver	1.0 +	3.0 +	2.0 +	4.0 +	3.0 +	-	4.0 +	Warning
onMouseUp	1.2 +	3.0 +	4.0 +	4.0 +	3.0 +	-	4.0 +	Warning
onRowEnter	-	3.0 +	-	4.0 +	-	-	-	-
onRowExit	-	3.0 +	-	4.0 +	-	-	-	-

Inheritance chain:

Element object, Input object, Node object

BUTTON object (Object/HTML)

An object that represents a special MSIE <BUTTON> element.

Availability:	DOM level – 1
	JavaScript – 1.5
	JScript – 3.0
	Internet Explorer – 4.0
	Netscape – 6.0

Inherits from:	Element object	
JavaScript syntax:	IE	*myBUTTON* = *myDocument*.all.*anElementID*
	IE	*myBUTTON* = *myDocument*.all.tags ("BUTTON")[*anIndex*]
	IE	*myBUTTON* = *myDocument*.all[*aName*]
	-	*myBUTTON* = *myDocument*.getElementById (*anElementID*)
	-	*myBUTTON* = *myDocument*.getElementsByName (*aName*)[*anIndex*]
	-	*myBUTTON* = *myDocument*.getElements ByTagName("BUTTON")[*anIndex*]
HTML syntax:	<BUTTON> ... </BUTTON>	
Argument list:	*anIndex*	A valid reference to an item in the collection
	aName	The NAME attribute of an element
	anElementID	The ID attribute of an element
Object properties:	accept, accessKey, alt, dataFld, dataFormatAs, dataSrc, form, name, status, tabIndex, type, value	
Object methods:	createTextRange()	
Event handlers:	onAfterUpdate, onBeforeUpdate, onBlur, onClick, onDblClick, onDragStart, onFilterChange, onFocus, onHelp, onKeyDown, onKeyPress, onKeyUp, onMouseDown, onMouseMove, onMouseOut, onMouseOver, onMouseUp, onResize, onRowEnter, onRowExit, onSelectStart	

This is an additional kind of button object, over and above that provided for the <INPUT TYPE="Button"> tag.

Warnings:

❑ This object is not the same as a Button object which is a convenience class that is really instantiated as an Input object. Netscape only supports Button (Input) objects and does not support BUTTON objects. MSIE supports both. The properties of each type of button object are different.

See also:	Element object, Element.isTextEdit, Form.elements[], FormElement object, Input object, Input.accessKey, onClick, TextRange object

Property	JavaScript	JScript	N	IE	Opera	DOM	HTML	Notes
accept	-	5.0 +	-	5.0 +	-	-	-	Warning
accessKey	1.5 +	3.0 +	6.0 +	4.0 +	-	1 +	-	Warning
alt	-	3.0 +	-	4.0 +	-	-	-	-
dataFld	1.5 +	3.0 +	6.0 +	4.0 +	-	1 +	-	Warning
dataFormatAs	1.5 +	3.0 +	6.0 +	4.0 +	-	1 +	-	Warning
dataSrc	1.5 +	3.0 +	6.0 +	4.0 +	-	1 +	-	Warning
form	1.5 +	3.0 +	6.0 +	4.0 +	-	1 +	-	Warning
name	1.5 +	3.0 +	6.0 +	4.0 +	-	1 +	-	-
status	1.5 +	3.0 +	6.0 +	4.0 +	-	1 +	-	Warning
tabIndex	1.5 +	3.0 +	6.0 +	4.0 +	-	1 +	-	Warning
type	1.5 +	3.0 +	6.0 +	4.0 +	-	1 +	-	ReadOnly
value	1.5 +	3.0 +	6.0 +	4.0 +	-	1 +	-	Warning

Method	JavaScript	JScript	N	IE	Opera	DOM	HTML	Notes
createTextRange()	1.5 +	3.0 +	6.0 +	4.0 +	-	1 +	-	Warning

Event name	JavaScript	JScript	N	IE	Opera	DOM	HTML	Notes
onAfterUpdate	-	3.0 +	-	4.0 +	-	-	-	-
onBeforeUpdate	-	3.0 +	-	4.0 +	-	-	-	-
onBlur	1.5 +	3.0 +	6.0 +	4.0 +	-	-	-	Warning
onClick	1.5 +	3.0 +	6.0 +	4.0 +	-	-	4.0 +	Warning
onDblClick	1.5 +	3.0 +	6.0 +	4.0 +	-	-	4.0 +	Warning
onDragStart	-	3.0 +	-	4.0 +	-	-	-	-
onFilterChange	-	3.0 +	-	4.0 +	-	-	-	-
onFocus	1.5 +	3.0 +	6.0 +	4.0 +	-	-	-	Warning
onHelp	-	3.0 +	-	4.0 +	-	-	-	Warning
onKeyDown	1.5 +	3.0 +	6.0 +	4.0 +	-	-	4.0 +	Warning
onKeyPress	1.5 +	3.0 +	6.0 +	4.0 +	-	-	4.0 +	Warning
onKeyUp	1.5 +	3.0 +	6.0 +	4.0 +	-	-	4.0 +	Warning
onMouseDown	1.5 +	3.0 +	6.0 +	4.0 +	-	-	4.0 +	Warning
onMouseMove	1.5 +	3.0 +	6.0 +	4.0 +	-	-	4.0 +	Warning
onMouseOut	1.5 +	3.0 +	6.0 +	4.0 +	-	-	4.0 +	Warning
onMouseOver	1.5 +	3.0 +	6.0 +	4.0 +	-	-	4.0 +	Warning
onMouseUp	1.5 +	3.0 +	6.0 +	4.0 +	-	-	4.0 +	Warning
onResize	1.5 +	3.0 +	6.0 +	4.0 +	-	-	-	Warning
onRowEnter	-	3.0 +	-	4.0 +	-	-	-	-
onRowExit	-	3.0 +	-	4.0 +	-	-	-	-
onSelectStart	-	3.0 +	-	4.0 +	-	-	-	-

Inheritance chain:

Element object, Node object

byte (Reserved word)

Reserved for future language enhancements.

A byte is a set of 8 adjacent binary digits (Bits). It is big enough to hold an 8 bit character code which will support the subset of 16 bit Unicode characters that most JavaScript users are likely to need, at least for developing scripts for use with the English language.

The least significant bit is called the low-order bit and the most significant bit is called the high-order bit. These do not necessarily map one to one to the bits stored in the memory of the computer which may be big-endian or little-endian. This is thankfully hidden from the JavaScript programmer who will need to operate on a standardized IEEE-754 bit pattern when working with binary values stored in Numeric primitive values.

The fact that the ECMAScript standard (edition 2) reserves this word for future use, suggests that some byte level support is expected to be added to the language at some time in the future.

This keyword also represents a Java data type and the byte keyword allows for the potential extension of JavaScript interfaces to access Java applet parameters and return values.

See also:	*char*, *IEEE 754*, LiveConnect, Reserved word

Cross-references:

ECMA 262 edition 2 – section – 7.4.3

ECMA 262 edition 3 – section – 7.5.3

C

Call Function/internal

An internal mechanism for executing function calls.

Availability:	ECMAScript edition – 2

This is the internal mechanism by which functions are implemented.

Objects supporting this method are called functions.

When they are called, they add themselves to the scope chain and any variables subsequently declared are added to that scope. Hence local objects belong to the function being executed.

Another name for the function being executed is the call object.

Warnings:

❑ The Global object does not have a Call property and you cannot therefore use it as a function.

See also:	Function property, Internal Method, *JSObject.call()*

Property attributes:

DontEnum, Internal.

Cross-references:

ECMA 262 edition 2 – section – 8.6.2

ECMA 262 edition 3 – section – 8.6.2

CanPut() (Function/internal)

Internal private function.

Availability:	ECMAScript edition – 2

This internal function returns a Boolean value to indicate whether the named property can be changed in the containing object.

If the property is found, the value of its ReadOnly attribute is checked. If it has a ReadOnly attribute, the result of CanPut() must be false. Otherwise, having found the property, the true result will be returned.

If the property does not exist in the receiving object, the prototype chain is walked until the property or a null prototype is encountered. At each inheritance level, the CanPut() function is used to determine the existence of the property.

If a null prototype is encountered, the result will be true, since the property can then be created in the original receiving object.

If the prototype is a host object that does not implement the CanPut() function, then false is returned as a result.

Because the prototype chain is walked extensively by the CanPut() function, if the prototype chain is not finite and terminated with a null at some stage, a recursive loop is built and the function never returns.

See also:	Internal Method

Property attributes:

Internal.

Cross-references:

ECMA 262 edition 2 – section – 8.6.2.3

ECMA 262 edition 3 – section – 8.6.2.3

CAPTION object (Object/HTML)

An object that represents the <CAPTION> HTML tag, which is used inside a <TABLE>.

Availability:	DOM level – 1 JavaScript – 1.5 JScript – 3.0 Internet Explorer – 4.0 Netscape – 6.0
Inherits from:	*Element object*
JavaScript syntax:	IE *myCAPTION = myDocument.all.anElementID*
	IE *myCAPTION = myDocument.all.tags* ("CAPTION") [*anIndex*]
	IE *myCAPTION = myDocument.all* [*aName*]
	- *myCAPTION = myDocument.getElementById* (*anElementID*)
	- *myCAPTION = myDocument.* getElementsByName (*aName*) [*anIndex*]
	- *myCAPTION = myDocument.getElementsBy* TagName ("CAPTION") [*anIndex*]
HTML syntax:	<CAPTION> ... </CAPTION>
Argument list:	*anIndex* A valid reference to an item in the collection
	aName The name attribute of an element
	anElementID The ID attribute of an element
Object properties:	align, vAlign
Event handlers:	onAfterUpdate, onBeforeUpdate, onBlur, onChange, onClick, onDblClick, onDragStart, onErrorUpdate, onFilterChange, onFocus, onHelp, onKeyDown, onKeyPress, onKeyUp, onMouseDown, onMouseMove, onMouseOut, onMouseOver, onMouseUp, onScroll, onSelect, onSelectStart

The caption forms an integral part of the table to which it belongs. It needs to be defined inside the <TABLE> tags.

The DOM level 1 standard describes these objects as TableCaptionElement objects.

See also:	*Element object*, style.captionSide, *TABLE object*, TABLE.caption, TABLE.createCaption(), TABLE.deleteCaption()

Property	JavaScript	JScript	N	IE	Opera	DOM	HTML	Notes
align	1.5 +	3.0 +	6.0 +	4.0 +	-	1 +	-	Warning, Deprecated
vAlign	-	3.0 +	-	4.0 +	-	-	-	Warning, Deprecated

Event name	JavaScript	JScript	N	IE	Opera	DOM	HTML	Notes
onAfterUpdate	-	3.0 +	-	4.0 +	-	-	-	-
onBeforeUpdate	-	3.0 +	-	4.0 +	-	-	-	-
onBlur	1.5 +	3.0 +	6.0 +	4.0 +	3.0 +	-	-	Warning
onChange	1.5 +	3.0 +	6.0 +	4.0 +	3.0 +	-	-	-
onClick	1.5 +	3.0 +	6.0 +	4.0 +	3.0 +	-	4.0 +	Warning
onDblClick	1.5 +	3.0 +	6.0 +	4.0 +	3.0 +	-	4.0 +	Warning
onDragStart	-	3.0 +	-	4.0 +	-	-	-	-
onErrorUpdate	-	3.0 +	-	4.0 +	-	-	-	-
onFilterChange	-	3.0 +	-	4.0 +	-	-	-	-
onFocus	1.5 +	3.0 +	6.0 +	4.0 +	3.0 +	-	-	Warning
onHelp	-	3.0 +	-	4.0 +	-	-	-	Warning
onKeyDown	1.5 +	3.0 +	6.0 +	4.0 +	3.0 +	-	4.0 +	Warning
onKeyPress	1.5 +	3.0 +	6.0 +	4.0 +	3.0 +	-	4.0 +	Warning
onKeyUp	1.5 +	3.0 +	6.0 +	4.0 +	3.0 +	-	4.0 +	Warning
onMouseDown	1.5 +	3.0 +	6.0 +	4.0 +	3.0 +	-	4.0 +	Warning
onMouseMove	1.5 +	3.0 +	6.0 +	4.0 +	-	-	4.0 +	Warning
onMouseOut	1.5 +	3.0 +	6.0 +	4.0 +	3.0 +	-	4.0 +	Warning
onMouseOver	1.5 +	3.0 +	6.0 +	4.0 +	3.0 +	-	4.0 +	Warning
onMouseUp	1.5 +	3.0 +	6.0 +	4.0 +	3.0 +	-	4.0 +	Warning
onScroll	-	3.0 +	-	4.0 +	-	-	-	-
onSelect	1.5 +	3.0 +	6.0 +	4.0 +	3.0 +	-	-	-
onSelectStart	-	3.0 +	-	4.0 +	-	-	-	-

Inheritance chain:

Element object, Node object

captureEvents() (Function)

Part of the Netscape 4 event propagation complex.

Availability:	JavaScript – 1.2 Netscape – 4.0 Deprecated	
Property/method value type:	`undefined`	
JavaScript syntax:	N	captureEvents (anEventMask)
	N	myObject.captureEvents (anEventMask)
	N	myWindow.captureEvents (anEventMask)
Argument list:	anEventMask	A mask constructed with the manifest event constants

Warnings:

❑ Since a bit mask is being used, this must be an int32 value. This suggests that there can only be 32 different Event types supported by this event propagation model.

❑ This capability is deprecated and is not supported in Netscape 6.0 anymore. It never was supported by MSIE, which implements a completely different event model. As it turns out, the DOM level 2 event model converges on the MSIE technique.

See also:	Document.captureEvents(), Document.releaseEvents(), Element.onevent, Event handler, Event management, Event propagation, Event type constants, Frame object, handleEvent(), Keyboard events, Layer.captureEvents(), Layer.releaseEvents(), onLoseCapture, onMouseMove, Window object, Window.captureEvents(), Window.releaseEvents(), Window.routeEvent()

Cross-references:

Wrox Instant JavaScript – page – 55

catch(...) (Function)

Part of the `try...catch...finally` error-handling mechanism.

Availability:	ECMAScript edition – 3 JavaScript – 1.5 JScript – 5.0 Internet Explorer – 5.0 Netscape – 6.0	
JavaScript syntax:	-	`catch(anError)`
Argument list:	`anError`	An instance of the `Error` object

The ECMAScript standard (edition 2) defined the `catch` keyword and reserves it for future use. Edition 3 mandates that this should now be supported in a compliant interpreter.

In anticipation of that, it is available in JavaScript version 1.4. This is also now supported in JScript version 5.0 as well.

Refer to the `try...catch...finally` topic for more details.

See also:	*Error object, EvalError object*, Exception handling, *finally ..., RangeError object, ReferenceError object, SyntaxError object, throw, try ... catch ... finally, TypeError object, URIError object*

Cross-references:

ECMA 262 edition 2 – section – 7.4.3

ECMA 262 edition 3 – section – 7.5.2

ECMA 262 edition 3 – section – 12.14

CDATASection object (Object/DOM)

Part of the extended interface that DOM describes for supporting non HTML content.

Availability:	DOM level – 1 JavaScript – 1.5 JScript – 5.0 Internet Explorer – 5.0 Netscape – 6.0
Inherits from:	*textNode object*

JavaScript syntax:	-	myCDATASection = myDocument.create CDATASection(someData)
Argument list:	someData	The data content for the new object

The extended interface supports various document forms other than HTML. This object is used to encapsulate marked up XML without needing to escape all of the markup characters.

You can test for the availability of this feature by means of the Implementation.hasFeature() method. In this case, test for a feature name of "XML" and a version value of "1.0".

See also:	Document.createCDATASection()

Inheritance chain:

CharacterData object, Node object, textNode object

char (Reserved word)

Reserved for future language enhancements.

The ECMAScript (edition 2) reserves the char keyword for future use. This suggests some additional C-like functionality may be added in the future. A char may be represented by a byte. However in JavaScript, characters are really double byte values since they encode a Unicode code point in each character.

This keyword also represents a Java data type and the char keyword allows for the potential extension of JavaScript interfaces to access Java applet parameters and return values.

See also:	byte, java.lang.Character, LiveConnect, Reserved word

Cross-references:

ECMA 262 edition 2 – section – 7.4.3

ECMA 262 edition 3 – section – 7.5.2

CharacterData object (Object/DOM)

A sub-class of the node object with extensions to support access to character data within the object.

Availability:	DOM level – 1 JavaScript – 1.5 JScript – 5.0 Internet Explorer – 5.0 Netscape – 6.0
Inherits from:	*Node object*
JavaScript syntax:	- *myCharacterData* = new CharacterData()
Object properties:	data, length
Object methods:	appendData(), deleteData(), insertData(), replaceData(), substringData()
See also:	*COMMENT object*

Property	JavaScript	JScript	N	IE	Opera	DOM	Notes
data	1.5 +	5.0 +	6.0 +	5.0 +	-	1 +	-
length	1.5 +	5.0 +	6.0 +	5.0 +	-	1 +	-

Method	JavaScript	JScript	N	IE	Opera	DOM	Notes
appendData()	1.5 +	5.0 +	6.0 +	5.0 +	-	1 +	-
deleteData()	1.5 +	5.0 +	6.0 +	5.0 +	-	1 +	-
insertData()	1.5 +	5.0 +	6.0 +	5.0 +	-	1 +	-
replaceData()	1.5 +	5.0 +	6.0 +	5.0 +	-	1 +	-
substringData()	1.5 +	5.0 +	6.0 +	5.0 +	-	1 +	-

Inheritance chain:

Node object

Checkbox object (Object/DOM)

C

A checkbox to be used in a form. It toggles as it is clicked, but is not related to other checkboxes in the way that radio buttons are related to one another in families.

Availability:	DOM level – 1
	JavaScript – 1.0
	JScript – 1.0
	Internet Explorer – 3.02
	Netscape – 2.0
	Opera – 3.0
Inherits from:	*Input object*
JavaScript syntax:	- `myCheckbox = myDocument.aFormName` `.anElementName`
	- `myCheckbox = myDocument.aFormName` `.elements[anItemIndex]`
	IE `myCheckbox =` `myDocument.all.anElementID`
	IE `myCheckbox = myDocument.all.tags` `("INPUT")[anIndex]`
	IE `myCheckbox = myDocument.all[aName]`
	- `myCheckbox = myDocument.forms` `[aFormIndex].anElementName`
	- `myCheckbox = myDocument.forms` `[aFormIndex].elements[anItemIndex]`
	- `myCheckbox = myDocument.getElementById` `(anElementID)`
	- `myCheckbox = myDocument.getElements` `ByName(aName)[anIndex]`
	- `myCheckbox = myDocument.getElements` `ByTagName("INPUT")[anIndex]`
HTML syntax:	`<INPUT TYPE="checkbox">`
Argument list:	`anIndex`	A valid reference to an item in the collection
	`aName`	The name attribute of an element
	`anElementID`	The ID attribute of an element
	`anItemIndex`	A valid reference to an item in the collection
	`aFormIndex`	A reference to a particular form in the forms collection
Object properties:	`checked, defaultChecked, indeterminate, status, type, value`
Object methods:	`handleEvent()`

JavaScript Programmer's Reference

Event handlers:	onAfterUpdate, onBeforeUpdate, onBlur, onClick, onDblClick, onErrorUpdate, onFilterChange, onFocus, onHelp, onKeyDown, onKeyPress, onKeyUp, onMouseDown, onMouseMove, onMouseOut, onMouseOver, onMouseUp, onRowEnter, onRowExit

Many properties, methods and event handlers are inherited from the Input object class. Refer to topics grouped with the "Input" prefix for details of common functionality across all sub-classes of the Input object super-class.

There isn't really a Checkbox object class but it is helpful when trying to understand the wide variety of input element types if we can reduce the complexity by discussing only the properties and methods of a checkbox. In actual fact, the object is represented as an item of the Input object class.

Checkboxes may be used in groups where each one has the same name. However, this breaks the mechanism by which a form element can be accessed associatively since there is now more than one object with the same name. The fix for this is to support an InputArray so that you can access the items with the same name from a collection.

Although Checkbox items should not deactivate other items in the same family in the way that Radio buttons do, you can relate their states to one another by means of the onclick event handler.

Unlike MSIE, Netscape does not support the defaultValue property or the select() method for this sub-class of the Input object.

Warnings:

❑ If you enumerate a form object which has several elements having the same name, in Netscape these will be represented by a single property of that name that refers to an InputArray. In MSIE, you will get multiple properties with the same name, but each will refer to a collection object. This is probably a bug in MSIE, which exhibits this behavior in version 5 for Macintosh and probably on other platforms too.

❑ Note that on MSIE, Input objects are actually INPUT objects because MSIE follows a general rule of naming object classes after the capitalized name of the HTML tag that instantiates them.

Example code:

```
<HTML>
<HEAD>
</HEAD>
<BODY>
<DIV ID="RESULT">?</DIV>
<FORM onClick="handleClick()">
<INPUT TYPE="checkbox" VALUE="A" NAME="BOX_A">Selection A<BR>
```

```
<INPUT TYPE="checkbox" VALUE="B" NAME="BOX_B">Selection B<BR>
<INPUT TYPE="checkbox" VALUE="C" NAME="BOX_C">Selection C<BR>
<INPUT TYPE="checkbox" VALUE="D" NAME="BOX_D">Selection D<BR>
</FORM>
<SCRIPT>
function handleClick()
{
    myString  = "Selection [";
    myString += event.srcElement.value;
    myString += "], State [";
    myString += event.srcElement.checked;
    myString += "]";
    document.all.RESULT.innerText = myString;
}
</SCRIPT>
</BODY>
</HTML>
```

See also:	*Element object*, `Form.elements[]`, *FormElement object*, *Input object*, `Input.accessKey`, `onClick`

Property	JavaScript	JScript	N	IE	Opera	DOM	HTML	Notes
checked	1.0 +	1.0 +	2.0 +	3.02 +	3.0 +	1 +	-	-
defaultChecked	1.0 +	1.0 +	2.0 +	3.02 +	3.0 +	1 +	-	-
indeterminate	-	3.0 +	-	4.0 +	-	-	-	-
status	-	3.0 +	-	4.0 +	-	-	-	Warning
type	1.1 +	1.0 +	3.0 +	3.02 +	3.0 +	1 +	-	ReadOnly
value	1.0 +	1.0 +	2.0 +	3.02 +	3.0 +	1 +	-	Warning

Method	JavaScript	JScript	N	IE	Opera	DOM	HTML	Notes
handleEvent()	1.2 +	-	4.0 +	-	-	-	-	-

Event name	JavaScript	JScript	N	IE	Opera	DOM	HTML	Notes
onAfterUpdate	-	3.0 +	-	4.0 +	-	-	-	-
onBeforeUpdate	-	3.0 +	-	4.0 +	-	-	-	-
onBlur	1.1 +	3.0 +	3.0 +	4.0 +	3.0 +	-	-	Warning
onClick	1.0 +	3.0 +	2.0 +	4.0 +	3.0 +	-	4.0 +	Warning
onDblClick	1.2 +	3.0 +	4.0 +	4.0 +	3.0 +	-	4.0 +	Warning
onErrorUpdate	-	3.0 +	-	4.0 +	-	-	-	-
onFilterChange	-	3.0 +	-	4.0 +	-	-	-	-
onFocus	1.0 +	3.0 +	2.0 +	4.0 +	3.0 +	-	-	Warning
onHelp	-	3.0 +	-	4.0 +	-	-	-	Warning
onKeyDown	1.2 +	3.0 +	4.0 +	4.0 +	3.0 +	-	4.0 +	Warning
onKeyPress	1.2 +	3.0 +	4.0 +	4.0 +	3.0 +	-	4.0 +	Warning

Table continued on following page

117

Event name	JavaScript	JScript	N	IE	Opera	DOM	HTML	Notes
onKeyUp	1.2 +	3.0 +	4.0 +	4.0 +	3.0 +	-	4.0 +	Warning
onMouseDown	1.2 +	3.0 +	4.0 +	4.0 +	3.0 +	-	4.0 +	Warning
onMouseMove	1.2 +	3.0 +	4.0 +	4.0 +	-	-	4.0 +	Warning
onMouseOut	1.1 +	3.0 +	3.0 +	4.0 +	3.0 +	-	4.0 +	Warning
onMouseOver	1.0 +	3.0 +	2.0 +	4.0 +	3.0 +	-	4.0 +	Warning
onMouseUp	1.2 +	3.0 +	4.0 +	4.0 +	3.0 +	-	4.0 +	Warning
onRowEnter	-	3.0 +	-	4.0 +	-	-	-	-
onRowExit	-	3.0 +	-	4.0 +	-	-	-	-

Inheritance chain:

Element object, Input object, Node object

ChildNodes object (Object/DOM)

A collection of all the children belonging to a DOM Node object.

Availability:	DOM level – 1 JavaScript – 1.5 JScript – 5.0 Internet Explorer – 5.0 Netscape – 6.0
JavaScript syntax:	- myChildNodes = myElement.childNodes

This is part of the internal DOM hierarchy model in the browser. There are several tree hierarchies supported and this one maintains a tree of parent-child node relationships across the document.

See also:	Element object, Element.childNodes[], Hierarchy of objects

Class (Property/internal)

Internal property that returns an object class.

Availability:	ECMAScript edition – 2

This internal property returns a string value containing the class name of the containing object.

Every object type must implement this property.

It is supported by all built-in native objects in an ECMA compliant JavaScript interpreter.

Host objects may supply any value as a `Class` identifying string. They may even masquerade as one of the built-in classes, but good sense suggests that if they do, then they must obey the protocol of that built-in class in precisely the same way as if they were a real built-in object. It's probably sensible for host implementers to avoid overloading the built-in class names like that.

At edition 2 of the ECMA standard, there is no publicly accessible method to retrieve this property in a script. However, the reserved keyword values suggest that this may be offered at a later revision of the standard.

See also: *Array.Class*, *Boolean.Class*, *class*, *Date.Class*, *Function.Class*, Internal Property, *Number.Class*, *Object.Class*, Reserved word, *String.Class*

Property attributes:

Internal.

Cross-references:

ECMA 262 edition 2 – section – 8.6.2

ECMA 262 edition 3 – section – 8.6.2

class (Reserved word)

Reserved for future language enhancements.

Although you cannot request the class of a particular object, you can probably establish what class it belongs to with the `typeof` operator.

This keyword also represents a Java object type and the `class` keyword allows for the potential extension of JavaScript interfaces to access Java applet parameters and return values.

See also: *Class*, Internal Property, *java.lang.Class*, LiveConnect, Reserved word, *typeof*

Cross-references:

ECMA 262 edition 2 – section – 7.4.3

ECMA 262 edition 2 – section – 11.4.3

ECMA 262 edition 3 – section – 7.5.3

ECMA 262 edition 3 – section – 11.4.3

CLASS="..." (HTML Tag Attribute)

A means of associating a tag with a style sheet class. Represented by the
className property of an Element object.

Availability:	DOM level – 1 JavaScript – 1.5 JScript – 3.0 Internet Explorer – 4.0 Netscape – 6.0

In MSIE, virtually any object can be associated with a style object by means of
the CLASS attribute. This is reflected into the className property of the object. It
is especially applicable to DOM related objects which are considered to be sub-
classed from the Element object. Netscape 6.0 brings that browser into line with
these capabilities.

See also:	DOM, Element object, Element.className, Element.style, STYLE object (1), style object (2)

client object (Object/NES)

A server-side object available in NES.

Availability:	JavaScript – 1.1 Netscape Enterprise Server – 2.0	
JavaScript syntax:	NES	client
HTML syntax:	client	
Object methods:	destroy(), expiration()	

One client object is created for each browser user. It is created when the user first
accesses the NES application and persists until some time after they have last visited.
A timeout allows the server to garbage collect these session objects and purge
them out. If a client comes back again later, a new object would need to be created.

Because there is no session object in Netscape Enterprise Server, this object serves
the purpose of maintaining session state as well as holding details of the client.

To maintain state across all session in an application, you should use the project
object discussed in a separate topic.

Client objects have a limited lifetime. It is configurable but typically they will
expire and be discarded after 10 minutes of inactivity.

See also:	Netscape Enterprise Server, project object, response.client, unwatch(), watch()

Method	JavaScript	JScript	NES	Notes
destroy()	1.1 +	-	2.0 +	-
expiration()	1.1 +	-	2.0 +	-

Clip object (Object/Navigator)

An object that represents a clip region within a layer.

Availability:	JavaScript – 1.2 Netscape – 4.0 Deprecated Netscape 6.0
JavaScript syntax:	N *myClip = myLayer.clip* N *myClip = myStyle.clip* N *myClip = myTextRectangle* N *myClip = myRect*
Object properties:	bottom, height, left, right, top, width

This object represents a clipping rectangle that the visible part of a display object is viewed through. This is most likely used with a layer object. The layer contents would be drawn off-screen and then that part which falls within the clipping rectangle would be displayed in the window.

This can be useful for performing wipes and making parts of a layer progressively visible within some kind of transition loop.

In the MSIE browser, these rectangular objects are manufactured as needed with the rect() constructor function.

Warnings:

❑ No longer supported in Netscape 6.0.

See also:	Layer.clip, *Rect object*, style.clip, *textRectangle object*

Property	JavaScript	JScript	N	IE	Opera	Notes
bottom	1.2 +	-	4.0 +	-	-	Warning, Deprecated
height	1.2 +	-	4.0 +	-	-	Warning, Deprecated
left	1.2 +	-	4.0 +	-	-	Warning, Deprecated
right	1.2 +	-	4.0 +	-	-	Warning, Deprecated
top	1.2 +	-	4.0 +	-	-	Warning, Deprecated
width	1.2 +	-	4.0 +	-	-	Warning, Deprecated

clipboardData object (Object/JScript)

An object that can be used with editing operations to provide script-driven access to the clipboard contents.

Availability:	JScript – 5.0 Internet Explorer – 5.0	
JavaScript syntax:	IE	*myClipboardData* = clipboardData
	IE	*myClipboardData* = myWindow.clipboardData
Object methods:	clearData(),getData(),setData()	

If you want to move data in and out of the clipboard on a Windows platform from within the MSIE browser, this object encapsulates the clipboard contents.

Refer to the dataTransfer object for a description of the clearData(), getData() and setData() methods that may also be used with the clipboardData object.

See also:	dataTransfer.clearData(), dataTransfer.getData(),Window.clipboardData

Method	JavaScript	JScript	N	IE	Opera	Notes
clearData()	-	5.0 +	-	5.0 +	-	-
getData()	-	5.0 +	-	5.0 +	-	-
setData()	-	5.0 +	-	5.0 +	-	-

Closure object (Object/internal)

A special kind of function object that preserves prototype inheritance and scope.

Availability:	JavaScript – 1.2 Netscape – 4.0	
JavaScript syntax:	N	*myClosure* = new Closure()
Object properties:	__parent__,__proto__	

This is a special kind of object, which maintains some contextual state information when it is created.

It can behave like a function, but is a kind of function wrapper that references a function and a scope. Since it inherits everything from the Function object, it can behave like a function and can be called as such.

Because it also stores the scope chain at the time it is manufactured, it can restore that scope chain when it is executed.

See also:	Lexical scoping

Property	JavaScript	JScript	N	IE	Opera	Notes
__parent__	1.2 +	-	4.0 +	-	-	-
__proto__	1.2 +	-	4.0 +	-	-	-

Closure() (Object/Navigator)

A Closure object constructor.

Availability:	JavaScript – 1.2 Netscape – 4.0	
JavaScript syntax:	N	new Closure(aFunction, aTarget)
Argument list:	aFunction	The declaration of a function
	aTarget	An object to associate the function with

This constructor is used internally to create a Closure object containing the function associated with a target object.

The Closure() constructor is used in Netscape 4 to create an event handler function that can be forced to run in a scope containing a target object.

Example code:

```
document.myform.myButton.onclick =
new Closure(
    function()
    {
        document.validated = false;
    },
    document.myform.myButton
);
```

See also:	Constructor function, constructor property, *Global object*, Object constant

clsid: URL (Request method)

Used by MSIE to locate ActiveX controls for the <OBJECT> tag.

A special request method for loading ActiveX objects from the locally stored object repository. This provides a portable cross platform, installation independent way to refer to the folder where you have installed shared ActiveX objects on your system. It is more or less equivalent to the file: request method but without the need to specify a path to the folder.

See also:	OBJECT.classid, URL

Code block delimiter {} (Delimiter)

A delimiting token for a block of executable script source text.

Availability:	ECMAScript edition – 2 JavaScript – 1.0 JScript – 1.0 Internet Explorer – 3.02 Netscape – 2.0 Netscape Enterprise Server – 2.0 Opera – 3.0	
JavaScript syntax:	-	aLabel: { someScript }
Argument list:	aLabel	An optional identifier to name the code block
	someScript	Some legal JavaScript source text

A block is a list of statements that form one syntactic unit enclosed in curly brace characters ({ }).

This is particularly useful in conditional execution and iterative execution. Both of those are expected to operate on a single syntactic unit. A block allows that single syntactic unit to be composed of multiple lines of source script text.

Because the curly brace characters are used to delimit a block of code that comprises a list of semi-colon terminated statements, you do not need to place any semi-colons after the closing curly brace.

A block of code is most often used like this with an iterator or conditional test to either call the same section of code repetitively or as the result of a conditional expression returning a true value.

In compiled languages, variables declared inside a block are sometimes local to that block and are garbage collected when the block exits. The ECMA standard indicates that variables created inside a code block will be global unless that code block is the body of a function. In ECMA compliant interpreters, a block does not instantiate a new execution context whereas in C language it does create a new scope within which the variables exist.

This means that variables created inside an 'if keyword' controlled compound statement will be function local or globally accessible according to whether the 'if keyword' is in a function or global code section.

Braces must be used in pairs. Although the JavaScript interpreters may forgive you when you miss out some language elements, very subtle and difficult to diagnose errors can occur if you misplace a brace character.

Modern text editors give you a lot of help when balancing pairs of braces.

The associativity is left to right.

Refer to the operator precedence topic for details of execution order.

At version 1.2 of JavaScript, you can name the code block and use the labeled form of the break keyword to exit the block prematurely.

See also:	Associativity, else if (...) ..., if(...) ..., if(...) ... else ..., Label, Operator Precedence, Punctuator

Cross-references:

ECMA 262 edition 2 – section – 12.5

ECMA 262 edition 3 – section – 12.1

Wrox *Instant JavaScript* – page – 18

COL object (Object/HTML)

An object that represents a <COL> HTML tag.

Availability:	DOM level – 1
	JavaScript – 1.5
	JScript – 3.0
	Internet Explorer – 4.0
	Netscape – 6.0
Inherits from:	*Element object*

JavaScript syntax:	IE	*myCOL* = *myDocument*.all.*anElementID*
	IE	*myCOL* = *myDocument*.all.tags("COL")[*anIndex*]
	IE	*myCOL* = *myDocument*.all[*aName*]
	-	*myCOL* = *myDocument*.getElementById (*anElementID*)
	-	*myCOL* = *myDocument*.getElementsByName (*aName*)[*anIndex*]
	-	*myCOL* = *myDocument*.getElementsByTagName ("COL")[*anIndex*]

HTML syntax:	<COL> ... </COL>	
Argument list:	*anIndex*	A valid reference to an item in the collection
	aName	The name attribute of an element
	anElementID	The ID attribute of an element

Object properties:	align, ch, chOff, span, vAlign, width
Event handlers:	onClick, onDblClick, onHelp, onKeyDown, onKeyPress, onKeyUp, onMouseDown, onMouseMove, onMouseOut, onMouseOver, onMouseUp

This object represents the <COL> tag which is used within <TABLE> constructs to provide a way of controlling an entire table column from a single definition. It is used in conjunction with a <COLGROUP> construct.

The HTML 4 specification describes functionality that currently none of the widely available browsers supports properly.

The DOM specification describes a HTMLTableColElement object which is the standardized interface to this class.

See also:	COLGROUP object, Element object, style.columnSpan, TABLE object, TABLE.rules, TableColElement object, TableColElement.align, TableColElement.ch, TableColElement.chOff, TableColElement.span, TableColElement.vAlign, TableColElement.width

Property	JavaScript	JScript	N	IE	Opera	DOM	HTML	Notes
align	1.5 +	3.0 +	6.0 +	4.0 +	-	1 +	-	-
ch	1.5 +	-	6.0 +	-	-	1 +	-	-
chOff	1.5 +	-	6.0 +	-	-	1 +	-	-
span	1.5 +	3.0 +	6.0 +	4.0 +	-	1 +	-	-
vAlign	1.5 +	3.0 +	6.0 +	4.0 +	-	1 +	-	-
width	1.5 +	3.0 +	6.0 +	4.0 +	-	1 +	-	-

Event name	JavaScript	JScript	N	IE	Opera	DOM	HTML	Notes
onClick	1.5 +	3.0 +	6.0 +	4.0 +	3.0 +	-	4.0 +	Warning
onDblClick	1.5 +	3.0 +	6.0 +	4.0 +	3.0 +	-	4.0 +	Warning
onHelp	-	3.0 +	-	4.0 +	-	-	-	Warning
onKeyDown	1.5 +	3.0 +	6.0 +	4.0 +	3.0 +	-	4.0 +	Warning
onKeyPress	1.5 +	3.0 +	6.0 +	4.0 +	3.0 +	-	4.0 +	Warning
onKeyUp	1.5 +	3.0 +	6.0 +	4.0 +	3.0 +	-	4.0 +	Warning
onMouseDown	1.5 +	3.0 +	6.0 +	4.0 +	3.0 +	-	4.0 +	Warning
onMouseMove	1.5 +	3.0 +	6.0 +	4.0 +	-	-	4.0 +	Warning
onMouseOut	1.5 +	3.0 +	6.0 +	4.0 +	3.0 +	-	4.0 +	Warning
onMouseOver	1.5 +	3.0 +	6.0 +	4.0 +	3.0 +	-	4.0 +	Warning
onMouseUp	1.5 +	3.0 +	6.0 +	4.0 +	3.0 +	-	4.0 +	Warning

Inheritance chain:

Element object, Node object

COLGROUP object (Object/HTML)

An object that represents the <COLGROUP> HTML tag.

Availability:	DOM level – 1 JavaScript – 1.5 JScript – 3.0 Internet Explorer – 4.0 Netscape – 6.0	
Inherits from:	*Element object*	
JavaScript syntax:	IE	*myCOLGROUP =* *myDocument.all.anElementID*
	IE	*myCOLGROUP = myDocument.all.tags* *("COLGROUP")[anIndex]*
	IE	*myCOLGROUP = myDocument.all[aName]*
	-	*myCOLGROUP = myDocument* *.getElementById(anElementID)*
	-	*myCOLGROUP = myDocument* *.getElementsByName(aName)[anIndex]*
	-	*myCOLGROUP = myDocument.getElements* *ByTagName("COLGROUP")[anIndex]*
HTML syntax:	<COLGROUP> ... </COLGROUP>	
Argument list:	*anIndex*	A valid reference to an item in the collection
	aName	The name attribute of an element
	anElementID	The ID attribute of an element

Object properties:	`align, ch, chOff, span, vAlign, width`
Event handlers:	`onClick, onDblClick, onHelp, onKeyDown, onKeyPress, onKeyUp, onMouseDown, onMouseMove, onMouseOut, onMouseOver, onMouseUp`

The <COL> and <COLGROUP> tags correspond to objects that represent the column or group of columns within a <TABLE> construct. Individual columns map to the COL object and groups of columns to the COLGROUP object. Attributes can be applied to a group of columns and overridden on an individual columns basis if necessary.

The DOM specification mentions an HTMLTableColElement object which provides the functionality of this class.

See also:	*COL object,* `style.columnSpan`, *TABLE object,* `TABLE.rules`, *TableColElement object,* `TableColElement.align`, `TableColElement.ch`, `TableColElement.chOff`, `TableColElement.span`, `TableColElement.vAlign`, `TableColElement.width`

Property	JavaScript	JScript	N	IE	Opera	DOM	HTML	Notes
align	1.5 +	3.0 +	6.0 +	4.0 +	-	1 +	-	-
ch	1.5 +	-	6.0 +	-	-	1 +	-	-
chOff	1.5 +	-	6.0 +	-	-	1 +	-	-
span	1.5 +	3.0 +	6.0 +	4.0 +	-	1 +	-	-
vAlign	1.5 +	3.0 +	6.0 +	4.0 +	-	1 +	-	-
width	1.5 +	3.0 +	6.0 +	4.0 +	-	1 +	-	-

Event name	JavaScript	JScript	N	IE	Opera	DOM	HTML	Notes
onClick	1.5 +	3.0 +	6.0 +	4.0 +	3.0 +	-	4.0 +	Warning
onDblClick	1.5 +	3.0 +	6.0 +	4.0 +	3.0 +	-	4.0 +	Warning
onHelp	-	3.0 +	-	4.0 +	-	-	-	Warning
onKeyDown	1.5 +	3.0 +	6.0 +	4.0 +	3.0 +	-	4.0 +	Warning
onKeyPress	1.5 +	3.0 +	6.0 +	4.0 +	3.0 +	-	4.0 +	Warning
onKeyUp	1.5 +	3.0 +	6.0 +	4.0 +	3.0 +	-	4.0 +	Warning
onMouseDown	1.5 +	3.0 +	6.0 +	4.0 +	3.0 +	-	4.0 +	Warning
onMouseMove	1.5 +	3.0 +	6.0 +	4.0 +	-	-	4.0 +	Warning
onMouseOut	1.5 +	3.0 +	6.0 +	4.0 +	3.0 +	-	4.0 +	Warning
onMouseOver	1.5 +	3.0 +	6.0 +	4.0 +	3.0 +	-	4.0 +	Warning
onMouseUp	1.5 +	3.0 +	6.0 +	4.0 +	3.0 +	-	4.0 +	Warning

Inheritance chain:

Element object, Node object

Collection object (Object/DOM)

An array of Element objects.

Availability:	DOM level – 1 JavaScript – 1.5 JScript – 3.0 Internet Explorer – 4.0 Netscape – 6.0 Opera – 3.0	
JavaScript syntax:	IE	myCollection = myDocument.all
	IE	myCollection = myDocument.children
	IE	myCollection = myDocument.filters
	-	myCollection = myDocument.get ElementsByName(aName)[anIndex]
	IE	myCollection = myElement.all
	IE	myCollection = myElement.children
	IE	myCollection = myElement.filters
	-	myCollection = myDocument .getElementsByTagName(aTag) [anIndex]
Argument list:	aName	The name attribute of an element
	anIndex	A valid reference to an item in the collection
	aTag	The name of a tag
Object properties:	length	
Object methods:	Item(), namedItem(), tags()	

A collection object is an enhancement to the basic array object to provide some additional searching capabilities for managing the contents of the document object model in a web browser.

Do not confuse DOM NodeList arrays with Enumerator or Collection objects. The NodeListitem() method is subtly different to the Enumerator.Item() method.

See also:	TABLE.cells[]

Property	JavaScript	JScript	N	IE	Opera	DOM	Notes
length	1.5 +	3.0 +	6.0 +	4.0 +	3.0 +	1 +	ReadOnly

Method	JavaScript	JScript	N	IE	Opera	DOM	Notes
Item()	1.5 +	3.0 +	6.0 +	4.0 +	5.0 +	1 +	Warning
namedItem()	1.5 +	5.0 +	6.0 +	5.0 +	5.0 +	1 +	-
tags()	-	3.0 +	-	4.0 +	-	-	-

Colon (:) (Delimiter)

A delimiter used with labels and conditional operators.

Availability:	ECMAScript edition – 2 JavaScript – 1.2 JScript – 3.0 Internet Explorer – 4.0 Netscape – 4.0

This delimiter is used with the case keyword and the default keyword in switch statement blocks.

Refer to the switch topic for details of how this is used.

See also:	switch(...) ... case: ... default: ...

Comma operator (,) (Delimiter)

An argument separator token.

Availability:	ECMAScript edition – 2 JavaScript – 1.0 JScript – 1.0 Internet Explorer – 3.02 Netscape – 2.0 Netscape Enterprise Server – 2.0 Opera – 3.0

The comma operator provides a way to evaluate several assignment expressions at once.

It is provided as a way to express the arguments to a function in a manner consistent with the ECMA standard.

It is also used in variable declaration lists to declare more than one variable with a single var statement.

Its most subtle use is to exploit the side effects of an expression without assigning the result of that expression to anything. This is actually so subtle as to confuse what it's actually doing. There is probably a simpler way to express the same functionality that probably doesn't execute any slower and is a lot easier to maintain.

The associativity is left to right. This means that the expressions should be executed in left to right order of appearance in the script source text. The result of the entire expression will be the evaluation of the last comma separated item. It is not good style to use a comma separated list as an RValue in an assignment to an LValue.

Example code:

```
// Declaring several variables
var e, c, d, x, y;

// Arguments in a for iterator header
for(a=0; a<10; a++, b++)
{
}

// Add c to d and assign the result to e with incrementing
// side effects
e = (x++, y++, c) + (z--, d)
```

See also:	Associativity, Comma expression, `Document.write()`, `Document.writeln()`, Operator Precedence, *var*

Cross-references:

ECMA 262 edition 2 – section – 11.14

ECMA 262 edition 3 – section – 11.14

Wrox *Instant JavaScript* – page – 21

Comment (// and /* ... */) (Delimiter)

Mark a multi-line comment block.

Availability:	ECMAScript edition – 2
	JavaScript – 1.0
	JScript – 1.0
	Internet Explorer – 3.02
	Netscape – 2.0
	Netscape Enterprise Server – 2.0
	Opera – 3.0
JavaScript syntax:	- `/* First line of comment text`
	- `Second line of comment text`
	- `Third line of comment text */`
	- `// Comment text`

There are two kinds of comment blocks supported by JavaScript. They each have a different kind of delimiter.

Single line comments commence with a pair of slash characters (//) and stop at the end of the current line.

Multi-line comments start with a slash-asterisk (/*) and finish at the first following asterisk-slash (*/). This means you cannot nest multiple line comment blocks inside one another. The disadvantage with that is that it is common practice in some languages to comment out sections of code by marking the start and end of the inactive sections as a multi-line comment block. This won't work if there are any multi-line comment blocks anywhere in this inactive block. A better technique, although slightly more cumbersome, is to use single line comments (//) to 'switch-off' the lines of code you want to deactivate. Thus:

```
//a = 1000;
//b = 2000;
//c = 3000;
```

See also:	Comment, Lexical convention, Line, Line terminator, Multi-line comment, Single line comment

Cross-references:

ECMA 262 edition 2 – section – 7.3

ECMA 262 edition 3 – section – 7.4

COMMENT object (Object/DOM)

An object that represents a section of HTML enclosed in comment delimiter tags.

Availability:	DOM level – 1 JavaScript – 1.5 JScript – 3.0 Internet Explorer – 4.0 Netscape – 6.0	
Inherits from:	*CharacterData object*	
JavaScript syntax:	IE	*myCOMMENT = myDocument*.all.*anElementID*
	IE	*myCOMMENT = myDocument*.all.tags ("COMMENT") [*anIndex*]
	IE	*myCOMMENT = myDocument*.all[*aName*]
	-	*myCOMMENT = myDocument*.getElementById (*anElementID*)
	-	*myCOMMENT = myDocument*.getElements ByName (*aName*) [*anIndex*]
	N	*myCOMMENT = myDocument*.createComment (*aString*)
	-	*myCOMMENT = myDocument*.getElements ByTagName ("COMMENT") [*anIndex*]

HTML syntax:	`<!-- ... -->`	
Argument list:	`anIndex`	An item within the collection
	`aString`	A comment string
	`aName`	The name of an element
	`anElementID`	The ID attribute of an element
Object properties:	`text`	
Object methods:	`click()`, `getAttribute()`, `removeAttribute()`, `setAttribute()`	
Collections:	`all[]`, `children[]`	

It is somewhat unlikely you would ever want to modify the contents of a comment tag. However, access to the text contained within it may be a way of passing hidden data values to your scripts without them being visible in the displayed page. Of course they would still be visible in the document source, but you might be able to avoid the creation of a `<FORM>` and hidden `<INPUT>` object.

Warnings:

❑ The DOM level 1 specification describes this as a `Comment` object, but MSIE implements it as a `COMMENT` object instead. You may need to be aware of this in case other platforms implement the DOM specified class exactly as it is intended.

See also:	*CharacterData object*, `Document.createComment()`, *Element object*, *Hiding scripts from old browsers*

Property	JavaScript	JScript	N	IE	Opera	DOM	Notes
text	-	3.0 +	-	4.0 +	-	-	-

Method	JavaScript	JScript	N	IE	Opera	DOM	Notes
click()	1.5 +	3.0 +	6.0 +	4.0 +	-	1 +	Warning
getAttribute()	1.5 +	3.0 +	6.0 +	4.0 +	-	1 +	Warning
removeAttribute()	1.5 +	3.0 +	6.0 +	4.0 +	-	1 +	Warning
setAttribute()	1.5 +	3.0 +	6.0 +	4.0 +	-	1 +	Warning

Inheritance chain:

`CharacterData` object, `Node` object

Concatenate then assign (+=) (Operator/assignment)

Concatenate two string operands and assign the result to the first. See addition for numeric values.

Availability:	ECMAScript edition – 2 JavaScript – 1.0 JScript – 1.0 Internet Explorer – 3.02 Netscape – 2.0
Property/method value type:	`Number primitive`
JavaScript syntax:	-

JavaScript syntax:	-	`anOperand1 += anOperand2`
Argument list:	`anOperand1`	A numeric value that can be assigned to
	`anOperand2`	Another numeric value

Concatenate the right operand to the left operand and assign the result to the left operand.

This is functionally equivalent to the expression:

```
anOperand1 = anOperand1 + anOperand2;
```

Although this is classified as an assignment operator, it is really a compound of an assignment and a concatenation operator.

It also works with numeric values and will add the second to the first.

The associativity is right to left.

Refer to the operator precedence topic for details of execution order.

The new value of *anOperand1* is returned as a result of the expression.

Warnings:

❑ The operand to the left of the operator must be an LValue. That is, it should be able to take an assignment and store the value.

See also:	*Add then assign (+=), Assign value (=),* Assignment expression, Assignment operator, Associativity, LValue, Operator Precedence

Cross-references:

ECMA 262 edition 2 – section – 11.13

ECMA 262 edition 3 – section – 11.13

Conditional code block (Pre-processor)

A pseudo pre-processor mechanism for conditionally executing code in MSIE.

There is an implementation of a C language inspired pre-processor in the MSIE JScript interpreter.

The usual pre-processor directives for conditional code use are reproduced here except that in C language they are prefixed with a hash symbol (#) and in JScript the commercial at sign (@) is used instead.

There are several directives and a set of predefined constants:

- ❑ @cc_on Statement
- ❑ @if Statement
- ❑ @set Statement
- ❑ @elif(...) ... Statement
- ❑ @else... Statement
- ❑ @end Statement
- ❑ @<variable_name> Reference
- ❑ @_alpha Pre-defined constant
- ❑ @_jscript Pre-defined constant
- ❑ @_jscript_build Pre-defined constant
- ❑ @_jscript_version Pre-defined constant
- ❑ @_mac Pre-defined constant
- ❑ @_mc680x0 Pre-defined constant
- ❑ @_PowerPC Pre-defined constant
- ❑ @_win16 Pre-defined constant
- ❑ @_win32 Pre-defined constant
- ❑ @_x86 Pre-defined constant

Warnings:

- ❑ This is not supported prior to MSIE version 4.

See also: *Pre-processing – @cc_on, Pre-processing – @elif(...) ..., Pre-processing – @else ..., Pre-processing – @end, Pre-processing – @if(...) ...*

Conditional comment (HTML Tag)

A portability trick that only works in Netscape.

Availability:	JavaScript – 1.2 Netscape – 4.0

Conditional comments use JavaScript entities to enclose a block of JavaScript and only execute it conditionally on some value being true.

It is accomplished by embedding a JavaScript entity with a logical expression evaluation in it. If the expression proves true then the <SCRIPT> HTML tag enclosed in the comment block is parsed, otherwise it is ignored.

This is how it's done. A conditional comment is formed by adding an ampersand character to the leading tag of a comment. Rather than use "<!--" the comment is introduced with "<!--&" instead. The comment is closed in the normal way with a trailing "-->" string. Inside the comment a <SCRIPT></SCRIPT> block is placed with some global code to be executed if called for.

Warnings:

❑ This only works in Netscape 4 or later which limits its usefulness somewhat. MSIE supports an alternative, but completely incompatible technique that only works inside the <SCRIPT> tag.

Example code:

```
<!--&{navigator.userAgent == "Mozilla/4.7 (Macintosh; I; PPC) "};
<SCRIPT>
document.write("Power Macintosh running Navigator 4.7");
</SCRIPT>
-->
```

See also:	Adding JavaScript to HTML

Conditionally execute (?:) (Operator/conditional)

Conditionally execute one code branch or another.

Availability:	ECMAScript edition – 2 JavaScript – 1.0 JScript – 1.0 Internet Explorer – 3.02 Netscape – 2.0 Netscape Enterprise Server – 2.0 Opera – 3.0	
Property/method value type:	Depends on arguments	
JavaScript syntax:	-	aCondition ? someCode : moreCode
Argument list:	aCondition	A relational or logical expression that yields true or false
	moreCode	Code that is executed if aCondition is false
	someCode	Code that is executed if aCondition is true

The two associated code blocks are executed according to the value yielded by a Boolean test on the first operand. If it is true, then the first code block is executed, otherwise the second is used.

The associativity is right to left.

Refer to the operator precedence topic for details of execution order.

This is sometimes called a Ternary operator, because it takes three operands.

Example code:

```
<HTML>
<HEAD></HEAD>
<BODY>
<SCRIPT>
mySwitch = false;
myResult = (mySwitch) ? "TRUE VALUE" : "FALSE VALUE" ;
document.write(myResult);
</SCRIPT>
</BODY>
</HTML>
```

See also:	Associativity, Conditional expression, Flow control, *if(...)* ..., *if(...) ... else ...*, Operator Precedence, Selection statement, Ternary operator

Cross-references:

ECMA 262 edition 2 – section – 11.12

ECMA 262 edition 3 – section – 11.12

Connection object (Object/NES)

An object that represents a connection from the server to the back-end database.

Availability:	JavaScript – 1.2 Netscape Enterprise Server – 3.0	
JavaScript syntax:	NES	*myConnection = myDbPool* .connection(*aName, aTimeout*)
Argument list:	*aName*	A connection name
	aTimeout	Timeout in seconds
Object properties:	prototype	
Object methods:	beginTransaction(), commitTransaction(), connected(), cursor(), execute(), majorErrorCode(), majorErrorMessage(), minorErrorCode(), minorErrorMessage(), release(), rollbackTransaction(), SQLTable(), storedProc(), toString()	

This object is used to maintain the connection state details between the Netscape Enterprise Server and the back-end database it is retrieving data from.

A connection object is created by calling the connection() method of the DbPool object.

Example code:

```
<SERVER>
// An example of how to create a connection object
// Based on the one in Wrox Professional JavaScript
myDbPool    = new DbPool("ODBC", "myDatabase", "", "", "");
myConnection = myDbPool.connection("ExampleConnection", 30);
myConnection.SQLTable("SELECT * FROM MY_TABLE");
</SERVER>
```

See also:	DbPool.connection(), Netscape Enterprise Server, *unwatch(), watch()*

Property	JavaScript	JScript	NES	Notes
prototype	1.2 +	-	3.0 +	-

Method	JavaScript	JScript	NES	Notes
beginTransaction()	1.2 +	-	3.0 +	-
commitTransaction()	1.2 +	-	3.0 +	-
connected()	1.2 +	-	3.0 +	-
cursor()	1.2 +	-	3.0 +	-
execute()	1.2 +	-	3.0 +	-
majorErrorCode()	1.2 +	-	3.0 +	-
majorErrorMessage()	1.2 +	-	3.0 +	-
minorErrorCode()	1.2 +	-	3.0 +	-
minorErrorMessage()	1.2 +	-	3.0 +	-
release()	1.2 +	-	3.0 +	-
rollbackTransaction()	1.2 +	-	3.0 +	-
SQLTable()	1.2 +	-	3.0 +	-
storedProc()	1.2 +	-	3.0 +	Warning
toString()	1.2 +	-	3.0 +	-

const (Reserved word)

Reserved for future language enhancements.

This keyword suggests that future standardization may support immutable constant values. This may allow stronger type casting of formal parameters in function prototypes.

See also:	Function prototype, Reserved word, Type, *volatile*

Cross-references:

ECMA 262 edition 2 – section – 7.4.3

ECMA 262 edition 3 – section – 7.5.3

Construct (Property/internal)

An object constructor call.

Availability:	ECMAScript edition – 2

The internal constructor is invoked via the new operator.

This is not implemented by all objects. Those that do support it are called constructor objects. In other languages these might be called factory objects.

Warnings:

❑ The global object does not have a Construct property and you cannot make copies of it with the new operator.

See also:	Constructor function, constructor property, Internal Method

Property attributes:

DontEnum.

Cross-references:

ECMA 262 edition 2 – section – 15

ECMA 262 edition 3 – section – 15.1.4

continue (Statement)

Force the next iteration of a loop.

Availability:	ECMAScript edition – 2 JavaScript – 1.0 JScript – 1.0 Internet Explorer – 3.0 Netscape – 2.0 Netscape Enterprise Server – 2.0 Opera – 3.0	
JavaScript syntax:	-	continue aLabelName;
	-	continue;
Argument list:	aLabelName	The name of a label associated with some code

The continue keyword is a jump statement. It is used in an iterator loop to proceed to the next cycle without executing the remaining lines in the statement block.

A continue statement can only legally exist inside a while or for loop in an ECMA compliant implementation. Implementations that provide additional iterator types may also honor the same behavior for the continue statement.

The continue statement would normally be executed conditionally, otherwise it would cause the remaining lines to be redundant since no execution flow would ever reach them. Compilers generally warn you about this, but JavaScript would likely simply ignore it.

The continue statement is obeyed by the smallest enclosing iterator loop.

At version 1.2 of JavaScript, the continue statement was enhanced to support a label as a continuing destination. When the continue is processed, it will jump to the start of the statement that has been labeled. If an iterator is labeled, then the continue is associated with that iterator. This mechanism can only be used in a while, for or for...in loop.

A labeled continue behaves differently according to the iterator it has been used in.

Warnings:

❑ In Netscape 4, there is a bug with labeled continue statements and do...while loops that causes the continue to vector to the top of the loop without testing the condition. This can set up an endless loop. You could work round this by creating a while loop and modifying the test condition.

❑ When the continue statement is used, its behavior inside a while loop suggests that a while loop is not exactly similar to a for loop. In a while loop, it simply runs the test condition again before deciding to loop or not. In a for loop, the incrementor gets executed again and then the test condition. You cannot perfectly simulate a for loop with a while loop if a continue statement is involved.

See also:	*break*, Completion type, *do ... while(...)*, *for(...) ...*, *for(... in ...) ...*, Iteration statement, Jump statement, Label, *return*, Scope chain, Statement, *while(...) ...*

Cross-references:

ECMA 262 edition 2 – section – 10.1.4

ECMA 262 edition 2 – section – 12.7

ECMA 262 edition 3 – section – 10.1.4

ECMA 262 edition 3 – section – 12.7

Wrox *Instant JavaScript* – page – 25

Cookie domain (Attribute)

An attribute that defines the domain scope of a cookie.

For security reasons, cookies can only be sent back to the web server the creating document originated from. However, in large web server farms, the web pages may be distributed for load balancing reasons. Because of this, the domain attribute provides a way to widen the scope to any machine within a domain.

Cookie expires (Attribute)

An attribute that defines the expiry date and time of a cookie.

The lifetime of a cookie is defined with this attribute. From JavaScript, you can set this attribute but you cannot read it since there is no real object model for the cookies.

To define this attribute, you add a name value pair to the cookie definition string whose name is "expires" and whose value is defined according to the `Date.toGMTString()` method.

A cookie only survives for the duration of the page in the browser unless you define an expiry date for it. If the expiry date is in the future when the browser exits, they will be remembered in a persistent cache inside the browser. If not, the cookie is discarded and unavailable next time you run the browser.

See also:	`Date.toGMTString()`

Cookie path (Attribute)

An attribute that defines the path scope of a cookie.

The scope of a cookie can be limited to a certain part of the document tree within the web server. By defining a node within the document hierarchy, the cookie will only be sent to the web server when requesting a page that exists at that path or lower down in any sub-directories within it.

Unless you specify this value, the cookie will by default be available to any pages in the same directory as the page that created it or in pages lower down in sub-directories. These might be referred to as sibling or child pages. The path value is usually modified to be more inclusive than the default settings.

Cookie secure (Attribute)

A Boolean attribute that defines whether a cookie is secure or not.

The secure attribute is a Boolean value that defines whether the secure protocol is required. If it is activated, then the cookie is only sent to a server when the secure `https:` protocol is used. To activate this facility simply add the secure attribute to the cookie.

Crypto object (Object/Navigator)

An object to manage cryptographic resources.

Availability:	JavaScript – 1.2 Netscape – 4.04	
JavaScript syntax:	N	crypto
Object properties:	constructor	
Object methods:	random(), signText()	

This object appears to be quite opaque. That seems to make sense as you wouldn't want security related information to be visible simply by enumerating the properties.

There appear to be no enumerable properties belonging to this object.

See also:	Window.crypto

Property	JavaScript	JScript	N	IE	Opera	Notes
constructor	1.2 +	-	4.04 +	-	-	-

Method	JavaScript	JScript	N	IE	Opera	Notes
random()	1.2 +	-	4.04 +	-	-	-
signText()	1.2 +	-	4.04 +	-	-	-

Cryptoki (Security related)

Part of the Netscape security facilities.

Cryptoki is pronounced crypto-key and is short for cryptographic token interface. It is provided by RSA Data Security, Inc and can be accessed from C language and Java.

See also:	Pkcs11 object

CSS (Standard)

Cascading Style Sheets.

In the early days of the web, page designers were intent on creating ever more complex HTML in an effort to be able to organize how the content would appear on every browser. It became important to be able to render the page with pixel perfect accuracy. This was not the original intent of HTML.

With the introduction of CSS, designers were given a much larger range of tools with which to control the appearance of web pages. For some time CSS level 1 was thought to be sufficient. Eventually this was superseded by CSS level 2.

The Netscape 4 browser supports a third alternative, that of JavaScript Style Sheets or JSS for short. With the release of Netscape 6.0 providing standards based support, JSS has no future and should not be used in any new projects. Our JSS coverage has accordingly been marked as deprecated.

CSS is constructed from packages of rules, which are assembled into style sheets.

There is no object model defined for style sheets as of DOM level 1. Until this is ratified in a later DOM specification, Netscape and MSIE continue to support mutually incompatible style sheet API specifications.

The DOM level 2 implementation of CSS style objects (the CSS Object model) provides a complex hierarchy of objects. These are only partly implemented in current browsers. The most complete implementation is in the MSIE browser, and even then the objects are factored differently and the classes named in an MSIE specific manner.

The DOM CSS suite is embodied in the following classes:

- CSSStyleSheet
- CSSRuleList
- CSSRule
- CSSStyleRule
- CSSMediaRule
- CSSFontFaceRule
- CSSPageRule
- CSSImportRule
- CSSCharsetRule
- CSSUnknownRule
- CSSStyleDeclaration
- CSSValue
- CSSPrimitiveValue
- CSSValueList
- RGBColor
- Rect
- Counter
- ViewCSS
- DocumentCSS
- DOMImplementationCSS
- ElementCSSInlineStyle
- CSS2Properties

See also:	*<STYLE>*, *CSS level 1*, *CSS level 2*, *CSS-P*, Dynamic HTML

CSS level 1 (Standard)

A standard for describing style sheets.

The CSS level 1 standard was issued in December 1996 and describes a simple formatting model intended mainly for screen based presentations. It makes available approximately 50 properties for controlling the appearance of a web page.

See also: *<STYLE>*, *CSS*, *CSS level 2*, JavaScript Style Sheets

Web-references:

http://www.w3.org/TR/REC-CSS1

CSS level 2 (Standard)

A standard for describing style sheets.

The CSS level 2 standard was presented around May 1998 and was based on the earlier CSS1 standard. It adds another 70 properties to the 50 already available with CSS level 1.

See also: *<STYLE>*, *CSS*, *CSS level 1*, *CSS-P*, Dynamic positioning

Web-references:

http://www.w3.org/TR/REC-CSS2

CSS-P (Standard)

Specifically and only the positional controls for HTML entities, nowadays folded into the CSS level 2 standard.

Warnings:

❑ The CSS-P specification allows that any tag can be positioned. However Netscape 4 only supports the positioning of elements that have an opening and closing tag. This means you cannot position control an IMG object on its own unless you encapsulate it correctly within the document. You can position control an IMG object if it is enclosed within a set of balanced <SPAN>, <DIV> or <A> HTML tags.

❑ Netscape 4 also converts any absolutely positioned <DIV> tags into layers. This means you can manipulate them as layers but this requires special script code that is only usable on version 4 of Netscape. This has completely changed on Netscape 6.0.

See also: *CSS*, *CSS level 2*, Dynamic positioning

currentStyle object (Object/JScript)

An object that represents the cascaded format and style of its parent object.

Availability:	JScript – 5.0 Internet Explorer – 5.0
Inherits from:	*style object*
JavaScript syntax:	IE `myCurrentStyle = myElement.currentStyle`
Object methods:	`getAttribute(), getExpression(), removeExpression(), setAttribute(), setExpression()`

Because the style values are cascaded from style sheet to style sheet and may include some inline styles as well as some explicit styles, objects need to maintain a current style value that is the result of all the inheritances applied on top of one another.

In addition they maintain a run-time style which reflects dynamic changes as well. The run-time style is based on the current style in the first place.

This represents the cascaded format and style of its parent object.

The properties belonging to this object correspond closely to those of the `style` object and so there is little point in discussing them again here. Refer to the `style` object property descriptions for details of the various properties.

See also:	`Element.currentStyle`, `Element.runtimeStyle`, *runtimeStyle object*, *style object (2)*

Method	JavaScript	JScript	N	IE	Opera	Notes
`getAttribute()`	-	5.0 +	-	5.0 +	-	-
`getExpression()`	-	5.0 +	-	5.0 +	-	-
`removeExpression()`	-	5.0 +	-	5.0 +	-	-
`setAttribute()`	-	5.0 +	-	5.0 +	-	-
`setExpression()`	-	5.0 +	-	5.0 +	-	-

Cursor object (Object/NES)

This object encapsulates a cursor that was returned from the database as a result of an SQL query.

Availability:	JavaScript – 1.1 Netscape Enterprise Server – 2.0	
JavaScript syntax:	NES	*myCursor* = Connection.cursor (*aQuery*)
	NES	*myCursor* = Database.cursor(*aQuery*)
Argument list:	*aQuery*	A valid SQL query for the database
Object properties:	<column_name>	
Object methods:	blobImage(), blobLink(), close(), columnName(), columns(), deleteRow(), insertRow(), next(), updateRow()	

You can construct a cursor object by requesting it via the Connection object or database object, both of which have cursor methods.

Example code:

```
<SERVER>
// An example cursor retrieved from a database
// Based on the example from Wrox Professional JavaScript
database.connect("ODBC", "myDatabase", "", "", "");
myCursor = database.cursor("SELECT * FROM MY_TABLE");
</SERVER>
```

See also:	Connection.cursor(), *database object*, database.cursor(), Netscape Enterprise Server, *unwatch(), watch()*

Property	JavaScript	JScript	NES	Notes
<column_name>	1.1 +	-	2.0 +	-

Method	JavaScript	JScript	NES	Notes
blobImage()	1.1 +	-	2.0 +	-
blobLink()	1.1 +	-	2.0 +	-
close()	1.1 +	-	2.0 +	-
columnName()	1.1 +	-	2.0 +	-
columns()	1.1 +	-	2.0 +	-
deleteRow()	1.1 +	-	2.0 +	-
insertRow()	1.1 +	-	2.0 +	-
next()	1.1 +	-	2.0 +	-
updateRow()	1.1 +	-	2.0 +	-

147

about: URL (Request method)
AbstractView object (Object/DOM)
ActiveXObject object (Object/JScript)
Add (+) (Operator/additive)
Add then assign (+=) (Operator/
assignment)

Data-tainting (Security related)

A mechanism for marking data in the client and controlling its use. An obsolete security work-around.

The data-tainting model was implemented in Netscape 3 but deprecated by version 4. It was never implemented in MSIE.

Rather than prevent access to data in other parts of the browser space, it allows full access even to private data. However, that access marked the data as tainted and any values that were derived from it were also tainted. Tainted data values could not be sent back to the server and in fact were not permitted to leave the client.

These capabilities were not used very much in production systems and have now been superseded by the signed scripts and privilege model.

Warnings:

❑ This is deprecated and should not be used in new projects.

See also:	Restricted access, Security policy, Signed scripts

database object (Object/NES)

An object that encapsulates the access to a back-end database from Netscape Enterprise Server.

Availability:	JavaScript - 1.1 Netscape Enterprise Server - 2.0
JavaScript syntax:	NES `database`
Object properties:	`prototype`
Object methods:	`beginTransaction()`, `commitTransaction()`, `connect()`, `connected()`, `cursor()`, `disconnect()`, `execute()`, `majorErrorCode()`, `majorErrorMessage()`, `minorErrorCode()`, `minorErrorMessage()`, `rollbackTransaction()`, `SQLTable()`, `storedProc()`, `storedProcArgs()`, `toString()`

The database object is always available through the `database` property of the `Global` object within the Netscape Enterprise Server session. Before using any other methods belonging to this object, you must first successfully connect to a database.

Until the `database` object has made a connection to the database, the only methods that have any meaning are `database.connect()` and `database.connected()`.

See also:	Cursor object, Netscape Enterprise Server, response.database, unwatch(), watch()

Property	JavaScript	JScript	NES	Notes
`prototype`	1.1 +	-	2.0 +	-

Method	JavaScript	JScript	NES	Notes
`beginTransaction()`	1.1 +	-	2.0 +	-
`commitTransaction()`	1.1 +	-	2.0 +	-
`connect()`	1.1 +	-	2.0 +	-
`connected()`	1.1 +	-	2.0 +	-
`cursor()`	1.1 +	-	2.0 +	-
`disconnect()`	1.1 +	-	2.0 +	-
`execute()`	1.1 +	-	2.0 +	Warning
`majorErrorCode()`	1.1 +	-	2.0 +	-
`majorErrorMessage()`	1.1 +	-	2.0 +	-

Method	JavaScript	JScript	NES	Notes
minorErrorCode()	1.1 +	-	2.0 +	-
minorErrorMessage()	1.1 +	-	2.0 +	-
rollbackTransaction()	1.1 +	-	2.0 +	-
SQLTable()	1.1 +	-	2.0 +	-
storedProc()	1.1 +	-	3.0 +	-
storedProcArgs()	1.1 +	-	3.0 +	-
toString()	1.1 +	-	2.0 +	-

dataTransfer object (Object/JScript)

An object used during drag and drop operations to provide access to data being dragged.

Availability:	JScript - 5.0 Internet Explorer - 5.0
JavaScript syntax:	IE *myDataTransfer =* *myEvent.dataTransfer*
Object properties:	dropEffect, effectAllowed
Object methods:	clearData(), getData(), setData()

This also assists with access to the clipboard while items are being dragged and dropped. You need to access this object via the dataTransfer property of the event object.

Operating this functionality is quite complex and you should check out the various examples covered in the documentation at the Microsoft developer web site.

See also:	Event.dataTransfer

Property	JavaScript	JScript	N	IE	Opera	Notes
dropEffect	-	5.0 +	-	5.0 +	-	-
effectAllowed	-	5.0 +	-	5.0 +	-	-

Method	JavaScript	JScript	N	IE	Opera	Notes
clearData()	-	5.0 +	-	5.0 +	-	-
getData()	-	5.0 +	-	5.0 +	-	-
setData()	-	5.0 +	-	5.0 +	-	-

D

Date object (Object/core)

An object of the class "Date".

Availability:	ECMAScript edition - 2 JavaScript - 1.0 JScript - 1.0 Internet Explorer - 3.02 Netscape - 2.0 Netscape Enterprise Server - 2.0 Opera - 3.0		
JavaScript syntax:	-	*myDate* = Date	
	N	*myDate* = *myEvent*.timeStamp	
	N	*myDate* = *myMouseEvent*.timeStamp	
	N	*myDate* = *myMutationEvent*.timeStamp	
	N	*myDate* = *myUIEvent*.timeStamp	
	-	*myDate* = new Date()	
Object properties:	constructor, length, prototype		
Class methods:	parse(), UTC()		
Object methods:	getDate(), getDay(), getFullYear(), getHours(), getMilliseconds(), getMinutes(), getMonth(), getSeconds(), getTime(), getTimezoneOffset(), getUTCDate(), getUTCDay(), getUTCFullYear(), getUTCHours(), getUTCMilliseconds(), getUTCMinutes(), getUTCMonth(), getUTCSeconds(), getVarDate(), getYear(), parse(), setDate(), setFullYear(), setHours(), setMilliseconds(), setMinutes(), setMonth(), setSeconds(), setTime(), setUTCDate(), setUTCFullYear(), setUTCHours(), setUTCMilliseconds(), setUTCMinutes(), setUTCMonth(), setUTCSeconds(), setYear(), toDateString(), toGMTString(), toLocaleDateString(), toLocaleString(), toLocaleTimeString(), toSource(), toString(), toTimeString(), toUTCString(), valueOf()		

A Date object contains a number that denotes a particular instant in time that is accurate to within a millisecond. The number value may also contain NaN, which indicates that the Date object does not represent a valid instant in time.

The prototype for the Date prototype object is the Object prototype object.

Instances of the Date object have no special properties beyond those they inherit from the Date.prototype object.

JavaScript version 1.2 and the ECMAScript standard both mandate additional methods that the Date object should support. These are generally useful when computing year numbers higher than 1999.

Warnings:

❑ The Date object is particularly bug prone in Netscape 2. If this browser version is important, you may need to provide significant amounts of date correcting logic or avoid the use of date values altogether.

Example code:

```
<!-- Display time since document loaded --->
<HTML>
<HEAD>
<SCRIPT>
window.myDate1 = new Date();
</SCRIPT>
</HEAD>
<BODY>
<DIV ID="TEXTCELL">
0000
</DIV>
<FORM>
<INPUT TYPE="button" VALUE="CLICK ME" onClick="clickMe()">
</FORM>
<SCRIPT>
function clickMe()
{
myDate2 = new Date();
myDelta = myDate2 - window.myDate1;
document.all.TEXTCELL.innerText = myDelta/1000;
}
</SCRIPT>
</BODY>
</HTML>
```

See also:	Broken down time, Browser version compatibility, Calendar time, Compatibility strategies, Date.Class, Date.length, Date.prototype, Event.timeStamp, java.util.Date, JellyScript, MakeDate(), MakeDay(), MakeTime(), Native object, Object object, Time range, Time value, TimeClip(), unwatch(), watch()

Property	JavaScript	JScript	N	IE	Opera	NES	ECMA	Notes
constructor	1.1 +	1.0 +	3.0 +	3.02 +	-	-	2 +	-
length	1.2 +	3.0 +	4.0 +	4.0 +	-	-	2 +	ReadOnly, DontEnum
prototype	1.1 +	3.0 +	3.0 +	4.0 +	3.0 +	2.0 +	2 +	ReadOnly, DontDelete, DontEnum

Method	JavaScript	JScript	N	IE	Opera	NES	ECMA	Notes
getDate()	1.0 +	1.0 +	2.0 +	3.02 +	3.0 +	2.0 +	2 +	-
getDay()	1.0 +	1.0 +	2.0 +	3.02 +	3.0 +	2.0 +	2 +	-
getFullYear()	1.2 +	3.0 +	4.0 +	4.0 +	-	-	2 +	-
getHours()	1.0 +	1.0 +	2.0 +	3.02 +	3.0 +	2.0 +	2 +	-
get Milliseconds()	1.2 +	3.0 +	4.0 +	4.0 +	-	-	2 +	-
getMinutes()	1.0 +	1.0 +	2.0 +	3.02 +	3.0 +	2.0 +	2 +	-
getMonth()	1.0 +	1.0 +	2.0 +	3.02 +	3.0 +	2.0 +	2 +	-
getSeconds()	1.0 +	1.0 +	2.0 +	3.02 +	3.0 +	2.0 +	2 +	-
getTime()	1.0 +	1.0 +	2.0 +	3.02 +	3.0 +	2.0 +	2 +	-
getTimezone Offset()	1.0 +	1.0 +	2.0 +	3.02 +	3.0 +	2.0 +	2 +	Warning
getUTCDate()	1.2 +	3.0 +	4.0 +	4.0 +	-	-	2 +	-
getUTCDay()	1.2 +	3.0 +	4.0 +	4.0 +	-	-	2 +	-
getUTCFull Year()	1.2 +	3.0 +	4.0 +	4.0 +	-	-	2 +	Warning
getUTCHours()	1.2 +	3.0 +	4.0 +	4.0 +	-	-	2 +	-
getUTC Milliseconds()	1.2 +	3.0 +	4.0 +	4.0 +	-	-	2 +	-
getUTC Minutes()	1.2 +	3.0 +	4.0 +	4.0 +	-	-	2 +	-
getUTCMonth()	1.2 +	3.0 +	4.0 +	4.0 +	-	-	2 +	-
getUTC Seconds()	1.2 +	3.0 +	4.0 +	4.0 +	-	-	2 +	-
getVarDate()	-	3.0 +	-	4.0 +	-	-	-	-
getYear()	1.0 +	1.0 +	2.0 +	3.02 +	3.0 +	2.0 +	2 +	Warning, Deprecated
parse()	1.0 +	1.0 +	2.0 +	3.02 +	3.0 +	2.0 +	2 +	-
setDate()	1.0 +	1.0 +	2.0 +	3.02 +	3.0 +	2.0 +	2 +	-
setFullYear()	1.2 +	3.0 +	4.0 +	4.0 +	-	-	2 +	-
setHours()	1.0 +	1.0 +	2.0 +	3.02 +	3.0 +	2.0 +	2 +	-
set Milliseconds()	1.2 +	3.0 +	4.0 +	4.0 +	-	-	2 +	-
setMinutes()	1.0 +	1.0 +	2.0 +	3.02 +	3.0 +	2.0 +	2 +	-
setMonth()	1.0 +	1.0 +	2.0 +	3.02 +	3.0 +	2.0 +	2 +	-
setSeconds()	1.0 +	1.0 +	2.0 +	3.02 +	3.0 +	2.0 +	2 +	-
setTime()	1.0 +	1.0 +	2.0 +	3.02 +	3.0 +	2.0 +	2 +	-
setUTCDate()	1.2 +	3.0 +	4.0 +	4.0 +	-	-	2 +	-
setUTC FullYear()	1.2 +	3.0 +	4.0 +	4.0 +	-	-	2 +	-
setUTCHours()	1.2 +	3.0 +	4.0 +	4.0 +	-	-	2 +	-
setUTC Milliseconds()	1.2 +	3.0 +	4.0 +	4.0 +	-	-	2 +	-
setUTC Minutes()	1.2 +	3.0 +	4.0 +	4.0 +	-	-	2 +	-

Method	JavaScript	JScript	N	IE	Opera	NES	ECMA	Notes
setUTCMonth()	1.2 +	3.0 +	4.0 +	4.0 +	-	-	2 +	-
setUTC Seconds()	1.2 +	3.0 +	4.0 +	4.0 +	-	-	2 +	-
setYear()	1.0 +	1.0 +	2.0 +	3.02 +	3.0 +	2.0 +	2 +	Warning, Deprecated
toDateString()	1.5 +	5.5 +	6.0 +	5.5 +	-	-	3 +	-
toGMTString()	1.0 +	1.0 +	2.0 +	3.02 +	3.0 +	2.0 +	2 +	Warning, Deprecated
toLocale DateString()	1.5 +	5.5 +	6.0 +	5.5 +	-	-	3 +	-
toLocale String()	1.0 +	1.0 +	2.0 +	3.02 +	3.0 +	2.0 +	2 +	-
toLocale TimeString()	1.5 +	5.5 +	6.0 +	5.5 +	-	-	3 +	-
toSource()	1.3 +	3.0 +	4.06 +	4.0 +	-	-	3 +	-
toString()	1.0 +	1.0 +	2.0 +	3.02 +	3.0 +	2.0 +	2 +	?
toTimeString()	1.5 +	5.5 +	6.0 +	5.5 +	-	-	3 +	-
toUTCString()	1.2 +	3.0 +	4.0 +	4.0 +	-	-	2 +	-
valueOf()	1.1 +	3.0 +	3.0 +	4.0 +	-	-	2 +	-

Cross-references:

ECMA 262 edition 2 - section - 10.1.5

ECMA 262 edition 2 - section - 15.9

ECMA 262 edition 2 - section - 15.9.6

ECMA 262 edition 3 - section - 10.1.5

ECMA 262 edition 3 - section - 15.9

O'Reilly *JavaScript Definitive Guide* - page - 48

Date() (Function)

A function that returns the current date.

Availability:	ECMAScript edition - 2 JavaScript - 1.0 JScript - 1.0 Internet Explorer - 3.02 Netscape - 2.0
Property/method value type:	String primitive
JavaScript syntax:	- Date()

This function returns a string primitive representing the current UTC time value.

When the Date() constructor is called as a function rather than in a new expression, it returns a string representing the current time (in UTC time). Note that when calling it as a function the arguments are all ignored and it is not equivalent to calling the Date() constructor in a new expression at all.

Effectively, the function call to a Date() constructor behaves as if you had coded this fragment of JavaScript in the script source text:

```
(new Date()).toString()
```

See also:	Cast operator, Constructor function, constructor property, Date constant, Date() constructor, Implicit conversion

Cross-references:

ECMA 262 edition 2 - section - 15.1.3.7

ECMA 262 edition 2 - section - 15.9.2

ECMA 262 edition 3 - section - 15.9.2

Date.Class (Property/internal)

Internal property that returns an object class.

Availability:	ECMAScript edition - 2

This is an internal property that describes the class that a Date object instance is a member of. The reserved words suggest that in the future, this property may be externalized.

See also:	Class, Date object

Property attributes:

DontEnum, Internal.

Cross-references:

ECMA 262 edition 2 - section - 8.6.2

ECMA 262 edition 2 - section - 15.9.3.1

ECMA 262 edition 3 - section - 8.6.2

Date.parse() (Method/static)

A class based factory method for converting strings to `Date` objects.

Availability:	ECMAScript edition - 2 JavaScript - 1.0 JScript - 1.0 Internet Explorer - 3.02 Netscape - 2.0 Netscape Enterprise Server - 2.0 Opera - 3.0
Property/method value type:	UTC time value

JavaScript syntax:	-	`Date.parse(aString)`
Argument list:	`aString`	A string containing a meaningful date value

The argument used with the `Date.parse()` method should process any string containing a sequence of characters that represents a meaningful date value. The `parse()` method then tokenizes that string and converts the value to a number in UTC time co-ordinates corresponding to the date and time in the string.

The string may be interpreted as a local time, UTC time, or a time in some other time zone depending on the contents of the string.

The result of this method is a UTC time value.

Example code:

```
<HTML>
<HEAD>
</HEAD>
<BODY>
<DIV ID="RESULT1">???</DIV>
<DIV ID="RESULT2">???</DIV>
<FORM>
<HR>
<SELECT ID="IN1">
<OPTION VALUE="Sun">Sunday
<OPTION VALUE="Mon">Monday
<OPTION VALUE="Tue">Tuesday
<OPTION VALUE="Wed">Wednesday
<OPTION VALUE="Thu">Thursday
<OPTION VALUE="Fri">Friday
<OPTION VALUE="Sat">Saturday
</SELECT>
<INPUT ID="IN2" TYPE="text" VALUE="1" SIZE="2">
<SELECT ID="IN3">
<OPTION VALUE="Jan">January
<OPTION VALUE="Feb">February
```

157

```
<OPTION VALUE="Mar">March
<OPTION VALUE="Apr">April
<OPTION VALUE="May">May
<OPTION VALUE="Jun">June
<OPTION VALUE="Jul">July
<OPTION VALUE="Aug">August
<OPTION VALUE="Sep">September
<OPTION VALUE="Oct">October
<OPTION VALUE="Nov">November
<OPTION VALUE="Dec">December
</SELECT>
<INPUT ID="IN4" TYPE="text" VALUE="2000" SIZE="4">
<INPUT ID="IN5" TYPE="text" VALUE="12" SIZE="2">:
<INPUT ID="IN6" TYPE="text" VALUE="00" SIZE="2">:
<INPUT ID="IN7" TYPE="text" VALUE="00" SIZE="2">
<INPUT ID="IN8" TYPE="text" VALUE="+0000" SIZE="5">
<HR>
<INPUT TYPE="button" VALUE="CLICK ME" onClick="clickMe()">
</FORM>
<SCRIPT>
function clickMe()
{
parseInput  = document.all.IN1.value;
parseInput += " ";
parseInput += document.all.IN2.value;
parseInput += " ";
parseInput += document.all.IN3.value;
parseInput += " ";
parseInput += document.all.IN4.value;
parseInput += " ";
parseInput += document.all.IN5.value;
parseInput += ":";
parseInput += document.all.IN6.value;
parseInput += ":";
parseInput += document.all.IN7.value;
parseInput += " ";
parseInput += document.all.IN8.value;
document.all.RESULT1.innerText = parseInput;

document.all.RESULT2.innerText = Date.parse(parseInput);
}
</SCRIPT>
</BODY>
</HTML>
```

See also: Cast operator, Date constant, `Date.constructor`

Cross-references:

ECMA 262 edition 2 - section - 15.9.4.2

ECMA 262 edition 3 - section - 15.9.4.2

Date.UTC() (Method/static)

A class based factory method for converting numeric values to `Date` objects.

D

Availability:		ECMAScript edition - 2 JavaScript - 1.0 JScript - 1.0 Internet Explorer - 3.02 Netscape - 2.0 Netscape Enterprise Server - 2.0 Opera - 3.0
Property/method value type:		UTC time in milliseconds
JavaScript syntax:	-	`Date.UTC(aYear, aMonth)`
	-	`Date.UTC(aYear, aMonth, aDate)`
	-	`Date.UTC(aYear, aMonth, aDate, anHour)`
	-	`Date.UTC(aYear, aMonth, aDate, anHour, aMinute)`
	-	`Date.UTC(aYear, aMonth, aDate, anHour, aMinute, aSecond)`
	- (JavaScript 1.3 +)	`Date.UTC(aYear, aMonth, aDate, anHour, aMinute, aSecond, aMillisecond)`
Argument list:	`aDate`	An optional date within the month value
	`aMillisecond`	An optional value between 0 and 999 milliseconds
	`aMinute`	An optional value between 0 and 59 minutes
	`aMonth`	An optional 0 to 11 month value
	`anHour`	A value between 0 and 23 hours
	`aSecond`	An optional value between 0 and 59 seconds
	`aYear`	A full year value
	`aValue`	A time in UTC milliseconds

This method returns a date value with the indicated date and time value.

When the `Date.UTC()` method is called, it interprets the arguments as UTC time values and returns a number representing the UTC time in milliseconds.

The value stored in the new date object depends on the argument values that are supplied. The arguments are all optional but are positional so if an argument is missing, it is assumed to be the last argument and so on.

Functionally, the algorithm that manufactures a new date value uses the internal `MakeDay()`, `MakeTime()` and `MakeDate()` methods that we describe elsewhere.

If the year value is less than 99, then the date creation adds 1900 to it and assumes the date is in the 20th century. To avoid millennium problems, always specify a full year number.

Where arguments are omitted, zero values are assumed for hours, minutes and seconds. When all three are missing, the time is assumed to be midnight.

An incomplete date with zero, one or two arguments will behave in an implementation dependant way and might yield a different result depending on the platform supporting the script interpreter.

See also: `Date(),Date.constructor,MakeDate(),MakeDay(), MakeTime(),TimeClip()`

Cross-references:

ECMA 262 edition 2 - section - 15.9.4.3

ECMA 262 edition 2 - section - 15.9.4.4

ECMA 262 edition 2 - section - 15.9.4.5

ECMA 262 edition 2 - section - 15.9.4.6

ECMA 262 edition 2 - section - 15.9.4.7

ECMA 262 edition 2 - section - 15.9.4.8

ECMA 262 edition 2 - section - 15.9.4.9

ECMA 262 edition 2 - section - 15.9.4.10

ECMA 262 edition 3 - section - 15.9.4.3

DbPool object (Object/NES)

An object of the class "DbPool" which provides a means of pooling connections to multiple databases.

Availability:	JavaScript - 1.2 Netscape Enterprise Server - 3.0

JavaScript syntax:	NES	`myDbPool = new DbPool();`
	NES	`myDbPool = new DbPool(aType,` `aServer, aUser, aPassword, aDb);`

	NES	`myDbPool = new DbPool(aType,`
		`aServer, aUser, aPassword, aDb,`
		`maxCon);`

	NES	`myDbPool = new DbPool(aType,`
		`aServer, aUser, aPassword, aDb,`
		`maxCon, aFlag);`

Argument list:	`aType`	A database type
	`aServer`	A data source name or server name
	`aUser`	A user identifier
	`aPassword`	A valid password for the user
	`aDb`	A database name if required by the data source
	`maxCon`	A number indicating maximum connections
	`aFlag`	Commit/rollback flag value
Object properties:	`prototype`	
Object methods:	`connect()`, `connected()`, `connection()`, `disconnect()`, `majorErrorCode()`, `majorErrorMessage()`, `minorErrorCode()`, `minorErrorMessage()`, `storedProcArgs()`, `toString()`	

In JavaScript 1.2, you can connect to multiple databases and reuse connections. Each database can have a pool of available and ready connections which can be created when needed.

A DbPool object is created in a similar way to when you connect a single `database` object to a database. In this case however, you create a new `DbPool` object each time so you could maintain connections to several databases which is not possible with a plain (JavaScript 1.1) database object.

To create an object instance of the DbPool class, use the new operator on the `DbPool()` constructor.

The database type would likely be one of:

❑ ORACLE

❑ SYBASE

❑ INFORMIX

❑ DB2

❑ ODBC

The server value would identify one of the available data source names.

The user and password details would correspond to valid users you have already created on your database server.

Likewise the database name although for some databases such as Oracle, this may be done through the data source description and so the argument should be left blank in that case.

The maximum number of connections depends on your licensing arrangements with your database supplier and the capacity of your server and whether it needs to share connections with other services.

The commit flag indicates whether to commit (true) or rollback (false) a pending transaction.

See also:	database.connect(), Netscape Enterprise Server, unwatch(), watch()

Property	JavaScript	JScript	NES	Notes
prototype	1.2 +	-	3.0 +	-

Method	JavaScript	JScript	NES	Notes
connect()	1.2 +	-	3.0 +	-
connected()	1.2 +	-	3.0 +	-
connection()	1.2 +	-	3.0 +	-
disconnect()	1.2 +	-	3.0 +	-
majorErrorCode()	1.2 +	-	3.0 +	-
majorErrorMessage()	1.2 +	-	3.0 +	-
minorErrorCode()	1.2 +	-	3.0 +	-
minorErrorMessage()	1.2 +	-	3.0 +	-
storedProcArgs()	1.2 +	-	3.0 +	-
toString()	1.2 +	-	3.0 +	-

DD object (Object/HTML)

An object that represents the <DD> HTML tag.

Availability:	DOM level - 1 JavaScript - 1.5 JScript - 3.0 Internet Explorer - 4.0 Netscape - 6.0	
Inherits from:	Element object	
JavaScript syntax:	IE	myDD = myDocument.all.anElementID
	IE	myDD = myDocument.all.tags ("DD")[anIndex]
	IE	myDD = myDocument.all[aName]
	-	myDD = myDocument.getElementById (anElementID)
	-	myDD = myDocument.getElementsByName (aName)[anIndex]
	-	myDD = myDocument .getElementsByTagName("DD")[anIndex]
HTML syntax:	<DD> ... </DD>	
Argument list:	anIndex	A reference to an element in a collection
	aName	An associative array reference
	anElementID	The ID value of an Element object
Object properties:	noWrap	
Event handlers:	onClick, onDblClick, onDragStart, onFilterChange, onHelp, onKeyDown, onKeyPress, onKeyUp, onMouseDown, onMouseMove, onMouseOut, onMouseOver, onMouseUp, onSelectStart	

This object represents the definition value of an item in a definition list. It corresponds to a related definition term maintained in an DT object. DT and DD objects are paired up and maintained together as a member of the DL collection.

The <DD> tag is a block-level tag. That means that it forces a line break before and after itself unless the DL is compacted.

See also:	DL object, DT object, Element object

Property	JavaScript	JScript	N	IE	Opera	HTML	Notes
noWrap	-	3.0 +	-	4.0 +	-	-	Warning

Event name	JavaScript	JScript	N	IE	Opera	HTML	Notes
onClick	1.5 +	3.0 +	6.0 +	4.0 +	-	4.0 +	Warning
onDblClick	1.5 +	3.0 +	6.0 +	4.0 +	-	4.0 +	Warning
onDragStart	-	3.0 +	-	4.0 +	-	-	-
onFilterChange	-	3.0 +	-	4.0 +	-	-	-
onHelp	-	3.0 +	-	4.0 +	-	-	Warning
onKeyDown	1.5 +	3.0 +	6.0 +	4.0 +	-	4.0 +	Warning
onKeyPress	1.5 +	3.0 +	6.0 +	4.0 +	-	4.0 +	Warning
onKeyUp	1.5 +	3.0 +	6.0 +	4.0 +	-	4.0 +	Warning
onMouseDown	1.5 +	3.0 +	6.0 +	4.0 +	-	4.0 +	Warning
onMouseMove	1.5 +	3.0 +	6.0 +	4.0 +	-	4.0 +	Warning
onMouseOut	1.5 +	3.0 +	6.0 +	4.0 +	-	4.0 +	Warning
onMouseOver	1.5 +	3.0 +	6.0 +	4.0 +	-	4.0 +	Warning
onMouseUp	1.5 +	3.0 +	6.0 +	4.0 +	-	4.0 +	Warning
onSelectStart	-	3.0 +	-	4.0 +	-	-	-

Inheritance chain:

Element object, Node object

Decimal point (.) (Delimiter)

A delimiter that marks the beginning of the fractional part of a floating point value.

Availability:	ECMAScript edition - 2 Opera - 3.0

A decimal point separates the integer and fractional parts of a floating point value. The character being used may need to alter depending on the locale of the hosting environment.

If your national language routines change the formatting of numbers, be aware that commas and dots mean different things.

A dot is really a decimal point. A comma is a thousands separator.

In some formatting regimes, thousands may be separated by a space character and a comma may be used in place of a dot (or vice versa).

Note also that it is a convention in financial reports to show negative values in parentheses but as a positive value.

All of this can make it difficult to parse numeric values that a user may enter into a text field.

Warnings:

❑ Localization of JavaScript implementations is still undergoing some development.

See also:	Floating point, Localization, Object property delimiter (.), Property accessor

Cross-references:

ECMA 262 edition 2 - section - 7.7.3

ECMA 262 edition 3 - section - 7.8.3

decodeURI() (Function)

This ECMA defined function can be used to decode an entire URI value that was encoded with the `encodeURI()` function.

Availability:	ECMAScript edition - 3 JavaScript - 1.5 JScript - 5.5 Internet Explorer - 5.5 Netscape - 6.0	
Property/method value type:	`String primitive`	
JavaScript syntax:	-	`decodeURI(anEncodedURI)`
Argument list:	`anEncodedURI`	A previously encoded URI

This function is the complement of the `encodeURI()` function that we describe elsewhere.

A string that might have been encoded with the `encodeURI()` function either locally or remotely can be converted back to a normal URI string with this function.

As far as ECMAScript is concerned, this supersedes the `unescape()` function which is flagged as deprecated functionality.

Note that the hash character (#) is not decoded.

See also:	`decodeURIComponent()`, `encodeURI()`, `encodeURIComponent()`, `escape()`, `unescape()`, URI handling functions

Cross-references:

ECMA 262 edition 3 - section - 15.1.3.1

165

decodeURIComponent() (Function)

This ECMA defined function can be used to decode a URI component value that was encoded with the `encodeURIComponent()` function.

Availability:	ECMAScript edition - 3 JavaScript - 1.5 JScript - 5.5 Internet Explorer - 5.5 Netscape - 6.0
Property/method value type:	`String primitive`
JavaScript syntax:	- `decodeURIComponent` `(anEncodedComponent)`
Argument list:	`anEncoded Component` A previously encoded component

This function is the complement of the `encodeURIComponent()` function that we describe elsewhere.

A string that might have been encoded with the `encodeURIComponent()` function either locally or remotely, can be converted back to a normal URI string with this function.

This enhances the encode/decode facilities of the compliant browser over and above what used to be available with `escape()`/`unescape()` functions.

See also:	`decodeURI()`, `encodeURI()`, `encodeURIComponent()`, `escape()`, `unescape()`, URI handling functions

Cross-references:

ECMA 262 edition 3 - section - 15.1.3.2

Decrement value (–) (Operator/postfix)

Pre or post decrementing operator.

Availability:	ECMAScript edition - 2 JavaScript - 1.0 JScript - 1.0 Internet Explorer - 3.02 Netscape - 2.0 Netscape Enterprise Server - 2.0 Opera - 3.0
Property/method value type:	`Number primitive`

JavaScript syntax:	-	--anOperand
	-	anOperand--
Argument list:	anOperand	A numeric value that can be decremented

The operand is decremented by one.

A pre-fixing decrementor will subtract 1 from the operand value before it is used in the expression.

A post-fixing decrementor will subtract 1 from the operand after it is used in the expression.

Be careful how you use this pre/post placement as you can easily generate 'off by one' errors in your algorithms by placing the operator on the wrong side of the operand.

This operator is more or less functionally equivalent to:

```
anOperand -= 1
```

…which is equivalent to:

```
anOperand = anOperand - 1
```

See also:	Additive expression, Additive operator, Increment value (++), Negation operator (-), Postfix decrement (--), Postfix expression, Postfix increment (++), Prefix decrement (--), Prefix expression, Prefix increment (++)

Cross-references:

ECMA 262 edition 2 - section - 11.3.2

ECMA 262 edition 3 - section - 11.3.2

DefaultValue() (Function/internal)

Internal private function.

Availability:	ECMAScript edition - 2

This internal function returns the default value for the object, given that the caller indicates a preferred result type in the hint argument.

The hint gives some suggestion to the receiving object about the preferred result type. This is a fairly ambiguous result. Generally if you ask for a string you will get a string. Asking for a number will generally yield a number. However, there are cases where the DefaultValue for an object cannot be rendered into the preferred type and you may generate a run-time error.

If you don't specify any hint value at all, the DefaultValue will first assume you want a Number unless the receiver is a Date object in which case it assumes a String is required.

See also:	Internal Method

Cross-references:

ECMA 262 edition 2 - section - 8.6.2.6

ECMA 262 edition 3 - section - 8.6.2.6

DEL object (Object/HTML)

An object that represents a <DEL> HTML tag within the document.

Availability:	DOM level - 1 JavaScript - 1.5 JScript - 3.0 Internet Explorer - 4.0 Netscape - 6.0	
Inherits from:	Element object	
JavaScript syntax:	IE	*myDEL* = *myDocument*.all.*anElementID*
	IE	*myDEL* = *myDocument*.all.tags ("DEL")[*anIndex*]
	IE	*myDEL* = myDocument.all[*aName*]
	-	*myDEL* = *myDocument*.getElementById (*anElementID*)
	-	*myDEL* = *myDocument*.getElementsByName (*aName*)[*anIndex*]
	-	*myDEL* = *myDocument* .getElementsByTagName("DEL")[*anIndex*]
HTML syntax:	<DEL> ... </DEL>	
Argument list:	*anIndex*	A reference to an element in a collection
	aName	An associative array reference
	anElementID	The ID value of an Element object
Object properties:	cite, dateTime	
Event handlers:	onClick, onDblClick, onDragStart, onFilterChange, onHelp, onKeyDown, onKeyPress, onKeyUp, onMouseDown, onMouseMove, onMouseOut, onMouseOver, onMouseUp, onSelectStart	

You can add markup to a document to strike through text as if it were deleted. This deleted text block can also have a citation reference that links to a description of why the deletion took place.

The DOM level 1 specification includes this in the ModElement object functionality.

See also:	Element object, INS object, ModElement object

Property	JavaScript	JScript	N	IE	Opera	DOM	HTML	Notes
cite	1.5 +	5.0 +	6.0 +	5.0 +	-	1 +	-	-
dateTime	1.5 +	5.0 +	6.0 +	5.0 +	-	1 +	-	-

Event name	JavaScript	JScript	N	IE	Opera	DOM	HTML	Notes
onClick	1.5 +	3.0 +	6.0 +	4.0 +	-	-	4.0 +	Warning
onDblClick	1.5 +	3.0 +	6.0 +	4.0 +	-	-	4.0 +	Warning
onDragStart	-	3.0 +	-	4.0 +	-	-	-	-
onFilterChange	-	3.0 +	-	4.0 +	-	-	-	-
onHelp	-	3.0 +	-	4.0 +	-	-	-	Warning
onKeyDown	1.5 +	3.0 +	6.0 +	4.0 +	-	-	4.0 +	Warning
onKeyPress	1.5 +	3.0 +	6.0 +	4.0 +	-	-	4.0 +	Warning
onKeyUp	1.5 +	3.0 +	6.0 +	4.0 +	-	-	4.0 +	Warning
onMouseDown	1.5 +	3.0 +	6.0 +	4.0 +	-	-	4.0 +	Warning
onMouseMove	1.5 +	3.0 +	6.0 +	4.0 +	-	-	4.0 +	Warning
onMouseOut	1.5 +	3.0 +	6.0 +	4.0 +	-	-	4.0 +	Warning
onMouseOver	1.5 +	3.0 +	6.0 +	4.0 +	-	-	4.0 +	Warning
onMouseUp	1.5 +	3.0 +	6.0 +	4.0 +	-	-	4.0 +	Warning
onSelectStart	-	3.0 +	-	4.0 +	-	-	-	-

Inheritance chain:

Element object, Node object

delete (Operator/unary)

Property deletion operator.

Availability:	ECMAScript edition - 2 JavaScript - 1.0 JScript - 3.0 Internet Explorer - 4.0 Netscape - 2.0 Netscape Enterprise Server - 2.0 Opera - 3.0

169

JavaScript syntax:	-	delete *anObject*
	-	delete *myArray*[*anIndex*]
	-	delete *myObject.aProperty*
Argument list:	*anIndex*	The index of the item to be deleted from the array
	anObject	An object to be deleted
	aProperty	An object property to be removed

The delete operator is used to delete a property from an object or delete a reference to an object. It can also be used to delete an element from an array.

Using the new operator creates a new object with a reference count of zero. Assigning that object creation to a variable increments the reference count. Saving it as an object property also increments the reference count. Storing it in an array does likewise.

All of these are simply references to the same object.

Deleting a variable containing a reference to an object decrements the reference count for that object.

The associativity is from right to left.

Refer to the operator precedence topic for details of execution order.

Warnings:

❑ The delete operator will not work with MSIE version 3.02 or earlier. It also won't work in Netscape 2.02.

❑ Netscape does not generate an error in version 3.0 if the delete operator is used but it is functionally ignored and does nothing.

❑ In JavaScript version 1.0 and version 1.1, the delete operator did not actually delete any object properties. Instead it set them to null. If you then subsequently tested for the existence of those properties, they might not prove false when you expect them to.

❑ In the JavaScript 1.2 implementation, in version 4 of Netscape , the behavior of the delete operator as it applies to variables is slightly different. Any variable declared with the var statement is considered to be permanent and cannot be deleted. This will generate an error if you try. This happens for the case when you enclose the script in <SCRIPT LANGUAGE="JAVASCRIPT1.2"> tags.

❑ There is some difference between Netscape and MSIE as to whether global variables can be deleted. The safest assumption is that they cannot, so to remain portable, your script should not try.

Example code:

```
// Create a new object
myObject = new Object;
// Then delete a reference to it
delete myObject;
```

See also:	Associativity, Garbage collection, Grouping operator ( ), JSObject.removeMember(), Memory leak, Object object, Operator Precedence, Property attribute, Reference counting, Unary expression, Unary operator, Variable statement

Cross-references:

ECMA 262 edition 2 - section - 11.1.4

ECMA 262 edition 2 - section - 11.4.1

ECMA 262 edition 3 - section - 11.4.1

Wrox *Instant JavaScript* - page - 21

Wrox *Instant JavaScript* - page - 28

Delete() (Function/internal)

Internal private function.

Availability:	ECMAScript edition - 2

This internal function removes the named property from the object.

This function does not walk the prototype inheritance chain. If it did and a shared property got deleted, that property would disappear from ALL the objects that shared it.

If the property does not exist in the receiving object, the Delete() is assumed to have been successful anyway and true is returned.

If the property is present but has the DontDelete attribute, it cannot be removed so false is returned.

If the property can be deleted, then it is removed and true is returned.

See also:	Internal Method

Cross-references:

ECMA 262 edition 2 - section - 8.6.2.5

ECMA 262 edition 3 - section - 8.6.2.5

Deprecated functionality (Pitfall)

Some language features are to be discontinued in later versions of the language.

Deprecated functionality describes a feature that is likely to be removed and should not be used in new developments.

There are various features that interpreter manufacturers add from time to time and which become standardized in a different and possibly better way, or that everyone agrees should be disregarded. Netscape's data-tainting functionality is a good example of a dead end that was introduced and withdrawn soon after.

The following is a list of such deprecated functionality that should be avoided:

❑ Data-tainting

❑ JavaScript extensions to HTML character entities

Warnings:

❑ If you use deprecated functionality, your script may fail when it is deployed on other platforms or when the platform it is hosted on is revised.

See also:	Definition, JavaScript entity, Obsolescent, Pitfalls

DHTML (Standard)

Dynamic HTML controlled by JavaScript. A fourth generation browser technology for dynamically altering the document that describes a web page.

You might be forgiven for thinking DHTML is a new kind of HTML. Actually it's not really. It's just plain old HTML code. What makes it dynamic are the supporting technologies that operate on it. Without them, there is nothing dynamic about HTML at all.

Principally, it's the JavaScript and CSS style sheet support that makes HTML dynamic and it's the access to the HTML through a Document Object Model that allows us to operate on the HTML in the document.

Things are complicated a little because the dynamism can be applied at the server end and really what we mean by DHTML is a client end activity. Server created HTML, even though it's done with JavaScript is not really DHTML.

Perhaps a less ambiguous description is CSS and DOM scripting. That allows some differentiation of the appearance vs. structural things you can accomplish with script driven documents.

See also:	Dynamic HTML

Dialog object (Object/JScript)

This is the `parent` object of a frame within a modal dialog window.

Availability:	JScript - 3.0 Internet Explorer - 4.0	
Inherits from:	`Window object`	
JavaScript syntax:	IE	`myDialog = myFrame.parent`
	IE	`myDialog = myWindow.parent`
Event handlers:	`onAfterPrint, onBeforePrint, onBeforeUnload, onBlur, onDragDrop, onError, onFocus, onHelp, onLoad, onMouseMove, onMove, onResize, onScroll, onUnload`	

To all intents and purposes this is a `window` object except that because it is modal it is placed on top of all other windows and until it is disposed of, no other browser windows can be accessed.

Some early documentation suggests that there are dialog sizing properties for this window type but this has not been confirmed to work.

On the new version 6.0 Netscape browser, there is the tantalizing possibility that the appearance of dialog boxes can be affected by altering the 'skin' of the browser. As yet, this does not appear to be scriptable or accessible from HTML. It is highly likely that internally the appearance is JavaScript driven. Historically, much of the internal behavior of Netscape has been controlled by `.js` files so this may change.

See also:	`Window.alert(), Window.confirm(), Window.parent, Window.prompt(), Window.showHelp(), Window.showModalDialog(), Window.showModelessDialog()`

Event name	JavaScript	JScript	N	IE	Opera	HTML	Notes
onAfterPrint	-	5.0 +	-	5.0 +	-	-	-
onBeforePrint	-	5.0 +	-	5.0 +	-	-	-
onBeforeUnload	-	3.0 +	-	4.0 +	-	-	-
onBlur	-	3.0 +	-	4.0 +	-	-	Warning
onDragDrop	-	-	-	-	-	-	-
onError	-	3.0 +	-	4.0 +	-	-	Warning

Table continued on following page

Event name	JavaScript	JScript	N	IE	Opera	HTML	Notes
onFocus	-	3.0 +	-	4.0 +	-	-	Warning
onHelp	-	3.0 +	-	4.0 +	-	-	Warning
onLoad	-	3.0 +	-	4.0 +	-	-	Warning
onMouseMove	-	3.0 +	-	4.0 +	-	4.0 +	Warning
onMove	-	-	-	-	-	-	-
onResize	-	3.0 +	-	4.0 +	-	-	Warning
onScroll	-	3.0 +	-	4.0 +	-	-	-
onUnload	-	3.0 +	-	4.0 +	-	-	Warning

Inheritance chain:

Window object

Dictionary object (Object/JScript)

A name-value collection object created by the Active X facilities.

Availability:	JScript - 3.0 Internet Explorer - 4.0
JavaScript syntax:	IE *myDictionary* = new ActiveXObject ("Scripting.Dictionary");
Object properties:	Count
Object methods:	Add(), Exists(), Item(), Items(), Key(), Keys(), Remove(), RemoveAll()

A Dictionary is a special kind of collection or array which allows you to access items using name and value pairs. This is functionally similar to using associative name indexing on a JavaScript array, so although this is not generally available, its fundamental usefulness is already provided in the native JavaScript implementation.

The Dictionary object provided JScript and Active X, has a few extra properties and methods to help manage the contents of the dictionary. These could be simulated fairly easily and added to the Array prototype to create your own portable Dictionary-like object.

Warnings:

❑ As this object needs to be created with the Active X facilities, it is not supported outside of the Windows environment. It is odd that such a useful object can only be constructed in this way and that it does not have a native JavaScript constructor. That at least would make it available in all platforms that JScript runs in.

❑ Note that the properties and methods for the Dictionary object all start with an upper case letter. This is not the common practice in JavaScript and may cause you a few run-time errors if you forget.

❑ There are some unusual syntactical constructs in this object. In particular, item and key methods that behave like properties. These are intended to provide an interface to replace an item in the dictionary or to rename a key. These methods would normally be made with several arguments to a single method, but instead they use a method to retrieve a reference to a Dictionary pocket and you can then assign a value to the reference that was returned.

Example code:

```
// Create a new dictionary
var myDictionary = new ActiveXObject("Scripting.Dictionary");
// Store some items in the dictionary
// (Melting Points of fats/waxes)
myDictionary.Add("Butter",       "28");
myDictionary.Add("Lard",         "36");
myDictionary.Add("MuttonTallow", "44");
myDictionary.Add("Beeswax",      "61");
myDictionary.Add("Stearin",      "71.6");
myDictionary.Add("ParaffinWax",  "38");
// Display one item if it exists
if(myDictionary.Exists("ParaffinWax"))
{
document.write("Paraffin Wax melts at ");
document.write(myDictionary.Item("ParaffinWax"));
document.write(" degrees Centigrade.");
}
// Remove an item
if(myDictionary.Exists("Stearin"))
{
myDictionary.Remove("Stearin");
}
// Change an item and its key
if(myDictionary.Exists("MuttonTallow"))
{
myDictionary.Item("MuttonTallow") = "40";
myDictionary.Key("MuttonTallow") = "BeefTallow";
}
// List all the items
myArray = (new VBArray(myDictionary.Keys())).toArray();
for(myEnum=0; myEnum<myArray.length; myEnum++)
{
document.write("Key value: ");
document.write(myArray[myEnum]);
document.write("Item value: ");
document.write(myDictionary.Item(myArray[myEnum]));
document.write("<BR>");
}
// Now discard the items in the array
myDictionary.RemoveAll();
```

See also:	ActiveX, ActiveXObject object

Property	JavaScript	JScript	N	IE	Opera	Notes
Count	-	3.0 +	-	4.0 +	-	ReadOnly

Method	JavaScript	JScript	N	IE	Opera	Notes
Add()	-	3.0 +	-	4.0 +	-	-
Exists()	-	3.0 +	-	4.0 +	-	-
Item()	-	3.0 +	-	4.0 +	-	Warning
Items()	-	3.0 +	-	4.0 +	-	-
Key()	-	3.0 +	-	4.0 +	-	-
Keys()	-	3.0 +	-	4.0 +	-	Warning
Remove()	-	3.0 +	-	4.0 +	-	-
RemoveAll()	-	3.0 +	-	4.0 +	-	-

DIR object (Object/HTML)

A somewhat deprecated object that is now superseded by the <UL> HTML tag and its object representation. This object represents the contents of a <DIR> HTML tag.

Availability:	DOM level - 1 JavaScript - 1.5 JScript - 3.0 Internet Explorer - 4.0 Netscape - 6.0	
Inherits from:	Element object	
JavaScript syntax:	IE	myDIR = myDocument.all.anElementID
	IE	myDIR = myDocument.all.tags ("DIR")[anIndex]
	IE	myDIR = myDocument.all[aName]
	-	myDIR = myDocument.getElementById (anElementID)
	-	myDIR = myDocument.getElementsByName (aName)[anIndex]
	-	myDIR = myDocument .getElementsByTagName("DIR")[anIndex]
HTML syntax:	<DIR> ... </DIR>	
Argument list:	anIndex	A reference to an element in a collection
	aName	An associative array reference
	anElementID	The ID value of an Element object
Object properties:	compact	
Event handlers:	onClick, onDblClick, onDragStart, onFilterChange, onHelp, onKeyDown, onKeyPress, onKeyUp, onMouseDown, onMouseMove, onMouseOut, onMouseOver, onMouseUp, onSelectStart	

The DOM level 1 specification refers to this as a DirectoryElement object.

See also:	Element object, UL object

Property	JavaScript	JScript	N	IE	Opera	DOM	HTML	Notes
compact	1.5 +	3.0 +	6.0 +	4.0 +	-	1 +	-	-

Event name	JavaScript	JScript	N	IE	Opera	DOM	HTML	Notes
onClick	1.5 +	3.0 +	6.0 +	4.0 +	-	-	4.0 +	Warning
onDblClick	1.5 +	3.0 +	6.0 +	4.0 +	-	-	4.0 +	Warning
onDragStart	-	3.0 +	-	4.0 +	-	-	-	-
onFilterChange	-	3.0 +	-	4.0 +	-	-	-	-
onHelp	-	3.0 +	-	4.0 +	-	-	-	Warning
onKeyDown	1.5 +	3.0 +	6.0 +	4.0 +	-	-	4.0 +	Warning
onKeyPress	1.5 +	3.0 +	6.0 +	4.0 +	-	-	4.0 +	Warning
onKeyUp	1.5 +	3.0 +	6.0 +	4.0 +	-	-	4.0 +	Warning
onMouseDown	1.5 +	3.0 +	6.0 +	4.0 +	-	-	4.0 +	Warning
onMouseMove	1.5 +	3.0 +	6.0 +	4.0 +	-	-	4.0 +	Warning
onMouseOut	1.5 +	3.0 +	6.0 +	4.0 +	-	-	4.0 +	Warning
onMouseOver	1.5 +	3.0 +	6.0 +	4.0 +	-	-	4.0 +	Warning
onMouseUp	1.5 +	3.0 +	6.0 +	4.0 +	-	-	4.0 +	Warning
onSelectStart	-	3.0 +	-	4.0 +	-	-	-	-

Inheritance chain:

Element object, Node object

DIV object (Object/HTML)

An object that represents a <DIV> block-level element.

Availability:	DOM level - 1 JavaScript - 1.5 JScript - 3.0 Internet Explorer - 4.0 Netscape - 6.0
Inherits from:	Element object
JavaScript syntax:	IE myDIV = myDocument.all.anElementID
	IE myDIV = myDocument.all.tags ("DIV")[anIndex]
	IE myDIV = myDocument.all[aName]
	- myDIV = myDocument.getElementById (anElementID)
	- myDIV = myDocument.getElementsByName (aName)[anIndex]
	- myDIV = myDocument .getElementsByTagName("DIV")[anIndex]

HTML syntax:	`<DIV> ... </DIV>`	
Argument list:	`anIndex`	A reference to an element in a collection
	`aName`	An associative array reference
	`anElementID`	The ID value of an Element object
Object properties:	`align, dataFld, dataFormatAs, dataSrc`	
Event handlers:	`onAfterUpdate, onBeforeUpdate, onBlur, onChange, onClick, onDblClick, onDragStart, onFocus, onHelp, onKeyDown, onKeyPress, onKeyUp, onMouseDown, onMouseMove, onMouseOut, onMouseOver, onMouseUp, onResize, onRowEnter, onRowExit, onScroll, onSelectStart`	

A `DIV` object is a means of building a block structured organization of a document that is custom designed. It is yet another means of building a hierarchical model if none of the existing models fits the structure you need. It is also a way of marking out blocks of a document to be treated as a styled area or perhaps a means of dynamically replacing or modifying document content in an easily controlled manner.

The `<DIV>` tag is a block-level tag. That means that it forces a line break before and after itself.

The example shows how to exchange the style values between two `<DIV>` blocks.

Warnings:

❏ In Netscape 4, a `<DIV>` object whose CSS style defines its positioning as absolute is then enumerated in the layers collection at an appropriate position in the document/layer hierarchy. This is confusing because a `<DIV>` is not a `<LAYER>`. Refer to the discussion about `Layer` objects in a separate topic for further details.

Example code:

```
<HTML>
<HEAD>
</HEAD>
<BODY>
<DIV ID="ONE" STYLE="background-color:RED">
The DIV block ONE
</DIV>
<DIV ID="TWO" STYLE="background-color:BLUE">
The DIV block TWO
</DIV>
<FORM>
<INPUT TYPE="button" VALUE="CLICK ME" onClick="clickMe()">
</FORM>
<SCRIPT>
function clickMe()
{
myStyle1 = document.all.ONE.style.cssText;
myStyle2 = document.all.TWO.style.cssText;
```

```
document.all.ONE.style.cssText = myStyle2;
document.all.TWO.style.cssText = myStyle1;
}
</SCRIPT>
</BODY>
</HTML>
```

See also: Element object, Hierarchy of objects, Layer object, LayerArray object

Property	JavaScript	JScript	N	IE	Opera	DOM	HTML	Notes
align	1.5 +	3.0 +	6.0 +	4.0 +	-	1 +	-	-
dataFld	1.5 +	3.0 +	6.0 +	4.0 +	-	1 +	-	Warning
dataFormatAs	1.5 +	3.0 +	6.0 +	4.0 +	-	1 +	-	Warning
dataSrc	1.5 +	3.0 +	6.0 +	4.0 +	-	1 +	-	Warning

Event name	JavaScript	JScript	N	IE	Opera	DOM	HTML	Notes
onAfterUpdate	-	3.0 +	-	4.0 +	-	-	-	-
onBeforeUpdate	-	3.0 +	-	4.0 +	-	-	-	-
onBlur	1.5 +	3.0 +	6.0 +	4.0 +	-	-	-	Warning
onChange	1.5 +	3.0 +	6.0 +	4.0 +	-	-	-	-
onClick	1.5 +	3.0 +	6.0 +	4.0 +	-	-	4.0 +	Warning
onDblClick	1.5 +	3.0 +	6.0 +	4.0 +	-	-	4.0 +	Warning
onDragStart	-	3.0 +	-	4.0 +	-	-	-	-
onFocus	1.5 +	3.0 +	6.0 +	4.0 +	-	-	-	Warning
onHelp	-	3.0 +	-	4.0 +	-	-	-	Warning
onKeyDown	1.5 +	3.0 +	6.0 +	4.0 +	-	-	4.0 +	Warning
onKeyPress	1.5 +	3.0 +	6.0 +	4.0 +	-	-	4.0 +	Warning
onKeyUp	1.5 +	3.0 +	6.0 +	4.0 +	-	-	4.0 +	Warning
onMouseDown	1.5 +	3.0 +	6.0 +	4.0 +	-	-	4.0 +	Warning
onMouseMove	1.5 +	3.0 +	6.0 +	4.0 +	-	-	4.0 +	Warning
onMouseOut	1.5 +	3.0 +	6.0 +	4.0 +	-	-	4.0 +	Warning
onMouseOver	1.5 +	3.0 +	6.0 +	4.0 +	-	-	4.0 +	Warning
onMouseUp	1.5 +	3.0 +	6.0 +	4.0 +	-	-	4.0 +	Warning
onResize	1.5 +	3.0 +	6.0 +	4.0 +	-	-	-	Warning
onRowEnter	-	3.0 +	-	4.0 +	-	-	-	-
onRowExit	-	3.0 +	-	4.0 +	-	-	-	-
onScroll	-	3.0 +	-	4.0 +	-	-	-	-
onSelectStart	-	3.0 +	-	4.0 +	-	-	-	-

Inheritance chain:

Element object, Node object

Divide (/) (Operator/multiplicative)

Divide one operand by another.

Availability:	ECMAScript edition - 2 JavaScript - 1.0 JScript - 1.0 Internet Explorer - 3.02 Netscape - 2.0 Netscape Enterprise Server - 2.0 Opera - 3.0
Property/method value type:	Number primitive
JavaScript syntax:	- anOperand1 / anOperand2
Argument list:	anOperand1 The dividend
	anOperand2 The divisor

The left-hand operand is divided by the right-hand operand and the quotient is returned.

The left operand is the dividend, and the right is the divisor. ECMAScript compliant interpreters do not perform integer division. The operand and results of all divisions are double-precision floating point numbers. All divisions are performed according to IEEE 754 specifications.

If either operand is NaN then the result is NaN.

The sign of the result is positive if both operands have the same sign and negative if the operands have different signs.

Division of an infinity by an infinity results in NaN.

Division of an infinity by zero results in an infinity. The sign is determined by the rule stated earlier.

Division of infinity by a non-zero finite value results in a signed infinity. The sign is determined as before.

Division of a finite value by infinity results in zero. The sign is determined as usual.

Division of a zero by a zero results in NaN.

Division of zero by any other finite value results in zero with the sign determined as normal.

Otherwise, where there is neither an infinity or zero involved and neither value is NaN, the quotient is computed and rounded to the nearest representable value. If the magnitude is too large to represent, it will overflow and become an infinity. If the magnitude is too small to represent, an underflow occurs and the result will be zero.

180

The associativity is from left to right.

Refer to the operator precedence topic for details of execution order.

See also:	Associativity, Divide then assign (/=), Double-precision, Multiplicative expression, Multiplicative operator, Operator Precedence, Remainder (%)

Cross-references:

ECMA 262 edition 2 - section - 11.5.2

ECMA 262 edition 2 - section - 11.13

ECMA 262 edition 3 - section - 11.5.2

Divide then assign (/=) (Operator/assignment)

Divide one operand by another and put the result in the first.

Availability:	ECMAScript edition - 2 JavaScript - 1.0 JScript - 1.0 Internet Explorer - 3.02 Netscape - 2.0 Netscape Enterprise Server - 2.0 Opera - 3.0	
Property/method value type:	Number primitive	
JavaScript syntax:	-	anOperand1 /= anOperand2
Argument list:	anOperand1	The dividend
	anOperand2	The divisor

Divide the left operand by the right operand and assign the quotient to the left operand.

This is functionally equivalent to the expression:

```
anOperand1 = anOperand1 / anOperand2;
```

Although this is classified as an assignment operator it is really a compound of an assignment and a multiplicative operator.

The associativity is from right to left.

Refer to the operator precedence topic for details of execution order.

The new value of anOperand1 is returned as a result of the expression.

Warnings:

❏ The operand to the left of the operator must be an LValue. That is, it should be able to take an assignment and store the value.

See also:	Assignment operator, Associativity, Divide (/), LValue, Multiplicative operator, Operator Precedence, Remainder (%)

Cross-references:

ECMA 262 edition 2 - section - 11.13

ECMA 262 edition 3 - section - 11.13

DL object (Object/HTML)

An object that represents a definition list defined by a <DL> HTML tag.

Availability:	DOM level - 1 JavaScript - 1.5 JScript - 3.0 Internet Explorer - 4.0 Netscape - 6.0	
Inherits from:	Element object	
JavaScript syntax:	IE	myDL = myDocument.all.anElementID
	IE	myDL = myDocument.all.tags("DL")[anIndex]
	IE	myDL = myDocument.all[aName]
	-	myDL = myDocument.getElementById (anElementID)
	-	myDL = myDocument.getElementsByName (aName)[anIndex]
	-	myDL = myDocument.getElementsByTagName ("DL")[anIndex]
HTML syntax:	<DL> ... </DL>	
Argument list:	anIndex	A reference to an element in a collection
	aName	An associative array reference
	anElementID	The ID value of an Element object
Object properties:	compact	
Event handlers:	onClick, onDblClick, onDragStart, onFilterChange, onHelp, onKeyDown, onKeyPress, onKeyUp, onMouseDown, onMouseMove, onMouseOut, onMouseOver, onMouseUp, onSelectStart	

Definition lists are collections of member definitions. The whole list is encapsulated in a DL object. Each member definition is constructed from a DT and a DD object which are maintained together.

The <DL> tag is a block-level tag. That means that it forces a line break before and after itself.

The DOM level 1 standard describes this as a DListElement object.

See also:	DD object, DT object, Element object

Property	JavaScript	JScript	N	IE	Opera	DOM	HTML	Notes
compact	1.5 +	3.0 +	6.0 +	4.0 +	-	1 +	-	-

Event name	JavaScript	JScript	N	IE	Opera	DOM	HTML	Notes
onClick	1.5 +	3.0 +	6.0 +	4.0 +	-	-	4.0 +	Warning
onDblClick	1.5 +	3.0 +	6.0 +	4.0 +	-	-	4.0 +	Warning
onDragStart	-	3.0 +	-	4.0 +	-	-	-	-
onFilterChange	-	3.0 +	-	4.0 +	-	-	-	-
onHelp	-	3.0 +	-	4.0 +	-	-	-	Warning
onKeyDown	1.5 +	3.0 +	6.0 +	4.0 +	-	-	4.0 +	Warning
onKeyPress	1.5 +	3.0 +	6.0 +	4.0 +	-	-	4.0 +	Warning
onKeyUp	1.5 +	3.0 +	6.0 +	4.0 +	-	-	4.0 +	Warning
onMouseDown	1.5 +	3.0 +	6.0 +	4.0 +	-	-	4.0 +	Warning
onMouseMove	1.5 +	3.0 +	6.0 +	4.0 +	-	-	4.0 +	Warning
onMouseOut	1.5 +	3.0 +	6.0 +	4.0 +	-	-	4.0 +	Warning
onMouseOver	1.5 +	3.0 +	6.0 +	4.0 +	-	-	4.0 +	Warning
onMouseUp	1.5 +	3.0 +	6.0 +	4.0 +	-	-	4.0 +	Warning
onSelectStart	-	3.0 +	-	4.0 +	-	-	-	-

Inheritance chain:

Element object, Node object

do ... while(...) (Iterator)

A variant of the while iterator that checks the condition after execution.

Availability:	ECMAScript edition - 2 JavaScript - 1.2 JScript - 3.0 Internet Explorer - 4.0 Netscape - 4.0 Netscape Enterprise Server - 2.0 Opera - 3.0	
JavaScript syntax:	-	aLabel: do { someCode } while (aCondition) ;
Argument list:	aCondition	This must prove true for a subsequent cycle to start
	aLabel	An optional identifier that names the loop
	someCode	The code that gets executed in the loop

A do loop is a variation on the while iterator. A while iterator checks the condition and only executes the code block if it is true. This means that a while loop may never execute even once. A do iterator checks the condition once the code has been executed. This ensures that a do iterator will perform at least one execution of the code block even if the condition proves false the first time it is tested.

ECMA edition 2 compliance merely states that it is a reserved word. At edition 3 of the ECMAScript standard, it is a fully supported requirement of compliance.

JavaScript version 1.2 anticipates this and provides it anyway.

If a labeled continue is used (available from version 1.2 of JavaScript), it is intended that execution should drop to the bottom of the loop and test the condition again before cycling or falling out.

Note carefully the line that increments the counter. If you leave it out, you create an endless loop and the browser locks you out. Maybe it will eventually crash but you may need to wait a long time.

Warnings:

❏ In Netscape 4, there is a bug with labeled continue statements and do ... while loops that causes the continue to vector to the top of the loop without testing the condition. This can set up an endless loop. You could work round this by creating a while loop and modifying the test condition.

Example code:

```
<HTML>
<HEAD>
</HEAD>
<BODY>
<SCRIPT>
myCounter = 10;
do
{
document.write(myCounter);
document.write("<BR>");
myCounter++;
}
while(myCounter < 35);
</SCRIPT>
</BODY>
</HTML>
```

See also:	continue, Flow control, for(...) ..., for(...in...)..., Label, Off by one errors, while(...)...

Cross-references:

ECMA 262 edition 2 - section - 7.4.3

ECMA 262 edition 3 - section - 7.5.2

ECMA 262 edition 3 - section - 12.6.1

Doctype object (Object/DOM)

An object that represents the document type DTD.

Availability:	DOM level - 1 JavaScript - 1.5 JScript - 5.5 Internet Explorer - 5.5 Netscape - 6.0
Inherits from:	Node object
JavaScript syntax:	IE *myDoctype* = *myDocument*.all.*anElementID*
	IE *myDoctype* = *myDocument*.all.tags ("DOCTYPE")[*anIndex*]
	IE *myDoctype* = *myDocument*.all[*aName*]
	- *myDoctype* = *myDocument*.doctype
	- *myDoctype* = *myDocument*.getElementById (*anElementID*)
	- *myDoctype* = *myDocument*.getElementsByName (*aName*)[*anIndex*]
	- *myDoctype* = *myDocument*.getElementsByTagName ("DOCTYPE")[*anIndex*]

185

HTML syntax:	`<!DOCTYPE>`	
Argument list:	`anIndex`	A reference to an element in a collection
	`aName`	An associative array reference
	`anElementID`	The ID value of an Element object
Object properties:	`name`	
Collections:	`entities[]`, `notations[]`	

Every document should own a Doctype object according to the DOM level 1 specification. This object encapsulates name and some collections that describe the DTD. Work is still underway on standardizing the XML and DTD requirements and this object is therefore likely to change in later versions of the DOM specification.

The DOM level 2 specification adds the following new properties:

❏ publicId

❏ systemId

❏ internalSubset

See also:	`Document.doctype`, `Element.document`, `Notation` object

Property	JavaScript	JScript	N	IE	Opera	DOM	Notes
`name`	1.5 +	5.5 +	6.0 +	5.5 +	-	1 +	ReadOnly

Inheritance chain:

`Node object`

Document (Object model)

An organized collection of objects that represent a document.

The document object is the foundation around which a scriptable interface to an HTML or XML document is constructed. This is sometimes referred to as the DOM and is subject to its own standardization exercise being managed by W3C and other interested parties.

The DOM has its origins in the MSIE version 4 browsers. Version 3 of MSIE and versions of Netscape prior to version 6 implement a more miscellaneous collection of objects that behave a bit like a DOM but are not really a standards compliant model.

There are areas where the so-called DOM support in each browser is so different as to render any script access to the document either problematical or virtually impossible with the same script. This means that you need to support parallel development of HTML and JavaScript to be able to cover both competing browsers.

Now that Netscape 6.0 converges on the same standards based DOM model as MSIE we can look forward to a much more portable future for our scripts. So long as we can disregard legacy versions and steer clear of the still quite large number of differences we should be able to do much more across different browsers without needing to code differently for each one. History suggests it is also equally likely that they will diverge in other areas where they introduce new features.

The starting point for the DOM hierarchy is the <HTML> HTML tag, although the <BODY> HTML tag is realistically the root of the DOM.

Until the version 5/6 browsers ship, the existing DOM support is referred to as Level 0. The current standard is level 1 and level 2 is on the horizon.

The basic approach to the DOM differs between the browsers on these points:

❑ Netscape prior to version 6.0 generally provides a constructor for every object type. MSIE only provides them for objects that you can reasonably instantiate. The new Netscape should comply with the DOM requirements and only provide constructors where they are mandated by the standard.

❑ MSIE implements an Element object on which most other DOM components are based. Netscape 6 implements a structured, DOM compliant model so this is implicit.

❑ The DOM hierarchy is organized in different ways. MSIE provides many reference vectors for locating parent and child objects to traverse the DOM tree. Netscape provides very few prior to version 6.0.

❑ MSIE provides an object to represent every tag. Its type is the tag name in upper case.

❑ On the down side, MSIE supports a DOM structure that resembles the DOM standard quite closely. However, many of its class names are incorrect. Netscape 6.0 supports a similar structure but uses the correct names for object classes. If you need to use class names in your scripts, beware!

Warnings:

❑ This is not supported at all on Netscape 2 and 3 or MSIE version 3. You should at least check for these browsers and generate a helpful warning message or skip round the requirement somehow.

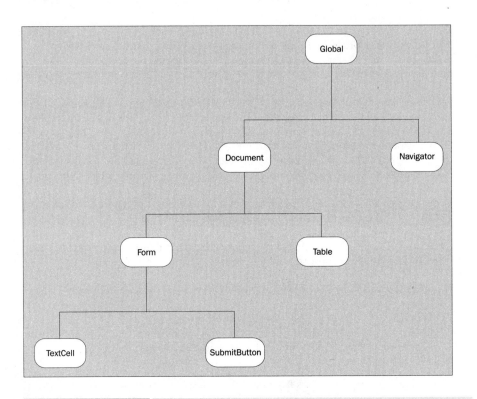

| See also: | Compatibility, Document object, DOM, Event handler scope |

Web-references:

http://msdn.microsoft.com/redirs/inetsdkredir.asp
http://www.w3.org/TR/WD-DOM/

Document object (Object/HTML)

An object that represents the document currently loaded into the window. This exposes the contents of the HTML document through a variety of collections and properties.

Availability:	DOM level - 1 JavaScript - 1.0 JScript - 1.0 Internet Explorer - 3.02 Netscape - 2.0 Opera - 3.0
Inherits from:	Element object

JavaScript syntax:	-	myDocument = document
	-	myDocument = document.documentElement
	IE	myDocument = myElement.document
	IE	myDocument = myElement.offsetParent
	-	myDocument = myElement.ownerDocument
	IE	myDocument = myElement.parentElement
	-	myDocument = myElement.parentNode
	-	myDocument = myFrame.document
	N	myDocument = myLayer.document
	-	myDocument = myWindow.document
	-	myDocument = opener.document
	-	myDocument = self.document

Argument list:	anIndex	An index that selects this document

Object properties: `<form_name>`, activeElement, alinkColor, background, bgColor, body, characterset, charset, cookie, defaultCharset, designMode, doctype, documentElement, domain, expando, fgColor, fileCreatedDate, fileModifiedDate, fileSize, height, implementation, lastModified, linkColor, location, parentWindow, protocol, readyState, referrer, selection, title, uniqueID, URL, vlinkColor, width

Object methods: attachEvent(), captureEvents(), clear(), close(), contextual(), createAttribute(), createCDATASection(), createComment(), createDocumentFragment(), createElement(), createEntityReference(), createProcessingInstruction(), createStyleSheet(), createTextNode(), detachEvent(), elementFromPoint(), execCommand(), getElementById(), getElementsByName(), getElementsByTagName(), getSelection(), handleEvent(), mergeAttrbutes(), open(), queryCommandEnabled(), queryCommandIndeterm(), queryCommandState(), queryCommandSupported(), queryCommandText(), queryCommandValue(), recalc(), releaseEvents(), routeEvent(), write(), writeln()

Functions: captureEvents(), releaseEvents(), routeEvent()

Event handlers: onAfterUpdate, onBeforeCut, onBeforeEditFocus, onBeforePaste, onBeforeUpdate, onClick, onContextMenu, onCut, onDblClick, onDrag, onDragEnd, onDragEnter, onDragLeave, onDragOver, onDragStart, onDrop, onErrorUpdate, onHelp, onKeyDown, onKeyPress, onKeyUp, onMouseDown, onMouseMove, onMouseOut, onMouseOver, onMouseUp, onPaste, onPropertyChange, onReadyStateChange, onRowEnter, onRowExit, onSelectStart, onStop

Collections: all[], anchors[], applets[], classes[], embeds[], forms[], frames[], ids[], images[], layers[], links[], plugins[], scripts[], styleSheets[], tags[]

The `document` object is the root of a hierarchy that describes the document in terms of objects, properties and methods that can operate on those objects.

The DOM level specification describes a core `Document` object and distinguishes that from the HTMLDocument that is a sub-class of it. However, the browsers do not make such a fine distinction and so Documents and HTMLDocuments are considered to be one and the same. This works because an HTMLDocument inherits the behavior of a DOM core Document object.

Documents and their child objects can respond to events by means of event handler functions. These are generally associated with one another by means of the HTML tag attributes that correspond to each event.

Although there is a superset of all event types, each object type only responds to a few of them.

The `document` object is based on the `Element` object, therefore it inherits all the properties and methods of that class and adds others itself.

The `document` object is basically derived initially from the <BODY> HTML tag although it contains some properties that are associated with the <HEAD> HTML tag and others from the <HTML> HTML tag that encloses the entire file. The document type header also affects properties in the `document` object.

Traversing the document object model in MSIE is quite straightforward. In Netscape prior to version 6.0 it is so difficult as to be virtually impossible. You can access certain parts of the DOM in earlier Netscape browsers by virtue of the forms, applets, embeds and other collections but you cannot access other parts of the DOM at all.

Event handling support via properties containing function objects was added to Anchor objects at version 1.1 of JavaScript and is significantly extended in Netscape 6.0 where it supports DOM level 2 capabilities.

Because you might refer to documents in many ways, possibly by means of object properties or as a property belonging to another window, it is not safe to assume that the document property belonging to the `Global` object is always the `document` object you are trying to access. Indeed, a document may belong to a window, frame, layer or Iframe and several may be accessible at once. Because of this, the object references in the syntax examples assume the object is being referred to via a variable called `myDocument` or `myObject` etc. In the object descriptions, the value `myDocument` is shown being assigned as a variable from the many alternative sources that you can obtain a document reference.

The DOM level specification deprecates the following properties in favor of their counterparts belonging to the `BODY` object:

❑ `alinkColor`

❑ `background`

❑ `bgColor`

❑ fgColor

❑ linkColor

❑ vlinkColor

The DOM level 2 specification adds the following methods:

❑ importNode()

❑ createElementNS()

❑ createAttributeNS()

❑ getElementsByTagNameNS()

❑ getElementById()

A new suite of functionality relating to the way documents are viewed is introduced at DOM level 2. This is embodied in the following classes:

❑ AbstractView

❑ DocumentView

DOM level 3 expects to add the following properties to the document object:

❑ actualEncoding

❑ encoding

❑ standalone

❑ strictErrorChecking

❑ version

It is also expected to add the following methods:

❑ adoptNode()

❑ getElementsByAttributeValue()

Warnings:

❑ There are a number of properties that are defined in both Netscape and MSIE browsers. There are also a few that each defines while the other doesn't. There is at least one (document.title) that is defined with different behavior in both browsers. Likewise the same is true of the support for different methods across the two browsers.

❑ With each release, they tend to support the extensions that the other introduced with its previous release but they also both introduce new and incompatible extensions each time as well.

191

See also: BODY object, Element.document, Form.handleEvent(), Frame object, HTML object, JavaScript Style Sheets, Layer.document, Node object, Node.ownerDocument, TextRange.queryCommandEnabled(), TextRange.queryCommandIndeterm(), TextRange.queryCommandState(), TextRange.queryCommandSupported(), TextRange.queryCommandText(), TextRange.queryCommandValue(), Window object, Window.document, Window.frames[], Window.opener

Property	JavaScript	JScript	N	IE	Opera	DOM	HTML	Notes
<form_name>	1.1 +	3.0 +	3.0 +	4.0 +	3.0 +	-	-	Warning
active Element	-	3.0 +	-	4.0 +	-	-	-	ReadOnly
alinkColor	1.0 +	1.0 +	2.0 +	3.02 +	3.0 +	0 +	-	Warning, Deprecated
background	-	-	-	-	-	0 +	-	Deprecated
bgColor	1.0 +	1.0 +	2.0 +	3.02 +	3.0 +	0 +	-	Warning, Deprecated
body	1.5 +	3.0 +	6.0 +	4.0 +	5.0 +	1 +	-	ReadOnly
characterset	1.5 +	-	6.0 +	-	-	-	-	-
charset	-	3.0 +	-	4.0 +	-	-	-	-
cookie	1.0 +	1.0 +	2.0 +	3.02 +	3.0 +	1 +	-	Warning
default Charset	-	3.0 +	-	4.0 +	-	-	-	Warning
designMode	-	5.0 +	-	5.0 +	-	-	-	Warning
doctype	1.5 +	3.0 +	6.0 +	4.0 +	-	1 +	-	Warning, ReadOnly
document Element	1.5 +	5.0 +	6.0 +	5.0 +	-	1 +	-	Warning, ReadOnly
domain	1.1 +	3.0 +	3.0 +	4.0 +	3.0 +	1 +	-	Warning, ReadOnly
expando	-	3.0 +	-	4.0 +	-	-	-	-
fgColor	1.0 +	1.0 +	2.0 +	3.02 +	3.0 +	0 +	-	Warning, Deprecated
file CreatedDate	-	3.0 +	-	4.0 +	-	-	-	ReadOnly
file ModifiedDate	-	3.0 +	-	4.0 +	-	-	-	ReadOnly
fileSize	-	3.0 +	-	4.0 +	-	-	-	ReadOnly
height	1.2 +	-	4.0 +	-	-	-	-	Warning
implementation	1.5 +	5.0 +	6.0 +	5.0 +	-	1 +	-	Warning, ReadOnly
lastModified	1.0 +	1.0 +	2.0 +	3.02 +	3.0 +	-	-	ReadOnly

Property	JavaScript	JScript	N	IE	Opera	DOM	HTML	Notes
linkColor	1.0 +	1.0 +	2.0 +	3.02 +	3.0 +	0 +	-	Warning, Deprecated
location	1.0 +	1.0 +	2.0 +	3.02 +	3.0 +	1 +	-	Warning, Deprecated
parentWindow	-	3.0 +	-	4.0 +	-	-	-	ReadOnly
protocol	-	1.0 +	-	3.02 +	-	-	-	ReadOnly
readyState	-	3.0 +	-	4.0 +	-	-	-	ReadOnly
referrer	1.0 +	1.0 +	2.0 +	3.02 +	3.0 +	1 +	-	Warning, ReadOnly
selection	-	3.0 +	-	4.0 +	-	-	-	Warning, ReadOnly
title	1.0 +	1.0 +	2.0 +	3.02 +	3.0 +	1 +	-	Warning
uniqueID	-	5.0 +	-	5.0 +	-	-	-	-
URL	1.1 +	3.0 +	3.0 +	4.0 +	3.0 +	1 +	-	ReadOnly
vlinkColor	1.0 +	1.0 +	2.0 +	3.02 +	3.0 +	0 +	-	Warning, Deprecated
width	1.2 +	-	4.0 +	-	-	-	-	Warning

Method	JavaScript	JScript	N	IE	Opera	DOM	HTML	Notes
attach Event()	-	5.0 +	-	5.0 +	-	-	-	-
capture Events()	1.2 +	-	4.0 +	-	-	-	-	Warning, Deprecated
clear()	1.0 +	1.0 +	2.0 +	3.02 +	5.0 +	-	-	Warning, Deprecated
close()	1.0 +	1.0 +	2.0 +	3.02 +	3.0 +	1 +	-	-
contextual()	1.2 +	-	4.0 +	-	-	-	-	Warning, Deprecated
create Attribute()	1.5 +	-	6.0 +	-	-	1 +	-	-
createCDATA Section()	1.5 +	-	6.0 +	-	-	1 +	-	-
create Comment()	1.5 +	-	6.0 +	-	-	1 +	-	-
createDocument Fragment()	1.5 +	-	6.0 +	-	-	1 +	-	-
create Element()	1.5 +	3.0 +	6.0 +	4.0 +	-	1 +	-	-
createEntity Reference()	1.5 +	-	6.0 +	-	-	1 +	-	-
create Processing Instruction()	1.5 +	-	6.0 +	-	-	1 +	-	-
createStyle Sheet()	-	3.0 +	-	4.0 +	-	-	-	Warning
createText Node()	1.5 +	5.0 +	6.0 +	5.0 +	-	1 +	-	-

Table continued on following page

JavaScript Programmer's Reference

D

Method	JavaScript	JScript	N	IE	Opera	DOM	HTML	Notes
detachEvent()	-	5.0 +	-	5.0 +	-	-	-	-
elementFromPoint()	-	3.0 +	-	4.0 +	-	-	-	-
execCommand()	-	3.0 +	-	4.0 +	-	-	-	Warning
getElementById()	1.5 +	5.0 +	6.0 +	5.0 +	5.0 +	1 +	-	-
getElementsByName()	1.5 +	5.0 +	6.0 +	5.0 +	5.0 +	1 +	-	Warning
getElementsByTagName()	1.5 +	5.0 +	6.0 +	5.0 +	-	1 +	-	-
getSelection()	1.2 +	-	4.0 +	-	-	-	-	Warning
handleEvent()	1.2 +	-	4.0 +	-	-	-	-	-
mergeAttrbutes()	1.0 +	1.0 +	2.0 +	3.02 +	3.0 +	1 +	-	Warning
open()	1.0 +	1.0 +	2.0 +	3.02 +	3.0 +	1 +	-	Warning
queryCommandEnabled()	-	3.0 +	-	4.0 +	-	-	-	Warning
queryCommandIndeterm()	-	3.0 +	-	4.0 +	-	-	-	Warning
queryCommandState()	-	3.0 +	-	4.0 +	-	-	-	Warning
queryCommandSupported()	-	3.0 +	-	4.0 +	-	-	-	Warning
queryCommandText()	-	3.0 +	-	4.0 +	-	-	-	Warning
queryCommandValue()	-	3.0 +	-	4.0 +	-	-	-	Warning
recalc()	-	5.0 +	-	5.0 +	-	-	-	-
releaseEvents()	1.2 +	-	4.0 +	-	-	-	-	-
routeEvent()	1.2 +	-	4.0 +	-	-	-	-	-
write()	1.0 +	1.0 +	2.0 +	3.02 +	3.0 +	1 +	-	Warning
writeln()	1.0 +	1.0 +	2.0 +	3.02 +	3.0 +	1 +	-	-

Event name	JavaScript	JScript	N	IE	Opera	DOM	HTML	Notes
onAfterUpdate	-	3.0 +	-	4.0 +	-	-	-	-
onBeforeCut	-	5.0 +	-	5.0 +	-	-	-	-
onBeforeEditFocus	1.0 +	1.0 +	2.0 +	3.02 +	3.0 +	1 +	-	Warning
onBeforePaste	-	5.0 +	-	5.0 +	-	-	-	-
onBeforeUpdate	-	3.0 +	-	4.0 +	-	-	-	-
onClick	1.0 +	1.0 +	2.0 +	3.02 +	3.0 +	-	4.0 +	Warning
onContextMenu	-	5.0 +	-	5.0 +	-	-	-	-
onCut	-	5.0 +	-	5.0 +	-	-	-	-
onDblClick	1.2 +	3.0 +	4.0 +	4.0 +	3.0 +	-	4.0 +	Warning

Event name	JavaScript	JScript	N	IE	Opera	DOM	HTML	Notes
onDrag	-	5.0 +	-	5.0 +	-	-	-	-
onDragEnd	-	5.0 +	-	5.0 +	-	-	-	-
onDragEnter	-	5.0 +	-	5.0 +	-	-	-	-
onDragLeave	-	5.0 +	-	5.0 +	-	-	-	-
onDragOver	-	5.0 +	-	5.0 +	-	-	-	-
onDragStart	-	3.0 +	-	4.0 +	-	-	-	-
onDrop	-	5.0 +	-	5.0 +	-	-	-	-
onError Update	-	3.0 +	-	4.0 +	-	-	-	-
onHelp	-	3.0 +	-	4.0 +	-	-	-	Warning
onKeyDown	1.2 +	3.0 +	4.0 +	4.0 +	3.0 +	-	4.0 +	Warning
onKeyPress	1.2 +	3.0 +	4.0 +	4.0 +	3.0 +	-	4.0 +	Warning
onKeyUp	1.2 +	3.0 +	4.0 +	4.0 +	3.0 +	-	4.0 +	Warning
onMouseDown	1.2 +	3.0 +	4.0 +	4.0 +	3.0 +	-	4.0 +	Warning
onMouseMove	1.2 +	3.0 +	4.0 +	4.0 +	-	-	4.0 +	Warning
onMouseOut	1.1 +	3.0 +	3.0 +	4.0 +	3.0 +	-	4.0 +	Warning
onMouseOver	1.0 +	1.0 +	2.0 +	3.0 +	3.0 +	-	4.0 +	Warning
onMouseUp	1.2 +	3.0 +	4.0 +	4.0 +	3.0 +	-	4.0 +	Warning
onPaste	-	5.0 +	-	5.0 +	-	-	-	-
onProperty Change	-	5.0 +	-	5.0 +	-	-	-	-
onReady StateChange	-	3.0 +	-	4.0 +	-	-	-	-
onRowEnter	-	3.0 +	-	4.0 +	-	-	-	-
onRowExit	-	3.0 +	-	4.0 +	-	-	-	-
onSelect Start	-	3.0 +	-	4.0 +	-	-	-	-
onStop	1.2 +	-	4.0 +	-	-	-	-	-

Inheritance chain:

Element object, Node object

Document.captureEvents() (Function)

Part of the Netscape 4 event propagation complex.

Availability:	JavaScript - 1.2 Netscape - 4.0 Deprecated	
Property/method value type:	undefined	
JavaScript syntax:	N	myDocument.captureEvents (anEventMask)
Argument list:	anEventMask	A mask constructed with the manifest event constants

This is part of the event management suite which allows events to be routed to handlers other than just the one that defaults to being associated with an event.

The events to be captured are signified by setting bits in a mask.

This method allows you to specify what events are to be routed to the receiving Document object.

The events are specified by using the bitwise OR operator to combine the required event mask constants into a mask that defines the events you want to capture. Refer to the Event Type Constants topic for a list of the event mask values.

A limitation of this technique is that ultimately, only 32 different kinds of events can be combined in this way and this may limit the number of events the browser can support. Since this is only supported by Netscape , the functionality is likely to be deprecated when the standards bodies agree on a standard way of handling events. Then we simply need to wait for the browser manufacturers to support the standardized behavior.

In the meantime, we shall have to implement scripts using this capability if we need to build complex event handling systems. A different script will be required for MSIE.

You may be able to factor your event handler so that you only have to make platform specific event dispatchers and can call common handling routines that can be shared between MSIE and Netscape .

The example copes with cross-browser execution in an interesting way.

Warnings:

❏ Since a bit mask is being used, this must be an int32 value. This suggests that there can only be 32 different Event types supported by this event propagation model.

❏ This capability is deprecated and is not supported in Netscape 6.0 anymore. It never was supported by MSIE which implements a completely different event model. As it turns out the DOM level 2 event model converges on the MSIE technique.

Example code:

```
// A portable keyboard event handler
// Provided by Jon Stephens
function handleKeypress(event)
{
var key;

if(document.layers)
{
key = event.which;
}
```

```
if(document.all)
{
event = window.event;
key   = event.keyCode;
}

alert("Key: " + String.fromCharCode(key) + "\nCharacter code: " +
key + ".");
}
if(document.layers)
{
document.captureEvents(Event.KEYPRESS);
}
document.onkeypress = handleKeypress;
```

See also:	captureEvents(), Document object, Document.releaseEvents(), Element.onevent, Event management, Event propagation, Event type constants, Frame object, Layer.captureEvents(), Layer.releaseEvents(), onMouseMove, Window object, Window.captureEvents(), Window.releaseEvents()

Document.handleEvent() (Function)

Pass an event to the appropriate handler for this object.

Availability:	JavaScript - 1.2 Netscape - 4.0	
Property/method value type:	undefined	
JavaScript syntax:	N	*myDocument*.handleEvent (*anEvent*)
Argument list:	*anEvent*	An event to be handled by this object

This applies to Netscape prior to version 6.0. From that release onwards, event management follows the guidelines in the DOM level 3 event specification.

On receipt of a call to this method, the receiving object will look at its available set of event handler functions and pass the event to an appropriately mapped handler function. It is essentially an event dispatcher that is granular down to the object level.

The argument value is an Event object that contains information about the event.

See also:	Document object, handleEvent()

Document.releaseEvents() (Function)

An alias for the `window.releaseEvents()` method.

Availability:	JavaScript - 1.2 Netscape - 4.0
Property/method value type:	`undefined`
JavaScript syntax:	N `myDocument.releaseEvents` `(anEventMask)`
Argument list:	`anEventMask` A mask defined with the manifest event constants

This is part of the Netscape 4 event management suite which allows events to be routed to handlers other than just the one that defaults to being associated with an event.

The events to be captured are signified by setting bits in a mask.

This method provides a means of indicating which events are no longer needing to be captured by the receiving `Document` object.

The events are specified by using the bitwise OR operator to combine the required event mask constants into a mask that defines the events you want to capture. Refer to the Event Type Constants topic for a list of the event mask values.

Since this is only supported by Netscape prior to version 6.0, the functionality is likely to be deprecated when the standards bodies agree on a standard way of handling events. In the meantime, we shall have to implement scripts using this capability if we need to build complex event handling systems that work on legacy browsers. A different script will be required for MSIE although it may be possible for Netscape 6.0 to share the same one.

You may be able to factor your event handler so that you only have to make platform specific event dispatchers and can call common handling routines that can be shared between MSIE and Netscape.

See also:	`captureEvents()`, `Document` object, `Document.captureEvents()`, `Element.onevent`, Event propagation, Event type constants, `Event.modifiers`, Frame object, `Layer.captureEvents()`, `Layer.releaseEvents()`, onMouseMove, Window object, `Window.releaseEvents()`

DocumentEvent (Object/DOM)

An interface that extends the `Document` object to support a DOM compliant event structure.

Availability:	DOM level - 2 JavaScript - 1.5 Netscape - 6.0
JavaScript syntax:	N *myDocumentEvent = myDocument*
Object methods:	`createEvent()`

This is not an object class that exists on its own. Rather it is an extension to the underlying Document object. It could be considered to be a sub-class of `Document` that inherits all the properties and methods of the `Document` class. Objects of this type are likely to report that they belong to the Document class rather than the DocumentEvent class although that may be implementation dependant.

The syntax listing shows that a DocumentEvent object is equal to a Document object although as is the case with Document, you cannot be certain which one of several possible documents you may have been passed if several windows, frames or layers are in use at once.

Method	JavaScript	JScript	N	IE	Opera	DOM	Notes
`createEvent()`	1.5 +	-	6.0 +	-	-	2 +	-

DocumentFragment object (Object/DOM)

The DOM specification calls this a lightweight or minimal document object. It can be used as a temporary store for a part of the document hierarchy.

Availability:	DOM level - 1 JavaScript - 1.5 Netscape - 6.0
Inherits from:	`Node object`
JavaScript syntax:	N *myDocumentFragment = myDocument* `.createDocumentFragment()`
See also:	`Document.createDocumentFragment()`, Node object

Inheritance chain:

Node object

DocumentStyle object (Object/DOM)

Added at DOM level 2 to support document related stylesheets.

Availability:	DOM level - 2 JavaScript - 1.5 Netscape - 6.0	
JavaScript syntax:	N	myDocumentStyle = new DocumentStyle()

This is a major upgrade in progress. At present the DOM level 2 standards run to several hundred pages and are extremely powerful.

The event model is supported by the Netscape 6.0 browser. Some (probably most) of the style model is supported by MSIE and Netscape 6.0 but there are some shortcomings. For instance, MSIE incorrectly names some properties and object types and it introduces some non-compliant extra methods and properties which are not portable.

The document styling interface is likely to be an area of major amounts of work on the next round of browser upgrades.

DOM mandates that this object should have a single property:

❏ styleSheets

Note that MSIE takes that property name and uses it as an object type. DOM mandates that the property should point at a StyleSheetList object and not a styleSheets object.

DOM (Standard)

A standardized model of a document built with objects.

The DOM standard is concerned with mapping document components to an object model which reflects the values defined in HTML tag attributes. These are visible to the script writer as object properties. In case of conflicts with reserved words and object names in the JavaScript context, any conflicting names will have the"html" prefix. An example is the "for" attribute which becomes the "htmlFor" property. The HTML tag that instantiated an object is reflected in the tagName property of each element object. All document elements derived from HTML tags are sub-classed from the Element class.

The W3C Document Object Model standard is being reviewed and updated to enhance the support of the document in the browser. There are several levels to this standard:

❏ Level 0 - The more or less de-facto situation with the version 4 browsers.

❏ Level 1 - Text, elements and attributes of HTML and XML.

❑ Level 2 - Views, traversals, events and stylesheets standardized.

❑ Level 3 - More work on events and the content model introduced.

❑ Future - Potential standardization of the security model and standardization of the context and environment in which the document exists.

Thankfully now that browsers are converging on the same standards the amount of duplicated effort will diminish over time as the older browsers are replaced. Netscape 6.0 is just beginning to ship. Beta versions of MSIE version 6.0 are imminent and Opera version 5 is likely to be similarly capable as regards DOM compliance. DOM level 1 seems to be roughly where we are at present.

Browser manufacturers make grand claims to be ECMAScript compliant as well as DOM compliant. This claim is somewhat suspect. Providing objects with the functionality of DOM specified classes but having different class names does not completely satisfy the requirements for DOM compliance. We may ultimately end up with objects being mirrored into duplicate instances under different class names to satisfy DOM class naming and to preserve legacy support.

MSIE at version 5 supports a DOM-like object model with Microsoft specific class names. Netscape 6 supports a highly DOM compliant object model with correct object class names. When testing the PR3 beta version of Netscape 6.0, it looked like several HTML tags instantiated objects of the same class when they should have been different but this may have gone away in the final release.

As browser manufacturers support more standardized interfaces we may be better off in some areas but are also likely to be inconsistent between the browsers in some new areas.

As the new levels are introduced and add new modules, they often extend the interfaces of existing classes. The DOM standard accomplishes this by defining new classes as if they were a sub-class of the object they extend. This provides some opportunity for implementors to name object classes incorrectly in early versions of their DOM support. For example, event handling extends the Document object to allow it to create new events. This would really be an extension of the Document object and would likely not be implemented by sub-classing Document to create a DocumentEvent object. Were that the way the implentor had chosen, we would have a DOM hierarchy model that had been structurally altered by the insertion of a new sub-class between Document and HTMLDocument and we already have enough confusion between those two object classes across browsers.

Warnings:

❑ The support for DOM in Netscape 4 is so vestigial that it cannot really be called a DOM implementation at all. This is corrected in Netscape 6.0 which supports DOM level 1 and additionally supports some DOM level 2 features to do with Event handling.

<table>
<tr><td>See also:</td><td>CLASS=" . . . ", Document, Document component, Dynamic
HTML, Element object, MutationEvent object, NamedNodeMap
object, Overview</td></tr>
</table>

Web-references:

http://www.w3c.org/DOM/

DOM - Level 0 (Standard)

The initial collation of document objects and properties from the de-facto HTML and JavaScript implementations.

The level 0 version of the DOM standard was compiled from the available functionality of the Netscape 3.0 and MSIE version 3.0 functionality. The principal input was derived from the HTML support provided by the browsers. As it stands, some attributes and methods are provided to support backwards compatability with these older browsers. Those items will likely become deprecated features and will in due course be withdrawn.

DOM - Level 1 (Standard)

A standardized model of a document built with objects.

The level 1 version of the DOM standard defines the complete content structure of the document.

This is implemented in the standard in two parts:

❑ DOM core functionality

❑ HTML functionality

The core functionality should apply to documents of a variety of types while the HTML functionality should only be supported in implementations that use HTML marked up documents.

In a fully compliant browser, you can expect to access all of the attributes names and values of each and every tag. There should be a high degree of consistency between HTML tag attribute sets and object properties and methods.

The document should then be represented as a tree of objects starting at the outermost <HTML> tag and all subsequent items being contained in a logical tree structured parent and child arrangement.

With the consistent compliance between HTML attributes and JavaScript object properties, there may still be a few catch-outs. For example, the namespaces may collide. An HTML attribute may correspond to a JavaScript reserved word and therefore it should not be used as a property or method name since they exist in the identifier namespace. Identifiers and JavaScript reserved words must not collide.

To work around this, some prefix will be added to the property names.

The Level 1 DOM support should also include some API support to locate objects by name without necessarily walking the document tree.

Warnings:

❑ The level 1 DOM specification is similar to but may be somewhat incompatible with the MSIE version 4 DOM implementation. Netscape 6.0 provides the most accurate and compliant implementation of DOM level 1 at the time of writing.

See also:	NamedNodeMap object

DOM - Level 2 (Standard)

A standardized model of a document built with objects.

The level 2 DOM is an enhancement on the level 1 support. It introduces additional properties and styles for document objects.

The standard is composed of the following modules:

❑ DOM core functionality

❑ HTML functionality

❑ Event handling

❑ Style specification

❑ Document views

❑ Traversal and range specification

The DOM level specification is now a 500 page document that maps the HTML specification to the ECMAScript and Java language bindings. Many additional objects are provided to assist in navigating the DOM hierarchy.

In general, the MSIE version 5 browser on Windows and Macintosh is the best and most complete implementation of DOM released for general use so far.

Netscape 5 never saw the light of day, and with Netscape 6, the development teams have a stated goal of going very aggressively for DOM standardization. Running the same inspection scripts on MSIE 5 and Netscape 6 reveals that the DOM implementations are structurally similar but that the DOM compliance is more robust in Netscape. This is because MSIE does not use the standardized class names fpr objects although the entity relations are more or less correct.

The differences between level 1 and level 2 basic support for DOM are as follows:

❏ Some new methods are added to the existing DOM interfaces and exceptions. This extends to about 30 minor changes.

❏ Many wholly new interfaces are added. These provide access to the HTML implementation, views on the document, additional StyleSheet support, new CSS support, Event handling support, traversals and ranges.

See also:	ECMAScript, MutationEvent object

DOM - Level 3 (Standard)

An improved model of the document object structure.

The level 3 DOM is an enhancement on the level 2 support. It introduces additional properties and interfaces for document objects.

The standard is composed of the following modules:

❏ DOM core functionality

❏ HTML functionality

❏ Event handling

❏ Style specification

❏ Document views

❏ Traversal and range specification

❏ Content model and archiving

The DOM level specification has grown again although not as much as it did at the level 2 version. Some changes to the Core and Events modules have taken place and a new module has been introduced to support content models and the ability to export and import documents between implementations.

Level 3 standardization is still very much a work in progress and as a whole the DOM standardization process is somewhat held back by work in other groups to do with XML and internationalization among other things. Progress is still being made and although there is much to do, many aspects of the DOM standard are now reasonably well defined and not likely to change.

It still remains for the browser manufacturers to catch up with the standard and in particular to use the same naming conventions for object classes instead of continually inventing their own.

See also:	ECMAScript

DOM Events (Standard)

A new modular part of the DOM standard introduced at level 2 and implemented in Netscape 6.

The DOM level 2 event model has been designed to be platform and language neutral. The standard describes bindings for Java and ECMAScript and it is applicable to other environments too.

The foundation on which DOM Events is constructed requires that DOM Core and DOM views are available too.

There are three main types of events:

❑   User interface related events such as those triggered by an input device. A key press or mouse click is an example.

❑   Logical events that may have been triggered via the UI but are more abstract. A focus change or element notification event is an example.

❑   Mutation events which are caused by some action that modified the structure of the document.

Events are captured in several ways depending on the implementation and context. For example, server-side events would be captured in a different way to those in a web browser.

In a structured document, a target element that receives an event may handle it or may choose to pass it upwards through the document hierarchy to its parent node. This is called event bubbling and was first provided in a web browser by MSIE. As of version 6, the same event model is used in Netscape which attempts to implement the entire DOM level 2 event capabilities as described in the standard.

Events can be cancelled. This can prevent them from bubbling upwards or from exercising some default behavior.

As an alternative to implementing an event bubbling technique, the DOM level 2 event model also provides for an event capturing approach where the highest ancestor object that registers a listener will receive the event before the target object. This traverses the document hierarchy from top to bottom and is the opposite of the bubbling technique which traverses from bottom to top.

EventTarget objects are not really objects in their own right although it is convenient to describe them thus in the DOM specification. An EventTarget is actually one of the already existing classes but when the DOM level 2 event model is implemented, the element objects that can react to events become EventTargets by inheriting the properties and methods of the EventTarget class as well as any others they inherit from their superclass.

Events are handled by registering EventListener functions. These are registered by the potential EventTargets. An EventTarget is simply an HTML instantiated object, or one that has been manufactured by script and placed into the display for the user to interact with.

See also:	Element object, Event, Event management, Event model, MutationEvent object

DontDelete (Property attribute)

An internal property attribute that prevents a property from being deleted.

Availability:	ECMAScript edition - 2
Property/method value type:	Boolean primitive

This attribute is set internally on properties by the host environment that the interpreter implementation is running in. When this attribute is set on a property, that property cannot be deleted by the script writer. This attribute is not normally exposed to the script level code.

See also:	DontEnumerate, ReadOnly

Cross-references:

ECMA 262 edition 2 - section - 11.4.1

DontEnumerate (Property attribute)

An internal property attribute that prevents a property from being enumerated.

Availability:	ECMAScript edition - 2
Property/method value type:	Boolean primitive

This attribute is set internally on properties by the host environment that the interpreter implementation is running in. When this attribute is set on a property, that property cannot be enumerated by the script writer. This attribute is not normally exposed to the script level code.

See also:	DontDelete, for (...in...) ..., ReadOnly

Cross-references:

ECMA 262 edition 2 - section - 12.6.3

ECMA 262 edition 3 - section - 12.6.4

D

double (Reserved word)

Reserved for future language enhancements.

Providing double as a reserved keyword suggests stronger data typing may be available in later versions of the ECMA standard.

This keyword also represents a Java data type and the double keyword allows for the potential extension of JavaScript interfaces to access Java applet parameters and return values.

See also:	float, Integer, java.lang.Double, LiveConnect, long, Reserved word, short

Cross-references:

ECMA 262 edition 2 - section - 7.4.3

ECMA 262 edition 3 - section - 7.5.3

Drive object (Object/JScript)

A special JScript object to represent a disk drive.

Availability:	JScript - 3.0 Internet Explorer - 4.0
JavaScript syntax:	IE *myDrive = myFileSystem.GetDrive()*
Object properties:	AvailableSpace, DriveLetter, DriveType, FileSystem, FreeSpace, IsReady, Path, RootFolder, SerialNumber, ShareName, TotalSize, VolumeName

This is an object that represents the disk drive that a file object is stored on in the Windows environment. This object is accessed via the GetDrive() method belonging to the FileSystem object.

See also:	FileSystem.GetDrive(), Folder.Drive

Property	JavaScript	JScript	N	IE	Opera	Notes
AvailableSpace	-	3.0 +	-	4.0 +	-	-
DriveLetter	-	3.0 +	-	4.0 +	-	-
DriveType	-	3.0 +	-	4.0 +	-	-
FileSystem	-	3.0 +	-	4.0 +	-	-
FreeSpace	-	3.0 +	-	4.0 +	-	-

Table continued on following page

207

Property	JavaScript	JScript	N	IE	Opera	Notes
IsReady	-	3.0 +	-.	4.0 +	-	-
Path	-	3.0 +	-	4.0 +	-	-
RootFolder	-	3.0 +	-	4.0 +	-	-
SerialNumber	-	3.0 +	-	4.0 +	-	-
ShareName	-	3.0 +	-	4.0 +	-	-
TotalSize	-	3.0 +	-·	4.0 +	-	-
VolumeName	-	3.0 +	-	4.0 +	-	-

Drives object (Object/JScript)

A collection of drives belonging to a file system.

Availability:	JScript - 3.0 Internet Explorer - 4.0	
JavaScript syntax:	IE	myDrives = myFileSystem.Drives
Object properties:	count	

The Drives object is a collection that needs to be used with an enumerator to access the individual drive items.

Example code:

```
// Instantiate a file system object
myFileSystem = new ActiveXObject("Scripting.FileSystemObject");
// Create an enumerator
myEnum = new Enumerator(myFileSystem.Drives);
// Traverse the Drives collection via the enumerator
for(; !myEnum.atEnd(); myEnum.moveNext())
{
processDrive(myEnum.item());
}
// A function to do something with each disk drive
function processDrive(aDrive)
{
...
}
```

See also:	FileSystem.Drives[]

Property	JavaScript	JScript	N	IE	Opera	Notes
count	-	3.0 +	-	4.0 +	-	-

DT object (Object/HTML)

An object that represents the content of a <DT> tag.

Availability:	JScript - 3.0 Internet Explorer - 4.0
Inherits from:	Element object
JavaScript syntax:	IE *myDT = myDocument*.all.*anElementID*
	IE *myDT = myDocument*.all.tags ("DT")[*anIndex*]
	IE *myDT = myDocument*.all[*aName*]
	- *myDT = myDocument*.getElementById (*anElementID*)
	- *myDT = myDocument*.getElementsByName (*aName*)[*anIndex*]
	- *myDT = myDocument*.getElementsByTagName ("DT")[*anIndex*]
HTML syntax:	<DT> ... </DT>
Argument list:	*anIndex* A reference to an element in a collection
	aName An associative array reference
	anElementID The ID value of an Element object
Object properties:	noWrap
Event handlers:	onClick, onDblClick, onDragStart, onFilterChange, onHelp, onKeyDown, onKeyPress, onKeyUp, onMouseDown, onMouseMove, onMouseOut, onMouseOver, onMouseUp, onSelectStart

This object represents the definition term of an item in a definition list. It corresponds to a related definition contained in a DD object. DT and DD objects are paired up and maintained together as a member of the DL collection.

The <DT> tag is a block-level tag. That means that it forces a line break before and after itself unless its enclosing <DL> tag uses its compact property.

See also:	DD object, DL object, Element object

Property	JavaScript	JScript	N	IE	Opera	DOM	HTML	Notes
noWrap	-	3.0 +	-	4.0 +	-	-	-	Warning

Event name	JavaScript	JScript	N	IE	Opera	DOM	HTML	Notes
onClick	-	3.0 +	-	4.0 +	-	-	4.0 +	Warning
onDblClick	-	3.0 +	-	4.0 +	-	-	4.0 +	Warning
onDragStart	-	3.0 +	-	4.0 +	-	-	-	-
onFilterChange	-	3.0 +	-	4.0 +	-	-	-	-
onHelp	-	3.0 +	-	4.0 +	-	-	-	Warning
onKeyDown	-	3.0 +	-	4.0 +	-	-	4.0 +	Warning
onKeyPress	-	3.0 +	-	4.0 +	-	-	4.0 +	Warning
onKeyUp	-	3.0 +	-	4.0 +	-	-	4.0 +	Warning
onMouseDown	-	3.0 +	-	4.0 +	-	-	4.0 +	Warning
onMouseMove	-	3.0 +	-	4.0 +	-	-	4.0 +	Warning
onMouseOut	-	3.0 +	-	4.0 +	-	-	4.0 +	Warning
onMouseOver	-	3.0 +	-	4.0 +	-	-	4.0 +	Warning
onMouseUp	-	3.0 +	-	4.0 +	-	-	4.0 +	Warning
onSelectStart	-	3.0 +	-	4.0 +	-	-	-	-

Inheritance chain:

Element object, Node object

DVB-MHP (Standard)

Digital Video Broadcasting - Multimedia Home Platform.

An emerging Digital TV platform standard, which may achieve some dominance in the future. Of interest to JavaScript users because it is being developed by Sun Microsystems as a platform in which a web browser could be hosted.

If that is the case, there may, by implication, be a JavaScript interpreter available for use.

See also:	Interpret

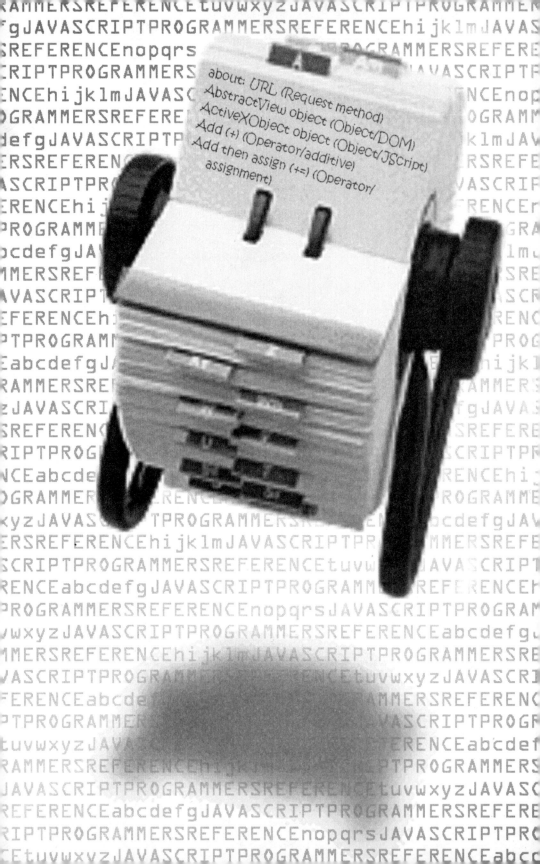

E

JavaScript Programmer's Reference

ECMA (Standard)

An international standards organization.

The European Computer Manufacturers Association (ECMA) has been developing standards for computing systems for many years.

You can obtain printed copies of their standards and in most cases you can download an electronic copy for your own use.

You should explore the ECMA web site for details of their activities and standards if you are developing compliant implementations or scripts.

See also:	Compliance, Conformance, ECMAScript, Implementation, *Opera*, Overview, Topic classification

Web-references:

ftp://ftp.ecma.ch/ mailto://documents@ecma.ch/ http://www.ecma.ch/

ECMAScript - edition 2 (Standard)

Specific conformance for ECMAScript at its second edition.

The character encoding support described in the second edition of the standard is very specific:

"A conforming implementation of the International standard shall interpret characters in conformance with the Unicode Standard, Version 2.0, and ISO/IEC 10646-1 with UCS-2 as the adopted encoding form, implementation level 3. If the adopted ISO/IEC 10646-1 subset is not otherwise specified, it is presumed to be the BMP subset, collection 300."

Other than typographical and editorial changes, little was added between the first and second editions of the ECMA standard. That means this edition becomes the foundation specification for the core language.

The principle features of this edition include:

- Arithmetic, string and logical operators
- Global and local variables managed via scope chains
- Core data types and objects (`Number`, `String`, `Boolean`)
- Core object types (`Date` and `Array`)
- Core numeric library support by means of the `Math` object
- Language flow control and keywords
- Object instantiation by means of constructors
- Inheritance supported via prototype chains

See also:	Compliance, Conformance, ECMAScript, Implementation

Cross-references:

ISO/IEC 10646-1 Information Technology -- Universal Multiple-Octet Coded Character Set (UCS), plus its amendments and technical corrigenda.

The Unicode Standard, Version 2.0, Addison-Wesley Publishing Co. ISBN: 0-201-48345-9

ECMAScript - edition 3 (Standard)

Specific conformance for ECMAScript at its third edition.

The character encoding support described in the third edition of the standard is somewhat more advanced than that in the second edition:

"A conforming implementation of this International standard shall interpret characters in conformance with the Unicode Standard, Version 2.1 or later, and ISO/IEC 10646-1 with either UCS-2 or UTF-16 as the adopted encoding form, implementation level 3. If the adopted ISO/IEC 10646-1 subset is not otherwise specified, it is presumed to be the BMP subset, collection 300. If the adopted encoding form is not otherwise specified, it is presumed to be the UTF-16 encoding form."

The third edition adds to the earlier versions in the following areas:

- Regular expressions
- Richer control statements
- Better string and array handling
- Exception handling improvements with `try`/`catch`
- Internationalization facilities
- Error objects for managing exceptions

ECMAScript edition 3 support is a feature of the MSIE/Jscript 5.5. upgrade and the new Netscape 6.0 release.

See also:	Compliance, Conformance, ECMAScript, Implementation

Cross-references:

ISO/IEC 10646-1 Information Technology -- Universal Multiple-Octet Coded Character Set (UCS), plus its amendments and technical corrigenda.

Unicode Technical Report #8, The Unicode Standard, Version 2.1.

ECMAScript version (Standard)

The version history for ECMAScript.

The version history of ECMAScript is slightly behind the current browser implementations. Versions of ECMAScript are defined as editions 2 and 3 of the standard. Edition 1 was superseded by edition 2, which made few functional changes. There were not enough to warrant revising the level of functionality.

ECMA edition 2 is roughly equivalent to JavaScript version 1.1, minus any HTML document modeling.

ECMA edition 3 is roughly equivalent to JavaScript 1.5 and JScript 5.5.

See also:	ECMAScript

Element object (Object/HTML)

A common name for an object that represents an HTML tag or container.

Availability:	DOM level – 1 JavaScript – 1.5 JScript – 3.0 Internet Explorer – 4.0 Netscape – 6.0	
Inherits from:	*Node object*	
JavaScript syntax:	IE	*myElement* = document.all(*anIndex*)
	IE	*myElement* = document.all.*anElementID*
	IE	*myElement* = document.all[*anIndex*]
	IE	*myElement* = document.children(*anIndex*)
	IE	*myElement* = document.children.*anElementID*

Table continued on following page

JavaScript syntax:	IE	*myElement* = document.children[*anIndex*]
	-	*myElement* = *myChildNodes*[*aName*]
	-	*myElement* = *myChildNodes*[*anIndex*]
	-	*myElement* = *myDocument*.getElementById (*anElementID*)
	-	*myElement* = *myDocument*.getElementsByName (*aName*)[*anIndex*]
	-	*myElement* = *myDocument*.createElement(*aTagName*)
	-	*myElement* = *myDocument*.documentElement
	-	*myElement* = *myDocument* .getElementsByTagName(*aTagName*)[*anIndex*]

HTML syntax:	<*anHTMLTag*>	
Argument list:	*anElementID*	The ID value for the required element
	anHTMLTag	A tag that represents a realizable concrete object
	anIndex	An index location in the collection
	aTagName	The name of an HTML tag to create an element for
	aName	An associative array reference

Object properties:	canHaveChildren, canHaveHTML, className, clientHeight, clientLeft, clientTop, clientWidth, contentEditable, currentStyle, dir, document, firstChild, hideFocus, id, innerHTML, innerText, isContentEditable, isDisabled, isTextEdit, lang, language, lastChild, nextSibling, nodeName, nodeType, nodeValue, offsetHeight, offsetLeft, offsetParent, offsetTop, offsetWidth, outerHTML, outerText, ownerDocument, parentElement, parentNode, parentTextEdit, previousSibling, readyState, recordNumber, runtimeStyle, scopeName, scrollHeight, scrollLeft, scrollTop, scrollWidth, sourceIndex, style, tagName, tagUrn, title, uniqueID
Object methods:	addBehavior(), applyElement(), blur(), clearAttributes(), click(), componentFromPoint(), contains(), doScroll(), focus(), getAdjacentText(), getAttribute(), getAttributeNode(), getElementsByTagName(), getExpression(), insertAdjacentHTML(), insertAdjacentText(), mergeAttributes(), normalize(), releaseCapture(), removeAttribute(), removeAttributeNode(), removeBehavior(), removeExpression(), replaceAdjacentText(), scrollIntoView(), setAttribute(), setAttributeNode(), setCapture(), setExpression()
Functions:	handleEvent()

Event handlers:	onClick, onDblClick, onHelp, onKeyDown, onKeyPress, onKeyUp, onMouseDown, onMouseMove, onMouseOut, onMouseOver, onMouseUp
Collections:	all[], attributes[], behaviorUrns[], childNodes[], children[], filters[]

The standard DOM hierarchy model specifies a variety of properties that should be available across the entire collection of objects. This suggests that all objects in the document would generally behave as if they were sub-classes of a master DOM element object.

DOM level 1 describes an Element object and an HTML object and makes a distinction between the two. JavaScript considers them to be one and the same within a web browser context.

In JavaScript 1.2 and MSIE 4, many HTML tags are represented as objects that have similar methods and properties. It is convenient also to model these as if they were sub-classes of a single super-class. Actually, Netscape at revision 4 does not really support this model very consistently, although it is a sound concept when studying the internals of the MSIE browser. Netscape 6.0 implements a much more robust and complete set of the DOM level 1 capabilities.

The Element object described here includes the behavior of the DOM Element object with some additional properties and methods that are common to many objects in the various browsers.

We call these Element objects. In other reference works they may be called DOM objects, DOM elements or HTML Elements. Trying to work out what kind of element you have is not always easy. Some objects will provide this with their toString() method. Others will need some inspection. You can look at constructor properties for help. Sometimes object.constructor.name will tell you what you need. This is not consistent across all the different kinds of objects, nor is the same technique applicable across all browsers.

By considering all the DOM and HTML Element objects as sub-classes of the Element object class, we can document their common behavior collectively and then deal with any specific behavior they may implement on a case by case basis.

We attempt to de-clutter the object descriptions by abstracting properties, methods, collections and events into a super-class wherever possible. This Element class does not really exist as a concrete class but it helps to understand the internals of the MSIE and Netscape 6.0 browsers in particular to model it like this. A couple of notable exceptions are the document object and window object classes which share some properties etc. with the Element class, but cannot easily be considered to be sub-classes of the Element class. Those properties and methods etc. are used in a contextually different way and may exhibit slightly different behavior, and so they merit being covered in separate (but similar) topics to the ones described as members of the Element topic set.

E

There is another special class and that is the `FormElement` object. These are sub-classes of the fundamental `Element` class, but are a super-class of all Form elements which represent <INPUT> tags. Many of these share common methods and properties in addition to the `Element` object functionality. Properties, methods, collections and events that relate to the `Input` object class are discussed under topics beginning with the phrase "Input" and are not duplicated here. However, they are listed here in the summary.

If you are inspecting objects with an enumeration loop, you may want to eliminate `Element` object properties so that your enumerator only lists special properties of the object you are inspecting. There is actually no object of the `Element` object type. We explored a great deal of the internal browser model by writing small fragments of JavaScript to walk through the properties of each object type. This yielded some properties that were hitherto undocumented and highlighted some differences between platforms and browsers.

In MSIE, there is a class for each type of HTML tag. There is also an `array` class for collections of each type of tag. For example, for an imaginary tag called <XXXX>, there will be an object class with the name `XXXX` which represents tags of that type regardless of whether they are upper or lower cased. There will also be an `XxxxArray` collection for that class which is yielded by this expression:

```
document.all.tags("XXXX")
```

If you create imaginary tags in your documents, MSIE won't render them nor will it create objects to represent them. However, the expression shown above will yield an empty collection of an appropriate type.

Versions of Netscape prior to 6.0 do not implement this mechanism because they manage its content with a different DOM construction technique. Netscape 6.0 and MSIE support a more consistent interface to all of the tags in a document. No version of Netscape provides the all[] collection.

If you want to examine the properties of `Element` objects you need to be able to isolate those properties that are inherited and those that are not. The example code for MSIE includes a function that you can use to exclude items that are inherited from `Element` objects as you enumerate the properties of an object. We used this to examine the undocumented structures within web content viewed in the browsers. There is also an attribute accessor function demonstrated here. The rest of the example demonstrates a framework for examining object properties.

The DOM level 2 specification adds the following new methods to support namespaces:

❑ `getAttributeNS()`

❑ `setAttributeNS()`

❑ `removeAttributeNS()`

❑ `getAttributeNodeNS()`

❑ `setAttributeNodeNS()`

❑ `getElementsByTagNameNS()`

❑ `hasAttribute()`

❑ `hasAttributeNS()`

DOM level 2 moves the `normalize()` method to the `Node` object but it is still available here through inheritance.

As the DOM standards advance and proliferate and the browser become more DOM standards compliant, a standards based approach to the documentation may become more appropriate. We have structured our coverage around a browser-centric approach.

`Element` objects will have other properties and methods are not included here because they are not yet implemented or fall outside the standard. The following properties are present in some implementations for example:

❑ onOffBehavior

❑ hasMedia

❑ syncMaster

These are part of the SMIL and HTML+TIME standards which are still in a state of evolution and therefore the behavior of the implementation may change.

Warnings:

❑ Be careful how you operate on these objects. Traversing the properties in a `for(...in...)` loop can recursively lock up your browser for some objects that represent high level parts of the DOM hierarchy.

Example code:

```
<HTML>
<HEAD></HEAD>
<BODY >
<IMG ID="IMAGE1" SRC="aaa.gif">
<TABLE CELLPADDING=2 CELLSPACING=2 BORDER=1>
<SCRIPT>
var myObject = document.getElementById("IMAGE1");
document.write(displayProperties(myObject));

// Display a table of enumerated properties
function displayProperties(anObject)
{
    var myOut = "";
    myOut += '<TR BGCOLOR="ANTIQUEWHITE">';
    myOut += "<TD>Object type</TD><TD>";
    myOut += typeof anObject;
    myOut += "</TD><TD>";
    myOut += anObject;
    myOut += "</TD><TD>Name</TD><TD>Specified</TD>";
    myOut += "<TD>Value</TD></TR>";

    for(myProp in anObject)
    {
        // Place a not symbol on this condition to see
```

219

```
          // non inherited properties
      if(isElementProperty(myProp))
      {
          myOut += "<TR><TD>";
          myOut += myProp;
          myOut += "</TD><TD>";
          myOut += typeof anObject[myProp];
          myOut += "</TD><TD>";
          myOut += displayableValue(myProp, anObject[myProp]);
          myOut += "</TD><TD>";
          myOut += getPropAttr(anObject, myProp, "name");
          myOut += "</TD><TD>";
          myOut += getPropAttr(anObject, myProp, "specified");
          myOut += "</TD><TD>";
          myOut += getPropAttr(anObject, myProp, "value");
          myOut += "</TD></TR>";
      }
   }

   return myOut;
}

// Prevent recursive displays
function displayableValue(aProperty, aValue)
{
   switch(aProperty)
   {
     case "innerHTML"     :
     case "innerText"     :
     case "outerHTML"     :
     case "outerText"     :
         return "**" + aProperty + "**";
   }
   return aValue;
}

// Element object property flag
function isElementProperty(aProperty)
{
   // Refer to isElementProperty() topic for code
}

// Property attribute accessor
function getPropAttr(anObject, aProp, anAttrib)
{
   // Refer to Element.attributes[] topic for code
}

</SCRIPT>
</TABLE>
</BODY>
</HTML>
```

See also:	*Attributes object*, `Document.all[]`, `Document.createElement()`, `Document.documentElement`, `isElementProperty()`, *Node object*

Property	JavaScript	JScript	N	IE	Opera	DOM	HTML	Notes
canHaveChildren	-	5.0 +	-	5.0 +	-	-	-	-
canHaveHTML	-	5.5 +	-	5.5 +	-	-	-	ReadOnly
className	1.5 +	3.0 +	6.0 +	4.0 +	-	1 +	-	Warning
clientHeight	-	3.0 +	-	4.0 +	-	-	-	Warning, ReadOnly
clientLeft	-	3.0 +	-	4.0 +	-	-	-	Warning, ReadOnly
clientTop	-	3.0 +	-	4.0 +	-	-	-	Warning, ReadOnly
clientWidth	-	3.0 +	-	4.0 +	-	-	-	Warning, ReadOnly
contentEditable	-	5.5 +	-	5.5 +	-	-	-	-
currentStyle	-	5.0 +	-	5.0 +	-	-	-	Warning
dir	1.5 +	5.0 +	6.0 +	5.0 +	-	1 +	-	-
document	-	3.0 +	-	4.0 +	5.0 +	-	-	Warning, ReadOnly
firstChild	1.5 +	5.0 +	6.0 +	5.0 +	-	1 +	-	-
hideFocus	-	5.5 +	-	5.5 +	-	-	-	-
id	1.5 +	3.0 +	6.0 +	4.0 +	-	1 +	-	Warning
innerHTML	1.5 +	3.0 +	6.0 +	4.0 +	-	-	-	Warning
innerText	-	3.0 +	-	4.0 +	-	-	-	Warning
isContentEditable	-	5.5 +	-	5.5 +	-	-	-	ReadOnly
isDisabled	-	5.5 +	-	5.5 +	-	-	-	ReadOnly
isTextEdit	-	3.0 +	-	4.0 +	-	-	-	ReadOnly
lang	1.5 +	3.0 +	6.0 +	4.0 +	-	1 +	-	-
language	-	3.0 +	-	4.0 +	-	-	-	-
lastChild	1.5 +	5.0 +	6.0 +	5.0 +	-	1 +	-	-
nextSibling	1.5 +	5.0 +	6.0 +	5.0 +	-	1 +	-	-
nodeName	1.5 +	5.0 +	6.0 +	5.0 +	-	1 +	-	ReadOnly
nodeType	1.5 +	5.0 +	6.0 +	5.0 +	-	1 +	-	ReadOnly
nodeValue	1.5 +	5.0 +	6.0 +	5.0 +	-	1 +	-	-
offsetHeight	-	3.0 +	-	4.0 +	-	-	-	Warning, ReadOnly
offsetLeft	-	3.0 +	-	4.0 +	5.0 +	-	-	Warning, ReadOnly
offsetParent	-	3.0 +	-	4.0 +	5.0 +	-	-	Warning, ReadOnly
offsetTop	-	3.0 +	-	4.0 +	5.0 +	-	-	Warning, ReadOnly
offsetWidth	-	3.0 +	-	4.0 +	-	-	-	Warning, ReadOnly
outerHTML	-	3.0 +	-	4.0 +	-	-	-	Warning
outerText	-	3.0 +	-	4.0 +	-	-	-	Warning

Table continued on following page

Property	JavaScript	JScript	N	IE	Opera	DOM	HTML	Notes
ownerDocument	1.5 +	5.0 +	6.0 +	5.0 +	-	1 +	-	ReadOnly
parentElement	-	3.0 +	-	4.0 +	-	-	-	ReadOnly
parentNode	1.5 +	5.0 +	6.0 +	5.0 +	5.0 +	1 +	-	ReadOnly
parentTextEdit	-	3.0 +	-	4.0 +	-	-	-	Warning, ReadOnly
previousSibling	1.5 +	5.0 +	6.0 +	5.0 +	-	1 +	-	-
readyState	-	3.0 +	-	4.0 +	-	-	-	ReadOnly
recordNumber	1.5 +	3.0 +	6.0 +	4.0 +	-	1 +	-	Warning
runtimeStyle	-	5.0 +	-	5.0 +	-	-	-	-
scopeName	-	5.0 +	-	5.0 +	-	-	-	-
scrollHeight	-	5.0 +	-	5.0 +	-	-	-	Warning, ReadOnly
scrollLeft	-	5.0 +	-	5.0 +	-	-	-	Warning
scrollTop	-	5.0 +	-	5.0 +	-	-	-	Warning
scrollWidth	-	5.0 +	-	5.0 +	-	-	-	Warning, ReadOnly
sourceIndex	-	3.0 +	-	4.0 +	-	-	-	Warning, ReadOnly
style	1.5 +	3.0 +	6.0 +	4.0 +	5.0 +	2 +	-	-
tagName	1.5 +	3.0 +	6.0 +	4.0 +	5.0 +	1 +	-	ReadOnly
tagUrn	-	5.0 +	-	5.0 +	-	-	-	-
title	1.5 +	3.0 +	6.0 +	4.0 +	-	1 +	-	Warning
uniqueID	-	5.0 +	-	5.0 +	-	-	-	ReadOnly

Method	JavaScript	JScript	N	IE	Opera	DOM	HTML	Notes
addBehavior()	-	5.0 +	-	5.0 +	-	-	-	-
applyElement()	-	5.0 +	-	5.0 +	-	-	-	Warning
blur()	1.5 +	3.0 +	6.0 +	4.0 +	-	1 +	-	Warning
clearAttributes()	-	5.0 +	-	5.0 +	-	-	-	Warning
click()	-	3.0 +	-	4.0 +	-	-	-	-
componentFromPoint()	-	5.0 +	-	5.0 +	-	-	-	-
contains()	-	3.0 +	-	4.0 +	5.0 +	-	-	-
doScroll()	-	5.0 +	-	5.0 +	-	-	-	-
focus()	1.5 +	3.0 +	6.0 +	4.0 +	-	1 +	-	Warning
getAdjacentText()	-	5.0 +	-	5.0 +	-	-	-	-
getAttribute()	1.5 +	3.0 +	6.0 +	4.0 +	5.0 +	1 +	-	Warning
getAttributeNode()	1.5 +	5.0 +	6.0 +	5.0 +	-	1 +	-	-
getElementsByTagName()	1.5 +	5.0 +	6.0 +	5.0 +	5.0 +	1 +	-	Warning
getExpression()	-	5.0 +	-	5.0 +	-	-	-	-
insertAdjacentHTML()	-	3.0 +	-	4.0 +	-	-	-	Warning
insertAdjacentText()	-	3.0 +	-	4.0 +	-	-	-	Warning
mergeAttributes()	-	5.0 +	-	5.0 +	-	-	-	-
normalize()	1.5 +	-	6.0 +	-	-	1 +	-	-
releaseCapture()	-	5.0 +	-	5.0 +	-	-	-	-
removeAttribute()	1.5 +	3.0 +	6.0 +	4.0 +	-	1 +	-	Warning
removeAttributeNode()	1.5 +	5.0 +	6.0 +	5.0 +	-	1 +	-	-

Method	JavaScript	JScript	N	IE	Opera	DOM	HTML	Notes
removeBehavior()	-	5.0 +	-	5.0 +	-	-	-	-
removeExpression()	-	5.0 +	-	5.0 +	-	-	-	-
replaceAdjacentText()	-	5.0 +	-	5.0 +	-	-	-	-
scrollIntoView()	-	3.0 +	-	4.0 +	-	-	-	-
setAttribute()	1.5 +	3.0 +	6.0 +	4.0 +	5.0 +	1 +	-	-
setAttributeNode()	1.5 +	5.0 +	6.0 +	5.0 +	-	1 +	-	-
setCapture()	-	5.0 +	-	5.0 +	-	-	-	-
setExpression()	-	5.0 +	-	5.0 +	-	-	-	-

Event name	JavaScript	JScript	N	IE	Opera	DOM	HTML	Notes
onClick	1.5 +	3.0 +	6.0 +	4.0 +	3.0 +	-	4.0 +	Warning
onDblClick	1.5 +	3.0 +	6.0 +	4.0 +	3.0 +	-	4.0 +	Warning
onHelp	-	3.0 +	-	4.0 +	-	-	-	Warning
onKeyDown	1.5 +	3.0 +	6.0 +	4.0 +	3.0 +	-	4.0 +	Warning
onKeyPress	1.5 +	3.0 +	6.0 +	4.0 +	3.0 +	-	4.0 +	Warning
onKeyUp	1.5 +	3.0 +	6.0 +	4.0 +	3.0 +	-	4.0 +	Warning
onMouseDown	1.5 +	3.0 +	6.0 +	4.0 +	3.0 +	-	4.0 +	Warning
onMouseMove	1.5 +	3.0 +	6.0 +	4.0 +	-	-	4.0 +	Warning
onMouseOut	1.5 +	3.0 +	6.0 +	4.0 +	3.0 +	-	4.0 +	Warning
onMouseOver	1.5 +	3.0 +	6.0 +	4.0 +	3.0 +	-	4.0 +	Warning
onMouseUp	1.5 +	3.0 +	6.0 +	4.0 +	3.0 +	-	4.0 +	Warning

Inheritance chain:

Node object

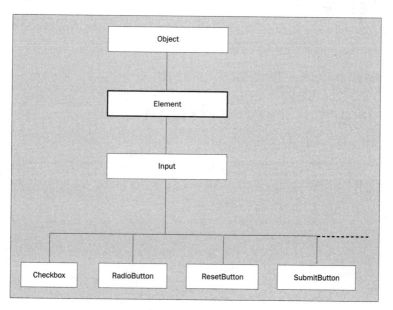

else ... (Keyword)

Part of the if...else conditional code execution mechanism.

Availability:	ECMAScript edition – 2 JavaScript – 1.0 JScript – 1.0 Internet Explorer – 3.02 Netscape – 2.0 Netscape Enterprise Server – 2.0
JavaScript syntax:	- `if(aCondition){someCode1}` `else{someCode2}`
Argument list:	`aCondition` A condition that tests true or false
	`someCode1` Code to be executed if the condition tests true
	`someCode2` Code to be executed if the condition tests false

This is an optional additional statement that can be added to an `if()` condition test to allow for some alternative code to be executed when the condition tests false. The true case will cause the first block of code to be executed, the false case will execute the second (that which follows the `else` keyword).

See also:	`else if(...)` ..., Flow control, *if(...) ...*, *if(...) ... else ...*, Selection statement, *switch(...) ... case: ... default: ...*

Cross-references:

ECMA 262 edition 2 – section – 12.5

ECMA 262 edition 3 – section – 12.5

Wrox *Instant JavaScript* – page – 23

EM object (Object/HTML)

An object representing the HTML content delimited by the <EM> tags.

Availability:	DOM level – 1 JavaScript – 1.5 JScript – 3.0 Internet Explorer – 4.0 Netscape – 6.0
Inherits from:	*Element object*

JavaScript syntax:	IE	`myEM = myDocument.all.anElementID`
	IE	`myEM = myDocument.all.tags("EM")[anIndex]`
	IE	`myEM = myDocument.all[aName]`
	-	`myEM = myDocument.getElementById (anElementID)`
	-	`myEM = myDocument.getElementsByName (aName)[anIndex]`
	-	`myEM = myDocument.getElementsByTagName ("EM")[anIndex]`
HTML syntax:	`<EM> ... </EM>`	
Argument list:	`anElementID`	The ID value of the element required
	`anIndex`	A reference to an element in a collection
	`aName`	An associative array reference
Event handlers:	`onClick, onDblClick, onDragStart, onFilterChange, onHelp, onKeyDown, onKeyPress, onKeyUp, onMouseDown, onMouseMove, onMouseOut, onMouseOver, onMouseUp, onSelectStart`	

`<EM>` tags and the objects that represent them are inline elements. Placing them into a document does not create a line break.

See also:	*Element object*

Event name	JavaScript	JScript	N	IE	Opera	DOM	HTML	Notes
onClick	1.5 +	3.0 +	6.0 +	4.0 +	3.0 +	-	4.0 +	Warning
onDblClick	1.5 +	3.0 +	6.0 +	4.0 +	3.0 +	-	4.0 +	Warning
onDragStart	-	3.0 +	-	4.0 +	-	-	-	-
onFilterChange	-	3.0 +	-	4.0 +	-	-	-	-
onHelp	-	3.0 +	-	4.0 +	-	-	-	Warning
onKeyDown	1.5 +	3.0 +	6.0 +	4.0 +	3.0 +	-	4.0 +	Warning
onKeyPress	1.5 +	3.0 +	6.0 +	4.0 +	3.0 +	-	4.0 +	Warning
onKeyUp	1.5 +	3.0 +	6.0 +	4.0 +	3.0 +	-	4.0 +	Warning
onMouseDown	1.5 +	3.0 +	6.0 +	4.0 +	3.0 +	-	4.0 +	Warning
onMouseMove	1.5 +	3.0 +	6.0 +	4.0 +	-	-	4.0 +	Warning
onMouseOut	1.5 +	3.0 +	6.0 +	4.0 +	3.0 +	-	4.0 +	Warning
onMouseOver	1.5 +	3.0 +	6.0 +	4.0 +	3.0 +	-	4.0 +	Warning
onMouseUp	1.5 +	3.0 +	6.0 +	4.0 +	3.0 +	-	4.0 +	Warning
onSelectStart	-	3.0 +	-	4.0 +	-	-	-	-

Inheritance chain:

`Element` object, `Node` object

<EMBED> (HTML Tag)

A mechanism for adding plugin functionality to a web browser.

Availability:	JavaScript - 1.0 JScript - 1.0 Internet Explorer - 3 Netscape - 2
Inherits from:	Element object

Netscape and MSIE encapsulate plugin/embedded objects in a different way. In MSIE they are objects of the EMBED class. In Netscape they are objects commonly referred to as belonging to the Plugin class.

Because of this, and because each browser supports different properties and methods for them, they will be discussed here as Embed objects for MSIE and Plugin objects for Netscape.

Warnings:

❏ Note that Netscape can talk to the plugins that are encapsulated with an <EMBED> tag, but the MSIE browser cannot. However MSIE will talks to plugins that are encapsulated with the <OBJECT> tag. Netscape has supported <OBJECT> tags, but somewhat unreliably. Version 6 should be more robust.

❏ The Macintosh platform does not support the <OBJECT> tag because the MSIE browser really expects and hopes that it will be used to encapsulate an ActiveX object. Since ActiveX objects are written to be compiled into X86 machine code, they can only be used on a Wintel platform.

❏ Because of this, the MSIE browser on the Macintosh does support some limited communication with <EMBED> tag plugins.

❏ Trying to find a platform and browser portable compromise for embedding plugins (especially for video playback) is an utterly lost cause right now. You will have to write browser specific modules and use the appropriate one.

See also:	Document.embeds[], *Embed object, EmbedArray object,* Plugin events, *Plugin object*

Inheritance chain:

Element object, Node object

Embed object (Object/HTML)

An object that represents an embedded item in MSIE.

Availability:	JavaScript – 1.0 JScript – 3.0 Internet Explorer – 4.0 Netscape – 2.0 Netscape Enterprise Server – 2.0 Opera – 3.0		
Inherits from:	*Element object*		
JavaScript syntax:	IE	`myEmbed = myDocument.all.anElementID`	
	IE	`myEmbed = myDocument.all.tags("EMBED")` `[anIndex]`	
	IE	`myEmbed = myDocument.all[aName]`	
	-	`myEmbed = myDocument.anElementName`	
	-	`myEmbed = myDocument.embeds[anIndex]`	
	-	`myEmbed = myDocument.getElementById` `(anElementID)`	
	-	`myEmbed = myDocument.getElementsByName` `(aName)[anIndex]`	
	-	`myEmbed = myEmbedArray[aName]`	
	-	`myEmbed = myEmbedArray[anIndex]`	
	-	`myEmbed = myDocument.` `getElementsByTagName("EMBED")[anIndex]`	
HTML syntax:	`<EMBED>`		
Argument list:	`anIndex`	A reference to an element in a collection	
	`aName`	An associative array reference	
	`anElementID`	The ID value of an `Element` object	
Object properties:	`accessKey`, `align`, `height`, `hidden`, `name`, `palette`, `pluginspage`, `readyState`, `src`, `tabIndex`, `units`, `width`		
Event handlers:	`onBlur`, `onClick`, `onDblClick`, `onFocus`, `onHelp`, `onKeyDown`, `onKeyPress`, `onKeyUp`, `onMouseDown`, `onMouseMove`, `onMouseOut`, `onMouseOver`, `onMouseUp`		

Netscape and MSIE encapsulate plugin/embedded objects in a different way. In MSIE they are objects of the EMBED class. In Netscape they are objects commonly referred to as belonging to the Plugin class, although they are really implemented as JavaObject objects. In MSIE, this is an ActiveX object.

There is additional confusion in that there is a plugins[] array that belongs to the document and another that belongs to the navigator object. They both contain collections of objects, but of different types. This is further confused by the fact that the document.plugins[] array is another name for the document.embeds[] array.

Because of this confusing situation, the best recommendation is that we refer to `document.embeds[]` and `navigator.plugins[]` and quietly ignore the `document.plugins[]` object. Furthermore we shall refer to `Plugin` objects as being something the browser can use to play embedded content and `Embed` objects will be an instance of a plugin that is alive and running in a document.

Warnings:

❑ Interacting with the properties of `Embed` objects in MSIE seems to work quite reliably. This is not the case with Netscape, which is prone to all kinds of strange behavior. However that may be version and platform specific and could depend greatly on the quality of what you are embedding.

❑ As an example, Video plugins work really well on one particular platform and are generally less optimal on others. Windows media player is great on Windows and lacking in reliability and quality on other platforms. QuickTime is brilliant on Macintosh and good on Windows, but it still suffers some instability. Real player is pretty good everywhere, but it works better as a player than it does as a plugin. Windows media player works well as a plugin on MSIE. QuickTime is good as both a plugin and a player, but its JavaScripting control is somewhat behind Real player. None of them share the remotest similarity as far as properties, parameters or JavaScript API calls are concerned. If only we could have some compatible video players, we could solve a lot of the embedding problems.

See also:	*<EMBED>*, `Document.embeds[]`, *Element object, EmbedArray object*, `Input.accessKey`, *Plugin object*

Property	JavaScript	JScript	N	IE	Opera	NES	DOM	HTML	Notes
accessKey	1.0 +	3.0 +	2.0 +	4.0 +	3.0 +	2.0 +	-	-	Warning
align	-	3.0 +	-	4.0 +	-	-	-	-	-
height	-	3.0 +	-	4.0 +	-	-	-	-	-
hidden	-	3.0 +	-	4.0 +	-	-	-	-	-
name	1.2 +	3.0 +	4.0 +	4.0 +	-	-	-	-	-
palette	-	3.0 +	-	4.0 +	-	-	-	-	ReadOnly
pluginspage	-	3.0 +	-	4.0 +	-	-	-	-	ReadOnly
readyState	-	3.0 +	-	4.0 +	-	-	-	-	ReadOnly
src	-	3.0 +	-	4.0 +	-	-	-	-	-
tabIndex	1.0 +	3.0 +	2.0 +	4.0 +	3.0 +	2.0 +	-	-	Warning
units	-	3.0 +	-	4.0 +	-	-	-	-	-
width	-	3.0 +	-	4.0 +	-	-	-	-	-

Event name	JavaScript	JScript	N	IE	Opera	NES	DOM	HTML	Notes
onBlur	1.1 +	3.0 +	3.0 +	4.0 +	3.0 +	-	-	-	Warning
onClick	1.0 +	3.0 +	2.0 +	4.0 +	3.0 +	-	-	4.0 +	Warning
onDblClick	1.2 +	3.0 +	4.0 +	4.0 +	3.0 +	-	-	4.0 +	Warning
onFocus	1.0 +	3.0 +	2.0 +	4.0 +	3.0 +	-	-	-	Warning
onHelp	-	3.0 +	-	4.0 +	-	-	-	-	Warning

Event name	JavaScript	JScript	N	IE	Opera	NES	DOM	HTML	Notes
onKeyDown	1.2 +	3.0 +	4.0 +	4.0 +	3.0 +	-	-	4.0 +	Warning
onKeyPress	1.2 +	3.0 +	4.0 +	4.0 +	3.0 +	-	-	4.0 +	Warning
onKeyUp	1.2 +	3.0 +	4.0 +	4.0 +	3.0 +	-	-	4.0 +	Warning
onMouseDown	1.2 +	3.0 +	4.0 +	4.0 +	3.0 +	-	-	4.0 +	Warning
onMouseMove	1.2 +	3.0 +	4.0 +	4.0 +	-	-	-	4.0 +	Warning
onMouseOut	1.1 +	3.0 +	3.0 +	4.0 +	3.0 +	-	-	4.0 +	Warning
onMouseOver	1.0 +	3.0 +	2.0 +	4.0 +	3.0 +	-	-	4.0 +	Warning
onMouseUp	1.2 +	3.0 +	4.0 +	4.0 +	3.0 +	-	-	4.0 +	Warning

Inheritance chain:

Element object, Node object

EmbedArray object (Object/browser)

A more appropriate name for a PluginArray that contains a collection of plugins within the current document.

Availability:	JavaScript – 1.1 JScript – 3.0 Internet Explorer – 4.0 Netscape – 3.0	
Inherits from:	*Object object*	
JavaScript syntax:	-	myEmbedArray = myDocument.embeds
	-	myEmbedArray = myDocument.plugins
Object properties:	length	

A collection of objects, each one representing a plugin that is embedded in the current page. The object being referred to is not the embedded data, but the plugin module that plays it.

Netscape and MSIE encapsulate plugin/embedded objects in a different way. In MSIE they are objects of the EMBED class. In Netscape they are objects commonly referred to as belonging to the Plugin class although they are really implemented as JavaObject objects. In MSIE, this is an ActiveX object.

There is additional confusion in that there is a plugins[] array that belongs to the document and another that belongs to the navigator object. They both contain collections of objects but of different types. This is further confused by the fact that the document.plugins[] array is another name for the document.embeds[] array.

Because of this confusing situation the best recommendation is that we refer to document.embeds[] and navigator.plugins[] and quietly ignore the document.plugins[] object. Furthermore we shall refer to Plugin objects as being something the browser can use to play embedded content and Embed objects will be an instance of a plugin that is alive and running in a document.

E

229

Warnings:

❏ Beware of confusion between `document.plugins` and `navigator.plugins`. The former relates to the plugins currently used in the document while the latter lists the plugins currently available and supported by the browser.

See also:	*<EMBED>*, *Collection object*, `Document.embeds[]`, `Document.plugins[]`, *Embed object*, *JavaObject object*, *Plugin object*, *PluginArray object*

Property	JavaScript	JScript	N	IE	Opera	HTML	Notes
length	1.1 +	3.0 +	3.0 +	4.0 +	-	-	ReadOnly

Inheritance chain:

`Object` object

Empty statement (;) (Statement)

A no-op 'do-nothing' statement.

Availability:	ECMAScript edition – 2 JavaScript – 1.0 JScript – 1.0 Internet Explorer – 3.02 Netscape – 2.0 Netscape Enterprise Server – 2.0	
JavaScript syntax:	-	;

An empty statement is signified by a semi-colon on a line by itself or a semi-colon following a semi-colon with no executable statements in between them.

The associativity is left to right.

Refer to the operator precedence topic for details of execution order.

Warnings:

❏ If you intentionally place an empty statement into your script, you should put a comment adjacent to it to make sure people realize you did it on purpose. They may remove it otherwise and you may have had a functional reason for putting it there such as to aid the parsing of the text inside a SCRIPT object.

❏ This sails awfully close to the territory of self modifying code which programmers have always loved to do and preachers of good programming style have said is a very bad thing.

❏ On the other hand, JavaScript supports the `eval()` function and you can't get closer to self modifying code than that.

| See also: | Associativity, Operator Precedence, *Semi-colon (;)*, Statement |

Cross-references:

ECMA 262 edition 2 – section – 12.3

ECMA 262 edition 3 – section – 12.3

encodeURI() (Function)

This ECMA defined function can be used to encode an entire URI value that can then be decoded with the `decodeURI()` function.

Availability:	ECMAScript edition – 3 JavaScript – 1.5 JScript – 5.5 Internet Explorer – 5.5 Netscape – 6.0	
Property/method value type:	`String primitive`	
JavaScript syntax:	-	`encodeURI(aURI)`
Argument list:	`aURI`	An unencoded URI

The `encodeURI()` function computes a new version of the string value it is passed. The new version has certain characters replaced with hexadecimal escape sequences. The string is expected to conform to the UTF-8 profile.

All character codes other than letters, numbers or a small set of special characters will be escaped.

These special characters are not transformed:

- ❏ Minus
- ❏ Underscore
- ❏ Period
- ❏ Exclamation-mark
- ❏ Tilde
- ❏ Single quote
- ❏ Opening and closing parentheses

Note that the hash character is also not encoded by this function.

| See also: | *decodeURI(), decodeURIComponent(), encodeURIComponent(), escape(), unescape(),* URI handling functions |

Cross-references:

ECMA 262 edition 3 – section – 15.1.3.3

231

encodeURIComponent() (Function)

This ECMA defined function can be used to encode a URI component value that can then be decoded with the `decodeURIComponent()` function.

Availability:	ECMAScript edition – 3 JavaScript – 1.5 JScript – 5.5 Internet Explorer – 5.5 Netscape – 6.0
Property/method value type:	`String primitive`
JavaScript syntax:	- `encodeURIComponent` `(aComponent)`
Argument list:	`aComponent` A URI component to be encoded

The `encodeURIComponent()` function is used to encode individual components belonging to a URI. You will need to deconstruct the URI yourself if you intend to call this function from your own scripts.

See also:	*decodeURI(), decodeURIComponent(), encodeURI(), escape(), unescape()*, URI handling functions

Cross-references:

ECMA 262 edition 3 – section – 15.1.3.4

Entity object (Object/DOM)

An entity is an item in an XML document. This object encapsulates the XML entity.

Availability:	DOM level – 1 JavaScript – 1.5 JScript – 5.0 Internet Explorer – 5.0 Netscape – 6.0
Inherits from:	*Node object*
JavaScript syntax:	- `myEntity = new Entity()`
Object properties:	`notationName, publicId, systemId`

DOM level 3 is expecting to add the following properties:

❑ actualEncoding

❑ encoding

❑ version

Property	JavaScript	JScript	N	IE	Opera	DOM	Notes
notationName	1.5 +	5.0 +	6.0 +	5.0 +	-	1 +	ReadOnly
publicId	1.5 +	5.0 +	6.0 +	5.0 +	-	1 +	ReadOnly
systemId	1.5 +	5.0 +	6.0 +	5.0 +	-	1 +	ReadOnly

Inheritance chain:

Node object

EntityReference object (Object/DOM)

A reference to an entity object in an XML document.

Availability:	DOM level – 1 JavaScript – 1.5 Netscape – 6.0
Inherits from:	*Node object*
JavaScript syntax:	N *myEntityReference = myDocument* `.createEntityReference(aName)`
Argument list:	*aName* The name of the entity to reference
See also:	`Document.createEntityReference()`

Inheritance chain:

Node object

enum (Reserved word)

Reserved for future language enhancements.

The provision of this keyword suggests that future versions of ECMAScript may support enumerated data types.

See also:	Reserved word, Type

Cross-references:

ECMA 262 edition 2 – section – 7.4.3

ECMA 262 edition 3 – section – 7.5.3

Enumerator object (Object/JScript)

A special object supported by MSIE for processing collections of objects.

Availability:	JScript – 3.0 Internet Explorer – 4.0	
JavaScript syntax:	IE	`myEnumerator = Enumerator`
	IE	`myEnumerator = new` `Enumerator(aCollection)`
Argument list:	`aCollection`	The collection to be enumerated
Object properties:	`constructor`	
Object methods:	`atEnd(), item(), moveFirst(), moveNext()`	

An `Enumerator` object provides a way to enumerate through all the objects in a collection (aka Array). You can create a new `Enumerator`, giving it your collection as an argument and can then access the items in the collection in a more sophisticated way than simply using a `for` loop.

You can use the `enumerator` to cycle through the items in a collection in much the same way as a `for(...in...)` loop would enumerate the properties. However, in some collections, objects have more than one entry. They may have an indexed entry and an associative entry. An `enumerator` should traverse the collection visiting each item only once. A `for` loop may visit objects several times.

The available set of methods and properties is somewhat limited compared with `enumerator` objects in other languages.

Because this is only available on MSIE and is severely dysfunctional on the Macintosh version of MSIE 5, its use is somewhat limited from the portability point of view. It is recommended that you avoid using it for the time being. Later, when it is more widely and reliably available, it may be more useful.

Do not confuse DOM `NodeList` arrays with `Enumerator` or `Collection` objects. The `NodeList item()` method is subtly different to the `Enumerator.Item()` method.

Warnings:

❑ When tested on MSIE 5 for Macintosh, this object exhibited some very odd behavior.

❑ When passed a `FormArray`, it complained that it was not a `Collection` object. When passed a `Collection` object (`document.all`) it still complained. However, when passed an `Array` object, it was happy to accept it. It would allow a new `Enumerator` to be created with no argument being passed to its constructor function.

❑ When examined, its constructor reported that it was a reference to a Date object.

❑ The object may only be usable on MSIE on the Windows platform until a later version of MSIE supports a corrected implementation.

❑ The naming convention for methods and properties of this object are capitalized in a very untypical way and you need to be aware of this in case you have trouble getting your enumerator to work properly.

Example code:

```
// Instantiate a file system object
myFileSystem = new ActiveXObject("Scripting.FileSystemObject");
// Create an enumerator
myEnum = new Enumerator(myFileSystem.Drives);
// Traverse the Drives collection via the enumerator
for(; !myEnum.atEnd(); myEnum.moveNext())
{
processDrive(myEnum.item());
}
// A function to do something with each disk drive
function processDrive(aDrive)
{
...
}
```

See also:	Collection object, Files object, NodeList object

Property	JavaScript	JScript	N	IE	Opera	Notes
constructor	-	3.0 +	-	4.0 +	-	Warning

Method	JavaScript	JScript	N	IE	Opera	Notes
atEnd()	-	3.0 +	-	4.0 +	-	-
item()	-	3.0 +	-	4.0 +	-	-
moveFirst()	-	3.0 +	-	4.0 +	-	-
moveNext()	-	3.0 +	-	4.0 +	-	-

Equal to (==) (Operator/equality)

Compare two operands for equality.

Availability:	ECMAScript edition – 2 JavaScript – 1.0 JScript – 1.0 Internet Explorer – 3.02 Netscape – 2.0 Netscape Enterprise Server – 2.0 Opera – 3.0

E

JavaScript Programmer's Reference

Property/method value type:	Boolean primitive	
JavaScript syntax:	-	*anOperand1* == *anOperand2*
Argument list:	*anOperand1*	A value that can reasonably be compared
	anOperand2	A value that can reasonably be compared with *anOperand1*

The result is the Boolean value true if anOperand1 is numerically or lexically equal to anOperand2, otherwise false is returned.

The equality operator is not always transitive. For example, two string objects may represent the same string value. Comparing the objects for equality will yield false because the references to the objects are being compared and not the object values themselves. However, forcing a string comparison may in fact yield a true value when testing for equality. Do this by converting the objects as part of the comparison process by type conversion or valueOf() methods.

Numeric values may require rounding to take place and testing for equality may be accurate down to a precision finer than your script cares about. You can set a precision value in a variable, then subtract the value you are comparing with from the absolute value of the comparee. If the difference is smaller than your precision value, then the two values are close enough to yield a match.

The associativity is left to right.

Refer to the operator precedence topic for details of execution order.

Refer to the Equality expression topic for a discussion on the ECMA standard definition of the equality testing rules.

Warnings:

❑ Be careful not to confuse the single equals with the double equals. Placing a single equals in place of a test for equality will assign the right hand value to the left hand operand and clobber the value accidentally. It will also force the relational expression to yield true as well. The interpreter may be forgiving enough that a run-time error isn't generated, but the side effects could be subtle and make it hard to diagnose the cause.

❑ A triple equals sign further complicates things as it is a test for identical type as well as equal value.

Example code:

```
// Fuzzy matching of numeric values
function almost_equal(aValue1, aValue2)
{
    var myPrecision = 1e-10;
    if((Math.abs(aValue1 - aValue2)) < myPrecision)
    {
        return(true);
    }
    return(false);
}
```

See also:	ASCII, Type conversion, *typeof*, *Unicode*

Cross-references:

ECMA 262 edition 2 – section – 11.9.1

ECMA 262 edition 3 – section – 11.9.1

Wrox *Instant JavaScript* – page – 36

Error handler (Interface)

Triggered by an error in the JavaScript execution.

JavaScript syntax:	-	`function anErrorHandler(aMessage, aURL, aLine) { someCode };`
Argument list:	`aLine`	The line number where the error occurred
	`aMessage`	The text of the error message
	`anErrorHandler`	An identifier name for the function
	`aURL`	The URL of the document containing the error
	`someCode`	The script source for the error handler

This is a means of trapping the errors in any script. You can activate an error handler in various ways. Placing this line at the top of your script will trap all errors within that script:

```
self.onerror = function() { return true };
```

Because the script always returns true, no error dialog will ever be displayed.

Here is a pseudo-code example of a better technique.

```
function HandleErrors(aMessage, aURL, aLine)
{
   //If we can handle the error with a piece of code
      return true;
   //Else we can't do anything
      return false;
}
self.onerror = HandleErrors;
```

An error handler should return true if the host environment can safely ignore the error and false if the environment needs to handle the error as normal.

See also:	Error, Error events, Semantic event, `Window.onerror`

Error object (Object/core)

An object that represents a custom error condition.

Availability:	ECMAScript edition – 3 JavaScript – 1.5 JScript – 5.0 Internet Explorer – 5.0 Netscape – 6.0
JavaScript syntax:	-	`myError = new Error()`
	-	`myError = new Error(aNumber)`
	-	`myError = new Error(aNumber, aText)`
Argument list:	`aNumber`	An error number
	`aText`	A text describing the error
Object properties:	`constructor`, `description`, `message`, `name`, `number`, `prototype`
Object methods:	`toString()`

This object is provided to create custom error codes for your application. The ECMA standard (edition 3) describes them as objects that are thrown as exceptions when a run-time error occurs.

These objects are passed as the first argument of the `catch()` function in a `try...catch` structure where you can inspect them and deal with the error.

Example code:

```
// Force an error condition
myError = new Error(100, "My user defined error text")
try
{
   throw myError;
}
catch(anErr)
{
   confirm(anErr.description);
}
finally
{
   alert("Sorted");
}
```

See also:	*catch(...), EvalError object, RangeError object, ReferenceError object, SyntaxError object, throw, try ... catch ... finally, TypeError object, URIError object*

Property	JavaScript	JScript	N	IE	Opera	NES	ECMA	Notes
constructor	1.5 +	5.0 +	6.0 +	5.0 +	-	-	3 +	DontEnum
description	-	5.0 +	-	5.0 +	-	-	-	Warning
message	1.5 +	5.5 +	6.0 +	5.5 +	-	-	3 +	Warning
name	1.5 +	5.5 +	6.0 +	5.5 +	-	-	3 +	-
number	1.5 +	5.0 +	6.0 +	5.0 +	-	-	-	-
prototype	1.5 +	5.0 +	6.0 +	5.0 +	3.0 +	2.0 +	3 +	ReadOnly, DontDelete, DontEnum

Method	JavaScript	JScript	N	IE	Opera	NES	ECMA	Notes
toString()	1.5 +	5.0 +	6.0 +	5.0 +	3.0 +	2.0 +	3 +	-

Cross-references:

ECMA 262 edition 3 – section – 15.1.4.9

ECMA 262 edition 3 – section – 15.11.1

ECMA 262 edition 3 – section – 15.11.2

JavaScript Programmer's Reference

E

Error() (Function)

An `Error` object constructor.

Availability:	ECMAScript edition – 3 JavaScript – 1.5 JScript – 5.0 Internet Explorer – 5.0 Netscape – 6.0	
JavaScript syntax:	-	`Error()`
	-	`Error(aNumber)`
	-	`Error(aNumber, aText)`
Argument list:	`aNumber`	An error number
	`aText`	A text describing the error

When the `Error()` constructor is called as a function, it creates and initializes a new `Error` object. The function call `Error()` is equivalent to the expression new `Error()` with the same arguments.

See also:	`Error.prototype`

Cross-references:

ECMA 262 edition 3 – section – 15.11.1

escape() (Function/global)

URL escape a text string.

Availability:	ECMAScript edition – 2 JavaScript – 1.0 JScript – 1.0 Internet Explorer – 3.02 Netscape – 2.0 Netscape Enterprise Server – 2.0 Opera – 3.0 Deprecated	
Property/method value type:	`String primitive`	
JavaScript syntax:	-	`escape(anInputString)`
	-	`escape(anInputString, aSwitch)`
Argument list:	`anInputString`	A string of un-escaped (normal) characters
	`aSwitch`	A switch that allows plus signs to be encoded or not

The `escape()` function computes a new version of the string value it is passed. The new version has certain characters replaced with hexadecimal escape sequences.

All character codes from zero to 32 (decimal) will be escaped.

All character codes above 126 will be escaped.

The table summarizes the characters below 127 that will be escaped.

Escape	Character
%09	Tab
%0A	Line feed
%0D	Carriage return
%20	space
%21	!
%22	"
%23	#
%24	$
%25	%
%26	&
%27	'
%28	(
%29	)
%3A	:
%3B	;
%3C	<
%3D	=
%3E	>
%3F	?
%5B	[
%5C	\
%5D	]
%5E	^
%60	`
%7B	{
%7C	|
%7D	}
%7E	~
%7F	Delete

For those characters that are replaced whose Unicode encoding is 0xFF or less, a two digit escape sequence of the form %xx is used. For those characters that are replaced whose Unicode character value is greater than 0xFF, a four-digit escape sequence of the form %uxxxx is used.

The encoding is partly based on the encoding described in document RFC1738. However the entire coding scheme goes beyond the scope of that RFC document.

Most non alphanumeric characters will be escaped. All control codes are and also the upper 128 of the 255 character codes that are normally used in a web browser will be escaped too. The example script generates a table of character codes that show how they are escaped. Note that control characters will be represented by a 'missing character' box, but on some platforms, special characters are mapped for display in these lower code points (0-31).

MSIE version 4 introduces Unicode support.

Netscape supports the optional second parameter to switch on the encoding of plus signs. You should place an integer 1 in this argument to activate plus encoding.

As far as ECMAScript is concerned, this is superceded in edition 3 with a set of generalized URI handling functions. The JScript 5.5 documentation refers to the escape() function as a deprecated feature.

Example code:

```javascript
// Create a 0-255 lookup table of escapes
document.write("<TABLE BORDER=1>");
document.write("<TR><TH>Index</TH>");
document.write("<TH>Char</TH>");
document.write("<TH>Escape</TH></TR>");
for(ii=0; ii<256; ii++)
{
    myBinary        = ii.toString(2);
    myBinaryPadding = "00000000".substr(1,(8-myBinary.length));

    myOctal         = ii.toString(8);
    myOctalPadding  = "000".substr(1,(3-myOctal.length));

    myHex           = ii.toString(16);
    myHexPadding    = "00".substr(1,(2-myHex.length));

    myChar          = String.fromCharCode(ii);

    document.write("<TR ALIGN=RIGHT><TD>");
    document.write(ii);
    document.write("</TD><TD>");
    document.write(" "+myChar);
    document.write("</TD><TD>");
    document.write(escape(myChar));
    document.write("</TD></TR>");
}
document.write("</TABLE>");
```

See also:	Cast operator, *decodeURI()*, *decodeURIComponent()*, *encodeURI()*, *encodeURIComponent()*, Function property, *Global object*, *unescape()*, URI handling functions

Cross-references:

ECMA 262 edition 2 – section – 15.1.2.4

ECMA 262 edition 3 – section – B.2.1

ftp://ftp.isi.edu/in-notes/

Escaped JavaScript quotes in HTML (Pitfall)

Closing quotes may appear when you least expect them.

If you are generating JavaScript calls from a database you might use one particular field as a quote delimited text parameter like this:

```
<A HREF="javascript:alert('Some text');">Click me</A>
```

Since the JavaScript call is inside a tag attribute, it is enclosed in double quotes. This means for starters that double quotes are a problem in your data if they appear.

You can get round this by enclosing any string constants in the JavaScript domain by using single quotes. JavaScript doesn't mind either. However, that means you get a problem when a single quote turns up in your data.

You might think that your output routines that get data from the database are doing very well by detecting the apostrophe and replacing it with ', however you might still be in trouble. Likewise if you escaped the double quote by using the HTML character entity descriptor. This is because the browser unescapes the page as it is loaded. This is extremely hard to diagnose because when you view the source, you see the character entities and not the characters they become.

You must ensure that your data extraction/insertion code places the database generated items into this scenario with JavaScript escapes and not HTML escapes.

Of course everywhere else in the document you need to escape things as HTML and not JavaScript.

This all applies vice versa by swapping the quotes around, although the escaped character entity value changes.

The example code illustrates a set of quoted strings that break and another set that work fine.

When they break, they cause a run-time error. In some cases they even prevent the status line from displaying the right thing.

Example code:

```
<HTML>
<HEAD>
</HEAD>
<BODY>
Watch the status bar as you roll over the link.<BR>
<HR>
Examples of broken quotes:<BR>
<BR>
<A HREF="javascript:alert('xxx'xxx');">Test 1.1</A><BR>
<A HREF="javascript:alert('xxx&#039;xxx');">Test 1.2</A><BR>
<A HREF='javascript:alert("xxx"xxx");'>Test 1.3</A><BR>
<A HREF='javascript:alert("xxx&#034;xxx");'>Test 1.4</A><BR>
<A HREF='javascript:alert("xxx\'xxx");'>Test 1.5</A><BR>
<A HREF="javascript:alert("xxx\"xxx");">Test 1.6</A><BR>
<HR>
These work fine:<BR>
<BR>
<A HREF="javascript:alert('xxx\'xxx');">Test 2.1</A><BR>
<A HREF="javascript:alert("xxx\"xxx");'>Test 2.2</A><BR>
<A HREF="javascript:alert('xxx&#034;xxx');">Test 2.3</A><BR>
<A HREF='javascript:alert("xxx&#039;xxx");'>Test 2.4</A><BR>
<A HREF="javascript:alert('xxx\047xxx');">Test 2.5</A><BR>
<A HREF="javascript:alert('xxx\x27xxx');">Test 2.6</A><BR>
<A HREF="javascript:alert('xxx\u0027xxx');">Test 2.7</A><BR>
<A HREF="javascript:alert('xxx\042xxx');">Test 2.8</A><BR>
<A HREF="javascript:alert('xxx\x22xxx');">Test 2.9</A><BR>
<A HREF="javascript:alert('xxx\u0022xxx');">Test 2.10</A><BR>
<HR>
</BODY>
</HTML>
```

See also:	HTML Character entity, Pitfalls, *String literal*

eval() (Function/global)

Execute some script source passed as an argument.

Availability:	ECMAScript edition – 2 JavaScript – 1.0 JScript – 1.0 Internet Explorer – 3.02 Netscape – 2.0 Opera – 3.0
Property/method value type:	Depends on the script source passed as an argument
JavaScript syntax:	-	eval(*aSourceText*)
Argument list:	*aSourceText*	A string value containing some syntactically correct script source code

When the `eval()` function is called, it expects a string to be passed to it as its single argument value. The contents of that string should be syntactically correct executable script source text.

The script code gets executed and any result it generates is returned. That value must be explicitly returned otherwise the result will be undefined.

Warnings:

❑ If the script source passed to the `eval()` function cannot be parsed without failure, a run-time error will result.

❑ Be careful how you let people pass values from outside into this function. It is feasible to provide a way for a user to type in some valid JavaScript and to then execute it for them in an `eval()` function. This can be dangerous, not only because it exposes all the variables in the script but also it may be possible to construct a JavaScript that when executed, talks back to the server that provided the page in the first place.

❑ It would be an unusual thing to do anyway, but the possibility may be there to compromise your server security. It rather depends on the security in the hosting environment. Possibly an `eval()` action is not permitted to do things that a non-user-modifiable script embedded in a web page can do. However, this is likely to be very implementation specific.

Example code:

```
// Create some script source
var scriptCode = "c = a * b";
var a = 5;
var b = 10;
var c = 2;
document.write(c);
document.write("<BR>");
eval(scriptCode);
document.write(c);
```

See also: Eval code, Function code, Function property, *function(...) ...*, *Global object, JSObject.eval()*, `Object.eval()`, `Window.setInterval()`, `Window.setTimeout()`

Property attributes:

DontEnum.

Cross-references:

ECMA 262 edition 2 – section – 10.1.2

ECMA 262 edition 2 – section – 15.1.2.1

ECMA 262 edition 3 – section – 10.1.2

ECMA 262 edition 3 – section – 15.1.2.1

Wrox *Instant JavaScript* – page – 28

EvalError object (Object/core)

A native error object based on the `Error` object.

Availability:	ECMAScript edition – 3 JavaScript – 1.5 Netscape – 6.0	
Inherits from:	*Error object*	
JavaScript syntax:	N	`myError = new EvalError()`
	N	`myError = new EvalError(aNumber)`
	N	`myError = new EvalError(aNumber, aText)`
Argument list:	`aNumber`	An error number
	`aText`	A text describing the error

This sub-class of the `Error` object is used when an exception is caused by using the global `eval()` function incorrectly.

See also:	*catch(...), Error object, RangeError object, ReferenceError object, SyntaxError object, throw, try ... catch ... finally, TypeError object, URIError object*

Inheritance chain:

`Error` object

Cross-references:

ECMA 262 edition 3 – section – 15.11.6.1

Event object (Object/DOM)

Early Netscape and MSIE browsers define different event object models. In MSIE, a single `Event` object is available globally and shared by all events.

Availability:	DOM level – 2 JavaScript – 1.2 JScript – 3.0 Internet Explorer – 4.0 Netscape – 4.0	
JavaScript syntax:	-	`myEvent = event`
	-	`myEvent = myWindow.event`
	N	`myEvent = myDocumentEvent.createEvent(aType)`

Argument list:	aType	An event type
Object properties:	altKey, bubbles, button, cancelable, cancelBubble, charCode, clientX, clientY, ctrlKey, currentTarget, data, dataFld, dataTransfer, eventPhase, fromElement, height, keyCode, layerX, layerY, modifiers, offsetX, offsetY, pageX, pageY, propertyName, qualifier, reason, recordset, repeat, returnValue, screenX, screenY, shiftKey, srcElement, srcFilter, srcUrn, target, timeStamp, toElement, type, which, width, x, y	
Class constants:	ABORT, ALT_MASK, AT_TARGET, BACK, BLUR, BUBBLING_PHASE, CAPTURING_PHASE, CHANGE, CLICK, CONTROL_MASK, DBLCLICK, DRAGDROP, ERROR, FOCUS, FORWARD, HELP, KEYDOWN, KEYPRESS, KEYUP, LOAD, LOCATE, META_MASK, MOUSEDOWN, MOUSEDRAG, MOUSEMOVE, MOUSEOUT, MOUSEOVER, MOUSEUP, MOVE, RESET, RESIZE, SCROLL, SELECT, SHIFT_MASK, SUBMIT, UNLOAD, XFER_DONE	
Object methods:	initEvent(), preventDefault(), stopPropagation()	
Collections:	bookmarks[], boundElements[]	

The event models in Netscape version 4 and MSIE version 4 support an Event object. However, both browsers support different properties for this object. It may be possible with some smart JavaScript code to normalize these to look like the same object model. You could either define your own or take one and emulate it in the other.

As well as being different, the Event object is passed to event handlers in a different way for each browser. Netscape version 4 passes the Event object as an argument. MSIE version 4 stores a reference to it in the global variable called event.

Netscape provides a set of Static constants that can be used to manufacture modifier masks. These can then be tested against the Event.modifiers property. These constants have names that all end with the suffix "_MASK". There are other constants provided so masks for event types can be made. These can be tested against the Event.type property.

MSIE does not support these static constants in the same way and uses fully spelled out event names as string primitive values for matching. This ultimately may be better because Netscape is constrained for space as regards bit values for new events. There are only 32 bits and most have already been allocated to event types.

As of version 6.0 of Netscape, the underlying event model is based on the DOM level 2 event module. This is fundamentally different to the support of events in earlier versions of the Netscape browser. DOM level 2 and Netscape 6.0 converge on the same basic model as MSIE. This adds some new properties, methods and static constants in accordance with the DOM specification. Some properties persist from earlier versions.

247

The DOM level 2 specification for events describes a category of HTMLEvents which it suggests is based on DOM level 0 capabilities. There is only a small amount of information about the event type strings and the event capabilities in the DOM level 2 context. No ECMAScript binding is described and because DOM level 0 has never been published as a standard, there is a little ambiguity about these events. The standardization is somewhat de-facto regarding them and in due course as the DOM event model evolves this should all become more consistent and more completely documented.

Warnings:

❑ Properties belonging to an Event object cannot be set in Netscape unless the script has the UniversalBrowserWrite privilege. You also cannot watch events in other windows if they are loaded from different sources unless the script also has the UniversalBrowserWrite privilege.

❑ The properties and methods supported by Netscape and MSIE differ greatly in name and function. You will need to be very careful when building sophisticated event management capabilities into your scripts.

❑ Netscape does not implement all of the events for which there are static constants defined.

Example code:

```
// List the event constants in Netscape.
// This does not work in MSIE.
d   = document;
e   = Event;
s1 = "<TR><TD>";
s2 = "</TD><TD>";
s3 = "</TD></TR>";
d.write("<TABLE BORDER=1>");
d.write(s1 + "MOUSEDOWN" + s2 + e.MOUSEDOWN + s3);
d.write(s1 + "MOUSEUP"   + s2 + e.MOUSEUP   + s3);
d.write(s1 + "MOUSEOVER" + s2 + e.MOUSEOVER + s3);
d.write(s1 + "MOUSEOUT"  + s2 + e.MOUSEOUT  + s3);
d.write(s1 + "MOUSEMOVE" + s2 + e.MOUSEMOVE + s3);
d.write(s1 + "CLICK"     + s2 + e.CLICK     + s3);
d.write(s1 + "DBLCLICK"  + s2 + e.DBLCLICK  + s3);
d.write(s1 + "KEYDOWN"   + s2 + e.KEYDOWN   + s3);
d.write(s1 + "KEYUP"     + s2 + e.KEYUP     + s3);
d.write(s1 + "KEYPRESS"  + s2 + e.KEYPRESS  + s3);
d.write(s1 + "DRAGDROP"  + s2 + e.DRAGDROP  + s3);
d.write(s1 + "FOCUS"     + s2 + e.FOCUS     + s3);
d.write(s1 + "BLUR"      + s2 + e.BLUR      + s3);
d.write(s1 + "SELECT"    + s2 + e.SELECT    + s3);
d.write(s1 + "CHANGE"    + s2 + e.CHANGE    + s3);
d.write(s1 + "RESET"     + s2 + e.RESET     + s3);
d.write(s1 + "SUBMIT"    + s2 + e.SUBMIT    + s3);
d.write(s1 + "LOAD"      + s2 + e.LOAD      + s3);
d.write(s1 + "UNLOAD"    + s2 + e.UNLOAD    + s3);
d.write(s1 + "ABORT"     + s2 + e.ABORT     + s3);
d.write(s1 + "ERROR"     + s2 + e.ERROR     + s3);
d.write(s1 + "MOVE"      + s2 + e.MOVE      + s3);
d.write(s1 + "RESIZE"    + s2 + e.RESIZE    + s3);
d.write("</TABLE>");
```

See also:	Element.onevent, Event bubbling, Event handler, *Event type constants*, Event.modifiers, Implementation.hasFeature(), *MouseEvent object*, Timer events, *UIEvent object, UniversalBrowserAccess, UniversalBrowserRead, UniversalBrowserWrite, unwatch(), watch(), Window.handleEvent()*

Property	JavaScript	JScript	N	IE	Opera	DOM	Notes
altKey	-	3.0 +	-	4.0 +	5.0 +	-	ReadOnly
bubbles	1.5 +	-	6.0 +	-	-	2 +	ReadOnly
button	-	3.0 +	-	4.0 +	-	-	Warning, ReadOnly
cancelable	1.5 +	-	6.0 +	-	-	2 +	ReadOnly
cancelBubble	-	3.0 +	-	4.0 +	5.0 +	-	-
charCode	-	3.0 +	-	4.0 +	-	-	-
clientX	-	3.0 +	-	4.0 +	5.0 +	-	ReadOnly
clientY	-	3.0 +	-	4.0 +	5.0 +	-	ReadOnly
ctrlKey	-	3.0 +	-	4.0 +	5.0 +	-	ReadOnly
current Target	1.5 +	-	6.0 +	-	5.0 +	2 +	ReadOnly
data	1.2 +	3.0 +	4.0 +	4.0 +	-	-	Warning, ReadOnly
dataFld	1.2 +	3.0 +	4.0 +	4.0 +	-	2 +	Warning
dataTransfer	-	5.0 +	-	5.0 +	-	-	-
eventPhase	1.5 +	-	6.0 +	-	-	2 +	ReadOnly
fromElement	-	3.0 +	-	4.0 +	-	-	ReadOnly
height	1.2 +	-	4.0 +	-	-	-	-
keyCode	-	3.0 +	-	4.0 +	-	-	Warning
layerX	1.2 +	-	4.0 +	-	-	-	Warning, ReadOnly
layerY	1.2 +	-	4.0 +	-	-	-	Warning, ReadOnly
modifiers	1.2 +	-	4.0 +	-	-	-	ReadOnly
offsetX	-	3.0 +	-	4.0 +	-	-	Warning, ReadOnly
offsetY	-	3.0 +	-	4.0 +	-	-	Warning, ReadOnly
pageX	1.2 +	-	4.0 +	-	-	-	ReadOnly
pageY	1.2 +	-	4.0 +	-	-	-	ReadOnly
propertyName	-	5.0 +	-	5.0 +	-	-	-
qualifier	1.2 +	3.0 +	4.0 +	4.0 +	-	2 +	Warning
reason	-	3.0 +	-	4.0 +	-	-	ReadOnly
recordset	1.2 +	3.0 +	4.0 +	4.0 +	-	2 +	Warning
repeat	-	5.0 +	-	5.0 +	-	-	-

Table continued on following page

Property	JavaScript	JScript	N	IE	Opera	DOM	Notes
returnValue	-	3.0 +	-	4.0 +	-	-	-
screenX	1.2 +	3.0 +	4.0 +	4.0 +	5.0 +	-	ReadOnly
screenY	1.2 +	3.0 +	4.0 +	4.0 +	5.0 +	-	ReadOnly
shiftKey	-	3.0 +	-	4.0 +	5.0 +	-	ReadOnly
srcElement	-	3.0 +	-	4.0 +	-	-	ReadOnly
srcFilter	-	3.0 +	-	4.0 +	-	-	ReadOnly
srcUrn	1.2 +	3.0 +	4.0 +	4.0 +	-	2 +	Warning
target	1.2 +	-	4.0 +	-	5.0 +	2 +	ReadOnly
timeStamp	1.5 +	-	6.0 +	-	-	2 +	Warning, ReadOnly
toElement	-	3.0 +	-	4.0 +	-	-	ReadOnly
type	1.2 +	3.0 +	4.0 +	4.0 +	5.0 +	2 +	ReadOnly
which	1.2 +	-	4.0 +	-	5.0 +	-	Warning, ReadOnly
width	1.2 +	-	4.0 +	-	-	-	-
x	1.2 +	3.0 +	4.0 +	4.0 +	-	-	ReadOnly
y	1.2 +	3.0 +	4.0 +	4.0 +	-	-	ReadOnly

Method	JavaScript	JScript	N	IE	Opera	DOM	Notes
initEvent()	1.5 +	-	6.0 +	-	-	2 +	-
preventDefault()	1.5 +	-	6.0 +	-	5.0 +	2 +	-
stopPropagation()	1.5 +	-	6.0 +	-	5.0 +	2 +	-

Event type constants (Constant/static)

Netscape defines a set of constants that represent event types.

Netscape provides some static properties of the Event object class that define mask values for event types. These can then be combined with a bitwise OR operator to build a mask that can be applied with the captureEvents() and releaseEvents() methods that are supported by Window, Document and Layer objects.

Here is a list of the available Event type constants:

Bit	Constant	Event type
2^0	MOUSEDOWN	The mouse button was pressed while the pointer was over the element.
2^1	MOUSEUP	The mouse button was released while the pointer was within the extent region of the element.
2^2	MOUSEOVER	The mouse has just moved over the extent region of the element.

Bit	Constant	Event type
2^3	MOUSEOUT	The mouse has just moved out of the extent region of the element.
2^4	MOUSEMOVE	The mouse was moved within the extent region of the element.
2^5	undefined	Reserved for future use.
2^6	CLICK	The element has been clicked on.
2^7	DBLCLICK	The element has been double clicked on.
2^8	KEYDOWN	A key was pressed while the element had focus.
2^9	KEYUP	A key was released while the element had focus.
2^10	KEYPRESS	A key was pressed and released again while the element had focus.
2^11	DRAGDROP	Some entity has been dragged over and dropped onto the element.
2^12	FOCUS	The element has had input focus restored to it.
2^13	BLUR	Window or input element has lost input focus.
2^14	SELECT	An item in a pop-up menu was selected.
2^15	CHANGE	The input element's value has changed.
2^16	RESET	The [RESET] button within a <FORM> was clicked.
2^17	SUBMIT	The [SUBMIT] button within a <FORM> was clicked.
2^18	undefined	Reserved for future use.
2^19	LOAD	An element (usually a <BODY> or <IMG>) has completed loading.
2^20	UNLOAD	The element (usually a <BODY>) is about to be unloaded.
2^21	undefined	Reserved for future use.
2^22	ABORT	Image loading was aborted.
2^23	ERROR	A script error has occurred.
2^24	undefined	Reserved for future use.
2^25	MOVE	The element (usually a Window) was moved.
2^26	RESIZE	The element (usually a Window) was resized.
2^27	undefined	Reserved for future use.
2^28	undefined	Reserved for future use.
2^29	undefined	Reserved for future use.
2^30	undefined	Reserved for future use.
2^31	undefined	Reserved for future use.

See also:	*captureEvents(), Document.captureEvents(), Document.releaseEvents(), Event object,* Event.eventPhase, Event.type, Keyboard events, *Layer.captureEvents(), Layer.releaseEvents(), Window.captureEvents(), Window.releaseEvents()*

E

EventCapturer object (Object/Navigator)

A special object that Netscape uses to grab events.

Availability:	JavaScript – 1.2 Netscape – 4.0	
JavaScript syntax:	N	`myEventCapturer = window.open()`

An object of this class is created when a `window.open()` method is executed in Netscape. Within the window, the `window` object is visible to the scripts running inside it. From outside, the creating script is handed an `EventCapturer` object as a handle on the window. In MSIE, you get a genuine `window` object back.

The properties of the Netscape `EventCapturer` object are difficult to inspect because they cannot be enumerated directly. The object, like many internal objects in Netscape has a constructor which can be inspected but the object is opaque otherwise.

Because the event manager complex is so new (and somewhat fragile in Netscape 6.0) it is hard to determine whether this is still true in that version. Some work needs to be done and a revised version of Netscape will be required before this can be verified.

See also:	*Window object*, `Window.open()`

EventException object (Object/DOM)

An object that describes the kind of event-based exception that has occurred.

Availability:	DOM level – 2 JavaScript – 1.5 Netscape – 6.0	
JavaScript syntax:	N	`myEventException = new EventException()`
Object properties:	code	
Class constants:	UNSPECIFIED_EVENT_TYPE_ERR	

During the processing of an event with its handler, some unexpected circumstance may cause an exception to occur. This is not quite the same as a `try ... catch` exception as defined in ECMAScript.

DOM level 2 describes an `EventException` object but it's not obvious how this would be associated with any JavaScript function that could be set up to catch it. The DOM level 2 event specification is founded on the principle that the implementation should be at least ECMAScript (third edition) compliant. This should ensure it has sophisticated enough error handling support to cope with an exception being thrown. Neither specification describes in detail exactly how this should happen and so it is likely that while we may have browsers that support a standard and consistent object model, we still have portability problems because they implement the surrounding infrastructure differently.

Assuming that a function handler were called, it would be passed a reference to an
EventException object from which it could obtain a code value that describes
the cause of the exception. Perhaps, the onError handler may be used to trap this
but an implementation might choose to provide an onException handler.

At DOM level 2, only the UNSPECIFIED_EVENT_TYPE_ERR is defined as a static
constant. This has the value 0. Other event types may be defined in later versions
of the DOM specification.

See also:	EventTarget.dispatchEvent()

Property	JavaScript	JScript	N	IE	Opera	DOM	Notes
code	1.5 +	-	6.0 +	-	-	2 +	-

EventListener object (Object/DOM)

A script function that is called when an event is triggered.

Availability:	DOM level – 2 JavaScript – 1.5 Netscape – 6.0
JavaScript syntax:	N	myEventListener = function Listener(anEvent) { ... }
Argument list:	anEvent	A placeholder argument

This is an event handler function which you can define in the script source text
and can then register as the listener for an event by means of the
addEventListener() and removeEventListener() methods belonging to
the EventTarget object.

The script function takes a single argument which is an Event object that is
instantiated as the event is triggered.

Warnings:

❑ If you copy a document node with the cloneNode() method, the copies will not
inherit the same listeners and you will need to add new listeners to handle any
events that are dispatched to the new copies of the nodes.

❑ HTML 4.0 describes a way to associate listeners with objects as they are
instantiated by means of the HTML tag attributes. However, to support multiple
listeners, the internal mechanisms no longer use the member attribute mechanism
for associating listeners with targets. This means that code that assigns values to
the onEventHandler property family may no longer work as expected if you
mix old and new style event handling techniques. Newer versions of browsers may
deprecate the old way and may in subsequent versions render it unsupported.

❑ The DOM level 2 event model is somewhat ambiguous about this part of the event handling complex. It describes an event listener as having a `handleEvent()` method which is called. It is not clear how you would add a `handleEvent()` method as a member of a function object which was itself the element that was registered to receive the event.

❑ There may be changes to this aspect of the event model in later DOM levels to better support HTML based event specification.

See also:	`EventTarget.addEventListener()`, *MutationEvent object*

EventTarget object (Object/DOM)

A set of properties and methods that extend the behavior of DOM nodes to support event handling.

Availability:	DOM level – 2
	JavaScript – 1.5
	Netscape – 6.0
JavaScript syntax:	N	`myEventTarget = myEvent.currentTarget`
	N	`myEventTarget = myEvent.target`
	N	`myEventTarget = myMouseEvent.currentTarget`
	N	`myEventTarget = myMouseEvent.relatedTarget`
	N	`myEventTarget = myMouseEvent.target`
	N	`myEventTarget = myMutationEvent.currentTarget`
	N	`myEventTarget = myMutationEvent.target`
	N	`myEventTarget = myUIEvent.currentTarget`
	N	`myEventTarget = myUIEvent.target`
Object methods:	`addEventListener()`, `dispatchEvent()`, `removeEventListener()`

Netscape version 6 introduces this capability and adds the `EventTarget` methods and properties to its `Node` objects. This provides the necessary tools for registering and deregistering event listeners and for dispatching an event to a `Node`.

See also:	`MouseEvent.initMouseEvent()`,
	`MouseEvent.relatedTarget`,
	`MutationEvent.initMutationEvent()`, *Node object*

Method	JavaScript	JScript	N	IE	Opera	DOM	Notes
addEventListener()	1.5 +	-	6.0 +	-	-	2 +	-
dispatchEvent()	1.5 +	-	6.0 +	-	-	2 +	-
removeEventListener()	1.5 +	-	6.0 +	-	-	2 +	-

export (Statement)

Export some properties to allow them to be imported into another execution context.

Availability:	ECMAScript edition – 2 JavaScript – 1.2 Netscape – 4.0 Netscape Enterprise Server – 3.0	
JavaScript syntax:	N	export *aFunction*;
	N	export *aProperty*;
Argument list:	*aFunction*	A function object to export
	aProperty	a named property

ECMAScript edition 2 suggests this is a future extension. As of the third edition of the ECMAScript standard it is still denoted as a reserved word.

Netscape 4 anticipates that a future standard will endorse this capability and provides it anyway.

This functionality allows layers to define handlers for themselves and then export them to allow other layers or windows to call them.

This facility is also useful to allow controlled access via the security policy. This can then allow an unsigned script to have access to content in a signed script's context.

This is good Object Oriented Programming technique on the grounds that hiding the private data and making a public interface available means code can be reused. This black-box approach is much used in languages such as Java, SmallTalk and Objective-C.

Warnings:

❑ This only works in Netscape version 4 when the LANGUAGE attribute is set to "JavaScript1.2". This will affect the behavior of the == and != operators as well.

❑ This can affect the security policy regarding the "same-signer" trustworthiness of a page.

❑ Be careful that you do not export a secure method or property and allow it to be executed or seen by insecure and untrusted non-signed scripts running in other windows.

JavaScript Programmer's Reference

E

Example code:

```
<HTML>
<HEAD></HEAD>
<BODY>
<SCRIPT>
var myLocalVariable;
function myLocalFunction()
{
    document.write("Test");
}
export myLocalVariable;
export myLocalFunction;
</SCRIPT>
</BODY>
</HTML>
```

See also:	*import, Same origin, Signed scripts*

Cross-references:

ECMA 262 edition 2 – section – 7.4.3

ECMA 262 edition 3 – section – 7.5.3

external object (Object/JScript)

Since MSIE can be embedded as a component into other applications, this object represents the object model of such a containing application.

Availability:	JScript – 3.0 Internet Explorer – 4.0	
JavaScript syntax:	IE	`myExternal = external`
	IE	`myExternal = myWindow.external`
Object properties:	`menuArguments`	

Object methods:	`AddChannel(),AddDesktopComponent(),`
	 `AddFavorite(),AddFavourite(),`
	 `AutoCompleteSaveForm(),AutoScan(),`
	 `ImportExportFavorites(),`
	 `ImportExportFavourites(),IsSubscribed(),`
	 `NavigateAndFind(),ShowBrowserUI()`	

Part of the MSIE on Windows environment object space. You should avoid using this facility if you want your scripts to be usable outside of the Windows environment.

To use this effectively, you need to know quite a bit about the application whose components you are calling in using this functionality. Each application has its own object model and unless you know how it works, making use of it will be a bit 'Hit and Miss'.

Warnings:

❑ Several methods for this object have arguments that are mandatory but may take empty strings or null values. This is somewhat diametrically opposed to the normal JavaScript behavior which dictates that unnecessary arguments are optional and can be assumed to be a default value when they are not present.

❑ By implementing methods with mandatory null or empty string values, Microsoft puts the script developer off balance and can cause unnecessary difficulty when developing scripts. Novices and even expert scripters may be caught out by this kind of implementation.

❑ You should always check the reference material if you are in any doubt as to how an API interface to a method is designed to work.

Property	JavaScript	JScript	N	IE	Opera	Notes
menuArguments	-	5.0 +	-	5.0 +	-	-

Method	JavaScript	JScript	N	IE	Opera	Notes
AddChannel()	-	5.0 +	-	5.0 +	-	-
AddDesktopComponent()	-	5.0 +	-	5.0 +	-	-
AddFavorite()	-	5.0 +	-	5.0 +	-	-
AddFavourite()	-	3.0 +	-	4.0 +	-	Warning
AutoCompleteSaveForm()	-	5.0 +	-	5.0 +	-	-
AutoScan()	-	5.0 +	-	5.0 +	-	-
ImportExportFavorites()	-	5.0 +	-	5.0 +	-	Warning
ImportExportFavourites()	-	3.0 +	-	4.0 +	-	Warning
IsSubscribed()	-	5.0 +	-	5.0 +	-	-
NavigateAndFind()	-	5.0 +	-	5.0 +	-	-
ShowBrowserUI()	-	5.0 +	-	5.0 +	-	Warning

E

JavaScript Programmer's Reference

false (Primitive value)

The Boolean false value.

Availability:	ECMAScript edition – 2
Property/method value type:	Boolean primitive

This is a Boolean primitive value representing the logically false state.

Conditional code execution depends on this value to signify the execution of a block of script code.

Warnings:

❑ Beware of a rather insidious effect when converting Boolean primitive values into objects. All objects yield the value true when converted back to a Boolean primitive. This also applies to a Boolean object having the value false.

❑ This if () test yields a true condition and selects the opposite branch to that which you would expect:

```
var myBoolean = new Boolean(false);

if(myBoolean)

{

  // This branch is called

}

else

{

  // You would have expected this one to be called

}
```

See also:	Boolean, Boolean, Boolean literal, Definition, true

Cross-references:

ECMA 262 edition 2 – section 9.2

ECMA 262 edition 2 – section 15.6

ECMA 262 edition 3 – section 9.2

ECMA 262 edition 3 – section 15.6

FIELDSET object (Object/HTML)

A field set within a form.

Availability:	DOM level – 1 JavaScript – 1.5 JScript – 3.0 Internet Explorer – 4.0 Netscape – 6.0	
Inherits from:	Element object	
JavaScript syntax:	IE	myFIELDSET = myDocument.all.anElementID
	IE	myFIELDSET = myDocument.all.tags ("FIELDSET")[anIndex]
	IE	myFIELDSET = myDocument.all[aName]
	-	myFIELDSET = myDocument.getElementById (anElementID)
	-	myFIELDSET = myDocument .getElementsByName(aName)[anIndex]
	-	myFIELDSET = myDocument.getElementsBy TagName("FIELDSET")[anIndex]
HTML syntax:	<FIELDSET> ... </FIELDSET>	
Argument list:	anIndex	A reference to an element in a collection
	aName	An associative array reference
	anElementID	The ID value of an Element object
Object properties:	accessKey, align, form, margin, tabIndex	
Event handlers:	onAfterUpdate, onBeforeUpdate, onBlur, onChange, onClick, onDblClick, onDragStart, onErrorUpdate, onFilterChange, onFocus, onHelp, onKeyDown, onKeyPress, onKeyUp, onMouseDown, onMouseMove, onMouseOut, onMouseOver, onMouseUp, onResize, onScroll, onSelect, onSelectStart	

A FIELDSET object represents a structured group of Input objects within a form. You can operate on them collectively. Grouping Input items might be useful for activating or hiding Input items without needing to access each one individually, which can be very useful if a form is undergoing rapid and continuous changes during its development. Controlling this with a FIELDSET allows the member elements to change without needing to modify your script.

See also:	Element object, Input object, Input.accessKey, Legend object

Property	JavaScript	JScript	N	IE	Opera	DOM	HTML	Notes
accessKey	1.5 +	3.0 +	6.0 +	4.0 +	-	1 +	-	-
align	-	3.0 +	-	4.0 +	-	-	-	-
form	1.5 +	3.0 +	6.0 +	4.0 +	-	1 +	-	-
margin	-	3.0 +	-	4.0 +	-	-	-	-
tabIndex	1.5 +	3.0 +	6.0 +	4.0 +	-	1 +	-	-

Event name	JavaScript	JScript	N	IE	Opera	DOM	HTML	Notes
onAfterUpdate	-	3.0 +	-	4.0 +	-	-	-	-
onBeforeUpdate	-	3.0 +	-	4.0 +	-	-	-	-
onBlur	1.5 +	3.0 +	6.0 +	4.0 +	-	-	-	Warning
onChange	1.5 +	3.0 +	6.0 +	4.0 +	-	-	-	-
onClick	1.5 +	3.0 +	6.0 +	3.0 +	-	-	4.0 +	Warning
onDblClick	1.5 +	3.0 +	6.0 +	4.0 +	-	-	4.0 +	Warning
onDragStart	-	3.0 +	-	4.0 +	-	-	-	-
onErrorUpdate	-	3.0 +	-	4.0 +	-	-	-	-
onFilterChange	-	3.0 +	-	4.0 +	-	-	-	-
onFocus	1.5 +	3.0 +	6.0 +	4.0 +	-	-	-	Warning
onHelp	-	3.0 +	-	4.0 +	-	-	-	Warning
onKeyDown	1.5 +	3.0 +	6.0 +	4.0 +	-	-	4.0 +	Warning
onKeyPress	1.5 +	3.0 +	6.0 +	4.0 +	-	-	4.0 +	Warning
onKeyUp	1.5 +	3.0 +	6.0 +	4.0 +	-	-	4.0 +	Warning
onMouseDown	1.5 +	3.0 +	6.0 +	4.0 +	-	-	4.0 +	Warning
onMouseMove	1.5 +	3.0 +	6.0 +	4.0 +	-	-	4.0 +	Warning
onMouseOut	1.5 +	3.0 +	6.0 +	4.0 +	-	-	4.0 +	Warning
onMouseOver	1.5 +	3.0 +	6.0 +	4.0 +	-	-	4.0 +	Warning
onMouseUp	1.5+	3.0 +	6.0 +	4.0 +	-	-	4.0 +	Warning
onResize	1.5 +	3.0 +	6.0 +	4.0 +	-	-	-	Warning
onScroll	-	3.0 +	-	4.0 +	-	-	-	-
onSelect	1.5 +	3.0 +	6.0 +	4.0 +	-	-	-	-
onSelectStart	-	3.0 +	-	4.0 +	-	-	-	-

Inheritance chain:

Element object, Node object

File object (Object/JScript)

A special JScript object representing a file on a locally mounted drive.

Availability:	JScript – 3.0 Internet Explorer – 4.0
JavaScript syntax:	IE `myFile = File`
	IE `myFile = new File(aName)`
	IE `myFile = myFileSystem.GetFile(aName)`
	IE `myFile = myFileSystem` `.CreateTextFile(aName, aFlag)`
	IE `myFile = myFileSystem.OpenTextFile` `(aName, aMode, aFlag, aFormat)`
Argument list:	`aName` The name of a file
	`aFlag` A flag indicating whether the file can be overwritten
	`aMode` An I/O mode for the file
	`aFormat` A format code indicating ASCII or Unicode content
Object properties:	`Attributes, dataFld, dataSrc, DateCreated, DateLastAccessed, DateLastModified, defaultValue, Drive, Name, ParentFolder, Path, recordNumber, ShortName, ShortPath, Size, Type, value`
Object methods:	`blur(), click(), Copy(), Delete(), focus(), Move(), OpenAsTextStream(), select()`
Event handlers:	`onBlur, onClick, onDblClick, onFocus`

This object is available in many contexts. On the server-side, it allows access to the server file-system. In that context it is available as part of the Netscape Enterprise Server product (see the separate `File` object entries for the NES version).

`File` objects may also exist client-side. Similar file-system access may be possible there as well, although you should not expect this to work from within your browser. It may be available as part of a desktop scripting environment.

Although they aren't instantiated as `File` objects, it is sometimes convenient to refer to a `File` object when we really mean to refer to an `Input` object whose `type` property is set to the "FILE" value.

Warnings:

❑ Be aware that `File` objects are not standardized and may offer different methods, properties and functions in each context. Furthermore, the same named methods, properties and functions may not yield the same results across all implementations.

❑ The JScript `File` object and the identically named Netscape Enterprise Server `File` object do not share any properties or methods. They are completely different implementations.

❑ The JScript `File` object is somewhat odd in that its properties and methods are spelled with a capital letter at the start of their name. This is not typical JavaScript or JScript usage so you should beware of capitalization when scripting `File` objects with JScript.

See also:	FileSystem object, FileSystem.CreateTextFile(), FileSystem.GetFile(), FileSystem.OpenTextFile(), Folder object

Property	JavaScript	JScript	N	IE	Opera	HTML	Notes
Attributes	-	3.0 +	-	4.0 +	-	-	-
dataFld	-	3.0 +	-	4.0 +	-	-	Warning
dataSrc	-	3.0 +	-	4.0 +	-	-	Warning
DateCreated	-	3.0 +	-	4.0 +	-	-	-
DateLastAccessed	-	3.0 +	-	4.0 +	-	-	-
DateLastModified	-	3.0 +	-	4.0 +	-	-	-
defaultValue	-	3.0 +	-	4.0 +	-	-	Warning
Drive	-	3.0 +	-	4.0 +	-	-	-
Name	-	3.0 +	-	4.0 +	-	-	-
ParentFolder	-	3.0 +	-	4.0 +	-	-	-
Path	-	3.0 +	-	4.0 +	-	-	-
recordNumber	-	3.0 +	-	4.0 +	-	-	Warning
ShortName	-	3.0 +	-	4.0 +	-	-	-
ShortPath	-	3.0 +	-	4.0 +	-	-	-
Size	-	3.0 +	-	4.0 +	-	-	-
Type	-	3.0 +	-	4.0 +	-	-	ReadOnly
value	-	3.0 +	-	4.0 +	-	-	Warning

Method	JavaScript	JScript	N	IE	Opera	HTML	Notes
blur()	-	3.0 +	-	4.0 +	-	-	Warning
click()	-	3.0 +	-	4.0 +	-	-	Warning
Copy()	-	3.0 +	-	4.0 +	-	-	-
Delete()	-	3.0 +	-	4.0 +	-	-	-
focus()	-	3.0 +	-	4.0 +	-	-	Warning
Move()	-	3.0 +	-	4.0 +	-	-	-
OpenAsTextStream()	-	3.0 +	-	4.0 +	-	-	-
select()	-	3.0 +	-	4.0 +	-	-	Warning

Event name	JavaScript	JScript	N	IE	Opera	HTML	Notes
onBlur	-	3.0 +	-	4.0 +	-	-	Warning
onClick	-	3.0 +	-	4.0 +	-	4.0 +	Warning
onDblClick	-	3.0 +	-	4.0 +	-	4.0 +	Warning
onFocus	-	3.0 +	-	4.0 +	-	-	Warning

File object (Object/NES)

An object that encapsulates a file on the local file system within the server.

Availability:	JavaScript – 1.1 Netscape Enterprise Server version – 2.0	
JavaScript syntax:	NES	myFile = File
	NES	myFile = new File(aName)
Argument list:	aName	A valid file name
Object methods:	byteToString(), clearError(), close(), eof(), error(), exists(), flush(), getLength(), getPosition(), open(), read(), readByte(), readln(), setPosition(), stringToByte(), write(), writeByte(), writeln()	

You can create a new instance of this class with the File() constructor.

Files tend to behave in a somewhat similar way in all languages and implementations. This generally means that they will read and write in 8 bit character sized elements. Beware of this as JavaScript is Unicode-based so file contents may not exactly mirror the in-memory representation of a string.

Warnings:

❑ Be careful not to confuse this with the JScript File object. The JScript object may be supported in a Microsoft server but the Netscape Enterprise Server supports an object with a mutually exclusive set of properties and methods and neither kind of File object has any chance of being portable between a Netscape Enterprise Server and a Microsoft server. There are so many other differences between their object models that it is a waste of time trying to write a portable server-side script.

See also:	Netscape Enterprise Server, unwatch(), watch()

Method	JavaScript	JScript	NES	Notes
byteToString()	1.1 +	-	2.0 +	-
clearError()	1.1 +	-	2.0 +	-
close()	1.1 +	-	2.0 +	-
eof()	1.1 +	-	2.0 +	-
error()	1.1 +	-	2.0 +	-
exists()	1.1 +	-	2.0 +	-
flush()	1.1 +	-	2.0 +	-
getLength()	1.1 +	-	2.0 +	-
getPosition()	1.1 +	-	2.0 +	-
open()	1.1 +	-	2.0 +	-
read()	1.1 +	-	2.0 +	-
readByte()	1.1 +	-	2.0 +	-
readln()	1.1 +	-	2.0 +	-
setPosition()	1.1 +	-	2.0 +	-
stringToByte()	1.1 +	-	2.0 +	-
write()	1.1 +	-	2.0 +	-
writeByte()	1.1 +	-	2.0 +	-
writeln()	1.1 +	-	2.0 +	-

file: URL (Request method)

Load a local file into a window.

This request method is useful for retrieving files from the local file system or can be used to display a window containing the HTML version of a directory in the client machine.

The file path values are platform dependant although web browsers tend to understand Unix path rules and convert them to the local platform specific conventions. MSIE doesn't do this quite as well when navigating local file systems.

On MSIE for Windows, you must specify a disk drive letter at least because the Unix root directory is not mapped. This presents network mapped drives and removable media all at the same peer level. So start with this:

```
file:c:\
```

MSIE is so well integrated into the Windows environment that it immediately recognizes that you are browsing the file system and goes into desktop explorer mode. This adds a folder icon to the toolbar and you can then navigate exactly as you would from the desktop.

The web browsers attempt to take this functionality across to other platforms and so on the Macintosh, with MSIE, try this:

```
file:/
```

MSIE version 5.0 does a much better job and is aware of local network zones and can see other machines connected via the AppleTalk protocol. Given that you can satisfy the security requirements you can browse a network of machines and keep shared documents on a workgroup server. On the Macintosh MSIE does a better job if the Finder has already mounted a shared volume on the desktop.

Using this technique you can also run applications provided the URL resolves to the name of an executable file. On Windows 98, this URL fires up the desktop calculator:

```
file:C:\Windows\Calc.exe
```

This means you can build a link on your page that activates local applications really easily. This works across platforms too. On the Macintosh, a functionally equivalent URL would be:

```
file://G3/APPS/Desk%20tools/Calculator%207.5
```

You may need to explore your hard disk to work out the paths to your installed applications. Don't forget that you need to use escaped URL values.

The same automated activation works for documents too. For example, locate an Excel spreadsheet and link to it from a document. When you click on the link, this will open Excel and load the document into it.

Older versions of Netscape Navigator are less capable of navigating the whole file system and initially start at the folder the browser application lives in. Netscape 6.0 exhibits a bug and this whole area of the browser needs more work before it is useful.

Accessing these capabilities from script is a little more tricky. `window.location.href` assignment effectively does the same thing on a Macintosh. On Windows, there are already capabilities for activating applications via the ActiveXObject and you need to use that technique because `window.location.href` does not like having applications loaded into browser frames.

Warnings:

❑ Be very careful what you browse on your system and how. You may corrupt your system although read only access is unlikely to cause any harm.

See also:	*javascript: URL, URL, view-source: URL*

Files object (Object/JScript)

A collection of files belonging together in a folder.

Availability:	JScript – 3.0 Internet Explorer – 4.0
JavaScript syntax:	IE `myFiles = myFolder.Files`
Object properties:	`Count`
Object methods:	`Item()`

This object is obtained by inspecting the `Files` property of a `Folder` object. The `Files` object is a collection containing objects that encapsulate the files in that folder. Each file is represented by a separate `File` object. You can then examine each of those objects to operate on them as you need to.

The `Files` object provides a method for searching and extracting a named `File` object within the collection and a property that yields the number of `File` objects in the collection.

You should be able to traverse the `Files` object using array indexing techniques or by means of an `Enumerator` object.

See also:	*Enumerator object*

Property	JavaScript	JScript	N	IE	Opera	Notes
`Count`	-	3.0 +	-	4.0 +	-	ReadOnly

Method	JavaScript	JScript	N	IE	Opera	Notes
`Item()`	-	3.0 +	-	4.0 +	-	-

FileSystem object (Object/JScript)

An object that represents an entire file system for a specific disk drive.

Availability:	JScript – 3.0 Internet Explorer – 4.0
JavaScript syntax:	IE `myFileSystem = myDrive.FileSystem`
	IE `myFileSystem = new ActiveXObject` `("Scripting.FileSystemObject")`

Object methods:	BuildPath(), CopyFile(), CopyFolder(), CreateFolder(), CreateTextFile(), DeleteFile(), DeleteFolder(), DriveExists(), FileExists(), FolderExists(), GetAbsolutePathName(), GetBaseName(), GetDrive(), GetDriveName(), GetExtensionName(), GetFile(), GetFileName(), GetFolder(), GetParentFolderName(), GetSpecialFolder(), GetTempName(), MoveFile(), MoveFolder(), OpenTextFile()
Collections:	Drives[]

When building scripts to run in the Windows environment, possibly for use with WSH, you may need to operate on files and folders within the file system hierarchy of the computer. This object encapsulates the file system so that you can operate on its methods and properties.

File systems may have been shared across from other computers but the network manager should make them appear identical to local drives. Foreign file systems should also be mapped to local drives and appear to have a structure that is familiar. However, there may be file name differences. Certain characters may be valid on one operating system and invalid on another or there may be different limitations on file name length and capitalization rules.

See also:	Drive.FileSystem, *File object*

Method	JavaScript	JScript	N	IE	Opera	Notes
BuildPath()	-	3.0 +	-	4.0 +	-	-
CopyFile()	-	3.0 +	-	4.0 +	-	-
CopyFolder()	-	3.0 +	-	4.0 +	-	-
CreateFolder()	-	3.0 +	-	4.0 +	-	-
CreateTextFile()	-	3.0 +	-	4.0 +	-	-
DeleteFile()	-	3.0 +	-	4.0 +	-	-
DeleteFolder()	-	3.0 +	-	4.0 +	-	-
DriveExists()	-	3.0 +	-	4.0 +	-	-
FileExists()	-	3.0 +	-	4.0 +	-	-
FolderExists()	-	3.0 +	-	4.0 +	-	-
GetAbsolute PathName()	-	3.0 +	-	4.0 +	-	-
GetBaseName()	-	3.0 +	-	4.0 +	-	-
GetDrive()	-	3.0 +	-	4.0 +	-	-
GetDriveName()	-	3.0 +	-	4.0 +	-	-
GetExtension Name()	-	3.0 +	-	4.0 +	-	-

Method	JavaScript	JScript	N	IE	Opera	Notes
GetFile()	-	3.0 +	-	4.0 +	-	-
GetFileName()	-	3.0 +	-	4.0 +	-	-
GetFolder()	-	3.0 +	-	4.0 +	-	-
GetParent FolderName()	-	3.0 +	-	4.0 +	-	-
GetSpecial Folder()	-	3.0 +	-	4.0 +	-	-
GetTempName()	-	3.0 +	-	4.0 +	-	-
MoveFile()	-	3.0 +	-	4.0 +	-	-
MoveFolder()	-	3.0 +	-	4.0 +	-	-
OpenTextFile()	-	3.0 +	-	4.0 +	-	-

FileUpload object (Object/DOM)

A text field in a form for entering the name of a file to be uploaded to the server.

Availability:	DOM level – 1 JavaScript – 1.0 JScript – 3.0 Internet Explorer – 4.0 Netscape – 2.0 Opera – 3.0
Inherits from:	*Input object*
JavaScript syntax:	- *myFileUpload = myDocument.aFormName.anElementName*
	- *myFileUpload = myDocument.aFormName .elements[anItemIndex]*
	IE *myFileUpload = myDocument.all.anElementID*
	IE *myFileUpload = myDocument.all.tags("INPUT")[anIndex]*
	IE *myFileUpload = myDocument.all[aName]*
	- *myFileUpload = myDocument.forms [aFormIndex].anElementName*
	- *myFileUpload = myDocument.forms [aFormIndex].elements[anItemIndex]*
	- *myFileUpload = myDocument.getElementById (anElementID)*
	- *myFileUpload = myDocument. getElementsByName(aName)[anIndex]*
	- *myFileUpload = myDocument.getElementsBy TagName("INPUT")[anIndex]*
HTML syntax:	<INPUT TYPE="file">

F

JavaScript Programmer's Reference

Argument list:	anItemIndex	A reference to an element in a collection
	anIndex	A reference to an element in a collection
	aName	An associative array reference
	anElementID	The ID value of an Element object
	aFormIndex	A reference to one specific form in the collection

Object properties:	accept, size, type, value

Object methods:	handleEvent(), select()

Event handlers:	onAfterUpdate, onBeforeUpdate, onBlur, onChange, onDragStart, onFilterChange, onFocus, onHelp, onKeyDown, onKeyPress, onKeyUp, onMouseDown, onMouseMove, onMouseOut, onMouseOver, onMouseUp, onResize, onRowEnter, onRowExit, onSelect, onSelectStart

Many properties, methods and event handlers are inherited from the Input object class. Refer to topics grouped with the "Input" prefix for details of common functionality across all subclasses of the Input object superclass.

There isn't really a FileUpload object class but it is helpful when trying to understand the wide variety of input element types if we can reduce the complexity by discussing only the properties and methods of a file upload. In actual fact, the object is represented as an item of the Input object class.

Unlike MSIE, Netscape Navigator does not support the defaultValue property or the select() method for this subclass of the Input object.

Warnings:

❑ To be able to upload a file under script control, you must have the UniversalFileRead privilege granted to the script.

See also:	Element object, FileUpload.handleEvent(), Form.elements[], Input object, Input.accessKey, onChange, UniversalFileRead

Property	JavaScript	JScript	N	IE	Opera	DOM	HTML	Notes
accept	-	5.0 +	-	5.0 +	-	-	-	-
size	1.0 +	3.0 +	2.0 +	4.0 +	-	-	-	-
type	1.1 +	3.0 +	3.0 +	4.0 +	3.0 +	1 +	-	ReadOnly
value	1.0 +	3.0 +	2.0 +	4.0 +	3.0 +	1 +	-	-

Method	JavaScript	JScript	N	IE	Opera	DOM	HTML	Notes
handleEvent()	1.2 +	-	4.0 +	-	-	-	-	-
select()	1.0 +	3.0 +	2.0 +	4.0 +	3.0 +	1 +	-	-

Event name	JavaScript	JScript	N	IE	Opera	DOM	HTML	Notes
onAfterUpdate	-	3.0 +	-	4.0 +	-	-	-	-
onBeforeUpdate	-	3.0 +	-	4.0 +	-	-	-	-
onBlur	1.1 +	3.0 +	3.0 +	4.0 +	3.0 +	-	-	Warning
onChange	1.0 +	3.0 +	2.0 +	4.0 +	3.0 +	-	-	-
onDragStart	-	3.0 +	-	4.0 +	-	-	-	-
onFilterChange	-	3.0 +	-	4.0 +	-	-	-	-
onFocus	1.0 +	3.0 +	2.0 +	4.0 +	3.0 +	-	-	Warning
onHelp	-	3.0 +	-	4.0 +	-	-	-	Warning
onKeyDown	1.2 +	3.0 +	4.0 +	4.0 +	3.0 +	-	4.0 +	Warning
onKeyPress	1.2 +	3.0 +	4.0 +	4.0 +	3.0 +	-	4.0 +	Warning
onKeyUp	1.2 +	3.0 +	4.0 +	4.0 +	3.0 +	-	4.0 +	Warning
onMouseDown	1.2 +	3.0 +	4.0 +	4.0 +	3.0 +	-	4.0 +	Warning
onMouseMove	1.2 +	3.0 +	4.0 +	4.0 +	-	-	4.0 +	Warning
onMouseOut	1.1 +	3.0 +	3.0 +	4.0 +	3.0 +	-	4.0 +	Warning
onMouseOver	1.0 +	3.0 +	2.0 +	4.0 +	3.0 +	-	4.0 +	Warning
onMouseUp	1.2 +	3.0 +	4.0 +	4.0 +	3.0 +	-	4.0 +	Warning
onResize	1.2 +	3.0 +	4.0 +	4.0 +	-	-	-	Warning
onRowEnter	-	3.0 +	-	4.0 +	-	-	-	-
onRowExit	-	3.0 +	-	4.0 +	-	-	-	-
onSelect	1.0 +	3.0 +	2.0 +	4.0 +	3.0 +	-	-	-
onSelectStart	-	3.0 +	-	4.0 +	-	-	-	-

Inheritance chain:

Element object, Input object, Node object

filter - Alpha() (Filter/visual)

A visual filter for controlling transparency.

Availability:	JScript – 3.0 Internet Explorer – 4.0
Object properties:	Enabled, Opacity, FinishOpacity, StartX, StartY, FinishX, FinishY, Style
Supported by objects:	A, ACRONYM, ADDRESS, B, BDO, BIG BLOCKQUOTE, body, BUTTON, CAPTION, CENTER, CITE, CODE, custom, DD, DFN, DIR, DIV, DL, DT, EM, FIELDSET, FONT, FORM, FRAME, Hn, I, IFRAME, IMG, INPUT, INS, KBD, LABEL, LEGEND, LI, MARQUEE, MENU, NOBR, OL, P, PLAINTEXT, PRE, Q, RT, RUBY, runtimeStyle, S, SAMP, SMALL, SPAN, STRIKE, STRONG, style, SUB, SUP, TABLE, TD, TEXTAREA, TH, TT, U, UL, VAR, XMP

This filter is used to define a transparency level with an optional gradient effect.

The `Enabled` property can be set true to switch on the effect of this filter or false to deactivate it.

The `Opacity` property describes the initial opacity value. The values 0 and 100 represent the full range of alpha levels with 0 being fully transparent to 100 being fully opaque.

When using a gradient, the `FinishOpacity` describes the opacity required on completion.

The `StartX` and `StartY` properties are the starting coordinates of the gradient.

The `FinishX` and `FinishY` properties are the ending coordinates of the gradient.

The `Style` property defines the kind of gradient to use for the alpha channel filter. The following kinds of gradient are supported:

Index	Description
0	Uniform alpha level defined by the opacity name=value pair. The entire element is rendered at the same opacity level.
1	A linear gradient is specified. The two opacity levels define the start and end gradient points while the start and finish coordinates define the gradient normal vector.
2	Radial gradient starting at the `StartX`, `StartY` position and using the two opacity values for range.
3	Rectangular gradient spanning the rectangle defined by the start and end coordinates and using the start and end opacity values.

There are two examples. One shows the creation of the filter from script, the other implements the same effect but shows the modification of an existing object defined by <STYLE> tags.

Warnings:

❑ Filters are defined in style sheets as if they were a function call with its arguments expressed as name=value pairs. This is not the typical way to define arguments so you should be aware of this anomaly when working with filters.

Example code:

```
<HTML>
<HEAD>
</HEAD>
<BODY onLoad="pulsateButton()">
<INPUT ID="MYBUTTON" TYPE="button" VALUE="Button">
<BR>
```

```
<SCRIPT>
var theOpacity = 0;
var theIncrement = 1;
function pulsateButton()
{
   theOpacity += theIncrement;

   myFilter = "Alpha(opacity="+theOpacity+")";
   document.all.MYBUTTON.style.filter = myFilter;
   if((theOpacity % 100) == 0)
   {
      theIncrement *= -1;
   }

   setTimeout("pulsateButton()", 5);
}
</SCRIPT>
</BODY>
</HTML>
------------------------------------------------------------------
<HTML>
<HEAD>
<STYLE>
INPUT.aFilter {filter:Alpha(Opacity=50);}
</STYLE>
</HEAD>
<BODY onLoad="pulsateButton()">
<INPUT ID="MYBUTTON" TYPE="button" VALUE="Button" CLASS="aFilter">
<BR>
<SCRIPT>
var theOpacity = 0;
var theIncrement = 1;
var theFilter = document.all.MYBUTTON.filters[0];
function pulsateButton()
{
   theOpacity += theIncrement;

   theFilter.opacity = theOpacity;
   if((theOpacity % 100) == 0)
   {
      theIncrement *= -1;
   }

   setTimeout("pulsateButton()", 5);
}
</SCRIPT>
</BODY>
</HTML>
```

| See also: | *Filter object*, style.filter |

Property	JavaScript	JScript	N	IE	Opera	Notes
Enabled	-	3.0 +	-	4.0 +	-	-
Opacity	-	3.0 +	-	4.0 +	-	Warning
FinishOpacity	-	3.0 +	-	4.0 +	-	Warning
StartX	-	3.0 +	-	4.0 +	-	Warning
StartY	-	3.0 +	-	4.0 +	-	Warning
FinishX	-	3.0 +	-	4.0 +	-	Warning
FinishY	-	3.0 +	-	4.0 +	-	Warning
Style	-	3.0 +	-	4.0 +	-	Warning

filter - AlphaImageLoader() (Filter/procedural)

An image is displayed in the object with some additional control over how it is displayed.

Availability:	JScript – 5.5 Internet Explorer – 5.5
Object properties:	Enabled, SizingMethod, Src
Supported by objects:	A, ACRONYM, ADDRESS, B, BDO, BIG BLOCKQUOTE, body, BUTTON, CAPTION, CENTER, CITE, CODE, custom, DD, DFN, DIR, DIV, DL, DT, EM, FIELDSET, FONT, FORM, FRAME, Hn, I, IFRAME, IMG, INPUT, INS, KBD, LABEL, LEGEND, LI, MARQUEE, MENU, NOBR, OL, P, PLAINTEXT, PRE, Q, RT, RUBY, runtimeStyle, S, SAMP, SMALL, SPAN, STRIKE, STRONG, style, SUB, SUP, TABLE, TD, TEXTAREA, TH, TT, U, UL, VAR, XMP

If you consider the content of the object and its background as two layers that are composited together, this filter interposes an additional image layer between them.

This layer can have its transparency adjusted as well as scaling and clipping to position the image where you want it.

The Enabled property can be set true to switch on the effect of this filter or false to deactivate it.

The SizingMethod property can be set to one of the following values:

❑ The crop value forces the image to be cropped to fit the HTML Element content's extent rectangle.

❑ The image value forces the HTML Element to be resized to accommodate the extent rectangle of the image file.

❑ The scale value forces the image to be scaled to fit the current extent rectangle for the HTML Element.

The `Src` property is mandatory and needs to point at a valid and absolute image URL value that can be loaded.

The example demonstrates these capabilities by cycling round all three settings using a `switch` case selector.

Example code:

```
<HTML><HEAD></HEAD>
<BODY>
<SCRIPT>
var theState = 0;
// Cycle the sizingMethod property to size the image.
function changeState(oObj)
{
    switch(theState)
    {
        case 0:
        theState = 1;
        CONTAINER.filters(0).sizingMethod = "image";
        oObj.innerText = 'Scale to fit';
        break;
        case 1:
        theState = 2;
        CONTAINER.filters(0).sizingMethod = "scale";
        oObj.innerText = 'Crop to fit';
        break;
        case 2:
        theState = 0;
        CONTAINER.filters(0).sizingMethod = "crop";
        oObj.innerText = 'Normal';
        break;
    }
}
</SCRIPT>
<DIV ID="CONTAINER" STYLE="position:absolute; left:140px; height:50;
width:50;
filter:progid:DXImageTransform.Microsoft.AlphaImageLoader(src='C:\Fi
lterTests\Logo150.gif', sizingMethod='scale');" >
</DIV>
<BUTTON onclick="changeState(this);">Scale to fit</BUTTON>
</BODY>
</HTML>
```

See also:	*Filter object*, Procedural surfaces, `style.filter`

Property	JavaScript	JScript	N	IE	Opera	Notes
Enabled	-	5.5 +	-	4.0 +	-	-
SizingMethod	-	5.5 +	-	5.5 +	-	-
Src	-	5.5 +	-	5.5 +	-	-

275

filter - Barn() (Filter/transition)

A transition effect with the appearance of barn doors opening or closing.

Availability:	JScript – 5.5 Internet Explorer – 5.5
Object properties:	Duration, Enabled, Motion, Orientation, Percent, status
Object methods:	apply(), play(), stop()

The Duration property controls the time it takes to playback the transition effect.

The Enabled property provides a way to activate or inhibit the filter from working by assigning the true or false value to it.

The Motion property can use the values in or out to determine the direction that the transition moves in.

The Orientation property indicates whether the effect is applied horizontally or vertically with the values horizontal or vertical.

The Percent property controls the point at which the effect can be halted to provide a static effect. The value can be between 0 and 100.

The status value can be read to determine the current disposition of the transition filter. It will return one of three values. The 0 value indicates the transition has stopped, 1 indicates that it is completed and 2 that it is still in progress.

The apply() method sets the transition effect to its initial condition.

The play() method executes the transition effect using the control values and taking the time specified in the duration value. You can override the duration property by passing an optional duration argument to this method when it is called.

The stop() method can be called at any time during the time the transition is running to halt the transition playback. This will also trigger the execution of an onFilterChange event handler if there is one defined.

The example shows the filter being applied in a continuous time-out loop.

Example code:

```
<HTML>
<HEAD>
</HEAD>
<BODY onLoad="switchState()">
<DIV ID="CONTAINER" STYLE="position:absolute; top: 0; left: 0;
width: 300; height:300;
filter:progid:DXImageTransform.Microsoft.Barn(orientation=vertical,
motion=out) ">
```

```
<DIV ID="DIV1" STYLE="position:absolute; top:50; left:10; width:240;
height:180;background:ivory">
<BR>
<BR>
<BR>
<HR>
<CENTER>
This is a DIV block containing text.
</CENTER>
<HR>
</DIV>
<DIV ID="DIV2" STYLE="visibility:hidden; position:absolute; top:50;
left:10; width:240; height:180; background:antiquewhite; ">
<CENTER>
<BR>
<IMG SRC="./Logo150.gif">
</CENTER>
</DIV>
</DIV>
<SCRIPT>
DIV1.style.visibility = "visible";
function switchState()
{
    CONTAINER.filters[0].Apply();
    if (DIV1.style.visibility == "visible")
    {
        DIV1.style.visibility = "hidden";
        DIV2.style.visibility = "visible";
    }
    else
    {
        DIV1.style.visibility = "visible";
        DIV2.style.visibility = "hidden";
    }
    CONTAINER.filters[0].Play();
    setTimeout("switchState()", 2000);
}
</SCRIPT>
</BODY>
</HTML>
```

See also:	*filter – Iris(), filter – RandomBars(), Filter object,* `style.filter`

Property	JavaScript	JScript	N	IE	Opera	Notes
Duration	-	5.5 +	-	5.5 +	-	-
Enabled	-	3.0 +	-	4.0 +	-	-
Motion	-	5.5 +	-	5.5 +	-	-
Orientation	-	5.5 +	-	5.5 +	-	-
Percent	-	5.5 +	-	5.5 +	-	-
status	-	5.5 +	-	5.5 +	-	-

277

Method	JavaScript	JScript	N	IE	Opera	Notes
apply()	-	5.5 +	-	5.5 +	-	-
play()	-	5.5 +	-	5.5 +	-	-
stop()	-	5.5 +	-	5.5 +	-	-

filter - BasicImage() (Filter/visual)

Controls the basic image display attributes of the containing HTML Element object.

Availability:	JScript – 5.5 Internet Explorer – 5.5
Object properties:	Enabled, GrayScale, Invert, Mask, MaskColor, Mirror, Opacity, Rotation, XRay
Supported by objects:	A, ACRONYM, ADDRESS, B, BDO, BIG BLOCKQUOTE, body, BUTTON, CAPTION, CENTER, CITE, CODE, custom, DD, DFN, DIR, DIV, DL, DT, EM, FIELDSET, FONT, FORM, FRAME, FRAMESET, Hn, I, IFRAME, IMG, INPUT, INS, KBD, LABEL, LEGEND, LI, MARQUEE, MENU, NOBR, OL, P, PLAINTEXT, PRE, Q, RT, RUBY, runtimeStyle, S, SAMP, SMALL, SPAN, STRIKE, STRONG, style, SUB, SUP, TABLE, TD, TEXTAREA, TH, TT, U, UL, VAR, XMP

This filter was added for version 5.5 of MSIE and consolidates the image handling capabilities of the filters in earlier versions of the MSIE browser.

The Enabled property turns the filter on and off by assigning the true or false value to it.

The GrayScale property replaces the functionality of the GrayScale() filter. Setting it to 1 discards the color information while zero makes it inactive.

The Invert property replaces the functionality of the Invert() filter. However, note that it inverts the value in the RGB color space and not the HSV color space that the deprecated Invert() filter used to use.

The Mask property replaces the functionality of the now deprecated Mask() filter. Any pixels set to transparent will be replaced by the color defined in the MaskColor operator. This means that MaskColor must be specified when the Mask operator is used.

The Mirror property replaces the deprecated FlipH() filter. The values 0 and 1 control whether the mirror effect is applied. To reproduce the effect of the FlipV() filter, use the Rotation operator first to rotate the element by 90 degrees.

The Opacity property can accept a floating point value between 0.0 and 1.0. 0.0 is completely transparent while 1.0 is completely opaque.

The Rotation property takes a set of values to specify which of the four cardinal directions to rotate the object. The value 0 corresponds to no rotation. Angles of 90, 180 and 270 degrees are indicated by the values 1,2 and 3 respectively. This does not provide a free rotate facility. You can use it in combination with the mirroring to perform Mirror flips other than a straightforward left to right mirror.

The XRay property displays the image taking the average of the red and green values of each pixel and then inverting it. This is not quite the same as an invert on the GrayScale value. It is also different to what the earlier XRay() filter provided according to the documentation. Earlier XRay() filters were documented as providing just an edge detected outline.

The example shows an image in its normal and XRay modes.

Example code:

```
<HTML>
<HEAD>
</HEAD>
<BODY>
Normal--&gt;
<IMG ID="NORMAL" SRC="./Logo150.gif">
X-Ray--&gt;
<IMG ID="MYIMAGE" SRC="./Logo150.gif">
<BR>
<SCRIPT>
myFilter = "progid:DXImageTransform.Microsoft.BasicImage(xray=1)";

document.all.MYIMAGE.style.filter = myFilter;
</SCRIPT>
</BODY>
</HTML>
```

See also:	color value, *filter – FlipH(), filter – FlipV(), filter – Grayscale(), filter – Invert(), filter – Mask(), filter – Matrix(), filter – XRay(), Filter object,* style.filter

Property	JavaScript	JScript	N	IE	Opera	Notes
Enabled	-	3.0 +	-	4.0 +	-	-
GrayScale	-	5.5 +	-	5.5 +	-	-
Invert	-	5.5 +	-	5.5 +	-	-
Mask	-	5.5 +	-	5.5 +	-	-
MaskColor	-	5.5 +	-	5.5 +	-	-
Mirror	-	5.5 +	-	5.5 +	-	-
Opacity	-	5.5 +	-	5.5 +	-	-
Rotation	-	5.5 +	-	5.5 +	-	-
XRay	-	5.5 +	-	5.5 +	-	-

filter - BlendTrans() (Filter/blend)

A blend filter for controlling transitions.

Availability:	JScript – 3.0 Internet Explorer – 4.0
Deprecated:	Yes

This blend transition filter is used to control the fading in and out of the filtered element. This would be used to create a dissolve effect.

The duration name=value pair specifies a floating point value in seconds which controls how quickly the effect should take place.

The use of this feature is deprecated in favor of the named transitions introduced in later versions of MSIE and which can be used as static or transitional effects.

Warnings:

❑ Filters are defined in style sheets as if they were a function call with its arguments expressed as name=value pairs. This is not the typical way to define arguments so you should be aware of this anomaly when working with filters.

See also:	*filter – RevealTrans(), Filter object,* `style.filter`, Transition

filter - Blinds() (Filter/transition)

A transition effect with the appearance of venetian blinds opening or closing.

Availability:	JScript – 5.5 Internet Explorer – 5.5
Object properties:	`bands, Direction, Duration, Enabled, Percent, status`
Object methods:	`apply(), play(), stop()`

This transition effect supports the following properties:

❑ The `bands` property defines the number of strips that the blinds filter will use for its transition effect. The value should be in the range 1 to 100.

❑ The `Direction` property determines which direction the transition should proceed. It accepts the values, left, right, up or down.

❑ The `Duration` property controls the time it takes to playback the transition effect.

❏ The `Enabled` property provides a way to activate or inhibit the filter from working by assigning the true or false value to it.

❏ The `Percent` property controls the point at which the effect can be halted to provide a static effect. The value can be between 0 and 100.

❏ The `status` property value can be read to determine the current disposition of the transition filter. It will return one of three values. The 0 value indicates the transition has stopped, 1 indicates that it is completed and 2 that it is still in progress.

The following methods are supported by this transition filter:

❏ The `apply()` method sets the transition effect to its initial condition.

❏ The `play()` method executes the transition effect using the control values and taking the time specified in the duration value. You can override the duration property by passing an optional duration argument to this method when it is called.

❏ The `stop()` method can be called at any time during the time the transition is running to halt the transition playback. This will also trigger the execution of an `onFilterChange` event handler if there is one defined.

The example runs continuously in a timeout loop.

Example code:

```
<HTML>
<HEAD>
</HEAD>
<BODY onLoad="switchState()">
<DIV ID="CONTAINER" STYLE="position:absolute; top: 0; left: 0;
width: 300; height:300;
filter:progid:DXImageTransform.Microsoft.Blinds(orientation=vertical
, motion=out) ">
<DIV ID="DIV1" STYLE="position:absolute; top:50; left:10; width:240;
height:180;background:ivory">
<BR>
<BR>
<BR>
<HR>
<CENTER>
This is a DIV block containing text.
</CENTER>
<HR>
</DIV>
<DIV ID="DIV2" STYLE="visibility:hidden; position:absolute; top:50;
left:10; width:240; height:180; background:antiquewhite; ">
<CENTER>
<BR>
<IMG SRC="./Logo150.gif">
</CENTER>
</DIV>
```

```
    </DIV>
    <SCRIPT>
    DIV1.style.visibility="visible";
    function switchState()
    {
        CONTAINER.filters[0].Apply();
        if (DIV1.style.visibility == "visible")
        {
            DIV1.style.visibility="hidden";
            DIV2.style.visibility="visible";
        }
        else
        {
            DIV1.style.visibility="visible";
            DIV2.style.visibility="hidden";
        }
        CONTAINER.filters[0].Play();
        setTimeout("switchState()", 2000);
    }
    </SCRIPT>
    </BODY>
    </HTML>
```

See also: *filter – CheckerBoard(), filter – Slide(), Filter object,* `style.filter`

Property	JavaScript	JScript	N	IE	Opera	Notes
bands	-	5.5 +	-	5.5 +	-	-
Direction	-	5.5 +	-	5.5 +	-	-
Duration	-	5.5 +	-	5.5 +	-	-
Enabled	-	5.5 +	-	5.5 +	-	-
Percent	-	5.5 +	-	5.5 +	-	-
status	-	5.5 +	-	5.5 +	-	-

Method	JavaScript	JScript	N	IE	Opera	Notes
apply()	-	5.5 +	-	5.5 +	-	-
play()	-	5.5 +	-	5.5 +	-	-
stop()	-	5.5 +	-	5.5 +	-	-

filter - Blur() (Filter/visual)

A visual filter for blurring objects.

Availability:	JScript – 3.0 Internet Explorer – 4.0
Object properties:	Enabled, MakeShadow, PixelRadius, ShadowOpacity
Supported by objects:	A, ACRONYM, ADDRESS, B, BDO, BIG BLOCKQUOTE, body, BUTTON, CAPTION, CENTER, CITE, CODE, custom, DD, DFN, DIR, DIV, DL, DT, EM, FIELDSET, FONT, FORM, FRAME, FRAMEST, Hn, I, IFRAME, IMG, INPUT, INS, KBD, LABEL, LEGEND, LI, MARQUEE, MENU, NOBR, OL, P, PLAINTEXT, PRE, Q, RT, RUBY, runtimeStyle, S, SAMP, SMALL, SPAN, STRIKE, STRONG, style, SUB, SUP, TABLE, TD, TEXTAREA, TH, TT, U, UL, VAR, XMP

This visual filter provides a way of adding motion blur to elements as they are drawn into the display. Versions of the MSIE browser prior to version 5.5 implement the MotionBlur() filter as a Blur() filter.

As of the IE 5.5 browser, the Blur effect provides a simple gaussian blur which is non-directional. The Previous motion blurring artifacts is now available with a specialized MotionBlur() filter.

From version 5.5 of MSIE, the properties supported by this filter have changed to this set:

❑ The Enabled property turns the blurring effect on and off when set to true or false, respectively.

❑ The MakeShadow property allows you to select between displaying the object as a shadow, or as its normal RGB values. Set to true to get a blurred shadow effect.

❑ The PixelRadius property takes a floating point value to indicate the radius of the blurring effect. The value ranges from 1.0 to 100.0 in pixels.

❑ The ShadowOpacity property takes a floating point value in the range 0.0 to 1.0 to indicate the opacity of the blurred image. The value 0.0 is completely transparent while 1.0 is completely opaque.

The example shows how to make a blurred shadow effect.

Warnings:

❑ Filters are defined in style sheets as if they were a function call with its arguments expressed as name=value pairs. This is not the typical way to define arguments so you should be aware of this anomaly when working with filters.

Example code:

```
<HTML>
<HEAD>
</HEAD>
<BODY>
Normal--&gt;
<IMG ID="NORMAL" SRC="./Logo150.gif">
Filtered--&gt;
<IMG ID="MYIMAGE" SRC="./Logo150.gif">
<BR>
<SCRIPT>
myFilter = "progid:DXImageTransform.Microsoft.Blur(makeshadow=true,
pixelradius=5.0, shadowopacity=0.5)";
document.all.MYIMAGE.style.filter = myFilter;
</SCRIPT>
</BODY>
</HTML>
```

See also:	*filter – MotionBlur(), Filter object,* `style.filter`

Property	JavaScript	JScript	N	IE	Opera	Notes
Enabled	-	3.0 +	-	4.0 +	-	-
MakeShadow	-	3.0 +	-	4.0 +	-	Warning
PixelRadius	-	3.0 +	-	4.0 +	-	Warning
ShadowOpacity	-	3.0 +	-	4.0 +	-	Warning

filter - CheckerBoard() (Filter/transition)

A transition effect with the appearance of checkerboard blinds opening or closing.

Availability:	JScript – 5.5 Internet Explorer – 5.5
Object properties:	Direction, Duration, Enabled, SquaresX, SquaresY

This transition effect supports the following properties:

❑ The Direction property determines which direction the transition should proceed. It accepts the values, left, right, up or down.

❑ The Duration property controls the time it takes to playback the transition effect.

❑ The Enabled property provides a way to activate or inhibit the filter from working by assigning the true or false value to it.

❑ The SquaresX and SquaresY properties describe how many squares the effect should use across the content being transitioned.

The example runs in a continuous loop.

Example code:

```
<HTML>
<HEAD>
</HEAD>
<BODY onLoad="switchState()">
<DIV ID="CONTAINER" STYLE="position:absolute; top: 0; left: 0;
width: 300; height:300;
filter:progid:DXImageTransform.Microsoft.CheckerBoard(direction=left
, squaresx=10, squaresy=10) ">
<DIV ID="DIV1" STYLE="position:absolute; top:50; left:10; width:240;
height:180;background:ivory">
<BR>
<BR>
<BR>
<HR>
<CENTER>
This is a DIV block containing text.
</CENTER>
<HR>
</DIV>
<DIV ID="DIV2" STYLE="visibility:hidden; position:absolute; top:50;
left:10; width:240; height:180; background:antiquewhite; ">
<CENTER>
<BR>
<IMG SRC="./Logo150.gif">
</CENTER>
</DIV>
</DIV>
<SCRIPT>
DIV1.style.visibility="visible";
function switchState()
{
    CONTAINER.filters[0].Apply();
    if (DIV1.style.visibility == "visible")
    {
        DIV1.style.visibility="hidden";
        DIV2.style.visibility="visible";
    }
    else
    {
        DIV1.style.visibility="visible";
        DIV2.style.visibility="hidden";
    }
    CONTAINER.filters[0].Play();
    setTimeout("switchState()", 2000);
}
</SCRIPT>
</BODY>
</HTML>
```

See also: *filter – Blinds(), Filter object,* `style.filter`

F

Property	JavaScript	JScript	N	IE	Opera	Notes
Direction	-	5.5 +	-	5.5 +	-	-
Duration	-	5.5 +	-	5.5 +	-	-
Enabled	-	5.5+	-	5.5 +	-	-
SquaresX	-	5.5 +	-	5.5 +	-	-
SquaresY	-	5.5 +	-	5.5 +	-	-

filter - Chroma() (Filter/visual)

A visual filter for chroma key effects.

Availability:	JScript – 3.0 Internet Explorer – 4.0
Object properties:	Enabled, Color
Supported by objects:	A, ACRONYM, ADDRESS, B, BDO, BIG BLOCKQUOTE, body, BUTTON, CAPTION, CENTER, CITE, CODE, custom, DD, DFN, DIR, DIV, DL, DT, EM, FIELDSET, FONT, FORM, FRAME, Hn, I, IFRAME, IMG, INPUT, INS, KBD, LABEL, LEGEND, LI, MARQUEE, MENU, NOBR, OL, P, PLAINTEXT, PRE, Q, RT, RUBY, runtimeStyle, S, SAMP, SMALL, SPAN, STRIKE, STRONG, style, SUB, SUP, TABLE, TD, TEXTAREA, TH, TT, U, UL, VAR, XMP

This visual filter provides a way to define a particular color as being transparent. This is sometimes called chroma keying (a technique much used in the television industry).

The Color property defines a hex triplet value which is deemed to be transparent for this element.

Version 5.5 of the MSIE browser adds the Enabled property which controls whether the effect is applied by means of the true and false value.

The example makes black the transparent color for the image.

Warnings:

❑ Filters are defined in style sheets as if they were a function call with its arguments expressed as name=value pairs. This is not the typical way to define arguments so you should be aware of this anomaly when working with filters.

❑ This can display some unattractive visual artifacts with images that have been compressed or dithered to reduce the number of colors available. It also does not work very well round the edges of anti-aliased images.

Example code:

```
<HTML>
<HEAD>
</HEAD>
<BODY>
Normal--&gt;
<IMG ID="NORMAL" SRC="./Logo150.gif">
Filtered--&gt;
<IMG ID="MYIMAGE" SRC="./Logo150.gif">
<BR>
<SCRIPT>
myFilter =
"progid:DXImageTransform.Microsoft.Chroma(color=#000000)";
document.all.MYIMAGE.style.filter = myFilter;
</SCRIPT>
</BODY>
</HTML>
```

See also:	Filter object, style.filter

Property	JavaScript	JScript	Nav	IE	Opera	Notes
Enabled	-	3.0 +	-	4.0 +	-	-
Color	-	3.0 +	-	4.0 +	-	Warning

filter - Compositor() (Filter/visual)

As content is added to an object, it can be colored to indicate it is changed content.

Availability:	JScript – 5.5 Internet Explorer – 5.5
Object properties:	Enabled, Function
Object methods:	apply(), play()
Supported by objects:	A, ACRONYM, ADDRESS, B, BDO, BIG BLOCKQUOTE, body, BUTTON, CAPTION, CENTER, CITE, CODE, custom, DD, DFN, DIR, DIV, DL, DT, EM, FIELDSET, FONT, FORM, FRAME, FRAMESET, Hn, I, IFRAME, IMG, INPUT, INS, KBD, LABEL, LEGEND, LI, MARQUEE, MENU, NOBR, OL, P, PLAINTEXT, PRE, Q, RT, RUBY, runtimeStyle, S, SAMP, SMALL, SPAN, STRIKE, STRONG, style, SUB, SUP, TABLE, TD, TEXTAREA, TH, TT, U, UL, VAR, XMP

Although this is implemented as a transitional effect, it actually only affects the display of an HTML element in a static manner.

F

JavaScript Programmer's Reference

287

The Function property provides a way to select a rule for displaying a pixel color based on the two corresponding pixels in the previous and new image content of the HTML element being filtered.

The actual function is selected by a numeric value as follows (as described by the MSDN scripting reference information):

Code	Operation	Description
0	CLEAR	Neither pixel value displayed.
1	MIN(A, B)	Show the less bright of the two pixels.
2	MAX(A, B)	Show the brighter of the two pixels.
3	A	*Input A* shown, *Input B* ignored.
4	A OVER B	*Input A* displayed over *Input B*. All of *Input A* is visible, and *Input B* shows through translucent regions of *Input A*.
5	A IN B	Display all parts of *Input A* that are contained in *Input B*. Only regions with nonzero alpha values for both images are visible, and no part of *Input B* shows through.
6	A OUT B	Display all parts of *Input A* that are not contained in *Input B*. No part of *Input B* is displayed.
7	A ATOP B	Display *Input A* covering *Input B*, with each sample scaled by the alpha channel of *Input B*.
8	A SUBTRACT B	Display *Input A* with the sample color values of *Input B* subtracted from the corresponding sample color values of *Input A*. The resulting color is scaled by the alpha values of *Input A*.
9	A ADD B	Display *Input A* with the sample color values of *Input B* added to the corresponding sample color values of *Input A*. The resulting color value is scaled by the alpha value of *Input A*.
10	A XOR B	Display pixels of each set of input where the two images do not overlap. Pixels that overlap are scaled by their inverse alpha value.
19	B	*Input B* shown, *Input A* ignored.
20	B OVER A	*Input B* displayed over *Input A* . All of *Input B* is visible, and *Input A* shows through translucent regions of *Input B*.
21	B IN A	Display all parts of *Input B* that are contained in *Input A*. Only regions with nonzero alpha values for both images are visible, and no part of *Input A* shows through.
22	B OUT A	Display all parts of *Input B* that are not contained in *Input A*. No part of *Input A* is displayed.

288

Code	Operation	Description
23	B ATOP A	Display *Input B* over *Input A*, with each sample scaled by the alpha channel of *Input A*.
24	B SUBTRACT A	Display *Input B* with the sample color values of *Input A* subtracted from the corresponding sample color values of *Input B*. The resulting color is scaled by the alpha values of *Input B*.
25	B ADD A	Display *Input B* with the sample color values of *Input A* added to the corresponding sample color values of *Input B*. The resulting color value is scaled by the alpha value of *Input B*.

The apply() method should be executed on the filter object to capture the initial (*state A*) image pixel map. Then the play() method can be applied after some changes have taken place. At this point the *state B* image can be determined and compared with the *state A* image.

Example code:

```
<HTML>
<HEAD>
</HEAD>
<BODY bgcolor=gray onload="loader()">
<BUTTON onClick="filterThing()">Click me</BUTTON>
<BR>
<DIV ID="CONTAINER"
STYLE="filter:progid:DXImageTransform.Microsoft.Compositor(function=
20); position:absolute; height:300; width:300">
<IMG SRC="./Logo150.gif" STYLE="position:absolute; left:50;
top:50;">
</DIV>
<SCRIPT>
function loader()
{
    CONTAINER.filters.item(0).Apply();
    CONTAINER.innerHTML = HIDDEN.innerHTML;
    CONTAINER.filters.item(0).Play();
}
function filterThing()
{
    CONTAINER.filters.item('DXImageTransform.Microsoft.Compositor')
.Function = 2;
}
</SCRIPT>
<DIV ID="HIDDEN" STYLE="display:none">
<IMG SRC="./Logo150.gif" STYLE="position:absolute; left:50;
top:50;">
<IMG SRC="./Logo150.gif" STYLE="position:absolute; left:70;
top:70;">
</DIV>
</BODY>
</HTML>
```

| See also: | Filter object, style.filter |

Property	JavaScript	JScript	N	IE	Opera	Notes
Enabled	-	5.5 +	-	5.5 +	-	-
Function	-	5.5 +	-	5.5 +	-	-

Method	JavaScript	JScript	N	IE	Opera	Notes
apply()	-	5.5 +	-	5.5 +	-	-
play()	-	5.5 +	-	5.5 +	-	-

filter - DropShadow() (Filter/visual)

A visual filter for creating drop shadows.

Availability:	JScript – 3.0 Internet Explorer – 4.0
Object properties:	Enabled, OffX, OffY, Positive , Color
Supported by objects:	A, ACRONYM, ADDRESS, B, BDO, BIG BLOCKQUOTE, body, BUTTON, CAPTION, CENTER, CITE, CODE, custom, DD, DFN, DIR, DIV, DL, DT, EM, FIELDSET, FONT, FORM, FRAME, Hn, I, IFRAME, IMG, INPUT, INS, KBD, LABEL, LEGEND, LI, MARQUEE, MENU, NOBR, OL, P, PLAINTEXT, PRE, Q, RT, RUBY, runtimeStyle, S, SAMP, SMALL, SPAN, STRIKE, STRONG, style, SUB, SUP, TABLE, TD, TEXTAREA, TH, TT, U, UL, VAR, XMP

This visual filter creates drop shadow effects. These are quite useful for lifting control elements out of the page to make them more readily visible.

The following properties are supported:

❑ The Enabled property was added at version 5.5 of MSIE to implement a consistent way of enabling/disabling filters by means of its true or false setting.

❑ The offx and offy properties define the magnitude and direction of the dropshadow.

❑ The positive property specifies whether all pixels or only visible pixels generate a drop shadow. Setting this value to 0 applies a shadow based on every pixel in the element. A value of 1 only shadows non-transparent pixels.

❑ The Color property provides a way to determine the drop shadow color. This is not available on earlier versions of the MSIE browser.

The example shows the effect of adding a drop shadow to an image. In this example, you will see that the shadow has a hard edge created by a point source of light – you may want to use the Blur filter to provide a more natural effect with soft edges.

Warnings:

❑ Filters are defined in style sheets as if they were a function call with its arguments expressed as name=value pairs. This is not the typical way to define arguments so you should be aware of this anomaly when working with filters.

Example code:

```
<HTML>
<HEAD>
</HEAD>
<BODY>
Normal--&gt;
<IMG ID="NORMAL" SRC="./Logo150.gif">
Filtered--&gt;
<IMG ID="MYIMAGE" SRC="./Logo150.gif">
<BR>
<SCRIPT>
myFilter = "progid:DXImageTransform.Microsoft.DropShadow(offx=10,
offy=10, positive=1, color=gray)";
document.all.MYIMAGE.style.filter = myFilter;
</SCRIPT>
</BODY>
</HTML>
```

See also:	color value, *Filter object*, style.filter

Property	JavaScript	JScript	N	IE	Opera	Notes
Enabled	-	3.0 +	-	4.0 +	-	-
OffX	-	3.0 +	-	4.0 +	-	Warning
OffY	-	3.0 +	-	4.0 +	-	Warning
Positive	-	3.0 +	-	4.0 +	-	Warning
Color	-	3.0 +	-	4.0 +	-	Warning

filter - Emboss() (Filter/visual)

Displays the image content of the HTML element as if it were an embossed effect.

Availability:	JScript – 5.5 Internet Explorer – 5.5
Object properties:	Enabled, Bias
Supported by objects:	A, ACRONYM, ADDRESS, B, BDO, BIG BLOCKQUOTE, body, BUTTON, CAPTION, CENTER, CITE, CODE, custom, DD, DFN, DIR, DIV, DL, DT, EM, FIELDSET, FONT, FORM, FRAME, FRAMESET, Hn, I, IFRAME, IMG, INPUT, INS, KBD, LABEL, LEGEND, LI, MARQUEE, MENU, NOBR, OL, P, PLAINTEXT, PRE, Q, RT, RUBY, runtimeStyle, S, SAMP, SMALL, SPAN, STRIKE, STRONG, style, SUB, SUP, TABLE, TD, TEXTAREA, TH, TT, U, UL, VAR, XMP

The grayscale values of the image are used as a height map, and an image is generated by using this height map with a light source to cast a shadow. The result is a grayscale image.

The following properties are supported:

❑ The `Enabled` property can be set to true or false to switch the filter on or off.

❑ The `Bias` property controls an intensity level that is added to the brightness of the embossed filter output. The value can range from -1.0 to 1.0 with brighter images as the value becomes more positive.

The example shows the application of an Emboss filter to an image. However when running tests, the `Bias` value did not seem to have any visible effect on MSIE 5.5 running on Windows 98.

Example code:

```
<HTML>
<HEAD>
</HEAD>
<BODY>
Normal--&gt;
<IMG ID="NORMAL" SRC="./Logo150.gif">
Filtered--&gt;
<IMG ID="MYIMAGE" SRC="./Logo150.gif">
<BR>
<SCRIPT>
myFilter = "progid:DXImageTransform.Microsoft.Emboss()";
document.all.MYIMAGE.style.filter = myFilter;
</SCRIPT>
</BODY>
</HTML>
```

See also:	filter – Engrave(), Filter object, `style.filter`

Property	JavaScript	JScript	N	IE	Opera	Notes
Enabled	-	5.5 +	-	5.5 +	-	-
Bias	-	5.5 +	-	5.5 +	-	-

filter - Engrave() (Filter/visual)

An effect that is the opposite of the embossed image appearance.

Availability:	JScript – 5.5 Internet Explorer – 5.5
Object properties:	Enabled, Bias

Supported by objects:	A, ACRONYM, ADDRESS, B, BDO, BIG BLOCKQUOTE, body, BUTTON, CAPTION, CENTER, CITE, CODE, custom, DD, DFN, DIR, DIV, DL, DT, EM, FIELDSET, FONT, FORM, FRAME, FRAMESST, Hn, I, IFRAME, IMG, INPUT, INS, KBD, LABEL, LEGEND, LI, MARQUEE, MENU, NOBR, OL, P, PLAINTEXT, PRE, Q, RT, RUBY, runtimeStyle, S, SAMP, SMALL, SPAN, STRIKE, STRONG, style, SUB, SUP, TABLE, TD, TEXTAREA, TH, TT, U, UL, VAR, XMP

This filter operates in a similar way to the Emboss() filter. In this case, the height information is inverted giving the effect of an engraved image.

The following properties are supported:

❑ The Enabled property can be set to true or false to switch the filter on or off.

❑ The Bias property controls an intensity level that is added to the brightness of the engraved filter output. The value can range from -1.0 to 1.0 with brighter images as the value becomes more positive.

The example shows the application of an Engrave filter to an image. However when running tests, the Bias value did not seem to have any visible effect on MSIE 5.5 running on Windows 98.

Example code:

```
<HTML>
<HEAD>
</HEAD>
<BODY>
Normal--&gt;
<IMG ID="NORMAL" SRC="./Logo150.gif">
Filtered--&gt;
<IMG ID="MYIMAGE" SRC="./Logo150.gif">
<BR>
<SCRIPT>
myFilter = "progid:DXImageTransform.Microsoft.Engrave()";
document.all.MYIMAGE.style.filter = myFilter;
</SCRIPT>
</BODY>
</HTML>
```

See also:	*filter – Emboss(), Filter object,* style.filter

Property	JavaScript	JScript	N	IE	Opera	Notes
Enabled	-	5.5 +	-	5.5 +	-	-
Bias	-	5.5 +	-	5.5 +	-	-

filter - Fade() (Filter/transition)

A transition effect with the appearance of a dissolve between two images.

Availability:	JScript – 5.5 Internet Explorer – 5.5
Object properties:	Duration, Enabled, Overlap, Percent, status
Object methods:	apply(), play(), stop()

This transition effect supports the following properties:

❑ The Duration property controls the time it takes to playback the transition effect.

❑ The Enabled property provides a way to activate or inhibit the filter from working by assigning the true or false value to it.

❑ The Overlap property is a floating point value from 0.0 to 1.0 that determines what proportion of the duration time both images should be partially visible.

❑ The Percent property controls the point at which the effect can be halted to provide a static effect. The value can be between 0 and 100.

❑ The status property value can be read to determine the current disposition of the transition filter. It will return one of three values. The 0 value indicates the transition has stopped, 1 indicates that it is completed and 2 that it is still in progress.

The following methods are supported by this transition filter:

❑ The apply() method sets the transition effect to its initial condition.

❑ The play() method executes the transition effect using the control values and taking the time specified in the duration value. You can override the duration property by passing an optional duration argument to this method when it is called.

❑ The stop() method can be called at any time during the time the transition is running to halt the transition playback. This will also trigger the execution of an onFilterChange event handler if there is one defined.

The example runs in a continuous loop.

Example code:

```
<HTML>
<HEAD>
</HEAD>
<BODY onLoad="switchState()">
```

```
<DIV ID="CONTAINER" STYLE="position:absolute; top: 0; left: 0;
width: 300; height:300;
filter:progid:DXImageTransform.Microsoft.Fade(duration=5, overlap=2)
">
<DIV ID="DIV1" STYLE="position:absolute; top:50; left:10; width:240;
height:180;background:ivory">
<BR>
<BR>
<BR>
<HR>
<CENTER>
This is a DIV block containing text.
</CENTER>
<HR>
</DIV>
<DIV ID="DIV2" STYLE="visibility:hidden; position:absolute; top:50;
left:10; width:240; height:180; background:antiquewhite; ">
<CENTER>
<BR>
<IMG SRC="./Logo150.gif">
</CENTER>
</DIV>
</DIV>
<SCRIPT>
DIV1.style.visibility="visible";
function switchState()
{
   CONTAINER.filters[0].Apply();
   if (DIV1.style.visibility == "visible")
   {
      DIV1.style.visibility="hidden";
      DIV2.style.visibility="visible";
   }
   else
   {
      DIV1.style.visibility="visible";
      DIV2.style.visibility="hidden";
   }
   CONTAINER.filters[0].Play();
   setTimeout("switchState()", 2000);
}
</SCRIPT>
</BODY>
</HTML>
```

See also:	*Filter object,* style.filter

Property	JavaScript	JScript	N	IE	Opera	Notes
Duration	-	5.5 +	-	5.5 +	-	-
Enabled	-	5.5 +	-	5.5 +	-	-
Overlap	-	5.5 +	-	5.5 +	-	-
Percent	-	5.5 +	-	5.5 +	-	-
status	-	5.5 +	-	5.5 +	-	-

Method	JavaScript	JScript	N	IE	Opera	Notes
apply()	-	5.5 +	-	5.5 +	-	-
play()	-	5.5 +	-	5.5 +	-	-
stop()	-	5.5 +	-	5.5 +	-	-

filter - FlipH() (Filter/visual)

A visual filter for horizontal mirror effects.

Availability:	JScript – 3.0 Internet Explorer – 4.0
Deprecated:	Yes

This visual filter is used for creating symmetrically mirrored copies of an element flipped on the horizontal axis. There are no properties to use with it.

The use of this filter is now deprecated in favor of the BasicImage() filter that was implemented with the IE 5.5 browser. You can also use the Matrix() filter in place of this.

Warnings:

❑ Filters are defined in style sheets as if they were a function call with its arguments expressed as name=value pairs. This is not the typical way to define arguments so you should be aware of this anomaly when working with filters.

See also:	filter – BasicImage(), filter – Matrix(), Filter object, style.filter

filter - FlipV() (Filter/visual)

A visual filter for vertical mirror effects.

Availability:	JScript – 3.0 Internet Explorer – 4.0
Deprecated:	Yes

This visual filter is used for creating symmetrically mirrored copies of an element flipped on the vertical axis. There are no properties to use with it.

The use of this filter is now deprecated in favor of the BasicImage() filter that was implemented with the IE 5.5 browser. You can also use the Matrix() filter in place of this.

Warnings:

❑ Filters are defined in style sheets as if they were a function call with its arguments expressed as name=value pairs. This is not the typical way to define arguments so you should be aware of this anomaly when working with filters.

See also:	*filter – BasicImage()*, *filter – Matrix()*, *Filter object*, `style.filter`

filter - Glow() (Filter/visual)

A visual filter for adding a glow effect.

Availability:	JScript – 3.0 Internet Explorer – 4.0
Object properties:	`Enabled, Color, Strength`
Supported by objects:	A, ACRONYM, ADDRESS, B, BDO, BIG BLOCKQUOTE, body, BUTTON, CAPTION, CENTER, CITE, CODE, custom, DD, DFN, DIR, DIV, DL, DT, EM, FIELDSET, FONT, FORM, FRAME, Hn, I, IFRAME, IMG, INPUT, INS, KBD, LABEL, LEGEND, LI, MARQUEE, MENU, NOBR, OL, P, PLAINTEXT, PRE, Q, RT, RUBY, runtimeStyle, S, SAMP, SMALL, SPAN, STRIKE, STRONG, style, SUB, SUP, TABLE, TD, TEXTAREA, TH, TT, U, UL, VAR, XMP

This visual filter adds a glow effect surrounding the filtered element.

The following properties are supported:

❑ The Enabled property was added for version 5.5 of MSIE to provide a consistent interface for controlling whether a filter is active. It takes the values true or false to enable or disable the filter.

❑ The color property defines the color value for the glow.

❑ The strength property sets the intensity of the glow with a value from 1 to 255.

The glow effect is demonstrated in the example.

Warnings:

❑ Filters are defined in style sheets as if they were a function call with its arguments expressed as name=value pairs. This is not the typical way to define arguments so you should be aware of this anomaly when working with filters.

Example code:

```
<HTML>
<HEAD>
</HEAD>
<BODY>
Normal--&gt;
<IMG ID="NORMAL" SRC="./Logo150.gif">
Filtered--&gt;
<IMG ID="MYIMAGE" SRC="./Logo150.gif">
<BR>
<SCRIPT>
myFilter = "progid:DXImageTransform.Microsoft.Glow(color=lightgreen,
strength=20)";
document.all.MYIMAGE.style.filter = myFilter;
</SCRIPT>
</BODY>
</HTML>
```

See also:	*Filter object,* `style.filter`

Property	JavaScript	JScript	N	IE	Opera	Notes
Enabled	-	3.0 +	-	4.0 +	-	-
Color	-	3.0 +	-	4.0 +	-	Warning
Strength	-	3.0 +	-	4.0 +	-	Warning

filter - Gradient() (Filter/procedural)

A procedural definition of a gradient effect.

Availability:	JScript – 5.5 Internet Explorer – 5.5
Object properties:	Enabled, StartColor, StartColorStr, EndColor, EndColorStr, GradientType
Supported by objects:	A, ACRONYM, ADDRESS, B, BDO, BIG BLOCKQUOTE, body, BUTTON, CAPTION, CENTER, CITE, CODE, custom, DD, DFN, DIR, DIV, DL, DT, EM, FIELDSET, FONT, FORM, FRAME, FRAMESET, Hn, I, IFRAME, IMG, INPUT, INS, KBD, LABEL, LEGEND, LI, MARQUEE, MENU, NOBR, OL, P, PLAINTEXT, PRE, Q, RT, RUBY, runtimeStyle, S, SAMP, SMALL, SPAN, STRIKE, STRONG, style, SUB, SUP, TABLE, TD, TEXTAREA, TH, TT, U, UL, VAR, XMP

The following properties can be used with this filter:

❏ The `Enabled` property can be set to true or false to control whether the Gradient() is used or not.

❏ The `StartColor` and `EndColor` properties can be specified as a 32 bit integer in decimal or hexadecimal notation. The extra 8 bits of information specify an alpha channel blending effect.

❏ The `GradientType` property selects the kind of gradient to apply. It simply controls the orientation of the gradient. A zero value specifies a vertical gradient while the 1 value specifies a horizontal gradient.

The example shows how to enable the gradient and select its direction interactively.

The `StartColorStr` and `EndColorStr` properties can be specified as a hexadecimal color value string including the alpha channel value. Color names may not work properly.

You should use `StartColor` or `StartColorStr` and `EndColor` or `EndColorStr` according to how you want to specify the start and end colors. This is another example of where the MSIE browser syntax breaks with the traditional color naming conventions and goes off in another direction. This lack of consistency even within a browser makes it more difficult for beginners to learn how to use these features.

Example code:

```
<HTML><HEAD></HEAD>
<BODY>
<SCRIPT>
var theState = 0;
var theGradientType = 0;
function selectGradientType()
{
    theGradientType = (theGradientType + 1) % 2;
    CONTAINER.filters(0).GradientType = theGradientType;
}

function switchState(anObject)
{
    switch(theState)
    {
        case 0:
            theState = 1;
            CONTAINER.filters(0).enabled = "true";
            anObject.innerText = 'Remove effect';
            break;
        case 1:
            theState = 0;
            CONTAINER.filters(0).enabled = "false";
            anObject.innerText = 'Apply effect';
```

299

```
            break;
        }
    }
</SCRIPT>
<BUTTON onclick="switchState(this);">Apply effect</BUTTON>
<BR>
<BUTTON onclick="selectGradientType();">Next style</BUTTON>
<BR>
<DIV ID="CONTAINER" STYLE="position:absolute; left:140px;
height:250; width:250;
filter:progid:DXImageTransform.Microsoft.Gradient(enabled='false',
startColorStr='#FF0000FF', endColorStr='#00FFFF00',
GradientType=0);">
<CENTER><BR><BR><BR>
<IMG SRC="./Logo150.gif">
</CENTER>
</DIV>
</BODY>
</HTML>
```

See also:	color value, *Filter object*, Procedural surfaces, `style.filter`

Property	JavaScript	JScript	N	IE	Opera	Notes
Enabled	-	5.5 +	-	5.5 +	-	-
StartColor	-	5.5 +	-	5.5 +	-	-
StartColorStr	-	5.5 +	-	5.5 +	-	-
EndColor	-	5.5 +	-	5.5 +	-	-
EndColorStr	-	5.5 +	-	5.5 +	-	-
GradientType	-	5.5 +	-	5.5 +	-	-

filter - GradientWipe() (Filter/transition)

A transition effect with the appearance of a wipe with a soft edge.

Availability:	JScript – 5.5 Internet Explorer – 5.5
Object properties:	Duration, Enabled, GradientSize, Motion, Percent, status, WipeStyle
Object methods:	apply(), play(), stop()

This transition effect supports the following properties:

❑ The Duration property controls the time it takes to playback the transition effect.

❑ The Enabled property provides a way to activate or inhibit the filter from working by assigning the true or false value to it.

❏ The GradientSize property indicates what proportion of the object is covered by the gradient band. The value is in the range 0.0 to 1.0 and is a floating point value.

❏ The Motion property can be defined as forward or reverse to indicate the direction of the transition.

❏ The Percent property controls the point at which the effect can be halted to provide a static effect. The value can be between 0 and 100.

❏ The status property value can be read to determine the current disposition of the transition filter. It will return one of three values. The 0 value indicates the transition has stopped, 1 indicates that it is completed and 2 that it is still in progress.

❏ The WipeStyle property is an integer value to determine which direction the gradient wipe travels. The value 0 selects a horizontal wipe while the value 1 selects a vertical wipe.

The following methods are supported by this transition filter:

❏ The apply() method sets the transition effect to its initial condition.

❏ The play() method executes the transition effect using the control values and taking the time specified in the duration value. You can override the duration property by passing an optional duration argument to this method when it is called.

❏ The stop() method can be called at any time during the time the transition is running to halt the transition playback. This will also trigger the execution of an onFilterChange event handler if there is one defined.

The example runs in a continuous loop. Note that you should ensure the loop is at least long enough to cope with the effect duration otherwise a jerky transition will result.

Example code:

```
<HTML>
<HEAD>
</HEAD>
<BODY onLoad="switchState()">
<DIV ID="CONTAINER" STYLE="position:absolute; top: 0; left: 0;
width: 300; height:300;
filter:progid:DXImageTransform.Microsoft.GradientWipe(duration=5,
gradientsize=0.4, motion=forward, wipestyle=0) ">
<DIV ID="DIV1" STYLE="position:absolute; top:50; left:10; width:240;
height:180;background:ivory">
<BR>
<BR>
<BR>
<HR>
<CENTER>
This is a DIV block containing text.
```

```
</CENTER>
<HR>
</DIV>
<DIV ID="DIV2" STYLE="visibility:hidden; position:absolute; top:50;
left:10; width:240; height:180; background:antiquewhite; "><CENTER>
<BR>
<IMG SRC="./Logo150.gif">
</CENTER>
</DIV>
</DIV>
<SCRIPT>
DIV1.style.visibility="visible";
function switchState()
{
   CONTAINER.filters[0].Apply();
   if (DIV1.style.visibility == "visible")
   {
      DIV1.style.visibility="hidden";
      DIV2.style.visibility="visible";
   }
   else
   {
      DIV1.style.visibility="visible";
      DIV2.style.visibility="hidden";
   }
   CONTAINER.filters[0].Play();
   setTimeout("switchState()", 7000);
}
</SCRIPT>
</BODY>
</HTML>
```

See also:	*Filter object*, `style.filter`

Property	JavaScript	JScript	N	IE	Opera	Notes
Duration	-	5.5 +	-	5.5 +	-	-
Enabled	-	5.5 +	-	5.5 +	-	-
GradientSize	-	5.5 +	-	5.5 +	-	-
Motion	-	5.5 +	-	5.5 +	-	-
Percent	-	5.5 +	-	5.5 +	-	-
status	-	5.5 +	-	5.5 +	-	-
WipeStyle	-	5.5 +	-	5.5 +	-	-

Method	JavaScript	JScript	N	IE	Opera	Notes
apply()	-	5.5 +	-	5.5 +	-	-
play()	-	5.5 +	-	5.5 +	-	-
stop()	-	5.5 +	-	5.5 +	-	-

filter - Grayscale() (Filter/visual)

A visual filter for converting to a grayscale appearance.

Availability:	JScript – 3.0 Internet Explorer – 4.0
Deprecated:	Yes

This visual filter removes all color information from the filtered element and displays it in grayscale mode only. There are no properties associated with it.

The use of this filter is now deprecated in favor of the `BasicImage()` filter that was implemented with the IE 5.5 browser.

Warnings:

❑ Filters are defined in style sheets as if they were a function call with its arguments expressed as name=value pairs. This is not the typical way to define arguments so you should be aware of this anomaly when working with filters.

See also:	*filter – BasicImage(), Filter object,* `style.filter`

filter - Inset() (Filter/transition)

A diagonal wipe across the image revealing the new image.

Availability:	JScript – 5.5 Internet Explorer – 5.5
Object properties:	`Duration, Enabled, Percent, status`
Object methods:	`apply(), play(), stop()`

This transition effect supports the following properties:

❑ The `Duration` property controls the time it takes to playback the transition effect.

❑ The `Enabled` property provides a way to activate or inhibit the filter from working by assigning the true or false value to it.

❑ The `Percent` property controls the point at which the effect can be halted to provide a static effect. The value can be between 0 and 100.

❑ The `status` property value can be read to determine the current disposition of the transition filter. It will return one of three values. The 0 value indicates the transition has stopped, 1 indicates that it is completed and 2 that it is still in progress.

F

The following methods are supported by this transition filter:

❑ The apply() method sets the transition effect to its initial condition.

❑ The play() method executes the transition effect using the control values and taking the time specified in the duration value. You can override the duration property by passing an optional duration argument to this method when it is called.

❑ The stop() method can be called at any time during the time the transition is running to halt the transition playback. This will also trigger the execution of an onFilterChange event handler if there is one defined.

There do not appear to be any values that control the direction of the inset which wipes diagonally rightwards and downwards. The example shows how to apply this in a cyclic manner.

Example code:

```
<HTML>
<HEAD>
</HEAD>
<BODY onLoad="switchState()">
<DIV ID="CONTAINER" STYLE="position:absolute; top: 0; left: 0;
width: 300; height:300;
filter:progid:DXImageTransform.Microsoft.Inset(duration=2) ">
<DIV ID="DIV1" STYLE="position:absolute; top:50; left:10; width:240;
height:180;background:ivory">
<BR>
<BR>
<BR>
<HR>
<CENTER>
This is a DIV block containing text.
</CENTER>
<HR>
</DIV>
<DIV ID="DIV2" STYLE="visibility:hidden; position:absolute; top:50;
left:10; width:240; height:180; background:antiquewhite; ">
<CENTER>
<BR>
<IMG SRC="./Logo150.gif">
</CENTER>
</DIV>
</DIV>
<SCRIPT>
DIV1.style.visibility="visible";
function switchState()
{
    CONTAINER.filters[0].Apply();
    if (DIV1.style.visibility == "visible")
    {
        DIV1.style.visibility="hidden";
        DIV2.style.visibility="visible";
```

```
    }
    else
    {
        DIV1.style.visibility="visible";
        DIV2.style.visibility="hidden";
    }
    CONTAINER.filters[0].Play();
    setTimeout("switchState()", 7000);
}
</SCRIPT>
</BODY>
</HTML>
```

See also:	*Filter object,* `style.filter`

Property	JavaScript	JScript	N	IE	Opera	Notes
Duration	-	5.5 +	-	5.5 +	-	-
Enabled	-	5.5 +	-	5.5 +	-	-
Percent	-	5.5 +	-	5.5 +	-	-
status	-	5.5 +	-	5.5 +	-	-

Method	JavaScript	JScript	N	IE	Opera	Notes
apply()	-	5.5 +	-	5.5 +	-	-
play()	-	5.5 +	-	5.5 +	-	-
stop()	-	5.5 +	-	5.5 +	-	-

filter - Invert() (Filter/visual)

A visual filter for inverting image colors.

Availability:	JScript – 3.0 Internet Explorer – 4.0
Deprecated:	Yes

This visual filter inverts the color value of every pixel in the filtered element.

There are several color models that could be used for this. The display is based around the RGB model and a printout would use the CMY or CMYK model. Inverting either of these would yield a different effect.

So, the browser will invert the colors using the HSV model. This should work consistently across all display mediums.

HSV stands for Hue, Saturation, and Value (which means brightness or luminosity in most cases).

The Hue value is represented by a color wheel where the colors are specified on an angular basis from 0 to 360 degrees. Opposite sides of the wheel yield complementary colors.

The Saturation value defines the amount of color. No color at all yields a purely grayscale appearance.

The Value or lightness axis defines how bright the pixel is.

So, inverting a pixel using HSV will perform these operations on discrete components of the color value:-

❑ Switch the color to one that is 180 degrees round the color wheel.

❑ Complement the saturation value. Unsaturated pixels become saturated and vice versa.

❑ Lightness is complemented making dark pixels light and vice versa.

Using this model to invert the pixels in an element should make it stand out clearly against a background.

There are no properties defined for this filter at present.

The use of this filter is now deprecated in favor of the `BasicImage()` filter that was implemented with the IE 5.5 browser.

Warnings:

❑ Filters are defined in style sheets as if they were a function call with its arguments expressed as `name=value` pairs. This is not the typical way to define arguments so you should be aware of this anomaly when working with filters.

See also:	*filter – BasicImage(), Filter object,* `style.filter`

filter - Iris() (Filter/transition)

A transition effect with the appearance of an iris opening or closing.

Availability:	JScript – 5.5 Internet Explorer – 5.5
Object properties:	`Duration, Enabled, IrisStyle, Motion, Percent, status`
Object methods:	`apply(), play(), stop()`

This transition effect supports the following properties:

❑ The `Duration` property controls the time it takes to playback the transition effect.

❑ The `Enabled` property provides a way to activate or inhibit the filter from working by assigning the true or false value to it.

❑ The `IrisStyle` property is used to define the shape of the iris that is opened or closed. It can be one of DIAMOND, CIRCLE, CROSS, PLUS, SQUARE or STAR.

❑ The `Motion` property can use the values in or out to determine the direction that the transition moves in.

❑ The `Percent` property controls the point at which the effect can be halted to provide a static effect. The value can be between 0 and 100.

❑ The `status` property value can be read to determine the current disposition of the transition filter. It will return one of three values. The 0 value indicates the transition has stopped, 1 indicates that it is completed and 2 that it is still in progress.

The following methods are supported by this transition filter:

❑ The `apply()` method sets the transition effect to its initial condition.

❑ The `play()` method executes the transition effect using the control values and taking the time specified in the duration value. You can override the duration property by passing an optional duration argument to this method when it is called.

❑ The `stop()` method can be called at any time during the time the transition is running to halt the transition playback. This will also trigger the execution of an `onFilterChange` event handler if there is one defined.

The example shows how to call this effect using a continuous loop.

Example code:

```
<HTML>
<HEAD>
</HEAD>
<BODY onLoad="switchState()">
<DIV ID="CONTAINER" STYLE="position:absolute; top: 0; left: 0;
width: 300; height:300;
filter:progid:DXImageTransform.Microsoft.Iris(duration=2,
motion=out, irisstyle=cross) ">
<DIV ID="DIV1" STYLE="position:absolute; top:50; left:10; width:240;
height:180;background:ivory">
<BR>
<BR>
<BR>
<HR>
<CENTER>
This is a DIV block containing text.
```

JavaScript Programmer's Reference

F

```
</CENTER>
<HR>
</DIV>
<DIV ID="DIV2" STYLE="visibility:hidden; position:absolute; top:50;
left:10; width:240; height:180; background:antiquewhite; ">
<CENTER>
<BR>
<IMG SRC="./Logo150.gif">
</CENTER>
</DIV>
</DIV>
<SCRIPT>
DIV1.style.visibility="visible";
function switchState()
{
   CONTAINER.filters[0].Apply();
   if (DIV1.style.visibility == "visible")
   {
      DIV1.style.visibility="hidden";
      DIV2.style.visibility="visible";
   }
   else
   {
      DIV1.style.visibility="visible";
      DIV2.style.visibility="hidden";
   }
   CONTAINER.filters[0].Play();
   setTimeout("switchState()", 5000);
}
</SCRIPT>
</BODY>
</HTML>
```

See also:	*filter – Barn()*, *Filter object*, `style.filter`

Property	JavaScript	JScript	N	IE	Opera	Notes
Duration	-	5.5 +	-	5.5 +	-	-
Enabled	-	5.5 +	-	5.5 +	-	-
IrisStyle	-	5.5 +	-	5.5 +	-	-
Motion	-	5.5 +	-	5.5 +	-	-
Percent	-	5.5 +	-	5.5 +	-	-
status	-	5.5 +	-	5.5 +	-	-

Method	JavaScript	JScript	N	IE	Opera	Notes
apply()	-	5.5 +	-	5.5 +	-	-
play()	-	5.5 +	-	5.5 +	-	-
stop()	-	5.5 +	-	5.5 +	-	-

filter - Light() (Filter/visual)

A visual filter for simulating a lighting model.

Availability:	JScript – 3.0 Internet Explorer – 4.0
Object properties:	Enabled
Object methods:	clear(), addAmbient(), addCone(), addPoint(), changeColor(), changeStrength(), moveLight()
Supported by objects:	A, ACRONYM, ADDRESS, B, BDO, BIG BLOCKQUOTE, body, BUTTON, CAPTION, CENTER, CITE, CODE, custom, DD, DFN, DIR, DIV, DL, DT, EM, FIELDSET, FONT, FORM, FRAME, Hn, I, IFRAME, IMG, INPUT, INS, KBD, LABEL, LEGEND, LI, MARQUEE, MENU, NOBR, OL, P, PLAINTEXT, PRE, Q, RT, RUBY, runtimeStyle, S, SAMP, SMALL, SPAN, STRIKE, STRONG, style, SUB, SUP, TABLE, TD, TEXTAREA, TH, TT, U, UL, VAR, XMP

This visual filter simulates the effect of a light source being played on the element.

The Enabled property is supported – it was added for version 5.5 of MSIE to provided a consistent way of controlling whether a filter was active or not.

There are also methods for defining the type of light source, the location of it, and its intensity. The light source color can also be specified. These methods are supported:

❑ The clear() method removes all currently defined light sources. It has no parameters. You should stack your light sources with this being the first one unless you want to accumulate the lighting effects during any dynamic updating.

❑ The addAmbient() method is used to add another ambient light source. The red, green, blue and strength parameter values describe its lighting properties. The parameters are presented in this order:

   ❑ Red intensity

   ❑ Green intensity

   ❑ Blue intensity

   ❑ Strength

❑ The addCone() method is used to to describe a directional light source. Its parameters include a description of the beam direction and spread. The parameters are presented in this order:

   ❑ Left coordinate of the light source

   ❑ Top coordinate of the light source

- ❏ Z-axis level of the light source
- ❏ Left coordinate of the target light focus
- ❏ Top coordinate of the target light focus
- ❏ Red intensity
- ❏ Green intensity
- ❏ Blue intensity
- ❏ Strength
- ❏ Spread

❏ The addPoint() method is used to describe a point light source. The parameters are presented in this order:

- ❏ Left coordinate of the light source
- ❏ Top coordinate of the light source
- ❏ Z-axis level of the light source
- ❏ Red intensity
- ❏ Green intensity
- ❏ Blue intensity
- ❏ Strength

❏ The color of a light source can be changed by calling the changeColor() method. The parameters are presented in this order:

- ❏ Light number
- ❏ Red intensity
- ❏ Green intensity
- ❏ Blue intensity
- ❏ Replace or accumulate color flag

❏ The intensity of the light impinging on the object can be modified for each light source with the changeStrength() method. The parameters are presented in this order:

- ❏ Light number
- ❏ Strength value
- ❏ Replace or accumulate strength flag

❏ The location of a light source can be modified with the moveLight() method. The parameters are presented in this order:

- ❏ Light number

- Left coordinate of the light source

- Top coordinate of the light source

- Z-axis level of the light source

- Relative or absolute move flag

The example demonstrates how several light sources can be combined and then moved in a mouseMove event loop to simulate the effect of a torchlight in a darkened room. The clear() function is necessary to avoid the light sources simply accumulating a lighting effect with each mouse move. The ambient light source raises the background illumination to a dull grey.

Warnings:

- Filters are defined in style sheets as if they were a function call with its arguments expressed as name=value pairs. This is not the typical way to define arguments so you should be aware of this anomaly when working with filters.

Example code:

```
<HTML>
<HEAD>
<STYLE>
.aFilter
{
    background-color:#FFFFFF;
    filter:light();
    position:absolute;
    top: 100;
    left: 100;
    color: cyan;
    height: 250;
    width: 250;
}
</STYLE>
</HEAD>
<BODY onMouseMove="myHandler()">
<DIV ID="EXAMPLE" CLASS="aFilter">
<BR><BR><BR>
<CENTER>
This text is highlighted<BR>
with a light source.
</CENTER>
</DIV>
<SCRIPT>
function myHandler()
{
    myLightX = 125;
    myLightY = 125;
    myLightZ = 1;
    myTargetX = event.x;
    myTargetY = event.y;
```

```
        myRed = 200;
        myGreen = 64;
        myBlue = 32;
        myStrength = 100;
        mySpread = 220;
        EXAMPLE.filters[0].clear();
        EXAMPLE.filters[0].addAmbient(64, 100, 10, 100);
        EXAMPLE.filters[0].addCone(myLightX, myLightY, myLightZ,
      myTargetX, myTargetY, myRed, myGreen, myBlue, myStrength, mySpread);
      }
      </SCRIPT>
      </BODY>
      </HTML>
```

See also:	Filter object, style.filter

Property	JavaScript	JScript	N	IE	Opera	Notes
Enabled	-	3.0 +	-	4.0 +	-	-

Method	JavaScript	JScript	N	IE	Opera	Notes
clear()	-	3.0 +	-	4.0 +	-	Warning
addAmbient()	-	3.0 +	-	4.0 +	-	Warning
addCone()	-	3.0 +	-	4.0 +	-	Warning
addPoint()	-	3.0 +	-	4.0 +	-	Warning
changeColor()	-	3.0 +	-	4.0 +	-	Warning
changeStrength()	-	3.0 +	-	4.0 +	-	Warning
moveLight()	-	3.0 +	-	4.0 +	-	Warning

filter - Mask() (Filter/visual)

A visual filter for creating a transparent mask.

Availability:	JScript – 3.0 Internet Explorer – 4.0
Deprecated:	Yes
Object properties:	Color

This visual filter is used for creating transparent masks. The transparent regions are defined by pixels set to the color value specified by the Color property.

The use of this filter is now deprecated in favor of the BasicImage() filter that was implemented with the IE 5.5 browser.

Warnings:

❑ Filters are defined in style sheets as if they were a function call with its arguments expressed as `name=value` pairs. This is not the typical way to define arguments so you should be aware of this anomaly when working with filters.

❑ According to the latest MSDN documentation, this filter appears to have been renamed as `MaskFilter()`.

See also:	*filter – BasicImage(), filter – MaskFilter(), Filter object,* `style.filter`

Property	JavaScript	JScript	N	IE	Opera	Notes
Color	-	3.0 +	-	4.0 +	-	Warning , Deprecated

filter - MaskFilter() (Filter/visual)

Uses the transparent color pixels of an object into a mask.

Availability:	JScript – 5.5 Internet Explorer – 5.5
Object properties:	`Enabled , Color`
Supported by objects:	A, ACRONYM, ADDRESS, B, BDO, BIG BLOCKQUOTE, body, BUTTON, CAPTION, CENTER, CITE, CODE, custom, DD, DFN, DIR, DIV, DL, DT, EM, FIELDSET, FONT, FORM, FRAME, Hn, I, IFRAME, IMG, INPUT, INS, KBD, LABEL, LEGEND, LI, MARQUEE, MENU, NOBR, OL, P, PLAINTEXT, PRE, Q, RT, RUBY, runtimeStyle, S, SAMP, SMALL, SPAN, STRIKE, STRONG, style, SUB, SUP, TABLE, TD, TEXTAREA, TH, TT, U, UL, VAR, XMP

This filter behaves differently according to whether a pixel in the HTML Element object being filtered is transparent or not.

Transparent pixels are added to the mask image. Non-transparent pixels are set to be transparent in the mask image.

The following properties are available to control this filter:

❑ The `Enabled` property provides a consistent means of controlling whether the filter is active or not. It can accept a value of true or false.

❑ The `Color` property defines the color value selected for the mask.

The example shows how a transparent GIF file can be used to cut out a shape with this filter.

Example code:

```
<HTML>
<HEAD>
</HEAD>
<BODY>
Normal--&gt;
<IMG ID="NORMAL" SRC="./Logo150.gif">
Filtered--&gt;
<IMG ID="MYIMAGE" SRC="./Logo150.gif">
<BR>
<SCRIPT>
myFilter =
"progid:DXImageTransform.Microsoft.MaskFilter(color=lightgreen,
strength=20)";
document.all.MYIMAGE.style.filter = myFilter;
</SCRIPT>
</BODY>
</HTML>
```

See also:	color value, *filter – Mask()*, *Filter object*, `style.filter`

Property	JavaScript	JScript	N	IE	Opera	Notes
Enabled	-	5.5 +	-	5.5 +	-	-
Color	-	5.5 +	-	5.5 +	-	-

filter - Matrix() (Filter/visual)

A means of applying sophisticated rotation, translate, and scaling effects to an image using matrix transformation.

Availability:	JScript – 5.5 Internet Explorer – 5.5
Object properties:	Enabled, M11, M12, M21, M22, Dx, Dy, SizingMethod, FilterType
Supported by objects:	A, ACRONYM, ADDRESS, B, BDO, BIG BLOCKQUOTE, body, BUTTON, CAPTION, CENTER, CITE, CODE, custom, DD, DFN, DIR, DIV, DL, DT, EM, FIELDSET, FONT, FORM, FRAME, FRAMESET< Hn, I, IFRAME, IMG, INPUT, INS, KBD, LABEL, LEGEND, LI, MARQUEE, MENU, NOBR, OL, P, PLAINTEXT, PRE, Q, RT, RUBY, runtimeStyle, S, SAMP, SMALL, SPAN, STRIKE, STRONG, style, SUB, SUP, TABLE, TD, TEXTAREA, TH, TT, U, UL, VAR, XMP

Matrix transformation of images provides the ability to do free rotation to any angle if you are prepared to do the trigonometrical math.

This matrix transformation provides the following possibilities:

❏ Scaling

❏ Rotation

❏ Flipping

The matrix transformations are based on a 2x2 matrix with an additional linear vector.

The following properties are supported:

❏ The `Enabled` property can be set to true or false to control whether the `Matrix()` filter is active or not.

❏ The `M11`, `M12`, `M21` and `M22` properties contain the four values that comprise the matrix. You can define values in each one of them on its own or you can perform more complex transforms by defining several at once.

❏ The `Dx` and `Dy` properties take floating point values and are used to move the resulting filtered output along a linear vector. This helps to simplify the transformation matrix and allows it to be implanted as a 2x2 matrix instead of a 2x3 or 3x3 matrix.

❏ The `FilterType` property is used to select a method for deriving the resulting filter output. This is necessary because when transforming objects with a matrix, you need to interpolate pixel values to fill in gaps. This operator can be defined as a bilinear or nearest neighbor interpolation function. The bilinear interpolation is better at the expense of needing more compute power. The nearest neighbor interpolation technique may be more useful for animated effects.

❏ The `sizingMethod` property determines how the results are displayed. They can either be clipped to fit the container or the container can be resized to accommodate the new size of the transformed output. The values are "clip to original" or "auto expand".

The following simple operations can be applied:

❏ Flip horizontal

❏ Flip vertical

❏ Resize

❏ Rotate

A horizontal flip can be accomplished with this code fragment:

```
myFilter.M11 -= myFilter.M11;

myFilter.M12 -= myFilter.M12;
```

F

JavaScript Programmer's Reference

315

A vertical flip can be accomplished with this code fragment:

```
myFilter.M21 -= myFilter.M21;

myFilter.M22 -= myFilter.M22;
```

A resize of the whole image can be accomplished like this:

```
myFilter.M11 *= aScaleFactor;

myFilter.M12 *= aScaleFactor;

myFilter.M21 *= aScaleFactor;

myFilter.M22 *= aScaleFactor;
```

A horizontal stretch can be done like this:

```
myFilter.M11 *= aScaleFactor;

myFilter.M12 *= aScaleFactor;
```

And a vertical stretch like this:

```
myFilter.M21 *= aScaleFactor;

myFilter.M22 *= aScaleFactor;
```

A rotation is a little more complex:

```
deg2radians = Math.PI * 2 / 360;

rad = deg * deg2radians;

costheta = Math.cos(rad);

sintheta = Math.sin(rad);

myFilter.M11 = costheta;

myFilter.M12 = -sintheta;

myFilter.M21 = sintheta;

myFilter.M22 = costheta;
```

The example demonstrates these transformations individually. Strange shearing effects can be achieved by modifying the coefficients of the rotation matrix. These introduce scaling artifacts which might be useful when fitting an image into a space, perhaps for designing some VRML-like projected surfaces without using VRML itself.

Example code:

```
<HTML>
<HEAD>
<STYLE>
.aFilter
{

filter:progid:DXImageTransform.Microsoft.Matrix(sizingMethod='auto
expand');
   position:absolute;
}
</STYLE>
</HEAD>
<BODY>
<TABLE BORDER=1>
<TR HEIGHT=160><TD>Normal--&gt;</TD><TD ALIGN=CENTER WIDTH=160>
<IMG ID="NORMAL" SRC="./Logo150.gif">
</TD></TR>
<TR HEIGHT=160><TD>Flip H--&gt;</TD><TD ALIGN=CENTER>
<IMG ID="FLIPH" CLASS="aFilter" SRC="./Logo150.gif">
</TD></TR>
<TR HEIGHT=160><TD>Flip V--&gt;</TD><TD>
<IMG ID="FLIPV" CLASS="aFilter" SRC="./Logo150.gif">
</TD></TR>
<TR HEIGHT=160><TD>Scale--&gt;</TD><TD ALIGN=CENTER>
<IMG ID="SCALE" CLASS="aFilter" SRC="./Logo150.gif">
</TD></TR>
<TR HEIGHT=160><TD>Scale--&gt;</TD><TD>
<IMG ID="ROTOR" CLASS="aFilter" SRC="./Logo150.gif">
</TD></TR>
</TABLE>
<SCRIPT>
FLIPH.filters.item(0).M11 *= -1;
FLIPH.filters.item(0).M12 *= -1;
FLIPH.style.top = 30+160;
FLIPH.style.left = 110;
FLIPV.filters.item(0).M21 *= -1;
FLIPV.filters.item(0).M22 *= -1;
FLIPV.style.top = 30+(160*2);
FLIPV.style.left = 110;
SCALE.filters.item(0).M11 *= 0.5;
SCALE.filters.item(0).M12 *= 0.5;
SCALE.filters.item(0).M21 *= 0.5;
SCALE.filters.item(0).M22 *= 0.5;
SCALE.style.top = 70+(160*3);
SCALE.style.left = 130;
myDeg2Rad = Math.PI*2/360;
myRadians = 30 * myDeg2Rad;
myCosine  = Math.cos(myRadians);
mySine    = Math.sin(myRadians);
ROTOR.filters.item(0).M11 = myCosine;
ROTOR.filters.item(0).M12 = -mySine;
ROTOR.filters.item(0).M21 = mySine;
ROTOR.filters.item(0).M22 = myCosine;
ROTOR.style.top = 20+(160*4);
ROTOR.style.left = 80;
</SCRIPT>
</BODY>
</HTML>
```

See also:		*filter – BasicImage(), filter – FlipH(), filter – FlipV(), Filter object,* `style.filter`				

Property	JavaScript	JScript	N	IE	Opera	Notes
Enabled	-	5.5 +	-	5.5 +	-	-
M11	-	5.5 +	-	5.5 +	-	-
M12	-	5.5 +	-	5.5 +	-	-
M21	-	5.5 +	-	5.5 +	-	-
M22	-	5.5 +	-	5.5 +	-	-
Dx	-	5.5 +	-	5.5 +	-	-
Dy	-	5.5 +	-	5.5 +	-	-
SizingMethod	-	5.5 +	-	5.5 +	-	-
FilterType	-	5.5 +	-	5.5 +	-	-

filter - MotionBlur() (Filter/visual)

An enhanced motion blur artifact that replaces the older `Blur()` filter functionality.

Availability:	JScript – 5.5 Internet Explorer – 5.5
Object properties:	Enabled, Add, Direction, Strength
Supported by objects:	A, ACRONYM, ADDRESS, B, BDO, BIG BLOCKQUOTE, body, BUTTON, CAPTION, CENTER, CITE, CODE, custom, DD, DFN, DIR, DIV, DL, DT, EM, FIELDSET, FONT, FORM, FRAME, Hn, I, IFRAME, IMG, INPUT, INS, KBD, LABEL, LEGEND, LI, MARQUEE, MENU, NOBR, OL, P, PLAINTEXT, PRE, Q, RT, RUBY, runtimeStyle, S, SAMP, SMALL, SPAN, STRIKE, STRONG, style, SUB, SUP, TABLE, TD, TEXTAREA, TH, TT, U, UL, VAR, XMP

This visual filter provides a way of adding motion blur to elements as they are drawn into the display.

The `Blur()` filter supplied with the version 4.0 of the MSIE browser was really a motion blur. At version 5.5 of MSIE, the filters have been enhanced and rationalized. The result is that the old `Blur()` filter has been renamed to `MotionBlur()` and a new `Blur()` filter has been introduced to provide a simpler gaussian blur effect without motion artifacts.

The following properties are supported by this filter:

❑ The `Enabled` property turns the motion blurring effect on and off by setting it to true or false.

❑ The `Add` property can have two values. If it is set to 1, it includes the original image as well as the blurred image. If the value 0 is defined, just the blurred effect is displayed.

❑ The `Direction` property defines the angle of the motion blur with respect to the original object. The value is specified in degrees from 0 to 359 moving clockwise as the values increase.

❑ The `Strength` property defines how many pixels distance to apply the blur effect.

The example shows an image with motion blur applied.

Example code:

```
<HTML>
<HEAD>
</HEAD>
<BODY>
Normal--&gt;
<IMG ID="NORMAL" SRC="./Logo150.gif">
Filtered--&gt;
<IMG ID="MYIMAGE" SRC="./Logo150.gif">
<BR>
<SCRIPT>
myFilter =
"progid:DXImageTransform.Microsoft.MotionBlur(direction=60,
strength=50, add=0)";
document.all.MYIMAGE.style.filter = myFilter;
</SCRIPT>
</BODY>
</HTML>
```

| See also: | *filter – Blur(), Filter object,* `style.filter` |

Property	JavaScript	JScript	N	IE	Opera	Notes
Enabled	-	5.5 +	-	5.5 +	-	-
Add	-	5.5 +	-	5.5 +	-	-
Direction	-	5.5 +	-	5.5 +	-	-
Strength	-	5.5 +	-	5.5 +	-	-

filter - Pixelate() (Filter/transition)

A transition effect with the appearance of a coarse pixelated dissolve.

Availability:	JScript – 5.5 Internet Explorer – 5.5
Object properties:	`Duration, Enabled, MaxSquare, Percent, status`
Object methods:	`apply(), play(), stop()`

This transition effect supports the following properties:

❑ The `Duration` property controls the time it takes to playback the transition effect.

❑ The `Enabled` property provides a way to activate or inhibit the filter from working by assigning the true or false value to it.

❑ The `MaxSquare` property indicates the largest possible size of a pixelated square. This can be in the range 2 to 50.

❑ The `Percent` property controls the point at which the effect can be halted to provide a static effect. The value can be between 0 and 100.

❑ The `status` property value can be read to determine the current disposition of the transition filter. It will return one of three values. The 0 value indicates the transition has stopped, 1 indicates that it is completed and 2 that it is still in progress.

The following methods are supported by this transition filter:

❑ The `apply()` method sets the transition effect to its initial condition.

❑ The `play()` method executes the transition effect using the control values and taking the time specified in the duration value. You can override the duration property by passing an optional duration argument to this method when it is called.

❑ The `stop()` method can be called at any time during the time the transition is running to halt the transition playback. This will also trigger the execution of an `onFilterChange` event handler if there is one defined.

The example demonstrates a gross pixelation transition effect.

Example code:

```
<HTML>
<HEAD>
</HEAD>
<BODY onLoad="switchState()">
```

```
<DIV ID="CONTAINER" STYLE="position:absolute; top: 0; left: 0;
width: 300; height:300;
filter:progid:DXImageTransform.Microsoft.Pixelate(duration=2,
maxsquare=50) ">
<DIV ID="DIV1" STYLE="position:absolute; top:50; left:10; width:240;
height:180;background:ivory">
<BR>
<BR>
<BR>
<HR>
<CENTER>
This is a DIV block containing text.
</CENTER>
<HR>
</DIV>
<DIV ID="DIV2" STYLE="visibility:hidden; position:absolute; top:50;
left:10; width:240; height:180; background:antiquewhite; ">
<CENTER>
<BR>
<IMG SRC="./Logo150.gif">
</CENTER>
</DIV>
</DIV>
<SCRIPT>
DIV1.style.visibility="visible";
function switchState()
{
    CONTAINER.filters[0].Apply();
    if (DIV1.style.visibility == "visible")
    {
        DIV1.style.visibility="hidden";
        DIV2.style.visibility="visible";
    }
    else
    {
        DIV1.style.visibility="visible";
        DIV2.style.visibility="hidden";
    }
    CONTAINER.filters[0].Play();
    setTimeout("switchState()", 5000);
}
</SCRIPT>
</BODY>
</HTML>
```

| See also: | *Filter object*, `style.filter` |

Property	JavaScript	JScript	N	IE	Opera	Notes
Duration	-	5.5 +	-	5.5 +	-	-
Enabled	-	5.5 +	-	5.5 +	-	-
MaxSquare	-	5.5 +	-	5.5 +	-	-
Percent	-	5.5 +	-	5.5 +	-	-
status	-	5.5 +	-	5.5 +	-	-

F

Method	JavaScript	JScript	N	IE	Opera	Notes
apply()	-	5.5 +	-	5.5 +	-	-
play()	-	5.5 +	-	5.5 +	-	-
stop()	-	5.5 +	-	5.5 +	-	-

filter - Pixelate() (Filter/visual)

An effect that simulates the pixellation achieved when lowering the display resolution of an image.

Availability:	JScript – 5.5 Internet Explorer – 5.5
Object properties:	Enabled, Duration, MaxSquare, Percent, status
Object methods:	apply(), play(), stop()
Supported by objects:	A, ACRONYM, ADDRESS, B, BDO, BIG BLOCKQUOTE, body, BUTTON, CAPTION, CENTER, CITE, CODE, custom, DD, DFN, DIR, DIV, DL, DT, EM, FIELDSET, FONT, FORM, FRAME, FRAMESET, Hn, I, IFRAME, IMG, INPUT, INS, KBD, LABEL, LEGEND, LI, MARQUEE, MENU, NOBR, OL, P, PLAINTEXT, PRE, Q, RT, RUBY, runtimeStyle, S, SAMP, SMALL, SPAN, STRIKE, STRONG, style, SUB, SUP, TABLE, TD, TEXTAREA, TH, TT, U, UL, VAR, XMP

Although this may be used as a static filter, it can also be used with the duration value, Apply(), Stop(), and Play() methods to control a transition effect.

The effect retains the current image size but takes groups of pixels and averages them and replaces the group with the average value. The effect is similar to that achieved by reducing the image and expanding it again without applying interpolation.

This can useful for greeking out some content that you don't want to display. For example, you can obscure facial features or car number plates in this way.

The following properties can be applied to this filter when it is used as a static visual effect (other transition control properties are not useful in this context):

❑ The Enabled property provides a way to activate or inhibit the filter from working by assigning the true or false value to it.

❑ The MaxSquare property defines the maximum width in pixels of a pixelated square. This is effectively the amount of pixelation that occurs.

❑ The Percent property sets the point in the overall transition effect at which to capture the transition and use it as a static filter effect.

The example demonstrates the pixelation filter applied as a static effect.

Example code:

```
<HTML>
<HEAD>
</HEAD>
<BODY>
Normal--&gt;
<IMG ID="NORMAL" SRC="./Logo150.gif">
Filtered--&gt;
<IMG ID="MYIMAGE" SRC="./Logo150.gif">
<BR>
<SCRIPT>
myFilter =
"progid:DXImageTransform.Microsoft.Pixelate(maxsquare=10)";
document.all.MYIMAGE.style.filter = myFilter;
</SCRIPT>
</BODY>
</HTML>
```

See also:	*Filter object,* `style.filter`

Property	JavaScript	JScript	N	IE	Opera	Notes
Enabled	-	5.5 +	-	5.5 +	-	-
Duration	-	5.5 +	-	5.5 +	-	-
MaxSquare	-	5.5 +	-	5.5 +	-	-
Percent	-	5.5 +	-	5.5 +	-	-
status	-	5.5 +	-	5.5 +	-	-

Method	JavaScript	JScript	N	IE	Opera	Notes
apply()	-	5.5 +	-	5.5 +	-	-
play()	-	5.5 +	-	5.5 +	-	-
stop()	-	5.5 +	-	5.5 +	-	-

filter - RadialWipe() (Filter/transition)

A transition effect with the appearance of a radar display wiping round.

Availability:	JScript – 5.5
	Internet Explorer – 5.5
Object properties:	`Duration, Enabled, Percent, status, WipeStyle`
Object methods:	`apply(), play(), stop()`

F

JavaScript Programmer's Reference

This transition effect supports the following properties:

❑ The Duration property controls the time it takes to playback the transition effect.

❑ The Enabled property provides a way to activate or inhibit the filter from working by assigning the true or false value to it.

❑ The Percent property controls the point at which the effect can be halted to provide a static effect. The value can be between 0 and 100.

❑ The status property value can be read to determine the current disposition of the transition filter. It will return one of three values. The 0 value indicates the transition has stopped, 1 indicates that it is completed and 2 that it is still in progress.

❑ The WipeStyle property is one of clock, wedge or radial which indicates the shape of the transition effect.

The following methods are supported by this transition filter:

❑ The apply() method sets the transition effect to its initial condition.

❑ The play() method executes the transition effect using the control values and taking the time specified in the duration value. You can override the duration property by passing an optional duration argument to this method when it is called.

❑ The stop() method can be called at any time during the time the transition is running to halt the transition playback. This will also trigger the execution of an onFilterChange event handler if there is one defined.

The example demonstrates the use of the clock version of the radial wipe.

Example code:

```
<HTML>
<HEAD>
</HEAD>
<BODY onLoad="switchState()">
<DIV ID="CONTAINER" STYLE="position:absolute; top: 0; left: 0;
width: 300; height:300;
filter:progid:DXImageTransform.Microsoft.RadialWipe(duration=2,
wipestyle=clock) ">
<DIV ID="DIV1" STYLE="position:absolute; top:50; left:10; width:240;
height:180;background:ivory">
<BR>
<BR>
<BR>
<HR>
<CENTER>
This is a DIV block containing text.
</CENTER>
<HR>
</DIV>
```

```
<DIV ID="DIV2" STYLE="visibility:hidden; position:absolute; top:50;
left:10; width:240; height:180; background:antiquewhite; ">
<CENTER>
<BR>
<IMG SRC="./Logo150.gif">
</CENTER>
</DIV>
</DIV>
<SCRIPT>
DIV1.style.visibility="visible";
function switchState()
{
    CONTAINER.filters[0].Apply();
    if (DIV1.style.visibility == "visible")
    {
        DIV1.style.visibility="hidden";
        DIV2.style.visibility="visible";
    }
    else
    {
        DIV1.style.visibility="visible";
        DIV2.style.visibility="hidden";
    }
    CONTAINER.filters[0].Play();
    setTimeout("switchState()", 5000);
}
</SCRIPT>
</BODY>
</HTML>
```

See also:	Filter object, style.filter

Property	JavaScript	JScript	N	IE	Opera	Notes
Duration	-	5.5 +	-	5.5 +	-	-
Enabled	-	5.5 +	-	5.5 +	-	-
Percent	-	5.5 +	-	5.5 +	-	-
status	-	5.5 +	-	5.5 +	-	-
WipeStyle	-	5.5 +	-	5.5 +	-	-

Method	JavaScript	JScript	N	IE	Opera	Notes
apply()	-	5.5 +	-	5.5 +	-	-
play()	-	5.5 +	-	5.5 +	-	-
stop()	-	5.5 +	-	5.5 +	-	-

F

JavaScript Programmer's Reference

325

filter - RandomBars() (Filter/transition)

A transition effect with the appearance of random bars sliding down.

Availability:	JScript – 5.5 Internet Explorer – 5.5
Object properties:	Duration, Enabled, Orientation, Percent, status
Object methods:	apply(), play(), stop()

This transition effect supports the following properties:

❑ The Duration property controls the time it takes to playback the transition effect.

❑ The Enabled property provides a way to activate or inhibit the filter from working by assigning the true or false value to it.

❑ The Orientation property indicates whether the effect is applied horizontally or vertically with the values horizontal or vertical.

❑ The Percent property controls the point at which the effect can be halted to provide a static effect. The value can be between 0 and 100.

❑ The status property value can be read to determine the current disposition of the transition filter. It will return one of three values. The 0 value indicates the transition has stopped, 1 indicates that it is completed and 2 that it is still in progress.

The following methods are supported by this transition filter:

❑ The apply() method sets the transition effect to its initial condition.

❑ The play() method executes the transition effect using the control values and taking the time specified in the duration value. You can override the duration property by passing an optional duration argument to this method when it is called.

❑ The stop() method can be called at any time during the time the transition is running to halt the transition playback. This will also trigger the execution of an onFilterChange event handler if there is one defined.

The example demonstrates the vertical orientation of this effect.

Example code:

```
<HTML>
<HEAD>
</HEAD>
<BODY onLoad="switchState()">
```

```
<DIV ID="CONTAINER" STYLE="position:absolute; top: 0; left: 0;
width: 300; height:300;
filter:progid:DXImageTransform.Microsoft.RandomBars(duration=2,
orientation=vertical) ">
<DIV ID="DIV1" STYLE="position:absolute; top:50; left:10; width:240;
height:180;background:ivory">
<BR>
<BR>
<BR>
<HR>
<CENTER>
This is a DIV block containing text.
</CENTER>
<HR>
</DIV>
<DIV ID="DIV2" STYLE="visibility:hidden; position:absolute; top:50;
left:10; width:240; height:180; background:antiquewhite; ">
<CENTER>
<BR>
<IMG SRC="./Logo150.gif">
</CENTER>
</DIV>
</DIV>
<SCRIPT>
DIV1.style.visibility="visible";
function switchState()
{
   CONTAINER.filters[0].Apply();
   if (DIV1.style.visibility == "visible")
   {
      DIV1.style.visibility="hidden";
      DIV2.style.visibility="visible";
   }
   else
   {
      DIV1.style.visibility="visible";
      DIV2.style.visibility="hidden";
   }
   CONTAINER.filters[0].Play();
   setTimeout("switchState()", 5000);
}
</SCRIPT>
</BODY>
</HTML>
```

| See also: | filter – Barn(), Filter object, style.filter |

Property	JavaScript	JScript	N	IE	Opera	Notes
Duration	-	5.5 +	-	5.5 +	-	-
Enabled	-	5.5 +	-	5.5 +	-	-
Orientation	-	5.5 +	-	5.5 +	-	-
Percent	-	5.5 +	-	5.5 +	-	-
status	-	5.5 +	-	5.5 +	-	-

327

Method	JavaScript	JScript	N	IE	Opera	Notes
apply()	-	5.5 +	-	5.5 +	-	-
play()	-	5.5 +	-	5.5 +	-	-
stop()	-	5.5 +	-	5.5 +	-	-

filter - RandomDissolve() (Filter/transition)

A transition effect with the appearance of a fine pixelated dissolve.

Availability:	JScript – 5.5 Internet Explorer – 5.5
Object properties:	Duration, Enabled, Percent, status
Object methods:	apply(), play(), stop()

This transition effect supports the following properties:

❑ The Duration property controls the time it takes to playback the transition effect.

❑ The Enabled property provides a way to activate or inhibit the filter from working by assigning the true or false value to it.

❑ The Percent property controls the point at which the effect can be halted to provide a static effect. The value can be between 0 and 100.

❑ The status property value can be read to determine the current disposition of the transition filter. It will return one of three values. The 0 value indicates the transition has stopped, 1 indicates that it is completed and 2 that it is still in progress.

The following methods are supported by this transition filter:

❑ The apply() method sets the transition effect to its initial condition.

❑ The play() method executes the transition effect using the control values and taking the time specified in the duration value. You can override the duration property by passing an optional duration argument to this method when it is called.

❑ The stop() method can be called at any time during the time the transition is running to halt the transition playback. This will also trigger the execution of an onFilterChange event handler if there is one defined.

Example code:

```
<HTML>
<HEAD>
</HEAD>
<BODY onLoad="switchState()">
<DIV ID="CONTAINER" STYLE="position:absolute; top: 0; left: 0;
width: 300; height:300;
filter:progid:DXImageTransform.Microsoft.RandomDissolve(duration=2)
">
<DIV ID="DIV1" STYLE="position:absolute; top:50; left:10; width:240;
height:180;background:ivory">
<BR>
<BR>
<BR>
<HR>
<CENTER>
This is a DIV block containing text.
</CENTER>
<HR>
</DIV>
<DIV ID="DIV2" STYLE="visibility:hidden; position:absolute; top:50;
left:10; width:240; height:180; background:antiquewhite; ">
<CENTER>
<BR>
<IMG SRC="./Logo150.gif">
</CENTER>
</DIV>
</DIV>
<SCRIPT>
DIV1.style.visibility="visible";
function switchState()
{
    CONTAINER.filters[0].Apply();
    if (DIV1.style.visibility == "visible")
    {
        DIV1.style.visibility="hidden";
        DIV2.style.visibility="visible";
    }
    else
    {
        DIV1.style.visibility="visible";
        DIV2.style.visibility="hidden";
    }
    CONTAINER.filters[0].Play();
    setTimeout("switchState()", 5000);
}
</SCRIPT>
</BODY>
</HTML>
```

See also: *Filter object,* `style.filter`

Property	JavaScript	JScript	N	IE	Opera	Notes
Duration	-	5.5 +	-	5.5 +	-	-
Enabled	-	5.5 +	-	5.5 +	-	-
Percent	-	5.5 +	-	5.5 +	-	-
status	-	5.5 +	-	5.5 +	-	-

Method	JavaScript	JScript	N	IE	Opera	Notes
apply()	-	5.5 +	-	5.5 +	-	-
play()	-	5.5 +	-	5.5 +	-	-
stop()	-	5.5 +	-	5.5 +	-	-

filter - RevealTrans() (Filter/reveal)

A reveal filter for controlling transitions.

Availability:	JScript – 3.0 Internet Explorer – 4.0
Deprecated:	Yes

This reveal filter controls a transition effect that specifies the kind of wipe to use between the hiding and showing of a filtered element.

The duration name=value pair is specified in the same way as for the blendTrans() filter. It specifies a floating point value in seconds which controls how quickly the effect should take place.

The transition-shape name=value pair specifies the kind of wipe effect to use. It is an integer value which defines the following wipe patterns:

index	Description
00	Box in
01	Box out
02	Circle in
03	Circle out
04	Wipe up
05	Wipe down
06	Wipe right
07	Wipe left
08	Vertical blinds

index	Description
09	Horizontal blinds
10	Checkerboard across
11	Checkerboard down
12	Random dissolve
13	Split vertical in
14	Split vertical out
15	Split horizontal in
16	Split horizontal out
17	Strips left down
18	Strips left up
19	Strips right down
20	Strips right up
21	Random bars horizontal
22	Random bars vertical
23	Random

These are loosely modelled on some of the standard SMPTE wipes and dissolves although the full complement is not available.

This is deprecated in favor of using named filters that provide the visual transition effect.

Warnings:

❑ Filters are defined in style sheets as if they were a function call with its arguments expressed as name=value pairs. This is not the typical way to define arguments so you should be aware of this anomaly when working with filters.

See also:	*filter – BlendTrans(), Filter object,* `style.filter`, Transition

filter - Shadow() (Filter/visual)

A visual filter for creating a shadow.

Availability:	JScript – 3.0 Internet Explorer – 4.0
Object properties:	`Enabled , Color, Direction`
Supported by objects:	A, ACRONYM, ADDRESS, B, BDO, BIG BLOCKQUOTE, body, BUTTON, CAPTION, CENTER, CITE, CODE, custom, DD, DFN, DIR, DIV, DL, DT, EM, FIELDSET, FONT, FORM, FRAME, Hn, I, IFRAME, IMG, INPUT, INS, KBD, LABEL, LEGEND, LI, MARQUEE, MENU, NOBR, OL, P, PLAINTEXT, PRE, Q, RT, RUBY, runtimeStyle, S, SAMP, SMALL, SPAN, STRIKE, STRONG, style, SUB, SUP, TABLE, TD, TEXTAREA, TH, TT, U, UL, VAR, XMP

This visual filter is used to define a shadow effect. The filtered element is displayed as a silhouette.

The following properties are available for use with this filter:

- The Enabled property was added at version 5.5 of the MSIE browser to provide a consistent way of enabling and disabling filters by assigning a true or false value to it.

- The color of the cast shadow is defined by the Color property and the Direction property specifies the angle of the shadow with respect to the original filtered element's location. This value is specified in degrees, measured in a clockwise direction from 0 to 359 as the values increase.

You may want more control over the shadow appearance and so other filters might be closer to the desired effect. This one is good for a simple shadow effect. The example shows it being applied to an image.

Warnings:

- Filters are defined in style sheets as if they were a function call with its arguments expressed as name=value pairs. This is not the typical way to define arguments so you should be aware of this anomaly when working with filters.

Example code:

```
<HTML>
<HEAD>
</HEAD>
<BODY>
Normal--&gt;
<IMG ID="NORMAL" SRC="./Logo150.gif">
Filtered--&gt;
<IMG ID="MYIMAGE" SRC="./Logo150.gif">
<BR>
<SCRIPT>
myFilter = "progid:DXImageTransform.Microsoft.Shadow(direction=120,
color=yellowgreen)";

document.all.MYIMAGE.style.filter = myFilter;
</SCRIPT>
</BODY>
</HTML>
```

See also: *Filter object,* style.filter, style.textShadow

Property	JavaScript	JScript	N	IE	Opera	Notes
Enabled	-	3.0 +	-	4.0 +	-	Warning
Color	-	3.0 +	-	4.0 +	-	Warning
Direction	-	3.0 +	-	4.0 +	-	Warning

filter - Slide() (Filter/transition)

A transition effect with the appearance of one image sliding over another.

Availability:	JScript – 5.5 Internet Explorer – 5.5
Object properties:	bands, Duration, Enabled, Percent, SlideStyle, status
Object methods:	apply(), play(), stop()

This transition effect supports the following properties:

❑ bands

❑ Duration

❑ Enabled

❑ Percent

❑ SlideStyle

❑ status

The bands property defines the number of strips that the sliding filter will use for its transition effect.

The Duration property controls the time it takes to playback the transition effect.

The Enabled property provides a way to activate or inhibit the filter from working by assigning the true or false value to it.

The Percent property controls the point at which the effect can be halted to provide a static effect. The value can be between 0 and 100.

The SlideStyle property indicates what sort of sliding effect is used. It can be one of HIDE, PUSH or SWAP.

The status value can be read to determine the current disposition of the transition filter. It will return one of three values. The 0 value indicates the transition has stopped, 1 indicates that it is completed and 2 that it is still in progress.

The following methods are supported by this transition filter:

❑ `apply()`

❑ `play()`

❑ `stop()`

The `apply()` method sets the transition effect to its initial condition.

The `play()` method executes the transition effect using the control values and taking the time specified in the duration value. You can override the `duration` property by passing an optional duration argument to this method when it is called.

The `stop()` method can be called at any time during the time the transition is running to halt the transition playback. This will also trigger the execution of an `onFilterChange` event handler if there is one defined.

The example shows one of the available variants of this filter.

Example code:

```
<HTML>
<HEAD>
</HEAD>
<BODY onLoad="switchState()">
<DIV ID="CONTAINER" STYLE="position:absolute; top: 0; left: 0;
width: 300; height:300;
filter:progid:DXImageTransform.Microsoft.Slide(duration=2, bands=5,
slidestyle=swap) ">
<DIV ID="DIV1" STYLE="position:absolute; top:50; left:10; width:240;
height:180;background:ivory">
<BR>
<BR>
<BR>
<HR>
<CENTER>
This is a DIV block containing text.
</CENTER>
<HR>
</DIV>
<DIV ID="DIV2" STYLE="visibility:hidden; position:absolute; top:50;
left:10; width:240; height:180; background:antiquewhite; ">
<CENTER>
<BR>
<IMG SRC="./Logo150.gif">
</CENTER>
</DIV>
</DIV>
<SCRIPT>
DIV1.style.visibility="visible";
function switchState()
{
```

```
    CONTAINER.filters[0].Apply();
    if (DIV1.style.visibility == "visible")
    {
        DIV1.style.visibility="hidden";
        DIV2.style.visibility="visible";
    }
    else
    {
        DIV1.style.visibility="visible";
        DIV2.style.visibility="hidden";
    }
    CONTAINER.filters[0].Play();
    setTimeout("switchState()", 5000);
}
</SCRIPT>
</BODY>
</HTML>
```

See also:	*filter – Blinds(), Filter object,* `style.filter`

Property	JavaScript	JScript	N	IE	Opera	Notes
bands	-	5.5 +	-	5.5 +	-	-
Duration	-	5.5 +	-	5.5 +	-	-
Enabled	-	3.0 +	-	4.0 +	-	-
Percent	-	5.5 +	-	5.5 +	-	-
SlideStyle	-	5.5 +	-	5.5 +	-	-
status	-	5.5 +	-	5.5 +	-	-

Method	JavaScript	JScript	N	IE	Opera	Notes
apply()	-	5.5 +	-	5.5 +	-	-
play()	-	5.5 +	-	5.5 +	-	-
stop()	-	5.5 +	-	5.5 +	-	-

filter - Spiral() (Filter/transition)

Reveals the new image with a spiral effect.

Availability:	JScript – 5.5 Internet Explorer – 5.5
Object properties:	Duration, Enabled, GridSizeX, GridSizeY, Percent, status
Object methods:	apply(), play(), stop()

JavaScript Programmer's Reference

F

This transition effect supports the following properties:

- ❏ Duration
- ❏ Enabled
- ❏ GridSizeX
- ❏ GridSizeY
- ❏ Percent
- ❏ status

The Duration property controls the time it takes to playback the transition effect.

The Enabled property provides a way to activate or inhibit the filter from working by assigning the true or false value to it.

The GridSizeX and GridSizeY properties indicate the granularity of the effect.

The Percent property controls the point at which the effect can be halted to provide a static effect. The value can be between 0 and 100.

The status value can be read to determine the current disposition of the transition filter. It will return one of three values. The 0 value indicates the transition has stopped, 1 indicates that it is completed and 2 that it is still in progress.

The following methods are supported by this transition filter:

- ❏ apply()
- ❏ play()
- ❏ stop()

The apply() method sets the transition effect to its initial condition.

The play() method executes the transition effect using the control values and taking the time specified in the duration value. You can override the duration property by passing an optional duration argument to this method when it is called.

The stop() method can be called at any time during the time the transition is running to halt the transition playback. This will also trigger the execution of an onFilterChange event handler if there is one defined.

The example shows how to apply this transition.

Example code:

```
<HTML>
<HEAD>
</HEAD>
<BODY onLoad="switchState()">
```

```
<DIV ID="CONTAINER" STYLE="position:absolute; top: 0; left: 0;
width: 300; height:300;
filter:progid:DXImageTransform.Microsoft.Spiral(duration=2,
gridsizex=10, gridsizey=10) ">
<DIV ID="DIV1" STYLE="position:absolute; top:50; left:10; width:240;
height:180;background:ivory">
<BR>
<BR>
<BR>
<HR>
<CENTER>
This is a DIV block containing text.
</CENTER>
<HR>
</DIV>
<DIV ID="DIV2" STYLE="visibility:hidden; position:absolute; top:50;
left:10; width:240; height:180; background:antiquewhite; ">
<CENTER>
<BR>
<IMG SRC="./Logo150.gif">
</CENTER>
</DIV>
</DIV>
<SCRIPT>
DIV1.style.visibility="visible";
function switchState()
{
   CONTAINER.filters[0].Apply();
   if (DIV1.style.visibility == "visible")
   {
      DIV1.style.visibility="hidden";
      DIV2.style.visibility="visible";
   }
   else
   {
      DIV1.style.visibility="visible";
      DIV2.style.visibility="hidden";
   }
   CONTAINER.filters[0].Play();
   setTimeout("switchState()", 5000);
}
</SCRIPT>
</BODY>
</HTML>
```

See also:	*filter – Zigzag(), Filter object,* `style.filter`

Property	JavaScript	JScript	N	IE	Opera	Notes
Duration	-	5.5 +	-	5.5 +	-	-
Enabled	-	3.0 +	-	4.0 +	-	-
GridSizeX	-	5.5 +	-	5.5 +	-	-
GridSizeY	-	5.5 +	-	5.5 +	-	-
Percent	-	5.5 +	-	5.5 +	-	-
status	-	5.5 +	-	5.5 +	-	-

Method	JavaScript	JScript	N	IE	Opera	Notes
apply()	-	5.5 +	-	5.5 +	-	-
play()	-	5.5 +	-	5.5 +	-	-
stop()	-	5.5 +	-	5.5 +	-	-

filter - Stretch() (Filter/transition)

A variation on a wipe effect except that the new image appears to stretch over the old one. The old one is squashed until it disappears.

Availability:	JScript – 5.5 Internet Explorer – 5.5
Object properties:	Duration, Enabled, Percent, status, StretchStyle
Object methods:	apply(), play(), stop()

This transition effect supports the following properties:

❑ Duration

❑ Enabled

❑ Percent

❑ status

❑ StretchStyle

The Duration property controls the time it takes to playback the transition effect.

The Enabled property provides a way to activate or inhibit the filter from working by assigning the true or false value to it.

The Percent property controls the point at which the effect can be halted to provide a static effect. The value can be between 0 and 100.

The status value can be read to determine the current disposition of the transition filter. It will return one of three values. The 0 value indicates the transition has stopped, 1 indicates that it is completed and 2 that it is still in progress.

The StretchStyle property describes the kind of effect that the transition uses. It can be one of HIDE, PUSH or SPIN.

The following methods are supported by this transition filter:

❑ apply()

❑ play()

❑ stop()

The `apply()` method sets the transition effect to its initial condition.

The `play()` method executes the transition effect using the control values and taking the time specified in the duration value. You can override the duration property by passing an optional duration argument to this method when it is called.

The `stop()` method can be called at any time during the time the transition is running to halt the transition playback. This will also trigger the execution of an `onFilterChange` event handler if there is one defined.

The example shows the spin variant of this effect.

Example code:

```
<HTML>
<HEAD>
</HEAD>
<BODY onLoad="switchState()">
<DIV ID="CONTAINER" STYLE="position:absolute; top: 0; left: 0;
width: 300; height:300;
filter:progid:DXImageTransform.Microsoft.Stretch(duration=2,
stretchstyle=spin) ">
<DIV ID="DIV1" STYLE="position:absolute; top:50; left:10; width:240;
height:180;background:ivory">
<BR>
<BR>
<BR>
<HR>
<CENTER>
This is a DIV block containing text.
</CENTER>
<HR>
</DIV>
<DIV ID="DIV2" STYLE="visibility:hidden; position:absolute; top:50;
left:10; width:240; height:180; background:antiquewhite; ">
<CENTER>
<BR>
<IMG SRC="./Logo150.gif">
</CENTER>
</DIV>
</DIV>
<SCRIPT>
DIV1.style.visibility="visible";
function switchState()
{
    CONTAINER.filters[0].Apply();
    if (DIV1.style.visibility == "visible")
    {
        DIV1.style.visibility="hidden";
        DIV2.style.visibility="visible";
    }
    else
    {
```

339

```
              DIV1.style.visibility="visible";
              DIV2.style.visibility="hidden";
        }
      CONTAINER.filters[0].Play();
      setTimeout("switchState()", 5000);
   }
   </SCRIPT>
   </BODY>
   </HTML>
```

See also:	*Filter object,* `style.filter`

Property	JavaScript	JScript	N	IE	Opera	Notes
Duration	-	5.5 +	-	5.5 +	-	-
Enabled	-	3.0 +	-	4.0 +	-	-
Percent	-	5.5 +	-	5.5 +	-	-
status	-	5.5 +	-	5.5 +	-	-
StretchStyle	-	5.5 +	-	5.5 +	-	-

Method	JavaScript	JScript	N	IE	Opera	Notes
apply()	-	5.5 +	-	5.5 +	-	-
play()	-	5.5 +	-	5.5 +	-	-
stop()	-	5.5 +	-	5.5 +	-	-

filter - Strips() (Filter/transition)

Reveals new image by sliding diagonal strips across the image.

Availability:	JScript – 5.5 Internet Explorer – 5.5
Object properties:	`Duration, Enabled, Motion, Percent, status`
Object methods:	`apply(), play(), stop()`

This transition effect supports the following properties:

❑ Duration

❑ Enabled

❑ Motion

❑ Percent

❑ status

The Duration property controls the time it takes to playback the transition effect.

The Enabled property provides a way to activate or inhibit the filter from working by assigning the true or false value to it.

The Motion property indicates which order and direction the transition moves in. The value can be one of leftdown, leftup, rightdown or rightup.

The Percent property controls the point at which the effect can be halted to provide a static effect. The value can be between 0 and 100.

The status value can be read to determine the current disposition of the transition filter. It will return one of three values. The 0 value indicates the transition has stopped, 1 indicates that it is completed and 2 that it is still in progress.

The following methods are supported by this transition filter:

❑ apply()

❑ play()

❑ stop()

The apply() method sets the transition effect to its initial condition.

The play() method executes the transition effect using the control values and taking the time specified in the duration value. You can override the duration property by passing an optional duration argument to this method when it is called.

The stop() method can be called at any time during the time the transition is running to halt the transition playback. This will also trigger the execution of an onFilterChange event handler if there is one defined.

One variant of this filter is demonstrated in the example.

Example code:

```
<HTML>
<HEAD>
</HEAD>
<BODY onLoad="switchState()">
<DIV ID="CONTAINER" STYLE="position:absolute; top: 0; left: 0;
width: 300; height:300;
filter:progid:DXImageTransform.Microsoft.Strips(duration=2,
motion=leftdown) ">
<DIV ID="DIV1" STYLE="position:absolute; top:50; left:10; width:240;
height:180;background:ivory">
<BR>
<BR>
<BR>
<HR>
<CENTER>
```

F

JavaScript Programmer's Reference

341

```
This is a DIV block containing text.
</CENTER>
<HR>
</DIV>
<DIV ID="DIV2" STYLE="visibility:hidden; position:absolute; top:50;
left:10; width:240; height:180; background:antiquewhite; ">
<CENTER>
<BR>
<IMG SRC="./Logo150.gif">
</CENTER>
</DIV>
</DIV>
<SCRIPT>
DIV1.style.visibility="visible";
function switchState()
{
   CONTAINER.filters[0].Apply();
   if (DIV1.style.visibility == "visible")
   {
      DIV1.style.visibility="hidden";
      DIV2.style.visibility="visible";
   }
   else
   {
      DIV1.style.visibility="visible";
      DIV2.style.visibility="hidden";
   }
   CONTAINER.filters[0].Play();
   setTimeout("switchState()", 5000);
}
</SCRIPT>
</BODY>
</HTML>
```

See also:	*Filter object*, `style.filter`

Property	JavaScript	JScript	N	IE	Opera	Notes
Duration	-	5.5 +	-	5.5 +	-	-
Enabled	-	3.0 +	-	4.0 +	-	-
Motion	-	5.5 +	-	5.5 +	-	-
Percent	-	5.5 +	-	5.5 +	-	-
status	-	5.5 +	-	5.5 +	-	-

Method	JavaScript	JScript	N	IE	Opera	Notes
apply()	-	5.5 +	-	5.5 +	-	-
play()	-	5.5 +	-	5.5 +	-	-
stop()	-	5.5 +	-	5.5 +	-	-

filter - Wave() (Filter/visual)

A visual filter for creating ripple effects.

Availability:	JScript – 3.0 Internet Explorer – 4.0
Object properties:	Enabled, Add, Freq, LightStrength, Phase, Strength
Supported by objects:	A, ACRONYM, ADDRESS, B, BDO, BIG, BLOCKQUOTE, body, BUTTON, CAPTION, CENTER, CITE, CODE, custom, DD, DEL, DFN, DIR, DIV, DL, DT, EM, FIELDSET, FONT, FORM, FRAME, Hn, I, IFRAME, IMG, INPUT, INS, KBD, LABEL, LEGEND, LI, MARQUEE, MENU, NOBR, OL, P, PLAINTEXT, PRE, Q, RT, RUBY, runtimeStyle, S, SAMP, SMALL, SPAN, STRIKE, STRONG, style, SUB, SUP, TABLE, TD, TEXTAREA, TH, TT, U, UL, VAR, XMP

This visual filter applies a rippled distortion effect to the filtered element. The effect is applied only along the vertical axis.

The following properties can be applied to this filter:

❑ Enabled

❑ Add

❑ Freq

❑ LightStrength

❑ Phase

❑ Strength

The Enabled property was introduced at version 5.5 of the MSIE browser to provide a consistent interface for activating and disabling filters by assigning the true or false value to it.

Like the MotionBlur() filter, the add property specifies whether the original unmodified image should be placed over the rippled copy. A value of 1 adds the original while a value of 0 displays only the rippled copy.

The freq property specifies the number of waves to be applied as the distorting effect is rendered.

The lightStrength property indicates the intensity of the light playing on the rippled surface with a value in the range 0 to 100.

The phase property defines the percentage offset for the sine wave curve in the range 0 to 100 which corresponds to an angular phase offset of 0 to 359 degrees.

343

The strength property defines the wave-rendering effect's intensity. This value must be between 0 and 255 with 0 providing no distortion and 255 causing a gross ripple effect.

The example shows this ripple effect being applied to an image.

Warnings:

❑ Filters are defined in style sheets as if they were a function call with its arguments expressed as name=value pairs. This is not the typical way to define arguments so you should be aware of this anomaly when working with filters.

Example code:

```
<HTML>
<HEAD>
</HEAD>
<BODY>
Normal--&gt;
<IMG ID="NORMAL" SRC="./Logo150.gif">
Filtered--&gt;
<IMG ID="MYIMAGE" SRC="./Logo150.gif">
<BR>
<SCRIPT>
myFilter = "progid:DXImageTransform.Microsoft.Wave(freq=6,
lightstrength=90, phase=60, add=1, strength=10)";

document.all.MYIMAGE.style.filter = myFilter;
</SCRIPT>
</BODY>
</HTML>
```

See also:	*Filter object,* style.filter

Property	JavaScript	JScript	N	IE	Opera	Notes
Enabled	-	3.0 +	-	4.0 +	-	-
Add	-	3.0 +	-	4.0 +	-	Warning
Freq	-	3.0 +	-	4.0 +	-	Warning
LightStrength	-	3.0 +	-	4.0 +	-	Warning
Phase	-	3.0 +	-	4.0 +	-	Warning
Strength	-	3.0 +	-	4.0 +	-	Warning

filter - Wheel() (Filter/transition)

Reveals the new image with a rotating spoked wheel effect.

Availability:	JScript – 5.5 Internet Explorer – 5.5
Object properties:	Duration, Enabled, Percent, spokes, status
Object methods:	apply(), play(), stop()

This transition effect supports the following properties:

❑ Duration

❑ Enabled

❑ Percent

❑ spokes

❑ status

The Duration property controls the time it takes to playback the transition effect.

The Enabled property provides a way to activate or inhibit the filter from working by assigning the true or false value to it.

The Percent property controls the point at which the effect can be halted to provide a static effect. The value can be between 0 and 100.

The spokes property indicates how many spokes there are in the cartwheel that is used for the transition effect. The value can range from 2 to 20 with 8 being a typical value.

The status value can be read to determine the current disposition of the transition filter. It will return one of three values. The 0 value indicates the transition has stopped, 1 indicates that it is completed and 2 that it is still in progress.

The following methods are supported by this transition filter:

❑ apply()

❑ play()

❑ stop()

The apply() method sets the transition effect to its initial condition.

The play() method executes the transition effect using the control values and taking the time specified in the duration value. You can override the duration property by passing an optional duration argument to this method when it is called.

The stop() method can be called at any time during the time the transition is running to halt the transition playback. This will also trigger the execution of an onFilterChange event handler if there is one defined.

This filter is demonstrated in the example.

Example code:

```
<HTML>
<HEAD>
</HEAD>
<BODY onLoad="swiitchState()">
<DIV ID="CONTAINER" STYLE="position:absolute; top: 0; left: 0;
width: 300; height:300;
filter:progid:DXImageTransform.Microsoft.Wheel(duration=2,
spokes=10) ">
<DIV ID="DIV1" STYLE="position:absolute; top:50; left:10; width:240;
height:180;background:ivory">
<BR>
<BR>
<BR>
<HR>
<CENTER>
This is a DIV block containing text.
</CENTER>
<HR>
</DIV>
<DIV ID="DIV2" STYLE="visibility:hidden; position:absolute; top:50;
left:10; width:240; height:180; background:antiquewhite; ">
<CENTER>
<BR>
<IMG SRC="./Logo150.gif">
</CENTER>
</DIV>
</DIV>
<SCRIPT>
DIV1.style.visibility="visible";
function swiitchState()
{
    CONTAINER.filters[0].Apply();
    if (DIV1.style.visibility == "visible")
    {
        DIV1.style.visibility="hidden";
        DIV2.style.visibility="visible";
    }
    else
    {
        DIV1.style.visibility="visible";
        DIV2.style.visibility="hidden";
    }
    CONTAINER.filters[0].Play();
    setTimeout("swiitchState()", 5000);
}
</SCRIPT>
</BODY>
</HTML>
```

See also:	*Filter object,* style.filter

346

Property	JavaScript	JScript	N	IE	Opera	Notes
Duration	-	5.5 +	-	5.5 +	-	-
Enabled	-	3.0 +	-	4.0 +	-	-
Percent	-	5.5 +	-	5.5 +	-	-
spokes	-	5.5 +	-	5.5 +	-	-
status	-	5.5 +	-	5.5 +	-	-

Method	JavaScript	JScript	N	IE	Opera	Notes
apply()	-	5.5 +	-	5.5 +	-	-
play()	-	5.5 +	-	5.5 +	-	-
stop()	-	5.5 +	-	5.5 +	-	-

filter - XRay() (Filter/visual)

A visual filter that displays only the element edges.

Availability:	JScript – 3.0 Internet Explorer – 4.0 Deprecated

This visual filter detects the visible edges of the filter element and only draws them. This might be useful for greeking a graphical object as it is dragged around with the cursor.

There are no properties for this filter.

The use of this filter is now deprecated in favor of the BasicImage() filter that was implemented with the version 5.5 MSIE browser.

Warnings:

❑ Filters are defined in style sheets as if they were a function call with its arguments expressed as name=value pairs. This is not the typical way to define arguments so you should be aware of this anomaly when working with filters.

See also:	*filter - BasicImage(), Filter object,* style.filter

filter - Zigzag() (Filter/transition)

Reveals the new image with a zigzag effect.

Availability:	JScript – 5.5 Internet Explorer – 5.5
Object properties:	Duration, Enabled, GridSizeX, GridSizeY, Percent, status
Object methods:	apply(), play(), stop()

This transition effect supports the following properties:

❑ Duration

❑ Enabled

❑ GridSizeX

❑ GridSizeY

❑ Percent

❑ status

The Duration property controls the time it takes to playback the transition effect.

The Enabled property provides a way to activate or inhibit the filter from working by assigning the true or false value to it.

The GridSizeX and GridSizeY properties indicate the granularity of the effect.

The Percent property controls the point at which the effect can be halted to provide a static effect. The value can be between 0 and 100.

The status value can be read to determine the current disposition of the transition filter. It will return one of three values. The 0 value indicates the transition has stopped, 1 indicates that it is completed and 2 that it is still in progress.

The following methods are supported by this transition filter:

❑ apply()

❑ play()

❑ stop()

The apply() method sets the transition effect to its initial condition.

The play() method executes the transition effect using the control values and taking the time specified in the duration value. You can override the duration property by passing an optional duration argument to this method when it is called.

The `stop()` method can be called at any time during the time the transition is running to halt the transition playback. This will also trigger the execution of an `onFilterChange` event handler if there is one defined.

This filter is demonstrated in the example.

Example code:

```
<HTML>
<HEAD>
</HEAD>
<BODY onLoad="switchState()">
<DIV ID="CONTAINER" STYLE="position:absolute; top: 0; left: 0;
width: 300; height:300;
filter:progid:DXImageTransform.Microsoft.ZigZag(duration=2,
gridsizex=15, gridsizey=15) ">
<DIV ID="DIV1" STYLE="position:absolute; top:50; left:10; width:240;
height:180;background:ivory">
<BR>
<BR>
<BR>
<HR>
<CENTER>
This is a DIV block containing text.
</CENTER>
<HR>
</DIV>
<DIV ID="DIV2" STYLE="visibility:hidden; position:absolute; top:50;
left:10; width:240; height:180; background:antiquewhite; ">
<CENTER>
<BR>
<IMG SRC="./Logo150.gif">
</CENTER>
</DIV>
</DIV>
<SCRIPT>
DIV1.style.visibility="visible";
function switchState()
{
   CONTAINER.filters[0].Apply();
   if (DIV1.style.visibility == "visible")
   {
      DIV1.style.visibility="hidden";
      DIV2.style.visibility="visible";
   }
   else
   {
      DIV1.style.visibility="visible";
      DIV2.style.visibility="hidden";
   }
   CONTAINER.filters[0].Play();
   setTimeout("switchState()", 5000);
}
</SCRIPT>
</BODY>
</HTML>
```

See also: *filter – Spiral(), Filter object,* `style.filter`

Property	JavaScript	JScript	N	IE	Opera	Notes
Duration	-	5.5 +	-	5.5 +	-	-
Enabled	-	3.0 +	-	4.0 +	-	-
GridSizeX	-	5.5 +	-	5.5 +	-	-
GridSizeY	-	5.5 +	-	5.5 +	-	-
Percent	-	5.5 +	-	5.5 +	-	-
status	-	5.5 +	-	5.5 +	-	-

Method	JavaScript	JScript	N	IE	Opera	Notes
apply()	-	5.5 +	-	5.5 +	-	-
play()	-	5.5 +	-	5.5 +	-	-
stop()	-	5.5 +	-	5.5 +	-	-

Filter object (Object/JScript)

A single filter object obtained from an element's filters array.

Availability:	JScript – 3.0 Internet Explorer – 4.0	
JavaScript syntax:	IE	*myFilter =* *myElement.*filters(*anIndex*)
	IE	*myFilter =* *myElement.*filters[*anIndex*]
	IE	*myFilter = myFilters[anIndex]*
Argument list:	*anIndex*	A reference to an element in a collection
Object properties:	enabled	

This object defines a visual effect that is used when the display is updated as the result of a change to the content of an element. The Filter object has properties that relate to the individual filters. There are some common properties (and methods) that are available to all filters and in some cases the same property name can mean different things depending on the filter being applied.

You should access the filter objects via the Filters collection because you may have the same filter type repeated for a cascading effect and so you need to be sure that you are addressing the right one.

There are three kinds of filters that can be applied to an object:

❑ Visual

❑ Reveal

❑ Blend

A visual filter is used to enhance the visual appearance of objects. Maybe to flip them over, add a glow effect or a drop shadow.

A reveal filter is used to apply a transition effect as the appearance changes.

A blend filter controls the speed at which a reveal filter is applied.

You can define more than one filter, they just need to be space separated from one another.

Here is a list of the procedural filter function names:

❏ AlphaImageLoader()
❏ Gradient()

Here is a list of the static filters supported at version 5.5 of the MSIE browser:

❏ Alpha()
❏ BasicImage()
❏ Blur()
❏ Chroma()
❏ Compositor()
❏ DropShadow()
❏ Emboss()
❏ Engrave()
❏ Glow()
❏ Light()
❏ MaskFilter()
❏ Matrix()
❏ MotionBlur()
❏ Pixelate() ·
❏ Shadow()
❏ Wave()

The old blendTrans() and revealTrans() filters are now replaced by these transition filters:

❏ Barn()
❏ Blinds()
❏ CheckerBoard()
❏ Fade()

351

- ❑ GradientWipe()
- ❑ Inset()
- ❑ Iris()
- ❑ Pixelate()
- ❑ RadialWipe()
- ❑ RandomBars()
- ❑ RandomDissolve()
- ❑ Slide()
- ❑ Spiral()
- ❑ Stretch()
- ❑ Strips()
- ❑ Wheel()
- ❑ Zigzag()

Filters are defined as if they were a sequence of space delimited function calls. They aren't really functions because their argument passing mechanism is not truly JavaScript based. Arguments to each filter function are defined as name=value pairs.

Refer to the specific topics on each filter function for details of what it does and how you can control it.

When using the filters in the context of the style object, the function name for each filter must be preceded by this string (although some less sophisticated filters seem to work without this):

```
"progid:DXImageTransform.Microsoft."
```

You can apply the filters directly as properties of the filter object that belongs to HTML element objects themselves.

Thus:

```
myFilter.Shadow(someAttributes)
```

Warnings:

- ❑ Filters are not supported in all versions of MSIE on the Macintosh. In fact they are not really well supported outside of the MSIE browser or the Win32 platform.

- ❑ There are various sources of documentation about these filters. There is some difference between them regarding the spelling of the filters names and the availability of the filters. The naming conventions are sometimes all lower case and at others a mixed upper- and lower-case. This suggests that the filter name parser may be case insensitive. This also applies to the name=value pairs that are passed as arguments to the filter functions.

❑ Certain filter functions are no longer included in the MSDN reference material and so they may be considered to be deprecated.

❑ We have conformed to the case style of the MSDN reference and have included all the filters that were covered in earlier references as well as those that have been added recently. Those that appear not to be in the MSDN reference anymore are marked as deprecated as follows:

> ❑ `FlipH()`
>
> ❑ `FlipV()`
>
> ❑ `Grayscale()`
>
> ❑ `Invert()`
>
> ❑ `Mask()`
>
> ❑ `XRay()`

❑ These are deprecated filters that used to provide blends and reveals:

> ❑ `BlendTrans()`
>
> ❑ `RevealTrans()`
>
> ❑ Note that the functionality and availability of the filters has changed significantly from version 4.0 to version 5.5 of the MSIE browser and the older deprecated filters have been assimilated into the functionality of the new filter set. No previously existing filter appearance has been lost but they do need to be operated differently.

See also:	`Element.filters[]`, `onFilterChange`, `style.filter`, `style.textShadow`, Transition

Property	JavaScript	JScript	N	IE	Opera	Notes
enabled	-	3.0 +	-	4.0 +	-	-

finally ... (Statement)

Part of the `try...catch...finally` error-handling mechanism.

Availability:	ECMAScript edition – 3 JavaScript – 1.5 JScript – 5.0 Internet Explorer – 5.0 Netscape – 6.0

The ECMAScript standard (edition 2) defined the `finally` keyword and reserves it for future use. At edition 3, it was made a required keyword.

In anticipation of that, it is available in JavaScript version 1.4. This is also now supported in JScript version 5.0 as well.

Refer to the `try...catch...finally` topic for more details.

Warnings:

❑ This is not available for use server-side with Netscape Enterprise Server 3.

See also:	catch(...), throw, try ... catch ... finally

Cross-references:

ECMA 262 edition 2 – section – 7.4.3

ECMA 262 edition 3 – section – 7.5.2

ECMA 262 edition 3 – section – 12.14

FindProxyForURL() (Function/proxy.pac)

The main function in a `proxy.pac` file.

Availability:	JavaScript – 1.2 Netscape – 4.0	
JavaScript syntax:	N	FindProxyForURL(*aFullURL*, *aHostname*)
Argument list:	*aFullURL*	The complete URL to be checked for proxy access
	aHostname	The hostname component of a URL for convenience

This function is called at request time for every URL. Therefore any lengthy and complex coding in here is going to be detrimental to the performance of your browser.

The `String` and `Math` object methods/functions are available in this context.

The return value from this function tells the browser how to reach the target URL.

For directly connected sites, the value "DIRECT" should be returned. This is usually appropriate for hosts within the same domain or on the same sub-net. The functions `isPlainHostName()` and `isInNet()` both return `true` for machines that should use DIRECT connection. However only one of them needs to return `true` for this to be the desired outcome. If both are `false`, then either a SOCKS gateway or PROXY server is needed.

For secure access using the HTTPS: protocol, the function might return "SOCKS" plus some details of the socks host and port to use. You may choose to perform secure access by some other means.

For the remaining cases, your script should probably return "PROXY" with details of the proxy server (or servers) to use. If more than one proxy server is returned, they are consulted in the order they are listed. This gives you an opportunity to add some load balancing logic if you care to. That is quite important if you have more than one proxy server, since you might return the proxies in the same order every time. That would more-or-less guarantee that the first one was loaded until it simply couldn't respond any more and the second would only kick in as a last resort. Randomizing the order in which they are presented ensures the work is fairly divided between them.

This function must return a very specific result. The following values are examples:

```
"DIRECT"

"SOCKS sockshost:1081"

"PROXY proxy1:1080 ; proxy2:1080"
```

Here we provide an example based on the one provided in the Wrox Instant JavaScript book (by Nigel MacFarlane) that illustrates all of these capabilities. The logic is unraveled to illustrate the selection technique at the expense of a minor performance hit.

Example code:

```
// Example proxy.pac file
// Example proxy.pac file
function FindProxyForURL(aFullURL, aHostname)
{
    // Check for hosts in the same domain as the client
    if(isPlainHostName(aHostname))
    {
        return "DIRECT";
    }
    // Check for hosts in the same IP sub-net
    if(isInNet(aHostname, "192.168.1.0"))
    {
        return "DIRECT";
    }
    // Check for secure http: protocol
    if(aFullURL.substring(0, 6) == "https:")
    {
        return "SOCKS sockshost:1081";
    }
    // Check for secure news protocol
    if(aFullURL.substring(0, 6) == "snews:")
    {
        return "SOCKS sockshost:1081";
    }
    // Return a randomly selected proxy list
    if(Math.random() < 0.5)
    {
```

```
            return "PROXY proxy1:1080 ; proxy2:1080";
      }
      else
      {
            return "PROXY proxy2:1080 ; proxy1:1080";
      }
}
```

See also:	*isInNet()*, *isPlainHostName()*, Proxies, *proxy.pac*

float (Reserved word)

Reserved for future language enhancements.

The inclusion of this reserved keyword in the ECMAScript standard suggests that future versions of ECMAScript may be more strongly typed.

This keyword also represents a Java data type and the `float` keyword allows for the potential extension of JavaScript interfaces to access Java applet parameters and return values.

See also:	*double*, Integer, *java.lang.Float*, LiveConnect, *long*, Reserved word, *short*

Cross-references:

ECMA 262 edition 2 – section – 7.4.3

ECMA 262 edition 3 – section – 7.5.3

Folder object (Object/JScript)

A special JScript folder object.

Availability:	JScript – 3.0 Internet Explorer – 4.0		
JavaScript syntax:	IE	*myFolder* = *myFile*.`ParentFolder`	
	IE	*myFolder* = *myFolder*.`ParentFolder`	
	IE	*myFolder* = *myFileSystem*.`CreateFolder`(*aPath*)	
	IE	*myFolder* = *myFileSystem*.`GetFolder`(*aPath*)	
	IE	*myFolder* = *myFileSystem*.`GetSpecialFolder`(*aNumber*)	
	IE	*myFolder* = *myFolders*.`Item`(*aPath*)	

Argument list:	aPath	The pathname of the folder to be created
	aNumber	A code referring to a special folder
Object properties:	Attributes, DateCreated, DateLastAccessed, DateLastModified, Drive, IsRootFolder, Name, ParentFolder, Path, ShortName, ShortPath, Size, SubFolders, Type	
Object methods:	Copy(), Delete(), Move()	
Collections:	Files[], SubFolders[]	

This is an object used in the Windows environment, probably as part of the WSH implementation to encapsulate a single folder within the file-system.

| **See also:** | *File object*, File.ParentFolder, FileSystem.CreateFolder(), FileSystem.GetFolder(), FileSystem.GetSpecialFolder(), Folder.ParentFolder, Folders.Add(), Folders.Item() |

Property	JavaScript	JScript	N	IE	Opera	Notes
Attributes	-	3.0 +	-	4.0 +	-	-
DateCreated	-	3.0 +	-	4.0 +	-	-
DateLastAccessed	-	3.0 +	-	4.0 +	-	-
DateLastModified	-	3.0 +	-	4.0 +	-	-
Drive	-	3.0 +	-	4.0 +	-	-
IsRootFolder	-	3.0 +	-	4.0 +	-	-
Name	-	3.0 +	-	4.0 +	-	-
ParentFolder	-	3.0 +	-	4.0 +	-	-
Path	-	3.0 +	-	4.0 +	-	-
ShortName	-	3.0 +	-	4.0 +	-	-
ShortPath	-	3.0 +	-	4.0 +	-	-
Size	-	3.0 +	-	4.0 +	-	-
SubFolders	-	3.0 +	-	4.0 +	-	-
Type	-	3.0 +	-	4.0 +	-	ReadOnly

Method	JavaScript	JScript	N	IE	Opera	Notes
Copy()	-	3.0 +	-	4.0 +	-	-
Delete()	-	3.0 +	-	4.0 +	-	-
Move()	-	3.0 +	-	4.0 +	-	-

Folders object (Object/JScript)

A special JScript object that contains a collection of Folder objects.

Availability:	JScript – 3.0 Internet Explorer – 4.0	
JavaScript syntax:	IE	myFileSystem.Folders
Object properties:	Count	
Object methods:	Add(), Item()	

You can access items in this array with the methods provided or you can create an Enumerator objects to index through the collection one object at a time.

Property	JavaScript	JScript	N	IE	Opera	Notes
Count	-	3.0 +	-	4.0 +	-	ReadOnly

Method	JavaScript	JScript	N	IE	Opera	Notes
Add()	-	3.0 +	-	4.0 +	-	-
Item()	-	3.0 +	-	4.0 +	-	-

FONT object (Object/HTML)

An object that represents a <FONT> tag.

Availability:	DOM level – 1 JavaScript – 1.5 JScript – 3.0 Internet Explorer – 4.0 Netscape – 6.0	
Inherits from:	*Element object*	
JavaScript syntax:	IE	myFONT = myDocument.all.anElementID
	IE	myFONT = myDocument.all .tags("FONT")[anIndex]
	IE	myFONT = myDocument.all[aName]
	-	myFONT = myDocument .getElementById(anElementID)
	-	myFONT = myDocument.getElementsByName (aName)[anIndex]
	-	myFONT = myDocument .getElementsByTagName("FONT")[anIndex]

HTML syntax:	<FONT> ... </FONT>	
Argument list:	*anIndex*	A reference to an element in a collection
	aName	An associative array reference
	anElementID	The ID value of an Element object
Object properties:	color, face, size	
Event handlers:	onClick, onDblClick, onDragStart, onFilterChange, onHelp, onKeyDown, onKeyPress, onKeyUp, onMouseDown, onMouseMove, onMouseOut, onMouseOver, onMouseUp, onSelectStart	

With this object, you can manipulate the appearance of text enclosed within the <FONT> tag and its corresponding </FONT> closure tag.

However, although this may be possible now, a more future-proof technique would be to modify the attributes of the style object associated with the block of text that is contained by this FONT object. Indeed, you may wish to replace the <FONT> tag with a <DIV> or <SPAN> tag and employ a CLASS="..." HTML tag attribute to attach the style object to it.

See also:	*Element object*

Property	JavaScript	JScript	N	IE	Opera	DOM	HTML	Notes
color	1.5 +	3.0 +	6.0 +	4.0 +	-	1 +	-	-
face	1.5 +	3.0 +	6.0 +	4.0 +	-	1 +	-	-
size	1.5 +	3.0 +	6.0 +	4.0 +	-	1 +	-	-

Event name	JavaScript	JScript	N	IE	Opera	DOM	HTML	Notes
onClick	1.5 +	3.0 +	6.0 +	4.0 +	-	-	4.0 +	Warning
onDblClick	1.5 +	3.0 +	6.0 +	4.0 +	-	-	4.0 +	Warning
onDragStart	-	3.0 +	-	4.0 +	-	-	-	-
onFilterChange	-	3.0 +	-	4.0 +	-	-	-	-
onHelp	-	3.0 +	-	4.0 +	-	-	-	Warning
onKeyDown	1.5 +	3.0 +	6.0 +	4.0 +	-	-	4.0 +	Warning
onKeyPress	1.5 +	3.0 +	6.0 +	4.0 +	-	-	4.0 +	Warning
onKeyUp	1.5 +	3.0 +	6.0 +	4.0 +	-	-	4.0 +	Warning
onMouseDown	1.5 +	3.0 +	6.0 +	4.0 +	-	-	4.0 +	Warning
onMouseMove	1.5 +	3.0 +	6.0 +	4.0 +	-	-	4.0 +	Warning
onMouseOut	1.5 +	3.0 +	6.0 +	4.0 +	-	-	4.0 +	Warning
onMouseOver	1.5 +	3.0 +	6.0 +	4.0 +	-	-	4.0 +	Warning
onMouseUp	1.2 +	3.0 +	6.0 +	4.0 +	-	-	4.0 +	Warning
onSelectStart	-	3.0 +	-	4.0 +	-	-	-	-

Inheritance chain:

Element object, Node object

for(...)...(Iterator)

An iterator mechanism – a loop construct.

Availability:	ECMAScript edition – 2 JavaScript – 1.0 JScript – 1.0 Internet Explorer – 3.02 Netscape – 2.0 Netscape Enterprise Server version – 2.0 Opera – 3.0	
JavaScript syntax:	-	aLabel: for(anInitializer; aCondition; aModifier)
Argument list:	aCondition	An expression that yields a Boolean value
	aLabel	An optional label to name the iterator
	aModifier	Modify the value being enumerated
	anInitializer	Assign the starting value

A for loop is established by setting up the control construct in the header and associating a statement block to be evaluated each time the loop is iterated.

The control construct in a for loop has three semicolon-separated expressions. They are all optional.

The first one initializes the enumerator. It can also declare and initialize a variable to be used for this purpose if one has not already been created.

The second is the condition to test for exit when the required number of loops has been iterated. The for() loop exits when this value becomes false. While it is true, the loop will continue to cycle.

The third is the incrementor (or decrementor if you prefer).

The code in the statement block can be completed early with the break, continue or return statements.

A break will cause the for() loop to drop out and execution to continue at the line following its statement block.

A continue statement will cycle to the next iteration and begin executing the statement block without executing the remaining lines in the block.

A return will exit the loop and its enclosing function and can only be used if the loop is executing inside a function block otherwise the return is meaningless.

You can understand how the `for()` loop works by considering how it can be restated as a `while()` loop.

```
for(anInitializer; aCondition; aModifier)
```

...can be recast as:

```
anInitializer;

while(aCondition)

{

someCode;

aModifier;

}
```

Although the items in the head of a `for()` iterator heading are optional, the semicolons must all be present to indicate the placement of any expressions in the heading.

There is an alternative construction called the `for...in...` statement which is especially useful for operating on objects. Refer to the `for...in...` topic for details.

At version 1.2 of JavaScript, a named continue can be used with this iterator. If the named continue is executed, control passes to the top of the named for loop. The increment expression is evaluated, then the test expression. If necessary the loop iterates once more.

Example code:

```
// Reccomended form
for(ii=0; ii<100; ii++)
{
    document.write("-");
}
// Possibly dangerous during maintenance
for(ii=0; ii<100; ii++)
document.write("-");
// Loop within a loop
for(ii=0; ii<100; ii++)
{
    for(jj=0; jj<ii; jj++)
    {
        document.write("-");
    }
document.write("<BR>");
}
// Loop forever doing some task
for(;;)
{
    animateSpinningGraphic();
}
```

See also:	*break, continue, do ... while(...)*, Flow control, *for(... in ...) ...*, Iteration statement, Label, *Off by one errors, while(...) ...*

Cross-references:

ECMA 262 edition 2 – section – 12.6.2

ECMA 262 edition 2 – section – 12.7

ECMA 262 edition 2 – section – 12.8

ECMA 262 edition 3 – section – 12.6.3

Wrox *Instant JavaScript* – page – 24

for(... in ...) ... (Iterator)

An iterator mechanism – a loop construct.

Availability:	ECMAScript edition – 2 JavaScript – 1.0 JScript – 5.0 Internet Explorer – 5.0 Netscape – 2.0 Netscape Enterprise Server version – 2.0 Opera – 3.0	
JavaScript syntax:	-	`aLabel: for(anLValue in anObject)` `{ someCode };`
Argument list:	`aLabel`	An optional label to identify the loop
	`anLValue`	A value that can be assigned to
	`anObject`	An object whose properties will be cycled
	`someCode`	Some code that executes each time round the loop

A `for...in` iteration statement is used to enumerate through the properties of an object.

The first item in the control construct is a container that a value can be assigned to. An `LValue` or Left-Hand Side expression in other words. The item following the in keyword, is the object whose properties are to be enumerated.

Each time round the loop, the name of an object property will be assigned to the `LValue` and it can then be used as an index to the property value in that object.

Properties that have the `DontEnum` attribute set will not be enumerated in this iteration statement.

During each iteration, the property name can be used as an array index key to extract the property value.

At version 1.2 of JavaScript, a named continue can be used with this iterator. If the named continue is executed, control passes to the top of the named for loop. The loop starts over with the next property name being assigned to the specified variable.

Warnings:

❑ It is often the case that some properties will not be enumerated with this mechanism. In particular, properties of host objects seem particularly prone to this problem.

Example code:

```
// Loop through the properties of an object only printing properties
// that have the string data type.
for(myProperty in myObject)
{
    if(typeof(myObject[myProperty]) == "string")
    {
        document.write(myProperty, myObject[myProperty]);
    }
}
```

See also:	*break,* Compound statement, *continue, do ... while(...),* DontEnumerate, Flow control, *for(...) ...,* Host object, Iteration statement, Label, *while(...) ...*

Cross-references:

ECMA 262 edition 2 – section – 11.1.2

ECMA 262 edition 2 – section – 12.6.3

ECMA 262 edition 2 – section – 12.7

ECMA 262 edition 2 – section – 12.8

ECMA 262 edition 3 – section – 12.6.4

ECMA 262 edition 3 – section – 12.7

ECMA 262 edition 3 – section – 12.8

Wrox *Instant JavaScript* – page – 34

Form object (Object/HTML)

An object representing an HTML <FORM> tag.

Availability:	DOM level – 1 JavaScript – 1.0 JScript – 1.0 Internet Explorer – 3.02 Netscape – 2.0 Opera – 3.0
Inherits from:	*Element object*
JavaScript syntax:	- `myForm = myDocument.aFormName`
	IE `myForm = myDocument.all.anElementID`
	IE `myForm =` `myDocument.all.tags("FORM")[anIndex]`
	IE `myForm = myDocument.all[aName]`
	- `myForm = myDocument.forms.aFormName`
	- `myForm = myDocument.forms[aFormName]`
	- `myForm = myDocument.forms[anIndex]`
	- `myForm =` `myDocument.getElementById(anElementID)`
	- `myForm = myDocument.getElementsByName` `(aName)[anIndex]`
	- `myForm = myDocument` `.getElementsByTagName("FORM")[anIndex]`
	- `myForm = myFormArray[aFormName]`
	- `myForm = myFormArray[anIndex]`
	- `myForm = myInputObject.form`
HTML syntax:	`<FORM> ... </FORM>`
Argument list:	`aFormName` The name of a form in the document
	`anIndex` A reference to an element in a collection
	`aName` An associative array reference
	`anElementID` The ID value of an Element object

Object properties:	`acceptCharset, accessKey, action,`
	`elements, encoding, enctype, length,`
	`method, name, tabIndex, target`

Object methods:	`handleEvent(), reset(), submit()`

Event handlers:	`onClick, onDblClick, onDragStart,`
	`onFilterChange, onHelp, onKeyDown, onKeyPress,`
	`onKeyUp, onMouseDown, onMouseMove, onMouseOut,`
	`onMouseOver, onMouseUp, onReset, onSelectStart,`
	`onSubmit`

Collections:	`elements[]`

Each <FORM> tag creates an object in the document.forms[] array. However even if the forms are given names, those names become properties within the document object and are not assigned as element names in the forms[] array. Because the associative naming is lacking, access to form objects at level 0 of the DOM may need some attention when the DOM becomes level 1.

In MSIE, the form details are collected in a FORM object rather than a Form object. It is these object naming differences that can cause some problems with scripts and it is possible that some implementations will actually make object class references case insensitive to avoid this problem.

Warnings:

❑ You can normally enumerate the properties in a Form object to access the Form input elements. However, if you place a <TEXTAREA> into a <FORM> then Netscape 4.7 on Macintosh will not enumerate the Form properties. The script halts but no error message is generated. MSIE has no problem enumerating a <FORM> containing a <TEXTAREA> tag.

See also:	*Collection object*, Document.<form_name>, Document.forms[], *Element object*, Element.all[], Form.elements[], Form.handleEvent(), Input.accessKey, Input.form, *Legend object*

Property	JavaScript	JScript	N	IE	Opera	DOM	HTML	Notes
acceptCharset	1.5 +	5.0 +	6.0 +	5.0 +	-	1 +	-	-
accessKey	1.0 +	1.0 +	2.0 +	3.02 +	3.0 +	1 +	-	Warning
action	1.0 +	1.0 +	2.0 +	3.02 +	3.0 +	1 +	-	Warning
elements	1.0 +	1.0 +	2.0 +	3.02 +	3.0 +	1 +	-	Warning
encoding	1.0 +	1.0 +	2.0 +	3.02 +	3.0 +	-	-	Warning
enctype	1.5 +	5.0 +	6.0 +	5.0 +	-	1 +	-	-
length	1.0 +	1.0 +	2.0 +	3.02 +	3.0 +	1 +	-	ReadOnly.
method	1.0 +	1.0 +	2.0 +	3.02 +	3.0 +	1 +	-	Warning
name	1.0 +	1.0 +	2.0 +	3.02 +	3.0 +	1 +	-	-
tabIndex	1.5 +	3.0 +	6.0 +	4.0 +	-	1 +	-	-
target	1.0 +	1.0 +	2.0 +	3.02 +	3.0 +	1 +	-	Warning

Method	JavaScript	JScript	N	IE	Opera	DOM	HTML	Notes
handleEvent()	1.2 +	-	4.0 +	-	-	-	-	-
reset()	1.1 +	3.0 +	3.0 +	4.0 +	3.0 +	1 +	-	-
submit()	1.0 +	1.0 +	2.0 +	3.02 +	3.0 +	1 +	-	-

Event name	JavaScript	JScript	N	IE	Opera	DOM	HTML	Notes
onClick	1.0 +	1.0 +	2.0 +	3.0 +	3.0 +	-	4.0 +	Warning
onDblClick	1.2 +	3.0 +	4.0 +	4.0 +	3.0 +	-	4.0 +	Warning
onDragStart	-	3.0 +	-	4.0 +	-	-	-	-
onFilterChange	-	3.0 +	-	4.0 +	-	-	-	-
onHelp	-	3.0 +	-	4.0 +	-	-	-	Warning
onKeyDown	1.2 +	3.0 +	4.0 +	4.0 +	3.0 +	-	4.0 +	Warning
onKeyPress	1.2 +	3.0 +	4.0 +	4.0 +	3.0 +	-	4.0 +	Warning
onKeyUp	1.2 +	3.0 +	4.0 +	4.0 +	3.0 +	-	4.0 +	Warning
onMouseDown	1.2 +	3.0 +	4.0 +	4.0 +	3.0 +	-	4.0 +	Warning
onMouseMove	1.2 +	3.0 +	4.0 +	4.0 +	-	-	4.0 +	Warning
onMouseOut	1.1 +	3.0 +	3.0 +	4.0 +	3.0 +	-	4.0 +	Warning
onMouseOver	1.0 +	1.0 +	2.0 +	3.0 +	3.0 +	-	4.0 +	Warning
onMouseUp	1.2 +	3.0 +	4.0 +	4.0 +	3.0 +	-	4.0 +	Warning
onReset	1.1 +	3.0 +	3.0 +	4.0 +	3.0 +	-	-	-
onSelectStart	-	3.0 +	-	4.0 +	-	-	-	-
onSubmit	1.1 +	3.0 +	3.0 +	4.0 +	3.0 +	-	-	-

Inheritance chain:

Element object, Node object

FormArray object (Object/browser)

The FormArray object is a collection of objects referring to the Form objects for the current document.

Availability:	JavaScript – 1.0 JScript – 3.0 Internet Explorer – 4.0 Netscape – 2.0
JavaScript syntax:	- myFormArray = myDocument.forms
Object properties:	length
Object methods:	item()

The array is constructed by taking the <FORM> tags in the document and building a unique Form object for each.

In MSIE, the FormArray is constructed by adding an element to the array for each Form object and setting its key to be the value of the NAME=" . . . " HTML tag attribute. For two named <FORM> tags, there will be only two entries in the array.

In Netscape, the array is constructed a little differently. First, the Form objects are created as was the case with MSIE. Then they are added to the array and can be accessed numerically. The `FormArray.length` property is then set according to the number of `Form` objects in the array. Then, additional elements are added to the FormArray to correspond to the NAME="..." HTML tag attribute. If you have this in your document:

```
<FORM NAME="ONE">

. . .

<FORM NAME="TWO">

. . .
```

Then your FormArray will contain these entries:

- ❏ 0 -> Form ONE
- ❏ 1 -> Form TWO
- ❏ ONE -> Form ONE
- ❏ TWO -> Form TWO

However the length property will still only return the value 2.

If you make both `<FORM>` tags identical, with the same NAME value, like this:

```
<FORM NAME="ONE">

. . .

<FORM NAME="ONE">

. . .
```

Then, you will get this array:

- ❏ 0 -> First form
- ❏ 1 -> Second form
- ❏ ONE -> Form ONE

The length value still reports 2 but if you enumerate the array contents in a `for(...in...)` loop, you get three entries now instead of four.

Regardless of how you define the forms in MSIE, it will always have the correct number of elements in the FormArray but they might have the same name. You can still access them numerically though.

Warnings:

❑ Although the FormArray is a collection, the MSIE 5.0 browser on the Macintosh will crash if you try to use the item() method on it.

❑ Be careful to avoid naming forms identically if you have more than one in a document. You still get the correct number of Form objects but accessing them via the FormArray may become problematic if you use the name attributes to locate them associatively.

See also:	*Collection object,* Document.forms[]

Property	JavaScript	JScript	N	IE	Opera	HTML	Notes
length	1.0 +	3.0 +	2.0 +	4.0 +	-	-	Warning, ReadOnly

Method	JavaScript	JScript	N	IE	Opera	HTML	Notes
item()	-	3.0 +	-	4.0 +	-	-	-

FormElement object (Object/browser)

An object representing an HTML <INPUT> tag in a <FORM>.

Availability:	JavaScript – 1.0 JScript – 1.0 Internet Explorer – 3.02 Netscape – 2.0
Inherits from:	*Input object*
JavaScript syntax:	IE *myFormElement =* *myDocument.*all.*anElementID*
	IE *myFormElement = myDocument.*all.tags ("INPUT")[*anIndex*]
	IE *myFormElement = myDocument.*all[*aName*]
	- *myFormElement =* *myDocument.*getElementById(*anElementID*)
	- *myFormElement = myDocument.*getElements ByName(*aName*)[*anIndex*]
	- *myFormElement = myForm.anElementName*
	- *myFormElement = myForm.*elements [*anItemIndex*]
	- *myFormElement = myForm*[*anIndex*]
	- *myFormElement = myFormElementsArray* [*anItemIndex*]
	- *myFormElement = myDocument* .getElementsByTagName("INPUT")[*anIndex*]

Argument list:	*anIndex*	A reference to an element in a collection
	aName	An associative array reference
	anElementID	The ID value of an Element object
	anItemIndex	A reference to a single item within the form elements array
Event handlers:	onAfterUpdate, onBeforeUpdate, onBlur, onChange, onClick, onDblClick, onFocus, onHelp, onKeyDown, onKeyPress, onKeyUp, onMouseDown, onMouseMove, onMouseOut, onMouseOver, onMouseUp, onRowEnter, onRowExit, onSelect	

This is a generic description of a form element object. The object will really be a concrete manifestation of a particular class but is available generally as an item in the elements array that belongs to the form.

Refer to the Input object topics for a more detailed description of FormElement functionality.

| See also: | *Button object, BUTTON object, Checkbox object, Element object,* Element.all[], Form.elements.length, Form.elements[], *Input object, Password object, RadioButton object, ResetButton object, Select object, SubmitButton object, TextCell object* |

Event name	JavaScript	JScript	N	IE	Opera	HTML	Notes
onAfterUpdate	-	3.0 +	-	4.0 +	-	-	-
onBeforeUpdate	-	3.0 +	-	4.0 +	-	-	-
onBlur	1.1 +	3.0 +	3.0 +	4.0 +	3.0 +	-	Warning
onChange	1.0 +	3.0 +	2.0 +	4.0 +	3.0 +	-	-
onClick	1.0 +	3.0 +	2.0 +	4.0 +	3.0 +	4.0 +	Warning
onDblClick	1.2 +	3.0 +	4.0 +	4.0 +	3.0 +	4.0 +	Warning
onFocus	1.0 +	3.0 +	2.0 +	4.0 +	3.0 +	-	Warning
onHelp	-	3.0 +	-	4.0 +	-	-	Warning
onKeyDown	1.2 +	3.0 +	4.0 +	4.0 +	3.0 +	4.0 +	Warning
onKeyPress	1.2 +	3.0 +	4.0 +	4.0 +	3.0 +	4.0 +	Warning
onKeyUp	1.2 +	3.0 +	4.0 +	4.0 +	3.0 +	4.0 +	Warning
onMouseDown	1.2 +	3.0 +	4.0 +	4.0 +	3.0 +	4.0 +	Warning
onMouseMove	1.2 +	3.0 +	4.0 +	4.0 +	-	4.0 +	Warning
onMouseOut	1.1 +	3.0 +	3.0 +	4.0 +	3.0 +	4.0 +	Warning
onMouseOver	1.0 +	3.0 +	2.0 +	4.0 +	3.0 +	4.0 +	Warning
onMouseUp	1.2 +	3.0 +	4.0 +	4.0 +	3.0 +	4.0 +	Warning
onRowEnter	-	3.0 +	-	4.0 +	-	-	-
onRowExit	-	3.0 +	-	4.0 +	-	-	-
onSelect	1.0 +	3.0 +	2.0 +	4.0 +	3.0 +	-	-

Inheritance chain:

Element object, Input object, Node object

Frame object (Object/DOM)

An object representing an HTML <FRAME> tag.

Availability:	DOM level – 1 JavaScript – 1.0 JScript – 1.0 Internet Explorer – 3.02 Netscape – 2.0 Opera – 3.0	
Inherits from:	*Window object*	
JavaScript syntax:	-	`myFrame = frame`
	-	`myFrame = frames[anIndex]`
	IE	`myFrame = myDocument.all.aFrameID`
	IE	`myFrame = myDocument.all.tags("FRAME")[anIndex]`
	IE	`myFrame = myDocument.all[aName]`
	-	`myFrame = myDocument.getElementById(anElementID)`
	-	`myFrame = myDocument.getElementsByName (aName)[anIndex]`
	-	`myFrame = myDocument.getElementsBy TagName("FRAME")[anIndex]`
	IE	`myFrame = myDocument.parentWindow`
	-	`myFrame = myFrameArray[anIndex]`
	-	`myFrame = parent`
	-	`myFrame = self`
	-	`myFrame = top`
	-	`myFrame = window`
HTML syntax:	`<FRAME>`	
Argument list:	`anIndex`	A reference to an element in a collection
	`aName`	An associative array reference
	`anElementID`	The ID value of an Element object
Object properties:	`borderColor, className, dataFld, dataSrc, defaultStatus, frameBorder, height, isTextEdit, lang, language, longDesc, marginHeight, marginWidth, name, noResize, parent, parentElement, parentTextEdit, scrolling, sourceIndex, src, style, tagName, title, top`	
Object methods:	`close(), contains(), getAttribute(), removeAttribute(), setAttribute()`	

Event handlers:	onAfterPrint, onBeforePrint, onBeforeUnload, onBlur, onDragDrop, onError, onFocus, onHelp, onLoad, onMouseMove, onMove, onResize, onScroll, onUnload
Collections:	all[], attributes[], children[]

The methods and properties of a frame are the same as those for a `window` object.

Note that MSIE supports a `FRAME` object as opposed to a `Frame` object for the management of frames within a frame-set.

DOM level 2 adds the following properties:

❑   contentDocument

Warnings:

❑   Be aware that if you store a reference to a `frame` object and the frame is closed, if you don't dispose of the reference to the `frame` object then it cannot be garbage collected. A `frame` object with no associated frame is not much use unless you need to keep the object persistent due to having added some properties to it. If this is the case, then arguably, the `frame` object was the wrong place to put such things.

| See also: | *BODY object, captureEvents(), Collection object, Document object,* `Document.activeElement,` *Document.captureEvents(),* `Document.frames[], Document.parentWindow,` *Document.releaseEvents(), Frames object, Global object, IFRAME object, Layer.captureEvents(), Layer.releaseEvents(),* `Layer.window, self` |

Property	JavaScript	JScript	N	IE	Opera	DOM	HTML	Notes
border Color	-	3.0 +	-	4.0 +	-	-	-	-
className	1.0 +	1.0 +	2.0 +	3.02 +	3.0 +	1 +	-	Warning
dataFld	1.0 +	1.0 +	2.0 +	3.02 +	3.0 +	1 +	-	Warning
dataSrc	1.0 +	1.0 +	2.0 +	3.02 +	3.0 +	1 +	-	Warning
default Status	1.0 +	1.0 +	2.0 +	3.02 +	-	-	-	-
frame Border	1.5 +	3.0 +	6.0 +	4.0 +	-	1 +	-	-
height	-	3.0 +	-	4.0 +	-	-	-	Warning
isText Edit	1.0 +	1.0 +	2.0 +	3.02 +	3.0 +	1 +	-	Warning
lang	1.0 +	1.0 +	2.0 +	3.02 +	3.0 +	1 +	-	Warning
language	1.0 +	1.0 +	2.0 +	3.02 +	3.0 +	1 +	-	Warning

Table continued on following page

F

Property	JavaScript	JScript	N	IE	Opera	DOM	HTML	Notes
longDesc	1.5 +	-	6.0 +	-	-	1 +	-	-
marginHeight	1.5 +	3.0 +	6.0 +	4.0 +	-	1 +	-	-
marginWidth	1.5 +	3.0 +	6.0 +	4.0 +	-	1 +	-	-
name	1.0 +	1.0 +	2.0 +	3.02 +	3.0 +	1 +	-	-
noResize	1.5 +	3.0 +	6.0 +	4.0 +	-	1 +	-	-
parent	1.0 +	1.0 +	2.0 +	3.02 +	3.0 +	-	-	-
parentElement	1.0 +	1.0 +	2.0 +	3.02 +	3.0 +	1 +	-	Warning
parentTextEdit	1.0 +	1.0 +	2.0 +	3.02 +	3.0 +	1 +	-	Warning
scrolling	1.5 +	3.0 +	2.0 +	3.0 +	-	1 +	-	Warning
sourceIndex	1.0 +	1.0 +	2.0 +	3.02 +	3.0 +	1 +	-	Warning
src	1.5 +	3.0 +	2.0 +	3.0 +	-	1 +	-	-
style	1.0 +	1.0 +	2.0 +	3.02 +	3.0 +	1 +	-	Warning
tagName	1.0 +	1.0 +	2.0 +	3.02 +	3.0 +	1 +	-	Warning
title	1.0 +	1.0 +	2.0 +	3.02 +	3.0 +	1 +	-	Warning
top	1.0 +	1.0 +	2.0 +	3.02 +	3.0 +	-	-	ReadOnly

Method	JavaScript	JScript	N	IE	Opera	DOM	HTML	Notes
close()	1.0 +	1.0 +	2.0 +	3.02 +	-	-	-	Warning
contains()	1.0 +	1.0 +	2.0 +	3.02 +	3.0 +	1 +	-	Warning
getAttribute()	1.0 +	1.0 +	2.0 +	3.02 +	3.0 +	1 +	-	Warning
removeAttribute()	1.0 +	1.0 +	2.0 +	3.02 +	3.0 +	1 +	-	Warning
setAttribute()	1.0 +	1.0 +	2.0 +	3.02 +	3.0 +	1 +	-	Warning

Event name	JavaScript	JScript	N	IE	Opera	DOM	HTML	Notes
onAfterPrint	-	5.0 +	-	5.0 +	-	-	-	-
onBeforePrint	-	5.0 +	-	5.0 +	-	-	-	-
onBeforeUnload	-	3.0 +	-	4.0 +	-	-	-	-
onBlur	1.1 +	3.0 +	3.0 +	4.0 +	3.0 +	-	-	Warning
onDragDrop	1.2 +	-	4.0 +	-	-	-	-	-
onError	1.1 +	3.0 +	3.0 +	4.0 +	3.0 +	-	-	Warning
onFocus	1.0 +	3.0 +	2.0 +	4.0 +	3.0 +	-	-	Warning
onHelp	-	3.0 +	-	4.0 +	-	-	-	Warning
onLoad	1.0 +	1.0 +	2.0 +	3.02 +	3.0 +	-	-	Warning
onMouseMove	1.2 +	3.0 +	4.0 +	4.0 +	-	-	4.0 +	Warning
onMove	1.2 +	-	4.0 +	-	-	-	-	-
onResize	1.2 +	3.0 +	4.0 +	4.0 +	-	-	-	Warning
onScroll	-	3.0 +	-	4.0 +	-	-	-	-
onUnload	1.0 +	1.0 +	2.0 +	3.02 +	3.0 +	-	-	Warning

Inheritance chain:

Window object

Frames object (Object/browser)

A collection of frames belonging to a document or window.

Availability:	JavaScript – 1.0 JScript – 1.0 Internet Explorer – 3.02 Netscape – 2.0 Opera – 3.0		
JavaScript syntax:	-	`myFrames = frames`	
	-	`myFrames = myDocument.frames`	
	-	`myFrames = myWindow.frames`	
Object properties:	`length`		
Object methods:	`item()`		

An array of `Frame` objects contained within the document or window.

If the `Frames` object were named consistent with the rest of MSIE, it might be called a `FrameArray` object.

Note that `Frame` objects is really another name for `Window` objects.

Each entry in the `Frames` object is a reference to a `Window` object for the specified frame.

Giving the individual frames a name with the `NAME="..."` HTML tag attribute does not feed through into the Frames array. The entries are simply numbered with their index value.

The `frames` property in Netscape points at a `Window` object rather than a `Frames` object. Although there is no Frames array in Netscape, the `Window` object acquires a length value which is the number of `Frame` objects. However, the frames are not enumerable by index number. We can simulate the functionality of the Frames array but to do this, we will need to enumerate all the properties of the `Window` object and eliminate the ones we don't want.

The example below illustrates how to enumerate through the properties of a `Window` object and extract only those which are valid `Frame` objects. The `toString` function forces the new array to pose as a new object class. This actually works in MSIE and Netscape and yields an array that is consistent in both browsers.

Warnings:

❑ The `frames` property in MSIE points at a Frames array object that is easy to enumerate and operate on by itself. In Netscape, the properties that would have been stored in the Frames array in MSIE are simply dumped into the global property space, and stored in a `Window` object. This not only makes them harder to find but much harder to operate on in a logical way. Yet again it illustrates the need for script developers to be aware of the finer points regarding the differences between MSIE and Netscape.

Example code:

```javascript
// Build a FrameArray in Netscape
var myIndex = 0;
var myFramesArray = new Array();
myFramesArray.toString = function () { return "[object FrameArray]";
}

for(var myProp in frames)
{
    if(isDesiredFrameObject(myProp, frames[myProp]))
    {
        myFramesArray[myIndex] = frames[myProp];
        myIndex++;
    }
}

// Select genuine frame objects
function isDesiredFrameObject(aProperty, anObject)
{
    if(toString(anObject) == "[object Window]")
    {
        switch(aProperty)
        {
            case "frames" :
            case "parent" :
            case "top"    :
            case "self"   :
                return false;
            default       :
                return true;
        }
    }
    return false;
}
```

See also: *Collection object,* `Document.frames[]`*, Frame object, Window object,* `Window.frames[]`

Property	JavaScript	JScript	N	IE	Opera	HTML	Notes
length	1.0 +	1.0 +	2.0 +	3.02 +	3.0 +	-	ReadOnly.

Method	JavaScript	JScript	N	IE	Opera	HTML	Notes
item()	1.0 +	1.0 +	2.0 +	3.02 +	3.0 +	-	Warning

FRAMESET object (Object/HTML)

An object that represents a <FRAMESET> tag.

Availability:	DOM level – 1 JavaScript – 1.5 JScript – 3.0 Internet Explorer – 3.0 Netscape – 2.0
Inherits from:	*<classname relation="parent">Element object</classname>*
JavaScript syntax:	IE *myFrameSET = myDocument.all.aFramesetID*
	IE *myFrameSET = myDocument.all.anElementID*
	IE *myFrameSET = myDocument.all.tags ("FRAMESET")[anIndex]*
	IE *myFrameSET = myDocument.all[aName]*
	- *myFrameSET = myDocument.getElementById(anElementID)*
	- *myFrameSET = myDocument .getElementsByName(aName)[anIndex]*
	- *myFrameSET = myDocument.getElementsBy TagName("FRAMESET")[anIndex]*
HTML syntax:	<FRAMESET> ... </FRAMESET>
Argument list:	*anIndex* A reference to an element in a collection
	aName An associative array reference
	anElementID The ID value of an Element object
Object properties:	accessKey, border, borderColor, cols, frameBorder, frameSpacing, rows, tabIndex
Event handlers:	onBeforeUnload, onClick, onDblClick, onHelp, onKeyDown, onKeyPress, onKeyUp, onLoad, onMouseDown, onMouseMove, onMouseOut, onMouseOver, onMouseUp, onResize, onUnload

This object encapsulates the top level frame-set in a multi-paned window. You need to be a little bit of cunning to access the object for the FRAMESET because normally you are running a script that lives inside one of its frames.

Logically, you might assume that a FRAMESET object has a property with a list of frames contained within it. Actually, you can navigate the hierarchy but it's via the usual DOM properties such as childNodes and firstChild etc.

The FRAMESET object can be a useful way of maintaining session state. Although it is only present in the MSIE browser, the Netscape browser can accomplish the same session store techniques with the global object that belongs to the document containing the frame-set.

See also:	*Element object*

Property	JavaScript	JScript	N	IE	Opera	DOM	HTML	Notes
accessKey	-	3.0 +	-	4.0 +	-	-	-	-
border	-	3.0 +	-	4.0 +	-	-	-	-
borderColor	-	3.0 +	-	4.0 +	-	-	-	-
cols	1.5 +	3.0 +	2.0 +	3.0 +	-	1 +	-	-
frameBorder	-	3.0 +	-	4.0 +	-	-	-	-
frameSpacing	-	3.0 +	-	4.0 +	-	-	-	-
rows	1.5 +	3.0 +	2.0 +	3.0 +	-	1 +	-	-
tabIndex	1.5 +	3.0 +	6.0 +	4.0 +	-	1 +	-	-

Event name	JavaScript	JScript	N	IE	Opera	DOM	HTML	Notes
onBeforeUnload	-	3.0 +	-	4.0 +	-	-	-	-
onClick	1.0 +	1.0 +	2.0 +	3.0 +	3.0 +	-	4.0 +	Warning
onDblClick	1.2 +	3.0 +	4.0 +	4.0 +	3.0 +	-	4.0 +	Warning
onHelp	-	3.0 +	-	4.0 +	-	-	-	Warning
onKeyDown	1.2 +	3.0 +	4.0 +	4.0 +	3.0 +	-	4.0 +	Warning
onKeyPress	1.2 +	3.0 +	4.0 +	4.0 +	3.0 +	-	4.0 +	Warning
onKeyUp	1.2 +	3.0 +	4.0 +	4.0 +	3.0 +	-	4.0 +	Warning
onLoad	1.0 +	1.0 +	2.0 +	3.02 +	3.0 +	-	-	Warning
onMouseDown	1.2 +	3.0 +	4.0 +	4.0 +	3.0 +	-	4.0 +	Warning
onMouseMove	1.2 +	3.0 +	4.0 +	4.0 +	-	-	4.0 +	Warning
onMouseOut	1.1 +	3.0 +	3.0 +	4.0 +	3.0 +	-	4.0 +	Warning
onMouseOver	1.0 +	1.0 +	2.0 +	3.0 +	3.0 +	-	4.0 +	Warning
onMouseUp	1.2 +	3.0 +	4.0 +	4.0 +	3.0 +	-	4.0 +	Warning
onResize	1.2 +	3.0 +	4.0 +	4.0 +	-	-	-	Warning
onUnload	1.0 +	1.0 +	2.0 +	3.02 +	3.0 +	-	-	Warning

Inheritance chain:

Element object, Node object

ftp: URL (Request method)

A request from a web browser to an ftp server to send a file.

This will download a file using the FTP protocol. In most respects it is very like accessing with HTTP. However, you may need to specify a user name and password.

See also:	*javascript:* URL, URL

Function object (Object/core)

An object of the class "Function".

Availability:	ECMAScript edition – 2
	JavaScript – 1.0
	JScript – 1.0
	Internet Explorer – 3.02
	Netscape – 2.0
	Netscape Enterprise Server version – 2.0
	Opera – 3.0
JavaScript syntax:	- *myFunction* = Function
	- *myFunction* = new Function()
Object properties:	arity, caller, constructor, length, prototype
Object methods:	apply(), call(), toSource(), toString(), valueOf()
Collections:	arguments[]

An instance of the class "Function" is created by using the new operator on the Function() constructor. The new object adopts the behavior of the built-in prototype object through the prototype-inheritance mechanisms.

All properties and functions of the prototype are available as if they were part of the instance.

Many built-in objects are functions. They can be invoked with arguments. Some of these are constructors. They are functions that are intended to be used with the new operator.

Function objects come in four varieties according to how they are implemented. They may be built in to the interpreter or may be provided as extensions in the script itself. The four types of functions are:

❑ Declared functions in script source text

❑ Anonymous functions built with the Function object constructor

❑ Implementation-supplied functions built into the host environment

❑ Internal functions built into the language

JavaScript has such relaxed syntax rules that it forgives the programmer if the arguments to a function are omitted. Instead, the interpreter will automatically pass the undefined value in place of the missing argument.

Every built-in function has the Function prototype object as the value returned by its internal Prototype property with the exception of the Function prototype object itself, which would return the Object prototype object.

The prototype for the Function prototype object is the Object prototype object.

If you want to create a function with no name, you can create your own `Function` object with the new operator. That function would have some script source associated with it and you can then call your function directly. Although it won't have a name, it would appear as if it did in the script source when you call it. However the name it would appear to have is actually the name of the variable containing the reference to it. Since it is an object, two variables can refer to the same object and you could call the same function under two different names. That might happen if you pass the function as an argument in the calling interface to another function. This is a way of implementing call-backs. You might build a comparator like this and pass it to a `sort()` function.

Creating function objects and referring to them in variables is somewhat like using an `eval()` function to execute script source that you have built in a string.

Example code:

```
// Create a function object
var myFunction = new Function("arg1, arg2", "return(arg1 * arg2);");

// And call it
document.write(myFunction(5, 10));
```

| See also: | Aggregate type, Anonymous function, `Arguments.callee`, `Arguments.caller`, Built-in function, Declared function, Execution context, Function call, *function(...) ...*, Function(), `Function.arity`, *Function.Class*, `Function.length`, `Function.prototype`, Implementation-supplied function, Internal function, JavaScript to Java values, `Native` object, *Object object*, Parameter |

Property	JavaScript	JScript	N	IE	Opera	NES	ECMA	Notes
arity	1.2 +	3.0 +	4.0 +	4.0 +	-	3.0 +	-	Warning, ReadOnly, DontDelete, DontEnum
caller	1.1 +	1.0 +	3.0 +	3.02 +	3.0 +	2.0 +	-	Warning, ReadOnly, DontEnum, Deprecated
constructor	1.1 +	1.0 +	3.0 +	3.02 +	-	-	2 +	DontEnum
length	1.1 +	1.0 +	4.0 +	3.02 +	-	-	2 +	Warning, ReadOnly, DontDelete, DontEnum, Deprecated
prototype	1.1 +	1.0 +	3.0 +	3.02 +	3.0 +	2.0 +	2 +	ReadOnly, DontDelete, DontEnum

Method	JavaScript	JScript	N	IE	Opera	NES	ECMA	Notes
apply()	1.3 +	5.5 +	4.06 +	5.5 +	-	-	3 +.	-
call()	1.3 +	5.5 +	4.06 +	5.5 +	-	-	3 +	-
toSource()	1.3 +	3.0 +	4.06 +	4.0 +	-	-	-	-
toString()	1.1 +	3.0 +	4.0 +	3.0 +	3.0 +	2.0 +	2 +	-
valueOf()	1.1 +	-	4.0 +	-	-	-	2 +	-

Cross-references:

ECMA 262 edition 2 – section – 10.1.1

ECMA 262 edition 2 – section – 10.2.4

ECMA 262 edition 2 – section – 13

ECMA 262 edition 2 – section – 15

ECMA 262 edition 2 – section – 15.3

ECMA 262 edition 3 – section – 10.1.1

ECMA 262 edition 3 – section – 13

ECMA 262 edition 3 – section – 15.3

O'Reilly *JavaScript Definitive Guide* – page – 42

Function() (Function)

A Function object constructor.

Availability:	ECMAScript edition – 2 JavaScript – 1.1 JScript – 1.0 Internet Explorer – 3.02 Netscape – 3.0	
Property/method value type:	Function object	
JavaScript syntax:	-	Function()
	-	Function(*someArguments*)
Argument list:	*someArguments*	Some formal parameters and a block of script source

When the Function constructor is called as a function, it creates and initializes a new function object. The function call Function() is equivalent to the expression new Function() with the same arguments.

The arguments supplied with the Function() constructor are all assumed to be parameters apart from the last one which is taken to be the body Source Script Text. If there is only one argument, then that is taken to be the body of the function.

See also:	Cast operator, Constructor function, constructor property, Function call, Function.prototype, Implicit conversion

Cross-references:

ECMA 262 edition 2 – section – 15.1.3.2

ECMA 262 edition 2 – section – 15.3.1

ECMA 262 edition 2 – section – 15.3.2.1

ECMA 262 edition 2 – section – 15.3.4.1

ECMA 262 edition 3 – section – 15.3.1

Function.Class (Property/internal)

Internal property that returns an object class.

Availability:	ECMAScript edition – 2

This is an internal property that describes the class that a Function object instance is a member of. The reserved words suggest that in the future, this property may be externalized.

See also:	*Class*, Function call, *Function object*

Property attributes:

DontEnum, Internal.

Cross-references:

ECMA 262 edition 2 – section – 8.6.2

ECMA 262 edition 2 – section – 15.3.2.1

ECMA 262 edition 3 – section – 8.6.2

function(...) ... (Declaration)

The description of a function in the script source text.

Availability:		ECMAScript edition – 2 JavaScript – 1.0 JScript – 1.0 Internet Explorer – 3.02 Netscape – 2.0 Netscape Enterprise Server version – 2.0 Opera – 3.0

JavaScript syntax:	-	`function anIdentifier`
		`(aParameter, ...) {`
		`scriptSource }`

Argument list:	`anIdentifier`	The name of the function being declared
	`aParameter`	One of the formal parameters to be passed to the function when it is called
	`scriptSource`	The source text for the script code that is executed when the function is called

A function declaration is a description of a function in the script source text. It provides the function name and a list of its arguments. It also provides a block of script code to be executed when the function is called.

Functions can be declared in the script source to add to the functions your script can make use of. When they are called, the prototype inheritance mechanism matches most local instances of the function having the name that the caller requests. This provides a way to override methods in parent prototypes or the global object.

When functions are declared in global and eval code, the new function object that is instantiated is added to the variable object for the owner of the script source text. It uses the function identifier as a name for the dictionary entry in the variable object. The functions are added in the order in which they appear in the Script Source Text and will replace any previously existing entry. Attributes are set according to the type of code being evaluated.

New functions can be added to the scripting environment as needed. They are described in the source script text with function declarators.

A function is declared with the function keyword, a set of parentheses enclosing its passed arguments and a block of executable code enclosed in curly braces.

Functions will always return a result but a function call can be cast to a void type to discard the resulting value. If you don't indicate a result to return yourself, the function mechanism would return the value undefined.

The internal mechanics of function declaration is to add a function property to the global object whose name is the function's identifier. The value of that property is a function object with the given parameter list and statement block.

If the function definition is part of the source text supplied to an eval function, then the function may be added to an internal activation object rather than the global object.

The act of executing or invoking a function is to call it.

Calling a function is accomplished by using the function property of an object as an RValue and appending the parentheses grouping operators with option arguments grouped within them.

Functions can be created and their script can refer to objects that don't yet exist, however you may not run them until the objects they refer to have been created. This is often the case with event handlers that are defined speculatively on the basis that they may be needed but in fact they may never be called at all.

As of JavaScript version 1.2, you can declare new functions anywhere in a script source text. Prior to this, you could only define them in global code but not inside any if() blocks, loop blocks or with blocks. In JavaScript version 1.2, functions can be declared inside these contexts and inside functions themselves. This means that function availability can be localized to only be usable within a function's context scope.

Warnings:

❑ Debugging namespace collisions between function and variable names can be difficult. For very large projects with many people working on shared code, you may want to establish some strict naming conventions to partition the namespace.

❑ This is an issue because function declarations occur before variable declarations. If you declare a variable with the same name as a function and assign a value to it the function will be inaccessible since you will have replaced the reference to its object with the value you just assigned to the variable.

❑ This will still happen even if the var declaration is placed sequentially earlier in the script block than the function declaration. The first pass declares and sets up the function. The second pass instantiates the variable.

❑ Remember that functions are created at compile (parse) time, and variables at run time.

Example code:

```
// Here is an example function declaration:
function circularArea (aRadius)
{
    someGlobalValue = aRadius;
    return(Math.pow(aRadius,2)*Math.PI);
}

// We are using functions belonging to the Math object to
// raise the passed in radius value to the power of 2
```

```
// and multiply the result by the constant value of PI.
// We can call this and assign its value like this:
myArea = circularArea(12);
alert(myArea);

// If we simply wanted to execute the function and discard its
// result we might use this form:
void circularArea(10000);

// The conseqence is just to set the global value but we don't
// do anything with the returned value.
```

See also: Formal Parameter List, Function.arguments[]

Cross-references:

ECMA 262 edition 2 – section – 10.1.1

ECMA 262 edition 2 – section – 10.1.3

ECMA 262 edition 2 – section – 10.1.6

ECMA 262 edition 2 – section – 13

ECMA 262 edition 2 – section – 15.3.2.1

ECMA 262 edition 3 – section – 10.1.1

ECMA 262 edition 3 – section – 13

ECMA 262 edition 3 – section – 15.3.2.1

Wrox *Instant JavaScript* – page – 26

about: URL (Request method)
AbstractView object (Object/DOM)
ActiveXObject object (Object/JScript)
Add (+) (Operator/additive)
Add then assign (+=) (Operator/assignment)

Get() (Function/internal)

Internal private function that is used to access public properties.

Availability:	ECMAScript edition – 2

This internal function is used to retrieve internal properties from objects.

If the property exists in the receiving object, its value will be returned.

If the property is not a member of the receiving object, then if the Prototype property for this object returns null, we have reached the top of the prototype chain so the property is undefined. The result will be the undefined value.

If the property does not exist, and there is a parent Prototype object, then the message is passed to that object for evaluation.

The Get internal function may indeed return a value when received by a Host object, even if that Host object would respond to the HasProperty function with a false result indicating that the property does not exist.

See also:	Accessor method, GetValue(), Internal Method

Cross-references:

ECMA 262 edition 2 – section – 8.6.2.1

ECMA 262 edition 3 – section – 8.6.2.1

GetBase() (Function/internal)

Internal private function.

Availability:	ECMAScript edition – 2

This internal function returns the base object component pointed at by the reference item passed as its argument.

A runtime error will be generated if the passed in object is not a reference item.

See also:	Reference

Cross-references:

ECMA 262 edition 2 – section – 8.7.1

ECMA 262 edition 3 – section – 8.7.1

GetObject() (Function)

A JScript function that returns a reference to an object representing a file belonging to an application on your system.

Availability:	JScript – 3.0 Internet Explorer – 4.0	
Property/method value type:	Automation object	
JavaScript syntax:	IE	GetObject(aLocation)
	IE	GetObject(aLocation, anObjectType)
	IE	GetObject (aLocation!aSubObject)
	IE	GetObject(aLocation! aSubObject, anObjectType)
Argument list:	anObjectType	What sort of application and object class type to be created
	aLocation	A path to the file for the object to be instantiated
	aSubObject	A fragment identifier for a sub-object within the file

When this function is called, the application may be activated to provide a remote interface to the file. You can also specify fragments within the file.

The path argument points at the file within the file system where the object you want reposes.

This is related to the `ActiveXObject()` constructor which creates an object that points at an application or document without loading a file to instantiate it.

The objects created by this function are called `Automation` objects.

The location value can have a fragment identifier delimited by an exclamation mark. With this for example, you can refer to one worksheet within an Excel document.

Example code:

```
// Locate an Excel spreadsheet
myWorkbook = GetObject("F:\\DOCUMENTS\\ACCOUNTS.XLS");
// Locate one worksheet within an Excel spreadsheet
myWorkSheet = GetObject("F:\\DOCUMENTS\\ACCOUNTS.XLS!sheet4");
```

See also:	`ActiveXObject()`

GetPropertyName() (Function/internal)

Internal private function.

Availability:	ECMAScript edition – 2

This internal function returns the property name component of the reference item passed in its argument.

A run time error is generated if the argument passed is not a reference item.

See also:	Reference

Cross-references:

ECMA 262 edition 2 – section – 8.7.2

ECMA 262 edition 3 – section – 8.7.2

GetValue() (Function/internal)

Internal private function.

Availability:	ECMAScript edition – 2

This internal function returns the value contained in the property belonging to the object pointed at by the reference item passed in its argument.

If the passed in argument is not a reference item, it is returned as the result.

If the object being referred to does not exist, a run-time error is generated.

Otherwise the usual Get() function behavior is invoked for the property named in the reference.

See also:	Get(), Reference

Cross-references:

ECMA 262 edition 2 – section – 8.7.3

ECMA 262 edition 3 – section – 8.7.1

Global object (Object/core)

A special type of object that is always available in the prototype chain.

Availability:	ECMAScript edition – 2 JavaScript – 1.0 JScript – 1.0 Internet Explorer – 3.0 Netscape – 2.0	
JavaScript syntax:	-	`myGlobal = document.parentWindow`
	-	`myGlobal = frame`
	-	`myGlobal = self`
	-	`myGlobal = window`
	-	`myGlobal = window.frames[anIndex]`
Argument list:	`anIndex`	A reference to a window object which is also a global object for that window

Object properties:	clientInformation, clipboardData, closed, crypto, defaultStatus, dialogArguments, dialogHeight, dialogLeft, dialogTop, dialogWidth, document, event, external, frame, frameRate, history, innerHeight, innerWidth, java, length, location, locationbar, Math, menubar, name, navigator, netscape, offScreenBuffering, opener, outerHeight, outerWidth, Packages, pageXOffset, pageYOffset, parent, personalbar, pkcs11, returnValue, screen, screenLeft, screenTop, screenX, screenY, scrollbars, secure, self, status, statusbar, sun, toolbar, top, window
Class constants:	Infinity, NaN, undefined
Object methods:	addClient(), addResponseHeader(), alert(), Array(), attachEvent(), back(), blob(), blur(), Boolean(), callC(), clearInterval(), clearTimeout(), close(), confirm(), Date(), debug(), deleteResponseHeader(), detachEvent(), disableExternalCapture(), enableExternalCapture(), escape(), eval(), execScript(), find(), flush, focus(), forward(), Function(), getOptionValue(), getOptionValueCount(), home(), isFinite(), isNaN(), moveBy(), moveTo(), navigate(), Number(), Object(), open(), parseFloat(), parseInt(), print(), prompt(), redirect(), registerCFunction(), resizeBy(), resizeTo(), scroll(), scrollBy(), scrollTo(), setHotkeys(), setInterval(), setResizable(), setTimeout(), setZOptions(), showHelp(), showModalDialog(), showModelessDialog(), ssjs_generateClientID(), ssjs_getCGIVariable(), ssjs_getClientID(), stop(), String(), typeof(), unescape(), write()
Functions:	atob(), btoa(), captureEvents(), handleEvent(), releaseEvents(), routeEvent()
Event handlers:	onAfterPrint, onBeforePrint, onBeforeUnload, onBlur, onDragDrop, onError, onFocus, onHelp, onLoad, onMove, onResize, onUnload
Collections:	frames[]

G

JavaScript Programmer's Reference

The Global object is unique and is created before any code is executed. In an ECMAScript compliant implementation it is where variables, methods, functions and properties are stored if you don't explicitly attach them to another object yourself. The member properties, methods, functions and variables are globally available because the Global object is placed into the scope chain of every execution context.

In a web browser, the Global object is also the Window object. In a server-side implementation, the Global object is probably the Response object but this is not mandatory. Other implementations will one of the host objects as the Global object but there is no defined and standard choice.

Since you don't ever use the keyword Global and can avoid using the keyword Window the properties and methods look as if they are part of the core language rather than members of an object. Web browsers are becoming more ECMAScript compliant as new versions are released.

The Global object is added to the scope chain of a program when it commences execution. Other built-in objects are accessible as initial properties of the global object. Some of these are added as core functionality and are available in all implementations. Others are added as host objects defined differently for each implementation.

When the Global object is created, it always has at least the following properties:

❏ Object object

❏ Function object

❏ Array object

❏ String object

❏ Boolean object

❏ Number object

❏ Date object

❏ Math object

❏ Value properties

❏ Utility function properties

❏ Additional host defined properties

Most of the properties initially provided by the Global object cannot be enumerated as their DontEnum attribute is set (at least in ECMA compliant implementations).

The initial properties soon change and are added to when the flow of control enters execution contexts and begins to process scripts.

The value properties that are initially set up in the Global object are listed in this table:

Name
Infinity
NaN

Refer to the discussion on each of the Value Properties for more details.

Some host implementations create aliases for the Global object and store those self referring aliases in the Global object when it is initialized. An example of this behavior is the window object created in some web browser host implementations of JavaScript.

There is one Global object for each window in a web browser. There is also one for each frame in a frame-set. This means that you can have Global objects that have global variables that are not shared with one another.

However, you can access them by referring to the parent object. This goes to an object context that contains the current frame. You can also access the top or outer window of a frame-set hierarchy directly.

Whether you can truly access objects in other windows or frames comes down to some basic security issues. Generally the security policy prevents access to code that arrives from different servers. You can legally get at values in pages served from the same host as your page was served from. It is unreasonable to be able to access variables in a page served from another host. This can lead to difficulties if you serve your site from multiple hosts. It isn't as limiting as all that though and there are ways to grant permission via the security policy in the browser.

Global objects support different sub-sets of the complete range of properties according to the context they are used. Server-side JavaScript won't support anything to do with window display and client-side (browser) JavaScript does not need to know about request-response handling.

If you want to access a Global object in another context, perhaps in a different window, you need to assign it to a variable. In the syntax listing this is illustrated by assigning references to Global objects to the *myGlobal* variable.

Warnings:

❑ You cannot use the Global object with the new operator to make a copy.

❑ You cannot call the Global object as a function.

❑ The value of the internal Prototype property of the Global object is implementation dependant. Since it contains the Object object as one of its children, it could not inherit its Prototype from there since that could set up an endlessly recurring loop of Prototype inheritors. It is likely that the Prototype of the Global object is null. If it is important that you know the value of this, then you should test it with a debugging script first. However, you may be writing non-portable code if you depend on the value that it indicates.

❑ In a web browser, the Window object serves as the Global object. It owns all the properties that you would expect the Global object to have in a core implementation. The hosting environment adds the other window-based properties.

See also:	escape(), eval(), Infinity, isFinite(), isNaN(), NaN, parseFloat(), parseInt(), typeof, undefined, unescape(), Window object

Property	JavaScript	JScript	N	IE	Opera	NES	ECMA	Notes
client Information	1.0 +	1.0 +	2.0 +	3.0 +	-	-	2 +	Warning
clipboardData	1.0 +	1.0 +	2.0 +	3.0 +	-	-	2 +	Warning
closed	1.0 +	1.0 +	2.0 +	3.0 +	-	-	2 +	Warning
crypto	1.0 +	1.0 +	2.0 +	3.0 +	-	-	2 +	Warning
defaultStatus	1.0 +	1.0 +	2.0 +	3.0 +	-	-	2 +	Warning
dialog Arguments	1.0 +	1.0 +	2.0 +	3.0 +	-	-	2 +	Warning
dialogHeight	1.0 +	1.0 +	2.0 +	3.0 +	-	-	2 +	Warning
dialogLeft	1.0 +	1.0 +	2.0 +	3.0 +	-	-	2 +	Warning
dialogTop	1.0 +	1.0 +	2.0 +	3.0 +	-	-	2 +	Warning
dialogWidth	1.0 +	1.0 +	2.0 +	3.0 +	-	-	2 +	Warning
document	1.0 +	1.0 +	2.0 +	3.0 +	-	-	2 +	Warning
event	1.0 +	1.0 +	2.0 +	3.0 +	-	-	2 +	Warning
external	1.0 +	1.0 +	2.0 +	3.0 +	-	-	2 +	Warning
frame	1.0 +	1.0 +	2.0 +	3.0 +	-	-	2 +	Warning
frameRate	1.0 +	1.0 +	2.0 +	3.0 +	-	-	2 +	Warning
history	1.0 +	1.0 +	2.0 +	3.0 +	-	-	2 +	Warning
innerHeight	1.0 +	1.0 +	2.0 +	3.0 +	-	-	2 +	Warning
innerWidth	1.0 +	1.0 +	2.0 +	3.0 +	-	-	2 +	Warning
java	1.0 +	1.0 +	2.0 +	3.0 +	-	-	2 +	Warning
length	1.0 +	1.0 +	2.0 +	3.0 +	-	-	2 +	Warning
location	1.0 +	1.0 +	2.0 +	3.0 +	-	-	2 +	Warning
locationbar	1.0 +	1.0 +	2.0 +	3.0 +	-	-	2 +	Warning
Math	1.0 +	1.0 +	2.0 +	3.0 +	-	-	2 +	Warning
menubar	1.0 +	1.0 +	2.0 +	3.0 +	-	-	2 +	Warning
name	1.0 +	1.0 +	2.0 +	3.0 +	-	-	2 +	Warning
navigator	1.0 +	1.0 +	2.0 +	3.0 +	-	-	2 +	Warning
netscape	1.0 +	1.0 +	2.0 +	3.0 +	-	-	2 +	Warning
offScreen Buffering	1.0 +	1.0 +	2.0 +	3.0 +	-	-	2 +	Warning
opener	1.0 +	1.0 +	2.0 +	3.0 +	-	-	2 +	Warning
outerHeight	1.0 +	1.0 +	2.0 +	3.0 +	-	-	2 +	Warning
outerWidth	1.0 +	1.0 +	2.0 +	3.0 +	-	-	2 +	Warning
Packages	1.0 +	1.0 +	2.0 +	3.0 +	-	-	2 +	Warning
pageXOffset	1.0 +	1.0 +	2.0 +	3.0 +	-	-	2 +	Warning
pageYOffset	1.0 +	1.0 +	2.0 +	3.0 +	-	-	2 +	Warning
parent	1.0 +	1.0 +	2.0 +	3.0 +	-	-	2 +	Warning
personalbar	1.0 +	1.0 +	2.0 +	3.0 +	-	-	2 +	Warning
pkcs11	1.0 +	1.0 +	2.0 +	3.0 +	-	-	2 +	Warning
returnValue	1.0 +	1.0 +	2.0 +	3.0 +	-	-	2 +	Warning
screen	1.0 +	1.0 +	2.0 +	3.0 +	-	-	2 +	Warning

Property	JavaScript	JScript	N	IE	Opera	NES	ECMA	Notes
screenLeft	1.0 +	1.0 +	2.0 +	3.0 +	-	-	2 +	Warning
screenTop	1.0 +	1.0 +	2.0 +	3.0 +	-	-	2 +	Warning
screenX	1.0 +	1.0 +	2.0 +	3.0 +	-	-	2 +	Warning
screenY	1.0 +	1.0 +	2.0 +	3.0 +	-	-	2 +	Warning
scrollbars	1.0 +	1.0 +	2.0 +	3.0 +	-	-	2 +	Warning
secure	1.0 +	1.0 +	2.0 +	3.0 +	-	-	2 +	Warning
self	1.0 +	1.0 +	2.0 +	3.0 +	-	-	2 +	Warning
status	1.0 +	1.0 +	2.0 +	3.0 +	-	-	2 +	Warning
statusbar	1.0 +	1.0 +	2.0 +	3.0 +	-	-	2 +	Warning
sun	1.0 +	1.0 +	2.0 +	3.0 +	-	-	2 +	Warning
toolbar	1.0 +	1.0 +	2.0 +	3.0 +	-	-	2 +	Warning
top	1.0 +	1.0 +	2.0 +	3.0 +	-	-	2 +	Warning
window	1.0 +	1.0 +	2.0 +	3.0 +	-	-	2 +	Warning

Method	JavaScript	JScript	N	IE	Opera	NES	ECMA	Notes
addClient()	1.0 +	1.0 +	2.0 +	3.0 +	-	-	2 +	Warning
addResponse Header()	1.0 +	1.0 +	2.0 +	3.0 +	-	-	2 +	Warning
alert()	1.0 +	1.0 +	2.0 +	3.0 +	-	-	2 +	Warning
Array()	1.0 +	1.0 +	2.0 +	3.0 +	-	-	2 +	Warning
attachEvent()	1.0 +	1.0 +	2.0 +	3.0 +	-	-	2 +	Warning
back()	1.0 +	1.0 +	2.0 +	3.0 +	-	-	2 +	Warning
blob()	1.0 +	1.0 +	2.0 +	3.0 +	-	-	2 +	Warning
blur()	1.0 +	1.0 +	2.0 +	3.0 +	-	-	2 +	Warning
Boolean()	1.0 +	1.0 +	2.0 +	3.0 +	-	-	2 +	Warning
callC()	1.0 +	1.0 +	2.0 +	3.0 +	-	-	2 +	Warning
clearInterval()	1.0 +	1.0 +	2.0 +	3.0 +	-	-	2 +	Warning
clearTimeout()	1.0 +	1.0 +	2.0 +	3.0 +	-	-	2 +	Warning
close()	1.0 +	1.0 +	2.0 +	3.0 +	-	-	2 +	Warning
confirm()	1.0 +	1.0 +	2.0 +	3.0 +	-	-	2 +	Warning
Date()	1.0 +	1.0 +	2.0 +	3.0 +	-	-	2 +	Warning
debug()	1.0 +	1.0 +	2.0 +	3.0 +	-	-	2 +	Warning
deleteResponse Header()	1.0 +	1.0 +	2.0 +	3.0 +	-	-	2 +	Warning
detachEvent()	1.0 +	1.0 +	2.0 +	3.0 +	-	-	2 +	Warning
disableExternal Capture()	1.0 +	1.0 +	2.0 +	3.0 +	-	-	2 +	Warning
enableExternal Capture()	1.0 +	1.0 +	2.0 +	3.0 +	-	-	2 +	Warning
escape()	1.0 +	1.0 +	2.0 +	3.0 +	-	-	2 +	Warning

Table continued on following page

G

JavaScript Programmer's Reference

Method	JavaScript	JScript	N	IE	Opera	NES	ECMA	Notes
eval()	1.0 +	1.0 +	2.0 +	3.0 +	-	-	2 +	Warning
execScript()	1.0 +	1.0 +	2.0 +	3.0 +	-	-	2 +	Warning
find()	1.0 +	1.0 +	2.0 +	3.0 +	-	-	2 +	Warning
flush	1.0 +	1.0 +	2.0 +	3.0 +	-	-	2 +	Warning
focus()	1.0 +	1.0 +	2.0 +	3.0 +	-	-	2 +	Warning
forward()	1.0 +	1.0 +	2.0 +	3.0 +	-	-	2 +	Warning
Function()	1.0 +	1.0 +	2.0 +	3.0 +	-	-	2 +	Warning
getOption Value()	1.0 +	1.0 +	2.0 +	3.0 +	-	-	2 +	Warning
getOption ValueCount()	1.0 +	1.0 +	2.0 +	3.0 +	-	-	2 +	Warning
home()	1.0 +	1.0 +	2.0 +	3.0 +	-	-	2 +	Warning
isFinite()	1.0 +	1.0 +	2.0 +	3.0 +	-	-	2 +	Warning
isNaN()	1.0 +	1.0 +	2.0 +	3.0 +	-	-	2 +	Warning
moveBy()	1.0 +	1.0 +	2.0 +	3.0 +	-	-	2 +	Warning
moveTo()	1.0 +	1.0 +	2.0 +	3.0 +	-	-	2 +	Warning
navigate()	1.0 +	1.0 +	2.0 +	3.0 +	-	-	2 +	Warning
Number()	1.0 +	1.0 +	2.0 +	3.0 +	-	-	2 +	Warning
Object()	1.0 +	1.0 +	2.0 +	3.0 +	-	-	2 +	Warning
open()	1.0 +	1.0 +	2.0 +	3.0 +	-	-	2 +	Warning
parseFloat()	1.0 +	1.0 +	2.0 +	3.0 +	-	-	2 +	Warning
parseInt()	1.0 +	1.0 +	2.0 +	3.0 +	-	-	2 +	Warning
print()	1.0 +	1.0 +	2.0 +	3.0 +	-	-	2 +	Warning
prompt()	1.0 +	1.0 +	2.0 +	3.0 +	-	-	2 +	Warning
redirect	1.0 +	1.0 +	2.0 +	3.0 +	-	-	2 +	Warning
registerC Function()	1.0 +	1.0 +	2.0 +	3.0 +	-	-	2 +	Warning
resizeBy()	1.0 +	1.0 +	2.0 +	3.0 +	-	-	2 +	Warning
resizeTo()	1.0 +	1.0 +	2.0 +	3.0 +	-	-	2 +	Warning
scroll()	1.0 +	1.0 +	2.0 +	3.0 +	-	-	2 +	Warning
scrollBy()	1.0 +	1.0 +	2.0 +	3.0 +	-	-	2 +	Warning
scrollTo()	1.0 +	1.0 +	2.0 +	3.0 +	-	-	2 +	Warning
setHotkeys()	1.0 +	1.0 +	2.0 +	3.0 +	-	-	2 +	Warning
setInterval()	1.0 +	1.0 +	2.0 +	3.0 +	-	-	2 +	Warning
setResizable()	1.0 +	1.0 +	2.0 +	3.0 +	-	-	2 +	Warning
setTimeout()	1.0 +	1.0 +	2.0 +	3.0 +	-	-	2 +	Warning
setZOptions()	1.0 +	1.0 +	2.0 +	3.0 +	-	-	2 +	Warning
showHelp()	1.0 +	1.0 +	2.0 +	3.0 +	-	-	2 +	Warning
showModal Dialog()	1.0 +	1.0 +	2.0 +	3.0 +	-	-	2 +	Warning
showModeless Dialog()	1.0 +	1.0 +	2.0 +	3.0 +	-	-	2 +	Warning

Method	JavaScript	JScript	N	IE	Opera	NES	ECMA	Notes
ssjs_generate ClientID()	1.0 +	1.0 +	2.0 +	3.0 +	-	-	2 +	Warning
ssjs_getCGI Variable()	1.0 +	1.0 +	2.0 +	3.0 +	-	-	2 +	Warning
ssjs_get ClientID()	1.0 +	1.0 +	2.0 +	3.0 +	-	-	2 +	Warning
stop()	1.0 +	1.0 +	2.0 +	3.0 +	-	-	2 +	Warning
String()	1.0 +	1.0 +	2.0 +	3.0 +	-	-	2 +	Warning
typeof()	1.0 +	1.0 +	2.0 +	3.0 +	-	-	2 +	Warning
unescape()	1.0 +	1.0 +	2.0 +	3.0 +	-	-	2 +	Warning
write()	1.0 +	1.0 +	2.0 +	3.0 +	-	-	2 +	Warning

Event name	JavaScript	JScript	N	IE	Opera	NES	ECMA	Notes
onAfterPrint	-	5.0 +	-	5.0 +	-	-	-	-
onBeforePrint	-	5.0 +	-	5.0 +	-	-	-	-
onBeforeUnload	-	3.0 +	-	4.0 +	-	-	-	-
onBlur	1.1 +	3.0 +	3.0 +	4.0 +	3.0 +	-	-	Warning
onDragDrop	1.2 +	-	4.0 +	-	-	-	-	-
onError	1.1 +	3.0 +	3.0 +	4.0 +	3.0 +	-	-	Warning
onFocus	1.0 +	3.0 +	2.0 +	4.0 +	3.0 +	-	-	Warning
onHelp	-	3.0 +	-	4.0 +	-	-	-	Warning
onLoad	1.0 +	1.0 +	2.0 +	3.02 +	3.0 +	-	-	Warning
onMove	1.2 +	-	4.0 +	-	-	-	-	-
onResize	1.2 +	3.0 +	4.0 +	4.0 +	-	-	-	Warning
onUnload	1.0 +	1.0 +	2.0 +	3.02 +	3.0 +	-	-	Warning

Cross-references:

ECMA 262 edition 2 – section – 10.1.5

ECMA 262 edition 2 – section – 15

ECMA 262 edition 3 – section – 10.1.5

ECMA 262 edition 3 – section – 15.1

goto (Reserved word)

Reserved for future language enhancements.

This keyword suggests that future versions of JavaScript may support the goto statement which will unconditionally go to a labelled portion of script source text. This also suggests that labels will need to be supported as well.

G

JavaScript Programmer's Reference

ECMA edition 3 already mandates that case and default labels are supported for the benefit of the switch() statement.

The ECMA standard notes that although it is reserved future use, an implementation is still compliant if it provides the appropriate functionality of these reserved keywords.

See also:	Jump statement, Label, Reserved word

Cross-references:

ECMA 262 edition 2 – section – 7.4.3

ECMA 262 edition 3 – section – 7.5.3

Greater than (>) (Operator/relational)

Compare two operands to determine which is nearer to +Infinity.

Availability:	ECMAScript edition – 2 JavaScript – 1.0 JScript – 1.0 Internet Explorer – 3.02 Netscape – 2.0 Netscape Enterprise Server version – 2.0 Opera – 3.0	
Property/method value type:	Boolean primitive	
JavaScript syntax:	-	anOperand1 > anOperand2
Argument list:	anOperand1	A value that can be compared numerically or lexically
	anOperand2	A compatible value

Returns true if the left operand is numerically greater than the right operand or is sorted later in the Unicode collating sequence when two string values are compared.

In numeric comparisons, the presence of NaN in either or both operands will yield undefined instead of true or false.

When comparing two strings, a prefixing plus sign is present, then a numeric coercion of a string takes place before the comparison. Numeric coercion takes place when either of the operands is numeric.

In ECMA compliant JavaScript implementations, string values are simply compared according to the Unicode character code point values with no attempt to provide the more complex semantically oriented definitions of character and string equality defined in the Unicode version 2.0 specification.

The associativity is left to right.

Refer to the operator precedence topic for details of execution order.

The result is the Boolean value true if *anOperand1* is numerically or lexically greater than *anOperand2* otherwise false is returned.

See also:	ASCII, Associativity, Equal to (==), Greater than or equal to (>=), Identically equal to (===), Less than (<), Less than or equal to (<=), Logical expression, Logical operator, NOT Equal to (!=), NOT Identically equal to (!==), Operator Precedence, Relational expression, Relational operator, Unicode

Cross-references:

ECMA 262 edition 2 – section – 11.8.2

ECMA 262 edition 2 – section – 11.8.5

ECMA 262 edition 3 – section – 11.8.2

ECMA 262 edition 3 – section – 11.8.5

Greater than or equal to (>=) (Operator/relational)

Compare two operands to determine which is nearer to +Infinity or whether they are equal.

Availability:	ECMAScript edition – 2 JavaScript – 1.0 JScript – 1.0 Internet Explorer – 3.02 Netscape – 2.0 Netscape Enterprise Server version – 2.0 Opera – 3.0	
Property/method value type:	Boolean primitive	
JavaScript syntax:	-	anOperand1 >= anOperand2
Argument list:	anOperand1	A value that can be compared numerically or lexically
	anOperand2	A compatible value

Returns true if the left operand is numerically greater than or equal to the right operand or is sorted later or identically in the Unicode collating sequence when two string values are compared.

In numeric comparisons, the presence of NaN in either or both operands will yield undefined instead of true or false.

When comparing two strings, a prefixing plus sign is present, then a numeric coercion of a string takes place before the comparison. Numeric coercion takes place when either of the operands is numeric.

In ECMA compliant JavaScript implementations, string values are simply compared according to the Unicode character code point values with no attempt to provide the more complex semantically oriented definitions of character and string equality defined in the Unicode version 2.0 specification.

The associativity is left to right.

Refer to the operator precedence topic for details of execution order.

The result is the Boolean value true if *anOperand1* is numerically or lexically greater than or equal to *anOperand2* otherwise false is returned.

See also:	ASCII, Associativity, Equal to (==), Greater than (>), Identically equal to (===), Less than (<), Less than or equal to (<=), Logical expression, Logical operator, NOT Equal to (!=), NOT Identically equal to (!==), Operator Precedence, Relational expression, Relational operator, Unicode

Cross-references:

ECMA 262 edition 2 – section – 11.8.4

ECMA 262 edition 3 – section – 11.8.4

Grouping operator ( ) (Delimiter)

A means of controlling precedence of evaluation in expressions.

Availability:	ECMAScript edition – 2

The grouping operator is a pair of parentheses placed around an expression or expressions to control the precedence of evaluation in expressions so that the sub-expressions are evaluated in the correct order. It is also used to enclose the arguments to a function or method.

Placing parentheses around expressions controls the order in which they are evaluated and can override the normal precedence that operators assume. This allows delete and typeof operations to be applied to expressions in parentheses for example.

Controlling the precedence of expressions allows operators with lower precedence to be evaluated ahead of the higher priority expression operators. For example:

```
A + B * C
```

by implication is executed like this:

```
A + (B * C)
```

A and B can be added before the multiplication like this:

```
(A + B) * C
```

This forces the addition to occur before the multiplication and is functionally equivalent to:

```
A*C + B*C
```

The associativity is left to right.

Refer to the operator precedence topic for details of execution order.

See also:	Associativity, delete, Function call operator ( ), Operator, Operator Precedence, Parentheses ( ), Primary expression, `typeof`

Cross-references:

ECMA 262 edition 2 – section – 11.1.4

ECMA 262 edition 3 – section – 11.1.6

about: URL (Request method)
AbstractView object (Object/DOM)
ActiveXObject object (Object/JScript)
Add (+) (Operator/additive)
Add then assign (+=) (Operator/
assignment)

handleEvent() (Function)

Pass an event to the appropriate handler for this object.

Availability:	JavaScript – 1.2 Netscape – 4.0	
Property/method value type:	`undefined`	
JavaScript syntax:	N	`handleEvent(anEvent)`
	N	`myWindow.handleEvent` `(anEvent)`
Argument list:	`anEvent`	An Event object

This applies to Netscape prior to version 6.0. From that release onwards, event management follows the guidelines in the DOM level 3 event specification.

This method is supported by all objects that respond to events. It is part of the event management suite which allows events to be routed to handlers other than just the one that defaults to being associated with an event.

On receipt of a call to this method, the receiving object will look at its available set of event handler functions and pass the event to an appropriately mapped handler function. It is essentially an event dispatcher that is granular down to the object level.

The argument value is an `Event` object that contains information about the event.

See also:	`Button.handleEvent()`, *captureEvents()*, `Checkbox.handleEvent()`, *Document.handleEvent()*, Event handler, Event management, `FileUpload.handleEvent()`, `Form.handleEvent()`, `Input.handleEvent()`, *Layer.handleEvent()*, `Password.handleEvent()`, `RadioButton.handleEvent()`, `ResetButton.handleEvent()`, *Window.handleEvent()*, *Window.routeEvent()*

Cross-references:

Wrox *Instant JavaScript* – page – 55

HasInstance() (Function/internal)

Internal private function to test for the existence of an instance.

Availability:	ECMAScript edition – 3

This internal function returns a Boolean value indicating whether the `function` object is the prototype of an instance object that is passed as an argument. If it is, then the function returns true.

This is an internal function very similar to the `Object.isPrototypeOf()` method.

See also:	`Object.isPrototypeOf()`

Cross-references:

ECMA 262 edition 3 – section – 15.3.5.3

HasProperty() (Function/internal)

Internal private function to test for the existence of a property.

Availability:	ECMAScript edition – 2

This internal function returns a Boolean value indicating whether the object contains the named property.

If the receiving object has the property, then the result is true.

If the receiving object does not, then the prototype chain is walked until the property is found or the chain is exhausted.

If a null prototype is found, the false value is returned.

Host objects may or may not strictly honor the intent of this internal function. The ECMA standard allows for the possibility that a host object may still properly manage `Get` and `Put` internal functions, even if the `HasProperty` function returns false for the properties being accessed.

To cope with that eventuality, ECMAScript edition 3 provides a way to test whether an object has a property of its own, but this test ignores the prototype inheritance. You might simulate that by walking up the prototype chain, testing objects as you go.

See also:	*Attribute object, Attributes object,* Host object, Internal Method, `Object.hasOwnProperty()`

Cross-references:

ECMA 262 edition 2 – section – 8.6.2.4

ECMA 262 edition 3 – section – 8.6.2.4

HEAD object (Object/HTML)

A special MSIE object that represents the head block of an HTML document.

Availability:	DOM level – 1 JavaScript – 1.5 JScript – 3.0 Internet Explorer – 4.0 Netscape – 6.0
Inherits from:	*Element object*
JavaScript syntax:	IE *myHEAD* = *myDocument*.all.*anElementID*
	IE *myHEAD* = *myDocument*.all.tags ("HEAD")[*anIndex*]
	IE *myHEAD* = *myDocument*.all[*aName*]
	- *myHEAD* = *myDocument*.getElementById (*anElementID*)
	- *myHEAD* = *myDocument*.getElementsByName (*aName*)[*anIndex*]
	- *myHEAD* = *myDocument*. getElementsByTagName("HEAD")[*anIndex*]
HTML syntax:	\<HEAD> ... \</HEAD>
Argument list:	*anIndex* A reference to an element in a collection
	aName An associative array reference
	anElementID The ID value of an Element object
Object properties:	profile, vAlign
Event handlers:	onClick, onDblClick, onHelp, onKeyDown, onKeyPress, onKeyUp, onMouseDown, onMouseMove, onMouseOut, onMouseOver, onMouseUp

This object inherits from HTML. It has a TITLE object as one of its children and its sibling is the BODY object that represents the contents of the <BODY> tag.

The CLASS tag attribute is supported by MSIE but serves no purpose other than maintaining consistency. You should avoid its use even though the reference is maintained within the corresponding HEAD object.

See also:	*BODY object, Element object,* HEAD.profile

Property	JavaScript	JScript	N	IE	Opera	DOM	HTML	Notes
profile	1.5 +	5.0 +	6.0 +	5.0 +	-	1 +	-	-
vAlign	-	3.0 +	-	4.0 +	-	-	-	Warning

403

Event name	JavaScript	JScript	N	IE	Opera	DOM	HTML	Notes
onClick	1.5 +	3.0 +	6.0 +	4.0 +	3.0 +	-	4.0 +	Warning
onDblClick	1.5 +	3.0 +	6.0 +	4.0 +	3.0 +	-	4.0 +	Warning
onHelp	-	3.0 +	-	4.0 +	-	-	-	Warning
onKeyDown	1.5 +	3.0 +	6.0 +	4.0 +	3.0 +	-	4.0 +	Warning
onKeyPress	1.5 +	3.0 +	6.0 +	4.0 +	3.0 +	-	4.0 +	Warning
onKeyUp	1.5 +	3.0 +	6.0 +	4.0 +	3.0 +	-	4.0 +	Warning
onMouseDown	1.5 +	3.0 +	6.0 +	4.0 +	3.0 +	-	4.0 +	Warning
onMouseMove	1.5 +	3.0 +	6.0 +	4.0 +	-	-	4.0 +	Warning
onMouseOut	1.5 +	3.0 +	6.0 +	4.0 +	3.0 +	-	4.0 +	Warning
onMouseOver	1.5 +	3.0 +	6.0 +	4.0 +	3.0 +	-	4.0 +	Warning
onMouseUp	1.5 +	3.0 +	6.0 +	4.0 +	3.0 +	-	4.0 +	Warning

Inheritance chain:

Element object, Node object

Hidden object (Object/DOM)

A field of data submitted with the form but not visible to the user.

Availability:	DOM level – 1 JavaScript – 1.0 JScript – 1.0 Internet Explorer – 3.02 Netscape – 2.0 Opera – 3.0
Inherits from:	*Input object*
JavaScript syntax:	-	*myHidden = myDocument.aFormName.anElementName*
	-	*myHidden = myDocument.aFormName .elements[anItemIndex]*
	IE	*myHidden = myDocument.all.anElementID*
	IE	*myHidden = myDocument.all.tags("INPUT")[anIndex]*
	IE	*myHidden = myDocument.all[aName]*
	-	*myHidden = myDocument.forms [aFormIndex].anElementName*
	-	*myHidden = myDocument.forms [aFormIndex].elements[anItemIndex]*
	-	*myHidden = myDocument.getElementById(anElementID)*
	-	*myHidden = myDocument .getElementsByName(aName)[anIndex]*
	-	*myHidden = myDocument.getElements ByTagName("INPUT")[anIndex]*

HTML syntax:	`<INPUT TYPE="hidden">`	
Argument list:	*anIndex*	A valid reference to an item in the collection
	aName	The `NAME` attribute of an element
	anElementID	The `ID` attribute of an element
	anItemIndex	A valid reference to an item in the collection
	aFormIndex	A reference to a particular form in the `forms` collection
Object properties:	`type`, `value`	
Event handlers:	`onAfterUpdate`, `onBeforeUpdate`, `onHelp`, `onRowEnter`, `onRowExit`	

Many properties, methods and event handlers are inherited from the `Input` object class. Refer to topics grouped with the "Input" prefix for details of common functionality across all sub-classes of the `Input` object super-class.

There isn't really a `Hidden` object class but it is helpful when trying to understand the wide variety of input element types if we can reduce the complexity by discussing only the properties and methods of a hidden field. In actual fact, the object is represented as an item of the `Input` object class.

`Hidden` objects don't respond to any events. They can't since they are not visible and therefore the user cannot interact with them to trigger one.

They may be accessed by event handling functions associated with the `Form` object but very little else.

Unlike MSIE, Netscape does not support the `defaultValue` property for this sub-class of the `Input` object. It also does not support the `onFocus` event, although why MSIE should support focus control onto a `Hidden` object is not clear.

Example code:

```
<HTML>
<HEAD>
</HEAD>
<BODY>
<DIV ID="RESULT">?</DIV>
<FORM>
    <INPUT TYPE="hidden" VALUE="A" NAME="BOX_A">
    <INPUT TYPE="hidden" VALUE="B" NAME="BOX_B">
    <INPUT TYPE="hidden" VALUE="C" NAME="BOX_C">
    <INPUT TYPE="hidden" VALUE="D" NAME="BOX_D">
    <INPUT TYPE="button" VALUE="Reveal" onClick="handleClick()">
</FORM>
<SCRIPT>
```

H

JavaScript Programmer's Reference

405

```
function handleClick()
{
    myString = "[";
    myString += document.forms[0].BOX_A.value;
    myString += "] [";
    myString += document.forms[0].BOX_B.value;
    myString += "] [";
    myString += document.forms[0].BOX_C.value;
    myString += "] [";
    myString += document.forms[0].BOX_D.value;
    myString += "]";
    document.all.RESULT.innerText = myString;
}
</SCRIPT>
</BODY>
</HTML>
```

See also:	Element object, `Form.elements[]`, *Input object*

Property	JavaScript	JScript	N	IE	Opera	DOM	Notes
type	1.1 +	3.0 +	3.0 +	4.0 +	3.0 +	1 +	ReadOnly
value	1.0 +	1.0 +	2.0 +	3.02 +	3.0 +	1 +	-

Event name	JavaScript	JScript	N	IE	Opera	DOM	Notes
onAfterUpdate	-	3.0 +	-	4.0 +	-	-	-
onBeforeUpdate	-	3.0 +	-	4.0 +	-	-	-
onHelp	-	3.0 +	-	4.0 +	-	-	Warning
onRowEnter	-	3.0 +	-	4.0 +	-	-	-
onRowExit	-	3.0 +	-	4.0 +	-	-	-

Inheritance chain:

Element object, Input object, Node object

Hiding scripts from old browsers (Pitfall)

Old browsers need to have script content disguised.

If you are presenting your HTML on the web to an audience that may use browsers that cannot cope with the <SCRIPT> tag, then you will need to hide the script inside the <SCRIPT> block. This is done by placing HTML comment tags around the script code.

This depends on the JavaScript interpreter providing some non-standardized behavior. That is, it needs to recognize the HTML comment opening tag as being some valid syntax, even though it is not really legal.

Beware that the closing HTML comment tag is placed on a line that itself is a JavaScript comment. However, you must also make sure that the closing </SCRIPT> tag is placed on a line of its own or the interpreter cannot see it and the <SCRIPT> block then becomes unterminated.

Example code:

```
<SCRIPT>
<!--
// Hide from older browsers
alert("some script here");
// end hiding -->
</SCRIPT>
```

See also:	COMMENT object, Pitfalls

Cross-references:

Wrox *Instant JavaScript* – page – 46

History object (Object/browser)

A history object owned by the window. This exposes information about URLs that have been visited previously.

Availability:	JavaScript – 1.0
	JScript – 1.0
	Internet Explorer – 3.02
	Netscape – 2.0
	Opera – 3.0
JavaScript syntax:	-	myHistory = history
	-	myHistory = myWindow.history
Object properties:	current, length, next, previous
Object methods:	back(), forward(), go()

Netscape version 4 provides access to the history array by signed scripts. Earlier versions of Netscape and MSIE do not provide this level of access and therefore the history object is limited in what you can do with it.

Some properties can be accessed by non-privileged scripts.

In Netscape, each element in the History object array is a String containing the URL for that item in the history. In MSIE, the objects are not accessible directly.

Warnings:

❏ The array elements and properties of this object cannot be accessed by JavaScript unless the script has the `UniversalBrowserRead` privilege granted to it.

❏ On Netscape, the `toString()` method is not correctly implemented and returns the value `"[object]"` instead of `"[object History]"`.

See also:	*Collection object, UniversalBrowserAccess, UniversalBrowserRead,* `Window.history`

Property	JavaScript	JScript	N	IE	Opera	DOM	Notes
current	1.1 +	-	3.0 +	-	3.0 +	-	Warning, ReadOnly
length	1.0 +	1.0 +	2.0 +	3.02 +	3.0 +	-	ReadOnly
next	1.1 +	-	3.0 +	-	3.0 +	-	Warning, ReadOnly
previous	1.1 +	-	3.0 +	-	3.0 +	-	Warning, ReadOnly

Method	JavaScript	JScript	N	IE	Opera	DOM	Notes
back()	1.0 +	1.0 +	2.0 +	3.02 +	3.0 +	-	-
forward()	1.0 +	1.0 +	2.0 +	3.02 +	3.0 +	-	-
go()	1.0 +	1.0 +	2.0 +	3.02 +	3.0 +	-	Warning

H<n> object (Object/HTML)

An object that represents the <H1> to <H6> tags.

Availability:	DOM level – 1 JavaScript – 1.5 JScript – 3.0 Internet Explorer – 4.0 Netscape – 6.0
Inherits from:	*Element object*
JavaScript syntax:	IE `myH1 = myDocument.all.anElementID`
	IE `myH1 = myDocument.all.tags("H1")[anIndex]`
	IE `myH1 = myDocument.all[aName]`
	- `myH1 = myDocument.getElementById (anElementID)`
	- `myH1 = myDocument.getElementsByName (aName)[anIndex]`
	- `myH1 = myDocument .getElementsByTagName("H1")[anIndex]`

HTML syntax:	<H1> ... </H1>, <H2> ... </H2>, <H3> ... </H3>, <H4> ... </H4>, <H5> ... </H5>, <H6> ... </H6>	
Argument list:	*anIndex*	A reference to an element in a collection
	aName	An associative array reference
	anElementID	The ID value of an Element object
Object properties:	align	
Event handlers:	onClick, onDblClick, onDragStart, onFilterChange, onHelp, onKeyDown, onKeyPress, onKeyUp, onMouseDown, onMouseMove, onMouseOut, onMouseOver, onMouseUp, onSelectStart	

The properties, methods, collections, and event handling support for the <H1> tag object are also provided for <H2> through <H6> tag objects as well. It is only necessary to document one of these object classes, although the other header types are each instantiated as objects of an appropriately named class in MSIE. The syntax examples illustrate the use of an <H1> tag object.

The <H1> through <H6> tags are block-level tags. That means that they force a line break before and after themselves.

The DOM level 1 specification refers to this and its sibling object types as a HeadingElement object.

See also:	*Element object*

Property	JavaScript	JScript	N	IE	Opera	DOM	HTML	Notes
align	1.5 +	3.0 +	6.0 +	4.0 +	-	1 +	-	-

Event name	JavaScript	JScript	N	IE	Opera	DOM	HTML	Notes
onClick	1.5 +	3.0 +	6.0 +	4.0 +	3.0 +	-	4.0 +	Warning
onDblClick	1.5 +	3.0 +	6.0 +	4.0 +	3.0 +	-	4.0 +	Warning
onDragStart	-	3.0 +	-	4.0 +	-	-	-	-
onFilterChange	-	3.0 +	-	4.0 +	-	-	-	-
onHelp	-	3.0 +	-	4.0 +	-	-	-	Warning
onKeyDown	1.5 +	3.0 +	6.0 +	4.0 +	3.0 +	-	4.0 +	Warning
onKeyPress	1.5 +	3.0 +	6.0 +	4.0 +	3.0 +	-	4.0 +	Warning
onKeyUp	1.5 +	3.0 +	6.0 +	4.0 +	3.0 +	-	4.0 +	Warning
onMouseDown	1.5 +	3.0 +	6.0 +	4.0 +	3.0 +	-	4.0 +	Warning
onMouseMove	1.5 +	3.0 +	6.0 +	4.0 +	-	-	4.0 +	Warning
onMouseOut	1.5 +	3.0 +	6.0 +	4.0 +	3.0 +	-	4.0 +	Warning
onMouseOver	1.5 +	3.0 +	6.0 +	4.0 +	3.0 +	-	4.0 +	Warning
onMouseUp	1.5 +	3.0 +	6.0 +	4.0 +	3.0 +	-	4.0 +	Warning
onSelectStart	-	3.0 +	-	4.0 +	-	-	-	-

Inheritance chain:

Element object, Node object

HR object (Object/HTML)

An object that represents an <HR> tag.

Availability:	DOM level – 1 JavaScript – 1.5 JScript – 3.0 Internet Explorer – 4.0 Netscape – 6.0
Inherits from:	*Element object*
JavaScript syntax:	IE `myHR = myDocument.all.anElementID`
	IE `myHR = myDocument.all.tags` `("HR")[anIndex]`
	IE `myHR = myDocument.all[aName]`
	\- `myHR = myDocument.getElementById` `(anElementID)`
	\- `myHR = myDocument.getElementsByName` `(aName)[anIndex]`
	\- `myHR = myDocument.getElementsByTagName` `("HR")[anIndex]`
HTML syntax:	`<HR>`
Argument list:	`anIndex` A reference to an element in a collection
	`aName` An associative array reference
	`anElementID` The ID value of an Element object
Object properties:	`align, color, noShade, size, width`

Event handlers:	`onClick, onDblClick, onDragStart,`
	`onFilterChange, onHelp, onKeyDown, onKeyPress,`
	`onKeyUp, onMouseDown, onMouseMove, onMouseOut,`
	`onMouseOver, onMouseUp, onSelectStart`

The <HR> tag is a block-level tag. That means that it forces a line break before and after itself.

See also:	*Element object*

Property	JavaScript	JScript	N	IE	Opera	DOM	HTML	Notes
`align`	1.5 +	3.0 +	6.0 +	4.0 +	* -	1 +	-	-
`color`	-	3.0 +	-	4.0 +	-	-	-	Warning
`noShade`	1.5 +	3.0 +	6.0 +	4.0 +	-	1 +	-	Warning
`size`	1.5 +	3.0 +	6.0 +	4.0 +	-	1 +	-	-
`width`	1.5 +	3.0 +	6.0 +	4.0 +	-	1 +	-	-

Event name	JavaScript	JScript	N	IE	Opera	DOM	HTML	Notes
onClick	1.5 +	3.0 +	6.0 +	4.0 +	3.0 +	-	4.0 +	Warning
onDblClick	1.5 +	3.0 +	6.0 +	4.0 +	3.0 +	-	4.0 +	Warning
onDragStart	-	3.0 +	-	4.0 +	-	-	-	-
onFilterChange	-	3.0 +	-	4.0 +	-	-	-	-
onHelp	-	3.0 +	-	4.0 +	-	-	-	Warning
onKeyDown	1.5 +	3.0 +	6.0 +	4.0 +	3.0 +	-	4.0 +	Warning
onKeyPress	1.5 +	3.0 +	6.0 +	4.0 +	3.0 +	-	4.0 +	Warning
onKeyUp	1.5 +	3.0 +	6.0 +	4.0 +	3.0 +	-	4.0 +	Warning
onMouseDown	1.5 +	3.0 +	6.0 +	4.0 +	3.0 +	-	4.0 +	Warning
onMouseMove	1.5 +	3.0 +	6.0 +	4.0 +	-	-	4.0 +	Warning
onMouseOut	1.5 +	3.0 +	6.0 +	4.0 +	3.0 +	-	4.0 +	Warning
onMouseOver	1.5 +	3.0 +	6.0 +	4.0 +	3.0 +	-	4.0 +	Warning
onMouseUp	1.5 +	3.0 +	6.0 +	4.0 +	3.0 +	-	4.0 +	Warning
onSelectStart	-	3.0 +	-	4.0 +	-	-	-	-

Inheritance chain:

Element object, Node object

.htc (File extension)

A file containing a behavior handler script for use in MSIE browsers.

This file contains an HTML Component (HTC). These used to be called scriptlets but have been evolved and renamed when used in an MSIE web browser. The Windows Script Host environment continues to use scriptlets but these have also evolved into something quite different to an HTC.

Refer to the Element.addBehavior() topic for a more detailed explanation of how these files are used.

See also:	<STYLE>, Element.addBehavior(), Scriptlet

HTML (Standard)

The standard notation for creating web pages.

HTML is short for HyperText Markup Language. It is a markup language belonging to the SGML (Standard Generalized Markup Language) family.

Currently, the HTML state of the art is framed in the HTML version 4.0 standard as defined by the World Wide Web Consortium (W3C). However, much web content is still presented in an HTML 3.2 conformant manner.

H

JavaScript Programmer's Reference

TV set-top boxes that employ HTML are generally built around an HTML 3.2 core which means that web content that needs to be deployed to the PC based browser and the TV viewer needs to be downgraded to be compatible with that standard version.

Browser manufacturers are still yet to release fully HTML 4.0 compliant browsers.

The strategic importance of HTML version 4.0 is to separate document content from presentation style. This means that certain techniques are deprecated in favor of the use of style sheets.

This adds much complexity to the JavaScript support since its API to those style controls is not as well standardized as the underlying Document Object Model (DOM). However, there is also significant flexibility in the new styling model, and to date, the MSIE browser has made great strides in implementing a robust styling model that provides many Dynamic HTML capabilities.

It is hoped that the forthcoming Netscape 6.0 might offer similar capabilities.

| **See also:** | Web browser |

HTML entity escape (Pitfall)

It looks like HTML but it isn't intended to be.

You can sometimes innocently include some text into your script that when presented with a `document.write()` gets completely misunderstood by the HTML parser. This will almost certainly be due to the presence of "<" and ">" characters in the output. It is likely that the browser will see what it thinks is a tag, but then ignore it according to the "I don't know what it is – so I won't display it" rule, as it won't be a recognized tag.

Use HTML escapes to output the character as intended.

This is important for the following characters if not for others:

< becomes <

> becomes >

& becomes &

| **See also:** | Pitfalls |

Cross-references:

Wrox *Instant JavaScript* – page – 46

HTML object (Object/HTML)

An object in MSIE that represents an <HTML> tag.

Availability:	DOM level – 1
	JavaScript – 1.5
	JScript – 3.0
	Internet Explorer – 4.0
	Netscape – 6.0
Inherits from:	*Element object*
JavaScript syntax:	IE `myHTML = myDocument.all.anElementID`
	IE `myHTML = myDocument.all.tags("HTML")[0]`
	IE `myHTML = myDocument.all.tags("HTML")` `[anIndex]`
	IE `myHTML = myDocument.all[aName]`
	IE `myHTML = myDocument.all[anIndex]`
	- `myHTML = myDocument.documentElement`
	- `myHTML = myDocument.getElementById` `(anElementID)`
	- `myHTML = myDocument.getElementsByName` `(aName)[anIndex]`
	- `myHTML = myDocument.getElementsByTagName` `("HTML")[anIndex]`
HTML syntax:	`<HTML> ... </HTML>`
Argument list:	`anIndex` A selector for one particular HTML element
	`aName` An associative array reference
	`anElementID` The ID value of an Element object
Object properties:	`title, version`
Event handlers:	`onClick, onDblClick, onHelp, onKeyDown,` `onKeyPress, onKeyUp, onMouseDown,` `onMouseMove, onMouseOut, onMouseOver,` `onMouseUp`

This object is otherwise known as the HTML object.

The <HTML> tag is a block-level tag, although it cannot be placed inside any other tag. Like the body tag, it is considered to be a block-level tag on grounds of its behavior in a framed context.

Warnings:

❑ Be careful how you operate on this object. Traversing its properties in a for (...in...) loop can recursively lock up your browser.

❑ The index value that points at this object in the all[] array for the document will be 0 if there is no DTD statement and 1 if there is. A correctly formed document should have a DTD statement. Use a dynamic mechanism for locating the object of type HTML instead of hardwiring the index value.

See also:	*Attributes object*, BODY.aLink, BODY.background, BODY.bgColor, BODY.link, BODY.text, BODY.vLink, *Document object*, Document.documentElement, Document.title, *Element object*

Property	JavaScript	JScript	N	IE	Opera	DOM	HTML	Notes
title	-	3.0 +	-	4.0 +	-	-	-	-
version	1.5 +	5.0 +	6.0 +	5.0 +	-	1 +	-	Warning, Deprecated

Event name	JavaScript	JScript	N	IE	Opera	DOM	HTML	Notes
onClick	1.0 +	1.0 +	2.0 +	3.0 +	3.0 +	-	4.0 +	Warning
onDblClick	1.2 +	3.0 +	4.0 +	4.0 +	3.0 +	-	4.0 +	Warning
onHelp	-	3.0 +	-	4.0 +	-	-	-	Warning
onKeyDown	1.2 +	3.0 +	4.0 +	4.0 +	3.0 +	-	4.0 +	Warning
onKeyPress	1.2 +	3.0 +	4.0 +	4.0 +	3.0 +	-	4.0 +	Warning
onKeyUp	1.2 +	3.0 +	4.0 +	4.0 +	3.0 +	-	4.0 +	Warning
onMouseDown	1.2 +	3.0 +	4.0 +	4.0 +	3.0 +	-	4.0 +	Warning
onMouseMove	1.2 +	3.0 +	4.0 +	4.0 +	-	-	4.0 +	Warning
onMouseOut	1.1 +	3.0 +	3.0 +	4.0 +	3.0 +	-	4.0 +	Warning
onMouseOver	1.0 +	1.0 +	2.0 +	3.0 +	3.0 +	-	4.0 +	Warning
onMouseUp	1.2 +	3.0 +	4.0 +	4.0 +	3.0 +	-	4.0 +	Warning

Inheritance chain:

Element object, Node object

http: URL (Request method)

A request from a web browser to a web server to send a document.

This requests a document from a web server. Most web traffic is requested this way.

See also:	*javascript: URL*, *URL*

https: URL (Request method)

A request from a web browser to a secure web server to send a document with an encrypted and secure protocol.

This requests a document from a secure web server. Your encryption code needs to be compatible and this may involve an exchange of security certificates.

See also:	*javascript: URL*, Security policy, URL

HyperLink object (Object/HTML)

Another name for the Url object.

Availability:	JavaScript – 1.0 JScript – 1.0 Internet Explorer – 3.02 Netscape – 2.0
Inherits from:	*Element object*
JavaScript syntax:	- *myHyperLink = myDocument.links[anIndex]*
Event handlers:	onClick, onDblClick, onHelp, onKeyDown, onKeyPress, onKeyUp, onMouseDown, onMouseMove, onMouseOut, onMouseOver, onMouseUp

In Netscape, links are stored in Url objects. These are distinctly different to Anchor objects.

MSIE does not distinguish between the two but since there is no constructor, it is hard to know what object type they are. Generally they are assumed to be Url objects.

Because the class name is Url in Netscape, the link objects are discussed in detail under that lexical topic location.

MSIE supports a LINK object class but this is a special object that stems from a styleSheet item. It doesn't support all the properties that a Url object does and is probably more concerned with managing the appearance of a Url object on the screen.

See also:	*Area object*, Element.all[], *LinkArray object*, URL, *Url object*

Event name	JavaScript	JScript	N	IE	Opera	DOM	HTML	Notes
onClick	1.0 +	1.0 +	2.0 +	3.0 +	3.0 +	-	4.0 +	Warning
onDblClick	1.2 +	3.0 +	4.0 +	4.0 +	3.0 +	-	4.0 +	Warning
onHelp	-	3.0 +	-	4.0 +	-	-	-	Warning
onKeyDown	1.2 +	3.0 +	4.0 +	4.0 +	3.0 +	-	4.0 +	Warning
onKeyPress	1.2 +	3.0 +	4.0 +	4.0 +	3.0 +	-	4.0 +	Warning
onKeyUp	1.2 +	3.0 +	4.0 +	4.0 +	3.0 +	-	4.0 +	Warning
onMouseDown	1.2 +	3.0 +	4.0 +	4.0 +	3.0 +	-	4.0 +	Warning
onMouseMove	1.2 +	3.0 +	4.0 +	4.0 +	-	-	4.0 +	Warning
onMouseOut	1.1 +	3.0 +	3.0 +	4.0 +	3.0 +	-	4.0 +	Warning
onMouseOver	1.0 +	1.0 +	2.0 +	3.0 +	3.0 +	-	4.0 +	Warning
onMouseUp	1.2 +	3.0 +	4.0 +	4.0 +	3.0 +	-	4.0 +	Warning

Inheritance chain:

Element object, Node object

about: URL (Request method)

AbstractView object (Object/DOM)

ActiveXObject object (Object/JScript)

Add (+) (Operator/additive)

Add then assign (+=) (Operator/ assignment)

I object (Object/HTML)

An object that represents the font style controlled by the `<I>` HTML tag.

Availability:	DOM level – 1 JScript – 3.0 Internet Explorer – 4.0 Deprecated
Inherits from:	*Element object*
JavaScript syntax:	IE `myI = myDocument.all.anElementID`
	IE `myI = myDocument.all.tags("I")` `[anIndex]`
	IE `myI = myDocument.all[aName]`
	- `myI = myDocument.getElementById` `(anElementID)`
	- `myI = myDocument.getElementsByName` `(aName)[anIndex]`
	- `myI = myDocument.getElementsByTagName` `("I")[anIndex]`
HTML syntax:	`<I> ... </I>`
Argument list:	`anIndex` A reference to an element in a collection
	`aName` An associative array reference
	`anElementID` The ID value of an element
Event handlers:	onClick, onDblClick, onDragStart, onFilterChange, onHelp, onKeyDown, onKeyPress, onKeyUp, onMouseDown, onMouseMove, onMouseOut, onMouseOver, onMouseUp, onSelectStart

`<I>` tags and the objects that represent them are inline elements. Placing them into a document does not create a line break.

See also:	Element object

Event name	JavaScript	JScript	N	IE	Opera	HTML	Notes
onClick	1.0 +	3.0 +	2.0 +	4.0 +	3.0 +	4.0 +	Warning
onDblClick	1.2 +	3.0 +	4.0 +	4.0 +	3.0 +	4.0 +	Warning
onDragStart	-	3.0 +	-	4.0 +	-	-	-
onFilterChange	-	3.0 +	-	4.0 +	-	-	-
onHelp	-	3.0 +	-	4.0 +	-	-	Warning
onKeyDown	1.2 +	3.0 +	4.0 +	4.0 +	3.0 +	4.0 +	Warning
onKeyPress	1.2 +	3.0 +	4.0 +	4.0 +	3.0 +	4.0 +	Warning
onKeyUp	1.2 +	3.0 +	4.0 +	4.0 +	3.0 +	4.0 +	Warning
onMouseDown	1.2 +	3.0 +	4.0 +	4.0 +	3.0 +	4.0 +	Warning
onMouseMove	1.2 +	3.0 +	4.0 +	4.0 +	-	4.0 +	Warning
onMouseOut	1.1 +	3.0 +	3.0 +	4.0 +	3.0 +	4.0 +	Warning
onMouseOver	1.0 +	3.0 +	2.0 +	4.0 +	3.0 +	4.0 +	Warning
onMouseUp	1.2 +	3.0 +	4.0 +	4.0 +	3.0 +	4.0 +	Warning
onSelectStart	-	3.0 +	-	4.0 +	-	-	-

Inheritance chain:

Element object, Node object

iCab (Web browser)

A web browser alternative to MSIE and Netscape Navigator.

The iCab web browser is only available on the Macintosh but has some interesting features not found in other products. It is developed by a small German company run by Alexander Clauss and Oliver Joppich. The browser was originally developed for use on the Atari platform.

The browser is compact, fast and standards based and can be downloaded free from the iCab web site (http://www.iCab.de). The current version is 2.1 and is available at the moment as a preview or Beta product (see web-references).

Earlier versions do not fully support JavaScript although implementation of a completely standards based version of the interpreter is expected in the final release. It also supports some of the browser specific tags that Netscape and Microsoft have added to their browsers. This is necessary to avoid the browser not being able to properly render the pages currently deployed on the web. However, iCab also has an HTML validator built in and this triggers an indicator on the screen when the page is non HTML 4.0 compliant. This shows up as a smiley face when the HTML is good and a frowning face when it's not. Clicking on the frowning face yields a report of the non-compliant HTML. This is a good browser for developers to use.

iCab supports some interesting features such as image and cookie filtering. This allows much finer control over image display than simply switching images on and off. By default, iCab is set up to not filter out banner ads, but by virtue of its awareness of standard banner ad image sizes it can prevent the display of banners leaving other graphics intact. It can also filter based on URL contents. Cookie filtering is also flexible and sophisticated.

The `<LINK REL="...">` and `<LINK REV="...">` tags are actively supported and provide some structural navigation when sites implement these tags properly.

Access the iCab web site for more details of special features.

See also:	Platform, Script execution, Web browser

Web-references:

http://www.icab.de/

ID="..." (HTML Tag Attribute)

MSIE document objects can be referenced conveniently with an ID name if it is added with this tag attribute.

Many objects are identified in the DOM hierarchy of the web browser by means of their id property. This value is defined as an HTML tag attribute.

Some objects can be accessed using a `<NAME="...">` HTML tag attribute instead of or as well as the `ID="..."` HTML tag attribute.

Netscape 4.0 supports ID access but only apparently for visible elements. Version 6.0 is much more consistent now that it supports the DOM standard properly.

See also:	`Document.ids[]`, `Document.layers[]`, `Document.scripts[]`, `Element.id`, `NAME="..."`

Identically equal to (===) (Operator/identity)

Compare two values for equality and identical type.

Availability:	ECMAScript edition – 3
	JavaScript – 1.3
	JScript – 1.0
	Internet Explorer – 3.02
	Netscape – 4.06

Table continued on following page

JavaScript Programmer's Reference

Property/method value type:	Boolean primitive	
JavaScript syntax:	-	anOperand1 === anOperand2
Argument list:	anOperand1	A value of a comparable type
	anOperand2	A value of the same type as operand 1

The two operands are compared and the Boolean true value is returned if they are equal and of the same type.

The equality operator is not always transitive. For example, two string objects may represent the same string value. Comparing the objects for equality will yield false because the references to the objects are being compared and not the object values themselves. However forcing a string comparison may in fact yield a true value when testing for equality. Do this by converting the objects as part of the comparison process by type conversion or valueOf() methods.

Numeric values may require rounding to take place, and testing for equality may be accurate down to a precision finer than your script cares about. You can set a precision value in a variable, then subtract the value you are comparing with from the absolute value of the comparee. If the difference is smaller than your precision value, then the two values are close enough to yield a match.

The associativity is from left to right.

Refer to the operator precedence topic for details of execution order.

The result is the Boolean value true if *anOperand1* is numerically or lexically equal to *anOperand2* and both operands are of the same type otherwise false is returned.

Warnings:

❑ Be careful not to confuse the single and double equals operators with the triple equals operator.

❑ Placing a single equals in place of a test for equality will assign the right-hand value to the left-hand operand and clobber the value accidentally. Placing a single equals sign instead of the identity operator has the same effect.

❑ Using the equality operator in place of the identity operator is more subtle. Sometimes the test will appear to work correctly because the values in the two objects could be the same. That would have failed the identity test because they may be equal but are not identical.

❑ The interpreter may be forgiving enough that a run-time error isn't generated but the side effects could be subtle and make it hard to diagnose the cause.

❑ This is not available for use server-side with Netscape Enterprise Server 3.

Example code:

```
<HTML>
<HEAD></HEAD>
<BODY>
<SCRIPT>
myObject1 = 100;
myObject2 = "100";
if(myObject1 == myObject2)
{
   document.write("Objects are equal<BR>");
}
else
{
   document.write("Objects are NOT equal<BR>");
}
if(myObject1 === myObject2)
{
   document.write("Objects are identical<BR>");
}
else
{
   document.write("Objects are NOT identical<BR>");
}
</SCRIPT>
</BODY>
</HTML>
```

See also: *ASCII*, Associativity, *Equal to (==)*, Equality expression, Equality operator, *Greater than (>), Greater than or equal to (>=),* Identity operator, JellyScript, *Less than (<), Less than or equal to (<=),* Logical expression, Logical operator, *NOT Equal to (!=), NOT Identically equal to (!==),* Operator Precedence, *Relational expression, Relational operator, typeof, Unicode*

Cross-references:

ECMA 262 edition 3 – section – 11.9.4

O'Reilly *JavaScript Definitive Guide* – page – 48

Wrox *Instant JavaScript* – page – 39

423

IEEE 754 (Standard)

An international standard for floating point number handling and storage in 8 bytes.

Availability:	ECMAScript edition – 2

The IEEE 754 standard defines the behaviour of a numeric environment in such a way that the computation should generate the same result across any compliant platforms.

It specifies the exact format for the storage and manipulation of the values. It also specifies bounding ranges for exponents and mantissas.

The standard describes how and when rounding should occur and the direction in which rounding takes place. Exceptions are also described and this determines how the NaN value is generated and propagated through expressions.

See also:	*byte*, Floating constant, *NaN*, Not a number, *Number*

Cross-references:

ECMA 262 edition 2 – section – 3

ECMA 262 edition 3 – section – 3

if(...)...(Selector)

A conditional execution mechanism.

Availability:	ECMAScript edition – 2 JavaScript – 1.0 JScript – 1.0 Internet Explorer – 3.02 Netscape – 2.0 Netscape Enterprise Server version – 2.0 Opera – 3.0	
JavaScript syntax:	-	`aLabel: if(aCondition) {` `someCode}`
Argument list:	`aCondition`	An expression that yields a Boolean value
	`aLabel`	An optional identifier to name the if block
	`someCode`	Some script source text that is executed if the condition tests true

The `if()` statement is used to conditionally execute a code block depending on the result of a conditional expression. This mechanism is called branching.

The expression in the parentheses is evaluated and cast to a Boolean value. If it yields a `true` value as a result, then the code in the associated block is executed. Otherwise, the code is ignored and execution continues at the line following the closing brace of the code block.

JavaScript allows you to omit the braces around the code block if the code is a single line. You must place the trailing semicolon on the line to delimit the script source text that is associated with the `if()` statement.

At version 1.2 of JavaScript, you can name the `if` statement and use the labeled form of the `break` keyword to exit the conditional code block prematurely.

Warnings:

❑ Beware of leaving the braces off the associated script source text as it is possible for this to be ambiguous to the reader and can lead to difficulties when adding more code to be executed conditionally. It can become easy to add a second line of code but still omit the braces. In that case, only the first line will be conditional but the second will always be executed regardless of the result of the `if()` condition. This can lead to completely unexpected behavior and is quite difficult to diagnose.

Example code:

```
// Recommended form
if(a == b)
{
    z = 100;
}
// Possibly dangerous during maintenance
if(a == b)
z = 100;
```

See also: *Code block delimiter {}*, Compound statement, *Conditionally execute (?:)*, *else ...*, `else if(...) ...`, Flow control, *if(...) ... else ...*, Obfuscation, Selection statement, Statement, *switch(...) ... case: ... default: ...*, *while(...) ...*

Cross-references:

ECMA 262 edition 2 – section – 12.5

ECMA 262 edition 2 – section – 12.6.1

ECMA 262 edition 3 – section – 12.5

Wrox *Instant JavaScript* – page – 22

if(...)...else...(Selector)

A conditional execution mechanism.

Availability:	ECMAScript edition – 2 JavaScript – 1.0 JScript – 1.0 Internet Explorer – 3.02 Netscape – 2.0 Netscape Enterprise Server version – 2.0 Opera – 3.0	
JavaScript syntax:	-	aLabel: if(aCondition) { someCode} else { someOtherCode)
Argument list:	aCondition	An expression that yields a Boolean value
	aLabel	An optional identifier to name the if block
	someCode	Some script source text that is executed if the condition tests true
	someOtherCode	Some script source text that is executed if the condition tests false

The if() ... else statement is used to conditionally execute one or other code block depending on the result of a conditional expression.

The expression in the parentheses is evaluated and cast to a Boolean value. If it yields a true value as a result, then the code in the first associated block is executed. Otherwise, the code in the first block is ignored and the code in the block following the else keyword is executed.

Each else keyword for which the associated if() is ambiguous will be associated with the nearest possible if() that would otherwise have no corresponding else.

At version 1.2 of JavaScript, you can name the if statement and use the labeled form of the break keyword to exit the conditional code block prematurely.

Example code:

```
// recommended form
if(a == b)
{
    z = 100;
}
else
{
    z = 200;
}
```

```
// Possibly dangerous during maintenance
if(a == b)
z = 100;
else
z = 200;
```

See also:	*Code block delimiter {},* Compound statement, *Conditionally execute (?:), else ...,* else if(...) ..., Flow control, *if(...) ...,* Selection statement, Statement, *switch(...) ... case: ... default: ...*

Cross-references:

ECMA 262 edition 2 – section – 12.5

ECMA 262 edition 3 – section – 12.5

Wrox *Instant JavaScript* – page – 22

IFRAME object (Object/HTML)

An object that represents an <IFRAME> tag.

Availability:	DOM level – 1 JavaScript – 1.2 JScript – 3.0 Internet Explorer – 4.0 Netscape – 6.0	
Inherits from:	*Element object*	
JavaScript syntax:	IE	`myIFRAME = myDocument.all.anElementID`
	IE	`myIFRAME = myDocument.all.tags ("IFRAME")[anIndex]`
	IE	`myIFRAME = myDocument.all[aName]`
	-	`myIFRAME = myDocument.aName`
	-	`myIFRAME = myDocument.getElementById (anElementID)`
	-	`myIFRAME = myDocument.getElementsByName (aName)[anIndex]`
	-	`myIFRAME = myDocument.getElementsBy TagName("IFRAME")[anIndex]`
HTML syntax:	`<IFRAME> ... </IFRAME>`	
Argument list:	`anIndex`	A reference to an element in a collection
	`aName`	An associative array reference
	`anElementID`	The ID value of an Element object

Object properties:	align, dataFld, dataSrc, frameBorder, frameSpacing, height, hspace, longDesc, marginHeight, marginWidth, name, noResize, scrolling, src, tabIndex, vspace, width
Event handlers:	onClick, onDblClick, onHelp, onKeyDown, onKeyPress, onKeyUp, onMouseDown, onMouseMove, onMouseOut, onMouseOver, onMouseUp

An <IFRAME> is a special MSIE supported tag that introduces an inline frame into a document that appears like a block structured element within the document text flow, accessible as a named frame object that belongs to the document.

Its properties appear to be all read only in the MSIE browser. Changing them seems to have no visible effect at all. The properties belonging to the object retain the values that you assign and return them when requested but the display does not change.

The DOM level 1 specification refers to IFRAME objects as IFrameElement objects and this makes them available in Netscape by virtue of its support for DOM level 1.

DOM level 2 adds the contentDocument property:

Warnings:

❑ Netscape does not support the <IFRAME> tag prior to version 6.0, but it does support an <ILAYER> tag, which describes an inline layer which is not the same thing but may provide a way to emulate the <IFRAME> functionality in some cases.

❑ MSIE seems to have trouble locating an IFRAME object in the document hierarchy, and you cannot refer to the object directly in the same way that you can with other objects.

❑ With an IFRAME object whose ID is "MYFRAME" this accessor works:

   ❑ document.all.MYFRAME

❑ But these accessors don't:

   ❑ document.MYFRAME

   ❑ MYFRAME

❑ Even worse, the IFRAME appears to float in some separate plane to its containing object. Placing an <IFRAME> inside a <DIV> block exhibits some very strange behavior. Its position seems locked to the top left of the <DIV> but its right edge seems to be able to flow outside the <DIV> area.

❑ Netscape 6.0, which implements IFRAME objects, does not appear to fare any better, exhibiting similarly strange behavior.

See also:	*Element object, Frame object, Window object*

Property	JavaScript	JScript	N	IE	Opera	DOM	HTML	Notes
align	1.5 +	3.0 +	6.0 +	4.0 +	-	1 +	-	Warning
dataFld	1.5 +	3.0 +	6.0 +	4.0 +	-	1 +	-	Warning
dataSrc	1.5 +	3.0 +	6.0 +	4.0 +	-	1 +	-	Warning
frameBorder	1.5 +	3.0 +	6.0 +	4.0 +	-	1 +	-	Warning
frameSpacing	-	3.0 +	-	4.0 +	-	-	-	Warning
height	1.5 +	3.0 +	6.0 +	4.0 +	-	1 +	-	Warning
hspace	-	3.0 +	-	4.0 +	-	-	-	Warning
longDesc	1.5 +	-	6.0 +	-	-	1 +	-	Warning
marginHeight	1.5 +	3.0 +	6.0 +	4.0 +	-	1 +	-	Warning
marginWidth	1.5 +	3.0 +	6.0 +	4.0 +	-	1 +	-	Warning
name	1.5 +	3.0 +	6.0 +	4.0 +	-	1 +	-	-
noResize	-	3.0 +	-	4.0 +	-	-	-	-
scrolling	1.5 +	3.0 +	6.0 +	4.0 +	-	1 +	-	-
src	1.5 +	3.0 +	6.0 +	4.0 +	-	1 +	-	-
tabIndex	1.5 +	3.0 +	6.0 +	4.0 +	-	1 +	-	-
vspace	-	3.0 +	-	4.0 +	-	-	-	Warning
width	1.5 +	3.0 +	6.0 +	4.0 +	-	1 +	-	Warning

Event name	JavaScript	JScript	N	IE	Opera	DOM	HTML	Notes
onClick	1.5+	1.0 +	2.0 +	3.0 +	3.0 +	-	4.0 +	Warning
onDblClick	1.5+	3.0 +	4.0 +	4.0 +	3.0 +	-	4.0 +	Warning
onHelp	-	3.0 +	-	4.0 +	-	-	-	Warning
onKeyDown	1.5 +	3.0 +	4.0 +	4.0 +	3.0 +	-	4.0 +	Warning
onKeyPress	1.5 +	3.0 +	4.0 +	4.0 +	3.0 +	-	4.0 +	Warning
onKeyUp	1.5 +	3.0 +	4.0 +	4.0 +	3.0 +	-	4.0 +	Warning
onMouseDown	1.5 +	3.0 +	4.0 +	4.0 +	3.0 +	-	4.0 +	Warning
onMouseMove	1.5 +	3.0 +	4.0 +	4.0 +	-	-	4.0 +	Warning
onMouseOut	1.5+	3.0 +	3.0 +	4.0 +	3.0 +	-	4.0 +	Warning
onMouseOver	1.5 +	1.0 +	2.0 +	3.0 +	3.0 +	-	4.0 +	Warning
onMouseUp	1.5+	3.0 +	4.0 +	4.0 +	3.0 +	-	4.0 +	Warning

Inheritance chain:

Element object, Node object

Image object (Object/HTML)

An object representing an HTML <IMG> tag in Netscape.

Availability:	DOM level – 1 JavaScript – 1.1 Netscape – 3.0 Opera – 3.0
Inherits from:	*Element object*

JavaScript syntax:		
	IE	*myImage* = *myDocument*.all.*anElementID*
	IE	*myImage* = *myDocument*.all.tags("IMG")[*anIndex*]
	IE	*myImage* = *myDocument*.all[*aName*]
	-	*myImage* = *myDocument*.*anImageName*
	-	*myImage* = *myDocument*.getElementById (*anElementID*)
	-	*myImage* = *myDocument*. getElementsByName(*aName*)[*anIndex*]
	-	*myImage* = *myDocument*.images[*anIndex*]
	-	*myImage* = *myImageArray*[*anIndex*]
	-	*myImage* = *myDocument*.getElements ByTagName("IMG")[*anIndex*]

HTML syntax:	<IMG>	
Argument list:	*anIndex*	A reference to an element in a collection
	aName	An associative array reference
	anElementID	The ID value of an Element object
Object properties:	border, complete, constructor, defaultValue, height, hspace, lowsrc, name, size, src, vspace, width, x, y	
Object methods:	select()	
Event handlers:	onAbort, onBlur, onClick, onDblClick, onError, onFocus, onHelp, onKeyDown, onKeyPress, onKeyUp, onLoad, onMouseDown, onMouseMove, onMouseOut, onMouseOver, onMouseUp	

The image object added at version 1.1 of JavaScript introduced the possibility of dynamically replacing images under script control.

Event handling support via properties containing function objects was added to Image objects at version 1.1 of JavaScript.

The image object supported by Netscape and the IMG object supported by MSIE are so different to each other that they are covered as separate objects. They share a few similarities but not many. By inspection, they are instances of different classes.

Warnings:

❏ In the MSIE browser, the images are instantiated inside IMG objects because they correspond to the IMG tag. There is an Image object created as another name for the same IMG tag and if you instantiate a new copy of it you get an IMG object. This means you should be careful when examining the constructors and class names of image objects, as their object type is not portable across platforms.

Example code:

```
<HTML>
<HEAD>
<SCRIPT>
function moved()
{
    document.all.ONE.width = event.x;
}
</SCRIPT>

</HEAD>
<BODY onMouseMove="moved()">
Move mouse horizontally to scale image<BR>
<IMG HEIGHT=40 ID="ONE" SRC="assets/image_9.gif">

</BODY>
</HTML>
```

See also:	*Background object*, Document.images[], Element.all[], *ImageArray object*, *IMG object*, *Input object*, Input.type, Web browser

Property	JavaScript	JScript	N	IE	Opera	DOM	HTML	Notes
border	1.1 +	-	3.0 +	-	3.0 +	1 +	-	-
complete	1.1 +	-	3.0 +	-	3.0 +	-	-	Warning, ReadOnly
constructor	1.1 +	-	3.0 +	-	-	-	-	-
defaultValue	1.1 +	-	3.0 +	-	3.0 +	1 +	-	Warning
height	1.1 +	-	3.0 +	-	3.0 +	1 +	-	ReadOnly
hspace	1.1 +	-	3.0 +	-	3.0 +	1 +	-	ReadOnly
lowsrc	1.1 +	-	3.0 +	-	3.0 +	1 +	-	-
name	1.1 +	-	3.0 +	-	3.0 +	1 +	-	-
size	1.1 +	-	3.0 +	-	3.0 +	1 +	-	Warning
src	1.1 +	-	3.0 +	-	3.0 +	1 +	-	-
vspace	1.1 +	-	3.0 +	-	3.0 +	1 +	-	ReadOnly
width	1.1 +	-	3.0 +	-	3.0 +	1 +	-	ReadOnly
x	1.1 +	-	3.0 +	-	-	-	-	ReadOnly
y	1.1 +	-	3.0 +	-	-	-	-	ReadOnly

JavaScript Programmer's Reference

431

Method	JavaScript	JScript	N	IE	Opera	DOM	HTML	Notes
select()	1.1 +	-	3.0 +	-	3.0 +	1 +	-	Warning

Event name	JavaScript	JScript	N	IE	Opera	DOM	HTML	Notes
onAbort	1.1 +	1.0 +	3.0 +	3.02 +	3.0 +	-	-	-
onBlur	1.1 +	3.0 +	3.0 +	4.0 +	3.0 +	-	-	Warning
onClick	1.1+	1.0 +	2.0 +	3.0 +	3.0 +	-	4.0 +	Warning
onDblClick	1.2 +	3.0 +	4.0 +	4.0 +	3.0 +	-	4.0 +	Warning
onError	1.1 +	3.0 +	3.0 +	4.0 +	3.0 +	-	-	Warning
onFocus	1.1+	3.0 +	2.0 +	4.0 +	3.0 +	-	-	Warning
onHelp	-	3.0 +	-	4.0 +	-	-	-	Warning
onKeyDown	1.2 +	3.0 +	4.0 +	4.0 +	3.0 +	-	4.0 +	Warning
onKeyPress	1.2 +	3.0 +	4.0 +	4.0 +	3.0 +	-	4.0 +	Warning
onKeyUp	1.2 +	3.0 +	4.0 +	4.0 +	3.0 +	-	4.0 +	Warning
onLoad	1.1+	1.0 +	2.0 +	3.02 +	3.0 +	-	-	Warning
onMouseDown	1.2 +	3.0 +	4.0 +	4.0 +	3.0 +	-	4.0 +	Warning
onMouseMove	1.2 +	3.0 +	4.0 +	4.0 +	-	-	4.0 +	Warning
onMouseOut	1.1 +	3.0 +	3.0 +	4.0 +	3.0 +	-	4.0 +	Warning
onMouseOver	1.1+	1.0 +	2.0 +	3.0 +	3.0 +	-	4.0 +	Warning
onMouseUp	1.2 +	3.0 +	4.0 +	4.0 +	3.0 +	-	4.0 +	Warning

Inheritance chain:

Element object, Node object

Image.Class (Property/internal)

Internal property that returns an object class.

This is an internal property that describes the class that an Image object instance is a member of. The reserved words suggest that in the future, this property may be externalized.

See also:	Web browser

Property attributes:

DontEnum, Internal.

ImageArray object (Object/browser)

A collection of image objects.

Availability:	JavaScript – 1.1 JScript – 3.0 Internet Explorer – 4.0 Netscape – 3.0
JavaScript syntax:	- *myImageArray = myDocument.images*
Object properties:	length
Object methods:	item()

The MSIE and Netscape browsers each maintain an ImageArray object, which is just a special case of the Array object. However, although they both store objects that represent images in that array, those image objects are quite different. For a start, in Netscape they are of the class "Image" while in MSIE they are of the class "IMG" (named after the HTML tag). This is fortunate in a way, because you can use this difference to detect what kind of object you are operating on if you need to perform complex image management activities.

For MSIE image objects refer to the IMG object topic and its properties.

For Netscape Navigator image objects refer to the Image object topic and its properties.

Warnings:

❑ Beware of the differences between the properties that MSIE and Netscape Navigator provide to support image management.

See also:	*Collection object*, Document.images[], *Image object, IMG object*

Property	JavaScript	JScript	N	IE	Opera	Notes
length	1.1 +	3.0 +	3.0 +	4.0 +	-	ReadOnly

Method	JavaScript	JScript	N	IE	Opera	Notes
item()	-	3.0 +	-	4.0 +	-	-

JavaScript Programmer's Reference

IMG object (Object/HTML)

The MSIE object wrapper for images.

Availability:	DOM level – 1 JavaScript – 1.2 JScript – 3.0 Internet Explorer – 4.0 Netscape – 3.0
Inherits from:	*Element object*

JavaScript syntax:	IE *myIMG* = *myDocument*.all.*anElementID*
	
	IE *myIMG* =
	     myDocument.all.tags("IMG")[*anIndex*]
	
	IE *myIMG* = *myDocument*.all[*aName*]
	
	- *myIMG* = *myDocument*.*anImageName*
	
	- *myIMG* =
	     myDocument.getElementById(*anElementID*)
	
	- *myIMG* = *myDocument*.getElementsByName
	     (*aName*)[*anIndex*]
	
	- *myIMG* = *myDocument*.images[*anIndex*]
	
	- *myIMG* = *myImageArray*[*anIndex*]
	
	- *myIMG* = *myDocument*.getElementsByTagName
	     ("IMG")[*anIndex*]

HTML syntax:	`<IMG> <INPUT TYPE="IMAGE">`
Argument list:	*anIndex* A reference to an element in a collection *aName* An associative array reference *anElementID* The ID value of an Element object
Object properties:	`accessKey, align, alt, border, complete, dataFld, dataFormatAs, dataSrc, defaultValue, dynsrc, fileCreatedDate, fileModifiedDate, fileSize, fileUpdatedDate, height, href, hspace, iccProfile, isMap, longDesc, loop, lowsrc, name, protocol, prototype, readyState, size, src, start, tabIndex, useMap, vspace, width`
Object methods:	`select()`
Event handlers:	`onAbort, onAfterUpdate, onBeforeUpdate, onBlur, onChange, onClick, onDataAvailable, onDataSetChanged, onDataSetComplete, onDblClick, onDragStart, onError, onFilterChange, onFocus, onHelp, onKeyDown, onKeyPress, onKeyUp, onLoad, onMouseDown, onMouseMove, onMouseOut, onMouseOver, onMouseUp, onResize, onRowEnter, onRowExit, onScroll, onSelectStart`

<IMG> tags and the objects that represent them are inline elements. Placing them into a document does not create a line break.

Event handling support via properties containing function objects was added to IMG objects at version 1.1 of JavaScript.

The DOM level 1 specification refers to this as an ImageElement object. Netscape implements an Image class with somewhat different properties. By inspecting their DOM attributes, you can see that they are instances of different classes.

See also:	*Element object, Image object, ImageArray object,* Input.accessKey

Property	JavaScript	JScript	N	IE	Opera	DOM	HTML	Notes
accessKey	1.5 +	3.0 +	3.0 +	4.0 +	-	1+	-	-
align	1.5 +	3.0 +	3.0 +	4.0 +	-	1+	-	-
alt	1.5 +	3.0 +	3.0 +	4.0 +	-	1+	-	-
border	1.5 +	3.0 +	3.0 +	4.0 +	-	1+	-	-
complete	-	3.0 +	-	4.0 +	-	-	-	ReadOnly
dataFld	1.5 +	3.0 +	3.0 +	4.0 +	-	1+	-	-
dataFormatAs	1.5 +	3.0 +	3.0 +	4.0 +	-	1+	-	-
dataSrc	1.5 +	3.0 +	3.0 +	4.0 +	-	1+	-	-
defaultValue	1.5 +	3.0 +	3.0 +	4.0 +	-	1+	-	-
dynsrc	-	3.0 +	-	4.0 +	-	-	-	Warning
file CreatedDate	-	3.0 +	-	4.0 +	-	-	-	ReadOnly
file ModifiedDate	-	3.0 +	-	4.0 +	-	-	-	ReadOnly
fileSize	-	3.0 +	-	4.0 +	-	-	-	ReadOnly
file UpdatedDate	-	3.0 +	-	4.0 +	-	-	-	ReadOnly
height	1.5 +	3.0 +	3.0 +	4.0 +	-	1+	-	-
href	-	3.0 +	-	4.0 +	-	-	-	-
hspace	1.5 +	3.0 +	3.0 +	4.0 +	-	1+	-	-
iccProfile	-	3.0 +	-	4.0 +	-	-	-	-
isMap	1.5 +	3.0 +	3.0 +	4.0 +	-	1+	-	-
longDesc	1.5 +	3.0 +	3.0 +	4.0 +	-	1+	-	Warning
loop	-	3.0 +	-	4.0 +	-	-	-	-
lowsrc	1.5 +	3.0 +	3.0 +	4.0 +	-	1+	-	-
name	1.5 +	3.0 +	3.0 +	4.0 +	-	1+	-	-
protocol	-	3.0 +	-	4.0 +	-	-	-	ReadOnly
prototype	-	3.0 +	-	4.0 +	-	-	-	ReadOnly
readyState	-	3.0 +	-	4.0 +	-	-	-	ReadOnly
size	1.5 +	3.0 +	3.0 +	4.0 +	-	1+	-	-
src	1.5 +	3.0 +	3.0 +	4.0 +	-	1+	-	-

Table continued on following page

Property	JavaScript	JScript	N	IE	Opera	DOM	HTML	Notes
start	-	3.0 +	-	4.0+	-	2 +	-	-
tabIndex	1.5 +	3.0 +	3.0 +	4.0 +	-	1 +	-	-
useMap	1.5 +	3.0 +	3.0 +	4.0 +	-	1 +	-	-
vspace	1.5 +	3.0 +	3.0 +	4.0 +	-	1 +	-	-
width	1.5 +	3.0 +	3.0 +	4.0 +	-	1 +	-	-

Method	JavaScript	JScript	N	IE	Opera	DOM	HTML	Notes
select()	1.5 +	3.0 +	3.0 +	4.0 +	-	1 +	-	-

Event name	JavaScript	JScript	N	IE	Opera	DOM	HTML	Notes
onAbort	1.5 +	3.0+	3.0+	4.0 +	3.0 +	-	-	-
onAfterUpdate	-	3.0 +	-	4.0 +	-	-	-	-
onBeforeUpdate	-	3.0 +	-	4.0 +	-	-	-	-
onBlur	1.5 +	3.0 +	3.0 +	4.0 +	3.0 +	-	-	Warning
onChange	1.5 +	3.0 +	3.0 +	4.0 +	3.0 +	-	-	-
onClick	1.5 +	3.0 +	3.0 +	4.0 +	3.0 +	-	4.0 +	Warning
onData Available	-	3.0 +	-	4.0 +	-	-	-	-
onData SetChanged	-	3.0 +	-	4.0 +	-	-	-	-
onData SetComplete	-	3.0 +	-	4.0 +	-	-	-	-
onDblClick	1.5 +	3.0 +	3.0 +	4.0 +	3.0 +	-	4.0 +	Warning
onDragStart	-	3.0 +	-	4.0 +	-	-	-	-
onError	1.5 +	3.0 +	3.0 +	4.0 +	3.0 +	-	-	Warning
onFilterChange	-	3.0 +	-	4.0 +	-	-	-	-
onFocus	1.5 +	3.0 +	3.0 +	4.0 +	3.0 +	-	-	Warning
onHelp	-	3.0 +	-	4.0 +	-	-	-	Warning
onKeyDown	1.5 +	3.0 +	3.0 +	4.0 +	3.0 +	-	4.0 +	Warning
onKeyPress	1.5 +	3.0 +	3.0 +	4.0 +	3.0 +	-	4.0 +	Warning
onKeyUp	1.5 +	3.0 +	3.0 +	4.0 +	3.0 +	-	4.0 +	Warning
onLoad	1.5 +	3.0 +	3.0 +	4.0 +	3.0 +	-	-	Warning
onMouseDown	1.5 +	3.0 +	3.0 +	4.0 +	3.0 +	-	4.0 +	Warning
onMouseMove	1.5 +	3.0 +	3.0 +	4.0 +	-	-	4.0 +	Warning
onMouseOut	1.5 +	3.0 +	3.0 +	4.0 +	3.0 +	-	4.0 +	Warning
onMouseOver	1.5 +	3.0 +	3.0 +	4.0 +	3.0 +	-	4.0 +	Warning
onMouseUp	1.5 +	3.0 +	3.0 +	4.0 +	3.0 +	-	4.0 +	Warning
onResize	1.5 +	3.0 +	3.0 +	4.0 +	-	-	-	Warning
onRowEnter	-	3.0 +	-	4.0 +	-	-	-	-
onRowExit	-	3.0 +	-	4.0 +	-	-	-	-
onScroll	-	3.0 +	-	4.0 +	-	-	-	-
onSelectStart	-	3.0 +	-	4.0 +	-	-	-	-

Inheritance chain:

Element object, Node object

Implementation object (Object/DOM)

A special core object that describes the DOM implementation.

Availability:	DOM level – 1 JavaScript – 1.5 JScript – 5.0 Internet Explorer – 5.0 Netscape – 6.0
JavaScript syntax:	- *myImplementation* = *myDocument*.implementation
Object methods:	hasFeature()

This is part of the DOM compliant implementation that MSIE now provides.

It has no enumerable properties and is a member of the Implementation object class. It describes the DOM implementation that is supported.

The DOM level 2 specification adds the following two methods:

❑ createDocumentType()

❑ createDocument()

Warnings:

❑ The DOM level 1 standard calls this a DOMImplementation object. MSIE calls it an Implementation object.

See also:	Document.implementation

Method	JavaScript	JScript	N	IE	Opera	DOM	Notes
hasFeature()	1.5 +	5.0 +	6.0 +	5.0 +	-	1 +	-

ImplicitParents (Attribute)

An internal attribute of a function object referred to by an object property.

Availability:	ECMAScript edition – 2

This internal attribute controls the way that the scope chain might be modified when an implementation defined function is being executed. If this attribute is set, then the list of objects defined by the 'this' value will be added to the scope chain after the implementation supplied activation object.

The difference between the behavior of the ImplicitParents and the ImplicitThis internal attributes is quite subtle and you should consult and fully understand the ECMA standard as it relates to them.

See also:	*ImplicitThis*

Cross-references:

ECMA 262 edition 2 – section – 10.1.1

ECMA 262 edition 2 – section – 10.2.4

ImplicitThis (Attribute)

An internal Function object property.

Availability:	ECMAScript edition – 2

This internal attribute controls the way that the scope chain might be modified when an implementation defined function is being executed. If this attribute is set, then the 'this' value will be added to the scope chain after the implementation supplied activation object.

The difference between the behavior of the ImplicitParents and the ImplicitThis internal attributes is quite subtle, and you should consult and fully understand the ECMA standard as it relates to them.

See also:	*ImplicitParents*

Cross-references:

ECMA 262 edition 2 – section – 10.1.1

ECMA 262 edition 2 – section – 10.2.4

import (Statement)

Import some properties that have been exported from another execution context.

Availability:	ECMAScript edition – 2 JavaScript – 1.2 JScript – 3.0 Internet Explorer – 4.0 Netscape – 3.0
JavaScript syntax:	-	import *anObject.aFunction*;
	-	import *anObject.aProperty*;

Argument list:	aFunction	A function object to import
	anObject	An object that is exporting some property values
	aProperty	A property value to import

ECMAScript edition 2 suggests this is a future extension. As of the third edition of the ECMAScript standard it is still denoted as a reserved word.

Navigator 4 anticipates that a future standard will endorse this capability and provides it anyway.

A layer might import a function exported by another layer so that they can exchange values or operate on one another.

The imported property name can include the wildcard asterisk character to match several properties.

Warnings:

❏ This only works in Netscape 4 when the LANGUAGE attribute is set to "JavaScript1.2". Using import will affect the behavior of the == and ! = operators as well.

❏ This can affect the security policy regarding the "same-signer" trustworthiness of a page.

See also:	*export, Same origin, Signed scripts*

Cross-references:

ECMA 262 edition 2 – section – 7.4.3

ECMA 262 edition 3 – section – 7.5.3

in (Operator/logical)

Test for the existence of a property in an object.

Availability:	ECMAScript edition – 3 JavaScript – 1.5 JScript – 5.0 Internet Explorer – 5.0 Netscape – 6.0
Property/method value type:	Boolean primitive
JavaScript syntax:	-	aProperty in anObject
Argument list:	aProperty	A specific property to test for the existence of

The object is examined to see if the property exists. If it does, then a Boolean `true` value is returned, otherwise the expression returns `false`.

This might be useful as a work-around for when you need to test for the existence of a property but to do so by referring to it directly might cause a run-time error.

Warnings:

❑   This is not available for use server-side with Netscape Enterprise Server 3.

Cross-references:

ECMA 262 edition 3 – section – 11.8.7

Increment value (++) (Operator/postfix)

Pre- or post-incrementing operator.

Availability:	ECMAScript edition – 2 JavaScript – 1.0 JScript – 1.0 Internet Explorer – 3.02 Netscape – 2.0 Netscape Enterprise Server version – 2.0 Opera – 3.0	
Property/method value type:	`Number primitive`	
JavaScript syntax:	-	*++anOperand*
	-	*anOperand++*
Argument list:	*anOperand*	A numeric value that can be incremented

The operand is incremented by 1.

A prefixing incrementor will add 1 to the operand value before it is used in an expression.

A postfixing incrementor will add 1 to the operand after it is used in an expression.

Be careful how you use this pre/post placement as you can easily generate 'off by one' errors in your algorithms by placing the operator on the wrong side of the operand.

This operator is more or less functionally equivalent to:

anOperand += 1

Which is equivalent to:

anOperand = anOperand + 1

See also:	*Add then assign (+=),* Additive expression, Additive operator, *Decrement value (--), Postfix expression, Postfix increment (++), Prefix expression*

Cross-references:

ECMA 262 edition 2 – section – 11.3.1

ECMA 262 edition 3 – section – 11.3.2

Infinity (Constant/static)

A literal constant whose type is a built-in primitive value.

Availability:	ECMAScript edition – 2 JavaScript – 1.3 JScript – 3.0 Internet Explorer – 4.0 Netscape – 4.06
Property/method value type:	Number primitive
JavaScript syntax:	- Infinity

The primitive value Infinity represents the positive infinite number value.

In JavaScript you can use the values positive infinity and negative infinity. They make reference to a global special variable called Infinity, and you can place an optional unary plus or unary minus in front to yield the positive and negative extremes.

If you are in an environment that does not have the Infinity value implemented, then you may be able to create one yourself like this:

```
var Infinity = 1e300 * 1e300;
```

You can check for infinity values with Number.POSITIVE_INFINITY and Number.NEGATIVE_INFINITY. They should be identical to Infinity and -Infinity which are properties of the Global object.

Note that although the type of result when testing the value Infinity or the copies available from the Number object is number, the value will print as "Inf" when displayed with a document.write() method.

Warnings:

❑ This constant is available as a property of the `global` object in MSIE version 4 but not in Netscape 4.

❑ This is not available for use server-side with Netscape Enterprise Server 3.

❑ Note that you can assign a new value to the `Infinity` property on some browsers. This is somewhat dangerous and may cause unpredictable results later on.

See also:	Arithmetic constant, Exception, *Global object*, Global special variable, *isFinite()*, *NaN*, *Number*, *Number*, *Number.NEGATIVE_INFINITY*, *Number.POSITIVE_INFINITY*, Range error, Special number values, Value property, Zero value

Property attributes:

`DontEnum`.

Cross-references:

ECMA 262 edition 2 – section – 4.3.22

ECMA 262 edition 2 – section – 15.1.1.2

ECMA 262 edition 3 – section – 4.3.22

ECMA 262 edition 3 – section – 15.1.1.2

Wrox *Instant JavaScript* – page – 14

Input object (Object/DOM)

Another name for a FormElement object.

Availability:	DOM level – 1 JavaScript – 1.0 JScript – 1.0 Internet Explorer – 3.02 Netscape – 2.0	
Inherits from:	*Element object*	
JavaScript syntax:	-	`myInput =` `myDocument.aFormName.anElementName`
	-	`myInput = myDocument.aFormName` `.elements[anItemIndex]`
	IE	`myInput = myDocument.all.anElementID`
	IE	`myInput =` `myDocument.all.tags("INPUT")[anIndex]`
	IE	`myInput = myDocument.all[aName]`
	-	`myInput = myDocument.forms[aFormIndex]` `.anElementName`

JavaScript syntax:	-	`myInput = myDocument.forms[aFormIndex]` `.elements[anItemIndex]`
	-	`myInput =` `myDocument.getElementById(anElementID)`
	-	`myInput = myDocument.getElementsByName` `(aName)[anIndex]`
	-	`myInput = myInputArray[aName]`
	-	`myInput = myInputArray[anIndex]`
	-	`myInput = myDocument.getElements` `ByTagName("INPUT")[anIndex]`
HTML syntax:	`<INPUT TYPE="aType">`	
Argument list:	`anIndex`	A valid reference to an item in the collection
	`aName`	The name attribute of an element
	`anElementID`	The ID attribute of an element
	`anItemIndex`	A valid reference to an item in the collection
	`aFormIndex`	A reference to a particular form in the forms collection
Object properties:	`accept, accessKey, align, alt, checked, dataFld, dataFormatAs, dataSrc, defaultChecked, defaultSelected, defaultValue, disabled, form, length, maxLength, name, readOnly, recordNumber, selected, selectedIndex, size, src, status, tabIndex, type, value`	
Object methods:	`blur(), click(), createTextRange(), focus(), handleEvent(), select()`	
Event handlers:	`onAfterUpdate, onBeforeUpdate, onBlur, onChange, onClick, onDblClick, onFocus, onHelp, onKeyDown, onKeyPress, onKeyUp, onMouseDown, onMouseMove, onMouseOut, onMouseOver, onMouseUp, onRowEnter, onRowExit, onSelect`	

This is a generic description of a form element object. The object will really be a concrete manifestation of a particular class, but is available generally as an item in the elements array that belongs to the form.

We have tried to conceive a general model of the object relationships in a browser, a difficult task – we document a general purpose class referred to as an `Element` object. Most displayable items in a document that are instantiated by an HTML tag can be considered to be sub-classes of the `Element` object.

Input objects, collectively, are a sub-class of the `Element` object class so to avoid over-duplicating the same coverage, properties, methods, events, and collections that are specific to `Input` objects are discussed here and are omitted from the discussion topics relating to the `Element` object. They are listed in the property, method, collection, and event summary for the `Element` object.

Likewise, under the Input object, those properties, method, collections, and events that apply generally to all kinds of Input objects are documented here but those that are specific to only a particular kind of Input object sub-class are covered under specific topics relating to that class.

Some properties and methods of the Input objects and its specific sub-classes are platform specific. The dataFld, dataSrc and dataFormatAs properties are only available in MSIE. Assigning event handlers to onevent... properties may also support different event sets in each browser platform.

MSIE supports an INPUT object class rather than an Input object class.

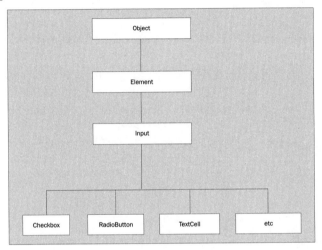

Warnings:

❑ Note that on MSIE, Input objects are actually INPUT objects because MSIE follows a general rule of naming object classes after the capitalised name of the HTML tag that instantiates them.

❑ Beware that although a small sub-set of the complete range of properties and methods are supported on all browsers, there are many properties and methods that are only available on one browser or another.

See also:	FIELDSET object, ISINDEX object, Label object, Legend object

Property	JavaScript	JScript	N	IE	Opera	DOM	HTML	Notes
accept	1.5 +	5.0 +	6.0 +	5.0 +	-	1 +	-	-
accessKey	1.5 +	3.0 +	6.0 +	4.0 +	-	1 +	-	-
align	1.5 +	3.0 +	6.0 +	4.0 +	-	1 +	-	-
alt	1.5 +	3.0 +	6.0 +	3.02 +	-	1 +	-	-
checked	1.0 +	1.0 +	2.0 +	3.02 +	3.0 +	1 +	-	-
dataFld	-	3.0 +	-	4.0 +	-	-	-	-

Property	JavaScript	JScript	N	IE	Opera	DOM	HTML	Notes
dataFormatAs	-	3.0 +	-	4.0 +	-	-	-	-
dataSrc	-	3.0 +	-	4.0 +	-	-	-	-
defaultChecked	1.0 +	1.0 +	2.0 +	3.02 +	3.0 +	1 +	-	-
default Selected	1.0 +	1.0 +	2.0 +	3.02 +	-	1 +	-	Warning
defaultValue	1.0 +	1.0 +	2.0 +	3.02 +	-	1 +	-	ReadOnly
disabled	1.5 +	3.0 +	6.0 +	4.0 +	-	1 +	-	-
form	1.0 +	1.0 +	2.0 +	3.02 +	3.0 +	1 +	-	ReadOnly
length	1.0 +	1.0 +	2.0 +	3.02 +	-	1 +	-	Warning
maxLength	1.5 +	3.0 +	6.0 +	4.0 +	-	1 +	-	-
name	1.5 +	5.5 +	6.0 +	5.5 +	3.0 +	1 +	-	-
readOnly	1.5 +	3.0 +	6.0 +	4.0 +	-	1 +	-	-
record Number	-	3.0 +	-	4.0 +	-	-	-	ReadOnly
selected	1.0 +	1.0 +	2.0 +	3.02 +	-	1 +	-	Warning
selectedIndex	1.0 +	1.0 +	2.0 +	3.02 +	-	1 +	-	Warning
size	1.0 +	1.0 +	2.0 +	3.02 +	-	1 +	-	-
src	1.5 +	3.0 +	6.0 +	4.0 +	-	1 +	-	-
status	1.0 +	1.0 +	2.0 +	3.02 +	-	1 +	-	Warning
tabIndex	1.5 +	3.0 +	6.0 +	4.0 +	-	1 +	-	-
type	1.1 +	1.0 +	3.0 +	3.02 +	3.0 +	1 +	-	ReadOnly
value	1.5 +	1.0 +	6.0 +	3.02 +	3.0 +	1 +	-	-

Method	JavaScript	JScript	N	IE	Opera	DOM	HTML	Notes
blur()	1.0 +	1.0 +	2.0 +	3.02 +	3.0 +	1 +	-	-
click()	1.0 +	3.0 +	2.0 +	4.0 +	3.0 +	1 +	-	-
create TextRange()	-	3.0 +	-	4.0 +	-	-	-	-
focus()	1.0 +	1.0 +	2.0 +	3.02 +	3.0 +	1 +	-	-
handleEvent()	1.2 +	-	4.0 +	-	-	-	-	-
select()	1.1 +	3.0 +	3.0 +	4.0 +	-	1 +	-	-

Event name	JavaScript	JScript	N	IE	Opera	DOM	HTML	Notes
onAfterUpdate	-	3.0 +	-	4.0 +	-	-	-	-
onBeforeUpdate	-	3.0 +	-	4.0 +	-	-	-	-
onBlur	1.1 +	3.0 +	3.0 +	4.0 +	3.0 +	-	-	Warning
onChange	1.0 +	3.0 +	2.0 +	4.0 +	3.0 +	-	-	-
onClick	1.0 +	1.0 +	2.0 +	3.02 +	3.0 +	-	4.0 +	Warning
onDblClick	1.2 +	3.0 +	4.0 +	4.0 +	3.0 +	-	4.0 +	Warning

Table continued on following page

JavaScript Programmer's Reference

Event name	JavaScript	JScript	N	IE	Opera	DOM	HTML	Notes
onFocus	1.0 +	3.0 +	2.0 +	4.0 +	3.0 +	-	-	Warning
onHelp	-	3.0 +	-	4.0 +	-	-	-	Warning
onKeyDown	1.2 +	3.0 +	4.0 +	4.0 +	3.0 +	-	4.0 +	Warning
onKeyPress	1.2 +	3.0 +	4.0 +	4.0 +	3.0 +	-	4.0 +	Warning
onKeyUp	1.2 +	3.0 +	4.0 +	4.0 +	3.0 +	-	4.0 +	Warning
onMouseDown	1.2 +	3.0 +	4.0 +	4.0 +	3.0 +	-	4.0 +	Warning
onMouseMove	1.2 +	3.0 +	4.0 +	4.0 +	-	-	4.0 +	Warning
onMouseOut	1.1 +	3.0 +	3.0 +	4.0 +	3.0 +	-	4.0 +	Warning
onMouseOver	1.0 +	1.0 +	2.0 +	3.02 +	3.0 +	-	4.0 +	Warning
onMouseUp	1.2 +	3.0 +	4.0 +	4.0 +	3.0 +	-	4.0 +	Warning
onRowEnter	-	3.0 +	-	4.0 +	-	-	-	-
onRowExit	-	3.0 +	-	4.0 +	-	-	-	-
onSelect	1.0 +	3.0 +	2.0 +	4.0 +	3.0 +	-	-	-

Inheritance chain:

Element object, Node object

InputArray object (Object/browser)

A collection of identically named input elements.

Availability:	JavaScript – 1.2 JScript – 3.0 Internet Explorer – 4.0 Netscape – 4.0
Inherits from:	*Collection object*
JavaScript syntax:	-	`myInputArray = myDocument` `.aFormName.anElementName`
	IE	`myInputArray =` `myDocument.all[aName]`
	-	`myInputArray = myDocument.forms` `[aFormIndex].anElementName`
	-	`myInputArray = myDocument.` `getElementsByName(aName)`
	-	`myInputArray = myDocument.` `getElementsByTagName("INPUT")`
Argument list:	*aName*	An associative array reference
	aFormIndex	A reference to a particular form in the forms collection
	anIndex	A valid reference to an item in the collection
Object properties:	length	

You may encounter this if you have several `Input` objects with the same name. It is better to make sure they have unique names.

Warnings:

❑ In Netscape, this array is of the type `InputArray`. However, in MSIE it is an object of type `Collection`. Be careful if your code depends on testing object types because you may find it breaks when used across the two browsers.

See also:	Input object

Property	JavaScript	JScript	Nav	IE	Opera	Notes
length	1.2 +	3.0 +	4.0 +	4.0 +	-	Warning

Inheritance chain:

`Collection` object

INS object (Object/HTML)

An object representing an `<INS>` tag in the document.

Availability:	JScript – 3.0
	Internet Explorer – 4.0
Inherits from:	Element object
JavaScript syntax:	IE `myINS = myDocument.all.anElementID`
	IE `myINS = myDocument.all.tags ("INS")[anIndex]`
	IE `myINS = myDocument.all[aName]`
	- `myINS = myDocument.getElementById (anElementID)`
	- `myINS = myDocument.getElementsByName (aName)[anIndex]`
	- `myINS = myDocument.getElementsBy TagName("INS")[anIndex]`
HTML syntax:	`<INS> ... </INS>`
Argument list:	`anIndex` A reference to an element in a collection
	`aName` An associative array reference
	`anElementID` The ID value of the object
Object properties:	`cite, dateTime`
Event handlers:	`onClick, onDblClick, onDragStart, onFilterChange, onHelp, onKeyDown, onKeyPress, onKeyUp, onMouseDown, onMouseMove, onMouseOut, onMouseOver, onMouseUp, onSelectStart`

This is a means of marking a section of the page that has been inserted since the previous version of the page. The appearance is styled to indicate the inserted text as distinct from the surrounding text. The cite property refers to a document that describes the reason for the insertion.

The DOM level 1 specification includes this in the ModElement object functionality.

See also:	DEL object, Element object, ModElement object

Property	JavaScript	JScript	N	IE	Opera	HTML	Notes
cite	-	5.0 +	-	5.0 +	-	-	-
dateTime	-	5.0 +	-	5.0 +	-	-	-

Event name	JavaScript	JScript	N	IE	Opera	HTML	Notes
onClick	1.0 +	1.0 +	2.0 +	4.0 +	3.0 +	4.0 +	Warning
onDblClick	1.2 +	3.0 +	4.0 +	4.0 +	3.0 +	4.0 +	Warning
onDragStart	-	3.0 +	-	4.0 +	-	-	-
onFilterChange	-	3.0 +	-	4.0 +	-	-	-
onHelp	-	3.0 +	-	4.0 +	-	-	Warning
onKeyDown	1.2 +	3.0 +	4.0 +	4.0 +	3.0 +	4.0 +	Warning
onKeyPress	1.2 +	3.0 +	4.0 +	4.0 +	3.0 +	4.0 +	Warning
onKeyUp	1.2 +	3.0 +	4.0 +	4.0 +	3.0 +	4.0 +	Warning
onMouseDown	1.2 +	3.0 +	4.0 +	4.0 +	3.0 +	4.0 +	Warning
onMouseMove	1.2 +	3.0 +	4.0 +	4.0 +	-	4.0 +	Warning
onMouseOut	1.1 +	3.0 +	3.0 +	4.0 +	3.0 +	4.0 +	Warning
onMouseOver	1.0 +	1.0 +	2.0 +	4.0 +	3.0 +	4.0 +	Warning
onMouseUp	1.2 +	3.0 +	4.0 +	4.0 +	3.0 +	4.0 +	Warning
onSelectStart	-	3.0 +	-	4.0 +	-	-	-

Inheritance chain:

Element object, Node object

instanceof (Operator/logical)

Checks to see if an object is an instance of another object.

Availability:	ECMAScript edition – 3
	JavaScript – 1.5
	JScript – 5.0
	Internet Explorer – 5.0
	Netscape – 6.0

Property/method value type:	Boolean primitive	
JavaScript syntax:	-	*anObject* instanceof *anotherObject*
Argument list:	*anObject*	The object to test
	anotherObject	The object to test against

The object referred to by the left operand is examined, and its type compared with the type of the object on the right. The object on the right should be an object with a constructor (that is, a class object) although this likely works with instances as well if they also have constructors inherited.

The ECMA standard (second edition) reserves this keyword for future use in anticipation of the JavaScript 1.4 implementation. That means that a compliant implementation does not need to support this feature.

This operator yields the true value if both objects are of the same class, otherwise it is false.

Warnings:

❑ Use with caution. Be aware that there are some bugs in the class instantiation of some objects in Netscape and MSIE. This may not always yield true when you expect it to.

❑ This is not available for use server-side with Netscape Enterprise Server 3.

See also:	Reserved word

Cross-references:

ECMA 262 edition 2 – section – 7.4.3

ECMA 262 edition 3 – section – 11.8.6

int (Reserved word)

Reserved for future language enhancements.

The provision of this reserved keyword suggests that future versions of the ECMAScript standard may provide for a stronger data-typing model than is currently available.

This keyword also represents a Java data type and the int keyword allows for the potential extension of JavaScript interfaces to access Java applet parameters and return values.

See also:	Identifier, *java.lang.Integer*, JavaScript language, Lexical element, LiveConnect, Reserved word, Type

Cross-references:

ECMA 262 edition 2 – section – 7.4.3

ECMA 262 edition 3 – section – 7.5.3

Internet Explorer (Web browser)

A Microsoft web browser product.

In this publication, we refer to this browser by the commonly used abbreviation MSIE.

Many values that MSIE exposes as JavaScript properties reflect the value of an HTML tag attribute. Likewise, many of its special objects are counterparts to the HTML tags.

Where the information is available, the version number where objects, properties and methods became accessible to JavaScript is indicated. In many cases, this may be a later version than when the instantiating HTML tag or attribute was first supported by the browser.

Because the Windows platform in particular and Microsoft products in general are componentized, the JScript interpreter can be replaced over the top of the Internet Explorer browser. This means that you can be running a version of JScript that is later than the browser version you are using. Scripts will work although they may not be able to exploit features of the later browser. For example, JScript 5.5 can be installed over the top of JScript 5.0 in a version 5.0 MSIE browser.

We wrote many scripts to inspect and enumerate various properties of the objects in the MSIE and Netscape browsers – the exposed object types and properties that were hitherto undocumented. They may have been available in earlier versions of the browser, however, where language elements were discovered for the first time, they are initially documented as being available from version 5 of MSIE. A limited amount of further testing was applied where it was suspected that language elements may have been available in earlier releases and the availability modified accordingly.

Because the MSIE browser is componentized to the extent that the JSscript interpreter is actually a separate installation to the MSIE browser, it is very difficult to arrive at a definitive version of JScript that correlates with a particular version of MSIE. For example, several different versions of JScript were extant with the version 3 MSIE browser.

Perhaps this may become less important as browsers converge on a single standard benchmark of functionality. For the time being, current practice suggests that version 4 browsers are rapidly being taken over by version 5 MSIE browsers. Version 2 and 3 of MSIE have declined to such small usage levels as to not require any further serious attempts to support them on new projects.

Refer to the JScript version topic for details of interpreter versus browser revisions.

Warnings:

- ❑ Version 3.02 has these problems with identifier names:

    - ❑ Do not use dollar signs in identifier names

    - ❑ Identifier names are caseless and this version cannot tell the difference between AAA and aaa

See also:	Browser version compatibility, Identifier, *JScript version*, Platform, Script execution, Web browser

Cross-references:

Wrox *Instant JavaScript* – page – 14

isFinite() (Function/global)

Test a numeric value for infinity.

Availability:	ECMAScript edition – 2 JavaScript – 1.3 JScript – 3.0 Internet Explorer – 4.0 Netscape – 4.06	
Property/method value type:	Boolean primitive	
JavaScript syntax:	-	isFinite(aValueToTest)
Argument list:	aValueToTest	A numeric value to check for validity

This is a built-in function to check for the infinity value. Because it is a member of the Global object, and the Global object is permanently in the prototype inheritance chain, you don't need to identify which object the function belongs to.

This applies the internal ToNumber operator to its argument, then returns true or false depending on whether the value is a finite number or not.

The result is true for a valid and finite numeric value and false if the value is NaN or one of the Infinities.

Warnings:

- ❑ This is not available for use server-side with Netscape Enterprise Server 3.

See also:	Enquiry functions, Function property, *Global object*, *Infinity*, Special type, *ToNumber*

Property attributes:

DontEnum.

Cross-references:

ECMA 262 edition 2 – section – 15.1.2.7

ECMA 262 edition 3 – section – 15.1.2.5

ISINDEX object (Object/HTML)

A deprecated object that represents the <ISINDEX> tag. Do not use this in new projects. This tag describes text entry field with an associated prompting text.

Availability:	DOM level – 1 JavaScript – 1.5 JScript – 3.0 Internet Explorer – 4.0 Netscape – 6.0 Deprecated
Inherits from:	*Element object*
JavaScript syntax:	IE `myISINDEX = myDocument.all.anElementID`
	IE `myISINDEX = myDocument.all.tags ("ISINDEX")[anIndex]`
	IE `myISINDEX = myDocument.all[aName]`
	- `myISINDEX = myDocument.getElementById(anElementID)`
	- `myISINDEX = myDocument. getElementsByName(aName)[anIndex]`
	- `myISINDEX = myDocument.getElementsBy TagName("ISINDEX")[anIndex]`
HTML syntax:	`<ISINDEX>`
Object properties:	`prompt, form`
Event handlers:	`onClick, onDblClick, onHelp, onKeyDown, onKeyPress, onKeyUp, onMouseDown, onMouseMove, onMouseOut, onMouseOver, onMouseUp`

Warnings:

❑ This element object is deprecated as of HTML version 4.0 and should not be used for any new projects. Refer to the <INPUT> tag and its corresponding objects for a better and more functional replacement.

See also:	Input object

Property	JavaScript	JScript	N	IE	Opera	DOM	HTML	Notes
prompt	1.5 +	3.0 +	6.0 +	4.0 +	-	1 +	-	Deprecated
form	1.5 +	3.0 +	6.0 +	4.0 +	-	1 +	-	ReadOnly, Deprecated
prompt	1.5 +	3.0 +	6.0 +	4.0 +	-	1 +	-	Deprecated

Event name	JavaScript	JScript	N	IE	Opera	DOM	HTML	Notes
onClick	1.5 +	3.0 +	6.0 +	4.0 +	3.0 +	-	4.0 +	Warning
onDblClick	1.5 +	3.0 +	6.0 +	4.0 +	3.0 +	-	4.0 +	Warning
onHelp	-	3.0 +	-	4.0 +	-	-	-	Warning
onKeyDown	1.5 +	3.0 +	6.0 +	4.0 +	3.0 +	-	4.0 +	Warning
onKeyPress	1.5 +	3.0 +	6.0 +	4.0 +	3.0 +	-	4.0 +	Warning
onKeyUp	1.5 +	3.0 +	6.0 +	4.0 +	3.0 +	-	4.0 +	Warning
onMouseDown	1.5 +	3.0 +	6.0 +	4.0 +	3.0 +	-	4.0 +	Warning
onMouseMove	1.5 +	3.0 +	6.0 +	4.0 +	-	-	4.0 +	Warning
onMouseOut	1.5 +	3.0 +	6.0 +	4.0 +	3.0 +	-	4.0 +	Warning
onMouseOver	1.5 +	3.0 +	6.0 +	4.0 +	3.0 +	-	4.0 +	Warning
onMouseUp	1.5 +	3.0 +	6.0 +	4.0 +	3.0 +	-	4.0 +	Warning

Inheritance chain:

Element object, Node object

isInNet() (Function/proxy.pac)

This is a convenience function for use with proxy.pac files.

Availability:	JavaScript – 1.2 Netscape – 4.0	
JavaScript syntax:	N	isInNet(aHostname, aSubNet)
Argument list:	aHostname	A host name whose IP address is compared with the sub-net
	aSubNet	A sub-net to test against the host IP address

This function performs a name to IP translation by means of an IP lookup. This involves connecting to a name server and waiting for its reply. This is not something you will want to do often as it can severely affect your performance.

Once the host IP address is known, it can be checked against the sub-net value and a true or false value returned.

The value true is returned if the host is a valid member of the sub-net and false if it is part of another sub-net.

See also:	FindProxyForURL(), isPlainHostName(), Proxies, proxy.pac

Cross-references:

Wrox *Instant JavaScript* – page – 58

isNaN() (Function/global)

Test a numeric value for validity.

Availability:	ECMAScript edition – 1 JavaScript – 1.3 JScript – 1.0 Internet Explorer – 3.02 Netscape – 2 Netscape Enterprise Server version – 2.0	
Property/method value type:	Boolean primitive	
JavaScript syntax:	-	isNaN(*aValueToTest*)
Argument list:	*aValueToTest*	A numeric value to be tested for validity

This is a built-in function to check for the Not-a-Number value. Because it is a member of the Global object, and the Global object is permanently in the prototype inheritance chain, you don't need to identify which object the function belongs to.

This applies the internal ToNumber operator to its argument and returns true or false depending on whether the value is a number or not.

The values may not always yield the result you expect.

These all yield a false value:

❑ "4"

❑ true

❑ false

❑ 100.00

❑ Infinity

❑ null

These all yield a `true` value:

- ❏ "4A"
- ❏ "true"
- ❏ "false"
- ❏ undefined

The result is `true` for valid numeric values and `false` for invalid numerics.

Warnings:

- ❏ This is not very useful on MSIE version 3.02 since it cannot understand what a `NaN` is in the first place.

- ❏ Although this was added to some browsers in version 1.0 of JavaScript, it was not available in all versions of Netscape until it was added to the Unix variants for JavaScript 1.1. Most browsers being used these days are at least version 1.1 compliant so this issue is becoming less important.

- ❏ Comparing the `NaN` value with anything using the `==` operator will always yield the Boolean `false` value.

See also:	Enquiry functions, Function property, *Global object*, *NaN*, *Number*, *Special type*, *ToNumber*

Property attributes:

`DontEnum`.

Cross-references:

ECMA 262 edition 2 – section – 15.1.2.6

ECMA 262 edition 3 – section – 15.1.2.4

Wrox *Instant JavaScript* – page – 15

Wrox *Instant JavaScript* – page – 28

ISO 3166 (Standard)

An ISO standard that identifies different countries.

The ISO 3166 standard is revised occasionally to add new country codes. The following table summarises the third edition of the standard. Note that some countries will have changed since this edition:

Code	Country
AD	Andorra
AE	United Arab Emirates
AF	Afghanistan
AG	Antigua and Barbuda
AI	Anguilla
AL	Albania
AN	Netherlands Antilles
AO	Angola
AQ	Antarctica
AR	Argentina
AS	American Samoa
AT	Austria
AU	Australia
AW	Aruba
BB	Barbados
BD	Bangladesh
BE	Belgium
BF	Burkina Faso
BG	Bulgaria
BH	Bahrain
BI	Burundi
BJ	Benin
BN	Brunei Darussalam
BO	Bolivia
BR	Brazil
BS	Bahamas
BT	Bhutan
BU	Burma
BV	Bouvet Island
BW	Botswana
BY	Byelorussian SSR
BZ	Belize
CA	Canada
CC	Cocos (Keeling) Islands
CF	Central African Republic
CG	Congo
CH	Switzerland

Code	Country
CI	Cote d'Ivoire
CK	Cook Islands
CL	Chile
CM	Cameroon
CN	China
CO	Colombia
CR	Costa Rica
CS	Czechoslovakia
CU	Cuba
CV	Cape Verde
CX	Christmas Island
CY	Cyprus
DD	German Democratic Republic
DE	Federal Republic Of Germany
DJ	Djibouti
DK	Denmark
DM	Dominica
DO	Dominican Republic
DZ	Algeria
EC	Ecuador
EG	Egypt
EH	Western Sahara
ES	Spain
ET	Ethiopia
FI	Finland
FJ	Fiji
FK	Falkland Islands
FM	Micronesia
FO	Faroe Islands
FR	France
GA	Gabon
GB	United Kingdom
GD	Grenada
GF	French Guiana
GH	Ghana
GI	Gibraltar
GL	Greenland

JavaScript Programmer's Reference

Table continued on following page

Code	Country
GM	Gambia
GN	Guinea
GP	Guadaloupe
GQ	Equatorial Guinea
GR	Greece
GT	Guatemala
GU	Guam
GW	Guinea-Bissau
GY	Guyana
HK	Hong Kong
HM	Heard and McDonald Islands
HN	Honduras
HT	Haiti
HU	Hungary
ID	Indonesia
IE	Ireland
IL	Israel
IN	India
IO	British Indian Ocean Territory
IQ	Iraq
IR	Islamic Republic Of Iran
IS	Iceland
IT	Italy
JM	Jamaica
JO	Jordan
JP	Japan
KE	Kenya
KH	Democratic Kampuchea
KI	Kiribati
KM	Comoros
KN	St Kitts And Nevis
KP	Democratic People's Republic Of Korea
KR	Republic Of Korea
KW	Kuwait
KY	Cayman Islands
LA	Lao People's Democratic Republic
LB	Lebanon

Code	Country
LC	Saint Lucia
LI	Lichtenstein
LK	Sri Lanka
LR	Liberia
LS	Lesotho
LU	Luxembourg
LY	Libyan Arab Jamahiriya
MA	Morocco
MC	Monaco
MG	Madagascar
MH	Marshall Islands
ML	Mali
MN	Mongolia
MO	Macau
MP	Northern Mariana Islands
MQ	Martinique
MR	Mauritania
MS	Montserrat
MT	Malta
MU	Mauritius
MV	Maldives
MW	Malawi
MX	Mexico
MY	Malaysia
MZ	Mozambique
NA	Namibia
NC	New Caledonia
NE	Niger
NF	Norfolk Island
NG	Nigeria
NI	Nicaragua
NL	Netherlands
NO	Norway
NP	Nepal
NR	Nauru
NU	Niue
NZ	New Zealand

Table continued on following page

JavaScript Programmer's Reference

Code	Country
OM	Oman
PA	Panama
PE	Peru
PF	French Polynesia
PG	Papua New Guinea
PH	Philippines
PK	Pakistan
PL	Poland
PM	St Pierre and Miquelon
PN	Pitcairn
PR	Puerto Rico
PT	Portugal
PW	Palau
PY	Paraguay
QA	Qatar
RE	Reunion
RO	Romania
RW	Rwanda
SA	Saudi Arabia
SB	Solomon Islands
SC	Seychelles
SD	Sudan
SE	Sweden
SG	Singapore
SH	St Helena
SJ	Svalbard and Jan Mayen Islands
SL	Sierra Leone
SM	San Marino
SN	Senegal
SO	Somalia
SR	Suriname
ST	Sao Tome and Principe
SU	Ussr Now Replaced By Individual Country Codes
SV	El Salvador
SY	Syrian Arab Republic
SZ	Swaziland
TC	Turks and Caicos Islands

Code	Country
TD	Chad
TF	French Southern Territories
TG	Togo
TH	Thailand
TK	Tokelau
TN	Tunisia
TO	Tonga
TP	East Timor
TR	Turkey
TT	Trinidad and Tobago
TV	Tuvalu
TW	Taiwan
TZ	United Republic Of Tanzania
UA	Ukraine SSR
UG	Uganda
UM	United States Minor Outlying Islands
US	United States
UY	Uruguay
VA	Vatican City State
VC	St Vincent and The Grenadines
VE	Venezuela
VG	British Virgin Islands
VI	Virgin Islands (US)
VN	Vietnam
VU	Vanuatu
WF	Wallis and Futuna Islands
WS	Samoa
YD	Democratic Yemen
YE	Yemen
YU	Yugoslavia
ZA	South Africa
ZM	Zambia
ZR	Zaire
ZW	Zimbabwe

See also:	Language codes, `Navigator.systemLanguage`, `Navigator.userLanguage`

isPlainHostName() (Function/proxy.pac)

This is a convenience function for use with `proxy.pac` files.

Availability:	JavaScript – 1.2 Netscape – 4.0
Property/method value type:	`Boolean primitive`
JavaScript syntax:	N	`isPlainHostName(aHostname)`
Argument list:	*aHostname* The name of a host to check

This function will check to see if the passed in hostname parameter is just a host name on its own or if it has a full domain specified too. This functionality can probably be simulated outside of a `proxy.pac` file by testing for the existence of a full stop within the passed hostname parameter.

This function returns true if the hostname parameter contains a plain host name with no domain specified. If the hostname parameter specifies a domain as well then this method returns false.

See also:	*FindProxyForURL(), isInNet(), proxy.pac*

Cross-references:

Wrox *Instant JavaScript* – page – 58

about: URL (Request method)
AbstractView object (Object/DOM)
ActiveXObject object (Object/JScript)
Add (+) (Operator/additive)
Add then assign (+=) (Operator/assignment)

.jar (File extension)

Java archive file.

JavaScript files normally have a .js file extension. In some rare cases, a .jar file may be used. This is really a Java archive file type.

It contains a collection of .js files and is normally requested with the ARCHIVE tag attribute in the <SCRIPT> tag.

A .jar file is a ZIP compressed archive of the .js files with a small amount of additional information that carries a manifest. The web browser extracts the manifest so that it can then index the archive to retrieve the items it needs. You can make a simple archive like this with a zip compression utility (for example, Winzip). There is nothing special about it other than making sure the names are consistent with what you refer to from a script or HTML document.

Archives are also useful for attaching digital signatures to scripts. The web reference points to a Netscape resource on archiving, including a link to a downloadable Signtool Archive generator tool.

See also:	*<SCRIPT ARCHIVE="...">*, File extensions, Security policy, Web browser

Cross-references:

O'Reilly *JavaScript Definitive Guide* – page – 390

Wrox *Instant JavaScript* – page – 3

Web-references:

http://developer.netscape.com/software/signedobj/

.java (File extension)

Java source file.

A very obscure situation is when JavaScript is hidden inside Java source code. In that case it will be contained in a file with a .java extension.

See also:	File extensions, Web browser

Cross-references:

Wrox *Instant JavaScript* – page – 3

java.awt (Java package)

A JavaPackage that represents the Abstract Windowing Toolkit.

Availability:	JavaScript – 1.1 Netscape – 3.0

The Abstract Windowing Toolkit is a set of Classes that provide a platform independent way to develop graphical user interfaces on your applets or Java applications. It was introduced quite early on in the Java history at version 1.0 and had some major additions at Java 1.1 and it has now been supplemented by the Swing components which override some AWT functionality but do not render it entirely obsolete.

java.awt.Button (Java class)

A JavaClass object that represents the java.awt.Button class.

Availability:	JavaScript – 1.1 Netscape – 3.0

Object methods:	action(), addNotify(), bounds(), checkImage(), createImage(), deliverEvent(), disable(), enable(), equals(), getBackground(), getClass(), getColorModel(), getFont(), getFontMetrics(), getForeground(), getGraphics(), getLabel(), getLocale(), getParent(), getPeer(), getToolkit(), gotFocus(), hashCode(), hide(), imageUpdate(), inside(), invalidate(), isEnabled(), isShowing(), isValid(), isVisible(), keyDown(), keyUp(), layout(), list(), locate(), location(), lostFocus(), minimumSize(), mouseDown(), mouseDrag(), mouseEnter(), mouseExit(), mouseMove(), mouseUp(), move(), nextFocus(), notify(), notifyAll(), paint(), paintAll(), postEvent(), preferredSize(), prepareImage(), print(), printAll(), removeNotify(), repaint(), requestFocus(), reshape(), resize(), setBackground(), setFont(), setForeground(), setLabel(), setVisible(), show(), size(), toString(), update(), validate(), wait()

This is a sub-class of the AWT Component Class. It describes a button labeled with a text legend which the user can click on. Clicking on the button initiates an action. Each button has an action associated with it and when it is clicked, it will generate an ActionEvent object.

Method	JavaScript	JScript	N	IE	Opera	Notes
action()	1.1 +	-	3.0 +	-	-	-
addNotify()	1.1 +	-	3.0 +	-	-	-
bounds()	1.1 +	-	3.0 +	-	-	-
checkImage()	1.1 +	-	3.0 +	-	-	-
createImage()	1.1 +	-	3.0 +	-	-	-
deliverEvent()	1.1 +	-	3.0 +	-	-	-
disable()	1.1 +	-	3.0 +	-	-	-
enable()	1.1 +	-	3.0 +	-	-	-
equals()	1.1 +	-	3.0 +	-	-	-
getBackground()	1.1 +	-	3.0 +	-	-	-
getClass()	1.1 +	-	3.0 +	-	-	-
getColorModel()	1.1 +	-	3.0 +	-	-	-
getFont()	1.1 +	-	3.0 +	-	-	-
getFontMetrics()	1.1 +	-	3.0 +	-	-	-
getForeground()	1.1 +	-	3.0 +	-	-	-
getGraphics()	1.1 +	-	3.0 +	-	-	-

Table continued on following page

J

JavaScript Programmer's Reference

Method	JavaScript	JScript	N	IE	Opera	Notes
getLabel()	1.1 +	-	3.0 +	-	-	-
getLocale()	1.1 +	-	3.0 +	-	-	-
getParent()	1.1 +	-	3.0 +	-	-	-
getPeer()	1.1 +	-	3.0 +	-	-	-
getToolkit()	1.1 +	-	3.0 +	-	-	-
gotFocus()	1.1 +	-	3.0 +	-	-	-
hashCode()	1.1 +	-	3.0 +	-	-	-
hide()	1.1 +	-	3.0 +	-	-	-
imageUpdate()	1.1 +	-	3.0 +	-	-	-
inside()	1.1 +	-	3.0 +	-	-	-
invalidate()	1.1 +	-	3.0 +	-	-	-
isEnabled()	1.1 +	-	3.0 +	-	-	-
isShowing()	1.1 +	-	3.0 +	-	-	-
isValid()	1.1 +	-	3.0 +	-	-	-
isVisible()	1.1 +	-	3.0 +	-	-	-
keyDown()	1.1 +	-	3.0 +	-	-	-
keyUp()	1.1 +	-	3.0 +	-	-	-
layout()	1.1 +	-	3.0 +	-	-	-
list()	1.1 +	-	3.0 +	-	-	-
locate()	1.1 +	-	3.0 +	-	-	-
location()	1.1 +	-	3.0 +	-	-	-
lostFocus()	1.1 +	-	3.0 +	-	-	-
minimumSize()	1.1 +	-	3.0 +	-	-	-
mouseDown()	1.1 +	-	3.0 +	-	-	-
mouseDrag()	1.1 +	-	3.0 +	-	-	-
mouseEnter()	1.1 +	-	3.0 +	-	-	-
mouseExit()	1.1 +	-	3.0 +	-	-	-
mouseMove()	1.1 +	-	3.0 +	-	-	-
mouseUp()	1.1 +	-	3.0 +	-	-	-
move()	1.1 +	-	3.0 +	-	-	-
nextFocus()	1.1 +	-	3.0 +	-	-	-
notify()	1.1 +	-	3.0 +	-	-	-
notifyAll()	1.1 +	-	3.0 +	-	-	-
paint()	1.1 +	-	3.0 +	-	-	-
paintAll()	1.1 +	-	3.0 +	-	-	-
postEvent()	1.1 +	-	3.0 +	-	-	-
preferredSize()	1.1 +	-	3.0 +	-	-	-

Method	JavaScript	JScript	N	IE	Opera	Notes
prepareImage()	1.1 +	-	3.0 +	-	-	-
print()	1.1 +	-	3.0 +	-	-	-
printAll()	1.1 +	-	3.0 +	-	-	-
removeNotify()	1.1 +	-	3.0 +	-	-	-
repaint()	1.1 +	-	3.0 +	-	-	-
requestFocus()	1.1 +	-	3.0 +	-	-	-
reshape()	1.1 +	-	3.0 +	-	-	-
resize()	1.1 +	-	3.0 +	-	-	-
setBackground()	1.1 +	-	3.0 +	-	-	-
setFont()	1.1 +	-	3.0 +	-	-	-
setForeground()	1.1 +	-	3.0 +	-	-	-
setLabel()	1.1 +	-	3.0 +	-	-	-
setVisible()	1.1 +	-	3.0 +	-	-	-
show()	1.1 +	-	3.0 +	-	-	-
size()	1.1 +	-	3.0 +	-	-	-
toString()	1.1 +	-	3.0 +	-	-	-
update()	1.1 +	-	3.0 +	-	-	-
validate()	1.1 +	-	3.0 +	-	-	-
wait()	1.1 +	-	3.0 +	-	-	-

java.awt.image (Java class)

A JavaClass object that represents the java.awt.image class.

Availability:	JavaScript – 1.1 Netscape – 3.0

This is an abstract class provided as the super-class of all classes that describe and encapsulate images within AWT. Because it is an abstract class, the methods are mostly place holders and will need to be overridden in the concrete classes that are sub-classed from this class.

java.lang (Java package)

The Java language package.

Availability:	JavaScript – 1.1 Netscape – 3.0	
Property/method value type:	JavaPackage object	
JavaScript syntax:	N	java.lang

This JavaPackage provides the main language support classes for Java. There are classes for handling variables, multi-threaded programming, system classes, string-handling and error/exception handler support.

It's not likely you would want to delve deeply into these issues but occasionally you may need to enquire of some readable attributes of a Java applet and this package may help.

java.lang.Boolean (Java class)

The Java Boolean class.

Availability:	JavaScript – 1.1 Netscape – 3.0
Property/method value type:	JavaObject object
Class properties:	FALSE, TRUE, TYPE
Class methods:	getBoolean(), valueOf()
Object methods:	booleanValue(), equals(), getClass(), hashCode(), notify(), notifyAll(), toString(), wait()

Support for Boolean primitives in Java.

Values of this type are visible to JavaScript as a JavaObject, which encapsulates the Java created value.

See also:	*boolean*, Java to JavaScript values, JavaScript to Java values

Method	JavaScript	JScript	N	IE	Opera	Notes
booleanValue()	1.1 +	-	3.0 +	-	-	-
equals()	1.1 +	-	3.0 +	-	-	-
getClass()	1.1 +	-	3.0 +	-	-	-
hashCode()	1.1 +	-	3.0 +	-	-	-
notify()	1.1 +	-	3.0 +	-	-	-
notifyAll()	1.1 +	-	3.0 +	-	-	-
toString()	1.1 +	-	3.0 +	-	-	-
wait()	1.1 +	-	3.0 +	-	-	-

java.lang.Character (Java class)

The Java Character class.

Availability:	JavaScript – 1.1 Netscape – 3.0
Property/method value type:	`JavaObject object`

Class properties:	`COMBINING_SPACING_MARK,`
	`CONNECTOR_PUNCTUATION, CONTROL,`
	`CURRENCY_SYMBOL, DASH_PUNCTUATION,`
	`DECIMAL_DIGIT_NUMBER,`
	`ENCLOSING_MARK, END_PUNCTUATION,`
	`FORMAT, LETTER_NUMBER,`
	`LINE_SEPARATOR, LOWERCASE_LETTER,`
	`MATH_SYMBOL, MAX_RADIX, MAX_VALUE,`
	`MIN_RADIX, MIN_VALUE,`
	`MODIFIER_LETTER, MODIFIER_SYMBOL,`
	`NON_SPACING_MARK, OTHER_LETTER,`
	`OTHER_NUMBER, OTHER_PUNCTUATION,`
	`OTHER_SYMBOL, PARAGRAPH_SEPARATOR,`
	`PRIVATE_USE, SPACE_SEPARATOR,`
	`START_PUNCTUATION, SURROGATE,`
	`TITLECASE_LETTER, TYPE, UNASSIGNED,`
	`UPPERCASE_LETTER`

Class methods:	`digit(), forDigit(),`
	`getNumericValue(), getType(),`
	`isDefined(), isDigit(),`
	`isIdentifierIgnorable(),`
	`isISOControl(),`
	`isJavaIdentifierPart(),`
	`isJavaIdentifierStart(),`
	`isJavaLetter(),`
	`isJavaLetterOrDigit(), isLetter(),`
	`isLetterOrDigit(), isLowerCase(),`
	`isSpace(), isSpaceChar(),`
	`isTitleCase(),`
	`isUnicodeIdentifierPart(),`
	`isUnicodeIdentifierStart(),`
	`isUpperCase(), isWhitespace(),`
	`toLowerCase(), toTitleCase(),`
	`toUpperCase()`

Object methods:	`charValue(), equals(), getClass(),`
	`hashCode(), notify(), notifyAll(),`
	`toString(), wait()`

Support for character based data in the Java environment.

Values of this type are visible to JavaScript as a JavaObject which encapsulates the Java created value.

See also:	*char*, Java to JavaScript values

Method	JavaScript	JScript	N	IE	Opera	Notes
charValue()	1.1 +	-	3.0 +	-	-	-
equals()	1.1 +	-	3.0 +	-	-	-
getClass()	1.1 +	-	3.0 +	-	-	-
hashCode()	1.1 +	-	3.0 +	-	-	-
notify()	1.1 +	-	3.0 +	-	-	-
notifyAll()	1.1 +	-	3.0 +	-	-	-
toString()	1.1 +	-	3.0 +	-	-	-
wait()	1.1 +	-	3.0 +	-	-	-

java.lang.Class (Java class)

The Java Class class.

Availability:	JavaScript – 1.1 Netscape – 3.0
Property/method value type:	JavaObject object
Class methods:	forName()

Support for access to the Java Classes that define the structure of objects.

Values of this type are visible to JavaScript as a JavaObject which encapsulates the Java created value.

You cannot instantiate new objects of this class because the constructor is not public.

See also:	*class*, Java to JavaScript values

Cross-references:

O'Reilly *JavaScript Definitive Guide* – page – 358

java.lang.Double (Java class)

The Java numeric double precision class.

Availability:	JavaScript – 1.1 Netscape – 3.0
Property/method value type:	JavaObject object
Class properties:	MAX_VALUE, MIN_VALUE, NaN, NEGATIVE_INFINITY, POSITIVE_INFINITY, TYPE

Class methods:	doubleToLongBits(), isInfinite(), isNaN(), longBitsToDouble(), toString(), valueOf()
Object methods:	byteValue(), doubleValue(), equals(), floatValue(), getClass(), hashCode(), intValue(), isInfinite(), isNaN(), longValue(), notify(), notifyAll(), shortValue(), toString(), wait()

Support for double precision floating point numbers.

Values of this type are visible to JavaScript as a JavaObject which encapsulates the Java created value.

See also:	*double*, Java to JavaScript values, JavaScript to Java values

Method	JavaScript	JScript	N	IE	Opera	Notes
byteValue()	1.1 +	-	3.0 +	-	-	-
doubleValue()	1.1 +	-	3.0 +	-	-	-
equals()	1.1 +	-	3.0 +	-	-	-
floatValue()	1.1 +	-	3.0 +	-	-	-
getClass()	1.1 +	-	3.0 +	-	-	-
hashCode()	1.1 +	-	3.0 +	-	-	-
intValue()	1.1 +	-	3.0 +	-	-	-
isInfinite()	1.1 +	-	3.0 +	-	-	-
isNaN()	1.1 +	-	3.0 +	-	-	-
longValue()	1.1 +	-	3.0 +	-	-	-
notify()	1.1 +	-	3.0 +	-	-	-
notifyAll()	1.1 +	-	3.0 +	-	-	-
shortValue()	1.1 +	-	3.0 +	-	-	-
toString()	1.1 +	-	3.0 +	-	-	-
wait()	1.1 +	-	3.0 +	-	-	-

java.lang.Float (Java class)

The Java floating point numeric class.

Availability:	JavaScript – 1.1 Netscape – 3.0
Property/method value type:	JavaObject object
Class properties:	MAX_VALUE, MIN_VALUE, NaN, NEGATIVE_INFINITY, POSITIVE_INFINITY, TYPE

Class methods:	`floatToIntBits(), intBitsToFloat(), isInfinite(), isNaN(), toString(), valueOf()`
Object methods:	`byteValue(), doubleValue(), equals(), floatValue(), getClass(), hashCode(), intValue(), isInfinite(), isNaN(), longValue(), notify(), notifyAll(), shortValue(), toString(), wait()`

Support for single precision floating point numbers.

Values of this type are visible to JavaScript as a JavaObject, which encapsulates the Java created value.

See also:	*float*, Java to JavaScript values

Method	JavaScript	JScript	N	IE	Opera	Notes
byteValue()	1.1 +	-	3.0 +	-	-	-
doubleValue()	1.1 +	-	3.0 +	-	-	-
equals()	1.1 +	-	3.0 +	-	-	-
floatValue()	1.1 +	-	3.0 +	-	-	-
getClass()	1.1 +	-	3.0 +	-	-	-
hashCode()	1.1 +	-	3.0 +	-	-	-
intValue()	1.1 +	-	3.0 +	-	-	-
isInfinite()	1.1 +	-	3.0 +	-	-	-
isNaN()	1.1 +	-	3.0 +	-	-	-
longValue()	1.1 +	-	3.0 +	-	-	-
notify()	1.1 +	-	3.0 +	-	-	-
notifyAll()	1.1 +	-	3.0 +	-	-	-
shortValue()	1.1 +	-	3.0 +	-	-	-
toString()	1.1 +	-	3.0 +	-	-	-
wait()	1.1 +	-	3.0 +	-	-	-

java.lang.Integer (Java class)

The Java integer numeric class.

Availability:	JavaScript – 1.1 Netscape – 3.0
Property/method value type:	`JavaObject object`
Class properties:	`MAX_VALUE, MIN_VALUE, TYPE`
Class methods:	`decode(), getInteger(), parseInt(), toBinaryString(), toHexString(), toOctalString(), toString(), valueOf()`

| Object methods: | byteValue(), doubleValue(), equals(), floatValue(), getClass(), hashCode(), intValue(), longValue(), notify(), notifyAll(), shortValue(), toString(), wait() |

Support for integer values in the Java environment.

Values of this type are visible to JavaScript as a JavaObject which encapsulates the Java created value.

| See also: | *int*, Java to JavaScript values |

Method	JavaScript	JScript	N	IE	Opera	Notes
byteValue()	1.1 +	-	3.0 +	-	-	-
doubleValue()	1.1 +	-	3.0 +	-	-	-
equals()	1.1 +	-	3.0 +	-	-	-
floatValue()	1.1 +	-	3.0 +	-	-	-
getClass()	1.1 +	-	3.0 +	-	-	-
hashCode()	1.1 +	-	3.0 +	-	-	-
intValue()	1.1 +	-	3.0 +	-	-	-
longValue()	1.1 +	-	3.0 +	-	-	-
notify()	1.1 +	-	3.0 +	-	-	-
notifyAll()	1.1 +	-	3.0 +	-	-	-
shortValue()	1.1 +	-	3.0 +	-	-	-
toString()	1.1 +	-	3.0 +	-	-	-
wait()	1.1 +	-	3.0 +	-	-	-

java.lang.Long (Java class)

The Java long numeric class.

Availability:	JavaScript – 1.1 Netscape – 3.0
Property/method value type:	JavaObject object
Class properties:	MAX_VALUE, MIN_VALUE, TYPE
Class methods:	getLong(), parseLong(), toBinaryString(), toHexString(), toOctalString(), toString(), valueOf()
Object methods:	byteValue(), doubleValue(), equals(), floatValue(), getClass(), hashCode(), intValue(), longValue(), notify(), notifyAll(), shortValue(), toString(), wait()

Support for long integer values in the Java environment.

Values of this type are visible to JavaScript as a JavaObject, which encapsulates the Java created value.

See also:	Java to JavaScript values, *long*

Method	JavaScript	JScript	N	IE	Opera	Notes
byteValue()	1.1 +	-	3.0 +	-	-	-
doubleValue()	1.1 +	-	3.0 +	-	-	-
equals()	1.1 +	-	3.0 +	-	-	-
floatValue()	1.1 +	-	3.0 +	-	-	-
getClass()	1.1 +	-	3.0 +	-	-	-
hashCode()	1.1 +	-	3.0 +	-	-	-
intValue()	1.1 +	-	3.0 +	-	-	-
longValue()	1.1 +	-	3.0 +	-	-	-
notify()	1.1 +	-	3.0 +	-	-	-
notifyAll()	1.1 +	-	3.0 +	-	-	-
shortValue()	1.1 +	-	3.0 +	-	-	-
toString()	1.1 +	-	3.0 +	-	-	-
wait()	1.1 +	-	3.0 +	-	-	-

java.lang.Object (Java class)

This is the super-class of all objects in the Java lang environment.

Availability:	JavaScript – 1.1 Netscape – 3.0
Property/method value type:	JavaObject object
Object methods:	equals(), getClass(), hashCode(), notify(), notifyAll(), toString(), wait()

Support for generic objects in the Java environment.

Methods and properties belonging to this object are inherited by objects such as the JavaArray object (as it appears to JavaScript).

This class is presented to the JavaScript programmer as a JavaObject object.

See also:	*JavaObject object*

Method	JavaScript	JScript	N	IE	Opera	Notes
equals()	1.1 +	-	3.0 +	-	-	-
getClass()	1.1 +	-	3.0 +	-	-	-
hashCode()	1.1 +	-	3.0 +	-	-	-
notify()	1.1 +	-	3.0 +	-	-	-
notifyAll()	1.1 +	-	3.0 +	-	-	-
toString()	1.1 +	-	3.0 +	-	-	-
wait()	1.1 +	-	3.0 +	-	-	-

Cross-references:

O'Reilly *JavaScript Definitive Guide* – page – 566

java.lang.String (Java class)

The Java String class.

Availability:	JavaScript – 1.1 Netscape – 3.0
Property/method value type:	JavaObject object
Class methods:	copyValueOf(), valueOf()
Object methods:	charAt(), compareTo(), concat(), endsWith(), equals(), equalsIgnoreCase(), getBytes(), getChars(), getClass(), hashCode(), indexOf(), intern(), lastIndexOf(), length(), notify(), notifyAll(), regionMatches(), replace(), startsWith(), substring(), toCharArray(), toLowerCase(), toString(), toUpperCase(), trim(), wait()

Support for string values in the Java environment.

Values of this type are visible to JavaScript as a JavaObject, which encapsulates the Java created value.

See also:	Java to JavaScript values, JavaScript to Java values, *String*

Method	JavaScript	JScript	N	IE	Opera	Notes
charAt()	1.1 +	-	3.0 +	-	-	-
compareTo()	1.1 +	-	3.0 +	-	-	-
concat()	1.1 +	-	3.0 +	-	-	-
endsWith()	1.1 +	-	3.0 +	-	-	-
equals()	1.1 +	-	3.0 +	-	-	-
equalsIgnoreCase()	1.1 +	-	3.0 +	-	-	-
getBytes()	1.1 +	-	3.0 +	-	-	-
getChars()	1.1 +	-	3.0 +	-	-	-
getClass()	1.1 +	-	3.0 +	-	-	-
hashCode()	1.1 +	-	3.0 +	-	-	-
indexOf()	1.1 +	-	3.0 +	-	-	-
intern()	1.1 +	-	3.0 +	-	-	-
lastIndexOf()	1.1 +	-	3.0 +	-	-	-
length()	1.1 +	-	3.0 +	-	-	-
notify()	1.1 +	-	3.0 +	-	-	-
notifyAll()	1.1 +	-	3.0 +	-	-	-
regionMatches()	1.1 +	-	3.0 +	-	-	-
replace()	1.1 +	-	3.0 +	-	-	-
startsWith()	1.1 +	-	3.0 +	-	-	-
substring()	1.1 +	-	3.0 +	-	-	-
toCharArray()	1.1 +	-	3.0 +	-	-	-
toLowerCase()	1.1 +	-	3.0 +	-	-	-
toString()	1.1 +	-	3.0 +	-	-	-
toUpperCase()	1.1 +	-	3.0 +	-	-	-
trim()	1.1 +	-	3.0 +	-	-	-
wait()	1.1 +	-	3.0 +	-	-	-

java.util (Java package)

The Java utility package.

Availability:	JavaScript – 1.1 Netscape – 3.0

This package provides a collection of classes and interfaces that are generally useful to the programmer. These fall into the following categories:

❑ Arrays

❑ Calender functions and date support

- ❏ Collections
- ❏ Event objects
- ❏ Mapping classes
- ❏ Random numbers
- ❏ Resource bundle support
- ❏ String tokenizer
- ❏ Timers
- ❏ Timer tasks

See also:	Method, Property

java.util.Date (Java class)

The Java Date object.

Availability:	JavaScript – 1.1 Netscape – 3.0
Class methods:	parse(), UTC()
Object methods:	after(), before(), equals(), getClass(), getDate(), getDay(), getHours(), getMinutes(), getMonth(), getSeconds(), getTime(), getTimezoneOffset(), getYear(), hashCode(), notify(), notifyAll(), setDate(), setHours(), setMinutes(), setMonth(), setSeconds(), setTime(), setYear(), toGMTString(), toLocaleString(), toString(), wait()

This class is an encapsulation of the machine date and time measured in milliseconds since January the 1st, 1970. Fortunately, this is the same reference time that the JavaScript standard (ECMA) prescribes.

See also:	*Date object, Universal coordinated time*

Method	JavaScript	JScript	N	IE	Opera	Notes
after()	1.1 +	-	3.0 +	-	-	-
before()	1.1 +	-	3.0 +	-	-	-
equals()	1.1 +	-	3.0 +	-	-	-
getClass()	1.1 +	-	3.0 +	-	-	-
getDate()	1.1 +	-	3.0 +	-	-	-
getDay()	1.1 +	-	3.0 +	-	-	-

Table continued on following page

J

JavaScript Programmer's Reference

479

Method	JavaScript	JScript	N	IE	Opera	Notes
getHours()	1.1 +	-	3.0 +	-	-	-
getMinutes()	1.1 +	-	3.0 +	-	-	-
getMonth()	1.1 +	-	3.0 +	-	-	-
getSeconds()	1.1 +	-	3.0 +	-	-	-
getTime()	1.1 +	-	3.0 +	-	-	-
getTimezone Offset()	1.1 +	-	3.0 +	-	-	-
getYear()	1.1 +	-	3.0 +	-	-	-
hashCode()	1.1 +	-	3.0 +	-	-	-
notify()	1.1 +	-	3.0 +	-	-	-
notifyAll()	1.1 +	-	3.0 +	-	-	-
setDate()	1.1 +	-	3.0 +	-	-	-
setHours()	1.1 +	-	3.0 +	-	-	-
setMinutes()	1.1 +	-	3.0 +	-	-	-
setMonth()	1.1 +	-	3.0 +	-	-	-
setSeconds()	1.1 +	-	3.0 +	-	-	-
setTime()	1.1 +	-	3.0 +	-	-	-
setYear()	1.1 +	-	3.0 +	-	-	-
toGMTString()	1.1 +	-	3.0 +	-	-	-
toLocale String()	1.1 +	-	3.0 +	-	-	-
toString()	1.1 +	-	3.0 +	-	-	-
wait()	1.1 +	-	3.0 +	-	-	-

JavaArray object (Object/Navigator)

A JavaScript data type that encapsulates a Java array.

Availability:	JavaScript – 1.1 Netscape – 3.0	
JavaScript syntax:	N	myJavaArray = myWindow.Packages
Object properties:	length	
Object methods:	toString()	

In Java, objects can be collected together into arrays. This is also true of JavaScript. However, as you might expect, some encapsulation of the Java array is necessary to be able to operate on it from a JavaScript environment. The JavaArray object does just this. It supports some JavaScript-like behavior in that it has a length property and can be accessed element by element using the JavaScript [ ] notation. JavaArray objects can be stacked to make multidimensional arrays and they can also be traversed with a for(...in...)... loop.

At version 1.4 of JavaScript, a `JavaArray` object inherits properties from the `java.lang.Object` super-class.

See also:	Array object, Collection object, Java to JavaScript values, JavaScript to Java values, LiveConnect, Window.Packages

Property	JavaScript	JScript	N	IE	Opera	Notes
length	1.1 +	-	3.0 +	-	-	ReadOnly

Method	JavaScript	JScript	N	IE	Opera	Notes
toString()	1.1 +	-	3.0 +	-	-	-

JavaClass object (Object/Navigator)

A JavaScript data type that encapsulates a Java Class.

Availability:	JavaScript – 1.1 Netscape – 3.0
JavaScript syntax:	N `myJavaClass = myWindow.Packages.java`

The static fields of the Java Class are presented as properties of the JavaClass object.

The static methods of the Java Class are presented as methods available to the JavaClass object. They may be presented as `JavaMethod` objects depending on how you access them from JavaScript.

The only properties and methods this object has correspond to the public properties and methods of the Java class that it represents. You can enumerate these properties in a loop.

Java classes are either stored in individual class files or are collected together into groups stored in a ZIP file. Groups of classes will be represented by a `JavaPackage` object. Each individual class is represented by a JavaClass object. The JavaClass objects belong to a parent `JavaPackage` object.

To operate on these objects, you really need to know something about the Java classes they encapsulate. There are many standard classes and some that may have been custom written for your project.

Example code:

```
<HTML>
<HEAD>
</HEAD>
<BODY>
```

```
<SCRIPT>
// Create a JavaScript object that encapsulates a Java Class
var myJavaDateClass  = Packages.java.util.Date;
var myJavaDateObject = new Packages.java.util.Date;
// Write the date to a web page
document.write(myJavaDateObject.toString());
// Write the same date value date to the Java console
java.lang.System.out.println(myJavaDateObject);
</SCRIPT>
</BODY>
</HTML>
```

See also:	JavaScript to Java values, LiveConnect, *Packages.java*, *Packages.netscape*, Window.Packages

Cross-references:

O'Reilly *JavaScript Definitive Guide* – page – 358

JavaObject object (Object/Navigator)

A JavaScript data type that encapsulates a Java object. These are generally going to be members of the Java component class

Availability:	JavaScript – 1.1 Netscape – 3.0
JavaScript syntax:	N *myJavaObject* = new java.lang.Object N *myJavaObject* = document.applets[*anIndex*];
Object properties:	description, filename, length, name
Object methods:	*booleanValue()*, destroy(), disable(), doubleValue(), enable(), getAppletContext(), getAppletInfo(), getBackground(), *getClass()*, getCodeBase(), getDocumentBase(), getLocale(), getParameter(), getParameterInfo(), getToolkit(), hide(), init(), isActive(), isEnabled(), isShowing(), isValid(), isVisible(), minimumSize(), refresh(), start(), stop(), toString()

To make any serious use of this object, you need to know a little Java – at least enough to be able to be familiar with the class structures and creating and modifying objects. If you know how to make your own applets then that is probably sufficient to get started with.

The public properties of the Java Class of which the JavaObject is an instance are presented as properties of the JavaObject object. A JavaObject also inherits the properties from the java.lang.Object Class and any other classes which are in its superclass hierarchy. These are generally available by means of accessor methods so they will likely be listed as methods rather than properties.

The public methods of the Java Class of which the JavaObject is an instance are presented as methods of the JavaObject object. A JavaObject also inherits the methods from the `java.lang.Object` Class and any other classes which are in its superclass hierarchy.

The only properties and methods this object has correspond to the public properties and methods of the Java object that it represents. You can enumerate the properties in a loop to inspect the interface to the object from your own scripts. Like this:

```
for(myProp in myJavaObject)
{
    document.write(myProp);
    document.write("<BR>");
}
for(myProp in myJavaObject){document.write(myProp);
    document.write("<BR>");
```

There may be some properties that are not revealed by this and you may need to resort to some Java documentation for further details. Properties and methods for the objects in Java are documented in more depth in *Java Programmer's Reference*, written by Grant Palmer and published by Wrox Press, which covers JDK 1.3 extensively.

To operate on the JavaObject objects, you really need to know something about the Java objects they encapsulate. There are many standard classes and some that may have been custom written for your project.

Beware that the object may report accessors that don't actually have any purpose in the object you have enumerated.

For properties and methods that apply to the `Applet` object in the context of an MSIE browser, examine the Applet object topic and its related items. This is documented separately because it does not support the same Java – JavaScript bridging mechanism and provides a mutually exclusive set of properties for communication with the `Applet` object.

Although JavaScript exposes a great many of the properties of an Applet by means of `Accessor` methods, it is probably not safe to call the more destructive of them from JavaScript. However, you may usefully want to use the various enquiry methods to find out about the Applet and its internals. Many of these `Accessor` methods yield other objects whose properties can also be inspected by using the same enumeration techniques.

Having examined some applets and other miscellaneous Java objects, a summary list of the accessor methods is presented at the head of this topic.

Some fragments of example code are given here and a couple of important methods are described in adjacent topics. Documenting all the interfaces to an Applet or Java object is so dependant on the object that you should refer to the Applet documentation and source and a Java reference manual for details of the internals of Java code.

J

JavaScript Programmer's Reference

Warnings:

❑ When JavaObject objects are used in JavaScript expressions, even though internally they may contain a value that could be represented by a JavaScript primitive type, they do not behave like that JavaScript primitive type. Instead, they behave according to the rules of the Java object type that contains the value. This can sometimes cause scripts to behave in unexpected ways, for example you might get a concatenation instead of a numeric addition. You should also explicitly test for values and not make assumptions that a null or undefined value is returned.

❑ The JavaObject in Netscape is notably unforgiving. Many other JavaScript objects will yield the value undefined if you ask for a property that does not exist. A JavaObject will generate a run-time error and so you cannot easily test for the existence of an unknown property.

❑ Some objects also support a strangely named function that is referred to by an enumerable but apparently unnamed property. It is exposed when you enumerate the properties in a for (...in...) loop and output their names with a document.write(). A property appears in the list that seems to have no name. Checking the property names with the typeof operator reports this as a string so it's not an undefined name. OK so let's measure its length. The suspect property reports a length of 6 in the example I was testing but it is still invisible. Here's where we try hunches and use our debugging instincts. Wrap the property name in the escape() function. That should tell us what weird characters are there. Voila. It reports that the name is now %3CInit%3E. So the name is the word Init wrapped in < and > characters, which explains why we couldn't see it. The web browser thought it was a tag and didn't recognize it so it was hidden.

❑ The second piece of example code shows how the properties were enumerated and how to display the hidden property name.

Example code:

```
// Output some text to the Java console
java.lang.System.out.println("Some text message");
// Create a JavaScript object that encapsulates a Java Object
var myJavaDateObject = new Packages.java.util.Date;
-------------------------------------------------------------
<!-- Debugging hidden property values -->
<HTML>
<HEAD>
</HEAD>
<BODY>
<TABLE BORDER=1>
<SCRIPT>
// Create a JavaScript object that encapsulates a Java Class
var myJavaDateClass = new Packages.java.util.Date;
// Now enumerate its properties
var myIndex = 0;
for(myProp in myJavaDateClass)
{
    document.write("<TR><TD>");
    document.write(myIndex);
    document.write("</TD><TD>");
```

```
        document.write(myProp);
        document.write("</TD><TD>");
        document.write(typeof(myProp));
        document.write("</TD><TD>");
        document.write(myProp.length);
        document.write("</TD><TD>");
        document.write(escape(myProp));
        document.write("</TD></TR>");

        myIndex++;
    }
    </SCRIPT>
    </TABLE>
    </BODY>
    </HTML>
```

See also:	*Applet object*, Document.applets[], Document.embeds[], *EmbedArray object*, Java to JavaScript values, *java.lang.Object*, *JavaObject.booleanValue()*, JavaScript to Java values, LiveConnect, *Packages.java*, *Packages.netscape*, Window.Packages

Property	JavaScript	JScript	N	IE	Opera	Notes
description	1.1 +	-	3.0 +	-	-	Warning
filename	1.1 +	-	3.0 +	-	-	Warning
length	1.1 +	-	3.0 +	-	-	Warning
name	1.1 +	-	3.0 +	-	-	Warning

Method	JavaScript	JScript	N	IE	Opera	Notes
booleanValue()	1.2 +	-	4.0 +	-	-	-
destroy()	1.1 +	-	3.0 +	-	-	Warning
disable()	1.1 +	-	3.0 +	-	-	Warning
doubleValue()	1.1 +	-	3.0 +	-	-	Warning
enable()	1.1 +	-	3.0 +	-	-	Warning
getAppletContext()	1.1 +	-	3.0 +	-	-	Warning
getAppletInfo()	1.1 +	-	3.0 +	-	-	Warning
getBackground()	1.1 +	-	3.0 +	-	-	Warning
getClass()	1.2 +	-	4.0 +	-	-	Warning
getCodeBase()	1.1 +	-	3.0 +	-	-	Warning
getDocumentBase()	1.1 +	-	3.0 +	-	-	Warning
getLocale()	1.1 +	-	3.0 +	-	-	Warning
getParameter()	1.1 +	-	3.0 +	-	-	Warning
getParameterInfo()	1.1 +	-	3.0 +	-	-	Warning
getToolkit()	1.1 +	-	3.0 +	-	-	Warning

Table continued on following page

J

JavaScript Programmer's Reference

Method	JavaScript	JScript	N	IE	Opera	Notes
hide()	1.1 +	-	3.0 +	-	-	Warning
init()	1.1 +	-	3.0 +	-	-	Warning
isActive()	1.1 +	-	3.0 +	-	-	Warning
isEnabled()	1.1 +	-	3.0 +	-	-	Warning
isShowing()	1.1 +	-	3.0 +	-	-	Warning
isValid()	1.1 +	-	3.0 +	-	-	Warning
isVisible()	1.1 +	-	3.0 +	-	-	Warning
minimumSize()	1.1 +	-	3.0 +	-	-	Warning
refresh()	1.1 +	-	3.0 +	-	-	Warning
start()	1.1 +	-	3.0 +	-	-	Warning
stop()	1.1 +	-	3.0 +	-	-	Warning
toString()	1.1 +	-	3.0 +	-	-	Warning

JavaObject.booleanValue() (Method/Java)

This is the value that is used when the JavaObject is used in a Boolean context.

Availability:	JavaScript – 1.2 Netscape – 4.0	
JavaScript syntax:	N	*myJavaObject*.booleanValue()

Java Boolean objects support this method. It is a Java method but it is analogous to the valueOf() method used on a JavaScript Boolean object.

Because all Java objects become members of the JavaObject class they respond to valueOf() and toString() but those can be overridden in the JavaScript environment. The booleanValue() method penetrates to the Java environment and is executed there with its result encapsulated. The valueOf() and toString() methods are executed in the JavaScript environment even if there is a corresponding Java method for each.

The example shows all three methods being invoked but the toString() and valueOf() are masked. Note that by masking toString(), valueOf() is affected too. That may not be common to all object types.

There are other similar methods to support different Java primitive data types when they are encapsulated in an object. Only this one is illustrated. The others are different only in the data type and the name they have.

Example code:

```
<HTML>
<HEAD>
</HEAD>
<BODY>
<SCRIPT>
// Create a JavaScript object that encapsulates a Java Class
var myJavaBooleanClass = new Packages.java.lang.Boolean(true);
// Mask the JavaScript environment values
myJavaBooleanClass.toString = mask;
// Write the object to a web page
document.write("toString() : ");
document.write(myJavaBooleanClass.toString());
document.write("<BR>");
document.write("valueOf() : ");
document.write(myJavaBooleanClass.valueOf());
document.write("<BR>");
document.write("booleanValue() : ");
document.write(myJavaBooleanClass.booleanValue());
document.write("<BR>");
// Masking function
function mask()
{
return "Masked";
}
</SCRIPT>
</BODY>
</HTML>
```

See also:	*JavaObject object*, LiveConnect

JavaObject.getClass() (Method/Java)

A JavaScript method for obtaining the class of a JavaObject.

Availability:	JavaScript – 1.2 Netscape – 4.0	
JavaScript syntax:	N	*myJavaObject*.getClass()

This returns the Java class of the encapsulated Java object. This is not necessarily the same as a JavaScript class name. In fact what is returned is an object reference to a class object which may need further work to extract the name of the class.

The example shows how a Java object is instantiated and then queried to as of its class. Using the LiveConnect, the getClass() method requests the class name from the Java code and then converts that to a JavaScript message. Inspecting the constructor of the new object and extracting its name property tells you what class JavaScript has wrapped around the Java object.

Warnings:

❑ Beware that you don't confuse this JavaScript getClass() method with the Java getClass() method. Although they have the same name, they yield a different result. The JavaScript method yields a JavaScript object of the class JavaClass. The Java method yields a Java object of the class java.lang.Class, which is not the same thing.

Example code:

```
<HTML>
<HEAD>
</HEAD>
<BODY>
<SCRIPT>
// Instantiate a Java object
myJavaString = new java.lang.String;
// Display its Java class
document.write("Java class : ");
document.write(myJavaString.getClass());
document.write("<BR><BR>");
// Display its JavaScript class
document.write("JavaScript class : ");
document.write(myJavaString.constructor.name);
document.write("<BR><BR>");
</SCRIPT>
</BODY>
</HTML>
```

See also:	LiveConnect

JavaPackage object (Object/Navigator)

A JavaScript data type that encapsulates a Java Package.

Availability:	JavaScript – 1.2 Netscape – 4.0	
JavaScript syntax:	N	myJavaPackage = myWindow.Packages

A collection of Java classes are represented as a package. The complete set of all available JavaPackages are contained within a single parent JavaPackage object. This constructs a hierarchy of JavaPackage and JavaClass objects.

The properties of the JavaPackage object are those that refer to any Java Class or Java Packages that belong to it. However, these are generally not enumerable so you do need to know what they are called before you can access them.

Because you cannot enumerate the properties of this object you won't be able to walk a Java package hierarchy with a script driven tree walker.

The JavaPackage tree structure resembles the directory structure that the Java class files are stored in. Some class files are collected into ZIP archives but even then the hierarchy is still intact and there will be one package that represents the ZIP file and corresponds to that node in the tree. Any arbitrary collection of classes will be represented by a `JavaPackage` object, regardless of how they are stored in the file system.

Example code:

```
// Create a JavaScript object that encapsulates a Java Package
var myJavaPackage = Packages.java.util;
```

See also: JavaScript to Java values, LiveConnect, *netscape.applet*, *Packages.java*, *Packages.netscape*, Window.java, Window.Packages, Window.sun

JavaScript entity (Pitfall)

This functionality is deprecated and should not be used in new projects.

The HTML character entities are useful for describing hard to type characters.

They are functionally similar to the back-quote substitutions that are available server-side with Netscape Enterprise Server.

MSIE version 3.0 introduced a means of passing JavaScript values into the HTML source space using a syntax that is similar to the character entity syntax. However, it is used in contexts that character entities were never intended to be used in. It is also advised as deprecated functionality in the HTML version 4.0 standard.

You might indicate an image width like this:

```
<IMG SRC="..." WIDTH="100">
```

The value for the image width can be taken from a JavaScript expression like this:

```
<IMG SRC="..." WIDTH="&{myWidth * myScaleFactor};">
```

This assumes that the values *myWidth* and *myScaleFactor* have already been defined in some earlier fragment of JavaScript.

The entity can be used to replace a single character in the tag attribute value so you can concatenate other characters such as percent signs if you use it in <HR> tags for example.

This functionality should be avoided and the usual client or server methods used to define the values in HTML tags.

Example code:

```
<HTML>
<BODY>
<FORM>
<INPUT TYPE="text" VALUE="&{top.name;}">
</FORM>
</BODY>
</HTML>
```

See also:	Adding JavaScript to HTML, *Backquote (`)*, *Deprecated functionality*, Pitfalls

Cross-references:

Wrox *Instant JavaScript* – page – 47

JavaScript interactive URL (Request method)

An interactive JavaScript statement executor.

Availability:	JavaScript – 1.0
	JScript – 3.0
	Internet Explorer – 4.0
	Netscape – 2.0

You can type short pieces of JavaScript source code into the location box and press return and the results will be executed in the document window.

For example, to see the value of some mathematical constants, you type these lines:

```
javascript:Math.PI

javascript:Math.LOG10

javascript:Number.MAX_VALUE

javascript:alert(top.location)
```

See also:	Bookmarklets, JavaScript Bookmark URLs, JavaScript debugger console, *javascript: URL*

Cross-references:

Wrox *Instant JavaScript* – page – 48

JavaScript version (Standard)

The version history for JavaScript.

JavaScript was initially developed by Netscape Communications and was originally called LiveScript 1.0. Around that time, the Java language was becoming more popular and, possibly as a marketing ploy, the name of LiveScript was changed to JavaScript. It was first available to the public in version 2.0 of Netscape.

Version	ECMA	Notes
LiveScript 1.0	No	The original precursor to JavaScript.
JavaScript 1.0	No	Netscape 2.0 implemented this. Now mostly obsolete.
JavaScript 1.1	Yes	Supported in Netscape 3.0 and Netscape Enterprise Server 2.0. Also supported in Opera 3.0. More robust and better support for arrays. Image replacement and access to plugin properties. Scroll control.
JavaScript 1.2	No	Netscape 4.0 to 4.05 added `RegExp`, `switch` and `delete`. `Screen` object and interval timer. `Window` `move` & `resize`. Object and array literals added.
JavaScript 1.3	Yes	Version 4.06 to 4.76 of Netscape adds better exception handling. Also supported by Netscape Enterprise Server 3.
JavaScript 1.4	Yes	Netscape version 5.0 (not widely released).
JavaScript 1.5	Yes	Netscape 6.0 (final beta stages at time of writing).

See also:	History, JavaScript language, *JScript version*, LiveScript

Cross-references:

O'Reilly *JavaScript Definitive Guide* – page – 3

Wrox *Instant JavaScript* – page – 3

javascript: URL (Request method)

Execute some JavaScript code instead of fetching a document.

When you specify a URL in a web browser, the intent is usually to fetch a document from a remote web server.

The javascript: URL method is used to execute a fragment of JavaScript code when the URL is requested.

You can use the javascript URL as follows:

- ❑ To call up the debugger console
- ❑ Interactively to execute statements
- ❑ As document source
- ❑ As bookmarks

The view-source: URL can be used in Netscape to call up a source view of a document under script control. It's not very portable and not much use for anything other than debugging.

These are all described in separate topics.

You can call up the JavaScript debugger by setting a document location to "javascript:", "livescript:" or "mocha:".

Looking at the internals of the Netscape browser, this debugging console is itself written in HTML with JavaScript dynamic actions.

Mostly, these special URLs will be useful for debugging – getting details of the disk cache may be useful for example. Pulling up the JavaScript debugger page if you detect an error in your script might also be a cool trick.

With a `javascript:` URL, you can also type the code directly into the location bar of your Netscape browser to see the results of evaluating it right away.

As of JavaScript version 1.1, you can use the void operator to discard the result of an expression.

This `javascript:` URL form is available in the WebTV set-top boxes effective from the Summer 2000 release. However, it cannot be typed in manually by the user as it can be in the desktop computer based web browsers.

Warnings:

- ❑ This technique does not work with MSIE 3.0.

- ❑ The JavaScript debugger is not present in MSIE at all although it may be possible to use the Visual J++ debugging tools if you have them installed.

- ❑ Almost too late for inclusion was a report that `History.back()` calls that worked in JScript 5.1 started to fail on upgrade to JScript 5.5 service pack 1. In the end it turned out to be related to calling a `javascript:` URL within an `<A HREF="...">` context. In earlier versions of MSIE, you could omit the single and double quotes around the URL. Version 5.5 is no longer forgiving that omission. This may affect other kinds of URL values and other HTML tag attributes in an MSIE 5.5 browser.

Example code:

```
<HTML>
<HEAD>
<SCRIPT>
function test()
{
alert("Test function called");
}
</SCRIPT>
</HEAD>
<BODY>
<DIV onClick="javascript:test();">Click on me</DIV>
</BODY>
</HTML>
```

See also: Adding JavaScript to HTML, Bookmarklets, JavaScript Bookmark URLs, JavaScript debugger console, JavaScript Document Source URL, JavaScript Image Source URL, *JavaScript interactive URL, mailbox: URL,* mailto: URL, URL, *void*

.js (File extension)

JavaScript include file.

You can include external shared fragments of JavaScript into a web page by calling in a .js file.

A .js file simply contains that JavaScript which would have been placed inside a <SCRIPT> tag.

In the case of the Netscape browser, it can store configuration and preferences data in .js files.

These .js files can also be used server-side with Netscape Enterprise Server. They can be compiled with the LiveWire JavaScript compiler and linked with the HTML to create .web files that Netscape Enterprise Server can deliver very quickly to a requesting client browser.

The MIME type for a .js file used to be application/x-javascript but is now text/javascript. Either should work but text/javascript is preferred. This may necessitate you carrying out some server configuration changes if you don't already serve this kind of file.

The file is included by specifying its URL with the SRC="..." HTML tag attribute. You must also include a closing </SCRIPT> tag because <SCRIPT> is a block level item.

J

Example code:

```
<SCRIPT SRC="http://www.mydomain.com/include.js">
</SCRIPT>
```

See also:	*<SCRIPT ARCHIVE="...">*, *<SCRIPT SRC="...">*, File extensions, Preferences, Source files, Web browser

Cross-references:

O'Reilly *JavaScript Definitive Guide* – page – 215

Wrox *Instant JavaScript* – page – 3

JScript version (Standard)

The version history for JScript.

Microsoft added scripting capabilities to version 3.0 of the MSIE browser. The JScript interpreter is perhaps named differently so that detractors would not accuse Microsoft of modifying the JavaScript language.

Version 1.0 of JScript was also available in Internet Information Server as well as the MSIE version 3.0 browser. That first version of JScript is broadly compatible with JavaScript version 1.0 although there are differences between them:

Interpreter	ECMA	Notes
JScript 1.0	No	Equivalent to JavaScript 1.0 and released with MSIE 3.0
JScript 1.1	No	Never released
JScript 1.2	No	Evidence of its existence but status unknown
JScript 2.0	No	Released with IIS 1.0
JScript 3.0	Yes	Equivalent to JavaScript 1.2 and Released with MSIE 4.0, IIS 4.0 and WSH 1.0 (some features are in MSIE 3.02)
JScript 4.0	Yes	Released with Visual Studio 6.0
JScript 5.0	Yes	Equivalent to JavaScript 1.5 and supported on all 32 bit Windows operatings systems with MSIE
JScript 5.1	Yes	Released with IIS 5.0 on Windows 2000
JScript 5.5	Yes	Released with MSIE 5.5

The JScript support in MSIE is excellent. However, if you limit yourself purely to the JavaScript sub-set, there are some limitations in the support. The language has been extended somewhat but not in the same way as Netscape Communications Inc provided enhancements to their interpreter.

If the JScript interpreter is re-installed without upgrading the browser, you may be using a version of JScript that is later than the browser. Scripts should work normally as long they do not exploit features of JScript that have changed. However, the scripts may not be able to access some new features of the later version. For example, JScript 5.5 can be installed over the top of JScript 5.0 in a version 5.0 MSIE browser. You get the later core language features but continue to use the old document model. This can get utterly confusing for script developers.

See also:	History, *Internet Explorer, JavaScript version*

Cross-references:

Wrox *Instant JavaScript* – page – 3

JSObject object (Java class)

A Java class that encapsulates JavaScript objects for access from Java code.

Availability:	JavaScript – 1.1 Netscape – 3.0
JavaScript syntax:	N `myJSObject = netscape.javascript` `.JSObject`
Class methods:	*getWindow()*
Object methods:	`call()`, `eval()`, `getMember()`, `getSlot()`, `removeMember()`, `setMember()`, `setSlot()`, `toString()`

This Java class is otherwise known as `netscape.javascript.JSObject` (to give it its full name within the Java context). This provides a way for Java code to interact fully with the JavaScript native environment.

`JSObject` is a sub-class of the generic Object class within Java. Its public interface defines the following methods and properties:

❑ `getWindow()`

❑ `getMember()`

❑ `getSlot()`

❑ `setMember()`

❑ `setSlot()`

❑ `removeMember()`

❑ `call()`

❑ `eval()`

❑ `toString()`

J

Note that these are hooks to Java methods although they may look like JavaScript methods.

When member properties and slot values are accessed from arrays, you get an `Object` object returned. If this object is really a JavaObject, then it will be unwrapped and the encapsulated Java object will be returned without its JavaScript wrapper. It will still be returned as an `Object` object but it can then be cast to a native Java object type rather than another JSObject.

The `setMember()` and `setSlot()` methods perform the converse although there are some subtle limitations.

Your Java development environment should give you plenty of help with the compilation of applets. The key point is that you have a copy of the `netscape.javascript.JSObject` class available for the applet to be linked against. This may involve setting your CLASSPATH to define where the Java classes are located. The file you need may be browser version specific. In Netscape Navigator version 4.0, the file is called `java40.jar` but it may be named differently in other versions. Where it is located also may depend on how and where you installed Netscape.

See also:	Java calling JavaScript, Java to JavaScript values, JavaScript embedded in Java, JavaScript to Java values, *JSObject.call()*, *JSObject.eval()*, *JSObject.getMember()*, *JSObject.getSlot()*, *JSObject.getWindow()*, *JSObject.removeMember()*, *JSObject.setMember()*, *JSObject.setSlot()*, *JSObject.toString()*, LiveConnect, *MAYSCRIPT*, *netscape.javascript.JSObject*

Method	JavaScript	JScript	N	IE	Opera	Notes
call()	1.1 +	-	3.0 +	-	-	-
eval()	1.1 +	-	3.0 +	-	-	-
getMember()	1.1 +	-	3.0 +	-	-	-
getSlot()	1.1 +	-	3.0 +	-	-	-
removeMember()	1.1 +	-	3.0 +	-	-	-
setMember()	1.1 +	-	3.0 +	-	-	-
setSlot()	1.1 +	-	3.0 +	-	-	-
toString()	1.1 +	-	3.0 +	-	-	-

Cross-references:

O'Reilly *JavaScript Definitive Guide* – page – 568-570

Wrox *Professional JavaScript* – page – 544

JSObject.call() (Java method)

Call a method in the JavaScript object from the Java environment.

Availability:	JavaScript – 1.1 Netscape – 3.0
Property/method value type:	`Object object`
Java syntax:	`myJSObject.call("aMethod",` `anArgArray)`
Argument list:	`aMethod` The name of a method to call
	`anArgArray` An array of arguments to pass to the method

This is the way in which a Java applet can call back to a JavaScript function in a page. Once you know the window, you can invoke methods that belong to it as well as access properties. This will always yield an `Object` object as a result.

There are quite restricted Java to JavaScript limitations on passing non-primitive values in the `arguments` array.

The values passed to JavaScript will conform to the following conversions as they are passed to the JSObject methods:

Java	JavaScript
java.lang.Boolean	JavaObject object
java.lang.Double	JavaObject object
java.lang.Integer	JavaObject object
java.lang.String	JavaObject object
netscape.javascript.JSObject	generic JavaScript object
all other Java objects	JavaObject object

The return values will conform to the following conversions as they are passed between the environments:

JavaScript	Java
boolean primitive	java.lang.Boolean
number primitive	java.lang.Double
string primitive	java.lang.String
JavaObject object	The encapsulated Java object unwrapped
all other JavaScript objects	netscape.javascript.JSObject

The result of this method call will be an `Object` object which needs to be cast to some other value for use in the Java environment.

| See also: | *Call*, Java to JavaScript values, JavaScript to Java values, *JSObject object*, *JSObject.eval()*, LiveConnect |

Cross-references:

Wrox *Professional JavaScript* – page – 542-3

JSObject.eval() (Java method)

A means of invoking native JavaScript eval() functionality.

Availability:	JavaScript – 1.1 Netscape – 3.0
Java syntax:	*myJSObject*.eval("*someScript*")
Argument list:	*someScript* Some valid JavaScript source

This is a much simpler way to execute JavaScript than by the call() method. Here there is no need to construct an array to pass in the method arguments.

The return values will conform to the following conversions as they are passed between the environments:

JavaScript	Java
boolean primitive	java.lang.Boolean
number primitive	java.lang.Double
string primitive	java.lang.String
JavaObject object	The encapsulated Java object unwrapped
all other JavaScript objects	netscape.javascript.JSObject

The JSObject.eval() method eliminates many of the parameter passing problems associated with the JSObject.call() method as far as type conversion is concerned. You will need to convert any parameters you want to pass into strings but this does allow you to pass primitive values which you simply cannot do with the JSObject.call() method.

| See also: | Eval code, *eval()*, JavaScript to Java values, *JSObject object*, *JSObject.call()*, LiveConnect |

JSObject.getMember() (Java method)

Returns the value of a named property of the object belonging to a JavaScript object to a calling in the Java environment.

Availability:	JavaScript – 1.1 Netscape – 3.0	
Property/method value type:	Object object	
Java syntax:	myJSObject.getMember("aMemberName")	
Argument list:	aMemberName	The name of a property belonging to the JSObjects.

As you read properties of JSObjects, you get more JSObjects returned. In this way, you can walk the document hierarchy to locate any item in the window referred to by the root JSObject.

The return values will conform to the following conversions as they are passed between the environments:

JavaScript	Java
boolean primitive	java.lang.Boolean
number primitive	java.lang.Double
string primitive	java.lang.String
JavaObject object	The encapsulated Java object unwrapped
all other JavaScript objects	netscape.javascript.JSObject

The result of this method call will be an Object object which needs to be cast to some other value for use in the Java environment.

See also:	JavaScript to Java values, *JSObject object*, LiveConnect

JSObject.getSlot() (Java method)

A means of accessing elements within an array encapsulated in a JSObject.

Availability:	JavaScript – 1.1 Netscape – 3.0	
Property/method value type:	Object object	
Java syntax:	myJSObject.getSlot(anIndex)	
Argument list:	anIndex	The array index equivalent to [anIndex].

The return values will conform to the following conversions as they are passed between the environments:

JavaScript	Java
boolean primitive	java.lang.Boolean
number primitive	java.lang.Double
string primitive	java.lang.String
JavaObject object	The encapsulated Java object unwrapped
all other JavaScript objects	netscape.javascript.JSObject

The result of this method call will be the element of the array at the slot location returned as an `Object` object which needs to be cast to some other value.

See also:	JavaScript to Java values, *JSObject object*, LiveConnect

JSObject.getWindow() (Java static method)

A static method to return a new JSObject that belongs to the window containing the applet.

Availability:	JavaScript – 1.1 Netscape – 3.0	
Property/method value type:	`JSObject object`	
JavaScript syntax:	N	`new JSObject(anApplet)`
Java syntax:	`myJSObject.getWindow(anApplet)`	
Argument list:	`anApplet`	The applet whose window is to be referenced by the new JSObject

When called from a Java applet, this method returns a new JSObject for the window containing the applet.

This is a way of creating a JSObject that relates to the correct window, that is, the one containing the applet. This factory method is called because there is no constructor for the JSObject class. It creates a JSObject appropriate for the applet whose reference is passed in its only parameter.

Example code:

```
// Create a JSObject for the applet we are running in
JSObject myJSObject = JSObject.getWindow(this);
```

See also:	*JSObject object*, LiveConnect

JSObject.removeMember() (Java method)

Remove a property from a JavaScript object.

Availability:	JavaScript – 1.1 Netscape – 3.0
Java syntax:	*myJSObject*.removeMember()

This is equivalent to the delete property mechanism in JavaScript.

See also:	*delete, JSObject object*, LiveConnect

JSObject.setMember() (Java method)

Store a new value in a property.

Availability:	JavaScript – 1.1 Netscape – 3.0	
Java syntax:	*myJSObject*.setMember("*aName*", "*aValue*")	
Argument list:	*aName*	The name of the property to be changed
	aValue	The new value to be stored in the property

This method allows the Java code to set a property of a JSObject to a new value. There is a minor limitation in that you must pass a Java object and cannot set a primitive value.

The values passed to JavaScript will conform to the following conversions as they are passed to the JSObject methods:

Java	JavaScript
java.lang.Boolean	JavaObject object
java.lang.Double	JavaObject object
java.lang.Integer	JavaObject object
java.lang.String	JavaObject object
netscape.javascript.JSObject	generic JavaScript object
all other Java objects	JavaObject object

See also:	Java to JavaScript values, *JSObject object*, LiveConnect

JSObject.setSlot() (Java method)

Store an element in the JavaScript array.

Availability:	JavaScript – 1.1 Netscape – 3.0
Java syntax:	`myJSObject.setSlot(anIndex, "aValue")`
Argument list:	`anIndex` The array index equivalent to [*anIndex*]
	`aValue` The new value to be stored in the array element

This method allows the Java code to set an element of a JavaScript array stored in a JSObject. There is a minor limitation in that you must pass a Java object and cannot set a primitive value.

The values passed to JavaScript will conform to the following conversions as they are passed to the JSObject methods:

Java	JavaScript
java.lang.Boolean	JavaObject object
java.lang.Double	JavaObject object
java.lang.Integer	JavaObject object
java.lang.String	JavaObject object
netscape.javascript.JSObject	generic JavaScript object
all other Java objects	JavaObject object

See also:	Java to JavaScript values, *JSObject object*, LiveConnect

JSObject.toString() (Java method)

Convert the object to a string value.

Availability:	JavaScript – 1.1 Netscape – 3.0
Java syntax:	`myJSObject.toString()`

The string equivalent value of the object is returned as a Java String.

See also:	JavaScript to Java values, *JSObject object*, LiveConnect, *ToString*, Type conversion

JSSClasses object (Object/JSS)

A collection of JavaScript Style Sheet classes.

Availability:	JavaScript – 1.2 Netscape – 4.0 Deprecated
JavaScript syntax:	N *myJSSClasses* = *myDocument*.classes
Object properties:	className

This style sheet control mechanism is becoming deprecated as it is only supported on Netscape 4.0 and will not be ratified by a W3C standard. It is not recommended that you use these facilities in new projects.

This object is somewhat like an array in that it contains a collection of objects that can be accessed associatively by name. However, unlike an array, it does not respond to the length property request. Also unlike an array, you cannot access it's members using index values.

The only meaningful property of this object is one of its array elements corresponding to a named class in the style sheet. That property is also associated with a named CLASS="..." attribute of an HTML tag in the document.

You cannot enumerate this object to inspect its properties.

Warnings:

❑ Deprecated for any further use. This was available only in Netscape 4.0 and is completely removed from Netscape 6.0.

See also:	Document.classes[]

Property	JavaScript	JScript	N	IE	Opera	Notes
className	1.2 +	-	4.0 +	-	-	Warning, Deprecated

Property attributes:

DontEnum.

JSSTag object (Object/JSS)

A single style object for use in Netscape 4.

Availability:	JavaScript – 1.2 Netscape – 4.0 Deprecated
JavaScript syntax:	N `myJSSTag = myDocument.classes` `.aClassName.aTagName`
	N `myJSSTag = myDocument` `.contextual(...)`
	N `myJSSTag = myDocument.ids` `.anElementName`
	N `myJSSTag = myDocument.tags` `.aTagName`
	N `myJSSTag = myJSSTags.aTagName`
Argument list:	`aClassName` A named class within the style sheet
	`anElementName` The value of a `NAME="..."` or `ID="..."` tag attribute
	`aTagName` The name of an HTML tag
Object properties:	`align, apply, background, backgroundColor, backgroundImage, bgColor, borderBottomWidth, borderColor, borderLeftWidth, borderRightWidth, borderStyle, borderTopWidth, clear, clip, color, display, fontFamily, fontSize, fontStyle, fontWeight, height, left, lineHeight, listStyleType, marginBottom, marginLeft, marginRight, marginTop, paddingBottom, paddingLeft, paddingRight, paddingTop, textAlign, textDecoration, textIndent, textTransform, top, verticalAlign, visibility, whiteSpace, width, zIndex`
Object methods:	`borderWidths(), margins(), paddings(), rgb()`

This is the Netscape 4.0 JSS equivalent of the DOM style object. You assign values to the properties of this object to define the styles according to the JSS rules. Browsers sometimes use different object types with incompatible properties and methods to represent the same thing. We cover them as distinctly different objects where it seems sensible. The Netscape 4.0 style settings are properties of a `JSSTag` object. Refer to the style object for details of the MSIE and Netscape 6.0 style control properties.

The property values for this object each represent a style attribute of an HTML tag.

To define a style setting with JSS, assign a value to this property according to the class name and tag name hierarchy.

These values are write only and must be defined in the `<HEAD>` of the document. You cannot read them back or change them after the `<BODY>` has commenced loading.

You cannot enumerate the properties of this object so it is impossible to inspect them. Indeed, after repeated attempts to access them, they appear to be write only properties.

Because you can only define them during the <HEAD> of a document they don't provide many helpful facilities as regards dynamic style control.

It is highly recommended that you refrain from using these JSS facilities in any new projects. They are deprecated now that Netscape 6.0 adopts a more standardized DOM based approach to style settings.

The CSS support in Netscape 4.0 is available up to CSS level 1. In MSIE and Netscape 6.0, much of CSS level 2 is available through its more sophisticated and easier to manage style model.

Warnings:

❏ Deprecated for any further use. This was available only in Netscape 4.0 and is completely removed from Netscape 6.0.

See also:	Document.contextual(), *JSSTags object, style object (2)*

Property	JavaScript	JScript	N	IE	Opera	CSS	Notes
align	1.2 +	-	4.0 +	-	-	-	Warning, Deprecated
apply	1.2 +	-	4.0 +	-	-	-	Warning, Deprecated
background	1.2 +	-	4.0 +	-	-	-	Warning, DontEnum, Deprecated
backgroundColor	1.2 +	-	4.0 +	-	-	1 +	Warning, Deprecated
backgroundImage	1.2 +	-	4.0 +	-	-	1 +	Warning, Deprecated
bgColor	1.2 +	-	4.0 +	-	-	-	Warning, DontEnum, Deprecated
borderBottomWidth	1.2 +	-	4.0 +	-	-	1 +	Warning, Deprecated
borderColor	1.2 +	-	4.0 +	-	-	1 +	Warning, Deprecated
borderLeftWidth	1.2 +	-	4.0 +	-	-	1 +	Warning, Deprecated
borderRightWidth	1.2 +	-	4.0 +	-	-	1 +	Warning, Deprecated
borderStyle	1.2 +	-	4.0 +	-	-	1 +	Warning, Deprecated

Table continued on following page

Property	JavaScript	JScript	N	IE	Opera	CSS	Notes
borderTopWidth	1.2 +	-	4.0 +	-	-	1 +	Warning, Deprecated
clear	1.2 +	-	4.0 +	-	-	1 +	Warning, Deprecated
clip	1.2 +	-	4.0 +	-	-	-	Warning, DontEnum, Deprecated
color	1.2 +	-	4.0 +	-	-	1 +	Warning, Deprecated
display	1.2 +	-	4.0 +	-	-	1 +	Warning, Deprecated
fontFamily	1.2 +	-	4.0 +	-	-	1 +	Warning, Deprecated
fontSize	1.2 +	-	4.0 +	-	-	1 +	Warning, Deprecated
fontStyle	1.2 +	-	4.0 +	-	-	1 +	Warning, Deprecated
fontWeight	1.2 +	-	4.0 +	-	-	1 +	Warning, Deprecated
height	1.2 +	-	4.0 +	-	-	1 +	Warning, Deprecated
left	1.2 +	-	4.0 +	-	-	-	Warning, DontEnum, Deprecated
lineHeight	1.2 +	-	4.0 +	-	-	1 +	Warning, Deprecated
listStyleType	1.2 +	-	4.0 +	-	-	1 +	Warning, Deprecated
marginBottom	1.2 +	-	4.0 +	-	-	1 +	Warning, Deprecated
marginLeft	1.2 +	-	4.0 +	-	-	1 +	Warning, Deprecated
marginRight	1.2 +	-	4.0 +	-	-	1 +	Warning, Deprecated
marginTop	1.2 +	-	4.0 +	-	-	1 +	Warning, Deprecated
paddingBottom	1.2 +	-	4.0 +	-	-	1 +	Warning, Deprecated
paddingLeft	1.2 +	-	4.0 +	-	-	1 +	Warning, Deprecated
paddingRight	1.2 +	-	4.0 +	-	-	1 +	Warning, Deprecated
paddingTop	1.2 +	-	4.0 +	-	-	1 +	Warning, Deprecated
textAlign	1.2 +	-	4.0 +	-	-	1 +	Warning, Deprecated

Property	JavaScript	JScript	N	IE	Opera	CSS	Notes
textDecoration	1.2 +	-	4.0 +	-	-	1 +	Warning, Deprecated
textIndent	1.2 +	-	4.0 +	-	-	1 +	Warning, Deprecated
textTransform	1.2 +	-	4.0 +	-	-	1 +	Warning, Deprecated
top	1.2 +	-	4.0 +	-	-	-	Warning, DontEnum, Deprecated
verticalAlign	1.2 +	-	4.0 +	-	-	1 +	Warning, Deprecated
visibility	1.2 +	-	4.0 +	-	-	-	Warning, DontEnum, Deprecated
whiteSpace	1.2 +	-	4.0 +	-	-	1 +	Warning, Deprecated
width	1.2 +	-	4.0 +	-	-	1 +	Warning, Deprecated
zIndex	1.2 +	-	4.0 +	-	-	-	Warning, DontEnum, Deprecated

Method	JavaScript	JScript	N	IE	Opera	CSS	Notes
borderWidths()	1.2 +	-	4.0 +	-	-	1 +	Warning, Deprecated
margins()	1.2 +	-	4.0 +	-	-	1 +	Warning, Deprecated
paddings()	1.2 +	-	4.0 +	-	-	1 +	Warning, Deprecated
rgb()	1.2 +	-	4.0 +	-	-	-	Warning, Deprecated

Property attributes:

DontEnum.

JSSTags object (Object/JSS)

Part of the Netscape Navigator style JSS rendering support.

Availability:	JavaScript – 1.2 Netscape – 4.0 Deprecated	
JavaScript syntax:	N	*myJSSTags = myDocument*.classes.*aClassName*
	N	*myJSSTags = myDocument*.ids.*anIdValue*
Argument list:	*aClassName*	The name of a style class
	anIdValue	The value of an ID="..." HTML tag attribute
Object properties:	<tagName>	

This object is somewhat like an array in that it contains a collection of objects that can be accessed associatively by name. However, unlike an array, it does not respond to the length property request. Also unlike an array, you cannot access its members using index values.

The only meaningful property of this object is one of its array elements corresponding to an HTML tag name. There is one item in this collection for each HTML tag.

This is part of the deprecated JSS support in Netscape 4.0. It is not recommended that you use these facilities in new projects.

You cannot enumerate this object to inspect its properties.

The document.tags object has properties that correspond to each of the stylable tags – for example, there is a document.tags.P, document.tags.B and document.tags.H1 object.

Each of those objects has properties such as borderWidth and color so you can set or get the property value.

Note that the tags object properties can be specified in mixed case as it is case insensitive. Its properties contain objects that correspond to HTML tags and therefore they also have case insensitive properties that correspond to each tag's attributes.

It's an interesting way to control style from JavaScript, but since it was only ever supported in Netscape 4.0 and is no longer available in Netscape 6.0 (which fully supports CSS), there is no future for JSS.

Warnings:

❏ This is sometimes called tags object but if you inspect the object with some script that reveals its constructor, you will see it is really a member of the JSSTags class.

❏ Deprecated for any further use. This was available only in Netscape 4.0 and is completely removed from Netscape 6.0.

See also:	Document.ids[], Document.tags[], JavaScript Style Sheets, *JSSTag object*, JSSTags.<tagName>

Property	JavaScript	JScript	N	IE	Opera	Notes
<tagName>	1.2 +	-	4.0 +	-	-	Warning , Deprecated

Property attributes:

DontEnum.

about: URL (Request method)
AbstractView object (Object/DOM)
ActiveXObject object (Object/JScript)
Add (+) (Operator/additive)
Add then assign (+=) (Operator/assignment)

KBD object (Object/HTML)

An object representing content to be displayed as if typed on the keyboard.

Availability:	DOM level – 1 JavaScript – 1.5 JScript – 3.0 Internet Explorer – 4.0 Netscape – 6.0
Inherits from:	*Element object*

JavaScript syntax:	IE *myKBD = myDocument.all.anElementID*
	IE *myKBD = myDocument.all.tags*
	      ("KBD")[anIndex]
	IE *myKBD = myDocument.all[aName]*
	- *myKBD = myDocument.getElementById*
	      (anElementID)
	- *myKBD = myDocument.getElementsByName*
	      (aName)[anIndex]
	- *myKBD = myDocument*
	      .getElementsByTagName("KBD")[anIndex]

HTML syntax:	`<KBD> ... </KBD>`
Argument list:	*anElementID* The ID attribute of the element required *anIndex* A reference to an element in a collection *aName* An associative array reference

Event handlers:	`onClick, onDblClick, onDragStart,`
	`onFilterChange, onHelp, onKeyDown, onKeyPress,`
	`onKeyUp, onMouseDown, onMouseMove, onMouseOut,`
	`onMouseOver, onMouseUp, onSelectStart`

The appearance of the content described by this object is likely to look similar to that enclosed in `<CODE>`, `<LISTING>` or `<PRE>` tags.

See also:	*Element object, LISTING object, PRE object*

Event name	JavaScript	JScript	N	IE	Opera	DOM	HTML	Notes
onClick	1.5 +	1.0 +	6.0 +	4.0 +	3.0 +	-	4.0 +	Warning
onDblClick	1.5 +	3.0 +	6.0 +	4.0 +	3.0 +	-	4.0 +	Warning
onDragStart	-	3.0 +	-	4.0 +	-	-	-	-
onFilterChange	-	3.0 +	-	4.0 +	-	-	-	-
onHelp	-	3.0 +	-	4.0 +	-	-	-	Warning
onKeyDown	1.5 +	3.0 +	6.0 +	4.0 +	3.0 +	-	4.0 +	Warning
onKeyPress	1.5 +	3.0 +	6.0 +	4.0 +	3.0 +	-	4.0 +	Warning
onKeyUp	1.5 +	3.0 +	6.0 +	4.0 +	3.0 +	-	4.0 +	Warning
onMouseDown	1.5 +	3.0 +	6.0 +	4.0 +	3.0 +	-	4.0 +	Warning
onMouseMove	1.5 +	3.0 +	6.0 +	4.0 +	-	-	4.0 +	Warning
onMouseOut	1.5 +	3.0 +	6.0 +	4.0 +	3.0 +	-	4.0 +	Warning
onMouseOver	1.5 +	1.0 +	6.0 +	4.0 +	3.0 +	-	4.0 +	Warning
onMouseUp	1.5 +	3.0 +	6.0 +	4.0 +	3.0 +	-	4.0 +	Warning
onSelectStart	-	3.0 +	-	4.0 +	-	-	-	-

Inheritance chain:

Element object, Node object

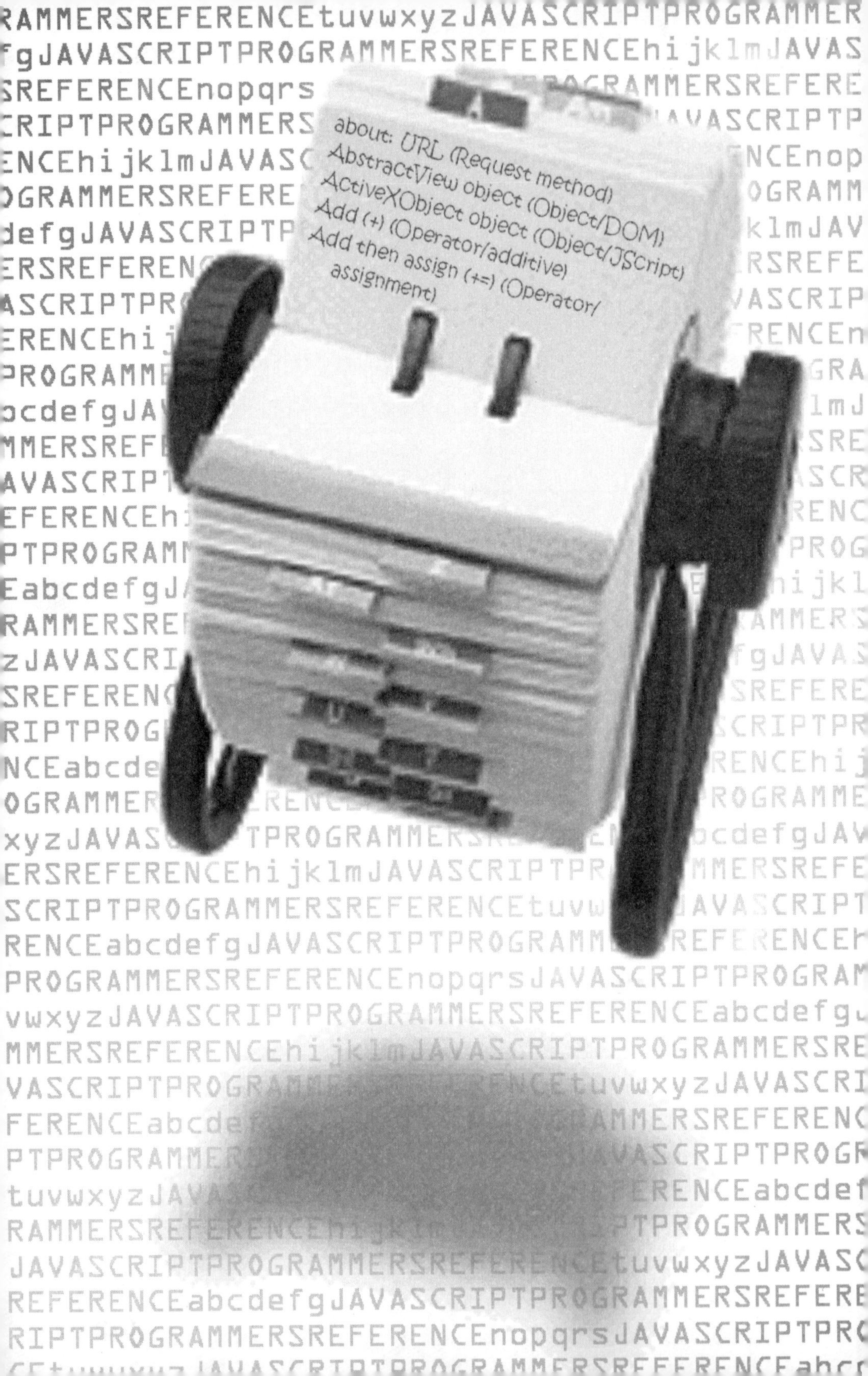
about: URL (Request method)
AbstractView object (Object/DOM)
ActiveXObject object (Object/JScript)
Add (+) (Operator/additive)
Add then assign (+=) (Operator/
assignment)

Label object (Object/HTML)

Adds a legend label to an input object.

Availability:	DOM level – 1 JavaScript – 1.5 JScript – 3.0 Internet Explorer – 4.0 Netscape version – 6.0
Inherits from:	*Element object*
JavaScript syntax:	IE `myLabel = myDocument.all.anElementID`
	IE `myLabel =` `myDocument.all.tags("LABEL")[anIndex]`
	IE `myLabel = myDocument.all[aName]`
	– `myLabel =` `myDocument.getElementById(anElementID)`
	– `myLabel = myDocument.getElementsByName` `(aName)[anIndex]`
	– `myLabel = myDocument.getElementsBy` `TagName("LABEL")[anIndex]`
HTML syntax:	`<LABEL> ... </LABEL>`
Argument list:	`anIndex` A reference to an element in a collection
	`aName` An associative array reference
	`anElementID` The ID value of an `Element` object
Object properties:	`accessKey, dataFld, dataFormatAs, dataSrc, form, htmlFor, tabIndex`
Object methods:	`blur(0), click(0)`
Event handlers:	`onBlur, onClick, onDblClick, onDragStart, onFilterChange, onFocus, onHelp, onKeyDown, onKeyPress, onKeyUp, onMouseDown, onMouseMove, onMouseOut, onMouseOver, onMouseUp, onSelectStart`

MSIE supports this object type with a LABEL object, and because we often don't need to know the specific class of an object, this does not cause us any significant problems with labels. But the inconsistent object class names across browsers may need to be standardized in a more reliable way in the future.

See also:	Element object, Input object, Input.accessKey

Property	JavaScript	JScript	N	IE	Opera	DOM	HTML	Notes
accessKey	1.5 +	3.0 +	6.0 +	4.0 +	-	1 +	-	-
dataFld	1.5 +	3.0 +	6.0 +	4.0 +	-	1 +	-	-
dataFormatAs	1.5 +	3.0 +	6.0 +	4.0 +	-	1 +	-	-
dataSrc	1.5 +	3.0 +	6.0 +	4.0 +	-	1 +	-	-
form	1.5 +	3.0 +	6.0 +	4.0 +	-	1 +	-	-
htmlFor	1.5 +	3.0 +	6.0 +	4.0 +	-	1 +	-	-
tabIndex	1.5 +	3.0 +	6.0 +	4.0 +	-	1 +	-	-

Method	JavaScript	JScript	N	IE	Opera	DOM	HTML	Notes
blur(0)	1.5 +	3.0 +	6.0 +	4.0 +	-	1 +	-	-
click(0)	1.5 +	3.0 +	6.0 +	4.0 +	-	1 +	-	-

Event name	JavaScript	JScript	N	IE	Opera	DOM	HTML	Notes
onBlur	1.5 +	3.0 +	6.0 +	4.0 +	-	-	-	Warning
onClick	1.5 +	3.0 +	6.0 +	4.0 +	-	-	4.0 +	Warning
onDblClick	1.5 +	3.0 +	6.0 +	4.0 +	-	-	4.0 +	Warning
onDragStart	-	3.0 +	-	4.0 +	-	-	-	-
onFilterChange	-	3.0 +	-	4.0 +	-	-	-	-
onFocus	1.5 +	3.0 +	6.0 +	4.0 +	-	-	-	Warning
onHelp	-	3.0 +	-	4.0 +	-	-	-	Warning
onKeyDown	1.5 +	3.0 +	6.0 +	4.0 +	-	-	4.0 +	Warning
onKeyPress	1.5 +	3.0 +	6.0 +	4.0 +	-	-	4.0 +	Warning
onKeyUp	1.5 +	3.0 +	6.0 +	4.0 +	-	-	4.0 +	Warning
onMouseDown	1.5 +	3.0 +	6.0 +	4.0 +	-	-	4.0 +	Warning
onMouseMove	1.5 +	3.0 +	6.0 +	4.0 +	-	-	4.0 +	Warning
onMouseOut	1.5 +	3.0 +	6.0 +	4.0 +	-	-	4.0 +	Warning
onMouseOver	1.5 +	3.0 +	6.0 +	4.0 +	-	-	4.0 +	Warning
onMouseUp	1.5 +	3.0 +	6.0 +	4.0 +	-	-	4.0 +	Warning
onSelectStart	-	3.0 +	-	4.0 +	-	-	-	-

Inheritance chain:

Element object, Node object

LANG="..." (HTML Tag Attribute)

A tag attribute that specifies the international language of some content.

This tag attribute allows the current national language to be overridden on a tag by tag basis if necessary. There are many values for international languages.

Refer to the Language codes topic for a list of language code values.

See also:	Element.lang, Language codes

Layer object (Object/Navigator)

An object representing an HTML <LAYER> tag.

Availability:	JavaScript – 1.2 Netscape version – 4.0 Deprecated	
JavaScript syntax:	N	*myLayer* = *myDocument*.*aLayerName*
	N	*myLayer* = *myLayerArray*[*anIndex*]
HTML syntax:	<ILAYER> <LAYER>	
Argument list:	*anIndex*	An index into the layer array
Object properties:	above, background, below, bgColor, clip, document, hidden, left, name, pageX, pageY, parentLayer, siblingAbove, siblingBelow, src, top, visibility, window, x, y, zIndex	
Object methods:	load(), moveAbove(), moveBelow(), moveBy(), moveTo(), moveToAbsolute(), offset(), resizeBy(), resizeTo()	
Functions:	captureEvents(), handleEvent(), releaseEvents(), routeEvent()	
Event handlers:	onBlur, onFocus, onLoad, onMouseOut, onMouseOver, onMouseUp	
Collections:	layers[]	

Each layer in Netscape is somewhat like a separate window or frame. This means it has its own document associated with it which can itself also contain layers. The individual objects cannot be positioned themselves but the layers they live in can be.

The Netscape Layer object has many properties that are similar to the MSIE Style object. However although they bear some similarities, they also have many differences. Furthermore a layer is not a style and therefore it is difficult to conveniently map one to the other and build cross platform solutions without constructing a compatibility layer.

517

Note that Netscape prior to version 6.0 instantiates an absolutely positioned <DIV> container as a Layer object.

Event handling support via properties containing function objects was added to Layer objects at version 1.1 of JavaScript.

The example demonstrates how to control a scrolling panel and do it in a way that is cross-browser compliant for MSIE and Netscape version 4. There are a lot of issues to deal with, not least the fact that Netscape supports layers but MSIE does not. It is necessary to use layers for scrolling in Netscape because you can only scroll windows or frames in Netscape if they have visible and active scrollbars. Also, the two browsers scroll vertically in opposing directions. If you are careful about the sizing of your objects, and relate the size of the window/frame the layer is drawn in, you can accomplish a continuous scrolling effect by duplicating items from the top of the list to the bottom. Then at an appropriate point, you can jump scroll back to the top of the list. If you do this right, it will appear as if the list is endless and scrolling gently in a continuous loop. This technique is a much simplified example taken from the Video On Demand console at http://www.bbc.co.uk/news where there is a panel showing a listing of live TV programs in a scrolling pane.

Warnings:

❑ If you are using layers to position items temporarily on the screen, then you should be careful when using absolute positioning. This can cause the layer to be absolutely positioned relative to the current mouse position and not the window border. The effect is that an item in the positioned layer will appear to follow the mouse as it is clicked. You may need to work out the mouse position and then calculate an offset to relocate the layer where you want it. You may be able to detect the mouse by removing focus from the layer that has the problem or it may be necessary to create an empty layer which can be safely attached to the mouse. All of these issues are Netscape 4 specific.

❑ Layers are no longer supported in Netscape 6.0.

Example code:

```
<HTML>
<HEAD>
<SCRIPT LANGUAGE="JavaScript">
// Initialize globals
var theScrollValue = 0;
var theMaxScroll = 50;
// Work out what kind of browser we are on
function getBrowserType()
{
    var myUserAgent;
    var myMajor;
    myUserAgent   = navigator.userAgent.toLowerCase();
    myMajor       = parseInt(navigator.appVersion);
    if( (myUserAgent.indexOf('mozilla')   != -1) &&
        (myUserAgent.indexOf('spoofer')   == -1) &&
```

```
            (myUserAgent.indexOf('compatible') == -1) &&
            (myUserAgent.indexOf('opera')      == -1) &&
            (myUserAgent.indexOf('webtv')      == -1)
         )
      {
         if (myMajor > 3)
         {
            return "nav4";
         }
         return "nav";
      }
      if (myUserAgent.indexOf("msie") != -1)
      {
         if (myMajor > 3)
         {
            return "ie4";
         }
         return "ie";
      }
      return "other";
}
// Start the correct scroller for this browser
function startScroller()
{
   eval(getBrowserType() + "_scrollPage()");
}
// Browser specific scroller (IE)
function ie4_scrollPage()
{
   self.scrollTo(0,theScrollValue);
   theScrollValue++;

   if(theScrollValue == theMaxScroll)
   {
      theScrollValue = 0;
   }

   setTimeout("ie4_scrollPage()", 100);
}
// Browser specific scroller (Navigator)
function nav4_scrollPage()
{
   self.document.layer1.moveTo(0,-theScrollValue);
   theScrollValue++;

   if(theScrollValue == theMaxScroll)
   {
      theScrollValue = 0;
   }
setTimeout("nav4_scrollPage()", 20);
}
</SCRIPT>
</HEAD>
<BODY ONLOAD="startScroller();">
<LAYER TOP=0 LEFT=0 NAME="layer1">
```

519

```
<TABLE CELLPADDING=0 CELLSPACING=0 BORDER=0>
<TR HEIGHT=25><TD VALIGN=TOP>Headline 1<BR></TD></TR>
<TR HEIGHT=25><TD VALIGN=TOP>Headline 2<BR></TD></TR>
<TR HEIGHT=25><TD VALIGN=TOP>Headline 3<BR></TD></TR>
<TR HEIGHT=25><TD VALIGN=TOP>Headline 4<BR></TD></TR>
<TR HEIGHT=25><TD VALIGN=TOP>Headline 5<BR></TD></TR>
<TR HEIGHT=25><TD VALIGN=TOP>Headline 6<BR></TD></TR>
</TABLE>
</LAYER>
</BODY></HTML>
```

See also:	*DIV object*, Layer.siblingAbove, Layer.siblingBelow, *LayerArray object, style object (2)*

Property	JavaScript	JScript	N	IE	Opera	Notes
above	1.2 +	-	4.0 +	-	-	Warning, ReadOnly, Deprecated
background	1.2 +	-	4.0 +	-	-	Warning, Deprecated
below	1.2 +	-	4.0 +	-	-	Warning, ReadOnly, Deprecated
bgColor	1.2 +	-	4.0 +	-	-	Warning, Deprecated
clip	1.2 +	-	4.0 +	-	-	Warning, Deprecated
document	1.2 +	-	4.0 +	-	-	Warning, ReadOnly, Deprecated
hidden	1.2 +	-	4.0 +	-	-	Warning, Deprecated
left	1.2 +	-	4.0 +	-	-	Warning, Deprecated
name	1.2 +	-	4.0 +	-	-	Warning, ReadOnly, Deprecated
pageX	1.2 +	-	4.0 +	-	-	Warning, Deprecated
pageY	1.2 +	-	4.0 +	-	-	Warning, Deprecated
parentLayer	1.2 +	-	4.0 +	-	-	Warning, ReadOnly, Deprecated
siblingAbove	1.2 +	-	4.0 +	-	-	Warning, ReadOnly, Deprecated
siblingBelow	1.2 +	-	4.0 +	-	-	Warning, ReadOnly, Deprecated
src	1.2 +	-	4.0 +	-	-	Warning, Deprecated
top	1.2 +	-	4.0 +	-	-	Warning, Deprecated
visibility	1.2 +	-	4.0 +	-	-	Warning, Deprecated
window	1.2 +	-	4.0 +	-	-	Warning, Deprecated
x	1.2 +	-	4.0 +	-	-	Warning, Deprecated
y	1.2 +	-	4.0 +	-	-	Warning, Deprecated
zIndex	1.2 +	-	4.0 +	-	-	Warning, Deprecated

Method	JavaScript	JScript	N	IE	Opera	Notes
load()	1.2 +	-	4.0 +	-	-	Warning, Deprecated
moveAbove()	1.2 +	-	4.0 +	-	-	Warning, Deprecated
moveBelow()	1.2 +	-	4.0 +	-	-	Warning, Deprecated
moveBy()	1.2 +	-	4.0 +	-	-	Warning, Deprecated
moveTo()	1.2 +	-	4.0 +	-	-	Warning, Deprecated
moveToAbsolute()	1.2 +	-	4.0 +	-	-	Warning, Deprecated
offset()	1.2 +	-	4.0 +	-	-	Warning, Deprecated
resizeBy()	1.2 +	-	4.0 +	-	-	Warning, Deprecated
resizeTo()	1.2 +	-	4.0 +	-	-	Warning, Deprecated

Event name	JavaScript	JScript	N	IE	Opera	Notes
onBlur	1.2 +	-	4.0 +	-	-	Warning
onFocus	1.2 +	-	4.0 +	-	-	Warning
onLoad	1.2 +	-	4.0 +	-	-	Warning
onMouseOut	1.2 +	-	4.0 +	-	-	Warning
onMouseOver	1.2 +	-	4.0 +	-	-	Warning
onMouseUp	1.2 +	-	4.0 +	-	-	Warning

Layer.captureEvents() (Function)

Part of the Netscape 4 event propagation complex.

Availability:	JavaScript – 1.2 Netscape version – 4.0 Deprecated
Property/method value type:	undefined
JavaScript syntax:	N	myLayer.captureEvents (anEventMask)
Argument list:	anEventMask	A mask constructed with the manifest event constants

This is part of the event management suite which allows events to be routed to handlers other than just the one that defaults to being associated with an event.

The events to be captured are signified by setting bits in a mask.

This method allows you to specify what events are to be routed to the receiving Layer object.

The events are specified by using the bitwise OR operator (|) to combine the required event mask constants into a mask that defines the events you want to capture. Refer to the Event Type Constants topic for a list of the event mask values.

A limitation of this technique is that ultimately, only 32 different kinds of events can be combined in this way and this may limit the number of events the browser can support. Since this is only supported by Netscape, the functionality is likely to be deprecated when the standards bodies agree on a standard way of handling events. Then we simply need to wait for the browser manufacturers to support the standardized behavior.

In the meantime, we shall have to implement scripts using this capability if we need to build complex event handling systems. A different script will be required for MSIE.

You may be able to factor your event handler so that you only have to make platform specific event dispatchers and can call common handling routines that can be shared between MSIE and Netscape.

Warnings:

❏ Since a bit mask is being used, this must be an `int32` value. This suggests that there can only be 32 different Event types supported by this event propagation model.

❏ This capability is deprecated and is not supported in Netscape version 6.0 anymore. It never was supported by MSIE which implements a completely different event model. As it turns out the DOM level 2 event model converges on the MSIE technique.

See also:	*captureEvents(), Document.captureEvents(), Document.releaseEvents(),* `Element.onevent`, *Event propagation, Event type constants, Frame object, Layer.releaseEvents(),* `onMouseMove`, *Window object, Window.captureEvents(), Window.releaseEvents()*

Layer.handleEvent() (Function)

Pass an event to the appropriate handler for this object.

Availability:	JavaScript – 1.2 Netscape version – 4.0 Deprecated	
Property/method value type:	`undefined`	
JavaScript syntax:	N	`myLayer.handleEvent(anEvent)`
Argument list:	`anEvent`	An event to be handled by this object

This applies to Netscape prior to version 6.0. From that release onwards, event management follows the guidelines in the DOM level 3 event specification.

On receipt of a call to this method, the receiving object will look at its available set of event handler functions and pass the event to an appropriately mapped handler function. It is essentially an event dispatcher that is granular down to the object level.

The argument value is an `Event` object that contains information about the event.

522

Warnings:

❑ No longer supported in Netscape 6.0.

See also:	handleEvent(), Layer.routeEvent()

Layer.releaseEvents() (Function)

Part of the Netscape 4 event propagation complex.

Availability:	JavaScript – 1.2 Netscape version – 4.0 Deprecated	
Property/method value type:	undefined	
JavaScript syntax:	N	myLayer.releaseEvents (anEventMask)
Argument list:	anEventMask	A mask defined with the manifest event constants

This is part of the event management suite which allows events to be routed to handlers other than just the one that defaults to being associated with an event.

The events to be captured are signified by setting bits in a mask.

This method provides a means of indicating which events are no longer needing to be captured by the receiving Layer object.

The events are specified by using the bitwise OR operator (|) to combine the required event mask constants into a mask that defines the events you want to capture. Refer to the Event Type Constants topic for a list of the event mask values.

Since this is only supported by Netscape, the functionality is likely to be deprecated when the standards bodies agree on a standard way of handling events. In the meantime, we shall have to implement scripts using this capability if we need to build complex event handling systems. A different script will be required for MSIE.

You may be able to factor your event handler so that you only have to make platform specific event dispatchers and can call common handling routines that can be shared between MSIE and Netscape.

Warnings:

❑ No longer supported in Netscape 6.0.

See also:	captureEvents(), Document.captureEvents(), Document.releaseEvents(), Element.onevent, Event propagation, Event type constants, Event.modifiers, Frame object, Layer.captureEvents(), onMouseMove, Window object, Window.releaseEvents()

Layer.routeEvent() (Function)

Part of the Netscape event propagation complex.

Availability:	JavaScript – 1.2 Netscape version – 4.0 Deprecated	
Property/method value type:	undefined	
JavaScript syntax:	N	myLayer.routeEvent(anEvent)
Argument list:	anEvent	An event object

Warnings:

❑ No longer supported in Netscape 6.0.

See also:	Layer.handleEvent(), Window.routeEvent()

LayerArray object (Object/Navigator)

An array containing a list of layers in the document.

Availability:	JavaScript – 1.2 Netscape version – 4.0 Deprecated	
JavaScript syntax:	N	myLayerArray = myDocument.layers
Object properties:	length	

Each item in this array corresponds to a <LAYER> tag in the document. This array also includes layers that are created in Netscape by setting the position attribute of an HTML <DIV> tag to absolute.

The layers in this array are ordered according to the order in which they appear in the document. Layers can be accessed associatively if they have been given an ID with the ID="..." or NAME="..." tag attribute. This means you can refer to an element whose ID is set to ABC by its unique name. Either as document.ABC or document layers["ABC"].

Warnings:

❑ There is a bug in the layer management code in Netscape. If a <LAYER> tag is placed into the document without an ID="..." or NAME="..." HTML tag attribute, it will increment the length count for the LayerArray but an object will not be placed into the array.

❑ Now if you try to enumerate through all the layers in the array using the length value, your enumeration loop will cause errors when it tries to access elements beyond the physical length of the array.

❑ To avoid this, you should always add NAME="..." HTML tag attributes to the <LAYER> tags to ensure the layers are stored in the array. ID="..." HTML tags are important and helpful when trying to access objects in MSIE and in Netscape 6.0.

❑ No longer supported in Netscape 6.0.

See also:	Collection object, DIV object, Document.layers[], Layer object, Layer.layers[]

Property	JavaScript	JScript	N	IE	Opera	Notes
length	1.2 +	-	4.0 +	-	-	Warning, ReadOnly, Deprecated

Legend object (Object/HTML)

The legend object relates to a field-set within a form.

Availability:	DOM level – 1 JavaScript – 1.5 JScript – 3.0 Internet Explorer – 4.0 Netscape version – 6.0 Deprecated
Inherits from:	Element object
JavaScript syntax:	IE myLegend = myDocument.all.anElementID
	IE myLegend = myDocument.all.tags("LEGEND")[anIndex]
	IE myLegend = myDocument.all[aName]
	- myLegend = myDocument.getElementById(anElementID)
	- myLegend = myDocument.getElementsByName(aName)[anIndex]
	- myLegend = myDocument.getElementsBy TagName("LEGEND")[anIndex]
HTML syntax:	<LEGEND> ... </LEGEND>
Argument list:	anIndex A reference to an element in a collection
	aName An associative array reference
	anElementID The ID value of an Element object
Object properties:	accessKey, align, form, padding, tabIndex
Event handlers:	onBlur, onChange, onClick, onDblClick, onDragStart, onFilterChange, onFocus, onHelp, onKeyDown, onKeyPress, onKeyUp, onMouseDown, onMouseMove, onMouseOut, onMouseOver, onMouseUp, onScroll, onSelectStart

L

JavaScript Programmer's Reference

This is the legend that is associated with the field-set. It must be placed immediately inside the <FIELDSET> containing HTML tags in the document source.

Now that CSS has become more widely available and is capable of doing the same thing, the Legend object has become deprecated.

See also:	Element object, FIELDSET object, Form object, Input object, Input.accessKey

Property	JavaScript	JScript	N	IE	Opera	DOM	HTML	Notes
accessKey	1.5 +	3.0 +	6.0 +	4.0 +	-	1 +	-	Deprecated
align	1.5 +	3.0 +	6.0 +	4.0 +	-	1 +	-	Warning, Deprecated
form	1.5 +	3.0 +	6.0 +	4.0 +	-	1 +	-	Deprecated
padding	-	3.0 +	-	4.0 +	-	-	-	-
tabIndex	1.5 +	3.0 +	6.0 +	4.0 +	-	1 +	-	Deprecated

Event name	JavaScript	JScript	N	IE	Opera	DOM	HTML	Notes
onBlur	1.5 +	3.0 +	6.0 +	4.0 +	-	-	-	Warning
onChange	1.5 +	3.0 +	6.0 +	4.0 +	-	-	-	-
onClick	1.5 +	3.0 +	6.0 +	3.0 +	-	-	4.0 +	Warning
onDblClick	1.5 +	3.0 +	6.0 +	4.0 +	-	-	4.0 +	Warning
onDragStart	-	3.0 +	-	4.0 +	-	-	-	-
onFilterChange	-	3.0 +	-	4.0 +	-	-	-	-
onFocus	1.5 +	3.0 +	6.0 +	4.0 +	-	-	-	Warning
onHelp	-	3.0 +	-	4.0 +	-	-	-	Warning
onKeyDown	1.5 +	3.0 +	6.0 +	4.0 +	-	-	4.0 +	Warning
onKeyPress	1.5 +	3.0 +	6.0 +	4.0 +	-	-	4.0 +	Warning
onKeyUp	1.5 +	3.0 +	6.0 +	4.0 +	-	-	4.0 +	Warning
onMouseDown	1.5 +	3.0 +	6.0 +	4.0 +	-	-	4.0 +	Warning
onMouseMove	1.5 +	3.0 +	6.0 +	4.0 +	-	-	4.0 +	Warning
onMouseOut	1.5 +	3.0 +	6.0 +	4.0 +	-	-	4.0 +	Warning
onMouseOver	1.5 +	3.0 +	6.0 +	4.0 +	-	-	4.0 +	Warning
onMouseUp	1.5 +	3.0 +	6.0 +	4.0 +	-	-	4.0 +	Warning
onScroll	-	3.0 +	-	4.0 +	-	-	-	-
onSelectStart	-	3.0 +	-	4.0 +	-	-	-	-

Inheritance chain:

Element object, Node object

Less than (<) (Operator/relational)

Compare two operands to determine which is nearer to -Infinity.

Availability:	ECMAScript edition – 2 JavaScript – 1.0 JScript – 1.0 Internet Explorer – 3.02 Netscape version – 2.0 Netscape Enterprise Server version – 2.0 Opera – 3.0
Property/method value type:	Boolean primitive
JavaScript syntax:	-	anOperand1 < anOperand2
Argument list:	anOperand1	A value that can be compared numerically or lexically
	anOperand2	A compatible value

Returns true if the left operand is numerically less than the right operand or is sorted earlier in the Unicode collating sequence when two string values are compared.

In numeric comparisons, the presence of NaN in either or both operands will yield undefined instead of true or false.

When comparing two strings, a prefixing plus sign is present, then a numeric coercion of a string takes place before the comparison. Numeric coercion takes place when either of the operands is numeric.

In ECMA compliant JavaScript implementations, string values are simply compared according to the Unicode character code point values with no attempt to provide the more complex semantically oriented definitions of character and string equality defined in the Unicode version 2.0 specification.

The associativity is from left to right.

Refer to the operator precedence topic for details of execution order.

The result is the Boolean value true if *anOperand1* is numerically or lexically less than *anOperand2*, otherwise false is returned.

See also:	*ASCII, Associativity, Equal to (==), Greater than (>), Greater than or equal to (>=), Identically equal to (===), Less than or equal to (<=)*, Logical expression, Logical operator, *NOT Equal to (!=), NOT Identically equal to (!==)*, Operator Precedence, *Relational expression, Relational operator, Unicode*

L

Cross-references:

ECMA 262 edition 2 – section – 11.8.1

ECMA 262 edition 2 – section – 11.8.5

ECMA 262 edition 3 – section – 11.8.1

ECMA 262 edition 3 – section – 11.8.5

Less than or equal to (<=) (Operator/relational)

Compare two operands to determine which is nearer to -Infinity or whether they are equal.

Availability:	ECMAScript edition – 2 JavaScript – 1.0 JScript – 1.0 Internet Explorer – 3.02 Netscape version – 2.0 Netscape Enterprise Server version – 2.0 Opera – 3.0	
Property/method value type:	Boolean primitive	
JavaScript syntax:	-	anOperand1 <= anOperand2
Argument list:	anOperand1	A value that can be compared numerically or lexically
	anOperand2	A compatible value

Returns `true` if the left operand is numerically less than or equal to the right operand or is sorted earlier or identically in the Unicode collating sequence when two string values are compared.

In numeric comparisons, the presence of NaN in either or both operands will yield undefined instead of `true` or `false`.

When comparing two strings, a prefixing plus sign is present, then a numeric coercion of a string takes place before the comparison. Numeric coercion takes place when either of the operands is numeric.

In ECMA compliant JavaScript implementations, string values are simply compared according to the Unicode character code point values with no attempt to provide the more complex semantically oriented definitions of character and string equality defined in the Unicode version 2.0 specification.

The associativity is from left to right.

Refer to the operator precedence topic for details of execution order.

The result is the Boolean value `true` if *anOperand1* is numerically or lexically less than or equal to *anOperand2*, otherwise `false` is returned.

See also:	ASCII, Associativity, *Equal to (==)*, *Greater than (>)*, *Greater than or equal to (>=)*, *Identically equal to (===)*, *Less than (<)*, Logical expression, Logical operator, *NOT Equal to (!=)*, *NOT Identically equal to (!==)*, Operator Precedence, *Relational expression*, *Relational operator*, Unicode

Cross-references:

ECMA 262 edition 2 – section – 11.8.3

ECMA 262 edition 2 – section – 11.8.5

ECMA 262 edition 3 – section – 11.8.3

ECMA 262 edition 3 – section – 11.8.5

LI object (Object/HTML)

An object that represents an <LI> object in the document.

Availability:	DOM level – 1 JavaScript – 1.5 JScript – 3.0 Internet Explorer – 4.0 Netscape version – 6.0	
Inherits from:	*Element object*	
JavaScript syntax:	IE	`myLI = myDocument.all.anElementID`
	IE	`myLI = myDocument.all.tags("LI")[anIndex]`
	IE	`myLI = myDocument.all[aName]`
	-	`myLI = myDocument.getElementById(anElementID)`
	-	`myLI = myDocument.getElementsByName(aName)[anIndex]`
	-	`myLI = myDocument.getElementsByTagName("LI")[anIndex]`
HTML syntax:	`<LI> ... </LI>`	
Argument list:	*anIndex*	A reference to an element in a collection
	aName	An associative array reference
	anElementID	The ID value of an Element object
Object properties:	`type, value`	

L

JavaScript Programmer's Reference

529

Event handlers:	onClick, onDblClick, onDragStart, onFilterChange, onHelp, onKeyDown, onKeyPress, onKeyUp, onMouseDown, onMouseMove, onMouseOut, onMouseOver, onMouseUp, onSelectStart

The <LI> tag is a block-level tag. That means that it forces a line break before and after itself.

The DOM level 1 specification refers to this as a LIElement object

See also:	Element object, OL.compact

Property	JavaScript	JScript	N	IE	Opera	DOM	HTML	Notes
type	1.5 +	3.0 +	6.0 +	4.0 +	-	1 +	-	-
value	1.5 +	3.0 +	6.0 +	4.0 +	-	1 +	-	-

Event name	JavaScript	JScript	N	IE	Opera	DOM	HTML	Notes
onClick	1.5 +	3.0 +	6.0 +	4.0 +	3.0 +	-	4.0 +	Warning
onDblClick	1.5 +	3.0 +	6.0 +	4.0 +	3.0 +	-	4.0 +	Warning
onDragStart	-	3.0 +	-	4.0 +	-	-	-	-
onFilterChange	-	3.0 +	-	4.0 +	-	-	-	-
onHelp	-	3.0 +	-	4.0 +	-	-	-	Warning
onKeyDown	1.5 +	3.0 +	6.0 +	4.0 +	3.0 +	-	4.0 +	Warning
onKeyPress	1.5 +	3.0 +	6.0 +	4.0 +	3.0 +	-	4.0 +	Warning
onKeyUp	1.5 +	3.0 +	6.0 +	4.0 +	3.0 +	-	4.0 +	Warning
onMouseDown	1.5 +	3.0 +	6.0 +	4.0 +	3.0 +	-	4.0 +	Warning
onMouseMove	1.5 +	3.0 +	6.0 +	4.0 +	-	-	4.0 +	Warning
onMouseOut	1.5 +	3.0 +	6.0 +	4.0 +	3.0 +	-	4.0 +	Warning
onMouseOver	1.5 +	3.0 +	6.0 +	4.0 +	3.0 +	-	4.0 +	Warning
onMouseUp	1.5 +	3.0 +	6.0 +	4.0 +	3.0 +	-	4.0 +	Warning
onSelectStart	-	3.0 +	-	4.0 +	-	-	-	-

Inheritance chain:

Element object, Node object

LINK object (Object/HTML)

An object that represents HTML <LINK> tags in documents.

Availability:	DOM level – 1 JavaScript – 1.5 JScript – 3.0 Internet Explorer – 4.0 Netscape version – 6.0
Inherits from:	*Element object*
JavaScript syntax:	IE *myLINK = myDocument.all.anElementID*
	IE *myLINK = myDocument.all.tags* *("LINK")[anIndex]*
	IE *myLINK = myDocument.all[aName]*
	– *myLINK = myDocument* *.getElementById(anElementID)*
	– *myLINK = myDocument.getElementsByName* *(aName)[anIndex]*
	– *myLINK = myLinkArray[anIndex]*
	– *myLINK = myDocument* *.getElementsByTagName("LINK")[anIndex]*
HTML syntax:	<LINK>
Argument list:	*anIndex* A reference to an element in a collection
	aName An associative array reference
	anElementID The ID value of an Element object
Object properties:	charset, disabled, href, hreflang, media, readyState, rel, rev, title, type
Event handlers:	onClick, onDblClick, onError, onHelp, onKeyDown, onKeyPress, onKeyUp, onLoad, onMouseDown, onMouseMove, onMouseOut, onMouseOver, onMouseUp, onReadyStateChange

The <LINK> tag is used to link in external style sheet files. You can link in CSS or JSS style sheets with this technique. It allows the style sheets to be shared among many documents and for the site appearance to be changed globally simply by modifying a single file.

When referring to style sheets, the REL attribute has the STYLESHEET value.

The TYPE attribute indicates that the style sheet is formatted as text and contains JavaScript source text.

The REL and TYPE attributes combined tell us it is a JSS file.

The HREF attribute points at the document containing the style sheet definition to be loaded at the <LINK> point in the calling document.

This a LINK object because it refers to a document that is accessed via a URL.

The <LINK> tag conveys no apparent visible effect on the document. It is considered to be an invisible tag.

MSIE supports a LINK object as a property of its styleSheet object.

Warnings:

❑ This object is related to but not identical to a Link object. It does share some property names but adds others.

❑ This a special MSIE object class although Netscape will probably support something functionally similar internally.

See also:	*Anchor object, Area object,* Document.anchors[], *Element object,* Element.all[], *LinkArray object, Location object,* String.link(), URL, *Url object*

Property	JavaScript	JScript	N	IE	Opera	DOM	HTML	Notes
charset	1.5 +	5.0 +	6.0 +	5.0 +	-	1 +	-	-
disabled	1.5 +	3.0 +	6.0 +	4.0 +	-	2 +	-	-
href	1.5 +	3.0 +	6.0 +	4.0 +	-	1 +	-	-
hreflang	1.5 +	5.0 +	6.0 +	5.0 +	-	1 +	-	-
media	1.5 +	3.0 +	6.0 +	4.0 +	-	1 +	-	Warning
readyState	-	3.0 +	-	4.0 +	-	-	-	ReadOnly
rel	1.5 +	3.0 +	6.0 +	4.0 +	-	1 +	-	-
rev	1.5 +	3.0 +	6.0 +	4.0 +	-	1 +	-	-
title	1.5 +	3.0 +	6.0 +	4.0 +	-	1 +	-	-
type	1.5 +	3.0 +	6.0 +	4.0 +	-	1 +	-	-

Event name	JavaScript	JScript	N	IE	Opera	DOM	HTML	Notes
onClick	1.5 +	3.0 +	6.0 +	4.0 +	3.0 +	-	4.0 +	Warning
onDblClick	1.5 +	3.0 +	6.0 +	4.0 +	3.0 +	-	4.0 +	Warning
onError	1.5 +	3.0 +	6.0 +	4.0 +	3.0 +	-	-	Warning
onHelp	-	3.0 +	-	4.0 +	-	-	-	Warning
onKeyDown	1.5 +	3.0 +	6.0 +	4.0 +	3.0 +	-	4.0 +	Warning
onKeyPress	1.5 +	3.0 +	6.0 +	4.0 +	3.0 +	-	4.0 +	Warning
onKeyUp	1.5 +	3.0 +	6.0 +	4.0 +	3.0 +	-	4.0 +	Warning
onLoad	1.5 +	3.0 +	6.0 +	4.0 +	3.0 +	-	-	Warning
onMouseDown	1.5 +	3.0 +	6.0 +	4.0 +	3.0 +	-	4.0 +	Warning
onMouseMove	1.5 +	3.0 +	6.0 +	4.0 +	-	-	4.0 +	Warning
onMouseOut	1.5 +	3.0 +	6.0 +	4.0 +	3.0 +	-	4.0 +	Warning
onMouseOver	1.5 +	3.0 +	6.0 +	4.0 +	3.0 +	-	4.0 +	Warning
onMouseUp	1.5 +	3.0 +	6.0 +	4.0 +	3.0 +	-	4.0 +	Warning
onReady StateChange	-	3.0 +	-	4.0 +	-	-	-	-

Inheritance chain:

Element object, Node object

LinkArray object (Object/browser)

A collection link object belonging to a document.

Availability:	JavaScript – 1.0 JScript – 3.0 Internet Explorer – 4.0 Netscape version – 2.0	
JavaScript syntax:	-	*myLinkArray = myDocument.links*
Object properties:	length	

This is a collection of Url objects. In Netscape, you can inspect the constructor to establish the class name which is masked by the toString() method of the Url object. In MSIE, you cannot get at the constructor so we have to assume that the object is a Url object.

Url objects are created when an <AREA> or <A> tag refers to a document. Anchors that are simply named locations within a document but which don't have an HREF get added to the anchors array but not to the links array.

Netscape prior to version 6.0 calls this a LinkArray (as opposed to a LinksArray which might be more appropriate). In MSIE it is just a Collection and in Netscape version 6.0 it has become an HTMLCollection because that is what DOM specifies it should be.

Warnings:

❑ Be careful not confuse the elements of this array with LINK objects. These are used in MSIE to support styling of Url objects on the screen. Other documentation may refer to Link objects but there is no evidence to support the existence of an object of that class. After inspection there appear to be Url objects in Netscape, LINK objects in MSIE and an object in MSIE that corresponds to the Netscape Url class but which provides no means of examining its constructor.

See also:	*Area object, Collection object,* Document.anchors[], Document.links[], *HyperLink object, LINK object, Url object*

Property	JavaScript	JScript	N	IE	Opera	HTML	Notes
length	1.0 +	3.0 +	2.0 +	4.0 +	-	-	ReadOnly

LinkStyle object (Object/DOM)

Added at DOM level 2 to support linked stylesheets.

Availability:	DOM level – 2 JavaScript – 1.5 Netscape version – 6.0
JavaScript syntax:	N *myLinkStyle* = new LinkStyle()

DOM level 2 specifies that this object should support the sheet property.

LISTING object (Object/HTML)

An object that represents the <LISTING> tag.

Availability:	JScript – 3.0 Internet Explorer – 4.0 Deprecated	
Inherits from:	*Element object*	
JavaScript syntax:	IE	*myLISTING* = *myDocument*.all.*anElementID*
	IE	*myLISTING* = *myDocument*.all.tags ("LISTING")[*anIndex*]
	IE	*myLISTING* = *myDocument*.all[*aName*]
	-	*myLISTING* = *myDocument*.getElementById (*anElementID*)
	-	*myLISTING* = *myDocument*.getElementsByName (*aName*)[*anIndex*]
	-	*myLISTING* = *myDocument*.getElementsBy TagName("LISTING")[*anIndex*]
HTML syntax:	<LISTING>	
Argument list:	*anIndex*	A reference to an element in a collection
	aName	An associative array reference
	anElementID	The ID value of an Element object
Event handlers:	onClick, onDblClick, onDragStart, onFilterChange, onHelp, onKeyDown, onKeyPress, onKeyUp, onMouseDown, onMouseMove, onMouseOut, onMouseOver, onMouseUp, onSelectStart	

The LISTING object is instantiated when the browser encounters a <LISTING> tag in the HTML for a document. This tag is used to enclose a section of text that should be presented as if it were a computer code listing.

The appearance will be similar to that rendered by a <CODE>, <PRE> or <KBD> tag.
Use of this tag is highly deprecated but it still persists in some legacy content.

See also:	Element object, KBD object, PRE object

Event name	JavaScript	JScript	N	IE	Opera	DOM	HTML	Notes
onClick	-	3.0 +	-	4.0 +	-	-	4.0 +	Warning
onDblClick	-	3.0 +	-	4.0 +	-	-	4.0 +	Warning
onDragStart	-	3.0 +	-	4.0 +	-	-	-	-
onFilterChange	-	3.0 +	-	4.0 +	-	-	-	-
onHelp	-	3.0 +	-	4.0 +	-	-	-	Warning
onKeyDown	-	3.0 +	-	4.0 +	-	-	4.0 +	Warning
onKeyPress	-	3.0 +	-	4.0 +	-	-	4.0 +	Warning
onKeyUp	-	3.0 +	-	4.0 +	-	-	4.0 +	Warning
onMouseDown	-	3.0 +	-	4.0 +	-	-	4.0 +	Warning
onMouseMove	-	3.0 +	-	4.0 +	-	-	4.0 +	Warning
onMouseOut	-	3.0 +	-	4.0 +	-	-	4.0 +	Warning
onMouseOver	-	3.0 +	-	4.0 +	-	-	4.0 +	Warning
onMouseUp	-	3.0 +	-	4.0 +	-	-	4.0 +	Warning
onSelectStart	-	3.0 +	-	4.0 +	-	-	-	-

Inheritance chain:

Element object, Node object

Location object (Object/DOM)

An object that represents the location of a document.

Availability:	DOM level – 1 JavaScript – 1.0 JScript – 1.0 Internet Explorer – 3.02 Netscape version – 2.0 Opera – 3.0
Inherits from:	Url object
JavaScript syntax:	- myLocation = myWindow.location
Object properties:	hash, host, hostname, href, pathname, port, protocol, search, target, text, x, y
Object methods:	assign(), reload(), replace()
Event handlers:	onClick, onDblClick, onHelp, onKeyDown, onKeyPress, onKeyUp, onMouseDown, onMouseMove, onMouseOut, onMouseOver, onMouseUp

This is a more or less portable encapsulation of a URL value and is most commonly used to describe the location of a document in a window. Changing its href property value has become the preferred means of loading a new document into a window or frame.

This is useful because it can also operate very conveniently across frame boundaries. That is, a script in one frame can modify the contents of another.

There are some security implications when accessing frames from different servers or domains. These can be overcome in Netscape by using signed scripts.

See also:	Anchor object, Area object, Document.location, LINK object, Map object, URL, Url object, Window.location, Window.navigate()

Property	JavaScript	JScript	N	IE	Opera	DOM	HTML	Notes
hash	1.0 +	1.0 +	2.0 +	3.02 +	3.0 +	1 +	-	-
host	1.0 +	1.0 +	2.0 +	3.02 +	3.0 +	1 +	-	-
hostname	1.0 +	1.0 +	2.0 +	3.02 +	3.0 +	1 +	-	-
href	1.0 +	1.0 +	2.0 +	3.02 +	3.0 +	1 +	-	-
pathname	1.0 +	1.0 +	2.0 +	3.02 +	3.0 +	1 +	-	-
port	1.0 +	1.0 +	2.0 +	3.02 +	3.0 +	1 +	-	-
protocol	1.0 +	1.0 +	2.0 +	3.02 +	3.0 +	1 +	-	ReadOnly
search	1.0 +	1.0 +	2.0 +	3.02 +	3.0 +	1 +	-	-
target	1.0 +	1.0 +	2.0 +	3.02 +	-	-	-	-
text	1.2 +	-	4.0 +	-	-	-	-	-
x	1.2 +	-	4.0 +	-	-	-	-	-
y	1.2 +	-	4.0 +	-	-	-	-	-

Method	JavaScript	JScript	N	IE	Opera	DOM	HTML	Notes
assign()	1.0 +	1.0 +	2.0 +	3.02 +	-	-	-	Warning, Deprecated
reload()	1.1 +	3.0 +	3.0 +	4.0 +	3.0 +	1 +	-	-
replace()	1.1 +	3.0 +	3.0 +	4.0 +	3.0 +	1 +	-	-

Event name	JavaScript	JScript	N	IE	Opera	DOM	HTML	Notes
onClick	1.0 +	1.0 +	2.0 +	3.0 +	3.0 +	-	4.0 +	Warning
onDblClick	1.2 +	3.0 +	4.0 +	4.0 +	3.0 +	-	4.0 +	Warning
onHelp	-	3.0 +	-	4.0 +	-	-	-	Warning
onKeyDown	1.2 +	3.0 +	4.0 +	4.0 +	3.0 +	-	4.0 +	Warning
onKeyPress	1.2 +	3.0 +	4.0 +	4.0 +	3.0 +	-	4.0 +	Warning
onKeyUp	1.2 +	3.0 +	4.0 +	4.0 +	3.0 +	-	4.0 +	Warnin
onMouseDown	1.2 +	3.0 +	4.0 +	4.0 +	3.0 +	-	4.0 +	Warning
onMouseMove	1.2 +	3.0 +	4.0 +	4.0 +	-	-	4.0 +	Warning
onMouseOut	1.1 +	3.0 +	3.0 +	4.0 +	3.0 +	-	4.0 +	Warning
onMouseOver	1.0 +	1.0 +	2.0 +	3.0 +	3.0 +	-	4.0 +	Warning
onMouseUp	1.2 +	3.0 +	4.0 +	4.0 +	3.0 +	-	4.0 +	Warning

Inheritance chain:

Element object, Node object, Url object

Lock object (Object/NES)

Provides a way of locking objects against multiple simultaneous access by several clients at once.

Availability:	JavaScript – 1.2 Netscape Enterprise Server version – 3.0	
JavaScript syntax:	NES	*myLock* = Lock
	NES	*myLock* = new Lock()
Object properties:	constructor, prototype	
Object methods:	isValid(), lock(), unlock()	

In a server back-end environment, you may have some objects which you share among several sessions. This means that they could be accessed on behalf of several clients all at once. You may want to prevent this happening by locking the object as the first client's request accesses it and then unlocking it again as the request handler for that client no longer needs access to it.

You can create new lock objects with the Lock() constructor.

It is good practice to unlock resources as soon as you can so that other processes can carry on running. You should not rely on the script exit handler unlocking the locks you place on objects.

Warnings:

❑ Be careful when you use locks. It is possible to place mutually exclusive locks on objects and introduce a deadlocking situation. There is a potential for this if your script is locking more than one object and the locks are not correctly nested.

❑ If you don't implement locks when necessary, you run the risk of run-time errors as your system can run out of resources.

See also:	Netscape Enterprise Server, *unwatch()*, *watch()*

Property	JavaScript	JScript	NES	Notes
constructor	1.2 +	-	3.0 +	-
prototype	1.2 +	-	3.0 +	-

Method	JavaScript	JScript	NES	Notes
isValid()	1.2 +	-	3.0 +	-
lock()	1.2 +	-	3.0 +	-
unlock()	1.2 +	-	3.0 +	-

Logical AND (&&) (Operator/logical)

Logical AND of two operands.

Availability:	ECMAScript edition – 2 JavaScript – 1.0 JScript – 1.0 Internet Explorer – 3.02 Netscape version – 2.0 Netscape Enterprise Server version – 2.0 Opera – 3.0
Property/method value type:	Boolean primitive
JavaScript syntax:	- anOperand1 && anOperand2
Argument list:	anOperand1 A Boolean value anOperand2 Another Boolean value

Traditionally in programming environments, the logical AND operator yields true only when both operands are true. However, the specifics of this are slightly different in JavaScript, and although the results may appear to be functionally the same, there is a subtle but important difference.

First, let's deal with the normal and expected behavior of a Logical AND operator. The truth table shows the result of this operator for two Boolean primitive values:

A	B	AND
false	false	false
false	true	false
true	false	false
true	true	true

Now, the implementation is expected to conform to the ECMA standard. This sets out the following method of evaluation for a Logical AND operator:

❑ Evaluate and convert the first operand using the ToBoolean() method.

❑ If it is false, then evaluate and return the second operand.

❑ Otherwise return the evaluation of the first operand.

To all intents and purposes the external perceived behavior is the same because another `ToBoolean()` conversion is likely to take place in the context that the expression is used – an `if()` statement or an outer logical expression for example.

The associativity is from left to right.

Refer to the operator precedence topic for details of execution order.

The result is the Boolean value `true` if both operands are true, otherwise Boolean `false` is returned.

Example code:

```
<HTML>
<HEAD></HEAD>
<BODY>
<TABLE BORDER=1 CELLPADDING=2>
<TR>
<TH>A</TH>
<TH>B</TH>
<TH>AND</TH>
</TR>
<SCRIPT>
for(a=0; a<2; a++)
{
    for(b=0; b<2; b++)
    {
        document.write("<TR ALIGN=CENTER><TD>");
        document.write(Boolean(a));
        document.write("</TD><TD>");
        document.write(Boolean(b));
        document.write("</TD><TD>");
        document.write(Boolean(a && b));
        document.write("</TD></TR>");
    }
}
</SCRIPT>
</TABLE>
</BODY>
</HTML>
```

See also: Associativity, Binary logical operator, *Bitwise AND (&)*, *Bitwise AND then assign (&=)*, Logical expression, Logical operator, Operator Precedence

Cross-references:

ECMA 262 edition 2 – section – 11.11

ECMA 262 edition 3 – section – 11.11

L

JavaScript Programmer's Reference

Logical NOT - complement (!) (Operator/logical)

Logical NOT operator.

Availability:	ECMAScript edition – 2 JavaScript – 1.0 JScript – 1.0 Internet Explorer – 3.02 Netscape version – 2.0 Netscape Enterprise Server version – 2.0 Opera – 3.0
Property/method value type:	Boolean primitive
JavaScript syntax:	- `! anOperand`
Argument list:	`anOperand` A Boolean value to be complemented

The result is the Boolean complement of the operand value.

The exclamation mark is the logical negation operator. The operand is evaluated and its result converted to a binary value. The value is then reversed and used to replace the expression in whatever context it has been used.

The truth table shows the result of this operator for a Boolean primitive value:

A	NOT
false	true
true	false

Although this is classified as a logical operator here, it is also classified as a unary operator since it only has one operand.

The associativity is from right to left.

Refer to the operator precedence topic for details of execution order.

Example code:

```
<HTML>
<HEAD></HEAD>
<BODY>
<TABLE BORDER=1 CELLPADDING=2>
<TR>
<TH>A</TH>
<TH>NOT</TH>
</TR>
<SCRIPT>
for(a=0; a<2; a++)
{
    document.write("<TR ALIGN=CENTER><TD>");
    document.write(Boolean(a));
    document.write("</TD><TD>");
    document.write(Boolean(!a));
    document.write("</TD></TR>");
}
</SCRIPT>
</TABLE>
</BODY>
</HTML>
```

See also:	Associativity, *Bitwise NOT – complement (~)*, Logical operator, *NOT Equal to (!=)*, Operator Precedence, Unary expression, Unary operator

Cross-references:

ECMA 262 edition 2 – section – 11.4.9

ECMA 262 edition 3 – section – 11.4.9

Logical OR (||) (Operator/logical)

Logical OR of two operands.

Availability:	ECMAScript edition – 2 JavaScript – 1.0 JScript – 1.0 Internet Explorer – 3.02 Netscape version – 2.0 Netscape Enterprise Server version – 2.0 Opera – 3.0	
Property/method value type:	Boolean primitive	
JavaScript syntax:	-	*anOperand1* || *anOperand2*
Argument list:	*anOperand1*	A Boolean value
	anOperand2	Another Boolean value

Traditionally in programming environments, the logical OR operator yields `true` when either or both of the operands are true. It yields `false` only when both are false. However, the specifics of this are slightly different in JavaScript and although the results may appear to be functionally the same, there is a subtle but important difference.

First, let's deal with the normal and expected behavior of a Logical OR operator. The truth table shows the result of this operator for two Boolean primitive values:

A	B	OR
false	false	false
false	true	true
true	false	true
true	true	true

Now, the implementation is expected to conform to the ECMA standard. This sets out the following method of evaluation for a Logical OR operator:

❑ Evaluate and convert the first operand using the ToBoolean() method.

❑ If it is true, then return that operand.

❑ Otherwise evaluate and return the second operand.

To all intents and purposes the external perceived behavior is the same because another ToBoolean() conversion is likely to take place in the context that the expression is used – an if() statement or an outer logical expression for example.

The associativity is from left to right.

Refer to the operator precedence topic for details of execution order.

Example code:

```
<HTML>
<HEAD></HEAD>
<BODY>
<TABLE BORDER=1 CELLPADDING=2>
<TR>
<TH>A</TH>
<TH>B</TH>
<TH>OR</TH>
</TR>
<SCRIPT>
for(a=0; a<2; a++)
{
    for(b=0; b<2; b++)
    {
        document.write("<TR ALIGN=CENTER><TD>");
        document.write(Boolean(a));
        document.write("</TD><TD>");
```

```
        document.write(Boolean(b));
        document.write("</TD><TD>");
        document.write(Boolean(a || b));
        document.write("</TD></TR>");
    }
}
</SCRIPT>
</TABLE>
</BODY>
</HTML>
```

See also:	Associativity, Binary logical operator, Logical operator, Operator Precedence

Cross-references:

ECMA 262 edition 2 – section – 11.11

ECMA 262 edition 3 – section – 11.11

Logical XOR (Operator/logical)

Logically exclusive OR of two values.

There isn't really an XOR logical operator, but the Bitwise XOR operator should work fine.

This is proven by evaluating the truth table in the example.

This seems to work fine even on MSIE where the sign bit exhibits some instability under Bitwise operations.

This is the truth table for two Boolean primitive values being operated on with the XOR operator.

A	B	XOR
false	false	false
false	true	true
true	false	true
true	true	false

Example code:

```
<HTML>
<HEAD></HEAD>
<BODY>
<TABLE BORDER=1 CELLPADDING=2>
<TR>
<TH>A</TH>
<TH>B</TH>
<TH>XOR</TH>
</TR>
<SCRIPT>
for(a=0; a<2; a++)
{
    for(b=0; b<2; b++)
    {
        document.write("<TR ALIGN=CENTER><TD>");
        document.write(Boolean(a));
        document.write("</TD><TD>");
        document.write(Boolean(b));
        document.write("</TD><TD>");
        document.write(Boolean(a ^ b));
        document.write("</TD></TR>");
    }
}
</SCRIPT>
</TABLE>
</BODY>
</HTML>
```

See also:	Bitwise XOR (^)

long (Reserved word)

Reserved for future language enhancements.

The inclusion of this reserved keyword in the ECMAScript standard suggests that future versions of ECMAScript may be more strongly typed.

This keyword also represents a Java data type and the long keyword allows for the potential extension of JavaScript interfaces to access Java applet parameters and return values.

See also:	double, float, Integer, java.lang.Long, LiveConnect, Reserved word, short

Cross-references:

ECMA 262 edition 2 – section – 7.4.3

ECMA 262 edition 3 – section – 7.5.3

about: URL (Request method)
AbstractView object (Object/DOM)
ActiveXObject object (Object/JScript)
Add (+) (Operator/additive)
Add then assign (+=) (Operator/assignment)

mailbox: URL (Request method)

Displays the Netscape Message Center window.

You can add keywords to access the individual components within the mailbox as necessary. The following are all valid URL values in Netscape:

- ❏ mailbox:
- ❏ mailbox:Inbox
- ❏ mailbox:Unsent%20Messages
- ❏ mailbox:Drafts
- ❏ mailbox:Templates
- ❏ mailbox:Sent
- ❏ mailbox:Trash

Each of these will spawn an additional window as required to display the relevant folder within the mailbox. Note that embedded spaces must be URL escaped for them to work. This mechanism does not seem to provide access to sub-folders.

Warnings:

- ❏ Although Netscape 6.0 supports this request method, its support is incomplete as of the first non-beta release.

See also:	*javascript:* URL, mailto: URL, *nethelp:* URL, *telnet:* URL, URL

<MAP TARGET="..."> (HTML Tag Attribute)

The frame or window to target by default with the links in an image map.

This is a non-standard tag attribute that is used as a means of linking frames and area maps. You should use <AREA TARGET="..."> instead of <MAP TARGET="..."> for portable applications.

Warnings:

❑ Because this is a non-standard HTML tag attribute, most implementations will not support the TARGET attribute on a <MAP> tag. In that case, apply the TARGET attribute to the <AREA> tags in the map instead.

See also:	Anchor.target, Form.target, Map.target, Window.frames[]

Deprecated usage:

Yes

Map object (Object/HTML)

An object that represents a <MAP> tag.

Availability:	DOM level – 1 JavaScript – 1.5 JScript – 3.0 Internet Explorer – 4.0 Netscape – 6.0
Inherits from:	*Element object*
JavaScript syntax:	IE *myMap = myDocument.all.anElementID*
	IE *myMap = myDocument.all.tags ("MAP")[anIndex]*
	IE *myMap = myDocument.all[aName]*
	- *myMap = myDocument.getElementById (anElementID)*
	- *myMap = myDocument.getElementsByName (aName)[anIndex]*
	- *myMap = myDocument .getElementsByTagName("MAP")[anIndex]*
HTML syntax:	<MAP>...</MAP>

Argument list:	anIndex	A reference to an element in a collection
	aName	An associative array reference
	anElementID	The ID value of an Element object
Object properties:	name, target	
Event handlers:	onClick, onDblClick, onHelp, onKeyDown, onKeyPress, onKeyUp, onMouseDown, onMouseMove, onMouseOut, onMouseOver, onMouseUp	
Collections:	areas[]	

The <MAP> tag in the HTML document source is a container for the <AREA> tags. These all belong to a parent Map object. This is a means of componentizing a client-side image map and building complex non-rectangular shaped areas.

See also:	A object, *Area object, Element object, Location object*

Property	JavaScript	JScript	N	IE	Opera	DOM	HTML	Notes
name	1.5 +	3.0 +	6.0 +	4.0 +	-	1 +	-	-
target	1.5 +	3.0 +	6.0 +	4.0 +	-	-	-	-

Event name	JavaScript	JScript	N	IE	Opera	DOM	HTML	Notes
onClick	1.5 +	3.0 +	6.0 +	4.0 +	3.0 +	-	4.0 +	Warning
onDblClick	1.5+	3.0 +	6.0 +	4.0 +	3.0 +	-	4.0 +	Warning
onHelp	-	3.0 +	-	4.0 +	-	-	-	Warning
onKeyDown	1.5 +	3.0 +	6.0 +	4.0 +	3.0 +	-	4.0 +	Warning
onKeyPress	1.5 +	3.0 +	6.0 +	4.0 +	3.0 +	-	4.0 +	Warning
onKeyUp	1.5 +	3.0 +	6.0 +	4.0 +	3.0 +	-	4.0 +	Warning
onMouseDown	1.5 +	3.0 +	6.0 +	4.0 +	3.0 +	-	4.0 +	Warning
onMouseMove	1.5 +	3.0 +	6.0 +	4.0 +	-	-	4.0 +	Warning
onMouseOut	1.5 +	3.0 +	6.0 +	4.0 +	3.0 +	-	4.0 +	Warning
onMouseOver	1.5 +	3.0 +	6.0 +	4.0 +	3.0 +	-	4.0 +	Warning
onMouseUp	1.5 +	3.0 +	6.0 +	4.0 +	3.0 +	-	4.0 +	Warning

Inheritance chain:

Element object, Node object

MARQUEE object (Object/HTML)

An object that represents a <MARQUEE> HTML tag.

Availability:	JScript – 3.0 Internet Explorer – 4.0
Inherits from:	*Element object*
JavaScript syntax:	IE *myMARQUEE* = *myDocument*.all.*anElementID*
	IE *myMARQUEE* = *myDocument*.all.tags ("MARQUEE")[*anIndex*]
	IE *myMARQUEE* = *myDocument*.all[*aName*]
	– *myMARQUEE* = *myDocument*.getElementById (*anElementID*)
	– *myMARQUEE* = *myDocument*.getElementsByName (*aName*)[*anIndex*]
	– *myMARQUEE* = *myDocument*. getElementsByTagName("MARQUEE")[*anIndex*]
HTML syntax:	<MARQUEE>
Argument list:	*anIndex* A reference to an element in a collection
	aName An associative array reference
	anElementID The ID value of an Element object
Object properties:	accessKey, behavior, bgColor, dataFld, dataFormatAs, dataSrc, direction, height, hspace, loop, scrollAmount, scrollDelay, tabIndex, trueSpeed, vspace, width
Object methods:	start(), stop()
Event handlers:	onAfterUpdate, onBlur, onBounce, onClick, onDblClick, onDragStart, onFilterChange, onFinish, onFocus, onHelp, onKeyDown, onKeyPress, onKeyUp, onMouseDown, onMouseMove, onMouseOut, onMouseOver, onMouseUp, onResize, onRowEnter, onRowExit, onScroll, onSelectStart, onStart

The MARQUEE object is only supported by MSIE and provides a means of quickly and easily generating a moving ticker display inside the window area. This can be accomplished with Netscape using layers and some interval timed JavaScript function calls to scroll the layer.

The MSIE MARQUEE object is a little more aware of Font Metrics than your average script access can achieve. This means making the MARQUEE bounce back and forth when the text hits the edge of the extent rectangle is a lot easier to accomplish in MSIE than in Netscape.

See also:	*Element object*, Input.accessKey

Property	JavaScript	JScript	N	IE	Opera	DOM	HTML	Notes
accessKey	-	3.0 +	-	4.0 +	-	-	-	-
behavior	-	3.0 +	-	4.0 +	-	-	-	-
bgColor	-	3.0 +	-	4.0 +	-	-	-	-
dataFld	-	3.0 +	-	4.0 +	-	-	-	-
dataFormatAs	-	3.0 +	-	4.0 +	-	-	-	-
dataSrc	-	3.0 +	-	4.0 +	-	-	-	-
direction	-	3.0 +	-	4.0 +	-	-	-	-
height	-	3.0 +	-	4.0 +	-	-	-	-
hspace	-	3.0 +	-	4.0 +	-	-	-	-
loop	-	3.0 +	-	4.0 +	-	-	-	-
scrollAmount	-	3.0 +	-	4.0 +	-	-	-	-
scrollDelay	-	3.0 +	-	4.0 +	-	-	-	-
tabIndex	-	3.0 +	-	4.0 +	-	-	-	-
trueSpeed	-	3.0 +	-	4.0 +	-	-	-	-
vspace	-	3.0 +	-	4.0 +	-	-	-	-
width	-	3.0 +	-	4.0 +	-	-	-	-

Method	JavaScript	JScript	N	IE	Opera	DOM	HTML	Notes
start()	-	3.0 +	-	4.0 +	-	-	-	-
stop()	-	3.0 +	-	4.0 +	-	-	-	-

Event name	JavaScript	JScript	N	IE	Opera	DOM	HTML	Notes
onAfterUpdate	-	3.0 +	-	4.0 +	-	-	-	-
onBlur	1.1 +	3.0 +	3.0 +	4.0 +	3.0 +	-	-	Warning
onBounce	-	3.0 +	-	4.0 +	-	-	-	-
onClick	1.0 +	3.0 +	4.0 +	3.0 +	3.0 +	-	4.0 +	Warning
onDblClick	1.2 +	3.0 +	4.0 +	4.0 +	3.0 +	-	4.0 +	Warning
onDragStart	-	3.0 +	-	4.0 +	-	-	-	-
onFilterChange	-	3.0 +	-	4.0 +	-	-	-	-
onFinish	-	3.0 +	-	4.0 +	-	-	-	-
onFocus	1.0 +	3.0 +	2.0 +	4.0 +	3.0 +	-	-	Warning
onHelp	-	3.0 +	-	4.0 +	-	-	-	Warning
onKeyDown	1.2 +	3.0 +	4.0 +	4.0 +	3.0 +	-	4.0 +	Warning
onKeyPress	1.2 +	3.0 +	4.0 +	4.0 +	3.0 +	-	4.0 +	Warning
onKeyUp	1.2 +	3.0 +	4.0 +	4.0 +	3.0 +	-	4.0 +	Warning
onMouseDown	1.2 +	3.0 +	4.0 +	4.0 +	3.0 +	-	4.0 +	Warning
onMouseMove	1.2 +	3.0 +	4.0 +	4.0 +	-	-	4.0 +	Warning
onMouseOut	1.1 +	3.0 +	3.0 +	4.0 +	3.0 +	-	4.0 +	Warning
onMouseOver	1.0 +	3.0 +	4.0 +	3.0 +	3.0 +	-	4.0 +	Warning

Table continued on following page

M

JavaScript Programmer's Reference

Event name	JavaScript	JScript	N	IE	Opera	DOM	HTML	Notes
onMouseUp	1.2 +	3.0 +	4.0 +	4.0 +	3.0 +	-	4.0 +	Warning
onResize	1.2 +	3.0 +	4.0 +	4.0 +	-	-	-	Warning
onRowEnter	-	3.0 +	-	4.0 +	-	-	-	-
onRowExit	-	3.0 +	-	4.0 +	-	-	-	-
onScroll	-	3.0 +	-	4.0 +	-	-	-	-
onSelectStart	-	3.0 +	-	4.0 +	-	-	-	-
onStart	-	3.0 +	-	4.0 +	-	-	-	-

Inheritance chain:

Element object, Node object

Math object (Object/core)

A globally available object containing a library of mathematical functions.

Availability:	ECMAScript edition – 2 JavaScript – 1.0 JScript – 1.0 Internet Explorer – 3.02 Netscape – 2.0 Netscape Enterprise Server version – 2.0 Opera – 3.0	
JavaScript syntax:	-	Math
Object properties:	constructor	
Class constants:	E, LN10, LN2, LOG10E, LOG2E, PI, SQRT1_2, SQRT2	
Functions:	abs(), acos(), asin(), atan(), atan2(), ceil(), cos(), exp(), floor(), log(), max(), min(), pow(), random(), round(), sin(), sqrt(), tan()	

The Math object is merely a single object owned by the Global object and which cannot be instantiated. It has some named properties, some of which are functions while others are constants.

The prototype for the Math prototype object is the Object prototype object.

Although it cannot be instantiated, it does have a constructor which in turn has a prototype property. By adding functions to that prototype, you can extend the capabilities of the Math object. Several examples are provided in nearby topics to illustrate the addition of extra trigonometric and hyperbolic functions.

Warnings:

❏ The Math object provides a collection of static constant values by way of properties belonging to the integral Math object. Because the mathematical mechanisms of any application tend to be provided by the operating system, you should find that between different browsers on any particular platform, the values that these constants yield will be very consistent.

❏ The ECMA standard lays down strict values for these properties and in general, the browser manufacturers try to comply – however, there is always the possibility that an implementation may use a non-compliant calculation.

❏ However, it may not be quite so reliable across platforms. You might enumerate one of these constants as you are authoring and then hard-code that value into your script. When that script is executed on another platform, even in the same browser, the internal mathematics support may yield a different value.

❏ You should always refer to the static constants using their symbolic names rather than hard-code a possibly platform dependant value into your script.

❏ Note for the trigonometric functions in general that certain implied identities cannot be assumed in JavaScript. For example:

❏ Math.sin(Math.PI/2) may not yield exactly 1

❏ Math.cos(Math.PI) may not return precisely zero

❏ Math.acos(0) may not return the same value as Math.PI

❏ Math.SQRT1_2 may not be exactly equal to the reciprocal of Math.SQRT2

See also:	Constant, Exponent-log function, *Global object*, Integer arithmetic, Java to JavaScript values, Native object, Object constant, *Object object*, Range error, Trigonometric function, Type conversion, *unwatch()*, *watch()*

Property	JavaScript	JScript	N	IE	Opera	NES	ECMA	Notes
constructor	1.0 +	1.0 +	2.0 +	3.02 +	-	-	-	-

Cross-references:

ECMA 262 edition 2 – section – 10.1.5

ECMA 262 edition 2 – section – 15.1.4.1

ECMA 262 edition 2 – section – 15.8

ECMA 262 edition 3 – section – 10.1.5

ECMA 262 edition 3 – section – 15.1.5.1

ECMA 262 edition 3 – section – 15.8

Math.abs() (Function)

The absolute value of a positive or negative number.

Availability:	ECMAScript edition – 2 JavaScript – 1.0 JScript – 1.0 Internet Explorer – 3.02 Netscape – 2.0 Netscape Enterprise Server version – 2.0 Opera – 3.0
Property/method value type:	`Number primitive`
JavaScript syntax:	- `Math.abs(aValue)`
Argument list:	`aValue` Some meaningful numeric value

This function returns the absolute value of the argument.

The absolute value of a number is its distance from zero.

In general, the result has the same magnitude as the argument but always has a positive sign.

Special boundary conditions that affect the results are:

Argument	Result
0	0
NaN	NaN
negative infinity	positive infinity

On some implementations, the absolute value of the most negative integer number may not be representable in the positive range.

This is not the same as `Number.MIN_VALUE` and `Number.MAX_VALUE`. They describe the largest and smallest possible positive floating point values.

Warnings:

- ❑ It is possible that due to the underlying implementation of the math library, the absolute value of the most negative number may not be representable and it may yield NaN instead.

Example code:

```
<HTML>
<HEAD></HEAD>
<BODY>
<SCRIPT>
for(myEnum = 1.5; myEnum > -2; myEnum -= 0.1)
{
    document.write(myEnum + " " + Math.abs(myEnum) + "<BR>");
}
</SCRIPT>
</BODY>
</HTML>
```

See also:	Integer arithmetic, Integer-value-remainder, *Math object*, *Math.ceil()*, *Math.floor()*, Type conversion

Cross-references:

ECMA 262 edition 2 – section – 15.8.2.1

ECMA 262 edition 3 – section – 15.8.2.1

Math.acos() (Function)

The inverse cosine of the passed in value.

Availability:	ECMAScript edition – 2 JavaScript – 1.0 JScript – 1.0 Internet Explorer – 3.02 Netscape – 2.0 Netscape Enterprise Server version – 2.0 Opera – 3.0
Property/method value type:	Number primitive
JavaScript syntax:	-	Math.acos(*aValue*)
Argument list:	*aValue*	Some meaningful numeric value

This function returns the arc cosine of the argument.

Special boundary conditions that affect the results are:

Argument	Result
1	0
greater than 1	NaN
less than -1	NaN
NaN	NaN

The exact value yielded by this function may vary slightly from implementation to implementation due to differences in the underlying precision of the implementation's math routines and the specific algorithm selected to evaluate this function.

The result of this method is the arc-cosine of the passed in value. The result is expressed in radians and ranges from 0 to pi.

Warnings:

❑ Note that `Math.acos(0)` may not return the same value as `Math.PI`.

See also:	Math object, Math.asin(), Math.atan(), Math.atan2(), Math.cos(), Math.PI, Math.sin(), Math.tan(), Trigonometric function

Cross-references:

ECMA 262 edition 2 – section – 15.8.2.2

ECMA 262 edition 3 – section – 15.8.2.2

Math.asin() (Function)

The inverse sine of the passed in value.

Availability:	ECMAScript edition – 2 JavaScript – 1.0 JScript – 1.0 Internet Explorer – 3.02 Netscape – 2.0 Netscape Enterprise Server version – 2.0 Opera – 3.0
Property/method value type:	Number primitive	
JavaScript syntax:	-	Math.asin(aValue)
Argument list:	aValue	Some meaningful numeric value

This function returns the arc sine of the argument.

Special boundary conditions that affect the results are:

Argument	Result
0	0
greater than 1	NaN
less than -1	NaN
NaN	NaN

The exact value yielded by this function may vary slightly from implementation to implementation due to differences in the underlying precision of the implementation's math routines and the specific algorithm selected to evaluate this function.

The result of this method is the arc-sine of the passed in value. The result is expressed in radians and ranges from -pi/2 to +pi/2.

See also:	Math object, Math.acos(), Math.atan(), Math.atan2(), Math.cos(), Math.sin(), Math.tan(), Trigonometric function

Cross-references:

ECMA 262 edition 2 – section – 15.8.2.3

ECMA 262 edition 3 – section – 15.8.2.3

Math.atan() (Function)

The inverse tangent of the passed in value.

Availability:	ECMAScript edition – 2 JavaScript – 1.0 JScript – 1.0 Internet Explorer – 3.02 Netscape – 2.0 Netscape Enterprise Server version – 2.0 Opera – 3.0	
Property/method value type:	Number primitive	
JavaScript syntax:	-	Math.atan(aValue)
Argument list:	aValue	Some meaningful numeric value

This function returns the arc tangent of the argument.

M

Special boundary conditions that affect the results are:

Argument	Result
0	0
minus infinity	-pi/2
NaN	NaN
plus infinity	+pi/2

The exact value yielded by this function may vary slightly from implementation to implementation due to differences in the underlying precision of the implementation's math routines and the specific algorithm selected to evaluate this function.

The result of this method is the arc-tangent of the passed in value. The result is expressed in radians and ranges from -pi/2 to +pi/2.

See also:	*Math object, Math.acos(), Math.asin(), Math.atan2(), Math.cos(), Math.sin(), Math.tan()*, Trigonometric function

Cross-references:

ECMA 262 edition 2 – section – 15.8.2.4

ECMA 262 edition 3 – section – 15.8.2.4

Math.atan2() (Function)

The inverse tangent of the slope of the two arguments.

Availability:	ECMAScript edition – 2 JavaScript – 1.0 JScript – 3.0 Internet Explorer – 4.0 Netscape – 2.0 Netscape Enterprise Server version – 2.0 Opera – 3.0	
Property/method value type:	`Number primitive`	
JavaScript syntax:	-	`Math.atan2(aValue1, aValue2)`
Argument list:	`aValue1`	Some meaningful numeric value
	`aValue2`	Some meaningful numeric value

This function computes the quotient of *aValue2/aValue1* and then returns the arc tangent of the result. It takes into account which quadrant the value falls into according to the signs of the two arguments.

It is provided in several languages other than JavaScript for those situations where very large numbers are involved.

Traditionally, for this function, the Y argument is placed first and the X argument second.

Special boundary conditions that affect the results are:

Argument1	Argument2	Result
+infinity	+infinity	+pi/4
+infinity	-infinity	+3pi/4
+infinity	non zero	+pi/2
-infinity	+infinity	-pi/4
-infinity	-infinity	-3pi/4
-infinity	non-zero	-pi/2
0	negative	pi * sign of Argument1
0	positive	0
< 0	-infinity	-pi
< 0	0	-pi/2
> 0	-infinity	+pi
> 0	0	+pi/2
Any value	NaN	NaN
NaN	Any value	NaN
non zero	+infinity	0

The exact value yielded by this function may vary slightly from implementation to implementation due to differences in the underlying precision of the implementation's math routines and the specific algorithm selected to evaluate this function.

The result of this method is the arc-tangent of the slope of the two arguments. The result is expressed in radians and ranges from -pi to +pi.

See also:	*Math object, Math.acos(), Math.asin(), Math.atan(), Math.cos(), Math.sin(), Math.tan()*, Trigonometric function

Cross-references:

ECMA 262 edition 2 – section – 15.8.2.5

ECMA 262 edition 3 – section – 15.8.2.5

M

Math.ceil() (Function)

The value rounded up to the next higher integer value.

Availability:	ECMAScript edition – 2 JavaScript – 1.0 JScript – 1.0 Internet Explorer – 3.02 Netscape – 2.0 Netscape Enterprise Server version – 2.0 Opera – 3.0
Property/method value type:	Number primitive
JavaScript syntax:	-　　　　Math.ceil(*aValue*)
Argument list:	*aValue*　　A meaningful numeric value

According to the ECMA standard, this function returns the smallest number value that is not less than the argument and is equal to a mathematical integer. If the argument is already an integer, the argument itself is returned.

Special boundary conditions that affect the results are:

Argument	Result
+infinity	+infinity
-1 < argument > 0	0
-infinity	-infinity
0	0
NaN	NaN

Note that if the value is negative, the magnitude decreases while it increases for positive numbers. The ceil of 25.4 is 26 whereas the ceil of -25.4 is -25.

The result is the input value rounded up to the next higher integer value.

Warnings:

❑ Other reference sources on this function differ as to its functionality. Some indicate that it rounds up to an integer, others that it rounds down. This suggests that some implementations may behave differently since they may use the available documentation to design their interpreter. The ECMA standard is probably the most reliable specification long term since manufacturers will attempt to build ECMA compliance into their implementations as a selling point.

❑ Recent browsers from Microsoft, Netscape and Opera are all compliant with the ECMA standard on this point.

❏ If you are uncertain, you should check the functionality by running some tests. For example, run the test for negative and positive values. Checking a few boundary conditions won't hurt either.

See also:	Integer, Integer arithmetic, Integer-value-remainder, *Math object*, *Math.abs()*, *Math.floor()*, *Math.round()*, *Number()*, *Remainder (%)*, *Remainder then assign (%=)*, Type conversion

Cross-references:

ECMA 262 edition 2 – section – 15.8.2.6

ECMA 262 edition 3 – section – 15.8.2.6

Math.cos() (Function)

The cosine of the input argument.

Availability:	ECMAScript edition – 2 JavaScript – 1.0 JScript – 1.0 Internet Explorer – 3.02 Netscape – 2.0 Netscape Enterprise Server version – 2.0 Opera – 3.0	
Property/method value type:	Number primitive	
JavaScript syntax:	-	`Math.cos(aValue)`
Argument list:	`aValue`	An angle measured in radians

This function returns the cosine of the argument. The argument must be expressed in radians.

Special boundary conditions that affect the results are:

Argument	Result
+infinity	NaN
-infinity	NaN
0	1
NaN	NaN

The exact value yielded by this function may vary slightly from implementation to implementation due to differences in the underlying precision of the implementation's math routines and the specific algorithm selected to evaluate this function.

M

Warnings:

❑ Note that `Math.cos(Math.PI)` may not return precisely zero.

See also:	Math object, Math.acos(), Math.asin(), Math.atan(), Math.atan2(), Math.PI, Math.sin(), Math.tan(), Trigonometric function

Cross-references:

ECMA 262 edition 2 – section – 15.8.2.7

ECMA 262 edition 3 – section – 15.8.2.7

Math.E (Constant/static)

A mathematical constant value.

Availability:	ECMAScript edition – 2 JavaScript – 1.0 JScript – 1.0 Internet Explorer – 3.02 Netscape – 2.0 Netscape Enterprise Server version – 2.0 Opera – 3.0
Property/method value type:	Number primitive
JavaScript syntax:	- Math.E

The numeric constant value for e, the base of natural logarithms.

The resulting value is approximately 2.718281828459045 (to 15 d.p.).

Warnings:

❑ The word approximately is used when describing the result because the mathematical accuracy of JavaScript implementations leaves something to be desired and there are some strange artifacts in some of the calculations.

See also:	Arithmetic constant, Exponent-log function, Floating point constant, Math object, Math.exp()

Property attributes:

ReadOnly, DontDelete, DontEnum.

Cross-references:

ECMA 262 edition 2 – section – 15.8.1.1

ECMA 262 edition 3 – section – 15.8.1.1

Math.exp() (Function)

The exponential function of the passed in argument.

Availability:	ECMAScript edition – 2 JavaScript – 1.0 JScript – 1.0 Internet Explorer – 3.02 Netscape – 2.0 Netscape Enterprise Server version – 2.0 Opera – 3.0
Property/method value type:	Number primitive
JavaScript syntax:	-	Math.exp(aValue)
Argument list:	aValue	A meaningful numeric value

This function returns the exponential function of the argument (e raised to the power of the argument, where e is the base of the natural logarithms).

Special boundary conditions that affect the results are:

Argument	Result
+infinity	+infinity
-infinity	0
0	1
NaN	NaN

The exact value yielded by this function may vary slightly from implementation to implementation due to differences in the underlying precision of the implementation's math routines and the specific algorithm selected to evaluate this function.

See also:	Exponent-log function, *Math object, Math.E,* *Math.LN10, Math.LN2, Math.log(), Math.LOG10E,* *Math.LOG2E*

Cross-references:

ECMA 262 edition 2 – section – 15.8.2.8

ECMA 262 edition 3 – section – 15.8.2.8

M

Math.floor() (Function)

The value is rounded down to the next integer.

Availability:	ECMAScript edition – 2 JavaScript – 1.0 JScript – 1.0 Internet Explorer – 3.02 Netscape – 2.0 Netscape Enterprise Server version – 2.0 Opera – 3.0	
Property/method value type:	Number primitive	
JavaScript syntax:	-	Math.floor(*aValue*)
Argument list:	*aValue*	A meaningful numeric value

Returns the greatest number value that is not greater than the argument and is equal to a mathematical integer. If the argument is already an integer, the argument itself is returned.

Special boundary conditions that affect the results are:

Argument	Result
+infinity	+infinity
-infinity	-infinity
0	0
0 < argument > 1	0
NaN	NaN

Note that if the value is negative, the magnitude increases while it decreases for positive numbers. The floor of 25.4 is 25 whereas the floor of -25.4 is -26.

The result is the input value rounded down to the next integer.

Warnings:

❑ Other reference sources on this function differ as to its functionality. Some indicate that it rounds up to an integer, others that it rounds down. However, all implementations appear to conform to the ECMA specified behavior.

See also:	Integer, Integer arithmetic, Integer-value-remainder, *Math object*, *Math.abs()*, *Math.ceil()*, *Math.round()*, *Number()*, *Remainder (%)*, *Remainder then assign (%=)*, Type conversion

Cross-references:

ECMA 262 edition 2 – section – 15.8.2.9

ECMA 262 edition 3 – section – 15.8.2.9

Math.LN10 (Constant/static)

A mathematical constant value.

Availability:	ECMAScript edition – 2 JavaScript – 1.0 JScript – 1.0 Internet Explorer – 3.02 Netscape – 2.0 Netscape Enterprise Server version – 2.0 Opera – 3.0
Property/method value type:	Number primitive
JavaScript syntax:	- Math.LN10

This constant provides the numeric value for the natural logarithm of 10.

The resulting value is approximately 2.302585092994046 (to 15 d.p.).

Warnings:

❑ The word approximately is used when describing the result because the mathematical accuracy of JavaScript implementations leaves something to be desired and there are some strange artifacts in some of the calculations.

See also:	Arithmetic constant, Exponent-log function, Floating point constant, *Math object*, *Math.exp()*

Property attributes:

ReadOnly, DontDelete, DontEnum.

Cross-references:

ECMA 262 edition 2 – section – 15.8.1.2

ECMA 262 edition 3 – section – 15.8.1.2

Math.LN2 (Constant/static)

A mathematical constant value.

Availability:	ECMAScript edition – 2 JavaScript – 1.0 JScript – 1.0 Internet Explorer – 3.02 Netscape – 2.0 Netscape Enterprise Server version – 2.0 Opera – 3.0
Property/method value type:	Number primitive
JavaScript syntax:	- Math.LN2

This constant provides the numeric value of the natural logarithm of 2.

The resulting value returned is approximately 0.693147180559945 (to 15 d.p.).

See also:	Arithmetic constant, Exponent-log function, Floating point constant, *Math object*, *Math.exp()*

Property attributes:

ReadOnly, DontDelete, DontEnum.

Cross-references:

ECMA 262 edition 2 – section – 15.8.1.3

ECMA 262 edition 3 – section – 15.8.1.3

Math.log() (Function)

The natural logarithm of the passed in value.

Availability:	ECMAScript edition – 2 JavaScript – 1.0 JScript – 1.0 Internet Explorer – 3.02 Netscape – 2.0 Netscape Enterprise Server version – 2.0 Opera – 3.0	
Property/method value type:	Number primitive	
JavaScript syntax:	-	Math.log(*aValue*)
Argument list:	*aValue*	A meaningful numeric value

This function returns the natural (base *e*) logarithm of the input argument.

This function is the inverse of the `Math.exp()` function.

Special boundary conditions that affect the results are:

Argument	Result
+infinity	+infinity
0	-infinity
1	0
< 0	NaN
NaN	NaN

The exact value yielded by this function may vary slightly from implementation to implementation due to differences in the underlying precision of the implementation's math routines and the specific algorithm selected to evaluate this function.

See also:	Exponent-log function, *Math object*, *Math.exp()*

Cross-references:

ECMA 262 edition 2 – section – 15.8.2.10

ECMA 262 edition 3 – section – 15.8.2.10

Math.LOG10E (Constant/static)

A mathematical constant value.

Availability:	ECMAScript edition – 2 JavaScript – 1.0 JScript – 1.0 Internet Explorer – 3.02 Netscape – 2.0 Netscape Enterprise Server version – 2.0 Opera – 3.0
Property/method value type:	Number primitive
JavaScript syntax:	- Math.LOG10E

This constant provides the numeric value for the base-10 logarithm of *e*, the base of natural logarithms.

Note that the value of `Math.LOG10E` is approximately the reciprocal of the value of `Math.LN10`.

The result returned is approximately 0.434294481903252 (to 15 d.p.).

Warnings:

❑ The word approximately is used when describing the result because the mathematical accuracy of JavaScript implementations leaves something to be desired and there are some strange artifacts in some of the calculations.

See also:	Arithmetic constant, Exponent-log function, Floating point constant, *Math object*, *Math.exp()*

Property attributes:

ReadOnly, DontDelete, DontEnum.

Cross-references:

ECMA 262 edition 2 – section – 15.8.1.5

ECMA 262 edition 3 – section – 15.8.1.5

Math.LOG2E (Constant/static)

A mathematical constant value.

Availability:	ECMAScript edition – 2 JavaScript – 1.0 JScript – 1.0 Internet Explorer – 3.02 Netscape – 2.0 Netscape Enterprise Server version – 2.0 Opera – 3.0
Property/method value type:	Number primitive
JavaScript syntax:	- Math.LOG2E

This constant provides the numeric value for the base-2 logarithm of e, the base of natural logarithms.

By inspection, the resulting value returned is 1.442695040888963 although this may vary from platform to platform.

Warnings:

❑ Note that the value of Math.LOG2E is approximately the reciprocal of the value of Math.LN2. The word approximately is used here because the mathematical accuracy of JavaScript implementations leaves something to be desired and there are some strange artifacts in some of the calculations.

See also:	Arithmetic constant, Exponent-log function, Floating point constant, *Math object*, *Math.exp()*

Property attributes:

ReadOnly, DontDelete, DontEnum.

Cross-references:

ECMA 262 edition 2 – section – 15.8.1.4

ECMA 262 edition 3 – section – 15.8.1.4

Math.max() (Function)

The maximum of the two or more input arguments is returned.

Availability:	ECMAScript edition – 2 JavaScript – 1.0 JScript – 1.0 Internet Explorer – 3.02 Netscape – 2.0 Netscape Enterprise Server version – 2.0 Opera – 3.0	
Property/method value type:	Number primitive	
JavaScript syntax:	-	Math.max(*aValue1*, *aValue2*, ...)
Argument list:	*aValue1*	Some meaningful numeric value
	aValue2	Some meaningful numeric value

Returns the larger of the two or more arguments.

Special boundary conditions that affect the results are:

Argument1	Argument2	Result
Any value	NaN	NaN
Any value	The same value	The value
larger	smaller	Argument1
NaN	Any value	NaN
smaller	larger	Argument2

See also:	*Math object*

Cross-references:

ECMA 262 edition 2 – section – 15.8.2.11

ECMA 262 edition 3 – section – 15.8.2.11

Math.min() (Function)

The minimum of the two or more input arguments is returned.

Availability:	ECMAScript edition – 2 JavaScript – 1.0 JScript – 1.0 Internet Explorer – 3.02 Netscape – 2.0 Netscape Enterprise Server version – 2.0 Opera – 3.0	
Property/method value type:	Number primitive	
JavaScript syntax:	-	Math.min(aValue1, aValue2, ...)
Argument list:	aValue1	Some meaningful numeric value
	aValue2	Some meaningful numeric value

This function returns the smaller of the two or more arguments.

Special boundary conditions that affect the results are:

Argument1	Argument2	Result
Any value	NaN	NaN
Any value	The same value	The value
larger	smaller	Argument2
NaN	Any value	NaN
smaller	larger	Argument1

See also:	*Math object*

Cross-references:

ECMA 262 edition 2 – section – 15.8.2.12

ECMA 262 edition 3 – section – 15.8.2.12

Math.PI (Constant/static)

A mathematical constant value.

Availability:	ECMAScript edition – 2 JavaScript – 1.0 JScript – 1.0 Internet Explorer – 3.02 Netscape – 2.0 Netscape Enterprise Server version – 2.0 Opera – 3.0	
Property/method value type:	`Number primitive`	
JavaScript syntax:	-	`Math.PI`

This constant provides the numeric value for pi, the ratio of the circumference of a circle to its diameter.

The resulting value returned is approximately 3.141592653589793 (to 15 d.p.).

Warnings:

❑ Note that `Math.sin(Math.PI/2)` may not yield exactly 1.

❑ Note that `Math.cos(Math.PI)` may not return precisely zero.

❑ Note that `Math.acos(0)` may not return the same value as `Math.PI`.

See also:	Arithmetic constant, Floating point constant, *Math object, Math.acos(), Math.cos(), Math.sin()*

Property attributes:

`ReadOnly`, `DontDelete`, `DontEnum`.

Cross-references:

ECMA 262 edition 2 – section – 15.8.1.6

ECMA 262 edition 3 – section – 15.8.1.6

Math.pow() (Function)

The result of raising a value to the power of another value.

Availability:	ECMAScript edition – 2 JavaScript – 1.0 JScript – 1.0 Internet Explorer – 3.02 Netscape – 2.0 Netscape Enterprise Server version – 2.0 Opera – 3.0	
Property/method value type:	`Number primitive`	
JavaScript syntax:	-	`Math.pow(aValue1, aValue2)`
Argument list:	`aValue1`	Some meaningful numeric value
	`aValue2`	Some meaningful numeric value

This function returns the result of raising the first argument to the power of the second.

Special boundary conditions that affect the results are:

Argument1	Argument2	Result
+0	< 0	+infinity
+infinity	< 0	0
+infinity	> 0	+infinity
-0	< 0 and is an even integer	+infinity
-0	< 0 and is an odd integer	-infinity
-infinity	< 0	0
-infinity	> 0 and is an even integer	+infinity
-infinity	> 0 and is an odd integer	-infinity
0	> 0	0
1	Any value	1
< 0 and finite	finite but non-integer	NaN
abs(arg) < 1	+infinity	0
abs(arg) < 1	-infinity	+infinity
abs(arg) == 1	+infinity	NaN
abs(arg) == 1	-infinity	NaN
abs(arg) > 1	+infinity	+infinity
abs(arg) > 1	-infinity	0
Any value	0	1
Any value	NaN	NaN
NaN	non-zero	NaN

The exact value yielded by this function may vary slightly from implementation to implementation due to differences in the underlying precision of the math routines, and the specific algorithm selected to evaluate this function.

The example shows a simple binary number converter which exhibits some instability in the most significant bit on some platforms.

Warnings:

❏ There are many boundary conditions that make this function hard to understand and therefore hard to diagnose if it goes wrong. Check both of the input arguments in case of doubt. They may have evaluated out to a strange boundary condition that yields unexpected results.

❏ Using MSIE on the Macintosh exhibits a instability when you raise 2 to the power 31 and test the resulting value in a bitwise expression. Netscape works correctly in this circumstance. This is demonstrated in the example.

Example code:

```
<HTML>
<HEAD>
</HEAD>
<BODY>
<SCRIPT>
document.write(-2 + " - " + binary32(-2) + "<BR>");
document.write(-1 + " - " + binary32(-1) + "<BR>");
document.write(0 + " - " + binary32(0) + "<BR>");
document.write(1 + " - " + binary32(1) + "<BR>");
document.write(2 + " - " + binary32(2) + "<BR>");
document.write(3 + " - " + binary32(3) + "<BR>");
function binary32(aValue)
{
    myArray = new Array(32);

    for(myEnum=0; myEnum<32; myEnum++)
    {
        if(aValue & Math.pow(2, myEnum))
        {
            myArray[31-myEnum] = "1";
        }
        else
        {
            myArray[31-myEnum] = "0";
        }
    }
    return myArray.join("");
}
</SCRIPT>
</BODY>
</HTML>
```

Cross-references:

ECMA 262 edition 2 – section – 15.8.2.13

ECMA 262 edition 3 – section – 15.8.2.13

Math.random() (Function)

Generate a pseudo-random value.

Availability:	ECMAScript edition – 2 JavaScript – 1.1 JScript – 1.0 Internet Explorer – 3.02 Netscape – 2.02 Netscape Enterprise Server version – 2.0 Opera – 3.0
Property/method value type:	Number primitive
JavaScript syntax:	- Math.random()

The Math.random() function generates and returns a pseudo-random value; a positive value between 0 and 1.

The resulting value is chosen randomly (or pseudo-randomly) depending on the implementation.

In any case, regardless of how it is selected, it should yield a uniform distribution over the range of possible values.

The exact value yielded by this function may vary slightly from implementation to implementation due to differences in the underlying precision of the implementation's math routines, and the specific algorithm selected to generate the random numbers.

Some implementations may provide a way to seed the random number sequence although the ECMAScript standard does not describe this capability.

Some implementations provide predictable series of random numbers that always start at the same seed point.

The algorithm and strategy is implementation dependant and the standard offers no recommendations as to which is best.

Warnings:

❑ Although this is noted as being available in Netscape 2.02, that only applies to the Unix platform. It wasn't widely available until JavaScript 1.1 was supported in Netscape 3.0 on the remaining platforms.

See also:	*Math object*, Pseudo-random numbers

Cross-references:

ECMA 262 edition 2 – section – 15.8.2.14

ECMA 262 edition 3 – section – 15.8.2.14

Math.round() (Function)

Rounds to the nearest integer value.

Availability:	ECMAScript edition – 2 JavaScript – 1.0 JScript – 1.0 Internet Explorer – 3.02 Netscape – 2.0 Netscape Enterprise Server version – 2.0 Opera – 3.0	
Property/method value type:	Number primitive	
JavaScript syntax:	-	Math.round(*aValue*)
Argument list:	*aValue*	A meaningful numeric value

This function returns the value that is closest to the argument and is a mathematical integer. It rounds the input value to the nearest integer value either rounding up or down as necessary.

If the input value is equidistant from two integer values, the result is rounded up towards positive infinity. If the argument is already an integer, the argument itself is returned.

Special boundary conditions that affect the results are:

Argument	Result
+infinity	+infinity
-0.5 < arg < 0.5	0
-infinity	-infinity
0	0
NaN	NaN

Note that `Math.round(3.5)` returns the value 4 while `Math.round(-3.5)` returns the value 3.

See also:	Integer arithmetic, Integer-value-remainder, *Math object*, *Math.ceil()*, *Math.floor()*, *Number()*, Type conversion

Cross-references:

ECMA 262 edition 2 – section – 15.8.2.15

ECMA 262 edition 3 – section – 15.8.2.15

Math.sin() (Function)

The sine of the passed in value.

Availability:	ECMAScript edition – 2 JavaScript – 1.0 JScript – 1.0 Internet Explorer – 3.02 Netscape – 2.0 Netscape Enterprise Server version – 2.0 Opera – 3.0
Property/method value type:	Number primitive
JavaScript syntax:	-	`Math.sin(aValue)`
Argument list:	aValue	An angle measured in radians

This function returns the sine of the input argument. The argument value must be expressed in radians.

Special boundary conditions that affect the results are:

Argument	Result
+infinity	NaN
-infinity	NaN
0	0
NaN	NaN

The exact value yielded by this function may vary slightly from implementation to implementation due to differences in the underlying precision of the implementation's math routines and the specific algorithm selected to evaluate this function.

Warnings:

❑ Note that `Math.sin(Math.PI/2)` may not yield exactly 1.

See also:	*Math object, Math.acos(), Math.asin(), Math.atan(), Math.atan2(), Math.cos(), Math.PI, Math.tan(),* Trigonometric function

Cross-references:

ECMA 262 edition 2 – section – 15.8.2.16

ECMA 262 edition 3 – section – 15.8.2.16

Math.sqrt() (Function)

The square root of the input argument.

Availability:	ECMAScript edition – 2 JavaScript – 1.0 JScript – 1.0 Internet Explorer – 3.02 Netscape – 2.0 Netscape Enterprise Server version – 2.0 Opera – 3.0	
Property/method value type:	`Number primitive`	
JavaScript syntax:	-	`Math.sqrt(aValue)`
Argument list:	`aValue`	A meaningful numeric value

This function computes the square root of the input argument.

Special boundary conditions that affect the results are:

Argument	Result
+infinity	+infinity
0	0
< 0	NaN
NaN	NaN

The exact value yielded by this function may vary slightly from implementation to implementation due to differences in the underlying precision of the math routines and the specific algorithm selected to evaluate this function.

See also:	*Math object, Math.pow()*

Cross-references:

ECMA 262 edition 2 – section – 15.8.2.17

ECMA 262 edition 3 – section – 15.8.2.17

Math.SQRT1_2 (Constant/static)

A mathematical constant value.

Availability:	ECMAScript edition – 2 JavaScript – 1.0 JScript – 1.0 Internet Explorer – 3.02 Netscape – 2.0 Netscape Enterprise Server version – 2.0 Opera – 3.0
Property/method value type:	Number primitive
JavaScript syntax:	- Math.SQRT1_2

This constant returns the numeric value of the square root of 0.5.

The resulting value returned is approximately 0.707106781186548 (to 15.d.p.).

Warnings:

❑ Note that the value of Math.SQRT1_2 is approximately the reciprocal of the value of Math.SQRT2. The word approximately is used here because the mathematical accuracy of JavaScript implementations leaves something to be desired and there are some strange artifacts in some of the calculations.

See also:	Arithmetic constant, Floating point constant, *Math object, Math.SQRT2*

Property attributes:

ReadOnly, DontDelete, DontEnum.

Cross-references:

ECMA 262 edition 2 – section – 15.8.1.7

ECMA 262 edition 3 – section – 15.8.1.7

Math.SQRT2 (Constant/static)

A mathematical constant value.

Availability:	ECMAScript edition – 2 JavaScript – 1.0 JScript – 1.0 Internet Explorer – 3.02 Netscape – 2.0 Netscape Enterprise Server version – 2.0 Opera – 3.0	
Property/method value type:	Number primitive	
JavaScript syntax:	-	Math.SQRT2

This constant provides the value of the square root of 2.

The resulting value returned is approximately 1.414213562373095 (to 15 d.p.).

Warnings:

❏ Note that Math.SQRT1_2 may not be exactly equal to the reciprocal of Math.SQRT2.

See also:	Arithmetic constant, Floating point constant, *Math object, Math.SQRT1_2*

Property attributes:

ReadOnly, DontDelete, DontEnum.

Cross-references:

ECMA 262 edition 2 – section – 15.8.1.8

ECMA 262 edition 3 – section – 15.8.1.8

M

JavaScript Programmer's Reference

Math.tan() (Function)

The tangent of the input argument.

Availability:	ECMAScript edition – 2 JavaScript – 1.0 JScript – 1.0 Internet Explorer – 3.02 Netscape – 2.0 Netscape Enterprise Server version – 2.0 Opera – 3.0
Property/method value type:	Number primitive
JavaScript syntax:	- Math.tan(aValue)
Argument list:	aValue An angle measured in radians

This function returns the tangent of the input argument. The argument value must be expressed in radians.

Special boundary conditions that affect the results are:

Argument	Result
+infinity	NaN
-infinity	NaN
0	0
NaN	NaN

The exact value yielded by this function may vary slightly from implementation to implementation due to differences in the underlying precision of the math routines and the specific algorithm selected to evaluate this function.

See also:	*Math object, Math.acos(), Math.asin(), Math.atan(), Math.atan2(), Math.cos(), Math.sin(),* Trigonometric function

Cross-references:

ECMA 262 edition 2 – section – 15.8.2.18

ECMA 262 edition 3 – section – 15.8.2.18

MAYSCRIPT (HTML Tag Attribute)

An attribute on the <APPLET> tag to allow Java to access the JavaScript object space.

This is an HTML tag attribute that can significantly affect the success or failure to run applets and plugins properly.

The MAYSCRIPT attribute must be present in the <APPLET> tag if you have applets that expect to communicate with JavaScript. This is a way of allowing applets to script under the behest of the web page author who may not be the person who programmed the applet. This way, the author has to know and expect the applet to connect to JavaScript before the applet is able to do so.

Without this attribute, an applet is not able to access the JSObject class and communicate with the JavaScript environment.

The MAYSCRIPT HTML tag attribute is not reflected into the JavaScript environment.

See also:	JavaScript embedded in Java, *JSObject object*

MediaList object (Object/DOM)

This object is added to DOM level 2 to support media lists in style sheets.

Availability:	DOM level – 2 JavaScript – 1.5 Netscape – 6.0
JavaScript syntax:	N	*myMedialist* = new MediaList()

DOM level 2 specifies the following properties for this object:

❑ mediaText

❑ length

DOM level 2 specifies these methods:

❑ item()

❑ deleteMedium()

❑ appendMedium()

MENU object (Object/HTML)

An object that represents the contents of a <MENU> tag.

Availability:	DOM level – 1 JavaScript – 1.5 JScript – 3.0 Internet Explorer – 4.0 Netscape – 6.0
Inherits from:	*Element object*
JavaScript syntax:	IE *myMENU = myDocument.all.anElementID* IE *myMENU = myDocument.all.tags ("MENU")[anIndex]* IE *myMENU = myDocument.all[aName]* – *myMENU = myDocument.getElementById (anElementID)* – *myMENU = myDocument.getElementsByName (aName)[anIndex]* – *myMENU = myDocument .getElementsByTagName("MENU")[anIndex]*
HTML syntax:	<MENU> ... </MENU>
Argument list:	*anIndex* A reference to an element in a collection *aName* An associative array reference *anElementID* The ID value of the element
Object properties:	compact
Event handlers:	onClick, onDblClick, onDragStart, onFilterChange, onHelp, onKeyDown, onKeyPress, onKeyUp, onMouseDown, onMouseMove, onMouseOut, onMouseOver, onMouseUp, onSelectStart

The DOM level 1 specification refers to this as a MenuElement object.

See also:	*Element object*

Property	JavaScript	JScript	N	IE	Opera	DOM	HTML	Notes
compact	1.5 +	3.0 +	6.0 +	4.0 +	-	1 +	-	-

Event name	JavaScript	JScript	N	IE	Opera	DOM	HTML	Notes
onClick	1.0 +	1.0 +	6.0 +	4.0 +	3.0 +	-	4.0 +	Warning
onDblClick	1.2 +	3.0 +	6.0 +	4.0 +	3.0 +	-	4.0 +	Warning
onDragStart	-	3.0 +	-	4.0 +	-	-	-	-
onFilterChange	-	3.0 +	-	4.0 +	-	-	-	-
onHelp	-	3.0 +	-	4.0 +	-	-	-	Warning
onKeyDown	1.2 +	3.0 +	6.0 +	4.0 +	3.0 +	-	4.0 +	Warning
onKeyPress	1.2 +	3.0 +	6.0 +	4.0 +	3.0 +	-	4.0 +	Warning
onKeyUp	1.2 +	3.0 +	6.0 +	4.0 +	3.0 +	-	4.0 +	Warning
onMouseDown	1.2 +	3.0 +	6.0 +	4.0 +	3.0 +	-	4.0 +	Warning
onMouseMove	1.2 +	3.0 +	6.0 +	4.0 +	-	-	4.0 +	Warning
onMouseOut	1.1 +	3.0 +	6.0 +	4.0 +	3.0 +	-	4.0 +	Warning
onMouseOver	1.0 +	1.0 +	6.0 +	4.0 +	3.0 +	-	4.0 +	Warning
onMouseUp	1.2 +	3.0 +	6.0 +	4.0 +	3.0 +	-	4.0 +	Warning
onSelectStart	-	3.0 +	-	4.0 +	-	-	-	-

Inheritance chain:

Element object, Node object

<META> (HTML Tag)

Document meta-information container.

Availability:	JavaScript – 1.2 Netscape – 4.0	
HTML syntax:	<META HTTP-EQUIV="aName" CONTENT="aValue">	
Argument list:	aName	A pseudo-header name
	aValue	A pseudo-header value

The <META> tag is a way of adding information about the document to the
document. This information is never intended for display to the user but helps the
browser and other server-side systems (and proxies) to manage the document.

There are many attributes to the <META> tag. We have only covered the ones that
are helpful in the context of script development here.

The items that are particularly useful to us are the HTTP_EQUIV and CONTENT
attributes. These are used to add information to the HTTP response body. The
browser can see these values in the <META> tag and interprets them as if they had
been part of the HTTP header.

So:

```
<META HTTP-EQUIV="name" CONTENT="value">
```

is understood to be equivalent to an HTTP header like this:

```
name: value
```

As far as JavaScript is concerned, there are two <META> tags that are useful.

This one defines the default scripting language:

```
<META HTTP-EQUIV="Content-Script-Type" CONTENT="text/JavaScript">
```

If you have access to the server mechanism, you might be able to effect the same things by forcing it to add this header to the response as it goes out:

```
Content-Script-Type: text/JavaScript
```

The second useful <META> tag is used to define the default style definition language. Given all the warnings about JSS not being portable and it having been deprecated, you could use this in your document <HEAD> block:

```
<META HTTP-EQUIV="Content-Style-Type" CONTENT="text/JavaScript">
```

Again, if you have access to the server mechanism, you might be able to add this header to the response as it goes out:

```
Content-Style-Type: text/JavaScript
```

Warnings:

❑ Since MSIE does not support JSS and Netscape ignores the tag variants, these <META> tags are of limited use.

See also:	*<SCRIPT LANGUAGE="...">*, *<SCRIPT>*, *<STYLE TYPE="...">*, *<STYLE>*, JavaScript Style Sheets, *META object*

Cross-references:

Wrox Instant JavaScript – page – 52

META object (Object/HTML)

An object that represents the contents of a <META> tag.

Availability:	DOM level – 1 JavaScript – 1.5 JScript – 3.0 Internet Explorer – 4.0 Netscape – 6.0
Inherits from:	*Element object*
JavaScript syntax:	IE `myMETA = myDocument.all.anElementID`
	IE `myMETA = myDocument.all.tags` `("META")[anIndex]`
	IE `myMETA = myDocument.all[aName]`
	- `myMETA = myDocument.getElementById` `(anElementID)`
	- `myMETA = myDocument.getElementsByName` `(aName)[anIndex]`
	- `myMETA = myDocument` `.getElementsByTagName("META")[anIndex]`
HTML syntax:	`<META>`
Argument list:	`anIndex` A reference to an element in a collection
	`aName` An associative array reference
	`anElementID` The ID value of an Element object
Object properties:	`charset, content, httpEquiv, name, scheme,` `url`

Event handlers:	`onClick, onDblClick, onHelp, onKeyDown,`
	`onKeyPress, onKeyUp, onMouseDown,`
	`onMouseMove, onMouseOut, onMouseOver,`
	`onMouseUp`

These tags and their corresponding object instantiations are used to convey hidden information about the document. This information might be useful to a search engine for example. Sometimes, the server uses the META information to control the way the pages are cached into a proxy. Likewise, a client browser may use these values to control the local caching and expiry times of a document.

There may be several META objects associated with a document. There is no collection object that provides an enumerable set containing only the META objects but you can traverse the `document.all[]` collection and extract them in MSIE or use the collection returned by the DOM compliant `document.getElementsByTagName("META")` method which is supported on Netscape 6.0 and recent versions of MSIE. It is possible you might know the unique `ID="..."` HTML tag attribute value in which case you can access the required object directly.

This is not currently supported at all in Netscape 4.0 although because it is part of the DOM specification, it is added to Netscape 6.0.

Warnings:

❑ Netscape 6.0 returns an undefined value for the charset property and incorrectly appends it to the content property

❑ For this meta tag:

```
<META http-equiv="Content-Type" content="text/html;
charset=iso-8859-1">
```

❑ Netscape Navigator 6.0 returns these values:

　　❑ myMeta.httpEquiv is defined as "Content-Type"

　　❑ myMeta.content is defined as "text/html; charset=8859-1"

　　❑ myMeta.charset is undefined

See also:	<META>, Element object, META.charset

Property	JavaScript	JScript	N	IE	Opera	DOM	HTML	Notes
charset	-	3.0 +	-	4.0 +	-	-	-	-
content	1.5 +	3.0 +	6.0 +	4.0 +	-	1 +	-	-
httpEquiv	1.5 +	3.0 +	6.0 +	4.0 +	-	1 +	-	-
name	1.5 +	3.0 +	6.0 +	4.0 +	-	1 +	-	-
scheme	1.5 +	5.0 +	6.0 +	5.0 +	-	1 +	-	-
url	-	3.0 +	-	4.0 +	-	-	-	-

Event name	JavaScript	JScript	N	IE	Opera	DOM	HTML	Notes
onClick	1.0 +	1.0 +	6.0 +	4.0 +	3.0 +	-	4.0 +	Warning
onDblClick	1.2 +	3.0 +	6.0 +	4.0 +	3.0 +	-	4.0 +	Warning
onHelp	-	3.0 +	-	4.0 +	-	-	-	Warning
onKeyDown	1.2 +	3.0 +	6.0 +	4.0 +	3.0 +	-	4.0 +	Warning
onKeyPress	1.2 +	3.0 +	6.0 +	4.0 +	3.0 +	-	4.0 +	Warning
onKeyUp	1.2 +	3.0 +	6.0 +	4.0 +	3.0 +	-	4.0 +	Warning
onMouseDown	1.2 +	3.0 +	6.0 +	4.0 +	3.0 +	-	4.0 +	Warning
onMouseMove	1.2 +	3.0 +	6.0 +	4.0 +	-	-	4.0 +	Warning
onMouseOut	1.1 +	3.0 +	6.0 +	4.0 +	3.0 +	-	4.0 +	Warning
onMouseOver	1.0 +	1.0 +	6.0 +	4.0 +	3.0 +	-	4.0 +	Warning
onMouseUp	1.2 +	3.0 +	6.0 +	4.0 +	3.0 +	-	4.0 +	Warning

Inheritance chain:

Element object, Node object

MimeType object (Object/browser)

An object representing a MIME type.

Availability:	JavaScript – 1.1 JScript – 3.0 Internet Explorer – 4.0 Netscape – 3.0	
JavaScript syntax:	-	*myMimeType = myWindow* *.navigator.mimeTypes[anIndex]*
	-	*myMimeType =* navigator.mimeTypes[*anIndex*]
	-	*myMimeType = myMimeTypeArray[anIndex]*
Argument list:	*anIndex*	A reference to an element in a collection
Object properties:	description, enabledPlugin, name, suffixes, type	
Collections:	suffixes[]	

The example code fragment will list all the available MIME types supported by the browser.

Example code:

```
// List the available mimeTypes in Netscape
for(ii=0; ii<navigator.mimeTypes.length; ii++)
{
    document.write(navigator.mimeTypes[ii].suffixes);
    document.write(" - ");
    document.write(navigator.mimeTypes[ii].type);
    document.write(" - ");
    document.write(navigator.mimeTypes[ii].description);
    document.write(" - ");

    if(navigator.mimeTypes[ii].enabledPlugin)
    {
        document.write(navigator.mimeTypes[ii].enabledPlugin.name);
    }
    else
    {
        document.write("<no_plugin>");
    }
    document.write("<BR>");
}
```

See also:	MIME types, *MimeTypeArray object*, Navigator.mimeTypes[]

M

JavaScript Programmer's Reference

Property	JavaScript	JScript	N	IE	Opera	HTML	Notes
description	1.1 +	3.0 +	3.0 +	4.0 +	-	-	ReadOnly
enabledPlugin	1.1 +	3.0 +	3.0 +	4.0 +	-	-	ReadOnly
name	1.5 +	5.0 +	6.0 +	5.0 +	-	-	ReadOnly
suffixes	1.1 +	3.0 +	3.0 +	4.0 +	-	-	-
type	1.1 +	3.0 +	3.0 +	4.0 +	-	-	ReadOnly

MimeTypeArray object (Object/browser)

A collection of `MimeType` objects.

Availability:	JavaScript – 1.1 JScript – 3.0 Internet Explorer – 4.0 Netscape – 3.0
JavaScript syntax:	-	`myMimeTypeArray = navigator.mimeTypes`
Object properties:	`length`

On MSIE, this array contains an element for each supported `MimeType` object that the browser can respond to.

Likewise on Netscape, a collection of somewhat different `MimeType` objects are available.

Warnings:

❑ MSIE prior to version 5.0 does not support this facility and returns the undefined value even though it has a place holder for the property.

❑ Note that Netscape 4.7 on Macintosh exhibits some careless `MimeType` instantiation with at least two of the items in this array.

❑ Item 50 does not exhibit an associative value because the type property for that `MimeType` is undefined. There is no apparent fix because the type property of a `MimeType` object is read only although there is no error generated when trying to assign a new value to it. The proper type value for this item should be `"application.gzip"`.

❑ Item 64 has a similar problem but just presents a null string rather than its index. This MimeType represents UU encoded files. It doesn't show up in the list of applications that map to file types in the Netscape preferences.

❑ This problem may be extant on other platforms although it is possible that the problems may be related to your user preference settings and the indices that have problems may not be the same number or `MimeType` values.

❑ The implications are that GZIP and UUencoded files are handled internally by the browser and therefore although it creates MimeType objects, they may not be derived from the preferences settings although changing your preferences may relocate these objects to different positions in the collection.

❑ Build an enumerator to examine the MimeType objects in the collection. You'll see a fragment of script that would do this in the example. There is no real fix for this other than to build some conditional check into any enumeration or iterative loop that examines the MimeTypes array.

❑ Note that Netscape 6.0 does not enumerate this collection properly and the example does not yield the correct result.

Example code:

```
// Inline this script fragment to display all mime types
// supported by your browser (except for NNav 6.0 which exhibits
// a strange bug.
for(myProp in navigator.mimeTypes)
{
   document.write(myProp);
   document.write("<BR>");
}
```

See also:	*Collection object, MimeType object,* `Navigator.mimeTypes[]`

Property	JavaScript	JScript	N	IE	Opera	HTML	Notes
length	1.1 +	3.0 +	3.0 +	4.0 +	-	-	ReadOnly

ModElement object (Object/DOM)

A DOM level 1 object that describes a modification to a document.

Availability:	DOM level – 1 JavaScript – 1.5 JScript – 3.0 Internet Explorer – 4.0 Netscape – 6.0
JavaScript syntax:	-	*myModElement* = new ModeElement()
Object properties:	cite, dateTime	

The MSIE browser implements deletions and insertions as separate object types (DEL and INS respectively). The DOM level 1 standard includes both in a single object class.

See also:	DEL object, INS object						

Property	JavaScript	JScript	N	IE	Opera	DOM	Notes
cite	1.5 +	5.0 +	6.0 +	5.0 +	-	1 +	-
dateTime	1.5 +	5.0 +	6.0 +	5.0 +	-	1 +	-

MouseEvent object (Object/DOM)

This is part of the DOM level 2 mouse event set.

Availability:	DOM level – 2 JavaScript – 1.5 Netscape – 6.0	
JavaScript syntax:	N	`myMouseEvent = new MouseEvent()`
Object properties:	altKey, bubbles, button, cancelable, clientX, clientY, ctrlKey, currentTarget, detail, eventPhase, metaKey, relatedTarget, screenX, screenY, shiftKey, target, timeStamp, type, view	
Object methods:	initEvent(), initMouseEvent(), initUIEvent(), preventDefault(), stopPropagation()	

The availability of the MouseEvent object handling can be determined with the Implementation.hasFeature() method call.

The available set of events is defined by HTML 4.0 and DOM level 0 with some additional events having been added. These event types are enumerated in the DOM level 2 specification and are:

❑ click

❑ mousedown

❑ mouseup

❑ mouseover

❑ mousemove

❑ mouseout

The contextual information is carried in the detail property which is inherited from the UIEvent object. This value is incremented for each complete mouse click cycle but is reset to zero if the mouse is moved, even if that happens between mousedown and mouseup.

This kind of event is a scenario where event bubbling is likely to be useful because the mouse may click on a pixel sized item which is a child of the object that is really receiving a higher level event.

See also:	*AbstractView object, Event object,* Implementation.hasFeature(), onClick, onMouseDown, onMouseMove, onMouseOut, onMouseOver, onMouseUp, *UIEvent object*

Property	JavaScript	JScript	Nav	IE	Opera	DOM	Notes
altKey	1.5 +	-	6.0 +	-	-	2 +	Warning, ReadOnly
bubbles	1.5 +	-	6.0 +	-	-	2 +	-
button	1.5 +	-	6.0 +	-	-	2 +	ReadOnly
cancelable	1.5 +	-	6.0 +	-	-	2 +	-
clientX	1.5 +	-	6.0 +	-	-	2 +	ReadOnly
clientY	1.5 +	-	6.0 +	-	-	2 +	ReadOnly
ctrlKey	1.5 +	-	6.0 +	-	-	2 +	ReadOnly
currentTarget	1.5 +	-	6.0 +	-	-	2 +	-
detail	1.5 +	-	6.0 +	-	-	2 +	-
eventPhase	1.5 +	-	6.0 +	-	-	2 +	-
metaKey	1.5 +	-	6.0 +	-	-	2 +	Warning, ReadOnly
relatedTarget	1.5 +	-	6.0 +	-	-	2 +	ReadOnly
screenX	1.5 +	-	6.0 +	-	-	2 +	ReadOnly
screenY	1.5 +	-	6.0 +	-	-	2 +	ReadOnly
shiftKey	1.5 +	-	6.0 +	-	-	2 +	ReadOnly
target	1.5 +	-	6.0 +	-	-	2 +	-
timeStamp	1.5 +	-	6.0 +	-	-	2 +	-
type	1.5 +	-	6.0 +	-	-	2 +	-
view	1.5 +	-	6.0 +	-	-	2 +	-

Method	JavaScript	JScript	Nav	IE	Opera	DOM	Notes
initEvent()	1.5 +	-	6.0 +	-	-	2 +	-
initMouseEvent()	1.5 +	-	6.0 +	-	-	2 +	-
initUIEvent()	1.5 +	-	6.0 +	-	-	2 +	-
preventDefault()	1.5 +	-	6.0 +	-	-	2 +	-
stopPropagation()	1.5 +	-	6.0 +	-	-	2 +	-

M

JavaScript Programmer's Reference

Multiply (*) (Operator/multiplicative)

Multiply one operand by another.

Availability:	ECMAScript edition – 2 JavaScript – 1.0 JScript – 1.0 Internet Explorer – 3.02 Netscape – 2.0 Netscape Enterprise Server version – 2.0 Opera – 3.0
Property/method value type:	Number primitive
JavaScript syntax:	-	anOperand1 * anOperand2
Argument list:	anOperand1	A value to be multiplied
	anOperand2	The multiplier value

The * operator performs multiplication, producing the product of its operands.

The multiplication is commutative. That means the operands being multiplied together can be arranged in any order without affecting the outcome as long as they are at the same precedence level. However, the multiplication may not always be associative in ECMAScript compliant interpreters due to finite precision in the evaluations. This means that placing parentheses around the operands may affect the outcome.

For example (A * B) * C may not evaluate identically to A * (B * C) to associative artifacts but A * B * C should be identical to B * C * A because of commutation.

The rules of floating point multiplication should be governed by the rules of IEEE 754 double-precision arithmetic.

If either operand is NaN then the result will be NaN.

The sign of the result is positive if both operands have the same sign, negative if the operands have different signs.

Multiplication of an infinite value by zero results in NaN.

Multiplication of infinity by infinity results in infinity. The sign is determined by the sign rules as normal.

Multiplying infinity by a finite non-zero value results in a signed infinity. The sign is determined as normal.

Otherwise, where neither an infinite value or NaN is involved, the product is computed and rounded to the nearest representable value. If the magnitude of the result is larger than the largest value the interpreter can cope with, an infinity of the appropriate sign is substituted. If the magnitude is too small to be represented, then a zero value is substituted.

Note that internally, zero values can be negative or positive and the sign may affect the result of subsequent computations.

The associativity is left to right.

Refer to the Operator Precedence topic for details of execution order.

See also:	Associativity, Multiplicative operator, *Multiply then assign (*=)*, Operator Precedence

Cross-references:

ECMA 262 edition 2 – section – 11.5.1

ECMA 262 edition 2 – section – 11.13

ECMA 262 edition 3 – section – 11.5.1

Multiply then assign (*=) (Operator/assignment)

Multiply two operands storing the result in the first.

Availability:	ECMAScript edition – 2 JavaScript – 1.0 JScript – 1.0 Internet Explorer – 3.02 Netscape – 2.0 Netscape Enterprise Server version – 2.0 Opera – 3.0	
Property/method value type:	Number primitive	
JavaScript syntax:	-	anOperand1 *= anOperand2
Argument list:	anOperand1	A value to be multiplied and then assigned into
	anOperand2	A multiplier value

Multiply the left operand by the right operand and assign the result to the left operand.

This is functionally equivalent to the expression:

anOperand1 = anOperand1 * anOperand2;

Although this is classified as an assignment operator it is really a compound of an assignment and a multiplicative operator.

The associativity is right to left.

Refer to the operator precedence topic for details of execution order.

The new value of *anOperand1* is returned as a result of the expression.

Warnings:

❑ The operand to the left of the operator must be an LValue. That is, it should be able to take an assignment and store the value.

See also:	*Assign value (=)*, Assignment expression, Assignment operator, Associativity, LValue, Multiplicative operator, *Multiply (*)*, Operator Precedence

Cross-references:

ECMA 262 edition 2 – section – 11.13

ECMA 262 edition 3 – section – 11.13

MutationEvent object (Object/DOM)

A notification that the document content has changed should trigger a mutation event which is described in one of these objects.

Availability:	DOM level – 2 JavaScript – 1.5 Netscape – 6.0
JavaScript syntax:	N *myMutationEvent* = new MutationEvent()
Object properties:	attrChange, attrName, bubbles, cancelable, currentTarget, eventPhase, newValue, prevValue, relatedNode, target, timeStamp, type
Class constants:	ADDITION, MODIFICATION, REMOVAL
Object methods:	initEvent(), initMutationEvent(), preventDefault(), stopPropagation()

The availability of the MutationEvent object handling can be determined with the Implementation.hasFeature() method call.

These event types are enumerated in the DOM level 2 specification and are:

- ❑ `DOMSubtreeModified`
- ❑ `DOMNodeInserted`
- ❑ `DOMNodeRemoved`
- ❑ `DOMNodeRemovedFromDocument`
- ❑ `DOMNodeInsertedIntoDocument`
- ❑ `DOMAttrModified`
- ❑ `DOMCharacterDataModified`

The DOM level 2 event module specification doesn't describe the binding of these events to event handlers so although this event model is implemented in Netscape 6.0, you may need to explore the event naming conventions to make effective use of it. Taking the event names and placing the `'on'` prefix in front of them and using that as a property name to which you can attach a handler function may work. The DOM level 2 event module also provides an `EventListener` registration which allows you to register event types with `EventTarget` objects, using the `addEventListener()` method.

The contextual information is carried in the `detail` property, and when it is present, will usually describe a reference to a node object or an attribute value.

When the document content is modified, a `MutationEvent` object is instantiated to carry a description of that change to the event handler.

Mutation events cannot be cancelled. This is because the DOM interface would become unwieldy if the document changes were not properly completed. This may change later when the DOM standard introduces transaction handling although the DOM level 2 event specification does not go to great lengths to explain in detail how that is likely to be implemented.

A cascading effect is very likely with a single DOM tree change causing a number of subsequent mutation events to be fired as lower portions of the tree are affected. The standard does not mandate any particular ordering of these events and leaves it to the implementation to control the sequence. This suggests that the cascaded mutations may occur in a different sequence depending on the browser. You should therefore design your event handler so that it can be called in a re-entrant and random order and that there should be no dependency on things being traversed in a predictable sequence.

See also:	DOM, DOM – Level 2, DOM Events, Event management, Event model, Event-driven model, EventListener object, `EventTarget.addEventListener()`, `Implementation.hasFeature()`

M

JavaScript Programmer's Reference

Property	JavaScript	JScript	N	IE	Opera	DOM	Notes
attrChange	1.5 +	-	6.0 +	-	-	2 +	ReadOnly
attrName	1.5 +	-	6.0 +	-	-	2 +	ReadOnly
bubbles	1.5 +	-	6.0 +	-	-	2 +	-
cancelable	1.5 +	-	6.0 +	-	-	2 +	-
currentTarget	1.5 +	-	6.0 +	-	-	2 +	-
eventPhase	1.5 +	-	6.0 +	-	-	2 +	-
newValue	1.5 +	-	6.0 +	-	-	2 +	ReadOnly
prevValue	1.5 +	-	6.0 +	-	-	2 +	ReadOnly
relatedNode	1.5 +	-	6.0 +	-	-	2 +	ReadOnly
target	1.5 +	-	6.0 +	-	-	2 +	-
timeStamp	1.5 +	-	6.0 +	-	-	2 +	-
type	1.5 +	-	6.0 +	-	-	2 +	-

Method	JavaScript	JScript	N	IE	Opera	DOM	Notes
initEvent()	1.5 +	-	6.0 +	-	-	2 +	-
initMutationEvent()	1.5 +	-	6.0 +	-	-	2 +	-
preventDefault()	1.5 +	-	6.0 +	-	-	2 +	-
stopPropagation()	1.5 +	-	6.0 +	-	-	2 +	-

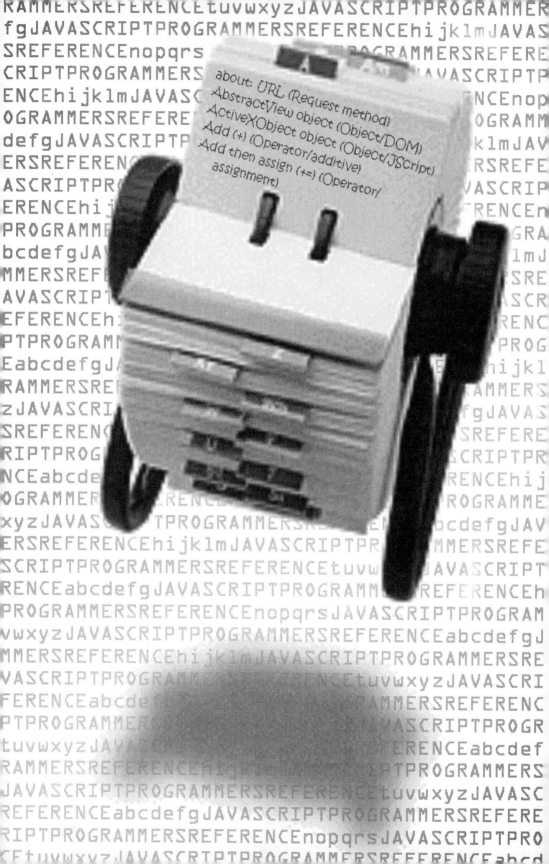

NamedNodeMap object (Object/DOM)

Where nodes have a name attribute, they can be presented as members of a NamedNodeMap collection object.

Availability:	DOM level – 1 JavaScript – 1.5 JScript – 5.0 Internet Explorer – 5.0 Netscape – 6.0
Inherits from:	*Array*
JavaScript syntax:	- *myNamedNodeMap = newNamedNodeMap()*
Object properties:	`length`
Object methods:	`getNamedItem(), item(),` `removeNamedItem(), setNamedItem()`

A `NamedNodeMap` is a collection of nodes that can be accessed by name. It does not inherit from NodeList, and DOM does not mandate any parentage. It will probably inherit from Collection or Array but this appears to be implementation dependant. A general purpose `Dictionary` class would be helpful as a starting point but these are not available in all implementations.

The nodes are not collated in any particular order and you can access them with a numeric index as well as by associative name.

This implies a namespacing issue and clearly there may be problems with your document if nodes share the same name and need to be collected into a NamedNodeList entity.

The DOM level 2 specification provides these new methods to cope with namespaces:

❑ `getNamedItemNS()`

❑ `setNamedItemNS()`

❑ `removeNamedItemNS()`

DOM 2 standardisation is not quite stable and no browsers support it yet. At this time, browsers have reached DOM level 1 capabilities and we can expect support for these namespace extensions in the next round of browser upgrades.

See also:	Collection object, DOM, DOM – Level 1, Node object, `Node.attributes[]`, NodeList object

Property	JavaScript	JScript	N	IE	Opera	DOM	Notes
length	1.5 +	5.0 +	6.0 +	5.0 +	-	1 +	-

Method	JavaScript	JScript	N	IE	Opera	DOM	Notes
getNamedItem()	1.5 +	5.0 +	6.0 +	5.0 +	-	1 +	-
item()	1.5 +	5.0 +	6.0 +	5.0 +	-	1 +	Warning
removeNamedItem()	1.5 +	5.0 +	6.0 +	5.0 +	-	1 +	-
setNamedItem()	1.5 +	5.0 +	6.0 +	5.0 +	-	1 +	-

Inheritance chain:

Array

Web-references:

http://www.w3.org/TR/REC-DOM-Level-1/level-one-core.html#ID-1074577549

NaN (Constant/static)

A literal constant whose type is a built-in primitive value.

Availability:	ECMAScript edition – 2 JavaScript – 1.3 JScript – 2.0 Internet Explorer – 4.0 Netscape – 4.06 Netscape Enterprise Server version – 2.0
Property/method value type:	Number primitive
JavaScript syntax:	- NaN

The primitive value NaN represents the IEEE 754 "Not-a-Number" value. This is returned when the result of an evaluation is known to yield a numeric value but its magnitude and sign is uncertain. Because the value is numeric but uncertain, you cannot compare NaN with anything else (including itself). However you can test for its existence with the isNaN() function.

In IEEE 754, there are many millions of possible values for NaN. In ECMA compliant JavaScript interpreters, they are all collected together and referred to as a single value. This means you cannot distinguish the reason for the NaN error as you may be able to in other languages that use IEEE 754 arithmetic.

It is possible in the hosting environment to provide additional facilities to determine what sort of NaN values you have. This is implementation dependant however and not part of the standard.

If you are in an environment that does not have the NaN value implemented, then you may be able to create one yourself like this:

```
var NaN = 0/0;
```

The value has existed since JavaScript 1.1 but it was given a property name in JavaScript 1.3. Therefore from a scripting point of view, its availability is defined as JavaScript 1.3 and not 1.1.

Warnings:

❑ Be careful not to assign your own values to this variable. You can corrupt it in some implementations. In MSIE version 5 for Macintosh, assigning a value to the global NaN value changes its setting but leaves Number.NaN unaffected. You cannot modify Number.NaN.

❑ Version 3.02 of MSIE with JScript version 1.0 silently converts NaN values to zero. It does not know what NaN is.

❑ Netscape 2.02 cannot tell the difference between null and undefined.

❑ This constant is available as a property of the global object in MSIE version 4 but not in Netscape 4.

See also:	Arithmetic constant, Exception, *Global object*, Global special variable, *IEEE 754*, *Infinity*, *isNaN()*, Not a Number, *null*, *Number*, *Number.NaN*, Range error, Special number values, Value property

Property attributes:

DontEnum.

Cross-references:

ECMA 262 edition 2 – section – 4.3.23

ECMA 262 edition 2 – section – 15.1.1.1

ECMA 262 edition 3 – section – 4.3.23

ECMA 262 edition 3 – section – 15.1.1.1

Wrox *Instant JavaScript* – page – 14

N

JavaScript Programmer's Reference

Navigator object (Object/browser)

An object that contains properties that describe the browser (aka User Agent or client).

Availability:	JavaScript – 1.0 JScript – 1.0 Internet Explorer – 3.02 Netscape – 2.0 Opera – 3.0

JavaScript syntax:	-	`myWindow.navigator`
	-	`navigator`

Object properties:	`appCodeName, appMinorVersion, appName,`
	`appVersion, browserLanguage, constructor,`
	`cookieEnabled, cpuClass, language,`
	`onLine, opsProfile, platform,`
	`securityPolicy, systemLanguage,`
	`userAgent, userLanguage, userProfile`

Object methods:	`javaEnabled(), plugins, preference(),` `savePreferences(), taintEnabled()`
Collections:	`mimeTypes[], plugins[]`

The `navigator` object is named after Netscape Navigator but is also present in other browsers since it has become the de facto standard way of enquiring as to a browser's provenance.

You can inspect the various properties belonging to the `navigator` object and establish the name and type of the browser, its version and the platform it is running on.

The `navigator` object is available as a property of the `window` and also the `global` object but it will be the same `navigator` object. There is only one and you cannot instantiate another.

As this object is persistent, you might add properties to it that can be passed from window to window. However this will only work on Netscape, because MSIE seems to initialize a new `navigator` object for each window. MSIE does allow you to add properties to `navigator` object but they are private to that window. Netscape shares them across windows. The example shows how to make this work.

You can accomplish the same thing in a cross-browser portable manner by using a frameset and storing properties in the top level frameset's `global` object. You can also (if security allows) write scripts to communicate between windows, in which case you may need to make sure the scripts are aware of multiple `document` objects as well as windows. This can get tricky and you may need to make sure the scripts run in the correct windows and return a value to a caller. This should ensure they run in the correct scope.

Netscape 6.0 provides a sidebar which you should expect to be persistent. There's a similar sidebar in MSIE too. Netscape clearly intends you to script its sidebar but right now the implementation is a bit buggy. It might be too much to hope for, but digging into the internals of these suggests that RDF is involved that may point to some commonality. Maybe we will be able to use the sidebar in the browsers as a repository for session storage, or persistent values that we can access from script, but it's not there and working yet.

Warnings:

❏ You cannot enumerate the properties of the `navigator` (clientInformation) object in MSIE version 4.5 for Macintosh. This may apply to other platform implementations of MSIE version 4.5 as well.

❏ The `navigator` object is much better supported in version 5.0 of MSIE for Macintosh, which was released in the Spring of 2000.

❏ The below example was found not to work on Netscape 6, due to bugs.

Example code:

```
<!-- Save this in navigator.html -->
<HTML>
<HEAD></HEAD>
<BODY>
<SCRIPT>
navigator.myNewProperty = "session global value";
open("navigator1.html")
</SCRIPT>
</BODY>
</HTML>
-----------------------------------------------------------------
<!-- Save this in  navigator1.html -->
<HTML>
<HEAD></HEAD>
<BODY>
<SCRIPT>
document.write(navigator.myNewProperty);
</SCRIPT>
</BODY>
</HTML>
```

See also:	Cross platform compatibility, `Window.navigator`

Property	JavaScript	JScript	N	IE	Opera	HTML	Notes
appCodeName	1.0 +	1.0 +	2.0 +	3.02 +	3.0 +	-	ReadOnly
appMinorVersion	-	3.0 +	-	4.0 +	-	-	Warning, ReadOnly
appName	1.0 +	1.0 +	2.0 +	3.02 +	3.0 +	-	ReadOnly

Table continued on following page

Property	JavaScript	JScript	N	IE	Opera	HTML	Notes
appVersion	1.0 +	1.0 +	2.0 +	3.02 +	3.0 +	-	ReadOnly
browserLanguage	-	3.0 +	-	4.0 +	-	-	Warning, ReadOnly
constructor	1.2 +	-	4.0 +	-	-	-	Warning
cookieEnabled	1.5 +	3.0 +	6.0 +	4.0 +	-	-	ReadOnly
cpuClass	-	3.0 +	-	4.0 +	-	-	ReadOnly
language	1.2 +	-	4.0 +	-	5.0 +	-	Warning, ReadOnly
onLine	-	3.0 +	-	4.0 +	-	-	ReadOnly
opsProfile	-	5.0 +	-	5.0 +	-	-	Warning, ReadOnly
platform	1.2 +	3.0 +	4.0 +	4.0 +	5.0 +	-	ReadOnly
securityPolicy	1.4 +	-	4.7 +	-	-	-	Warning, ReadOnly
systemLanguage	-	3.0 +	-	4.0 +	-	-	Warning, ReadOnly
userAgent	1.0 +	1.0 +	2.0 +	3.02 +	3.0 +	-	Warning, ReadOnly
userLanguage	-	3.0 +	-	4.0 +	-	-	Warning, ReadOnly
userProfile	-	3.0 +	-	4.0 +	-	-	ReadOnly

Method	JavaScript	JScript	N	IE	Opera	HTML	Notes
javaEnabled()	1.1 +	3.0 +	3.0 +	4.0 +	3.0 +	-	-
plugins	1.0 +	1.0 +	2.0 +	3.02 +	3.0 +	-	Warning
preference()	1.2 +	3.0 +	4.0 +	4.0 +	-	-	Warning
savePreferences()	1.2 +	-	4.0 +	-	-	-	Warning
taintEnabled()	1.1 +	3.0 +	3.0 +	4.0 +	5.0 +	-	Warning, Deprecated

Negation operator (-) (Operator/unary)

Negate an operand's value.

Availability:	ECMAScript edition – 2 JavaScript – 1.0 JScript – 1.0 Internet Explorer – 3.02 Netscape – 2.0 Netscape Enterprise Server – 2.0 Opera – 3.0
Property/method value type:	Number primitive
JavaScript syntax:	- -anOperand
Argument list:	anOperand A numeric value that can be negated

The operand is evaluated and converted to a numeric value. The result is negated.

A positive value becomes negative and a negative value becomes positive.

This is functionally equivalent to:

```
anOperand *= -1
```

...which is equivalent to:

```
anOperand = anOperand * -1
```

...and also:

```
anOperand = 0 - anOperand
```

Although this is classified as a unary operator, its functionality is really that of an additive operator.

The associativity is from right to left.

Refer to the operator precedence topic for details of execution order.

See also:	*Add (+)*, Additive expression, Additive operator, Associativity, *Decrement value (--)*, Operator Precedence, *Subtract (-)*, Unary operator

Cross-references:

ECMA 262 edition 2 – section – 11.4.7

ECMA 262 edition 3 – section – 11.4.7

nethelp: URL (Request method)

A special URL access mode for Netscape help screens.

Availability:	JavaScript – 1.2 Netscape – 4.0

This is a special request method provided by the Netscape browser to gain access to local client-side help resources. The resources are loaded from files that live in a help folder within the folder containing the browser application. You can access the files with a text editor and study how they work. They are just plain HTML and JavaScript, however they provide a quite helpful embedded help system. In a large enterprise where you control the deployment of the browsers, you may want to augment the browser help with some internal help pages. You might want to add details of your help desk and how to contact them for instance.

N

JavaScript Programmer's Reference

These special URLs are not present in MSIE although there will be some internal resources in that browser which may provide customization opportunities in a similar way. Indeed, Microsoft provide an administrator kit which you can use to customize the browser installation.

You may also be able to obtain admin tools from Netscape and Microsoft to carry out legitimate customizations on the browsers before deploying them throughout your organization.

This can be called from JavaScript by setting the `location.href` of a window to a valid `nethelp: location`.

Here are some examples:

URL	Description
nethelp:netscape/home:start_here	Front page of the help system
nethelp:netscape/collabra:HELP_SEC_CERTS_CRYPTOMODS	Security help
nethelp:netscape/collabra:HELP_SEC_CERTS_ISSUERS	Security help
nethelp:netscape/collabra:HELP_SEC_INFO	Security help
nethelp:netscape/collabra:HELP_SEC_PASS_UNSET	Security help
nethelp:netscape/collabra:HELP_SEC_PREFS_APPLET	Security help
nethelp:netscape/collabra:HELP_SEC_PREFS_MESSENGER	Security help
nethelp:netscape/collabra:HELP_SEC_PREFS_NAVIGATOR	Security help

Mostly, these special URLs will be useful for debugging. Getting details of the disk cache for example may be useful. Pulling up the JavaScript debugger page if you detect an error in your script might also be a cool trick.

This appears to have changed somewhat in Netscape 6.0 which is likely to provide a whole range of new possibilities. Once the browser is fully debugged and working we can spend many happy hours inspecting it to discover them.

Warnings:

❑ This is not present in MSIE at all. It displays help using a completely different mechanism altogether.

See also: *about: URL, javascript: URL, mailbox: URL,* `mailto:` URL, URL

Cross-references:

Wrox *Professional JavaScript* – page – 359

Netscape Navigator (Web browser)

One of the two major web browser platforms.

Netscape have made the source of the Communicator product available (which includes the Navigator browser). You can download this from the Netscape web site and participate in the development of the browser project. Netscape 6.0 is only just released for public use but is likely to contain some bugs.

We refer to this browser consistently as Netscape regardless of whether you are running Communicator or any other packaged version.

Here is a brief guide to versions of Netscape vs. JavaScript:

Netscape	JavaScript
2.0	JavaScript 1.0
3.0	JavaScript 1.1
4.0 to 4.05	JavaScript 1.2
4.06 to 4.75	JavaScript 1.3
5.0	JavaScript 1.4
6.0	JavaScript 1.5

Note that version 5.0 never shipped although if you search on the web you can find some installable binaries which may satisfy your curiosity regarding browser history. Some reports suggest that those version 5.0 browsers only supported JavaScript 1.3. Because Mozilla is factored into components, it's feasible that you could build any version of the browser with whatever version of JavaScript you want.

Many values that Netscape exposes as JavaScript properties reflect the value of an HTML tag attribute. Likewise, many of its special objects are counterparts to the HTML tags. However it does not map objects so completely or consistently to HTML tags as the MSIE browser. Nor does it support the attributes and style mechanisms as elegantly.

Where the information is available, we have indicated the version number of JavaScript (or JScript) when HTML tags and attributes became accessible as objects or properties. In many cases, this may be a later version than when the instantiating HTML tag or attribute was first supported by the browser.

We constructed many scripts to inspect and enumerate the various properties of the objects in the MSIE and Netscape browsers. These uncovered many object types and properties that were hitherto undocumented. They might have been available in earlier versions of the browser. However, where language elements were discovered for the first time, they are initially documented as being available from version 4 of Netscape . A limited amount of further testing was applied where it was suspected that language elements may have been available in earlier releases and the availability modified accordingly.

N

JavaScript Programmer's Reference

607

Version 5 of Netscape was scrapped because its codebase became too unwieldy to work with. There seems little point in documenting its peculiarities. Netscape version 6.0 was in beta trials and until PR3 was so unstable and crash prone that most of our testing bore little fruit. Right at the point where content was being finalized for publication Netscape 6.0 was released as a final product. It is clearly still a work in progress and there are quite a few non-working components. It looks good though. The potential for exercising the DOM standard document navigation is really exciting. There is a great deal yet to discover about the new browser and it will stabilize as bugs get fixed and new releases are shipped.

Perhaps browser versions may become less important as they converge on a single standard benchmark of functionality. For the time being, current practice suggests that version 4 browsers of both traditions are rapidly being taken over by version 5 MSIE browsers. Versions 2 and 3 of MSIE and Netscape have declined to such small usage levels as to not require any further serious attempts to support them on new projects. Netscape 6.0 may win back some market share but only if its bugs are fixed quickly. Version 6.0 of MSIE is about to go to beta testers and the standards bodies are still some way ahead of the browser manufacturers so there is a long way to go yet.

Warnings:

❑   Netscape 2.02 does not cope gracefully with dollar signs in identifier names.

See also:	Identifier, Platform, Script execution, Undocumented features, Web browser

Cross-references:

Wrox *Instant JavaScript* – page – 14

Web-references:

http://www.mozilla.org/ http://www.netscape.com/
http://home.netscape.com/browsers/6/index.html

netscape.applet (Java package)

The root node of the Java hierarchy where the applets are built. A shortcut to the `Packages.netscape.applet` package.

Availability:	JavaScript – 1.1 Netscape – 3.0

This property returns a Java package that is encapsulated inside a JavaScript object belonging to the `JavaPackage` class.

You need to know quite a lot about the underlying Java objects to make use of this because the properties and methods it supports are not exposed in an enumerable fashion. This means you would have difficulty in writing a JavaScript inspector to examine these objects.

See also:	*JavaPackage object*

netscape.javascript.JSObject (Java class)

The full definition of the JSObject class for encapsulating JavaScript objects in Java. A shortcut to the `Packages.netscape.javascript.JSObject` class.

Availability:	JavaScript – 1.1 Netscape – 3.0
Class methods:	`getWindow()`

Values of this type are visible to JavaScript as the encapsulated object that was originally passed to Java. Effectively, the wrapper is removed.

Note that you cannot use this as a constructor. There wouldn't be any point anyway because you can create JavaScript objects within the JavaScript environment; there is no need to go through the Java bridge to accomplish that.

See also:	Java calling JavaScript, Java to JavaScript values, JavaScript to Java values, *JSObject object*

netscape.lck (Java package)

A configuration file as used in older versions of Netscape . Not to be confused with `Packages.netscape`.

Availability:	JavaScript – 1.1 Netscape – 3.0

This is provided as support for preference management in older versions of Netscape .

See also:	Preferences

Cross-references:

Wrox *Instant JavaScript* – page – 59

N

JavaScript Programmer's Reference

netscape.security.PrivilegeManager (Java class)

Part of the Netscape security model implemented with Java.

Availability:	JavaScript – 1.1 Netscape – 3.0
Class properties:	EQUAL, NO_SUBSET, PROPER_SUBSET, SIGNED_APPLET_DBNAME, TEMP_FILENAME, theDebugLevel
Class methods:	checkPrivilegeEnabled(), checkPrivilegeGranted(), disablePrivilege(), enablePrivilege(), enableTarget(), getMyPrincipals(), getPrivilegeManager(), getSystemPrincipal(), revertPrivilege()
Object methods:	disablePrivilege(), enablePrivilege(), getPrivilegeTableFromStack()

Because the Netscape security model is based on the Java security model, the Netscape browser requests its privileges through the Java mechanisms. These are encapsulated in a class that you can access from inside JavaScript.

The downside of this is that there is no meaningful value returned when the request is made. If the request for a privilege is denied, the error causes a Java exception, which is difficult to trap from JavaScript. It is possible that more recent browser versions will support an exception handling mechanism.

See also:	*PrivilegeManager object, Requesting privileges, UniversalBrowserAccess, UniversalBrowserRead, UniversalBrowserWrite, UniversalFileRead, UniversalPreferencesRead, UniversalPreferencesWrite, UniversalSendMail*

Method	JavaScript	JScript	N	IE	Opera	Notes
disablePrivilege()	1.1 +	-	3.0 +	-	-	-
enablePrivilege()	1.1 +	-	3.0 +	-	-	-
getPrivilege TableFromStack()	1.1 +	-	3.0 +	-	-	-

new (Operator/unary)

An object construction operator.

Availability:	ECMAScript edition – 2 JavaScript – 1.0 JScript – 1.0 Internet Explorer – 3.02 Netscape – 2.0 Netscape Enterprise Server – 2.0 Opera – 3.0	
Property/method value type:	An object whose type depends on the constructor	
JavaScript syntax:	-	`myObject = new aConstructor`
	-	`myObject = new anObject (someArguments)`
Argument list:	`aConstructor`	An object constructor function
	`anObject`	An object to clone
	`someArguments`	A collection of initial values for the new instance

The new operator creates a new instance of the object it is operating on.

As the object is created, the receiver's Construct method is called with no arguments passed to it. Any initialization is only carried out by the Construct method.

The associativity is from right to left.

Refer to the operator precedence topic for details of execution order.

Typically this would be used to instantiate core objects of the following types:

❑ Array

❑ Boolean

❑ Date

❑ Function

❑ Number

❑ Object

❑ RegExp

❑ String

This can also be used to instantiate some host objects.

N

See also:	Array(), Associativity, Boolean(), Date(), Function(), Left-Hand-Side expression, List type, Number(), Object(), Operator Precedence, RegExp(), String()

Cross-references:

ECMA 262 edition 2 – section – 11.2.2

ECMA 262 edition 2 – section – 11.2.4

ECMA 262 edition 2 – section – 15

ECMA 262 edition 3 – section – 11.2.2

Wrox *Instant JavaScript* – page – 15

Wrox *Instant JavaScript* – page – 21

Newline (Escape sequence)

A means of introducing line breaks into string content texts.

Availability:	ECMAScript edition – 2

The newline escape sequence \n can be placed in string literals if you want to break the output text over more than one line.

Warnings:

❑ Do not use a line terminator even with a backslash to escape it. In other words, don't think that placing a backslash as the last character of a line will hide the line terminator. While that may work in other languages, it won't work in JavaScript.

See also:	Escape sequence (\), Line terminator

Cross-references:

ECMA 262 edition 2 – section – 7.2

ECMA 262 edition 2 – section – 7.7.4

ECMA 262 edition 3 – section – 7.3

Newlines are not <BR> tags (Pitfall)

Newline in a script does not display a line break in HTML output.

Because HTML is fairly freely formatted, you have to explicitly tell it when a line break is to appear. You can do this with a variety of block-level tags. It's most likely done with a <BR> or <P> tag.

When you use the document.write() method, you need to explicitly include the necessary <BR> or <P> tags otherwise the HTML output that gets displayed will all run onto a single line. Placing a \n Newline escape into the output may make the HTML source look nice but it won't affect the displayed output.

A line break is also introduced when you use block structured elements in the HTML. Here is a list of common HTML tags that do this (there are others too):

- <BLOCKQUOTE>
- <BODY>
-
- <DD>
- <DL>
- <DIV>
- <DT>
- <H1> etc
- <HR>
- <HTML>
- <LI>
- <OBJECT>
- <OL>
- <P>
- <PRE>
- <UL>

See also:	Pitfalls

Cross-references:

Wrox *Instant JavaScript* – page – 46

news: URL (Request method)

A request from a web browser to a news server to send a document.

Use the browser to download and browse some news content.

Warnings:

❑ This is only allowed under script control if the script has the UniversalSendMail privilege.

See also:	*javascript: URL, UniversalSendMail*, URL

Node object (Object/DOM)

A node is the primary component from which documents are built (in the context of a DOM hierarchy).

Availability:	DOM level – 1 JavaScript – 1.5 JScript – 5.0 Internet Explorer – 5.0 Netscape – 6.0
JavaScript syntax:	- `myNode = myMutationEvent.relatedNode`

Object properties:	`firstChild, lastChild, nextSibling,`
	`nodeName, nodeType, nodeValue,`
	`ownerDocument, parentNode,`
	`previousSibling`

Class constants:	`ATTRIBUTE_NODE, CDATA_SECTION_NODE,`
	`COMMENT_NODE, DOCUMENT_FRAGMENT_NODE,`
	`DOCUMENT_NODE, DOCUMENT_TYPE_NODE,`
	`ELEMENT_NODE, ENTITY_NODE,`
	`ENTITY_REFERENCE_NODE, NOTATION_NODE,`
	`PROCESSING_INSTRUCTION_NODE, TEXT_NODE`

Object methods:	`appendChild(), cloneNode(),`
	`hasChildNodes(), insertBefore(),`
	`removeChild(), replaceChild()`

Collections:	`attributes[], childNodes[]`

Here is a list of the available node types:

Constant	Type	Description
undefined	null	A member of the attributes collection
ELEMENT_NODE	1	HTML element object node
ATTRIBUTE_NODE	2	HTML tag attribute object
TEXT_NODE	3	Text object node
CDATA_SECTION_NODE	4	CDATA section
ENTITY_REFERENCE_NODE	5	Entity reference
ENTITY_NODE	6	Entity node
PROCESSING_INSTRUCTION_NODE	7	Processing instruction node
COMMENT_NODE	8	Comment node
DOCUMENT_NODE	9	Document object
DOCUMENT_TYPE_NODE	10	Doctype object
DOCUMENT_FRAGMENT_NODE	11	Document fragment node
NOTATION_NODE	12	Notation node

The DOM level 2 specification adds the following methods:

❑ supports()

❑ normalize()

It also adds the following properties:

❑ namespaceURI

❑ prefix

❑ localName

At DOM level 3, the interface to the Node object is expected to evolve further to allow nodes to be compared and to be able to extract a serialized version of a DOM tree branch into a string primitive. This functionality is still under review as this is being written. The following additional properties are expected to be supported:

❑ baseURI

❑ textContent

❑ key

N

DOM level 3 is expected to add the following methods to the `Node` object:

- ❑ `compareDocumentOrder()`
- ❑ `compareTreePosition()`
- ❑ `isSameNode()`
- ❑ `lookupNamespacePrefix()`
- ❑ `lookupNamespaceURI`
- ❑ `normalizeNS()`
- ❑ `setUserData()`
- ❑ `getUserData()`

If the implementation supports the DOM level 2 event model (this is the case with Netscape 6.0), then the `Node` object should also support the methods and properties defined by the EventTarget object.

See also:	`Attribute.nodeType`, *Document object*, *DocumentFragment object*, *Element object*, *EventTarget object*, `MutationEvent.initMutationEvent()`, `MutationEvent.relatedNode`, *NamedNodeMap object*, `Node.firstChild`, `Node.insertBefore()`, `Node.lastChild`, `Node.nextSibling`, `Node.parentNode`, `Node.previousSibling`

Property	JavaScript	JScript	N	IE	Opera	DOM	Notes
firstChild	1.5 +	5.0 +	6.0 +	5.0 +	-	1 +	-
lastChild	1.5 +	5.0 +	6.0 +	5.0 +	-	1 +	-
nextSibling	1.5 +	5.0 +	6.0 +	5.0 +	-	1 +	-
nodeName	1.5 +	5.0 +	6.0 +	5.0 +	-	1 +	-
nodeType	1.5 +	5.0 +	6.0 +	5.0 +	-	1 +	-
nodeValue	1.5 +	5.0 +	6.0 +	5.0 +	-	1 +	-
ownerDocument	1.5 +	5.0 +	6.0 +	5.0 +	-	1 +	-
parentNode	1.5 +	5.0 +	6.0 +	5.0 +	-	1 +	-
previousSibling	1.5 +	5.0 +	6.0 +	5.0 +	-	1 +	-

Method	JavaScript	JScript	N	IE	Opera	DOM	Notes
appendChild()	1.5 +	5.0 +	6.0 +	5.0 +	-	1 +	-
cloneNode()	1.5 +	5.0 +	6.0 +	5.0 +	-	1 +	-
hasChildNodes()	1.5 +	5.0 +	6.0 +	5.0 +	-	1 +	-
insertBefore()	1.5 +	5.0 +	6.0 +	5.0 +	-	1 +	-
removeChild()	1.5 +	5.0 +	6.0 +	5.0 +	-	1 +	-
replaceChild()	1.5 +	5.0 +	6.0 +	5.0 +	-	1 +	-

NodeList object (Object/DOM)

A generic collection of nodes, not presented in any particular order.

Availability:	DOM level – 1 JavaScript – 1.5 JScript – 5.0 Internet Explorer – 5.0 Netscape – 6.0	
JavaScript syntax:	-	*myNodeList = myDocument.* *getElementsByTagName(aTagName)*
Argument list:	*aTagName*	The name of an HTML tag
Object properties:	length	
Object methods:	item()	

This object is based on an `Array` object and contains a set of `Node` items contained within a DOM hierarchy.

Do not confuse DOM `NodeList` arrays with `Enumerator` or `Collection` objects. The `NodeListitem()` method is subtly different to the `Enumerator.Item()` method.

See also:	*Collection object,* `Document.getElementsByTagName()`, `Element.getElementsByTagName()`, *Enumerator* *object, NamedNodeMap object,* `Node.childNodes[]`

Property	JavaScript	JScript	N	IE	Opera	DOM	Notes
length	1.5 +	5.0 +	6.0 +	5.0 +	3.0 +	1 +	ReadOnly.

Method	JavaScript	JScript	N	IE	Opera	DOM	Notes
item()	1.5 +	5.0 +	6.0 +	5.0 +	-	1 +	-

NOFRAMES object (Object/HTML)

An object that represents the content of a <NOFRAMES> tag.

Availability:	JScript – 3.0 Internet Explorer – 4.0
Inherits from:	*Element object*

N

JavaScript Programmer's Reference

JavaScript syntax:	IE	`myNOFRAMES = myDocument.all.anElementID`
	IE	`myNOFRAMES = myDocument.all.tags ("NOFRAMES")[anIndex]`
	IE	`myNOFRAMES = myDocument.all[aName]`
	-	`myNOFRAMES = myDocument.getElementById (anElementID)`
	-	`myNOFRAMES = myDocument.getElementsByName (aName)[anIndex]`
	-	`myNOFRAMES = myDocument .getElementsByTagName("NOFRAMES") [anIndex]`

HTML syntax:	`<NOFRAMES>...</NOFRAMES>`	
Argument list:	`anIndex`	A reference to an element in a collection
	`aName`	An associative array reference
	`anElementID`	The ID value of an Element object
Object properties:	`accessKey, tabIndex, dir`	
Event handlers:	`onClick, onDblClick, onHelp, onKeyDown, onKeyPress, onKeyUp, onMouseDown, onMouseMove, onMouseOut, onMouseOver, onMouseUp`	

This was added to the MSIE browser at revision 4. It is a sub-class of the basic `Element` object and therefore shares many properties with other objects in the MSIE browser. Although it is implemented as an Element, it is not a DOM specified item.

See also:	*Element object, NOSCRIPT object*

Property	JavaScript	JScript	N	IE	Opera	DOM	HTML	Notes
accessKey	-	3.0 +	-	4.0 +	-	-	-	-
tabIndex	-	3.0 +	-	4.0 +	-	-	-	-
dir	-	5.0 +	-	5.0 +	-	-	-	-

Event name	JavaScript	JScript	N	IE	Opera	DOM	HTML	Notes
onClick	-	3.0 +	-	4.0 +	-	-	4.0 +	Warning
onDblClick	-	3.0 +	—	4.0 +	-	-	4.0 +	Warning
onHelp	-	3.0 +	-	4.0 +	-	-	-	Warning
onKeyDown	-	3.0 +	—	4.0 +	-	-	4.0 +	Warning
onKeyPress	-	3.0 +	—	4.0 +	-	-	4.0 +	Warning
onKeyUp	-	3.0 +	—	4.0 +	-	-	4.0 +	Warning
onMouseDown	-	3.0 +	—	4.0 +	-	-	4.0 +	Warning
onMouseMove	-	3.0 +	-	4.0 +	-	-	4.0 +	Warning
onMouseOut	-	3.0 +	—	4.0 +	-	-	4.0 +	Warning
onMouseOver	-	3.0 +	-	4.0 +	-	-	4.0 +	Warning
onMouseUp	—	3.0 +	-	4.0 +	-	-	4.0 +	Warning

Inheritance chain:

Element object, Node object

<NOSCRIPT> (HTML Tag)

A special tag that allows browsers that don't support scripting to display alternative content.

Availability:	JavaScript – 1.1
	JScript – 3.0
	Internet Explorer – 4.0
	Netscape – 3.0

Browsers that support the <SCRIPT> tag, should also support the <NOSCRIPT> tag. However, their support for the <NOSCRIPT> tag should be to hide or ignore anything between the <NOSCRIPT> tag and its corresponding </NOSCRIPT> closure.

Warnings:

❑ This is not supported by Netscape 2.

See also:	*<SCRIPT>*, Compatibility

NOSCRIPT object (Object/HTML)

An object representing the <NOSCRIPT> tag.

Availability:	JScript – 3.0
	Internet Explorer – 4.0
Inherits from:	*Element object*
JavaScript syntax:	IE `myNOSCRIPT = myDocument.all.anElementID`
	IE `myNOSCRIPT = myDocument.all.tags` `("NOSCRIPT")[anIndex]`
	IE `myNOSCRIPT = myDocument.all[aName]`
	- `myNOSCRIPT = myDocument.getElementById` `(anElementID)`
	- `myNOSCRIPT = myDocument.getElementsByName` `(aName)[anIndex]`

	- `myNOSCRIPT =`
	`myDocument.getElementsByTagName`
	`("NOSCRIPT")[anIndex]`

HTML syntax:	`<NOSCRIPT> ... </NOSCRIPT>`

N

JavaScript Programmer's Reference

Argument list:	anIndex	A reference to an element in a collection
	aName	An associative array reference
	anElementID	The ID value of an Element object
Object properties:	accessKey, tabIndex, dir	
Event handlers:	onClick, onDblClick, onHelp, onKeyDown, onKeyPress, onKeyUp, onMouseDown, onMouseMove, onMouseOut, onMouseOver, onMouseUp	

This was added to the MSIE browser at revision 4. It is a sub-class of the basic Element object and therefore shares many properties with other objects in the MSIE browser. Although it is implemented as an Element, it is not a DOM specified item.

See also:	Element object, NOFRAMES object

Property	JavaScript	JScript	N	IE	Opera	DOM	HTML	Notes
accessKey	-	3.0 +	-	4.0 +	-	-	-	-
tabIndex	-	3.0 +	-	4.0 +	-	-	-	-
dir	-	5.0 +	-	5.0 +	-	-	-	-

Event name	JavaScript	JScript	N	IE	Opera	DOM	HTML	Notes
onClick	-	3.0 +	-	4.0 +	-	-	4.0 +	Warning
onDblClick	-	3.0 +	-	4.0 +	-	-	4.0 +	Warning
onHelp	-	3.0 +	-	4.0 +	-	-	-	Warning
onKeyDown	-	3.0 +	-	4.0 +	-	-	4.0 +	Warning
onKeyPress	-	3.0 +	-	4.0 +	-	-	4.0 +	Warning
onKeyUp	-	3.0 +	-	4.0 +	-	-	4.0 +	Warning
onMouseDown	-	3.0 +	-	4.0 +	-	-	4.0 +	Warning
onMouseMove	-	3.0 +	-	4.0 +	-	-	4.0 +	Warning
onMouseOut	-	3.0 +	-	4.0 +	-	-	4.0 +	Warning
onMouseOver	-	3.0 +	-	4.0 +	-	-	4.0 +	Warning
onMouseUp	-	3.0 +	-	4.0 +	-	-	4.0 +	Warning

Inheritance chain:

Element object, Node object

NOT Equal to (!=) (Operator/equality)

Compare two operands for inequality.

Availability:	ECMAScript edition – 2 JavaScript – 1.0 JScript – 1.0 Internet Explorer – 3.02 Netscape – 2.0 Netscape Enterprise Server – 2.0 Opera – 3.0	
Property/method value type:	Boolean primitive	
JavaScript syntax:	-	*anOperand1* != *anOperand2*
Argument list:	*anOperand1*	A value to be compared
	anOperand2	Another value to be compared

The two operands are compared, and the Boolean `true` value is returned if they are not equal, otherwise `false` if they are equal. Note that JavaScript will attempt to convert both operands to the same type for comparison.

When testing for inequality, the following rule is invariant:

```
A != B
```

is equivalent to:

```
!(A == B)
```

Also, the rule of positioning allows that:

```
A == B
```

is identical to:

```
B == A
```

(Apart from the fact that exchanging the operands in this way alters the order in which they are evaluated.)

Exchanging the operands may have undesirable side effects if they are expressions. For example, they may call functions and test the results. If the functions are not totally independent of one another, you may get unexpected results.

The associativity is from left to right.

Refer to the operator precedence topic for details of execution order.

N

JavaScript Programmer's Reference

Refer to the Equality expression topic for a discussion on the ECMA standard definition of the equality testing rules.

The truth table shows the result of this operator for a Boolean primitive value:

A	NOT
false	true
true	false

See also:	ASCII, Associativity, *Equal to (==)*, Equality expression, Equality operator, *Greater than (>)*, *Greater than or equal to (>=)*, *Identically equal to (===)*, *Less than (<)*, *Less than or equal to (<=)*, Logical expression, *Logical NOT – complement (!)*, Logical operator, *NOT Identically equal to (!==)*, Operator Precedence, *Relational expression*, *Relational operator, typeof, Unicode*

Cross-references:

ECMA 262 edition 2 – section – 11.9.2

ECMA 262 edition 2 – section – 11.9.3

ECMA 262 edition 3 – section – 11.9.2

ECMA 262 edition 3 – section – 11.9.3

NOT Identically equal to (!==) (Operator/identity)

Compare two values for non-equality and identical type.

Availability:	ECMAScript edition – 3 JavaScript – 1.3 JScript – 1.0 Internet Explorer – 3.02 Netscape – 4.06	
Property/method value type:	Boolean primitive	
JavaScript syntax:	-	anOperand1 !== anOperand2
Argument list:	anOperand1	A value to be compared
	anOperand2	Another value of the same type to be compared

The two operands are compared and Boolean `false` is returned if both values are equal, and of the same type, otherwise Boolean `true` is returned.

The associativity is from left to right.

Refer to the operator precedence topic for details of execution order.

Warnings:

❑ This is not available for use server-side with Netscape Enterprise Server 3.

Example code:

```
<HTML>
<HEAD></HEAD>
<BODY>
<SCRIPT>
myObject1 = 100;
myObject2 = "100";
if(myObject1 != myObject2)
{
document.write("Objects are NOT equal<BR>");
}
else
{
document.write("Objects are equal<BR>");
}
if(myObject1 !== myObject2)
{
document.write("Objects are NOT identical<BR>");
}
else
{
document.write("Objects are identical<BR>");
}
</SCRIPT>
</BODY>
</HTML>
```

See also: *ASCII*, Associativity, *Equal to (==)*, Equality expression, Equality operator, *Greater than (>)*, *Greater than or equal to (>=)*, *Identically equal to (===)*, Identity operator, JellyScript, *Less than (<)*, *Less than or equal to (<=)*, Logical expression, Logical operator, *NOT Equal to (!=)*, Operator Precedence, *Relational expression, Relational operator, typeof, Unicode*

Cross-references:

ECMA 262 edition 3 – section – 11.9.5

Wrox *Instant JavaScript* – page – 39

N

JavaScript Programmer's Reference

623

Notation object (Object/DOM)

Notations are decalred in the DTD and are encapsulated in these `Notation` objects.

Availability:	DOM level – 1 JavaScript – 1.5 JScript – 5.0 Internet Explorer – 5.0 Netscape – 6.0
Inherits from:	*Node object*
JavaScript syntax:	- *myNotation = new Notation()*
Object properties:	`publicId, systemId`
See also:	*Doctype object*, `Doctype.notations[]`

Property	JavaScript	JScript	N	IE	Opera	DOM	Notes
`publicId`	1.5 +	5.0 +	6.0 +	5.0 +	-	1 +	ReadOnly
`systemId`	1.5 +	5.0 +	6.0 +	5.0 +	-	1 +	ReadOnly

Inheritance chain:

Node object

null (Primitive value)

A built-in primitive value.

Availability:	ECMAScript edition – 2 JScript – 5.0 Internet Explorer – 5.0
Property/method value type:	`Null primitive`
JavaScript syntax:	IE `null`

The `null` value is a primitive value that represents the `null`, empty or non-existent reference.

This is equivalent to the Java `null` data type when passing values back and forth between JavaScript and Java.

If you don't have a null keyword, you may be able to simulate a null value like this:

```
var null = (void 0);
```

The null and undefined values are subtly different. An empty thing is not the same as a non-existent thing. However in a browser it is difficult to distinguish between them.

The null value is now provided in some browsers as a built-in keyword, but the undefined value is not.

See also:	Cast operator, JavaScript to Java values, LiveConnect, *NaN*, *undefined*

Cross-references:

ECMA 262 edition 2 – section – 4.3.11

ECMA 262 edition 3 – section – 4.3.11

O'Reilly *JavaScript Definitive Guide* – page – 47

null (Type)

A native built-in type.

Availability:	ECMAScript edition – 2
Property/method value type:	Null primitive

The type null has exactly one value, called null.

You can use this value when testing for the undefined state of variables and objects in browsers that do not support an explicit undefined value, to test for in logical expressions.

See also:	Cast operator, Special type, Type

Cross-references:

ECMA 262 edition 2 – section – 4.3.12

ECMA 262 edition 2 – section – 8.2

ECMA 262 edition 3 – section – 4.3.12

ECMA 262 edition 3 – section – 8.2

Wrox *Instant JavaScript* – page – 14

Null literal (Primitive value)

A literal constant whose type is a built-in primitive value.

Availability:	ECMAScript edition – 2 JavaScript – 1.5 JScript – 5.0 Internet Explorer – 5.0 Netscape – 6.0
Property/method value type:	`Null primitive`
JavaScript syntax:	- `null`

The `null` literal is a value that represents the `null` or undefined state. It only has one value.

Name
null

The `null` value is sometimes used in place of other values. For example, in some browser based interpreters, there is no specific value for the undefined condition. However, you can work around this by testing for `null`. Strictly speaking they are distinctly different values with different semantic meanings. Even so, the trick works well enough for most practical purposes.

Use null in place of undefined when testing for the existence of entities.

See also:	Literal, Range error, Token, *undefined*

Cross-references:

ECMA 262 edition 2 – section – 7.7.1

ECMA 262 edition 3 – section – 7.8.1

Number (Primitive value)

A built-in primitive value.

Availability:	ECMAScript edition – 2
Property/method value type:	`Number primitive`

A `number` value is a member of the type `Number` and is a direct representation of a number.

It is basically a floating point number and there is no special integer number class. Integers are simply floating point values with a zero fractional part.

Numbers can be expressed as integers or floating point values. They can be expressed in decimal, octal or hexadecimal notation. They can also be expressed in exponential form.

Typical limits for the number type allow for very large number values. You can find out what the maximum value is by requesting the `MAX_VALUE` property from the built-in `Number` object. It will probably give you a value in the region of 1 followed by some 300 or more zeros. The smallest value is some 300 decimal places past the decimal point.

Actually the limits are 1.79e308 down to 5e-324 and both can be positive or negative.

There are special constants for the values `Infinity` and `NaN`. The `Infinity` value can be positive or negative. The `NaN` value represents a quantity that is known to be numeric but is not a valid value for the implementation. It can be tested for with the `isNaN()` function.

See also:	Cast operator, Floating constant, *Infinity*, *isNaN()*, JavaScript to Java values, *Number.MAX_VALUE*, *Number.MIN_VALUE*, Primitive value

Cross-references:

ECMA 262 edition 2 – section – 4.3.19

ECMA 262 edition 3 – section – 4.3.19

Wrox *Instant JavaScript* – page – 14

Number (Type)

A native built-in type.

Availability:	ECMAScript edition – 2
Property/method value type:	`Number primitive`

The number type defines objects that represent numbers and include the IEEE 754 NaN values in the set if the implementation is fully ECMA compliant.

The number range is huge, representing the double precision 64 bit IEEE 754 set of values.

The IEEE 754 standard defines a large number of values that are considered to be not an actual number, and should be represented as NaN. Some implementations of IEEE 754 allow you to tell the difference between an overflow error and a divide by zero error. In JavaScript, all of these values are represented by a single NaN value and you cannot distinguish between them. The JavaScript NaN value is globally defined as a variable.

The Number type includes the values positive and negative Infinity and, internally at least, positive and negative zero are represented as two distinct values.

See also:	Cast operator, Data Type, Floating point, Fundamental data type, Hexadecimal value, *IEEE 754*, *Infinity*, Integer, *NaN*, Octal value, Primitive value, *ToBoolean*, *ToInt32*, *ToNumber*, *ToObject*, *ToPrimitive*, *ToUint16*, *ToUint32*, Type, Type conversion, valueOf()

Cross-references:

ECMA 262 edition 2 – section – 4.3.19

ECMA 262 edition 2 – section – 8.5

ECMA 262 edition 3 – section – 4.3.20

ECMA 262 edition 3 – section – 8.5

O'Reilly *JavaScript Definitive Guide* – page – 34

Number object (Object/core)

An object of the class "Number".

Availability:	ECMAScript edition – 2 JavaScript – 1.1 JScript – 1.0 Internet Explorer – 3.02 Netscape – 3.0 Netscape Enterprise Server version – 2.0 Opera – 3.0	
JavaScript syntax:	-	`myNumber = new Number()`
	-	`myNumber = Number`
Object properties:	`constructor, prototype`	
Class constants:	`MAX_VALUE, MIN_VALUE, NaN,` `NEGATIVE_INFINITY, POSITIVE_INFINITY`	

Object methods:	`toExponential(), toFixed(),`
	`toLocaleString(), toPrecision(),`
	`toSource(), toString(), valueOf()`	

An instance of the class "Number" is created by using the new operator on the Number() constructor. The new object adopts the behavior of the built-in prototype object through the prototype-inheritance mechanisms.

All properties and methods of the prototype are available as if they were part of the instance.

A number object is a member of the type Object and is an instance of the built-in Number object.

Number objects are created by cloning the built-in Number object. This is done by calling the Number constructor with the new operator being applied to an existing number object. Thus:

```
myNumber = new Number(1000);
```

A number object can be coerced to a number value and can be used anywhere where a number value would be expected.

Programmers familiar with object oriented techniques may prefer to use the number object while procedural language programmers may implement the same functionality with a number value instead.

This is an example of the flexibility of JavaScript in its ability to accommodate a variety of users from different backgrounds.

The prototype for the Number prototype object is the Object prototype object.

You might want to add useful methods to the Number.prototype to output numbers in unusual formats. For example you could implement a roman numeral conversion method. Adding that to the prototype would let you output year numbers in classical formats.

Warnings:

❑ The Number object provides a collection of static constant values by way of properties belonging to the integral Number object. Because the mathematical mechanisms of any application tend to be provided by the operating system, you should find that between different browsers on any particular platform, the values that these constants yield will be very consistent.

❑ The ECMA standard lays down strict values for these properties and in general the browser manufacturers try to comply but there is always the possibility that an implementation may use a non-compliant calculation.

❑ However, it may not be quite so reliable across platforms. You might enumerate one of these constants as you are authoring and then hard-code that value into your script. When that script is executed on another platform, even in the same browser, the internal numeric support may yield a different value.

❑ You should always refer to the static constants using their symbolic names and not define them yourself, unless you are certain that the script is running on a platform that does not already define the constant value.

See also:	Constant, Limits, `Native` object, *Number.Class*, `Number.prototype`, *Object object*

Property	JavaScript	JScript	N	IE	Opera	NES	ECMA	Notes
constructor	1.1 +	1.0 +	3.0 +	3.02 +	-	-	2 +	-
prototype	1.1 +	1.0 +	3.0 +	3.02 +	3.0 +	2.0 +	2 +	DontDelete, DontEnum

Method	JavaScript	JScript	N	IE	Opera	NES	ECMA	Notes
toExponential()	1.5 +	5.5 +	6.0 +	5.5 +	-	-	3 +	-
toFixed()	1.5 +	5.5 +	6.0 +	5.5 +	-	-	3 +	-
toLocaleString()	1.5 +	5.5 +	6.0 +	5.5 +	-	-	3 +	Warning
toPrecision()	1.5 +	5.5 +	6.0 +	5.5 +	-	-	3 +	-
toSource()	1.3 +	-	4.06 +	-	-	-	3 +	-
toString()	1.1 +	1.0 +	3.0 +	3.02 +	3.0 +	-	2 +	-
valueOf()	1.1 +	3.0 +	3.0 +	4.0 +	-	-	2 +	-

Cross-references:

ECMA 262 edition 2 – section – 4.3.20

ECMA 262 edition 2 – section – 10.1.5

ECMA 262 edition 2 – section – 15.7

ECMA 262 edition 3 – section – 4.3.21

ECMA 262 edition 3 – section – 10.1.5

ECMA 262 edition 3 – section – 15.7

Wrox *Instant JavaScript* – page – 33

Number() (Function)

A Number type convertor.

Availability:	ECMAScript edition – 2 JavaScript – 1.2 JScript – 1.0 Internet Explorer – 3.02 Netscape – 4.0
Property/method value type:	Number primitive
JavaScript syntax:	-	*Number()*
	-	Number(*aValue*)
Argument list:	*aValue*	A value to be converted to a number

When the Number() constructor is called as a function, it will perform a type conversion.

The following values are yielded as a result of calling Number() as a function:

Value	Result
No value	0
Undefined	Returns NaN
Null	0
Boolean false	0
Boolean true	1
Number	No conversion, the input value is returned unchanged.
Non-numeric string	NaN
Numeric string	The numeric value rounded down if the number of digits exceeds the numeric accuracy specified by Number.MAX_VALUE.
Object	Internally, a conversion to one of the primitive types happens followed by a conversion from that type to a number. Some objects will return a number that is readily usable others will return something that cannot be converted and NaN will result.

The result is a number value that is equivalent to the value of the passed in argument. If the argument is omitted the value 0 is returned.

Warnings:

❏ When converting strings to numbers, the number of digits in the numeric string is significant. If it exceeds the accuracy that the numeric storage can cope with, the value needs to be rounded before conversion. This is an area where the implementations are notoriously weak. MSIE apparently does a better job than Netscape. However, both are undergoing revision and it's possible that the new versions of each will cope better than the older ones did.

See also:	Cast operator, Constructor function, constructor property, Implicit conversion, *Math.ceil()*, *Math.floor()*, *Math.round()*, Number.prototype, *String()*

Cross-references:

ECMA 262 edition 2 – section – 15.1.3.6

ECMA 262 edition 2 – section – 15.7.1

ECMA 262 edition 3 – section – 15.7.1

Wrox *Instant JavaScript* – page – 36

N

Number.Class (Property/internal)

Internal property that returns an `object` class.

Availability:	ECMAScript edition – 2

This is an internal property that describes the class that a `Number` object instance is a member of. The reserved words suggest that in the future, this property may be externalized.

See also:	*Class, Number object*

Property attributes:

DontEnum, Internal.

Cross-references:

ECMA 262 edition 2 – section – 8.6.2

ECMA 262 edition 2 – section – 15.7.2.1

ECMA 262 edition 3 – section – 8.6.2

Number.MAX_VALUE (Constant/static)

A mathematical constant value.

Availability:	ECMAScript edition – 2 JavaScript – 1.1 JScript – 1.0 Internet Explorer – 3.02 Netscape – 3.0 Netscape Enterprise Server version – 2.0 Opera – 3.0	
Property/method value type:	Number primitive	
JavaScript syntax:	-	Number.MAX_VALUE

This is a constant value representing the largest realizable positive finite value of the `Number` type.

The value is approximately $1.7976931348623157e+308$.

Warnings:

❑ The word approximately is used when describing the result, because the mathematical accuracy of JavaScript implementations leaves something to be desired and there are some strange artifacts in some of the calculations.

See also:	Arithmetic constant, Floating point constant, *Number*, `Number.constructor`, Special number values

Property attributes:

`ReadOnly, DontDelete, DontEnum.`

Cross-references:

ECMA 262 edition 2 – section – 15.7.3.2

ECMA 262 edition 3 – section – 15.7.3.2

O'Reilly *JavaScript Definitive Guide* – page – 37

Number.MIN_VALUE (Constant/static)

A mathematical constant value.

Availability:	ECMAScript edition – 2 JavaScript – 1.1 JScript – 1.0 Internet Explorer – 3.02 Netscape – 3.0 Netscape Enterprise Server version – 2.0 Opera – 3.0
Property/method value type:	`Number primitive`
JavaScript syntax:	- `Number.MIN_VALUE`

This is a constant value representing the smallest realizable non-zero positive value of the Number type.

The resulting value is approximately 5e-324.

Warnings:

❑ Although the `MAX_VALUE` is generally correct across implementations there are variations in the value of the `MIN_VALUE` constant.

See also:	Arithmetic constant, Floating point constant, *Number*, Number.constructor, Special number values

N

JavaScript Programmer's Reference

633

Property attributes:

ReadOnly, DontDelete, DontEnum.

Cross-references:

ECMA 262 edition 2 – section – 15.7.3.3

ECMA 262 edition 3 – section – 15.7.3.3

O'Reilly *JavaScript Definitive Guide* – page – 37

Number.NaN (Constant/static)

A mathematical constant value.

Availability:	ECMAScript edition – 2 JavaScript – 1.1 JScript – 1.0 Internet Explorer – 3.02 Netscape – 3.0 Netscape Enterprise Server version – 2.0 Opera – 3.0	
Property/method value type:	Number primitive	
JavaScript syntax:	-	Number.NaN

This is a value representing invalid numeric values. It should be identical to the NaN value provided by the Global object in an ECMA compliant implementation. Refer to the coverage of the NaN topic for full details.

However, it is generally considered unreliable to compare against NaN values with a simple equality test. To reliably test whether a numeric value is NaN or a good numeric value, use the isNaN() function and select an appropriate action according to its result.

See also:	Arithmetic constant, *NaN*, Number.constructor, Special number values

Property attributes:

ReadOnly, DontDelete, DontEnum.

Cross-references:

ECMA 262 edition 2 – section – 15.7.3.4

ECMA 262 edition 3 – section – 15.7.3.4

O'Reilly *JavaScript Definitive Guide* – page – 37

Number.NEGATIVE_INFINITY (Constant/static)

A mathematical constant value.

Availability:	ECMAScript edition – 2 JavaScript – 1.1 JScript – 1.0 Internet Explorer – 3.02 Netscape – 3.0 Netscape Enterprise Server version – 2.0 Opera – 3.0
Property/method value type:	Number primitive
JavaScript syntax:	- Number.NEGATIVE_INFINITY

This is a constant representing the value negative infinity. It should be identical to a negative sign placed in front of the Infinity value provided as a property of the Global object in an ECMA compliant implementation. Refer to the Infinity topic for further discussion.

Warnings:

❑ Netscape 2.02 does not understand what Number.NEGATIVE_INFINITY is.

See also:	Arithmetic constant, *Infinity*, Number.constructor, Special number values

Property attributes:

ReadOnly, DontDelete, DontEnum.

Cross-references:

ECMA 262 edition 2 – section – 15.7.3.5

ECMA 262 edition 3 – section – 15.7.3.5

O'Reilly *JavaScript Definitive Guide* – page – 37

Wrox *Instant JavaScript* – page – 15

N

JavaScript Programmer's Reference

635

Number.POSITIVE_INFINITY (Constant/static)

A mathematical constant value.

Availability:	ECMAScript edition – 2 JavaScript – 1.1 JScript – 1.0 Internet Explorer – 3.02 Netscape – 3.0 Netscape Enterprise Server version – 2.0 Opera – 3.0
Property/method value type:	Number primitive
JavaScript syntax:	- Number.POSITIVE_INFINITY

This is a constant value representing positive infinity. It should be identical to the Infinity value provided as a property of the Global object in an ECMA compliant implementation. Refer to the Infinity topic for further discussion.

Warnings:

❑ Netscape 2.02 does not understand what Number.POSITIVE_INFINITY is.

See also:	Arithmetic constant, *Infinity*, Number.constructor, Special number values

Property attributes:

ReadOnly, DontDelete, DontEnum.

Cross-references:

ECMA 262 edition 2 – section – 15.7.3.6

ECMA 262 edition 3 – section – 15.7.3.6

O'Reilly *JavaScript Definitive Guide* – page – 37

Wrox *Instant JavaScript* – page – 15

Numeric literal (Primitive value)

A literal constant whose type is a built-in primitive value.

Availability:	ECMAScript edition – 2
Property/method value type:	Number primitive

Numeric literals are constant numeric values expressed in Decimal, Hexadecimal or Octal notation.

Numeric values can be integer or floating point.

Floating point values can be specified with exponential notation.

Hexadecimal values must always be integers, thus:

❑ 0xFF

❑ 0XABCD

Octal values must always be integers, must start with a zero and contain only the characters 0-7.

The standard does not mandate any particular rounding technique but recommends the use of IEEE 754 standard numeric computation. This standard has been in existence for some time now and is likely to be the foundation numeric computation standard in most platforms.

See also:	Floating constant, Implicit conversion, Literal, Number formats (.)

Cross-references:

ECMA 262 edition 2 – section – 7.7.3

ECMA 262 edition 3 – section – 7.8.3

about: URL (Request method)
AbstractView object (Object/DOM)
ActiveXObject object (Object/JScript)
Add (+) (Operator/additive)
Add then assign (+=) (Operator/
assignment)

Object (Type)

A native built-in type.

Availability:	ECMAScript edition – 2

An Object is an unordered collection of properties. Each property consists of a name, a value and a set of attributes.

See also:	Alias, Data Type, Definition, Internal Method, Internal Property, *Object object*, Property, Property attribute, Type

Cross-references:

ECMA 262 edition 2 – section – 8.6

ECMA 262 edition 3 – section – 8.6

Wrox *Instant JavaScript* – page – 28

Object object (Object/core)

An object of the class "Object".

Availability:	ECMAScript edition – 2 JavaScript – 1.1 JScript – 3.0 Internet Explorer – 4.0 Netscape – 3.0 Netscape Enterprise Server version – 2.0 Opera browser – 3.0
JavaScript syntax:	-	`myObject = new Object()`
	-	`myObject = Object`

Object properties:	__parent__, __proto__, constructor, name, prototype
Object methods:	assign(), eval(), hasOwnProperty(), isPrototypeOf(), propertyIsEnumerable(), toLocaleString(), toSource(), toString(), unwatch(), valueOf(), watch()

An instance of the class "Object" is created by using the new operator on the Object() constructor. The new object adopts the behavior of the built-in prototype object through the prototype-inheritance mechanisms.

All properties and methods of the prototype are available as if they were part of the instance.

An Object is a member of the type Object. It is an unordered collection of properties, each of which may contain a primitive value, another object or a function.

The constructor is invoked by the new operator or by calling it as a Constructor function. For example:

```
new String("Some Text");
```

This will create a new object of the String type. You can invoke the constructor without the new operator but the consequences will depend on the constructor as to what it will yield as a result. In the case of the String data type, the constructor could be invoked like this:

```
String("Some Text");
```

However, you would get a primitive string as a result from this and not a String object. JavaScript is somewhat forgiving and you may not notice this happening until later on when it becomes important that you have a String object and not a simple string.

Because this object is the topmost parent object in the prototype inheritance hierarchy, all other object classes inherit its methods and properties. However, in some cases they will get overridden or nulled out.

DOM level 2 adds the following properties:

```
contentDocument
```

Although JavaScript is object based, it does not support true object oriented classes such as the ones you find in C++, Smalltalk, Java or Objective C. Instead, it provides Constructor mechanisms which create objects by allocating space for them in memory and assigning initial values to their properties.

All functions, including constructors are themselves objects, however not all objects are constructors. Each constructor has a Prototype property that is used to facilitate inheritance based on the prototype. It also provides for shared properties which is similar to but not the same as the Class properties that you find in true object oriented languages.

Externally, the objects in JavaScript exhibit most of the attributes of a class based object oriented system and some commentators argue that this qualifies JavaScript as being a genuine object oriented system. However I think the following points declassify it as a truly object oriented system, meaning that it is an "object-like" system:

❑ Global variables and the scope chain mechanism

❑ Prototype based inheritance

❑ Creation of multiple objects and calling them within a single script

❑ Object data is not truly private

It's a close enough call that JavaScript 2.0 may well move it into the class based object oriented category at which time the prototype inheritance would be replaced with super-class/sub-class mechanisms and the arguments become null and void.

Warnings:

❑ Be very careful not to confuse this generic top-level core object with the object that MSIE instantiates to represent an <OBJECT> tag. MSIE creates OBJECT objects for that purpose but also supports Object objects. For this reason, it may be the case that interpreters cannot become case insensitive when matching class names. If they did, then it would be impossible to distinguish between Object and OBJECT class names.

See also:	Aggregate type, *Array object, Boolean object, Date object, delete,* *Function object, Math object,* Native object, *Number object, Object,* OBJECT object, Object(), *Object(), Object.Class,* Object.prototype, *String object, userDefined object*

Property	JavaScript	JScript	N	IE	Opera	NES	ECMA	Notes
__parent__	1.2 +	-	4.0 +	-	-	-	-	-
__proto__	1.2 +	-	4.0 +	-	-	-	-	-
constructor	1.1 +	3.0 +	3.0 +	4.0 +	3.0 +	-	2 +	-
name	-	5.5 +	-	5.5 +	-	-	-	-
prototype	1.1 +	3.0 +	3.0 +	4.0 +	3.0 +	-	2 +	Warning, ReadOnly, DontDelete, DontEnum

Method	JavaScript	JScript	N	IE	Opera	NES	ECMA	Notes
assign()	1.1 +	-	3.0 +	-	-	-	-	Warning, Deprecated
eval()	1.1 +	3.0 +	3.0 +	4.0 +	3.0 +	2.0 +	-	Warning, Deprecated
hasOwnProperty()	1.5 +	5.5 +	6.0 +	5.5 +	-	-	3 +	-

Table continued on following page

O

Method	JavaScript	JScript	N	IE	Opera	NES	ECMA	Notes
isPrototype Of()	1.5 +	5.5 +	6.0 +	5.5 +	-	-	3 +	-
propertyIs Enumerable()	1.5 +	5.5 +	6.0 +	5.5 +	-	-	3 +	-
toLocale String()	1.5 +	5.5 +	6.0 +	5.5 +	-	-	3 +	Warning
toSource()	1.3 +	3.0 +	4.06 +	4.0 +	-	-	-	Warning
toString()	1.1 +	3.0 +	3.0 +	4.0 +	3.0 +	-	2 +	-
unwatch()	1.2 +	-	4.0 +	-	-	3.0 +	-	Warning
valueOf()	1.1 +	3.0 +	3.0 +	4.0 +	3.0 +	2.0 +	2 +	-
watch()	1.2 +	-	4.0 +	-	-	3.0 +	-	Warning

Cross-references:

ECMA 262 edition 2 – section – 4.2.1

ECMA 262 edition 2 – section – 4.3.3

ECMA 262 edition 2 – section – 10.1.5

ECMA 262 edition 2 – section – 15.2

ECMA 262 edition 3 – section – 4.2.1

ECMA 262 edition 3 – section – 4.3.3

ECMA 262 edition 3 – section – 10.1.5

ECMA 262 edition 3 – section – 15.2

O'Reilly *JavaScript Definitive Guide* – page – 44

Wrox *Instant JavaScript* – page – 28

Object() (Function)

An Object object constructor.

Availability:	ECMAScript edition – 2 JavaScript – 1.1 JScript – 1.0 Internet Explorer – 3.02 Netscape – 3.0
Property/method value type:	An object of a type that depends on the passed in argument
JavaScript syntax:	- Object()
	- Object(*aValue*)
Argument list:	*aValue* A value to be stored in the new object

The Object Constructor can be called as a function. When this happens, the value passed in undergoes a type conversion.

In an ECMA compliant implementation, the Object constructor function uses the ToObject conversion. However, it handles the input values, undefined and null, as special cases and creates a new object as if the constructor had been used with the new operator.

The table summarizes the results based on the input value data types.

Value	Result
No argument	Creates a new empty object as if new Object() had been called.
null	Creates a new empty object as if new Object(null) had been called.
undefined	Creates a new empty object as if new Object(undefined) had been called.
Boolean	Creates a new boolean object whose default value is the input value.
Number	Creates a new number object whose default value is the input value.
String	Creates a new string object whose default value is the input value.
Object	No conversion, the input value is returned unchanged.

See also:	Cast operator, Constructor function, constructor property, Implicit conversion, *Object object*

Cross-references:

ECMA 262 edition 2 – section – 15.1.1

ECMA 262 edition 2 – section – 15.1.3.1

ECMA 262 edition 2 – section – 15.2.2.2

ECMA 262 edition 3 – section – 15.2

Object.Class (Property/internal)

Internal property that returns an object class.

Availability:	ECMAScript edition – 2

This is an internal property that describes the class that an `Object` object instance is a member of. The reserved words suggest that in the future, this property may be externalized.

See also:	*Class, Object object*

Property attributes:

DontEnum, Internal.

Cross-references:

ECMA 262 edition 2 – section – 8.6.2

ECMA 262 edition 2 – section – 15.2.2.1

ECMA 262 edition 3 – section – 8.6.2

Object property delimiter (.) (Delimiter)

A token to delimit object properties from their object.

Availability:	ECMAScript edition – 2 JavaScript – 1.0 JScript – 1.0 Internet Explorer – 3.0 Netscape – 2.0 Netscape Enterprise Server version – 2.0 Opera browser – 3.0	
JavaScript syntax:	-	`myObject.aProperty`
	-	`myObject.aProperty.aProperty`
Argument list:	`aProperty`	The identifier name of property to be accessed

The dot delimits properties and objects. It can find properties of properties of objects too.

The associativity is left to right.

Refer to the operator precedence topic for details of execution order.

You can also access the property values as if the object were an array. This:

`anObject.aProperty`

is equivalent to:

`anObject["aProperty"]`

The result will be the value of the property when it is an RValue or a reference to the property when it is an LValue.

See also:	Associativity, *Decimal point (.)*, Operator Precedence, Postfix operator

Cross-references:

ECMA 262 edition 2 – section – 8.6

ECMA 262 edition 2 – section – 11.2

ECMA 262 edition 3 – section – 8.6

ECMA 262 edition 3 – section – 11.2.1

Wrox *Instant JavaScript* – page – 28

OBJECT object (Object/HTML)

This is an object that encapsulates an ActiveX plugin. Do not confuse it with the Object object that is the super-class of all objects in JavaScript.

Availability:	DOM level – 1 JavaScript – 1.5 JScript – 3.0 Internet Explorer – 4.0 Netscape – 6.0	
Inherits from:	*Element object*	
JavaScript syntax:	IE	`myOBJECT = myDocument.all.anElementID`
	IE	`myOBJECT = myDocument.all.tags` `("OBJECT")[anIndex]`
	IE	`myOBJECT = myDocument.all[aName]`
	-	`myOBJECT = myDocument.applets[anIndex]`
	-	`myOBJECT = myDocument.getElementById` `(anElementID)`
	-	`myOBJECT = myDocument.getElementsByName` `(aName)[anIndex]`
	-	`myOBJECT = myDocument.` `getElementsByTagName("OBJECT")[anIndex]`
HTML syntax:	`<OBJECT>...</OBJECT>`	
Argument list:	`anIndex`	A reference to an element in a collection
	`aName`	An associative array reference
	`anElementID`	The ID value of an Element object

O

Object properties:	accessKey, align, altHtml, archive, border, classid, code, codeBase, codeType, data, dataFld, dataSrc, declare, form, height, hspace, name, object, readyState, standby, tabIndex, type, useMap, vspace, width
Event handlers:	onAfterUpdate, onBeforeUpdate, onBlur, onClick, onDataAvailable, onDataSetChanged, onDataSetComplete, onDblClick, onDragStart, onError, onErrorUpdate, onFilterChange, onFocus, onHelp, onKeyDown, onKeyPress, onKeyUp, onMouseDown, onMouseMove, onMouseOut, onMouseOver, onMouseUp, onReadyStateChange, onRowEnter, onRowExit, onSelectStart

This is an object representing an <OBJECT> HTML tag.

The <OBJECT> tag is a block-level tag. That means that it forces a line break before and after itself.

This object is specific to the MSIE browser when it runs on the Windows operating system. No other browser supports ActiveX as well as MSIE and no other operating system properly or completely supports the ActiveX infrastructure.

The events handled, the properties and the methods of this object will depend on the kind of ActiveX object that is created.

The DOM level 1 specification refers to this as an ObjectElement object.

Warnings:

❑ Be very careful not to confuse this object with the generic top level core Object object that is the super-class of all objects in the interpreter.

❑ This is the object that MSIE instantiates to represent an <OBJECT> tag. MSIE creates OBJECT objects for that purpose but also supports Object objects. For this reason, it may be the case that interpreters cannot become case insensitive when matching class names. If they did, then it would be impossible to distinguish between Object and OBJECT class names.

❑ Creating an OBJECT class when an Object class already exists must have been a moment of insanity in an otherwise mostly excellent browser implementation project.

See also:	*ActiveXObject object*, Document.applets[], *Element object*, Input.accessKey, *Object object*

Property	JavaScript	JScript	N	IE	Opera	DOM	HTML	Notes
accessKey	1.5 +	3.0 +	6.0 +	4.0 +	-	1 +	-	Warning
align	1.5 +	3.0 +	6.0 +	4.0 +	-	1 +	-	-
altHtml	-	3.0 +	-	4.0 +	-	-	-	-
archive	1.5 +	-	6.0 +	-	-	1 +	-	Deprecated
border	1.5 +	3.0 +	6.0 +	4.0 +	-	1 +	-	-
classid	-	3.0 +	-	4.0 +	-	-	-	ReadOnly
code	1.5 +	3.0 +	6.0 +	4.0 +	-	1 +	-	-
codeBase	1.5 +	3.0 +	6.0 +	4.0 +	-	1 +	-	-
codeType	1.5 +	3.0 +	6.0 +	4.0 +	-	1 +	-	-
data	1.5 +	3.0 +	6.0 +	4.0 +	-	1 +	-	ReadOnly
dataFld	1.5 +	3.0 +	6.0 +	4.0 +	-	1 +	-	Warning
dataSrc	1.5 +	3.0 +	6.0 +	4.0 +	-	1 +	-	Warning
declare	1.5 +	-	6.0 +	-	-	1 +	-	-
form	1.5 +	3.0 +	6.0 +	4.0 +	-	1 +	-	ReadOnly
height	1.5 +	3.0 +	6.0 +	4.0 +	-	1 +	-	-
hspace	1.5 +	3.0 +	6.0 +	4.0 +	-	1 +	-	-
name	-	5.5 +	-	5.5 +	-	-	-	-
object	-	3.0 +	-	4.0 +	-	-	-	ReadOnly
readyState	-	3.0 +	-	4.0 +	-	-	-	ReadOnly
standby	1.5 +	-	6.0 +	-	-	1 +	-	-
tabIndex	1.5 +	3.0 +	6.0 +	4.0 +	-	1 +	-	-
type	1.5 +	3.0 +	6.0 +	4.0 +	-	1 +	-	-
useMap	1.5 +	-	6.0 +	-	-	1 +	-	-
vspace	1.5 +	3.0 +	6.0 +	4.0 +	-	1 +	-	-
width	1.5 +	3.0 +	6.0 +	4.0 +	-	1 +	-	-

Event name	JavaScript	JScript	N	IE	Opera	DOM	HTML	Notes
onAfter Update	-	3.0 +	-	4.0 +	-	-	-	-
onBefore Update	-	3.0 +	-	4.0 +	-	-	-	-
onBlur	1.5 +	3.0 +	6.0 +	4.0 +	3.0 +	-	-	Warning
onClick	1.5 +	3.0 +	6.0 +	4.0 +	3.0 +	-	4.0 +	Warning
onData Available	-	3.0 +	-	4.0 +	-	-	-	-
onData SetChanged	-	3.0 +	-	4.0 +	-	-	-	-
onDataSet Complete	-	3.0 +	-	4.0 +	-	-	-	-
onDblClick	1.5 +	3.0 +	6.0 +	4.0 +	3.0 +	-	4.0 +	Warning
onDragStart	-	3.0 +	-	4.0 +	-	-	-	-
onError	1.5 +	3.0 +	6.0 +	4.0 +	3.0 +	-	-	Warning

Table continued on following page

O

JavaScript Programmer's Reference

Event name	JavaScript	JScript	N	IE	Opera	DOM	HTML	Notes
onErrorUpdate	-	3.0 +	-	4.0 +	-	-	-	-
onFilterChange	-	3.0 +	-	4.0 +	-	-	-	-
onFocus	1.5 +	3.0 +	6.0 +	4.0 +	3.0 +	-	-	Warning
onHelp	-	3.0 +	-	4.0 +	-	-	-	Warning
onKeyDown	1.5 +	3.0 +	6.0 +	4.0 +	3.0 +	-	4.0 +	Warning
onKeyPress	1.5 +	3.0 +	6.0 +	4.0 +	3.0 +	-	4.0 +	Warning
onKeyUp	1.5 +	3.0 +	6.0 +	4.0 +	3.0 +	-	4.0 +	Warning
onMouseDown	1.5 +	3.0 +	6.0 +	4.0 +	3.0 +	-	4.0 +	Warning
onMouseMove	1.5 +	3.0 +	6.0 +	4.0 +	-	-	4.0 +	Warning
onMouseOut	1.5 +	3.0 +	6.0 +	4.0 +	3.0 +	-	4.0 +	Warning
onMouseOver	1.5 +	3.0 +	6.0 +	4.0 +	3.0 +	-	4.0 +	Warning
onMouseUp	1.5 +	3.0 +	6.0 +	4.0 +	3.0 +	-	4.0 +	Warning
onReadyStateChange	-	3.0 +	-	4.0 +	-	-	-	-
onRowEnter	-	3.0 +	-	4.0 +	-	-	-	-
onRowExit	-	3.0 +	-	4.0 +	-	-	-	-
onSelectStart	-	3.0 +	-	4.0 +	-	-	-	-

Inheritance chain:

Element object, Node object

Web-references:

http://www.w3.org/pub/WWW/TR/WD-object.htm

Off by one errors (Pitfall)

An error caused by missing the target value by one.

These kind of errors are caused by the following:

❑ Forgetting that an index is zero based and assuming it begins at 1. This typically affects arrays and strings.

❑ Enumerating through a range of values and testing for equality with the target value rather than testing that you are still less than the target value. This is typically a problem when you build for loops.

See also:	*Array index delimiter ([ ]), Array.slice(), do ... while(...), for(...* *) ..., Pitfalls, while(...) ...*

OL object (Object/HTML)

An object that represents the ordered list contained in an <OL> tag.

Availability:	DOM level – 1 JavaScript – 1.5 JScript – 3.0 Internet Explorer – 4.0 Netscape – 6.0	
Inherits from:	*Element object*	
JavaScript syntax:	IE	myOL = *myDocument*.all.*anElementID*
	IE	myOL = *myDocument*.all.tags ("OL")[*anIndex*]
	IE	myOL = *myDocument*.all[*aName*]
	-	myOL = *myDocument*.getElementById (*anElementID*)
	-	myOL = *myDocument*.getElementsByName (*aName*)[*anIndex*]
	-	myOL = *myDocument*.getElementsByTagName ("OL")[*anIndex*]
HTML syntax:	<OL>...</OL>	
Argument list:	*anIndex*	A reference to an element in a collection
	aName	An associative array reference
	anElementID	The ID value of an Element object
Object properties:	compact, start, type	
Event handlers:	onClick, onDblClick, onDragStart, onFilterChange, onHelp, onKeyDown, onKeyPress, onKeyUp, onMouseDown, onMouseMove, onMouseOut, onMouseOver, onMouseUp, onSelectStart	

The <OL> tag is a block-level tag. That means that it forces a line break before and after itself.

The DOM level 1 standard describes this as a HTMLOListElement object.

See also:	*Element object, UL object*

Property	JavaScript	JScript	N	IE	Opera	DOM	HTML	Notes
compact	1.5 +	3.0 +	6.0 +	4.0 +	-	1 +	-	Warning
start	1.5 +	3.0 +	6.0 +	4.0 +	-	1 +	-	Warning
type	1.5 +	3.0 +	6.0 +	4.0 +	-	1 +	-	-

O

Event name	JavaScript	JScript	N	IE	Opera	DOM	HTML	Notes
onClick	1.5 +	3.0 +	6.0 +	4.0 +	3.0 +	-	4.0 +	Warning
onDblClick	1.5 +	3.0 +	6.0 +	4.0 +	3.0 +	-	4.0 +	Warning
onDragStart	-	3.0 +	-	4.0 +	-	-	-	-
onFilterChange	-	3.0 +	-	4.0 +	-	-	-	-
onHelp	-	3.0 +	-	4.0 +	-	-	-	Warning
onKeyDown	1.5 +	3.0 +	6.0 +	4.0 +	3.0 +	-	4.0 +	Warning
onKeyPress	1.5 +	3.0 +	6.0 +	4.0 +	3.0 +	-	4.0 +	Warning
onKeyUp	1.5 +	3.0 +	6.0 +	4.0 +	3.0 +	-	4.0 +	Warning
onMouseDown	1.5 +	3.0 +	6.0 +	4.0 +	3.0 +	-	4.0 +	Warning
onMouseMove	1.5 +	3.0 +	6.0 +	4.0 +	-	-	4.0 +	Warning
onMouseOut	1.5 +	3.0 +	6.0 +	4.0 +	3.0 +	-	4.0 +	Warning
onMouseOver	1.5 +	3.0 +	6.0 +	4.0 +	3.0 +	-	4.0 +	Warning
onMouseUp	1.5 +	3.0 +	6.0 +	4.0 +	3.0 +	-	4.0 +	Warning
onSelectStart	-	3.0 +	-	4.0 +	-	-	-	-

Inheritance chain:

Element object, Node object

Opera (Web browser)

A web browser alternative to MSIE and Netscape.

The Opera web browser is an alternative browser to the Netscape and MSIE browsers on the Windows platform. It is highly standards based, and as a result has gained much respect. However, because many pages do not contain strictly standard content, you should quality check your site on this browser to ensure its compliance. Using Opera as a reference browser can significantly improve the likelihood of your site continuing top work in the future as all browsers are likely to converge on the functionality embodied in the standards.

Details of what is supported in (the freely downloadable) version 5 can be found at the web reference below.

See also:	ECMA, ECMAScript, Platform, Script execution, Web browser

Web-references:

http:www.opera.com/opera5/

OptGroupElement object (Object/HTML)

A means of grouping options together into logical sets.

Availability:	DOM level – 1 JavaScript – 1.5 JScript – 5.0 Internet Explorer – 5.0 Netscape – 6.0
Inherits from:	*Element object*
JavaScript syntax:	IE myOPTGROUP = *myDocument*.all.*anElementID*
	IE *myOPTGROUP* = *myDocument*.all.tags ("OPTGROUP")[*anIndex*]
	IE *myOPTGROUP* = *myDocument*.all[*aName*]
	-- *myOPTGROUP* = *myDocument*.getElementById (*anElementID*)
	-- *myOPTGROUP* = *myDocument* .getElementsByName(*aName*)[*anIndex*]

	-- myOPTGROUP =
	      myDocument.getElementsByTagName
	      ("OPTGROUP")[*anIndex*]

HTML syntax:	<OPTGROUP>...</OPTGROUP>
Argument list:	*anElementID* The ID value of the element required
	anIndex A reference to an element in a collection
	aName An associative array reference
Object properties:	disabled, label
Event handlers:	onClick, onDblClick, onHelp, onKeyDown, onKeyPress, onKeyUp, onMouseDown, onMouseMove, onMouseOut, onMouseOver, onMouseUp

Property	JavaScript	JScript	N	IE	Opera	DOM	HTML	Notes
disabled	1.5 +	5.0 +	6.0 +	5.0 +	-	1 +	-	-
label	1.5 +	5.0 +	6.0 +	5.0 +	-	1 +	-	-

Event name	JavaScript	JScript	N	IE	Opera	DOM	HTML	Notes
onClick	1.5 +	5.0 +	6.0 +	5.0 +	3.0 +	-	4.0 +	Warning
onDblClick	1.5 +	5.0 +	6.0 +	5.0 +	3.0 +	-	4.0 +	Warning
onHelp	-	5.0 +	-	5.0 +	-	-	-	Warning
onKeyDown	1.5 +	5.0 +	6.0 +	5.0 +	3.0 +	-	4.0 +	Warning
onKeyPress	1.5 +	5.0 +	6.0 +	5.0 +	3.0 +	-	4.0 +	Warning

Table continued on following page

O

JavaScript Programmer's Reference

651

Event name	JavaScript	JScript	N	IE	Opera	DOM	HTML	Notes
onKeyUp	1.5 +	5.0 +	6.0 +	5.0 +	3.0 +	-	4.0 +	Warning
onMouseDown	1.5 +	5.0 +	6.0 +	5.0 +	3.0 +	-	4.0 +	Warning
onMouseMove	1.5 +	5.0 +	6.0 +	5.0 +	-	-	4.0 +	Warning
onMouseOut	1.5 +	5.0 +	6.0 +	5.0 +	3.0 +	-	4.0 +	Warning
onMouseOver	1.5 +	5.0 +	6.0 +	5.0 +	3.0 +	-	4.0 +	Warning
onMouseUp	1.5 +	5.0 +	6.0 +	5.0 +	3.0 +	-	4.0 +	Warning

Inheritance chain:

Element object, Node object

Option object (Object/HTML)

One of a set of objects belonging to a select object in a form.

Availability:	DOM level – 1 JavaScript – 1.0 JScript – 1.0 Internet Explorer – 3.02 Netscape – 2.0 Netscape Enterprise Server version – 2.0 Opera – 3.0	
Inherits from:	*Element object*	
JavaScript syntax:	-	*myOption = myDocument.aFormName* *.aSelectorName.options[anIndex]*
	-	*myOption = myDocument.aFormName* *.elements[anItemIndex].options[anIndex]*
	IE	*myOption = myDocument.all.anElementID*
	IE	*myOption = myDocument.all.anElementID* *.elements[anIndex].options[anIndex]*
	IE	*myOption = myDocument.all* *.anElementID.options[anIndex]*
	IE	*myOption = myDocument.all.tags* *("OPTION")[anIndex]*
	IE	*myOption = myDocument.all[aName]*
	-	*myOption = myDocument.forms[aFormIndex]* *.aSelectorName.options[anIndex]*
	-	*myOption = myDocument.forms[aFormIndex]* *.elements[anIndex].options[anIndex]*
	-	*myOption = myDocument* *.getElementById(anElementID)*
	-	*myOption = myDocument* *.getElementsByName(aName)[anIndex]*

JavaScript syntax:	-	`myOption = myForm.aSelectorName` `.options[anIndex]`
	-	`myOption = myForm.elements` `[anItemIndex].options[anIndex]`
	-	`myOption = myOptionsArray[anIndex]`
	-	`myOption = mySelector.options[anIndex]`
	-	`myOption = myDocument.` `getElementsByTagName("OPTION")[anIndex]`
HTML syntax:	`<OPTION>...</OPTION>`	
Argument list:	`anIndex`	A valid reference to an item in the collection
	`anItemIndex`	A valid reference to an item in the collection
	`aName`	The name attribute of an element
	`aFormIndex`	A reference to a particular form in the forms collection
	`anElementID`	The ID attribute of an element
Object properties:	`defaultSelected, form, index, label,` `prototype, selected, text, value`	

Event handlers:	`onClick, onDblClick, onHelp, onKeyDown,`
	`onKeyPress, onKeyUp, onMouseDown,`
	`onMouseMove, onMouseOut, onMouseOver,`
	`onMouseUp`	

In Netscape, this sub-class of the `Input` object supports a couple of properties that may not be available on other platforms.

The DOM level 1 specification calls this object type an `OptionElement` object.

Warnings:

❏ In Netscape, this object is easy to confuse with the `Select` object to which the options belong. Be careful to maintain the correct structural relationship between `Select` popup menus and their option sets.

❏ Netscape 6.0 PR3 exhibited some instabilities in the support of this object. However it is not certain whether the bug is still outstanding on the final release as well. The problem seemed related to the creation of new `Option` objects by means of the constructor. This is not something that everyone is going to be doing on all their pages so its not likely to be a show stopper unless it's just that one thing you need to use.

See also:	Form.elements[], *Input object*, *OptionsArray object*, response.getOptionValue(), response.getOptionValueCount(), *Select object*

O

JavaScript Programmer's Reference

Property	JavaScript	JScript	N	IE	Opera	NES	DOM	HTML	Notes
default Selected	1.1 +	1.0 +	3.0 +	3.02 +	3.0 +	2.0 +	1 +	-	-
form	1.0 +	1.0 +	2.0 +	3.02 +	3.0 +	2.0 +	1 +	-	Warning
index	1.0 +	1.0 +	2.0 +	3.02 +	-	-	-	-	ReadOnly
label	1.5 +	-	6.0 +	-	-	-	1 +	-	-
prototype	1.0 +	1.0 +	2.0 +	3.02 +	-	2.0 +	-	-	Warning
selected	1.0 +	1.0 +	2.0 +	3.02 +	3.0 +	2.0 +	1 +	-	-
text	1.0 +	1.0 +	2.0 +	3.02 +	3.0 +	2.0 +	1 +	-	ReadOnly
value	1.2 +	3.0 +	4.0 +	4.0 +	3.0 +	2.0 +	1 +	-	-

Event name	JavaScript	JScript	N	IE	Opera	NES	DOM	HTML	Notes
onClick	1.0 +	1.0 +	2.0 +	3.0 +	3.0 +	-	-	4.0 +	Warning
onDblClick	1.2 +	3.0 +	4.0 +	4.0 +	3.0 +	-	-	4.0 +	Warning
onHelp	-	3.0 +	-	4.0 +	-	-	-	-	Warning
onKeyDown	1.2 +	3.0 +	4.0 +	4.0 +	3.0 +	-	-	4.0 +	Warning
onKeyPress	1.2 +	3.0 +	4.0 +	4.0 +	3.0 +	-	-	4.0 +	Warning
onKeyUp	1.2 +	3.0 +	4.0 +	4.0 +	3.0 +	-	-	4.0 +	Warning
onMouseDown	1.2 +	3.0 +	4.0 +	4.0 +	3.0 +	-	-	4.0 +	Warning
onMouseMove	1.2 +	3.0 +	4.0 +	4.0 +	-	-	-	4.0 +	Warning
onMouseOut	1.1 +	3.0 +	3.0 +	4.0 +	3.0 +	-	-	4.0 +	Warning
onMouseOver	1.0 +	1.0 +	2.0 +	3.0 +	3.0 +	-	-	4.0 +	Warning
onMouseUp	1.2 +	3.0 +	4.0 +	4.0 +	3.0 +	-	-	4.0 +	Warning

Inheritance chain:

Element object, Node object

OptionsArray object (Object/browser)

A collection object that belongs to a select popup.

Availability:	JavaScript – 1.0 JScript – 1.0 Internet Explorer – 3.02 Netscape – 2.0
JavaScript syntax:	- `myOptionsArray = mySelector.options`
Object properties:	length
Object methods:	add(), item(), remove(), select()

Warnings:

❑ Netscape 6.0 implements this in a DOM compliant manner. That means the object type is an `HTMLCollection` object. This is a generic object type and there are no special methods or properties added to it. The things you might previously have done with an `OptionsArray` object are not going to work.

❑ MSIE appears to implement this as a `NodeList` although you cannot tell because it doesn't make a constructor or prototype available for you to inspect.

See also:	*Collection object, Option object, Select object,* Select.options[]

Property	JavaScript	JScript	N	IE	Opera	HTML	Notes
length	1.0 +	1.0 +	2.0 +	3.02 +	-	-	ReadOnly

Method	JavaScript	JScript	N	IE	Opera	HTML	Notes
add()	-	3.0 +	-	4.0 +	-	-	-
item()	-	3.0 +	-	4.0 +	-	-	-
remove()	-	3.0 +	-	4.0 +	-	-	-
select()	-	3.0 +	-	4.0 +	-	-	-

O

about: URL (Request method)
AbstractView object (Object/DOM)
ActiveXObject object (Object/JScript)
Add (+) (Operator/additive)
Add then assign (+=) (Operator/
assignment)

P object (Object/HTML)

An object that encapsulates a paragraph delimited by a `<P>` tag.

Availability:	DOM level – 1 JavaScript – 1.5 JScript – 3.0 Internet Explorer – 4.0 Netscape – 6.0
Inherits from:	*Element object*

JavaScript syntax:	IE `myP = myDocument.all.anElementID`
	
	IE `myP =`
	`myDocument.all.tags("P")[anIndex]`
	
	IE `myP = myDocument.all[aName]`
	
	\- `myP = myDocument.getElementByID`
	`(anElementID)`
	
	\- `myP = myDocument.getElementsByName`
	`(aName)[anIndex]`
	
	\- `myP = myDocument.getElementsByTagName`
	`("P")[anIndex]`

HTML syntax:	`<P>`, `<P>...</P>`
Argument list:	`anIndex` A reference to an element in a collection `aName` An associative array reference `anElementID` The ID value of an `Element` object
Object properties:	`align`

Event handlers:	`onClick, onDblClick, onDragStart,`
	`onFilterChange, onHelp, onKeyDown,`
	`onKeyPress, onKeyUp, onMouseDown,`
	`onMouseMove, onMouseOut, onMouseOver,`
	`onMouseUp, onSelectStart`

The `<P>` tag is a block-level tag. That means that it forces a line break before and after itself.

The DOM level 1 specification refers to this as a `Paragraph` object.

See also:	Element object

Property	JavaScript	JScript	N	IE	Opera	DOM	HTML	Notes
align	1.5 +	3.0 +	6.0 +	4.0 +	-	1 +	-	-

Event name	JavaScript	JScript	N	IE	Opera	DOM	HTML	Notes
onClick	1.5 +	3.0 +	6.0 +	4.0 +	-	-	4.0 +	Warning
onDblClick	1.5 +	3.0 +	6.0 +	4.0 +	-	-	4.0 +	Warning
onDragStart	-	3.0 +	-	4.0 +	-	-	-	-
onFilterChange	-	3.0 +	-	4.0 +	-	-	-	-
onHelp	-	3.0 +	-	4.0 +	-	-	-	Warning
onKeyDown	1.5 +	3.0 +	6.0 +	4.0 +	-	-	4.0 +	Warning
onKeyPress	1.5 +	3.0 +	6.0 +	4.0 +	-	-	4.0 +	Warning
onKeyUp	1.5 +	3.0 +	6.0 +	4.0 +	-	-	4.0 +	Warning
onMouseDown	1.5 +	3.0 +	6.0 +	4.0 +	-	-	4.0 +	Warning
onMouseMove	1.5 +	3.0 +	6.0 +	4.0 +	-	-	4.0 +	Warning
onMouseOut	1.5 +	3.0 +	6.0 +	4.0 +	-	-	4.0 +	Warning
onMouseOver	1.5 +	3.0 +	6.0 +	4.0 +	-	-	4.0 +	Warning
onMouseUp	1.5 +	3.0 +	6.0 +	4.0 +	-	-	4.0 +	Warning
onSelectStart	-	3.0 +	-	4.0 +	-	-	-	-

Inheritance chain:

Element object, Node object

.pac (File extension)

Proxy lookup conversion file.

This is a script container for a small and compact JavaScript function that returns a computed value indicating whether to proxy serve a URL or not.

See also:	Proxies, proxy.pac

Cross-references:

Wrox Instant JavaScript – page – 58

Packages.java (Java package)

A package containing a collection of generic Java classes maintained as a package.

Availability:	JavaScript – 1.1 Netscape – 3.0 Opera – 3.0

An example of a Package reference is the Java Date class stored in the `java.util` package.

To access this from JavaScript you would use this kind of construction:

```
myJavaClass = Packages.java.util.Date;
```

That mode of access would yield a reference to the Class and would produce a `JavaClass` object in the JavaScript environment. To create an instance and yield an object of that class, use the class as a constructor. Like this:

```
myJavaObject = new Packages.java.util.Date;
```

That would create a `JavaObject` object in the JavaScript environment.

If necessary, you may want to access a collection of Classes which is called a Package. Here is how to create a JavaScript environment's `JavaPackage` object:

```
myJavaPackage = Packages.java.util;
```

See also:	*JavaClass object, JavaObject object, JavaPackage object,* `Window.java`

Packages.netscape (Java package)

A package containing a collection of Netscape defined Java classes maintained as a package.

Availability:	JavaScript – 1.1 Netscape – 3.0 Opera – 3.0

This is a code support for Java applets that use LiveConnect to access JavaScript from within the Java context.

See also:	*JavaClass object, JavaObject object, JavaPackage object,* `Window.netscape`

P

JavaScript Programmer's Reference

ParamElement object (Object/HTML)

An object that encapsulates one of the parameters passed to an OBJECT object from its <PARAM> tags.

Availability:	DOM level – 1 JavaScript – 1.5 JScript – 5.0 Internet Explorer – 5.0 Netscape – 6.0
Inherits from:	*Element object*
JavaScript syntax:	IE *myParam = myDocument.all.anElementID*
	IE *myParam = myDocument.all.tags* *("PARAMETER")[anIndex]*
	IE *myParam = myDocument.all.[aName]*
	- *myParam = myDocument.getElementByID* *(anElementID)*
	- *myParam = myDocument.getElementsByName* *(aName)[anIndex]*

	- *myParam =*
	     myDocument.getElementsByTagName
	     ("PARAMETER")[anIndex]

HTML syntax:	<PARAM>
Argument list:	*anElementID* The ID value of the element required
	anIndex A reference to an element in a collection
	aName An associative array reference
Object properties:	name, type, value, valueType
Event handlers:	onClick, onDblClick, onHelp, onKeyDown, onKeyPress, onKeyUp, onMouseDown, onMouseMove, onMouseOut, onMouseOver, onMouseUp

This is a new object introduced with the DOM specification. Its full name is HTMLParamElement. It can only exist as a child element within a block structured <OBJECT> tag.

Property	JavaScript	JScript	N	IE	Opera	DOM	HTML	Notes
name	1.5 +	5.0 +	6.0 +	5.0 +	-	1 +	-	-
type	1.5 +	5.0 +	6.0 +	5.0 +	-	1 +	-	-
value	1.5 +	5.0 +	6.0 +	5.0 +	-	1 +	-	-
valueType	1.5 +	5.0 +	6.0 +	5.0 +	-	1 +	-	-

Event name	JavaScript	JScript	N	IE	Opera	DOM	HTML	Notes
onClick	1.5 +	5.0 +	6.0 +	5.0 +	-	-	4.0 +	Warning
onDblClick	1.5 +	5.0 +	6.0 +	5.0 +	-	-	4.0 +	Warning
onHelp	-	5.0 +	-	5.0 +	-	-	-	Warning
onKeyDown	1.5 +	5.0 +	6.0 +	5.0 +	-	-	4.0 +	Warning
onKeyPress	1.5 +	5.0 +	6.0 +	5.0 +	-	-	4.0 +	Warning
onKeyUp	1.5 +	5.0 +	6.0 +	5.0 +	-	-	4.0 +	Warning
onMouseDown	1.5 +	5.0 +	6.0 +	5.0 +	-	-	4.0 +	Warning
onMouseMove	1.5 +	5.0 +	6.0 +	5.0 +	-	-	4.0 +	Warning
onMouseOut	1.5 +	5.0 +	6.0 +	5.0 +	-	-	4.0 +	Warning
onMouseOver	1.5 +	5.0 +	6.0 +	5.0 +	-	-	4.0 +	Warning
onMouseUp	1.5 +	5.0 +	6.0 +	5.0 +	-	-	4.0 +	Warning

Inheritance chain:

Element object, Node object

Parentheses ( ) (Delimiter)

A precedence of execution control mechanism.

Availability:	ECMAScript edition – 2 JavaScript – 1.0 JScript – 1.0 Internet Explorer – 3.02 Netscape – 2.0 Netscape Enterprise Server version – 2.0 Opera – 3.0

Expression evaluation order is controlled by enclosing expressions in parentheses.

See also:	*Grouping operator ( )*

Cross-references:

ECMA 262 edition 2 – section – 11.1.4

ECMA 262 edition 3 – section – 11.1.6

P

JavaScript Programmer's Reference

parseFloat() (Function/global)

Parse a string to extract a floating point value.

Availability:	ECMAScript edition – 2 JavaScript – 1.0 JScript – 1.0 Internet Explorer – 3.02 Netscape – 2.0 Netscape Enterprise Server – 2.0 Opera – 3.0	
Property/method value type:	`Number primitive`	
JavaScript syntax:	-	`parseFloat (aNumericString)`
Argument list:	`aNumericString`	A meaningful numeric value

The `parseFloat()` function returns a numeric value is returned, unless the string cannot be resolved to a meaningful value in which case NaN is returned instead.

It produces a number value dictated by interpreting the contents of the string as if it were a decimal literal value. During conversion `parseFloat()` ignores leading white space characters so you don't have to remove them from the string before conversion takes place.

Note that `parseFloat()` will only process the leading portion of the string. As soon as it encounters an invalid floating point numeric character it will assume the scanning is complete. It will then silently ignore any remaining characters in the input argument.

See also:	`Cast` operator, *Global object, parseInt(), String concatenate (+)*

Property attributes:

`DontEnum`.

Cross-references:

ECMA 262 edition 2 – section – 15.1.2.3

ECMA 262 edition 3 – section – 15.1.2.3

parseInt() (Function/global)

Parse a string to extract an integer value.

Availability:	ECMAScript edition – 2 JavaScript – 1.0 JScript – 1.0 Internet Explorer – 3.02 Netscape – 2.0 Netscape Enterprise Server – 2.0 Opera – 3.0
Property/method value type:	Number primitive
JavaScript syntax:	-	parseInt (*aNumericString*, *aRadixValue*)
Argument list:	*aNumericString*	A string that comprises a meaningful numeric value
	aRadixValue	A numeric value indicating the radix for conversion

The parseInt() function produces an integer value dictated by interpreting the string argument according to the specified radix. It can happily cope with hexadecimal values specified with the leading 0x or 0X notation. During conversion parseInt() will remove any leading white space characters. You don't need to do that to the string before parsing it.

Note also that parseInt() may only interpret the leading portion of a string. As soon as it encounters an invalid integer numeric character it will assume the scanning is complete. It will then silently ignore any remaining characters in the input argument.

Typical radix values are:

❏   2 – Binary

❏   8 – Octal

❏   10 – Decimal

❏   16 – Hexadecimal

The result of this function call is an integer value, unless the string cannot be resolved to a meaningful value in which case NaN is returned instead.

See also:	Cast operator, Function property, *Global object*, *parseFloat()*, *String concatenate (+)*

P

Property attributes:

DontEnum.

Cross-references:

ECMA 262 edition 2 – section – 15.1.2.2

ECMA 262 edition 3 – section – 15.1.2.2

Password object (Object/DOM)

A text field in a form that echoes bullets instead of the typed character. Behaves as if it were a text cell but you cannot see what was typed.

Availability:	DOM level – 1 JavaScript – 1.0 JScript – 1.0 Internet Explorer – 3.02 Netscape – 2.0 Opera – 3.0	
Inherits from:	*Input object*	
JavaScript syntax:	-	*myPassword = myDocument.aFormName* *.anElementName*
	-	*myPassword = myDocument.aFormName* *.elements[anItemIndex]*
	IE	*myPassword = myDocument.all.anElementID*
	IE	*myPassword = myDocument.all.tags* *("INPUT")[anIndex]*
	IE	*myPassword = myDocument.all[aName]*
	-	*myPassword = myDocument.forms[aFormIndex]* *.anElementName*
	-	*myPassword = myDocument.forms[aFormIndex]* *.elements[anItemIndex]*
	-	*myPassword = myDocument.getElementByID* *(anElementID)*
	-	*myPassword = myDocument.getElementsByName* *(aName)[anIndex]*
	-	*myPassword =* *myDocument.getElementsByTagName* *("INPUT")[anIndex]*
HTML syntax:	<INPUT TYPE="password">	

Argument list:	*anIndex*	A valid reference to an item in the collection
	aName	The name attribute of an element
	anElementID	The ID attribute of an element
	anItemIndex	A valid reference to an item in the collection
	aFormIndex	A reference to a particular form in the forms collection
Object properties:	`maxLength, readOnly, size, type, value`	
Object methods:	`handleEvent(), select()`	
Event handlers:	`onAfterUpdate, onBeforeUpdate, onBlur, onChange, onFilterChange, onFocus, onHelp, onKeyDown, onKeyPress, onKeyUp, onMouseDown, onMouseMove, onMouseOut, onMouseOver, onMouseUp, onResize, onRowEnter, onRowExit, onSelect, onSelectStart`	

Many properties, methods and event handlers are inherited from the `Input` object class. Refer to topics grouped with the "Input" prefix for details of common functionality across all sub-classes of the `Input` object super-class.

Event handling support via properties containing function objects was added to `Password` objects at version 1.1 of JavaScript.

Some implementations will not allow JavaScript to read the password string that the user has entered. This is good. You might imagine otherwise on the grounds that you'd expect then that JavaScript won't be able to validate the password. If you think about this for a minute you'll realize that view source in a web browser exposes your entire security checking regime. It's actually quite sensible to disallow JavaScript from inspecting the Password field. But then, all the user has to do is run a different browser – one that does access the contents of the Password field.

Realistically the validation of the password can only be done back at the server anyway and, other than some simple range checking in the client-end, access to password values from JavaScript is of doubtful use.

| See also: | *Element object*, `Form.elements[]`, *FormElement object*, *Input object*, `Input.accessKey`, `onBlur`, `onChange`, `onFocus`, `Password.handleEvent()` |

Property	JavaScript	JScript	N	IE	Opera	DOM	HTML	Notes
maxLength	-	3.0 +	-	4.0 +	-	-	-	-
readOnly	-	3.0 +	-	4.0 +	-	-	-	ReadOnly
size	-	3.0 +	-	4.0 +	-	-	-	Warning
type	1.1 +	3.0 +	3.0 +	4.0 +	3.0 +	1 +	-	ReadOnly
value	1.0 +	1.0 +	2.0 +	3.02 +	3.0 +	1 +	-	-

Method	JavaScript	JScript	N	IE	Opera	DOM	HTML	Notes
handleEvent()	1.2 +	-	4.0 +	-	-	-	-	-
select()	1.0 +	1.0 +	2.0 +	3.02 +	3.0 +	1 +	-	-

Event name	JavaScript	JScript	N	IE	Opera	DOM	HTML	Notes
onAfterUpdate	-	3.0 +	-	4.0 +	-	-	-	-
onBeforeUpdate	-	3.0 +	-	4.0 +	-	-	-	-
onBlur	1.1 +	3.0 +	3.0 +	4.0 +	3.0 +	-	-	Warning
onChange	1.0 +	3.0 +	2.0 +	4.0 +	3.0 +	-	-	-
onFilterChange	-	3.0 +	-	4.0 +	-	-	-	-
onFocus	1.0 +	3.0 +	2.0 +	4.0 +	3.0 +	-	-	Warning
onHelp	-	3.0 +	-	4.0 +	-	-	-	Warning
onKeyDown	1.2 +	3.0 +	4.0 +	4.0 +	3.0 +	-	4.0 +	Warning
onKeyPress	1.2 +	3.0 +	4.0 +	4.0 +	3.0 +	-	4.0 +	Warning
onKeyUp	1.2 +	3.0 +	4.0 +	4.0 +	3.0 +	-	4.0 +	Warning
onMouseDown	1.2 +	3.0 +	4.0 +	4.0 +	3.0 +	-	4.0 +	Warning
onMouseMove	1.2 +	3.0 +	4.0 +	4.0 +	-	-	4.0 +	Warning
onMouseOut	1.1 +	3.0 +	3.0 +	4.0 +	3.0 +	-	4.0 +	Warning
onMouseOver	1.0 +	1.0 +	2.0 +	3.0 +	3.0 +	-	4.0 +	Warning
onMouseUp	1.2 +	3.0 +	4.0 +	4.0 +	3.0 +	-	4.0 +	Warning
onResize	1.2 +	3.0 +	4.0 +	4.0 +	-	-	-	Warning
onRowEnter	-	3.0 +	-	4.0 +	-	-	-	-
onRowExit	-	3.0 +	-	4.0 +	-	-	-	-
onSelect	1.0 +	3.0 +	2.0 +	4.0 +	3.0 +	-	-	-
onSelectStart	-	3.0 +	-	4.0 +	-	-	-	-

Inheritance chain:

Element object, Input object, Node object

Cross-references:

O'Reilly *JavaScript Definitive Guide* – page – 645

PDF (Standard)

A de facto standard for portable documents which is owned by Adobe Inc.

JavaScript is used inside Acrobat 4.0 as a forms handling language. This provides a scripting environment in which you can manipulate the form data whose layout is defined by PostScript but whose content can then be 'activated' by JavaScript. There are a few minor limitations imposed due to the fact that Acrobat is not a web browser. There are also several additional objects provided to support the PDF forms environment.

| See also: | Host environment, Platform, Script execution |

Web-references:

http://www.pdfzone.com/pdfs/PDFSPEC13.PDF

Pkcs11 object (Object/Navigator)

A hitherto undocumented object type supported by Netscape.

Availability:	JavaScript – 1.2 Netscape – 4.04	
JavaScript syntax:	N	`myPkcs11 = myWindow.pkcs11`
	N	`myPkcs11 = pkcs11`

The Pkcs11 object is part of the security model built into Netscape. It is otherwise known as Cryptoki and is provided by RSA Data Security, Inc.

They implement a C language API that has now been mapped to Java as well. According to the Netscape web site, it is not a fully-fledged object oriented API, but can be readily understood by programmers already familiar with Cryptoki.

According to the release notes, Netscape 4.04 added support for the FORTEZZA PKCS#11 module for making use of the FORTEZZA Crypto Card and FORTEZZA cryptographic algorithms (KEA and Skipjack) when using SSL and S/MIME. Although a link was provided for more details, it appears that the support documents may have been moved or deleted.

| See also: | *Cryptoki*, `Window.pkcs11` |

Property attributes:

`ReadOnly`.

Web-references:

http://developer.netscape.com/support/faqs/pkcs_11.html

P

JavaScript Programmer's Reference

667

Plugin object (Object/browser)

An object representing a plugin.

Availability:	JavaScript – 1.1 JScript – 3.0 Internet Explorer – 4.0 Netscape – 3.0 Opera – 3.0	
JavaScript syntax:	-	`myPlugin = document.plugins[anIndex]`
	N	`myPlugin = navigator.plugins[anIndex]`
	-	`myPlugin = myPluginArray[anIndex]`
HTML syntax:	`<APPLET> <EMBED> <OBJECT>`	
Argument list:	`anIndex`	A reference to an element in a collection
Object properties:	`description, filename, length, name`	
Object methods:	`isActive(), refresh()`	

Netscape and MSIE encapsulate plugin/embedded objects in a different way. In MSIE they are objects of the `EMBED` class. In Netscape they are objects commonly referred to as belonging to the `Plugin` class although they are really implemented as `JavaObject` objects. In MSIE, this is an `ActiveX` object.

There is additional confusion in that there is a `plugins[]` array that belongs to the document and another than belongs to the `navigator` object. They both contain collections of objects but of different types. This is further confused by the fact that the `document.plugins[]` array is another name for the `document.embeds[]` array.

Because of this confusing situation, the best recommendation is that we refer to `document.embeds[]` and `navigator.plugins[]` and quietly ignore the `document.plugins[]` array. Furthermore we shall refer to `Plugin` objects as being something the browser can use to play embedded content and `Embed` objects will be an instance of a plugin that is alive and running in a document.

Warnings:

❑ Do not confuse `Plugin` and `Embed` objects with one another. `Plugin` objects are owned by the `navigator.plugins` array. `Embed` objects are owned by the `document.embeds` array.

See also:	*<EMBED>, Collection object, Embed object, EmbedArray object,* Glue code, Java, `Navigator.plugins[]`, *Plugin events, PluginArray object*

Property	JavaScript	JScript	N	IE	Opera	HTML	Notes
description	1.1 +	3.0 +	3.0 +	4.0 +	3.0 +	-	ReadOnly
filename	1.1 +	3.0 +	3.0 +	4.0 +	3.0 +	-	ReadOnly
length	1.1 +	3.0 +	3.0 +	4.0 +	3.0 +	-	Warning, ReadOnly
name	1.1 +	3.0 +	3.0 +	4.0 +	3.0 +	-	ReadOnly

Method	JavaScript	JScript	N	IE	Opera	HTML	Notes
isActive()	1.3 +	-	4.7 +	-	-	-	-
refresh()	1.1 +	-	3.0 +	-	3.0 +	-	-

PluginArray object (Object/browser)

A collection of plugin modules that the browser can use to playback embedded content.

Availability:	JavaScript – 1.1 JScript – 3.0 Internet Explorer – 4.0 Netscape – 3.0 Opera – 3.0	
JavaScript syntax:	IE	`myPluginArray = document.plugins`
	N	`myPluginArray = navigator.plugins`
Object properties:	`length`	
Object methods:	`item()`, `refresh()`	

Netscape and MSIE encapsulate plugin/embedded objects in a different way. In MSIE they are objects of the EMBED class. In Netscape they are objects commonly referred to as belonging to the Plugin class although they are really implemented as JavaObject objects. In MSIE, this is an ActiveX object.

There is additional confusion in that there is a plugins[] array that belongs to the document and another that belongs to the navigator object. They both contain collections of objects but of different types. This is further confused by the fact that the document.plugins[] array is another name for the document.embeds[] array.

Due to this confusing situation, the best recommendation is that we refer to document.embeds[] and navigator.plugins[] and quietly ignore the document.plugins[] array. Furthermore we shall refer to Plugin objects as being something the browser can use to play embedded content and Embed objects will be an instance of a plugin that is alive and running in a document.

P

Warnings:

❑ Beware of confusion between document.plugins and navigator.plugins. One relates to the plugins currently used in the document while the other lists the plugins currently available and supported by the browser.

❑ In Netscape 4.7 for Macintosh, there is a strange enumeration problem. Immediately after starting the Netscape browser, when you enumerate the properties of the netscape.plugins PluginArray object, it appears to have no properties at all. If you explicitly ask for the length property, you will get a value. During investigation, it returned the value 8 but this will depend on the number of plugins you have installed.

❑ Now, this suggests that you should be able to access the plugins individually by index number. As soon as you access one of the plugins by its numeric index, Netscape also adds an entry using the plugin name so you can access it associatively. However, you can also enumerate the item you just created until the browser clears the array (probably when the application exits). So, although you cannot enumerate the plugins from cold, you can enumerate the ones that you have accessed by index value.

❑ Sending a refresh message to a plugin object also allows it to be enumerable. Based on this idea, a short fragment of code is given in the example which will force the plugins to all be added to the collection as associative items which can then be enumerated.

❑ MSIE allows the plugins to be enumerated and the length property is also enumerable. However, the plugins can only accessed by their numeric index.

❑ To make this properly portable then, execute the bug fix code and access plugins by their numeric index and your scripts should then be reasonably portable.

Example code:

```
// Execute this in Netscape to fix the
// navigator.plugins enumeration bug
for(ii=0; ii<navigator.plugins.length; ii++)
{
navigator.plugins[ii].refresh;
}
```

See also:	Collection object, EmbedArray object, Navigator.plugins[], Plugin object

Property	JavaScript	JScript	N	IE	Opera	HTML	Notes
length	1.1 +	3.0 +	3.0 +	4.0 +	-	-	Warning, ReadOnly

Method	JavaScript	JScript	N	IE	Opera	HTML	Notes
item()	-	3.0 +	-	4.0 +	-	-	-
refresh()	1.1 +	-	3.0 +	-	3.0 +	-	-

Positive value (+) (Operator/unary)

Indicate positive value or numeric cast a non-numeric value.

Availability:	ECMAScript edition – 2 JavaScript – 1.0 JScript – 1.0 Internet Explorer – 3.02 Netscape – 2.0 Netscape Enterprise Server – 2.0 Opera – 3.0	
Property/method value type:	`Number primitive`	
JavaScript syntax:	-	`+anOperand`
Argument list:	`anOperand`	A value that can reasonably be converted to a number

The operand is evaluated and converted to a numeric value.

A positive value is unchanged.

A negative value is unchanged.

A string value will be converted to a numeric value and replaced in context.

Although this is classified as a unary operator, its functionality is really that of an additive operator.

The result will be the value of the operand, cast to a numeric type.

See also:	Additive operator, Unary operator

Cross-references:

ECMA 262 edition 2 – section – 11.4.6

ECMA 262 edition 3 – section – 11.4.6

P

Postfix decrement (–) (Operator/postfix)

Decrement after access.

Availability:	ECMAScript edition – 2 JavaScript – 1.0 JScript – 1.0 Internet Explorer – 3.02 Netscape – 2.0
Property/method value type:	`Number primitive`

JavaScript syntax:	-	`anOperand--`
Argument list:	`anOperand`	A numeric value that can be decremented

The operand is decremented by 1.

The operand is evaluated first and is then decremented when the evaluation is completed.

The associativity is from right to left.

Refer to the operator precedence topic for details of execution order.

See also:	Associativity, *Decrement value (--)*, Operator Precedence, *Postfix expression*, Postfix operator, *Prefix decrement (--)*, *Prefix expression*

Cross-references:

ECMA 262 edition 2 – section – 11.3.2

ECMA 262 edition 3 – section – 11.3.2

Postfix expression (Operator/postfix)

Increment or decrement an operand after access.

Availability:	ECMAScript edition – 2
Property/method value type:	`Number primitive`

Postfix expressions operate on Left-Hand-Side (sometimes called LValue) expressions.

There are two postfix operators:

❑ ++ performs a numeric increment on the operand.

❑ -- performs a numeric decrement on the operand.

These can also be classified as additive operators and because they modify a value in place, they also imply that an assignment takes place as well.

See also:	Additive operator, Assignment operator, *Decrement value (--)*, Expression, *Increment value (++)*, *Postfix decrement (--)*, *Postfix increment (++)*, *Prefix expression*

Cross-references:

ECMA 262 edition 2 – section – 11.3

ECMA 262 edition 3 – section – 11.3

Postfix increment (++) (Operator/postfix)

Increment after access.

Availability:	ECMAScript edition – 2 JavaScript – 1.0 JScript – 1.0 Internet Explorer – 3.02 Netscape – 2.0	
Property/method value type:	Number primitive	
JavaScript syntax:	-	anOperand++
Argument list:	anOperand	An incrementable numeric value

The operand is incremented by 1.

The operand is evaluated first and is then incremented when the evaluation is completed.

The associativity is from right to left.

Refer to the operator precedence topic for details of execution order.

See also:	Associativity, *Decrement value (--)*, *Increment value (++)*, Operator Precedence, *Postfix expression*, Postfix operator, *Prefix expression*

P

Cross-references:

ECMA 262 edition 2 – section – 11.3.1

ECMA 262 edition 3 – section – 11.3.1

PRE object (Object/HTML)

An object that encapsulates the content of a <PRE> tag.

Availability:	DOM level – 1 JavaScript – 1.5 JScript – 3.0 Internet Explorer – 4.0 Netscape – 6.0
Inherits from:	*Element object*
JavaScript syntax:	IE *myPRE* = *myDocument*.all.*anElementID*
	IE *myPRE* = *myDocument*.all.tags ("PRE")[*anIndex*]
	IE *myPRE* = *myDocument*.all[*aName*]
	- *myPRE* = *myDocument*.getElementByID (*anElementID*)
	- *myPRE* = *myDocument*.getElementsByName (*aName*)[*anIndex*]
	- *myPRE* = *myDocument* .getElementsByTagName("PRE")[*anIndex*]
HTML syntax:	<PRE> ... </PRE>
Argument list:	*anIndex* A reference to an element in a collection
	aName An associative array reference
	anElementID The ID value of an Element object
Object properties:	width
Event handlers:	onClick, onDblClick, onDragStart, onFilterChange, onHelp, onKeyDown, onKeyPress, onKeyUp, onMouseDown, onMouseMove, onMouseOut, onMouseOver, onMouseUp, onSelectStart

The <PRE> tag is a block-level tag. That means that it forces a line break before and after itself.

See also:	*Element object, KBD object, LISTING object,* style.overflow

Property	JavaScript	JScript	N	IE	Opera	DOM	HTML	Notes
width	1.5 +	3.0 +	6.0 +	4.0 +	-	1+	-	-

Event name	JavaScript	JScript	N	IE	Opera	DOM	HTML	Notes
onClick	1.5 +	3.0 +	6.0 +	4.0 +	-	-	4.0 +	Warning
onDblClick	1.5 +	3.0 +	6.0 +	4.0 +	-	-	4.0 +	Warning
onDragStart	-	3.0 +	-	4.0 +	-	-	-	-
onFilterChange	-	3.0 +	-	4.0 +	-	-	-	-
onHelp	-	3.0 +	-	4.0 +	-	-	-	Warning
onKeyDown	1.5 +	3.0 +	6.0 +	4.0 +	-	-	4.0 +	Warning
onKeyPress	1.5 +	3.0 +	6.0 +	4.0 +	-	-	4.0 +	Warning
onKeyUp	1.5 +	3.0 +	6.0 +	4.0 +	-	-	4.0 +	Warning
onMouseDown	1.5 +	3.0 +	6.0 +	4.0 +	-	-	4.0 +	Warning
onMouseMove	1.5 +	3.0 +	6.0 +	4.0 +	-	-	4.0 +	Warning
onMouseOut	1.5 +	3.0 +	6.0 +	4.0 +	-	-	4.0 +	Warning
onMouseOver	1.5 +	3.0 +	6.0 +	4.0 +	-	-	4.0 +	Warning
onMouseUp	1.5 +	3.0 +	6.0 +	4.0 +	-	-	4.0 +	Warning
onSelectStart	-	3.0 +	-	4.0 +	-	-	-	-

Inheritance chain:

Element object, Node object

Pre-processing - /*@ ... @*/ (Delimiter)

A special form of the comment delimiters for enclosing pre-processor directives.

Availability:	JScript – 3.0 Internet Explorer – 4.0	
JavaScript syntax:	IE	/*@someDirectives@*/
Argument list:	someDirectives	One or more pre-processor directives

This form of the comment delimiters is important when you need to use the JScript pre-processor directives. Enclosing them in a comment block hides them from non-compliant browsers and script interpreters.

The pre-processor directive has the following general format:

```
@<some_keyword>
```

To hide it within comments, you need to modify it so it resembles this general form:

```
/*@<some_keyword> @*/
```

There are special requirements for enclosing entire blocks of code when the conditional inclusion directives are used. Refer to the @if topic for more details.

It seems to be convention to place a space character in front of the closing @*/ comment delimiter. This may not be strictly necessary for functional reasons but aids the readability of the directives when placed into portable code.

See also:	@*/, Pre-processing, Pre-processing - @<variable_name>, Pre-processing - @_alpha, Pre-processing - @_jscript, Pre-processing - @_jscript_build, Pre-processing - @_jscript_version, Pre-processing - @_mac, Pre-processing - @_mc680x0, Pre-processing - @_PowerPC, Pre-processing - @_win16, Pre-processing - @_win32, Pre-processing - @_x86, Pre-processing - @cc_on, Pre-processing - @elif(...) ..., Pre-processing - @else ..., Pre-processing - @end, Pre-processing - @if(...) ..., Pre-processing - @set

Pre-processing - @<variable_name> (Pre-processor)

A special pre-processor variable container.

Availability:	JScript – 3.0 Internet Explorer – 4.0	
Property/method value type:	User defined	
JavaScript syntax:	IE	@aVariable
	IE	@aVariable=aValue
Argument list:	aValue	A value to be assigned
	aVariable	A variable created with the @set directive

The pre-processor sub-system supports the definition and use of a special kind of variable. These are defined and modified with the @set pre-processor directive.

Once created, the variable can be used anywhere in the code, like this:

```
myString = "***" + @myvariable;
```

If you intend to hide this directive inside some comments, it must be done like this:

```
/*@myvariable @*/
```

See also:	Pre-processing, *Pre-processing – /*@ ... @*/*

Pre-processing - @_alpha (Pre-processor)

A pre-processor constant indicating whether the script is running in a DEC alpha workstation.

Availability:	JScript – 3.0 Internet Explorer – 4.0
Property/method value type:	Boolean primitive
JavaScript syntax:	IE	@_alpha

This pre-processor constant yields true when used on a DEC alpha processor and NaN otherwise.

Since MSIE only runs on Macintosh and Windows platforms, and a DEC alpha is not a Macintosh, there is an implication here that this will be true only when MSIE is running on Windows NT on a DEC alpha. It should also be the case that the @_win32 directive returns true as well.

If you intend to hide this directive inside some comments, it must be done like this:

```
/*@_alpha @*/
```

See also:	Pre-processing, *Pre-processing – /*@ ... @*/*

P

Pre-processing - @_jscript (Pre-processor)

A pre-processor constant indicating whether the script is executing in a JScript interpreter.

Availability:	JScript – 3.0 Internet Explorer – 4.0
Property/method value type:	Boolean primitive
JavaScript syntax:	IE	@_jscript

This preprocessor constant yields true if the script is running in a genuine Microsoft JScript interpreter, and NaN if it is JavaScript but not JScript.

These directives may have been defined with a @ symbol rather than a # symbol for reasons of consistency across a variety of Microsoft platforms. Therefore, this directive may be useful to be able to conditionally include script source that depends on the kind of interpreter being used.

For now this directive will always return the true value when used in the MSIE browser.

If you intend to hide this directive inside some comments, it must be done like this:

```
/*@_jscript @*/
```

See also:	Pre-processing, *Pre-processing – /*@ ... @*/*

Pre-processing - @_jscript_build (Pre-processor)

A pre-processor constant indicating the build version of the JScript environment.

Availability:	JScript – 3.0
	Internet Explorer – 4.0
Property/method value type:	Number primitive
JavaScript syntax:	IE @_jscript_build

This pre-processor constant returns the build number of the interpreter (but not the browser) in which the script is running.

For example, in version 5.0 of MSIE for Macintosh, the browser build number is 2022 but the JScript build number reported by this pre-processor directive is 3715.

If you intend to hide this directive inside some comments, it must be done like this:

```
/*@_jscript_build @*/
```

Warnings:

❑ Oddly enough, in version 4.5 of MSIE, the value reported is also 3715 even though the build number of the browser is 0408 and is therefore much older.

❑ Because both versions of the browser were tested in the same machine, it is possible that by installing the MSIE 5 browser, some components of the browser are stored in the System folder. These may well have overwritten components that the version 4.5 browser was using and so you need to be aware of the possibility of MSIE browsers exhibiting odd behavior due to the way the application is factored into components. In fact this is confirmed by the fact that the `@_jscript_version` directive reports JScript 5 from within MSIE 4.5 which is not correct. Other aspects of the interpreter that interact with the browser core may exhibit JScript 3 functionality. So installing MSIE 5 on a Macintosh over the top of an MSIE 4.5 yields an interesting hybrid variant of the version 4.5 browser. Performing upgrades of your browser and JScript components on a Windows platform may yield similar hybrid variants.

❑ Don't test browser versions to conditionally execute JSCript version specific code.

❑ The Netscape browser code is contained more integrally within its own application space and you may be able to have several versions of that browser without any subtle interaction between low level shared library modules.

❑ You may assume the version of the interpreter tells you something useful but don't assume any other implications regarding browser versions based on the interpreter version.

See also:	Pre-processing, *Pre-processing – /*@ ... @*/*

Pre-processing - @_jscript_version (Pre-processor)

A pre-processor constant indicating the version number of the JScript interpreter.

Availability:	JScript – 3.0 Internet Explorer – 4.0	
Property/method value type:	Number primitive	
JavaScript syntax:	IE	@_jscript_version

This pre-processor constant provides the version number of the interpreter (but not the browser) in which the script is running.

For example, in version 5.0 of MSIE for Macintosh, the version of JScript expected is version 5.0 and you do get the value 5 reported by this directive.

If you intend to hide this directive inside some comments, it must be done like this:

```
/*@_jscript_version @*/
```

Warnings:

❑ As is the case with the `@_jscript_build` directive, this one may be affected by the installation history of your workstation.

❑ Installing MSIE 5 on a Macintosh over the top of an MSIE 4.5 yields an interesting hybrid variant of the version 4.5 browser. Due to the component nature of Microsoft browsers and interpreters, the same is true on the Windows platform and you can very easily find the versions of browser and JScript interpreter have diverged as a result of installing another application that may upgrade some shared components.

❑ You may assume the version of the interpreter tells you something useful but don't assume any other implications regarding browser versions based on the interpreter version or vice versa. Test the thing you need to know about and do not assume that the browser and interpreter are directly related to one another.

❑ The version history tables suggest they are related but this simply lists the versions of JScript that were shipped as part of the browser install kit for a fresh and complete installation.

See also:	Pre-processing, *Pre-processing – /*@ ... @*/*

Pre-processing - @_mac (Pre-processor)

A pre-processor constant indicating whether the script is running in a Macintosh workstation.

Availability:	JScript – 3.0 Internet Explorer – 4.0	
Property/method value type:	`Boolean primitive`	
JavaScript syntax:	IE	`@_mac`

This directive should yield the value true when tested on any Macintosh system.

In MSIE version 5, it yields the value NaN which is what you would expect on a non-Macintosh system.

If you intend to hide this directive inside some comments, it must be done like this:

```
/*@_mac @*/
```

Warnings:

❑ This does not appear to work in MSIE 5 for Macintosh.

See also:	Pre-processing, *Pre-processing – /*@ ... @*/*

Pre-processing - @_mc680x0 (Pre-processor)

A pre-processor constant indicating whether the system contains a Motorola 68000 CPU.

Availability:	JScript – 3.0 Internet Explorer – 4.0	
Property/method value type:	Boolean primitive	
JavaScript syntax:	IE	@_mc680x0

This directive should yield the value true when tested on any older pre-Power PC equipped Macintosh system and NaN when tested on a modern Power PC machine.

In MSIE version 5, it yields the value NaN regardless of the CPU, which is what you would expect on a non 68K equipped system.

If you intend to hide this directive inside some comments, it must be done like this:

```
/*@_mc680x0 @*/
```

Warnings:

❑ This does not appear to work in MSIE 5 for Macintosh.

See also:	Pre-processing, *Pre-processing – /*@ ... @*/*

Pre-processing - @_PowerPC (Pre-processor)

A pre-processor constant indicating whether the system contains a Motorola PowerPC CPU.

Availability:	JScript – 3.0 Internet Explorer – 4.0	
Property/method value type:	Boolean primitive	
JavaScript syntax:	IE	@_PowerPC

This directive should yield the value true when tested on any newer Power PC equipped Macintosh system and NaN when tested on an older 68K machine.

P

JavaScript Programmer's Reference

In MSIE version 5, it yields the value NaN regardless of the CPU, which is what you would expect on a non-Power PC system.

If you intend to hide this directive inside some comments, it must be done like this:

```
/*@_PowerPC @*/
```

Warnings:

❑ This does not appear to work in MSIE 5 for Macintosh.

❑ Be careful with capitalization on this directive, none of the others seem to require capital letters but this one does.

See also:	Pre-processing, *Pre-processing – /*@ ... @*/*

Pre-processing - @_win16 (Pre-processor)

A pre-processor constant indicating whether the script is running in a 16 bit Windows environment.

Availability:	JScript – 3.0 Internet Explorer – 4.0	
Property/method value type:	Boolean primitive	
JavaScript syntax:	IE	@_win16

This directive should yield the value true when tested on any older 16 bit Windows system.

If you intend to hide this directive inside some comments, it must be done like this:

```
/*@_win16 @*/
```

See also:	Pre-processing, *Pre-processing – /*@ ... @*/*

Pre-processing - @_win32 (Pre-processor)

A pre-processor constant indicating whether the script is running in a 32 bit Windows environment.

Availability:	JScript – 3.0 Internet Explorer – 4.0	
Property/method value type:	Boolean primitive	
JavaScript syntax:	IE	@_win32

This directive should yield the value true when tested on any modern 32 bit Windows system.

If you intend to hide this directive inside some comments, it must be done like this:

```
/*@_win32 @*/
```

See also:	Pre-processing, *Pre-processing – /*@ ... @*/*

Pre-processing - @_x86 (Pre-processor)

A pre-processor constant indicating whether the system contains an Intel X-86 series CPU.

Availability:	JScript – 3.0 Internet Explorer – 4.0
Property/method value type:	`Boolean primitive`
JavaScript syntax:	IE `@_x86`

This directive should yield the value true when tested on any system equipped with an Intel X86 CPU. It should yield NaN on any non-Intel system and always read NaN on a Macintosh.

If you intend to hide this directive inside some comments, it must be done like this:

```
/*@_x86 @*/
```

See also:	Pre-processing, *Pre-processing – /*@ ... @*/*

Pre-processing - @cc_on (Pre-processor)

A switch to activate the pre-processor phase of the script interpreter.

Availability:	JScript – 3.0 Internet Explorer – 4.0
JavaScript syntax:	IE `@cc_on`

The pre-processor directives will not work unless they are first activated by placing this directive near the top of the script.

If you intend to hide this directive inside some comments, it must be done like this:

```
/*@cc_on @*/
```

See also:	*Conditional code block*, Pre-processing, *Pre-processing – /*@ ... @*/*

P

JavaScript Programmer's Reference

683

Pre-processing - @elif(...) ... (Pre-processor)

An optional else-if pre-processor token.

Availability:	JScript – 3.0 Internet Explorer – 4.0
JavaScript syntax:	IE ... @elif(*aCondition*) ...
Argument list:	*aCondition* A pre-processor supported condition test

This can be used in a conditional code block to indicate a supplementary conditional block.

Refer to the @if() topic for more details.

If you intend to hide this directive inside some comments, you must place the comment around the entire construct and not the individual pre-processor directives.

See also:	*Conditional code block*, Pre-processing, *Pre-processing – /*@ ... @*/*

Pre-processing - @else ... (Pre-processor)

Part of the conditional code use directive.

Availability:	JScript – 3.0 Internet Explorer – 4.0
JavaScript syntax:	IE ... @else ...

This can be used in a conditional code block to indicate an alternative conditional block.

Refer to the @if() topic for more details.

If you intend to hide this directive inside some comments, you must place the comment around the entire construct and not the individual pre-processor directives.

See also:	*Conditional code block*, Pre-processing, *Pre-processing – /*@ ...* *@*/*

Pre-processing - @end (Pre-processor)

Terminator for a conditional code block.

Availability:	JScript – 3.0 Internet Explorer – 4.0
JavaScript syntax:	IE ... @end

This should be used to terminate a conditional code block.

Refer to the @if() topic for more details.

If you intend to hide this directive inside some comments, you must place the comment around the entire construct and not the individual pre-processor directives.

See also:	*Conditional code block,* Pre-processing, *Pre-processing – /*@ ... @*/*

Pre-processing - @if(...) ... (Pre-processor)

Conditionally include a block of code.

Availability:	JScript – 3.0 Internet Explorer – 4.0	
JavaScript syntax:	IE	@if(*aCondition*) *someCode* @elif(*aCondition*) *someCode* @else *someCode* @end
	IE	@if(*aCondition*) *someCode* @elif(*aCondition*) *someCode* @end
	IE	@if(*aCondition*) *someCode* @else *someCode* @end
	IE	@if(*aCondition*) *someCode* @end
Argument list:	*aCondition*	A condition that yields a Boolean value
	someCode	A block of code that is conditionally included

The @if() directive is very flexible having two optional associated directives (@elif() and @else) which provide a variety of different configurations.

The simplest form is where a section of code is included or not. That would be organized like this:

```
@if(anExpression)

. . .

someCode

. . .

@end
```

If the expression yields a true value then the code will be included, otherwise it will be skipped, as if it had been completely commented out.

The next most complex form is to place an alternative section of code in the conditional section and have that used when the expression yields a false value. That would be laid out like this:

```
@if(anExpression)

. . .

someCode

. . .

@else

. . .

someOtherCode

. . .

@end
```

The result of the expression selects one block of code or the other.

A third and somewhat more complex configuration allows a series of conditions to be tested. This is somewhat like a switch tree although it is a little less elegant in its presentation. You can test for several conditions and include an appropriate block of code for the one that holds true. However, only one will be selected. This is accomplished with the @elif() directive. This is only tested when a prior @if() or @elif() test proves false.

```
Here is an configuration that tests for three possible conditions:

@if(anExpression)

. . .

someCode
```

```
...

@elif(anExpression)

...

someCode

...

@elif(anExpression)

...

someCode

...

@end
```

Note in this form, there is no alternative block of code associated with an `@else` directive. One of these expressions must prove true for any code to be included. If none of them prove true, then the entire conditional block is ignored.

The final configuration provides a fall-back alternative code block and is constructed like this:

```
@if(anExpression)

...

someCode

...

@elif(anExpression)

...

someCode

...

@elif(anExpression)

...

someCode

...

@else

...
```

```
someOtherCode

...

@end
```

You may be able to nest these directives but it is recommended that you avoid complexity when building conditional code structures as it makes the code more difficult to maintain.

If you intend to hide this directive inside some comments, it must be done like this:

```
/*@if(anExpression)

...

someCode

...

@elif(anExpression)

...

someCode

...

@elif(anExpression)

...

someCode

...

@else

...

someOtherCode

...

@end @*/
```

See also: *Conditional code block*, Pre-processing, *Pre-processing – /*@ ... @*/*

Pre-processing - @set (Pre-processor)

Set the contents of a pre-processor variable.

Availability:	JScript – 3.0 Internet Explorer – 4.0	
JavaScript syntax:	IE	`@set aVariable=aValue`
Argument list:	`aValue`	A value to assign
	`aVariable`	A pre-processor variable name

You can define variables that exist in the namespace of the pre-processor and which can then be used as if they were directives that you had created. For example, you might test some complex set of conditions and set a variable so that you can simply test for its existence later. Or you might use that variable in some fragment of code as a manifest constant, perhaps to specify the size of an array or a flag to activate some capability.

You should note that these pre-processor directives will likely not survive from one script block to another or for any duration in the time domain. They are not variables in the sense of a script variable.

To create a new pre-processor variable, use the `@set` directive, name the variable and assign a value to it, like this:

```
@set @myvariable=1000
```

You can then use the variable in the source text like this:

```
document.write(@myvariable);
```

You may need to experiment to establish how long one of these variables actually persists. It is unlikely to still be defined when an event handler is called. However, that event handler may have been interpreted and stored when the script was loaded, in which case the variable would have been replaced by its value at that time.

If you intend to hide this directive inside some comments, it must be done like this:

```
/*@set @myvariable=1000 @*/
```

See also:	Pre-processing, *Pre-processing – /*@ ... @*/*

P

JavaScript Programmer's Reference

Prefix decrement (--) (Operator/prefix)

Decrement an operand before access.

Availability:	ECMAScript edition – 2 JavaScript – 1.0 JScript – 1.0 Internet Explorer – 3.02 Netscape – 2.0
Property/method value type:	Number primitive
JavaScript syntax:	-	--anOperand
Argument list:	anOperand	A numeric value that can be decremented

The operand is evaluated, converted to a numeric value and decremented by 1.

Although this is classified as a unary operator, its functionality is really that of an additive operator.

The associativity is from right to left.

Refer to the operator precedence topic for details of execution order.

See also:	Additive operator, Arithmetic operator, Associativity, *Decrement value (--)*, Operator Precedence, *Postfix decrement (--)*, *Prefix expression*, Prefix operator, Unary expression

Cross-references:

ECMA 262 edition 2 – section – 11.4.5

ECMA 262 edition 2 – section – 11.6.3

ECMA 262 edition 3 – section – 11.4.5

Prefix expression (Operator/prefix)

Increment or decrement an operand before access.

Availability:	ECMAScript edition – 2
Property/method value type:	Number primitive

Prefix expressions operate on Left-Hand-Side (sometimes called LValue) expressions.

There are two prefix operators:

❏ ++ performs a numeric increment on the operand.

❏ -- performs a numeric decrement on the operand.

These can also be classified as additive operators and because they modify a value in place, they also imply that an assignment takes place as well.

See also:	Additive operator, Assignment operator, *Decrement value (--)*, Expression, *Increment value (++)*, *Postfix decrement (--)*, *Postfix expression*, *Postfix increment (++)*, *Prefix decrement (--)*, *Prefix increment (++)*

Cross-references:

ECMA 262 edition 2 – section – 11.3

ECMA 262 edition 3 – section – 11.3

Prefix increment (++) (Operator/prefix)

Increment an operand before access.

Availability:	ECMAScript edition – 2 JavaScript – 1.0 JScript – 1.0 Internet Explorer – 3.02 Netscape – 2.0 Netscape Enterprise Server – 2.0 Opera – 3.0	
Property/method value type:	Number primitive	
JavaScript syntax:	-	++anOperand
Argument list:	anOperand	An incrementable numeric value

The operand is evaluated, converted to a numeric value and incremented by 1.

Although this is classified as a unary operator, its functionality is really that of an additive operator.

The associativity is from right to left.

P

Refer to the operator precedence topic for details of execution order.

See also:	Additive operator, Arithmetic operator, Associativity, *Decrement value (--)*, Operator Precedence, *Prefix expression*, Prefix operator, Unary expression

Cross-references:

ECMA 262 edition 2 – section – 11.4.4

ECMA 262 edition 2 – section – 11.6.3

ECMA 262 edition 3 – section – 11.4.4

PrivilegeManager object (Java class)

A Java class that administers privileges.

Availability:	JavaScript – 1.2 Netscape – 4.0
JavaScript syntax:	N *myPrivilegeManager =* `netscape.security.PrivilegeManager`
Object methods:	`disablePrivilege(), enablePrivilege()`

Because the Netscape security model is based on the Java security model, the Netscape browser requests its privileges through the Java mechanisms. These are encapsulated in a class that you can access from inside JavaScript.

The downside of this is that there is no meaningful value returned when the request is made. If the request for a privilege is denied, the error causes a Java exception that is difficult to trap from JavaScript. It is possible that more recent browser versions will support an exception handling mechanism.

There are two principle methods that are useful here, one to request the privilege and the other to relinquish it.

❑ `enablePrivilege()` – Requests the privilege passed as a string argument

❑ `disablePrivilege()` – Relinquishes the privilege based on a string argument

It is good practice to disable the privilege as soon as you no longer need it. In any case the privilege is given up when the function that requested it exits.

Trying to examine an instance of this class leads to some interesting run-time errors. That is perhaps understandable since the object is involved with keeping things secret. Even after requesting privileges, you cannot examine the internals of an instance of this class.

See also:	netscape.security.PrivilegeManager, Requesting privileges, UniversalBrowserAccess, UniversalBrowserRead, UniversalBrowserWrite, UniversalFileRead, UniversalPreferencesRead, UniversalPreferencesWrite, UniversalSendMail

Method	JavaScript	JScript	N	IE	Opera	Notes
disablePrivilege()	1.2 +	-	4.0 +	-	-	-
enablePrivilege()	1.2 +	-	4.0 +	-	-	-

ProcessingInstruction object (Object/DOM)

Part of the DOM level support for XML that relates to the handling of a processing instruction embedded in the text of the document.

Availability:	DOM level – 1 JavaScript – 1.5 JScript – 5.0 Internet Explorer – 5.0 Netscape – 6.0
Inherits from:	Node object
JavaScript syntax:	- myProcessingInstruction = new ProcessingInstruction()
Object properties:	data, target
See also:	Document.createProcessingInstruction()

Property	JavaScript	JScript	N	IE	Opera	DOM	Notes
data	1.5 +	5.0 +	6.0 +	5.0 +	-	1 +	-
target	1.5 +	5.0 +	6.0 +	5.0 +	-	1 +	ReadOnly

Inheritance chain:

Node object

project object (Object/NES)

A server-side host object provided inside NES. This object represents a running application inside the server.

Availability:	JavaScript – 1.1 Netscape Enterprise Server – 2.0
JavaScript syntax:	NES `project`
Object methods:	`lock()`, `unlock()`

The `client` object provides a means of maintaining state during a client session. This object is used for maintaining state across all sessions running in a single application. There may be several applications running in a server.

If you need to maintain state across the entire server then you need to access the `server` object which is discussed in a separate topic.

See also:	*client object*, Netscape Enterprise Server, `response.project`, *server object, unwatch(), watch()*

Method	JavaScript	JScript	NES	Notes
`lock()`	1.1 +	-	2.0 +	-
`unlock()`	1.1 +	-	2.0 +	-

proxy.pac (Special file)

This is a special file containing rules for accessing sites through proxy servers.

If you are using a browser inside a firewall, you will likely reach the Internet by using a proxy server. This is a special kind of web server that spans or bridges the firewall and fetches things across the Internet for you.

Generally these proxy servers will also limit access or log details of everything you fetch.

You can operate with no proxies, manually defined proxies or automatic proxies in the case of Netscape.

When you select Automatic mode, you are connecting in to a piece of JavaScript code that can work out whether to use a proxy or not and if so, which one.

In this context, some language features may be unavailable but then others are provided to assist in the deconstruction of URL values, and are only available in this context.

The only purpose of a `proxy.pac` file is to define the content of the `FindProxyForURL()` function.

The `proxy.pac` file can be retrieved from any location that can be defined by a URL. This means it could be a local file on your desktop or served directly by a web server inside your firewall. In theory it could be served by a web server outside your firewall so long as your firewall had a 'hole' in it to allow you to gain direct access to the server. That could lead to problems where the file you pull back might thereafter prevent access to that location, and it obviates the whole purpose of having a firewall in the first place.

Providing this file on a local web server inside your firewall means that it can be shared by all your Netscape browser users and maintained from a central location. This is not very much use if you only have one user but when you have 500 it is a great time saver. However, the downside is that if you publish a broken `proxy.pac` file, all of your users go offline as soon as their browsers download it.

You cannot browse a `proxy.pac` file with a Netscape browser, however you might be able to download one with MSIE if you are curious to see what it looks like.

To set this mechanism working, you need to go to the proxy configuration panel in your browser preferences and choose automatic proxy configuration. Then you need to type in the URL where the `proxy.pac` file lives.

See also:	*.pac*, File extensions, *FindProxyForURL()*, *isInNet()*, *isPlainHostName()*, Proxies

Cross-references:

Wrox *Instant JavaScript* – page – 57

Put() (Function/internal)

Internal private function.

Availability:	ECMAScript edition – 2

This internal function is used to store a new value into an internal property.

The property is set or not according to the result of the CanPut() function for the property. If the property does not exist, then a new property is created with its attributes set to an empty condition.

The Put() internal function may indeed allow a property value to be changed when received by a host object, even if that host object would respond to the HasProperty() function with a false result indicating that the property does not exist.

See also:	Internal Method, *PutValue()*

P

Property attributes:

Internal.

Cross-references:

ECMA 262 edition 2 – section – 8.6.2.2

ECMA 262 edition 3 – section – 8.6.2.2

put() (Method/internal)

Write publicly accessible properties.

Availability:	ECMAScript edition – 2

Used to store new values into publicly exposed properties.

See also:	Accessor method

Cross-references:

ECMA 262 edition 2 – section – 8.6.2.2

ECMA 262 edition 3 – section – 8.6.2.2

PutValue() (Function/internal)

Internal private function.

Availability:	ECMAScript edition – 2

This internal function stores a value in the property belonging to the reference item passed as its argument.

A run-time error is generated if the passed in argument is not a reference item.

If the target object does exist, the usual Put() function logic is invoked to store the value in the object property.

If the target object does not exist, then the property is added to the global object and takes the value that is passed as a new value.

See also:	*Global object, Put(),* Reference

Property attributes:

Internal.

Cross-references:

ECMA 262 edition 2 – section – 8.7.4

ECMA 262 edition 3 – section – 8.7.2

about: URL (Request method)
AbstractView object (Object/DOM)
ActiveXObject object (Object/JScript)
Add (+) (Operator/additive)
Add then assign (+=) (Operator/assignment)

RadioButton object (Object/DOM)

A toggle button that acts together with a group of radio buttons in a family.
Clicking one deselects any others in the group. These are used in forms to choose
one item from a set.

Availability:		DOM level – 1 JavaScript – 1.0 JScript – 1.0 Internet Explorer – 3.02 Netscape – 2.0 Opera – 3.0
Inherits from:		*Input object*
JavaScript syntax:	-	*myRadioButton =* *myDocument.aFormName.anElementName*
	-	*myRadioButton = myDocument.aFormName.* `elements`[*anItemIndex*]
	IE	*myRadioButton =* *myDocument.*`all.`*anElementID*
	IE	*myRadioButton = myDocument.*`all.tags` `("INPUT")`[*anIndex*]
	IE	*myRadioButton = myDocument.*`all`[*aName*]
	-	*myRadioButton = myDocument.*`forms` [*aFormIndex*]*.anElementName*
	-	*myRadioButton = myDocument.*`forms` [*aFormIndex*]*.*`elements`[*anItemIndex*]
	-	*myRadioButton =* *myDocument.*`getElementById`(*anElementID*)
	-	*myRadioButton = myDocument* `.getElementsByName`(*aName*)[*anIndex*]
	-	*myRadioButton = myDocument.*`get` `ElementsByTagName("INPUT")`[*anIndex*]

Table continued on following page

HTML syntax:	`<INPUT TYPE="radio">`	
Argument list:	*anIndex*	A valid reference to an item in the collection
	aName	The name attribute of an element
	anElementID	The ID attribute of an element
	anItemIndex	A valid reference to an item in the collection
	aFormIndex	A reference to a particular form in the `forms` collection
Object properties:	`checked, defaultChecked, status, type, value`	
Object methods:	`handleEvent()`	
Event handlers:	`onAfterUpdate, onBeforeUpdate, onBlur, onClick, onDblClick, onErrorUpdate, onFilterChange, onFocus, onHelp, onKeyDown, onKeyPress, onKeyUp, onMouseDown, onMouseMove, onMouseOut, onMouseOver, onMouseUp, onRowEnter, onRowExit`	

Many properties, methods, and event handlers are inherited from the Input object class. Refer to topics grouped with the "Input" prefix for details of common functionality across all sub-classes of the Input object super-class.

There isn't really a RadioButton object class but it is helpful when trying to understand the wide variety of input element types if we can reduce the complexity by discussing only the properties and methods of a radio button. In actual fact, the object is represented as an item of the Input object class.

The RadioButton sub-class of the Input object does not support the select() method or the defaultValue property except on MSIE.

Example code:

```
<HTML>
<HEAD>
</HEAD>
<BODY>
<DIV ID="RESULT">?</DIV>
<FORM onClick="handleClick()">
<INPUT TYPE="radio" VALUE="A" NAME="SET">Selection A<BR>
<INPUT TYPE="radio" VALUE="B" NAME="SET">Selection B<BR>
<INPUT TYPE="radio" VALUE="C" NAME="SET">Selection C<BR>
<INPUT TYPE="radio" VALUE="D" NAME="SET">Selection D<BR>
</FORM>
<SCRIPT>
// Code for IE only
function handleClick()
```

```
    {
        myString   = "[";
        myString += document.forms[0].elements[0].checked;
        myString += "] [";
        myString += document.forms[0].elements[1].checked;
        myString += "] [";
        myString += document.forms[0].elements[2].checked;
        myString += "] [";
        myString += document.forms[0].elements[3].checked;
        myString += "]";
        document.all.RESULT.innerText = myString;
    }
    </SCRIPT>
    </BODY>
    </HTML>
```

See also:	Element object, Form.elements[], FormElement object, Input object, Input.accessKey, onClick, RadioButton.handleEvent()

Property	JavaScript	JScript	N	IE	Opera	DOM	Notes
checked	1.0 +	1.0 +	2.0 +	3.02 +	3.0 +	1 +	-
defaultChecked	1.0 +	1.0 +	2.0 +	3.02 +	3.0 +	1 +	-
status	-	3.0 +	-	4.0 +	-	-	-
type	1.1 +	3.0 +	3.0 +	4.0 +	3.0 +	1 +	ReadOnly
value	1.0 +	1.0 +	2.0 +	3.02 +	3.0 +	1 +	Warning

Method	JavaScript	JScript	N	IE	Opera	DOM	Notes
handleEvent()	1.2 +	-	4.0 +	-	-	-	-

Event name	JavaScript	JScript	N	IE	Opera	DOM	Notes
onAfterUpdate	-	3.0 +	-	4.0 +	-	-	-
onBeforeUpdate	-	3.0 +	-	4.0 +	-	-	-
onBlur	1.1 +	3.0 +	3.0 +	4.0 +	3.0 +	-	Warning
onClick	1.0 +	1.0 +	2.0 +	3.0 +	3.0 +	-	Warning
onDblClick	1.2 +	3.0 +	4.0 +	4.0 +	3.0 +	-	Warning
onErrorUpdate	-	3.0 +	-	4.0 +	-	-	-
onFilterChange	-	3.0 +	-	4.0 +	-	-	-
onFocus	1.0 +	3.0 +	2.0 +	4.0 +	3.0 +	-	Warning
onHelp	-	3.0 +	-	4.0 +	-	-	Warning
onKeyDown	1.2 +	3.0 +	4.0 +	4.0 +	3.0 +	-	Warning
onKeyPress	1.2 +	3.0 +	4.0 +	4.0 +	3.0 +	-	Warning

Table continued on following page

R

JavaScript Programmer's Reference

Event name	JavaScript	JScript	N	IE	Opera	DOM	Notes
onKeyUp	1.2 +	3.0 +	4.0 +	4.0 +	3.0 +	-	Warning
onMouseDown	1.2 +	3.0 +	4.0 +	4.0 +	3.0 +	-	Warning
onMouseMove	1.2 +	3.0 +	4.0 +	4.0 +	-	-	Warning
onMouseOut	1.1 +	3.0 +	3.0 +	4.0 +	3.0 +	-	Warning
onMouseOver	1.0 +	1.0 +	2.0 +	3.0 +	3.0 +	-	Warning
onMouseUp	1.2 +	3.0 +	4.0 +	4.0 +	3.0 +	-	Warning
onRowEnter	-	3.0 +	-	4.0 +	-	-	-
onRowExit	-	3.0 +	-	4.0 +	-	-	-

Inheritance chain:

Element object, Input object, Node object

RangeError object (Object/core)

A native error object based on the Error object.

Availability:	ECMAScript edition – 3 JavaScript – 1.5 Netscape – 6.0	
Inherits from:	&Error object	
JavaScript syntax:	N	myError = new RangeError()
	N	myError = new RangeError(aNumber)
	N	myError = new RangeError(aNumber, aText)
Argument list:	aNumber	An error number
	aText	Text describing the error

This sub-class of the Error object is used when an exception is caused by a numeric value exceeding its allowable range.

See also:	catch(...), Error object, EvalError object, ReferenceError object, SyntaxError object, throw, try ... catch ... finally, TypeError object, URIError object

Inheritance chain:

Error object

Cross-references:

ECMA 262 edition 3 – section – 15.1.4.11

ECMA 262 edition 3 – section – 15.11.6.2

ReadOnly (Property attribute)

An internal property attribute that controls whether a property value can be changed.

Availability:	ECMAScript edition – 2
Property/method value type:	`Boolean primitive`

This is intended to prevent the script from modifying a property value.

You should note however that this does not mean that the property must always be ReadOnly. There may be times when the hosting environment changes the ReadOnly settings for a property.

Generally, the ReadOnly state would not change very often but the standard mandates that it does not mean constant and unchanging, only that while the ReadOnly state is true, the property should be locked out against any attempts to change its value.

Note that this is not the ReadOnly property that belongs to a Form Input element. That is intended to stop the user from altering the current state of an input item.

See also:	*DontDelete, DontEnumerate,* `Input.readOnly`

Cross-references:

ECMA 262 edition 2 – section – 8.6.1

ECMA 262 edition 3 – section – 8.6.1

Rect object (Object/browser)

A rectangle object used for Layer clip rectangles.

Availability:	JavaScript – 1.2 Netscape – 4.0
JavaScript syntax:	N `myRect = myLayer.clip` N `myRect = myStyle.clip`
Object properties:	`bottom, height, left, right, top, width`

This object represents a clipping rectangle that the visible part of a display object is viewed through. This is most likely used with a `layer` object. The layer contents would be drawn off-screen and then that part which falls within the clipping rectangle would be displayed in the window.

This can be useful for performing wipes and making parts of a layer progressively visible within some kind of transition loop.

In the MSIE browser, these rectangular objects are manufactured as needed with the `rect()` constructor function.

These rectangles are not the same as you can create with the `getBoundingClientRect()` method, which applies to a `TextRange` object. That method creates `TextRectangle` which responds differently to the pixel rectangle we have here.

See also:	*Clip object*, `Layer.clip`, `style.clip`, `TextRange.getBoundingClientRect()`, *textRectangle object*

Property	JavaScript	JScript	N	IE	Opera	HTML	Notes
bottom	1.2 +	-	4.0 +	-	-	-	-
height	1.2 +	-	4.0 +	-	-	-	-
left	1.2 +	-	4.0 +	-	-	-	-
right	1.2 +	-	4.0 +	-	-	-	-
top	1.2 +	-	4.0 +	-	-	-	-
width	1.2 +	-	4.0 +	-	-	-	-

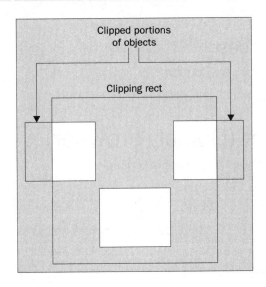

ReferenceError object (Object/core)

A native error object based on the `Error` object.

Availability:	ECMAScript edition – 3 JavaScript – 1.5 Netscape – 6.0	
Inherits from:	*Error object*	
JavaScript syntax:	N	`myError = new ReferenceError()`
	N	`myError = new` `ReferenceError(aNumber)`
	N	`myError = new` `ReferenceError(aNumber, aText)`
Argument list:	*aNumber*	An error number
	aText	Text describing the error

This sub-class of the `Error` object is used when an exception is caused by an incorrect reference being made to an object.

See also:	*catch(...), Error object, EvalError object, RangeError object, SyntaxError object, throw, try ... catch ... finally, TypeError object, URIError object*

Inheritance chain:

`Error` object

Cross-references:

ECMA 262 edition 3 – section – 15.1.4.12

ECMA 262 edition 3 – section – 15.11.6.3

RegExp object (Object/core)

An object that encapsulates regular expressions.

Availability:	ECMAScript edition – 3 JavaScript – 1.2 JScript – 3.0 Internet Explorer – 4.0 Netscape – 4.0 Netscape Enterprise Server – 3.0 Opera 5.0

JavaScript syntax:	-	$myRegExp$ = RegExp
	-	$myRegExp$ = new RegExp()
	-	$myRegExp$ = RegExp($aPattern$)
	-	$myRegExp$ = RegExp($aPattern$, $someAttribs$)
Argument list:	$aPattern$	A regular expression pattern
	$someAttribs$	One or more regular expression attributes
Class properties:	\$n, index, input, lastMatch, lastParen, leftContext, multiline, rightContext	
Object properties:	\$&, \$', \$*, \$+, \$_, \$`, constructor, global, ignoreCase, index, lastIndex, prototype, source	
Object methods:	compile(), exec(), test(), toSource(), toString()	

The RegExp object implements some class (or static) methods which is fairly untypical of classes that support a constructor. There are also instance methods and properties.

Warnings:

❑ The static properties of a regular expression object do not conform to the same static scoping rules as the rest of JavaScript. Their static or class based properties are dynamically scoped and available in the scope chain from which they are executed. This is not the same as the scope rules for functions which dictates that they run in the scope in which they are declared and not the scope from which they are called. This means that if a regular expression object is accessed in a function declared in one frame, when that function is called, the static properties are modified for the global built-in regular expression object that belongs to the calling frame, avoiding all manner of multithreaded simultaneous execution problems that would be difficult to deal with if the scoping rules for regular expression objects were the same as the rest of JavaScript.

❑ In Netscape, many properties of the RegExp built-in object are enumerable but they are not available in this way in MSIE.

❑ IE 5 does not properly support the RegExp object on the Macintosh platform. Many properties such as lastMatch, leftContext, etc. return an undefined value regardless of the RegExp result.

Example code:

```
// Create a RegExp object using a constructor
var myRegExp = new RegExp("sque[ea]ky", "g");
// Create the same RegExp object with a reg exp literal
var myRegExp = /sque[ea]ky/g;
```

See also:	Function scope, RegExp pattern – character literal, RegExp(), *RegExp.multiline, unwatch(), watch()*

Property	JavaScript	JScript	N	IE	Opera	NES	ECMA	Notes
$&	1.2 +	3.0 +	4.0 +	4.0 +	5.0 +	3.0 +	3 +	Warning
$ '	1.2 +	3.0 +	4.0 +	4.0 +	5.0 +	3.0 +	3 +	Warning
$*	1.2 +	3.0 +	4.0 +	4.0 +	5.0 +	3.0 +	3 +	Warning
$+	1.2 +	3.0 +	4.0 +	4.0 +	5.0 +	3.0 +	3 +	Warning
$_	1.2 +	3.0 +	4.0 +	4.0 +	5.0 +	3.0 +	-	-
$`	1.2 +	3.0 +	4.0 +	4.0 +	5.0 +	3.0 +	3 +	Warning
constructor	1.2 +	3.0 +	4.0 +	4.0 +	5.0 +	-	3 +	-
global	1.2 +	3.0 +	4.0 +	4.0 +	5.0 +	3.0 +	3 +	ReadOnly
ignoreCase	1.2 +	5.5 +	4.0 +	5.5 +	5.0 +	3.0 +	3 +	ReadOnly
index	-	3.0 +	-	4.0 +	5.0 +	-	-	-
lastIndex	1.2 +	3.0 +	4.0 +	4.0 +	5.0 +	3.0 +	3 +	Warning
prototype	1.2 +	3.0 +	4.0 +	4.0 +	5.0 +	-	3 +	-
source	1.2 +	3.0 +	4.0 +	4.0 +	5.0 +	3.0 +	3 +	ReadOnly

Method	JavaScript	JScript	N	IE	Opera	NES	ECMA	Notes
compile()	1.2 +	3.0 +	4.0 +	4.0 +	5.0 +	3.0 +	-	-
exec()	1.2 +	3.0 +	4.0 +	4.0 +	5.0 +	3.0 +	3 +	Warning
test()	1.2 +	3.0 +	4.0 +	4.0 +	5.0 +	3.0 +	3 +	-
toSource()	1.3 +	-	4.06 +	-	-	-	-	-
toString()	1.2 +	3.0 +	4.0 +	4.0 +	5.0 +	-	3 +	-

Cross-references:

ECMA 262 edition 3 – section – 15.1.4.8

ECMA 262 edition 3 – section – 15.10.3

ECMA 262 edition 3 – section – 15.10.4

RegExp.$n (Property/static)

A property of the global RegExp object.

Availability:	ECMAScript edition – 3 JavaScript – 1.2 JScript – 3.0 Internet Explorer – 4.0 Netscape – 4.0 Netscape Enterprise Server – 3.0 Opera 5.0

Table continued on following page

R

JavaScript syntax:	-	RegExp.$1
	-	RegExp.$2
	-	RegExp.$3
	-	RegExp.$4
	-	RegExp.$5
	-	RegExp.$6
	-	RegExp.$7
	-	RegExp.$8
	-	RegExp.$9

There are nine similarly named properties whose name is a dollar symbol followed by a single digit, each of these holding text matched by a sub-expression (in parentheses) for the most recent match.

The ECMAScript edition 3 specification suggests that the range of values for this is $01 to $99 and for an implementation to be ECMA compliant, it should support that range of possibilities, as well as the $1 to $9 values.

Warnings:

❑ Since this is a class property (a static property), it belongs to the global built-in RegExp object. This means it is shared by all RegExp object instances and therefore is very transient and will be overwritten as soon as the next regular expression is evaluated. If you want to preserve the value, you will need to copy it immediately your regular expression has evaluated and before you call another.

❑ Note that there are only 9 of these. If you create a complex pattern that has more than 9 sub-expressions, you won't be able to access the sub-expressions above the ninth one unless the implementation is fully compliant with ECMAScript edition 3.

❑ Early versions of MSIE did not fully support this numbered property mechanism.

See also:	RegExp pattern – grouping, RegExp pattern – references, RegExp.exec(), RegExp.test()

Property attributes:

ReadOnly.

Cross-references:

ECMA 262 edition 3 – section – 15.5.4.11

RegExp.input (Property/static)

A property of the global `RegExp` object.

Availability:	JavaScript – 1.2
	JScript – 3.0
	Internet Explorer – 4.0
	Netscape – 4.0
	Netscape Enterprise Server – 3.0
	Opera 5.0

JavaScript syntax:	-	`RegExp.input`

A default string to search when the `exec()` and `test()` methods are called with no arguments.

You can set this and then call the `RegExp.exec()` or `RegExp.test()` methods without passing a string argument value. They will then use this property of the built-in global `RegExp` object as their target search string.

Warnings:

❑ This behaves slightly differently in JavaScript version 1.2 in Netscape.

❑ Since this is a class property (a static property), it belongs to the global built-in `RegExp` object. This means it is shared by all `RegExp` object instances and therefore is very transient and will be overwritten as soon as the next regular expression is evaluated. If you want to preserve the value, you will need to copy it immediately your regular expression has evaluated and before you call another.

❑ In Netscape 4, event handlers for `FormElement` objects in a web page form automatically load the input property of the built-in `RegExp` object as the event handlers are fired. Hence, you should not rely on the input property remaining consistent once your function call exits. Set it immediately before you need to parse the string and do not bank on it being there later.

❑ This property was not supported fully in IE 4 as it was read only. The work-around was to always pass in a value to the `exec()` method when it is invoked.

See also:	`RegExp.exec()`, `RegExp.test()`

R

RegExp.lastMatch (Property/static)

A property of the global `RegExp` object.

Availability:	JavaScript – 1.2 JScript – 5.5 Internet Explorer – 5.5 Netscape – 4.0 Netscape Enterprise Server – 3.0 Opera – 5.0	
JavaScript syntax:	-	`RegExp.lastMatch`

This property returns the most recently matched text.

Warnings:

❑ Since this is a class property (a static property), it belongs to the global built-in `RegExp` object. This means it is shared by all `RegExp` object instances and therefore is very transient and will be overwritten as soon as the next regular expression is evaluated. If you want to preserve the value, you will need to copy it immediately after your regular expression has been evaluated and before you call another.

See also:	`RegExp.exec()`, `RegExp.test()`, `RegExp["$&"]`

Property attributes:

`ReadOnly`.

RegExp.lastParen (Property/static)

A property of the global `RegExp` object.

Availability:	JavaScript – 1.2 JScript – 5.5 Internet Explorer – 5.5 Netscape – 4.0 Netscape Enterprise Server – 3.0 Opera – 5.0	
JavaScript syntax:	-	`RegExp.lastParen`

This property returns the text matched by the last sub-expression which was part of the most recent match. It will contain a null or undefined value if there was no previous match.

Warnings:

❑ Since this is a class property (a static property), it belongs to the global built-in `RegExp` object. This means it is shared by all `RegExp` object instances and therefore is very transient and will be overwritten as soon as the next regular expression is evaluated. If you want to preserve the value, you will need to copy it immediately after your regular expression has been evaluated and before you call another.

See also:	RegExp pattern – grouping, RegExp pattern – references, `RegExp.exec()`, `RegExp.test()`, `RegExp["$+"]`

Property attributes:

`ReadOnly`.

RegExp.leftContext (Property/static)

A property of the global `RegExp` object.

Availability:	JavaScript – 1.2 JScript – 5.5 Internet Explorer – 5.5 Netscape – 4.0 Netscape Enterprise Server – 3.0 Opera – 5.0	
JavaScript syntax:	-	`RegExp.leftContext`

This property returns the text to the left of the most recent match.

Warnings:

❑ Since this is a class property (a static property), it belongs to the global built-in `RegExp` object. This means it is shared by all `RegExp` object instances and therefore is very transient and will be overwritten as soon as the next regular expression is evaluated. If you want to preserve the value, you will need to copy it immediately after your regular expression has been evaluated and before you call another.

See also:	`RegExp.exec()`, `RegExp.test()`, `RegExp["$`"]`

Property attributes:

`ReadOnly`.

RegExp.multiline (Property/static)

A regular expression attribute to control the scope of the pattern.

Availability:	ECMAScript edition – 3 JavaScript – 1.2 JScript – 5.5 Internet Explorer – 5.5 Netscape – 4.0 Netscape Enterprise Server – 3.0 Opera – 5	
Property/method value type:	`Boolean primitive`	
JavaScript syntax:	-	`RegExp.multiline = aBoolean`
Argument list:	`aBoolean`	A switch to set the property true or false

When you want the regular expression to apply to multiple lines separated by newline characters, this property should be set to `true`. When it is `false` the pattern is applied only to a single line.

Warnings:

❑ In JavaScript version 1.2 in Netscape, this is the only way to set the pattern to operate on multiple lines.

❑ The 'm' attribute is provided in JavaScript version 1.3 in some implementations.

❑ Note that client-side JavaScript used in Netscape 4 will set the multi-line property to `true` when it is used in an event handler for a `TextArea` object. The value is restored to whatever it was beforehand on exiting the handler. This suggests that you should explicitly set the multi-line property to the value you require when you parse a regular expression. You cannot rely on the stability of any value you may have stored in that attribute previously.

❑ Since this is a class property (a static property), it belongs to the global built-in `RegExp` object. This means it is shared by all `RegExp` object instances and therefore is very transient and will be overwritten as soon as the next regular expression is evaluated. If you want to preserve the value, you will need to copy it immediately before your regular expression has been evaluated and before you call another.

Example code:

```
RegExp.multiline = true;
RegExp.multiline = false;
```

See also:	*RegExp object*, RegExp pattern – attributes, RegExp pattern – position, `RegExp.exec()`, `RegExp.test()`, `RegExp["$*"]`

Cross-references:

ECMA 262 edition 3 – section – 15.10.7.4

RegExp.rightContext (Property/static)

A property of the global `RegExp` object.

Availability:	JavaScript – 1.2 JScript – 5.5 Internet Explorer – 5.5 Netscape – 4.0 Netscape Enterprise Server – 3.0 Opera – 5	
JavaScript syntax:	-	`RegExp.rightContext`

This property returns the text to the right of the most recent match.

Warnings:

❑ Since this is a class property (a static property), it belongs to the global built-in `RegExp` object. This means it is shared by all `RegExp` object instances and therefore is very transient and will be overwritten as soon as the next regular expression is evaluated. If you want to preserve the value, you will need to copy it immediately after your regular expression has been evaluated and before you call another.

See also:	`RegExp.exec()`, `RegExp.test()`, `RegExp["$'"]`

Property attributes:

`ReadOnly`.

Regular expression (Definition)

A means of matching patterns of text in string values.

Regular expressions are a way of describing a pattern match that can be used to select a group of characters from an input string. This usually then leads on to replacing them with some other set of characters. It is analogous to the find and replace capability in a word processor.

JavaScript version 1.2 introduced regular expression support by way of a specialized object, a utility that UNIX developers have long known about and used. It has migrated into many desktop applications now and has become a somewhat portable way of matching text strings with one another and performing edits on them. The regular expression syntax adopted by JavaScript version 1.2 emulates that which is commonly used in Perl interpreters, specifically the syntax that is supported is generally called Perl version 4. In JavaScript version 1.3, the regular expression syntax was expanded to support Perl version 5 syntax.

Regular expressions are managed by creating a RegExp object with the RegExp() constructor. RegExp objects support a literal syntax and can be created on the fly without needing a constructor call which makes them extremely convenient to deploy.

The ECMAScript standard ratifies regular expressions in the third edition. They were not present in the second edition.

Warnings:

❑ Regular expressions are still an area of concern when developing portable content. For example, they are completely unsupported on the WebTV platform as of the Summer 2000 release of the JellyScript interpreter.

See also:	Fundamental data type, JellyScript, RegExp pattern, RegExp pattern – character literal, RegExp(), RegExp.exec(), String.match(), String.replace(), String.search(), String.split()

Cross-references:

O'Reilly JavaScript Definitive Guide – page – 49

Relational expression (Definition)

Relational expressions yield a Boolean result.

Availability:	ECMAScript edition – 2
Property/method value type:	Boolean primitive

Relational expressions yield a Boolean result according to the relational test of the values either side of the operator.

Numerical values are compared according to sign and magnitude while string values are compared according to the Unicode collating sort sequence.

Relational operators will attempt to convert both arguments to a Number, and if at least one argument can be converted to a Number then the other will be forced to be a Number for comparison purposes. If both arguments are Strings or string-like objects, the relational test will be String-based.

If a prefixing plus sign is present, then a numeric coercion of a string takes place before the comparison.

Example code:

```
// Force a string comparison
myResult = (a+'' <= b+'');
// Force a numeric comparison
myResult = (a-0 <= b-0);
// Force a Boolean comparison
myResult = (!a <= !b);
```

| See also: | *Equal to (==)*, Equality expression, Expression, *Greater than (>)*, *Greater than or equal to (>=)*, *Identically equal to (===)*, *Less than (<)*, *Less than or equal to (<=)*, *NOT Equal to (!=)*, *NOT Identically equal to (!==)*, *Relational operator*, Type conversion |

Cross-references:

ECMA 262 edition 2 – section – 11.8

ECMA 262 edition 3 – section – 11.8

Wrox Instant JavaScript – page – 37

Wrox Instant JavaScript – page – 39

Relational operator (Definition)

Relational operators are used to create relational expressions.

R

| Availability: | ECMAScript edition – 2 |
| Property/method value type: | Boolean primitive |

Relational operators are used in relational expressions and always yield a Boolean result.

Although generally considered to be members of the relational operator set, equality and non-equality tests are classified as equality operators in the ECMA standard.

JavaScript Programmer's Reference

The following table lists all operators that could be loosely classified or specifically classified as relational operators:

Operator	Description
==	Equal to
===	Identically equal to
!=	NOT equal to
!==	NOT identically equal to
<	Less than
<=	Less than or equal to
>	Greater than
>=	Greater than or equal to

It follows that all equality operators are generally classifiable as relational operators and all relational operators are members of the set of logical operators, since they all yield a Boolean value as a result.

See also:	*Equal to* (==), Equality operator, *Greater than* (>), *Greater than or equal to* (>=), *Identically equal to* (===), *Less than* (<), *Less than or equal to* (<=), *NOT Equal to* (!=), *NOT Identically equal to* (!==), *Relational expression*

Cross-references:

ECMA 262 edition 2 – section – 11.8

ECMA 262 edition 3 – section – 11.8

Wrox *Instant JavaScript* – page – 19

Remainder (%) (Operator/multiplicative)

Divide one operand by another and yield the remainder.

Availability:	ECMAScript edition – 2 JavaScript – 1.0 JScript – 1.0 Internet Explorer – 3.02 Netscape – 2.0 Netscape Enterprise Server – 2.0 Opera – 3.0
Property/method value type:	Number primitive

JavaScript syntax:	-	anOperand1 % anOperand2
Argument list:	anOperand1	The dividend value
	anOperand2	The divisor value

The % operator yields the remainder after dividing the left operand by the right. This is otherwise known as the modulo or modulus operator.

In an ECMAScript compliant interpreter, the remainder is a floating point value and, unlike the C and C++ languages, the input operands can also be floating point values.

The result of performing a remainder on floating point values is not the same as the IEEE 754 remainder operation. IEEE 754 mandates a remainder computed via a rounding division whereas ECMA mandates a truncating remainder. In ECMAScript the remainder behaves similarly to the Java integer remainder operator and is analogous to the fmod() library function in C language compilers.

The behavior in an ECMA compliant JavaScript implementation should obey these rules:

If either operand is NaN then the result is NaN.

The sign of the result is the same as the sign of the dividend (the operand on the left).

If the dividend is an infinity, the result is NaN.

If the divisor is zero, the result is NaN.

If the dividend is a finite value and the divisor is infinity, the result equals the dividend.

If the dividend is zero and the divisor is finite, the result is zero.

Otherwise, as long as neither an infinity, zero or NaN is involved, the floating remainder is calculated like this. The dividend n is divided by the divisor d to produce a quotient, q. The quotient is forced to be an integer and multiplied again by d and the result subtracted from n to yield the remainder. Thus:

```
q = n/d

r = n - (d * q)
```

The value q will be forced to be an integer although the resulting value r may not be.

The associativity is left to right.

Refer to the operator precedence topic for details of execution order.

Warnings:

❏ JScript version 1.0 truncates floating point values to integers before applying the
remainder operator. This means that the expression 5.5 % 2.2 yields the value 1.

See also:	Arithmetic operator, Associativity, *Divide (/)*, *Divide then assign (/=)*, Integer arithmetic, Integer-value-remainder, *Math.ceil()*, *Math.floor()*, Multiplicative expression, Multiplicative operator, Operator Precedence, *Remainder then assign (%=)*

Cross-references:

ECMA 262 edition 2 – section – 11.5.3

ECMA 262 edition 2 – section – 11.13

ECMA 262 edition 3 – section – 11.5.3

Wrox *Instant JavaScript* – page – 19

Remainder then assign (%=) (Operator/assignment)

Divide one operand by another, leaving the remainder in the first.

Availability:	ECMAScript edition – 2 JavaScript – 1.0 JScript – 1.0 Internet Explorer – 3.02 Netscape – 2.0 Netscape Enterprise Server – 2.0 Opera – 3.0	
Property/method value type:	`Number primitive`	
JavaScript syntax:	-	`anOperand1 %= anOperand2`
Argument list:	*anOperand1*	The dividend value where the result is also assigned
	anOperand2	The divisor value

Divide the left operand by the right operand and assign the remainder to
the left operand.

This is functionally equivalent to the expression:

```
anOperand1 = anOperand1 % anOperand2;
```

Although this is classified as an assignment operator it is really a compound of an assignment and a multiplicative operator.

The associativity is right to left.

Refer to the operator precedence topic for details of execution order.

The new value of anOperand1 is returned as a result of the expression.

Warnings:

❑ The operand to the left of the operator must be an LValue. That is, it should be able to take an assignment and store the value.

See also:	Arithmetic operator, *Assign value (=)*, Assignment expression, Assignment operator, Associativity, Integer arithmetic, Integer-value-remainder, LValue, *Math.ceil()*, *Math.floor()*, Multiplicative operator, Operator Precedence, *Remainder (%)*

Cross-references:

ECMA 262 edition 2 – section – 11.13

ECMA 262 edition 3 – section – 11.13

request object (Object/NES)

A server-side object maintained by NES for each HTTP: request.

Availability:	JavaScript – 1.1 Netscape Enterprise Server – 2.0	
JavaScript syntax:	NES	request
Object properties:	<input_name>, <urlExtension>, agent, imageX, imageY, ip, method, protocol	

Whenever a user requests a page from a Netscape Enterprise Server, a request object is created to manage storage methods and properties for that request. When the request is returned, the object can be destroyed as it will have no further use.

The request object contains details of the URL, form data and search criteria. This is the way that you access the data in a form submit for example.

R

There are other properties belonging to this object that can tell you a lot about the client and what is happening there.

The ASP server also supports a `Request` object, whose name is capitalized. It's there for the same purpose and manages the incoming requests from the clients' browsers.

Warnings:

❑ The `Request` object supported by ASP is quite different to that supported by NES. Since the tag introducer is quite different for each server-side system, it is unlikely you'll deploy common scripts across NES and ASP running on IIS.

See also:	Netscape Enterprise Server, `response.client`, `response.request`, *unwatch()*, *watch()*

Property	JavaScript	JScript	NES	Notes
`<input_name>`	1.1 +	-	2.0 +	-
`<urlExtension>`	1.1 +	-	2.0 +	-
`agent`	1.1 +	-	2.0 +	-
`imageX`	1.1 +	-	2.0 +	-
`imageY`	1.1 +	-	2.0 +	-
`ip`	1.1 +	-	2.0 +	Warning
`method`	1.1 +	-	2.0 +	-
`protocol`	1.1 +	-	2.0 +	-

Requesting privileges (Security related)

Your script needs to request privileges when it requires them.

So long as you can sign scripts for Netscape, you can then make requests for privileges when those scripts run. This is done by means of the privilege manager.

Because the Netscape security model is based on the Java security model, the Netscape browser requests its privileges through the Java mechanisms. These are encapsulated in a class that you can access from inside JavaScript.

The downside of this is that there is no meaningful value returned when the request is made. If the request for a privilege is denied, the error causes a Java exception which is difficult to trap from JavaScript. It is possible that new browser versions will support an exception handling mechanism.

There are two principal methods that are useful here, one to request the privilege and the other to relinquish it.

`enablePrivilege()` – Requests the privilege passed as a string argument

`disablePrivilege()` – Relinquishes the privilege based on a string argument

Example code:

```
// Request the file reading privilege
netscape.security.PrivilegeManager.enablePrivilege
("UniversalFileRead")
```

See also:	*netscape.security.PrivilegeManager, PrivilegeManager object,* `PrivilegeManager.disablePrivilege()`, `PrivilegeManager.enablePrivilege()`, *Signed scripts, UniversalBrowserAccess, UniversalBrowserRead, UniversalBrowserWrite, UniversalFileRead, UniversalPreferencesRead, UniversalPreferencesWrite, UniversalSendMail*

ResetButton object (Object/DOM)

A button in a form that will reset the form fields to their default values.

Availability:	DOM level – 1 JavaScript – 1.0 JScript – 1.0 Internet Explorer – 3.02 Netscape – 2.0 Opera – 3.0	
Inherits from:	*Input object*	
JavaScript syntax:	-	`myResetButton =` `myDocument.aFormName.anElementName`
	-	`myResetButton =` `myDocument.aFormName.elements[anItemIndex]`
	IE	`myResetButton = myDocument.all.anElementID`
	IE	`myResetButton =` `myDocument.all.tags("INPUT")[anIndex]`
	IE	`myResetButton = myDocument.all[aName]`
	-	`myResetButton =` `myDocument.forms[aFormIndex].anElementName`
	-	`myResetButton = myDocument.forms` `[aFormIndex].elements[anItemIndex]`
	-	`myResetButton =` `myDocument.getElementById(anElementID)`
	-	`myResetButton = myDocument` `.getElementsByName(aName)[anIndex]`
	-	`myResetButton = myDocument` `.getElementsByTagName("INPUT")[anIndex]`

Table continued on following page

R

JavaScript Programmer's Reference

HTML syntax:	`<INPUT TYPE="reset">`	
Argument list:	*anIndex*	A valid reference to an item in the collection
	aName	The name attribute of an element
	anElementID	The ID attribute of an element
	anItemIndex	A valid reference to an item in the collection
	aFormIndex	A reference to a particular form in the forms collection
Object properties:	`type, value`	
Object methods:	`handleEvent()`	
Event handlers:	`onAfterUpdate, onBeforeUpdate, onBlur, onClick, onDblClick, onFilterChange, onFocus, onHelp, onKeyDown, onKeyPress, onKeyUp, onMouseDown, onMouseMove, onMouseOut, onMouseOver, onMouseUp, onRowEnter, onRowExit`	

Many properties, methods, and event handlers are inherited from the `Input` object class. Refer to topics grouped with the "Input" prefix for details of common functionality across all sub-classes of the `Input` object super-class.

There isn't really a `ResetButton` object class but it is helpful when trying to understand the wide variety of input element types if we can reduce the complexity by discussing only the properties and methods of a reset button. In actual fact, the object is represented as an item of the `Input` object class.

Event handling support via properties containing function objects was added to `ResetButton` objects at version 1.1 of JavaScript.

Unlike MSIE, Netscape does not support the `defaultValue` property or the `select()` method in this sub-class of the `Input` object.

See also:	*Element object*, `Form.elements[]`, *FormElement object*, *Input object*, `Input.accessKey`, `onClick`, `ResetButton.handleEvent()`

Property	JavaScript	JScript	N	IE	Opera	DOM	Notes
type	1.1 +	3.0 +	3.0 +	4.0 +	3.0 +	1 +	ReadOnly
value	1.0 +	1.0 +	2.0 +	3.02 +	3.0 +	1 +	Warning

Method	JavaScript	JScript	N	IE	Opera	DOM	Notes
handleEvent()	1.2 +	-	4.0 +	-	-	-	-

Event name	JavaScript	JScript	N	IE	Opera	DOM	Notes
onAfterUpdate	-	3.0 +	-	4.0 +	-	-	-
onBeforeUpdate	-	3.0 +	-	4.0 +	-	-	-
onBlur	1.1 +	3.0 +	3.0 +	4.0 +	3.0 +	-	Warning
onClick	1.0 +	1.0 +	2.0 +	3.0 +	3.0 +	-	Warning
onDblClick	1.2 +	3.0 +	4.0 +	4.0 +	3.0 +	-	Warning
onFilterChange	-	3.0 +	-	4.0 +	-	-	-
onFocus	1.0 +	3.0 +	2.0 +	4.0 +	3.0 +	-	Warning
onHelp	-	3.0 +	-	4.0 +	-	-	Warning
onKeyDown	1.2 +	3.0 +	4.0 +	4.0 +	3.0 +	-	Warning
onKeyPress	1.2 +	3.0 +	4.0 +	4.0 +	3.0 +	-	Warning
onKeyUp	1.2 +	3.0 +	4.0 +	4.0 +	3.0 +	-	Warning
onMouseDown	1.2 +	3.0 +	4.0 +	4.0 +	3.0 +	-	Warning
onMouseMove	1.2 +	3.0 +	4.0 +	4.0 +	-	-	Warning
onMouseOut	1.1 +	3.0 +	3.0 +	4.0 +	3.0 +	-	Warning
onMouseOver	1.0 +	1.0 +	2.0 +	3.0 +	3.0 +	-	Warning
onMouseUp	1.2 +	3.0 +	4.0 +	4.0 +	3.0 +	-	Warning
onRowEnter	-	3.0 +	-	4.0 +	-	-	-
onRowExit	-	3.0 +	-	4.0 +	-	-	-

Inheritance chain:

Element object, Input object, Node object

response object (Object/NES)

Part of the server-side support for JavaScript. This is the Global object in NES.

Availability:	JavaScript – 1.1 Netscape Enterprise Server – 2.0	
JavaScript syntax:	NES	response
Object properties:	client, database, project, request, server	
Object methods:	addClient(), addResponseHeader(), blob(), callC(), debug(), deleteResponseHeader(), flush(), getOptionValue(), getOptionValueCount(), redirect(), registerCFunction(), ssjs_generateClientID(), ssjs_getCGIVariable(), ssjs_getClientID(), trace(), write()	

The response object in NES is the global object as well. This means the methods and properties that belong to the global object also belong to the response.

R

JavaScript Programmer's Reference

723

Because it is the global object there is no explicit way of referring to it.

We have collated all the response object methods and properties together in a group to aid the rapid location of related topics. Additional index entries are provided for the properties and methods as they would be addressed as members of the global object.

Warnings:

❑ The Response object is the Global object in a NES request-response context.

See also:	Netscape Enterprise Server, *unwatch()*, *watch()*

Property	JavaScript	JScript	NES	Notes
client	1.1 +	-	2.0 +	-
database	1.1 +	-	2.0 +	-
project	1.1 +	-	2.0 +	-
request	1.1 +	-	2.0 +	-
server	1.1 +	-	2.0 +	-

Method	JavaScript	JScript	NES	Notes
addClient()	1.1 +	-	2.0 +	-
addResponseHeader()	1.2 +	-	3.0 +	-
blob()	1.1 +	-	2.0 +	-
callC()	1.1 +	-	2.0 +	-
debug()	1.1 +	-	2.0 +	-
deleteResponseHeader()	1.2 +	-	3.0 +	-
flush()	1.1 +	-	2.0 +	-
getOptionValue()	1.1 +	-	2.0 +	-
getOptionValueCount()	1.1 +	-	2.0 +	-
redirect()	1.1 +	-	2.0 +	-
registerCFunction()	1.1 +	-	2.0 +	-
ssjs_generateClientID()	1.2 +	-	3.0 +	-
ssjs_getCGIVariable()	1.2 +	-	3.0 +	-
ssjs_getClientID()	1.2 +	-	3.0 +	-
trace()	1.1 +	-	2.0 +	-
write()	1.2 +	-	3.0 +	-

ResultSet object (Object/NES)

This is part of the database access suite in Netscape Enterprise Server. It is returned by a stored procedure call.

Availability:	JavaScript – 1.2 Netscape Enterprise Server – 3.0	
JavaScript syntax:	NES	`myResultSet = myStProc.resultSet();`
Object properties:	`prototype`	
Object methods:	`close(), columnName(), columns(), next()`	

When you call a stored procedure in a RDBMS, you don't always get back a sequence of records in the same layout and structure as when you just do a simple SQL select style query.

An SQL query would return a series of records separated by newline characters. A stored procedure might return a mixed collection of records of different types.

A `ResultSet` object is created by asking the `Stproc` object for it when the stored procedure has been called and returned from the database.

The traversing mechanisms provided with a result set allow you to move forwards through the data but you cannot move backwards. Also, you can only read values from a result set as opposed to a `cursor` which allows you to update it and write new values back.

Example code:

```
<SERVER>
// An example derived from Wrox Professional JavaScript
database.connect("ODBC", "myDatabase", "me", "myPassword", "");
myStoredProc = database.storedProc("myProcedure", 40);
myResultSet = myStoredProc.resultSet();
</SERVER>
```

See also:	`database.storedProc()`, Netscape Enterprise Server, `Stproc.resultSet()`, *unwatch()*, *watch()*

Property	JavaScript	JScript	NES	Notes
prototype	1.2 +	-	3.0 +	-

Method	JavaScript	JScript	NES	Notes
close()	1.2 +	-	3.0 +	-
columnName()	1.2 +	-	3.0 +	-
columns()	1.2 +	-	3.0 +	-
next()	1.2 +	-	3.0 +	-

R

return (Statement)

Return control back to the caller of a function.

Availability:	ECMAScript edition – 2 JavaScript – 1.0 JScript – 1.0 Internet Explorer – 3.02 Netscape – 2.0 Netscape Enterprise Server – 2.0 Opera – 3.0	
JavaScript syntax:	-	`return(anExpression);`
	-	`return anExpression;`
	-	`return;`
Argument list:	*anExpression*	A value to return to the function caller

A `return` keyword is a jump statement. It is used to unconditionally exit from a function, pass back a result, and make execution flow to the caller of the function.

When the `return` statement is executed, the execution context is disposed of and removed from the stack. Execution continues at the point in the caller where the function was invoked. The function is replaced by the value being returned.

If the function is not being assigned to an `LValue` or Left Hand Side expression or has been cast to a `void` type, the result will be discarded.

If the expression is omitted in the `return` statement, the `undefined` value is returned in its place. While compiled languages are far more particular about the presence or absence of this expression, JavaScript is far more forgiving.

Functions that return undefined values are likely to be used as procedures rather than functions. A procedure is invoked as a statement that stands alone. The intent of a function is to return a result that will be substituted in its place.

It is considered illegal for the `return` statement to be present in any statement block other than that belonging to a function. However it can exist inside the statement block associated with a conditional statement or iterator statement as long as they themselves are within a function block. They may be nested more than one level deep but must ultimately belong to a function.

Warnings:

❑ It is considered to be a syntax error to use the `return` statement anywhere other than in a function body.

❑ You will not get the return value back properly if there is a line terminator between the return keyword and the value it was supposed to return. There is a temptation to break long strings over several lines like this:

```
return

"A very long string goes here ...";
```

❑ This will return the value undefined and not the string you intended to return. It is probably better style to assign the string to a variable and return that but there are implications there of string construction-destruction, garbage collection, and potential memory leaks and to trade those problems off it's best to try and eliminate string creation and memory usage if possible.

Example code:

```
// Declare a procedure with an implied return
function aProcedure()
{
    document.write("Hello");
}
// Declare a procedure that returns an undefined value
function anotherProcedure()
{
    alert("Click OK to continue");
    return;
}
// Declare a function that returns a result
function aRealFunction()
{
    return 1000;
}
// Use the functions and procedures
aProcedure();
anotherProcedure();
x = aRealFunction();
```

See also: *break*, Completion type, *continue, function(...) ...*, Iteration statement, Jump statement, Statement

Cross-references:

ECMA 262 edition 2 – section – 12.9

ECMA 262 edition 3 – section – 12.9

Wrox Instant JavaScript – page – 27

rgb() (Function)

A special color definition function used in style sheet color specifications.

Availability:	JavaScript – 1.5 JScript – 3.0 Internet Explorer – 4.0 Netscape – 6.0	
JavaScript syntax:	-	`rgb(rValue gValue bValue)`
Argument list:	`bValue`	Blue intensity
	`gValue`	Green intensity
	`rValue`	Red intensity

The values are separated by spaces and you must specify all three. This value can then be used in the property assignment for a `style` property that controls color. You can use it in any position where a color value would be used.

See also:	Color value, `style.backgroundColor`, `style.borderColor`, `style.color`, `style.outlineColor`

RUBY object (Object/HTML)

A ruby is an annotation or pronunciation guide for a string of text. The string of text annotated with a ruby is referred to as the base.

Availability:	JScript – 5.0 Internet Explorer – 5.0	
Inherits from:	*Element object*	
JavaScript syntax:	IE	`myRuby = myDocument.all.anElementID`
	IE	`myRuby = myDocument.all.tags ("RUBY")[anIndex]`
	IE	`myRuby = myDocument.all[aName]`
	-	`myRuby = myDocument.getElement ById(anElementID)`
	-	`myRuby = myDocument.getElements ByName(aName)[anIndex]`
	-	`myRuby = myDocument.getElements ByTagName("RUBY")[anIndex]`
Argument list:	`anIndex`	A reference to an element in a collection
	`aName`	An associative array reference
	`anElementID`	The ID value of an Element object
Collections:	`all[]`, `attributes[]`, `childNodes[]`, `children[]`, `filters[]`	

To create a RUBY object, you use the <RUBY> HTML tag like this:

```
<RUBY>

Some base text

<RT>Some ruby text

</RUBY>
```

The <RT> tag creates an RT object.

See also:	*Element object,* style.rubyAlign, style.rubyOverhang, style.rubyPosition

Inheritance chain:

Element object, Node object

rule object (Object/DOM)

An object that contains a single CSS styling rule.

Availability:	DOM level – 2 JavaScript – 1.5 JScript – 3.0 Internet Explorer – 4.0 Netscape – 6.0	
JavaScript syntax:	IE	*myRule = myDocument*.all .*aStyleSheetID*.rules[*anIndex*]
	IE	*myRule = myStyleSheet*.rules[*anIndex*]
	IE	*myRule = mySelectorArray*[*anIndex*]
	-	*myRule = myDocument*.styleSheets [*anIndex*].cssRules[*anIndex*]
Argument list:	*anIndex*	A reference to an element in a collection
Object properties:	cssText, parentStyleSheet, readOnly, runtimeStyle, selectorText, style	

This is referred to as a selector and one or more declarations within a cascading style sheet (CSS). It is supported by MSIE.

DOM level 2 calls this a CSSRule object. It also describes a CSSStyleRule object as a sub-class of that object. The MSIE browser implements both as a single class. The CSSRule class maintains the following named constants:

Value	Name	DOM
0	UNKNOWN_RULE	2
1	STYLE_RULE	2
2	CHARSET_RULE	2
3	IMPORT_RULE	2
4	MEDIA_RULE	2
5	FONT_FACE_RULE	2
6	PAGE_RULE	2

DOM level 2 specifies these additional properties:

❑ `type`

❑ `parentRule`

See also:	`Document.styleSheets[]`, *SelectorArray object*, *StyleSheet object*, `StyleSheet.rules[]`

Property	JavaScript	JScript	N	IE	Opera	DOM	Notes
cssText	1.5 +	5.0 +	6.0 +	5.0 +	-	2 +	-
parentStyleSheet	1.5 +	5.0 +	6.0 +	5.0 +	-	2 +	-
readOnly	-	3.0 +	-	3.0 +	-	-	ReadOnly
runtimeStyle	-	5.0 +	-	5.0 +	-	-	-
selectorText	1.5 +	3.0+	6.0 +	4.0+	-	2 +	ReadOnly
style	1.5 +	5.0 +	6.0 +	5.0 +	-	2 +	-

runtimeStyle object (Object/JScript)

A style that applies to an object at run-time and overrides other style settings.

Availability:	JScript – 5.0 Internet Explorer – 5.0
Inherits from:	*style object*
JavaScript syntax:	IE *myRuntimeStyle = myElement*.runtimeStyle
Object methods:	getAttribute(), getExpression(), removeExpression(), setAttribute(), setExpression()

This represents the cascaded format and style of its parent object. The value in this object overrides global style sheets, inline styles and HTML tag attribute values. It overwrites the values provided by `currentStyle` objects but not those supplied by the `style` object.

The properties belonging to this object correspond closely to those of the `style` object and so there is little point in discussing them again here. Refer to the `style` object property descriptions for details of the various properties.

Because the style values are cascaded from style sheet to style sheet and may include some inline styles as well as some explicit styles, objects need to maintain a current style value that is the result of all the inheritances applied on top of one another.

In addition they maintain a run-time style which reflects dynamic changes as well. The `runtimeStyle` is based on the `currentStyle` originally.

See also:	*currentStyle object*, `Element.currentStyle`, `Element.runtimeStyle`, *style object (2)*

Method	JavaScript	JScript	N	IE	Opera	Notes
getAttribute()	-	5.0 +	-	5.0 +	-	-
getExpression()	-	5.0 +	-	5.0 +	-	-
removeExpression()	-	5.0 +	-	5.0 +	-	-
setAttribute()	-	5.0 +	-	5.0 +	-	-
setExpression()	-	5.0 +	-	5.0 +	-	-

R

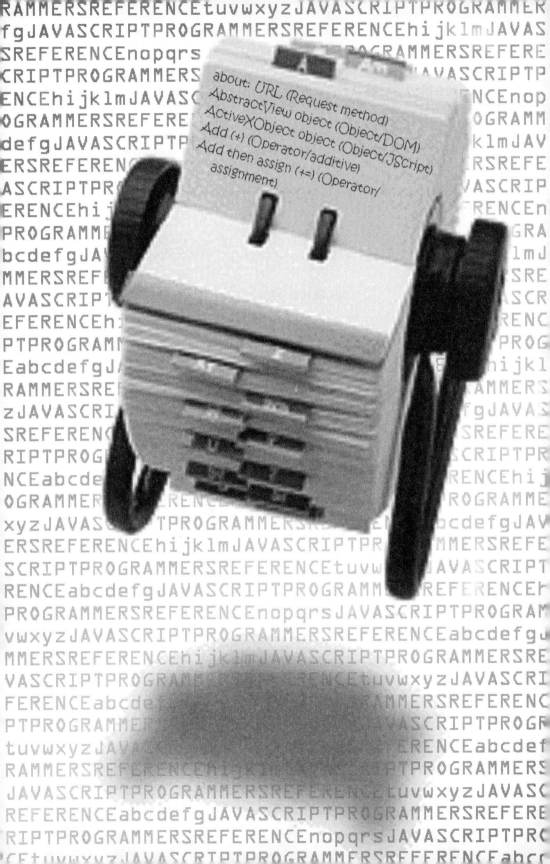

about: URL (Request method)
AbstractView object (Object/DOM)
ActiveXObject object (Object/JScript)
Add (+) (Operator/additive)
Add then assign (+=) (Operator/
assignment)

Same origin (Security related)

A policy for granting access across window boundaries.

The same origin policy is a foundational concept as far as browser security is concerned. Put simply, it states that a script can access the contents of another window or frame if the HREF for that target was loaded from the same host at the same IP port number and with the same protocol.

This ensures that http: pages cannot read https: content and that pages served by a web server on port 80 cannot read values from a potentially different web server on port 80 for example. Both of those also require that the host be the same.

This can be circumvented with UniversalBrowserRead privilege which allows properties to be read from windows containing objects that were from a different origin. The UniversalBrowserWrite property allows those objects with a different origin to be modified. Granting both would allow a script to read and write properties in a window with a different origin.

The same origin policy applies to most but not all properties of a window. It does apply to almost every property belonging to a document object.

You can allow documents from different origins to access properties belonging to your window and document but you need to provide a public API to let them do this. You can alias the private properties by publishing them as user defined values.

You can also relax the same origin policy as far as hostnames are concerned by setting the domain property. You could set the domain value inside a document as long as it is a genuine fragment of the host name. If you do this in two documents, both served from different hosts belonging to a higher level domain that is the same, the same origin policy is relaxed when the domain value is identical for both documents.

Warnings:

❑ The common domain access relaxation technique only works for JavaScript version 1.1 and higher.

See also:	export, import, Security policy, Signed scripts, UniversalBrowserAccess, UniversalBrowserRead, UniversalBrowserWrite

Screen object (Object/browser)

An object that represents the screen display and its rendering capabilities.

Availability:	JavaScript – 1.2 JScript – 3.0 Internet Explorer – 4.0 Netscape – 4.0 Opera – 5.0	
JavaScript syntax:	-	myScreen = myWindow.screen
	-	myScreen = screen
Object properties:	availHeight, availLeft, availTop, availWidth, bufferDepth, colorDepth, fontSmoothingEnabled, height, pixelDepth, updateInterval, width	

The properties of this object describe the physical attributes of the display screen the browser is currently operating in. The values reflected by users of desktop computers will describe a much higher resolution than a WebTV set-top box, for example. Other set-top boxes for use with TV should conform to the same resolution but it is likely that they will all vary slightly from one another.

Warnings:

❑ Some documentation resources have referred to this object as a screen object rather than a Screen object. Note the capitalization. When examined, we found that several browsers spell the object with a capital S.

See also:	JellyScript, Window.screen

Property	JavaScript	JScript	N	IE	Opera	HTML	Notes
availHeight	1.2 +	3.0 +	4.0 +	4.0 +	5.0+	-	ReadOnly
availLeft	1.2 +	-	4.0 +	-	-	-	ReadOnly
availTop	1.2 +	-	4.0 +	-	-	-	ReadOnly
availWidth	1.2 +	3.0 +	4.0 +	4.0 +	5.0+	-	ReadOnly
bufferDepth	▪	3.0 +	▪	4.0 +	▪	▪	▪
colorDepth	1.2 +	3.0 +	4.0 +	4.0 +	5.0+	-	ReadOnly

Property	JavaScript	JScript	N	IE	Opera	HTML	Notes
fontSmoothing Enabled	-	3.0 +	-	4.0 +	-	-	-
height	1.2 +	3.0 +	4.0 +	4.0 +	5.0+	-	ReadOnly
pixelDepth	1.2 +	-	4.0 +	-	5.0+	-	ReadOnly
updateInterval	-	3.0 +	-	4.0 +	-	-	-
width	1.2 +	3.0 +	4.0 +	4.0 +	5.0+	-	ReadOnly

SCRIPT object (Object/HTML)

An object that represents a <SCRIPT> block within the document.

Availability:	DOM level – 1 JavaScript – 1.5 JScript – 3.0 Internet Explorer – 4.0 Netscape – 6.0
Inherits from:	*Element object*

JavaScript syntax:	IE `mySCRIPT = myDocument.all.anElementID`
	IE `mySCRIPT = myDocument.all.tags`
	     `("SCRIPT")[anIndex]`
	IE `mySCRIPT = myDocument.all[aName]`
	- `mySCRIPT = myDocument.getElementById`
	     `(anElementID)`
	- `mySCRIPT = myDocument.getElementsByName`
	     `(aName)[anIndex]`
	- `mySCRIPT = myDocument.getElements`
	     `ByTagName("SCRIPT")[anIndex]`

HTML syntax:	`<SCRIPT>...</SCRIPT>`
Argument list:	`anIndex` A reference to an element in a collection `aName` An associative array reference `anElementID` The ID value of an Element object
Object properties:	charset, defer, event, htmlFor, readyState, recordNumber, src, text, type
Event handlers:	onClick, onDblClick, onError, onHelp, onKeyDown, onKeyPress, onKeyUp, onLoad, onMouseDown, onMouseMove, onMouseOut, onMouseOver, onMouseUp, onReadyStateChange

Given that you can access a SCRIPT object, you may be tempted to write some self-modifying code. This is not recommended. You should be able to accomplish everything you need to do in that respect with an eval() method and that would be more widely supported across browsers.

Accessing the script block may be useful to ascertain whether a particular function is available although you should know that since you wrote the page yourself. On the other hand, if you imported a script block with a reference to a .js file, you may not know the provenance of its contents.

In the example, the source text is extracted from a script block and executed with an eval() function. The variable value is set according to the evaluated script which replaces the default value.

Warnings:

❑ This is not supported by Netscape Navigator prior to version 6.0.

Example code:

```
<HTML>
<HEAD></HEAD>
<BODY>
<SCRIPT ID="ONE">
block = "ONE";
</SCRIPT>
<SCRIPT ID="TWO">
block = "TWO";
</SCRIPT>
<SCRIPT ID="THREE">
block = "THREE";
</SCRIPT>
<SCRIPT ID="FOUR">
block = "FOUR";
mySourceText = eval(document.scripts.THREE.text);

document.write(block);
</SCRIPT>
</BODY>
</HTML>
```

See also:	Document.scripts[], *Element object*

Property	JavaScript	JScript	N	IE	Opera	DOM	HTML	Notes
charset	1.5 +	-	6.0 +	-	-	1 +	-	Warning
defer	1.5 +	3.0 +	6.0 +	4.0 +	-	1 +	-	Warning
event	1.5 +	3.0 +	6.0 +	4.0 +	-	1 +	-	Warning, ReadOnly
htmlFor	1.5 +	3.0 +	6.0 +	4.0 +	-	1 +	-	Warning, ReadOnly
readyState	-	3.0 +	-	4.0 +	-	-	-	ReadOnly
recordNumber	-	3.0 +	-	4.0 +	-	-	-	Warning, ReadOnly
src	1.5 +	3.0 +	6.0 +	4.0 +	-	1 +	-	Warning, ReadOnly
text	1.5 +	3.0 +	6.0 +	4.0 +	-	1 +	-	Warning, ReadOnly
type	1.5 +	3.0 +	6.0 +	4.0 +	-	1 +	-	Warning, ReadOnly

Event name	JavaScript	JScript	N	IE	Opera	DOM	HTML	Notes
onClick	1.5 +	3.0 +	6.0 +	4.0 +	-	-	4.0 +	Warning
onDblClick	1.5+	3.0 +	6.0 +	4.0 +	-	-	4.0 +	Warning
onError	1.5 +	3.0 +	6.0 +	4.0 +	-	-	-	Warning
onHelp	-	3.0 +	-	4.0 +	-	-	-	Warning
onKeyDown	1.5 +	3.0 +	6.0 +	4.0 +	-	-	4.0 +	Warning
onKeyPress	1.5 +	3.0 +	6.0 +	4.0 +	-	-	4.0 +	Warning
onKeyUp	1.5 +	3.0 +	6.0 +	4.0 +	-	-	4.0 +	Warning
onLoad	1.5 +	3.0 +	6.0 +	4.0 +	-	-	-	Warning
onMouseDown	1.5 +	3.0 +	6.0 +	4.0 +	-	-	4.0 +	Warning
onMouseMove	1.5 +	3.0 +	6.0 +	4.0 +	-	-	4.0 +	Warning
onMouseOut	1.5 +	3.0 +	6.0 +	4.0 +	-	-	4.0 +	Warning
onMouseOver	1.5 +	3.0 +	6.0 +	4.0 +	-	-	4.0 +	Warning
onMouseUp	1.5 +	3.0 +	6.0 +	4.0 +	-	-	4.0 +	Warning
onReady StateChange	-	3.0 +	-	4.0 +	-	-	-	-

Inheritance chain:

Element object, Node object

<SCRIPT SRC="..."> (HTML Tag Attribute)

The URL to access an insertable fragment of JavaScript contained in an include file.

Availability:	JavaScript – 1.1 JScript – 3.0 Internet Explorer – 4.0 Netscape – 3.0
HTML syntax:	<SCRIPT SRC="..."></SCRIPT>
Argument list:	... A URL to reach an includable .js file

This provides a way to include JavaScript from an external file and share some common functionality among several pages. No data is transported from page to page apart from that which is in the included file as assignment statements so this is not a means of maintaining state between pages.

Although this behaves in the same way as script that is in the HTML page itself, some people prefer not to call this inline code because it's held in a separate file. It depends whether you are referring to the location of the code when you use the term inline or whether you are talking about how it is executed; included script code is executed inline.

You can refer to javascript .js files on your local client-side hard disk as long as the page is not being requested from a web server. To access a local client file in a page coming from a web server would be to break the security regimes established to prevent client systems being hacked by intruders.

This is a really useful technique for debugging because you can build an entire library of object disassembly and diagnostic tools and include them in a script block which you can then eliminate when the code goes into production use.

A lot of the undocumented features of the browsers were uncovered in this way.

Warnings:

❑ Included files sometimes do not work as expected. Browsers do not always support the capability, or may not be configured to accept the application/x-JavaScript MIME type as an executable file with a .js file extension.

❑ Note also that although you can examine the properties of SCRIPT objects within the MSIE browser, the SCRIPT objects that are created as a result of a SRC="..." include will not enumerate their properties without causing a run-time error in your script.

Example code:

```
<SCRIPT SRC="include.js">
</SCRIPT>
------------------------------------------------------------
// This content goes into include.js
function getBrowserType()
{
    var myUserAgent;
    var myMajor;
    myUserAgent  = navigator.userAgent.toLowerCase();
    myMajor      = parseInt(navigator.appVersion);
    if( (myUserAgent.indexOf('mozilla')    != -1) &&
        (myUserAgent.indexOf('spoofer')    == -1) &&
        (myUserAgent.indexOf('compatible') == -1) &&
        (myUserAgent.indexOf('opera')      == -1) &&
        (myUserAgent.indexOf('webtv')      == -1)
      )
    {
        return "N";
    }
    if (myUserAgent.indexOf("msie") != -1)
    {
        return "msie";
    }
    return "other";
}
```

See also: *.js, <SCRIPT ARCHIVE="...">, <SCRIPT>,* Adding JavaScript to HTML, File extensions, Inline script, MIME types, SCRIPT.src, Security policy

Cross-references:

Wrox *Instant JavaScript* – page – 42

<SCRIPT TYPE="..."> (HTML Tag Attribute)

The MIME type for a block of script code.

Availability:	JavaScript – 1.2 JScript – 3.0 Internet Explorer – 4.0 Netscape – 4.0	
HTML syntax:	<SCRIPT TYPE="..."> *someCode* </SCRIPT>	
Argument list:	...	A MIME type that signifies JavaScript source text
	someCode	Some script source text

This is an alternative method of selecting the interpreter to be used for the
<SCRIPT> block. It has limited support prior to the version 4.0 browsers and so it
may be less portable for a while.

Warnings:

❑ If a browser does not understand this attribute and if there is not a corresponding
LANGUAGE attribute that it does understand, it is possible that the script block will
be ignored and the script code may not be executed.

Example code:

```
<SCRIPT TYPE="text/JavaScript">
document.write("Basic functionality")
</SCRIPT>
```

See also:	*<SCRIPT LANGUAGE="...">*, *<SCRIPT>*, *<STYLE TYPE="...">*, MIME types, SCRIPT.type, StyleSheet.type, *text/JavaScript*

Cross-references:

Wrox *Instant JavaScript* – page – 42

</SCRIPT> (Pitfall)

Problems with closing <SCRIPT> tags.

You cannot use the string '</SCRIPT>' within an inline JavaScript fragment. Even if it is enclosed inside quotation marks, it will still be seen by the parser and interpreted as a closure to the <SCRIPT> tag. You will need to hide it by constructing the string from component parts and using concatenation techniques to manufacture the string you need.

If you need to say this:

```
var myScriptTag = '</SCRIPT>';
```

...then you should do this:

```
var myScriptTag = '<' + '/SCRIPT' + '>';
```

...which should hide the tag from the parser.

Another alternative is to escape the slash character with a backslash like this:

```
var myScriptTag = '<\/SCRIPT>';
```

Look at that previous line carefully, and see how the forward slash is preceded by a backslash. After a long day cranking code out that might look like an upper case V, so it might be best to use the concatenation technique.

See also:	<SCRIPT>, Pitfalls

Cross-references:

Wrox *Instant JavaScript* – page – 45

<SCRIPT ARCHIVE="..."> (HTML Tag Attribute)

The URL to access an archive containing insertable fragments of JavaScript contained in a single file.

Availability:	JavaScript – 1.2 JScript – 3.0 Internet Explorer – 4.0 Netscape – 4.0 Opera – 5.0	
HTML syntax:	<SCRIPT ARCHIVE="..." SRC="..."></SCRIPT>	
Argument list:	...	A URL to reach an includable .js or .jar file

This tag attribute allows an archive file to be specified. This allows a whole collection of .js files to be shipped as a single unit. The required .js file can then be included by extracting it from the archive. If the archive is requested from the web server, it will likely persist in the cache and therefore some time is saved by collecting these archives and referring to items contained within them.

The ARCHIVE tag attribute has no use on its own in this context and you must use it with the SRC attribute.

Archives are called .jar files and are basically a zip-compressed collection of .js files. You will probably find one of the Java development environments contains all the tools you need to create these archives in a straightforward way. Actually you don't need anything more complex than a text editor and a zip compression tool.

You can do this manually if you follow these steps:

❑ Create your collection of .js files

❑ Collect them into a zipped archive file whose file extension is .jar

❑ Construct some HTML to include them

❑ Call the functions as needed

Refer to the example for script and HTML code. Create the two files test1.js and test2.js and store them in an archive called test.jar. Then create test.html with its <SCRIPT> tags to call in the files from the archive. When you run it, you can see both functions are called during the document.write() methods.

Example code:

```
// Save this into file test1.js
function test1()
{
    return "Test 1";
}
------------------------------------------------------------
// Save this into file test2.js
function test2()
{
    return "Test 2";
}
------------------------------------------------------------
<!-- Save this as file test.html -->
<HTML>
<HEAD>
<SCRIPT ARCHIVE="./test.jar" SRC="test1.js"></SCRIPT>
<SCRIPT ARCHIVE="./test.jar" SRC="test2.js"></SCRIPT>
</HEAD>
<BODY>
<SCRIPT>
document.write(test1());
```

S

JavaScript Programmer's Reference

```
document.write("<BR>");
document.write(test2());
document.write("<BR>");
</SCRIPT>
</BODY>
</HTML>
```

See also:	.jar, .js, <SCRIPT SRC="...">, <SCRIPT>, Adding JavaScript to HTML, File extensions, Inline script, MIME types, Security policy

<SCRIPT EVENT="..."> (HTML Tag Attribute)

A tag attribute to associate a script block with an event to be handled.

Availability:	JScript – 3.0 Internet Explorer – 4.0

This HTML tag attribute is quite useful when using ActiveX controls in web pages. You can use this to attach a fragment of script to an event so that the screen gets updated.

Here is a skeleton of some HTML that attaches a script to an object that has been embedded:

```
<SCRIPT FOR="Xbutton" EVENT="Click()">

// Do some kind of stuff in here as a

// result of the ActiveX calling this

<SCRIPT>

<OBJECT ID="Xbutton" CLASSID="..." CODEBASE="..." STYLE="...">

<PARAM NAME="..." VALUE="...">

</OBJECT>
```

The CLASSID, CODEBASE, and other parameters depend on the ActiveX control you are embedding. The point to make here is that as the page is loaded, the control will be displayed and when the user clicks on it, the browser makes the association by mapping the FOR="..." HTML tag attribute in the <SCRIPT> tag to the ID="..." attribute of the <OBJECT> tag. Then the event that the control triggers is mapped to the EVENT="..." HTML tag attribute of the <SCRIPT> tag.

You can create a whole set of <SCRIPT> blocks, one for each event and control you expect to use. This means the browser does the mapping and dispatching of events for you.

See also:	<SCRIPT>, Event handler in <SCRIPT>, Script execution

<SCRIPT ID="..."> (HTML Tag Attribute)

Script blocks can be given ID values so they can be identified within the document scripts array.

If you can identify a script block by its ID value, you should be able to locate the object and at least read the contents of the script block. Some browsers may let you change the script block but it has always been recommended practice to avoid self-modifying code.

See also:	`Document.scripts[]`

<SCRIPT LANGUAGE="..."> (HTML Tag Attribute)

The required version of JavaScript to interpret the enclosed code.

HTML syntax:	`<SCRIPT LANGUAGE="..."> someCode </SCRIPT>`	
Argument list:	`...`	The script language to use for this block of script source
	`someCode`	Some script source text

As you embed the script code into an HTML page with the `<SCRIPT>` tag, you can indicate by means of the LANGUAGE attribute which version of JavaScript (or indeed other scripting languages) the interpreter should use to process the script. This is subtle and allows various aspects of the language to be switched so that they behave differently according to the version selection.

It also provides a way to hide JavaScript written according to newer syntax conventions from older browsers that cannot cope with it. In general, you should always try to specify the lowest version of JavaScript to achieve maximum portability.

JavaScript version 1.2 implemented some different capabilities regarding equality tests where the operands were different types. Selecting `LANGUAGE="JavaScript"` as opposed to `LANGUAGE="JavaScript1.2"` affects how these tests are carried out when the script is executed.

The following values are legal for the `<SCRIPT>` tag's LANGUAGE attribute:

Attribute Value	**Description**
Nothing, attribute omitted	Basic JavaScript functionality
`JavaScript`	Basic JavaScript functionality
`JavaScript1.1`	Version 1.1 language capabilities

Table continued on following page

Attribute Value	Description
JavaScript1.2	Version 1.2 language capabilities
JavaScript1.3	Version 1.3 language capabilities
JavaScript1.4	Version 1.4 language capabilities
JavaScript1.5	Version 1.5 language capabilities
VBScript	Visual BASIC scripting in MSIE browsers
Tcl	In the HTML 4.0 specification, Tcl is used as an example

The example below will display the text 1.3 in a Netscape 4.7 browser and the value 1.4 in version 5 of MSIE for Macintosh.

Note with this technique that you should ensure you test for a high enough version. The browsers will execute the versions indicated. If you only test up to version 1.2, then the variable assignment is never going to reflect a 1.4 version capability.

Warnings:

❑ If a browser does not support the specified language, it may not execute the script block, even with a degraded version of the interpreter.

❑ Be aware that Netscape 4 supports some special capabilities in JavaScript version 1.2 mode that are not strictly correct according to the ECMA standard nor are they compatible with earlier versions of Netscape Navigator and other browsers. If you find that you need to turn on JavaScript version 1.2 with the LANGUAGE attribute, check your scripts for portability very carefully.

Example code:

```
<!-- JavaScript version detector --->
<HTML>
<HEAD>
<SCRIPT LANGUAGE="JavaScript">    myVersion = "Generic";</SCRIPT>
<SCRIPT LANGUAGE="JavaScript1.0"> myVersion = "1.0";</SCRIPT>
<SCRIPT LANGUAGE="JavaScript1.1"> myVersion = "1.1";</SCRIPT>
<SCRIPT LANGUAGE="JavaScript1.2"> myVersion = "1.2";</SCRIPT>
<SCRIPT LANGUAGE="JavaScript1.3"> myVersion = "1.3";</SCRIPT>
<SCRIPT LANGUAGE="JavaScript1.4"> myVersion = "1.4";</SCRIPT>
<SCRIPT LANGUAGE="JavaScript1.5"> myVersion = "1.5";</SCRIPT>
</HEAD>
<BODY>
<SCRIPT>
document.write(myVersion);
</SCRIPT>
</BODY>
</HTML>
```

See also:	*<META>*, *<SCRIPT TYPE="...">*, *<SCRIPT>*, Compatibility, Element.language

Cross-references:

Wrox *Instant JavaScript* – page – 42

<SCRIPT> (HTML Tag)

A container for JavaScript in an HTML page.

HTML syntax:	<SCRIPT> *someCode* </SCRIPT>	
Argument list:	*someCode*	Some script source text

The <SCRIPT> tag is how the JavaScript code is embedded into a web page. There are several ways to do this. Note that the <SCRIPT> tag must have an associated closing </SCRIPT> tag at the end of the script source text. The following attributes may be useful:

❑ LANGUAGE

❑ SRC

❑ ARCHIVE

❑ TYPE

You can place the <SCRIPT> tag in the <HEAD> or <BODY> section of the page.

In the <HEAD> context, it is expected to provide some support to the rest of the page so you might place useful functions and event handlers here. You can also put some global code here and it will get executed inline, probably initializing some global variables. The intent is for the <HEAD> block to contain only meta-information about the document. This implies you should not place a document.write() method into the <HEAD> area such that it will be executed during page loading. However, both the Netscape and MSIE browsers will allow the document.write() if it is called during page loading even if it is located in the <HEAD> block.

It makes some sense to be sure that if you do a document.write() in the <HEAD> block, that you make sure it writes something sensible. For example, you can write the document title from a script that is executed inline. If you just write some textual output, the browsers are at least smart enough to place it into the page body.

Because JavaScript is interpreted, it needs to have any functions declared before they are called. However, this means they must be declared chronologically before they are called. This is not the same as positionally defining them before they are called because the page content may be traversed several times. For example, an event handler can probably be placed anywhere because very few events happen before the </BODY> closure happens. Nevertheless, it is still probably good practice to locate any functions that you can in <SCRIPT> blocks placed in the <HEAD> area.

You can place <SCRIPT> tags throughout the <BODY> of the document. These might also contain functions but are more likely to contain inline code to be executed as the page is loading. Although they are in different <SCRIPT> tag blocks, they are all conceptually part of the same script.

S

JavaScript Programmer's Reference

If your inline script code is going to do any `document.write()` calls to modify the HTML as the page is loaded, then this is the optimum place to put the code. It's quite sensible to break the code into smaller `<SCRIPT>` blocks and place them appropriately throughout the document. If the code starts to become complicated, then factor some of it into functions placed in the `<HEAD>` area and then call it as needed from the `<BODY>` area.

If you are using a frame-set, you can put the `<SCRIPT>` block after the `<HEAD>` tag but before the `<FRAMESET>` tag. You could write the entire `<FRAMESET>` description at this point using `document.write()` methods. You could do that with the entire `<BODY>` content too.

You can break your script code into smaller blocks, each one associated with a different `<SCRIPT></SCRIPT>` area and, if necessary, each can be executed in a different version of JavaScript. They will each have a different execution context and the scope chain may be affected, although global variables should be reachable from anywhere.

When the browser encounters a `<SCRIPT>` tag, it pauses the processing of the HTML page description and executes the `<SCRIPT>` tag's source code. That may affect subsequent HTML output anyway, and may generate some HTML to be placed into the page at the point where the `<SCRIPT>` block appears. Any lengthy script evaluation is going to slow down the display of your page. You should defer any lengthy processing until you can use some sleight of hand to hide it. For example, perhaps you can wait until the `<BODY>` tag is closed and then activate some processing with a `<BODY ONLOAD="...">` handler. This may be an issue if you are using included `.js` files since they will need to be requested and fetched from a web server.

You can build event handlers and associate them with the event by means of the `<SCRIPT>` tag attributes, but this only works in MSIE.

Warnings:

❑ Be aware that if you place `<SCRIPT>` blocks inside the `<HEAD>` of a document, you may be able to initialize some data structures but you certainly won't be able to access any objects that belong to the `<BODY>` since they won't yet exist.

❑ Note that during page loading, until you have reached the closing `</BODY>` tag, the page may be in some intermediate state where objects and memory locations are not locked down. This may cause some difficulties in writing to the document or changing the content of `<DIV>` blocks. In particular, you cannot inline `document.write()` into the content of an `<OBJECT>` block. Until the page is completed, the `<OBJECT>` is not properly linked into a structure in which you can access it from JavaScript, this is the case with MSIE version 4 browsers, at least.

Example code:

```
<HTML>
<HEAD>
</HEAD>
<BODY>
<SCRIPT>
myResult = 100;
myExpr = myResult %= 1000;
document.write(myResult);
document.write("<BR>");
document.write(myExpr);
document.write("<BR>");
</SCRIPT>
</BODY>
</HTML>
```

See also:	</SCRIPT>, <META>, <NOSCRIPT>, <SCRIPT ARCHIVE="...">, <SCRIPT EVENT="...">, <SCRIPT LANGUAGE="...">, <SCRIPT SRC="...">, <SCRIPT TYPE="...">, <STYLE TYPE="...">, Adding JavaScript to HTML, Document.scripts[], Host environment, HTML file, *String*, Web browser

Cross-references:

Wrox *Instant JavaScript* – page – 42

ScriptArray object (Object/browser)

A collection of script blocks belonging to a document.

Availability:	JScript – 3.0 Internet Explorer – 4.0
JavaScript syntax:	IE *myScriptArray = myDocument*.scripts
Object properties:	length
Object methods:	item()

In the example, the document contains several script blocks. The script source is extracted and formatted with an escape() function and line breaks are reinserted by means of the String.split() and Array.join() methods.

Warnings:

❑ This is not supported by Netscape Navigator.

Example code:

```
<HTML>
<HEAD></HEAD>
<BODY>
<TABLE BORDER=1>
<TH>Index</TH>
<TH>ID</TH>
<TH>Text</TH>
<SCRIPT ID="ONE">
block1 = "ONE";
</SCRIPT>
<SCRIPT ID="TWO">
block2 = "TWO";
</SCRIPT>
<SCRIPT ID="THREE">block3 = "THREE";</SCRIPT>
<SCRIPT ID="FOUR">
block4 = "FOUR";
myLength = document.scripts.length;
for (myEnumerator=0; myEnumerator<myLength; myEnumerator++ )
{
    mySourceText = escape(document.scripts[myEnumerator].text);
    myArray = mySourceText.split("%0D");

    document.write("<TR><TD>");
    document.write(myEnumerator);
    document.write("</TD><TD>");
    document.write(document.scripts[myEnumerator].id);
    document.write("</TD><TD>");
    document.write(myArray.join("%0D<BR>"));
    document.write("</TD></TR>");
}
</SCRIPT>
</TABLE>
</BODY>
</HTML>
```

See also: *Collection object*, `Document.scripts[]`, `ScriptArray.length`

Property	JavaScript	JScript	N	IE	Opera	HTML	Notes
length	-	3.0 +	-	4.0 +	-	-	Warning, ReadOnly

Method	JavaScript	JScript	N	IE	Opera	HTML	Notes
item()	-	3.0 +	-	4.0 +	-	-	-

ScriptEngine() (Function)

A special MSIE globally available function that describes the scripting engine currently installed for use with the browser.

Availability:	JScript – 2.0 Internet Explorer – 4.0	
Property/method value type:	String primitive	
JavaScript syntax:	IE	ScriptEngine()

The following values will be returned by this function depending on the context in which it is called:

❑ JScript

❑ VBA

❑ VBScript

See also:	Navigator.appMinorVersion

ScriptEngineBuildVersion() (Function/global)

A special MSIE globally available function that describes the build version of the scripting engine currently installed for use with the browser.

Availability:	JScript – 2.0 Internet Explorer – 4.0
Property/method value type:	String primitive

This is only available in the MSIE browser. It is useful if you are developing scripts and it is possible that you could build a reference to this into a form that is submitted as part of an error handler. That way you might determine what the error is, what caused it and note the build number of the script interpreter. This may then yield a pattern. An essential part of the fault diagnosis process involves the search for a pattern in the failures of a system. It is very possible that a certain build of the interpreter could manifest a bug which is not present in other builds.

See also:	Navigator.appMinorVersion

S

Select object (Object/HTML)

A drop-down menu containing a list of <OPTION> items. These are used in forms to build menus and pop-ups. They may select single items or multiple items.

Availability:	DOM level – 1 JavaScript – 1.0 JScript – 1.0 Internet Explorer – 3.02 Netscape – 2.0 Opera – 3.0	
Inherits from:	*Element object*	
JavaScript syntax:	IE	mySelect = *myDocument*.all.*anElementID*
	IE	mySelect = *myDocument*.all.*anElementID* .elements[*anIndex*]
	IE	mySelect = *myDocument*.all.tags ("SELECT")[*anIndex*]
	IE	mySelect = *myDocument*.all[*aName*]
	-	mySelect = *myDocument*.getElementById (*anElementID*)
	-	mySelect = *myDocument* .getElementsByName(*aName*)[*anIndex*]
	-	mySelect = *myDocument*.getElementsBy TagName("SELECT")[*anIndex*]
	-	mySelect = *myForm*.*aSelectName*
	-	mySelect = *myForm*.elements[*anIndex*]
	-	mySelect = myForm[*anIndex*]
HTML syntax:	<SELECT>...</SELECT>	
Argument list:	*anIndex*	A valid reference to an item in the collection
	aName	The name attribute of an element
	anElementID	The ID attribute of an element
	aFormIndex	A reference to a particular form in the forms collection
Object properties:	accessKey, dataFld, dataSrc, form, length, multiple, selectedIndex, size, tabIndex, type, value	
Object methods:	add(), remove(), tags()	
Event handlers:	onAfterUpdate, onBeforeUpdate, onBlur, onChange, onDragStart, onFilterChange, onFocus, onHelp, onKeyDown, onKeyPress, onKeyUp, onMouseDown, onMouseMove, onMouseOut, onMouseOver, onMouseUp, onResize, onRowEnter, onRowExit, onSelectStart	
Collections:	options[]	

Many properties, methods, and event handlers are inherited from the `Input` object class. Refer to topics grouped with the "Input" prefix for details of common functionality across all sub-classes of the `Input` object super-class.

Unusually, there actually is a `Select` object class where most other kinds of input are instances of an `Input` object.

Event handling support via properties containing function objects was added to `Select` popup objects at version 1.1 of JavaScript.

Unlike MSIE, the Netscape Navigator implementation of this object type does not support the `click()` method.

The MSIE instance of this object is actually a `SELECT` object and not a `Select` object. This is another example of class naming differences between browsers that may cause problems later.

Warnings:

❑ Note that this `FormElement` object type does not have a `value` property. You may need to make allowances for that in generic form object handlers. Its value is reflected by the option item that is currently selected. This `FormElement` object is not a sub-class of the `Input` object as many other `FormElements` are.

Example code:

```
<HTML>
<HEAD>
</HEAD>
<BODY>
<DIV ID="RESULT">???</DIV>
<FORM>
<HR>
<SELECT ID="IN1">
<OPTION VALUE="0">Sunday
<OPTION VALUE="1">Monday
<OPTION VALUE="2">Tuesday
<OPTION VALUE="3">Wednesday
<OPTION VALUE="4">Thursday
<OPTION VALUE="5">Friday
<OPTION VALUE="6">Saturday
</SELECT>
<INPUT TYPE="button" VALUE="CLICK ME" onClick="clickMe()">
</FORM>
<SCRIPT>
//MSIE Only
function clickMe()
{
    selectedValue  = document.all.IN1.value;
    document.all.RESULT.innerText = selectedValue;
}
</SCRIPT>
</BODY>
</HTML>
```

JavaScript Programmer's Reference

See also: *Element object*, `Form.elements[]`, *FormElement object*, *Input object*, `Input.accessKey`, `onChange`, *Option object*, *OptionsArray object*, `response.getOptionValue()`, `response.getOptionValueCount()`

Property	JavaScript	JScript	N	IE	Opera	DOM	HTML	Notes
accessKey	1.0 +	1.0 +	2.0 +	3.02 +	3.0 +	1 +	-	Warning
dataFld	1.0 +	1.0 +	2.0 +	3.02 +	3.0 +	1 +	-	Warning
dataSrc	1.0 +	1.0 +	2.0 +	3.02 +	3.0 +	1 +	-	Warning
form	1.0 +	1.0 +	2.0 +	3.02 +	3.0 +	1 +	-	Warning
length	1.0 +	1.0 +	2.0 +	3.02 +	3.0 +	1 +	-	ReadOnly
multiple	1.5 +	3.0 +	6.0 +	4.0 +	-	1 +	-	-
selectedIndex	1.0 +	1.0 +	2.0 +	3.02 +	3.0 +	1 +	-	-
size	1.5 +	3.0 +	6.0 +	4.0 +	-	1 +	-	-
tabIndex	1.0 +	1.0 +	2.0 +	3.02 +	3.0 +	1 +	-	Warning
type	1.1 +	3.0 +	3.0 +	4.0 +	3.0 +	1 +	-	ReadOnly
value	1.5 +	3.0 +	6.0 +	4.0 +	-	1 +	-	-

Method	JavaScript	JScript	N	IE	Opera	DOM	HTML	Notes
add()	1.5 +	3.0 +	6.0 +	4.0 +	-	1 +	-	-
remove()	1.5 +	3.0 +	6.0 +	4.0 +	-	1 +	-	-
tags()	-	3.0 +	-	4.0 +	-	-	-	-

Event name	JavaScript	JScript	N	IE	Opera	DOM	HTML	Notes
onAfterUpdate	-	3.0 +	-	4.0 +	-	-	-	-
onBeforeUpdate	-	3.0 +	-	4.0 +	-	-	-	-
onBlur	1.1 +	3.0 +	3.0 +	4.0 +	3.0 +	-	-	Warning
onChange	1.0 +	3.0 +	2.0 +	4.0 +	3.0 +	-	-	-
onDragStart	-	3.0 +	-	4.0 +	-	-	-	-
onFilterChange	-	3.0 +	-	4.0 +	-	-	-	-
onFocus	1.0 +	3.0 +	2.0 +	4.0 +	3.0 +	-	-	Warning
onHelp	-	3.0 +	-	4.0 +	-	-	-	Warning
onKeyDown	1.2 +	3.0 +	4.0 +	4.0 +	3.0 +	-	4.0 +	Warning
onKeyPress	1.2 +	3.0 +	4.0 +	4.0 +	3.0 +	-	4.0 +	Warning
onKeyUp	1.2 +	3.0 +	4.0 +	4.0 +	3.0 +	-	4.0 +	Warning
onMouseDown	1.2 +	3.0 +	4.0 +	4.0 +	3.0 +	-	4.0 +	Warning
onMouseMove	1.2 +	3.0 +	4.0 +	4.0 +	-	-	4.0 +	Warning

752

Event name	JavaScript	JScript	N	IE	Opera	DOM	HTML	Notes
onMouse Out	1.1 +	3.0 +	3.0 +	4.0 +	3.0 +	-	4.0 +	Warning
onMouse Over	1.0 +	1.0 +	2.0 +	3.0 +	3.0 +	-	4.0 +	Warning
onMouseUp	1.2 +	3.0 +	4.0 +	4.0 +	3.0 +	-	4.0 +	Warning
onResize	1.2 +	3.0 +	4.0 +	4.0 +	-	-	-	Warning
onRow Enter	-	3.0 +	-	4.0 +	-	-	-	-
onRowExit	-	3.0 +	-	4.0 +	-	-	-	-
onSelect Start	-	3.0 +	-	4.0 +	-	-	-	-

Inheritance chain:

Element object, Node object

Selection object (Object/browser)

An object representing a user selection in the current window.

Availability:	JScript – 3.0 Internet Explorer – 4.0
JavaScript syntax:	IE *mySelection* = *myDocument*.selection
Object properties:	type
Object methods:	clear(), createRange(), empty()

This object represents a portion of the document in the current window that is currently highlighted, having been selected by the user or by a script. The selection is operated on by means of a TextRange object. This object is created by calling a createRange() method on the Selection object. This step is necessary because a selection cannot by its very nature persist very long so a TextRange object encapsulates its value into a persistent store so it can be operated on even though the original selection may have been deselected.

In Netscape Navigator, an entirely different technique is used that involves the document.getSelection() method.

Because it is easy to deselect the highlighted text by clicking on some other active object in the page, you will need to access the selection inside an event handler that is triggered by the selection action itself. This might be done quite effectively in an onSelectStart handler.

Warnings:

❑ Selection objects do not appear to be functional on any version of MSIE for the Macintosh. This may be because the the TextRange objects have not been mapped to the Macintosh cut and paste architecture.

See also:	Document.getSelection(), Document.selection, Password.select(), *TextRange object*

Property	JavaScript	JScript	N	IE	Opera	HTML	Notes
type	-	3.0 +	-	4.0 +	-	-	ReadOnly

Method	JavaScript	JScript	N	IE	Opera	HTML	Notes
clear()	-	3.0 +	-	4.0 +	-	-	-
createRange()	-	3.0 +	-	4.0 +	-	-	-
empty()	-	3.0 +	-	4.0 +	-	-	-

SelectorArray object (Object/browser)

A collection of style sheet rules.

Availability:	JScript – 3.0 Internet Explorer – 4.0
JavaScript syntax:	IE *mySelectorArray = myStyleSheet*.rules
Object properties:	length
Object methods:	item()

This is sometimes referred to as a rules object which is not strictly true. It is often so named because it is referenced by the rules property of a stylesheet.

DOM level 2 describes this object as a CSSRuleList object. It implies it is a sub-class of the Collection object and therefore it supports the item() method.

See also:	*Collection object, rule object,* rule.selectorText, StyleSheet.rules[]

Property	JavaScript	JScript	N	IE	Opera	HTML	Notes
length	-	3.0 +	-	4.0 +	-	-	ReadOnly

Method	JavaScript	JScript	N	IE	Opera	HTML	Notes
item()	-	3.0 +	-	4.0 +	-	-	-

Semicolon (;) (Delimiter)

Semicolon characters are used to mark the end of a statement.

Availability:	ECMAScript edition – 2 JavaScript – 1.0 JScript – 1.0 Internet Explorer – 3.02 Netscape – 2.0 Netscape Enterprise Server version – 2.0 Opera – 3.0	
JavaScript syntax:	-	*aStatement;*
Argument list:	*aStatement*	A JavaScript statement

Semicolon characters are used to mark the end of a statement, separating one from another.

JavaScript is somewhat forgiving and will place semicolons into the script automatically as needed except in some rare cases. Refer to the discussion on Automatic Semicolon Insertion for more details.

Placing two semicolons one after the other indicates a null statement. A line terminator can separate them and an optional comment is also permitted.

See also:	Automatic semi-colon insertion, *Empty statement (;)*, Expression statement, Line terminator, Statement, *var*

Cross-references:

ECMA 262 edition 2 – section – 12.2

ECMA 262 edition 2 – section – 12.3

ECMA 262 edition 2 – section – 12.4

ECMA 262 edition 3 – section – 12.2

ECMA 262 edition 3 – section – 12.3

ECMA 262 edition 3 – section – 12.4

Wrox *Instant JavaScript* – page – 18

S

JavaScript Programmer's Reference

SendMail object (Object/NES)

An object that encapsulates an outgoing e-mail message.

Availability:	JavaScript – 1.2 Netscape Enterprise Server version – 3.0
JavaScript syntax:	NES *mySendMail* = SendMail
	NES *mySendMail* = new SendMail()
Object properties:	Bcc, Body, Cc, constructor, ErrorsTo, From, Organization, prototype, ReplyTo, Smtpserver, Subject, To
Object methods:	errorCode(), errorMessage(), send()

This provides a way for the Netscape Enterprise Server to send e-mail messages as a result of a client request.

You create a new message handling object with the SendMail() constructor. Then you define where it is going to be sent, its subject matter and content by storing string values in its various properties.

Finally, you transmit the message via an SMTP server with the send() method.

Example code:

```
<SERVER>
mySendMail = new SendMail();
mySendMail.Smtpserver = "mailhost";
mySendMail.To = "someone@somewhere.com";
mySendMail.From = "me@here.com";
mySendMail.Subject = "A test message";
mySendMail.Body = "Some body text";
mySendMail.send();
</SERVER>
```

See also:	Netscape Enterprise Server, SendMail(), *unwatch(), watch()*

Property	JavaScript	JScript	NES	Notes
Bcc	1.2 +	-	3.0 +	-
Body	1.2 +	-	3.0 +	-
Cc	1.2 +	-	3.0 +	-
constructor	1.2 +	-	3.0 +	-
ErrorsTo	1.2 +	-	3.0 +	-
From	1.2 +	-	3.0 +	-
Organization	1.2 +	-	3.0 +	-

Property	JavaScript	JScript	NES	Notes
prototype	1.2 +	-	3.0 +	-
ReplyTo	1.2 +	-	3.0 +	-
Smtpserver	1.2 +	-	3.0 +	-
Subject	1.2 +	-	3.0 +	-
To	1.2 +	-	3.0 +	-

Method	JavaScript	JScript	NES	Notes
errorCode()	1.2 +	-	3.0 +	-
errorMessage()	1.2 +	-	3.0 +	-
send()	1.2 +	-	3.0 +	-

server object (Object/NES)

An object that represents the server in server-side JavaScript implementations.

Availability:	JavaScript – 1.1 Netscape Enterprise Server version – 2.0	
JavaScript syntax:	NES	server
Object properties:	agent, host, hostname, port, protocol	
Object methods:	lock(), unlock()	

This is a server-side host object representing the server. There is only one and you cannot instantiate it although you can make references to it. All users on the web server share this object.

This is an object that allows you to share values across all sessions running in all applications across the entire server. The locking facilities permit you to lock resources while you are using them.

Because this applies server-wide, there is even more reason to ensure you lock objects for the minimum of time and relinquish the locks as soon as possible. It is quite feasible to completely stall the whole server by locking a vital resource during the processing of a single client request. The effect of this is to make your server a single-threaded non-concurrent session server. That is, it will only actually serve one client request at a time.

See also:	Netscape Enterprise Server, *project object*, response.server, *unwatch()*, *watch()*

Property	JavaScript	JScript	NES	Notes
agent	1.1 +	-	2.0 +	-
host	1.1 +	-	2.0 +	-
hostname	1.1 +	-	2.0 +	-
port	1.1 +	-	2.0 +	-
protocol	1.1 +	-	2.0 +	-

Method	JavaScript	JScript	NES	Notes
lock()	1.1 +	-	2.0 +	Warning
unlock()	1.1 +	-	2.0 +	-

Cross-references:

Wrox *Instant JavaScript* – page – 65

Wrox *Instant JavaScript* – page – 67

short (Reserved word)

Reserved for future language enhancements.

The inclusion of this reserved keyword in the ECMAScript standard suggests that future versions of ECMAScript may be more strongly typed.

This keyword also represents a Java data type and the short keyword allows for the potential extension of JavaScript interfaces to access Java applet parameters and return values.

See also:	*double, float,* Integer, LiveConnect, *long,* Reserved word

Cross-references:

ECMA 262 edition 2 – section – 7.4.3

ECMA 262 edition 3 – section – 7.5.3

Sidebar object (Object/Navigator)

A new object introduced with Netscape 6.0 to manage the left side navigation bar.

Availability:	JavaScript – 1.5 Netscape – 6.0	
JavaScript syntax:	N	myWindow.sidebar
	N	sidebar

This is a new object which needs to be explored as we get to know the Netscape Navigator 6.0 browser. It encapsulates the behavior and appearance of the sidebar frame on the left of the browser window.

See also:	Window.sidebar

Signed scripts (Security related)

A means of giving scripts a privilege to access secure content.

Netscape Navigator allows scripts to have digital signatures attached to them. These signatures can control the level of privilege that a script is allowed to have in a web browser. This is ultimately under user control but if the user allows, the scripts can be secured at source.

The signature combines the identity of the signatory and a checksum of the content. The content cannot be modified without invalidating the checksum and hence voiding the signature.

It would be difficult to establish the exact security criteria beforehand, so Netscape Navigator forces scripts to request the privileges they need. Then, you can allow or deny the access which can be stored and mapped against the identity of the person signing the script. This means a security policy can gradually be established by training the browser to recognize and make decisions on access. Initially, no access is available but after some time, your browser preferences will contain a very sophisticated set of rules that govern the access to the secure values.

To sign your scripts, you will need additional tools and utilities. These are available from Netscape and should form part of your publishing pipeline.

An alternative is to serve your scripts separately from a secure server. Scripts served in this way will be assumed to have been signed by the secure server itself.

As a way round the inconvenience of signing scripts after every minor correction, you can sign the codebase of a script. This means you can establish a security setting for scripts from a specific web server. It is slightly less secure than signing a checksum but more convenient during development. It is recommended that proper signing be used once the script changes are less frequent and the development process is complete, as the scripts will be more stable and signing will be carried out less frequently. With some automation in the publishing work flow, you may be able to sign scripts as part of the releasing procedure that your developers employ.

S

JavaScript Programmer's Reference

759

Your web page may contain more than one script. For signed script access control to work, all of the scripts on a page must be signed. If an unsigned script is present, it defeats the entire signing status of the whole page. Scripts can be signed by more than one person. Netscape Navigator will try and find the highest most complete coverage of the scripts in a page. Ideally it will find a particular signer who has signed all of the scripts. Other signers may have conferred a higher level of security but not on all of the scripts. The more complete coverage will prevail.

Although these fairly strict same signer policies apply to the scripts within a window, scripts in multiple windows may operate under a slightly relaxed policy. The "same signer" policy is a variation of the "same origin" policy. Different signers cause the browser to behave as if the pages were from different origins. Both scripts may have rights to request `UniversalBrowserRead` access which might work around the problem.

Unsigned scripts have quite restricted access to window properties for windows that contain signed scripts. This means that untrusted and insecure scripts cannot access secure data by subverting an already trusted script.

Warnings:

❑ MSIE version 4 does not support the Netscape Navigator privilege model. Therefore scripts are always unprivileged. The MSIE security model is based on zones. This is a fairly coarse grained approach and simply allows scripts to be executed or not as a whole. The Netscape Navigator model allows access to be controlled object by object.

❑ Being so closely related to the MSIE browser, the WebTV box also does not support signed scripts.

See also:	*AuthentiCode*, Code signing, *Data-tainting, export, import,* JellyScript, *Requesting privileges, Same origin*

Web-references:

http://developer.netscape.com/software/signedobj/
http://developer.netscape.com/library/documentation/signedobj/signtool/

snews: URL (Request method)

A request from a web browser to a secure news server to send a document.

Use the browser to download and browse some content from a secure news site.

See also:	*javascript: URL*, Security policy, URL

SPAN object (Object/HTML)

An object that encapsulates the contents of an inline <SPAN> tag.

Availability:	JScript – 3.0 Internet Explorer – 4.0
Inherits from:	*Element object*
JavaScript syntax:	IE *mySPAN* = *myDocument*.all.*anElementID*
	IE *mySPAN* = *myDocument*.all.tags("SPAN") [*anIndex*]
	IE *mySPAN* = *myDocument*.all[*aName*]
	- *mySPAN* = *myDocument*.getElementById (*anElementID*)
	- *mySPAN* = *myDocument*.getElementsByName (*aName*)[*anIndex*]
	- *mySPAN* = *myDocument* .getElementsByTagName("SPAN")[*anIndex*]
HTML syntax:	<SPAN>...</SPAN>
Argument list:	*anIndex* A reference to an element in a collection
	aName An associative array reference
	anElementID The ID value of the object
Object properties:	dataFld, dataFormatAs, dataSrc
Event handlers:	onBlur, onClick, onDblClick, onDragStart, onFilterChange, onHelp, onKeyDown, onKeyPress, onKeyUp, onMouseDown, onMouseMove, onMouseOut, onMouseOver, onMouseUp, onSelectStart

<SPAN> tags and the objects that represent them are inline elements. Placing them into a document does not create a line break.

Note that a positioned <SPAN> element will appear as a member of the document.layers[] collection in Netscape 4.

The example shows how properties of <SPAN> blocks can be moved from one to another. In this example, the background color of each block is moved along to the next in a cyclic manner as the mouse is clicked:

Example code:

```
<HTML>
<HEAD>
</HEAD>
<BODY>
<SPAN ID="AAA" STYLE="background-color:RED">ONE</SPAN>
<SPAN ID="BBB" STYLE="background-color:BLUE">TWO</SPAN>
```

```
<SPAN ID="CCC" STYLE="background-color:GREEN">THREE</SPAN>
<SPAN ID="DDD" STYLE="background-color:CYAN">FOUR</SPAN>
<SPAN ID="EEE" STYLE="background-color:YELLOW">FIVE</SPAN>
<SPAN ID="FFF" STYLE="background-color:GRAY">SIX</SPAN>
<FORM>
<INPUT TYPE="button" VALUE="CLICK ME" onClick="clickMe()">
</FORM>
<SCRIPT>
//IE only
function clickMe()
{
    mySpans = document.all.tags("SPAN");
    myStyle1 = mySpans[mySpans.length-1].style.cssText;

    for(myEnum=0; myEnum<mySpans.length; myEnum++)
    {
        myStyle2 = mySpans[myEnum].style.cssText;
        mySpans[myEnum].style.cssText = myStyle1;
        myStyle1 = myStyle2;
    }
}
</SCRIPT>
</BODY>
</HTML>
```

See also:	*Element object*

Property	JavaScript	JScript	N	IE	Opera	DOM	HTML	Notes
dataFld	-	3.0 +	-	4.0 +	-	-	-	-
dataFormatAs	-	3.0 +	-	4.0 +	-	-	-	-
dataSrc	-	3.0 +	-	4.0 +	-	-	-	-

Event name	JavaScript	JScript	N	IE	Opera	DOM	HTML	Notes
onBlur	-	3.0 +	-	4.0 +	-	-	-	Warning
onClick	-	3.0 +	-	4.0 +	-	-	4.0 +	Warning
onDblClick	-	3.0 +	-	4.0 +	-	-	4.0 +	Warning
onDragStart	-	3.0 +	-	4.0 +	-	-	-	-
onFilterChange	-	3.0 +	-	4.0 +	-	-	-	-
onHelp	-	3.0 +	-	4.0 +	-	-	-	Warning
onKeyDown	-	3.0 +	-	4.0 +	-	-	4.0 +	Warning
onKeyPress	-	3.0 +	-	4.0 +	-	-	4.0 +	Warning
onKeyUp	-	3.0 +	-	4.0 +	-	-	4.0 +	Warning
onMouseDown	-	3.0 +	-	4.0 +	-	-	4.0 +	Warning
onMouseMove	-	3.0 +	-	4.0 +	-	-	4.0 +	Warning
onMouseOut	-	3.0 +	-	4.0 +	-	-	4.0 +	Warning
onMouseOver	-	3.0 +	-	4.0 +	-	-	4.0 +	Warning
onMouseUp	-	3.0 +	-	4.0 +	-	-	4.0 +	Warning
onSelectStart	-	3.0 +	-	4.0 +	-	-	-	-

Inheritance chain:

Element object, Node object

762

Status code (Result value/NES)

Many of the NES supported methods return a status code that is consistently defined across all objects and methods.

The following methods will return a status code:

- ❑ `database.execute()`
- ❑ `database.beginTransaction()`
- ❑ `database.commitTransaction()`
- ❑ `database.rollbackTransaction()`
- ❑ `cursor.insertRow()`
- ❑ `cursor.updateRow()`
- ❑ `cursor.deleteRow()`

The status codes are summarized in the table:

Code	Meaning
00	No error
01	Out of memory
02	Object was never initialized
03	Type conversion error
04	Database not registered
05	Error reported by database engine
06	Message from database engine
07	Error from database vendor's library
08	Lost connection
09	End of fetch
10	Invalid use of object
11	Column does not exist
12	Bounds error – invalid positioning within object
13	Unsupported feature
14	Null reference parameter
15	Database object not found
16	Required information missing
17	Object cannot support multiple readers
18	Object cannot support deletes
19	Object cannot support inserts
20	Object cannot support updates (1)

Table continued on following page

S

JavaScript Programmer's Reference

Code	Meaning
21	Object cannot support updates (2)
22	Object cannot support indices
23	Object cannot be dropped
24	Incorrect connection supplied
25	Object cannot support privileges
26	Object cannot support cursors
27	Unable to open

Status codes 5 and 7 are significant. It depends on the database being used as to which is important.

Status code 5 is important for Oracle and ODBC.

Status code 7 is important for Informix and Sybase.

If these values are detected, then the major and minor error codes and messages can be inspected for further help in diagnosing the problems.

See also:	`Connection.majorErrorCode()`, `Connection.majorErrorMessage()`, `Connection.minorErrorCode()`, `Connection.minorErrorMessage()`, `Cursor.deleteRow()`, `Cursor.insertRow()`, `Cursor.updateRow()`, `database.beginTransaction()`, `database.commitTransaction()`, `database.execute()`, `database.majorErrorCode()`, `database.majorErrorMessage()`, `database.minorErrorCode()`, `database.minorErrorMessage()`, `database.rollbackTransaction()`, Error handling

Stproc object (Object/NES)

An object that encapsulates a call to a stored procedure on a database from a Netscape Enterprise Server.

Availability:	JavaScript – 1.2 Netscape Enterprise Server version – 3.0	
JavaScript syntax:	NES	`myStproc = database.storedProc (aProcName, aProcParm);`
	NES	`myStproc = myConnection.storedProc (aProcName, aProcParm)`
Argument list:	`aProcName`	The name of a stored procedure to call
	`aProcParm`	A parameter value to pass to the stored procedure

Object properties:	prototype
Object methods:	close(), outParamCount(), outParameters(), resultSet(), returnValue()

This object provides a container to manage the call to the stored procedure and somewhere that the results can be made available for further processing by your scripts.

You create Stproc objects by requesting them from the database or connection objects that are accessing the target database you are interested in.

Example code:

```
<SERVER>
// An example derived from Wrox Professional JavaScript
database.connect("ODBC", "myDatabase", "me", "myPassword", "");
myStproc = database.storedProc("myProcedure", 40);
</SERVER>
```

See also:	Connection.storedProc(), Netscape Enterprise Server

Property	JavaScript	JScript	NES	Notes
prototype	1.2 +	-	3.0 +	-

Method	JavaScript	JScript	NES	Notes
close()	1.2 +	-	3.0 +	-
outParamCount()	1.2 +	-	3.0 +	-
outParameters()	1.2 +	-	3.0 +	-
resultSet()	1.2 +	-	3.0 +	-
returnValue()	1.2 +	-	3.0 +	-

String (Primitive value)

A built-in primitive value.

Availability:	ECMAScript edition – 2
Property/method value type:	String primitive

A string value is a member of the type String and is a finite ordered sequence of zero or more Unicode characters. There is no way to represent a single character other than by means of a very short string.

A string is not an array of characters as it would be in the C language. It is also not mutable as the other object data types that are passed by reference are. Strings are immutable and therefore to change one, you must manufacture a new string and discard the old one. This can lead to memory leaks.

Strings can contain any Unicode character code point, however, many are not available on even the most international keyboard and must be escaped. You will need to check that the host environment can render the international symbols correctly if you use them.

Strings can be delimited by either single or double quotes. This can be very useful for the occasions when a fragment of JavaScript is contained within some HTML.

Refer to the String literal topic for a list of escape characters and more information on defining string values.

Warnings:

❑ Beware that the HTML escaping rules come into play when JavaScript is contained within HTML quote delimited name-value pairs in tags and you must be careful to escape any characters within scripts using the JavaScript escape mechanisms and not the HTML escape mechanisms. JavaScript inside <SCRIPT> tags may also be affected by the host environment's escaping mechanisms.

See also:	<SCRIPT>, Cast operator, *java.lang.String*, JavaScript to Java values, *String concatenate (+)*, *String literal*

Cross-references:

ECMA 262 edition 2 – section – 4.3.16

ECMA 262 edition 3 – section – 4.3.16

Wrox *Instant JavaScript* – page – 14

String (Type)

A native built-in type.

Availability:	ECMAScript edition – 2
Property/method value type:	`String primitive`

Entities of type `String` are collections of zero or more Unicode characters.

A string is arranged so that the characters in it can be accessed by their position. The leftmost character is considered to be at position 0 and the right most character is therefore at a position whose value is 1 less than the length of the string.

This is convenient when processing strings in a `for()` loop since you can check the enumerator against the length and as long as it is less than the length and is a positive value, it is indexing within the string.

Zero length strings are a special case.

Strings can only be accessed read only. You cannot change the contents of a string, you can only replace it with another.

Warnings:

❑ You cannot reference strings with negative position values.

See also:	Cast operator, Data Type, Fundamental data type, *String concatenate (+)*, *toString()*, Type, Type conversion, *Unicode*

Cross-references:

ECMA 262 edition 2 – section – 4.3.17

ECMA 262 edition 2 – section – 6

ECMA 262 edition 2 – section – 8.4

ECMA 262 edition 3 – section – 4.3.17

ECMA 262 edition 3 – section – 8.4

O'Reilly *JavaScript Definitive Guide* – page – 38

O'Reilly *JavaScript Definitive Guide* – page – 50

String concatenate (+) (Operator/string)

Join two string values together.

Availability:	ECMAScript edition – 2 JavaScript – 1.0 JScript – 1.0 Internet Explorer – 3.02 Netscape – 2.0 Netscape Enterprise Server version – 2.0 Opera – 3.0	
Property/method value type:	`String primitive`	
JavaScript syntax:	-	`aString1 + aString2`
Argument list:	`aString1`	A string value
	`aString2`	Another string value

S

When the operands are a pair of strings, the plus sign will concatenate them together. This yields a single string combining both values joined end to end.

The string concatenation is not commutative. That is, the position of the two operands will affect the outcome if they are exchanged.

The addition/concatenation operator looks at the arguments and if either is a `String` already or preferentially converts to one, then a concatenation occurs. If neither argument prefers to be a `String` then a `Number` conversion happens and the values are added.

The associativity is left to right.

Refer to the operator precedence topic for details of execution order.

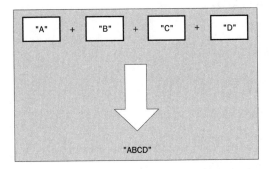

Warnings:

❑ Some conversion of type will occur if a mixture of data types is used in certain contexts.

❑ In string concatenations, when either of the operands is a string, the result will be a string concatenation. The same does not apply when relational expressions are involved when the subtraction operator can be used to coerce a string value into a numeric type.

See also: Add (+), Additive operator, `Array.join()`, `Array.toString()`, Associativity, Operator Precedence, *parseFloat()*, *parseInt()*, *String value*, *String type*, *String literal*, *String object*, String operator, `String.split()`, *ToString*, *toString()*, Type conversion

Cross-references:

ECMA 262 edition 2 – section – 11.6.1

ECMA 262 edition 3 – section – 11.6.1

Wrox *Instant JavaScript* – page – 37

String literal (Primitive value)

A literal constant whose type is a built-in primitive value.

Availability:	ECMAScript edition – 2
Property/method value type:	`String primitive`

A string literal is zero or more characters enclosed in matching single or double quotes. Each character may be represented by an escape sequence.

You can escape special characters with special escape sequences. You can also escape any character and specify it by its octal, hexadecimal or Unicode equivalent code point. Note that the octal values will be in the range 0 to 377 and the hexadecimal values will be in the range 0 to FF. The octal and hexadecimal escapes can only cover the first 256 character codes, some of which are control codes and should not be used anyway. The Unicode escape gives access to the full 65536 character codes in the Unicode set. Although you can specify octal or hexadecimal values, there is presently no standardized decimal based escape mechanism. You'll just have to learn octal or hexadecimal unfortunately.

Here are the valid common escape sequences:

Escape Sequence	Name	Symbol
\"	Double Quote	"
\'	Single Quote (Apostrophe)	'
\\	Backslash	\
\a	Audible alert (MSIE displays the letter a)	<BEL>
\b	Backspace (ignored silently in MSIE)	<BS>
\f	Form Feed (ignored silently in MSIE)	<FF>
\n	Line Feed (Newline – MSIE inserts a space)	<LF>
\r	Carriage Return (MSIE inserts a space)	<CR>
\t	Horizontal Tab (MSIE inserts a space)	<HT>
\v	Vertical Tab (MSIE displays the letter v)	<VT>
\0nn	Octal escape	-
\042	Double Quote	"
\047	Single Quote (Apostrophe)	'
\134	Backslash	\
\xnn	Hexadecimal escape	-
\x22	Double Quote	"
\x27	Single Quote (Apostrophe)	'
\x5C	Backslash	\

Table continued on following page

S

Escape Sequence	Name	Symbol
\unnnn	Unicode escape	-
\u0022	Double Quote	"
\u0027	Single Quote (Apostrophe)	'
\u005C	Backslash	\
\uFFFE	A special Unicode sentinel character for flagging byte reversed text	-
\uFFFF	A special Unicode sentinel character	-

Here are some example string literals:

```
myString = "James Bond";

myString = 'Another String';

myString = 'A string with double " quotes';

myString = "He's got a single quote";
```

The characters in the quotes are converted to a String primitive value and will replace the expression in the context in which it has been used. This would normally be an assignment of a variable or perhaps part of a relational expression.

There are circumstances in HTML documents where JavaScript string delimiters may need to be single quotes because the fragment of JavaScript is already enclosed in double quotes that are part of the HTML source code space.

For example:

```
<A HREF="javascript:passStringValue('ABCDEF');">ABCDEF</A>;
```

You can use double quotes without breaking the syntax rules of the HTML page containing the JavaScript.

You can exchange the pairs of quotes around between the contexts but it is good to stick with one or the other. It tends to work out that double quotes are used in HTML which forces single quotes to be used in the JavaScript fragments that are placed into HTML tag attributes.

This is discussed with examples in the "Escaped JavaScript quotes in HTML" topic.

Warnings:

❑ If you use quotes in JavaScript that you plan to use inside HTML, then be sensible about the use of single and double quotes. Often you will find that double quotes will break even though they are enclosed in single quotes when you include them in an HREF for an anchor. For example, this can break because the double quotes are seen by the HTML parser:

```
<A HREF="javascript:handleClick('bad " quotes');">
```

❏ Put an escape round the quotes. Sometimes a backslash is appropriate and sometimes an HTML character entity depending on who you are trying to hide the quotes from.

❏ Be careful if you use HTML escape sequences such as ' in JavaScript string literals. Some implementations will unescape that string in the JavaScript context and not the HTML context hoped for. That will restore the single quote inside the JavaScript string literal causing a run-time error. You should escape single quotes with a backslash.

❏ You cannot include a line terminator within a string literal. Instead use a newline (\n) escape sequence.

❏ Currency symbols are notoriously non-portable. Check that your target audience can display international currency symbols before using GB pounds or Euro symbols. Although these are defined in the standards, they are often missing from the installed character sets.

| See also: | Escape sequence (\), *Escaped JavaScript quotes in HTML*, Identifier, Implicit conversion, Line terminator, Literal, *String, String concatenate (+), Unicode* |

Cross-references:

ECMA 262 edition 2 – section – 7.7.3

ECMA 262 edition 2 – section – 7.7.4

ECMA 262 edition 3 – section – 7.8.4

O'Reilly *JavaScript Definitive Guide* – page – 38

String object (Object/core)

An object of the class "String".

Availability:	ECMAScript edition – 2 JavaScript – 1.0 JScript – 1.0 Internet Explorer – 3.02 Netscape – 2.0 Netscape Enterprise Server version – 2.0 Opera – 3.0	
JavaScript syntax:	-	myString = new String()
	-	myString = String
Object properties:	constructor, length, prototype	
Class methods:	*fromCharCode()*	

Object methods:	anchor(), big(), blink(), bold(), charAt(), charCodeAt(), concat(), fixed(), fontcolor(), fontsize(), fromCharCode(), indexOf(), italics(), lastIndexOf(), link(), localeCompare(), match(), replace(), search(), slice(), small(), split(), strike(), sub(), substr(), substring(), sup(), toLocaleLowerCase(), toLocaleUpperCase(), toLowerCase(), toSource(), toString(), toUpperCase(), valueOf()

An instance of the class "String" is created by using the new operator on the String() constructor. The new object adopts the behavior of the built-in prototype object through the prototype-inheritance mechanisms.

All properties and methods of the prototype are available as if they were part of the instance.

A String object is a member of the type Object.

Cloning the built-in String object creates new String objects. This is done by calling the String constructor with the new operator being applied to an existing String object, thus:

```
myString = new String("a string of text");
```

A String object can be coerced to a string value and can be used anywhere where a string value would be expected.

Programmers familiar with object oriented techniques may prefer to use the String object while procedural language programmers may implement the same functionality with a string value instead.

This is an example of the flexibility of JavaScript in its ability to accommodate a variety of users from different backgrounds.

The prototype for the String prototype object is the Object prototype object.

In Netscape Navigator, you can traverse a string as if it were an array and access characters individually by their index position in the array. This doesn't work in MSIE.

See also:	Native object, *Object object*, *String concatenate (+)*, *String.Class*, String.length, String.prototype, *unwatch()*, *watch()*

Property	JavaScript	JScript	N	IE	Opera	NES	ECMA	Notes
constructor	1.0 +	1.0 +	2.0 +	3.02 +	-	-	2 +	-
length	1.0 +	1.0 +	2.0 +	3.02 +	3.0 +	2.0 +	2 +	ReadOnly, DontDelete, DontEnum
prototype	1.1 +	3.0 +	3.0 +	4.0 +	3.0 +	3.0 +	2 +	-

Method	JavaScript	JScript	N	IE	Opera	NES	ECMA	Notes
anchor()	1.0 +	1.0 +	2.0 +	3.02 +	3.0 +	2.0 +	-	-
big()	1.0 +	1.0 +	2.0 +	3.02 +	3.0 +	2.0 +	-	Deprecated
blink()	1.0 +	1.0 +	2.0 +	3.02 +	3.0 +	2.0 +	-	Deprecated
bold()	1.0 +	1.0 +	2.0 +	3.02 +	3.0 +	2.0 +	-	Deprecated
charAt()	1.0 +	1.0 +	2.0 +	3.02 +	3.0 +	2.0 +	2 +	-
charCodeAt()	1.2 +	5.5 +	4.0 +	5.5 +	3.0 +	3.0 +	2 +	Warning
concat()	1.2 +	3.0 +	4.0 +	4.0 +	-	3.0 +	3 +	-
fixed()	1.0 +	1.0 +	2.0 +	3.02 +	3.0 +	2.0 +	-	Deprecated
fontcolor()	1.0 +	1.0 +	2.0 +	3.02 +	3.0 +	2.0 +	-	Deprecated
fontsize()	1.0 +	1.0 +	2.0 +	3.02 +	3.0 +	2.0 +	-	Deprecated
fromCharCode()	1.2 +	3.0 +	4.0 +	4.0 +	3.0 +	3.0 +	3 +	-
indexOf()	1.0 +	1.0 +	2.0 +	3.02 +	3.0 +	2.0 +	2 +	-
italics()	1.0 +	1.0 +	2.0 +	3.02 +	3.0 +	2.0 +	-	Deprecated
lastIndexOf()	1.0 +	1.0 +	2.0 +	3.02 +	3.0 +	2.0 +	2 +	-
link()	1.0 +	1.0 +	2.0 +	3.02 +	3.0 +	2.0 +	-	-
localeCompare()	1.5 +	5.5 +	6.0 +	5.5 +	-	-	3 +	-
match()	1.2 +	3.0 +	4.0 +	4.0 +	-	-	3 +	Warning
replace()	1.2 +	3.0 +	4.0 +	4.0 +	-	-	3 +	Warning
search()	1.2 +	3.0 +	4.0 +	4.0 +	-	-	3 +	Warning
slice()	1.2 +	3.0 +	4.0 +	4.0 +	-	2.0 +	3 +	-
small()	1.0 +	1.0 +	2.0 +	3.02 +	3.0 +	2.0 +	-	Deprecated
split()	1.1 +	3.0 +	3.0 +	4.0 +	3.0 +	2.0 +	2 +	-
strike()	1.0 +	1.0 +	2.0 +	3.02 +	3.0 +	2.0 +	-	-
sub()	1.0 +	1.0 +	2.0 +	3.02 +	3.0 +	2.0 +	-	Deprecated
substr()	1.2 +	3.0 +	4.0 +	4.0 +	-	3.0 +	3 +	-
substring()	1.0 +	1.0 +	2.0 +	3.02 +	3.0 +	2.0 +	2 +	-
sup()	1.0 +	1.0 +	2.0 +	3.02 +	3.0 +	2.0 +	-	Deprecated
toLocaleLowerCase()	1.5 +	5.5 +	6.0 +	5.5 +	3.0 +	2.0 +	3 +	-
toLocaleUpperCase()	1.5 +	5.5 +	6.0 +	5.5 +	3.0 +	2.0 +	3 +	-
toLowerCase()	1.0 +	1.0 +	2.0 +	3.02 +	3.0 +	2.0 +	2 +	-
toSource()	1.3 +	3.0 +	4.06 +	4.0 +	-	-	3 +	-
toString()	1.3 +	1.0 +	4.06 +	3.02 +	-	-	2 +	-
toUpperCase()	1.0 +	1.0 +	2.0 +	3.02 +	3.0 +	2.0 +	2 +	-
valueOf()	1.1 +	3.0 +	3.0 +	4.0 +	-	-	2 +	-

S

Cross-references:

ECMA 262 edition 2 – section – 4.3.18

ECMA 262 edition 2 – section – 10.1.5

ECMA 262 edition 2 – section – 15.5

ECMA 262 edition 3 – section – 4.3.18

ECMA 262 edition 3 – section – 15.5

Wrox *Instant JavaScript* – page – 33

String() (Function)

A String object constructor called as a function.

Availability:	ECMAScript edition – 2 JavaScript – 1.2 JScript – 1.0 Internet Explorer – 3.02 Netscape – 4.0	
Property/method value type:	`String primitive`	
JavaScript syntax:	-	`String()`
	-	`String(aValue)`
Argument list:	`aValue`	Some value to be converted to a string

When `String()` is called as a function rather than a constructor, it performs a type conversion.

The internal `ToString` conversion facilities are used for type conversion with the additional handling of a missing argument provided by the constructor itself.

Value	Result
No argument	An empty string "".
undefined	`"undefined"`.
null	`"null"`.
Boolean	If the argument is true, then the result is `"true"` otherwise the result is `"false"`.
Number	Special cases are provided for NaN and Infinity where `"NaN"` and `"Infinity"` will be returned. Otherwise the string is a textual representation of the value.
String	No conversion, the input value is returned unchanged.
Object	An internal conversion to a primitive takes place followed by a conversion from that primitive to a string. Some objects will return a string value that is immediately useful.

The result of calling this function is a string version of the value passed in. If there is no value passed in argument an empty string is returned.

Warnings:

❏ Converting numbers to strings can yield some strange effects due to rounding errors. Taking a numeric value and simply converting it is fairly reliable. However, the result of a numeric expression, being cast to a string directly rather than to a number variable and thence to a string seems to expose some weaknesses in the arithmetic in some implementations.

See also:	Cast operator, Constructor function, constructor property, Implicit conversion, *Number()*

Cross-references:

ECMA 262 edition 2 – section – 15.1.3.4

ECMA 262 edition 2 – section – 15.5.1

ECMA 262 edition 3 – section – 15.5.1

Wrox *Instant JavaScript* – page – 36

String.Class (Property/internal)

Internal property that returns an object class.

Availability:	ECMAScript edition – 2

This is an internal property that describes the class that a `String` object instance is a member of. The reserved words suggest that in the future this property may be externalized.

See also:	*Class, String object*

Property attributes:

`DontEnum`, `Internal`.

Cross-references:

ECMA 262 edition 2 – section – 8.6.2

ECMA 262 edition 2 – section – 15.5.2.1

ECMA 262 edition 3 – section – 8.6.2

String.fromCharCode() (Method/static)

A class-based factory method for converting numeric character codes to `String` objects.

Availability:	ECMAScript edition – 3 JavaScript – 1.2 JScript – 3.0 Internet Explorer – 4.0 Netscape – 4.0 Netscape Enterprise Server version – 3.0 Opera – 3.0
Property/method value type:	`String primitive`
JavaScript syntax:	- `String.fromCharCode(aChar0, aChar1, aChar2, ...)`
Argument list:	`aCharN` a character code value.

This constructs a new string from a sequence of Unicode character code point values each passed as a separate argument.

This is a static method so called because it belongs to the `String()` constructor and not any of the string objects. This means it is analogous to a class method in other object oriented environments.

Example code:

```
<HTML>
<HEAD>
</HEAD>
<BODY>
<SCRIPT>
document.write(String.fromCharCode(72, 69, 76, 76, 79));
</SCRIPT>
</BODY>
</HTML>
```

See also:	Arithmetic type, Cast operator, Character handling, Character testing, Character-case mapping, `File.byteToString()`, Java to JavaScript values, Keyboard events, `onKeyDown`, `String.charCodeAt()`, `String.constructor`, *ToUint16*, *Window.atob()*, *Window.btoa()*

Cross-references:

ECMA 262 edition 2 – section – 15.5.3.2

ECMA 262 edition 3 – section – 15.5.3.2

776

STRONG object (Object/HTML)

An object representing the HTML content delimited by the <STRONG> tags.

Availability:	JScript – 3.0 Internet Explorer – 4.0
Inherits from:	*Element object*
JavaScript syntax:	IE *mySTRONG* = *myDocument*.all.*anElementID*
	IE *mySTRONG* = *myDocument*.all.tags ("STRONG")[*anIndex*]
	IE *mySTRONG* = *myDocument*.all[*aName*]
	- *mySTRONG* = *myDocument*.getElementById (*anElementID*)
	- *mySTRONG* = *myDocument* .getElementsByName(*aName*)[*anIndex*]
	- *mySTRONG* = *myDocument*.getElements ByTagName("STRONG")[*anIndex*]
HTML syntax:	<STRONG> ... </STRONG>
Argument list:	*anElementID* The ID value of the element required
	anIndex A reference to an element in a collection
	aName An associative array reference
Event handlers:	onClick, onDblClick, onDragStart, onFilterChange, onHelp, onKeyDown, onKeyPress, onKeyUp, onMouseDown, onMouseMove, onMouseOut, onMouseOver, onMouseUp, onSelectStart

<STRONG> tags and the objects that represent them are inline elements. Placing them into a document does not create a line break.

See also:	*Element object*

Event name	JavaScript	JScript	N	IE	Opera	DOM	HTML	Notes
onClick	-	3.0 +	-	4.0 +	-	-	4.0 +	Warning
onDblClick	-	3.0 +	-	4.0 +	-	-	4.0 +	Warning
onDragStart	-	3.0 +	-	4.0 +	-	-	-	-
onFilterChange	-	3.0 +	-	4.0 +	-	-	-	-
onHelp	-	3.0 +	-	4.0 +	-	-	-	Warning
onKeyDown	-	3.0 +	-	4.0 +	-	-	4.0 +	Warning
onKeyPress	-	3.0 +	-	4.0 +	-	-	4.0 +	Warning
onKeyUp	-	3.0 +	-	4.0 +	-	-	4.0 +	Warning
onMouseDown	-	3.0 +	-	4.0 +	-	-	4.0 +	Warning

Table continued on following page

Event name	JavaScript	JScript	N	IE	Opera	DOM	HTML	Notes
onMouseMove	-	3.0 +	-	4.0 +	-	-	4.0 +	Warning
onMouseOut	-	3.0 +	-	4.0 +	-	-	4.0 +	Warning
onMouseOver	-	3.0 +	-	4.0 +	-	-	4.0 +	Warning
onMouseUp	-	3.0 +	-	4.0 +	-	-	4.0 +	Warning
onSelectStart	-	3.0 +	-	4.0 +	-	-	-	-

Inheritance chain:

Element object, Node object

STYLE object (1) (Object/HTML)

An object that encapsulates the <STYLE> tag in the document source as opposed to the internally created style objects manufactured from CSS style sheet contents.

Availability:	DOM level – 1 JavaScript – 1.5 JScript – 3.0 Internet Explorer – 4.0 Netscape – 6.0	
Inherits from:	*Element object*	
JavaScript syntax:	IE	*mySTYLE = myDocument.all.anElementID*
	IE	*mySTYLE =* *myDocument.all.tags("STYLE")[anIndex]*
	IE	*mySTYLE = myDocument.all[aName]*
	-	*mySTYLE = myDocument.getElementById* *(anElementID)*
	-	*mySTYLE = myDocument.getElementsByName* *(aName)[anIndex]*
	-	*mySTYLE = myDocument.getElements* *ByTagName("STYLE")[anIndex]*
HTML syntax:	<STYLE>...</STYLE>	
Argument list:	*anIndex*	A reference to an element in a collection
	aName	An associative array reference
	anElementID	The ID value of an Element object
Object properties:	disabled, media, readyState, type	
Event handlers:	onClick, onDblClick, onError, onHelp, onKeyDown, onKeyPress, onKeyUp, onLoad, onMouseDown, onMouseMove, onMouseOut, onMouseOver, onMouseUp, onReadyStateChange	

The <STYLE> tag conveys no apparent visible effect on the document. It is considered to be an invisible tag.

778

Warnings:

❑ Be careful not to confuse this DOM object with the internal CSS `style` object that MSIE supports. The STYLE object is instantiated by the <STYLE> tag and is defined in the DOM standard. The `style` object is based on the CSS attributes.

See also:	CLASS="...", Element object

Property	JavaScript	JScript	N	IE	Opera	DOM	HTML	Notes
disabled	1.5 +	3.0 +	6.0 +	4.0 +	-	1 +	-	Warning
media	1.5 +	3.0 +	6.0 +	4.0 +	-	1 +	-	-
readyState	-	3.0 +	-	4.0 +	-	-	-	ReadOnly.
type	1.5 +	3.0 +	6.0 +	4.0 +	-	1 +	-	-

Event name	JavaScript	JScript	N	IE	Opera	DOM	HTML	Notes
onClick	1.5+	3.0 +	6.0 +	4.0+	-	-	4.0 +	Warning
onDblClick	1.5 +	3.0 +	6.0 +	4.0 +	-	-	4.0 +	Warning
onError	1.5 +	3.0 +	6.0 +	4.0 +	-	-	-	Warning
onHelp	-	3.0 +	-	4.0 +	-	-	-	Warning
onKeyDown	1.5 +	3.0 +	6.0 +	4.0 +	-	-	4.0 +	Warning
onKeyPress	1.5 +	3.0 +	6.0 +	4.0 +	-	-	4.0 +	Warning
onKeyUp	1.5 +	3.0 +	6.0 +	4.0 +	-	-	4.0 +	Warning
onLoad	1.5 +	3.0 +	6.0 +	4.0 +	-	-	-	Warning
onMouseDown	1.5 +	3.0 +	6.0 +	4.0 +	-	-	4.0 +	Warning
onMouseMove	1.5 +	3.0 +	6.0 +	4.0 +	-	-	4.0 +	Warning
onMouseOut	1.5 +	3.0 +	6.0 +	4.0 +	-	-	4.0 +	Warning
onMouseOver	1.5 +	3.0 +	6.0 +	3.0 +	-	-	4.0 +	Warning
onMouseUp	1.5 +	3.0 +	6.0 +	4.0 +	-	-	4.0 +	Warning
onReady StateChange	-	3.0 +	-	4.0 +	-	-	-	-

Inheritance chain:

Element object, Node object

style object (2) (Object/CSS)

An object that represents an individual style element within a style sheet.

Availability:	DOM level – 2 JavaScript – 1.5 JScript – 3.0 Internet Explorer – 4.0 Netscape – 6.0 Opera – 5.0	
Inherits from:	*Element object*	
JavaScript syntax:	IE	`myStyle = myDocument.all` `.anElementID.style`
	-	`myStyle = myElement.style`
Argument list:	*aClassName*	The value in a `CLASS="..."` tag attribute.
	anElementName	The value in a `NAME="..."` or `ID="..."` tag attribute
	aTagName	An HTML tag name
Object properties:	azimuth, background, backgroundAttachment, backgroundColor, backgroundImage, backgroundPosition, backgroundPositionX, backgroundPositionY, backgroundRepeat, behavior, border, borderBottom, borderBottomColor, BorderBottomStyle, borderBottomWidth, borderCollapse, borderColor, borderLeft, borderLeftColor, borderLeftStyle, borderLeftWidth, borderRight, borderRightColor, borderRightStyle, borderRightWidth, borderSpacing, borderStyle, borderTop, borderTopColor, borderTopStyle, borderTopWidth, borderWidth, bottom, boxSizing, captionSide, cellSpacing, clear, clip, color, colorProfile, columnSpan, content, counterIncrement, counterReset, cssFloat, cssText, cue, cueAfter, cueBefore, cursor, direction, display, elevation, emptyCells, filter, float, floatStyle, font, fontFamily, fontSize, fontSizeAdjust, fontStretch, fontStyle, fontVariant, fontWeight, height, imeMode, important, layoutGrid, layoutGridChar, layoutGridCharSpacing, layoutGridLine, layoutGridMode, layoutGridType, left, length, letterSpacing, lineBreak, lineHeight, listStyle, listStyleImage, listStylePosition, listStyleType, margin, marginBottom, marginLeft, marginRight, marginTop, markerOffset, marks, maxHeight, maxWidth, minHeight, minWidth, orphans, outline, outlineColor, outlineStyle, outlineWidth, overflow, overflowX, overflowY, padding, paddingBottom, paddingLeft, paddingRight, paddingTop, page, pageBreakAfter, pageBreakBefore, pageBreakInside, pause, pauseAfter, pauseBefore, pitch, pitchRange, pixelBottom, pixelHeight, pixelLeft, pixelRight, pixelTop, pixelWidth, playDuring, posBottom, posHeight, position, posLeft, posRight, posTop, posWidth, quotes, renderingIntent, richness,		

Object properties:	right, rowSpan, rubyAlign, rubyOverhang, rubyPosition, scrollbar3dLightColor, scrollbarArrowColor, scrollbarBaseColor, scrollbarDarkShadowColor, scrollbarFaceColor, scrollbarHighlightColor, scrollbarShadowColor, size, speak, speakDate, speakHeader, speakNumeral, speakPunctuation, speakTime, speechRate, stress, styleFloat, tableLayout, textAlign, textAutospace, textDecoration, textDecorationBlink, textDecorationLineThrough, textDecorationNone, textDecorationOverline, textDecorationUnderline, textIndent, textJustify, textKashidaSpace, textShadow, textTransform, textUnderlinePosition, top, unicodeBidi, verticalAlign, visibility, voiceFamily, volume, whiteSpace, widows, width, wordBreak, wordSpacing, wordWrap, writingMode, zIndex, zoom
Object methods:	getAttribute(), getExpression(), item(), removeExpression(), setAttribute(), setExpression()
Event handlers:	onClick, onDblClick, onHelp, onKeyDown, onKeyPress, onKeyUp, onMouseDown, onMouseMove, onMouseOut, onMouseOver, onMouseUp

DOM level 2 mandates that this object should really be called a CSS2Properties object and not a style object. It has become known as a style object due to the Element property name that points at it.

The style objects supported by MSIE and Netscape Navigator 4.x are quite different. For a start, the style objects are associated with each element in MSIE and are accessible quite easily via the style property. For Netscape Navigator 4, the style properties are documented under the JSSTag object. JSS style control permits the definition of element styles before an element has been instantiated into the document. You cannot use JSS to make dynamic style alterations.

With the release of Netscape 6.0, the style manipulation is virtually the same across both browsers. This works in both MSIE and Netscape 6 now:

```
document.getElementById("anID").style.backgroundColor="#003366";
```

Nearly all the attributes described in CSS level 1 and 2 are now supported by the style object. Because the codebase in Netscape 6.0 is totally new and it has only just been released, you may experience some minor instability in its support for styles.

When you look at the properties of the style object, you will observe that there are many alternative ways to define properties. This is quite commonplace where Microsoft define an interface to an object themselves or enhance one that has been defined by someone else (W3C or Netscape perhaps). For example, you can specify border attributes for all four borders but there are also separately defined attributes for each border. Although it's not that confusing, it does mean that there are a lot of additional keywords to learn and, from a parsing point of view, the more keywords there are, the slower the parser is going to be. It also means that programmers will employ a variety of different techniques which then forces the competing browser manufacturers to support the Microsoft extensions too.

Minimalist design is obviously not a priority here. Arguably there are benefits from this approach, too, and some people prefer having a variety of alternative ways to script around a problem. The `style` object could have been just as flexible with fewer properties at the expense of having scripts with a few more lines.

In the case of the border attributes, we might easily have coped with having a single border attribute that applied to all four sides because there are relatively few circumstances where we would want a different border on each side of a cell. On the other hand, we would then have lost some functionality so perhaps having individually addressable sides is beneficial but then we could have omitted the collective reference leading to a need to explicitly define all four. At least this way, everyone's needs are catered for.

The properties for this object may apply styles to a variety of object types. Some are very specifically applicable to only a particular sub-set of objects. You should generally assume that the style attribute can apply to objects of any kind unless the property description topic enumerates a set of objects. In that case, the style attribute should only be applied to those object types and will likely be ignored by others. There is a possibility that applying a completely inappropriate styling to an object may cause problems or unpredictable behavior.

Warnings:

❑ Note that the object type for MSIE is a `style` object spelled without capitalization. The corresponding object type for Netscape 4 is a `JSSTag` object.

❑ MSIE also supports a `STYLE` object, which is instantiated by the `<STYLE>` tag. This is an object that represents an inline style element within the HTML of the document.

See also: *CLASS="…", Collection object, currentStyle object, Element object,* `Element.currentStyle`, `Element.style`, *JSSTag object, Layer object,* `rule.style`, *runtimeStyle object*

Property	JavaScript	JScript	N	IE	Opera	DOM	CSS	HTML	Notes
azimuth	-	-	-	-	-	2 +	2 +	-	Warning
background	1.5 +	3.0 +	6.0 +	4.0 +	5.0 +	2 +	1 +	-	-
background Attachment	1.5 +	3.0 +	6.0 +	4.0 +	-	2 +	1 +	-	Warning
background Color	1.5 +	3.0 +	6.0 +	4.0 +	5.0 +	2 +	1 +	-	-
background Image	1.5 +	3.0 +	6.0 +	4.0 +	5.0 +	2 +	1 +	-	-
background Position	1.5 +	3.0 +	6.0 +	4.0 +	-	2 +	2 +	-	Warning
background PositionX	1.5 +	3.0 +	6.0 +	4.0 +	-	-	Proposed +	-	-
background PositionY	1.5 +	3.0 +	6.0 +	4.0 +	-	-	Proposed +	-	-
background Repeat	1.5 +	3.0 +	6.0 +	4.0 +	-	2 +	1 +	-	-
behavior	1.5 +	3.0 +	6.0 +	4.0 +	-	2 +	-	-	Warning

Property	JavaScript	JScript	N	IE	Opera	DOM	CSS	HTML	Notes
border	1.5 +	3.0 +	6.0 +	4.0 +	-	2 +	1 +	-	-
border Bottom	1.5 +	3.0 +	6.0 +	4.0 +	-	2 +	1 +	-	-
border BottomColor	1.5 +	3.0 +	6.0 +	4.0 +	-	2 +	2 +	-	-
Border BottomStyle	1.5 +	3.0 +	6.0 +	4.0 +	-	2 +	2 +	-	-
border BottomWidth	1.5 +	3.0 +	6.0 +	4.0 +	-	2 +	1 +	-	-
border Collapse	1.5 +	5.0 +	6.0 +	5.0 +	-	2 +	2 +	-	Warning
borderColor	1.5 +	3.0 +	6.0 +	4.0 +	-	2 +	1 +	-	-
borderLeft	1.5 +	3.0 +	6.0 +	4.0 +	-	2 +	1 +	-	-
border LeftColor	1.5 +	3.0 +	6.0 +	4.0 +	-	2 +	2 +	-	-
border LeftStyle	1.5 +	3.0 +	6.0 +	4.0 +	-	2 +	2 +	-	-
border LeftWidth	1.5 +	3.0 +	6.0 +	4.0 +	-	2 +	1 +	-	-
borderRight	1.5 +	3.0 +	6.0 +	4.0 +	-	2 +	1 +	-	-
border RightColor	1.5 +	3.0 +	6.0 +	4.0 +	-	2 +	2 +	-	-
border RightStyle	1.5 +	3.0 +	6.0 +	4.0 +	-	2 +	2 +	-	-
border RightWidth	1.5 +	3.0 +	6.0 +	4.0 +	-	2 +	1 +	-	-
border Spacing	1.5 +	5.0 +	6.0 +	5.0 +	-	2 +	-	-	Warning
borderStyle	1.5 +	3.0 +	6.0 +	4.0 +	-	2 +	1 +	-	Warning
borderTop	1.5 +	3.0 +	6.0 +	4.0 +	-	2 +	1 +	-	-
border TopColor	1.5 +	3.0 +	6.0 +	4.0 +	-	2 +	2 +	-	-
border TopStyle	1.5 +	3.0 +	6.0 +	4.0 +	-	2 +	2 +	-	-
border TopWidth	1.5 +	3.0 +	6.0 +	4.0 +	-	2 +	1 +	-	-
borderWidth	1.5 +	3.0 +	6.0 +	4.0 +	-	2 +	1 +	-	-
bottom	1.5 +	5.0 +	6.0 +	5.0 +	-	2 +	2 +	-	-
boxSizing	-	5.0 +	-	5.0 +	-	-	-	-	-
captionSide	1.5 +	5.0 +	6.0 +	5.0 +	-	2 +	2 +	-	-
cellSpacing	-	-	-	-	-	-	2 +	-	Warning
clear	1.5 +	3.0 +	6.0 +	4.0 +	-	2 +	1 +	-	-
clip	1.5 +	3.0 +	6.0 +	4.0 +	-	2 +	2 +	-	Warning
color	1.5 +	3.0 +	6.0 +	4.0 +	5.0 +	2 +	1 +	-	-
color Profile	-	5.0 +	-	5.0 +	-	-	-	-	-
columnSpan	-	-	-	-	-	-	2 +	-	Warning
content	1.5 +	5.0 +	6.0 +	5.0 +	-	2 +	2 +	-	-
counter Increment	1.5 +	5.0 +	6.0 +	5.0 +	-	2 +	-	-	-
counter Reset	1.5 +	5.0 +	6.0 +	5.0 +	-	2 +	-	-	-
cssFloat	1.5 +	5.0 +	6.0 +	5.0 +	-	2 +	-	-	-
cssText	-	3.0 +	-	4.0 +	-	-	-	-	ReadOnly

Table continued on following page

783

Property	JavaScript	JScript	N	IE	Opera	DOM	CSS	HTML	Notes
cue	-	-	-	-	-	2 +	2 +	-	Warning
cueAfter	-	-	-	-	-	2 +	2 +	-	Warning
cueBefore	-	-	-	-	-	2 +	2 +	-	Warning
cursor	1.5 +	3.0 +	6.0 +	4.0 +	-	2 +	2 +	-	-
direction	1.5 +	5.0 +	6.0 +	5.0 +	-	2 +	2 +	-	-
display	1.5 +	3.0 +	6.0 +	4.0 +	-	2 +	1 +	-	-
elevation	-	-	-	-	-	2 +	2 +	-	Warning
emptyCells	1.5 +	5.0 +	6.0 +	5.0 +	-	2 +	-	-	-
filter	-	3.0 +	-	4.0 +	-	-	Proposed +	-	Warning
float	-	3.0 +	-	4.0 +	-	-	1 +	-	Warning
floatStyle	-	5.0 +	-	5.0 +	-	-	-	-	-
font	1.5 +	3.0 +	6.0 +	4.0 +	-	2 +	1 +	-	-
fontFamily	1.5 +	3.0 +	6.0 +	4.0 +	-	2 +	1 +	-	-
fontSize	1.5 +	3.0 +	6.0 +	4.0 +	-	2 +	1 +	-	Warning
fontSize Adjust	1.5 +	5.0 +	6.0 +	5.0 +	-	2 +	2 +	-	-
fontStretch	1.5 +	5.0 +	6.0 +	5.0 +	-	2 +	-	-	-
fontStyle	1.5 +	3.0 +	6.0 +	4.0 +	-	2 +	1 +	-	Warning
fontVariant	1.5 +	3.0 +	6.0 +	4.0 +	-	2 +	1 +	-	-
fontWeight	1.5 +	3.0 +	6.0 +	4.0 +	-	2 +	1 +	-	-
height	1.5 +	3.0 +	6.0 +	4.0 +	-	2 +	1 +	-	Warning
imeMode	-	5.0 +	-	5.0 +	-	-	Proposed +	-	-
important	-	3.0 +	-	4.0 +	-	-	1 +	-	-
layoutGrid	-	5.0 +	-	5.0 +	-	-	Proposed +	-	-
layout GridChar	-	5.0 +	-	5.0 +	-	-	Proposed +	-	-
layoutGrid CharSpacing	-	5.0 +	-	5.0 +	-	-	Proposed +	-	-
layout GridLine	-	5.0 +	-	5.0 +	-	-	Proposed +	-	-
layout GridMode	-	5.0 +	-	5.0 +	-	-	Proposed +	-	-
layout GridType	-	5.0 +	-	5.0 +	-	-	Proposed +	-	-
left	1.5 +	3.0 +	6.0 +	4.0 +	5.0 +	2 +	2 +	-	-
length	-	5.0 +	-	5.0 +	-	-	-	-	ReadOnly
letter Spacing	1.5 +	3.0 +	6.0 +	4.0 +	-	2 +	1 +	-	-
lineBreak	-	5.0 +	-	5.0 +	-	-	Proposed +	-	-
lineHeight	1.5 +	3.0 +	6.0 +	4.0 +	-	2 +	1 +	-	-
listStyle	1.5 +	3.0 +	6.0 +	4.0 +	-	2 +	1 +	-	-
listStyle Image	1.5 +	3.0 +	6.0 +	4.0 +	-	2 +	1 +	-	-
listStyle Position	1.5 +	3.0 +	6.0 +	4.0 +	-	2 +	1 +	-	-
listStyle Type	1.5 +	3.0 +	6.0 +	4.0 +	-	2 +	1 +	-	-
margin	1.5 +	3.0 +	6.0 +	4.0 +	-	2 +	1 +	-	Warning
margin Bottom	1.5 +	3.0 +	6.0 +	4.0 +	-	2 +	1 +	-	-
marginLeft	1.5 +	3.0 +	6.0 +	4.0 +	-	2 +	1 +	-	-

Property	JavaScript	JScript	N	IE	Opera	DOM	CSS	HTML	Notes
marginRight	1.5 +	3.0 +	6.0 +	4.0 +	-	2 +	1 +	-	-
marginTop	1.5 +	3.0 +	6.0 +	4.0 +	-	2 +	1 +	-	-
marker Offset	1.5 +	5.0 +	6.0 +	5.0 +	-	2 +	-	-	-
marks	1.5 +	5.0 +	6.0 +	5.0 +	-	2 +	2 +	-	-
maxHeight	1.5 +	5.0 +	6.0 +	5.0 +	-	2 +	2 +	-	-
maxWidth	1.5 +	5.0 +	6.0 +	5.0 +	-	2 +	2 +	-	-
minHeight	1.5 +	5.0 +	6.0 +	5.0 +	-	2 +	2 +	-	-
minWidth	1.5 +	5.0 +	6.0 +	5.0 +	-	2 +	2 +	-	-
orphans	1.5 +	5.0 +	6.0 +	5.0 +	-	2 +	2 +	-	-
outline	1.5 +	5.0 +	6.0 +	5.0 +	-	2 +	-	-	-
outline Color	1.5 +	5.0 +	6.0 +	5.0 +	-	2 +	-	-	-
outline Style	1.5 +	5.0 +	6.0 +	5.0 +	-	2 +	-	-	-
outline Width	1.5 +	5.0 +	6.0 +	5.0 +	-	2 +	-	-	-
overflow	1.5 +	3.0 +	6.0 +	4.0 +	-	2 +	2 +	-	Warning
overflowX	1.5 +	5.0 +	6.0 +	5.0 +	-	-	-	-	-
overflowY	1.5 +	5.0 +	6.0 +	5.0 +	-	-	-	-	-
padding	1.5 +	3.0 +	6.0 +	4.0 +	-	2 +	1 +	-	Warning
padding Bottom	1.5 +	3.0 +	6.0 +	4.0 +	-	2 +	1 +	-	-
paddingLeft	1.5 +	3.0 +	6.0 +	4.0 +	-	2 +	1 +	-	-
padding Right	1.5 +	3.0 +	6.0 +	4.0 +	-	2 +	1 +	-	-
paddingTop	1.5 +	3.0 +	6.0 +	4.0 +	-	2 +	1 +	-	-
page	1.5 +	5.5 +	6.0 +	5.5 +	-	2 +	-	-	-
pageBreak After	1.5 +	3.0 +	6.0 +	4.0 +	-	2 +	2 +	-	Warning
pageBreak Before	1.5 +	3.0 +	6.0 +	4.0 +	-	2 +	2 +	-	-
pageBreak Inside	1.5 +	5.0 +	6.0 +	5.0 +	-	2 +	-	-	-
pause	-	-	-	-	-	2 +	2 +	-	Warning
pauseAfter	-	-	-	-	-	2 +	2 +	-	Warning
pauseBefore	-	-	-	-	-	2 +	2 +	-	Warning
pitch	-	-	-	-	-	2 +	2 +	-	Warning
pitchRange	-	-	-	-	-	2 +	2 +	-	Warning
pixelBottom	-	5.0 +	-	5.0 +	-	-	-	-	-
pixelHeight	-	3.0 +	-	4.0 +	5.0 +	-	-	-	-
pixelLeft	-	3.0 +	-	4.0 +	5.0 +	-	-	-	-
pixelRight	-	5.0 +	-	5.0 +	-	-	-	-	-
pixelTop	-	3.0 +	-	4.0 +	5.0 +	-	-	-	-
pixelWidth	-	3.0 +	-	4.0 +	5.0 +	-	-	-	-
playDuring	-	-	-	-	-	2 +	2 +	-	Warning
posBottom	-	5.0 +	-	5.0 +	-	-	-	-	-
posHeight	-	3.0 +	-	4.0 +	-	-	-	-	-

Table continued on following page

Property	JavaScript	JScript	N	IE	Opera	DOM	CSS	HTML	Notes
position	1.5 +	3.0 +	6.0 +	4.0 +	-	2 +	2 +	-	Warning, ReadOnly
posLeft	-	3.0 +	-	4.0 +	-	-	-	-	-
posRight	-	5.0 +	-	5.0 +	-	-	-	-	-
posTop	-	3.0 +	-	4.0 +	-	-	-	-	-
posWidth	-	3.0 +	-	4.0 +	-	-	-	-	-
quotes	1.5 +	5.0 +	6.0 +	5.0 +	-	2 +	-	-	-
rendering Intent	-	5.0 +	-	5.0 +	-	-	-	-	-
richness	-	-	-	-	-	2 +	2 +	-	Warning
right	1.5 +	5.0 +	6.0 +	5.0 +	-	2 +	2 +	-	-
rowSpan	-	-	-	-	-	-	2 +	-	-
rubyAlign	-	5.0 +	-	5.0 +	-	-	Proposed +	-	-
ruby Overhang	-	5.0 +	-	5.0 +	-	-	Proposed +	-	-
ruby Position	-	5.0 +	-	5.0 +	-	-	Proposed +	-	-
scrollbar3d LightColor	-	5.5 +	-	5.5 +	-	-	-	-	-
scrollbar ArrowColor	-	5.5 +	-	5.5 +	-	-	-	-	-
scrollbar BaseColor	-	5.5 +	-	5.5 +	-	-	-	-	-
scrollbar DarkShadow Color	-	5.5 +	-	5.5 +	-	-	-	-	-
scrollbar FaceColor	-	5.5 +	-	5.5 +	-	-	-	-	-
scrollbar Highlight Color	-	5.5 +	-	5.5 +	-	-	-	-	-
scrollbar ShadowColor	-	5.5 +	-	5.5 +	-	-	-	-	-
size	-	-	-	-	-	2 +	2 +	-	-
speak	-	-	-	-	-	2 +	2 +	-	Warning
speakDate	-	-	-	-	-	-	2 +	-	Warning
speakHeader	-	-	-	-	-	2 +	2 +	-	Warning
speak Numeral	-	-	-	-	-	2 +	2 +	-	Warning
speak Punctuation	-	-	-	-	-	2 +	2 +	-	Warning
speakTime	-	-	-	-	-	-	2 +	-	Warning
speechRate	-	-	-	-	-	2 +	2 +	-	Warning
stress	-	-	-	-	-	2 +	2 +	-	Warning
styleFloat	1.5 +	3.0 +	6.0 +	4.0 +	-	-	-	-	-
tableLayout	1.5 +	5.0 +	6.0 +	5.0 +	-	2 +	2 +	-	-
textAlign	1.5 +	3.0 +	6.0 +	4.0 +	-	2 +	1 +	-	Warning
text Autospace	-	5.0 +	-	5.0 +	-	-	Proposed +	-	-
text Decoration	1.5 +	3.0 +	6.0 +	4.0 +	-	2 +	1 +	-	-
text Decoration Blink	1.5 +	3.0 +	6.0 +	4.0 +	-	-	Proposed +	-	Warning

Property	JavaScript	JScript	N	IE	Opera	DOM	CSS	HTML	Notes
text Decoration LineThrough	1.5 +	3.0 +	6.0 +	4.0 +	-	-	Proposed +	-	Warning
text Decoration None	1.5 +	3.0 +	6.0 +	4.0 +	-	-	Proposed +	-	Warning
text Decoration Overline	1.5 +	3.0 +	6.0 +	4.0 +	-	-	Proposed +	-	Warning
text Decoration Underline	1.5 +	3.0 +	6.0 +	4.0 +	-	-	Proposed +	-	Warning
textIndent	1.5 +	3.0 +	6.0 +	4.0 +	-	2 +	1 +	-	Warning
textJustify	-	5.0 +	-	5.0 +	-	-	Proposed +	-	-
textKashida Space	-	5.5 +	-	5.5 +	-	-	Proposed +	-	-
textShadow	1.5 +	5.0 +	6.0 +	5.0 +	-	2 +	2 +	-	-
text Transform	1.5 +	3.0 +	6.0 +	4.0 +	-	2 +	1 +	-	-
text Underline Position	-	5.5 +	-	5.5 +	-	-	Proposed +	-	-
top	1.5 +	3.0 +	6.0 +	4.0 +	5.0 +	2 +	2 +	-	-
unicodeBidi	1.5 +	5.0 +	6.0 +	5.0 +	-	2 +	-	-	-
vertical Align	1.5 +	3.0 +	6.0 +	4.0 +	-	2 +	1 +	-	-
visibility	1.2 +	3.0 +	4.0 +	4.0 +	5.0 +	2 +	2 +	-	-
voiceFamily	-	-	-	-	-	2 +	2 +	-	Warning
volume	-	-	-	-	-	2 +	2 +	-	Warning
whiteSpace	1.5 +	5.5 +	6.0 +	5.5 +	-	2 +	1 +	-	Warning
widows	1.5 +	5.0 +	6.0 +	5.0 +	-	2 +	2 +	-	-
width	1.5 +	3.0 +	6.0 +	4.0 +	-	2 +	1 +	-	Warning
wordBreak	-	5.0 +	-	5.0 +	-	-	Proposed +	-	-
wordSpacing	1.5 +	3.0 +	6.0 +	4.01 +	-	2 +	1 +	-	Warning
wordWrap	-	5.5 +	-	5.5 +	-	-	Proposed +	-	-
writingMode	-	5.5 +	-	5.5 +	-	-	Proposed +	-	-
zIndex	1.5 +	3.0 +	6.0 +	4.0 +	5.0 +	2 +	2 +	-	Warning
zoom	-	5.5 +	-	5.5 +	-	-	-	-	-

Method	JavaScript	JScript	N	IE	Opera	DOM	CSS	HTML	Notes
getAttribute()	1.5 +	3.0 +	6.0 +	4.0 +	-	-	-	-	Warning
get Expression()	-	5.0 +	-	5.0 +	-	-	-	-	-
item()	-	3.0 +	-	4.0 +	-	-	-	-	-
remove Expression()	-	5.0 +	-	5.0 +	-	-	-	-	-
setAttribute()	1.5 +	5.0 +	6.0 +	5.0 +	-	-	-	-	-
set Expression()	-	5.0 +	-	5.0 +	-	-	-	-	-

Event name	JavaScript	JScript	N	IE	Opera	DOM	CSS	HTML	Notes
onClick	1.5 +	3.0 +	6.0 +	4.0 +	5.0 +	-	-	4.0 +	Warning
onDblClick	1.5 +	3.0 +	6.0 +	4.0 +	5.0 +	-	-	4.0 +	Warning
onHelp	-	3.0 +	-	4.0 +	-	-	-	-	Warning
onKeyDown	1.5 +	3.0 +	6.0 +	4.0 +	5.0 +	-	-	4.0 +	Warning
onKeyPress	1.5 +	3.0 +	6.0 +	4.0 +	5.0 +	-	-	4.0 +	Warning
onKeyUp	1.5 +	3.0 +	6.0 +	4.0 +	5.0 +	-	-	4.0 +	Warning
onMouseDown	1.5 +	3.0 +	6.0 +	4.0 +	5.0 +	-	-	4.0 +	Warning
onMouseMove	1.5 +	3.0 +	6.0 +	4.0 +	-	-	-	4.0 +	Warning
onMouseOut	1.5 +	3.0 +	6.0 +	4.0 +	5.0 +	-	-	4.0 +	Warning
onMouseOver	1.5 +	3.0 +	6.0 +	4.0 +	5.0 +	-	-	4.0 +	Warning
onMouseUp	1.5 +	3.0 +	6.0 +	4.0 +	5.0 +	-	-	4.0 +	Warning

Inheritance chain:

Element object, Node object

style.zOrder (Pitfall)

In some documentation, this property is described as an alternative way of controlling the Z ordered location of the styled object.

Warnings:

❑ So far, no examples of this property have been located. Use the zIndex property.

See also:	style.zIndex

<STYLE> (HTML Tag)

Style controls can be effected from JavaScript code.

The style mechanisms allow the content and the appearance of the document to be separated. The style sheet can now define the appearance of the page. This also means that styles can be shared and if your server is up to the task, you can serve a different style sheet according to the user agent value defined by the requesting browser.

Currently, CSS1 styling is widely used and CSS2 is gaining acceptance.

As far as we are concerned with JavaScript, we either need to create a style or apply it to part of a document. To create a style in Netscape Navigator 4 we use JSSS (JavaScript Style Sheets), which is functionally equivalent to CSS1. However JSSS is completely unavailable in any other browser, including Netscape Navigator 6.0 and its use for scripts is discouraged.

See also:	*.htc, <META>, <STYLE TYPE="...">, CSS, CSS level 1, CSS level 2*, `Document.attachEvent()`, `Document.detachEvent()`, JavaScript Style Sheets, `Window.attachEvent()`, `Window.detachEvent()`

Cross-references:

Wrox *Instant JavaScript* – page – 50

<STYLE TYPE="..."> (HTML Tag Attribute)

The mime type for a block of JSSS style code.

Availability:	JavaScript – 1.2 JScript – 3.0 Internet Explorer – 4.0 Netscape – 4.0	
Deprecated:	Yes	
HTML syntax:	`<STYLE TYPE="..."> some JSSS Code </STYLE>`	
Argument list:	...	A MIME type that signifies JavaScript source text.
	someCode	Some script based style text

The same MIME type values that apply to the `<SCRIPT>` tag are also used for the `<STYLE>` tag when this attribute is applied.

When this JavaScript style sheet is evaluated, the interpreter adds the document to the scope chain so that the tags, classes and ids properties of the document object can be accessed directly as if they were global values. This saves accessing them with the document object prefix. Thus:

`document.tags` becomes `tags`

`document.classes` becomes `classes`

`document.ids` becomes `ids`

Warnings:

❑ This functionality is removed from Netscape Navigator 6.0.

See also:	<META>, <SCRIPT TYPE="...">, <SCRIPT>, <STYLE>, Adding JavaScript to HTML, JavaScript Style Sheets, MIME types, SCRIPT.type, StyleSheet.type, *text/JavaScript*

Cross-references:

Wrox *Instant JavaScript* – page – 50

StyleSheet object (Object/DOM)

An object that represents a style sheet.

Availability:	DOM level – 2 JavaScript – 1.5 JScript – 3.0 Internet Explorer – 4.0 Netscape – 6.0	
JavaScript syntax:	-	*myStyleSheet* = *myDocument*.styleSheets[*anIndex*]
	IE	*myStyleSheet* = *myDocument*.createStyleSheet()
Argument list:	*anIndex*	A valid reference to an item in the collection
Object properties:	cssText, disabled, href, id, media, ownerNode, owningElement, owningNode, parentStyleSheet, readOnly, title, type	
Object methods:	addImport(), addRule(), removeRule()	
Collections:	cssRules[], imports[], rules[]	

A stylesheet contains many individual style objects which are managed as a collection. These stylesheet objects are created by means of the <STYLE> HTML tag or are imported with the <LINK> tag. They can also be created by means of the @import statement inside a style definition.

The Document.styleSheets[] collection contains a reference for every styleSheet object in the document.

Beware that a STYLE object and a style object are different things. A STYLE object is instantiated by the <STYLE> HTML tag and contains properties that reflect its attributes.

This is quite different to a style object which is a member of a styleSheet and describes the rules for a particular style.

DOM level 2 adds the following properties:

❑ `title`

❑ `media`

❑ `ownerRule`

It also adds the following methods:

❑ `insertRule()`

❑ `deleteRule()`

Warnings:

❑ Note that MSIE 5 incorrectly names this object class as `styleSheet` instead of `StyleSheet` (note the capitalization).

See also:	`Document.createStyleSheet()`, `Document.styleSheets[]`, `Element.style`, *rule object*, `Style` *sheet*, *StyleSheetList object*

Property	JavaScript	JScript	N	IE	Opera	DOM	Notes
cssText	-	5.0 +	-	5.0 +	-	-	-
disabled	1.5 +	3.0 +	6.0 +	4.0 +	-	2 +	-
href	1.5 +	3.0 +	6.0 +	4.0 +	-	2 +	ReadOnly
id	-	5.0 +	-	5.0 +	-	-	ReadOnly
media	1.5 +	3.0 +	6.0 +	4.0 +	-	2 +	Warning, ReadOnly
ownerNode	1.5 +	-	6.0 +	-	-	2 +	ReadOnly
owningElement	-	3.0 +	-	4.0 +	-	-	ReadOnly
owningNode	-	5.0 +	-	5.0 +	-	-	Warning, ReadOnly
parentStyleSheet	1.5 +	3.0 +	6.0 +	4.0 +	-	2 +	ReadOnly
readOnly	1.5 +	3.0 +	6.0 +	4.0 +	-	-	ReadOnly
title	1.5 +	3.0 +	6.0 +	4.0 +	-	2 +	Warning, ReadOnly
type	1.5 +	3.0 +	6.0 +	4.0 +	-	2 +	ReadOnly

Method	JavaScript	JScript	N	IE	Opera	DOM	Notes
addImport()	-	3.0 +	-	4.0 +	-	-	-
addRule()	-	3.0 +	-	4.0 +	-	-	-
removeRule()	-	5.0 +	-	5.0 +	-	-	-

S

StyleSheetList object (Object/DOM)

An array of style sheet objects provided by MSIE.

Availability:	DOM level – 2 JavaScript – 1.5 JScript – 5.0 Internet Explorer – 5.0 Netscape – 6.0
JavaScript syntax:	- `myStyleSheets = myDocument.styleSheets`
Object properties:	`length`
Object methods:	`item()`

Warnings:

❑ MSIE inconsistently names this as a `styleSheets` object rather than a `StyleSheets`, `StyleSheetCollection` or `StyleSheetArray` object.

❑ DOM level 2 describes this as a `StyleSheetList` which is more consistent. Because this is a collection, DOM allows for the `item()` method to be supported.

See also:	*Collection object*, `Document.styleSheets[]`, *StyleSheet object*

Property	JavaScript	JScript	N	IE	Opera	DOM	Notes
`length`	1.5 +	5.0 +	6.0 +	5.0 +	-	2 +	ReadOnly

Method	JavaScript	JScript	N	IE	Opera	DOM	Notes
`item()`	1.5 +	5.0 +	6.0 +	5.0 +	-	2 +	-

SubmitButton object (Object/DOM)

A button in a form that submits the form to the server.

Availability:	DOM level – 1 JavaScript – 1.0 JScript – 1.0 Internet Explorer – 3.02 Netscape – 2.0 Opera – 3.0
Inherits from:	*Input object*

JavaScript syntax:	-	*mySubmitButton = myDocument.aFormName.anElementName*
	-	*mySubmitButton = myDocument.aFormName* `.elements[`*anItemIndex*`]`
	IE	*mySubmitButton =* *myDocument*`.all.`*anElementID*
	IE	*mySubmitButton =* *myDocument*`.all.tags("INPUT")[`*anIndex*`]`
	IE	*mySubmitButton = myDocument*`.all[`*aName*`]`
	-	*mySubmitButton = myDocument*`.forms` `[`*aFormIndex*`].`*anElementName*
	-	*mySubmitButton = myDocument*`.forms` `[`*aFormIndex*`].elements[`*anItemIndex*`]`
	-	*mySubmitButton =* *myDocument*`.getElementById(`*anElementID*`)`
	-	*mySubmitButton = myDocument* `.getElementsByName(`*aName*`)[`*anIndex*`]`
	-	*mySubmitButton = myDocument* `.getElementsByTagName("INPUT")[`*anIndex*`]`

HTML syntax:	`<INPUT TYPE="submit">`	
Argument list:	*anIndex*	A valid reference to an item in the collection
	aName	The name attribute of an element
	anElementID	The ID attribute of an element
	anItemIndex	A valid reference to an item in the collection
	aFormIndex	A reference to a particular form in the `forms` collection

Object properties:	`type, value`
Object methods:	`handleEvent()`
Event handlers:	`onAfterUpdate, onBeforeUpdate, onBlur,` `onClick, onDblClick, onFilterChange,` `onFocus, onHelp, onKeyDown, onKeyPress,` `onKeyUp, onMouseDown, onMouseMove,` `onMouseOut, onMouseOver, onMouseUp,` `onRowEnter, onRowExit`

Many properties, methods, and event handlers are inherited from the `Input` object class. Refer to topics grouped with the "Input" prefix for details of common functionality across all subclasses of the `Input` object superclass.

There isn't really a `SubmitButton` object class but it is helpful when trying to understand the wide variety of input element types if we can reduce the complexity by discussing only the properties and methods of a submit button. In actual fact, the object is represented as an item of the `Input` object class.

S

Event handling support via properties containing function objects was added to SubmitButton objects at version 1.1 of JavaScript.

Unlike MSIE, Netscape Navigator does not support the select() method or defaultValue property for this subclass of the Input object.

Example code:

```
<HTML>
<HEAD>
</HEAD>
<BODY>
<FORM>
<SELECT ID="IN1">
<OPTION VALUE="-1">Please select an item
<OPTION VALUE="0">Sunday
<OPTION VALUE="1">Monday
<OPTION VALUE="2">Tuesday
<OPTION VALUE="3">Wednesday
<OPTION VALUE="4">Thursday
<OPTION VALUE="5">Friday
<OPTION VALUE="6">Saturday
</SELECT>
<INPUT ID="SUBMIT" TYPE="Submit" VALUE="CLICK ME"
onClick="clickMe()">
</FORM>
<SCRIPT>
//MSIE only
function clickMe()
{
    selectedValue = document.all.IN1.value;

    if(selectedValue == -1)
    {
        alert("You must select an item first!");
    }
    else
    {
        document.all.SUBMIT.click()
    }
}
</SCRIPT>
</BODY>
</HTML>
```

See also: *Element object*, Form.elements[], *FormElement object*, *Input object*, Input.accessKey, onClick, SubmitButton.handleEvent()

Property	JavaScript	JScript	N	IE	Opera	DOM	HTML	Notes
type	1.1 +	3.0 +	3.0 +	4.0 +	3.0 +	1 +	-	ReadOnly
value	1.0 +	1.0 +	2.0 +	3.02 +	3.0 +	1 +	-	Warning

Method	JavaScript	JScript	N	IE	Opera	DOM	HTML	Notes
handleEvent()	1.2 +	-	4.0 +	-	-	-	-	-

Event name	JavaScript	JScript	N	IE	Opera	DOM	HTML	Notes
onAfterUpdate	-	3.0 +	-	4.0 +	-	-	-	-
onBeforeUpdate	-	3.0 +	-	4.0 +	-	-	-	-
onBlur	1.1 +	3.0 +	3.0 +	4.0 +	3.0 +	-	-	Warning
onClick	1.0 +	1.0 +	2.0 +	3.0 +	3.0 +	-	4.0 +	Warning
onDblClick	1.2 +	3.0 +	4.0 +	4.0 +	3.0 +	-	4.0 +	Warning
onFilterChange	-	3.0 +	-	4.0 +	-	-	-	-
onFocus	1.0 +	3.0 +	2.0 +	4.0 +	3.0 +	-	-	Warning
onHelp	-	3.0 +	-	4.0 +	-	-	-	Warning
onKeyDown	1.2 +	3.0 +	4.0 +	4.0 +	3.0 +	-	4.0 +	Warning
onKeyPress	1.2 +	3.0 +	4.0 +	4.0 +	3.0 +	-	4.0 +	Warning
onKeyUp	1.2 +	3.0 +	4.0 +	4.0 +	3.0 +	-	4.0 +	Warning
onMouseDown	1.2 +	3.0 +	4.0 +	4.0 +	3.0 +	-	4.0 +	Warning
onMouseMove	1.2 +	3.0 +	4.0 +	4.0 +	-	-	4.0 +	Warning
onMouseOut	1.1 +	3.0 +	3.0 +	4.0 +	3.0 +	-	4.0 +	Warning
onMouseOver	1.0 +	1.0 +	2.0 +	3.0 +	3.0 +	-	4.0 +	Warning
onMouseUp	1.2 +	3.0 +	4.0 +	4.0 +	3.0 +	-	4.0 +	Warning
onRowEnter	-	3.0 +	-	4.0 +	-	-	-	-
onRowExit	-	3.0 +	-	4.0 +	-	-	-	-

Inheritance chain:

Element object, Input object, Node object

Subtract (-) (Operator/additive)

Subtract the right operand from the left operand.

Availability:	ECMAScript edition – 2 JavaScript – 1.0 JScript – 1.0 Internet Explorer – 3.02 Netscape – 2.0 Netscape Enterprise Server – 2.0 Opera– 3.0

Property/method value type:	Number primitive	
JavaScript syntax:	-	*anOperand1 - anOperand2*
Argument list:	*anOperand1*	A numeric value to be subtracted from
	anOperand2	A numeric value to be subtracted

Subtraction is indicated when two operands are separated by a minus sign.

The value on the right is subtracted from the value on the left. The result is the difference between the two values.

Subtraction behaves identically to addition, as if the formula:

```
a - b
```

...had become:

```
a + (-b)
```

The associativity is left to right.

Refer to the operator precedence topic for details of execution order.

See also:	*Add (+)*, Additive operator, Arithmetic operator, *Assign value (=)*, Assignment expression, Associativity, *Negation operator (-)*, Operator Precedence, *Subtract then assign (-=)*

Cross-references:

ECMA 262 edition 2 – section – 11.6.2

ECMA 262 edition 2 – section – 11.6.3

ECMA 262 edition 3 – section – 11.6.2

Subtract then assign (-=)
(Operator/assignment)

Subtract the right value from the left, modifying the left-hand value.

Availability:	ECMAScript edition – 2 JavaScript – 1.0 JScript – 1.0 Internet Explorer – 3.02 Netscape – 2.0

796

Property/method value type:	Number primitive	
JavaScript syntax:	-	*anLValue -= anOperand*
Argument list:	*anLValue*	An operand that can be assigned into
	anOperand	A value to subtract

Subtract the right operand from the left operand and assign the result to the left operand.

This is functionally equivalent to the expression:

```
anOperand1 = anOperand1 - anOperand2;
```

Although this is classified as an assignment operator it is really a compound of an assignment and an additive operator.

The associativity is right to left.

Refer to the operator precedence topic for details of execution order.

The new value of *anOperand1* is returned as a result of the expression.

Warnings:

❑ The operand to the left of the operator must be an LValue. That is, it should be able to take an assignment and store the value.

See also:	*Add then assign (+=)*, Additive operator, Arithmetic operator, Assignment operator, Associativity, Operator Precedence, *Subtract (-)*

Cross-references:

ECMA 262 edition 2 – section – 11.13

ECMA 262 edition 3 – section – 11.13

switch(...) ... case: ... default: ... (Selector)

Select one of a set of cases according to a switch value.

Availability:	ECMAScript edition – 3 JavaScript – 1.2 JScript – 3.0 Internet Explorer – 4.0 Netscape – 4.0 Netscape Enterprise Server – 3.0	
JavaScript syntax:	-	switch(aValue) { aCaseTree }
Argument list:	aCaseTree	A set of case statements to be selected
	aValue	An integer value used as a selector

The switch statement evaluates its expression and selects a labeled statement block for execution according to the value resulting from the expression.

If there is no match, then a default case is used.

Each labeled case should be terminated by a break keyword to avoid the execution dropping down through into the handler for the next case in the script source. On the other hand, this may be what you intend and so omitting the break keyword allows several cases to be matched and handled with a common fragment of code.

The use of switch is illustrated in the example. The value enclosed in parentheses is evaluated and its result is used as a selector. It looks for a matching case label and executes the code in that block. If it does not match, it uses the default block (if there is one).

Unlike the ANSI C version of switch, the JavaScript one will match strings as well as integers.

The break; statements prevent the code from dropping down into the next block.

The following are all legal case labels:

```
case 0:

case 100*23:

case "abc":

case "aaa" + "bbb":

case Number.NaN:
```

The C language environment dictates that a `switch` statement must be capable of supporting at least 256 individual cases. The ECMAScript standard does not define a limit.

You need to be careful when nesting `switch` statements. The `case` labels will be subordinate to the closest enclosing `switch` given the rules of precedence and block structuring of the code. Case labels must be unique within a single `switch` mechanism but can duplicate `case` values in other `switch` structures within the same or an enclosing code block.

Warnings:

❑ Primitive values are allowed as selectors but objects, arrays and functions are not. You could wrap them with `toString()` or `valueOf()` functions though. However the results may be slightly unpredictable unless you thoroughly test the effects of those functions in all your target implementations.

❑ The value `document.forms.length` is valid for use in a `case` label at JavaScript version 1.2 but may not be later. The values really do have to be constant and it's possible that a later version of the interpreter may check the read-only attribute of any property value that is used in this context.

Example code:

```
// An example switch statement
switch(myValue)
{
    case 1:        document.write("one");
    break;
    case 'too':    document.write("two");
    break;
    default:       document.write("unknown");
    break;
}
```

See also:	*break, Colon (:), else ..., Flow control, if(...) ..., if(...) ... else ..., Selection statement*

Cross-references:

ECMA 262 edition 2 – section – 7.4.3

ECMA 262 edition 3 – section – 7.5.2

ECMA 262 edition 3 – section – 12.11

SyntaxError object (Object/core)

A native error object based on the `Error` object.

Availability:	ECMAScript edition – 3 JavaScript – 1.5 Netscape – 6.0
Inherits from:	*Error object*
JavaScript syntax:	N `myError = new SyntaxError()`
	N `myError = new SyntaxError(aNumber)`
	N `myError = new SyntaxError` `(aNumber, aText)`
Argument list:	`aNumber` An error number
	`aText` A text describing the error

This subclass of the `Error` object is used when an exception is caused by a script source text parsing error.

See also:	*catch(...), Error object, EvalError object, RangeError object, ReferenceError object, throw, try ... catch ... finally, TypeError object, URIError object*

Inheritance chain:

`Error` object

Cross-references:

ECMA 262 edition 3 – section – 15.1.4.13

ECMA 262 edition 3 – section – 15.11.6.4

TABLE object (Object/HTML)

An object that represents a table within a document.

Availability:	DOM level – 1 JavaScript – 1.5 JScript – 3.0 Internet Explorer – 4.0 Netscape – 6.0
Inherits from:	*Element object*
JavaScript syntax:	IE `myTABLE = myDocument.all.anElementID`
	IE `myTABLE = myDocument.all.aTableID`
	IE `myTABLE = myDocument.all.tags` `("TABLE")[anIndex]`
	IE `myTABLE = myDocument.all[aName]`
	- `myTABLE = myDocument.getElementById` `(anElementID)`
	- `myTABLE = myDocument.getElementsByName` `(aName)[anIndex]`
	- `myTABLE = myDocument.` `getElementsByTagName("TABLE")[anIndex]`
HTML syntax:	`<TABLE> ... </TABLE>`
Argument list:	`anIndex` A reference to an element in a collection
	`aName` An associative array reference
	`anElementID` The ID value of an Element object

Object properties:	`align, background, bgColor, border, borderColor,`
	`borderColorDark, borderColorLight, caption,`
	`cellPadding, cellSpacing, cols, dataFld,`
	`dataPageSize, dataSrc, frame, height, rules,`
	`summary, tabIndex, tFoot, tHead, width`

Object methods:	createCaption(), createTFoot(), createTHead(), deleteCaption(), deleteRow(), deleteTFoot(), deleteTHead(), insertRow(), nextPage(), previousPage(), refresh()
Event handlers:	onAfterUpdate, onBeforeUpdate, onBlur, onClick, onDblClick, onDragStart, onFilterChange, onFocus, onHelp, onKeyDown, onKeyPress, onKeyUp, onMouseDown, onMouseMove, onMouseOut, onMouseOver, onMouseUp, onResize, onRowEnter, onRowExit, onScroll, onSelectStart
Collections:	cells[], rows[], tBodies[]

Tables are a hierarchical means of describing a two-dimensional array of cells containing HTML.

Generally speaking the DOM compliant browsers provide a more sophisticated model of the table for access under control of a JavaScript program.

There are a set of related object types that need to be understood to utilize tables most effectively:

❑ CAPTION

❑ COL

❑ COLGROUP

❑ TBODY

❑ TD

❑ TFOOT

❑ TH

❑ THEAD

❑ TR

The following style object properties should also be considered:

❑ style.captionSide

❑ style.cellSpacing

❑ style.columnSpan

❑ style.emptyCells

❑ style.rowSpan

❑ style.tableLayout

See also:	CAPTION object, COL object, COLGROUP object, Element object, Element.offsetParent, style.captionSide, style.cellSpacing, style.columnSpan, style.emptyCells, style.rowSpan, style.tableLayout

804

Property	JavaScript	JScript	N	IE	Opera	DOM	HTML	Notes
align	1.5 +	3.0 +	6.0 +	4.0 +	-	1 +	-	-
background	-	3.0 +	-	4.0 +	-	-	-	-
bgColor	1.5 +	3.0 +	6.0 +	4.0 +	-	1 +	-	-
border	1.5 +	3.0 +	6.0 +	4.0 +	-	1 +	-	-
borderColor	-	3.0 +	-	4.0 +	-	-	-	-
borderColorDark	-	3.0 +	-	4.0 +	-	-	-	-
border ColorLight	-	3.0 +	-	4.0 +	-	-	-	-
caption	1.5 +	3.0 +	6.0 +	4.0 +	-	1 +	-	Warning, ReadOnly
cellPadding	1.5 +	3.0 +	6.0 +	4.0 +	-	1 +	-	-
cellSpacing	1.5 +	3.0 +	6.0 +	4.0 +	-	1 +	-	-
cols	-	3.0 +	-	4.0 +	-	-	-	-
dataFld	1.5 +	3.0 +	6.0 +	4.0 +	-	1 +	-	-
dataPageSize	-	3.0 +	-	4.0 +	-	-	-	-
dataSrc	1.5 +	3.0 +	6.0 +	4.0 +	-	1 +	-	-
frame	1.5 +	3.0 +	6.0 +	4.0 +	-	1 +	-	-
height	1.5 +	3.0 +	6.0 +	4.0 +	-	-	-	-
rules	1.5 +	3.0 +	6.0 +	4.0 +	-	1 +	-	Warning
summary	1.5 +	-	6.0 +	-	-	1 +	-	-
tabIndex	1.5 +	3.0 +	6.0 +	4.0 +	-	1 +	-	-
tFoot	1.5 +	3.0 +	6.0 +	4.0 +	-	1 +	-	ReadOnly
tHead	1.5 +	3.0 +	6.0 +	4.0 +	-	1 +	-	ReadOnly
width	1.5 +	3.0 +	6.0 +	4.0 +	-	1 +	-	-

Method	JavaScript	JScript	N	IE	Opera	DOM	HTML	Notes
createCaption()	1.5 +	3.0 +	6.0 +	4.0 +	-	1 +	-	-
createTFoot()	1.5 +	3.0 +	6.0 +	4.0 +	-	1 +	-	-
createTHead()	1.5 +	3.0 +	6.0 +	4.0 +	-	1 +	-	-
deleteCaption()	1.5 +	3.0 +	6.0 +	4.0 +	-	1 +	-	-
deleteRow()	1.5 +	3.0 +	6.0 +	4.0 +	-	1 +	-	-
deleteTFoot()	1.5 +	3.0 +	6.0 +	4.0 +	-	1 +	-	-
deleteTHead()	1.5 +	3.0 +	6.0 +	4.0 +	-	1 +	-	-
insertRow()	1.5 +	3.0 +	6.0 +	4.0 +	-	1 +	-	-
nextPage()	-	3.0 +	-	4.0 +	-	-	-	-
previousPage()	-	3.0 +	-	4.0 +	-	-	-	-
refresh()	-	3.0 +	-	4.0 +	-	-	-	-

Event name	JavaScript	JScript	N	IE	Opera	DOM	HTML	Notes
onAfterUpdate	-	3.0 +	-	4.0 +	-	-	-	-
onBeforeUpdate	-	3.0 +	-	4.0 +	-	-	-	-
onBlur	1.5 +	3.0 +	6.0 +	4.0 +	3.0 +	-	-	Warning
onClick	1.5 +	3.0 +	6.0 +	4.0 +	3.0 +	-	4.0 +	Warning
onDblClick	1.5 +	3.0 +	6.0 +	4.0 +	3.0 +	-	4.0 +	Warning
onDragStart	-	3.0 +	-	4.0 +	-	-	-	-
onFilterChange	-	3.0 +	-	4.0 +	-	-	-	-
onFocus	1.5 +	3.0 +	6.0 +	4.0 +	3.0 +	-	-	Warning
onHelp	-	3.0 +	-	4.0 +	-	-	-	Warning
onKeyDown	1.5 +	3.0 +	6.0 +	4.0 +	3.0 +	-	4.0 +	Warning
onKeyPress	1.5 +	3.0 +	6.0 +	4.0 +	3.0 +	-	4.0 +	Warning
onKeyUp	1.5 +	3.0 +	6.0 +	4.0 +	3.0 +	-	4.0 +	Warning
onMouseDown	1.5 +	3.0 +	6.0 +	4.0 +	3.0 +	-	4.0 +	Warning
onMouseMove	1.5 +	3.0 +	6.0 +	4.0 +	-	-	4.0 +	Warning
onMouseOut	1.5 +	3.0 +	6.0 +	4.0 +	3.0 +	-	4.0 +	Warning
onMouseOver	1.5 +	3.0 +	6.0 +	4.0 +	3.0 +	-	4.0 +	Warning
onMouseUp	1.5 +	3.0 +	6.0 +	4.0 +	3.0 +	-	4.0 +	Warning
onResize	1.5 +	3.0 +	6.0 +	4.0 +	-	-	-	Warning
onRowEnter	-	3.0 +	-	4.0 +	-	-	-	-
onRowExit	-	3.0 +	-	4.0 +	-	-	-	-
onScroll	-	3.0 +	-	4.0 +	-	-	-	-
onSelectStart	-	3.0 +	-	4.0 +	-	-	-	-

Inheritance chain:

Element object, Node object

TableColElement object (Object/HTML)

A means of accessing cells in a particular column of the table without needing to traverse the rows.

Availability:	DOM level – 1 JavaScript – 1.5 JScript – 5.0 Internet Explorer – 5.0 Netscape – 6.0
Inherits from:	*Element object*
JavaScript syntax:	- *myTableColElement* = new TableColElement()
Object properties:	align, ch, chOff, span, vAlign, width
Event handlers:	onClick, onDblClick, onHelp, onKeyDown, onKeyPress, onKeyUp, onMouseDown, onMouseMove, onMouseOut, onMouseOver, onMouseUp

	See also:	COL object, COLGROUP object, TABLE object

Property	JavaScript	JScript	N	IE	Opera	DOM	HTML	Notes
align	1.5 +	5.0 +	6.0 +	5.0 +	-	1 +	-	-
ch	1.5 +	5.0 +	6.0 +	5.0 +	-	1 +	-	-
chOff	1.5 +	5.0 +	6.0 +	5.0 +	-	1 +	-	-
span	1.5 +	5.0 +	6.0 +	5.0 +	-	1 +	-	-
vAlign	1.5 +	5.0 +	6.0 +	5.0 +	-	1 +	-	-
width	1.5 +	5.0 +	6.0 +	5.0 +	-	1 +	-	-

Event name	JavaScript	JScript	N	IE	Opera	DOM	HTML	Notes
onClick	1.5 +	5.0 +	6.0 +	5.0 +	-	-	4.0 +	Warning
onDblClick	1.5 +	5.0 +	6.0 +	5.0 +	-	-	4.0 +	Warning
onHelp	-	5.0 +	-	5.0 +	-	-	-	Warning
onKeyDown	1.5 +	5.0 +	6.0 +	5.0 +	-	-	4.0 +	Warning
onKeyPress	1.5 +	5.0 +	6.0 +	5.0 +	-	-	4.0 +	Warning
onKeyUp	1.5 +	5.0 +	6.0 +	5.0 +	-	-	4.0 +	Warning
onMouseDown	1.5 +	5.0 +	6.0 +	5.0 +	-	-	4.0 +	Warning
onMouseMove	1.5 +	5.0 +	6.0 +	5.0 +	-	-	4.0 +	Warning
onMouseOut	1.5 +	5.0 +	6.0 +	5.0 +	-	-	4.0 +	Warning
onMouseOver	1.5 +	5.0 +	6.0 +	5.0 +	-	-	4.0 +	Warning
onMouseUp	1.5 +	5.0 +	6.0 +	5.0 +	-	-	4.0 +	Warning

Inheritance chain

Element object, Node object

taint() (Function/global)

A method for controlling secure access to data values.

Availability:	JavaScript – 1.1
	Netscape – 3.0
	Deprecated

This was removed at version 1.2 of JavaScript. If you encounter it in a script you are maintaining, it is probably wise to seek how it can be removed, otherwise it is likely to cause a run-time error.

Warnings:

❏ DO NOT USE THIS FUNCTION!

See also:	Navigator.taintEnabled(), untaint()

JavaScript Programmer's Reference

T

TBODY object (Object/HTML)

An object that encapsulates a `<TBODY>` tag within a `<TABLE>` block.

Availability:	DOM level – 1 JavaScript – 1.5 JScript – 3.0 Internet Explorer – 4.0 Netscape – 6.0	
Inherits from:	*Element object*	
JavaScript syntax:	IE	`myTBODY = myDocument.all.anElementID`
	IE	`myTBODY = myDocument.all.tags("TBODY")[anIndex]`
	IE	`myTBODY = myDocument.all[aName]`
	-	`myTBODY = myDocument.getElementById(anElementID)`
	-	`myTBODY = myDocument.getElementsByName(aName)[anIndex]`
	-	`myTBODY = myTable.tBodies[anIndex]`
	-	`myTBODY = myDocument.getElementsByTagName("TBODY")[anIndex]`
HTML syntax:	`<TBODY> ... </TBODY>`	
Argument list:	`anIndex`	A reference to an element in a collection
	`aName`	An associative array reference
	`anElementID`	The ID value of an Element object
Object properties:	`accessKey, align, bgColor, chOff, rows, tabIndex,` `vAlign`	

Event handlers:	`onClick, onDblClick, onDragStart,`
	`onFilterChange, onHelp, onKeyDown, onKeyPress,`
	`onKeyUp, onMouseDown, onMouseMove, onMouseOut,`
	`onMouseOver, onMouseUp, onSelectStart`	

Collections:	`rows[]`	

Each table owns at least one TBODY object which is created by default even if you don't enclose some rows within `<TBODY>` tags. Additional TBODY objects can be created to break the table into sections if you need to.

The TBODY object represents that part of the table which excludes any footer or header cells.

You can access TBODY objects by their ID HTML tag attribute in the DOM hierarchy or by selecting them from the tBodies[] collection belonging to their parent TABLE object.

Warnings:

❑ Note that on some versions of the MSIE browser on the Macintosh platform, you cannot access the innerHTML, innerText, outerHTML or outerText properties of a TBODY object.

See also:	*Element object*, Input.accessKey, *TABLE object*, TABLE.rules, TABLE.tBodies[], *TD object*, *TR object*

Property	JavaScript	JScript	N	IE	Opera	DOM	HTML	Notes
accessKey	1.5 +	3.0 +	6.0 +	4.0 +	-	1+	-	Warning
align	1.5 +	3.0 +	6.0 +	4.0 +	-	1+	-	-
bgColor	1.5 +	3.0 +	6.0 +	4.0 +	-	1+	-	-
chOff	1.5 +	3.0 +	6.0 +	4.0 +	-	1+	-	Warning
rows	1.5 +	3.0 +	6.0 +	4.0 +	-	1+	-	Warning
tabIndex	1.5 +	3.0 +	6.0 +	4.0 +	-	1+	-	Warning
vAlign	1.5 +	3.0 +	6.0 +	4.0 +	-	1+	-	-

Event name	JavaScript	JScript	N	IE	Opera	DOM	HTML	Notes
onClick	1.5 +	3.0 +	6.0 +	4.0 +	-	-	4.0 +	Warning
onDblClick	1.5 +	3.0 +	6.0 +	4.0 +	-	-	4.0 +	Warning
onDragStart	-	3.0 +	-	4.0 +	-	-	-	-
onFilterChange	-	3.0 +	-	4.0 +	-	-	-	-
onHelp	-	3.0 +	-	4.0 +	-	-	-	Warning
onKeyDown	1.5 +	3.0 +	6.0 +	4.0 +	-	-	4.0 +	Warning
onKeyPress	1.5 +	3.0 +	6.0 +	4.0 +	-	-	4.0 +	Warning
onKeyUp	1.5 +	3.0 +	6.0 +	4.0 +	-	-	4.0 +	Warning
onMouseDown	1.5 +	3.0 +	6.0 +	4.0 +	-	-	4.0 +	Warning
onMouseMove	1.5 +	3.0 +	6.0 +	4.0 +	-	-	4.0 +	Warning
onMouseOut	1.5 +	3.0 +	6.0 +	4.0 +	-	-	4.0 +	Warning
onMouseOver	1.5 +	3.0 +	6.0 +	4.0 +	-	-	4.0 +	Warning
onMouseUp	1.5 +	3.0 +	6.0 +	4.0 +	-	-	4.0 +	Warning
onSelectStart	-	3.0 +	-	4.0 +	-	-	-	-

T

Inheritance chain:

Element object, Node object

TD object (Object/HTML)

An object that encapsulates a single cell described by a <TD> tag.

Availability:	DOM level – 1 JavaScript – 1.5 JScript – 3.0 Internet Explorer – 4.0 Netscape – 6.0
Inherits from:	*Element object*
JavaScript syntax:	IE *myTD* = *myDocument*.all.*anElementID*
	IE *myTD* = *myDocument*.all.tags("TD")[*anIndex*]
	IE *myTD* = *myDocument*.all[*aName*]
	- *myTD* = *myDocument*.getElementById(*anElementID*)
	- *myTD* = *myDocument* .getElementsByName(*aName*)[*anIndex*]
	- *myTD* = *myDocument* .getElementsByTagName("TD")[*anIndex*]
HTML syntax:	<TD> ... </TD>
Argument list:	*anIndex* A reference to an element in a collection
	aName An associative array reference
	anElementID The ID value of an Element object
Object properties:	abbr, accessKey, align, axis, background, bgColor, borderColor, borderColorDark, borderColorLight, cellIndex, ch, chOff, colSpan, headers, height, noWrap, rowSpan, scope, tabIndex, vAlign, width
Event handlers:	onAfterUpdate, onBeforeUpdate, onBlur, onClick, onDblClick, onDragStart, onFilterChange, onHelp, onKeyDown, onKeyPress, onKeyUp, onMouseDown, onMouseMove, onMouseOut, onMouseOver, onMouseUp, onResize, onRowEnter, onRowExit, onSelectStart

This object is instantiated by a <TD> tag that encloses the content of a single data cell.

Some of the property values in this object may be inherited from parent objects such as TABLE, TR and TBODY.

Warnings:

❏ Note that on some versions of the MSIE browser on the Macintosh platform, you cannot access the innerHTML, innerText, outerHTML or outerText properties of a TD object.

See also:	Element object, Input.accessKey, TABLE object, TBODY object, TH object, TR object

Property	JavaScript	JScript	N	IE	Opera	DOM	HTML	Notes
abbr	1.5 +	-	6.0 +	-	-	1 +	-	-
accessKey	1.5 +	3.0 +	6.0 +	4.0 +	-	1 +	-	Warning
align	1.5 +	3.0 +	6.0 +	4.0 +	-	1 +	-	-
axis	1.5 +	-	6.0 +	-	-	1 +	-	-
background	-	3.0 +	-	4.0 +	-	-	-	-
bgColor	1.5 +	3.0 +	6.0 +	4.0 +	-	1 +	-	-
borderColor	-	3.0 +	-	4.0 +	-	-	-	-
border ColorDark	-	3.0 +	-	4.0 +	-	-	-	-
border ColorLight	-	3.0 +	-	4.0 +	-	-	-	-
cellIndex	1.5 +	3.0 +	6.0 +	4.0 +	-	1 +	-	Warning, ReadOnly
ch	1.5 +	-	6.0 +	-	-	1 +	-	-
chOff	1.5 +	-	6.0 +	-	-	1 +	-	-
colSpan	1.5 +	3.0 +	6.0 +	4.0 +	-	1 +	-	Warning
headers	1.5 +	-	6.0 +	-	-	1 +	-	-
height	1.5 +	3.0 +	6.0 +	4.0 +	-	1 +	-	-
noWrap	1.5 +	3.0 +	6.0 +	4.0 +	-	1 +	-	Warning
rowSpan	1.5 +	3.0 +	6.0 +	4.0 +	-	1 +	-	-
scope	1.5 +	-	6.0 +	-	-	1 +	-	-
tabIndex	1.5 +	3.0 +	6.0 +	4.0 +	-	1 +	-	Warning
vAlign	1.5 +	3.0 +	6.0 +	4.0 +	-	1 +	-	-
width	1.5 +	3.0 +	6.0 +	4.0 +	-	1 +	-	-

Event name	JavaScript	JScript	N	IE	Opera	DOM	HTML	Notes
onAfterUpdate	-	3.0 +	-	4.0 +	-	-	-	-
onBeforeUpdate	-	3.0 +	-	4.0 +	-	-	-	-
onBlur	1.5 +	3.0 +	6.0 +	4.0 +	-	-	-	Warning
onClick	1.5 +	3.0 +	6.0 +	4.0 +	-	-	4.0 +	Warning
onDblClick	1.5 +	3.0 +	6.0 +	4.0 +	-	-	4.0 +	Warning
onDragStart	-	3.0 +	-	4.0 +	-	-	-	-
onFilterChange	-	3.0 +	-	4.0 +	-	-	-	-
onHelp	-	3.0 +	-	4.0 +	-	-	-	Warning

Table continued on following page

JavaScript Programmer's Reference

T

Event name	JavaScript	JScript	N	IE	Opera	DOM	HTML	Notes
onKeyDown	1.5 +	3.0 +	6.0 +	4.0 +	-	-	4.0 +	Warning
onKeyPress	1.5 +	3.0 +	6.0 +	4.0 +	-	-	4.0 +	Warning
onKeyUp	1.5 +	3.0 +	6.0 +	4.0 +	-	-	4.0 +	Warning
onMouseDown	1.5 +	3.0 +	6.0 +	4.0 +	-	-	4.0 +	Warning
onMouseMove	1.5 +	3.0 +	6.0 +	4.0 +	-	-	4.0 +	Warning
onMouseOut	1.5 +	3.0 +	6.0 +	4.0 +	-	-	4.0 +	Warning
onMouseOver	1.5 +	3.0 +	6.0 +	4.0 +	-	-	4.0 +	Warning
onMouseUp	1.5 +	3.0 +	6.0 +	4.0 +	-	-	4.0 +	Warning
onResize	1.5 +	3.0 +	6.0 +	4.0 +	-	-	-	Warning
onRowEnter	-	3.0 +	-	4.0 +	-	-	-	-
onRowExit	-	3.0 +	-	4.0 +	-	-	-	-
onSelectStart	-	3.0 +	-	4.0 +	-	-	-	-

Inheritance chain:

Element object, Node object

telnet: URL (Request method)

Open up a telnet client to do terminal mode access.

Open a telnet application and connect to the telnet port on the target server. You should be asked for a username and password. This will then give you access to a command line interface on the target host as long as you are validated.

See also:	*javascript: URL*, *mailbox: URL*, Security policy, URL

text/JavaScript (MIME type)

A MIME type that indicates the content is a JavaScript source text.

This is otherwise known as application/x-javascript, although text/JavaScript should be used.

See also:	*<SCRIPT TYPE="...">*, *<STYLE TYPE="...">*, MIME types

TEXTAREA object (Object/DOM)

A multiple line text cell in a form.

Availability:	DOM level – 1 JavaScript – 1.0 JScript – 1.0 Internet Explorer – 3.02 Netscape – 2.0 Opera – 3.0
Inherits from:	*Input object*

JavaScript syntax:	IE *myTEXTAREA = myDocument.all.anElementID*
	IE *myTEXTAREA =*
	     myDocument.all.tags("TEXTAREA")[anIndex]
	IE *myTEXTAREA = myDocument.all[aName]*
	- *myTEXTAREA = myDocument.getElementById
	    (anElementID)*
	- *myTEXTAREA = myDocument.getElementsByName
	    (aName)[anIndex]*
	- *myTEXTAREA = myDocument.
	    getElementsByTagName("TEXTAREA")[anIndex]*

HTML syntax:	`<TEXTAREA> ... </TEXTAREA>`
Argument list:	*anIndex* A reference to an element in a collection *aName* An associative array reference *anElementID* The ID value of an `Element` object
Object properties:	`cols, readOnly, rows, type, value, wrap`
Object methods:	`handleEvent(), select()`

Event handlers:	`onAfterUpdate, onBeforeUnload, onBeforeUpdate,`
	`onBlur, onChange, onDragStart, onErrorUpdate,`
	`onFilterChange, onFocus, onHelp, onKeyDown,`
	`onKeyPress, onKeyUp, onMouseDown, onMouseMove,`
	`onMouseOut, onMouseOver, onMouseUp, onRowEnter,`
	`onRowExit, onScroll, onSelect, onSelectStart`

JavaScript Programmer's Reference

T

Many properties, methods and event handlers are inherited from the `Input` object class. Refer to topics grouped with the "Input" prefix for details of common functionality across all sub-classes of the `Input` object super-class.

Untypically, there actually is a TEXTAREA class supported by MSIE. Most other kinds of input are simply an instance of the `Input` object class. Netscape prior to version 6.0 internally represents this object as a sub-class of the `Input` object even though it is created by a different HTML tag.

Event handling support via properties containing function objects was added to TEXTAREA objects at version 1.1 of JavaScript, but this will have changed to reflect the new DOM event model for Netscape 6.0.

Unlike MSIE, the Netscape 4 implementation of this sub-class of the Input object does not support the click() method or the onSelect event.

The example below seems to be supported by all browsers apart from Netscape 6.0. On this browser, the escape sequence \x0D needs to be changed to \n in order for the example to work.

Example code:

```
<HTML>
<HEAD>
</HEAD>
<BODY>
<FORM>
Type some lines of text into the text area, click the button and
they will be sorted.<BR><BR>
<TEXTAREA VALUE="" NAME="BOX_A" ROWS=15 COLS=39></TEXTAREA><BR>
<INPUT TYPE="button" VALUE="Reveal" onClick="handleClick()">
</FORM>
<SCRIPT>
function handleClick()
{
    myString = document.forms[0].BOX_A.value;
    myArray = myString.split("\x0D");
    myArray.sort();
    document.forms[0].BOX_A.value = myArray.join("\x0D");
}
</SCRIPT>
</BODY>
</HTML>
```

See also: *Element object*, Element.isTextEdit, Form.elements[], *Input object*, Input.accessKey, onChange, onKeyDown, onKeyPress, onKeyUp, TEXTAREA.handleEvent(), *TextRange object*

Property	JavaScript	JScript	N	IE	Opera	DOM	HTML	Notes
cols	1.5 +	3.0 +	6.0 +	4.0 +	-	1 +	-	-
readOnly	1.5 +	3.0 +	6.0 +	4.0 +	-	1 +	-	ReadOnly
rows	1.5 +	3.0 +	6.0 +	4.0 +	-	1 +	-	-
type	1.1 +	3.0 +	3.0 +	4.0 +	3.0 +	1 +	-	ReadOnly
value	1.0 +	1.0 +	2.0 +	3.02 +	3.0 +	1 +	-	-
wrap	-	3.0 +	-	4.0 +	-	-	-	-

Method	JavaScript	JScript	N	IE	Opera	DOM	HTML	Notes
handleEvent()	1.2 +	-	4.0 +	-	-	-	-	-
select()	1.0 +	1.0 +	2.0 +	3.02 +	3.0 +	1 +	-	-

Event name	JavaScript	JScript	N	IE	Opera	DOM	HTML	Notes
onAfterUpdate	-	3.0 +	-	4.0 +	-	-	-	-
onBeforeUnload	-	3.0 +	-	4.0 +	-	-	-	-
onBeforeUpdate	-	3.0 +	-	4.0 +	-	-	-	-
onBlur	1.1 +	3.0 +	3.0 +	4.0 +	3.0 +	-	-	Warning
onChange	1.0 +	3.0 +	2.0 +	4.0 +	3.0 +	-	-	-
onDragStart	-	3.0 +	-	4.0 +	-	-	-	-
onErrorUpdate	-	3.0 +	-	4.0 +	-	-	-	-
onFilterChange	-	3.0 +	-	4.0 +	-	-	-	-
onFocus	1.0 +	3.0 +	2.0 +	4.0 +	3.0 +	-	-	Warning
onHelp	-	3.0 +	-	4.0 +	-	-	-	Warning
onKeyDown	1.2 +	3.0 +	4.0 +	4.0 +	3.0 +	-	4.0 +	Warning
onKeyPress	1.2 +	3.0 +	4.0 +	4.0 +	3.0 +	-	4.0 +	Warning
onKeyUp	1.2 +	3.0 +	4.0 +	4.0 +	3.0 +	-	4.0 +	Warning
onMouseDown	1.2 +	3.0 +	4.0 +	4.0 +	3.0 +	-	4.0 +	Warning
onMouseMove	1.2 +	3.0 +	4.0 +	4.0 +	-	-	4.0 +	Warning
onMouseOut	1.1 +	3.0 +	3.0 +	4.0 +	3.0 +	-	4.0 +	Warning
onMouseOver	1.0 +	1.0 +	2.0 +	3.02 +	3.0 +	-	4.0 +	Warning
onMouseUp	1.2 +	3.0 +	4.0 +	4.0 +	3.0 +	-	4.0 +	Warning
onRowEnter	-	3.0 +	-	4.0 +	-	-	-	-
onRowExit	-	3.0 +	-	4.0 +	-	-	-	-
onScroll	-	3.0 +	-	4.0 +	-	-	-	-
onSelect	1.0 +	3.0 +	2.0 +	4.0 +	3.0 +	-	-	-
onSelectStart	-	3.0 +	-	4.0 +	-	-	-	-

Inheritance chain:

Element object, Input object, Node object

TextCell object (Object/DOM)

A single line text cell in a form.

Availability:	DOM level – 1 JavaScript – 1.0 JScript – 1.0 Internet Explorer – 3.02 Netscape – 2.0 Opera – 3.0	
Inherits from:	*Input object*	
JavaScript syntax:	-	`myTextCell =` `myDocument.aFormName.anElementName`
	-	`myTextCell = myDocument.` `aFormName.elements[anItemIndex]`
	IE	`myTextCell = myDocument.all.anElementID`
	IE	`myTextCell = myDocument.all.tags("INPUT")` `[anIndex]`
	IE	`myTextCell = myDocument.all[aName]`
	-	`myTextCell = myDocument.forms` `[aFormIndex].anElementName`
	-	`myTextCell = myDocument.forms[aFormIndex]` `.elements[anItemIndex]`
	-	`myTextCell = myDocument.getElementById` `(anElementID)`
	-	`myTextCell = myDocument.getElementsByName` `(aName)[anIndex]`
	-	`myTextCell = myDocument` `.getElementsByTagName("INPUT")[anIndex]`
HTML syntax:	`<INPUT TYPE="text">`	
Argument list:	`anIndex`	A valid reference to an item in the collection
	`aName`	The NAME attribute of an element
	`anElementID`	The ID attribute of an element
	`anItemIndex`	A valid reference to an item in the collection
	`aFormIndex`	A reference to a particular form in the forms collection
Object properties:	`maxLength, readOnly, size, type, value`	
Object methods:	`handleEvent(), select()`	

Event handlers:	`onAfterUpdate, onBeforeUpdate, onBlur, onChange,`
	`onFilterChange, onFocus, onHelp, onKeyDown,`
	`onKeyPress, onKeyUp, onMouseDown, onMouseMove,`
	`onMouseOut, onMouseOver, onMouseUp, onRowEnter,`
	`onRowExit, onSelect`	

Many properties, methods, and event handlers are inherited from the `Input` object class. Refer to topics grouped with the "Input" prefix for details of common functionality across all sub-classes of the `Input` object super-class.

There isn't really a `TextCell` object class, but it is helpful when trying to understand the wide variety of input element types if we can reduce the complexity by discussing only the properties and methods of a text cell. In actual fact, the object is represented as an item·of the `Input` object class.

Event handling support via properties containing function objects was added to `TextCell` objects at version 1.1 of JavaScript.

The Netscape implementation of this sub-class of the `Input` object does not support as wide a variety of events as the MSIE implementation. In particular, the keyboard events are not supported.

The WebTV set-top box does not support the `onkeypress` event handler for this object type prior to the Summer 2000 release.

Example code:

```
<HTML>
<HEAD>
</HEAD>
<BODY>
<DIV ID="RESULT">?</DIV>
<FORM>
<INPUT TYPE="text" VALUE="" NAME="BOX_A"><BR>
<INPUT TYPE="text" VALUE="" NAME="BOX_B"><BR>
<INPUT TYPE="text" VALUE="" NAME="BOX_C"><BR>
<INPUT TYPE="text" VALUE="" NAME="BOX_D"><BR><BR>
<INPUT TYPE="button" VALUE="Reveal" onClick="handleClick()">
</FORM>
<SCRIPT>
function handleClick()
{
   myString  = "[";
   myString += document.forms[0].elements.BOX_A.value;
   myString += "] [";
   myString += document.forms[0].elements.BOX_B.value;
   myString += "] [";
   myString += document.forms[0].elements.BOX_C.value;
   myString += "] [";
   myString += document.forms[0].elements.BOX_D.value;
   myString += "]";
   document.all.RESULT.innerText = myString;
}
</SCRIPT>
</BODY>
</HTML>
```

See also: *Element object,* `Element.isTextEdit,` `Form.elements[],` *FormElement object, Input object,* `Input.accessKey,` *JellyScript,* `onChange, onKeyDown, onKeyPress, onKeyUp,` `TextCell.handleEvent(),` *TextRange object*

JavaScript Programmer's Reference

T

Property	JavaScript	JScript	N	IE	Opera	DOM	HTML	Notes
maxLength	-	3.0 +	-	4.0 +	-	-	-	-
readOnly	-	3.0 +	-	4.0 +	-	-	-	ReadOnly
size	-	3.0 +	-	4.0 +	-	-	-	Warning
type	1.1 +	3.0 +	3.0 +	4.0 +	3.0 +	1 +	-	ReadOnly
value	1.0 +	1.0 +	2.0 +	3.02 +	3.0 +	1 +	-	-

Method	JavaScript	JScript	N	IE	Opera	DOM	HTML	Notes
handleEvent()	1.2 +	-	4.0 +	-	-	-	-	-
select()	1.0 +	1.0 +	2.0 +	3.02 +	3.0 +	1 +	-	-

Event name	JavaScript	JScript	N	IE	Opera	DOM	HTML	Notes
onAfterUpdate	-	3.0 +	-	4.0 +	-	-	-	-
onBeforeUpdate	-	3.0 +	-	4.0 +	-	-	-	-
onBlur	1.1 +	3.0 +	3.0 +	4.0 +	3.0 +	-	-	Warning
onChange	1.0 +	3.0 +	2.0 +	4.0 +	3.0 +	-	-	-
onFilterChange	-	3.0 +	-	4.0 +	-	-	-	-
onFocus	1.0 +	3.0 +	2.0 +	4.0 +	3.0 +	-	-	Warning
onHelp	-	3.0 +	-	4.0 +	-	-	-	Warning
onKeyDown	1.2 +	3.0 +	4.0 +	4.0 +	3.0 +	-	4.0 +	Warning
onKeyPress	1.2 +	3.0 +	4.0 +	4.0 +	3.0 +	-	4.0 +	Warning
onKeyUp	1.2 +	3.0 +	4.0 +	4.0 +	3.0 +	-	4.0 +	Warning
onMouseDown	1.2 +	3.0 +	4.0 +	4.0 +	3.0 +	-	4.0 +	Warning
onMouseMove	1.2 +	3.0 +	4.0 +	4.0 +	-	-	4.0 +	Warning
onMouseOut	1.1 +	3.0 +	3.0 +	4.0 +	3.0 +	-	4.0 +	Warning
onMouseOver	1.0 +	1.0 +	2.0 +	3.02 +	3.0 +	-	4.0 +	Warning
onMouseUp	1.2 +	3.0 +	4.0 +	4.0 +	3.0 +	-	4.0 +	Warning
onRowEnter	-	3.0 +	-	4.0 +	-	-	-	-
onRowExit	-	3.0 +	-	4.0 +	-	-	-	-
onSelect	1.0 +	3.0 +	2.0 +	4.0 +	3.0 +	-	-	-

Inheritance chain:

Element object, Input object, Node object

textNode object (Object/DOM)

A string of text represented as a node within the document hierarchy.

Availability:	DOM level – 1 JavaScript – 1.5 JScript – 5.0 Internet Explorer – 5.0 Netscape – 6.0	
Inherits from:	*CharacterData object*	
JavaScript syntax:	IE	`myTextNode = myDocument.all.tags ("TEXT") [anIndex]`
	-	`myTextNode = myDocument. createTextNode(someData)`
Argument list:	`someData`	Textual content for the text node
	`anIndex`	A selector within a collection of text nodes
Object properties:	`data, length`	
Object methods:	`splitText()`	

The MSIE browser models the document as a collection of nodes. Clearly, an HTML tag corresponds to an object. However, what isn't so obvious is that the text in between HTML tags is collected together and represented by a `textNode` object.

These `textNodes` are generally accessible as child objects belonging to an object instantiated by an HTML tag.

For example:

`AAA<P>BBB<P>CCC`

Can be accessed as follows:

The `<P>` tags are objects which are members of the `document.getElementsByTagName("P")` collection. The text "BBB" is referenced through the `firstChild` property of the `P` object instantiated by the first `<P>` tag. The text "CCC" is a `textNode` object referenced via the `firstChild` property of the second `<P>` tag.

The DOM level 3 specification is expected to add the following method to the `textNode` object:

❑ `isWhitespaceInElementContent()`

See also:	`Attribute.nodeName, Document.createTextNode()`

Property	JavaScript	JScript	N	IE	Opera	DOM	Notes
data	1.5 +	5.0 +	6.0 +	5.0 +	-	1 +	-
length	1.5 +	5.0 +	6.0 +	5.0 +	-	1 +	ReadOnly

Method	JavaScript	JScript	N	IE	Opera	DOM	Notes
splitText()	1.5 +	5.0 +	6.0 +	5.0 +	-	1 +	-

Inheritance chain:

CharacterData object, Node object

TextRange object (Object/JScript)

An object that represents part of the text stream of an HTML document.

Availability:	JScript – 3.0 Internet Explorer – 4.0
Inherits from:	*Element object*
JavaScript syntax:	IE *myTextRange =* *myElement.*createTextRange()
Object properties:	boundingHeight, boundingLeft, boundingTop, boundingWidth, htmlText, text
Object methods:	collapse(), compareEndPoints(), duplicate(), execCommand(), expand(), findText(), getBookmark(), getBoundingClientRect(), getClientRects(), inRange(), isEqual(), move(), moveEnd(), moveStart(), moveToBookmark(), moveToElementText(), moveToPoint(), parentElement(), pasteHTML(), queryCommandEnabled(), queryCommandIndeterm(), queryCommandState(), queryCommandSupported(), queryCommandText(), queryCommandValue(), select(), setEndPoint()

The main purpose of a TextRange object is to encapsulate that part of the document text that depends on the user having used the mouse to select a portion of text. A TextRange object can also encapsulate an insertion point in the text of a document.

An insertion point is encapsulated by creating a TextRange object that is of zero length.

A new `TextRange` object is instantiated with the `createTextRange()` method which can be applied to the following object types which can contain selectable text:

❑ BODY

❑ TextCell

❑ TEXTAREA

The `TextCell` and `TEXTAREA` objects are members of the `Form` Element category, sometimes called `Input` Elements.

When you have created a `TextRange` object, you can then manipulate its properties to select just that portion of text in the document that you want.

Once you have marked the text you want within the start and end points, you can replace the content of the `TextRange` with the `pasteHTML()` method to operate on the text in the document. However, there may be limitations on when and how you can do this depending on the extent of the `TextRange` object's boundaries.

Warnings:

❑ There are platform limitations to the `TextRange` object that mean it is only functional on the Windows platform within MSIE. This limits the audience for your ingenuity in using it, but within a captive environment, this capability can still be useful.

See also:	BODY.createTextRange(), *Button object*, *BUTTON object*, Element.isTextEdit, Element.parentTextEdit, Input.createTextRange(), *Selection object*, selection.createRange(), *TEXTAREA object*, *TextCell object*

Property	JavaScript	JScript	N	IE	Opera	Notes
boundingHeight	-	3.0 +	-	4.0 +	-	ReadOnly
boundingLeft	-	3.0 +	-	4.0 +	-	ReadOnly
boundingTop	-	3.0 +	-	4.0 +	-	ReadOnly
boundingWidth	-	3.0 +	-	4.0 +	-	ReadOnly
htmlText	-	3.0 +	-	4.0 +	-	ReadOnly
text	-	3.0 +	-	4.0 +	-	-

Method	JavaScript	JScript	N	IE	Opera	Notes
collapse()	-	3.0 +	-	4.0 +	-	-
compareEndPoints()	-	3.0 +	-	4.0 +	-	-
duplicate()	-	3.0 +	-	4.0 +	-	-
execCommand()	-	3.0 +	-	4.0 +	-	-
expand()	-	3.0 +	-	4.0 +	-	-

Table continued on following page

JavaScript Programmer's Reference

T

Method	JavaScript	JScript	N	IE	Opera	Notes
findText()	-	3.0 +	-	4.0 +	-	-
getBookmark()	-	3.0 +	-	4.0 +	-	-
getBoundingClientRect()	-	5.0 +	-	5.0 +	-	-
getClientRects()		5.0 +	-	5.0 +	-	-
inRange()	-	3.0 +	-	4.0 +	-	-
isEqual()	-	3.0 +	-	4.0 +	-	-
move()	-	3.0 +	-	4.0 +	-	-
moveEnd()	-	3.0 +	-	4.0 +	-	Warning
moveStart()	-	3.0 +	-	4.0 +	-	Warning
moveToBookmark()	-	3.0 +	-	4.0 +	-	-
moveToElementText()	-	3.0 +	-	4.0 +	-	-
moveToPoint()	-	3.0 +	-	4.0 +	-	-
parentElement()	-	3.0 +	-	4.0 +	-	-
pasteHTML()	-	3.0 +	-	4.0 +	-	-
queryCommandEnabled()	-	3.0 +	-	4.0 +	-	-
queryCommandIndeterm()	-	3.0 +	-	4.0 +	-	-
queryCommandState()	-	3.0 +	-	4.0 +	-	-
queryCommandSupported()	-	3.0 +	-	4.0 +	-	-
queryCommandText()	-	3.0 +	-	4.0 +	-	-
queryCommandValue()	-	3.0 +	-	4.0 +	-	-
select()	-	3.0 +	-	4.0 +	-	-
setEndPoint()	-	3.0 +	-	4.0 +	-	-

Inheritance chain:

Element object, Node object

textRectangle object (Object/JScript)

The extent rectangle that encloses a TextRange object.

Availability:	JScript – 5.0 Internet Explorer – 5.0	
JavaScript syntax:	IE	myTextRectangle = myTextRange .getBoundingClientRect()
Object properties:	bottom, left, right, top	

This is a close relation to the rect object. This is a special case, used for describing rectangles on the screen which are the bounding extent rectangles for TextRange objects.

You shouldn't try to modify the properties of this object directly. It's intended for you to read to establish where on the screen the TextRange is located.

See also:	Clip object, Rect object, TextRange.getBoundingClientRect(), TextRange.getClientRects()					

Property	JavaScript	JScript	N	IE	Opera	Notes
bottom	-	5.0 +	-	5.0 +	-	-
left	-	5.0 +	-	5.0 +	-	-
right	-	5.0 +	-	5.0 +	-	-
top	-	5.0 +	-	5.0 +	-	-

TextStream object (Object/JScript)

An object that represents an I/O text stream. Very useful in a server-side context.

Availability:	JScript – 2.0 Internet Explorer – 4.0
JavaScript syntax:	IE *myTextStream =* *myFile*.OpenAsTextStream()
	IE *myTextStream = myFileSystem*. OpenTextFile(*aName*, *aMode*, *aFlag*, *aFormat*)
Argument list:	*aName* The name of the file to be created
	aFlag A flag indicating whether the file can be created if necessary
	aMode An access mode for the file
	aFormat A format control for the file
Object properties:	AtEndOfLine, AtEndOfStream, Column, Line
Object methods:	Close(), Read(), ReadAll(), ReadLine(), Skip(), SkipLine(), Write(), WriteBlankLines(), WriteLine()

This object is a wrapper for a file when opened for I/O. With this object you can read and write to the file.

Files can be opened via methods belonging to the File object or by requesting that the FileSystem object open a named file. Both techniques yield the same kind of TextStream object.

See also:	Active Server Pages, File.OpenAsTextStream(), FileSystem.OpenTextFile()

JavaScript Programmer's Reference

T

Property	JavaScript	JScript	N	IE	Opera	Notes
AtEndOfLine	-	2.0 +	-	4.0 +	-	-
AtEndOfStream	-	2.0 +	-	4.0 +	-	-
Column	-	2.0 +	-	4.0 +	-	-
Line	-	2.0 +	-	4.0 +	-	-

Method	JavaScript	JScript	N	IE	Opera	Notes
Close()	-	2.0 +	-	4.0 +	-	-
Read()	-	2.0 +	-	4.0 +	-	-
ReadAll()	-	2.0 +	-	4.0 +	-	-
ReadLine()	-	2.0 +	-	4.0 +	-	-
Skip()	-	2.0 +	-	4.0 +	-	-
SkipLine()	-	2.0 +	-	4.0 +	-	-
Write()	-	2.0 +	-	4.0 +	-	-
WriteBlankLines()	-	2.0 +	-	4.0 +	-	-
WriteLine()	-	2.0 +	-	4.0 +	-	-

TFOOT object (Object/HTML)

An object that encapsulates a <TFOOT> tag within a <TABLE> block.

Availability:	DOM level – 1 JavaScript – 1.5 JScript – 3.0 Internet Explorer – 4.0 Netscape – 6.0
Inherits from:	*Element object*
JavaScript syntax:	IE *myTFOOT* = *myDocument*.all.*anElementID*
	IE *myTFOOT* = *myDocument*.all.tags ("TFOOT")[*anIndex*]
	IE *myTFOOT* = *myDocument*.all[*aName*]
	- *myTFOOT* = *myDocument*.getElementById (*anElementID*)
	- *myTFOOT* = *myDocument*.getElementsByName (*aName*)[*anIndex*]
	- *myTFOOT* = *myDocument*. getElementsByTagName("TFOOT")[*anIndex*]
HTML syntax:	<TFOOT> ... </TFOOT>

Argument list:	anIndex	A reference to an element in a collection
	aName	An associative array reference
	anElementID	The ID value of an Element object
Object properties:	align, bgColor, ch, chOff, vAlign	
Object methods:	deleteRow(), insertRow()	
Event handlers:	onClick, onDblClick, onDragStart, onFilterChange, onHelp, onKeyDown, onKeyPress, onKeyUp, onMouseDown, onMouseMove, onMouseOut, onMouseOver, onMouseUp, onSelectStart	
Collections:	rows[]	

A table must contain one and only one TFOOT object. If you don't create one automatically, the TABLE object instantiates one for you but it would be empty.

The TFOOT object is instantiated by a <TFOOT> HTML tag. This is a means of marking off a section at the bottom of the table so that the rows can be grouped together and operated on separately to the table body.

The DOM level 1 standard calls for the implementation of a TableSectionElement object which includes both TFOOT and THEAD in its capabilities.

Warnings:

❑ Some earlier versions of MSIE for Macintosh have very limited capabilities implemented for this object. You cannot access any of the HTML or text contained in the object, nor the rows collection.

See also:	Element object, TABLE object, TABLE.createTFoot(), TABLE.deleteTFoot(), TABLE.rules, TABLE.tFoot, THEAD object, TR object

Property	JavaScript	JScript	N	IE	Opera	DOM	HTML	Notes
align	1.5 +	3.0 +	6.0 +	4.0 +	-	1 +	-	-
bgColor	1.5 +	3.0 +	6.0 +	4.0 +	-	1 +	-	-
ch	1.5 +	-	6.0 +	-	-	1 +	-	-
chOff	1.5 +	-	6.0 +	-	-	1 +	-	-
vAlign	1.5 +	3.0 +	6.0 +	4.0 +	-	1 +	-	-

Method	JavaScript	JScript	N	IE	Opera	DOM	HTML	Notes
deleteRow()	1.5 +	3.0 +	6.0 +	4.0 +	-	1 +	-	-
insertRow()	1.5 +	3.0 +	6.0 +	4.0 +	-	1 +	-	-

Event name	JavaScript	JScript	N	IE	Opera	DOM	HTML	Notes
onClick	1.5 +	3.0 +	6.0 +	4.0 +	3.0 +	-	4.0 +	Warning
onDblClick	1.5 +	3.0 +	6.0 +	4.0 +	3.0 +	-	4.0 +	Warning
onDragStart	-	3.0 +	-	4.0 +	-	-	-	-
onFilterChange	-	3.0 +	-	4.0 +	-	-	-	-
onHelp	-	3.0 +	-	4.0 +	-	-	-	Warning
onKeyDown	1.5 +	3.0 +	6.0 +	4.0 +	3.0 +	-	4.0 +	Warning
onKeyPress	1.5 +	3.0 +	6.0 +	4.0 +	3.0 +	-	4.0 +	Warning
onKeyUp	1.5 +	3.0 +	6.0 +	4.0 +	3.0 +	-	4.0 +	Warning
onMouseDown	1.5 +	3.0 +	6.0 +	4.0 +	3.0 +	-	4.0 +	Warning
onMouseMove	1.5 +	3.0 +	6.0 +	4.0 +	-	-	4.0 +	Warning
onMouseOut	1.5 +	3.0 +	6.0 +	4.0 +	3.0 +	-	4.0 +	Warning
onMouseOver	1.5 +	3.0 +	6.0 +	4.0 +	3.0 +	-	4.0 +	Warning
onMouseUp	1.5 +	3.0 +	6.0 +	4.0 +	3.0 +	-	4.0 +	Warning
onSelectStart	-	3.0 +	-	4.0 +	-	-	-	-

Inheritance chain:

Element object, Node object

TH object (Object/HTML)

An object that encapsulates a <TH> table header cell.

Availability:	DOM level – 1 JavaScript – 1.5 JScript – 3.0 Internet Explorer – 4.0 Netscape – 6.0	
Inherits from:	*Element object*	
JavaScript syntax:	IE	myTH = myDocument.all.anElementID
	IE	myTH = myDocument.all.tags("TH")[anIndex]
	IE	myTH = myDocument.all[aName]
	-	myTH = myDocument.getElementById(anElementID)
	-	myTH = myDocument.getElementsByName(aName)[anIndex]
	-	myTH = myDocument.getElementsByTagName("TH")[anIndex]

HTML syntax:	`<TH> ... </TH>`
Argument list:	`anIndex` A reference to an element in a collection
	`aName` An associative array reference
	`anElementID` The `ID` value of an `Element` object
Object properties:	`abbr`, `align`, `axis`, `background`, `bgColor`, `borderColor`, `borderColorDark`, `borderColorLight`, `cellIndex`, `ch`, `chOff`, `colSpan`, `headers`, `height`, `noWrap`, `rowSpan`, `scope`, `vAlign`, `width`
Event handlers:	`onAfterUpdate`, `onBeforeUnload`, `onBlur`, `onClick`, `onDblClick`, `onDragStart`, `onFilterChange`, `onHelp`, `onKeyDown`, `onKeyPress`, `onKeyUp`, `onMouseDown`, `onMouseMove`, `onMouseOut`, `onMouseOver`, `onMouseUp`, `onResize`, `onRowEnter`, `onRowExit`, `onSelectStart`

This object is instantiated by a <TH> tag that encloses the content of a single data cell. This cell is formatted differently to a TD cell because a TH cell is considered to be a table header cell whereas a TD cell is a table data cell.

Some of the property values in this object may be inherited from parent objects such as TABLE, TR and TBODY.

See also:	*Element object, TABLE object, TD object*

Property	JavaScript	JScript	N	IE	Opera	DOM	HTML	Notes
abbr	1.5 +	-	6.0 +	-	-	1 +	-	-
align	1.5 +	3.0 +	6.0 +	4.0 +	-	1 +	-	-
axis	1.5 +	-	6.0 +	-	-	1 +	-	-
background	-	3.0 +	-	4.0 +	-	-	-	-
bgColor	1.5 +	3.0 +	6.0 +	4.0 +	-	1 +	-	-
borderColor	-	3.0 +	-	4.0 +	-	-	-	-
border ColorDark	-	3.0 +	-	4.0 +	-	-	-	-
border ColorLight	-	3.0 +	-	4.0 +	-	-	-	-
cellIndex	1.5 +	3.0 +	6.0 +	4.0 +	-	1 +	-	ReadOnly
ch	1.5 +	-	6.0 +	-	-	1 +	-	-
chOff	1.5 +	-	6.0 +	-	-	1 +	-	-
colSpan	1.5 +	3.0 +	6.0 +	4.0 +	-	1 +	-	Warning
headers	1.5 +	-	6.0 +	-	-	1 +	-	-
height	1.5 +	3.0 +	6.0 +	4.0 +	-	1 +	-	-
noWrap	1.5 +	3.0 +	6.0 +	4.0 +	-	1 +	-	Warning
rowSpan	1.5 +	3.0 +	6.0 +	4.0 +	-	1 +	-	-
scope	1.5 +	-	6.0 +	-	-	1 +	-	-
vAlign	1.5 +	3.0 +	6.0 +	4.0 +	-	1 +	-	-
width	1.5 +	3.0 +	6.0 +	4.0 +	-	1 +	-	-

T

Event name	JavaScript	JScript	N	IE	Opera	DOM	HTML	Notes
onAfterUpdate	-	3.0 +	-	4.0 +	-	-	-	-
onBeforeUnload	-	3.0 +	-	4.0 +	-	-	-	-
onBlur	1.5 +	3.0 +	6.0 +	4.0 +	3.0 +	-	-	Warning
onClick	1.5 +	3.0 +	6.0 +	4.0 +	3.0 +	-	4.0 +	Warning
onDblClick	1.5 +	3.0 +	6.0 +	4.0 +	3.0 +	-	4.0 +	Warning
onDragStart	-	3.0 +	-	4.0 +	-	-	-	-
onFilterChange	-	3.0 +	-	4.0 +	-	-	-	-
onHelp	-	3.0 +	-	4.0 +	-	-	-	Warning
onKeyDown	1.5 +	3.0 +	6.0 +	4.0 +	3.0 +	-	4.0 +	Warning
onKeyPress	1.5 +	3.0 +	6.0 +	4.0 +	3.0 +	-	4.0 +	Warning
onKeyUp	1.5 +	3.0 +	6.0 +	4.0 +	3.0 +	-	4.0 +	Warning
onMouseDown	1.5 +	3.0 +	6.0 +	4.0 +	3.0 +	-	4.0 +	Warning
onMouseMove	1.5 +	3.0 +	6.0 +	4.0 +	-	-	4.0 +	Warning
onMouseOut	1.5 +	3.0 +	6.0 +	4.0 +	3.0 +	-	4.0 +	Warning
onMouseOver	1.5 +	3.0 +	6.0 +	4.0 +	3.0 +	-	4.0 +	Warning
onMouseUp	1.5 +	3.0 +	6.0 +	4.0 +	3.0 +	-	4.0 +	Warning
onResize	1.5 +	3.0 +	6.0 +	4.0 +	-	-	-	Warning
onRowEnter	-	3.0 +	-	4.0 +	-	-	-	-
onRowExit	-	3.0 +	-	4.0 +	-	-	-	-
onSelectStart	-	3.0 +	-	4.0 +	-	-	-	-

Inheritance chain:

Element object, Node object

THEAD object (Object/HTML)

An object that encapsulates a <THEAD> tag within a <TABLE> block.

Availability:	DOM level – 1 JavaScript – 1.5 JScript – 3.0 Internet Explorer – 4.0 Netscape – 6.0	
Inherits from:	*Element object*	
JavaScript syntax:	IE	*myTHEAD* = *myDocument*.all.*anElementID*
	IE	*myTHEAD* = *myDocument*.all.tags("THEAD")[*anIndex*]
	IE	*myTHEAD* = *myDocument*.all[*aName*]
	-	*myTHEAD* = *myDocument*.getElementById (*anElementID*)
	-	*myTHEAD* = *myDocument*.getElementsByName (*aName*)[*anIndex*]
	-	*myTHEAD* = *myDocument*. getElementsByTagName("THEAD")[*anIndex*]

HTML syntax:	`<THEAD> ... </THEAD>`	
Argument list:	`anIndex`	A reference to an element in a collection
	`aName`	An associative array reference
	`anElementID`	The ID value of an `Element` object
Object properties:	`align, bgColor, ch, chOff, vAlign`	
Object methods:	`deleteRow(), insertRow()`	
Event handlers:	`onClick, onDblClick, onDragStart,` `onFilterChange, onHelp, onKeyDown, onKeyPress,` `onKeyUp, onMouseDown, onMouseMove, onMouseOut,` `onMouseOver, onMouseUp, onSelectStart`	
Collections:	`rows[]`	

A table must contain one and only one THEAD object. If you don't create one automatically, the TABLE object instantiates one for you, but it will be empty.

The THEAD object is instantiated by a `<THEAD>` HTML tag. This is a means of marking off a section at the top of the table so that the rows can be grouped together and operated on separately to the table body.

The DOM level 1 standard calls for the implementation of a `TableSectionElement` object which includes both TFOOT and THEAD in its capabilities.

See also:	*Element object, TABLE object,* `TABLE.createTHead()`, `TABLE.deleteTHead()`, `TABLE.rules`, `TABLE.tHead`, *TFOOT object, TR object*

Property	JavaScript	JScript	N	IE	Opera	DOM	HTML	Notes
`align`	1.5 +	3.0 +	6.0 +	4.0 +	-	1 +	-	-
`bgColor`	1.5 +	3.0 +	6.0 +	4.0 +	-	1 +	-	-
`ch`	1.5 +	-	6.0 +	-	-	1 +	-	-
`chOff`	1.5 +	-	6.0 +	-	-	1 +	-	-
`vAlign`	1.5 +	3.0 +	6.0 +	4.0 +	-	1 +	-	-

Method	JavaScript	JScript	N	IE	Opera	DOM	HTML	Notes
`deleteRow()`	1.5 +	3.0 +	6.0 +	4.0 +	-	1 +	-	-
`insertRow()`	1.5 +	3.0 +	6.0 +	4.0 +	-	1 +	-	-

JavaScript Programmer's Reference

T

Event name	JavaScript	JScript	N	IE	Opera	DOM	HTML	Notes
onClick	1.5 +	3.0 +	6.0 +	4.0 +	3.0 +	-	4.0 +	Warning
onDblClick	1.5 +	3.0 +	6.0 +	4.0 +	3.0 +	-	4.0 +	Warning
onDragStart	-	3.0 +	-	4.0 +	-	-	-	-
onFilterChange	-	3.0 +	-	4.0 +	-	-	-	-
onHelp	-	3.0 +	-	4.0 +	-	-	-	Warning
onKeyDown	1.5 +	3.0 +	6.0 +	4.0 +	3.0 +	-	4.0 +	Warning
onKeyPress	1.5 +	3.0 +	6.0 +	4.0 +	3.0 +	-	4.0 +	Warning
onKeyUp	1.5 +	3.0 +	6.0 +	4.0 +	3.0 +	-	4.0 +	Warning
onMouseDown	1.5 +	3.0 +	6.0 +	4.0 +	3.0 +	-	4.0 +	Warning
onMouseMove	1.5 +	3.0 +	6.0 +	4.0 +	-	-	4.0 +	Warning
onMouseOut	1.5 +	3.0 +	6.0 +	4.0 +	3.0 +	-	4.0 +	Warning
onMouseOver	1.5 +	3.0 +	6.0 +	4.0 +	3.0 +	-	4.0 +	Warning
onMouseUp	1.5 +	3.0 +	6.0 +	4.0 +	3.0 +	-	4.0 +	Warning
onSelectStart	-	3.0 +	-	4.0 +	-	-	-	-

Inheritance chain:

Element object, Node object

this (Keyword)

A reference to the receiving object.

Availability:	ECMAScript edition – 2 JavaScript – 1.0 JScript – 1.0 Internet Explorer – 3.02 Netscape – 2.0 Netscape Enterprise Server – 2.0 Opera – 3.0	
Property/method value type:	An object	
JavaScript syntax:	-	this

Every active execution context owns a this value. It is used for self-referring script statements.

The specific this value of an execution context depends on the caller and the type of code being executed. This is determined on entry to an execution context. The this value associated with an execution context is immutable and therefore cannot be changed from a script.

A this value is considered to be a primary expression.

The this keyword is often used inside function bodies that are registered with a prototype. When it is executed, the function can refer to its owning object without having to know what sort of object it is. We can use this to write a function that can be used with several kinds of object.

If the this keyword is used inside an event handler, it refers to the object that the event belongs to. We can exploit this to build event handlers that support many objects and can be called by different event types.

If the this keyword is used outside of all functions (in global code) it refers to the Global object. A this property used in a script will therefore return that Global object. In fact it will return an object of type Window.

Other object types will be returned according the context in which the property is applied.

The example shows how the this keyword can be used to enhance the prototype of an object.

Example code:

```
<HTML>
<HEAD>
</HEAD>
<BODY>
<SCRIPT>
// See what the scope rules define for 'this'
document.write(this);
document.write("<BR>");
document.write(typeof this);
document.write("<BR>");

// Create a user defined prototype
function AnimalClass()
{
    return "Animal";
}

function Animal(aSpecies, aHabitat)
{
    this.species  = aSpecies;
    this.habitat  = aHabitat;
    this.toString = AnimalClass;
}

// Instantiate an animal
myAnimal = new Animal("Cow", "Field");
document.write("Object: "  + myAnimal + "<BR>");
document.write("Species: " + myAnimal.species + "<BR>");
document.write("Habitat: " + myAnimal.habitat + "<BR>");
</SCRIPT>
</BODY>
</HTML>
```

JavaScript Programmer's Reference

T

See also: Execution context, Method, Primary expression, Reference

Cross-references:

ECMA 262 edition 2 – section – 10.1.6

ECMA 262 edition 2 – section – 10.1.7

ECMA 262 edition 2 – section – 11.1.1

ECMA 262 edition 3 – section – 10.1.6

ECMA 262 edition 3 – section – 10.1.7

ECMA 262 edition 3 – section – 11.1.1

Wrox *Instant JavaScript* – page – 30

Wrox *Instant JavaScript* – page – 53

throw (Statement)

Throw a custom exception in the hope it will be caught by an error handler.

Availability:	ECMAScript edition – 3 JavaScript – 1.5 JScript – 5.0 Internet Explorer – 5.0 Netscape – 6.0

The throw statement provides a way to create an exception which will be passed to an associated catch() handler in a try...catch structure. It is really intended to be used in that context, but you can use it outside of a try...catch structure and trap the exception with the normal onError event handling support.

You can use this mechanism to generate an error, perhaps as a result of testing some value. Placing a throw statement into your code will force the error handling to be invoked. However if you use it outside of a try...catch block, the browser error handling will generate an error due to there being no way of catching the thrown event. It forces an error dialog, but not the one you wanted. You need to use a throw with a try...catch block to force the catch code to be called.

You can work around this by assigning an error handler function to the onerror property and making sure that the error handler returns a Boolean true value to signify that the error has no further processing required.

Warnings:

❏ This is not supported by Netscape Enterprise Server 3, and so its error handling capabilities are not available server-side.

❏ When using MSIE version 5 on the Macintosh platform, if you set the LANGUAGE HTML tag attribute of the enclosing <SCRIPT> tag to JScript 1.3, this handler will not be invoked properly.

❏ The example below, while supported on Netscape 6.0, does not seem to be supported on Internet Explorer 5.0 or 5.5.

Example code:

```
<HTML>
<HEAD>
</HEAD>
<BODY>
<SCRIPT>
// Define an error handler function
function myErrHandler(anException)
{
    alert("An error happened and was caught by this handler.");
    return true;
}

// Register the error handler
onerror = myErrHandler;

// Throw an exception
throw "ERR";
</SCRIPT>
</BODY>
</HTML>
```

See also:	catch(...), Error object, EvalError object, Exception handling, finally ..., RangeError object, ReferenceError object, SyntaxError object, try ... catch ... finally, TypeError object, URIError object

Cross-references:

ECMA 262 edition 2 – section – 7.4.3

ECMA 262 edition 3 – section – 7.5.2

ECMA 262 edition 3 – section – 12.13

<TITLE> (HTML Tag)

A tag that encloses the title block in a document header. It corresponds to the MSIE TITLE object.

The <TITLE> tag conveys no apparent visible effect on the document. It is considered to be an invisible tag, although its value does appear in the window heading bar.

Warnings:

❑ Be careful not to confuse this with the TITLE attribute of an HTML tag and its corresponding Element object's title property. They are just a means of naming objects and associating specific tags with specific objects.

See also:	Document.title, *TITLE object*

TITLE object (Object/HTML)

An MSIE object that represents the <TITLE> block of a document.

Availability:	DOM level – 1 JavaScript – 1.5 JScript – 3.0 Internet Explorer – 4.0 Netscape – 6.0
Inherits from:	*Element object*
JavaScript syntax:	IE *myTITLE* = document.all.tags("TITLE")[0]
	IE *myTITLE* = document.all[*anIndex*]
	IE *myTITLE* = *myDocument*.all.*anElementID*
	IE *myTITLE* = *myDocument*.all.tags("TITLE")[*anIndex*]
	IE *myTITLE* = *myDocument*.all[*aName*]
	– *myTITLE* = *myDocument*.getElementById(*anElementID*)
	– *myTITLE* = *myDocument*.getElementsByName(*aName*)[*anIndex*]
	– *myTITLE* = *myDocument*.getElementsByTagName("TITLE")[*anIndex*]
HTML syntax:	<TITLE> ... </TITLE>
Argument list:	*anIndex* A reference to an element in a collection
	aName An associative array reference
	anElementID The ID value of an Element object

834

Object properties:	text
Event handlers:	onClick, onDblClick, onHelp, onKeyDown, onKeyPress, onKeyUp, onMouseDown, onMouseMove, onMouseOut, onMouseOver, onMouseUp

The <TITLE> tag conveys no apparent visible effect on the document. It is considered to be an invisible tag although its value does appear in the window heading bar.

See also:	<TITLE>, Document.title

Property	JavaScript	JScript	N	IE	Opera	DOM	HTML	Notes
text	1.5 +	3.0 +	6.0 +	4.0 +	-	1 +	-	ReadOnly

Event name	JavaScript	JScript	N	IE	Opera	DOM	HTML	Notes
onClick	1.5 +	3.0 +	6.0 +	4.0 +	3.0 +	-	4.0 +	Warning
onDblClick	1.5 +	3.0 +	6.0 +	4.0 +	3.0 +	-	4.0 +	Warning
onHelp	-	3.0 +	-	4.0 +	-	-	-	Warning
onKeyDown	1.5 +	3.0 +	6.0 +	4.0 +	3.0 +	-	4.0 +	Warning
onKeyPress	1.5 +	3.0 +	6.0 +	4.0 +	3.0 +	-	4.0 +	Warning
onKeyUp	1.5 +	3.0 +	6.0 +	4.0 +	3.0 +	-	4.0 +	Warning
onMouseDown	1.5 +	3.0 +	6.0 +	4.0 +	3.0 +	-	4.0 +	Warning
onMouseMove	1.5 +	3.0 +	6.0 +	4.0 +	-	-	4.0 +	Warning
onMouseOut	1.5 +	3.0 +	6.0 +	4.0 +	3.0 +	-	4.0 +	Warning
onMouseOver	1.5 +	3.0 +	6.0 +	4.0 +	3.0 +	-	4.0 +	Warning
onMouseUp	1.5 +	3.0 +	6.0 +	4.0 +	3.0 +	-	4.0 +	Warning

Inheritance chain:

Element object, Node object

ToBoolean (Operator/internal)

An internal operator for converting values.

Availability:	ECMAScript edition – 2

This internal operator converts the public types to Boolean values.

The ToBoolean operator converts its argument to a value of type Boolean according to the following table:

Input Type	Result
Undefined	Always false
Null	Always false
Boolean	No conversion, the input value is returned unchanged
Number	The result is false if the argument is 0 or NaN otherwise it is true
String	Zero length strings return false otherwise the result is true
Object	Always true

See also:	Cast operator, Conversion, Implicit conversion, Logical operator, *Number*, Type conversion

Property attributes:

Internal.

Cross-references:

ECMA 262 edition 2 – section – 9.2

ECMA 262 edition 3 – section – 9.2

ToInt32 (Operator/internal)

An internal operator for converting values.

Availability:	ECMAScript edition – 2

This internal operator converts its input value to a 32 bit signed integer value.

See also:	Cast operator, Conversion, Implicit conversion, *Number*, Type conversion

Property attributes:

Internal.

Cross-references:

ECMA 262 edition 2 – section – 9.5

ECMA 262 edition 3 – section – 9.5

ToInteger (Operator/internal)

An internal operator for converting values.

Availability:	ECMAScript edition – 2

This internal operator converts values to integers.

See also:	Cast operator, Conversion, Implicit conversion, Type conversion

Property attributes:

Internal.

Cross-references:

ECMA 262 edition 2 – section – 9.4

ECMA 262 edition 3 – section – 9.4

ToNumber (Operator/internal)

An internal operator for converting values.

Availability:	ECMAScript edition – 2

This internal operator converts its argument to an appropriate numeric value.

The ToNumber operator converts its input values according to the following table:

Input Type	Result
Undefined	Returns NaN.
Null	0.
Boolean	1 if true, 0 if false.
Number	No conversion, the input value is returned unchanged.
String	The value of a sequence of characters that can reasonably be converted to a number, and if not then NaN is returned.
Object	Internally, a conversion to one of the primitive types happens followed by a conversion from that type to a number. Some objects will return a number that is readily usable. Others will return something that cannot be converted and NaN will result.

T

The string scanning algorithm copes with spelled out special values such as Infinity and exponential values, and can scan integers in Octal and Hexadecimal notation as well as decimal.

See also:	Cast operator, Conversion, Implicit conversion, *isFinite()*, *isNaN()*, *Number*, Type conversion

Cross-references:

ECMA 262 edition 2 – section – 9.3

ECMA 262 edition 3 – section – 9.3

ToObject (Operator/internal)

An internal operator for converting values.

Availability:	ECMAScript edition – 2

This internal operator converts its input argument into an object.

The ToObject operator converts its input arguments according to the following table:

Input Type	Result
Undefined	Generates a run-time error.
Null	Generates a run-time error.
Boolean	Creates a new Boolean object whose default value is the input value.
Number	Creates a new Number object whose default value is the input value.
String	Creates a new String object whose default value is the input value.
Object	No conversion, the input value is returned unchanged.

See also:	Cast operator, Conversion, Implicit conversion, *Number*, Type conversion

Cross-references:

ECMA 262 edition 2 – section – 9.9

ECMA 262 edition 3 – section – 9.9

http://cm.bell-labs.com/cm/cs/doc/90/4-10.ps.gz

http://cm.bell-labs.com/netlib/fp/dtoa.c.gz

http://cm.bell-labs.com/netlib/fp/g_fmt.c.gz

838

ToPrimitive (Operator/internal)

An internal operator for converting values.

Availability:	ECMAScript edition – 2

This operator converts objects to primitive values.

The ToPrimitive operator takes a value argument and an optional preferred type argument and converts its input to a primitive type from an object representation.

Input Type	Result
Undefined	No conversion, the input value is returned unchanged.
Null	No conversion, the input value is returned unchanged.
Boolean	No conversion, the input value is returned unchanged.
Number	No conversion, the input value is returned unchanged.
String	No conversion, the input value is returned unchanged.
Object	The default value defined by the object's internal DefaultValue method is returned. A coercion to the preferred type happens and is context dependant on where the result is being assigned.

See also:	Cast operator, Conversion, Implicit conversion, *Number*, Type conversion

Cross-references:

ECMA 262 edition 2 – section – 8.6.2.6

ECMA 262 edition 2 – section – 9.1

ECMA 262 edition 3 – section – 8.6.2.6

ECMA 262 edition 3 – section – 9.1

ToString (Operator/internal)

Return a string primitive version of an object.

Availability:	ECMAScript edition – 2

This internal operator converts its input argument to a string.

JavaScript Programmer's Reference

T

The ToString operator converts its input arguments according to the following table:

Input Type	Result
Undefined	"undefined".
Null	"null".
Boolean	If the argument is true, then the result is "true" otherwise the result is "false".
Number	Special cases are provided for NaN and Infinity where "NaN" and "Infinity" will be returned. Otherwise the string is a textual representation of the value. The string is formatted into decimal or exponential formats as determined by the magnitude of the value.
String	No conversion, the input value is returned unchanged.
Object	An internal conversion to a primitive takes place followed by a conversion from that primitive to a string. Some objects will return a string value that is immediately useful.

Warnings:

❑ In Microsoft environments, this is available most of the time but does not work for certain objects. In particular, there may some objects in WSH for which it is not supported.

See also:	Cast operator, Conversion, Implicit conversion, *JSObject.toString()*, *String concatenate (+)*, *toString()*, Type conversion

Cross-references:

ECMA 262 edition 2 – section – 9.8

ECMA 262 edition 3 – section – 9.8

toString() (Function/global)

Returns a string representation of the receiving object.

Availability:	JavaScript – 1.1 JScript – 3.0 Internet Explorer – 4.0 Netscape – 3.0	
Property/method value type:	String primitive	
JavaScript syntax:	-	*myObject*.toString()
	-	*myObject*.toString(*aRadix*)
Argument list:	aRadix	Radix conversion can be applied when the receiver is a number

The generic behavior of this method is to return a String primitive representation of the receiving object. It is generally overridden on a class by class basis due to objects containing such different properties and values.

The `ToString` internal operator is called. This doesn't usually tell you very much. The default `toString()` handlers may be different for the built-in classes, but all you'll likely get from a class you create yourself will be the string "[object Object]".

You will need to override the `toString()` function that is provided by default and add your own. This should be added to the prototype of your class.

The generic version of the `toString()` method may be useful when debugging. You can use the `apply()` method to force its use on objects you are trying to inspect and which may have overridden the `toString()` method themselves.

This method is supported by virtually every object by virtue of the fact that it is available as a method of the `Global` object in Netscape. Therefore it gets inherited into the scope chain for every script and function (method).

Warnings:

❑ At JavaScript version 1.2 in the Netscape version 4 browser, there is a slight difference in the way that `toString()` works. It will output all the nested objects that are joined by properties. This gave rise to a technique for deep-copying objects. However, it wasn't ECMA compliant and it no longer works in Netscape as of JavaScript 1.3.

❑ It might still work if you set the language version to JavaScript 1.2, but it's unreliable, not portable and definitely not going to work in Netscape 6.0. If you are exploiting it, you need to find an alternative because your scripts are going to break.

See also:	`Array.toString()`, `Boolean.toString()`, Conversion, `Date.toString()`, `Error.toString()`, `Function.toString()`, `Number.toString()`, `Object.toString()`, `prototype.toString()`, `RegExp.toString()`, *String*, *String concatenate* (+), `String.toString()`, *ToString*

ToUint16 (Operator/internal)

An internal operator for converting values.

Availability:	ECMAScript edition – 2

This internal operator converts its input argument into an unsigned 16 bit integer value.

See also:	`Cast` operator, Conversion, Implicit conversion, *Number*, *String.fromCharCode()*, Type conversion

JavaScript Programmer's Reference

T

Cross-references:

ECMA 262 edition 2 – section – 9.7

ECMA 262 edition 3 – section – 9.7

ToUint32 (Operator/internal)

An internal operator for converting values.

Availability:	ECMAScript edition – 2

This internal operator converts its input argument to an unsigned 32 bit integer.

See also:	Cast operator, Conversion, Implicit conversion, *Number*, Type conversion

Cross-references:

ECMA 262 edition 2 – section – 9.6

ECMA 262 edition 3 – section – 9.6

TR object (Object/HTML)

An object that encapsulates the row content of a table contained in a `<TR>` tag.

Availability:	DOM level – 1 JavaScript – 1.5 JScript – 3.0 Internet Explorer – 4.0 Netscape – 6.0
Inherits from:	*Element object*
JavaScript syntax:	IE `myTR = myDocument.all.anElementID`
	IE `myTR =` `myDocument.all.tags("TR")[anIndex]`
	IE `myTR = myDocument.all[aName]`
	- `myTR = myDocument.getElementById` `(anElementID)`
	- `myTR = myDocument.getElementsByName` `(aName)[anIndex]`
	- `myTR = myDocument.getElementsByTagName` `("TR")[anIndex]`
HTML syntax:	`<TR> ... </TR>`

Argument list:	anIndex	A reference to an element in a collection
	aName	An associative array reference
	anElementID	The ID value of an Element object
Object properties:	align, bgColor, borderColor, borderColorDark, borderColorLight, ch, chOff, rowIndex, sectionRowIndex, vAlign	
Object methods:	deleteCell(), insertCell()	
Event handlers:	onBlur, onClick, onDblClick, onDragStart, onFilterChange, onHelp, onKeyDown, onKeyPress, onKeyUp, onMouseDown, onMouseMove, onMouseOut, onMouseOver, onMouseUp, onSelectStart	
Collections:	cells[]	

Tables are a two-dimensional array of cells divided first into rows and then into columns. To access a particular cell, you locate its row first and then index along the cells in a row to find the one you want.

Rows are enclosed in <TR> tags which instantiate a TR object. The TR objects in a table are available as members of the rows[] collection.

They are also available in the rows[] collections that belong to TFOOT, TBODY and THEAD objects if the rows have been grouped inside tags that instantiate those objects.

You can access the cells in a row by using the cells[] collection that belongs to the TR object for the row you are interested in.

Warnings:

❑ Some earlier versions of the MSIE browser did not support access to the innerHTML property and related content when used on the Macintosh platform.

See also:	Element object, TABLE object, TABLE.deleteRow(), TABLE.insertRow(), TBODY object, TD object, TFOOT object, THEAD object

Property	JavaScript	JScript	N	IE	Opera	DOM	HTML	Notes
align	1.5 +	3.0 +	6.0 +	4.0 +	-	1+	-	-
bgColor	1.5 +	3.0 +	6.0 +	4.0 +	-	1+	-	-
borderColor	-	3.0 +	-	4.0 +	-	-	-	-
borderColorDark	-	3.0 +	-	4.0 +	-	-	-	-
borderColorLight	-	3.0 +	-	4.0 +	-	-	-	-
ch	1.5 +	-	6.0 +	-	-	1+	-	-
chOff	1.5 +	-	6.0 +	-	-	1+	-	-
rowIndex	1.5 +	3.0 +	6.0 +	4.0 +	-	1+	-	ReadOnly
sectionRowIndex	1.5 +	3.0 +	6.0 +	4.0 +	-	1+	-	ReadOnly
vAlign	1.5 +	3.0 +	6.0 +	4.0 +	-	1+	-	-

Method	JavaScript	JScript	N	IE	Opera	DOM	HTML	Notes
deleteCell()	1.5 +	3.0 +	6.0 +	4.0 +	-	1 +	-	-
insertCell()	1.5 +	3.0 +	6.0 +	4.0 +	-	1 +	-	-

Event name	JavaScript	JScript	N	IE	Opera	DOM	HTML	Notes
onBlur	1.5 +	3.0 +	6.0 +	4.0 +	3.0 +	-	-	Warning
onClick	1.5 +	3.0 +	6.0 +	4.0 +	3.0 +	-	4.0 +	Warning
onDblClick	1.5 +	3.0 +	6.0 +	4.0 +	3.0 +	-	4.0 +	Warning
onDragStart	-	3.0 +	-	4.0 +	-	-	-	-
onFilterChange	-	3.0 +	-	4.0 +	-	-	-	-
onHelp	-	3.0 +	-	4.0 +	-	-	-	Warning
onKeyDown	1.5 +	3.0 +	6.0 +	4.0 +	3.0 +	-	4.0 +	Warning
onKeyPress	1.5 +	3.0 +	6.0 +	4.0 +	3.0 +	-	4.0 +	Warning
onKeyUp	1.5 +	3.0 +	6.0 +	4.0 +	3.0 +	-	4.0 +	Warning
onMouseDown	1.5 +	3.0 +	6.0 +	4.0 +	3.0 +	-	4.0 +	Warning
onMouseMove	1.5 +	3.0 +	6.0 +	4.0 +	-	-	4.0 +	Warning
onMouseOut	1.5 +	3.0 +	6.0 +	4.0 +	3.0 +	-	4.0 +	Warning
onMouseOver	1.5 +	3.0 +	6.0 +	4.0 +	3.0 +	-	4.0 +	Warning
onMouseUp	1.5 +	3.0 +	6.0 +	4.0 +	3.0 +	-	4.0 +	Warning
onSelectStart	-	3.0 +	-	4.0 +	-	-	-	-

Inheritance chain:

Element object, Node object

true (Primitive value)

The Boolean true value.

Availability:	ECMAScript edition – 2
Property/method value type:	Boolean primitive

This is a Boolean primitive value representing the logically true state.

Conditional code execution depends on this value to signify the execution of a block of script code.

See also:	Boolean, Boolean, Boolean literal, Definition, false

Cross-references:

ECMA 262 edition 2 – section – 9.2

ECMA 262 edition 2 – section – 15.6

ECMA 262 edition 3 – section – 9.2

ECMA 262 edition 3 – section – 15.6

try ... catch ... finally (Statement)

A mechanism for attempting to execute some potentially problematic code with a means of catching the exception and continuing execution.

Availability:	ECMAScript edition – 3
	JavaScript – 1.5
	JScript – 5.0
	Internet Explorer – 5.0
	Netscape – 6.0

This was introduced in JavaScript 1.4 and JScript 5.0. The intention is to provide a way to execute a section of code in the `try` block and then if it has a problem, some recovery action can trap the error and handle it gracefully.

There are three basic sections.

The `try` statement is followed by a block of code enclosed in braces that may be problematic. Indeed, the problems may not be script based errors but may be the result of testing for some condition. That may lead to a custom exception being thrown.

If an exception of any kind happens in the `try` block, execution is immediately passed to the `catch()` function following.

The `catch` function is passed an `Error` object containing details of the kind of exception that has occurred.

When the `catch` function completes, execution drops into the block of code associated with the `finally` statement. In the case of the `try` block not having any exceptional behavior, at the end of that block execution also drops into the `finally` code block, bypassing the `catch` function altogether. So the `finally` code gets executed always after the `try` block.

You might use the `finally` block to tidy up or discard some unwanted objects.

In the example, the `try` block makes sure two values are presented in the correct order. If they are not in the right order, an exception is thrown and during the exception handling, they are swapped over. We put up an alert and set a flag that is presented in the output just to be sure it really happened like that.

JavaScript Programmer's Reference

T

Warnings:

❑ The functionality is not supported in Netscape prior to version 6.0.

❑ This is not supported by Netscape Enterprise Server 3 and so its error handling capabilities are not available server-side.

Example code:

```
<HTML>
<HEAD>
</HEAD>
<BODY>
<SCRIPT>
testThrow(100, 200);
testThrow(300, 100);
function testThrow(arg1, arg2)
{
    var switched = "NO";

    // Force an error condition
    try
    {
        if(arg1 < arg2)
        {
            throw "Wrong order";
        }
    }
    catch(myErr)
    {
        alert(myErr);
        var temp = arg1;
        arg1 = arg2;
        arg2 = temp;
        switched = "YES"
    }
    finally
    {
        document.write("Biggest : "  + arg1 + "<BR>");
        document.write("Smallest : " + arg2 + "<BR>");
        document.write("Switched : " + switched + "<BR>");
        document.write("<BR>");
    }
}
</SCRIPT>
</BODY>
</HTML>
```

See also:	catch(...), Error object, EvalError object, Exception handling, finally ..., RangeError object, ReferenceError object, SyntaxError object, throw, TypeError object, URIError object

Cross-references:

ECMA 262 edition 2 – section – 7.4.3

ECMA 262 edition 3 – section – 7.5.2

ECMA 262 edition 3 – section – 12.14

TT object (Object/HTML)

An object that represents the font style controlled by the `<TT>` HTML tag.

Availability:	JScript – 3.0 Internet Explorer – 4.0 Deprecated
Inherits from:	*Element object*
JavaScript syntax:	IE `myTT = myDocument.all.anElementID`
	IE `myTT = myDocument.all.tags("TT")[anIndex]`
	IE `myTT = myDocument.all[aName]`
	- `myTT = myDocument.getElementById (anElementID)`
	- `myTT = myDocument.getElementsByName (aName)[anIndex]`
	- `myTT = myDocument.getElementsByTagName ("TT")[anIndex]`
HTML syntax:	`<TT> ... </TT>`
Argument list:	`anIndex` A reference to an element in a collection
	`aName` An associative array reference
	`anElementID` The ID value of an `Element` object

Event handlers:	`onClick, onDblClick, onDragStart,`
	`onFilterChange, onHelp, onKeyDown, onKeyPress,`
	`onKeyUp, onMouseDown, onMouseMove, onMouseOut,`
	`onMouseOver, onMouseUp, onSelectStart`

`<TT>` tags and the objects that represent them are inline elements. Placing them into a document does not create a line break.

See also:	*Element object*

T

Event name	JavaScript	JScript	N	IE	Opera	DOM	HTML	Notes
onClick	-	3.0 +	-	4.0 +	3.0 +	-	4.0 +	Warning
onDblClick	-	3.0 +	-	4.0 +	3.0 +	-	4.0 +	Warning
onDragStart	-	3.0 +	-	4.0 +	-	-	-	-
onFilterChange	-	3.0 +	-	4.0 +	-	-	-	-
onHelp	-	3.0 +	-	4.0 +	-	-	-	Warning
onKeyDown	-	3.0 +	-	4.0 +	3.0 +	-	4.0 +	Warning
onKeyPress	-	3.0 +	-	4.0 +	3.0 +	-	4.0 +	Warning
onKeyUp	-	3.0 +	-	4.0 +	3.0 +	-	4.0 +	Warning
onMouseDown	-	3.0 +	-	4.0 +	3.0 +	-	4.0 +	Warning
onMouseMove	-	3.0 +	-	4.0 +	-	-	4.0 +	Warning
onMouseOut	-	3.0 +	-	4.0 +	3.0 +	-	4.0 +	Warning
onMouseOver	-	3.0 +	-	4.0 +	3.0 +	-	4.0 +	Warning
onMouseUp	-	3.0 +	-	4.0 +	3.0 +	-	4.0 +	Warning
onSelectStart	-	3.0 +	-	4.0 +	-	-	-	-

Inheritance chain:

Element object, Node object

TypeError object (Object/core)

A native error object based on the Error object.

Availability:	ECMAScript edition – 3 JavaScript – 1.5 Netscape – 6.0	
Inherits from:	Error object	
JavaScript syntax:	N	myError = new TypeError()
	N	myError = new TypeError(aNumber)
	N	myError = new TypeError(aNumber, aText)
Argument list:	aNumber	An error number
	aText	A text describing the error

This sub-class of the Error object is used when an exception is caused by an operand having an unexpected data type.

See also:	catch(...), Error object, EvalError object, RangeError object, ReferenceError object, SyntaxError object, throw, try ... catch ... finally, URIError object

Inheritance chain:

Error object

Cross-references:

ECMA 262 edition 3 – section – 15.1.4.14

ECMA 262 edition 3 – section – 15.11.6.5

typeof (Operator/unary)

An operator that yields the type of an operand.

Availability:	ECMAScript edition – 2 JavaScript – 1.1 JScript – 1.0 Internet Explorer – 3.02 Netscape – 3.0 Opera – 3.0	
Property/method value type:	String primitive	
JavaScript syntax:	-	typeof anOperand
	-	typeof (anOperand)
Argument list:	anOperand	An object or variable to check for type

This operator produces a string that contains the operand's type.

The typeof operator inspects the operand and returns a string representing its type. The operand is not evaluated. There are times when this is advantageous and can avoid a run-time error.

The string value returned depends on the operand type being evaluated. The typeof operator returns these values:

Type	Result
Undefined	"undefined"
Infinity	"number"
NaN	"number"
Null	"object"
Boolean primitive	"boolean"
Number primitive	"number"
String primitive	"string"

Table continued on following page

JavaScript Programmer's Reference

T

Type	Result
Boolean() constructor	"boolean"
Date() constructor	"string"
Number() constructor	"number"
RegExp() constructor	"undefined"
String() constructor	"string"
Boolean object instance	"object"
Date object instance	"object"
Math object instance	"object"
Number object instance	"object"
RegExp object instance	"object"
String object instance	"object"
Generic object instance	"object"
Object not supporting a call interface	"object"
Object that supports a call interface	"function"
Other host objects	Implementation defined
typeof any value	"string"

Note that the values returned are lower case and are not an exact match for the class of the operand. String objects and primitive strings are both described as having a typeof "string" for instance.

In some documentation the typeof operator is referred to as a function. Since it has optional parentheses and the operand is passed as an argument, it behaves as if it were a function.

The typeof operator is one of the few ways in which you can use the contents of a variable that is not yet defined. It will yield the undefined type for variables that have not yet had a value assigned to them. And thus you can determine if it is safe to use them as an RValue in an assignment expression.

The associativity is right to left.

Refer to the operator precedence topic for details of execution order.

In JavaScript version 1.1, you can determine the difference between the undefined and null values.

In JavaScript version 1.3, the === operator will detect the difference.

You cannot distinguish between different kinds of objects. To do that you can compare the object constructor property with one of the built-in types. You can ask the constructor property (if there is one) for its name. Sometimes a toString() conversion on the object will yield a function name and occasionally you may need to check prototype values or test for the existence of properties. If all else fails, you have to assume that it's just an object of arbitrary type.

Warnings:

❏ The `typeof` operator is not available in Netscape version 2.02.

❏ In Microsoft environments, this is available most of the time, but does not work for certain objects. In particular, there may some objects in WSH for which it is not supported.

Example code:

```
// Testing a string value
var aString = 'String text';
document.write(typeof(aString));      // Yields "string"

// Testing variables that exist but are not yet assigned
var aVar1;
document.write(typeof aVar1);      // Yields "undefined"

// Testing variables that do not yet exist
document.write(typeof aVar2 );      // Yields "undefined"
```

See also:	Associativity, Cast operator, *class*, Enquiry functions, *Equal to (==)*, *Global object*, *Grouping operator ( )*, *Identically equal to (===)*, *NOT Equal to (!=)*, *NOT Identically equal to (!==)*, Object inspector, Operator, Operator Precedence, Reference, Special type, Unary expression, Unary operator, *void*

Cross-references:

ECMA 262 edition 2 – section – 11.1.4

ECMA 262 edition 2 – section – 11.4.3

ECMA 262 edition 3 – section – 11.4.3

O'Reilly JavaScript Definitive Guide – page – 47

Wrox *Instant JavaScript* – page – 21

Wrox *Instant JavaScript* – page – 22

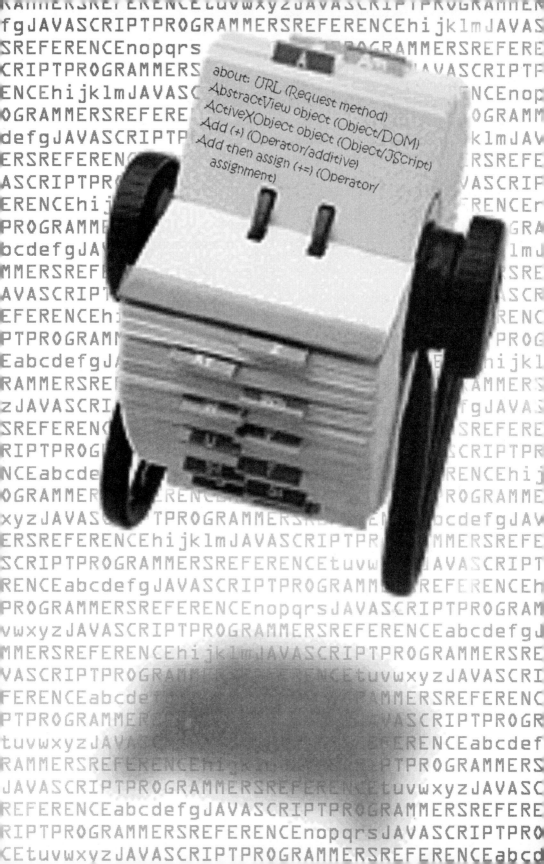

U object (Object/HTML)

An object that represents the font style controlled by the <U> HTML tag.

Availability:	DOM level – 1 JavaScript – 1.5 JScript – 3.0 Internet Explorer – 4.0 Netscape – 6.0 Deprecated
Inherits from:	*Element object*

JavaScript syntax:	IE *myU = myDocument.all.anElementID*
	
	IE *myU =*
	    myDocument.all.tags("U")[anIndex]
	
	IE *myU = myDocument.all[aName]*
	
	- *myU = myDocument.getElementById
	    (anElementID)*
	
	- *myU = myDocument.getElementsByName
	    (aName)[anIndex]*
	
	- *myU = myDocument.getElementsByTagName
	    ("U")[anIndex]*

HTML syntax:	<U> ... </U>
Argument list:	*anIndex* A reference to an element in a collection *aName* An associative array reference *anElementID* The ID value of an Element object
Event handlers:	onClick, onDblClick, onDragStart, onFilterChange, onHelp, onKeyDown, onKeyPress, onKeyUp, onMouseDown, onMouseMove, onMouseOut, onMouseOver, onMouseUp, onSelectStart

<U> tags and the objects that represent them are inline elements. Placing them into a document does not create a line break.

See also:	Element object

Event name	JavaScript	JScript	N	IE	Opera	DOM	HTML	Notes
onClick	1.5 +	3.0 +	6.0 +	4.0 +	-	-	4.0 +	Warning
onDblClick	1.5 +	3.0 +	6.0 +	4.0 +	-	-	4.0 +	Warning
onDragStart	-	3.0 +	-	4.0 +	-	-	-	-
onFilterChange	-	3.0 +	-	4.0 +	-	-	-	-
onHelp	-	3.0 +	-	4.0 +	-	-	-	Warning
onKeyDown	1.5 +	3.0 +	6.0 +	4.0 +	-	-	4.0 +	Warning
onKeyPress	1.5 +	3.0 +	6.0 +	4.0 +	-	-	4.0 +	Warning
onKeyUp	1.5 +	3.0 +	6.0 +	4.0 +	-	-	4.0 +	Warning
onMouseDown	1.5 +	3.0 +	6.0 +	4.0 +	-	-	4.0 +	Warning
onMouseMove	1.5 +	3.0 +	6.0 +	4.0 +	-	-	4.0 +	Warning
onMouseOut	1.5 +	3.0 +	6.0 +	4.0 +	-	-	4.0 +	Warning
onMouseOver	1.5 +	3.0 +	6.0 +	4.0 +	-	-	4.0 +	Warning
onMouseUp	1.5 +	3.0 +	6.0 +	4.0 +	-	-	4.0 +	Warning
onSelectStart	-	3.0 +	-	4.0 +	-	-	-	-

Inheritance chain:

Element object, Node object

UIEvent object (Object/DOM)

This is part of the DOM level 2 user interface event set.

Availability:	DOM level – 2 JavaScript – 1.5 Netscape version – 6.0	
Inherits from:	Event object	
JavaScript syntax:	N	myUIEvent = new UIEvent()
Object properties:	detail, view	
Object methods:	initUIEvent()	

The availability of the UIEvent object handling can be determined with the Implementation.hasFeature() method call.

The available set of events is defined by HTML 4.0 and DOM level 0 with some additional events having been added. These event types are enumerated in the DOM level 2 specification and are:

- ❑ DOMFocusIn

- ❑ DOMFocusOut

- ❑ DOMActivate

See also:	*AbstractView object*, *Event object*, `Implementation.hasFeature()`, *MouseEvent object*, `onBlur`, `onClick`, `onFocus`

Property	JavaScript	JScript	N	IE	Opera	DOM	Notes
`detail`	1.5 +	-	6.0 +	-	-	2 +	ReadOnly
`view`	1.5 +	-	6.0 +	-	-	2 +	ReadOnly

Method	JavaScript	JScript	N	IE	Opera	DOM	Notes
`initUIEvent()`	1.5 +	-	6.0 +	-	-	2 +	-

Inheritance chain:

Event object

UL object (Object/HTML)

An object that encapsulates an unordered list in a `<UL>` tag.

Availability:	DOM level – 1 JavaScript – 1.5 JScript – 3.0 Internet Explorer – 4.0 Netscape – 6.0
Inherits from:	*Element object*
JavaScript syntax:	IE `myUL = myDocument.all.anElementID`
	IE `myUL = myDocument.all.tags ("UL")[anIndex]`
	IE `myUL = myDocument.all[aName]`
	- `myUL = myDocument.getElementById (anElementID)`
	- `myUL = myDocument.getElementsByName (aName)[anIndex]`
	- `myUL = myDocument.getElementsByTagName ("UL")[anIndex]`
HTML syntax:	`<UL> ... </UL>`

JavaScript Programmer's Reference

U

Argument list:	anIndex	A reference to an element in a collection
	aName	An associative array reference
	anElementID	The ID value of an Element object
Object properties:	compact, start, type	
Event handlers:	onClick, onDblClick, onDragStart, onFilterChange, onHelp, onKeyDown, onKeyPress, onKeyUp, onMouseDown, onMouseMove, onMouseOut, onMouseOver, onMouseUp, onSelectStart	

The <UL> tag is a block-level tag. That means that it forces a line break before and after itself.

The DOM level 1 standard describes this as a UListElement object.

See also:	DIR object, Element object, OL object

Property	JavaScript	JScript	N	IE	Opera	DOM	HTML	Notes
compact	1.5 +	3.0 +	6.0 +	4.0 +	-	1+	-	-
start	1.5 +	3.0 +	6.0 +	4.0 +	-	1+	-	-
type	1.5 +	3.0 +	6.0 +	4.0 +	-	1+	-	-

Event name	JavaScript	JScript	N	IE	Opera	DOM	HTML	Notes
onClick	1.5 +	3.0 +	6.0 +	4.0 +	-	-	4.0 +	Warning
onDblClick	1.5 +	3.0 +	6.0 +	4.0 +	-	-	4.0 +	Warning
onDragStart	-	3.0 +	-	4.0 +	-	-	-	-
onFilterChange	-	3.0 +	-	4.0 +	-	-	-	-
onHelp	-	3.0 +	-	4.0 +	-	-	-	Warning
onKeyDown	1.5 +	3.0 +	6.0 +	4.0 +	-	-	4.0 +	Warning
onKeyPress	1.5 +	3.0 +	6.0 +	4.0 +	-	-	4.0 +	Warning
onKeyUp	1.5 +	3.0 +	6.0 +	4.0 +	-	-	4.0 +	Warning
onMouseDown	1.5 +	3.0 +	6.0 +	4.0 +	-	-	4.0 +	Warning
onMouseMove	1.5 +	3.0 +	6.0 +	4.0 +	-	-	4.0 +	Warning
onMouseOut	1.5 +	3.0 +	6.0 +	4.0 +	-	-	4.0 +	Warning
onMouseOver	1.5 +	3.0 +	6.0 +	4.0 +	-	-	4.0 +	Warning
onMouseUp	1.5 +	3.0 +	6.0 +	4.0 +	-	-	4.0 +	Warning
onSelectStart	-	3.0 +	-	4.0 +	-	-	-	-

Inheritance chain:

Element object, Node object

undefined (Constant/static)

A literal constant whose type is a built-in primitive value.

Availability:	ECMAScript edition – 2
	JavaScript – 1.3
	JScript – 5.5
	Internet Explorer – 5.5
	Netscape – 4.06
Property/method value type:	Undefined primitive

The undefined value is a primitive value that is returned when a variable has not yet been assigned a value.

In some implementations this value compares equal to the null value. They are not actually the same but this can sometimes provide a work-around for those implementations that do not provide a way to explicitly test for an undefined value.

If a variable is declared and no value is assigned to it, then it will contain the undefined value. It will exist and can be referred to in expressions and will affect them to the extent they can be affected by the value 'undefined'.

If a variable has never been declared and it is referred to, a run-time error will result. It does not exist let alone contain the 'undefined' value. There is one instance where referring to a non-existent variable does not generate an error, and that is to use it as an LValue in an assignment. Only the = operator can be used. The prefix and postfix increment/decrement operators should yield an error and so should the compound assignment operators, since the value to the left does not exist until after the assignment has taken place.

You cannot create an 'undefined' value explicitly in older interpreters since there is no keyword to yield it as a constant. This is more of a problem with MSIE which only supported the undefined keyword as of version 5.5 while Netscape has supported it since JavaScript 1.3. If you need to, you can manufacture one of your own with this expression:

```
undefined = (void 0);
```

This whole area is somewhat mysterious and the (void 0) simulation really creates a null value which some browsers cannot distinguish from the undefined value.

Warnings:

❑ Some implementations do not provide adequate protection against you corrupting this value. Be careful not to assign your own values to this variable. It will lead to unpredictable results if you do.

❑ This is not available for use server-side with Netscape Enterprise Server 3.

JavaScript Programmer's Reference

U

Example code:

```
// Assuming a or b has not been declared, this generates an error
a += 10;
// This doesn't
a = 10;
// This does
alert(b);
```

See also:	Exception, *Global object*, *null*, *Null literal*, Range error, *void*

Cross-references:

ECMA 262 edition 2 – section – 4.3.9

ECMA 262 edition 3 – section – 4.3.9

O'Reilly *JavaScript Definitive Guide* – page – 47

undefined type (Type)

A native built-in type.

Availability:	ECMAScript edition – 2
Property/method value type:	Undefined primitive

The type undefined has exactly one value, called undefined. It is returned by variables that have not yet been assigned with a value.

This value is also returned in some browsers when referring to a part of the document object model that is non-existent.

Sending a subsequent message to values that are currently undefined results in a run-time error.

See also:	Cast operator, Special type, Type

Cross-references:

ECMA 262 edition 2 – section – 4.3.10

ECMA 262 edition 2 – section – 8.1

ECMA 262 edition 3 – section – 4.3.10

ECMA 262 edition 3 – section – 8.1

Wrox *Instant JavaScript* – page – 14

unescape() (Function/global)

Un-URL-escape a string.

Availability:	ECMAScript edition – 2 JavaScript – 1.0 JScript – 1.0 Internet Explorer – 3.02 Netscape – 2.0 Opera – 3.0 Deprecated	
Property/method value type:	String primitive	
JavaScript syntax:	-	unescape(*anInputString*)
Argument list:	*anInputString*	A string to be converted

This function is the complement of the escape() function described in its own topic elsewhere.

A string that might have been escaped with the escape() function either locally or remotely can be converted back to a normal unescaped string with this function.

This function has Unicode support in MSIE version 4.

As far as ECMAScript is concerned, this is superceded in edition 3 with a set of generalized URI handling functions. The JScript 5.5 documentation refers to this as a deprecated feature.

See also:	Cast operator, *decodeURI()*, *decodeURIComponent()*, *encodeURI()*, *encodeURIComponent()*, *escape()*, Function property, *Global object*, URI handling functions

Property attributes:

DontEnum.

Cross-references:

ECMA 262 edition 2 – section – 15.1.2.5

ECMA 262 edition 3 – section – B.2.2

Unicode (Standard)

A character encoding standard.

Availability:	ECMAScript edition – 2

The Unicode standard is derived originally from ASCII. ASCII was an 8 bit coded character set with a limited number of individual character values. Unicode is a 16 bit coding that supports all the required characters for the major languages of the world, plus the technical symbols in common use.

Implementations of JavaScript that conform to the ECMA 262 standard must interpret character values in accordance with the Unicode Standard, version 2.0, and ISO/IEC 10646-1 with UCS-2 (Universal Character Set) as the adopted encoding form, implementation level 3. If the adopted 10646 subset is not indicated, then it should be assumed to be the BMP subset, collection 300.

For most usage, the character set will be the lower 128 characters that roughly correspond to the ASCII character table. However, internationalization and localization work in progress suggests that non-English speaking users should be able to declare identifiers in their own natural language with its particular character sets and special symbols. Internet web site domain name standards are undergoing some revision to support double byte characters. The ECMAScript edition 3 improves support for handling localized strings, numbers, and dates.

The Unicode standard is due for updating to a new edition as the version 2.0 is somewhat old now and does not support Euro currency symbols among other things. A version 3.0 standard is reported to be on the way.

Unicode characters are more properly referred to as code points.

See also:	Character set, Character-case mapping, Control character, *Equal to* (==), *Greater than* (>), *Greater than or equal to* (>=), *Identically equal to* (===), isLower(), isUpper(), *Less than* (<), *Less than or equal to* (<=), Locale-specific behavior, Multi-byte character, *NOT Equal to* (!=), *NOT Identically equal to* (!==), String, String literal

Cross-references:

ECMA 262 edition 2 – section – 2

ECMA 262 edition 2 – section – 6

ECMA 262 edition 3 – section – 2

ECMA 262 edition 3 – section – 6

O'Reilly *JavaScript Definitive Guide* – page – 30

Web-references:

ftp://unicode.org/
mail_list://unicode-request@unicode.org/
mailto://unicode-inc@unicode.org/
http://www.unicode.org/

Universal coordinated time (Standard)

A universal standard time that is synchronized to GMT.

The universal coordinated time (AKA Universel Temps Cordonne – UTC) is a standard time value that is based on an atomic clock, measured and calibrated according to astronomical observations of pulsars.

UTC is synchronized to Greenwich Mean Time which is coincident with the location of the zero meridian.

Local time at any point on the earth's surface is computed relative to UTC by adding a positive or negative offset to UTC. In general, the offsets are measured in complete hours of 60 minutes duration.

However there are some locations in the world where the offset is a fractional offset in hours. As a general rule, each hour corresponds to a movement of 15 degrees further away from the meridian. This is not completely strict since China spans almost 4 hours in terms of distance but is entirely in one time-zone based on the time in Peking.

Some Islamic countries do not adopt the same time scale in any case, choosing instead to measure the time from sunrise to sunset as 12 hours. Since days wax and wane according to the season, this can cause some difficulty in converting local time to UTC and vice versa.

See also:	Broken down time, Calendar time, Date and time, Daylight savings time adjustment, *java.util.Date*, Time value

UniversalBrowserAccess (Security privilege)

A combination of both read and write access.

This is a combination of everything that `UniversalBrowserRead` and `UniversalBrowserWrite` provide access control for in a single privilege.

See also:	*about: URL, Event object,* `Event.data`, *History object, netscape.security.PrivilegeManager,* `onDragDrop`, *PrivilegeManager object,* `PrivilegeManager.disablePrivilege()`, `PrivilegeManager.enablePrivilege()`, *Requesting privileges,* Restricted access, *Same origin,* Security policy, self, `Window.close()`

U

UniversalBrowserRead (Security privilege)

A privilege to grant read access to browser internals.

Gives a script permission to read the properties of windows whose content comes from different origins. This also controls script access to the `history` object among other things. Other internal browser state information that is accessible via the about: URL is also controlled by this privilege.

This privilege is also necessary to read the `data` property of an `event` object that is passed to the `ondragdrop()` event handler.

See also:	*about: URL, Event object,* `Event.data`, *History object,* `History.current`, *netscape.security.PrivilegeManager,* `onDragDrop`, *PrivilegeManager object,* `PrivilegeManager.disablePrivilege()`, `PrivilegeManager.enablePrivilege()`, *Requesting privileges,* Restricted access, *Same origin,* Security policy

UniversalBrowserWrite (Security privilege)

A privilege that grants the ability to write to internal browser values.

This property allows scripts to close windows. Without this privilege, if a script opens a window, it cannot create a window that is smaller than 100 pixels square. Scripts without this privilege also cannot move a window off-screen, create one that is larger than the screen or create a window that lacks a title-bar. Conferring this privilege allows scripts to do all these things. Without it, scripts cannot hide from view or carry on running when the user thinks they have stopped.

This privilege grants the script permission to hide or show the various window furniture (menu-bar, status-line, scroll-bars, tool-bar, location-bar, directory-bar or personal-bar). Without it, scripts cannot change the visibility of these items.

It also affects event management. You cannot watch events in other windows if they come from different sources without this privilege and you cannot set `event` object properties without it either. The occasional bug in a browser lets you get round the security in odd ways.

This is how to put a toolbar back onto a window that didn't have one. You are supposed to require privileges to do it but it sometimes works regardless:

```
open('', '_top', 'status=0,toolbar=1');
```

Putting a toolbar back lets you view source because the menu is reinstated too.

See also:	*netscape.security.PrivilegeManager, PrivilegeManager object,* `PrivilegeManager.disablePrivilege()`, `PrivilegeManager.enablePrivilege()`, *Requesting privileges,* Restricted access, *Same origin,* Security policy

UniversalFileRead (Security privilege)

A privilege to grant access to read a file in the file system.

If your script has this privilege, it can then select a file in the client file-system and upload it to the server by means of a `FileUpload` object. This is done by setting the `value` property of that `FileUpload` object.

If this capability is activated, the contents of any file on the local file-system can be presented to a CGI script running on a web server.

See also:	*FileUpload object*, `FileUpload.value`, *netscape.security.PrivilegeManager*, *PrivilegeManager object*, `PrivilegeManager.disablePrivilege()`, `PrivilegeManager.enablePrivilege()`, *Requesting privileges*, Restricted access, Security policy

UniversalPreferencesRead (Security privilege)

A privilege that allows access to preferences information.

This privilege controls read access to preference settings. Scripts without it cannot see user preference settings. It arbitrates the use of the `Navigator.preference()` method in read mode.

See also:	`History.next`, `History.previous`, `Navigator.preference()`, *netscape.security.PrivilegeManager*, *PrivilegeManager object*, `PrivilegeManager.disablePrivilege()`, `PrivilegeManager.enablePrivilege()`, *Requesting privileges*, Restricted access, Security policy

UniversalPreferencesWrite (Security privilege)

A privilege that grants the ability to change preferences settings.

This privilege controls whether scripts can change the current user preference settings. It controls the use of the `Navigator.preference()` method.

See also:	`Navigator.preference()`, `Navigator.savePreferences()`, *netscape.security.PrivilegeManager*, *PrivilegeManager object*, `PrivilegeManager.disablePrivilege()`, `PrivilegeManager.enablePrivilege()`, *Requesting privileges*, Restricted access, Security policy

JavaScript Programmer's Reference

U

863

UniversalSendMail (Security privilege)

A privilege that grants the permission to send mail.

This controls whether a `mailto:` or `news:` URL can be used when submitting a form. A confirmation dialog affirmative response is required if this privilege is not granted to the script.

The result of this is an e-mail or Usenet news article is submitted that contains the user's e-mail address.

See also:	`mailto:` URL, *netscape.security.PrivilegeManager, news:* URL, *PrivilegeManager object,* `PrivilegeManager.disablePrivilege()`, `PrivilegeManager.enablePrivilege()`, *Requesting privileges,* Restricted access, Security policy

untaint() (Function/global)

A deprecated method for controlling secure access to data values.

Availability:	JavaScript – 1.1 Netscape version – 3.0 Deprecated

This was removed at version 1.2 of JavaScript. If you encounter it in a script you are maintaining, it is probably wise to seek to have it removed otherwise it is likely to cause a run-time error.

Warnings:

❑ DO NOT USE THIS FUNCTION!

See also:	`Navigator.taintEnabled()`, *taint()*

unwatch() (Function/global)

Un-set a watch-point for a named property of an object.

Availability:	JavaScript – 1.2 Netscape – 4.0	
JavaScript syntax:	N	*myObject*.unwatch(*aProperty*)
Argument list:	*aProperty*	A property to cease watching

This method is provided to ease the task of debugging JavaScript.

It is provided to disconnect the watcher that was set up with the watch() method.

Its calling circumstances are identical and you simply need to provide a complementary unwatch() to deactivate the effects of a watch().

The new event model supported by Netscape version 6.0 and that is already available in MSIE 5.0 presents a propertyName property that belongs to the Event object. You can inspect that during an onPropertyChanged event and achieve the same watch()/unwatch() behavior.

See also:	Event, Event handler, Event management, Event model, *Event object*, onPropertyChange, *watch()*

Cross-references:

Wrox *Instant JavaScript* – page – 56

URIError object (Object/core)

A native error object based on the Error object.

Availability:	ECMAScript edition – 3 JavaScript – 1.5 Netscape – 6.0	
JavaScript syntax:	N	*myError* = new URIError()
	N	*myError* = new URIError(*aNumber*)
	N	*myError* = new URIError(*aNumber*, *aText*)
Argument list:	*aNumber*	An error number
	aText	A text describing the error
Object properties:	description, message, name, number	
Object methods:	toString()	

JavaScript Programmer's Reference

U

This sub-class of the Error object is used when an exception is caused by one of the URI handler functions being used inappropriately.

See also:	*catch(...), Error object, EvalError object, RangeError object, ReferenceError object, SyntaxError object, throw, try ... catch ... finally, TypeError object*

Property	JavaScript	JScript	N	IE	Opera	NES	ECMA	Notes
description	1.5 +	-	6.0 +	-	-	-	3 +	-
message	1.5 +	-	6.0 +	-	-	-	3 +	-
name	1.5 +	-	6.0 +	-	-	-	3 +	-
number	1.5 +	-	6.0 +	-	-	-	3 +	-

Method	JavaScript	JScript	N	IE	Opera	NES	ECMA	Notes
toString()	1.5 +	-	6.0 +	-	-	-	3 +	-

Cross-references:

ECMA 262 edition 3 – section – 15.1.4.15

ECMA 262 edition 3 – section – 15.11.6.6

Url object (Object/HTML)

An object that represents URLs in Netscape but which has extensions in MSIE.

Availability:	JavaScript – 1.0 JScript – 1.0 Internet Explorer – 3.02 Netscape – 2.0 Opera – 3.0
Inherits from:	*Element object*
JavaScript syntax:	-	myUrl = myDocument.links[anIndex]
Argument list:	anIndex	A reference to an element in a collection
Object properties:	charset, coords, hash, host, hostname, href, hreflang, Methods, mimeType, name, nameProp, pathname, port, protocol, protocolLong, rel, rev, search, shape, tabIndex, target, text, type, urn, x, y
Event handlers:	onClick, onDblClick, onHelp, onKeyDown, onKeyPress, onKeyUp, onMouseDown, onMouseMove, onMouseOut, onMouseOver, onMouseUp

Objects of this type are contained in the `document.links[]` array.

Event handling support via properties containing function objects was added to `Url` objects at version 1.1 of JavaScript.

See also:	Anchor object, Area object, Document.links[], HyperLink object, LINK object, LinkArray object, Location object, String.anchor(), String.link(), Url.hash, Url.host, Url.hostname, Url.href, Url.name, Url.pathname, Url.port, Url.protocol, Url.search, Url.target, Url.text

Property	JavaScript	JScript	N	IE	Opera	DOM	HTML	Notes
charset	-	-	-	-	-	-	-	-
coords	1.0 +	1.0 +	2.0 +	3.02 +	-	-	-	-
hash	1.0 +	1.0 +	2.0 +	3.02 +	3.0 +	-	-	Warning
host	1.0 +	1.0 +	2.0 +	3.02 +	3.0 +	-	-	-
hostname	1.0 +	1.0 +	2.0 +	3.02 +	3.0 +	-	-	Warning
href	1.0 +	1.0 +	2.0 +	3.02 +	3.0 +	1 +	-	-
hreflang	-	-	-	-	-	-	-	-
Methods	-	3.0 +	-	4.0 +	-	-	-	-
mimeType	-	3.0 +	-	4.0 +	-	-	-	-
name	1.5 +	1.0 +	6.0 +	3.02 +	-	-	-	Warning
nameProp	-	3.0 +	-	4.0 +	-	-	-	-
pathname	1.0 +	1.0 +	2.0 +	3.02 +	3.0 +	-	-	-
port	1.0 +	1.0 +	2.0 +	3.02 +	3.0 +	-	-	Warning
protocol	1.0 +	1.0 +	2.0 +	3.02 +	3.0 +	-	-	-
protocolLong	-	3.0 +	-	4.0 +	-	-	-	-
rel	1.5 +	3.0 +	6.0 +	4.0 +	-	1 +	-	-
rev	1.5 +	3.0 +	6.0 +	4.0 +	-	1 +	-	-
search	1.0 +	1.0 +	2.0 +	3.02 +	3.0 +	-	-	-
shape	1.0 +	1.0 +	2.0 +	3.02 +	-	1 +	-	-
tabIndex	1.0 +	1.0 +	2.0 +	3.02 +	3.0 +	-	-	-
target	1.0 +	1.0 +	2.0 +	3.02 +	3.0 +	1 +	-	-
text	1.2 +	-	4.0 +	-	-	-	-	Warning
type	1.5 +	3.0 +	6.0 +	4.0 +	-	1 +	-	-
urn	-	3.0 +	-	4.0 +	-	-	-	-
x	1.2 +	-	4.0 +	-	-	-	-	Warning, Deprecated
y	1.2 +	-	4.0 +	-	-	-	-	Warning, Deprecated

Event name	JavaScript	JScript	N	IE	Opera	DOM	HTML	Notes
onClick	1.0 +	1.0 +	2.0 +	3.0 +	3.0 +	-	4.0 +	Warning
onDblClick	1.2 +	3.0 +	4.0 +	4.0 +	3.0 +	-	4.0 +	Warning
onHelp	-	3.0 +	-	4.0 +	-	-	-	Warning
onKeyDown	1.2 +	3.0 +	4.0 +	4.0 +	3.0 +	-	4.0 +	Warning
onKeyPress	1.2 +	3.0 +	4.0 +	4.0 +	3.0 +	-	4.0 +	Warning
onKeyUp	1.2 +	3.0 +	4.0 +	4.0 +	3.0 +	-	4.0 +	Warning
onMouseDown	1.2 +	3.0 +	4.0 +	4.0 +	3.0 +	-	4.0 +	Warning
onMouseMove	1.2 +	3.0 +	4.0 +	4.0 +	-	-	4.0 +	Warning
onMouseOut	1.1 +	3.0 +	3.0 +	4.0 +	3.0 +	-	4.0 +	Warning
onMouseOver	1.0 +	1.0 +	2.0 +	3.0 +	3.0 +	-	4.0 +	Warning
onMouseUp	1.2 +	3.0 +	4.0 +	4.0 +	3.0 +	-	4.0 +	Warning

Inheritance chain:

Element object, Node object

userDefined object (Object/DOM)

You can define your own objects in several different ways.

Availability:	DOM level – 1 JavaScript – 1.5 JScript – 5.0 Internet Explorer – 5.0 Netscape – 6.0
JavaScript syntax:	-　　*myObject* = new Function()
	-　　*myObject* = new Object()

Aside from the ways in which you can create custom objects with your own constructor functions, you can also create your own HTML tags to make custom document elements.

Objects are instantiated from HTML tags and assume a class name from the HTML tag names in the document. So you can invent your own tags that become objects in the document model in MSIE, and inherit some basic capabilities from the environment. Netscape introduces this functionality at version 6.0.

See also:	*Object object*

userProfile object (Object/JScript)

An object that encapsulates a user's profile within the system.

Availability:	JScript – 3.0 Internet Explorer – 4.0
JavaScript syntax:	IE *myUserProfile* = navigator.userProfile
Object methods:	addReadRequest(), clearRequest(), doReadRequest(), getAttribute()

Through this object, a script can access details about the user from the profile that the system maintains.

This is accomplished by the arcane method of queueing requests for access. Then having queued all the requests, you can then ask the user for permission with a single dialog.

If the user grants permission, you can then access the userProfile values after which the request queue can be cleared.

Warnings:

❑ This is not fully supported on some versions of MSIE for Macintosh.

See also:	userProfile.addReadRequest(), userProfile.clearRequest(), userProfile.doReadRequest(), userProfile.getAttribute()

Method	JavaScript	JScript	N	IE	Opera	Notes
AddReadRequest()	-	3.0 +	-	4.0 +	-	-
clearRequest()	-	3.0 +	-	4.0 +	-	-
doReadRequest()	-	3.0 +	-	4.0 +	-	-
getAttribute()	-	3.0 +	-	4.0 +	-	Warning

JavaScript Programmer's Reference

U

about: URL (Request method)
AbstractView object (Object/DOM)
ActiveXObject object (Object/JScript)
Add (+) (Operator/additive)
Add then assign (+=) (Operator/
assignment)

var (Declaration)

A variable declarator.

Availability:	ECMAScript edition – 2 JavaScript – 1.0 JScript – 1.0 Internet Explorer- 3.02 Netscape – 2.0 Netscape Enterprise Server – 2.0 Opera – 3.0	
JavaScript syntax:	-	var *anIdentifier*
	-	var *anIdentifier* = *anInitialVaue*
	-	var *anIdentifier* = *anInitialVaue, anIdentifier* = *anInitialVaue, ...*
	-	var *anIdentifier,* *anIdentifier, ...*
Argument list:	*anIdentifier*	The name of a variable
	anInitialVaue	An initial value for the variable

The var keyword prefaces a list of variable declarations. The list is terminated by a semicolon.

Variables can be initialized in the declaration list that can declare a single variable or several at once.

If the var statement occurs inside a function declaration, the variables are defined with a scope that is local to that function body. Otherwise they are defined with global scope and are created as members of the Global object. When they are created as global variables, they take on the DontDelete property attributes.

Variables are created when an execution scope is entered. A block does not indicate a new execution scope so variables cannot be created local to a code block unless it is a function body. That means they are not local to an if(), while() or for() block of compound statements.

V

When variables are created, they are initialized to contain the value undefined. If an initializer is added to the variable declaration, the value is assigned when the var statement is executed, which may be some time after the execution scope has caused the variable to be created.

Warnings:

❑ If you fail to declare a variable with the var keyword, you will end up creating a global variable automatically. If the variable should only have local scope and duration within a function, then you may want to avoid this.

❑ You should use local variables as often as possible to avoid unwanted side effects.

Example code:

```
<HTML>
<HEAD>
</HEAD>
<BODY>
<SCRIPT>
var myGlobalVariable = 100;
function mLocalScope()
{
    var myLocalVariable = 200;
}
</SCRIPT>
</BODY>
</HTML>
```

See also: = *(Assign)*, *Assign value (=)*, Assignment expression, Assignment operator, *Comma operator (,)*, Compound statement, *function(...) ...*, *Global object*, Initialization, *Semicolon (;)*, Statement, Variable Declaration, Variable statement

Cross-references:

ECMA 262 edition 2 – section – 10.1.3

ECMA 262 edition 2 – section – 12.2

ECMA 262 edition 3 – section – 10.1.3

ECMA 262 edition 3 – section – 12.2

VBArray object (Object/JScript)

A special JScript object for interacting with Visual Basic or VBScript array data.

Availability:	JScript – 3.0 Internet Explorer- 4.0	
JavaScript syntax:	IE	*myVBArray* = new VBArray()
	IE	*myVBArray* = new VBArray(*aVisBasArray*)
	IE	*myVBArray* = VBArray
Argument list:	*aVisBasArray*	An array created inside Visual Basic or VBScript
Object methods:	dimensions(), getItem(), lbound(), toArray(), ubound()	

Because VBScript is only available on the Windows platform, this object has limited use in portable applications.

You might find it useful in an intranet scenario where you have total control over which browsers are deployed to the users. In that case, you know that your pages will be viewed on a compatible platform and can happily use this object with impunity.

Warnings:

❑ Because the Visual Basic interpreter is only available on a limited number of platforms, this functionality is likely to be limited only to those pages that need to work on the MSIE browser in a Windows environment. This technique is unlikely to work in any other context.

Example code:

```
<!-- An example taken from Wrox: Professional JavaScript -->
<SCRIPT LANGUAGE="VBScript">
function getArray()
dim arrVB(1)
arrVB(0) = 100
arrVB(1) = 250
getArray = arrVB
End function
</SCRIPT>
<SCRIPT LANGUAGGE="JavaScript">
var vbArr = new VBArray(getArray());
</SCRIPT>
```

Method	JavaScript	JScript	N	IE	Opera	Notes
dimensions()	-	3.0 +	-	4.0 +	-	-
getItem()	-	3.0 +	-	4.0 +	-	-
lbound()	-	3.0 +	-	4.0 +	-	-
toArray()	-	3.0 +	-	4.0 +	-	-
ubound()	-	3.0 +	-	4.0 +	-	-

vCard object (Object/JScript)

This is an object accessible only through the user preferences interface in the MSIE browser.

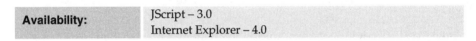

Availability:	JScript – 3.0
	Internet Explorer – 4.0

The vCard object is the parent object that contains all the user preferences settings.

There are basically three kinds of properties:

❑ Those that are members of the vCard.Business object

❑ Those that are members of the vCard.Home object

❑ Those that are members of the vCard object directly

Here is a list of all the user preference attributes that you can request:

❑ vCard.Business.City

❑ vCard.Business.Country

❑ vCard.Business.Fax

❑ vCard.Business.Phone

❑ vCard.Business.State

❑ vCard.Business.StreetAddress

❑ vCard.Business.URL

❑ vCard.Business.Zipcode

❑ vCard.Cellular

❑ vCard.Company

❑ vCard.Department

❑ vCard.DisplayName

❑ vCard.Email

❑ vCard.FirstName

874

- ❏ vCard.Home.City
- ❏ vCard.Home.Country
- ❏ vCard.Home.Fax
- ❏ vCard.Home.Phone
- ❏ vCard.Home.State
- ❏ vCard.Home.StreetAddress
- ❏ vCard.Home.Zipcode
- ❏ vCard.Homepage
- ❏ vCard.JobTitle
- ❏ vCard.LastName
- ❏ vCard.MiddleName
- ❏ vCard.Notes
- ❏ vCard.Office
- ❏ vCard.Pager

See also: `Navigator.userProfile, userProfile.addReadRequest(),`
`userProfile.getAttribute()`

view-source: URL (Request method)

You can use this for debugging in both Netscape and MSIE.

This is a useful debugging aid in some circumstances. Sometimes it is hard to download a file and this may give you a workaround.

To display a window containing the HTML version of a directory in the client machine, try this:

```
view-source:/
```

It works at least on Netscape version 4.7 on a Macintosh. It likely works on other platforms and versions of Netscape too.

The top level directory is the folder in which Netscape lives.

On a Macintosh at least, you can append a disk volume name, like this:

```
view-source:/MacintoshHD/
```

Beyond that you can build a path to any document in the Macintosh system, including this, which is very interesting.

```
view-source:/MacintoshHD/System%20Folder/System
```

JavaScript Programmer's Reference

V

This displays a preferences file:

```
view-source:
/MacintoshHD/System%20Folder/Preferences/Fetch%20Shortcuts
```

With this level of read access to your client machine, you might be able to browse various file content that normally you wouldn't have time to do. Point at a file and its data is visible right there on the screen in a browser window.

Warnings:

❑ Be very careful what you browse and how. This may void your warranty. Your mileage may vary. You may corrupt your system although read only access is unlikely to cause any harm.

See also:	*file: URL, javascript: URL*, URL

void (Operator/unary)

Force an undefined value to replace an operand.

Availability:	ECMAScript edition – 2 JavaScript – 1.1 JScript – 2.0 Internet Explorer – 4.0 Netscape – 3.0 Opera – 3.0	
Property/method value type:	Undefined primitive	
JavaScript syntax:	-	void (*anExpression*)
	-	void *anExpression*
Argument list:	*anExpression*	An expression to be evaluated

The void operator is used to allow the operand to be evaluated in the normal way (perhaps it is an expression or function call) but to force an undefined value to be returned in its place.

A very useful place for this is when you create JavaScript: URLs. Making sure the result of the expression is void helps the browser cope with the fact you are calling a script and not fetching a document. Don't use void however if you want the result of the JavaScript execution to be used as the content of a window.

This shows how to use void in a click handler:

```
<a HREF="javascript:void(callHandler('testString'));">
```

876

This shows how to force JavaScript result data into a window:

```
<a HREF="javascript:'<HR>Some text here</HR>'">
```

You can also use the `void` operator to manufacture an undefined value in older browsers that have no keyword already defined. The expression (void 0) is just such a value. This is unnecessary now that JScript 5.5 supports an undefined value in compliance with ECMA edition 2.

The associativity is from right to left.

Refer to the operator precedence topic for details of execution order.

This keyword also represents a Java data type and the `void` keyword allows for the potential extension of JavaScript interfaces to access Java applet parameters and return values.

This technique is also useful if you want to evaluate an expression merely for the benefit of its side effects and without any interest in the value it returns.

Warnings:

❑ The `void` keyword is not available in Netscape version 2.02, or MSIE version 3.02 or earlier versions of either.

Example code:

```
<HTML>
<HEAD>
</HEAD>
<BODY>
<SCRIPT>
if(document.myUndefinedProperty == (void 0))
{
    document.write("An undefined property has been referenced");
}
else
{
    document.write("A defined property was used");
}
</SCRIPT>
</BODY>
</HTML>
```

See also:	Assignment expression, Associativity, *javascript: URL*, LiveConnect, Operator, Operator Precedence, *typeof*, Unary expression, Unary operator, *undefined*

V

Cross-references:

ECMA 262 edition 2 – section – 11.4.2

ECMA 262 edition 3 – section – 11.4.2

Wrox *Instant JavaScript* – page – 21

volatile (Reserved word)

Reserved for future language enhancements.

The addition of this operator suggests that volatile identifiers may be supported in a later version of the ECMAScript standard.

See also:	*const*, Reserved word

Cross-references:

ECMA 262 edition 2 – section – 7.4.3

ECMA 262 edition 3 – section – 7.5.3

about: URL (Request method)
AbstractView object (Object/DOM)
ActiveXObject object (Object/JScript)
Add (+) (Operator/additive)
Add then assign (+=) (Operator/
assignment)

WAP (Standard)

Wireless Application Protocol.

This is a popular standard for use in mobile computing devices. It uses a derivative of the JavaScript standard language called WScript. This is constructed within a framework called WML which is built around a structure organized like a stack of cards rather than pages although the linkages between them are similar.

At the time of writing, this standard has become somewhat popular but there is already talk of it only being a transitory system. Future mobile computing devices may use something more sophisticated and therefore WAP may become less popular. Ultimately it will be made obsolete by a new standard.

See also:	Interpret, *WML*, *WScript*

watch() (Function/global)

Set a watch-point for a named property of an object.

Availability:	JavaScript – 1.2 Netscape – 4.0	
JavaScript syntax:	N	*myObject.watch(aProperty, aHandler)*
Argument list:	*aHandler*	A handler that gets called when the property changes
	aProperty	A property to watch

This method is provided to ease the task of debugging JavaScript.

It provides a general purpose way to call an unconnected function when a property value is changed. The function does not need to be called explicitly. The function that gets called has a particular API, which passes the following values:

❑ Property name

❑ Old value

❑ New value

It gets an opportunity to modify the new value or veto the change by returning the old value. Whatever value is returned is stored in the property. You can carry out other JavaScript tasks during this property call although it is probably best to avoid making changes to other property values with watch-points that call the same handler, because you could set up a recursive loop.

If you invoke the watch() method without specifying a receiving object, as if it were a function, you are actually setting watch-points on global object properties. Since this is where global variables live, you can monitor them as easily as object properties.

The new event model supported by Netscape 6.0 and that already available in MSIE 5.0 present a propertyName property that belongs to the Event object. You can inspect that during an onPropertyChanged event and achieve the same watch()/unwatch() behavior.

Example code:

```
<HTML>
<HEAD>
</HEAD>
<BODY>
<SCRIPT>
// Code works with Netscape 4+ only
// Define initial value for property
var XXX = 10;
// Define watch handler function
function watchHandler(aProp, anOldVal, aNewVal)
{
    var myText = "";

    myText += "Property name ...: ";
    myText += aProp;
    myText += "\n";

    myText += "Old value .......: ";
    myText += anOldVal;
    myText += "\n";

    myText += "New value .......: ";
    myText += aNewVal;
    myText += "\n";
    alert(myText);
    return aNewVal;
```

```
}
// Register the watch handler
watch("XXX", watchHandler);
</SCRIPT>
Some body text
<SCRIPT>
// Modify the property to trigger the watch handler
XXX = 1000;
</SCRIPT>
</BODY>
</HTML>
```

See also:	Event, Event handler, Event management, Event model, *Event object*, onPropertyChange, *unwatch()*, *Watchpoint handler*

Cross-references:

Wrox *Instant JavaScript* – page – 56

Watchpoint handler (Interface)

The handler that is connected to a watch point has a special pre-defined API specification.

JavaScript syntax:	-	function anId(aProp, oldVal, newVal) { someCode; return actualVal}
Argument list:	actualVal	The value that will be placed into the property
	anId	A name for your handler function
	aProp	A formal parameter to pass the property name in
	newVal	A formal parameter to pass the new value in
	oldVal	A formal parameter to pass the old value in

Your handler function is passed to the watch() method belonging to the object whose property you want to monitor.

When that property changes, your handler will be called.

You will be passed the following:

❑ The property name

❑ The old value

❑ The new value

Whatever you return from this handler will be stored in the property and will become its new value. This means you can return the old value, forcing the property to be read-only. You might change the new value to something else. Perhaps you would force the value to be all uppercase regardless of how it had been specified. You may even want to display an alert to warn the operator that the property is being changed.

See also:	*watch()*

while(...) ... (Iterator)

An iterator mechanism – a loop construct.

Availability:	ECMAScript edition – 2 JavaScript – 1.0 JScript – 1.0 Internet Explorer – 3.02 Netscape – 2.0 Netscape Enterprise Server version – 2.0 Opera – 3.0	
JavaScript syntax:	-	`while ( aCondition )` `{ someCode }`
	-	`aLabel: while ( aCondition )` `{ someCode }`
Argument list:	`aCondition`	If true, the loop cycles once more
	`aLabel`	An optional identifier name for the loop
	`someCode`	The code that gets looped

Although the `while()` statement is an iterator, it is functionally related to the `if()` statement since it will execute the statement block only as long as the condition evaluates to `true`.

The difference between `if()` and `while()` is that `if()` only processes the statement block once whereas `while()` processes the statement block repeatedly until something causes the condition enclosed in parentheses to evaluate to `false`.

A while loop tests the condition before execution of each pass through the loop. If a do loop is supported by the implementations, it would test the condition after each pass through the loop.

A `break` statement can be used to terminate a `while()` iterator prematurely, perhaps within a conditional test that is supplementary to the one in the `while()` heading.

A `continue` statement can be used to initiate the next cycle of the `while()` iterator.

The unlabeled form is more commonly used and was available from earlier releases of the JavaScript and JScript interpreters. Labeling was added later at version 1.2 but is not often used.

If a labeled continue is used, the condition is tested again, and the loop will cycle if necessary.

Warnings:

❑ Make sure that something in the statement block will cause the test condition to change to false otherwise you will create an endless loop that can never exit. How this is dealt with depends on what you are doing in the loop and whether the implementation can detect an endless loop situation. It is likely the process containing the JavaScript interpreter will either stall and hang or a run-time error may result. In extreme cases, the hosting application may crash and on some platforms, the entire system may halt. At the very least, you could expect memory and CPU usage to go up while the loop runs. On a multi-user system, you may be able to use an administrator account to kill the offending process.

Example code:

```
// An enumerator built with a while statement
var a = 10;
while(a > 0)
{
document.write("*");
a--;
}
// A labelled enumerator
a = 0;
head: while(a < 20)
{
document.write(a);
a++;
if(a > 10)
{
continue head;
}
document.write("*<BR>");
}
```

See also:	*break*, Compound statement, *continue, do ... while(...)*, Flow control, *for(...) ..., for(... in ...) ..., if(...) ...*, Iteration statement, Label, Obfuscation, *Off by one errors*

Cross-references:

ECMA 262 edition 2 – section – 12.6.1

ECMA 262 edition 2 – section – 12.7

ECMA 262 edition 2 – section – 12.8

ECMA 262 edition 3 – section – 12.6.2

Wrox *Instant JavaScript* – page – 23

Wrox *Instant JavaScript* – page – 25

Window object (Object/browser)

An object representing a window or frame. This object exposes methods, properties, and events associated with it to the script.

Availability:	JavaScript – 1.0 JScript – 1.0 Internet Explorer – 3.02 Netscape – 2.0 Opera – 3.0	
JavaScript syntax:	-	`myWindow = aFrameName`
	-	`myWindow = frames[anIndex]`
	-	`myWindow = opener`
	-	`myWindow = parent`
	-	`myWindow = self`
	-	`myWindow = top`
	-	`myWindow = window`
	-	`myWindow = window.open()`
	IE	`myWindow = document.parentWindow`
	IE	`myWindow = frame`
Argument list:	`anIndex`	An index to a `window` object
	`aFrameName`	The name of a frame in the window
Object properties:	`clientInformation, clipboardData, closed, crypto, defaultStatus, dialogArguments, dialogHeight, dialogLeft, dialogTop, dialogWidth, document, event, external, frame, frameRate, history, innerHeight, innerWidth, java, length, location, locationbar, Math, menubar, name, navigator, netscape, offScreenBuffering, opener, outerHeight, outerWidth, Packages, pageXOffset, pageYOffset, parent, personalbar, pkcs11, returnValue, screen, screenLeft, screenTop, screenX, screenY, scrollbars, secure, self, sidebar, status, statusbar, sun, toolbar, top, window`	

Object methods:	alert(), attachEvent(), back(), blur(), clearInterval(), clearTimeout(), close(), confirm(), detachEvent(), disableExternalCapture(), enableExternalCapture(), execScript(), find(), focus(), forward(), home(), moveBy(), moveTo(), navigate(), open(), print(), prompt(), resizeBy(), resizeTo(), scroll(), scrollBy(), scrollTo(), setHotkeys(), setInterval(), setResizable(), setTimeout(), setZOptions(), showHelp(), showModalDialog(), showModelessDialog(), stop()
Functions:	*atob(), btoa(), captureEvents(), handleEvent(), releaseEvents(), routeEvent()*
Event handlers:	onAfterPrint, onBeforePrint, onBeforeUnload, onBlur, onDragDrop, onError, onFocus, onHelp, onLoad, onMouseMove, onMove, onResize, onScroll, onUnload
Collections:	frames[]

The window object was introduced when JavaScript was made available at version 1.0. It has been revised several times and is likely to gain new functionality with every release.

This object is added to the scope chain as the global object when scripts are executed in a web browser. This means that the properties and methods are available without needing the window prefix.

In a web browser this IS the global object. Adding properties (variables) during script execution adds them to the window object for the window in which the page containing the script is loaded.

The window represents the browser container that the document object lives in.

Since the on-screen window persists as long as the window is open, you might think it may be a useful place to store some session state data between documents. Clearly, storing session data in a document object is no use if the document is going to be discarded and replaced. However, anything created by a script belonging to a window is going to get zapped when the document goes away, so you cannot store persistent values in the window object like that because the global object for a web page is recreated each time a page is loaded.

Storing session state data is best accomplished with a frame-set and some accessor scripts that are called within it.

Event handling support via properties containing function objects was added to window objects in version 1.1 of JavaScript.

W

Warnings:

❏ Be aware that if you store a reference to a window object and the window is closed, if you don't dispose of the reference to the window object then it cannot be garbage collected. A window object with no associated window is not much use unless you need to keep the object persistent due to having added some properties to it. If this is the case, then, arguably, the window object was the wrong place to put such things.

See also:	BODY object, captureEvents(), Collection object, Document object, Document.activeElement, Document.captureEvents(), Document.frames[], Document.parentWindow, Document.releaseEvents(), EventCapturer object, Frame object, Frames object, Global object, IFRAME object, Layer.captureEvents(), Layer.releaseEvents(), Layer.window, self, Window.frame

Property	JavaScript	JScript	N	IE	Opera	HTML	Notes
client Information	-	3.0 +	-	4.0 +	-	-	Warning, ReadOnly, DontEnum
clipboardData	-	5.0 +	-	5.0 +	-	-	-
closed	1.1 +	3.0 +	3.0 +	4.0 +	3.0 +	-	Warning, ReadOnly
crypto	1.2 +	-	4.04 +	-	-	-	ReadOnly
defaultStatus	1.0 +	1.0 +	2.0 +	3.02 +	3.0 +	-	Warning
dialog Arguments	-	3.0 +	-	4.0 +	-	-	ReadOnly
dialogHeight	-	3.0 +	-	4.0 +	-	-	-
dialogLeft	-	3.0 +	-	4.0 +	-	-	-
dialogTop	-	3.0 +	-	4.0 +	-	-	-
dialogWidth	-	3.0 +	-	4.0 +	-	-	-
document	1.0 +	1.0 +	2.0 +	3.02 +	3.0 +	-	Warning, ReadOnly
event	-	3.0 +	-	4.0 +	-	-	Warning, ReadOnly
external	-	5.0 +	-	5.0 +	-	-	-
frame	-	5.0 +	-	5.0 +	-	-	Warning, ReadOnly
frameRate	1.2 +	-	4.0 +	-	-	-	ReadOnly
history	1.1 +	3.0 +	3.0 +	4.0 +	3.0 +	-	Warning, ReadOnly
innerHeight	1.2 +	-	4.0 +	-	5.0 +	-	Warning
innerWidth	1.2 +	-	4.0 +	-	5.0 +	-	Warning
java	1.1 +	-	3.0 +	-	-	-	ReadOnly

Property	JavaScript	JScript	N	IE	Opera	HTML	Notes
length	1.0 +	3.0 +	2.0 +	4.0 +	3.0 +	-	ReadOnly
location	1.0 +	1.0 +	2.0 +	3.02 +	3.0 +	-	Warning, ReadOnly
locationbar	1.2 +	-	4.0 +	-	5.0 +	-	Warning, ReadOnly
Math	1.0 +	1.0 +	2.0 +	3.02 +	3.0 +	-	Warning
menubar	1.2 +	-	4.0 +	-	-	-	Warning, ReadOnly
name	1.0 +	1.0 +	2.0 +	3.02 +	3.0 +	-	Warning
navigator	1.0 +	3.0 +	2.0 +	4.0 +	3.0 +	-	Warning, ReadOnly
netscape	1.1 +	-	3.0 +	-	-	-	ReadOnly
offScreen Buffering	1.2 +	3.0 +	4.0 +	4.0 +	-	-	Warning
opener	1.1 +	3.0 +	3.0 +	4.0 +	3.0 +	-	Warning, ReadOnly
outerHeight	1.2 +	-	4.0 +	-	5.0 +	-	Warning, ReadOnly
outerWidth	1.2 +	-	4.0 +	-	5.0 +	-	Warning, ReadOnly
Packages	1.1 +	-	3.0 +	-	3.0 +	-	ReadOnly
pageXOffset	1.2 +	-	4.0 +	-	5.0 +	-	ReadOnly
pageYOffset	1.2 +	-	4.0 +	-	5.0 +	-	ReadOnly
parent	1.0 +	1.0 +	2.0 +	3.02 +	3.0 +	-	Warning, ReadOnly
personalbar	1.2 +	-	4.0 +	-	-	-	Warning, ReadOnly
pkcs11	1.2 +	-	4.04 +	-	-	-	ReadOnly
returnValue	-	3.0 +	-	4.0 +	-	-	Warning
screen	1.2 +	3.0 +	4.0 +	4.0 +	5.0 +	-	Warning, ReadOnly
screenLeft	-	5.0 +	-	5.0 +	-	-	ReadOnly
screenTop	-	5.0 +	-	5.0 +	-	-	ReadOnly
screenX	1.2 +	-	4.0 +	-	-	-	-
screenY	1.2 +	-	4.0 +	-	-	-	-
scrollbars	1.2 +	-	4.0 +	-	-	-	Warning, ReadOnly
secure	1.2 +	-	4.0 +	-	-	-	ReadOnly
self	1.0 +	1.0 +	2.0 +	3.02 +	3.0 +	-	ReadOnly
sidebar	1.5 +	-	6.0 +	-	-	-	-
status	1.0 +	1.0 +	2.0 +	3.02 +	3.0 +	-	Warning
statusbar	1.2 +	-	4.0 +	-	-	-	Warning, ReadOnly

Table continued on following page

JavaScript Programmer's Reference

W

Property	JavaScript	JScript	N	IE	Opera	HTML	Notes
sun	1.1 +	-	3.0 +	-	-	-	ReadOnly
toolbar	1.2 +	-	4.0 +	-	-	-	Warning, ReadOnly
top	1.0 +	1.0 +	2.0 +	3.02 +	3.0 +	-	Warning, ReadOnly
window	1.0 +	1.0 +	2.0 +	3.02 +	3.0 +	-	Warning, ReadOnly

Method	JavaScript	JScript	N	IE	Opera	HTML	Notes
alert()	1.0 +	1.0 +	2.0 +	3.02 +	3.0 +	-	Warning
attachEvent()	-	5.0 +	-	5.0 +	-	-	Warning
back()	1.2 +	-	4.0 +	-	-	-	Warning
blur()	1.1 +	3.0 +	3.0 +	4.0 +	3.0 +	-	Warning
clearInterval()	1.2 +	3.0 +	4.0 +	4.0 +	-	-	Warning
clearTimeout()	1.0 +	1.0 +	2.0 +	3.02 +	3.0 +	-	Warning
close()	1.0 +	1.0 +	2.0 +	3.02 +	3.0 +	-	Warning
confirm()	1.0 +	1.0 +	2.0 +	3.02 +	3.0 +	-	-
detachEvent()	-	5.0 +	-	5.0 +	-	-	-
disableExternalCapture()	1.2 +	-	4.0 +	-	-	-	Warning
enableExternalCapture()	1.2 +	-	4.0 +	-	-	-	Warning
execScript()	-	3.0 +	-	4.0 +	-	-	-
find()	1.2 +	-	4.0 +	-	-	-	-
focus()	1.1 +	3.0 +	3.0 +	4.0 +	3.0 +	-	Warning
forward()	1.2 +	-	4.0 +	-	-	-	Warning
home()	1.2 +	-	4.0 +	-	-	-	-
moveBy()	1.2 +	3.0 +	4.0 +	4.0 +	-	-	Warning
moveTo()	1.2 +	3.0 +	4.0 +	4.0 +	-	-	Warning
navigate()	-	1.0 +	-	3.02 +	-	-	Warning
open()	1.0 +	1.0 +	2.0 +	3.02 +	3.0 +	-	Warning
print()	1.2 +	5.0 +	4.0 +	5.0 +	-	-	Warning
prompt()	1.0 +	1.0 +	2.0 +	3.02 +	3.0 +	-	Warning
resizeBy()	1.2 +	3.0 +	4.0 +	4.0 +	-	-	Warning
resizeTo()	1.2 +	3.0 +	4.0 +	4.0 +	-	-	Warning
scroll()	1.1 +	3.0 +	3.0 +	4.0 +	3.0 +	-	Warning, Deprecated
scrollBy()	1.2 +	3.0 +	4.0 +	4.0 +	-	-	Warning
scrollTo()	1.2 +	3.0 +	4.0 +	4.0 +	-	-	Warning
setHotkeys()	1.2 +	-	4.0 +	-	-	-	Warning
setInterval()	1.2 +	3.0 +	4.0 +	4.0 +	-	-	Warning
setResizable()	1.2 +	-	4.0 +	-	-	-	Warning

Method	JavaScript	JScript	N	IE	Opera	HTML	Notes
setTimeout()	1.0 +	1.0 +	2.0 +	3.02 +	3.0 +	-	Warning
setZOptions()	1.2 +	-	4.0 +	-	-	-	Warning
showHelp()	-	3.0 +	-	4.0 +	-	-	Warning
showModal Dialog()	-	3.0 +	-	4.0 +	-	-	Warning
showModeless Dialog()	-	5.0 +	-	5.0 +	-	-	-
stop()	1.2 +	-	4.0 +	-	-	-	Warning

Event name	JavaScript	JScript	N	IE	Opera	HTML	Notes
onAfterPrint	-	5.0 +	-	5.0 +	-	-	-
onBeforePrint	-	5.0 +	-	5.0 +	-	-	-
onBeforeUnload	-	3.0 +	-	4.0 +	-	-	-
onBlur	1.1 +	3.0 +	3.0 +	4.0 +	3.0 +	-	Warning
onDragDrop	1.2 +	-	4.0 +	-	-	-	-
onError	1.1 +	3.0 +	3.0 +	4.0 +	3.0 +	-	Warning
onFocus	1.0 +	3.0 +	2.0 +	4.0 +	3.0 +	-	Warning
onHelp	-	3.0 +	-	4.0 +	-	-	Warning
onLoad	1.0 +	1.0 +	2.0 +	3.02 +	3.0 +	-	Warning
onMouseMove	1.2 +	3.0 +	4.0 +	4.0 +	-	4.0 +	Warning
onMove	1.2 +	-	4.0 +	-	-	-	-
onResize	1.2 +	3.0 +	4.0 +	4.0 +	-	-	Warning
onScroll	-	3.0 +	-	4.0 +	-	-	-
onUnload	1.0 +	1.0 +	2.0 +	3.02 +	3.0 +	-	Warning

Window.atob() (Function)

Decode some base-64 encoded data.

Availability:	JavaScript – 1.2 Netscape – 4.0	
Property/method value type:	String primitive	
JavaScript syntax:	N	atob(aBase64String)
	N	myWindow.atob(aBase64String)
Argument list:	aBase64String	A string containing base-64 encoded data

This function provides a means of decoding base-64 encoded values which represent an encoded form of some binary data. This encoding can be applied to text too but is most useful where you have a block of non-textual content.

JavaScript Programmer's Reference

W

The base-64 data is decoded and converted to a block of binary data. This is then stored in a string primitive and returned to the caller as the result of the method.

To extract the binary data from the string, you will need to parse the string a character at a time and extract the numeric character value with the `String.charCodeAt()` method. You can modify the binary data directly by storing numeric values at each character position.

Note that the string will contain a sequence of 8 bit bytes and so you will need to be careful to range-limit any values that you store in the binary string.

The result is a block of binary data in a string primitive. This is somewhat cumbersome and not likely to be much used outside of a mail-reading client.

See also:	`String.charAt()`, `String.charCodeAt()`, String.fromCharCode(), Window.btoa()

Window.btoa() (Function)

Encode some data into base-64 form.

Availability:	JavaScript – 1.2 Netscape – 4.0	
Property/method value type:	`String primitive`	
JavaScript syntax:	N	`btoa(aBinaryString)`
	N	`myWindow.btoa` `(aBinaryString)`
Argument list:	`aBinaryString`	A string of binary data to be encoded

This function will encode the string passed as an argument and return a base-64 encoded version. Base-64 encoding is used to convert binary data into a form that survives transmission across a network, so the data passed in its input argument is really binary data. It is carried in a string value because JavaScript doesn't support a special binary container. However, JavaScript strings will happily accept 8 bit values and you can therefore store binary data in them. You would normally create the string of binary data by means of the `String.fromCharCode()` static method.

The result is a string of binary data escaped in such a way that it will survive a serial transfer through an "old-fashioned" connection. Network drivers and serial interfacing technology makes this technique largely redundant and there can be few genuine applications for this other than to decode information from legacy systems or to interface to them somehow from a web browser. The functionality has very limited portability and will likely be deprecated at some stage in the future.

See also:	String.fromCharCode(), Window.atob()

Window.captureEvents() (Function)

Part of the Netscape Navigator 4 event propagation complex.

Availability:	JavaScript – 1.2 Netscape – 4.0	
Deprecated:	JavaScript – 1.5 Netscape – 6.0	
Property/method value type:	undefined	
JavaScript syntax:	N	captureEvents (anEventMask)
	N	myWindow.captureEvents (anEventMask)
Argument list:	anEventMask	A mask constructed with the manifest event constants

This is part of the event management suite which allows events to be routed to handlers other than just the one that defaults to being associated with an event.

The events to be captured are signified by setting bits in a mask.

This method allows you to specify what events are to be routed to the receiving window object.

The events are specified by using the bitwise OR operator to combine the required event mask constants into a mask that defines the events you want to capture. Refer to the Event Type Constants topic for a list of the event mask values.

A limitation of this technique is that, ultimately, only 32 different kinds of events can be combined in this way and this may limit the number of events the browser can support. If you need to build complex event handling systems in Netscape Navigator 4.x, you will have to implement scripts using this technique. A different script will be required for MSIE.

You may be able to factor your event handler so that you only have to make platform specific event dispatchers and can call common handling routines that can be shared between MSIE and Netscape Navigator.

This method is supported by virtually every object by virtue of the fact that it is available as a method of the Global object in Netscape Navigator. Therefore it gets inherited into the scope chain for every script and function (method).

Warnings:

❑ Since a bit mask is being used, this must be an int32 value. This suggests that there can only be 32 different event types supported by this event propagation model.

❑ This capability is deprecated and is not supported in Netscape 6.0 . It has never been supported by MSIE which implements a completely different event model. As it turns out, the DOM level 2 event model converges on the MSIE technique.

JavaScript Programmer's Reference

W

Example code:

```
// Build and setup a mask for several events
myEventMask = Event.KEYDOWN | Event.MOUSEDOWN | Event.RESET;
window.captureEvents(myEventMask);
function EventHandler(anEventObject)
{
//... some event handling code here
}
window.onkeydown    = EventHandler;
window.onmousedown = EventHandler;
window.onreset      = EventHandler;
```

See also:	*captureEvents()*, *Document.captureEvents()*, `Element.onevent`, Event propagation, *Event type constants*, *Frame object*, *Layer.captureEvents()*, *onMouseMove*, *Window object*, *Window.releaseEvents()*

Window.handleEvent() (Function)

Pass an event to the appropriate handler for the window.

Availability:	JavaScript – 1.2 Netscape – 4.0	
Property/method value type:	`undefined`	
JavaScript syntax:	N	`handleEvent(anEvent)`
	N	`myWindow.handleEvent (anEvent)`
Argument list:	`anEvent`	An event to be handled by this object

This applies to Netscape Navigator prior to version 6.0. From that release onwards, event management follows the guidelines in the DOM level 2 event specification.

On receipt of a call to this method, the receiving object will look at its available set of event handler functions and pass the event to an appropriately mapped handler function. It is essentially an event dispatcher that is granular down to the object level.

The argument value is an `event` object that contains information about the event.

See also:	*Event object*, Event propagation, *Frame object*, *handleEvent()*, `SubmitButton.handleEvent()`, `TEXTAREA.handleEvent()`, `TextCell.handleEvent()`, *Window object*, *Window.routeEvent()*

Window.releaseEvents() (Function)

Part of the Netscape Navigator 4 event propagation complex.

Availability:	JavaScript – 1.2 Netscape – 4.0	
Property/method value type:	`undefined`	
JavaScript syntax:	N	`myWindow.releaseEvents (anEventMask)`
	N	`releaseEvents (anEventMask)`
Argument list:	*anEventMask*	A mask defined with the manifest event constants

This is part of the event management suite which allows events to be routed to handlers other than just the one that defaults to being associated with an event.

The events to be captured are signified by setting bits in a mask.

This method provides a means of indicating which events are no longer needing to be captured by the receiving window object.

The events are specified by using the bitwise OR operator to combine the required event mask constants into a mask that defines the events you want to capture. Refer to the Event Type Constants topic for a list of the event mask values.

We have to implement scripts using this capability if we need to build complex event handling systems on Netscape 4.x. A different script will be required for MSIE.

You may be able to factor your event handler so that you only have to make platform specific event dispatchers and can call common handling routines that can be shared between MSIE and Netscape Navigator.

See also:	*captureEvents(), Document.captureEvents(), Document.releaseEvents(),* `Element.onevent,` *Event* names, *Event* propagation, *Event type constants,* `Event.modifiers,` *Frame object, Layer.captureEvents(), Layer.releaseEvents(),* `onMouseMove,` *Window object, Window.captureEvents()*

Window.routeEvent() (Function)

Part of the Netscape Navigator 4 event propagation complex.

Availability:	JavaScript – 1.2 Netscape – 4.0	
Property/method value type:	`undefined`	
JavaScript syntax:	N	`myWindow.routeEvent (anEvent)`
	N	`routeEvent(anEvent)`
Argument list:	*anEvent*	An event object

W

This is part of the event management suite which allows events to be routed to handlers other than just the one that defaults to being associated with an event.

Depending on the current setting of the event type mask for the receiving object, an event may be available for processing with this method. An initial mask that enumerates the events to be received might have been set up with the captureEvents() method. Then perhaps sometime later, some of those events may have been deselected by means of the releaseEvents() method. The remaining mask defines the finite set of events that will be visible to the object.

So, when a suitable event arrives and is captured, it can be passed on to the appropriately mapped event handler function belonging to the next object in the event handling hierarchy or to another handler belonging to the receiving object.

This means that an event can be processed via several handlers within an object before being passed to the next object in sequence. The order in which handlers and objects are visited by the event is controlled by Netscape Navigator. However, whether the event is passed on or not is controlled by the script in the handler. If it chooses not to pass on the event, then no subsequent handlers will see it, nor will any other objects.

This trickle down effect is somewhat clumsy and uncontrolled. You can gain some control over the way that events are propagated with the handleEvent() method and applying it to the various objects that need to take the event. This does disperse the event handling around the scripts somewhat and can be difficult to maintain.

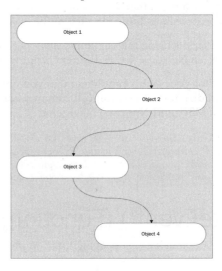

Warnings:

❑ This entire mechanism may become obsolete when the W3C standardizes the event handling process for the Document Object Model.

See also: captureEvents(), Event handler, Event management, Event propagation, *Frame object, handleEvent(), Layer.routeEvent(), Window object, Window.handleEvent()*

with ... (Statement)

Adds an object to the front of the scope chain for use in the following block of script code.

Availability:	ECMAScript edition – 2 JavaScript – 1.0 JScript – 1.0 Internet Explorer – 3.02 Netscape – 2.0 Netscape Enterprise Server – 2.0 Opera – 3.0	
JavaScript syntax:	-	with(anObject) { someCode };
Argument list:	someCode	Some code to execute with the enhanced scope chain
	anObject	A reference to an object to add to the scope chain

This statement is provided as a convenience mechanism to simplify your script code and save time and trouble.

When a statement executes, your line of script is running in one context or another. Each context is created and destroyed as functions are called and exit respectively. The contexts are added to an inheritance chain, which allows variables to be shared globally or locally.

The with keyword adds an object to the front of the scope chain for the current execution context. This saves you having to describe the full object reference since it is placed in the scope chain and always available and implicitly provided by JavaScript when resolving references to identifiers.

The code in the statement block is then executed while this augmented scope chain is in place. The object that is added to the scope chain is computed by the expression value in parentheses.

When the statement block is executed, the scope chain is restored to its original condition. This happens regardless of how the statement block is completed. Although the ECMA standard is ambiguous on this point, the implication is that a break might be appropriate in this context. A continue or return in the statement block would be inappropriate unless perhaps the with() construct is used within an iterator or function. Because of this ambiguity, you may find this behaves differently according to the implementation you are using.

The with statement can save you the effort of typing object names over and over again.

Warnings:

❑ Even though it is very convenient, it is considered somewhat bad form to use this construct. The code is hard to optimize inside the interpreter, which means it will likely run more slowly. Functions and variables instantiated inside a with block do not behave consistently, so it is recommended that you avoid using this construct.

Example code:

```
// Create a new object
var myObject = new Object;
// Add a property containing another object
myObject.itsObject = new Object;
// Add a property to that object
myObject.itsObject.someProperty = "String text";
// Now enhance the scope chain
with(myObject.itsObject)
{
    document.write(someProperty);
}
```

See also: Identifier, Identifier resolution, Scope chain, Statement

Cross-references:

ECMA 262 edition 2 – section – 10.1.4

ECMA 262 edition 2 – section – 12.10

ECMA 262 edition 3 – section – 10.1.4

ECMA 262 edition 3 – section – 12.10

Wrox *Instant JavaScript* – page – 35

WML (Standard)

Wireless Mark-up Language.

This is the markup language used to describe cards (analogous to pages) in a wireless mobile device. This is the framework in which the WScript code will run. This is variously referred to as WScript and WMLScript and should not be confused with the WScript that Microsoft refer to as being a component of WSH.

See also: Interpret, *WAP*, *WScript*

WScript (Standard)

Otherwise known as WMLScript or WAP Script – a variation of JavaScript for use in mobile devices.

This is the somewhat modified version of JavaScript, which is used in WAP mobile devices such as cellphones.

Warnings:

❑ Be aware that Microsoft have implemented a WScript object as part of the WSH environment. That object has absolutely nothing to do with WAP or mobile telecommunications. It is a container for an object model that is fundamental to WSH.

See also:	Host environment, Interpret, Platform, Script execution, WAP, WML

WScript object (Object/WSH)

An object that represents the object model of the WSH framework.

Availability:	JScript – 3.0	
JavaScript syntax:	WSH	WScript
Object properties:	Application, Arguments, FullName, Name, Network, Path, ScriptFullName, ScriptName, StdErr, StdIn, StdOut, Version	
Object methods:	CreateObject(), DisconnectObject(), Echo(), GetObject(), Quit(), Sleep()	

Property	JavaScript	JScript	HTML	Notes
Application	-	3.0 +	-	-
Arguments	-	3.0 +	-	-
FullName	-	3.0 +	-	-
Name	-	3.0 +	-	-
Network	-	3.0 +	-	-
Path	-	3.0 +	-	-
ScriptFullName	-	3.0 +	-	-
ScriptName	-	3.0 +	-	-
StdErr	-	3.0 +	-	-
StdIn	-	3.0 +	-	-
StdOut	-	3.0 +	-	-
Version	-	3.0 +	-	-

Method	JavaScript	JScript	HTML	Notes
CreateObject()	-	3.0 +	-	-
DisconnectObject()	-	3.0 +	-	-
Echo()	-	3.0 +	-	-
GetObject()	-	3.0 +	-	-
Quit()	-	3.0 +	-	-
Sleep()	-	3.0 +	-	-

JavaScript Programmer's Reference

W

wysiwyg: (Request method)

Special URL method to handle page content when resized in Netscape Navigator.

If a page is generated using JavaScript, then if the page is subsequently resized, this special method is used to encapsulate the previous page location and invoke special handling to ensure that the page is printed properly.

about: URL (Request method)
AbstractView object (Object/DOM)
ActiveXObject object (Object/JScript)
Add (+) (Operator/additive)
Add then assign (+=) (Operator/
   assignment)

XML (Standard)

Extensible Mark-up Language.

This is gradually becoming commonplace as a way to exchange data between systems. It is also supported by the MSIE browser and you can load in XML documents directly.

It is the future direction that HTML will evolve towards, beginning with XHTML.

This topic is the entry point to a complete new subject area. It's too vast to attempt to cover it meaningfully in just a few pages and yes, it's probably going to become one of the most important parts of the web programming landscape.

Refer to the Wrox *Professional XML* for details of how to use it in earnest. Here we will just scratch on the surface to begin to see what it looks like.

This creates a new XML document via ActiveX:

```
myXMLDoc = new ActiveXObject("Microsoft.XMLDOM");
```

Having created it, now we can load the contents of a URL into the object:

```
myXMLDoc.load("http://xmlserver.domain.com/reports.xml");
```

This is useful because one big problem with JavaScript in a web browser is that it's very hard to download a data file from a web server to a script without having to work around lots of security issues. This might solve that problem a lot more elegantly.

Now we can begin to look at the contents of the file and extract information from it.

```
myXMLDoc.loadXML("JoeSmith");
```

Now that we have acquired the document we can use the DOM navigation techniques that already work for HTML documents to walk through the XML structures:

```
var myXMLNodeList = myXMLDoc.getElementsByTagName(strNodeName);
```

XML object (Object/JScript)

An object that represents a block of XML page content within an HTML document.

Availability:	JScript – 5.0 Internet Explorer version – 5.0	
Inherits from:	*Element object*	
JavaScript syntax:	IE	`myXML =` `myDocument.all.anElementID`
	IE	`myXML = myDocument.all` `.tags("XML")[anIndex]`
	IE	`myXML = myDocument.all[aName]`
	-	`myXML = myDocument` `.getElementById(anElementID)`

	-	`myXML = myDocument`
		`.getElementsByName`
		`(aName)[anIndex]`

	-	`myXML = myDocument`
		`.getElementsByTagName`
		`("XML")[anIndex]`

Argument list:	`anIndex`	A reference to an element in a collection
	`aName`	An associative array reference
	`anElementID`	The `ID` value of an `Element` object
Object properties:	`canHaveHTML, defer, event, htmlFor, src,` `text, type`	

Event handlers:	`onDataAvailable, onDatasetChanged,`
	`onDatasetComplete, onReadyStateChange,`
	`onRowEnter, onRowExit, onRowsDelete,`
	`onRowsInserted`	

The MSIE browser can now cope with pages delivered as arbitrary blocks of XML. If it encounters an <XML> tag, then it will instantiate one of these objects to provide JavaScript binding to it. This can also be used to build a small island of XML based content in the middle of an HTML page.

The XML data can sit in an HTML page like this:

```
<XML ID="myBlock">

<METADATA>

<OWNER>Wrox</OWNER>

<DATATYPE>Example</DATATYPE>

<ABSTRACT>This is an example block of text</ABSTRACT>

</METADATA>

</XML>
```

Accessing the `text` property of the `XML` object will return all the inner text inside it. To access the components you will need to access the `XMLDocument` property to expose a DOM document interface. This can be explored using DOM compatible methods and properties.

See also:	Document.readyState, onRowEnter, onRowExit

Property	JavaScript	JScript	Nav	IE	Opera	Notes
canHaveHTML	-	5.0 +	-	5.0 +	-	-
defer	-	5.0 +	-	5.0 +	-	-
event	-	5.0 +	-	5.0 +	-	-
htmlFor	-	5.0 +	-	5.0 +	-	-
src	-	5.0 +	-	5.0 +	-	-
text	-	5.0 +	-	5.0 +	-	-
type	-	5.0 +	-	5.0 +	-	-

Event name	JavaScript	JScript	Nav	IE	Opera	Notes
onDataAvailable	-	3.0 +	-	4.0 +	-	-
onDatasetChanged	-	3.0 +	-	4.0 +	-	-
onDatasetComplete	-	3.0 +	-	4.0 +	-	-
onReadyStateChange	-	3.0 +	-	4.0 +	-	-
onRowEnter	-	3.0 +	-	4.0 +	-	-
onRowExit	-	3.0 +	-	4.0 +	-	-
onRowsDelete	-	3.0 +	-	4.0 +	-	-
onRowsInserted	-	3.0 +	-	4.0 +	-	-

Inheritance chain:

`Element` object, `Node` object

Web-references:

http://msdn.microsoft.com/xml/xmlguide/dom-guide-document.asp

about: URL (Request method)
AbstractView object (Object/DOM)
ActiveXObject object (Object/JScript)
Add (+) (Operator/additive)
Add then assign (+=) (Operator/assignment)

Symbols

= (Assign) (Operator/assignment)

Assign the right value to the left operand.

Availability:	ECMAScript edition – 2 JavaScript – 1.0 JScript – 1.0 Internet Explorer – 3.02 Netscape – 2.0 Netscape Enterprise Server – 2.0 Opera – 3.0
Property/method value type:	Depends on right value

Warnings:

❑ The operand to the left of the operator must be an LValue. That is, it should be able to take an assignment and store the value.

❑ Be careful not to confuse the single equals with the double equals. Placing a double equals in place of an assignment will not assign the value and may be considered to be a syntax error, since it may perform a comparison in entirely the wrong context. The interpreter may be forgiving enough that a run-time error isn't generated though, but the side effects could be subtle and make it hard to diagnose the cause.

See also:	*Assign value (=)*, Assignment operator, *Equal to (==)*, Equality operator, LValue, *var*, Variable statement

Cross-references:

ECMA 262 edition 2 – section – 11.13

ECMA 262 edition 2 – section – 12.2

ECMA 262 edition 3 – section – 11.13

ECMA 262 edition 3 – section – 12.2

@*/ (Pre-processor)

The closing pre-processor directive comment delimiter.

Availability:	JScript – 3.0 Internet Explorer – 4.0	
JavaScript syntax:	IE	`/*@someDirectives@*/`
Argument list:	`someDirectives`	One or more directives

See also:	Pre-processing, *Pre-processing – /*@ ... @*/*

! object (Object/HTML)

An object representing a `<!DOCTYPE>` DTD statement tag at the front of a document.

Availability:	DOM level – 1 JScript – 5.0 Internet Explorer – 5.0	
Inherits from:	*Element object*	
JavaScript syntax:	IE	`myDoctype = myDocument.all.tags("!")[0]`
	IE	`myDoctype = myDocument.all[anIndex]`
	IE	`myDoctype = myDocument.getElementById (anElementID)`
	IE	`myDoctype = myDocument .getElementsByName(aName)[anIndex]`
	IE	`myDoctype = myDocument.doctype`
	IE	`myDoctype = myDocument.getElements ByTagName("!")[anIndex]`
HTML syntax:	`<!DOCTYPE aDocumentDescription>`	
Argument list:	`aDocumentDescription`	A reference to a DTD for this document
	`anIndex`	A reference to an element in a collection
	`aName`	An associative array reference
	`anElementID`	The `ID` value of an `Element` object
Object properties:	`accessKey, tabIndex`	
Event handlers:	`onClick, onDblClick, onHelp, onKeyDown, onKeyPress, onKeyUp, onMouseDown, onMouseMove, onMouseOut, onMouseOver, onMouseUp`	

The MSIE implementation creates an object that has a constructor name that suggests its class is "!". This is very odd, and if you intend to do any work on object classes, then naming a class with what might be interpreted as a special character in the script source may lead to some problems.

This is really a Doctype object and is specified in the DOM standard as a <!DOCTYPE> element.

The recommended means of access is to retrieve the value of the doctype property of the document you want to operate on. This is normally document.doctype for the current window but in the case of multiple frames, layers or windows you may be referring to the doctype of a different document object.

This object appears to inherit all of the properties of an HTML element.

See also:	!.tabIndex, Document.doctype, *Element object*, Input.accessKey

Property	JavaScript	JScript	N	IE	Opera	DOM	HTML	Notes
accessKey	-	5.0 +	-	5.0 +	-	1 +	-	-
tabIndex	-	5.0 +	-	5.0 +	-	-	-	Warning

Event name	JavaScript	JScript	N	IE	Opera	DOM	HTML	Notes
onClick	-	5.0 +	-	5.0 +	-	-	4.0 +	Warning
onDblClick	-	5.0 +	-	5.0 +	-	-	4.0 +	Warning
onHelp	-	5.0 +	-	5.0 +	-	-	-	Warning
onKeyDown	-	5.0 +	-	5.0 +	-	-	4.0 +	Warning
onKeyPress	-	5.0 +	-	5.0 +	-	-	4.0 +	Warning
onKeyUp	-	5.0 +	-	5.0 +	-	-	4.0 +	Warning
onMouseDown	-	5.0 +	-	5.0 +	-	-	4.0 +	Warning
onMouseMove	-	5.0 +	-	5.0 +	-	-	4.0 +	Warning
onMouseOut	-	5.0 +	—	5.0 +	-	-	4.0 +	Warning
onMouseOver	-	5.0 +	-	5.0 +	-	-	4.0 +	Warning
onMouseUp	—	5.0 +	—	5.0 +	—	-	4.0 +	Warning

Inheritance chain:

Element object, Node object

about: URL (Request method)
AbstractView object (Object/DOM)
ActiveXObject object (Object/JScript)
Add (+) (Operator/additive)
Add then assign (+=) (Operator/assignment)

Cross Reference by Entry Type

Each entry in this reference has a type or class, for example, 'object/HTML' for the A object. This cross-reference is ordered by entry type, with corresponding entries listed alphabetically beneath.

The collections, events, methods and properties entry types are slightly different because they list the collection, event, method or property name first and the actual entry name (which incorporates the object name) second.

Collections, events, methods and properties often have their own detailed entries, but information on browser support for them is also provided in the entry for the object to which they belong. References to both entries are listed where they exist.

An asterisk is used to show which entries are in the book. Entries without an asterisk will be found on the CD only.

Advice (see also Pitfall, Useful tip)
Adding JavaScript to HTML
Associative array indexing
Bookmarklets
Browser detection
Browser version compatibility
Character handling
Color value
Compatibility strategies
Cookie
Copying objects
Debugging - client side
Defensive coding
E-mail containing JavaScript
JavaScript Bookmark URLs
JavaScript debugger console
News posts containing JavaScript
Obfuscation
Pitfalls

ASP tag
<% ... %> (Server side code block)

Attribute
Cookie domain*
Cookie expires*
Cookie path*
Cookie secure*
Cookie value
ImplicitParents*
ImplicitThis*

Background (see also Definition, Overview, Standard)
ECMAScript
History
Overview
Version History

Collection
all[], Document.all[]
all[], Element.all[]
anchors[], Document.anchors[]
applets[], Document.applets[]
areas[]
areas[], Map.areas[]
arguments[]
arguments[], Function.arguments[]
attributes[], Element.attributes[]
attributes[], Node.attributes[]
behaviorUrns[], Element.behaviorUrns[]
bookmarks[], Event.bookmarks[]
boundElements[], Event.boundElements[]
cells[], TABLE.cells[]
cells[], TR.cells[]
childNodes[], Element.childNodes[]
childNodes[], Node.childNodes[]
children[], Element.children[]
classes[], Document.classes[]
controlRange[], BODY.controlRange[]
cssRules[], StyleSheet.cssRules[]
Drives[], FileSystem.Drives[]
elements[], Form.elements[]
embeds[], Document.embeds[]
entities[], Doctype.entities[]
Files[], Folder.Files[]
filters[], Element.filters[]
forms[], Document.forms[]
frames[]
frames[], Document.frames[]
frames[], Window.frames[]
ids[], Document.ids[]
images[], Document.images[]
imports[], StyleSheet.imports[]
layers[], Document.layers[]
layers[], Layer.layers[]
links[], Document.links[]
mimeTypes[], Navigator.mimeTypes[]
notations[], Doctype.notations[]
options[], Select.options[]

Collection (continued)

plugins[], Document.plugins[]
plugins[], Navigator.plugins[]
rows[], TABLE.rows[]
rows[], TBODY.rows[]
rows[], TFOOT.rows[]
rows[], THEAD.rows[]
rules[], StyleSheet.rules[]
scripts[], Document.scripts[]
styleSheets[], Document.styleSheets[]
SubFolders[], Folder.SubFolders[]
suffixes[], MimeType.suffixes[]
tags[], Document.tags[]
tBodies[], TABLE.tBodies[]

Constant/static

Event type constants*
Global.undefined
Infinity*
Math.E*
Math.LN10*
Math.LN2*
Math.LOG10E*
Math.LOG2E*
Math.PI*
Math.SQRT1_2*
Math.SQRT2*
NaN*
Number.MAX_VALUE*
Number.MIN_VALUE*
Number.NaN*
Number.NEGATIVE_INFINITY*
Number.POSITIVE_INFINITY*
undefined*

Constructor

ActiveXObject()
Anchor()
Applet()
Array()
Boolean()
Date()
DbPool()
Enumerator()
Error()
File()
Function()
Image()
Layer()
Lock()
Number()
Object()
Option()
RegExp()
SendMail()
String()
VBArray()

Declaration

Array literal
function(...) ...*
var*

Definition (see also Background, Overview, Standard)

Accessor method
Additive expression
Additive operator
Adornments
Aggregate type
Alias
Anonymous code
Anonymous function
argc parameter
Argument
Argument list
argv parameter
Arithmetic constant
Arithmetic operator
Arithmetic type
Array simulation
Assignment expression
Assignment operator
Associativity
Aural style sheets
Automatic semi-colon insertion
Basic type
BeanConnect
Behavior
Big endian
Binary bitwise operator
Binary logical operator
Binary operator
Binding
Bit
Bit-field
Bitwise expression
Bitwise operator
Bitwise shift operator
Block-level tag
Broken down time
Browser wars
Built-in function
Built-in method
Built-in object
By reference
By value
Calendar time
Call a function
Call by reference
Call by value
Call-back event
Calling event handlers
Case Sensitivity
Cast operator
Category of an object
CGI Driven JavaScript
Character constant
Character display semantics
Character entity
Character set
Character testing
Character value
Class method
Class variable

Definition (continued)

Implementation-supplied code
Implementation-supplied function
Implicit conversion
Included JavaScript files
Inheritance
Initialization
Inline script
Inline tags
Input event
Input-output
Instance method
Instance variable
Instantiating Function
Integer
Integer arithmetic
Integer constant
Integer promotion
Integer-value-remainder
Internal function
Internal Method
Internal Property
Interpret
Interval handlers
Intrinsic events
Invoke a function
Iteration statement
Java
Java calling JavaScript
Java exception events
Java method calls
Java method data conversion
Java to JavaScript values
JavaScript Document Source URL
JavaScript embedded in Java
JavaScript Image Source URL
JavaScript Style Sheets
JavaScript to Java values
JellyScript
JSS
Jump statement
Keyboard events
Keyword
Label
Language codes
Left-Hand-Side expression
Length units
Letter
Lexical convention
Lexical scoping
Limits
Line
Line terminator
List type
Literal
Little endian
Local time
Local time zone adjustment
Locale-specific behavior
Localization
Logical constant
Logical entity
Logical expression
Logical operator
Low order bit
LValue
main() function

Mathematics
Measurement units
Member
Memory allocation
Memory leak
Memory management
Metacharacter
Method
MIME types
Minima-maxima
Money
Mouse events
Multi-byte character
Multi-dimensional arrays
Multi-line comment
Multiplicative expression
Multiplicative operator
Namespace
Native feature
Native object
Nondigit
Not a number
Null statement
Number formats (.)
Numerical limits
Object
Object constant
Object literal
Object model
Obsolescent
Octal value
Operator
Operator Precedence
Parameter
Pattern matching
Platform
Plugin compatibility issues
Plugin events
Polymorphic
Portability
Postfix operator
Power function
Precedence
Preferences
Prefix operator
Pre-processing
Primary expression
Primitive value
Printing character
Privileges
Procedural surfaces
Procedure
Program
Property
Property accessor
Property attribute
Property name
Property value
Prototype Based Inheritance
Prototype chain
Prototype object
prototype property
prototype.constructor
prototype.toString()
Proxies
Pseudo-random numbers
Punctuator

Delimiter

Delimiter (continued)
Object property delimiter (.)*
Parentheses ( )*
Pre-processing - /*@ ... @*/*
Quotation mark (" and ')
Semi-colon (;)*

Environment variable
CLASSPATH

Escape sequence
Newline*

Event handler
on ...
onAbort
onAbort, Image object*
onAbort, IMG object*
onAfterPrint
onAfterPrint, Dialog object*
onAfterPrint, Frame object*
onAfterPrint, Global object*
onAfterPrint, Window object*
onAfterUpdate
onAfterUpdate, Applet object*
onAfterUpdate, Area object*
onAfterUpdate, BODY object*
onAfterUpdate, Button object*
onAfterUpdate, BUTTON object*
onAfterUpdate, CAPTION object*
onAfterUpdate, Checkbox object*
onAfterUpdate, DIV object*
onAfterUpdate, Document object*
onAfterUpdate, FIELDSET object*
onAfterUpdate, FileUpload object*
onAfterUpdate, FormElement object*
onAfterUpdate, Hidden object*
onAfterUpdate, IMG object*
onAfterUpdate, Input object*
onAfterUpdate, MARQUEE object*
onAfterUpdate, OBJECT object*
onAfterUpdate, Password object*
onAfterUpdate, RadioButton object*
onAfterUpdate, ResetButton object*
onAfterUpdate, Select object*
onAfterUpdate, SubmitButton object*
onAfterUpdate, TABLE object*
onAfterUpdate, TD object*
onAfterUpdate, TEXTAREA object*
onAfterUpdate, TextCell object*
onAfterUpdate, TH object*
onBack
onBeforeCopy
onBeforeCut
onBeforeCut, Document object*
onBeforeEditFocus
onBeforeEditFocus, Document object*
onBeforePaste
onBeforePaste, Document object*
onBeforePrint
onBeforePrint, Dialog object*
onBeforePrint, Frame object*
onBeforePrint, Global object*
onBeforePrint, Window object*
onBeforeUnload

onBeforeUnload, BODY object*
onBeforeUnload, Dialog object*
onBeforeUnload, Frame object*
onBeforeUnload, FRAMESET object*
onBeforeUnload, Global object*
onBeforeUnload, TEXTAREA object*
onBeforeUnload, TH object*
onBeforeUnload, Window object*
onBeforeUpdate
onBeforeUpdate, Applet object*
onBeforeUpdate, Area object*
onBeforeUpdate, BODY object*
onBeforeUpdate, Button object*
onBeforeUpdate, BUTTON object*
onBeforeUpdate, CAPTION object*
onBeforeUpdate, Checkbox object*
onBeforeUpdate, DIV object*
onBeforeUpdate, Document object*
onBeforeUpdate, FIELDSET object*
onBeforeUpdate, FileUpload object*
onBeforeUpdate, FormElement object*
onBeforeUpdate, Hidden object*
onBeforeUpdate, IMG object*
onBeforeUpdate, Input object*
onBeforeUpdate, OBJECT object*
onBeforeUpdate, Password object*
onBeforeUpdate, RadioButton object*
onBeforeUpdate, ResetButton object*
onBeforeUpdate, Select object*
onBeforeUpdate, SubmitButton object*
onBeforeUpdate, TABLE object*
onBeforeUpdate, TD object*
onBeforeUpdate, TEXTAREA object*
onBeforeUpdate, TextCell object*
onBlur
onBlur, A object
onBlur, Applet object*
onBlur, Area object*
onBlur, Button object*
onBlur, BUTTON object*
onBlur, CAPTION object*
onBlur, Checkbox object*
onBlur, Dialog object*
onBlur, DIV object*
onBlur, Embed object*
onBlur, FIELDSET object*
onBlur, File object*
onBlur, FileUpload object*
onBlur, FormElement object*
onBlur, Frame object*
onBlur, Global object*
onBlur, Image object*
onBlur, IMG object*
onBlur, Input object*
onBlur, Label object*
onBlur, Layer object*
onBlur, Legend object*
onBlur, MARQUEE object*
onBlur, OBJECT object*
onBlur, Password object*
onBlur, RadioButton object*
onBlur, ResetButton object*
onBlur, Select object*
onBlur, SPAN object*
onBlur, SubmitButton object*
onBlur, TABLE object*
onBlur, TD object*

onBlur, TEXTAREA object*
onBlur, TextCell object*
onBlur, TH object*
onBlur, TR object*
onBlur, Window object*
onBounce
onBounce, MARQUEE object*
onChange
onChange, BODY object*
onChange, CAPTION object*
onChange, DIV object*
onChange, FIELDSET object*
onChange, FileUpload object*
onChange, FormElement object*
onChange, IMG object*
onChange, Input object*
onChange, Legend object*
onChange, Password object*
onChange, Select object*
onChange, TEXTAREA object*
onChange, TextCell object*
onClick
onClick, ! object*
onClick, A object
onClick, ABBR object
onClick, ACRONYM object
onClick, ADDRESS object
onClick, Anchor object*
onClick, Applet object*
onClick, Area object*
onClick, B object
onClick, BASE object*
onClick, BASEFONT object*
onClick, BDO object*
onClick, BGSOUND object*
onClick, BIG object
onClick, BLOCKQUOTE object*
onClick, BODY object*
onClick, BR object*
onClick, Button object*
onClick, BUTTON object*
onClick, CAPTION object*
onClick, CENTER object
onClick, Checkbox object*
onClick, CITE object
onClick, CODE object
onClick, COL object*
onClick, COLGROUP object*
onClick, DD object*
onClick, DEL object*
onClick, DFN object
onClick, DIR object*
onClick, DIV object*
onClick, DL object*
onClick, Document object*
onClick, DT object*
onClick, Element object*
onClick, EM object*
onClick, Embed object*
onClick, FIELDSET object*
onClick, File object*
onClick, FONT object*
onClick, Form object*
onClick, FormElement object*
onClick, FRAMESET object*
onClick, HEAD object*
onClick, H<n> object*

onClick, HR object*
onClick, HTML object*
onClick, HyperLink object*
onClick, I object*
onClick, IFRAME object*
onClick, Image object*
onClick, IMG object*
onClick, Input object*
onClick, INS object*
onClick, ISINDEX object*
onClick, KBD object*
onClick, Label object*
onClick, Legend object*
onClick, LI object*
onClick, LINK object*
onClick, LISTING object*
onClick, Location object*
onClick, Map object*
onClick, MARQUEE object*
onClick, MENU object*
onClick, META object*
onClick, NOFRAMES object*
onClick, NOSCRIPT object*
onClick, OBJECT object*
onClick, OL object*
onClick, OptGroupElement object*
onClick, Option object*
onClick, P object*
onClick, ParamElement object*
onClick, PLAINTEXT object
onClick, PRE object*
onClick, Q object
onClick, RadioButton object*
onClick, ResetButton object*
onClick, S object
onClick, SAMP object
onClick, SCRIPT object*
onClick, SMALL object
onClick, SPAN object*
onClick, STRIKE object
onClick, STRONG object*
onClick, STYLE object (1)*
onClick, style object (2)*
onClick, SUB object
onClick, SubmitButton object*
onClick, SUP object
onClick, TABLE object*
onClick, TableColElement object*
onClick, TBODY object*
onClick, TD object*
onClick, TextRange object*
onClick, TFOOT object*
onClick, TH object*
onClick, THEAD object*
onClick, TITLE object*
onClick, TR object*
onClick, TT object*
onClick, U object*
onClick, UL object*
onClick, Url object*
onClick, VAR object
onContentReady
onContextMenu
onContextMenu, Document object*
onCopy
onCut
onCut, Document object*

917

Event handler (continued)

onDataAvailable
onDataAvailable, Applet object*
onDataAvailable, Area object*
onDataAvailable, BODY object*
onDataAvailable, IMG object*
onDataAvailable, OBJECT object*
onDataAvailable, XML object*
onDataSetChanged
onDataSetChanged, Applet object*
onDataSetChanged, Area object*
onDataSetChanged, BODY object*
onDataSetChanged, IMG object*
onDatasetChanged, OBJECT object*
onDataSetChanged, XML object*
onDataSetComplete
onDataSetComplete, Applet object*
onDataSetComplete, Area object*
onDataSetComplete, BODY object*
onDataSetComplete, IMG object*
onDatasetComplete, OBJECT object*
onDataSetComplete, XML object*
onDblClick
onDblClick, ! object*
onDblClick, A object
onDblClick, ABBR object
onDblClick, ACRONYM object
onDblClick, ADDRESS object
onDblClick, Applet object*
onDblClick, Area object*
onDblClick, B object
onDblClick, BASE object*
onDblClick, BASEFONT object*
onDblClick, BDO object*
onDblClick, BGSOUND object*
onDblClick, BIG object
onDblClick, BLOCKQUOTE object*
onDblClick, BODY object*
onDblClick, BR object*
onDblClick, Button object*
onDblClick, BUTTON object*
onDblClick, CAPTION object*
onDblClick, CENTER object
onDblClick, Checkbox object*
onDblClick, CITE object
onDblClick, CODE object
onDblClick, COL object*
onDblClick, COLGROUP object*
onDblClick, DD object*
onDblClick, DEL object*
onDblClick, DFN object
onDblClick, DIR object*
onDblClick, DIV object*
onDblClick, DL object*
onDblClick, Document object*
onDblClick, DT object*
onDblClick, Element object*
onDblClick, EM object*
onDblClick, Embed object*
onDblClick, FIELDSET object*
onDblClick, File object*
onDblClick, FONT object*
onDblClick, Form object*
onDblClick, FormElement object*
onDblClick, FRAMESET object*
onDblClick, HEAD object*
onDblClick, H<n> object*

onDblClick, HR object*
onDblClick, HTML object*
onDblClick, HyperLink object*
onDblClick, I object*
onDblClick, IFRAME object*
onDblClick, Image object*
onDblClick, IMG object*
onDblClick, Input object*
onDblClick, INS object*
onDblClick, ISINDEX object*
onDblClick, KBD object*
onDblClick, Label object*
onDblClick, Legend object*
onDblClick, LI object*
onDblClick, LINK object*
onDblClick, LISTING object*
onDblClick, Location object*
onDblClick, Map object*
onDblClick, MARQUEE object*
onDblClick, MENU object*
onDblClick, META object*
onDblClick, NOFRAMES object*
onDblClick, NOSCRIPT object*
onDblClick, OBJECT object*
onDblClick, OL object*
onDblClick, OptGroupElement object*
onDblClick, Option object*
onDblClick, P object*
onDblClick, ParamElement object*
onDblClick, PLAINTEXT object*
onDblClick, PRE object*
onDblClick, Q object
onDblClick, RadioButton object*
onDblClick, ResetButton object*
onDblClick, S object
onDblClick, SAMP object
onDblClick, SCRIPT object*
onDblClick, SMALL object
onDblClick, SPAN object*
onDblClick, STRIKE object
onDblClick, STRONG object*
onDblClick, STYLE object (1)*
onDblClick, style object (2)*
onDblClick, SUB object
onDblClick, SubmitButton object*
onDblClick, SUP object
onDblClick, TABLE object*
onDblClick, TableColElement object*
onDblClick, TBODY object*
onDblClick, TD object*
onDblClick, TextRange object*
onDblClick, TFOOT object*
onDblClick, TH object*
onDblClick, THEAD object*
onDblClick, TITLE object*
onDblClick, TR object*
onDblClick, TT object*
onDblClick, U object*
onDblClick, UL object*
onDblClick, Url object*
onDblClick, VAR object
onDocumentReady
onDrag
onDrag, Document object*
onDragDrop
onDragDrop, Dialog object*
onDragDrop, Frame object*

onDragDrop, Global object*
onDragDrop, Window object*
onDragEnd
onDragEnd, Document object*
onDragEnter
onDragEnter, Document object*
onDragLeave
onDragLeave, Document object*
onDragOver
onDragOver, Document object*
onDragStart
onDragStart, ACRONYM object
onDragStart, ADDRESS object
onDragStart, B object
onDragStart, BIG object
onDragStart, BLOCKQUOTE object*
onDragStart, BODY object*
onDragStart, BUTTON object*
onDragStart, CAPTION object*
onDragStart, CENTER object
onDragStart, CITE object
onDragStart, CODE object
onDragStart, DD object*
onDragStart, DEL object*
onDragStart, DFN object
onDragStart, DIR object*
onDragStart, DIV object*
onDragStart, DL object*
onDragStart, Document object*
onDragStart, DT object*
onDragStart, EM object*
onDragStart, FIELDSET object*
onDragStart, FileUpload object*
onDragStart, FONT object*
onDragStart, Form object*
onDragStart, H<n> object*
onDragStart, HR object*
onDragStart, I object*
onDragStart, IMG object*
onDragStart, INS object*
onDragStart, KBD object*
onDragStart, Label object*
onDragStart, Legend object*
onDragStart, LI object*
onDragStart, LISTING object*
onDragStart, MARQUEE object*
onDragStart, MENU object*
onDragStart, OBJECT object*
onDragStart, OL object*
onDragStart, P object*
onDragStart, PLAINTEXT object
onDragStart, PRE object*
onDragStart, Q object
onDragStart, S object
onDragStart, SAMP object
onDragStart, Select object*
onDragStart, SMALL object
onDragStart, SPAN object*
onDragStart, STRIKE object
onDragStart, STRONG object*
onDragStart, SUB object
onDragStart, SUP object
onDragStart, TABLE object*
onDragStart, TBODY object*
onDragStart, TD object*
onDragStart, TEXTAREA object*
onDragStart, TFOOT object*

onDragStart, TH object*
onDragStart, THEAD object*
onDragStart, TR object*
onDragStart, TT object*
onDragStart, U object*
onDragStart, UL object*
onDragStart, VAR object
onDrop
onDrop, Document object*
onError
onError, Dialog object*
onError, Frame object*
onError, Global object*
onError, Image object*
onError, IMG object*
onError, LINK object*
onError, OBJECT object*
onError, SCRIPT object*
onError, STYLE object (1)*
onError, Window object*
onErrorUpdate
onErrorUpdate, Applet object*
onErrorUpdate, Area object*
onErrorUpdate, BODY object*
onErrorUpdate, Button object*
onErrorUpdate, CAPTION object*
onErrorUpdate, Checkbox object*
onErrorUpdate, Document object*
onErrorUpdate, FIELDSET object*
onErrorUpdate, OBJECT object*
onErrorUpdate, RadioButton object*
onErrorUpdate, TEXTAREA object*
onFilterChange
onFilterChange, ACRONYM object
onFilterChange, ADDRESS object
onFilterChange, B object
onFilterChange, BIG object
onFilterChange, BLOCKQUOTE object*
onFilterChange, BODY object*
onFilterChange, Button object*
onFilterChange, BUTTON object*
onFilterChange, CAPTION object*
onFilterChange, CENTER object
onFilterChange, Checkbox object*
onFilterChange, CITE object
onFilterChange, CODE object
onFilterChange, DD object*
onFilterChange, DEL object*
onFilterChange, DFN object
onFilterChange, DIR object*
onFilterChange, DL object*
onFilterChange, DT object*
onFilterChange, EM object*
onFilterChange, FIELDSET object*
onFilterChange, FileUpload object*
onFilterChange, FONT object*
onFilterChange, Form object*
onFilterChange, H<n> object*
onFilterChange, HR object*
onFilterChange, I object*
onFilterChange, IMG object*
onFilterChange, INS object*
onFilterChange, KBD object*
onFilterChange, Label object*
onFilterChange, Legend object*
onFilterChange, LI object*
onFilterChange, LISTING object*

Event handler (continued)

onFilterChange, MARQUEE object*
onFilterChange, MENU object*
onFilterChange, OBJECT object*
onFilterChange, OL object*
onFilterChange, P object*
onFilterChange, Password object*
onFilterChange, PLAINTEXT object
onFilterChange, PRE object*
onFilterChange, Q object
onFilterChange, RadioButton object*
onFilterChange, ResetButton object*
onFilterChange, S object
onFilterChange, SAMP object
onFilterChange, Select object*
onFilterChange, SMALL object
onFilterChange, SPAN object*
onFilterChange, STRIKE object
onFilterChange, STRONG object*
onFilterChange, SUB object
onFilterChange, SubmitButton object*
onFilterChange, SUP object
onFilterChange, TABLE object*
onFilterChange, TBODY object*
onFilterChange, TD object*
onFilterChange, TEXTAREA object*
onFilterChange, TextCell object*
onFilterChange, TFOOT object*
onFilterChange, TH object*
onFilterChange, THEAD object*
onFilterChange, TR object*
onFilterChange, TT object*
onFilterChange, U object*
onFilterChange, UL object*
onFilterChange, VAR object
onFinish
onFinish, MARQUEE object*
onFocus
onFocus, A object
onFocus, Applet object*
onFocus, Area object*
onFocus, Button object*
onFocus, BUTTON object*
onFocus, CAPTION object*
onFocus, Checkbox object*
onFocus, Dialog object*
onFocus, DIV object*
onFocus, Embed object*
onFocus, FIELDSET object*
onFocus, File object*
onFocus, FileUpload object*
onFocus, FormElement object*
onFocus, Frame object*
onFocus, Global object*
onFocus, Image object*
onFocus, IMG object*
onFocus, Input object*
onFocus, Label object*
onFocus, Layer object*
onFocus, Legend object*
onFocus, MARQUEE object*
onFocus, OBJECT object*
onFocus, Password object*
onFocus, RadioButton object*
onFocus, ResetButton object*
onFocus, Select object*
onFocus, SubmitButton object*

onFocus, TABLE object*
onFocus, TEXTAREA object*
onFocus, TextCell object*
onFocus, Window object*
onForward
onHelp
onHelp, ! object*
onHelp, A object
onHelp, ABBR object
onHelp, ACRONYM object
onHelp, ADDRESS object
onHelp, Applet object*
onHelp, Area object*
onHelp, B object
onHelp, BASE object*
onHelp, BASEFONT object*
onHelp, BDO object*
onHelp, BGSOUND object*
onHelp, BIG object
onHelp, BLOCKQUOTE object*
onHelp, BODY object*
onHelp, BR object*
onHelp, Button object*
onHelp, BUTTON object*
onHelp, CAPTION object*
onHelp, CENTER object
onHelp, Checkbox object*
onHelp, CITE object
onHelp, CODE object
onHelp, COL object*
onHelp, COLGROUP object*
onHelp, DD object*
onHelp, DEL object*
onHelp, DFN object
onHelp, Dialog object*
onHelp, DIR object*
onHelp, DIV object*
onHelp, DL object*
onHelp, Document object*
onHelp, DT object*
onHelp, Element object*
onHelp, EM object*
onHelp, Embed object*
onHelp, FIELDSET object*
onHelp, FileUpload object*
onHelp, FONT object*
onHelp, Form object*
onHelp, FormElement object*
onHelp, Frame object*
onHelp, FRAMESET object*
onHelp, Global object*
onHelp, HEAD object*
onHelp, Hidden object*
onHelp, H<n> object*
onHelp, HR object*
onHelp, HTML object*
onHelp, HyperLink object*
onHelp, I object*
onHelp, IFRAME object*
onHelp, Image object*
onHelp, IMG object*
onHelp, Input object*
onHelp, INS object*
onHelp, ISINDEX object*
onHelp, KBD object*
onHelp, Label object*
onHelp, Legend object*

onHelp, LI object*
onHelp, LINK object*
onHelp, LISTING object*
onHelp, Location object*
onHelp, Map object*
onHelp, MARQUEE object*
onHelp, MENU object*
onHelp, META object*
onHelp, NOFRAMES object*
onHelp, NOSCRIPT object*
onHelp, OBJECT object*
onHelp, OL object*
onHelp, OptGroupElement object*
onHelp, Option object*
onHelp, P object*
onHelp, ParamElement object*
onHelp, Password object*
onHelp, PLAINTEXT object
onHelp, PRE object*
onHelp, Q object
onHelp, RadioButton object*
onHelp, ResetButton object*
onHelp, S object
onHelp, SAMP object
onHelp, SCRIPT object*
onHelp, Select object*
onHelp, SMALL object
onHelp, SPAN object*
onHelp, STRIKE object
onHelp, STRONG object*
onHelp, STYLE object (1)*
onHelp, style object (2)*
onHelp, SUB object
onHelp, SubmitButton object*
onHelp, SUP object
onHelp, TABLE object*
onHelp, TableColElement object*
onHelp, TBODY object*
onHelp, TD object*
onHelp, TEXTAREA object*
onHelp, TextCell object*
onHelp, TextRange object*
onHelp, TFOOT object*
onHelp, TH object*
onHelp, THEAD object*
onHelp, TITLE object*
onHelp, TR object*
onHelp, TT object*
onHelp, U object*
onHelp, UL object*
onHelp, Url object*
onHelp, VAR object
onHelp, Window object*
onKeyDown
onKeyDown, ! object*
onKeyDown, A object
onKeyDown, ABBR object
onKeyDown, ACRONYM object
onKeyDown, ADDRESS object
onKeyDown, Applet object*
onKeyDown, Area object*
onKeyDown, B object
onKeyDown, BASE object*
onKeyDown, BASEFONT object*
onKeyDown, BDO object*
onKeyDown, BGSOUND object*
onKeyDown, BIG object

onKeyDown, BLOCKQUOTE object*
onKeyDown, BODY object*
onKeyDown, BR object*
onKeyDown, Button object*
onKeyDown, BUTTON object*
onKeyDown, CAPTION object*
onKeyDown, CENTER object
onKeyDown, Checkbox object*
onKeyDown, CITE object
onKeyDown, CODE object
onKeyDown, COL object*
onKeyDown, COLGROUP object*
onKeyDown, DD object*
onKeyDown, DEL object*
onKeyDown, DFN object
onKeyDown, DIR object*
onKeyDown, DIV object*
onKeyDown, DL object*
onKeyDown, Document object*
onKeyDown, DT object*
onKeyDown, Element object*
onKeyDown, EM object*
onKeyDown, Embed object*
onKeyDown, FIELDSET object*
onKeyDown, FileUpload object*
onKeyDown, FONT object*
onKeyDown, Form object*
onKeyDown, FormElement object*
onKeyDown, FRAMESET object*
onKeyDown, HEAD object*
onKeyDown, H<n> object*
onKeyDown, HR object*
onKeyDown, HTML object*
onKeyDown, HyperLink object*
onKeyDown, I object*
onKeyDown, IFRAME object*
onKeyDown, Image object*
onKeyDown, IMG object*
onKeyDown, Input object*
onKeyDown, INS object*
onKeyDown, ISINDEX object*
onKeyDown, KBD object*
onKeyDown, Label object*
onKeyDown, Legend object*
onKeyDown, LI object*
onKeyDown, LINK object*
onKeyDown, LISTING object*
onKeyDown, Location object*
onKeyDown, Map object*
onKeyDown, MARQUEE object*
onKeyDown, MENU object*
onKeyDown, META object*
onKeyDown, NOFRAMES object*
onKeyDown, NOSCRIPT object*
onKeyDown, OBJECT object*
onKeyDown, OL object*
onKeyDown, OptGroupElement object*
onKeyDown, Option object*
onKeyDown, P object*
onKeyDown, ParamElement object*
onKeyDown, Password object*
onKeyDown, PLAINTEXT object
onKeyDown, PRE object*
onKeyDown, Q object
onKeyDown, RadioButton object*
onKeyDown, ResetButton object*
onKeyDown, S object

921

Event handler (continued)

onKeyDown, SAMP object
onKeyDown, SCRIPT object*
onKeyDown, Select object*
onKeyDown, SMALL object
onKeyDown, SPAN object*
onKeyDown, STRIKE object
onKeyDown, STRONG object*
onKeyDown, STYLE object (1)*
onKeyDown, style object (2)*
onKeyDown, SUB object
onKeyDown, SubmitButton object*
onKeyDown, SUP object
onKeyDown, TABLE object*
onKeyDown, TableColElement object*
onKeyDown, TBODY object*
onKeyDown, TD object*
onKeyDown, TEXTAREA object*
onKeyDown, TextCell object*
onKeyDown, TextRange object*
onKeyDown, TFOOT object*
onKeyDown, TH object*
onKeyDown, THEAD object*
onKeyDown, TITLE object*
onKeyDown, TR object*
onKeyDown, TT object*
onKeyDown, U object*
onKeyDown, UL object*
onKeyDown, Url object*
onKeyDown, VAR object
onKeyPress
onKeyPress, ! object*
onKeyPress, A object
onKeyPress, ABBR object
onKeyPress, ACRONYM object
onKeyPress, ADDRESS object
onKeyPress, Applet object*
onKeyPress, Area object*
onKeyPress, B object
onKeyPress, BASE object*
onKeyPress, BASEFONT object*
onKeyPress, BDO object*
onKeyPress, BGSOUND object*
onKeyPress, BIG object
onKeyPress, BLOCKQUOTE object*
onKeyPress, BODY object*
onKeyPress, BR object*
onKeyPress, Button object*
onKeyPress, BUTTON object*
onKeyPress, CAPTION object*
onKeyPress, CENTER object
onKeyPress, Checkbox object*
onKeyPress, CITE object
onKeyPress, CODE object
onKeyPress, COL object*
onKeyPress, COLGROUP object*
onKeyPress, DD object*
onKeyPress, DEL object*
onKeyPress, DFN object
onKeyPress, DIR object*
onKeyPress, DIV object*
onKeyPress, DL object*
onKeyPress, Document object*
onKeyPress, DT object*
onKeyPress, Element object*
onKeyPress, EM object*
onKeyPress, Embed object*

onKeyPress, FIELDSET object*
onKeyPress, FileUpload object*
onKeyPress, FONT object*
onKeyPress, Form object*
onKeyPress, FormElement object*
onKeyPress, FRAMESET object*
onKeyPress, HEAD object*
onKeyPress, H<n> object*
onKeyPress, HR object*
onKeyPress, HTML object*
onKeyPress, HyperLink object*
onKeyPress, I object*
onKeyPress, IFRAME object*
onKeyPress, Image object*
onKeyPress, IMG object*
onKeyPress, Input object*
onKeyPress, INS object*
onKeyPress, ISINDEX object*
onKeyPress, KBD object*
onKeyPress, Label object*
onKeyPress, Legend object*
onKeyPress, LI object*
onKeyPress, LINK object*
onKeyPress, LISTING object*
onKeyPress, Location object*
onKeyPress, Map object*
onKeyPress, MARQUEE object*
onKeyPress, MENU object*
onKeyPress, META object*
onKeyPress, NOFRAMES object*
onKeyPress, NOSCRIPT object*
onKeyPress, OBJECT object*
onKeyPress, OL object*
onKeyPress, OptGroupElement object*
onKeyPress, Option object*
onKeyPress, P object*
onKeyPress, ParamElement object*
onKeyPress, Password object*
onKeyPress, PLAINTEXT object
onKeyPress, PRE object*
onKeyPress, Q object
onKeyPress, RadioButton object*
onKeyPress, ResetButton object*
onKeyPress, S object
onKeyPress, SAMP object
onKeyPress, SCRIPT object*
onKeyPress, Select object*
onKeyPress, SMALL object
onKeyPress, SPAN object*
onKeyPress, STRIKE object
onKeyPress, STRONG object*
onKeyPress, STYLE object (1)*
onKeyPress, style object (2)*
onKeyPress, SUB object
onKeyPress, SubmitButton object*
onKeyPress, SUP object
onKeyPress, TABLE object*
onKeyPress, TableColElement object*
onKeyPress, TBODY object*
onKeyPress, TD object*
onKeyPress, TEXTAREA object*
onKeyPress, TextCell object*
onKeyPress, TextRange object*
onKeyPress, TFOOT object*
onKeyPress, TH object*
onKeyPress, THEAD object*
onKeyPress, TITLE object*

onKeyPress, TR object*
onKeyPress, TT object*
onKeyPress, U object*
onKeyPress, UL object*
onKeyPress, Url object*
onKeyPress, VAR object
onKeyUp
onKeyUp, ! object*
onKeyUp, A object
onKeyUp, ABBR object
onKeyUp, ACRONYM object
onKeyUp, ADDRESS object
onKeyUp, Applet object*
onKeyUp, Area object*
onKeyUp, B object
onKeyUp, BASE object*
onKeyUp, BASEFONT object*
onKeyUp, BDO object*
onKeyUp, BGSOUND object*
onKeyUp, BIG object
onKeyUp, BLOCKQUOTE object*
onKeyUp, BODY object*
onKeyUp, BR object*
onKeyUp, Button object*
onKeyUp, BUTTON object*
onKeyUp, CAPTION object*
onKeyUp, CENTER object
onKeyUp, Checkbox object*
onKeyUp, CITE object
onKeyUp, CODE object
onKeyUp, COL object*
onKeyUp, COLGROUP object*
onKeyUp, DD object*
onKeyUp, DEL object*
onKeyUp, DFN object
onKeyUp, DIR object*
onKeyUp, DIV object*
onKeyUp, DL object*
onKeyUp, Document object*
onKeyUp, DT object*
onKeyUp, Element object*
onKeyUp, EM object*
onKeyUp, Embed object*
onKeyUp, FIELDSET object*
onKeyUp, FileUpload object*
onKeyUp, FONT object*
onKeyUp, Form object*
onKeyUp, FormElement object*
onKeyUp, FRAMESET object*
onKeyUp, HEAD object*
onKeyUp, H<n> object*
onKeyUp, HR object*
onKeyUp, HTML object*
onKeyUp, HyperLink object*
onKeyUp, I object*
onKeyUp, IFRAME object*
onKeyUp, Image object*
onKeyUp, IMG object*
onKeyUp, Input object*
onKeyUp, INS object*
onKeyUp, ISINDEX object*
onKeyUp, KBD object*
onKeyUp, Label object*
onKeyUp, Legend object*
onKeyUp, LI object*
onKeyUp, LINK object*
onKeyUp, LISTING object*

onKeyUp, Location object*
onKeyUp, Map object*
onKeyUp, MARQUEE object*
onKeyUp, MENU object*
onKeyUp, META object*
onKeyUp, NOFRAMES object*
onKeyUp, NOSCRIPT object*
onKeyUp, OBJECT object*
onKeyUp, OL object*
onKeyUp, OptGroupElement object*
onKeyUp, Option object*
onKeyUp, P object*
onKeyUp, ParamElement object*
onKeyUp, Password object*
onKeyUp, PLAINTEXT object
onKeyUp, PRE object*
onKeyUp, Q object
onKeyUp, RadioButton object*
onKeyUp, ResetButton object*
onKeyUp, S object
onKeyUp, SAMP object
onKeyUp, SCRIPT object*
onKeyUp, Select object*
onKeyUp, SMALL object
onKeyUp, SPAN object*
onKeyUp, STRIKE object
onKeyUp, STRONG object*
onKeyUp, STYLE object (1)*
onKeyUp, style object (2)*
onKeyUp, SUB object
onKeyUp, SubmitButton object*
onKeyUp, SUP object
onKeyUp, TABLE object*
onKeyUp, TableColElement object*
onKeyUp, TBODY object*
onKeyUp, TD object*
onKeyUp, TEXTAREA object*
onKeyUp, TextCell object*
onKeyUp, TextRange object*
onKeyUp, TFOOT object*
onKeyUp, TH object*
onKeyUp, THEAD object*
onKeyUp, TITLE object*
onKeyUp, TR object*
onKeyUp, TT object*
onKeyUp, U object*
onKeyUp, UL object*
onKeyUp, Url object*
onKeyUp, VAR object
onLoad
onLoad, Applet object*
onLoad, Area object*
onLoad, Dialog object*
onLoad, Frame object*
onLoad, FRAMESET object*
onLoad, Global object*
onLoad, Image object*
onLoad, IMG object*
onLoad, Layer object*
onLoad, LINK object*
onLoad, SCRIPT object*
onLoad, STYLE object (1)*
onLoad, Window object*
onLoseCapture
onMouseDown
onMouseDown, ! object*
onMouseDown, A object

923

Event handler (continued)

onMouseDown, ABBR object
onMouseDown, ACRONYM object
onMouseDown, ADDRESS object
onMouseDown, Anchor object*
onMouseDown, Applet object*
onMouseDown, Area object*
onMouseDown, B object
onMouseDown, BASE object*
onMouseDown, BASEFONT object*
onMouseDown, BDO object*
onMouseDown, BGSOUND object*
onMouseDown, BIG object
onMouseDown, BLOCKQUOTE object*
onMouseDown, BODY object*
onMouseDown, BR object*
onMouseDown, Button object*
onMouseDown, BUTTON object*
onMouseDown, CAPTION object*
onMouseDown, CENTER object
onMouseDown, Checkbox object*
onMouseDown, CITE object
onMouseDown, CODE object
onMouseDown, COL object*
onMouseDown, COLGROUP object*
onMouseDown, DD object*
onMouseDown, DEL object*
onMouseDown, DFN object
onMouseDown, DIR object*
onMouseDown, DIV object*
onMouseDown, DL object*
onMouseDown, Document object*
onMouseDown, DT object*
onMouseDown, Element object*
onMouseDown, EM object*
onMouseDown, Embed object*
onMouseDown, FIELDSET object*
onMouseDown, FileUpload object*
onMouseDown, FONT object*
onMouseDown, Form object*
onMouseDown, FormElement object*
onMouseDown, FRAMESET object*
onMouseDown, HEAD object*
onMouseDown, H<n> object*
onMouseDown, HR object*
onMouseDown, HTML object*
onMouseDown, HyperLink object*
onMouseDown, I object*
onMouseDown, IFRAME object*
onMouseDown, Image object*
onMouseDown, IMG object*
onMouseDown, Input object*
onMouseDown, INS object*
onMouseDown, ISINDEX object*
onMouseDown, KBD object*
onMouseDown, Label object*
onMouseDown, Legend object*
onMouseDown, LI object*
onMouseDown, LINK object*
onMouseDown, LISTING object*
onMouseDown, Location object*
onMouseDown, Map object*
onMouseDown, MARQUEE object*
onMouseDown, MENU object*
onMouseDown, META object*
onMouseDown, NOFRAMES object*
onMouseDown, NOSCRIPT object*

onMouseDown, OBJECT object*
onMouseDown, OL object*
onMouseDown, OptGroupElement object*
onMouseDown, Option object*
onMouseDown, P object*
onMouseDown, ParamElement object*
onMouseDown, Password object*
onMouseDown, PLAINTEXT object
onMouseDown, PRE object*
onMouseDown, Q object
onMouseDown, RadioButton object*
onMouseDown, ResetButton object*
onMouseDown, S object
onMouseDown, SAMP object
onMouseDown, SCRIPT object*
onMouseDown, Select object*
onMouseDown, SMALL object
onMouseDown, SPAN object*
onMouseDown, STRIKE object
onMouseDown, STRONG object*
onMouseDown, STYLE object (1)*
onMouseDown, style object (2)*
onMouseDown, SUB object
onMouseDown, SubmitButton object*
onMouseDown, SUP object
onMouseDown, TABLE object*
onMouseDown, TableColElement object*
onMouseDown, TBODY object*
onMouseDown, TD object*
onMouseDown, TEXTAREA object*
onMouseDown, TextCell object*
onMouseDown, TextRange object*
onMouseDown, TFOOT object*
onMouseDown, TH object*
onMouseDown, THEAD object*
onMouseDown, TITLE object*
onMouseDown, TR object*
onMouseDown, TT object*
onMouseDown, U object*
onMouseDown, UL object*
onMouseDown, Url object*
onMouseDown, VAR object
onMouseDrag
onMouseMove
onMouseMove, ! object*
onMouseMove, A object
onMouseMove, ABBR object
onMouseMove, ACRONYM object
onMouseMove, ADDRESS object
onMouseMove, Applet object*
onMouseMove, Area object*
onMouseMove, B object
onMouseMove, BASE object*
onMouseMove, BASEFONT object*
onMouseMove, BDO object*
onMouseMove, BGSOUND object*
onMouseMove, BIG object
onMouseMove, BLOCKQUOTE object*
onMouseMove, BODY object*
onMouseMove, BR object*
onMouseMove, Button object*
onMouseMove, BUTTON object*
onMouseMove, CAPTION object*
onMouseMove, CENTER object
onMouseMove, Checkbox object*
onMouseMove, CITE object
onMouseMove, CODE object

onMouseMove, COL object*
onMouseMove, COLGROUP object*
onMouseMove, DD object*
onMouseMove, DEL object*
onMouseMove, DFN object
onMouseMove, Dialog object*
onMouseMove, DIR object*
onMouseMove, DIV object*
onMouseMove, DL object*
onMouseMove, Document object*
onMouseMove, DT object*
onMouseMove, Element object*
onMouseMove, EM object*
onMouseMove, Embed object*
onMouseMove, FIELDSET object*
onMouseMove, FileUpload object*
onMouseMove, FONT object*
onMouseMove, Form object*
onMouseMove, FormElement object*
onMouseMove, Frame object*
onMouseMove, FRAMESET object*
onMouseMove, HEAD object*
onMouseMove, H<n> object*
onMouseMove, HR object*
onMouseMove, HTML object*
onMouseMove, HyperLink object*
onMouseMove, I object*
onMouseMove, IFRAME object*
onMouseMove, Image object*
onMouseMove, IMG object*
onMouseMove, Input object*
onMouseMove, INS object*
onMouseMove, ISINDEX object*
onMouseMove, KBD object*
onMouseMove, Label object*
onMouseMove, Legend object*
onMouseMove, LI object*
onMouseMove, LINK object*
onMouseMove, LISTING object*
onMouseMove, Location object*
onMouseMove, Map object*
onMouseMove, MARQUEE object*
onMouseMove, MENU object*
onMouseMove, META object*
onMouseMove, NOFRAMES object*
onMouseMove, NOSCRIPT object*
onMouseMove, OBJECT object*
onMouseMove, OL object*
onMouseMove, OptGroupElement object*
onMouseMove, Option object*
onMouseMove, P object*
onMouseMove, ParamElement object*
onMouseMove, Password object*
onMouseMove, PLAINTEXT object
onMouseMove, PRE object*
onMouseMove, Q object
onMouseMove, RadioButton object*
onMouseMove, ResetButton object*
onMouseMove, S object
onMouseMove, SAMP object
onMouseMove, SCRIPT object*
onMouseMove, Select object*
onMouseMove, SMALL object
onMouseMove, SPAN object*
onMouseMove, STRIKE object
onMouseMove, STRONG object*
onMouseMove, STYLE object (1)*

onMouseMove, style object (2)*
onMouseMove, SUB object
onMouseMove, SubmitButton object*
onMouseMove, SUP object
onMouseMove, TABLE object*
onMouseMove, TableColElement object*
onMouseMove, TBODY object*
onMouseMove, TD object*
onMouseMove, TEXTAREA object*
onMouseMove, TextCell object*
onMouseMove, TextRange object*
onMouseMove, TFOOT object*
onMouseMove, TH object*
onMouseMove, THEAD object*
onMouseMove, TITLE object*
onMouseMove, TR object*
onMouseMove, TT object*
onMouseMove, U object*
onMouseMove, UL object*
onMouseMove, Url object*
onMouseMove, VAR object
onMouseMove, Window object*
onMouseOut
onMouseOut, ! object*
onMouseOut, A object
onMouseOut, ABBR object
onMouseOut, ACRONYM object
onMouseOut, ADDRESS object
onMouseOut, Anchor object*
onMouseOut, Applet object*
onMouseOut, Area object*
onMouseOut, B object
onMouseOut, BASE object*
onMouseOut, BASEFONT object*
onMouseOut, BDO object*
onMouseOut, BGSOUND object*
onMouseOut, BIG object
onMouseOut, BLOCKQUOTE object*
onMouseOut, BODY object*
onMouseOut, BR object*
onMouseOut, Button object*
onMouseOut, BUTTON object*
onMouseOut, CAPTION object*
onMouseOut, CENTER object
onMouseOut, Checkbox object*
onMouseOut, CITE object
onMouseOut, CODE object
onMouseOut, COL object*
onMouseOut, COLGROUP object*
onMouseOut, DD object*
onMouseOut, DEL object*
onMouseOut, DFN object
onMouseOut, DIR object*
onMouseOut, DIV object*
onMouseOut, DL object*
onMouseOut, Document object*
onMouseOut, DT object*
onMouseOut, Element object*
onMouseOut, EM object*
onMouseOut, Embed object*
onMouseOut, FIELDSET object*
onMouseOut, FileUpload object*
onMouseOut, FONT object*
onMouseOut, Form object*
onMouseOut, FormElement object*
onMouseOut, FRAMESET object*
onMouseOut, HEAD object*

925

Event handler (continued)

onMouseOut, H<n> object*
onMouseOut, HR object*
onMouseOut, HTML object*
onMouseOut, HyperLink object*
onMouseOut, I object*
onMouseOut, IFRAME object*
onMouseOut, Image object*
onMouseOut, IMG object*
onMouseOut, Input object*
onMouseOut, INS object*
onMouseOut, ISINDEX object*
onMouseOut, KBD object*
onMouseOut, Label object*
onMouseOut, Layer object*
onMouseOut, Legend object*
onMouseOut, LI object*
onMouseOut, LINK object*
onMouseOut, LISTING object*
onMouseOut, Location object*
onMouseOut, Map object*
onMouseOut, MARQUEE object*
onMouseOut, MENU object*
onMouseOut, META object*
onMouseOut, NOFRAMES object*
onMouseOut, NOSCRIPT object*
onMouseOut, OBJECT object*
onMouseOut, OL object*
onMouseOut, OptGroupElement object*
onMouseOut, Option object*
onMouseOut, P object*
onMouseOut, ParamElement object*
onMouseOut, Password object*
onMouseOut, PLAINTEXT object
onMouseOut, PRE object*
onMouseOut, Q object
onMouseOut, RadioButton object*
onMouseOut, ResetButton object*
onMouseOut, S object
onMouseOut, SAMP object
onMouseOut, SCRIPT object*
onMouseOut, Select object*
onMouseOut, SMALL object
onMouseOut, SPAN object*
onMouseOut, STRIKE object
onMouseOut, STRONG object*
onMouseOut, STYLE object (1)*
onMouseOut, style object (2)*
onMouseOut, SUB object
onMouseOut, SubmitButton object*
onMouseOut, SUP object
onMouseOut, TABLE object*
onMouseOut, TableColElement object*
onMouseOut, TBODY object*
onMouseOut, TD object*
onMouseOut, TEXTAREA object*
onMouseOut, TextCell object*
onMouseOut, TextRange object*
onMouseOut, TFOOT object*
onMouseOut, TH object*
onMouseOut, THEAD object*
onMouseOut, TITLE object*
onMouseOut, TR object*
onMouseOut, TT object*
onMouseOut, U object*
onMouseOut, UL object*

onMouseOut, Url object*
onMouseOut, VAR object
onMouseOver
onMouseOver, ! object*
onMouseOver, A object
onMouseOver, ABBR object
onMouseOver, ACRONYM object
onMouseOver, ADDRESS object
onMouseOver, Anchor object*
onMouseOver, Applet object*
onMouseOver, Area object*
onMouseOver, B object
onMouseOver, BASE object*
onMouseOver, BASEFONT object*
onMouseOver, BDO object*
onMouseOver, BGSOUND object*
onMouseOver, BIG object
onMouseOver, BLOCKQUOTE object*
onMouseOver, BODY object*
onMouseOver, BR object*
onMouseOver, Button object*
onMouseOver, BUTTON object*
onMouseOver, CAPTION object*
onMouseOver, CENTER object
onMouseOver, Checkbox object*
onMouseOver, CITE object
onMouseOver, CODE object
onMouseOver, COL object*
onMouseOver, COLGROUP object*
onMouseOver, DD object*
onMouseOver, DEL object*
onMouseOver, DFN object
onMouseOver, DIR object*
onMouseOver, DIV object*
onMouseOver, DL object*
onMouseOver, Document object*
onMouseOver, DT object*
onMouseOver, Element object*
onMouseOver, EM object*
onMouseOver, Embed object*
onMouseOver, FIELDSET object*
onMouseOver, FileUpload object*
onMouseOver, FONT object*
onMouseOver, Form object*
onMouseOver, FormElement object*
onMouseOver, FRAMESET object*
onMouseOver, HEAD object*
onMouseOver, H<n> object*
onMouseOver, HR object*
onMouseOver, HTML object*
onMouseOver, HyperLink object*
onMouseOver, I object*
onMouseOver, IFRAME object*
onMouseOver, Image object*
onMouseOver, IMG object*
onMouseOver, Input object*
onMouseOver, INS object*
onMouseOver, ISINDEX object*
onMouseOver, KBD object*
onMouseOver, Label object*
onMouseOver, Layer object*
onMouseOver, Legend object*
onMouseOver, LI object*
onMouseOver, LINK object*
onMouseOver, LISTING object*
onMouseOver, Location object*
onMouseOver, Map object*

onMouseOver, MARQUEE object*
onMouseOver, MENU object*
onMouseOver, META object*
onMouseOver, NOFRAMES object*
onMouseOver, NOSCRIPT object*
onMouseOver, OBJECT object*
onMouseOver, OL object*
onMouseOver, OptGroupElement object*
onMouseOver, Option object*
onMouseOver, P object*
onMouseOver, ParamElement object*
onMouseOver, Password object*
onMouseOver, PLAINTEXT object
onMouseOver, PRE object*
onMouseOver, Q object
onMouseOver, RadioButton object*
onMouseOver, ResetButton object*
onMouseOver, S object
onMouseOver, SAMP object
onMouseOver, SCRIPT object*
onMouseOver, Select object*
onMouseOver, SMALL object
onMouseOver, SPAN object*
onMouseOver, STRIKE object
onMouseOver, STRONG object*
onMouseOver, STYLE object (1)*
onMouseOver, style object (2)*
onMouseOver, SUB object
onMouseOver, SubmitButton object*
onMouseOver, SUP object
onMouseOver, TABLE object*
onMouseOver, TableColElement object*
onMouseOver, TBODY object*
onMouseOver, TD object*
onMouseOver, TEXTAREA object*
onMouseOver, TextCell object*
onMouseOver, TextRange object*
onMouseOver, TFOOT object*
onMouseOver, TH object*
onMouseOver, THEAD object*
onMouseOver, TITLE object*
onMouseOver, TR object*
onMouseOver, TT object*
onMouseOver, U object*
onMouseOver, UL object*
onMouseOver, Url object*
onMouseOver, VAR object
onMouseUp
onMouseUp, ! object*
onMouseUp, A object
onMouseUp, ABBR object
onMouseUp, ACRONYM object
onMouseUp, ADDRESS object
onMouseUp, Anchor object*
onMouseUp, Applet object*
onMouseUp, Area object*
onMouseUp, B object
onMouseUp, BASE object*
onMouseUp, BASEFONT object*
onMouseUp, BDO object*
onMouseUp, BGSOUND object*
onMouseUp, BIG object
onMouseUp, BLOCKQUOTE object*
onMouseUp, BODY object*
onMouseUp, BR object*
onMouseUp, Button object*
onMouseUp, BUTTON object*

onMouseUp, CAPTION object*
onMouseUp, CENTER object
onMouseUp, Checkbox object*
onMouseUp, CITE object
onMouseUp, CODE object
onMouseUp, COL object*
onMouseUp, COLGROUP object*
onMouseUp, DD object*
onMouseUp, DEL object*
onMouseUp, DFN object
onMouseUp, DIR object*
onMouseUp, DIV object*
onMouseUp, DL object*
onMouseUp, Document object*
onMouseUp, DT object*
onMouseUp, Element object*
onMouseUp, EM object*
onMouseUp, Embed object*
onMouseUp, FIELDSET object*
onMouseUp, FileUpload object*
onMouseUp, FONT object*
onMouseUp, Form object*
onMouseUp, FormElement object*
onMouseUp, FRAMESET object*
onMouseUp, HEAD object*
onMouseUp, H<n> object*
onMouseUp, HR object*
onMouseUp, HTML object*
onMouseUp, HyperLink object*
onMouseUp, I object*
onMouseUp, IFRAME object*
onMouseUp, Image object*
onMouseUp, IMG object*
onMouseUp, Input object*
onMouseUp, INS object*
onMouseUp, ISINDEX object*
onMouseUp, KBD object*
onMouseUp, Label object*
onMouseUp, Layer object*
onMouseUp, Legend object*
onMouseUp, LI object*
onMouseUp, LINK object*
onMouseUp, LISTING object*
onMouseUp, Location object*
onMouseUp, Map object*
onMouseUp, MARQUEE object*
onMouseUp, MENU object*
onMouseUp, META object*
onMouseUp, NOFRAMES object*
onMouseUp, NOSCRIPT object*
onMouseUp, OBJECT object*
onMouseUp, OL object*
onMouseUp, OptGroupElement object*
onMouseUp, Option object*
onMouseUp, P object*
onMouseUp, ParamElement object*
onMouseUp, Password object*
onMouseUp, PLAINTEXT object
onMouseUp, PRE object*
onMouseUp, Q object
onMouseUp, RadioButton object*
onMouseUp, ResetButton object*
onMouseUp, S object
onMouseUp, SAMP object
onMouseUp, SCRIPT object*
onMouseUp, Select object*
onMouseUp, SMALL object

927

Event handler (continued)

onMouseUp, SPAN object*
onMouseUp, STRIKE object
onMouseUp, STRONG object*
onMouseUp, STYLE object (1)*
onMouseUp, style object (2)*
onMouseUp, SUB object
onMouseUp, SubmitButton object*
onMouseUp, SUP object
onMouseUp, TABLE object*
onMouseUp, TableColElement object*
onMouseUp, TBODY object*
onMouseUp, TD object*
onMouseUp, TEXTAREA object*
onMouseUp, TextCell object*
onMouseUp, TextRange object*
onMouseUp, TFOOT object*
onMouseUp, TH object*
onMouseUp, THEAD object*
onMouseUp, TITLE object*
onMouseUp, TR object*
onMouseUp, TT object*
onMouseUp, U object*
onMouseUp, UL object*
onMouseUp, Url object*
onMouseUp, VAR object
onMove
onMove, Dialog object*
onMove, Frame object*
onMove, Global object*
onMove, Window object*
onPaste
onPaste, Document object*
onPropertyChange
onPropertyChange, Document object*
onReadyStateChange
onReadyStateChange, Applet object*
onReadyStateChange, Area object*
onReadyStateChange, Document object*
onReadyStateChange, LINK object*
onReadyStateChange, OBJECT object*
onReadyStateChange, SCRIPT object*
onReadyStateChange, STYLE object (1)*
onReadyStateChange, XML object*
onReset
onReset, Form object*
onResize
onResize, Applet object*
onResize, Area object*
onResize, BUTTON object*
onResize, Dialog object*
onResize, DIV object*
onResize, FIELDSET object*
onResize, FileUpload object*
onResize, Frame object*
onResize, FRAMESET object*
onResize, Global object*
onResize, IMG object*
onResize, MARQUEE object*
onResize, Password object*
onResize, Select object*
onResize, TABLE object*
onResize, TD object*
onResize, TH object*
onResize, Window object*
onRowEnter
onRowEnter, Applet object*

onRowEnter, Area object*
onRowEnter, BODY object*
onRowEnter, Button object*
onRowEnter, BUTTON object*
onRowEnter, Checkbox object*
onRowEnter, DIV object*
onRowEnter, Document object*
onRowEnter, FileUpload object*
onRowEnter, FormElement object*
onRowEnter, Hidden object*
onRowEnter, IMG object*
onRowEnter, Input object*
onRowEnter, MARQUEE object*
onRowEnter, OBJECT object*
onRowEnter, Password object*
onRowEnter, RadioButton object*
onRowEnter, ResetButton object*
onRowEnter, Select object*
onRowEnter, SubmitButton object*
onRowEnter, TABLE object*
onRowEnter, TD object*
onRowEnter, TEXTAREA object*
onRowEnter, TextCell object*
onRowEnter, TH object*
onRowEnter, XML object*
onRowExit
onRowExit, Applet object*
onRowExit, Area object*
onRowExit, BODY object*
onRowExit, Button object*
onRowExit, BUTTON object*
onRowExit, Checkbox object*
onRowExit, DIV object*
onRowExit, Document object*
onRowExit, FileUpload object*
onRowExit, FormElement object*
onRowExit, Hidden object*
onRowExit, IMG object*
onRowExit, Input object*
onRowExit, MARQUEE object*
onRowExit, OBJECT object*
onRowExit, Password object*
onRowExit, RadioButton object*
onRowExit, ResetButton object*
onRowExit, Select object*
onRowExit, SubmitButton object*
onRowExit, TABLE object*
onRowExit, TD object*
onRowExit, TEXTAREA object*
onRowExit, TextCell object*
onRowExit, TH object*
onRowExit, XML object*
onRowsDelete
onRowsDelete, XML object*
onRowsInserted
onRowsInserted, XML object*
onScroll
onScroll, BODY object*
onScroll, CAPTION object*
onScroll, Dialog object*
onScroll, DIV object*
onScroll, FIELDSET object*
onScroll, Frame object*
onScroll, IMG object*
onScroll, Legend object*
onScroll, MARQUEE object*
onScroll, TABLE object*

onScroll, TEXTAREA object*
onScroll, Window object*
onSelect
onSelect, CAPTION object*
onSelect, FIELDSET object*
onSelect, FileUpload object*
onSelect, FormElement object*
onSelect, Input object*
onSelect, Password object*
onSelect, TEXTAREA object*
onSelect, TextCell object*
onSelectStart
onSelectStart, A object
onSelectStart, ACRONYM object
onSelectStart, ADDRESS object
onSelectStart, B object
onSelectStart, BIG object
onSelectStart, BLOCKQUOTE object*
onSelectStart, BODY object*
onSelectStart, BUTTON object*
onSelectStart, CAPTION object*
onSelectStart, CENTER object
onSelectStart, CITE object
onSelectStart, CODE object
onSelectStart, DD object*
onSelectStart, DEL object*
onSelectStart, DFN object
onSelectStart, DIR object*
onSelectStart, DIV object*
onSelectStart, DL object*
onSelectStart, Document object*
onSelectStart, DT object*
onSelectStart, EM object*
onSelectStart, FIELDSET object*
onSelectStart, FileUpload object*
onSelectStart, FONT object*
onSelectStart, Form object*
onSelectStart, H<n> object*
onSelectStart, HR object*
onSelectStart, I object*
onSelectStart, IMG object*
onSelectStart, INS object*
onSelectStart, KBD object*
onSelectStart, Label object*
onSelectStart, Legend object*
onSelectStart, LI object*
onSelectStart, LISTING object*
onSelectStart, MARQUEE object*
onSelectStart, MENU object*
onSelectStart, OBJECT object*
onSelectStart, OL object*
onSelectStart, P object*
onSelectStart, Password object*
onSelectStart, PLAINTEXT object
onSelectStart, PRE object*
onSelectStart, Q object
onSelectStart, S object
onSelectStart, SAMP object
onSelectStart, Select object*
onSelectStart, SMALL object
onSelectStart, SPAN object*
onSelectStart, STRIKE object
onSelectStart, STRONG object*
onSelectStart, SUB object
onSelectStart, SUP object
onSelectStart, TABLE object*
onSelectStart, TBODY object*

onSelectStart, TD object*
onSelectStart, TEXTAREA object*
onSelectStart, TFOOT object*
onSelectStart, TH object*
onSelectStart, THEAD object*
onSelectStart, TR object*
onSelectStart, TT object*
onSelectStart, U object*
onSelectStart, UL object*
onSelectStart, VAR object
onStart
onStart, MARQUEE object*
onStop
onStop, Document object*
onSubmit
onSubmit, Form object*
onUnload
onUnload, BODY object*
onUnload, Dialog object*
onUnload, Frame object*
onUnload, FRAMESET object*
onUnload, Global object*
onUnload, Window object*

External code call
` (Backquote)
Backquote (`)*

File extension (see also Special file)
.cfg
.cgi
.htc*
.htm
.html
.jar*
.java*
.js*
.jsc
.jse
.jsh
.lck
.pac*
.shtm
.shtml
.stm
.web

Filter/blend
BlendTrans()
filter - BlendTrans()*

Filter/procedural
filter - AlphaImageLoader()*
filter - Gradient()*

Filter/reveal
filter - RevealTrans()*
RevealTrans()

Filter/transition
Barn()
Blinds()

929

Filter/transition (continued)

CheckerBoard()
Fade()
filter - Barn()*
filter - Blinds()*
filter - CheckerBoard()*
filter - Fade()*
filter - GradientWipe()*
filter - Inset()*
filter - Iris()*
filter - Pixelate()*
filter - RadialWipe()*
filter - RandomBars()*
filter - RandomDissolve()*
filter - Slide()*
filter - Spiral()*
filter - Stretch()*
filter - Strips()*
filter - Wheel()*
filter - Zigzag()*
GradientWipe()
Inset()
Iris()
Pixelate()
RadialWipe()
RandomBars()
RandomDissolve()
Slide()
Spiral()
Stretch()
Strips()
Wheel()
Zigzag()

Filter/visual

Alpha()
AlphaImageLoader()
BasicImage()
Blur()
Chroma()
Compositor()
DropShadow()
Emboss()
Engrave()
filter - Alpha()*
filter - BasicImage()*
filter - Blur()*
filter - Chroma()*
filter - Compositor()*
filter - DropShadow()*
filter - Emboss()*
filter - Engrave()*
filter - FlipH()*
filter - FlipV()*
filter - Glow()*
filter - Grayscale()*
filter - Invert()*
filter - Light()*
filter - Mask()*
filter - MaskFilter()*
filter - Matrix()*
filter - MotionBlur()*
filter - Pixelate()*
filter - Shadow()*
filter - Wave()*
filter - XRay()*

FlipH()
FlipV()
Glow()
Gradient()
Grayscale()
Invert()
Light()
Mask()
MaskFilter()
Matrix()
MotionBlur()
Pixelate()
Shadow()
Wave()
XRay()

Function

abs()*, Math.abs()*
acos()*, Math.acos()*
Array()*
asin()*, Math.asin()*
atan()*, Math.atan()*
atan2()*, Math.atan2()*
atob()*, Window.atob()*
Boolean()*
btoa()*, Window.btoa()*
captureEvents()*
captureEvents()*,
    Document.captureEvents()*
captureEvents()*, Layer.captureEvents()*
captureEvents()*,
    Window.captureEvents()*
catch(...)*
ceil()*, Math.ceil()*
cos()*, Math.cos()*
Date()*
decodeURI()*
decodeURIComponent()*
encodeURI()*
encodeURIComponent()*
Error()*
exp()*, Math.exp()*
floor()*, Math.floor()*
Function()*
getClass()
GetObject()*
handleEvent()*
handleEvent()*, Document.handleEvent()*
handleEvent()*, Layer.handleEvent()*
handleEvent()*, Window.handleEvent()*
Image()
log()*, Math.log()*
max()*, Math.max()*
min()*, Math.min()*
Number()*
Object()*
pow()*, Math.pow()*
random(), Crypto.random()
random()*, Math.random()*
RegExp()
releaseEvents()
releaseEvents()*,
    Document.releaseEvents()*
releaseEvents()*, Layer.releaseEvents()*
releaseEvents()*, Window.releaseEvents()*
rgb()*
round()*, Math.round()*

routeEvent()
routeEvent(), Document.routeEvent()
routeEvent()*, Layer.routeEvent()*
routeEvent()*, Window.routeEvent()*
ScriptEngine()*
signText(), Crypto.signText()
sin()*, Math.sin()*
sqrt()*, Math.sqrt()*
String()*
tan()*, Math.tan()*

Function/global
escape()*
eval()*
isFinite()*
isNaN()*
parseFloat()*
parseInt()*
ScriptEngineBuildVersion()*
ScriptEngineMajorVersion()
ScriptEngineMinorVersion()
taint()*
toString()*
unescape()*
untaint()*
unwatch()*
watch()*

Function/internal
Call*
CanPut()*
DefaultValue()*
Delete()*
Get()*
GetBase()*
GetPropertyName()*
GetValue()*
HasInstance()*
HasProperty()*
Put()*
PutValue()*

Function/proxy.pac
FindProxyForURL()*
isInNet()*
isPlainHostName()*

HTML Tag
<EMBED>*
<META>*
<NOSCRIPT>*
<SCRIPT>*
<STYLE>*
<TITLE>*
Conditional comment*
HTML Comment tag (<!-- ... -->)

HTML Tag Attribute
<MAP TARGET="...">*
<SCRIPT ARCHIVE="...">*
<SCRIPT EVENT="...">*
<SCRIPT FOR="...">
<SCRIPT ID="...">*
<SCRIPT LANGUAGE="...">*

<SCRIPT SRC="...">*
<SCRIPT TYPE="...">*
<STYLE TYPE="...">*
CLASS="..."*
HTTP-EQUIV="..."
ID="..."*
LANG="..."*
MAYSCRIPT*
NAME="..."

Interface
Error handler*
Watchpoint handler*

Iterator
do ... while(...)*
for(...) ...*
for(... in ...) ...*
while(...) ...*

Java class
java.awt.Button*
java.awt.image*
java.lang.Boolean*
java.lang.Character*
java.lang.Class*
java.lang.Double*
java.lang.Float*
java.lang.Integer*
java.lang.Long*
java.lang.Object*
java.lang.String*
java.util.Date*
JSObject object*
netscape.javascript.JSObject*
netscape.plugin.Plugin
netscape.security.PrivilegeManager*
PrivilegeManager object*

Java method
call()*, JSObject.call()*
eval()*, JSObject.eval()*
getMember()*, JSObject.getMember()*
getSlot()*, JSObject.getSlot()*
removeMember()*,
    JSObject.removeMember()*
setMember()*, JSObject.setMember()*
setSlot()*, JSObject.setSlot()*
toString()*, JSObject.toString()*

Java method/static
JSObject.getWindow()*

Java package
java.awt*
java.lang*
java.util*
netscape
netscape.applet*
netscape.cfg
netscape.javascript
netscape.lck*
netscape.plugin

Java package (continued)

netscape.security
Packages.java*
Packages.netscape*
Packages.netscape.javascript
Packages.netscape.plugin
Packages.sun
sun

Keyword

else ...*
in ...
this*

Label

case ... :
default:

Method

action(), java.awt.Button*
add(), Area object*
add(), Area.add()
Add(), Dictionary object*
Add(), Dictionary.Add()
Add(), Folders object*
Add(), Folders.Add()
add(), OptionsArray object*
add(), OptionsArray.add()
add(), Select object*
add(), Select.add()
addAmbient(), filter - Light()*
addBehavior(), Element object*
addBehavior(), Element.addBehavior()
AddChannel(), external object*
AddChannel(), external.AddChannel()
addClient(), Global object*
addClient(), response object*
addClient(), response.addClient()
addCone(), filter - Light()*
AddDesktopComponent(), external object*
AddDesktopComponent(),
　external.AddDesktopComponent()
addEventListener(), EventTarget object*
addEventListener(),
　EventTarget.addEventListener()
AddFavorite(), external object*
AddFavorite(), external.AddFavorite()
addImport(), StyleSheet object*
addImport(), StyleSheet.addImport()
addNotify(), java.awt.Button*
addPoint(), filter - Light()*
addReadRequest(), userProfile object*
addReadRequest(),
　userProfile.addReadRequest()
addResponseHeader(), Global object*
addResponseHeader(), response object*
addResponseHeader(),
　response.addResponseHeader()
addRule(), StyleSheet object*
addRule(), StyleSheet.addRule()
after(), java.util.Date*
alert()
alert(), Global object*
alert(), Window object*
alert(), Window.alert()

anchor(), String object*
anchor(), String.anchor()
appendChild(), Node object*
appendChild(), Node.appendChild()
appendData(), CharacterData object*
appendData(), CharacterData.appendData()
apply(), filter - Barn()*
apply(), filter - Blinds()*
apply(), filter - Compositor()*
apply(), filter - Fade()*
apply(), filter - GradientWipe()*
apply(), filter - Inset()*
apply(), filter - Iris()*
apply(), filter - Pixelate()*
apply(), filter - Pixelate()*
apply(), filter - RadialWipe()*
apply(), filter - RandomBars()*
apply(), filter - RandomDissolve()*
apply(), filter - Slide()*
apply(), filter - Spiral()*
apply(), filter - Stretch()*
apply(), filter - Strips()*
apply(), filter - Wheel()*
apply(), filter - Zigzag()*
apply(), Function object*
apply(), Function.apply()
applyElement(), Element object*
applyElement(), Element.applyElement()
Array()*
Array(), Global object*
assign(), Location object*
assign(), Location.assign()
assign(), Object object*
assign(), Object.assign()
atEnd(), Enumerator object*
atEnd(), Enumerator.atEnd()
atob()
atob()*, Window.atob()*
attachEvent()
attachEvent(), Document object*
attachEvent(), Document.attachEvent()
attachEvent(), Global object*
attachEvent(), Window object*
attachEvent(), Window.attachEvent()
AutoCompleteSaveForm(), external object*
AutoCompleteSaveForm(),
　external.AutoCompleteSaveForm()
AutoScan(), external object*
AutoScan(), external.AutoScan()
back()
back(), Global object*
back(), History object*
back(), History.back()
back(), Window object*
back(), Window.back()
before(), java.util.Date*
beginTransaction(), Connection object*
beginTransaction(),
　Connection.beginTransaction()
beginTransaction(), database object*
beginTransaction(),
　database.beginTransaction()
big(), String object*
big(), String.big()
blink(), String object*
blink(), String.blink()
blob(), Global object*

blob(), response object*
blob(), response.blob()
blobImage(), blob object*
blobImage(), blob.blobImage()
blobImage(), Cursor object*
blobImage(), Cursor.blobImage()
blobLink(), blob object*
blobLink(), blob.blobLink()
blobLink(), Cursor object*
blobLink(), Cursor.blobLink()
blur()
blur(), Anchor object*
blur(), Element object*
blur(), File object*
blur(), Global object*
blur(), Input object*
blur(), Label object*
blur(), Window object*
blur(), Anchor.blur()
blur(), Input.blur()
blur(), Window.blur()
bold(), String object*
bold(), String.bold()
Boolean()*
Boolean(), Global object*
booleanValue(), java.lang.Boolean*
booleanValue(), JavaObject object*
booleanValue()*,
    JavaObject.booleanValue()*
borderWidths(), JSSTag object*
borderWidths(), JSSTag.borderWidths()
bounds(), java.awt.Button*
btoa()
btoa()*, Window.btoa()*
BuildPath(), FileSystem object*
BuildPath(), FileSystem.BuildPath()
byteToString(), File object*
byteToString(), File.byteToString()
byteValue(), java.lang.Double*
byteValue(), java.lang.Float*
byteValue(), java.lang.Integer*
byteValue(), java.lang.Long*
call(), Function object*
call(), Function.call()
call(), JSObject object*
call()*, JSObject.call()*
callC(), Global object*
callC(), response object*
callC(), response.callC()
captureEvents()*
captureEvents(), Document object*
captureEvents()*,
    Document.captureEvents()*
captureEvents()*, Layer.captureEvents()*
captureEvents()*,
    Window.captureEvents()*
changeColor(), filter - Light()*
changeStrength(), filter - Light()*
charAt(), java.lang.String*
charAt(), String object*
charAt(), String.charAt()
charCodeAt(), String object*
charCodeAt(), String.charCodeAt()
charValue(), java.lang.Character*
checkImage(), java.awt.Button*
clear(), Document object*
clear(), Document.clear()

clear(), filter - Light()*
clear(), Selection object*
clear(), selection.clear()
clearAttributes(), Element object*
clearAttributes(), Element.clearAttributes()
clearData(), clipboardData object*
clearData(), dataTransfer object*
clearData(), dataTransfer.clearData()
clearError(), File object*
clearError(), File.clearError()
clearInterval()
clearInterval(), Global object*
clearInterval(), Window object*
clearInterval(), Window.clearInterval()
clearRequest(), userProfile object*
clearRequest(), userProfile.clearRequest()
clearTimeout()
clearTimeout(), Global object*
clearTimeout(), Window object*
clearTimeout(), Window.clearTimeout()
click(), BLOCKQUOTE object*
click(), COMMENT object*
click(), Element object*
click(), Element.click()
click(), File object*
click(), Input object*
click(), Input.click()
click(), Label object*
client.destroy()
cloneNode(), Node object*
cloneNode(), Node.cloneNode()
close()
close(), Cursor object*
close(), Cursor.close()
close(), Document object*
close(), Document.close()
close(), File object*
close(), File object*
close(), File.close()
close(), Frame object*
close(), Frame.close()
close(), Global object*
close(), ResultSet object*
close(), ResultSet.close()
Close(), Stproc object*
Close(), Stproc.close()
close(), TextStream object*
close(), TextStream.Close()
close(), Window object*
close(), Window.close()
collapse(), TextRange object*
collapse(), TextRange.collapse()
columnName(), Cursor object*
columnName(), Cursor.columnName()
columnName(), ResultSet object*
columnName(), ResultSet.columnName()
columns(), Cursor object*
columns(), Cursor.columns()
columns(), ResultSet object*
columns(), ResultSet.columns()
commitTransaction(), Connection object*
commitTransaction(),
    Connection.commitTransaction()
commitTransaction(), database object*
commitTransaction(),
    database.commitTransaction()
compareEndPoints(), TextRange object*

Method

Method (continued)

compareEndPoints(),
  TextRange.compareEndPoints()
compareTo(), java.lang.String*
compile(), RegExp object*
compile(), RegExp.compile()
componentFromPoint(), Element object*
componentFromPoint(),
  Element.componentFromPoint()
concat(), Array object*
concat(), Array.concat()
concat(), java.lang.String*
concat(), String object*
concat(), String.concat()
confirm()
confirm(), Global object*
confirm(), Window object*
confirm(), Window.confirm()
connect(), database object*
connect(), database.connect()
connect(), DbPool object*
connect(), DbPool.connect()
connected(), Connection object*
connected(), Connection.connected()
connected(), database object*
connected(), database.connected()
connected(), DbPool object*
connected(), DbPool.connected()
connection(), DbPool object*
connection(), DbPool.connection()
contains(), Element object*
contains(), Element.contains()
contains(), Frame object*
contextual()
contextual(), Document object*
contextual(), Document.contextual()
Copy(), File object*
Copy(), File.Copy()
Copy(), Folder object*
Copy(), Folder.Copy()
CopyFile(), FileSystem object*
CopyFile(), FileSystem.CopyFile()
CopyFolder(), FileSystem object*
CopyFolder(), FileSystem.CopyFolder()
createAttribute(), Document object*
createAttribute(),
  Document.createAttribute()
createCaption(), TABLE object*
createCaption(), TABLE.createCaption()
createCDATASection(), Document object*
createCDATASection(),
  Document.createCDATASection()
createComment(), Document object*
createComment(),
  Document.createComment()
createControlRange(), BODY object*
createControlRange(),
  BODY.createControlRange()
createDocumentFragment(), Document
  object*
createDocumentFragment(),
  Document.createDocumentFragment()
createElement(), Document object*
createElement(),
  Document.createElement()
createEntityReference(), Document object*

createEntityReference(),
  Document.createEntityReference()
createEvent(), DocumentEvent*
createEvent(),
  DocumentEvent.createEvent()
CreateFolder(), FileSystem object*
CreateFolder(), FileSystem.CreateFolder()
createImage(), java.awt.Button*
CreateObject(), WScript object*
CreateObject(), WScript.CreateObject()
createProcessingInstruction(), Document
  object*
createProcessingInstruction(),
  Document.createProcessingInstruction()
createRange(), Selection object*
createRange(), selection.createRange()
createStyleSheet(), Document object*
createStyleSheet(),
  Document.createStyleSheet()
CreateTextFile(), FileSystem object*
CreateTextFile(),
  FileSystem.CreateTextFile()
createTextNode(), Document object*
createTextNode(),
  Document.createTextNode()
createTextRange(), BODY object*
createTextRange(),
  BODY.createTextRange()
createTextRange(), BUTTON object*
createTextRange(), Input object*
createTextRange(), Input.createTextRange()
createTFoot(), TABLE object*
createTFoot(), TABLE.createTFoot()
createTHead(), TABLE object*
createTHead(), TABLE.createTHead()
cursor(), Connection object*
cursor(), Connection.cursor()
cursor(), database object*
cursor(), database.cursor()
Date()*
Date(), Global object*
debug(), Global object*
debug(), response object*
debug(), response.debug()
Delete(), File object*
Delete(), File.Delete()
Delete(), Folder object*
Delete(), Folder.Delete()
deleteCaption(), TABLE object*
deleteCaption(), TABLE.deleteCaption()
deleteCell(), TR object*
deleteCell(), TR.deleteCell()
deleteData(), CharacterData object*
deleteData(), CharacterData.deleteData()
DeleteFile(), FileSystem object*
DeleteFile(), FileSystem.DeleteFile()
DeleteFolder(), FileSystem object*
DeleteFolder(), FileSystem.DeleteFolder()
deleteResponseHeader(), Global object*
deleteResponseHeader(), response object*
deleteResponseHeader(),
  response.deleteResponseHeader()
deleteRow(), Cursor object*
deleteRow(), Cursor.deleteRow()
deleteRow(), TABLE object*
deleteRow(), TABLE.deleteRow()

deleteRow(), TFOOT object*
deleteRow(), TFOOT.deleteRow()
deleteRow(), THEAD object*
deleteRow(), THEAD.deleteRow()
deleteTFoot(), TABLE object*
deleteTFoot(), TABLE.deleteTFoot()
deleteTHead(), TABLE object*
deleteTHead(), TABLE.deleteTHead()
deliverEvent(), java.awt.Button*
destroy(), client object*
destroy(), JavaObject object*
destroy(), netscape.plugin.Plugin
detachEvent()
detachEvent(), Document object*
detachEvent(), Document.detachEvent()
detachEvent(), Global object*
detachEvent(), Window object*
detachEvent(), Window.detachEvent()
dimensions(), VBArray object*
dimensions(), VBArray.dimensions()
disable(), java.awt.Button*
disable(), JavaObject object*
disableExternalCapture()
disableExternalCapture(), Global object*
disableExternalCapture(), Window object*
disableExternalCapture(),
    Window.disableExternalCapture()
disablePrivilege(),
    netscape.security.PrivilegeManager*
disablePrivilege(), PrivilegeManager
    object*
disablePrivilege(),
    PrivilegeManager.disablePrivilege()
disconnect(), database object*
disconnect(), database.disconnect()
disconnect(), DbPool object*
disconnect(), DbPool.disconnect()
DisconnectObject(), WScript object*
DisconnectObject(),
    WScript.DisconnectObject()
dispatchEvent(), EventTarget object*
dispatchEvent(),
    EventTarget.dispatchEvent()
doReadRequest(), userProfile object*
doReadRequest(),
    userProfile.doReadRequest()
doScroll(), Element object*
doScroll(), Element.doScroll()
doubleValue(), java.lang.Double*
doubleValue(), java.lang.Float*
doubleValue(), java.lang.Integer*
doubleValue(), java.lang.Long*
doubleValue(), JavaObject object*
DriveExists(), FileSystem object*
DriveExists(), FileSystem.DriveExists()
duplicate(), TextRange object*
duplicate(), TextRange.duplicate()
Echo(), WScript object*
Echo(), WScript.Echo()
elementFromPoint(), Document object*
elementFromPoint(),
    Document.elementFromPoint()
empty(), Selection object*
empty(), selection.empty()
enable(), java.awt.Button*
enable(), JavaObject object*
enableExternalCapture()

enableExternalCapture(), Global object*
enableExternalCapture(), Window object*
enableExternalCapture(),
    Window.enableExternalCapture()
enablePrivilege(),
    netscape.security.PrivilegeManager*
enablePrivilege(), PrivilegeManager object*
enablePrivilege(),
    PrivilegeManager.enablePrivilege()
endsWith(), java.lang.String*
eof(), File object*
eof(), File.eof()
equals(), java.awt.Button*
equals(), java.lang.Boolean*
equals(), java.lang.Character*
equals(), java.lang.Double*
equals(), java.lang.Float*
equals(), java.lang.Integer*
equals(), java.lang.Long*
equals(), java.lang.Object*
equals(), java.lang.String*
equals(), java.util.Date*
equals(), netscape.plugin.Plugin
equalsIgnoreCase(), java.lang.String*
error(), File object*
error(), File.error()
errorCode(), SendMail object*
errorCode(), SendMail.errorCode()
errorMessage(), SendMail object*
errorMessage(), SendMail.errorMessage()
escape(), Global object*
etAttribute(), COMMENT object*
etData(), clipboardData object*
eval(), Global object*
eval(), JSObject object*
eval(), JSObject.eval()*
eval(), Object object*
eval(), Object.eval()
exec(), RegExp object*
exec(), RegExp.exec()
execCommand(), Document object*
execCommand(),
    Document.execCommand()
execCommand(), TextRange object*
execCommand(),
    TextRange.execCommand()
execScript()
execScript(), Global object*
execScript(), Window object*
execScript(), Window.execScript()
execute(), Connection object*
execute(), Connection.execute()
execute(), database object*
execute(), database.execute()
Exists(), Dictionary object*
Exists(), Dictionary.Exists()
exists(), File object*
exists(), File.exists()
expand(), TextRange object*
expand(), TextRange.expand()
expiration(), client object*
expiration(), client.expiration()
FileExists(), FileSystem object*
FileExists(), FileSystem.FileExists()
find()
find(), Global object*
find(), Window object*

Method (continued)

find(), Window.find()
findText(), TextRange object*
findText(), TextRange.findText()
fixed(), String object*
fixed(), String.fixed()
floatValue(), java.lang.Double*
floatValue(), java.lang.Float*
floatValue(), java.lang.Integer*
floatValue(), java.lang.Long*
flush, Global object*
flush(), File object*
flush(), File object*
flush(), File.flush()
flush(), response object*
flush(), response.flush()
focus()
focus(), Anchor object*
focus(), Anchor.focus()
focus(), Element object*
focus(), File object*
focus(), Global object*
focus(), Input object*
focus(), Input.focus()
focus(), Window object*
focus(), Window.focus()
FolderExists(), FileSystem object*
FolderExists(), FileSystem.FolderExists()
fontcolor(), String object*
fontcolor(), String.fontcolor()
fontsize(), String object*
fontsize(), String.fontsize()
forward()
forward(), Global object*
forward(), History object*
forward(), History.forward()
forward(), Window object*
forward(), Window.forward()
fromCharCode(), String object*
fromCharCode()*, String.fromCharCode()*
Function()*
Function(), Global object*
GetAbsolutePathName(), FileSystem
   object*
GetAbsolutePathName(),
   FileSystem.GetAbsolutePathName()
getAdjacentText(), Element object*
getAdjacentText(),
   Element.getAdjacentText()
getAppletContext(), JavaObject object*
getAppletInfo(), JavaObject object*
getAttribute(), BASEFONT object*
getAttribute(), currentStyle object*
getAttribute(), Element object*
getAttribute(), Element.getAttribute()
getAttribute(), Frame object*
getAttribute(), runtimeStyle object*
getAttribute(), style object (2)*
getAttribute(), style.getAttribute()
getAttribute(), userProfile object*
getAttribute(), userProfile.getAttribute()
getAttributeNode(), Element object*
getAttributeNode(),
   Element.getAttributeNode()
getBackground(), java.awt.Button*
getBackground(), JavaObject object*

GetBaseName(), FileSystem object*
GetBaseName(),
   FileSystem.GetBaseName()
getBookmark(), TextRange object*
getBookmark(), TextRange.getBookmark()
getBoundingClientRect(), TextRange
   object*
getBoundingClientRect(),
   TextRange.getBoundingClientRect()
getBytes(), java.lang.String*
getChars(), java.lang.String*
getClass()
getClass(), java.awt.Button*
getClass(), java.lang.Boolean*
getClass(), java.lang.Character*
getClass(), java.lang.Double*
getClass(), java.lang.Float*
getClass(), java.lang.Integer*
getClass(), java.lang.Long*
getClass(), java.lang.Object*
getClass(), java.lang.String*
getClass(), java.util.Date*
getClass(), JavaObject object*
getClass(), JavaObject.getClass()*
getClass(), netscape.plugin.Plugin
getClientRects(), TextRange object*
getClientRects(),
   TextRange.getClientRects()
getCodeBase(), JavaObject object*
getColorModel(), java.awt.Button*
getData(), dataTransfer object*
getData(), dataTransfer.getData()
getDate(), Date object*
getDate(), Date.getDate()
getDate(), java.util.Date*
getDay(), Date object*
getDay(), Date.getDay()
getDay(), java.util.Date*
getDocumentBase(), JavaObject object*
GetDrive(), FileSystem object*
GetDrive(), FileSystem.GetDrive()
GetDriveName(), FileSystem object*
GetDriveName(),
   FileSystem.GetDriveName()
getElementById(), Document object*
getElementById(),
   Document.getElementById()
getElementsByName(), Document object*
getElementsByName(),
   Document.getElementsByName()
getElementsByTagName(), Document
   object*
getElementsByTagName(),
   Document.getElementsByTagName()
getElementsByTagName(), Element object*
getElementsByTagName(),
   Element.getElementsByTagName()
getExpression(), currentStyle object*
getExpression(), Element object*
getExpression(), Element.getExpression()
getExpression(), runtimeStyle object*
getExpression(), style object (2)*
getExpression(), style.getExpression()
GetExtensionName(), FileSystem object*
GetExtensionName(),
   FileSystem.GetExtensionName()
GetFile(), FileSystem object*

GetFile(), FileSystem.GetFile()
GetFileName(), FileSystem object*
GetFileName(), FileSystem.GetFileName()
GetFolder(), FileSystem object*
GetFolder(), FileSystem.GetFolder()
getFont(), java.awt.Button*
getFontMetrics(), java.awt.Button*
getForeground(), java.awt.Button*
getFullYear(), Date object*
getFullYear(), Date.getFullYear()
getGraphics(), java.awt.Button*
getHours(), Date object*
getHours(), Date.getHours()
getHours(), java.util.Date*
getItem(), VBArray object*
getItem(), VBArray.getItem()
getLabel(), java.awt.Button*
getLength(), File object*
getLength(), File.getLength()
getLocale(), java.awt.Button*
getLocale(), JavaObject object*
getMember(), JSObject object*
getMember(), JSObject.getMember()*
getMilliseconds(), Date object*
getMilliseconds(), Date.getMilliseconds()
getMinutes(), Date object*
getMinutes(), Date.getMinutes()
getMinutes(), java.util.Date*
getMonth(), Date object*
getMonth(), Date.getMonth()
getMonth(), java.util.Date*
getNamedItem(), NamedNodeMap object*
getNamedItem(),
    NamedNodeMap.getNamedItem()
GetObject()*
GetObject(), WScript object*
GetObject(), WScript.GetObject()
getOptionValue(), Global object*
getOptionValue(), response object*
getOptionValue(),
    response.getOptionValue()
getOptionValueCount(), Global object*
getOptionValueCount(), response object*
getOptionValueCount(),
    response.getOptionValueCount()
getParameter(), JavaObject object*
getParameterInfo(), JavaObject object*
getParent(), java.awt.Button*
GetParentFolderName(), FileSystem
    object*
GetParentFolderName(),
    FileSystem.GetParentFolderName()
getPeer(), java.awt.Button*
getPeer(), netscape.plugin.Plugin
getPosition(), File object*
getPosition(), File.getPosition()
getPrivilegeTableFromStack(),
    netscape.security.PrivilegeManager*
getSeconds(), Date object*
getSeconds(), Date.getSeconds()
getSeconds(), java.util.Date*
getSelection(), Document object*
getSelection(), Document.getSelection()
getSlot(), JSObject object*
getSlot(), JSObject.getSlot()*
GetSpecialFolder(), FileSystem object*

GetSpecialFolder(),
    FileSystem.GetSpecialFolder()
GetTempName(), FileSystem object*
GetTempName(),
    FileSystem.GetTempName()
getTime(), Date object*
getTime(), Date.getTime()
getTime(), java.util.Date*
getTimezoneOffset(), Date object*
getTimezoneOffset(),
    Date.getTimezoneOffset()
getTimezoneOffset(), java.util.Date*
getToolkit(), java.awt.Button*
getToolkit(), JavaObject object*
getUTCDate(), Date object*
getUTCDate(), Date.getUTCDate()
getUTCDay(), Date object*
getUTCDay(), Date.getUTCDay()
getUTCFullYear(), Date object*
getUTCFullYear(), Date.getUTCFullYear()
getUTCHours(), Date object*
getUTCHours(), Date.getUTCHours()
getUTCMilliseconds(), Date object*
getUTCMilliseconds(),
    Date.getUTCMilliseconds()
getUTCMinutes(), Date object*
getUTCMinutes(), Date.getUTCMinutes()
getUTCMonth(), Date object*
getUTCMonth(), Date.getUTCMonth()
getUTCSeconds(), Date object*
getUTCSeconds(), Date.getUTCSeconds()
getVarDate(), Date object*
getVarDate(), Date.getVarDate()
getWindow(), netscape.plugin.Plugin
getWindow(), JSObject.getWindow()*
getYear(), Date object*
getYear(), Date.getYear()
getYear(), java.util.Date*
go(), History object*
go(), History.go()
gotFocus(), java.awt.Button*
handleEvent()*
handleEvent(), Button object*
handleEvent(), Button.handleEvent()
handleEvent(), Checkbox object*
handleEvent(), Checkbox.handleEvent()
handleEvent(), Document object*
handleEvent(), Document.handleEvent()*
handleEvent(), FileUpload object*
handleEvent(), FileUpload.handleEvent()
handleEvent(), Form object*
handleEvent(), Form.handleEvent()
handleEvent(), Input object*
handleEvent(), Input.handleEvent()
handleEvent(), Layer.handleEvent()*
handleEvent(), Password object*
handleEvent(), Password.handleEvent()
handleEvent(), RadioButton object*
handleEvent(), RadioButton.handleEvent()
handleEvent(), ResetButton object*
handleEvent(), ResetButton.handleEvent()
handleEvent(), SubmitButton object*
handleEvent(), SubmitButton.handleEvent()
handleEvent(), TEXTAREA object*
handleEvent(), TEXTAREA.handleEvent()
handleEvent(), TextCell object*

Method (continued)

Method (continued)

moveToAbsolute(), Layer.moveToAbsolute()
moveToBookmark(), TextRange object*
moveToBookmark(),
 TextRange.moveToBookmark()
moveToElementText(), TextRange object*
moveToElementText(),
 TextRange.moveToElementText()
moveToPoint(), TextRange object*
moveToPoint(), TextRange.moveToPoint()
namedItem(), Collection object*
namedItem(), Collection.namedItem()
navigate()
navigate(), Global object*
navigate(), Window object*
navigate(), Window.navigate()
NavigateAndFind(), external object*
NavigateAndFind(),
 external.NavigateAndFind()
next(), Cursor object*
next(), Cursor.next()
next(), ResultSet object*
next(), ResultSet.next()
nextFocus(), java.awt.Button*
nextPage(), TABLE object*
nextPage(), TABLE.nextPage()
normalize(), Element object*
normalize(), Element.normalize()
notify(), java.awt.Button*
notify(), java.lang.Boolean*
notify(), java.lang.Character*
notify(), java.lang.Double*
notify(), java.lang.Float*
notify(), java.lang.Integer*
notify(), java.lang.Long*
notify(), java.lang.Object*
notify(), java.lang.String*
notify(), java.util.Date*
notify(), netscape.plugin.Plugin
notifyAll(), java.awt.Button*
notifyAll(), java.lang.Boolean*
notifyAll(), java.lang.Character*
notifyAll(), java.lang.Double*
notifyAll(), java.lang.Float*
notifyAll(), java.lang.Integer*
notifyAll(), java.lang.Long*
notifyAll(), java.lang.Object*
notifyAll(), java.lang.String*
notifyAll(), java.util.Date*
notifyAll(), netscape.plugin.Plugin
Number()*
Number(), Global object*
Object()*
Object(), Global object*
offset(), Layer object*
offset(), Layer.offset()
open()
open(), Document object*
open(), Document.open()
open(), File object*
open(), File object*
open(), File.open()
open(), Global object*
open(), Window object*
open(), Window.open()
OpenAsTextStream(), File object*

OpenAsTextStream(),
 File.OpenAsTextStream()
OpenTextFile(), FileSystem object*
OpenTextFile(), FileSystem.OpenTextFile()
outParamCount(), Stproc object*
outParamCount(), Stproc.outParamCount()
outParameters(), Stproc object*
outParameters(), Stproc.outParameters()
paddings(), JSSTag object*
paddings(), JSSTag.paddings()
paint(), java.awt.Button*
paintAll(), java.awt.Button*
parentElement(), TextRange object*
parentElement(),
 TextRange.parentElement()
parse(), Date object*
parse(), Date.parse()*
parseFloat(), Global object*
parseInt(), Global object*
pasteHTML(), TextRange object*
pasteHTML(), TextRange.pasteHTML()
play(), filter - Barn()*
play(), filter - Blinds()*
play(), filter - Compositor()*
play(), filter - Fade()*
play(), filter - GradientWipe()*
play(), filter - Inset()*
play(), filter - Iris()*
play(), filter - Pixelate()*
play(), filter - Pixelate()*
play(), filter - RadialWipe()*
play(), filter - RandomBars()*
play(), filter - RandomDissolve()*
play(), filter - Slide()*
play(), filter - Spiral()*
play(), filter - Stretch()*
play(), filter - Strips()*
play(), filter - Wheel()*
play(), filter - Zigzag()*
plugins, Navigator object*
pop(), Array object*
pop(), Array.pop()
postEvent(), java.awt.Button*
preference(), Navigator object*
preference(), Navigator.preference()
preferredSize(), java.awt.Button*
prepareImage(), java.awt.Button*
preventDefault(), Event object*
preventDefault(), Event.preventDefault()
preventDefault(), MouseEvent object*
preventDefault(), MutationEvent object*
previousPage(), TABLE object*
previousPage(), TABLE.previousPage()
print()
print(), Global object*
print(), java.awt.Button*
print(), Window object*
print(), Window.print()
printAll(), java.awt.Button*
prompt()
prompt(), Global object*
prompt(), Window object*
prompt(), Window.prompt()
propertyIsEnumerable(), Object object*
propertyIsEnumerable(),
 Object.propertyIsEnumerable()

push(), Array object*
push(), Array.push()
put()*
querycommandEnabled(), Document
object*
querycommandEnabled(),
Document.querycommandEnabled()
querycommandEnabled(), TextRange
object*
querycommandEnabled(),
TextRange.querycommandEnabled()
querycommandIndeterm(), Document
object*
querycommandIndeterm(),
Document.querycommandIndeterm()
querycommandIndeterm(), TextRange
object*
querycommandIndeterm(),
TextRange.querycommandIndeterm()
querycommandState(), Document object*
querycommandState(),
Document.querycommandState()
querycommandState(), TextRange object*
querycommandState(),
TextRange.querycommandState()
querycommandSupported(), Document
object*
querycommandSupported(),
Document.querycommandSupported()
querycommandSupported(), TextRange
object*
querycommandSupported(),
TextRange.querycommandSupported()
querycommandText(), Document object*
querycommandText(),
Document.querycommandText()
querycommandText(), TextRange object*
querycommandText(),
TextRange.querycommandText()
querycommandValue(), Document object*
querycommandValue(),
Document.querycommandValue()
querycommandValue(), TextRange object*
querycommandValue(),
TextRange.querycommandValue()
Quit(), WScript object*
Quit(), WScript.Quit()
random(), Crypto object*
random(), Crypto.random()
random(), Math.random()*
read(), File object*
read(), File object*
read(), File.read()
Read(), TextStream object*
Read(), TextStream.Read()
ReadAll(), TextStream object*
ReadAll(), TextStream.ReadAll()
readByte(), File object*
readByte(), File object*
readByte(), File.readByte()
ReadLine(), TextStream object*
ReadLine(), TextStream.ReadLine()
readln(), File object*
readln(), File.readln()
recalc(), Document object*
recalc(), Document.recalc()
redirect, Global object*

redirect(), response object*
redirect(), response.redirect()
refresh(), JavaObject object*
refresh(), Navigator.plugins.refresh()
refresh(), Plugin object*
refresh(), Plugin.refresh()
refresh(), PluginArray object*
refresh(), PluginArray.refresh()
refresh(), TABLE object*
refresh(), TABLE.refresh()
regionMatches(), java.lang.String*
registerCFunction(), Global object*
registerCFunction(), response object*
registerCFunction(),
response.registerCFunction()
release(), Connection object*
release(), Connection.release()
releaseCapture(), Element object*
releaseCapture(), Element.releaseCapture()
releaseEvents()
releaseEvents(), Document object*
releaseEvents(),
Document.releaseEvents()*
releaseEvents(), Layer.releaseEvents()*
releaseEvents(), Window.releaseEvents()*
reload(), Location object*
reload(), Location.reload()
Remove(), Dictionary object*
Remove(), Dictionary.Remove()
remove(), OptionsArray object*
remove(), OptionsArray.remove()
remove(), Select object*
remove(), Select.remove()
RemoveAll(), Dictionary object*
RemoveAll(), Dictionary.RemoveAll()
removeAttribute(), CENTER object
removeAttribute(), COMMENT object*
removeAttribute(), Element object*
removeAttribute(),
Element.removeAttribute()
removeAttribute(), Frame object*
removeAttributeNode(), Element object*
removeAttributeNode(),
Element.removeAttributeNode()
removeBehavior(), Element object*
removeBehavior(),
Element.removeBehavior()
removeChild(), Node object*
removeChild(), Node.removeChild()
removeEventListener(), EventTarget object*
removeEventListener(),
EventTarget.removeEventListener()
removeExpression(), currentStyle object*
removeExpression(), Element object*
removeExpression(),
Element.removeExpression()
removeExpression(), runtimeStyle object*
removeExpression(), style object (2)*
removeExpression(),
style.removeExpression()
removeMember(), JSObject object*
removeMember(),
JSObject.removeMember()*
removeNamedItem(), NamedNodeMap
object*
removeNamedItem(),
NamedNodeMap.removeNamedItem()

Method (continued)

removeNotify(), java.awt.Button*
removeRule(), StyleSheet object*
removeRule(), StyleSheet.removeRule()
repaint(), java.awt.Button*
replace(), java.lang.String*
replace(), Location object*
replace(), Location.replace()
replace(), String object*
replace(), String.replace()
replaceAdjacentText(), Element object*
replaceAdjacentText(),
    Element.replaceAdjacentText()
replaceChild(), Node object*
replaceChild(), Node.replaceChild()
replaceData(), CharacterData object*
replaceData(), CharacterData.replaceData()
requestFocus(), java.awt.Button*
reset(), Form object*
reset(), Form.reset()
reshape(), java.awt.Button*
resize(), java.awt.Button*
resizeBy()
resizeBy(), Global object*
resizeBy(), Layer object*
resizeBy(), Layer.resizeBy()
resizeBy(), Window object*
resizeBy(), Window.resizeBy()
resizeTo()
resizeTo(), Global object*
resizeTo(), Layer object*
resizeTo(), Layer.resizeTo()
resizeTo(), Window object*
resizeTo(), Window.resizeTo()
resultSet(), Stproc object*
resultSet(), Stproc.resultSet()
returnValue(), Stproc object*
returnValue(), Stproc.returnValue()
reverse(), Array object*
reverse(), Array.reverse()
rgb(), JSSTag object*
rgb(), JSSTag.rgb()
rollbackTransaction(), Connection object*
rollbackTransaction(),
    Connection.rollbackTransaction()
rollbackTransaction(), database object*
rollbackTransaction(),
    database.rollbackTransaction()
routeEvent(), Document object*
savePreferences(), Navigator object*
savePreferences(),
    Navigator.savePreferences()
scroll()
scroll(), Global object*
scroll(), Window object*
scroll(), Window.scroll()
scrollBy()
scrollBy(), Global object*
scrollBy(), Window object*
scrollBy(), Window.scrollBy()
scrollIntoView(), Element object*
scrollIntoView(), Element.scrollIntoView()
scrollTo()
scrollTo(), Global object*
scrollTo(), Window object*
scrollTo(), Window.scrollTo()
search(), String object*

search(), String.search()
select(), File object*
select(), FileUpload object*
select(), FileUpload.select()
select(), Image object*
select(), IMG object*
select(), Input object*
select(), Input.select()
select(), OptionsArray object*
select(), OptionsArray.select()
select(), Password object*
select(), Password.select()
select(), TEXTAREA object*
select(), TEXTAREA.select()
select(), TextCell object*
select(), TextCell.select()
select(), TextRange object*
select(), TextRange.select()
send(), SendMail object*
send(), SendMail.send()
setAttribute(), COMMENT object*
setAttribute(), currentStyle object*
setAttribute(), Element object*
setAttribute(), Element.setAttribute()
setAttribute(), Frame object*
setAttribute(), runtimeStyle object*
setAttribute(), style object (2)*
setAttribute(), style.setAttribute()
setAttributeNode(), Element object*
setAttributeNode(),
    Element.setAttributeNode()
setBackground(), java.awt.Button*
setCapture(), Element object*
setCapture(), Element.setCapture()
setData(), clipboardData object*
setData(), dataTransfer object*
setData(), dataTransfer.setData()
setDate(), Date object*
setDate(), java.util.Date*
setDate(), Date.setDate()
setEndPoint(), TextRange object*
setEndPoint(), TextRange.setEndPoint()
setExpression(), currentStyle object*
setExpression(), Element object*
setExpression(), Element.setExpression()
setExpression(), runtimeStyle object*
setExpression(), style object (2)*
setExpression(), style.setExpression()
setFont(), java.awt.Button*
setForeground(), java.awt.Button*
setFullYear(), Date object*
setFullYear(), Date.setFullYear()
setHotkeys()
setHotkeys(), Global object*
setHotkeys(), Window object*
setHotkeys(), Window.setHotkeys()
setHours(), Date object*
setHours(), Date.setHours()
setHours(), java.util.Date*
setInterval()
setInterval(), Global object*
setInterval(), Window object*
setInterval(), Window.setInterval()
setLabel(), java.awt.Button*
setMember(), JSObject object*
setMember(), JSObject.setMember()*
setMilliseconds(), Date object*

Method (continued)

stop(), filter - Slide()*
stop(), filter - Spiral()*
stop(), filter - Stretch()*
stop(), filter - Strips()*
stop(), filter - Wheel()*
stop(), filter - Zigzag()*
stop(), Global object*
stop(), JavaObject object*
stop(), MARQUEE object*
stop(), MARQUEE.stop()
stop(), Window object*
stop(), Window.stop()
stopPropagation(), Event object*
stopPropagation(), Event.stopPropagation()
stopPropagation(), MouseEvent object*
stopPropagation(), MutationEvent object*
storedProc(), Connection object*
storedProc(), Connection.storedProc()
storedProc(), database object*
storedProc(), database.storedProc()
storedProcArgs(), database object*
storedProcArgs(),
   database.storedProcArgs()
storedProcArgs(), DbPool object*
storedProcArgs(), DbPool.storedProcArgs()
strike(), String object*
strike(), String.strike()
String()*
String(), Global object*
stringToByte(), File object*
stringToByte(), File.stringToByte()
sub(), String object*
sub(), String.sub()
submit(), Form object*
submit(), Form.submit()
substr(), String object*
substr(), String.substr()
substring(), java.lang.String*
substring(), String object*
substring(), String.substring()
substringData(), CharacterData object*
substringData(),
   CharacterData.substringData()
sup(), String object*
sup(), String.sup()
tags(), Collection object*
tags(), Collection.tags()
tags(), rows object
tags(), Select object*
tags(), Select.tags()
taintEnabled(), Navigator object*
taintEnabled(), Navigator.taintEnabled()
test(), RegExp object*
test(), RegExp.test()
toArray(), VBArray object*
toArray(), VBArray.toArray()
toCharArray(), java.lang.String*
toDateString(), Date object*
toDateString(), Date.toDateString()
toExponential(), Number object*
toExponential(), Number.toExponential()
toFixed(), Number object*
toFixed(), Number.toFixed()
toGMTString(), Date object*
toGMTString(), Date.toGMTString()
toGMTString(), java.util.Date*
toLocaleDateString(), Date object*

toLocaleDateString(),
   Date.toLocaleDateString()
toLocaleLowerCase(), String object*
toLocaleLowerCase(),
   String.toLocaleLowerCase()
toLocaleString(), Array object*
toLocaleString(), Array.toLocaleString()
toLocaleString(), Date object*
toLocaleString(), Date.toLocaleString()
toLocaleString(), java.util.Date*
toLocaleString(), Number object*
toLocaleString(), Number.toLocaleString()
toLocaleString(), Object object*
toLocaleString(), Object.toLocaleString()
toLocaleTimeString(), Date object*
toLocaleTimeString(),
   Date.toLocaleTimeString()
toLocaleUpperCase(), String object*
toLocaleUpperCase(),
   String.toLocaleUpperCase()
toLowerCase(), java.lang.String*
toLowerCase(), String object*
toLowerCase(), String.toLowerCase()
toPrecision(), Number object*
toPrecision(), Number.toPrecision()
toSource(), Array object*
toSource(), Array.toSource()
toSource(), Boolean object*
toSource(), Boolean.toSource()
toSource(), Date object*
toSource(), Date.toSource()
toSource(), Function object*
toSource(), Function.toSource()
toSource(), Number object*
toSource(), Number.toSource()
toSource(), Object object*
toSource(), Object.toSource()
toSource(), RegExp object*
toSource(), RegExp.toSource()
toSource(), String object*
toSource(), String.toSource()
toString(), Array object*
toString(), Array.toString()
toString(), Boolean object*
toString(), Boolean.toString()
toString(), Connection object*
toString(), Connection.toString()
toString(), database object*
toString(), database.toString()
toString(), Date object*
toString(), Date.toString()
toString(), DbPool object*
toString(), DbPool.toString()
toString(), Error object*
toString(), Error.toString()
toString(), Function object*
toString(), Function.toString()
toString(), java.awt.Button*
toString(), java.lang.Boolean*
toString(), java.lang.Character*
toString(), java.lang.Double*
toString(), java.lang.Float*
toString(), java.lang.Integer*
toString(), java.lang.Long*
toString(), java.lang.Object*
toString(), java.lang.String*
toString(), java.util.Date*
toString(), JavaArray object*

toString(), JavaArray.toString()
toString(), JavaObject object*
toString(), JSObject object*
toString(), JSObject.toString()*
toString(), netscape.plugin.Plugin
toString(), Number object*
toString(), Number.toString()
toString(), Object object*
toString(), Object.toString()
toString(), RegExp object*
toString(), RegExp.toString()
toString(), String object*
toString(), String.toString()
toString(), URIError object*
toTimeString(), Date object*
toTimeString(), Date.toTimeString()
toUpperCase(), java.lang.string*
toUpperCase(), String object*
toUpperCase(), String.toUpperCase()
toUTCString(), Date object*
toUTCString(), Date.toUTCString()
trace(), response object*
trace(), response.trace()
trim(), java.lang.String*
typeof(), Global object*
ubound(), VBArray object*
ubound(), VBArray.ubound()
unescape(), Global object*
unlock(), Lock object*
unlock(), Lock.unlock()
unlock(), project object*
unlock(), project.unlock()
unlock(), server object*
unlock(), server.unlock()
unshift(), Array object*
unshift(), Array.unshift()
unwatch(), Object object*
unwatch(), Object.unwatch()
update(), java.awt.Button*
updateRow(), Cursor object*
updateRow(), Cursor.updateRow()
UTC(), Date.UTC()*
validate(), java.awt.Button*
valueOf()
valueOf(), Array object*
valueOf(), Array.valueOf()
valueOf(), Boolean object*
valueOf(), Boolean.valueOf()
valueOf(), Date object*
valueOf(), Date.valueOf()
valueOf(), Function object*
valueOf(), Function.valueOf()
valueOf(), Number object*
valueOf(), Number.valueOf()
valueOf(), Object object*
valueOf(), Object.valueOf()
valueOf(), String object*
valueOf(), String.valueOf()
wait(), java.awt.Button*
wait(), java.lang.Boolean*
wait(), java.lang.Character*
wait(), java.lang.Double*
wait(), java.lang.Float*
wait(), java.lang.Integer*
wait(), java.lang.Long*
wait(), java.lang.Object*
wait(), java.lang.String*

wait(), java.util.Date*
wait(), netscape.plugin.Plugin
watch(), Object object*
watch(), Object.watch()
write(), Document object*
write(), Document.write()
write(), File object*
write(), File object*
write(), File.write()
write(), Global object*
write(), response object*
write(), response.write()
Write(), TextStream object*
Write(), TextStream.Write()
WriteBlankLines(), TextStream object*
WriteBlankLines(),
    TextStream.WriteBlankLines()
writeByte(), File object*
writeByte(), File.writeByte()
WriteLine(), TextStream object*
WriteLine(), TextStream.WriteLine()
writeln(), Document object*
writeln(), Document.writeln()
writeln(), File object*
writeln(), File object*
writeln(), File.writeln()

Method/internal
put()*

Method/Java
booleanValue(),
    JavaObject.booleanValue()*
getClass(), JavaObject.getClass()*

Method/static
parse(), Date.parse()*
UTC(), Date.UTC()*
fromCharCode(), String.fromCharCode()*

MIME type
text/JavaScript*

Object model
ASP*
Browser
Document*
WSH

Object/browser
Background object*
EmbedArray object*
FormArray object*
FormElement object*
FormElementsArray object
FrameArray object
Frames object*
History object*
ImageArray object*
InputArray object*
LinkArray object*
MimeType object*
MimeTypeArray object*

Object/browser (continued)

Navigator object*
OptionsArray object*
Plugin object*
PluginArray object*
Rect object*
Screen object*
ScriptArray object*
Selection object*
SelectorArray object*
Window object*

Object/core

Arguments object*
Array object*
Boolean object*
Date object*
Error object*
EvalError object*
Function object*
Global object*
Math object*
Number object*
Object object*
RangeError object*
ReferenceError object*
RegExp object*
String object*
SyntaxError object*
TypeError object*
URIError object*

Object/CSS

style object (2)*

Object/DOM

AbstractView object*
AnchorArray object*
AppletArray object*
Attr object*
Attribute object*
Attributes object*
Button object*
CDATASection object*
CharacterData object*
Checkbox object*
ChildNodes object*
Collection object*
COMMENT object*
Doctype object*
DocumentEvent*
DocumentFragment object*
DocumentStyle object*
DocumentType object
DOMImplementation object
Entity object*
EntityReference object*
Event object*
EventException object*
EventListener object*
EventTarget object*
FileUpload object*
Frame object*
Hidden object*
Implementation object*

Input object*
LinkStyle object*
Location object*
MediaList object*
ModElement object*
MouseEvent object*
MutationEvent object*
NamedNodeMap object*
Node object*
NodeList object*
Notation object*
OptionElement object
Password object*
ProcessingInstruction object*
RadioButton object*
ResetButton object*
rule object*
StyleSheet object*
StyleSheetList object*
SubmitButton object*
TableSectionElement object
Text object
TEXTAREA object*
TextCell object*
textNode object*
UIEvent object*
userDefined object*

Object/HTML

! object*
<!-- ... --> (Comment block)
A object
ABBR object
ACRONYM object
ADDRESS object
Anchor object*
Applet object*
Area object*
B object
BASE object*
BASEFONT object*
BDO object*
BGSOUND object*
BIG object
BLOCKQUOTE object*
BODY object*
BR object*
BUTTON object*
CAPTION object*
CENTER object
CITE object
CODE object
COL object*
COLGROUP object*
DD object*
DEL object*
DFN object
DIR object*
DIV object*
DL object*
Document object*
DT object*
Element object*
EM object*
Embed object*
FIELDSET object*
FONT object*

Form object*
FRAMESET object*
H<n> object*
HEAD object*
HR object*
HTML object*
HyperLink object*
I object*
IFRAME object*
Image object*
IMG object*
INS object*
ISINDEX object*
KBD object*
Label object*
Legend object*
LI object*
LINK object*
LISTING object*
Map object*
MARQUEE object*
MENU object*
META object*
NOFRAMES object*
NOSCRIPT object*
OBJECT object*
OL object*
OptGroupElement object*
Option object*
P object*
ParamElement object*
PLAINTEXT object
PRE object*
Q object
RT object
RUBY object*
S object
SAMP object
SCRIPT object*
Select object*
SMALL object
SPAN object*
STRIKE object
STRONG object*
STYLE object (1)*
SUB object
SUP object
TABLE object*
TableColElement object*
TBODY object*
TD object*
TFOOT object*
TH object*
THEAD object*
TITLE object*
TR object*
TT object*
U object*
UL object*
Url object*
VAR object
XMP object

Object/internal

Activation object
Call object
Closure object*

Object/JScript

ActiveXObject object*
Automation object
clipboardData object*
currentStyle object*
dataTransfer object*
Dialog object*
Dictionary object*
Drive object*
Drives object*
Enumerator object*
external object*
File object*
Files object*
FileSystem object*
Filter object*
Filters object
Folder object*
Folders object*
runtimeStyle object*
TextRange object*
textRectangle object*
TextStream object*
userProfile object*
VBArray object*
vCard object*
XML object*

Object/JSS

JSSClasses object*
JSSTag object*
JSSTags object*

Object/Navigator

Bar object*
Clip object*
Closure()*
Crypto object*
EventCapturer object*
JavaArray object*
JavaClass object*
JavaMethod object
JavaObject object*
JavaPackage object*
Layer object*
LayerArray object*
Pkcs11 object*
Sidebar object*

Object/NES

blob object*
client object*
Connection object*
Cursor object*
database object*
DbPool object*
File object*
Lock object*
project object*
request object*
response object*
ResultSet object*
SendMail object*
server object*
Stproc object*

Object/WSH
WScript object*

Operator/additive
- (Minus)
+ (Add)
Add (+)*
Minus (-)
Subtract (-)*

Operator/assignment
%= (Modulo assign)
&= (Bitwise AND assign)
*= (Multiply assign)
/= (Divide assign)
^= (Bitwise XOR assign)
|= (Bitwise OR assign)
+= (Add assign)
<<= (Bitewise shift left assign)
 = (Assign)*
-= (Minus assign)
>>= (Bitwise shift right assign)
>>>= (Bitwise unsigned shift right assign)
Add then assign (+=)*
Assign value (=)*
Bitwise AND then assign (&=)*
Bitwise OR then assign (|=)*
Bitwise shift left then assign (<<=)*
Bitwise shift right and assign (>>=)*
Bitwise unsigned shift right and assign
 (>>>=)*
Bitwise XOR and assign (^=)*
Concatenate then assign (+=)*
Divide then assign (/=)*
Minus then assign (-=)
Multiply then assign (*=)*
Remainder then assign (%=)*
Subtract then assign (-=)*

Operator/bitwise
& (Bitwise AND)
^ (Bitwise XOR)
| (Bitwise OR)
~ (Bitwise NOT)
<< (Bitwise shift left)
>> (Bitwise shift right)
>>> (Bitwise unsigned shift right)
Bitwise AND (&)*
Bitwise NOT - complement (~)*
Bitwise OR (|)*
Bitwise shift left (<<)*
Bitwise shift right (>>)*
Bitwise unsigned shift right (>>>)*
Bitwise XOR (^)*
Left shift
Right shift

Operator/conditional
?: (Conditional block)
Conditionally execute (?:)*

Operator/equality
!= (NOT equal)
== (Equal to)
Equal to (==)*
NOT Equal to (!=)*

Operator/identity
!== (NOT identical)
=== (Identical to)
Exactly equal to (===)
Identically equal to (===)*
NOT Identically equal to (!==)*
Strictly equal to (===)

Operator/internal
ToBoolean*
ToInt32*
ToInteger*
ToNumber*
ToObject*
ToPrimitive*
ToString*
ToUint16*
ToUint32*

Operator/logical
! (Logical NOT)
&& (Logical AND)
|| (Logical OR)
in*
instanceof*
Logical AND (&&)*
Logical NOT - complement (!)*
Logical OR (||)*
Logical XOR*

Operator/multiplicative
% (Modulo/remainder)
* (Multiply)
/ (Divide)
Divide (/)*
Modulo
Multiply (*)*
Remainder (%)*

Operator/postfix
-- (Post decrement)
++ (Post increment)
Decrement value (--)*
Increment value (++)*
Postfix decrement (--)*
Postfix expression*
Postfix increment (++)*

Operator/prefix
-- (Pre decrement)
++ (Pre increment)
Prefix decrement (--)*
Prefix expression*
Prefix increment (++)*

Operator/relational
< (Less than)
<= (Less than or equal to)
> (Greater than)
>= (Greater than or equal to)
Greater than (>)*
Greater than or equal to (>=)*
Less than (<)*
Less than or equal to (<=)*

Operator/string
+ (Concatenate)
Concatenate (+)
String concatenate (+)*

Operator/unary
- (Unary minus)
+ (Unary plus)
delete*
Negation operator (-)*
new*
Positive value (+)*
typeof*
void*

Overview (see also Background, Definition)
Character-case mapping
Compliance
JavaScript language
Lexical element
Pointers
Topic classification

Pitfall (see also Advice, Useful tip)
</SCRIPT>*
Bar.visibility*
Deprecated functionality*
Escaped JavaScript quotes in HTML*
Hiding scripts from old browsers*
HTML entity escape*
JavaScript entity*
Newlines are not <BR> tags*
Off by one errors*
style.zOrder*

Pre-processor
@*/*
@_alpha
@_jscript
@_jscript_build
@_jscript_version
@_mac
@_mc680x0
@_PowerPC
@_win16
@_win32
@_x86
@<variable_name>
@cc_on
@elif(...) ...
@else ...
@end
@if(...) ...
@set
Conditional code block*
Pre-processing - @_alpha*
Pre-processing - @_jscript*
Pre-processing - @_jscript_build*
Pre-processing - @_jscript_version*
Pre-processing - @_mac*
Pre-processing - @_mc680x0*
Pre-processing - @_PowerPC*
Pre-processing - @_win16*

Pre-processing - @_win32*
Pre-processing - @_x86*
Pre-processing - @<variable_name>*
Pre-processing - @cc_on*
Pre-processing - @elif(...) ...*
Pre-processing - @else ...*
Pre-processing - @end*
Pre-processing - @if(...) ...*
Pre-processing - @set*

Primitive value
Boolean literal*
Boolean*
false*
Null literal*
null*
Number*
Numeric literal*
String literal*
String*
true*

Product
Active Server Pages
ActiveX
ADO
ASP
fdlibm
IIS
Internet Information Server
LiveConnect
LiveScript
LiveWire
NES
Netscape Enterprise Server
Nombas ScriptEase
Perl Connect
ScriptEase
Windows Script Host
WSH

Property
!.tabIndex
$', RegExp object*
$&, RegExp object*
$*, RegExp object*
$_, RegExp object*
$_, RegExp.$_
$`, RegExp object*
$+, RegExp object*
__parent__
__parent__, Closure object*
__parent__, Closure.__parent__
__parent__, Object object*
__parent__, Object.__parent__
__proto__
__proto__, Closure object*
__proto__, Closure.__proto__
__proto__, Object object*
__proto__, Object.__proto__
<column_name>, Cursor object*
<column_name>, Cursor.<column_name>
<form_name>, Document object*
<form_name>, Document.<form_name>
<input_name>, request object*

Property (continued)

<input_name>, request.<input_name>
<tagName>, JSSTags object*
<tagName>, JSSTags.<tagName>
<urlExtension>, request object*
<urlExtension>, request.<urlExtension>
abbr, TD object*
abbr, TD.abbr
abbr, TH object*
abbr, TH.abbr
above, Layer object*
above, Layer.above
accept, BUTTON object*
accept, BUTTON.accept
accept, FileUpload object*
accept, FileUpload.accept
accept, Input object*
accept, Input.accept
acceptCharset, Form object*
acceptCharset, Form.acceptCharset
accessKey, ! object*
accessKey, A object
accessKey, Anchor object*
accessKey, Anchor.accessKey
accessKey, Applet object*
accessKey, Area object*
accessKey, Area.accessKey
accessKey, BODY object*
accessKey, BUTTON object*
accessKey, Embed object*
accessKey, FIELDSET object*
accessKey, Form object*
accessKey, FRAMESET object*
accessKey, FRAMESET.accessKey
accessKey, IMG object*
accessKey, Input object*
accessKey, Input.accessKey
accessKey, Label object*
accessKey, Legend object*
accessKey, MARQUEE object*
accessKey, NOFRAMES object*
accessKey, NOSCRIPT object*
accessKey, OBJECT object*
accessKey, Select object*
accessKey, TBODY object*
accessKey, TD object*
action, Form object*
action, Form.action
activeElement, Document object*
activeElement, Document.activeElement
Add, filter - MotionBlur()*
Add, filter - Wave()*
agent, request object*
agent, request.agent
agent, server object*
agent, server.agent
align, Applet object*
align, Applet.align
align, CAPTION object*
align, CAPTION object*
align, CAPTION.align
align, COL object*
align, COL.align
align, COLGROUP object*
align, COLGROUP.align
align, DIV object*
align, DIV.align

align, Embed object*
align, Embed.align
align, FIELDSET object*
align, FIELDSET.align
align, H<n> object*
align, H<n>.align
align, HR object*
align, HR.align
align, IFRAME object*
align, IFRAME.align
align, IMG object*
align, IMG.align
align, Input object*
align, Input.align
align, JSSTag object*
align, JSSTag.align
align, Legend object*
align, Legend.align
align, OBJECT object*
align, OBJECT.align
align, P object*
align, P.align
align, TABLE object*
align, TABLE.align
align, TableColElement object*
align, TableColElement.align
align, TBODY object*
align, TBODY.align
align, TD object*
align, TD.align
align, TFOOT object*
align, TFOOT.align
align, TH object*
align, TH.align
align, THEAD object*
align, THEAD.align
align, TR object*
align, TR.align
aLink, BODY object*
aLink, BODY.aLink
alinkColor, Document object*
alinkColor, Document.alinkColor
alt, Applet object*
alt, Applet.alt
alt, Area object*
alt, Area.alt
alt, BUTTON object*
alt, BUTTON.alt
alt, IMG object*
alt, IMG.alt
alt, Input object*
alt, Input.alt
altHTML, Applet object*
altHTML, Applet.altHTML
altHtml, OBJECT object*
altHtml, OBJECT.altHtml
altKey, Event object*
altKey, Event.altKey
altKey, MouseEvent object*
altKey, MouseEvent.altKey
appCodeName, Navigator object*
appCodeName, Navigator.appCodeName
Application, WScript object*
Application, WScript.Application
apply, JSSTag object*
apply, JSSTag.apply
appMinorVersion, Navigator object*

appMinorVersion,
  Navigator.appMinorVersion
appName, Navigator object*
appName, Navigator.appName
appVersion, Navigator object*
appVersion, Navigator.appVersion
archive, Applet object*
archive, Applet.archive
archive, OBJECT object*
archive, OBJECT.archive
Arguments, WScript object*
Arguments, WScript.Arguments
arity, Function object*
arity, Function.arity
AtEndOfLine, TextStream object*
AtEndOfLine, TextStream.AtEndOfLine
AtEndOfStream, TextStream object*
AtEndOfStream,
  TextStream.AtEndOfStream
attrChange, MutationEvent object*
attrChange, MutationEvent.attrChange
Attributes, File object*
Attributes, File.Attributes
Attributes, Folder object*
Attributes, Folder.Attributes
attrName, MutationEvent object*
attrName, MutationEvent.attrName
AvailableSpace, Drive object*
AvailableSpace, Drive.AvailableSpace
availHeight, Screen object*
availHeight, Screen.availHeight
availLeft, Screen object*
availLeft, Screen.availLeft
availTop, Screen object*
availTop, Screen.availTop
availWidth, Screen object*
availWidth, Screen.availWidth
axis, TD object*
axis, TD.axis
axis, TH object*
axis, TH.axis
azimuth, style object (2)*
azimuth, style.azimuth
background, BODY object*
background, BODY.background
background, Document object*
background, Document.background
background, JSSTag object*
background, Layer object*
background, Layer.background
background, style object (2)*
background, style.background
background, TABLE object*
background, TABLE.background
background, TD object*
background, TD.background
background, TH object*
background, TH.background
backgroundAttachment, style object (2)*
backgroundAttachment,
  style.backgroundAttachment
backgroundColor, JSSTag object*
backgroundColor, JSSTag.backgroundColor
backgroundColor, style object (2)*
backgroundColor, style.backgroundColor
backgroundImage, JSSTag object*
backgroundImage,
  JSSTag.backgroundImage

backgroundImage, style object (2)*
backgroundImage, style.backgroundImage
backgroundPosition, style object (2)*
backgroundPosition,
  style.backgroundPosition
backgroundPositionX, style object (2)*
backgroundPositionX,
  style.backgroundPositionX
backgroundPositionY, style object (2)*
backgroundPositionY,
  style.backgroundPositionY
backgroundRepeat, style object (2)*
backgroundRepeat,
  style.backgroundRepeat
balance, BGSOUND object*
balance, BGSOUND.balance
bands, filter - Blinds()*
bands, filter - Slide()*
Bcc, SendMail object*
Bcc, SendMail.Bcc
behavior, MARQUEE object*
behavior, MARQUEE.behaviour
behavior, style object (2)*
behavior, style.behavior
below, Layer object*
below, Layer.below
bgColor, BODY object*
bgColor, BODY.bgColor
bgColor, Document object*
bgColor, Document.bgColor
bgColor, JSSTag object*
bgColor, Layer object*
bgColor, Layer.bgColor
bgColor, MARQUEE object*
bgColor, MARQUEE.bgColor
bgColor, TABLE object*
bgColor, TABLE.bgColor
bgColor, TBODY object*
bgColor, TBODY.bgColor
bgColor, TD object*
bgColor, TD.bgColor
bgColor, TFOOT object*
bgColor, TFOOT.bgColor
bgColor, TH object*
bgColor, TH.bgColor
bgColor, THEAD object*
bgColor, THEAD.bgColor
bgColor, TR object*
bgColor, TR.bgColor
bgProperties, BODY object*
bgProperties, BODY.bgProperties
Bias, filter - Emboss()*
Bias, filter - Engrave()*
body, Document object*
body, Document.body
Body, SendMail object*
Body, SendMail.Body
border, FRAMESET object*
border, FRAMESET.border
border, Image object*
border, Image.border
border, IMG object*
border, IMG.border
border, OBJECT object*
border, OBJECT.border
border, style object (2)*
border, style.border
border, TABLE object*

Property (continued)

border, TABLE.border
borderBottom, style object (2)*
borderBottom, style.borderBottom
borderBottomColor, style object (2)*
borderBottomColor,
  style.borderBottomColor
BorderBottomStyle, style object (2)*
borderBottomStyle,
  style.borderBottomStyle
borderBottomWidth, JSSTag object*
borderBottomWidth,
  JSSTag.borderBottomWidth
borderBottomWidth, style object (2)*
borderBottomWidth,
  style.borderBottomWidth
borderCollapse, style object (2)*
borderCollapse, style.borderCollapse
borderColor, Frame object*
borderColor, Frame.borderColor
borderColor, FRAMESET object*
borderColor, FRAMESET.borderColor
borderColor, JSSTag object*
borderColor, JSSTag.borderColor
borderColor, style object (2)*
borderColor, style.borderColor
borderColor, TABLE object*
borderColor, TABLE.borderColor
borderColor, TD object*
borderColor, TD.borderColor
borderColor, TH object*
borderColor, TH.borderColor
borderColor, TR object*
borderColor, TR.borderColor
borderColorDark, TABLE object*
borderColorDark, TABLE.borderColorDark
borderColorDark, TD object*
borderColorDark, TD.borderColorDark
borderColorDark, TH object*
borderColorDark, TH.borderColorDark
borderColorDark, TR object*
borderColorDark, TR.borderColorDark
borderColorLight, TABLE object*
borderColorLight, TABLE.borderColorLight
borderColorLight, TD object*
borderColorLight, TD.borderColorLight
borderColorLight, TH object*
borderColorLight, TH.borderColorLight
borderColorLight, TR object*
borderColorLight, TR.borderColorLight
borderLeft, style object (2)*
borderLeft, style.borderLeft
borderLeftColor, style object (2)*
borderLeftColor, style.borderLeftColor
borderLeftStyle, style object (2)*
borderLeftStyle, style.borderLeftStyle
borderLeftWidth, JSSTag object*
borderLeftWidth, JSSTag.borderLeftWidth
borderLeftWidth, style object (2)*
borderLeftWidth, style.borderLeftWidth
borderRight, style object (2)*
borderRight, style.borderRight
borderRightColor, style object (2)*
borderRightColor, style.borderRightColor
borderRightStyle, style object (2)*
borderRightStyle, style.borderRightStyle
borderRightWidth, JSSTag object*

borderRightWidth,
  JSSTag.borderRightWidth
borderRightWidth, style object (2)*
borderRightWidth, style.borderRightWidth
borderSpacing, style object (2)*
borderSpacing, style.borderSpacing
borderStyle, JSSTag object*
borderStyle, JSSTag.borderStyle
borderStyle, style object (2)*
borderStyle, style.borderStyle
borderTop, style object (2)*
borderTop, style.borderTop
borderTopColor, style object (2)*
borderTopColor, style.borderTopColor
borderTopStyle, style object (2)*
borderTopStyle, style.borderTopStyle
borderTopWidth, JSSTag object*
borderTopWidth, JSSTag.borderTopWidth
borderTopWidth, style object (2)*
borderTopWidth, style.borderTopWidth
borderWidth, style object (2)*
borderWidth, style.borderWidth
bottom, Clip object*
bottom, Clip.bottom
bottom, Rect object*
bottom, Rect.bottom
bottom, style object (2)*
bottom, style.bottom
bottom, textRectangle object*
bottom, textRectangle.bottom
bottomMargin, BODY object*
bottomMargin, BODY.bottomMargin
boundingHeight, TextRange object*
boundingHeight, TextRange.boundingHeight
boundingLeft, TextRange object*
boundingLeft, TextRange.boundingLeft
boundingTop, TextRange object*
boundingTop, TextRange.boundingTop
boundingWidth, TextRange object*
boundingWidth, TextRange.boundingWidth
boxSizing, style object (2)*
boxSizing, style.boxSizing
browserLanguage, Navigator object*
browserLanguage,
  Navigator.browserLanguage
browserLanguage,
  Navigator.browserLanguage
bubbles, Event object*
bubbles, Event.bubbles
bubbles, MouseEvent object*
bubbles, MutationEvent object*
bufferDepth, Screen object*
bufferDepth, Screen.bufferDepth
button, Event object*
button, Event.button
button, MouseEvent object*
button, MouseEvent.button
callee, Arguments object*
callee, Arguments.callee
caller, Arguments object*
caller, Arguments.caller
caller, Function object*
caller, Function.caller
cancelable, Event object*
cancelable, Event.cancelable
cancelable, MouseEvent object*
cancelable, MutationEvent object*

cancelBubble, Event object*
cancelBubble, Event.cancelBubble
canhaveChildren, Element object*
canhaveChildren,
   Element.canhaveChildren
canhaveHTML, Element object*
canhaveHTML, Element.canhaveHTML
canhaveHTML, XML object*
caption, TABLE object*
caption, TABLE.caption
captionSide, style object (2)*
captionSide, style.captionSide
Cc, SendMail object*
Cc, SendMail.Cc
cellIndex, TD object*
cellIndex, TD.cellIndex
cellIndex, TH object*
cellIndex, TH.cellIndex
cellPadding, TABLE object*
cellPadding, TABLE.cellPadding
cellSpacing, style object (2)*
cellSpacing, style.cellSpacing
cellSpacing, TABLE object*
cellSpacing, TABLE.cellSpacing
ch, COL object*
ch, COL.ch
ch, COLGROUP object*
ch, COLGROUP.ch
ch, TableColElement object*
ch, TableColElement.ch
ch, TD object*
ch, TD.ch
ch, TFOOT object*
ch, TFOOT.ch
ch, TH object*
ch, TH.ch
ch, THEAD object*
ch, THEAD.ch
ch, TR object*
ch, TR.ch
characterset, Document object*
characterset, Document.characterset
charCode, Event object*
charCode, Event.charCode
charset, Anchor object*
charset, Anchor.charset
charset, Document object*
charset, Document.charset
charset, LINK object*
charset, LINK.charset
charset, META object*
charset, META.charset
charset, SCRIPT object*
charset, SCRIPT.charset
charset, Url object*
charset, Url.charset
checked, Checkbox object*
checked, Checkbox.checked
checked, Input object*
checked, Input.checked
checked, RadioButton object*
checked, RadioButton.checked
chOff, COL object*
chOff, COL.chOff
chOff, COLGROUP object*
chOff, COLGROUP.chOff
chOff, TableColElement object*

chOff, TableColElement.chOff
chOff, TBODY object*
chOff, TD object*
chOff, TD.chOff
chOff, TFOOT object*
chOff, TFOOT.chOff
chOff, TH object*
chOff, TH.chOff
chOff, THEAD object*
chOff, THEAD.chOff
chOff, TR object*
chOff, TR.chOff
cite, BLOCKQUOTE object*
cite, BLOCKQUOTE.cite
cite, DEL object*
cite, DEL.cite
cite, INS object*
cite, INS.cite
cite, ModElement object*
cite, ModElement.cite
cite, Q object
classes
classid, OBJECT object*
classid, OBJECT.classid
className, Element object*
className, Element.className
className, Frame object*
className, JSSClasses object*
className, JSSClasses.className
clear, BR object*
clear, BR.clear
clear, JSSTag object*
clear, JSSTag.clear
clear, style object (2)*
clear, style.clear
client, response object*
client, response.client
clientHeight, Element object*
clientHeight, Element.clientHeight
clientInformation
clientInformation, Global object*
clientInformation, Window object*
clientInformation, Window.clientInformation
clientLeft, Element object*
clientLeft, Element.clientLeft
clientTop, Element object*
clientTop, Element.clientTop
clientWidth, Element object*
clientWidth, Element.clientWidth
clientX, Event object*
clientX, Event.clientX
clientX, MouseEvent object*
clientX, MouseEvent.clientX
clientY, Event object*
clientY, Event.clientY
clientY, MouseEvent object*
clientY, MouseEvent.clientY
clip, JSSTag object*
clip, Layer object*
clip, Layer.clip
clip, style object (2)*
clip, style.clip
clip.bottom, Layer.clip.bottom
clip.bottom, style.clip.bottom
clip.height, Layer.clip.height
clip.left, Layer.clip.left
clip.left, style.clip.left

Property (continued)

Property (continued)

counterIncrement, style.counterIncrement
counterReset, style object (2)*
counterReset, style.counterReset
cpuClass, Navigator object*
cpuClass, Navigator.cpuClass
crypto
crypto, Global object*
crypto, Window object*
crypto, Window.crypto
cssFloat, style object (2)*
cssFloat, style.cssFloat
cssText, rule object*
cssText, rule.cssText
cssText, style object (2)*
cssText, style.cssText
cssText, StyleSheet object*
cssText, StyleSheet.cssText
ctrlKey, Event object*
ctrlKey, Event.ctrlKey
ctrlKey, MouseEvent object*
ctrlKey, MouseEvent.ctrlKey
cue, style object (2)*
cue, style.cue
cueAfter, style object (2)*
cueAfter, style.cueAfter
cueBefore, style object (2)*
cueBefore, style.cueBefore
current, History object*
current, History.current
currentStyle, Element object*
currentStyle, Element.currentStyle
currentTarget, Event object*
currentTarget, Event.currentTarget
currentTarget, MouseEvent object*
currentTarget, MutationEvent object*
cursor, style object (2)*
cursor, style.cursor
data, CharacterData object*
data, CharacterData.data
data, Event object*
data, Event.data
data, OBJECT object*
data, OBJECT.data
data, ProcessingInstruction object*
data, ProcessingInstruction.data
data, textNode object*
data, textNode.data
database, response object*
database, response.database
dataFld, A object
dataFld, Anchor object*
dataFld, Anchor.dataFld
dataFld, Applet object*
dataFld, BUTTON object*
dataFld, DIV object*
dataFld, Event object*
dataFld, File object*
dataFld, Frame object*
dataFld, IFRAME object*
dataFld, IMG object*
dataFld, Input object*
dataFld, Input.dataFld
dataFld, Label object*
dataFld, MARQUEE object*
dataFld, OBJECT object*
dataFld, Select object*

dataFld, SPAN object*
dataFld, TABLE object*
dataFormatAs, BUTTON object*
dataFormatAs, DIV object*
dataFormatAs, IMG object*
dataFormatAs, Input object*
dataFormatAs, Input.dataFormatAs
dataFormatAs, Label object*
dataFormatAs, MARQUEE object*
dataFormatAs, SPAN object*
dataPageSize, TABLE object*
dataPageSize, TABLE.dataPageSize
dataSrc, A object
dataSrc, Anchor object*
dataSrc, Anchor.dataSrc
dataSrc, Applet object*
dataSrc, BUTTON object*
dataSrc, DIV object*
dataSrc, File object*
dataSrc, Frame object*
dataSrc, IFRAME object*
dataSrc, IMG object*
dataSrc, Input object*
dataSrc, Input.dataSrc
dataSrc, Label object*
dataSrc, MARQUEE object*
dataSrc, OBJECT object*
dataSrc, Select object*
dataSrc, SPAN object*
dataSrc, TABLE object*
dataTransfer, Event object*
dataTransfer, Event.dataTransfer
DateCreated, File object*
DateCreated, File.DateCreated
DateCreated, Folder object*
DateCreated, Folder.DateCreated
DateLastAccessed, File object*
DateLastAccessed, File.DateLastAccessed
DateLastAccessed, Folder object*
DateLastAccessed,
    Folder.DateLastAccessed
DateLastModified, File object*
DateLastModified, File.DateLastModified
DateLastModified, Folder object*
DateLastModified, Folder.DateLastModified
dateTime, DEL object*
dateTime, DEL.dateTime
dateTime, INS object*
dateTime, INS.dateTime
dateTime, ModElement object*
dateTime, ModElement.dateTime
declare, OBJECT object*
declare, OBJECT.declare
defaultCharset, Document object*
defaultCharset, Document.defaultCharset
defaultChecked, Checkbox object*
defaultChecked, Checkbox.defaultChecked
defaultChecked, Input object*
defaultChecked, Input.defaultChecked
defaultChecked, RadioButton object*
defaultChecked,
    RadioButton.defaultChecked
defaultSelected, Input object*
defaultSelected, Option object*
defaultSelected, Option.defaultSelected
defaultStatus
defaultStatus, Frame object*

Property (continued)

defaultStatus, Frame.defaultStatus
defaultStatus, Global object*
defaultStatus, Window object*
defaultStatus, Window.defaultStatus
defaultValue, File object*
defaultValue, Image object*
defaultValue, IMG object*
defaultValue, Input object*
defaultValue, Input.defaultValue
defer, SCRIPT object*
defer, SCRIPT.defer
defer, XML object*
defer, XML.defer
description, Error object*
description, Error.description
description, JavaObject object*
description, MimeType object*
description, MimeType.description
description, Plugin object*
description, Plugin.description
description, URIError object*
designMode, Document object*
designMode, Document.designMode
detail, MouseEvent object*
detail, UIEvent object*
detail, UIEvent.detail
dialogArguments
dialogArguments, Global object*
dialogArguments, Window object*
dialogArguments, Window.dialogArguments
dialogHeight
dialogHeight, Global object*
dialogHeight, Window object*
dialogHeight, Window.dialogHeight
dialogLeft
dialogLeft, Global object*
dialogLeft, Window object*
dialogLeft, Window.dialogLeft
dialogTop
dialogTop, Global object*
dialogTop, Window object*
dialogTop, Window.dialogTop
dialogWidth
dialogWidth, Global object*
dialogWidth, Window object*
dialogWidth, Window.dialogWidth
dir, BDO object*
dir, BDO.dir
dir, Element object*
dir, Element.dir
dir, NOFRAMES object*
dir, NOFRAMES.dir
dir, NOSCRIPT object*
dir, NOSCRIPT.dir
Direction, filter - Blinds()*
Direction, filter - CheckerBoard()*
Direction, filter - MotionBlur()*
Direction, filter - Shadow()*
direction, MARQUEE object*
direction, MARQUEE.direction
direction, style object (2)*
direction, style.direction
disabled, Input object*
disabled, Input.disabled
disabled, LINK object*
disabled, LINK.disabled

disabled, OptGroupElement object*
disabled, OptGroupElement.disabled
disabled, STYLE object (1)*
disabled, STYLE.disabled
disabled, StyleSheet object*
disabled, StyleSheet.disabled
display, JSSTag object*
display, JSSTag.display
display, style object (2)*
display, style.display
doctype, Document object*
doctype, Document.doctype
document
document, Element object*
document, Element.document
document, Global object*
document, Layer object*
document, Layer.document
document, Window object*
document, Window.document
documentElement, Document object*
documentElement,
    Document.documentElement
domain, Document object*
domain, Document.domain
Drive, File object*
Drive, File.Drive
Drive, Folder object*
Drive, Folder.Drive
DriveLetter, Drive object*
DriveLetter, Drive.DriveLetter
DriveType, Drive object*
DriveType, Drive.DriveType
dropEffect, dataTransfer object*
dropEffect, dataTransfer.dropEffect
Duration, filter - Barn()*
Duration, filter - Blinds()*
Duration, filter - CheckerBoard()*
Duration, filter - Fade()*
Duration, filter - GradientWipe()*
Duration, filter - Inset()*
Duration, filter - Iris()*
Duration, filter - Pixelate()*
Duration, filter - Pixelate()*
Duration, filter - RadialWipe()*
Duration, filter - RandomBars()*
Duration, filter - RandomDissolve()*
Duration, filter - Slide()*
Duration, filter - Spiral()*
Duration, filter - Stretch()*
Duration, filter - Strips()*
Duration, filter - Wheel()*
Duration, filter - Zigzag()*
Dx, filter - Matrix()*
Dy, filter - Matrix()*
dynsrc, IMG object*
dynsrc, IMG.dynsrc
effectAllowed, dataTransfer object*
effectAllowed, dataTransfer.effectAllowed
elements, Form object*
elements.length, Form.elements.length
elevation, style object (2)*
elevation, style.elevation
emptyCells, style object (2)*
emptyCells, style.emptyCells
Enabled, filter - Alpha()*
Enabled, filter - AlphaImageLoader()*

Property (continued)

form, Input.form
form, ISINDEX object*
form, ISINDEX.form
form, Label object*
form, Legend object*
form, OBJECT object*
form, OBJECT.form
form, Option object*
form, Select object*
frame
frame, Global object*
frame, TABLE object*
frame, TABLE.frame
frame, Window object*
frame, Window.frame
frameBorder, Frame object*
frameBorder, Frame.frameBorder
frameBorder, FRAMESET object*
frameBorder, FRAMESET.frameBorder
frameBorder, IFRAME object*
frameBorder, IFRAME.frameBorder
frameRate
frameRate, Global object*
frameRate, Window object*
frameRate, Window.frameRate
frameSpacing, FRAMESET object*
frameSpacing, FRAMESET.frameSpacing
frameSpacing, IFRAME object*
frameSpacing, IFRAME.frameSpacing
FreeSpace, Drive object*
FreeSpace, Drive.FreeSpace
Freq, filter - Wave()*
From, SendMail object*
From, SendMail.From
fromElement, Event object*
fromElement, Event.fromElement
FullName, WScript object*
FullName, WScript.FullName
Function, filter - Compositor()*
global, RegExp object*
global, RegExp.global
GradientSize, filter - GradientWipe()*
GradientType, filter - Gradient()*
GrayScale, filter - BasicImage()*
GridSizeX, filter - Spiral()*
GridSizeX, filter - Zigzag()*
GridSizeY, filter - Spiral()*
GridSizeY, filter - Zigzag()*
hash, A object
hash, Anchor object*
hash, Anchor.hash
hash, Area object*
hash, Area.hash
hash, Location object*
hash, Location.hash
hash, Url object*
hash, Url.hash
headers, TD object*
headers, TD.headers
headers, TH object*
headers, TH.headers
height, Applet object*
height, Applet.height
height, Clip object*
height, Clip.height
height, Document object*

height, Document.height
height, Embed object*
height, Embed.height
height, Event object*
height, Event.height
height, Frame object*
height, Frame.height
height, IFRAME object*
height, IFRAME.height
height, Image object*
height, Image.height
height, IMG object*
height, IMG.height
height, JSSTag object*
height, JSSTag.height
height, MARQUEE object*
height, MARQUEE.height
height, OBJECT object*
height, OBJECT.height
height, Rect object*
height, Rect.height
height, Screen object*
height, Screen.height
height, style object (2)*
height, style.height
height, TABLE object*
height, TABLE.height
height, TD object*
height, TD.height
height, TH object*
height, TH.height
hidden, Embed object*
hidden, Embed.hidden
hidden, Layer object*
hidden, Layer.hidden
hideFocus, Element object*
hideFocus, Element.hideFocus
history
history, Global object*
history, Window object*
history, Window.history
host, A object
host, Anchor object*
host, Anchor.host
host, Area object*
host, Area.host
host, Location object*
host, Location.host
host, server object*
host, server.host
host, Url object*
host, Url.host
hostname, A object
hostname, Anchor object*
hostname, Anchor.hostname
hostname, Area object*
hostname, Area.hostname
hostname, Location object*
hostname, Location.hostname
hostname, server object*
hostname, server.hostname
hostname, Url object*
hostname, Url.hostname
href, A object
href, Anchor object*
href, Anchor.href
href, Area object*

href, Area.href
href, BASE object*
href, BASE.href
href, IMG object*
href, IMG.href
href, LINK object*
href, LINK.href
href, Location object*
href, Location.href
href, StyleSheet object*
href, StyleSheet.href
href, Url object*
href, Url.href
hreflang, Anchor object*
hreflang, Anchor.hreflang
hreflang, LINK object*
hreflang, LINK.hreflang
hreflang, Url object*
hreflang, Url.hreflang
hspace, Applet object*
hspace, Applet.hspace
hspace, IFRAME object*
hspace, IFRAME.hspace
hspace, Image object*
hspace, Image.hspace
hspace, IMG object*
hspace, IMG.hspace
hspace, MARQUEE object*
hspace, MARQUEE.hspace
hspace, OBJECT object*
hspace, OBJECT.hspace
htmlFor, Label object*
htmlFor, Label.htmlFor
htmlFor, SCRIPT object*
htmlFor, SCRIPT.htmlFor
htmlFor, XML object*
htmlText, TextRange object*
htmlText, TextRange.htmlText
httpEquiv, META object*
httpEquiv, META.httpEquiv
iccProfile, IMG object*
iccProfile, IMG.iccProfile
id, Element object*
id, Element.id
id, StyleSheet object*
id, StyleSheet.id
ids
ignoreCase, RegExp object*
ignoreCase, RegExp.ignoreCase
imageX, request object*
imageX, request.imageX
imageY, request object*
imageY, request.imageY
imeMode, style object (2)*
imeMode, style.imeMode
implementation, Document object*
implementation, Document.implementation
important, style object (2)*
important, style.important
indeterminate, Checkbox object*
indeterminate, Checkbox.indeterminate
index, Array object*
index, Array.index
index, Option object*
index, Option.index
index, RegExp object*
index, RegExp.index

innerHeight
innerHeight, Global object*
innerHeight, Window object*
innerHeight, Window.innerHeight
innerHTML, Element object*
innerHTML, Element.innerHTML
innerText, Element object*
innerText, Element.innerText
innerWidth
innerWidth, Global object*
innerWidth, Window object*
innerWidth, Window.innerWidth
input, Array object*
input, Array.input
Invert, filter - BasicImage()*
ip, request object*
ip, request.ip
IrisStyle, filter - Iris()*
isContentEditable, Element object*
isContentEditable,
   Element.isContentEditable
isDisabled, Element object*
isDisabled, Element.isDisabled
isMap, IMG object*
isMap, IMG.isMap
IsReady, Drive object*
IsReady, Drive.IsReady
IsRootFolder, Folder object*
IsRootFolder, Folder.IsRootFolder
isTextEdit, Element object*
isTextEdit, Element.isTextEdit
isTextEdit, Frame object*
java
java, Global object*
java, Window object*
java, Window.java
keyCode, Event object*
keyCode, Event.keyCode
label, OptGroupElement object*
label, OptGroupElement.label
label, Option object*
label, Option.label
lang, Element object*
lang, Element.lang
lang, Frame object*
language, Element object*
language, Element.language
language, Frame object*
language, Navigator object*
language, Navigator.language
lastChild, Element object*
lastChild, Element.lastChild
lastChild, Node object*
lastChild, Node.lastChild
lastIndex, RegExp object*
lastIndex, RegExp.lastIndex
lastModified, Document object*
lastModified, Document.lastModified
layerX, Event object*
layerX, Event.layerX
layerY, Event object*
layerY, Event.layerY
layoutGrid, style object (2)*
layoutGrid, style.layoutGrid
layoutGridChar, style object (2)*
layoutGridChar, style.layoutGridChar

959

Property (continued)

layoutGridCharSpacing, style object (2)*
layoutGridCharSpacing,
   style.layoutGridCharSpacing
layoutGridLine, style object (2)*
layoutGridLine, style.layoutGridLine
layoutGridMode, style object (2)*
layoutGridMode, style.layoutGridMode
layoutGridType, style object (2)*
layoutGridType, style.layoutGridType
left, Clip object*
left, Clip.left
left, JSSTag object*
left, Layer object*
left, Layer.left
left, Rect object*
left, Rect.left
left, style object (2)*
left, style.left
left, textRectangle object*
left, textRectangle.left
leftMargin, BODY object*
leftMargin, BODY.leftMargin
length
length, AnchorArray object*
length, AnchorArray.length
length, AppletArray object*
length, AppletArray.length
length, Arguments object*
length, Arguments.length
length, Array object*
length, Array.length
length, Attributes object*
length, Attributes.length
length, CharacterData object*
length, CharacterData.length
length, Collection object*
length, Collection.length
length, Date object*
length, Date.length
length, EmbedArray object*
length, EmbedArray.length
length, Filters object
length, Filters.length
length, Form object*
length, Form.length
length, FormArray object*
length, FormArray.length
length, FormElementsArray object
length, FormElementsArray.length
length, FrameArray object
length, FrameArray.length
length, Frames object*
length, Frames.length
length, Function object*
length, Function.length
length, Global object*
length, History object*
length, History.length
length, ImageArray object*
length, ImageArray.length
length, Input object*
length, InputArray object*
length, JavaArray object*
length, JavaArray.length
length, JavaObject object*
length, LayerArray object*

length, LayerArray.length
length, LinkArray object*
length, LinkArray.length
length, MimeTypeArray object*
length, MimeTypeArray.length
length, NamedNodeMap object*
length, NamedNodeMap.length
length, NodeList object*
length, NodeList.length
length, OptionsArray object*
length, OptionsArray.length
length, Plugin object*
length, Plugin.length
length, PluginArray object*
length, PluginArray.length
length, rows object
length, ScriptArray object*
length, ScriptArray.length
length, Select object*
length, Select.length
length, SelectorArray object*
length, SelectorArray.length
length, String object*
length, String.length
length, style object (2)*
length, style.length
length, StyleSheetList object*
length, StyleSheetList.length
length, textNode object*
length, textNode.length
length, Window object*
length, Window.length
letterSpacing, style object (2)*
letterSpacing, style.letterSpacing
LightStrength, filter - Wave()*
Line, TextStream object*
Line, TextStream.Line
lineBreak, style object (2)*
lineBreak, style.lineBreak
lineHeight, JSSTag object*
lineHeight, JSSTag.lineHeight
lineHeight, style object (2)*
lineHeight, style.lineHeight
link, BODY object*
link, BODY.link
linkColor, Document object*
linkColor, Document.linkColor
listStyle, style object (2)*
listStyle, style.listStyle
listStyleImage, style object (2)*
listStyleImage, style.listStyleImage
listStylePosition, style object (2)*
listStylePosition, style.listStylePosition
listStyleType, JSSTag object*
listStyleType, JSSTag.listStyleType
listStyleType, style object (2)*
listStyleType, style.listStyleType
location
location, Document object*
location, Document.location
location, Global object*
location, Window object*
location, Window.location
locationbar
locationbar, Global object*
locationbar, Window object*
locationbar, Window.locationbar

longDesc, Frame object*
longDesc, Frame.longDesc
longDesc, IFRAME object*
longDesc, IFRAME.longDesc
longDesc, IMG object*
longDesc, IMG.longDesc
loop, BGSOUND object*
loop, BGSOUND.loop
loop, IMG object*
loop, IMG.loop
loop, MARQUEE object*
loop, MARQUEE.loop
lowsrc, Image object*
lowsrc, Image.lowsrc
lowsrc, IMG object*
lowsrc, IMG.lowsrc
M11, filter - Matrix()*
M12, filter - Matrix()*
M21, filter - Matrix()*
M22, filter - Matrix()*
MakeShadow, filter - Blur()*
margin, FIELDSET object*
margin, FIELDSET.margin
margin, style object (2)*
margin, style.margin
marginBottom, JSSTag object*
marginBottom, JSSTag.marginBottom
marginBottom, style object (2)*
marginBottom, style.marginBottom
marginHeight, Frame object*
marginHeight, Frame.marginHeight
marginHeight, IFRAME object*
marginHeight, IFRAME.marginHeight
marginLeft, JSSTag object*
marginLeft, JSSTag.marginLeft
marginLeft, style object (2)*
marginLeft, style.marginLeft
marginRight, JSSTag object*
marginRight, JSSTag.marginRight
marginRight, style object (2)*
marginRight, style.marginRight
marginTop, JSSTag object*
marginTop, JSSTag.marginTop
marginTop, style object (2)*
marginTop, style.marginTop
marginWidth, Frame object*
marginWidth, Frame.marginWidth
marginWidth, IFRAME object*
marginWidth, IFRAME.marginWidth
markerOffset, style object (2)*
markerOffset, style.markerOffset
marks, style object (2)*
marks, style.marks
Mask, filter - BasicImage()*
MaskColor, filter - BasicImage()*
Math, Global object*
Math, Window object*
maxHeight, style object (2)*
maxHeight, style.maxHeight
maxLength, Input object*
maxLength, Input.maxLength
maxLength, Password object*
maxLength, Password.maxLength
maxLength, TextCell object*
maxLength, TextCell.maxLength
MaxSquare, filter - Pixelate()*
MaxSquare, filter - Pixelate()*

maxWidth, style object (2)*
maxWidth, style.maxWidth
media, LINK object*
media, LINK.media
media, STYLE object (1)*
media, STYLE.media
media, StyleSheet object*
media, StyleSheet.media
menuArguments, external object*
menuArguments, external.menuArguments
menubar
menubar, Global object*
menubar, Window object*
menubar, Window.menubar
message, Error object*
message, Error.message
message, URIError object*
metaKey, MouseEvent object*
metaKey, MouseEvent.metaKey
method, Form object*
method, Form.method
method, request object*
method, request.method
Methods, A object
Methods, Anchor object*
Methods, Anchor.Methods
Methods, Url object*
Methods, Url.Methods
mimeType, A object
mimeType, Anchor object*
mimeType, Anchor.mimeType
mimeType, Url object*
mimeType, Url.mimeType
minHeight, style object (2)*
minHeight, style.minHeight
minWidth, style object (2)*
minWidth, style.minWidth
Mirror, filter - BasicImage()*
modifiers, Event object*
modifiers, Event.modifiers
Motion, filter - Barn()*
Motion, filter - GradientWipe()*
Motion, filter - Iris()*
Motion, filter - Strips()*
multiple, Select object*
multiple, Select.multiple
name
name, Anchor object*
name, Anchor.name
name, Applet object*
name, Applet.name
name, Area object*
name, Area.name
name, Attribute object*
name, Attribute.name
name, BUTTON object*
name, BUTTON.name
name, Doctype object*
name, Doctype.name
name, Embed object*
name, Embed.name
name, Error object*
Name, Error.name
Name, File object*
Name, File.Name
Name, Folder object*
name, Folder.Name

Property (continued)

name, Form object*
name, Form.name
name, Frame object*
name, Frame.name
name, Global object*
name, IFRAME object*
name, IFRAME.name
name, Image object*
name, Image.name
name, IMG object*
name, IMG.name
name, Input object*
name, Input.name
name, JavaObject object*
name, Layer object*
name, Layer.name
name, Map object*
name, Map.name
name, META object*
name, META.name
name, MimeType object*
name, MimeType.name
name, Object object*
name, OBJECT object*
name, Object.name
name, OBJECT.name
name, ParamElement object*
name, ParamElement.name
name, Plugin object*
name, Plugin.name
name, URIError object*
name, Url object*
name, Url.name
name, Window object*
Name, Window.name
Name, WScript object*
name, WScript.Name
nameProp, A object
nameProp, Anchor object*
nameProp, Anchor.nameProp
nameProp, Url object*
nameProp, Url.nameProp
navigator
navigator, Global object*
navigator, Window object*
navigator, Window.navigator
netscape, Global object*
netscape, Window object*
netscape, Window.netscape
Network, WScript object*
Network, WScript.Network
newValue, MutationEvent object*
newValue, MutationEvent.newValue
next, History object*
next, History.next
nextSibling, Element object*
nextSibling, Element.nextSibling
nextSibling, Node object*
nextSibling, Node.nextSibling
nodeName, Attribute object*
nodeName, Attribute.nodeName
nodeName, Element object*
nodeName, Element.nodeName
nodeName, Node object*
nodeName, Node.nodeName
nodeType, Attribute object*

nodeType, Attribute.nodeType
nodeType, Element object*
nodeType, Element.nodeType
nodeType, Node object*
nodeType, Node.nodeType
nodeValue, Attribute object*
nodeValue, Attribute.nodeValue
nodeValue, Element object*
nodeValue, Element.nodeValue
nodeValue, Node object*
nodeValue, Node.nodeValue
noHref, Area object*
noHref, Area.noHref
noResize, Frame object*
noResize, Frame.noResize
noResize, IFRAME object*
noResize, IFRAME.noResize
noShade, HR object*
noShade, HR.noShade
notationName, Entity object*
notationName, Entity.notationName
noWrap, BODY object*
noWrap, BODY.noWrap
noWrap, DD object*
noWrap, DD.noWrap
noWrap, DT object*
noWrap, DT.noWrap
noWrap, TD object*
noWrap, TD.noWrap
noWrap, TH object*
noWrap, TH.noWrap
number, Error object*
number, Error.number
number, URIError object*
object, Applet object*
object, Applet.object
object, OBJECT object*
object, OBJECT.object
offScreenBuffering
offScreenBuffering, Global object*
offscreenBuffering, Window object*
offscreenBuffering,
   Window.offscreenBuffering
offsetHeight, Element object*
offsetHeight, Element.offsetHeight
offsetLeft, Element object*
offsetLeft, Element.offsetLeft
offsetParent, Element object*
offsetParent, Element.offsetParent
offsetTop, Element object*
offsetTop, Element.offsetTop
offsetWidth, Element object*
offsetWidth, Element.offsetWidth
offsetX, Event object*
offsetX, Event.offsetX
offsetY, Event object*
offsetY, Event.offsetY
OffX, filter - DropShadow()*
OffY, filter - DropShadow()*
onblur, Window.onblur
ondragdrop, Window.ondragdrop
onerror, Window.onerror
onevent, Element.onevent
onevent, Input.onevent
onfocus, Window.onfocus
onLine, Navigator object*
onLine, Navigator.onLine

onload, Window.onload
onmove, Window.onmove
onresize, Window.onresize
onunload, Window.onunload
Opacity, filter - Alpha()*
Opacity, filter - BasicImage()*
opener
opener, Global object*
opener, Window object*
opener, Window.opener
opsProfile, Navigator object*
opsProfile, Navigator.opsProfile
Organization, SendMail object*
Organization, SendMail.Organization
Orientation, filter - Barn()*
Orientation, filter - RandomBars()*
orphans, style object (2)*
orphans, style.orphans
outerHeight
outerHeight, Global object*
outerHeight, Window object*
outerHeight, Window.outerHeight
outerHTML, Element object*
outerHTML, Element.outerHTML
outerText, Element object*
outerText, Element.outerText
outerWidth
outerWidth, Global object*
outerWidth, Window object*
outerWidth, Window.outerWidth
outline, style object (2)*
outline, style.outline
outlineColor, style object (2)*
outlineColor, style.outlineColor
outlineStyle, style object (2)*
outlineStyle, style.outlineStyle
outlineWidth, style object (2)*
outlineWidth, style.outlineWidth
overflow, style object (2)*
overflow, style.overflow
overflowX, style object (2)*
overflowX, style.overflowX
overflowY, style object (2)*
overflowY, style.overflowY
Overlap, filter - Fade()*
ownerDocument, Element object*
ownerDocument, Element.ownerDocument
ownerDocument, Node object*
ownerDocument, Node.ownerDocument
ownerNode, StyleSheet object*
ownerNode, StyleSheet.ownerNode
owningElement, StyleSheet object*
owningElement, StyleSheet.owningElement
owningNode, StyleSheet object*
owningNode, StyleSheet.owningNode
Packages
Packages, Global object*
Packages, Window object*
Packages, Window.Packages
padding, Legend object*
padding, Legend.padding
padding, style object (2)*
padding, style.padding
paddingBottom, JSSTag object*
paddingBottom, JSSTag.paddingBottom
paddingBottom, style object (2)*
paddingBottom, style.paddingBottom

paddingLeft, JSSTag object*
paddingLeft, JSSTag.paddingLeft
paddingLeft, style object (2)*
paddingLeft, style.paddingLeft
paddingRight, JSSTag object*
paddingRight, JSSTag.paddingRight
paddingRight, style object (2)*
paddingRight, style.paddingRight
paddingTop, JSSTag object*
paddingTop, JSSTag.paddingTop
paddingTop, style object (2)*
paddingTop, style.paddingTop
page, style object (2)*
page, style.page
pageBreakAfter, style object (2)*
pageBreakAfter, style.pageBreakAfter
pageBreakBefore, style object (2)*
pageBreakBefore, style.pageBreakBefore
pageBreakInside, style object (2)*
pageBreakInside, style.pageBreakInside
pageX, Event object*
pageX, Event.pageX
pageX, Layer object*
pageX, Layer.pageX
pageXOffset
pageXOffset, Global object*
pageXOffset, Window object*
pageXOffset, Window.pageXOffset
pageY, Event object*
pageY, Event.pageY
pageY, Layer object*
pageY, Layer.pageY
pageYOffset
pageYOffset, Global object*
pageYOffset, Window object*
pageYOffset, Window.pageYOffset
palette, Embed object*
palette, Embed.palette
parent
parent, Frame object*
parent, Frame.parent
parent, Global object*
parent, Window object*
parent, Window.parent
parentElement, Element object*
parentElement, Element.parentElement
parentElement, Frame object*
ParentFolder, File object*
ParentFolder, File.ParentFolder
ParentFolder, Folder object*
ParentFolder, Folder.ParentFolder
parentLayer, Layer object*
parentLayer, Layer.parentLayer
parentNode, Element object*
parentNode, Element.parentNode
parentNode, Node object*
parentNode, Node.parentNode
parentStyleSheet, rule object*
parentStyleSheet, rule.parentStyleSheet
parentStyleSheet, StyleSheet object*
parentStyleSheet,
    StyleSheet.parentStyleSheet
parentTextEdit, Element object*
parentTextEdit, Element.parentTextEdit
parentTextEdit, Frame object*
parentWindow, Document object*

Property (continued)

parentWindow, Document.parentWindow
Path, Drive object*
Path, Drive.Path
Path, File object*
Path, File.Path
Path, Folder object*
Path, Folder.Path
Path, WScript object*
Path, WScript.Path
pathname, A object
pathname, Anchor object*
pathname, Anchor.pathname
pathname, Area object*
pathname, Area.pathname
pathname, Location object*
pathname, Location.pathname
pathname, Url object*
pathname, Url.pathname
pause, style object (2)*
pause, style.pause
pauseAfter, style object (2)*
pauseAfter, style.pauseAfter
pauseBefore, style object (2)*
pauseBefore, style.pauseBefore
Percent, filter - Barn()*
Percent, filter - Blinds()*
Percent, filter - Fade()*
Percent, filter - GradientWipe()*
Percent, filter - Inset()*
Percent, filter - Iris()*
Percent, filter - Pixelate()*
Percent, filter - Pixelate()*
Percent, filter - RadialWipe()*
Percent, filter - RandomBars()*
Percent, filter - RandomDissolve()*
Percent, filter - Slide()*
Percent, filter - Spiral()*
Percent, filter - Stretch()*
Percent, filter - Strips()*
Percent, filter - Wheel()*
Percent, filter - Zigzag()*
personalbar
personalbar, Global object*
personalbar, Window object*
personalbar, Window.personalbar
Phase, filter - Wave()*
pitch, style object (2)*
pitch, style.pitch
pitchRange, style object (2)*
pitchRange, style.pitchRange
pixelBottom, style object (2)*
pixelBottom, style.pixelBottom
pixelDepth, Screen object*
pixelDepth, Screen.pixelDepth
pixelHeight, style object (2)*
pixelHeight, style.pixelHeight
pixelLeft, style object (2)*
pixelLeft, style.pixelLeft
PixelRadius, filter - Blur()*
pixelRight, style object (2)*
pixelRight, style.pixelRight
pixelTop, style object (2)*
pixelTop, style.pixelTop
pixelWidth, style object (2)*
pixelWidth, style.pixelWidth
pkcs11, Global object*

pkcs11, Window object*
pkcs11, Window.pkcs11
platform, Navigator object*
platform, Navigator.platform
playDuring, style object (2)*
playDuring, style.playDuring
pluginspage, Embed object*
pluginspage, Embed.pluginspage
port, A object
port, Anchor object*
port, Anchor.port
port, Area object*
port, Area.port
port, Location object*
port, Location.port
port, server object*
port, server.port
port, Url object*
port, Url.port
posBottom, style object (2)*
posBottom, style.posBottom
posHeight, style object (2)*
posHeight, style.posHeight
position, style object (2)*
position, style.position
Positive , filter - DropShadow()*
posLeft, style object (2)*
posLeft, style.posLeft
posRight, style object (2)*
posRight, style.posRight
posTop, style object (2)*
posTop, style.posTop
posWidth, style object (2)*
posWidth, style.posWidth
previous, History object*
previous, History.previous
previousSibling, Element object*
previousSibling, Element.previousSibling
previousSibling, Node object*
previousSibling, Node.previousSibling
prevValue, MutationEvent object*
prevValue, MutationEvent.prevValue
profile, HEAD object*
profile, HEAD.profile
project, response object*
project, response.project
prompt, ISINDEX object*
prompt, ISINDEX object*
prompt, ISINDEX.prompt
propertyName, Event object*
propertyName, Event.propertyName
protocol, A object
protocol, Anchor object*
protocol, Anchor.protocol
protocol, Area object*
protocol, Area.protocol
protocol, Document object*
protocol, Document.protocol
protocol, IMG object*
protocol, IMG.protocol
protocol, Location object*
protocol, Location.protocol
protocol, request object*
protocol, request.protocol
protocol, server object*
protocol, server.protocol
protocol, Url object*

protocol, Url.protocol
protocolLong, A object
protocolLong, Anchor object*
protocolLong, Anchor.protocolLong
protocolLong, Url object*
protocolLong, Url.protocolLong
prototype, Array object*
prototype, Array.prototype
prototype, Boolean object*
prototype, Boolean.prototype
prototype, Connection object*
prototype, Connection.prototype
prototype, Cursor.prototype
prototype, database object*
prototype, database.prototype
prototype, Date object*
prototype, Date.prototype
prototype, DbPool object*
prototype, DbPool.prototype
prototype, Error object*
prototype, Error.prototype
prototype, File object*
prototype, File.prototype
prototype, Function object*
prototype, Function.prototype
prototype, IMG object*
prototype, IMG.prototype
prototype, Lock object*
prototype, Lock.prototype
prototype, Number object*
prototype, Number.prototype
prototype, Object object*
prototype, Object.prototype
prototype, Option object*
prototype, Option.prototype
prototype, RegExp object*
prototype, RegExp.prototype
prototype, ResultSet object*
prototype, ResultSet.prototype
prototype, SendMail object*
prototype, SendMail.prototype
prototype, Stproc object*
prototype, Stproc.prototype
prototype, String object*
prototype, String.prototype
publicId, Entity object*
publicId, Entity.publicId
publicId, Notation object*
publicId, Notation.publicId
qualifier, Event object*
quotes, style object (2)*
quotes, style.quotes
readOnly, Input object*
readOnly, Input.readOnly
readOnly, Password object*
readOnly, Password.readOnly
readOnly, rule object*
readOnly, rule.readOnly
readOnly, StyleSheet object*
readOnly, StyleSheet.readOnly
readOnly, TEXTAREA object*
readOnly, TEXTAREA.readOnly
readOnly, TextCell object*
readOnly, TextCell.readOnly
readyState, Document object*
readyState, Document.readyState
readyState, Element object*

readyState, Element.readyState
readyState, Embed object*
readyState, Embed.readyState
readyState, IMG object*
readyState, IMG.readyState
readyState, LINK object*
readyState, LINK.readyState
readyState, OBJECT object*
readyState, OBJECT.readyState
readyState, SCRIPT object*
readyState, SCRIPT.readyState
readyState, STYLE object (1)*
readyState, STYLE.readyState
reason, Event object*
reason, Event.reason
recordNumber, Anchor object*
recordNumber, Anchor.recordNumber
recordNumber, BODY object*
recordNumber, BODY.recordNumber
recordNumber, Element object*
recordNumber, File object*
recordNumber, Input object*
recordNumber, Input.recordNumber
recordNumber, SCRIPT object*
recordNumber, SCRIPT.recordNumber
recordset, Event object*
referrer, Document object*
referrer, Document.referrer
RegExp["$&"]
rel, A object
rel, Anchor object*
rel, Anchor.rel
rel, LINK object*
rel, LINK.rel
rel, Url object*
rel, Url.rel
relatedNode, MutationEvent object*
relatedNode, MutationEvent.relatedNode
relatedTarget, MouseEvent object*
relatedTarget, MouseEvent.relatedTarget
renderingIntent, style object (2)*
renderingIntent, style.renderingIntent
repeat, Event object*
repeat, Event.repeat
ReplyTo, SendMail object*
ReplyTo, SendMail.ReplyTo
request, response object*
request, response.request
returnValue
returnValue, Event object*
returnValue, Event.returnValue
returnValue, Global object*
returnValue, Window object*
returnValue, Window.returnValue
rev, Anchor object*
rev, Anchor.rev
rev, LINK object*
rev, LINK.rev
rev, Url object*
rev, Url.rev
richness, style object (2)*
richness, style.richness
right, Clip object*
right, Clip.right
right, Rect object*
right, Rect.right
right, style object (2)*

965

Property (continued)

right, style.right
right, textRectangle object*
right, textRectangle.right
rightMargin, BODY object*
rightMargin, BODY.rightMargin
RootFolder, Drive object*
RootFolder, Drive.RootFolder
Rotation, filter - BasicImage()*
rowIndex, TR object*
rowIndex, TR.rowIndex
rows, FRAMESET object*
rows, FRAMESET.rows
rows, TBODY object*
rows, TEXTAREA object*
rows, TEXTAREA.rows
rowSpan, style object (2)*
rowSpan, style.rowSpan
rowSpan, TD object*
rowSpan, TD.rowSpan
rowSpan, TH object*
rowSpan, TH.rowSpan
rubyAlign, style object (2)*
rubyAlign, style.rubyAlign
rubyOverhang, style object (2)*
rubyOverhang, style.rubyOverhang
rubyPosition, style object (2)*
rubyPosition, style.rubyPosition
rules, TABLE object*
rules, TABLE.rules
runtimeStyle, Element object*
runtimeStyle, Element.runtimeStyle
runtimeStyle, rule object*
runtimeStyle, rule.runtimeStyle
scheme, META object*
scheme, META.scheme
scope, TD object*
scope, TD.scope
scope, TH object*
scope, TH.scope
scopeName, Element object*
scopeName, Element.scopeName
screen
screen, Global object*
screen, Window object*
screen, Window.screen
screenLeft
screenLeft, Global object*
screenLeft, Window object*
screenLeft, Window.screenLeft
screenTop
screenTop, Global object*
screenTop, Window object*
screenTop, Window.screenTop
screenX
screenX, Event object*
screenX, Event.screenX
screenX, Global object*
screenX, MouseEvent object*
screenX, MouseEvent.screenX
screenX, Window object*
screenX, Window.screenX
screenY
screenY, Event object*
screenY, Event.screenY
screenY, Global object*
screenY, MouseEvent object*

screenY, MouseEvent.screenY
screenY, Window object*
screenY, Window.screenY
ScriptFullName, WScript object*
ScriptFullName, WScript.ScriptFullName
ScriptName, WScript object*
ScriptName, WScript.ScriptName
scroll, BODY object*
scroll, BODY.scroll
scrollAmount, MARQUEE object*
scrollAmount, MARQUEE.scrollAmount
scrollbar3dLightColor, style object (2)*
scrollbar3dLightColor,
  style.scrollbar3dLightColor
scrollbarArrowColor, style object (2)*
scrollbarArrowColor,
  style.scrollbarArrowColor
scrollbarBaseColor, style object (2)*
scrollbarBaseColor,
  style.scrollbarBaseColor
scrollbarDarkShadowColor, style object
  (2)*
scrollbarDarkShadowColor,
  style.scrollbarDarkShadowColor
scrollbarFaceColor, style object (2)*
scrollbarFaceColor,
  style.scrollbarFaceColor
scrollbarHighlightColor, style object (2)*
scrollbarHighlightColor,
  style.scrollbarHighlightColor
scrollbars
scrollbars, Global object*
scrollbars, Window object*
scrollbars, Window.scrollbars
scrollbarShadowColor, style object (2)*
scrollbarShadowColor,
  style.scrollbarShadowColor
scrollDelay, MARQUEE object*
scrollDelay, MARQUEE.scrollDelay
scrollHeight, Element object*
scrollHeight, Element.scrollHeight
scrolling, Frame object*
scrolling, Frame.scrolling
scrolling, IFRAME object*
scrolling, IFRAME.scrolling
scrollLeft, Element object*
scrollLeft, Element.scrollLeft
scrollTop, Element object*
scrollTop, Element.scrollTop
scrollWidth, Element object*
scrollWidth, Element.scrollWidth
search, A object
search, Anchor object*
search, Anchor.search
search, Area object*
search, Area.search
search, Location object*
search, Location.search
search, Url object*
search, Url.search
sectionRowIndex, TR object*
sectionRowIndex, TR.sectionRowIndex
secure
secure, Global object*
secure, Window object*
secure, Window.secure
securityPolicy, Navigator object*

securityPolicy, Navigator.securityPolicy
selected, Input object*
selected, Option object*
selected, Option.selected
selectedIndex, Input object*
selectedIndex, Select object*
selectedIndex, Select.selectedIndex
selection, Document object*
selection, Document.selection
selectorText, rule object*
selectorText, rule.selectorText
self
self, Global object*
self, Window object*
self, Window.self
SerialNumber, Drive object*
SerialNumber, Drive.SerialNumber
server, response object*
server, response.server
ShadowOpacity, filter - Blur()*
shape, Anchor object*
shape, Anchor.shape
shape, Area object*
shape, Area.shape
shape, Url object*
shape, Url.shape
ShareName, Drive object*
ShareName, Drive.ShareName
shiftKey, Event object*
shiftKey, Event.shiftKey
shiftKey, MouseEvent object*
shiftKey, MouseEvent.shiftKey
ShortName, File object*
ShortName, File.ShortName
ShortName, Folder object*
ShortName, Folder.ShortName
ShortPath, File object*
ShortPath, File.ShortPath
ShortPath, Folder object*
ShortPath, Folder.ShortPath
siblingAbove, Layer object*
siblingAbove, Layer.siblingAbove
siblingBelow, Layer object*
siblingBelow, Layer.siblingBelow
sidebar, Window object*
sidebar, Window.sidebar
size, BASEFONT object*
size, BASEFONT.size
Size, File object*
Size, File.Size
size, FileUpload object*
size, FileUpload.size
Size, Folder object*
Size, Folder.Size
size, FONT object*
size, FONT.size
size, HR object*
size, HR.size
size, Image object*
size, IMG object*
size, Input object*
size, Input.size
size, Password object*
size, Password.size
size, Select object*
size, Select.size
size, style object (2)*

size, style.size
size, TextCell object*
size, TextCell.size
SizingMethod, filter - AlphaImageLoader()*
SizingMethod, filter - Matrix()*
SlideStyle, filter - Slide()*
Smtpserver, SendMail object*
Smtpserver, SendMail.Smtpserver
source, RegExp object*
source, RegExp.source
sourceIndex, Element object*
sourceIndex, Element.sourceIndex
sourceIndex, Frame object*
span, COL object*
span, COL.span
span, COLGROUP object*
span, COLGROUP.span
span, TableColElement object*
span, TableColElement.span
speak, style object (2)*
speak, style.speak
speakDate, style object (2)*
speakDate, style.speakDate
speakHeader, style object (2)*
speakHeader, style.speakHeader
speakNumeral, style object (2)*
speakNumeral, style.speakNumeral
speakPunctuation, style object (2)*
speakPunctuation, style.speakPunctuation
speakTime, style object (2)*
speakTime, style.speakTime
specified, Attribute object*
specified, Attribute.specified
speechRate, style object (2)*
speechRate, style.speechRate
spokes, filter - Wheel()*
SquaresX, filter - CheckerBoard()*
SquaresY, filter - CheckerBoard()*
src, Applet object*
src, Applet.src
src, Background object*
src, Background.src
src, BGSOUND object*
src, BGSOUND.src
src, Embed object*
src, Embed.src
Src, filter - AlphaImageLoader()*
src, Frame object*
src, Frame.src
src, IFRAME object*
src, IFRAME.src
src, Image object*
src, Image.src
src, IMG object*
src, IMG.src
src, Input object*
src, Input.src
src, Layer object*
src, Layer.src
src, SCRIPT object*
src, SCRIPT.src
src, XML object*
src, XML.src
srcElement, Event object*
srcElement, Event.srcElement
srcFilter, Event object*
srcFilter, Event.srcFilter

967

Property (continued)

srcUrn, Event object*
standby, OBJECT object*
standby, OBJECT.standby
start, IMG object*
start, IMG.start
start, OL object*
start, OL.start
start, UL object*
StartColor, filter - Gradient()*
StartColorStr, filter - Gradient()*
StartX, filter - Alpha()*
StartY, filter - Alpha()*
status
status, BUTTON object*
status, Checkbox object*
status, Checkbox.status
status, filter - Barn()*
status, filter - Blinds()*
status, filter - Fade()*
status, filter - GradientWipe()*
status, filter - Inset()*
status, filter - Iris()*
status, filter - Pixelate()*
status, filter - Pixelate()*
status, filter - RadialWipe()*
status, filter - RandomBars()*
status, filter - RandomDissolve()*
status, filter - Slide()*
status, filter - Spiral()*
status, filter - Stretch()*
status, filter - Strips()*
status, filter - Wheel()*
status, filter - Zigzag()*
status, Global object*
status, Input object*
status, RadioButton object*
status, RadioButton.status
status, Window object*
status, Window.status
statusbar
statusbar, Global object*
statusbar, Window object*
statusbar, Window.statusbar
StdErr, WScript object*
StdErr, WScript.StdErr
StdIn, WScript object*
StdIn, WScript.StdIn
StdOut, WScript object*
StdOut, WScript.StdOut
Strength, filter - Glow()*
Strength, filter - MotionBlur()*
Strength, filter - Wave()*
stress, style object (2)*
stress, style.stress
StretchStyle, filter - Stretch()*
style, Element object*
style, Element.style
Style, filter - Alpha()*
style, Frame object*
style, rule object*
style, rule.style
styleFloat, style object (2)*
styleFloat, style.styleFloat
SubFolders, Folder object*
Subject, SendMail object*
Subject, SendMail.Subject

suffixes, MimeType object*
summary, TABLE object*
summary, TABLE.summary
sun, Global object*
sun, Window object*
sun, Window.sun
systemId, Entity object*
systemId, Entity.systemId
systemId, Notation object*
systemId, Notation.systemId
systemLanguage, Navigator object*
systemLanguage,
    Navigator.systemLanguage
tabIndex, ! object*
tabIndex, A object
tabIndex, Anchor object*
tabIndex, Anchor.tabIndex
tabIndex, Applet object*
tabIndex, Area object*
tabIndex, Area.tabIndex
tabIndex, BODY object*
tabIndex, BODY.tabIndex
tabIndex, BUTTON object*
tabIndex, Embed object*
tabIndex, FIELDSET object*
tabIndex, Form object*
tabIndex, Form.tabIndex
tabIndex, FRAMESET object*
tabIndex, FRAMESET.tabIndex
tabIndex, IFRAME object*
tabIndex, IFRAME.tabIndex
tabIndex, IMG object*
tabIndex, Input object*
tabIndex, Input.tabIndex
tabIndex, Label object*
tabIndex, Legend object*
tabIndex, MARQUEE object*
tabIndex, NOFRAMES object*
tabIndex, NOSCRIPT object*
tabIndex, OBJECT object*
tabIndex, OBJECT.tabIndex
tabIndex, Select object*
tabIndex, TABLE object*
tabIndex, TBODY object*
tabIndex, TD object*
tabIndex, Url object*
tableLayout, style object (2)*
tableLayout, style.tableLayout
tagName, Element object*
tagName, Element.tagName
tagName, Frame object*
tags
tagUrn, Element object*
tagUrn, Element.tagUrn
target, A object
target, Anchor object*
target, Anchor.target
target, Area object*
target, Area.target
target, BASE object*
target, BASE.target
target, Event object*
target, Event.target
target, Form object*
target, Form.target
target, Location object*
target, Location.target

Property (continued)

Type, File.Type
type, FileUpload object*
type, FileUpload.type
Type, Folder object*
Type, Folder.Type
type, Hidden object*
type, Hidden.type
type, Input object*
type, Input.type
type, LI object*
type, LI.type
type, LINK object*
type, LINK.type
type, MimeType object*
type, MimeType.type
type, MouseEvent object*
type, MutationEvent object*
type, OBJECT object*
type, OBJECT.type
type, OL object*
type, OL.type
type, ParamElement object*
type, ParamElement.type
type, Password object*
type, Password.type
type, RadioButton object*
type, RadioButton.type
type, ResetButton object*
type, ResetButton.type
type, SCRIPT object*
type, SCRIPT.type
type, Select object*
type, Select.type
type, Selection object*
type, selection.type
type, STYLE object (1)*
type, STYLE.type
type, StyleSheet object*
type, StyleSheet.type
type, SubmitButton object*
type, SubmitButton.type
type, TEXTAREA object*
type, TEXTAREA.type
type, TextCell object*
type, TextCell.type
type, UL object*
type, UL.type
type, Url object*
type, Url.type
type, XML object*
type, XML.type
unicodeBidi, style object (2)*
unicodeBidi, style.unicodeBidi
uniqueID, Document object*
uniqueID, Document.uniqueID
uniqueID, Element object*
uniqueID, Element.uniqueID
units, Embed object*
units, Embed.units
updateInterval, Screen object*
updateInterval, Screen.updateInterval
URL, Document object*
URL, Document.URL
url, META object*
url, META.url
urn, Anchor object*

urn, Anchor.urn
urn, Url object*
urn, Url.urn
useMap, IMG object*
useMap, IMG.useMap
useMap, OBJECT object*
useMap, OBJECT.useMap
userAgent, Navigator object*
userAgent, Navigator.userAgent
userLanguage, Navigator object*
userLanguage, Navigator.userLanguage
userProfile, Navigator object*
userProfile, Navigator.userProfile
vAlign, CAPTION object*
vAlign, CAPTION object*
vAlign, CAPTION.vAlign
vAlign, COL object*
vAlign, COL.vAlign
vAlign, COLGROUP object*
vAlign, COLGROUP.vAlign
vAlign, HEAD object*
vAlign, HEAD.vAlign
vAlign, TableColElement object*
vAlign, TableColElement.vAlign
vAlign, TBODY object*
vAlign, TBODY.vAlign
vAlign, TD object*
vAlign, TD.vAlign
vAlign, TFOOT object*
vAlign, TFOOT.vAlign
vAlign, TH object*
vAlign, TH.vAlign
vAlign, THEAD object*
vAlign, THEAD.vAlign
vAlign, TR object*
vAlign, TR.vAlign
value, Attribute object*
value, Attribute.value
value, Button object*
value, BUTTON object*
value, Button.value
value, BUTTON.value
value, Checkbox object*
value, Checkbox.value
value, File object*
value, FileUpload object*
value, FileUpload.value
value, Hidden object*
value, Hidden.value
value, Input object*
value, Input.value
value, LI object*
value, LI.value
value, Option object*
value, Option.value
value, ParamElement object*
value, ParamElement.value
value, Password object*
value, Password.value
value, RadioButton object*
value, RadioButton.value
value, ResetButton object*
value, ResetButton.value
value, Select object*
value, Select.value
value, SubmitButton object*
value, SubmitButton.value

value, TEXTAREA object*
value, TEXTAREA.value
value, TextCell object*
value, TextCell.value
valueType, ParamElement object*
valueType, ParamElement.valueType
version, HTML object*
version, HTML.version
Version, WScript object*
Version, WScript.Version
verticalAlign, JSSTag object*
verticalAlign, JSSTag.verticalAlign
verticalAlign, style object (2)*
verticalAlign, style.verticalAlign
view, MouseEvent object*
view, UIEvent object*
view, UIEvent.view
visibility, JSSTag object*
visibility, Layer object*
visibility, Layer.visibility
visibility, style object (2)*
visibility, style.visibility
visible, Bar object*
visible, Bar.visible
vLink, BODY object*
vLink, BODY.vLink
vlinkColor, Document object*
vlinkColor, Document.vlinkColor
voiceFamily, style object (2)*
voiceFamily, style.voiceFamily
volume, BGSOUND object*
volume, BGSOUND.volume
volume, style object (2)*
volume, style.volume
VolumeName, Drive object*
VolumeName, Drive.VolumeName
vspace, Applet object*
vspace, Applet.vspace
vspace, IFRAME object*
vspace, IFRAME.vspace
vspace, Image object*
vspace, Image.vspace
vspace, IMG object*
vspace, IMG.vspace
vspace, MARQUEE object*
vspace, MARQUEE.vspace
vspace, OBJECT object*
vspace, OBJECT.vspace
which, Event object*
which, Event.which
whiteSpace, JSSTag object*
whiteSpace, JSSTag.whiteSpace
whiteSpace, style object (2)*
whiteSpace, style.whiteSpace
widows, style object (2)*
widows, style.widows
width, Applet object*
width, Applet.width
width, Clip object*
width, Clip.width
width, COL object*
width, COL.width
width, COLGROUP object*
width, COLGROUP.width
width, Document object*
width, Document.width
width, Embed object*

width, Embed.width
width, Event object*
width, Event.width
width, HR object*
width, HR.width
width, IFRAME object*
width, IFRAME.width
width, Image object*
width, Image.width
width, IMG object*
width, IMG.width
width, JSSTag object*
width, JSSTag.width
width, MARQUEE object*
width, MARQUEE.width
width, OBJECT object*
width, OBJECT.width
width, PRE object*
width, PRE.width
width, Rect object*
width, Rect.width
width, Screen object*
width, Screen.width
width, style object (2)*
width, style.width
width, TABLE object*
width, TABLE.width
width, TableColElement object*
width, TableColElement.width
width, TD object*
width, TD.width
width, TH object*
width, TH.width
window
window, Global object*
window, Layer object*
window, Layer.window
window, Window object*
window, Window.window
WipeStyle, filter - GradientWipe()*
WipeStyle, filter - RadialWipe()*
wordBreak, style object (2)*
wordBreak, style.wordBreak
wordSpacing, style object (2)*
wordSpacing, style.wordSpacing
wordWrap, style object (2)*
wordWrap, style.wordWrap
wrap, TEXTAREA object*
wrap, TEXTAREA.wrap
writingMode, style object (2)*
writingMode, style.writingMode
x, Anchor object*
x, Anchor.x
x, Area object*
x, Area.x
x, Event object*
x, Event.x
x, Image object*
x, Image.x
x, Layer object*
x, Layer.x
x, Location object*
x, Location.x
x, Url object*
x, Url.x
XMLDocument, XML.XMLDocument
XRay, filter - BasicImage()*

Property (continued)
y, Anchor object*
y, Anchor.y
y, Area object*
y, Area.y
y, Event object*
y, Event.y
y, Image object*
y, Image.y
y, Layer object*
y, Layer.y
y, Location object*
y, Location.y
y, Url object*
y, Url.y
zIndex, JSSTag object*
zIndex, Layer object*
zIndex, Layer.zIndex
zIndex, style object (2)*
zIndex, style.zIndex
zoom, style object (2)*
zoom, style.zoom

Property attribute
DontDelete*
DontEnumerate*
ReadOnly*

Property/internal
Array.Class*
Boolean.Class*
Class*
Construct*
Date.Class*
Function.Class*
Image.Class*
Number.Class*
Object.Class*
String.Class*

Property/static
$n (Numbered argument)
$n, RegExp.$n*
input, RegExp.input*
lastMatch, RegExp.lastMatch*
lastParent, RegExp.lastParent*
leftContext, RegExp.leftContext*
multiline, RegExp.multiline*
rightContext, RegExp.rightContext*
RegExp["$'"]
RegExp["$*"]
RegExp["$`"]
RegExp["$+"]

Request method
about: URL*
clsid: URL*
file: URL*
ftp: URL*
http: URL*
https: URL*
JavaScript interactive URL*
javascript: URL*
livescript: URL

mailbox: URL*
mailto: URL
mocha: URL
nethelp: URL*
news: URL*
snews: URL*
telnet: URL*
view-source: URL*
wysiwyg:*

Reserved word
abstract
boolean*
byte*
char*
class*
const*
debugger
double*
enum*
extends
final
float*
goto*
implements
int*
interface
long*
native
package
private
protected
public
short*
static
super
synchronized
throws
transient
volatile*

Security privilege
UniversalBrowserAccess*
UniversalBrowserRead*
UniversalBrowserWrite*
UniversalFileRead*
UniversalPreferencesRead*
UniversalPreferencesWrite*
UniversalSendMail*

Security related
AuthentiCode*
Cryptoki*
Data-tainting*
Requesting privileges*
Same origin*
Signed scripts*

Selector (see also Label)
else if(...) ...
if(...) ... else ...*
if(...) ...*
switch(...) ... case: ... default: ...*

Simulated functionality
isAlnum()
isAlpha()
isCtrl()
isDigit()
isElementProperty()
isGraph()
isLower()
isObjectEqual()
isODigit()
isPrint()
isPunct()
isSpace()
isUpper()
isXDigit()
Math.cosec()
Math.cosh()
Math.cot()
Math.sec()
Math.sinh()

Special file (see also File extension)
config.jsc
preferences.js
prefs.js
proxy.pac*

Standard (see also Background, Definition, Overview)
ASCII*
ATVEF*
CSS level 1*
CSS level 2*
CSS*
CSS-P*
DHTML*
DOM - Level 0*
DOM - Level 1*
DOM - Level 2*
DOM - Level 3*
DOM Events*
DOM*
DVB-MHP*
ECMA*
ECMAScript - edition 2*
ECMAScript - edition 3*
ECMAScript version*
HTML*
IEEE 754*
ISO 3166*
ISO 639
JavaScript version*
JScript version*
PDF*
Unicode*
Universal coordinated time*
UTC
WAP*
WML*
WScript*
XML*

Statement
Block { }
break*
continue*
Empty statement (;)*
export*
finally ...*
import*
return*
throw*
try ... catch ... finally*
with ...*

Time calculation
Date from time
Date number
Day from year
Day number
Day within year
Days in year
In leap year
MakeDate()
MakeDay()
MakeTime()
Month from time
Month number
Time from year
Time value
Time within day
TimeClip()
Week day
Year from time
Year number

Type
Boolean*
null*
Number*
Object*
String*
undefined type*

Useful tip (see also Advice, Pitfall)
Determining the object type
Image animation
Image preloading
Object inspector
Off-screen image caching
Queue manipulation
Server-side browser detection
Stack manipulation
Static variable

Web browser
iCab*
Internet Explorer*
MSIE
Netscape Navigator*
Opera*

about: URL (Request method)
AbstractView object (Object/DOM)
ActiveXObject object (Object/JScript)
Add (+) (Operator/additive)
Add then assign (+=) (Operator/assignment)

Associated Titles

Beginning XML

wrox

This book explains and demonstrates XML and related technologies. This is the exciting new way of marking up and manipulating data within your applications. XML is platform independent and versatile, meaning that it is rapidly becoming a major technology. Anywhere that data is exchanged between applications or tiers is a potential application for XML. This book will teach you how to use it in your data exchange applications – on the web, for e-commerce or in n-tier architectures – by explaining XML theory, reinforced with plenty of practical examples and real life solutions.

- XML syntax and writing well formed XML

- Using namespaces in XML

- Adding style with CSS and XSL

Summary of contents

Chapter 1:	What is XML?
Chapter 2:	Well Formed XML
Chapter 3:	Cascading Style Sheets
Chapter 4:	XML in the Browser and Beyond - XSLT
Chapter 5:	XSLT - The Gory Details
Chapter 6:	The Document Object Model (DOM)
Chapter 7:	The Simple API for XML (SAX)
Chapter 8:	Namespaces
Chapter 9:	Basic Valid XML - DTDs
Chapter 10:	Valid XML - Schemas
Chapter 11:	Advanced Valid XML
Chapter 12:	Linking XML
Chapter 13:	XML and Databases
Chapter 14:	Other Uses for XML
Chapter 15:	Case Study 1
Chapter 16:	Case Study 2
Chapter 17:	Case Study 3

Kurt Cagle
Dave Gibbons
David Hunter
Nikola Ozu
Jonathan Pinnock
Paul Spencer

1-861003-41-2

June 2000

US$ 39.99
C$ 59.95
£ 28.99

Associated Titles

Beginning Active Server Pages 3.0

David Buser
Jon Duckett
Brian Francis
John Kauffman
Juan T Llibre
David Sussman
Chris Ullman

1-861003-38-2

December 1999

US$ 39.99
C$ 59.95
£ 28.99

If you're looking for a way to create attractive, intelligent web pages or, if you're just looking for a way to extend your HTML know-how, then ASP is an effective way to acheive your goals. With ASP, you can customize your web pages to be more dynamic, more efficient and more responsive to your users. It's not just a technology, though - to get the best out of ASP, you'll be using it in tandem with HTML, and with one or more of the web's simple scripting languages. The book will teach you everything you need to create useful real-world applications on the web.

●   Teaches VBScript as an integral part of learning to use ASP

●   Describes how to make your pages more dynamic with HTML and script code

●   Covers writing and debugging script code

Summary of contents

JavaScript is the language of the Web. Used for programming all major browsers, JavaScript gives you the ability to enhance your web site by creating interactive, dynamic and personalized pages. Our focus in this book is on client-side scripting, but JavaScript is also hugely popular as a scripting language in server-side environments, a subject that we cover in later chapters. Beginning JavaScript assumes no prior knowledge of programming languages, and teaches you all the fundamental concepts that you need as you progress. After covering the core JavaScript language, you'll move on to learn about more advanced techniques, including Dynamic HTML, using cookies, debugging techniques, and server-side scripting with ASP. By the end of this book, you will have mastered the art of using JavaScript to create dynamic and professional-looking web pages. Whether you want to pick up some programming skills, or want to find out how to transfer your existing programming knowledge to the Web, then this book is for you. All you need is a text editor (like Notepad) and a browser, and you're ready to go!

- Fundamental programming concepts
- Comprehensive practical tutorial in JavaScript
- Cross-browser scripting, including Netscape 6

Paul Wilton

1-861004-06-0

December 2000

US$ 39.99
C$ 59.95
£ 30.99

Summary of contents

Associated Titles

Professional JavaScript

This book covers the broad spectrum of programming JavaScript - from the core language to browser applications and server-side use to stand-alone and embedded JavaScript. It includes a guide to the language - when where and how to get the most out of JavaScript - together with practical case studies demonstrating JavaScript in action. Coverage is bang up-to-date, with discussion of compatibility issues and version differences, and the book concludes with a comprehensive reference section. This book is for programmers who want to bring their JavaScript programming skills to the cutting edge, and for any programmer looking for a comprehensive compendium of techniques and an up-to-date JavaScript reference. It will also be of use to experienced programmers who want to learn JavaScript or leverage its power for a specific purpose.

- Core, client-side and server-side JavaScript
- JavaScript and the Web
- Dynamic HTML

Andrea Chiarelli
James R De Carli
Sing Li
Nigel McFarlane
Stuart Updegrave
Mark Wilcox
Paul Wilton
Cliff Wootton

1-861002-70-X

September 1999

US$ 49.99
C$ 74.95
£ 35.99

Summary of contents

PHP is a rapidly growing Web technology which enables web designers to build dynamic, interactive web applications, incorporating information from a host of databases, and including features such as e-mail integration and dynamically generated images. PHP4 added tons of features to make web application development even easier, and this book will show you how to make the most of the language's powerful capabilities. This book is a complete tutorial in PHP's language features and functionality, beginning with the basics and building up to the design and construction of complex data-driven websites. Fully working examples in the book include a directory-style web search engine, a mailing list management system, a web based file editor, and a graphical online shopping mall guidebook.

- Complete tutorial in the PHP language
- Installation guide and troubleshooting tips
- Introduction to relational databases and MySQL

Jon Blank
Wankyu Choi
Allan Kent
Ganesh Prasad
Chris Ullman

1-861003-73-0

October 2000

US$ 39.99
C$ 59.95
£ 28.99

Summary of contents

Susanne Clark
Antonio De Donatis
Adrian Kingsley-Hughes
Kathie Kingsley-Hughes
Brian Matsik
Erick Nelson
Piotr Prussak
Daniel Read
Carsten Thomsen
Stuart Updegrave
Paul Wilton

1-861002-71-8

October 1999

US$ 29.99
C$ 44.95
£ 21.99

VBScript is one of Microsoft's scripting languages, which can be employed in a variety of ways - from client-side scripting in Internet Explorer to server-side programming in ASP and the new Microsoft Windows Script Host. The language itself has been gradually increasing in power and flexibility, and the newest release, represents a huge increase in functionality and effectiveness. This book will be useful for anyone who wishes to get to grips with VBScript. Whether you've just played around with HTML and want to find out about the world of programming, or whether you're an experienced programmer who needs to learn the VBScript language in order to work with the Windows Script Host or develop ASP pages, this book will show you the way. No prior knowledge of programming is assumed.

- Complete guide to the VBScript language and its syntax

- Up-to-date details of the most recent scripting engines for Internet Explorer, ASP and the Windows Script Host

- Coverage of the new features in VBScript 5, including constructing classes, specific data-types and using regular expressions

Summary of contents

about: URL (Request method)
AbstractView object (Object/DOM)
ActiveXObject object (Object/JScript)
Add (+) (Operator/additive)
Add then assign (+=) (Operator/assignment)

p2p.wrox.com
The programmer's resource centre

A unique free service from Wrox Press
with the aim of helping programmers to help each other

Wrox Press aims to provide timely and practical information to today's programmer.
P2P is a list server offering a host of targeted mailing lists where you can share
knowledge with your fellow programmers and find solutions to your problems.
Whatever the level of your programming knowledge, and whatever technology you
use, P2P can provide you with the information you need.

ASP
Support for beginners and professionals, including a resource
page with hundreds of links, and a popular ASP+ mailing list.

DATABASES
For database programmers, offering support on SQL Server,
mySQL, and Oracle.

MOBILE
Software development for the mobile market is growing rapidly.
We provide lists for the several current standards, including WAP,
WindowsCE, and Symbian.

JAVA
A complete set of Java lists, covering beginners,
professionals,and server-side programmers (including JSP,
servlets and EJBs)

.NET
Microsoft's new OS platform, covering topics such as ASP+, C#,
and general .Net discussion.

VISUAL BASIC
Covers all aspects of VB programming, from programming Office
macros to creating components for the .Net platform.

WEB DESIGN
As web page requirements become more complex, programmer
sare taking a more important role in creating web sites. For these
programmers, we offer lists covering technologies such as Flash,
Coldfusion, and JavaScript.

XML
Covering all aspects of XML, including XSLT and schemas.

OPEN SOURCE
Many Open Source topics covered including PHP, Apache, Perl,
Linux, Python and more.

FOREIGN LANGUAGE
Several lists dedicated to Spanish and German speaking
programmers, categories include .Net, Java, XML, PHP and XML.

How To Subscribe

Simply visit the P2P site, at **http://p2p.wrox.com/**

Select the 'FAQ' option on the side menu bar for more information about the
subscription process and our service.

WROX PRESS INC.

Wrox writes books for you. Any suggestions, or ideas
about how you want information given in your
ideal book will be studied by our team.
Your comments are always valued at Wrox.

Free phone in USA 800-USE-WROX
Fax (312) 893 8001

UK Tel. (0121) 687 4100   Fax   (0121) 687 4101

NB. If you post the bounce back card below in the UK, please send it to:
Wrox Press Ltd., Arden House, 1102 Warwick Road, Acocks Green, Birmingham. B27 6BH. UK.

Name

Address

City _____ State/Region

Country _____ Postcode/Zip

E-mail

Occupation

How did you hear about this book?

☐ Book review (name)

☐ Advertisement (name)

☐ Recommendation

☐ Catalog

☐ Other

Where did you buy this book?

☐ Bookstore (name) _____ City

☐ Computer Store (name)

☐ Mail Order

☐ Other

What influenced you in the
purchase of this book?

☐ Cover Design

☐ Contents

☐ Other (please specify)

What did you find most useful about this book?

What did you find least useful about this book?

Please add any additional comments.

What other subjects will you buy a computer
book on soon?

What is the best computer book you have used this year?

How did you rate the overall
contents of this book?

☐ Excellent   ☐ Good

☐ Average   ☐ Poor

*Note: This information will only be used to keep you updated
about new Wrox Press titles and will not be used for any other
purpose or passed to any other third party.*

wrox

PROGRAMMER TO PROGRAMMER™